William Wenman Seward

Topographia hibernica

The topography of Ireland: Antient and modern

William Wenman Seward

Topographia hibernica
The topography of Ireland: Antient and modern

ISBN/EAN: 9783337270346

Printed in Europe, USA, Canada, Australia, Japan

Cover: Foto ©Andreas Hilbeck / pixelio.de

More available books at **www.hansebooks.com**

TOPOGRAPHIA HIBERNICA;

OR THE

TOPOGRAPHY OF IRELAND,

ANTIENT AND MODERN.

GIVING A COMPLETE VIEW OF THE

CIVIL AND ECCLESIASTICAL STATE

OF

THAT KINGDOM;

WITH ITS

Antiquities, Natural Curiofities, Trade, Manufactures, Extent and Population. Its Counties, Baronies, Cities, Boroughs, Parliamentary Reprefentation and Patronage; Antient Diftricts and their original Proprietors. Poft, Market, and Fair Towns; Bifhopricks, Ecclefiaftical Benefices, Abbies, Monafteries, Caftles, Ruins, Private-Seats, and remarkable Buildings. Mountains, Rivers, Lakes, Mineral-Springs, Bays and Harbours, with the Latitude and Longitude of the principal Places, and their Diftances from the Metropolis, and from each other. Hiftorical Anecdotes, and remarkable Events.

THE WHOLE

Alphabetically arranged and carefully collected.

WITH

AN APPENDIX,

Containing fome additional Places and Remarks, and feveral ufeful Tables.

By WM. WENMAN SEWARD, Efq;

DUBLIN: Printed by ALEX. STEWART, No. 86, *Bride-ftreet*, 1795.

T O

THE MOST PUISSANT PRINCE

Wm. Robert DUKE of LEINSTER,

Marquefs and Earl of Kildare, Earl of Offaley, Vifc. Leinfter
of Taplow, and Baron of Offaley in Ireland.

Vifcount Leinfter of Taplow in Great-Britain.

One of His Majefty's Moft Honorable Privy Council, a Knight
of the Illuftrious Order of St. Patrick, &c. &c.

The following Work

(By His Grace's Permiffion)

Is moft refpectfully Dedicated, By

His Lordfhips Dutiful and Obliged

Humble Servant,

Wm. Wenman Seward.

THE general approbation with which the plan of the HIBERNIAN GAZETTEER was favored by the public, induced the author to purfue it on a more extenfive fcale. The following work however (except in the mere form of alphabetical arrangement) is materially different from the former, as it contains the defcription of feveral hundred additional places, and has been enlarged and improved throughout, with the utmoft care and attention. We think it unneceffary to point out the obvious utility of fuch an undertaking; we fubmit the merit of our defign and the execution of it, to the judgment of an indulgent and impartial public: a few words however may not be improper to fhew the method we adopted in this compilation.

As the diftances of places from the capital has been differently reprefented in our maps, we have as far as poffible ftated it in every inftance, from the beft and lateft furveys, and on this occafion we have chiefly followed Meffrs. *Taylor* and *Skinner*. But there are feveral inftances where for want of actual furvey, we have been obliged to put down the diftance by computation: in fuch cafe a critical exactnefs cannot be expected. It is neceffary to obferve, that wherever the diftance may be faid to vary, according to different roads, we have mentioned that which was neareft to the metropolis. This indeed often occurs, and the difference may be fometimes confiderable; thus, from Dublin to Wexford by *Broad-ferry*, is fomewhat above 66 miles: but by *Ennifcorthy* it is 71;—again,—from Dublin to Youghal by *Cork* is 108, but by *Tallagh* 115 miles.

With refpect to the *Names* of places, we have followed what appeared to be the moft *ufual* orthography; having frequently found great diverfity both in the maps and the authors we confulted; the fame uncertainty attends their etymology, concerning which writers not only differ, but often appear more whimfical than fatisfactory.

The *Extent* and *Population* of the feveral *Counties* have been likewife fubjects of controverfy: we have taken *Doctor Beaufort* for our guide, (in the memoir of his new and elegant map of this kingdom,) as he is not only the *lateft*, but we think the moft accurate authority on them points; we acknowledge to have received much affiftance from that work, which has appeared fince our publication of the HIBERNIAN GAZETTEER.

The *Patronage* of *Boroughs*, has been ftated from the beft information we could procure: but as that is liable to perpetual alteration, it cannot be imagined that this work could continue always correct in that particular.

The principal *Harbours* in this kingdom have been particularly noticed, with ufeful inftructions for navigating them: a matter highly ferviceable to fea-men and traders frequenting our coafts: the *Latitude* and *Longitude* of feveral chief-towns, have been corrected from actual obfervations lately made; and the *Fair-days* have been fully and accurately inferted.

It muft, we apprehend, be acknowledged that the mere collection and arrangement of the following places (which amount to about *Six Thoufand*) was a matter of fome ufe, and no inconfiderable difficulty: but our labour was not confined to this. In our enquiry into the Antiquities, Situation, Soil, Produce, Manufactures, natural Curiofities, &c. of particular places, we had a variety of authors to examine, compare, and fometimes

A a

times

times correct; but after all the care that has been taken in the execution of our design, we are neither so ignorant or so vain, as not to feel and acknowledge, that a work of this nature, even from the ablest hands, must admit of frequent improvement and additional information, in proportion as new discoveries are made and alterations take place in the state of this country. We claim no greater merit therefore, than that of having collected into one view, what before lay scattered in a confused and almost endless variety of materials: and should superior abilities be at any time employed in a similar undertaking, we have the pleasing assurance that our labours must contribute to facilitate the task: and we may at least take credit for the original attempt.

An ingenious writer to whom we are indebted for several remarks, very justly observes, that "innumerable and almost unsurmountable difficulties attend the elucidation of the *antient* Topography of Ireland; little or no information relative to this subject is to be obtained from foreign, and not much from our domestic writers." All we could do therefore was to consult the best authorities which such circumstances afforded: and amongst others we must confess how considerably we are indebted to the late Mr. Archdall's *Monastic. Hibernic.* and *Doctor Ledwich's* antiquities of this country.

We have added at the end of the work, an appendix containing some additional remarks and several useful tables, particularly a table of the *First-fruits* of the several benefices in Ireland, as taxed in the King's books, faithfully transcribed from the original record, in the chief Remembrancer's office: and also a table shewing the cross-distances, between the principal trading and post towns in this kingdom.

Upon the whole, we have no doubt, but from those who are acquainted with the nature and trouble of the present work, we shall meet with much indulgence for any imperfections; they will know the difficulties we had to encounter, and it is probable they will rather commend us for having done so much, than censure us for not having done more.

E R R A T A.

TITLE, AGHABOE, (near the end) for *Aghaboy*, read *Aghaboe*.
ALLEN, for *or Isle*, read *in Isle*, &c.
ANNA LIFFEY, for *to* Kildare, read *towards* Kildare.
BALLYCASSIDY, for *Daughters*, read *Daughtons*.
BIRR, for *wherein*, read *where in*.
CROM, for *Butterabo*, read *Buttlerabo*.
DUMOGHADEIRNE, read *Dungohdeirne*.
DUNBRODY, (line 3) dele *of*
GREEN-CASTLE, for *bar. Mourne, same county*, read *bar. Mourne, co. Down, same prov.*
ISRALONG, read *Istealong*.
IVEAGH, (line 7) for *Coclepaig*, read *Coalhpaig*.
KERRY, (line 3) for *tron*, read *from*.
KILKENNY, (col. 2) for *stile*, read *pile*.
MONASTEREVAN, (line 20) for *families*, read *family* (line 21) for *earle* read *marquis*.

Some other errors may have escaped the Press, which the reader is requested to correct.

TOPOGRAPHIA HIBERNICA.

ABACCY, otherwife called *Ardquin*; this village is fit. in bar. Ardes, co. Down, prov. Ulfter: having a handfome feat near the lake of Strangford. 'Tis held by a bifhop's leafe, which has continued in the family of the *Echlins* for many generations, even before the rebellion of 1641. Ardquin is a corrupted word from *Ard-Cuan*, fignifying a height over the lough Strangford, formerly called lough Cuan: according to the antient foundation of the feat, which was a caftle and dwelling houfe inclofed within a rampart, and ftanding boldly over the lake on a pretty high hill. The other name *Abaccy* feems to imply, as if thefe lands belonged to fome abbey, or that an abbey formerly ftood there: perhaps the priory of Eynes, (the fituation of which is not now to be found) might have ftood near this place; Ardquin is now a rectory in dioc. of Down.

ABBERT, fit. near Caftleblakeney, prov. Con.

ABBEY-BOYLE, fee *Boyle*.

ABBEY-DEIRG, fit. in bar. Moydoe, co. Longford, prov. Leinfter. A priory for regular canons was founded here, under the invocation of St. Peter, by Gorman O'Quin, in the reign of king *John*; it was granted at the fuppreffion to Nicholas Aylmer. In 1255, Brendan Magoduig, bifhop of Ardagh, was interred here.

ABBEY-FEALE, a fmall market town in bar. Connello, co. Limerick, prov. Munfter: fo called from the river Feal, which runs thro' it, and a celebrated monaftery formerly erected

here; it is now a vicarage in dioc. of Limerick. Fairs are held here on 29 June and 18 Oct. Diftance from Dublin 123 miles. One mile beyond Abbey-Feale, are the ruins of *Purt-caftle*.

ABBEY-GORMAGAN, a village in bar. Longford, co. Galway, prov. Connaught. It is now a vicarage in dioc. of Ardfert.

ABBEY-KNOCKMOY, a fair town in co. Galway, prov. Connaught. Fair day, 21 Auguft in every year.

ABBEY-LARAGH, a vicarage in dioc. of Ardagh, fit. in bar. Granard, co. Longford, prov. Leinfter.

ABBEY-MAHON, fit. near the bay of Court-macfherry, in bar. Ibawn and Barryroe, co. Cork, prov. Munfter. Here are the ruins of an antient abbey founded by the Benedictine monks at their own expence. The lord Barry gave them 18 plow lands, which conftitute the *parifh* of Abbeymahon; but this eftate was only given them 'till the building was finifhed; for foon after, the diffolution of monafteries took place, and thefe lands were feized into the hands of the crown; this is a rectory in dioc. of Rofs.

ABBEY-ODORNEY, a village fit. in bar. Clanmaurice, co. Kerry, prov. Munfter, near 141 miles from Dublin; where are the ruins of an abbey near the river *Brick*. It was founded in 1154, and fupplied with monks, from the Ciftertian abbey of Magis, in the co. Limerick.

ABBEY-

Abbey-Shrule, or *Abbey-Shreole*, a fair town in bar. *Shreule*, co. Longford, prov. Leinster; where an abbey was founded by one O'Ferral for Ciftertian monks. Fairs held on the first Wed. after Trinity-fund. this is a rectory in dioc. of Ardagh —Also a place in bar. Moygeeth, co. Westmeath, prov. Leinster. —Also the ruins of a once superb abbey, fit. at Shrule in co. Mayo, prov. Connaught: otherwise called *Burrifhrule* or *Burrifhroole*, and antiently *Barafsule*.

Abington, fit. near Limerick, co. Limerick, prov. Munfter.

Abby, fit. in bar. Coftello, co. Mayo, prov. Connaught.

Abby-Leix, fit. in bar. *Cullinagh*, Queen's co. prov. Leinfter; it was called *Abbey-Leix* from a Ciftertian abbey founded there, A. D. 1183, by one of the O'More's, near the river *Nore*, about 3 miles diftant from *Lifbigny*; this place is now a vicarage in dioc. of Leighlin. Thomas Vefey was created vifc. *de Vefci* of Abby-Leix in 1776.

Abby-Shruer, or *Abyfhreor*, fit. in bar. Carbury, co. Cork, prov. Munfter.

Abby-Shrule, fee *Abbey-Shrule*.

Abby-Side, fit. in bar. Decies without Drum, co. Waterford, prov. Munfter.

Abby-Strowry, now a vicarage in dioc. of Rofs, fit. in bar. Carbery, co. Cork, prov. Munfter.

Abhanmore, or the great river; a fmall river rifing in the upper lake of Glendaloch, in the co. Wicklow; from whence taking a S. E. courfe, thro' a glen formerly covered with wood, it falls into the fea at Arklow. The river Black-water, or Broad-water, in the co. of Waterford, is named by Ptolemy *Daurona*, but by Nacham it is called *Abhan-more*.

Abingdon or *Abington*, a fair town fit. in bar. Owneybeg, co. Limerick, prov. Munfter, about 7 miles E. of Limerick: its antient name was *Withencia* or *Wothency*, famous for an abbey which ftood there, of which *John O'Mulrain* was the laft abbot; queen Elizabeth, in the 5th year of her reign, granted this abbey for ever, with certain lands, to Peter Walth in capite, at the yearly rent of 57l. 2s. 3d. This abbey was founded by Theobald Fitz-Walter, lord of Carrick, in 1205: he was interred here in 1206. It is now a rectory in the dioc. of Emly. Diftance from Dublin about 91 miles. Fair days 27 May and 31 Aug. 5 miles beyond it are the ruins of a church.

Abboy, fee *Athboy*.

Abylane. fit. in bar. Granard, co. Longford. prov. Leinfter.

Acclare, fee *Athclare*.

Achadbhoe, fee *Aghaboe*.

Achadchaon, fee *Achonry*.

Achadfinglass, an abbey on the E. of the river Barrow, in bar. Idrone, co Carlow, prov. Leinfter: of which St. Finton was abbot. This abbey was pillaged by the Danes, A. D. 864.

Achadfodhair, fee *Aghagower*.

Achadoe, otherwife called *Aghadse*, a bifhop's fee in the co. Kerry, prov. Munfter, united to Limerick and Ardfert. Nothing remains of this place but the ruined walls of the cathedral, and one of the antient round towers, which ftands about 8 miles S. E. of *Tralee*. Aoah fon of Conor fon of Auliff Mor O'Donoghue, died in 1231, and was buried in his old abbey of *Aghadoe*, according to the Munfter annals.

Acharrow, a village in bar. Carbury, co. Sligo, prov. Connaught.

Achilbeg, fee *Achill-Ifles*.

Achill, a parifh and village in bar. Erris, co. Mayo, prov. Connaught.—Also an ifland in bar. Burrifhoole, in fame county.

Achill-head, a promontory fit. on coaft of co. Mayo, prov. Connaught.

Achill-isles, two iflands, one of which ftretches out into the Atlantic oceah, and the other lies adjoining to it, in Clew bay, co. Mayo, prov. Connaught. They are high coarfe land; the name fignifies Eagles iflands, from the great refort of eagles thither. Lat. 54 : 00, lon. 10 : 11. One of thefe iflands is diftinguifhed by the name of *Achilbeg*.

Achonry, a bifhop's fee united to Killala, having a village in it of fame name, which is now a rectory in that dioc. and fit. in bar. Leney, co. Sligo, prov. Connaught, about 16 miles S. W of Sligo, Lat. 54 : 00, lon. 9 : 8. St. *Finian* bifhop of Clonard, founded a church here about the year 530; the fcite was granted by a dynaft of the antient diftrict of *Luigny*, now the bar. of Leney before-mentioned. This church and monaftery were afterwards given by the founder to St. *Cruimthair Nathy*, who was made bifhop thereof, and of the neighbouring diftrict of Luigny; whence the bifhops of Achonry in the antient Irifh annals, are generally called bifhops of Luigny. This bifhoprick remained a diftinct diocefe 'till the year 1607, when it was united to that of Killala; it was antiently called *Achadchaon* or *Achadconre*, and is rated in the king's books at 10l. per. ann. but with Killala is worth 2000l.

Acoill, antiently fit. near *Teamor* or *Tarah*, in co. Meath, prov. Leinfter. At this place *Elim* at the head of the provincial kings of Ireland, was defeated in battle by *Tuathal Teachmar*, A. D. 130, and an end put to the fecond Attacotic war.

Acton, a fair town in bar. Orior, co. Armagh,

magh, prov. Ulfter, where fairs are held on 4 May and 11 December.

ADAIR, an antient town 8 miles diftant from Limerick, and 102 from Dublin, pleafantly fit. in bar. Cofhma, co. Limerick, prov. Munfter, having a good bridge over the river Maige, which river is navigable for large boats. Here are the ruins of feveral churches and convents, rendered elegant by ivy, which almoft covers them; in this town was a ftrong caftle of the earl of Defmond. The large and very perfect ruins of the Trinitarian friary ftill remain at Adair, with other pieces of antiquity, which prove this to have been a place of importance. This friary was founded in the reign of Edward Ift. by John earl of Kildare, Nov. 4th. in 37th. queen Eliz. it was granted with other premifes to fir H. Wallop, knt. The entrance into it was by a low gate on the W. fide, which is yet ftanding. On the S. fide of the river an Auguftinian friary was alfo founded, which was called the Black-abbey; and great part of it remains in good prefervation. Adair is now a vicarage in dioc. of Limerick. Fairs are held here 27 March and 14 Oct.

ADAMSTOWN, fit. in bar. Balruddery, co. Dublin, prov. Leinfter. — Alfo a rectory in dioc. of Ferns, fit. in bar. Bantry, co. Wexford, prov. Leinfter.

ADAR-RIVER, fit. in bar. Gallen, co. Mayo, prov. Connaught.

ADDERGOULE, fit. in bar. Tirawly, co. Mayo, prov. Connaught, now a vicarage in dioc. of Killala.—Alfo a place in bar. Downamore, co. Galway, prov. Connaught, which is alfo a vicarage in dioc. of Tuam.

ADNITH, a vicarage in dioc. of Cafhel, fit. in bar. Eliogurty, co. Tipperary, prov. Munft.

ADRAGOAL, a place fo called fit. in Bantry bay, co. Cork, prov. Munfter, probably fo named from a clan of the Gauls or Celtiberi who landed here. It is remarkable for its cataract. Ardgoal or Argyle in Scotland is the fame name. A colony of the before-mentioned clan failed from Ireland to the Weftern Ifles, and gave the county of Argyle in Scotland their name. They called that country *Gael Albenich*, from old Albania; and thofe of Ireland *Gael Erinich*; each retaining to this day a fimilarity of language, manners and cuftoms.

ADRISTON, fit. in bar. Forth, co. Carlow, prov. Leinfter.

ADROS, an ifland in the Irifh fea, mentioned by Ptolemy, and called by him *Advi Deferta*, by Pliny corruptly written *Andros*, by others *Edri*, and by Rich. Cirenceft. *Edria*; Ware takes it for *Begeari*, one of the Saltees on the coaft of Wexford. Adros feems a corruption

from the Britifh word *Adar*, which fignifies birds; whence *Inis Adar*, birds ifland, in old Saxon. It is now vulgarly denominated *Ireland's Eye*, and is fit. N. of the hill of Hoath, the *Ben Hadar* of the antients.

AFFADOWN, a pleafant feat in co. Cork, prov. Munfter, about 3 miles W. of Skibbereen, adorned with good gardens and plantations. The jaw bone of a whale forms the fide pofts and arch of a gateway, large enough for a coach to drive through, altho' fome part is buried in the earth. Near it on a rifing ground, is a round tower, on the top of which is a lanthorn; from this is a profpect of the adjacent coafts and iflands, with the ruins of feveral old caftles.

AFFANE, a parifh in bar. Decies without Drum, co. Wexford, prov. Munfter, now a vicarage in dioc. of Lifmore. On the Ift. Feb. 1564, a bloody conflict was fought at this place between the earls of Ormond and Defmond, where the latter had 300 men killed. *Affane* has been famous for the beft cherries perhaps in Ireland, which were firft planted here by fir *Walter Raleigh*, who brought them from the *Canary-iflands*. The moft remarkable place in this parifh is *Drumana*, the feat of lord *Grandifon*: the houfe is built on the foundation of an antient caftle, that formerly was the chief feat of the *Fitzgeralds* of *Decies*; the caftle with all its furniture was burned down by the Irifh. Fairs are held at the village of *Affane* 14 May, 12 Aug. and 22 Nov.

AFFANE-BRIDGE, fit. in bar. Dundalk, co. Louth, prov. Leinfter.

AFFARREL, fit. near *Tallagh*, co. Dublin, prov. Leinfter.

AGHABOE or *Aughaboe*, a village fit. in bar. Upper Offory, Queen's co. prov. Leinfter, 58 miles from Dublin. The Irifh name is *Achadboe* or *Aghavoe*, i. e. *the field of oxen*; it was formerly an open plain, where St. *Canice*, the fon of *Laidec*, an eminent poet, founded a monaftery towards the clofe of the 6th century, in which he died on the 11 Oct. 599. Near the fcite of this monaftery a church was built about 1052, and the fhrine of St. *Canice* placed therein; on which the fee of Offory was tranflated to this place, from Ely. O'Carrol in the King's county. Here it continued 'till about the end of the reign of Henry IId. when it was tranflated to Kilkenny, by *Felis O'Dullany*, bifhop of Offory. *Aghaboe* was no inconfiderable place, even at the clofe of the laft century: but the only remains of its former confequence now vifible, are the church and ruins of a Dominican abbey, founded by one of the *M'Gilla Padruices*, antient chiefs, and anceftors of the prefent earl of Offory. This town, with the fhrine and reliques of St. *Canice*, were

burned.

burned by the villainy of *Dennis M'Gillpatrick*, 13th. May, 1346. The monastery was granted 43 queen *Eliz.* to Florence Fitzpatrick. *Aghboe* is now a vicarage in dioc. of Offory. Fairs held 1 and 2 Aug. and 21 and 22 Oct.

AGHABOG, fit. according to *Scale, Hib. Atl.* in bar. Monaghan, co. Monaghan, prov. Ulfter; *Dr. Beaufort* places it in bar. Dartree, in fame co. It is a rectory in dioc. of Clogher.

AGHABOLLOGE, an antient village in bar. Mufkerry, co. Cork, prov. Munfter, having an old church, near which is a celebrated well. In the church yard is a ftone called *St. Olan's cap*, by which the vulgar people fwear on all common occafions: and they pretend, if this ftone was carried away, it would return to its old ftation. This place is a rectory in dioc. of Cloyne.

AGHACREW. fit. near Oldcaftle, co. Meath, prov. Leinfter.—Alfo a rectory in dioc. of Cafhel. fit. in bar. Kilnemanna, co. Tipperary, prov. Munfter.

AGHACROSS, a rectory in dioc. of Cloyne, fit. in bar. Condons, co. Cork, prov. Munfter.

AGHADA, a rectory in dioc. of Cloyne, fit. in bar. Imokilly, co. Cork, prov. Munfter.

AGHADE, a curacy in dioc. of Leighlin, fit. in bar. Ravilly, co. Carlow, prov. Leinfter.

AGHADERRIG, fit. in bar. Upper Iveach, co. Down, prov. Ulfter. It is a vicarage in dioc. of Dromore.

AGHADOE, fee *Achadoe*.

AGHADOWN, a vicarage in dioc. of Rofs, fit. in bar. Carbery, co. Cork, prov. Munfter. Fairs held here on 6 May and 2 Oct.

AGHADOWY, fit. in bar. Colerain, co. Londonderry, prov. Ulfter. It is a rectory in dioc. of Derry—Alfo a river in bar. Colerain, co. Londonderry, prov. Ulfter.

AGHAGALLEN, a vicarage in dioc. of Connor, fit. in bar. Maffareen, co. Antrim, prov. Ulfter.

AGHAGOWER, (antiently called *Achadfobhair*) a plain comprehending the prefent bar. of Morifk, in the co. Mayo, prov. Connaught. In this place St. Patrick founded a church and placed St. *Senach*, one of his difciples over it, in confequence of which it continued an epifcopal fee for many years, but was at length united to that of *Tuam*, and is now only a parifh church, and the head of a rural deanery. Here is one of the antient round towers.—Dr. *Beaufort* mentions a vicarage of this name in bar. Burrifhoole, fame county.

AGHALEAGH, fit. near Lough Earn, in bar. Knockniny, co. Fermanagh, prov. Ulfter, and adjoining the co. Cavan.

AGHALEE, a village in bar. Maffareen, co. Antrim, prov. Ulfter, now a vicarage in dioc. of Dromore.

AGHALOW, a rectory in dioc. of Armagh, fit. in bar. Dungannon, co. Tyrone, prov. Ulfter.

AGHALURCHER, a rectory in dioc. of Clogher, fit. in bar. Magheraftephana, co. Fermanagh, prov. Ulfter.

AGHAMISH, fit. in bar. Conillo, co. Limerick, prov. Munfter.

AGHAMORE, the remains of a fmall abbey founded in the 7th century, fit. near the mouth of the river Kenmare, in co. Kerry, prov. Munfter. The land here, together with the ifland of *Scariff*, is the property of the earl of Orrery, adjoining to which lord Carberry has alfo a confiderable eftate.—Alfo a monaftery erected by St. *Patrick* for his difciple St. *Loarn*, which was fit. near the borders of Rofcommon, in bar. Coftello, co. Mayo, prov. Connaught. It is now a parifh church in the deanery of Mayo.

AGHAMY, fit. in co. Kilkenny, prov. Leinft.

AGHANCON, a rectory in dioc. of Killaloe, fit. in bar. Ballibrit, King's co. prov. Leinfter.

AGHANILLY *caftle*, fit. in bar. Ibacene, co. Cork, prov. Munfter.

AGHARNEY, a rectory in dioc. of Offory, fit. in bar. Gallmoy, co. Kilkenny, prov. Leinfter.

AGHASKER, fit. in bar. Kilconnel, co. Galway, prov. Connaught.

AGHAVALLIN, a parifh in dioc. of Ardfert, bar. Iraghticonnor, co. Kerry, prov. Munfter, half vicarial; the church here is in repair: patronage in the *Stoughton* family.

AGHAVEA, a rectory in dioc. of Clogher, fit. in bar. Magheraftephana, co. Fermanagh, prov. Ulfter.

AGHAVILLER, or *Aghavuller*, a rectory in dioc. of Offory, fit. in bar. Knocktopher, co. Kilkenny, prov. Leinfter. Here was one of the antient round towers, of which part only is now remaining.

AGHAVOE, fee *Aghabee*.

AGHAVOURE, a rectory in dioc. of Tuam, fit. in bar. Coftello, co. Mayo, prov. Connau.

AGHCLARE, a fair town in co. Mayo, prov. Connaught. Fair days 14 Aug. and 12 Dec.

AGHENISH, fit. in bar. Kilmacrenan, co. Donegal, prov. Ulfter.—Alfo an ifland fit. in bar. Conillo, co. Limerick, prov. Munfter.

AGHENTEAN, fit. in bar. Clogher, co. Tyrone, prov. Ulfter.

AGHER, a rectory in dioc. of Meath, fit. in bar. Deece, co. Meath, prov. Leinfter.

AGHERN, a vicarage in dioc. of Cloyne, fit. in bar. Killnatallon, co. Cork, prov. Munft.

AGHERTON, a rectory in dioc. of Connor, fit. in the liberties of Colerain, co. Londonderry, prov. Ulfter.

AGHILLS,

ACHILLS, certain loughs, fit. near Skibbereen, co. Cork, prov. Munster; fo called by the Irish: They abound with trout and eels, and fome have fmall floating iflands, which fwim from one fide to the other.

AGHINAGH, a rectory in dioc. of Cloyne, fit. in bar. Mufkerry, co. Cork, prov. Munster.

AGHINNIS, a feat of lord Belmore's at Caledon, co. Tyrone, prov. Ulfter.

AGHIVEY, a river in bar. Colerain, co. Londonderry, prov. Ulfter.

AGHMACART, fit. 4 miles W. of Durrow in bar. upper Offory, Queen's co. prov. Leinfter. An abbey is faid to have been founded here about A. D. 550, on the fcite of which, O'Dempfey founded a priory for canons regular; feveral ruinous parts of this building ftill remain. Dr. Pococke, whilft bifhop of Offory, had part of thefe ruins repaired for divine fervice, which is now the parifh church, and a vicarage in the dioc. of Offory.

AGHMARTYR, fit. in bar. upper Offory, Queen's co. prov. Leinfter.

AGHNABOY, fit. in bar. Monaghan, co. Monaghan, prov. Ulfter.

AGHNAMULLIN, a rectory in dioc. of Clogher, fit. in bar. Cremourne, co. Monaghan, prov. Ulfter.

AGHNAMULT, a rectory in dioc. of Offory, fit. in bar. Shillogher, co. Kilkenny, prov. Leinfter.

AGHNANEEDLE, a rectory in dioc. of Killaloe, fit. in bar. upper Ormond, co. Tipperary, prov. Munster.

AGHNENGIN, fit. in bar. Kilmacrenan, co. Donegal, prov. Ulfter.

AGHNISH-POINT, a cape in bar. Kiltartan, co. Galway, prov. Connaught.

AGHOGHILL, or Ahogill, a rectory in dioc. of Conner, fit. in bar. Toome, co. Antrim, prov. Ulfter, 94 miles from Dublin.——Fairs held here 4 June, 26 Aug. and 5 Dec.

AGHOLD, a rectory in dioc. of Leighlin, fit. in bar. Shillelagh, co. Wicklow, prov. Leinfter.

AGHOUR, a rectory in dioc. of Offory, fit. in bar. Crannagh, co. Kilkenny, prov. Leinfter.

AGHRIM, a fair town in co. Wicklow, prov. Leinfter, 35 miles from Dublin. Fair days, 22 June, 22 Nov. and the 4th Tuefday in Dec. Alfo a village in co. Galway, prov. Connaught, 75 miles from Dublin; it is a vicarage in dioc. of Ardfert, and famous for the battle fought there 12th July, 1691, between the English and Irish forces, in which the latter were defeated, and M. St. Ruth their commander, kill'd. There is alfo a vicarage of fame name, in dioc. of Elphin, fit. in bar. Boyle, co. Rofcommon, prov. Connaught.

AGHRIS-POINT, a cape in bar. Tyreragh, co. Sligo, prov. Connaught.

AGLISH, a vicarage in dioc. of Lifmore, fit. in bar. Decies within Drum, co. Waterford, prov. Munster.——Here are the remains of an antient fquare building, called by the Irish Clough; it confifts of a high wall, with a tower at each angle; on the fouth fide is a gateway formerly defended by a portcullis; round the walls are ranges of fpike-holes, and on the top are the remains of battlements; the towers were the only parts of this building, which have been roofed; the whole feems to have been an antient piece of regular fortification, fuch as have been in ufe, before the invention of fire arms: tradition fays, that this place was built by king John, as an half-way ftage, betwixt the counties Cork and Waterford. It is diftant above 100 miles from Dublin.—— There is likewife a place of the fame name, fit. in bar. Magunihy, co. Kerry, prov. Munster; which is a vicarage in dioc. of Ardfert. Another in bar. Carragh, co. Mayo, prov. Connaught, which is a vicarage in the dioc. of Tuam; and a fourth in bar. Barrett's, co. Cork, prov. Munster; which is a vicarage in dioc. Cork.

AGLISH-CLOGHAN, a rectory in dioc. of Killaloe, fit. in bar. Lower Ormond, co. Tipperary, prov. Munster.

AGLISH-DRANINA, a rectory in dioc. of Cloyne, fit. in bar. Orrery, co. Cork, prov. Munster.

AGNAMALEEN, fit. in bar. Gorey, co. Wexford, prov. Leinfter.

AHADOE, fit. in co. Cork, prov. Munster, 111 Miles from Dublin.

AHAMORE-INN, a village in bar. Drumahire, co. Limerick, prov. Connaught.

AHAMPLISH, a vicarage in dioc. Elphin, bar. Carbury, co. Sligo, prov. Connaught.

AHANA, a vicarage in dioc. of Elphin, fit. in bar. Tyraghrill, co. Sligo, prov. Connaught.

AHARAH, a vicarage in dioc. of Ardagh, fit. in bar. Shrowle, co. Longford, prov. Leinfter.

AHARCROSS, a fair town in co. Cork, prov. Munster. Fairs held 20th Jan. and 3d Oct.

AHASCRAGH, a rectory in dioc. of Elphin, fit. in bar. Killconnell, co. Galway, prov. Connaught: diftant 78 miles from Dublin.—— Fairs held here on Eafter Monday; Wednefday after Trinity; 25 Aug. and 24 Nov.

AHOGILL, fee Aghogill.

AILE, a river fit. in bar. Burrifhoole, co. Mayo, prov. Connaught.

AILEACH or Ailich-Neid, a rath or caftle of O'Neills, 3 miles N. of Derry, prov Ulfter, It is afferted to have been erected by the great Hy Naillia, on his fettlement in the N. of Ireland, in the 4th century, the name fignifies the Eagle's neft; and the place is of the fame conftruction, as thofe monuments of antiquity, commonly called Danifh forts: It was laid in

ruins

ruins by Mortogh Mor O'Brien, in 1101.

AILECH-MOR, fit. in dioc. of Elphin, co. Roscommon, prov. Connaught. Here Donnal the fon of Crimthan, a difciple of faint Patrick, was head of a monaftery.

AIR-HILL, fit. near Rofcrea, co. Tipperary, prov. Munfter.

ALAND'S-BAY, fit. in bar. Gualtiere, co. Waterford, prov. Munfter.

ALDBOROUGH, fit. in upper Ormond, co. Tipperary, prov. Munfter; it gives title of earl to the noble family of Stratford.

ALDERG, a curacy in dioc. of Dublin, fit. in bar. Newcaftle, co. Dublin, prov. Leinfter.

ALLADOWN, fit. in bar. Carberry, co. Cork, prov. Munfter.

ALLAGHMORE, fit. in bar. Carberry, co. Cork, prov. Munfter.

ALLEN, or *Ifle of Allen*, a village in bar. great Connell, co. Kildare, prov. Leinfter. It gives title of *Vifcount* to the noble family of *Allen*.

ALLEN'S-TOWN, fit. in bar. Kells, co. Meath, prov. of Leinfter.

ALLICANT, fit. near Caftleblakeney, co. Galway, prov. Connaught.

ALLOW, a river in bar. Duhallow, co. Cork, prov. Munfter.

ALL-SAINTS, a chapelry, in dioc. of Raphoe, co. Donegal, prov. Ulfter.

ALLYN, a lake fo called, fit. in bar. Dromahaire, co. Leitrim, prov. Connaught.

ALMAR, a fair town, in co. Limerick, prov. Munfter. Fair days, 11 and 12 of May, July and Dec. Alfo a rectory in dioc. of Meath, fit. in bar. Rathconrath, co. Weftmeath, prov. Leinfter.

ALMORITIA, fit. near Mullingar, co. Weftmeath, prov. Leinfter.

ALNAPEST, mountains, fit. in bar. Raphoe, co. Donegal, prov. Ulfter.

ALTAMIRA, fit. to the N. W. of Lifcarrol, co. Cork, prov. Munfter. It is an elegant feat, with a neat houfe, and pretty improvements, commanding an extenfive profpect to the Eaft.

ALTERCLON, fit. near Rofs, co. Cork, prov. Munfter.

ALTHAM, fit. in co. Cork, prov. Munfter; it gives title of Baron to the family of Annefley, (earl Mountnorris) fo created 14 Feb. 1680.

ALTIDORE, fit. near Newtown-mount-kennedy, co. Wicklow, prov. Leinfter.

ALTIMORE, fit. in bar. Dungannon, co. Tyrone, prov. Ulfter.

ALUA-LOUGH, fit. in bar. Mufkerry, co. Cork, prov. Munfter.

AMBROSE-TOWN, a rectory in dioc. of Ferns; fit. in bar. Bargie, co. Wexford, prov. Leinfter.

ANADORN, fee *Annadorn*.

ANAGH, fee *Annagh*.

ANAHILT, a rectory in dioc. of Dromore, fit. 3 miles S. of Hillfborough, in bar. *lower Iveach*, co. Down, prov. Ulfter. The church was built at the expence of Archdeacon Thomas Smyth, when rector of that parifh; it was confecrated on St. Peter's day, 1741.— There is a large bog near this place, abounding with groufe, green plover, wild geefe, ducks, fnipes, curliews, godwits and plenty of hares. Quarries of the grit kind of ftone have been dug up here; and in the W. ditch of the church-yard, was found a pair of querns or hand-mills, of 9 inches diameter. Alfo in the lands bordering the church, were found ammunition balls of about a pound weight; and half a fmall hollow ball, like a granade: from whence it has been conjectured, that the old church and churchyard here, were formerly ufed in troublefome times, as a place of ftrength: tho' thefe things might have been dropt in the rout of an army, and poffibly in that of fir Phelim O'Neil, at Lifburn, in 1641, when he was obliged to throw his two field-pieces into the river *Lagan*.

ANALEE, a river in bar. Tullagharvey, co. Cavan, prov. Ulfter.

ANARAP, fit. near Tynan, in co. Armagh, prov. Ulfter.

ANCLES, fit. in bar. Monaghan, co. Monaghan, prov. Ulfter.

ANDLY's-CASTLE, fit. in bar. Lecale, co. Down, prov. Ulfter.

ANEGROVE, fit. near Rofcrea, in co. Tipperary, prov. Munfter.

ANFIELD, fit. in bar. Ifleagh, co. Tipperary, prov. Munfter.

ANGALIA, fee *Annaly*.

ANGER-ROCK, fit. off the coaft of the bar. of Lecale, co. Down, prov. Ulfter.

ANGLESBOROUH, a fair town in co. Limerick, prov. Munfter: fairs held 26 Apr. July, Sept. and Nov.

ANNACLOY, a place fit. S. of Kilmore on a branch of Strangford lake, in co. Down, prov. of Ulfter.

ANNACOTTY, a village in co. Limerick, prov. Munfter, 91 miles diftant from Dublin.

ANNADORN or *Anadorn*, a fair town, fit. in bar. Kinelearty, co. Down, prov. Ulfter: fairs held 14 May, and 8 Nov. Here was the principal feat of the *Macartanes*.—Alfo the name of a river, which rifes from this place, (called alfo *Black-Staff river*) which takes a S. W. courfe, and falls into the N. end of the inner bay of Dundrum; over which river, clofe to the bay, a bridge is erected for the convenience of travellers.

ANNADOWN, fit. in bar. Clare, co. Galway, prov. Connaught. An abbey was founded
here

here, in a remote age, of which St. *Meldan* was abbot, so early as the 7th century : his feast is observed on the 7th Feb.—This place is now a vicarage, in dioc. of Tuam.

ANNADUFF, a rectory, in dioc. of Ardagh, fit. in bar. Leitrim, prov. Connaught ; otherwise called *Annaghduff*. An abbey was erected here in 766.

ANNAGELIFFE, a vicarage, in dioc. of Kilmore, fit. in bar. Loughtree, co. Cavan, prov. Ulster.

ANNAGH (or *Anagh*) a pretty village near Charleville, co. Cork, prov. Munster. Here stood a strong castle, that in the wars of 1641, was for four years garrison'd at the expence of fir Philip Perceval, bart. and by its situation, (being then in the midst of a bog) was deemed impregnable ; but it was at last taken in 1645, by treachery, and the whole garrison put to the sword, in cold blood, by order of the lord Castleconnel, who then commanded the Irish army, consisting of 5000 horse and foot; and was an inveterate enemy to fir Philip Perceval, because he had refused to give him his daughter in marriage before the war. This castle was demolished by the earl of Egmont, who drained the ground, built the village of Annagh, and established the linen manufacture therein.—This is also the name of a place in bar. Inishowen, co. Donegal, prov. Ulster.—Also in bar. Lower Ormond, co. Tipperary, prov. Munster.—Also in bar. Tullaghgarry, co. Cavan, prov. Ulster.—Also a town in bar. upper Iveagh, co. Down, prov. Ulster ; lat. 54: 19, lon. 6: 46.—Likewise in bar. Igrin, co. Kilkenny, prov. Leinster.—And in bar. Costello, co. Mayo, prov. Connaught.—There is also a peninsula of same name in bar. Erris, in same co.—And two islands, one in the same barony ; and another in bar. Tyrawly, in same co.—also a village in bar. Drumahare, co. Leitrim, prov. Connaught.—also a rectory in dioc. of Ardfert, fit in bar. Corcaguinny, co. Kerry, prov. Munster.

ANNAGHDUFF, see *Annaduff*.

ANNAHOLE, fit. by the coast of the bar. of Mourne, co. Down, prov. Ulster.

ANAKEEN, fit. in bar. Clare, co. Galway, prov. Connaught.

ANNA-LIFFY, a river rising in co. Wicklow, prov. Leinster, from whence it runs W. to Kildare, then winding N. E. passes thro' the city and co. Dublin, and falls a little below Dublin, into the Irish channel.

ANNALONG, a river and small harbour in co. Down, prov. Ulster ; sometimes called *Islealong* : the village of same name, fit. near this harbour, is distant about 69 miles from Dublin.

ANNALY, or *Angalia*, is a district comprehending the antient N. Teffia, and the present co. Long. prov. Lein. the chiefs of this district, were formerly denominated *Hy Ferghael*, (or the prince of the men of *Ghael*,) by corruption, O'Ferral. The descendants of this antient family were in possession of the N. W. and S. parts of the co. Longford, on the commencement of the last century, but were dispossess'd of the E. parts by the English settlers, the *Tuites* and *Dellameres*. Annaly was also called *Conmacne*: and gives title of baron to the family of *Gore*.

ANNATRIM, fit. in bar. upper Ossory, Queen's co. prov. Leinster.—here is now a parish church, where an abbey was founded in 550 by St. *Mochoemore*, alias *Pulcherius*.

ANNA-DAN Islands; fit in bar. Moycullen, co. Galway, prov. Connaught.

ANNER. fit. in co. Tipperary, prov. Munster. It gives title of baron to the family of Carleton, the Rt. honourable Hugh Carleton, chief justice of his majesties court of common pleas in Ireland, being created baron Carleton of Anner 17 Sep. 1789.

ANNGROVE, a fair town in co. Cork, prov. Munster :—fairs held 25 Mar. 25 May, 15 Aug. 29 Sept. and 26 Dec.

ANNISCAVERY, fit. in bar. O'Neland, co. Armagh, prov. Ulster.

ANNVILLE, fit. near *Rathangan*, co. Kildare, prov. Leinster, where are excellent flower mills, erected by Mr. John Montgomery.

ANTICURBRIDGE, fit. in co. Antrim, prov. Ulster.

ANTRIM, the most N. E. county of the prov. of Ulster; it is bounded E. and N. by the sea, S. by the county Down, and W. by the counties Londonderry and Tyrone. It contains about 387,200 acres, 77 parishes, 8 baronies, and 5 boroughs, and returns 10 members to parliament, also gives title of earl to the noble family of *Mc. Donnell.* — Its extent from N. to S. is 44 miles, and from E. to W. 24 ; number of houses 29,122, and inhabitants 160,000.—Its baronies are Massareen, Antrim, Toome, Kilconwuy, Dunluce, Cary, Glenarm, and Belfast, exclusive of the county of the town of Carrickfergus. It is watered by many small rivers, and it's chief mountains are those of Slenish and Knocklaid. In this as in the other northern counties the linen is the principal manufacture, the ⅞ wide linens of this co. are chiefly bleached and finished in the neighbourhood of Ballymena and Antrim ; some few of the finest sorts are finished in the neighbourhood of Belfast ; many of the ⅞ wide linens are bleached in the interior parts of the co. but the greatest part of that width and those of the best quality are bleached near Belfast and Lisburn, and finished in the highest order, together with the principal part of the yard-wides, which compose a very large share

of

of the trade of the prov. which is eftimated at £263,200 yearly.—The principal antient families of this diftrict were the *O'Neil's*, *Mc. Donald's*, *O'Hara's* and *O'Sheil's*.——Antrim is the name alfo of a borough, market, fair and poft town, the capital of this county, fit. at the N. end of Loughneagh 13 miles W. of Carrickfergus, and about 84 N. of Dublin, lat. 54:45. lon. 6:26. Fair days 12 May and Nov. This borough fends two members to parliament propriet. the earl of Maffareen. It has a ftately caftle, long the refidence of the illuftrious family of Skeffington, whofe title is derived from the barons Maffareen in this co.—here is one of the antient round towers——an abbey alfo was founded here by *Durtract*, a difciple of St. Patrick; it is now a vicarage in the dioc. of Connor——there is alfo a barony of fame name in this county which is bounded by the baronies Glanarin, Belfaft, Toome, and Kilconway.

ANY, a vicarage in the dioc. of Limerick, this village is fit. about 12 miles S. E. of that town, on a pleafant river, in the bar. fmall county, co. Limerick, prov. Munfter. A friary for Eremites, following the rule of St. Auguftine, was founded here in the reign of Henry 2nd. — On the 21 June 23 Eliz. a leafe was made to Edw. Abfley and I. and M. Abfley of this friary for the term of 40 years, at the annual rent of 47*l.* 7*s.* 6*d.*—the ruins of this building are ftill vifible. Here we find a noble caftle adjoining the river, and a fmaller one in the village, both of which belonged to the earl of Defmond.

AOIBH-LIATHAIN, part of the antient diftrict called by the Irifh antiquaries, *Dergtenach* and *Corcaduibhne*, and by Ptolemy *Vodic*, the chiefs of which obtained the name of *Hy Lehane*, from whence *O'Lehane*, a branch of which family obtained the appellation of *O'Anamhchadha*. They were difpoffefs'd by the Barries; whence their country was denominated Barrymore: now a bar. in co. Cork, prov. Munfter.

AONACH, an antient town in lower Ormond, and capital of the antient diftrict of Eoganacht Aine Cliach, now *Nenagh* in co. Tipperary, prov. Munfter. Near this place Brien fon of Mahon Menevy O'Brien in 1370, obtained a compleat victory over his uncle Turlogh, affifted by the Englith forces, under the command of the earl of Defmond, from which battle he obtained the fir-name of Brian Catha-an-Aonaig, or Brian of the battle of Nenagh.

APPLESHIELD, fit. in bar. Atherdee, co. Louth, prov. Leinfter.

ARADH-CLIACH, a diftrict in co. Tipperary, prov. Munfter, the antient proprietors of which were the O'Briens.

ARAGLIN, fit. in bar. Coffmore, co. Waterford, prov. Munfter: alfo a river of fame name fit. in bar. Condons, co. Cork, prov. Munfter.

ARBELLA, a fmall village in co. Kerry, prov. Munfter, fit. about 138 miles from Dublin; a mile beyond which are the ruins of Ballycarthy caftle.

ARBOE, or *Ardboe*, a rec. in dioc. of Armagh, fit. in bar. Dungannon, co. Tyrone, prov. Ulfter. This village is but poor, and fit. on the river Ballinderry, two miles W. of Loughneagh. A noble and celebrated monaftery was founded there by St. Colman, whofe reliques were long preferved in it; but it was deftroyed by fire in 1166—there ftill remain here the walls of an old church, with a crofs about 15 feet high, on which are feveral infcriptions.

ARCHDALE, a *Caftle* in bar. Lurge, co. Fermanagh, prov. Ulfter.

ARCHERSTOWN, fit. in bar. Delvin, co Weftmeath, prov. Leinfter.

ARCHIME, fit. in bar. Kilmacrenan, co. Donegal, prov. Ulfter.

ARD, an antient diftrict in the N. W. part of the co. Tipperary, prov. Munfter; comprehending originally both upper and lower Ormond, being generally denominated *Eogan Ara*, whofe antient chiefs were called from thence Egan-ara, or Owen-ara; and fometimes Mc. Egan, whofe defcendants were in poffeffion of the northern parts of Lower Ormond in the beginning of the laft century. But the fouthern, or upper Ormond in an early period, appertained to another branch of the fame family, called Hy Dun-Eogan (by corruption O'Donegan)— O'Donegan was difpoffefs'd of his territory in 1318 by the defcendants of Brien Rua king of Thomond, who from thence were called the O'Briens of Ara; and who remained in poffeffion of the greateft part of it, in the beginning of the laft century.

ARDAGH, a village, alfo a bifhop's fee, fit. about 6 miles S. W. of Edgworthftown, in the bar. of fame name, county Longford, prov. Leinfter. There are fairs held here on 5 Apr. and 26 Aug. This fee extends into part of fix counties, viz. Cavan, Leitrim, Sligo, Rofcommon, Longford, and Meath. The church is one of the moft antient in Ireland. St. Mæll, a difciple of St. Patrick and his fifter's fon, is faid to have been placed over this church before the year 454, as bifhop and abbot.—In 1658, it was united to the bifhoprick of Killmore, but in 1692, Dr. Ulyffes Burgh, was appointed to it feparately. Upon his death, in the fame year, it was united to Killmore, and continued fo 'till Dr. Hort was promoted from thofe fees to the archbifhoprick of Tuam in 1741, when they were again feparated, and *Ardagh* was annexed to the archbifhoprick; which union has continued ever fince, though the dioc. of Elphin intervenes between them. The bifhoprick of *Ardagh* is rated in the king's books, at 11*l.* per. Ann.

and

and *Tuam* at 50*l.* but they are worth 4000*l.* The only remains of the cathedral is part of a wall, built with large ftones, which from its prefent appearance, muft have been, when entire, a very fmall building. There is alfo another place of fame name, near Ruthkeale, in bar. Conillo, co. Limerick, prov. Munfter, where there are fairs held on 11 May, 14 Aug. and 21 Nov.— Lat. 53 : 34 lon. 8 : 8. —— Alfo a town in co. Leitrim, prov. Connaught ; lat. 53 : 56 lon. 8 : 22.—Alfo a village in bar. Carberry, co. Cork, prov. Munfter, lat. 51 : 32 lon. 9 : 16.—Alfo a village in bar. Morgallion, co. Meath, prov. Leinfter, lat. 53 : 54 lon. 7 : 14 : — And alfo a vicarage in dioc. of Killala, fit. in bar. Tyrawly, co. Mayo, prov. Connaught.

ARDAMINE, a curacy in dioc. of Ferns, fit. in bar. Ballagheen, co. Wexford, prov. Leinft.

ARDARAGH, a fair town in co. Donegal prov. Ulfter. — Fairs held 15 May, 1 Aug. 1 Nov. and 22 Dec.

ARDART, fee *Ardfert*.

ARDBOE, fee *Arboe*.

ARDBRACCAN, a neat village in bar. Navan, co. Meath, prov. Leinfter, the place of refidence of the bifhops of Meath. It takes its name from *St. Braccan*, who was abbot here: The abbey was plunder'd by the Danes in 886, and again in 940. Ardbraccan ftands 3 miles W. of Navan, and about 25 N. W. of Dublin, lat. 53 : 40, lon. 7. 0. It has a handfome church and charter fchool, the latter was endowed by the late Dr. Maule, lord bifhop of Meath, with two acres of land belonging to the fee, rent free in perpetuity, whereon the fchool houfe is built—He granted alfo a leafe of 18 acres more, contiguous to the fame, at 5*s.* per. acre, for which he took no rent during his incumbency, and renewed without fine. The late Samuel Gerrard efq, of Clangill, in the co. Meath, bequeathed 40 fhillings per. Ann. for 40 years towards the fupport of this fchool, to be paid by the then Mr. Thomas Gerrard of Lifcarton, in fame co.

ARDCANDRISK, a rectory in dioc. of Ferns, fit. in bar. Shelmaliere, co. Wexford, prov. Leinfter.

ARDCANNY, a rectory in dioc. of Limerick, fit. in bar. Kenry, co. Limerick, prov. Munfter.

ARDCARNE, a village and vicarage in dioc. of Elphin, fit. in bar. Boyle, co. Rofcommon, prov. Connaught.

ARDCATH, a vicarage in dioc. of Meath, fit. in bar. Duleek, co. Meath, prov. Leinfter.

ARDCAVAN, a curacy in dioc. of Ferns, fit. in bar. Shelmaliere, co. Wexford, prov. Leinfter.

ARDCLEAVE, or *Ardcleave*, a village in bar. Coleraine, co. Londonderry, prov. Ulfter.

ARDCLINNIS, fit. in bar. Glenarm, co. Antrim,

prov. Ulfter, otherwife called *Ardeclinnis* or *Ardelinnis*. It is a rectory in dioc. of Connor.

ARDCOLLUM, a rectory in dioc. of Lifmore, fit. in bar. Iffa and Offa, co. Tipperary, prov. Munfter.

ARDCOLM, a curacy in dioc. of Ferns, fit. in bar. Shelmaliere, co. Wexford, prov. Leinfter.

ARDCRONEY, a rectory in dioc. of Killaloe, fit. in bar. lower Ormond, co. Tipperary, prov. Munfter.

ARDEA, a *Caftle*, fit. in bar. Clanfrought, co. Kerry, prov. Munfter. It is kept in repair and inhabited.—Alfo a rectory in dioc. of Kildare, fit. in bar. Portnehinch, Queen's co. prov. Leinfter.

ARDEATH, a fair town in the co. Meath, prov. Leinfter.—Fairs held 7 May, 21 June and 27 Oct.

ARDECLEAVE, fee *Ardcleave*.

ARDECLINNIS, fee *Ardclinnis*.

ARDEE, or *Atherdee*, a borough, market and poft-town, fit. in bar. of fame name, in co. Louth prov. Leinfter, 34 miles N. W. of Dublin, lat. 53 : 50½, lon. 6 : 40. —— Fairs held 6 June 20 Aug. 23 Oct. and 17 Dec. It fends 2 members to parliament : patronage in the Ruxton family.——This place gives title of *Baron* to the family of Brabazon, earls of Meath. Roger Pippard, lord of Ardee, erected a magnificent caftle here, and founded a friary for crouched friars of the order of St. Auguftin, A. D. 1207.—A carmelite friary was alfo founded here in the reign of Edw. 1ft, the church of which filled with men, women and children, was burn'd to afhes in 1315, by the Scots and Irifh, under the command of Edw. Bruce. — Ardee is now a vicarage in the dioc. of Armagh. — The bar. of Ardee, is bounded by the baronies of Louth and Ferrard, the Irifh fea, and part of the counties Monaghan and Meath. *Ardee* is alfo the name of a parifh and village, fit. on the river Barrow, about a mile S., of Athy, co. Kildare, prov. Leinfter: it was once a town commanding a ford and pafs over the river, on the great fouthern road to Dublin; and antiently called *Athardriogh*, or the ford of the royal-height, being fit. on a rifing ground, and is celebrated for a battle fought here in the 10th century, between the Irifh and the Danes. It feems to have been a Danifh ftation, as a rath or fort ftill remains called *Dunbrin*, on the W. fide of the river, commanding the ford, in which a great number of Danifh coins have been found. The town was fit. oppofite the fort, on the E. fide of the river; feveral ftreets of which may ftill be traced, particularly one called Botharbollagher, or the ftreet of the great road, leading to the town of Ardfcul. Here, after the arrival of the Englifh, a caftle was erected, in which was a garrifon in the reign of Queen Eliz. and a number

ber

her of her coins were found on the old fcite.—
This town fell into decay on the eftablifhment
of Athy: the only remains now vifible are the
rath and the ruins of a church: the road alfo
which led thro' it is ftill obfervable on both
fides of the river for fome miles; and feems to
have been paved.

ARDELINIS, fee *Ardelinnis*.

ARDERAGH, fit. in bar. Carberry, co. Cork,
prov. Munfter.

ARDERE, fit. in co. Sligo, prov. Connaught.

ARDERONY, fit. in bar. lower-Ormond, co.
Tipperary, prov. Munfter.

ARDES, an antient bar. in co. Down, prov.
Ulfter, bounded E. and S. by St. George's
channel, W. for the moft part by the lake
Strangford, and N. by Carrickfergus-bay. The
whole territory was antiently called the heights
of Ulfter, near the eaftern fea; *Ard* fignifying
high in Irifh. This place produces large quantities of barley, and a kind of oats called light-
foot-oats; here is good marl and the *ore-weed*,
from which they make much kelp. Several
Englifh families, particularly the *Savages*,
fettled here as early as the 12th century, under
John De Courcy, and maintained themfelves
a long time in a flourifhing condition.—Ardes
bar. was antiently a co. in itfelf, for we find
by a patent roll of 1ft Hen. 4th (A. D. 1400)
in Bermingham's tower, that the faid king
granted to Robert Fitz Jordan Savage, the office of Sheriff of the Ardes in Ulfter.

ARDFERT, a borough town and bifhop's fee
in bar. Clanmorris, co. Kerry, prov. Munfter,
diftant from Dublin 144 miles; lat. 52 : 10,
lon. 9 : 40.—Fairs held here on 27 March,
Whitfun monday and 9 July.—The family of
Crofbie, (now earl of Glandore,) was created
Vifc. Crofbie, of *Ardfert*, in 1771. This borough
returns two members to parliament—patron,
the earl of Glandore, who has his country
refidence at this place. The fee is faid to have
been founded by St. *Ert*, in the 5th century;
it was otherwife called *Ardart*, and was fuccef-
fively governed by its own bifhops, 'till 1663,
when it was united with Aghadoe to the fee of
Limerick. St. *Brendan* or *Brandon* erected a
fumptuous monaftery here, in the 6th century:
in 1089 the abbey and town were deftroyed by
fire; the town was again reduced to afhes by
Cormac O'Cullen in 1151; it fuffered the
fame fate in 1179, and the abbey was totally
deftroyed. Thomas lord Kerry founded a monaftery here in 1253, probably on the fcite of
the antient abbey, the date of the foundation
is infcribed over the great gate, and the founder
was interred here in 1280. The ruins of the
nave and choir of the cathedral, (which is
dedicated to St. Brandon) is but 26 yards long
and 10 broad; the E. window was large and

lightfome, being 26 feet high; the church was
demolifhed in the wars of 1641, it has a number of grave-ftones, one of which has the
effigy of a bifhop carved in relievo, lying in
his pontificals, faid to have been the tomb of
bifhop *Stack*, who died in 1488. In this cathedral are the remains of a fine figure in alto
relievo, of St. Brandon; oppofite the end of
the church are the ruins of one of the antient
round towers, it was 120 feet high; a great
part of which fell down in 1770. Behind lord
Glandore's houfe, over an arch, is an infcription in relief, done in a mafterly manner;
but the characters are unknown, nor could it
be decyphered even by that excellent orientalift
and antiquarian, Dr. Pococke, late bifhop of
Offory: it appears to bear fome refemblance
to the Ethiopic character.—The fee of Ardfert
is rated in the king's books, at 12*l* 13*s* 4*d* per
ann. but united with Limerick, is worth 3,500*l*.

ARDFIELD, a vicarage in dioc. of Rofs, fit.
in bar. Ibawn, co. Cork, prov. Munfter.

ARDFINNAN, a rectory in dioc. of Lifmore,
fit. in bar. Iffa and Offa, co. Tipperary, prov.
Munfter; having the ruins of an old caftle
built on a rock, which overlooks the river
Suir; it was erected by king John, (fon of
Henry 2d) when he was earl of Moreton, and
lord of Ireland, in 1186.—St. Finian founded
an abbey here, which was plundered and
burnt by the Englifh forces in 1178.—A monaftery was alfo founded here, for conventual
francifcans.

ARDGLAS, fit. in bar. Slieumargy, Queen's
co. prov. Leinfter; about 4 miles N. of Carlow.—Its name imports a high green hill.—Tho'
it is called *Ardglas church*, it is now a Roman
catholic chapel, built, as tradition reports,
above 100 years ago by a lady of the family
of the *Hartpoles*, who have a large property
in its vicinity. It is erected in the form of a
crofs and thatched; in one arm of the crofs
is a fmall chapel, wherein the antient family
of the *Graces* have their interment; this family
are defcended from the Graces who came over
with *Strongbow*, and are fubfcribing witneffes
to the earl of Pembroke's charter to St. John's,
Kilkenny, A. D. 1220. Branches of them
fettled at Ballylinch, at Carney, and Leighan
in the co. Tipperary, and at Shanganagh,
afterwards called *Gracefield*, in the Queen's co.

ARDGLASS, a rectory in the dioc. of Cloyn;
now a decayed, but once a principal town in
the bar. Lecale, co. Down, prov. Ulfter.—Here
is a long range of building in the caftle ftile,
called by the inhabitants, *the new works*; altho'
they have no tradition for what ufe they were
intended; it is fit. clofe by the harbour, a
rocky fhore, and wafhed by the fea on its N.
end and on the rere; its front is to the W.

it

it extends 250 feet in length, in breadth only 24; the thickness of the walls 3 feet. It has three towers in front joined to it, one at each end and one at the centre, which shews the design uniform and elegant. It has been divided into 18 different apartments, and the same number above, with a stair-case in the centre; each of the towers has three rooms, 10 feet square, with broad flagged floors, so contrived and lodged in the walls, that they support each other without any timber; each apartment on the ground floor, had a small gothic door, and a large square window, which seems to denote they were shops or ware-rooms, occupied at some very early period, by merchants who came from sea. Here were no fire places; the rooms on the ground floor have been 7 feet high, the upper rooms but 6½, in each of which rooms is a small water-closet, the flue of which runs down thro' the wall, and was washed at bottom by the sea.—Within 10 feet of the south tower of this building stands a square castle, called *Horn-castle*, from the great quantity of ox, deer, and cow horns found about it; 'tis 40 feet by 30, consists of two stories, and from the fire places and other marks, appears to have been the kitchen and dining-hall belonging to the merchants.—Near to this is another small castle, called the Cowed castle.—King's castle is a large building, now in repair and inhabited, it stands W. and over the principal gate to the land side.—Jordan's castle stands in the centre of the town, and appears to have been the citadel; it is a very elegant pile, and tho' it has stood upwards of 180 years without a roof, not a stone of it has failed; at the door is a fine spring-well; there are the remains of other castles and gates, whose names are lost: It is observable, that so late as the beginning of Cha. 1st. reign, the duties of the port of Ardglass were let to farm. This place lies 7 miles N. E. of Downpatrick; it formerly gave title of earl to the family of *Cromwell*, as it has since given that of viscount to the family of *Barrington*.—*Ardhol church* which was near it, was antiently the parish church of Ardglass, but it was defecrated by a cruel murder, committed by the Macartanes, on the whole congregation, at a Christmas midnight mass: there is a very curious natural cave, with a very large entrance on the shore, within the N. E. point of Ardglass harbour.

ARDGROOM, a *harbour*, in co. Kerry, prov. Munster.

ARDHOL-CHURCH, sit. near *Ardglass*, in bar. Lecale, co. Down, prov. Ulster.—It was antiently the parish church of Ardglass, but was defecrated by a cruel murder committed by the Macartanes, on the whole congregation, at a Christmas midnight mass.

ARDIONICE, sit. in co. Down, prov. Ulster. Here was a Franciscan friary, but the time of it's foundation is unknown.

ARDINAN, sit. at the mouth of the river Ban, in co. Londonderry, prov. Ulster.

ARDISTOWN, sit. in bar. Ardes, co. Down, prov. Ulster.

ARDKEEN, sit. in bar. Ravilly, co. Carlow, prov. Leinster. Also a place near Newtown-Ardes, co. Down, prov. Ulster.

ARDLIMORE, sit. in bar. Tyraghrill, co. Sligo, prov. Connaught.

ARDMACNASCA, sit. by Lough-Neagh, co. Antrim, prov. Ulster. An abbey was founded here by *Laifrean*, who died 25 Oct. 650.

ARDMAGH, fee *Armagh*.

ARDMAGIL, sit. in bar. Kenoght, co. Londonderry, prov. Ulster.

ARDMAIL, sit. in bar. Middlethird, co. Tipperary, prov. Munster.

ARDMAN, sit. in bar. Ballaghkeen, co. Wexford, prov. Leinster; also in bar. Colerain, co. Londonderry, prov. Ulster.

ARDMILLAN, a place where a Challybeate water was difcovered in the bar. of Castlereagh, close on the edge of the bar. of Duffrin; and by the lake Strangford: about midway between Killileagh, and Newtown, in co. Down, prov. Ulster.

ARDMORE, a village and rectory belonging to the dioc. of Lismore, sit. in bar. Decies, within Drum, co. Waterford, prov. Munster. The name signifies a great eminence: it was antiently an episcopal fee, erected by faint *Declan*, the first bishop of it, in the infancy of the Irish church; and confirmed by St. Patrick in the synod of Cashel, held in 448.—St. Declan was born in this co. and was of the family of the *Desii*.—There are at present the remains of two antient churches belonging to Ardmore: one sit. on the edge of a cliff near the sea, which is quite in ruins, near which on the strand, they shew you St. Declan's stone, which they say swam miraculously from Rome, conveying upon it St. Declan's bell and vestments. The other church stands about a mile N. W. of the former: it has some curious figures in alto relievo; and by its appearance seems very antient. Here is one of the antient round towers. Ardmore was antiently a Danish settlement, for thereabouts are several vestiges of that people: as circular entrenchments, &c. There is at present the stump of an old castle: not long since was a much larger one, which is taken down. There is also another place of this name, in bar. Belfast, co. Antrim, prov. Ulster.—And one sit. near Youghal in co. Cork, prov. Munster.

ARDMORE-BAY, sit. in bar. Decies within Drum, co. Waterford, prov. Munster.

ARDMORE-HEAD, a noted promontory on the coast of Ireland, which forms the E. side of
Youghal

Youghal harbour, fit. in co. Waterford, prov. Munfter.

ARDMOY, fee *Armoy.*

ARDMULCHAN, fit. near Painftown, in bar. *Duleek,* co. Meath, prov. Leinfter. A perpetual chantry of one prieft was eftablifhed here in the church of St. Mary; who was conftantly to celebrate fervice therein.—*Archd. Monaft.*—It is now according to Dr. Beaufort a rectory in the dioc. of Meath, he names it *Ardmulcan,* and places it in the barony of Skreen or Skrine, fame co.

ARDNACRANA, fit. in co. Weftmeath, prov. Leinfter; a monaftery founded for Carmelites, in the 14 century, by Rt. Dillon of Drumrany. On 20 Mar. 1545, the lands were granted to Sir Rt. Dillon of Newtown, and in the grant they are called the friars preachers of *Athnecarne.*

ARDNAGEHY, a rectory in dioc. of Cork, fit. in bar. Barrymore, co. Cork, prov. Munfter.

ARDNAGLASS *village* and *bay,* fit. near Sligo, in co. Sligo, prov. Connaught. 'Tis fometimes written *Ainaglafs.*

ARDNAREE, otherwife called *Arnaree,* a fair town in co. Mayo, prov. Connaught—fairs held 20 June, 10 Oct. and 13 Dec. A monaftery for Eremites, following the rule of St. Auguftin, was built here in 1427.

ARDNECARNE, fee *Ardnacrana.*

ARDNECLAW, fit. in bar. Middlethird, co. Waterford, prov. Munfter.

ARDNORCHER or *Ardnurcher,* fit. in bar. Moycafhel or Moyafhel, co. Weftmeath, prov. Leinfter. It is alfo called *Horfe-leap.*—Here was an antient ftately ftructure, founded by Sir Hugh de Lacey; tradition fays, that in this place and during the building thereof, the faid Sir Hugh was treacheroufly flain by a common labourer; as he was ftooping down to give fome directions to his workmen, who beat out his brains with a fpade: this gentleman, it is faid, was low and fmall of ftature, and from thence nick-named *Petite,* and from him the *Petits* of this country claim their defcent. Ardnorcher is a vicarage in dioc. of Meath.

ARDNURCHER, fee *Ardnorcher.*

ARDOYNE, fit. in bar. Shillelagh, co. Wicklow, prov. Leinfter.

ARDPATRICK, a fair town in bar. Cofhlea, co. Limerick, prov. Munfter, 19 miles S. of Limerick city. St. Patrick founded an abbey here, of which fcarce any hiftorical account can be found. Fair days, 17 March, 25 Apr. 22 Sept. and 17 Nov.——Alfo a village in bar. Louth, co. Louth, prov. Leinfter; where a church was erected by St. Patrick.

ARDQUIN, a rectory in dioc. of Down; fit. in bar. Ardes, co. Down, prov. Ulfter. The word is a corruption of *Ard-Cuan,* fignifying a height over the lake Strangford, formerly called lough Cuan. This place is otherwife

called Abacey, and has a handfome feat; which has continued in the family of *Echlin* for many generations, even before the rebellion of 1641

ARDRA, fit. near the fea, in co. Donegal, prov. Ulfter; about 131 miles from Dublin: it is a chapelry in the dioc. of Raphoe.—Alfo a village fit. near *Millgrove,* in Kings co. prov. Leinfter; having a good bridge, over the *Violet-river.*

ARDRAHIN, a fair town in bar. Dunkellin, co. Galway, prov. Connaught. Fair days 21 May, 12 Sept. and 12 Nov. It is a vicarage in the dioc. of Kilmacduagh.

ARDREE, a curacy in dioc. of Dublin. fit. in bar. Kilkea, co. Kildare, prov. Leinfter.

ARDRISTAN, a curacy in dioc. of Leighlin, fit. in bar. Ravilly, co. Carlow, prov. Leinfter.

ARDRUMEN, fit. in bar. Longford. co. Longford, prov. Leinfter.

ARDRUSS, fit. in co. Sligo, prov. Connaught.

ARDRY, fit. in bar. Antrim, co. Antrim, prov. Ulfter.

ARDS, a village in bar. Kilmacrenan, co. Donegal, prov. of Ulfter.—Alfo a bar. otherwife called *Ardes,* fit. in co. Down, prov. Ulfter. This bar. is bounded by that of Caftlereagh, the Irifh fea and the lake Strangford. See *Ardes.*

ARDSALLAGH, a fair town in co. Rofcommon, prov. Connaught. Fair days, 1 Jan. 1 Wed. O. S. in May, 30 July and 19 Oct.—— Alfo a village in bar. Navan, co. Meath. prov. Leinfter; 'tis fit. on the river Boyne: St. Finian founded a monaftery here, and died 12 Dec. 563. This is now a rectory in dioc. of Meath, and gives title to the family of *Ludlow,* created vif. Prefton of Ardfallagh, co. Meath, in 1760.

ARDSALLIS, fit. in bar. Burrin, co. Clare, prov. Munfter. This is one of the principal horfe fairs in Ireland.

ARDSCOL, fee *Mote of Ardfeol.*

ARDSEINLIS, fit. in bar. Tyreragh, co. Sligo, prov. Connaught. St. Patrick built a nunnery here, for St. Lalloca, the fifter of St. Mæll.

ARDSKEAGH, a rectory in dioc. Cloyne, fit. in bar. Condons, co. Cork, prov. Munfter.

ARDSRATH, fee *Rathlure.*

ARDSTRAW, a village and rectory in dioc. of Derry, fit. in bar. Strabane, co. Tyrone, prov. Ulfter: 97 miles from Dublin.

ARDTERMAN, fit. in co. Sligo, prov. Connaught.

ARDTREAGH,-CHURCH, fit. about 3 miles from Stewart's-Town, co. Tyrone, prov. Ulfter.

ARDTULLY, fit. in bar. Clanfrought and parifh of Kilgarvan, co. Kerry, prov. Munfter; near which are the veftigia of an antient building, which was by tradition a religious
houfe,

houſe, called *Monaſter ni-Oriel*, i. e. the abbey of Oriel. A caſtle was erected here about A. D. 1180.

ARDVARNEY, otherwiſe called *Ardvirney* or *Ardvary*: a *Church*, ſit. in bar. Lurge, near Enniſkillen, co. Fermanagh, prov. Ulſter.

ARGETROSS, an antient copper mine, in the mountains near the river Nore, whence ſilver was extracted; and according to antiquaries, money firſt coined in Ireland by Enius Kuber. It ſtood in lower Oſſory, and is ſuppoſed to be the modern village of Rathbeagh, ſit. within 5 miles of Kilkenny, and 3 of Ballyragget, in co. Kilkenny, prov. Leinſter. It is otherwiſe written *Argiodroſs*.

ARGITA RIVER, the antient name of a river or lough, in the N. of Ireland, mentioned by *Ptolemy*, and thought by ſome to be Lough Swilly, by others the river Ban, which proceeds from Lough Neagh: The word ſeems to be a corruption from the Britiſh Ergid or Ergit, which ſignifies literally the mouth or opening of the land, and therefore may be any bay: But Richard Cirenceſter thinks it is Lough Swilly, which is by no means improbable, as the form of that bay agrees perfectly with the ſignification of the word.

ARIGIDEEN, a river ſit. in co. Cork, prov. Munſter; the name ſignifies the ſilver river or ſtream: It diſcharges itſelf into the bay of Courtmacſherry.

ARIGNA-MINES, ſit. in bar. Drumahare, co. Leitrim, prov. Connaught. An extenſive Iron manufactory has been lately eſtabliſhed here, on the eſtate of Thomas Tenniſon eſq; by Meſſrs. O'Reilly of Dublin; from which they are diſtant about 100 miles.

ARKLOW, a vicarage in dioc. of Dublin, and neat market town, ſit. in bar. of ſame name, co. Dublin, prov. Leinſter: 12 miles S. of Wicklow, and 36 from Dublin: lat. 51 : 41 lon. 6 : 35. Fairs held 14 May, 9 Aug. 25 Sept. and 15 Nov. It lies on the river *Oroca*, near the Iriſh channel Here are the ruins of a caſtle of the late earls of Ormond, and a barrack for 2 companies of foot. Theobald Fitz-Walter founded a monaſtery here for Dominican friars; he died 26 Sept. 1285, and was here interred; a tomb, with his ſtatue thereupon, was erected over him; large ruins of this once famous ſtructure ſtill remain. At Arklow is a charter ſchool, to which the late lady viſc. Allen gave 20 acres of land and one of bog in perpetuity, and alſo £50 towards the building: the late alderman Bowen alſo bequeathed to this ſchool £10 per. Ann. to be paid out of the rent, ariſing out of Brian's holding in Arklow, during the continuance of the leaſe, which was made in 1745 for 3 lives or 31 years. Arklow has a haven for ſmall

D

craft. There are ſand banks hereabouts, called *Arklow banks*: the bar. of Arklow is bounded by the bar. of Newcaſtle and Balinacour, the co. of Wexford, and the Iriſh ſea. It gives title of baron to the family of *Butler*.

ARLES, a village ſit. in Queen's co. prov. Leinſter. Here is a Romiſh chapel by the ſide of the high-road which paſſes thro' this place, and it is remarkable that it has a burial place belonging to it, regularly walled in.

ARMAGH, there is a county, city and bar. of this name all in prov. Ulſter. The county of Armagh is bounded N. by L. Neagh, S. by Louth, W. by Tyrone and Monaghan, and E. by Down.—It contains 20 pariſhes, and 5 bar. viz. thoſe of O'Neiland, Armagh, Tyranny, Fews and Orior, and ſends 6 members to parliament. Its length from N. to S. is 25 miles, the breadth from E to W. 15 miles, having 21,983 houſes, in which there cannot be fewer than 120,000, inhabitants. In this county there is very little flat ground, but the gentle hills which diverſify the face of it, are covered in general with a very rich ſoil; except a ridge of mountains which run acroſs it, called *the Fews*. It has great improvements, and is principally inhabited by Proteſtants, and may be eſteemed the moſt populous county in Ireland. The linen trade of this county is eſtimated at £299,900 yearly: ——— Its weekly market is the beſt in Ulſter for 9, 10 and 11 hundreds of the beſt fabric. The bleach-greens of this co. are principally ſit. in the neighbourhood of Armagh and Keady, where they finiſh thoſe ſtrong yard-wide linens called "*ſtout Armaghs*," which are in great repute:—The moſt antient families of this co. are the O'Neils, O'Hanlons, Acheſons, and Brownlows. The *town of Armagh*, (formerly a celebrated city) and now a bor. market and poſt-town, where the aſſizes are held for this co. is ſit. about 30 miles S. of Londonderry and 62 N. of Dublin; on the river *Blackwater*. It ſends two members to parliament, patronage in the primate; and holds fairs on 28 May, 10 July, 12 Aug. Tueſday before 10th Oct. and 20 Nov.—lat. 54; 20½; lon 7 : 12;—It is an archbiſhoprick, the ſee of which extends into parts of 5 counties, viz. Armagh, Londonderry, Tyrone, Louth and Meath; it is charged in the king's books at 400l. per Ann. but is worth 8000l. The cathedral was antiently called *Druim-Sailec*, i. e. the church built with willows, and was founded by St. Patrick, who fixed his ſee here about A. D. 445.—In the years 670, and 687, it was nearly conſumed by fire; and on the arrival of the Danes, was frequently plundered by theſe pirates, its inhabitants put to the ſword, and the greater part of its books and records taken away and deſtroyed; an irreparable loſs to the eccleſiaſtical and civil hiſtory

and

and antiquities of Ireland. During these calamities the cathedral church being often destroyed, and as frequently repaired, was in the year 1262, rebuilt nearly in its present form by *Patrick O'Scanlan*, then bishop; whose successor, *Nicholas M'Molissa*, added to it several rich gifts and emoluments. It was made an archbishoprick in 1152, and continues to retain its dignity as metropolitan see of all Ireland:—In A. D. 1013, the bodies of king *Brian Boromh*, and his son *Murchaid*, with the heads of *Conaing* his nephew, and of *Mothlan* prince of the Decies, who fell in the battle of Clontarf, were brought hither with great funeral pomp, from the monastery of *Swords*.—The king was interred on the N. side of the great church, in a stone coffin by itself; and *Murchaid* and the head of *Conaing*, in another coffin on the S. side. In the market place of this town is a cross of two stones, with old basso relievos, representing Christ on the cross between two thieves; and some ingenious fret-work. Here are the the ruins of some abbeys—and a large and handsome barracks—the town has been considerably improved by his grace Dr. Rich: Robinson, Baron Rokeby, the present primate, who has erected several churches; also a superb palace, a school, library, and observatory, at his own expence. A charter-school was founded here in 1758, and endowed with a rent charge of 40*l.* per Ann. by Mrs. Drelincourt, widow of Dr. Drelincourt, dean of Armagh. His grace the then primate and the corporation of Armagh gave 20 acres of good land for the scite and accommodation of the school, rent free for ever.

ARMAGHBREGAGH, a fair-town in co. Meath, prov. Leinster.—Fairs held 19 May, 19 July, 24 Oct. and 7 Dec.

ARMAR's-HOLE, sit. in co. Down, prov. Ulster, so called from one James Armar being murder'd there by his son, about the year 1701, who deservedly suffer'd for the fact at the ensuing assizes.—'Tis a large hole on the brow of a hill, not far from the sea side: near it and not far from *Bealachancir-pass*, is a deep narrow cave wrought by the violence of the surges into a rock of flint.

ARMOY, or *Ardmoy*, a fair-town in bar. Carey, co. Antrim, prov. Ulster, fairs held 25 Jan. 25 Feb. 29 Mar. 25 May, 12 Nov. and 25 Dec. About 3 miles beyond Armoy church, near a plantation of trees, are some remarkable ruins of a castle.—This church, which is a vicarage in dioc. of Connor, is distant about 109 miles from Dublin; here one of the antient round towers has been erected.

ARNAGLASS, see *Ardnaglass*.

ARNAGRAGH, sit. in bar. Kilkenny-west, co. Westmeath, prov. Leinster.

ARNAREE, see *Ardnaree*.

ARNOES-VALE, sit. near Rostrevor, co. Down, prov. Ulster.

ARRA, a half bar. joined to that of *Owen*, sit. co Tipperary, prov. Munster; sometimes called *Owen* and *Arra*.

ARRAGELL, sit. in bar. Colerain, co. Londonderry, prov. Ulster: *St. Columb*, founded a monastery here, which is now a parish church in the diocese of Derry.

ARRAN, according to *Mr. Echard*, is a bar. in co. Galway, prov. Connaught; but we find none such in any present map or survey.

ARRAN-ISLES, the *(Canganij of Ptolemy)* sit. on the W. coast of Ireland, in the mouth of Galway-bay, co. Galway, prov. Connaught.—They are very fruitful, and produce a small kind of oats without any husk; and are remarkable for the stoutest calves in the county.—They are called the S. Isles of *Arran*, and gave title of earl to the noble family of *Butler*, lately extinct, and afterwards to that of Gore; they are three in number. — Lat. 53 : 00 : Lon. 10 : 00 : The largest of these Isles was called *Arranmore*, where several of the antient Irish saints were buried; whence it also obtained the name of *Arranancim*; the inhabitants are still persuaded that in a clear day, they can see from this coast *Hy Brasail*, or the inchanted Island, the paradise of the pagan Irish, and concerning which, they relate a number of romantic stories; these are called the south Isles of *Arran*, to distinguish them from another Island of the same name called the N. Isle of *Arran*, sit. on the coast of the co. Donegal, prov. Ulster, lat. 55: 00, long. 8 : 50.——At the greater Isle of *Arran* is *Dun-angus*, sit. on a high cliff over the sea; it is a circle of monstrous stones without cement, capable of containing 200 Cows.—Tradition says that *Angus*, king of Cashel, about the year 490, granted this Island to *St. Enna*, to build ten churches on. In 1020 the abbey erected here was destroyed by fire; and in 1081, this place was pillaged by the Danes: In 1334, the Isles of *Arran* and *Bophin* were plunder'd and burnt, and hostages were taken from thence by sir John D'Arcy, lord justice of Ireland, who surrounded the Island with a fleet of 56 sail.

ARRANMORE island,—there are two islands of this name, one in bar. Boylagh, co. Donegal, prov. Ulster; the other in bar. Moycullen, co. Galway, prov. Connaught; the latter is a rectory in the dioc of Tuam.

ARRIGLE *mountains*, sit. in bar. Kilmacrenan, co. Donegal. prov. Ulster.

ARROW *lough* and *river*, sit. in bar. Tyraghrill, co. Sligo, prov. Connaught; this lough is about 8 miles long, of a very irregular form, and full of islands; the river proceeding from it, runs northward to Ballysadere, and rushes at once into the sea in a stupendous cataract.

ARTANE,

ARTANE, an agreeable village, two miles and an half distant from the castle of Dublin, and about half a mile beyond the earl of Charlemont's seat, at Marino, in co. Dublin, prov. Leinster; the air is peculiarly wholesome, and instances of longevity are here very frequent: here are the fragments of an old church, overgrown with ivy, and venerable in its ruins; the church yard, full of antique tomb-stones, merits attention.

ARTAVER, sit. near Lough Garn, in bar. Boyle, co. Roscommon, prov. Connaught.

ARTHRAMEN, sit. in co. Wexford, prov. Leinster.

ARTHUR'S-TOWN, sit. near Ardee, co. Louth, prov. Leinster.

ARTIKELEY, sit. in bar. Kenought, co. Londonderry, prov. Ulster.

ARTRAMONT, a rectory in dioc. of Ferns, sit. in bar. Shelmaliere, co. Wexford, prov. Leinster.

ARTREA, a rectory in dioc. of Armagh, sit. in bar. Dungannon, co. Tyrone, prov. Ulster.

ARVAGH, a village in bar. of Tullaghronoho, co. Cavan, prov. Ulster.

ASDEE, sit. in bar. Iraghticonnor, co. Kerry, prov. Munster:—these lands with many others thereabout, (as *Carrigfoil*, &c.) were forfeited by the O'Connors of Kerry; partly in queen Eliz.'s time, and partly in 1641; and were, after the restoration of the royal family, granted to the University of Dublin. Near Asdee is a large enclosure of stone, called in Irish. a *Baun*, formerly built as a place of strength, to prevent cattle from being carried off by an enemy.

ASHBURY, sit. near Roscrea, co. Tipperary, prov. Munster.

ASHFIELD, sit. near Castleblakeney, co. Galway, prov. Connaught:—also, a place near Clonard, in co. Meath, prov. Leinster.

ASHGROVE, sit. in bar. Iverk, co. Kilkenny: another in bar. Balruddery, co. Dublin; both in prov. Leinster.

ASHPARK, sit. near Roscommon, co. Roscommon, prov. Connaught.

ASHROW-ABBEY, sit. near Ballyshannon, in co. Donegal, prov. Ulster; this piece of antiquity is worth attention; some of the gilding in the vault of the cloister is still visible. It was founded by Roderick O'Cananan, in 1178, and in 1377 the abbey was consumed by fire.

ASKEATON, see *Askeyton*.

ASKEYTON, or *Askeaton*, an antient borough town, in bar. Connello, co. Limerick, prov. Munster; sit. 16 miles W. of Limerick, and 110 from Dublin; lat. 52:26, lon. 9:20. It is now a vicarage in the dioc. of Limerick; it returns two members to parliament; patronage in the earl of Carrick, and the *Massey*

family; and holds fairs on 30th July, and 9th Oct. 'tis seated on the river *Shannon*, on the influx of the river *Deel* and is famous for its castle, built by the earl of Desmond, and one of the most beautiful and perfect abbeys in Ireland; the latter was of such consequence, that a provincial chapter of the order was held there in 1564.

ASSEY, a rectory in dioc. of Meath, sit. in bar. Deece, co. Meath, prov. Leinster.

ASTRAKO, sit. in bar. Boylagh, co. Donegal, prov. Ulster.

ATERITH, see *Athenry*.

ATHA, see *Rath-crayhan*.

ATHADDY, sit. in co. Carlow, prov. Leinster; about the year 1151, an abbey was founded here by Dermod, the son of Murchad, king of Leinster; for nuns of the order of St. Augustin.

ATHASSEL-ABBEY, sit. in bar. Clanwilliam, co. Tipperary, prov. Munster; here are the elegant remains of an Augustine priory, founded by *William Fitzadelm de Burke*, about A. D. 1200; it lies 3 miles distant from Cashel, and was dedicated to Edmund, the king and martyr; it is now a rectory in the dioc. of Cashel. *Fitzadelm* was steward to Henry 2d, and ancestor to the illustrious family of *De Burgho*; he died about 1204, and was here interred.—To this place, Richard, the red earl of Ulster, retreated from the world, after entertaining the nobility assembled at Kilkenny, in 1326, he died shortly after.—The choir of this priory, is 44 feet by 26, the nave was of the same breadth with the choir, supported by lateral ailes; by the external walls it measures 117 feet in length; in the S. W. corner is a small chapel; the steeple was square and lofty, and the cloisters were large; many curious sculptures, it is supposed, lie here concealed under the rubbish, as some have been lately discovered.—A castle was erected here about the year 1180; and in 1329, the town of Athassel was burnt to the ground.

ATHBOY, a borough and market town, in bar. Lune, co. Meath, prov. Leinster, sit. 3 miles S. W. of Trim, and 28 N. W. from Dublin; lat. 53:20, long. 7.2.—It has fairs on 4th May. 4th Aug. and 7th Nov. and sends two members to parliament; patron, Mr. *Bligh*. It is a vicarage in the dioc. of Meath; here was a friary of the order of the B. V. of mount Carmel.—A mile from Athboy, on the right, are the ruins of a church; and on the left, those of a castle.

ATHEAL, sit. in bar. Conillo, co. Limerick, prov. Munster.

ATHCLARE, sit. in bar. Ferrard, co. Louth, prov. Leinster; otherwise called *Acclare*.

ATHDORN,

ATHDORN, sit. in bar. Coshma, co. Limerick, prov. Munster; lat. 52:24, long. 9:7.

ATHENASSY, a rectory in dioc. of Limerick, sit. in bar. Small-county, co. Limerick, prov. Munster.

ATHENREE, see *Athenry*.

ATHENRY, or *Athenree*, an antient borough or corporate town in the bar. of same name in co Galway, prov. Connaught. It was formerly called *Aterith*, and is governed by a Portrieve; it gives title of baron to the family of *Bermingham*, premier baron of Ireland.——It is a post and fair town—has a barrack for three companies, and stands 8 miles E. of Galway, and 61 W. from Dublin. It sends two members to Parliment: patronage in the *Blakeney* family. lat. 53:14, lon. 8:48.—Fairs held 5 May, 2 July, and 28 Oct. Athenry was antiently called *Bealatha*, i. e. the place of beal on the waters; 'twas destroyed in 1133 by Conor O'Brien.——Here was a Dominican friary, which with other buildings was consumed by fire in 1432, also a Francisean friary was founded here in 1464 by Thomas earl of Kildare: it is now a rectory in the dioc. of Tuam. The bar. of Athenry is bounded by the baronies of Clare, Doonkillen, Loughrea, Leitrim, Longford, Clonnacowen, Kilconnel, Tiaquin and Downamore.

ATHERDEE, see *Ardee*.

ATHGOE sit. in bar. Newcastle, co. Dublin, prov. Leinster.

ATHLACCA, a village in bar. Coshma, co. Limerick, prov. Munster. It is a vicarage in dioc. of Limerick.

ATHLAGGIN, a village in bar. Clare, co. Galway, prov. Connaught.

ATHLEAGUE, a fair town in bar. Athlone, co. Roscommon, prov. Connaught: fairs held 11 July, 24 Sep.——distance from Dublin 73 miles.—*Mayleffa O'Hannyn*, who was abbot of this place, died A. D. 1266—it is now a vicarage in dioc. of Elphin.

ATHLONE, a vicarage in dioc. of Meath: it was formerly a bishoprick, but is now a borough, market and fair town, sit. on both banks of the river Shannon, partly in the bar. of *Athlone* and partly in that of Brawny—this town being part in the co. Roscommon, prov. Connaught, and part in the co. Westmeath, prov. Leinster, which co. are here united by a bridge, in the middle of which was erected a fair monument, with some figures well cut in marble: together with Queen Eliz's. escutcheon of arms, and some inscriptions declaring the time and the founders of the building. On the corner of the castle wall, was a tower founded by king John, on a parcel of land belonging to St Peter's Abbey—It was built on a high raised hill, resembling a Danish fort or rath. On the side of the castle that faced the river, there were

apartments which served for the residence of the lord president of Connaught, and governor of the castle: the middle tower was for the repository of warlike provisions. Since the presidency was dissolved, the castle with its demesnes and revenues were granted in fee to the grandson of lord Ranelagh, who was president of Connaught in 1641; but all the beauty and strength of this place is now decayed: the whole town having been destroyed by fire, during the fury of the war, in the rebellion of that year. Here were antiently two convents or monasteries, the one on the Connaught side called St. Peter's; the other on Westmeath side, for Franciscans, founded by *Cathal Cruyarig* (i. e. of the *red first*) but he did not live to finish it, that being done by sir *Henry Dillon* in 1244, who lies buried here.—Athlone gave title of earl to the family of *Ginkle*, as a reward for the general of that name, having passed the river Shannon in the face of the Irish army 1691, who were then strongly entrenched on the opposite shore. There are generally two troops of horse and 4 companies of foot quartered here; and it is a noted pass from the prov. of Leinster into that of Connaught: it is governed by a sovereign, bailiffs, and recorder—and sends two members to parliament—patronage in the families of *Handcock*, and *St. George*. —— Fairs held on the first Monday after twelve days after old Christmas day, 21 Mar. Wednesday before Ascension day, and 1st Monday in Sept. lat. 53:23½ distance from Dublin 59 miles.—Near Athlone is a chalybeate water of an excellent quality. The bar. of Athlone lies in the prov. of Connaught, and is bounded by Lough Ree, the river Shannon, and the baronies Roscommon, Ballinoe and Moycarne, and part of the co. Galway.

ATHLUMNEY, sit. near Navan, in bar. Skryne, co. Meath, prov. Leinster. Here are the ruins of the castle and church of Athlumney, once a noble structure, and said to have been burnt by one M'Guire, who dreaded the approach of Cromwell, after his taking Drogheda. This is now a vicarage in dioc. of Meath.

ATH-MAIGHNE, (or the plain of the shallow water) a place in co. Westmeath, prov. Leinster; but where is uncertain.—It is however distinguished by a bloody battle fought there between Turlough O'Brien king of Munster, and Turlogh O'Connor king of Connaught, in 1152; when O'Connor was entirely defeated, with the loss of 9 chiefs, and 900 common men.——*Ath Maighne* was probably a little to the N. of Lough Derrevarragh, in the parish of Maina, and half bar. of Fore.

ATHNECARNE otherwise called *Ardnacrana*, sit. in co. Westmeath, prov. Leinster. A Carmelite friary, according to some, or a Dominican friary, according to others, was founded here

ATHY

in the 14th. century, by Robert Dillon, of Drumrany, the lands of which were, on the 20 Nov. 1545, granted to sir Robert Dillon, of Newtown.

ATHNET, a rectory in dioc. of Limerick, sit. in bar. Coshma, co Limerick, prov. Munster.

ATHNOWEN, a rectory in dioc. of Cork, sit. in bar. Muskerry, co. Cork, prov. Munster.

ATHTACKA, a village in bar. Coshma, co. Limerick, prov. Munster.

ATHY, a borough, market and post-town, sit. in bar. of Narragh and Rheban, co. Kildare, prov. Leinster: it stands on the river Barrow, 10 miles S. of Kildare, and 32 S. W. from Dublin: it returns 2 members to parliament: patronage in the duke of Leinster. Fairs held 17 March, 25 Apr. 9 June, 25 July, 10 of Oct. and 11 Dec. Lat. 52 : 59 : 45" lon. 6 : 56 : 30" W. of Greenwich, and 42' W. of Dublin.—The neighbouring country is pleasant, a lime-stone soil, better adapted for agriculture than pasturage. The place where the town stands was an antient ford leading from the principality of Leix, in Queen's co. to that of Celleagh or Cuellan, in co. Kildare. According to Keating, a battle was fought here in the 2d. or 3d. century, between the people of Munster, and those of Leix, under Laviseagh Cean Mordha. This town owes its foundation to two monasteries erected on different sides of the river, at the entrance of an extensive wood, in the 13th. century. That on the W. side of the river, was founded by Richard de St. Michael, lord of Rheban, under the invocation of St John, for crouched friars; it was at the dissolution granted in Aug. 1575 to Anthony Power, which reverting to the crown, was granted by statute 17 and 18 of Charles the 2d. to dame Mary Meredith: part of the walls of the church still remain. The monastery on the E. side was founded in 1253 for Dominicans, by the families of *Boisel*, and *Hogan*; it was granted with its appurtenances, 24th January, 35th of Henry the 8th, A. D. 1544, to Martin Pelles in capite for ever, at the annual rent of 2s. 8d. Irish money: no remains of this abbey now exist, except the postern gate, commonly and corruptly called Preston's gate. In 1308, the town was burned by the Irish; and in 1309, John lord de Bonneville, slain near the town of Arstol or Ascul, was interred in the church of the abbey of St. John. In 1315, Athy was plundered by the Scots under Robert Bruce, who gained the battle of Ascul, in which were slain Hamond le Grace and sir William Prendergrest, and on the side of the Scots, sir Fergus Andressan and sir Walter Murry; all of whom were buried in the Dominican abbey. In 13th of James 1st. A. D. 1615, that king granted a charter, constituting the market-town of Athy a borough, &c. to be governed

E

by a recorder, sovereign, two bailiffs and a town-clerk; it is now alternately with *Naas*, the assizes town for the co. Kildare; it is a vicarage also in the dioc. of Dublin. The church was erected about 1740, the county-court-house sometime after, and the barracks about 25 or 30 years since; here is also a Roman Catholic chapel, and a Quaker's meeting house; also a public school for the classics, with a subscription of 40l. viz. 20l. from the duke of Leinster, 15l. from the corporation, and 5l. from the representatives of —— Weldon esq. Gerald the 8th earl of Kildare, for the purpose of securing the English pale, erected several castles, and amongst others that of Athy, at the foot of the bridge, about the year 1506, of which there only now remains a tower. In 1575, this castle was repaired and enlarged by one William White, from whence it obtained the name of White's castle: the remaining tower is now used as a prison, being an appendage to the co. goal of Naas. In 1642, the earl of Ormond arrived in this town, with 3000 foot and 500 horse, to relieve the neighbouring garrisons of Carlow, Maryborough and Ballynakill, &c.—In 1648, the Irish, under *Owen Roe O'Neil*, were in possession of it; but it was taken in 1650, by colonels Hewson and Reynolds. Near Athy is *Woodstock castle*, which had been built about the time of the foundation of St. John's abbey, by Richard St. Michael, lord of Rheban, as an appendage to the palatinate of Dunnamaes, granted to the earl of Pembroke. About the year 1424, Thomas the 7th earl of Kildare, then lord *Offaly*, married Dorothea, daughter of Anthony More of Leix; and with her obtained the manors of Rheban and Woodstock; and in them erected a court baron, and court leet, which are still held.

ATTANAGH, a rectory in dioc. of Ossory, sit. in bar. upper Ossory, Queen's co. prov. Leinster.

ATTEMAS, a vicarage in dioc. of Achonry, sit. in bar. Gallen, co. Mayo, prov. Connaught.

AUDLEY-CASTLE, in co. Down, prov. Ulster, boldly sit. on an eminence, commanding a prospect of the whole lake of Strangford, to the very N. end of it at Newtown, and is built on a tongue of land, hanging over the lake. It was erected by one of the *Audleys*, who settled here under John de Courcy, in the infancy of the English government; and which family is not long extinct.

AUDLEY-ROAD, sit in co. Down, prov. Ulster; it forms a part of Strangford bay, on the W. side; where ships may lie safely.

AUGHABOE, see *Aghaixe*.

AUGHADOE or *Aghadoe*, see *Achadoe*.

AUGHANLOO, a rectory in dioc. of Derry, sit. in bar. Kenoght, co Londonderry, prov. Ulster. AUGHA-

Aughanunchin, a rectory in dioc. of Raphoe, fit. in bar. Kilmacrenan, co. Donegal, prov. Ulster.

Aughdediff, fit. in bar. Kilmacrenan, co. Donegal, prov. Ulster.

Aughebutt, fit. in bar. Antrim, co. Antrim, prov. Ulster.

Augher, a borough town in bar. Clogher, co. Tyrone, prov. Ulster ; fit. 12 miles S. W. of Dungannon, and 75 miles from Dublin.—Lat. 54 : 24, lon. 7 : 20. It holds fairs 28th March, 12th of May, 14th of Aug. and 12th Nov. Sends 2 members to parliament. Proprietor lord *Caledon.*

Augheraghan, fit. in bar. Killyan, co. Galway, prov. Connaught.

Aughnacloy, a fair town fit. by the river Blackwater, in bar. Dungannon, co. Tyrone, prov. Ulster ; in which fairs are held on 6 Jan. 14 May, 5 July, 10 Oct. and the second Thursday in Nov. distant from Dublin 71 miles. About two miles beyond Aughnacloy is *Lifmore fort,* now in ruins.

Aughnishe, a rectory in dioc. of Raphoe, fit. in bar. Kilmacrenan, co. Donegal, prov. Ulster.

Aughrim, or *Aghrim,* fit. in co. Galway, prov. Connaught ; famous for the battle fought there at *Kilcomodon-hill,* on the 12 July 1691, between the Irish forces, under king James 2d, commanded by M. St. Ruth, and the forces of king William 3d, commanded by general Ginkle, in which the latter proved victorious. St. Ruth, was killed in this engagement, together with 7,000 of his men ; but of the English, only 600 ; the victory was the more remarkable, as the English army confisted of no more than 18,000 men ; whereas the Irish were computed at 20,000 foot and 5,000 horse and dragoons. The Irish also loft 9 pieces of cannon, all their ammunition, tents and baggage, most of their small arms, which they threw away to expedite their flight, with eleven standards and 32 pair of colours. — Aughrim is distant from Dublin, about 75 miles.

Aughterard, a small town in co. Galway, prov. Connaught; having a barrack in it.

Ausoba, the antient name of a river in the W. of Connaught, mentioned by Ptolemy, and fuppofed by Ware to be the river Galvia, in co. Galway ; but by Camden and Baxter, *Loughsrb* : — It is indeed extremely difficult to ascertain its exact fituation ; Richard of Cirencefter, makes it *Clew-bay,* in co. Mayo, but as it was a place frequented by foreign merchants, the bay of Galway feems the most probable place.—— It is also called *Aufona.*

Ausona, fee *Aufoba.*

Austrinum, a promontory in the S. of Ireland, mentioned by Rich: Cirenceft : it is the fame as the notium of Ptolemy, and thought by Camden to be *Beer-head,* but most probably it was *Miffen-head* at the entrance of Dunmanusbay, in bar. Carbery, co. Cork, prov. Munster.

Auteræ, an antient city mentioned by Ptolemy, as the capital of the Auterii, who are thought by fome to be the inhabitants of the co. Galway and Rofcommon, prov. Connaught.

Avenmore, otherwife called Blackwater, a river in co. Kerry, prov. Munster. — Alfo a river in the co. Wicklow, prov. Leinster, otherwife called *Avonmore.*

Avondale, a handfome feat, fit. on the river Avenmore, co. Wicklow, prov. Leinster : it lies near Rathdrum, and exhibits a beautiful diverfity of fcenery in the higheft perfection.

Awbeg, a river.fit. in co. Cork, prov. Munster.

Awin-Banna, a river in bar. Gorey, co. Wexford, prov. Leinster.

Awin Buy, a river in bar. Kinalea, county Cork, prov. Munster.

Awin-Ea, a river in bar. Boylagh, co. Donegal, prov. Ulster.

Awin-Gorm, a river in bar. Leney, co. Sligo, prov. Connaught.

Awin-More, a river in bar. Tirawly, co. Mayo, prov. Connaught.—Alfo another in bar. Leney, co. Sligo, fame prov.

Awin-Ure, a river in bar. Rofcommon, co. Rofcommon, prov. Connaught.

Awn, otherwife *Emly,* or *Elmly,* a village in bar. Clanwilliam, co. Tipperary, prov. Munster, lat. 52 : 20, long. 8 : 42.—Its antient name was *Imleach-jobhuir,* or the land of the lake of the western diftrict. It is fit. about 14 miles W. of Cafhel, on the borders of a lake, and was formerly a bifhoprick, under the name of *Emly,* founded by *St. Albe,* towards the clofe of the 4th century, fome years before the arrival of St. Patrick : the church was afterwards tranflated to Cafhel.—The city was plundered by robbers in 1125, and the mitre of *St. Albe* burned : it was alfo deftroyed by fire in 1192, but was afterwards rebuilt, and continued a confiderable town for feveral ages ; even 'till the time of Hen. 8th, in whofe reign *Thomas Hurly,* bifhop of *Emly,* erected a college for fecular priefts, but the only remains at prefent of this antient, and perhaps firft ecclefiaftical city in Ireland, are the ruins of a church, fome walls, a large unhewn stone crofs, and a holy well.—The fee of *Emly* was united to that of Cafhel in 1568.

Aylrue, fit. in bar. Clanderlaw, co. Clare, prov. Munster.

B A.

BADONEY. There are two rectories of this name in the dioc. of Derry, called *upper* and *lower* Badoney; each sit. in bar. Strabane, co. Tyrone, prov. Ulster.

BAG and BUN-POINT, sit. near Feathard, co. Wexford, prov. Leinster.

BAGATELLE, sit. near Clonard, co. Meath, prov. Leinster.

BAGENBON-HEAD, a cape in bar. Shelburne, co. Wexford, prov. Leinster.

BAGGATROT-CASTLE, sit. in co. Dublin, prov. Leinster, about 1½ mile from the castle of Dublin. Scarce any remains of this antient strong hold are now visible: it was formerly extensive and important, and the scene of several severe engagements. It held out for some time against the parliament's forces headed by *Oliver Cromwell*; but that experienced commander taking it by storm, demolished the greatest part of it, leaving only one tower or battlement standing. Since that time it has been gradually decaying, and now exhibits but a very small remnant of its former greatness: the upper part, which threaten'd destruction to passengers, was in 1785 taken down, and the remaining part of the tower filled up with rubbish, and closed at the top; in which state it now remains.

BAGNAL, a name for the town of *Newry*, in co. Down, prov. Ulster; so called in remembrance of Marshal *Bagnal*.

BAGNAL'S-ARMS, a place so called, within two miles of Carlow, and 41 from Dublin; prov. Leinster.

BAGNAL'S-BRIDGE, sit. in bar. Idrone, co. Carlow, prov. Leinster, 47 miles distant from Dublin.

BAGNAL'S-TOWN, or *Bagnel's-town*, sit. in co. Carlow, prov. Leinster, 3 miles south of Leighlin-bridge: it was intended to have been erected into one of the best towns in the kingdom, by the name of *Versailles*. A magnificent square court-house, and several other buildings were raised, with stone of different kinds, intermixed with marble: over the river Barrow it has a beautiful bridge. It was the intent of the proprietor to have brought the great road thro' this town, instead of *Loughlin's-town*; but he failed in the attempt, and a stop was put to the farther progress of the buildings, after an immense expense incurred.

BAILLIEBOROUGH, sit. in bar. Clonchee, co. Cavan, prov. Ulster, 43 miles from Dublin, a mile beyond which is a very pleasant lough, and nearer to it is *Baillieborough-castle*. There is a challybeate spring at this place; and fairs are held 17 Feb. 17 May, 15 June, 17 Aug. 14 Oct. and 17 Nov.

BAILLYBORROW, sit. near Kells, co. Meath, prov. Leinster.

BALBRIGGEN, a small sea port town, much improved by the late baron *Hamilton*, and sit. in bar. Balruddery, co. Dublin, prov. Leinster— distant between 15 and 16 miles from Dublin. It is principally supported by its fishery; a cotton manufactory is also established here; and a pier has been built, by parliamentary encouragement, within which ships of 200 tons can lay their broad sides, and unload on the quay. Such vessels bring coals and culm from *Wales* and other places. The base of the pier is 18 feet thick, and on the outside is a considerable rampart of great fragments of rock, sunk to defend the pier against the waves. Fairs are held here 29 April, and Sep. Half a mile from Balbriggen are the ruins of *Bremore Castle*.

BALCARRA, sit. in co. Mayo, prov. Connaught, 115 miles from Dublin, within a mile and half of which are the ruins of two castles.

BALDONGAN, sit. in bar. Balruddery, co. Dublin, prov. Leinster, about 14 miles from the Metropolis, and two miles from Rush. Here was once a famous castle, now in ruins: boldly sit. on a rising ground, and commanding an extensive prospect. It consists on the W. end of two square towers, with a parapet in front, covering a passage between each; from these towers a regular building is carried on each side, but narrower: to which a similar tower is joined at the N. E. angle; but at the S. E. angle is only a small tower, in which are the stairs leading to the battlements. On the front are the arms of the lords of Howth. This place, tradition says, has been at different times a friary and a nunnery: that whilst it was in the latter capacity, it was besieged by a party of armed men, whereupon the nuns, in a fit of despair, threw themselves from the windows. It appears to have been erected in the 13th century, and intended rather as a lordly habitation than a place of defence: It was the seat of *Rd. Bermingham Esq.* whose sister and heiress *Ann*, married *Sir Chr. St. Lawrence*, lord of *Howth*, who died 20 Apr. 1542, when this castle became the property of the *Howth* family. Oliver Cromwel batter'd this castle from his ships, and many of the balls have been found in digging near it. A few feet S. E. from the square, is a small chapel with a large chancel; and on the W. end a square steeple, with stairs leading to the top, where there are two apertures for bells. Adjoining the chapel is a cemetery, in which are several tomb stones.

BALDOYLE or *Bulldoyle*, a large fishing village, in bar. Coolock, co. Dublin, prov. Leinster; about 6 miles from the metropolis; pleasantly
sit.

fit. or a branch of St. George's channel. It is extremely delightful in the summer season, and well accommodated for the purpose of bathing. The air is pure but keen, the place standing much exposed: it enjoys a good prospect of Howth, Ireland's eve, and Lambay island: and is a curacy in the dioc. of Dublin.

BALDWIN'S-TOWN, fit. in bar. Bargie, co. Wexford, prov. Leinster; 79 miles from Dublin.

BALEEK, a village in bar. Fews, co. Armagh, prov. Ulster.

BALEGART, fit. near Drogheda, prov. Leinster.

BALFEIGHAN, a village in bar. Deece, co. Meath, prov. Leinster: It is a rectory in dioc. of Meath.

BALINAGAR, fit. in co. Galway, prov. Connaught; 83 miles from Dublin, within a mile and half of which, are the ruins of an antient abbey.

BALINTRA, fit. in co. Roscommon, prov. Connaught, 83 miles and an half from Dublin; three miles and an half from this place, on the side of *Lough Allen*, are the ruins of Currag church.

BALISLAND, fit. in bar Shillelagh, co. Wicklow, prov. Leinster.

BALL, or *Balla*, see *Ballagh*.

BALLA, or *Ball*, see *Ballagh*.

BALLAGAN, fit. in bar. Dundalk, co. Louth, prov Leinster.

BALLAGAN-POINT, a cape fit. in bar. Dundalk, co. Louth, prov. Leinster. It is otherwise written Ballaghan-point.

BALLAGDAREEN, see *Ballaghadireen*.

BALLAGEEN or *Bolloghkeen*, a bar. in co. Wexford, prov. Leinster, in which is a village of same name.

BALLAGH, fit. in bar. Balruddery, co. Dublin, prov. Leinster.—Also a village otherwise called *Balla* or *Ball*, fit. in bar. Clanmorris, co. Mayo, prov. Connaught, 107 miles from Dublin, where an abbey was erected by *St. Mochuo*, generally called *Cronan*; he died 30th March 637, at the age of 75 years. Here is one of the antient round towers and a celebrated holy well. This place is a vicarage in dioc. of Tuam, and has fairs on the 11 June, 24 of Sep. and 7 Nov.

BALLAGHADIREEN, fit. in bar. Costello. co. Mayo. prov. Connaught, 89 miles from Dublin; within 2½ miles of which are the ruins of a castle. This village is otherwise called *Ballagdareen*, and holds fairs on 25th March, 1st May, 23d of June, 1st Aug. 7th Sep. 1st Nov. and 22d of Dec.

BALLAGHANERY BAY, fit. in co. Down, prov. Ulster.

BALLAGHAN-POINT, see *Ballagan point*.

BALLAGHEEN, see *Ballageen*.

BALLAGHMORE, a village in bar. Ossory, Queen's co. prov. Leinster. Here are the ruins of a castle, and within a few miles are the remains of Monaincha abbey. According to Dr. Beaufort, there is a vicarage of this name in dioc. of Dublin, fit. in bar. Kilkea and Moone, co. Kildare, prov. Leinster.

BALLAGHNEED, fit. in co. Tyrone, prov. Ulster; 78 miles from Dublin.

BALLAGH-TOBIN, fit. near Callan, in bar. Kells, co. Kilkenny, prov. Leinster. It is a rectory in dioc. of Ossory.

BALLAGHY: There are 3 villages of this name. The 1st in bar. Leney, co. Sligo, prov. Connaught; about 20 miles S. of Sligo, and 105 from Dublin: lat. 53 : 48, lon. 8 : 55.—The 2d in co. Mayo, fame prov. 97 miles from Dublin.——The 3d in bar. Loughlinsholen, co. Londonderry, prov. Ulster; 92 miles from Dublin: where are fairs on the 12th May and Nov.

BALLAN, a vicarage in dioc. of Leighlin, fit. in bar. Forth, co. Carlow, prov. Leinster.

BALLANAGOR, fit. in bar. Dunluce, co. Antrim, prov. Ulster.

BALLANAGORE, fit. near Kilbeggan, co. Westmeath, prov. Leinster.

BALLANALIE, otherwise called *St. Johnstown*, fit. in co. Longford, prov. Leinster.

BALLANE, a vicarage in dioc. of Clonfert, fit. in bar. Athenry, co. Galway, prov. Connaught.

BALLARD'S-POINT, a cape in bar. Ibrickan, co. Clare, prov. Munster.

BALLASEDERE or *Ballasodare*, fit. in co. Sligo, prov. Connaught, 100 miles from Dublin; where there is a waterfall, with very magnificent ruins of an antient abbey. The river here breaks over the rocks in a most romantic manner, from edge to edge, in many falls, before it comes to the principal one, which is about 14 feet perpendicular: the scenery about it is bold, the features of the mountains are great, and *Knocknaree* in full relief: if the falls were thro' a dark wood, the scenery would be amongst the finest in the world. This place is also written *Ballysedere*.

BALLDERIN, fit. near Roscommon, co. Roscommon, prov. Connaught.

BALLEA-CASTLE, a large ruin, fit. one mile W. of Carigaline, in co. Cork, prov. Munster.

BALLEEK, see *Belleek*.

BALLEE, a rectory in dioc. of Down, fit. in bar. Lecale, co. Down, prov. Ulster.

BALLEGUARCY, fit. in co. Leitrim, prov. Connaught.—A monastery for conventual franciscans, was founded here in 1518, by *Cornelius O'Brien*.

BALLENGARY, fit. near Ardfert, in co. Kerry, prov. Munster; here is the mouth of the river Shannon.

Shannon, and the ſcite of an old fort, ſeparated from the country by a chaſm of a prodigious depth, thro' which the waves drive, the noiſe of which is ſo great when the wind ſets in W. S. W. as to be heard at many miles diſtance; and hereby the country people foretell the approaching ſtate of the weather.

BALLGATHRINO, ſit. in bar. Ferrard, co. Louth, prov. Leinſter.

BALLGREEN, ſit. near Drogheda, co. Louth, prov. Leinſter.

BALLGRIFFIN, ſit. in bar. Coòlock, co. Dublin, prov. Leinſter.

BALLIALOGH, ſit. near Randal's-town, co. Antrim, prov. Ulſter.

BALLIBOFY, a fair town in co. Donegal, prov. Ulſter; fair days 21 May and 24 Dec. 'Tis ſit. in bar. Raphoe, 113 miles from Dublin, and otherwiſe written *Ballibofey*. Four miles from it are the ruins of a caſtle.

BALLIBOGHAN-ABBEY, (now in ruins) was ſit. near Clonard, in co. Meath, prov. Leinſter: it was for ſome time called the priory *de Laude Dei*, and was founded in the 12th century by *Jordan Comin*, for canons of St. Auguſtin; in the beginning of 1446 it was conſumed by fire. It is otherwiſe called *Ballybogan*; and is now a curacy in dioc. of Meath.

BALLIBOUGHAN, ſit. in co. Mayo, prov. Connaught.

BALLIBRACK, ſit. in half bar. Rathdown, co. Dublin, prov. Leinſter.

BALLIBREGAN, ſit. in bar. Cranagh, co. Kilkenny, prov. Leinſter.

BALLIBUR, ſit. in bar. Shelilogher, co. Kilkenny, prov. Leinſter.

BALLICARY, ſit. near Sligo bay, co. Sligo, prov. Connaught.

BALLICLARE, a fair town in co. Antrim, prov. Ulſter; fairs held 2d Tueſday O. S. in May, July and Nov.

BALLICLOGH, a fair town in co. Cork, prov. Munſter; fairs held 5 Aug. 19 Sept. and 6 Oct.

BALLIDONNELL, ſit. in bar. Arklow, co. Wicklow, prov. Leinſter.

BALLIDORE, ſit. in bar. Morifk, co. Mayo, prov. Connaught.

BALLIDUAN-WEST, a fair town in co. Clare, prov. Munſter; fairs held 24 June and Nov.

BALLIELLIN, ſit. in bar. Idrone, co. Carlow, prov. Leinſter.

BALLIGIBBERT, ſit. in bar. Glenarm, co. Antrim, prov. Ulſter.

BALLIHANESS, a fair town in co. Mayo, prov. Connaught. Fairs held 1 June, 2 July, 22 Sept. and 29 Oct.

BALLIHOUGHTER, ſit. near Elphin, co. Roſcommon, prov. Connaught.

BALLIKERRY, ſit. in Rathlin iſland, co. Antrim, prov. Ulſter.

F

BALLILEAGUE, a fair town in co. Roſcommon, prov. Connaught. Fairs held on the day after Trinity Sunday, and 3 Monday O. S. in Oct.

BALLIMACLOGHNA, ſee *Kellymount*.

BALLIMOE, a tract of land divided into two parts or baronies, each called the barony of half Ballymoe, they are reſpectively ſit. in the co. Galway and Roſcommon, prov. Connaught; in the latter is a ſmall village called Ballimoe.

BALLIMONEY, ſee *Bullymoney*.

BALLIMOON, ſee *Ballymoon*.

BALLIMORE, ſit. in bar. Rathconrath, co. Weſtmeath, prov. Leinſter, 50 miles from Dublin; 'tis a market and fair town ſeated on the W. ſide of lough Scuddy.—Here was formerly a ſtrong garriſon of the Engliſh forces, towards the latter end of the wars of 1641; this garriſon ſeated on the ſkirts of the lake, was divided from the main land by a deep and large graff, with ramparts of earth and bulwarks; the ditch was carried ſo low as to receive 3 or 4 feet of the reſtagnant water of the lake, over which was by a draw-bridge the entry into the fort; this was the chief fortreſs of this county, ſeated midway between Mullingar and Athlone, being about 10 miles diſtant from each:——adjoining to this place, is the old diſſolved monaſtery of *Plary*: Ballymore is now a curacy in the dioc. of Meath, and was famous for its abbey of the order of Gilbertines, founded in the 12th century: and in 1338, *Theobald de Vernon*, lord of the manor, obtained a grant of a weekly Saturday market, and a fair to be held for 15 days:—an antient abbey is ſaid to have been founded here, in or before the year 700:—there is alſo a rectory of ſame name, in dioc. of Ferns, ſit. in bar. Forth, co. Wexford, prov. Leinſter.

BALLIMORE-EUSTACE, ſee *Ballymore Euſtace*.

BALLIMOTE, ſit. in bar. Corran, co. Sligo, prov. Connaught; 5 miles E. of *Achonry*:——here the ſept of *M'Donogh* built a ſmall monaſtery, for franciſcan friars of the third order; the remains of it are at the lower end of the town, and the E. window is remarkably curious.

BALLIMULTON, ſit. in bar. Upper Oſſory, Queen's co. prov. Leinſter.

BALLINA, a poſt town, ſit. in bar. Tiravly, co. Mayo, prov. Connaught, 120 miles from Dublin, and 14 miles N. of Caſtlebar; lat. 54:4. lon. 9:10. It holds fairs on 12 May, 3 June and 12 Aug. two miles beyond it are the ruins of Connor caſtle; and a little farther, the ruins of *Roſerk-Abbey*.—Alſo a village of ſame name in bar. Balagheen, co. Wexford, prov. Leinſter.—And another in bar. Doonkillen, co. Galway, prov. Connaught.

BALLINABOY, a curacy in dioc. of Cork, ſit. in bar. Kinalea, co. Cork, prov. Munſter.

BALLIN-

BALLINACARGY, fit. in bar. Moygoifh, co. Weftmeath; prov. Leinfter, near 46 miles from Dublin; near which is a fine feat belonging to lord *Sunderlin*. Alfo a village in bar. Tullagh-arvey, co. Cavan, prov. Ulfter.

BALLINACARIG, a fair town in co. Cavan, prov. Ulfter. Fairs held 12 Feb. 12 May, 6 Aug. and 22 Nov.—Alfo a village in co. Wicklow prov. Leinfter.—And alfo a vicarage in dioc. of Leighlin, fit. in bar. Catherlough, co. Carlow, prov. Leinfter.

BALLINACHORA, fit. near *Middletown*, co. Cork, prov. Munfter. Where is a high fepulchral Mount, being one of the antient tumuli.

BALLINACLASH, fit. according to Mr. *Scale*, in bar. *Arklow*, but placed by Dr. *Beaufort* in bar. *Ballinacor*, in co. Wicklow, prov. Leinfter.

BALLINACLOGH, a rectory in dioc. of Emly, fit. in bar. Coonagh, co. Limerick, prov. Munfter. Alfo a vicarage in dioc. of Killala. fit. in bar. upper Ormond, co. Tipperary, prov. Munfter.

BALLINACOR, fee *Ballynacour*.

BALLINACOURTENY, a vicarage in dioc. of Tuam, fit. in bar. Dunkellin, co. Galway, prov. Connaught.

BALLINACOURTY, fee *Ballynacourty*.

BALLINACREAGH, a village in bar. Carbury, co. Cork, prov. Munfter.

BALLINAFAD, fit. in bar. Tiraghrill, co. Sligo, prov. Connaught, about 88 miles from Dublin; on the left of which are the ruins of a caftle, and 3 miles beyond it, are the ruins of *Ballindown-abbey*. Alfo a fair town in co. Rofcommon, prov. Connaught: fair day 27 Aug.

BALLINAFEAGH, a vicarage in dioc. of Dublin, fit. in bar. Claine, co. Kildare, prov. Leinfter.

BALLINAGAR, fit. in bar. Gefhill, King's co. prov. Leinfter: 41 miles from Dublin, within 3 miles of which are the ruins of a church.

BALLINAGH, a fair town in co. Cavan, prov. Ulfter: fairs held Thurfday before Eafter, 5 June, and Aug. 2 Oct. and 21 Dec.

BALLINAGLISH, a vicarage in dioc. of Killala, fit. in bar. of Tirawly, co. Mayo, prov. Connaught.

BALLINAGULLOCK, a vicarage in dioc. of Ferns, fit. in bar. Bargie, co. Wexford, prov. Leinfter.

BALLINAHAGLISH, a vicarage in dioc. of Ardfert, fit. in bar. Truachnacmy, co. Kerry, prov. Munfter.

BALLINAHINCH, fee *Ballynahinch*.

BALLINAKELLY, fee *Ballynakelly*.

BALLINAKILL, fee *Ballynakill*.

BALLINALACK, fit. in bar. Corkerry, co. Weftmeath, prov. Leinfter, near 47 miles from Dublin; within a mile of which are the ruins of a caftle.

BALLINAMULLARD, a village fit. in bar. Tyrefkennedy, co. Fermanagh, prov. Ulfter. Fairs held 12 Feb. 5 Apr. and Aug. and 21 Oct. It is otherwife written *Ballinamullard*.

BALLINAMONA, fee *Ballynamona*.

BALLINAMORE, fee *Ballynamore*.

BALLINAMULLARD, fee *Ballinamallard*.

BALLINANAGHT, fit. in co. Cavan, prov. Ulfter, above 54 miles from Dublin, within about 2 miles of which are the ruins of Ballintemple church.

BALLINARD, a vicarage in dioc. of Emly, fit. in bar. Small co. co. Limerick, prov. Munfter.

BALLINASLOE, a poft and fair town, fit. in bar. Clonmacow, co. Galway, prov. Connaught, near 72 miles from Dublin, remarkable for it's great fairs of wool, cattle &c. fairs 27 March, 4 Jul. and from 5 to 9 Oct. lat. 52: 48 lon. 7: 42.

BALLINASKELLIG, fee *Ballynafkellig*

BALLINAVAR, a fair town in co. Cork, prov. Munfter—fairs held on 4 Sept.

BALLINCALLA, a rectory in dioc. of Tuam, fit. in bar. Kilmain, co. Mayo. prov. Connaught.

BALLINCARRAGH *mountains*; fit. in bar. Erris, co. Mayo, prov. Connaught.

BALLINCLARE, a fair town in co. Kerry, prov. Munfter, fairs held 1 May and 4 Oct.

BALLINCOLLY, a large caftle fit. 4 miles from Cork, prov. Munfter. It was an antient feat of the *Barretts*. Anno 1600, W. Barrett of Ballincolly fubmitted to the Queen's mercy, having been concerned in Defmond's rebellion. This caftle was garrifoned by Cromwell; and in the late wars, for king James the 2d.—it is built on a rock, and flanked with towers at each angle.

BALLINDAGGIN, fit. in co. Mayo, prov. Connaught, near 100 miles from Dublin. Fairs held here 23 May, 22 Jul. 11 Oct. and 7 Dec.

BALLINDEE, a rectory in dioc. of Cork, fit. in bar. Carbury, co. Cork, prov. Munfter.

BALLINDERRY, a fair town fit. in bar. Ballinacor, co. Wicklow, prov. Leinfter——fairs held 21 April, 21 Aug. 29 Oct. firft Monday in Nov. and 2 Dec. Alfo a place in bar. Maffareen, co. Antrim, prov. Ulfter, diftant 73 miles from Dublin: near which are the ruins of *Portmore caftle*, and about a mile from it the ruins of a church—This is a vicarage in dioc. of Connor.—Alfo a river in bar. Tyrone, and a rectory of fame name in dioc. of Armagh, and bar. of Loughlinfholen, both fit. in co Londonderry, prov. Ulfter.

BALLINDINE, a village in bar. Clanmorris, co. Mayo, prov. Connaught.

BALLINDOWN, fit. in bar. Ballinahinch, co. Galway, prov. Connaught. It is a rectory in dioc. of Tuam—Alfo the name of an antient abbey now in ruins, fit. near Ballinafad, co. Sligo, prov. Connaught; it was founded in

1227 by the family of *Mc Donogh*; it's poffeffions were affigned to *Ed. Crofton.*

BALLINDRAIT, a village fit. in bar. Raphoe, co. Donegal, prov. Ulfter; diftant about 104 miles from Dublin.

BALLINDRENAN, fit. in bar. Ballycowen, King's co. prov. Leinfter.

BALLINDROGHED, fee *Bridgetown.*

BALLINECUR, fit. in bar. Delvin, co. Weftmeath, prov. Leinfter.

BALLINEEN, a village in bar. Carbery, co. Cork, prov. Munfter.

BALLINEFAGH, a vicarage in dioc. of Kildare, fit. in bar. Claine, co. Kildare, prov. Leinfter.

BALLINEGILL, fit. in bar. Scarewalfh, co. Wexford, prov. Leinfter.

BALLINEGROSS-CHURCH, fit. in co. Weftmeath, prov. Leinfter : it was built at the charge of the bar. and confecrated by the Rt. rev. *Henry Jones,* lord bifhop of *Meath,* in 1680; the patron thereof was *Walter Pollard, efq;* who beftowed the ground thereof, and a handfome church-yard for it.

BALLINESAGART, fit. in bar. Dungannon, co. Tyrone, prov. Ulfter : a monaftery was founded here in 1489, for Francifcans of the third order, by *Con O' Neal.*

BALLTINGADDY, a rectory in dioc. of Limerick, fit. in bar. Cofhlea, co. Limerick, prov. Munfter.

BALLINGARRY, a rectory in dioc. of Emly, fit. in bar. Cofhlea, co. Limerick, prov. Munfter ; diftant about 122 miles from Dublin : fairs held Eafter Monday, Whitfun Monday, 4 July and 5 of Dec.—There is alfo a vicarage of fame name, in bar. Connello, belonging to the dioc. of Limerick.—Alfo a place in bar. lower Ormond, co. Tipperary, prov. Munfter ; diftant near 71 miles from Dublin : which holds fairs on Whitfun-Monday, 23 July, 11 of Nov. and Dec.—Another place of this name is in co. Kerry, prov. Munfter, about 2 miles N. of *Ballyheigh* : it is a fmall caftle, built by col. *David Crofby,* together with fome intrenchments, as a defence to a narrow ifthmus that led to a fmall peninfula ; whither he retired with feveral Englifh families, during the wars of 1641, to avoid the fury of the Irifh : he built feveral houfes for them in the ifthmus, and caufed 2 covered ways to be made, from the caftle to a draw-bridge, which formed the peninfula, in order to have his people pafs and repafs with fecurity ; as he was fupplied by the means of the earl of *Inchiquin's* friends, with provifions from the co. Clare fide of the river Shannon, by water, he was enabled to defend the place above a year, when at length the draw-bridge being treacheroufly let down by one Kelly whom he had in his fervice, the

Irifh gained admiffion into the fortrefs ; nor did he hear any thing of the matter, (being then ill of the gout) until he was informed thereof by his niece ; in this condition he ftood on his defence in his chamber for fome time, and at laft obtained quarter with fome difficulty ; they conveyed him to the caftle of Ballybeggan near Tralee ; where, notwithftanding the capitulation, they formed a defign to murder him, which they would have put in execution, if he had not been privately carried off by his nephews, *Mc. Elligot* and *Mc. Gilly-Cuddy,* his fifter's fons, then colonels in the Irifh army.— This caftle was one of the laft garrifons in the Englifh hands, that held out in the co. Kerry.

BALLINGARRY CRAMER, a fair town in co. Limerick, prov. Munfter ; where fairs are held 15 Apr. and 30 Aug.

BALLINGATE or *Bolingate,* fit. in bar. Shillelagh, co. Wicklow, prov. Leinfter.

BALLINGRANY-BRIDGE, fit. over the river Vincion, in co. Sligo, prov. Connaught.

BALLINLAW, fit. near the junction of the river Barrow and Suir, in co. Kilkenny, prov. Leinfter.

BALLINLEY, fit. near a rivulet of that name in bar. Tyreragh, co. Sligo, prov. Connaught ; where are the ruins of an abbey.

BALLINLINE, fit. near *Old Rofs,* in co. Wexford, prov. Leinfter.

BALLINLONDRY, a rectory in dioc. of Emly, fit. in bar. Cofhlea, co. Limerick, prov. Munfter.

BALLINLOUGH, a fmall town in the parifh of Anahilt, co Down, prov. Ulfter.—Alfo a village in bar. Ballintobar, co. Rofcommon, prov. Connaught, diftant near 90 miles from Dublin ; where are fairs held 31 May, 5 July, 26 Sep. and 31 Oct. This place is fometimes called *Belonlagh.*—Alfo the name of a village in bar. Delvin, co. Weftmeath, prov. Leinfter.

BALLINODE, a village in bar. Monaghan, co. Monaghan, prov. Ulfter.———Alfo in bar. Carbury, co. Sligo, prov. Connaught.

BALLINOE, a rectory in dioc. of Cloyne, fit. in bar. Killnataloon, co. Cork, prov. Munfter.

BALLINOLLIGAN, fit. in bar. Glenarm, co. Antrim, prov. Ulfter.

BALLINPHELIC, a fair town in co. Cork, prov. Munfter ; fair days 9 June and 10 Oct. There is a fulphereo-chailybeate water at this place.

BALLINRINK, fit. in bar. Faffadining, co. Kilkenny, prov. Leinfter.

BALLINROBE, fit. in bar. Kilmain, co. Mayo, prov. Connaught, 110 miles from Dublin ; 'tis a market and poft-town, in which the affizes are fometimes held, and has a barrack for 2 companies of foot ; 'tis alfo a rectory in dioc. of Tuam. Lat. 53 : 40, lon. 9 : 10. Here are the ruins of a once celebrated abbey, and near

them

them is a charter school, by the banks of Lough Sky. A troop of horse is generally quarter'd here. Fairs held Whitfun Monday and 5 Dec.

BALLINSALDIN, fit. in bar. Ballaghkeen, co. Wexford, prov. Leinfter.

BALLINSPIDLE, a fair town in co. Cork, prov. Munfter—fairs held 14 and 15 May, 25 and 26 Sept.

BALLINTANE, fit. near Rofs, in co. Wexford, prov. Leinfter

BALLINTEAGUE, fit. in co. Kildare, prov. Leinfter. Here is a large bog thro' which the grand canal leading from Dublin to Monafter-evan paffes, and on the bank of which ftand the remains of *Ballinteague caftle.*

BALLINTEMPLE, a feat in the King's co.——alfo in co. Carlow—alfo a village in bar. Arklow, co. Wicklow, all in prov. Leinfter: the latter is a vicarage in dioc. of Dublin.—There is alfo a vicarage of this name in dioc. of Kilmore, fit. in bar. Clomaghan, co. Cavan, prov. Ulfter; and a rectory in dioc. of Cafhel, fit. in bar. Kilnemanna, co. Tipperary, prov. Munfter.

BALLINTOBBER, a bar. having in it a village of fame name, fit. in co. Rofcommon, prov. Connaught. The latter is a rectory in dioc. of Elphin, fit. 78 miles from Dublin.——Fairs held 25 Aug. here are remarkable ruins of the former refidence of fome of the princes of Connaught. — There is likewife another village fo called, fit. in bar. Carragh, co. Mayo, prov. Connaught; here are the ruins of a very antient abbey, which exhibits a fine fpecimen of Gothic architecture; the rafters, if they may be fo termed, being formed of hewn ftone, indented into each other in a very regular manner. It was founded by Carhal O'Conogher, king of Connaught about A. D. 1216. John Rourke of Tirawly was murdered in this abbey by David FitzBurke, his nephew, in A. D. 1506.

BALLINTOCHAN, fit. in bar. Idrone, co. Carlow, prov. Leinfter.

BALLINTOGHER, a fair town fit. in bar. Tyraghrill, co. Sligo, prov. Connaught, 105 miles from Dublin.—Fair days 8 June, 28 Ju. 17 Oct. 8 Dec. — Within about two miles of it are the ruins of three different caftles.

BALLINTOY, fit. in bar. Carey, co. Antrim, prov. Ulfter, 150 miles from Dublin; where fairs are held on 3 Jun. 4 Sep. and 14 Oct. This place has a tolerable good bay.——In the year 1756, a vein of coal was difcovered near it, which has been wrought with fuch effect, as to fupply the falt-works here and at Port-rufh and Coleraine. Ballintoy is a rectory in dioc. of Connor.

BALLINTRA, a fair town in bar. Tyrhugh, co. Donegal, prov. Ulfter, near 106 miles from Dublin. Fair days 1 Feb. 25 Mar. 20 May,

31 July, 2 Oct. and 30 Nov. Alfo a village in bar. Boylagh in fame co.

BALLINURE, fee *Ballynure.*

BALLINVARRY, a village in bar. Gallan, co. Mayo, prov. Connaught.

BALLINVOHER, a rectory in dioc. of Ardfert, fit. in bar. Corkaguinny, co. Kerry, prov. Munfter.

BALLINVROONY, a fair town in co. Cork, prov. Munfter. Fair days, 10 May, Sept. and Nov.

BALLISALLAGH, fit. in bar. Arklow, co. Wicklow, prov. Leinfter.

BALLITORE, fee *Ballytore.*

BALLIVADY, fit. in bar. Glenarm, co. Antrim, prov. Ulfter.

BALLNALEE, (otherwife called St John's town) fit. in co. Longford, prov. Leinfter.

BALLNELIN, fit. in co. Mayo, prov. Connaught.

BALLONESTEAR, fit. in bar. Shelmaliere, co. Wexford, prov. Leinfter.

BALLOW, fit. in bar. Belfaft, co. Antrim, prov. Ulfter.

BALLOY, fit. in bar. Ferrard, co. Louth, prov. Leinfter.

BALLRATH, fit. in bar. Duleek, co. Meath, prov. Leinfter.

BALLRICHAN, a pleafant peninfula, fit. 2 miles from Dundalk, in bar. Dundalk, co. Louth, prov. Leinfter, in which are remaining evident marks of a Druid's grove or dwelling. To form a more perfect idea of it, according to the accounts given us of the feats and habitations of thofe men, we are to imagine it was once furrounded with fine old oaks; forming within an awful folemn fhade.—The entrance is marked by large ftone pillars, with circles of great ftones. Here is likewife fome indication of a fepulchre or family burial place. This choice fpot of ground is fuppofed to have been the fupreme feat of the Drew, or arch-Druid: this place is fometimes written Ballriggan. Here alfo are the remains of a caftle, fit. on a rifing ground, between two winding rivers; having the mountain of *Slievegullion,* to the N. *caftle-rock* on the W. and that of *Caftle-town* E. of it. It belongs to lord Limerick, and is of a remarkable conftruction, inclofed within a walled court, capable of containing a large body of men. Here is a fubterraneous cave, and a fpacious vault under it, which feems to have had fome communication with a Sally-port, directing towards the banks of the river, which are here very fteep and high.

BALLRIGGAN, fee *Ballrichan.*

BALL'S-BRIDGE, a village in co. Dublin, prov. Leinfter; one mile and a half from Dublin caftle. It is fit. on a broad but fhallow ftream, that iffues from the mountains, near *Fock-brook,*

brook, and falls into the bay of Dublin a little below this place. Here is a very confiderable manufactory for printing linens and cottons, &c.

BALL's-GROVE, a handfome feat pleafantly fit. on the river Boyne, near Drogheda, in co. Louth, prov. Leinfter.

BALL's-MILLS, fit. in bar. Dundalk, co. Louth, prov. Leinfter.

BALLUG-CASTLE, fit. near Caftlerath, in co. Louth, prov. Leinfter.

BALLYADAMS, a bar. with a village in it of fame name, fit. in Queen's co. prov. Leinfter; the latter is a rectory in dioc. of Leighlin.

BALLYADEN, fit. in bar. Ballaghkeen, co. Wexford, prov. Leinfter.

BALLYAGHRAN, a village in the liberties of Colerain, fit. in co. Londonderry, prov. Ulfter.

BALLYANE, a rectory in dioc. of Ferns, fit. in bar. Bantry, co. Wexford, prov. Leinfter.

BALLYARTHUR, fit. in bar. Arklow, co. Wicklow, prov. Leinfter. —— Above 30 miles from Dublin.

BALLYBACK, fit. near Duncannon fort, co. Wexford, prov. Leinfter.

BALLYBACON, a vicarage in dioc. of Lifmore, fit. in bar. Iffa, co. Tipperary, prov. Munfter.

BALLYBAR, fit. in bar. Carlow, co. Carlow, prov. Leinfter.

BALLYBARRACK, a rectory in dioc. of Armagh, fit. in bar. Dundalk, co. Louth, prov. Leinfter.

BALLYBAY, fit. in co. Monaghan, prov. Ulfter, 53 miles from Dublin; fairs held 1 Jan. Thurfd. before Eafter, 5 July and 2 Oct.

BALLYBEACON, a rectory within the deanery of Ardfinane, in co. Waterford, prov. Munfter. The church is in ruins.—Alfo a ridge of mountains in bar. Offa, co. Tipperary, prov. Munfter, called Ballybeacon, or Ballybacon mountains; they join the co.'s Waterford and Tipperary.

BALLYBEG, fit. near *Buttevant*, in bar. Orrery, co. Cork, prov. Munfter; here was a monaftery of Auguftinians, founded A. D. 1237, and dedicated to St. Thomas, by William de Barry, being endowed by his fon David, who founded the friary of Buttevant; it is now a rectory in dioc. of Cloyne :—the lands belonging to this abbey contained 2060 Irifh acres, and by a valuation taken in 1622, were only worth 60l. per Ann. at the fame time the tythe and glebe belonging to it were valued at 200l. per Ann. more.—Some part of the building, particularly the fteeple, which was ftrong, and the E. window of the chancel, have outlived the injuries of time; by the holes which remain in the vaulted roof of the fteeple, there were here a chime of bells; the traces of the foundation, and part of a high round tower, de-

tached a confiderable way to the S. W. (faid to have been once a part of this fabric) fhew it to have been a very large and magnificent ftructure. — There is alfo a village of fame name in bar. Eliogurty, co. Tipperary, prov. Munfter.

BALLYBEG-CASTLE, fit. at the village of Ballybeg, on the confines of the co. Waterford and Tipperary, prov. Munfter; within a few miles of Ballybacon mountains.

BALLYBEGGAN, fit. 2 miles E. by N. from Tralee, co. Kerry, prov. Munfter; it had formerly been a high and ftrong caftle, but was reduced during the wars in king James the 2d's time, when it was a noted pafs between Tralee and Caftle-ifland. In the grounds hereabout, is a dark kind of grey marble, veined with white fpots of a fparry matter, which has been raifed in very large blocks.

BALLYBOFEY, fee *Ballybofy*.

BALLYBOG, a large tract of the parifh of Kilcrogan, co. Kerry, prov. Munfter; in which the late Dr. *Nath. Bland* had a neat lodge, and a great number of unprofitable acres, which he endeavoured to reclaim at a confiderable expence.

BALLYBOGAN, a fair town in bar. Moyfenrath, co. Meath, prov. Leinfter; it is a curacy in dioc. of Meath; fairs held 25th Sept.

BALLYBOGHILL, or *Ballybohill*, fit. in bar. Balruddery, co. Dublin, prov. Leinfter; 10½ miles from Dublin; it is a curacy in dioc. of Dublin; here are the ruins of the church.

BALLYBORO, fit. in bar. Bantry, co. Wexford, prov. Leinfter.

BALLYBORRIS, a village in bar. Idrone, co. Carlow, prov. Leinfter.

BALLYBOUGH, a village in the vicinity of Dublin; it is otherwife called *Ballybough-bridge*, from a bridge erected over the river here; at which place is a white-flint-glafs houfe, with extenfive and convenient offices: 1½ mile from Dublin.

BALLYBOUGHT, a vicarage in dioc. of Dublin, fit. in co. Wicklow, prov. Leinfter.

BALLYBOY, a bar. having in it a market, fair and poft town of fame name, fit. in King's co. prov. Leinfter, 56 miles from Dublin; it has a weekly market on Saturday, and alfo the firft day of every month from May to Nov. inclufive. Lat. 53 : 12, lon. 7 : 50; fairs held 4 May, 21 Aug. and 6 Dec. It is a vicarage in dioc. of Meath; the river contiguous to it is called the *Silver river*.

BALLYBRAZIL, a curacy in dioc. of Ferns, fit. in bar. Shelburne, co. Wexford, prov. Leinfter.

BALLYBRINAN, or *Ballybrennan*, a rectory in dioc. of Ferns, fit. in bar. Forth, co. Wexford, prov. Leinfter.

BALLY-

BALLYBRITT, a bar. with a village of same name, sit. in King's co. prov. Leinster. Lat. 52:55, lon. 8:13.

BALLYBRITTAIN, sit. in bar. Coole's-town, King's co. prov. Leinster. The pasturage here is remarkably good, rich and fertile ; on the lands is an old castle, contiguous to the dwelling house of *Mr. Inman.*

BALLYBRITTAS, sit. in bar. Portnehinch, Queen's co. prov. Leinster, 33 miles from Dublin. At that part of the village called *Old Ballybrittas,* is a Presbyterian meeting house ; and in a field adjoining it, stand the remains of a large mansion or castle which belonged to the O'Dempsy's, lords of *Glanmalliere :* it felt the severity of Cromwell's attacks, who played his cannon upon it from an opposite hill.

BALLYBROON, a fair town in co. Limerick, prov. Munster ; fairs held custom free on 12 June and 13 Oct. It is a rectory in dioc. of Emly.

BALLYBURK, a village in bar. Carragh, co. Mayo, prov. Connaught.

BALLYBURLY, sit. in bar. Warren's-town, King's co. prov. Leinster.

BALLYBURNY, sit. in bar. Clunlonan, co. Westmeath, prov. Leinster.

BALLYBURRIS, sit. in bar. Idrone, co. Carlow, prov. Leinster.

BALLYCAHAN, a rectory in dioc. of Limerick, sit. in bar. Poblebrien, co. Limerick, prov. Munster.

BALLYCALLEN, a rectory in dioc. of Ossory, sit. in bar. Crannagh, co. Kilkenny, prov. Leinster.

BALLYCAM-BAY, sit. near Killough, co. Down, prov. Ulster ; at the extremity of which is a beautiful grotto under a hill ; and at the bottom thereof is a well 7 feet deep and intensely cold, which always continues the same, and is fed by a water perpetually oozing from the top of the cave, thro' a vein of lime-stone.

BALLYCANNON, sit. in bar. Ikeath, co. Kildare, prov. Leinster.

BALLYCANOE or *Ballycanow,* sit. in bar. Gorey, co. Wexford, prov. Leinster, about 49 miles from Dublin, and 4 from Gorey ; it is a rectory in dioc. of Ferns. Fairs held 23 April, 25 July, 21 Sept. 2 Oct. and 30 Nov.

BALLYCARBERRY-CASTLE, sit. in the parish of Cahir, co. Kerry, prov. Munster, by whom erected is not known ; there is a large fleur de lis carved on a stone on the inside.

BALLYCARICKEEN, sit. in bar. Scarawalsh, co. Wexford. prov. Leinster.

BALLYCARNEY, a fair town in bar. Scarawalsh, co. Wexford, prov. Leinster ; fairs held 16 March and 26 May.

BALLYCAROGE or *Ballykecroge,* sit. in parish Killosinta, co. Waterford, prov. Munster,

where are fairs annually on 2 Oct. Here are the remains of a castle which formerly belonged to the family of the *Walshes.* In an adjacent brook to the W. the country people shew a large rock, which they call *Clough Lowrish,* i. e. the speaking stone, and relate a fabulous account of its speaking at a certain time, in contradiction to a person who swore by it in a lie.

BALLYCARRY, sit. in co. Antrim, prov. Ulster, 92 miles from Dublin. Fairs held 21 June, 2 Friday O. S. in Aug. and 31 Oct.

BALLYCASHEDY, see *Ballicassidy.*

BALLYCASHIN, a parish so called, sit. in co. Waterford, prov. Munster.

BALLYCASSIDY, a village sit. about 4 miles N. W. of Enniskillen, co. Fermanagh, prov. Ulster. Here are subterraneous caves called *the Daughters,* being the curious work of nature ; the entrance is by a large arch 25 feet high ; the roof is rock, composed of various pieces in regular order. The name is sometimes written *Ballycashedy.* This place lies near *Lough Earn,* and according to Mr. Scale's Hiber. Atlas, is in the bar. *Tureskennedy,* but Dr. Beaufort places it in bar. *Lurge.*

BALLYCASTLE, sit. in bar. Cary, co. Antrim, prov. Ulster, 113 miles from Dublin ; it is a port and post-town about 30 miles N. of Carrickfergus, and noted for its adjacent collieries, and a pier built by parliamentary encouragement. Lat. 52 : 12, lon. 6 : 40. Fair days 15 July, 25 Aug. 3 Nov. and 1 Dec. Near it is a Challybeate spring. Here is a charter school for about 40 children ; it was endowed by *Hugh Boyd,* esq. with 20 acres of land, rent free for ever ; and his mother the late Mrs. *Rose Boyd* bequeathed 20 l. towards its support. The pits here produce a coal somewhat like that of Whitehaven, but swifter in burning and of a more ardent heat ; and altho' they are in the greatest abundance, yet the want of a safe and commodious harbour to ship them, prevents their being work'd up as they might be, to an extent fully equal to the supply of the nation. This town has been almost the creation of one man (Mr. Boyd) who died some years ago : the different fossils commonly sit. above the coal of this place, are iron-stone, black-slate, grey, brown or yellowish sand-stone, and bassaltes, (called here *whinstone* ;) In 1770 the miners in pushing forward an adit toward the bed of coal, at an unexplored part of the Ballycastle cliff, unexpectedly broke thro' the rock into a narrow choaked up passage, which being examined, discovered a complete gallery that had been carried on several hundred yards to the bed of coal, and branched off into chambers, where miners had carried on their different works ; pillars were left at proper distances : some remains of tools, and even baskets used in the

works

works were difcovered; but in fuch a decayed ftate, that on being touched, they immediately crumbled into pieces: as it feems impoffible to determine with precifion the early period when thefe works were carried on, the difcovery furnifhes us with additional proof that Ireland was not deftitute of arts and fciences in times of remote antiquity. Here was alfo an antient caftle, to the E. of which is an old building called the abbey, in the chapel of which is the following infcription, " In dei deiparæquæ virgini honorem, illuftriffimus ac nobiliffimus dominus Randolphus Mc. Donnell, comes de Antrim, hoc facellum fieri curavit, A. D. 1612.

BALLYCLARE, a village in bar. Belfaft, co. Antrim, prov. Ulfter.

BALLYCLEAVE, a fair town in co. Kerry, prov. Munfter; fair days, 1 May, 2 Aug. 6 Oct. 1 Dec.

BALLYCLERIHAN, a rectory in dioc. of Cafhrel, fit. in co. Tipperary, prov. Munfter; fairs held annually on 30 Sept.

BALLYCLOG, a rectory in dioc. of Armagh, fit. in bar. Dungannon, co. Tyrone, prov. Ulfter.

BALLYCLOGHY, a vicarage in dioc. of Emly, fit. in bar. Small-county, co. Limerick, prov. Munfter.

BALLYCLOUGH, a village in bar. Orrery, co. Cork, prov. Munfter; within about one mile of *Mallow*. Here is a church and a caftle, the latter was built by a family of the *Barrys*, which went by the name of *Mac Robifon*: fome years ago, there was a chalybeate fpa in this place, in good repute, but it is now neglected, being overflowed by an adjacent brook. Ballyclough is now a vicarage in dioc. of Cloyne.

BALLYCLUG, a vicarage in dioc. of Connor, fit. in bar. Antrim, co. Antrim, prov. Ulfter.

BALLYCOMMON, a rectory in dioc. of Kildare, fit. in bar. Philipftown, King's co. prov. Leinfter.

BALLYCONNELL, a village in bar. Tullalagh, co. Cavan, prov. Ulfter; above 67 miles from Dublin, and about 11 miles N. E. of Cavan. Lat. 54:6, lon. 7:50. Fair days, 13 Feb. 17 Mar. 16 May, 24 June, 29 July, 26 Sept. 25 Oct.

BALLYCOPLAND, a town land fo called, which lies oppofite Copland Ifles, in co. Down, prov. Ulfter; thefe iflands lie in Carrickfergus bay; and they, as well as the town land we fpeak of, received their names from a family of the *Coplands*, long fince extinct; who fettled in that part of the kingdom, in the time of *John de Courcy*, in the 12th century.

BALLYCORA, a village in bar. Imokilly, co. Cork, prov. Munfter. Lat. 51:47, lon. 8:25.

BALLYCORMACK, a rectory in dioc. of Ferns, fit. in bar. Bargie, co. Wexford, prov. Leinfter.

BALLYCORR, a rectory in dioc. of Connor, fit. in bar. Antrim, co. Antrim, prov. Ulfter.

BALLYCORRY, a village in bar. Belfaft, co. Antrim, prov. Ulfter.

BALLYCOTTON, a bay, with a fmall ifland and village of fame name, fit. in bar. Imokilly, co. Cork, prov. Munfter; the bay is about 4 miles from Cloyne, and is large, but dangerous; 'tis remarkable for the largeft flat-fifhe when the tide is out, the ftrand is fuppofed to be the firft in Europe. There are hereabouts the ruins of fome caftles and a church; the entire village is inhabited by fifhermen; the ifland lies oppofite and near the coaft.

BALLYCOWAN, or *Ballycowen*, a bar. having in it a village of fame name, fit. in King's co. prov. Leinfter. Fairs held 31 July.

BALLYCROGE, a rectory in dioc. of Leighlin, fit. in bar. Catherlough, co. Carlow, prov. Leinfter.

BALLYCROY, fit. in bar. Erris, co. Mayo, prov. Connaught.

BALLYCULLEN, fit. in co. Down, prov. Ulfter.

BALLYCULTER, a rectory in dioc. of Down, fit. in bar. Lecale, co. Down, prov. Ulfter.

BALLYCUMBER, a village fit. in bar. Garrycaftle, King's co. prov. Leinfter; about 51 miles from Dublin; a mile beyond which is the church, feated on a hill. Fair days, 2 May, and 1 Dec.

BALLYCURRANCY, a rectory in dioc. of Cloyne, fit. in bar. Barrymore, co. Cork, prov. Munfter.

BALLYCURRIS, fit. in bar. Coolock, co. Dublin, prov. Leinfter.

BALLYCUSLAN, a rectory in dioc. of Ardfert; fit. in bar. Truachnacmy, co. Kerry, prov. Munfter.

BALLYDANGAN, fit. between Balinafloe and Athlone, in co. Rofcommon, prov. Connaught.

BALLYDARGAN, an inconfiderable place on the W. fide of the road leading from Killough to Downpatrick, in co. Down, prov. Ulfter.

BALLYDARTAN, fit. in bar. Forth, co. Carlow, prov. Leinfter.

BALLYDAVID, a *cape*, fit. in bar. Corkaguinny, co. Kerry, prov. Munfter.

BALLYDEHOB, a fair town in co. Cork, prov. Munfter; fairs held on Eafter Tuefday and 10 Oct.

BALLYDELOUGHY, a vicarage in dioc. of Cloyne, fit. in bar. Fermoy, co. Cork, prov. Munfter.

BALLYDEROON, a *caftle* in co. Cork, prov. Munfter, fit. on a pleafant fpot, between the junction of the rivers Funcheon and Araglin.

BALLYDEROWEN, fit. in bar. Tyraghrill, co. Sligo, prov. Connaught.

BALLYDESMOND, (now called *Ballydivilin*,) a caftle in co. Cork, prov. Munfter; boldly erected

erected on a rock, projecting over the sea, at the place called Ballydivilin bay.

BALLYDEVELIN-BAY, (or *Ballidivilin,*) fit. in bar. Carbery, co. Cork, prov. Munfter.

BALLYDONAGAN-BAY, (fometimes called *Ballydonaghan,*) fit. in bar. Beer and Bantry, co. Cork, prov. Munfter.

BALLYDONELLAN, fit. in bar. Leitrim, co. Galway, prov. Connaught.

BALLYDONNELL, a village in bar. Fermoy, co. Cork, prov. Munfter.—Alfo a vicarage in dioc. of Dublin, fit. in bar. Arklow, co. Wicklow, prov. Leinfter.

BALLYDOUGAN, fit. S. of *Hollymount,* on the verge of Lake Strangford, co. Down, prov. Ulfter. Here was formerly a large ftone houfe, with a draw-bridge and turret for defence; burned down by the treachery of Irifh fervants, in 1641.

BALLYDUFF, a village in Queen's co. prov. Leinfter; where are the ruins of a church.—Alfo a curacy in dioc. of Ardfert, fit. in bar. Corkaguinny, co. Kerry, prov. Munfter.

BALLYELA-BAY, fit. in bar. Corcomroe, co. Clare, prov. Munfter.

BALLYELLIN, a vicarage in dioc. of Leighlin, fit. in bar. St. Mullens, co. Carlow, prov. Leinfter.

BALLYELLIS, fit. in bar. Scarawalfh, co. Wexford, prov. Leinfter.

BALLYENN, fit. in bar. Cofhmore and Cofhbride, near the river Blackwater, in co. Waterford, prov. Munfter.

BALLYEO, an antient name for the town of *Slane,* in co. Meath, prov. Leinfter; fit. on the Northern bank of the river Boyne: the word is derived from *Bally* a town and *Eo* a grave. This place was alfo called *Fir Feic,* derived according to Dr. Beaufort from *Ferta-fir-bheitheach,* or the graves of the herdfmen; from a number of thefe people being flain here in battle, and buried in this place; and from this circumftance perhaps came the prefent name *Slane* or *Slain.* Here St. Patrick pitched his tent the night before his arrival at the court of *Tarah;* at which, early in the morning, he lighted up that fire which gave fo much aftonifhment to the Druids and affembly of the ftates. A monaftery and bifhoprick were afterwards founded in this place by *St. Eire* or *Erc.*

BALLYESTON, a village in bar. Antrim, co. Antrim, prov. Ulfter.

BALLYEVIL, fit. near Killeigh, in bar. Gifhil, King's co. prov. Leinfter; the feat of David Cooke, efq.

BALLYFARMOT or *Ballyfermot,* a very pleafant but fmall village fit. in bar. Newcaftle, co. Dublin, prov. Leinfter; diftant about ¼ mile from *Chapelizod:* hereare the remains of an old church and caftle. This place is a curacy in the dioc. of Dublin.

BALLYFERNON, a village in bar. Boyle, co. Rofcommon, prov. Connaught.

BALLYFERRIS, fit. in bar. Ardes, co. Down, prov. Ulfter. Here is a cape ufually called *Ballyferris point.*

BALLYFIARD, a vicarage in dioc. of Cork, fit. in bar. Kinalea, co. Cork, prov. Munfter.

BALLYFIN, a village in bar. Maryborough, Queen's co. prov. Leinfter; to which belongs a chapel in the dioc. of Leighlin: here is a handfome feat.

BALLYFORAN, fit. in bar. Athlone, co. Rofcommon, prov. Connaught; 71 miles from Dublin. Fairs held 8 Feb. firft Thurfday O. S. in April, 19 May, 6 July, 19 Sep. 21 Oct. and 3 Thurfday in Dec.

BALLYFOYLE, a rectory in dioc. of Cork, fit. in bar. Kinalea, co. Cork, prov. Munfter.

BALLYGAD, a village fit. near Carigallen, in bar. Carigallen, co. Leitrim, prov. Connaught.

BALLYGADDY, fit. in co. Galway, prov. Connaught: here are the remains of one of the antient round towers.

BALLYGALL, fit. near Finglafs, co. Dublin, prov. Leinfter.

BALLYGAMBOON, fit. in co. Kerry, prov. Munfter. Here is an orchard in which are fingle apple trees, that have produced 3 hogfheads of cyder each; the diameter of the oppofite boughs of one tree was meafured, the extremities of which were 50 feet afunder, which, if confidered as the diameter of a circle, the fuperficial content will be 1964 fquare feet, or 218 fquare yards, which is the quantity of ground that this tree covers; and if we fuppofe that a horfe when ftanding, takes up the fpace of ground equal to 3 fquare yards, then there may ftand no lefs than 72 horfes under the drip of this apple tree.

BALLYGARRON-CASTLE, fit. in co. Waterford, prov. Munfter; faid to have been built by one *Gay;* it has no very antient appearance, and feems to have been deftroyed in the wars of king James the 2d.

BALLYGARRY, a fmall caftle in co. Kerry, prov. Munfter; near 2 miles N. of *Ballyheigh;* near which is the elegant feat of *Caftle-Shannon.*

BALLYGART or *Billygarth,* a rectory in dioc. of Meath, fit. in bar. Duleek, co. Meath, prov. Leinfter.

BALLYGAWLY, a village fit. in bar. Clogher, co. Tyrone, prov. Ulfter; 74 miles from Dublin: fairs held 5 June, 2 Sep. and Nov. 4 miles from this place is *Starbog-fpa.*

BALLYGAWLY-MOUNTAINS, fit. in bar. Clogher, co. Tyrone, prov. Ulfter.

BALLYGELLY-HEAD, a cape in bar. Glenarm, co. Antrim, prov. Ulfter.

BALLYGLASS, fit. near Belleek, co. Mayo, prov. Connaught.

BALLY-

BALLYGOBBIN, fee *Bantry*.

BALLYGOREEN, a fair town in co. Cork, prov. Munfter; fairs held 24 June, 25 July and 28 Dec.

BALLYGORRY, fit. in bar. Newcaftle, co. Wicklow, prov. Leinfter.

BALLYGOURNEY, a rectory in dioc. of Cloyne, fit. in bar. Imokilly, co. Cork, prov. Munfter.

BALLYGRACE, fit. in bar. Balruddery, co. Dublin, prov. Leinfter.

BALLYGRANY or *Ballygranny*, a village in bar. Tyraghrill, co. Sligo, prov. Connaught.

BALLYGRENAN-CASTLE, fit. within 1 mile of *Bruff*, co. Limerick, prov. Munfter.

BALLYGRIFFIN, a rectory in dioc. of Cafhel, fit. in bar. Clanwilliam, co. Tipperary, prov. Munfter.

BALLYGUNN, a vicarage in dioc. of Offory, fit. in bar. Ida, co. Kilkenny, prov. Leinfter.

BALLYGUNKER, a village and rectory in dioc. of Waterford, fit. in bar Gualtiere, co. Waterford, prov. Munfter, thro' which the road leads to *Paffage*. Fairs held 19 Sep. This parifh is bounded on the N. by the river *Suir*, on the S. with *Kilmacleague*, on the W. and N. W. with the parifh of *Bifhop's-court*, and *Ballenckill*, and on the E. with *Killmacombe*, and *Kill-Saint-Nicholas*.

BALLYHACK, fit. in bar. Shelburne, co. Wexford, prov. Leinfter; 91½ miles from Dublin. Fairs, Thurfday after Trin. Sunday, 25 Mar. and July, 24 Aug. and 29 Sept. Here was a commandery which belonged to the grand priory of Kilmainham: it was fubordinate to that of *Kilcloghan*.

BALLYHALBERT, a village in bar. Ardes, co. Down, prov. Ulfter; 86 miles from Dublin. Here are two Prefbyterian meeting houfes, one of the *new*, and the other of the *old-light*. Near this village is the old parifh of St. Andrew, where was formerly an abbey of Benedictine monks, founded by *John de Courcy*, and was known by the name of the *Black-abbey*; the poffeffions of which were granted to the lord *Clanebay*, and from him came by affignment to the lord vifc. *Ardes*.

BALLYHALY, fit. in bar. Forth, co. Wexford, prov. Leinfter.

BALLYHANNES, fee *Ballyhannis*.

BALLYHARA, fit. in bar. Nethercrofs, co. Dublin, prov. Leinfter.

BALLYHARTY, fit. in bar. Bargie, co. Wexford, prov. Leinfter.

BALLYHASSIK, a fair town in co. Cork, prov. Munfter. Fair days, 1 May, 29 June, 10 Aug. and 29 Sept.

BALLYHAUNIS, a village in bar. Coftello, co. Mayo, prov. Connaught; near 94 miles from Dublin, otherwife called *Ballyhannes*. Here are the ruins of a monaftery, founded for Auguftinian friars by the family of *Nan*. Fairs held 1 June, 2 July, 22 Sept. and 29 Oct.

BALLYHAVELL, fit. in bar. Drumahare, co. Leitrim, prov. Connaught.

BALLYHAVEN-ROAD, fit. near Strangfordbay, co. Down, prov. Ulfter. Here is a rock funk juft before it, to avoid which, the failor muft bring the faddle of the two hills which are on the W. fhore, oppofite to him; and then he may go in fafely; but care muft be taken not to come nearer than in 4 fathom water, the ground being every where foul and ftoney.

BALLYHAYS, a village in bar. Loughtee, co. Cavan, prov. Ulfter; above 57 miles from Dublin: three miles beyond it are the ruins of a church. Fairs held 1 Mar. 18 May, 13 July, 30 Aug. 6 Nov. and 13 Dec.

BALLYHEAGUE, a vicarage in dioc. of Ferns, fit. in bar. Shelmaliere, co. Wexford, prov. Leinfter.

BALLYHEAN, a rectory in dioc. of Tuam, fit. in bar. Carragh, co. Mayo, prov. Connaught. Fair days, 4 July and 20 Aug.

BALLYHEEN, a fair town in co. Cork, prov. Munfter; where fairs are held from 2 to 9 Oct.

BALLYHEIGH-BAY, fit. in bar. Clanmaurice, co. Kerry, prov. Munfter. The ftrand here is about 5 miles long, and in fine weather a very pleafant ride: the coaft is compofed of feveral fand hills, on which a long fedgy grafs grows in confiderable quantities, which contributes greatly to prevent the havock and devaftation the fea fometimes makes in the banks. —— The fhore is very flat, and being expofed to the weftern ocean, and the winds from that quarter, a very heavy fea with dreadful breakers roll in upon it, which makes it extremely dangerous for veffels, which muft ftrike the ground a great way from the coaft, and are thereby loft with all their people; fo that, mariners ought to endeavour to proceed to the Northward of Kerryhead, by which means they may gain the mouth of the river Shannon. There is alfo a *village* here called Ballyheigh, which is a rectory in dioc. of Ardfert.

BALLY-HENRY-ROAD, fit. in Strangford-bay, co. Down, prov. Ulfter; where fhips may lie out of the force of the current.

BALLYHIBBUCK, a fair town in co. Kilkenny, prov. Leinfter. Fair day 25 Sept.

BALLYHIGHLAND, a fair town in co. Cavan, prov. Ulfter. Fairs held on the day before Trin. Sunday.

BALLYHINCH, a fair town in co. Kilkenny, prov. Leinfter. Fair held 9 July.

BALLYHIRE, fit. in bar. Forth, co. Wexford, prov. Leinfter.

BALLYHOLM-BAY, fit. in co. Down, prov. Ulfter; between Carrickfergus-bay, and Copland Iflands.

BALLYHOOLY, a fair town in bar. Fermoy, co. Cork, prov. Munfter: above 111 miles from

from Dublin; Fair day 26 Aug. It is a small but pleasant village, having a new and elegant church; it stands over the river Black-water, and commands a delightful view of a country highly wooded, and embellished by art. This is a vicarage in dioc. of Cloyne.

BALLYHOWEL, a village in bar. Drumahire, co. Leitrim, prov. Connaught.

BALLYHUBBACK, fit. in bar. Talbot's-town, co. Wicklow, prov. Leinster.

BALLYHUSKARD, a rectory in dioc. of Ferns, fit. in bar. Ballaghkeen, co. Wexford, prov. Leinster.

BALLY-JAMES-DUFF, fit. in bar. Castleraghan, co. Cavan, prov. Ulster; 45 miles from Dublin. Fairs held 7 May, 17 July, 26 Oct. and 21 Dec.

BALLYINGLY, a curacy in dioc. of Ferns, fit. in bar. Shelmaliere, co. Wexford, prov. Leinster.

BALLYKEALY, an antient castle of the *Fitzmaurices*, in co. Kerry, prov. Munster. It stands 2 miles N. of Ardfert, and gave title of baron to a younger branch of that family.

BALLYKEAN, fit. in bar. Tinehinch, Queen's co. prov. Leinster.

BALLYKELLY, fit. in bar. Kenoght, co. Londonderry, prov. Ulster; above 125 miles from Dublin. Here is a charter school, toward the establishment of which, the late Rt. Hon. earl of Tyrone granted to the incorporated Society 40 acres of land for 60 years, renewable, at 20s. per Ann.

BALLYKEOGE, fit. near the river Slaney, co. Wexford, prov. Leinster.

BALLYKERAN, a village in bar. Brawny, co. Westmeath, prov. Leinster.

BALLYKFROGE, fit. in bar. Decies without Drum, co. Waterford, prov. Munster.

BALLYKET, a fair town in co. Clare, prov. Munster; fairs held Thursday before Whit-Sunday, 4 July, 17 Aug. and 1 Dec. It is distant about 141 miles from Dublin.

BALLYKIELTY, fit. in bar. Gorey, co. Wexford, prov. Leinster.

BALLYKILLCAVAN, fit. in bar. Stradbally, Queen's co. prov. Leinster.

BALLYKILLCOURSEY, fit. in bar. Killcoursy, King's co. prov. Leinster.

BALLYKILLEN, fit. in King's co. prov. Leinster; about 30 miles from Dublin: here is a large mount or rath.

BALLYKILLY, a village, fit. at Bear-island, co. Cork, prov. Munster.

BALLYKINE, fit. in bar. Arklow, co. Wicklow, prov. Leinster. An abbey was founded here by a brother of St. *Kevin.* (probably St. *Dangan;*) and the feat of Mr. Whaley, called *Whaley-abbey,* has been erected on the antient fite.

BALLYKNOCKAM, fit. between the bar. Ballybritt and Clonlisk, in King's co. prov. Leinst.

BALLYKNOCKAN, fit. in bar. Cullinagh, Queen's co. prov. Leinster.

BALLYLAGHAN, fit. in bar. Gallen, co. Mayo, prov. Connaught; about 110 miles from Dublin.

BALLYLAHEEN, fit. in bar. Upper-third, co. Waterford, prov. Munster.

BALLYLAMEEN, a vicarage in dioc. of Lismore, fit. in bar. Upper-third, co. Waterford, prov. Munster.

BALLYLANY-ISLAND, fit. in bar. Ballynahinch, co. Galway, prov. Connaught.

BALLYLASS-BAY, fit. in bar. Tyrawly, co. Mayo, prov. Connaught.

BALLYLAUGHAN CASTLE, one of the antient castles of the kings of Leinster, of which they had three; fit. near Wexford mountains. The first called Claghamon, was near the river Cloady, in co. Wexford. The second, (another large ruin) at Garey-hill, near the church of Drimefen. The third was Ballylaughan; both the latter are near Laughlin bridge, co. Carlow, prov. Leinster.

BALLY-LEAN-CLIATH, or *Lean-cliath,* i. e. the fishing harbour; an antient name of the town and harbour of Dublin: Lean-cliath, or Leam-cliath, is derived from *Lean* or *Leam,* a harbour; and *cliath* or *cliabth,* which literally signifies a hurdle, or any thing made of wicker work. It also signified certain wiers made of hurdles, and placed in rivers and bays by the antien: Irish, for the purpose of taking fish; whence any river or bay, having these wiers placed in them, generally had the name of Cliath or Cliabth added to them, to signify the establishment of a fishery. Dublin therefore, being originally built on or near one of these harbours, was antiently called Bally-lean-cliath, i. e. the town on the fishing harbour, and not (as frequently translated) the town on hurdles. Vide *Baxter, Harris* and *Beauford.*

BALLYLEE, fit. in bar. Kiltartan, co. Galway, prov. Connaught.

BALLYLEEDY, fit. in co. Down, prov. Ulster.

BALLYLEENY, fit. in co. Galway, prov. Connaught.

BALLYLEMON fit. in co. Waterford, prov. Munster: antiently the feat of fir Richard Osborne, bart. where it is faid he kept a feraglio of women, from whence this place had its name; *Bally* signifying a town, and *Lemon* a kept mistress. Excellent marl has been discovered here in an adjacent bog, upon searching for which, the horns and skeleton of a Moose-deer were found; which came into the possession of the then earl of Grandison.

BALLYLENNAN, a curacy in dioc. of Ferns, fit. in bar. Shelmaliere, co. Wexford, prov. Leinst.

BALLY-

BALLYLINCH, fit. near Thomaftown, co. Kilkenny, prov. Leinfter.—Alfo a place in co. Cavan, prov. Ulfter, where an antient religious houfe or hofpital was eftablifhed ; but there are no traces of its hiftory, nor any account of its founder.

BALLYLINNY, a vicarage in dioc. of Connor, fit. in bar. Belfaft, co. Antrim, prov. Ulfter.

BALLYLOGLOE, a vicarage in dioc. of Meath, fit. in bar. Clonlonan, co. Weftmeath, prov. Leinfter.

BALLYLOHAN, fit. in bar. Ballyadams, Queen's co. prov. Leinfter.

BALLYLONGFORD, a village fit. in bar. Irraghticonnor, co. Kerry, prov. Munfter, 128 miles from Dublin ; within half a mile of it are the noble ruins of Liflatin abbey.

BALLYLOSCAN, a vicarage in dioc. of Offory, fit. in bar. Crannagh, co. Kilkenny, prov. Leinfter.

BALLYLOSHRAN, fit. near Taghman, co. Wexford, prov. Leinfter.

BALLYLURGAN, fit. in bar. Dundalk, co. Louth, prov. Leinfter.

BALLYNAN, a neat village, fit. in Queen's co. prov. Leinfter.

BALLYMACADANE, fit. in the high road to Bandon, within 4 miles of Cork, co. Cork, prov. Munfter. Here an abbey was founded by *Cormac M'Carthy*, about the year 1450, part of the walls of the building ftill remain.

BALLYMACANDAN, otherwife now called *Thomaftown* ; fit. in co. Kilkenny, prov. Leinfter ; by the river *Newre*. The name fignifies in Englifh the town of *Anthony*, having been built by Thomas Fitzanthony, an Englifh gentleman who came over with Henry 2d. It is an antient borough, and fends 2 members to parliament ; patron, lord *Clifden*. It was accounted formerly a very rich place, but is at prefent wore to a vifible decay. The church is part of an old abbey, in the ruins of which is a monftrous tomb ftone, which the country people fay covers the body of a giant ; and the inhabitants infift that one of their kings had lain buried here, feveral ages before this kingdom fubmitted to the Englifh. There is a good bridge over the river, and from this place to Waterford, the ftream is navigable for fmall veffels. On a high hill that overlooks the town, ftand the remains of a very large monaftery of Auguftinian friars. This is a poft and fair town ; diftant from Dublin near 59 miles. Fair day 25 May.

BALLYMACART, a vicarage in dioc. of Lifmore, fit. in bar. Decies within Drum, co. Waterford, prov. Munfter.

BALLYMACELLIGOT, a rectory in dioc. of

Ardfert, fit. in bar. Truaghnacmy, co. Kerry, prov. Munfter.

BALLYMACHUGH, a vicarage in dioc. of Ardagh, fit in bar. Clonmaghan, co Cavan, prov. Ulfter.

BALLYMACKY, a rectory in dioc. of Killaloe, fit. in bar. upper Ormond, co. Tipperary, prov. Munfter.

BALLYMACODA, fit. near Caftlemartyr, in co. Cork, prov. Munfter. Here is a caftle which was built in 1521.

BALLYMACORMACK, a rectory in dioc. of Ardagh, fit. in bar. Ardagh, co. Longford, prov. Leinfter.

BALLYMACPATRICK *caftle*, fit. near *Fermoy*, in co. Cork, prov. Munfter ; it was built by the *Condons*, on a rifing ground above the river Black-water.

BALLYMACSWINEY, fit. in bar. Kilmacrenan, co. Donegal, prov. Ulfter ; a monaftery was founded here by *Macfwiney*, for friars of the order of St. Francis. Part of the building is yet extant.

BALLYMACUS, fit. in bar. Bantry, co. Wexford, prov. Leinfter.

BALLYMACWARD, a vicarage in dioc. of Clonfert, fit. in bar. Tiaquin, co. Galway, prov. Connaught.

BALLYMACWILLIAM, a rectory in dioc. of Kildare, fit. in bar. Warren's-town, King's co. prov. Leinfter.

BALLYMADDOCK, fit. in bar. Stradbally, Queen's co. prov. Leinfter. Here are the ruins of an antient caftle.

BALLYMADUN, fit. in bar. Balruddery, co. Dublin, prov. Leinfter. In 1542 this was the feat of Robert Prefton efq. The ruins of an antient abbey appear here, and there was alfo the cell of an anchorite. This place is a vicarage in dioc. of Dublin.

BALLYMAGANNY, a village in bar. Half-fowre, co. Meath, prov. Leinfter.

BALLYMAGARY, fit. in bar. Dunluce, co. Antrim, prov. Ulfter.

BALLYMAGARVY, a vicarage in dioc. of Meath, fit. in bar. Duleek, co. Meath, prov. Leinfter.

BALLYMAGLASSON, a rectory in dioc. of Meath, fit. in bar. Ratoath, co. Meath, prov. Leinfter.

BALLYMAGORRY, a village in bar. Strabane, co. Tyrone, prov. Ulfter.

BALLYMAGOWRAN, a fair town in bar. Tullaghah, co. Cavan, prov. Ulfter, fairs held 23 May, 12 Aug. and 23 Nov.

BALLYMAHON, a market and poft town, fit. near the river Inny, in bar. Rathcline, co. Longford, prov. Leinfter ; 52¼ miles from Dublin. Lat. 53 : 31, long. 7 : 58 ; fair days, ir May, 11 Aug. 21 Nov. and Thursday before Ath Wednesday.

BALLYMAKENNY, a rectory in dioc. of Armagh, fit. within the co. of the town of Drogheda, in co. Louth, prov. Leinfter.

BALLYMALOE-CASTLE, fit. in co. Cork, prov. Munfter; 'tis now a good feat, but was ruinated in 1641; after which it was repaired, and fome new buildings added. In the hall of this caftle are two pair of the horns of Moofe deer, one of which meafured from tip to tip 10 feet 3 inches; the breadth of the palm 32 inches; from the vertex or the head to the nofe 20 inches. Adjoining this caftle, are fome good gardens and plantations.

BALLYMALONY, fit. in co. Clare, prov. Munfter, 92¼ miles from Dublin.

BALLYMALUS CASTLE, feated on the river Lane, co. Kerry, prov. Munfter; faid to have been built by the Moriarties.

BALLYMANEY, a rectory in dioc. of Kildare, fit. in bar. Great-Connel, co. Kildare, prov. Leinfter. Fairs held 5 Apr. 21 Aug and 1 Nov.

BALLYMANLAGH, fit. in co. Tipperary, prov. Munfter; 91 miles from Dublin.

BALLYMANE's, fit. in bar. Rallynacour, co. Wicklow, prov. Leinfter.

BALLYMARTLE, a rectory in dioc. of Cork, fit. in bar. Kinalea, co. Cork, prov. Munfter.

BALLYMASCANLAN, a curacy in dioc. of Armagh, fit. in bar. Dundalk, co. Louth, prov. Leinfter; near 44 miles from Dublin. Near this place is a ftone of a moft enormous fize, incumbent upon three others. It is thought to weigh between 30 and 40 tons, and by the inhabitants of the country, called the giants-load. At Ballymafcanlan, the Englifh army under Duke Schomberg, was encamped in 1690, which proved fatal to numbers.

BALLYMASCAW, fit. in co. Down, prov. Ulfter.

BALLYMASCORNEY, fit. in bar. Uppercrofs, co. Dublin, prov. Leinfter.

BALLYMEGARRY, fit. in co. Tyrone, prov. Ulfter; 104 miles from Dublin.

BALLYMENA, a curacy in dioc. of Clogher, fit. in bar. Toome, co. Antrim, prov. Ulfter; 20 miles N. W. of Belfaft, and 93¼ N. of Dublin. Lat. 54 : 52, lon. 6 : 30. Fair days 26 July, and 21 Oct. Within a ¼ mile of this place, on a rifing ground, oppofite Gilgorin caftle is a fettlement of Moravian brethren, at a place called Grace hill, which is well worthy a traveller's attention.

BALLYMERAGH, fit. in co. Down, prov. Ulfter.

BALLYMEN, fit. near Wexford hay, co. Wexford, prov. Leinfter.

BALLYMODIN, a vicarage in dioc. of Cork, fit. in bar. Kinalmeaky, co. Cork, prov. Munfter.

BALLYMOE, a fair town in co. Galway, prov. Connaught; fairs held on 2 Thurfday in May, and on 25 Oct.—There is alfo a bar. of fame name in this prov. divided between the counties Galway and Rofcommon, diftinguifhed between each into half Ballymoe.

BALLYMONEY, a rectory in dioc. of Connor, fit. in bar. Dunluce, co. Antrim, prov. Ulfter; 107 miles from Dublin. It is a market, fair and poft-town: lat 55 : 4, lon. 6 : 50. Here is a feat of lord Hilliborough. Fairs held 6 May, 10 July and 10 Oct.—Alfo a rectory in dioc. of Cork, fit. in bar. Carberry, co. Cork, prov. Munfter.

BALLIMONY, fit. in bar. Atherdee, co. Louth, prov. Leinfter.

BALLYMOON or Ballimeen, a caftle fit. on the road to Ennifcorthy, 5 miles from Laughlin bridge, in bar. Idrone, co. Carlow, prov. Leinfter. It was properly that fpecies of building denominated a Bawn, ferving principally for the fecurity of cattle, and appertained to the Cavanaghs; being placed in a wild, barren country, it ferved to defend the pafs from the mountains, as well as a fecurity for the cattle of the diftrict; the walls, rudely built of mountain ftone, were originally about 30 feet high, and are ftill about 20, inclofing an area of 110 feet fquare, on the S. fide in the entrance defended by a portcullis; on the right of which are newel ftairs leading to the parapet and battlements on the top of the wall: on the E. fide was a tower, which contained the principal apartments, having 3 ftories, each containing a room 25 feet by 16, to which conducted a newel ftair: on the W. fide was another tower: on the N. fide are 3 fmall apartments, afcended to by fteps in the wall; each apartment is 12 feet by 6, and has a fire-place and one window in form of a crofs, fmall, and which does not appear to have been glazed: within the area were wells and other conveniencies, now filled up. The building is fit. on a high and rocky field, without either ditch or mould, nor doth there appear to have been either wood or habitation near it. This caftle, from the architecture and ornaments, feems to be of the 14 century.

BALLYMORE (otherwife called Ballymoreloughfeway) a fmall market and poft-town in co. Weftmeath, prov. Leinfter. This place was famous for its abbey of the order of Gilbertines, founded in the 12th century. In 1388 Theobald De Vernon, lord of the manor, obtaine a grant of a weekly market, and a fair for 15 days to be held there. Fair days Whitfun-Monday and 14 Oct. It is diftant 47 miles from Dublin. Lat. 53 : 27, lon. 7 : 40. Near it is the diffolved monaftery monaſtery of Mary. It is ſometimes written *Ballimore*.

BALLYMOREEN otherwiſe called *Ballymurrin*, a vicarage in dioc. of Caſhel, ſit. in bar. Eliogurty, co. Tipperary, prov. Munſter; 68 miles from Dublin. Not far from this are the ruins of *Moycarty caſtle*.

BALLYMORE-EUSTACE, (i. e. *the great town of Euſtace*) ſit. on the river Liffey about 17½ miles from Dublin, in bar. Newcaſtle, co. Dublin, prov. Leinſter: it has a handſome bridge over the river, and is in a pleaſant ſituation; but the town which was formerly larger, is now much decayed; owing to the great Southern road, which for ages led thro' this place, being now turned by the way of Kilcullen bridge. It is a vicarage in the dioc. of Dublin; and a market and poſt-town. Fairs held 26 Aug. and 29 Oct. Near it is a large common and ground mark'd out for horſe races; alſo a moſt beautiful natural caſcade, formed by a river that riſes in the co. Wicklow and falls into the river Liffey. Here are the ruins of a fine old caſtle, formerly a place of great ſtrength, built by *Euſtace* the head of an antient family in this county, from whom the town takes its name. The late lord Mountcaſhel built here a neat lodge, and made ſome pretty improvements.

BALLYMOTE, a fair town in co. Galway, prov. Connaught; fairs held 21 Oct. and 16 Nov.—Alſo a fair town in co. Sligo, prov. Connaught; fairs held on the laſt Monday in Jan. 11 May, 1 Monday O. S. in June, 3 Sep. 1 Monday O. S. in Nov. and 2 Monday O. S. in Dec. In this place is an extenſive linen manufactory; and alſo one of the largeſt old caſtles in Ireland, flank'd by 6 towers of great ſtrength.

BALLYMOUNT, ſit. in bar. Coolock, co. Dublin, prov. Leinſter; where are ſome antient ruins.

BALLYMULLALON, ſit. in co. Roſcommon, prov. Connaught; 64 miles from Dublin.

BALLYMULLART, ſit. in co. Fermanagh, prov. Ulſter; the church of which is diſtant 101 miles from Dublin. ¼ mile from it are the ruins of a caſtle.

BALLYMULVY, ſit. in bar. Rathline, co. Longford, prov. Leinſter.

BALLYMURRIN, ſee *Ballymoreen*.

BALLYMURRY, a fair town in co. Roſcommon, prov. Connaught; above 69 miles from Dublin. Fair days 10 May and 15 Aug.

BALLYMURTOGH, ſit. near the river Proca, in co. Wicklow, prov. Leinſter. Here is a copper mine, which was formerly wrought and yielded vaſt profit; but on account of a diſſention among the proprietors, it had been diſuſed for ſome years; which occaſioned other adventurers to ſink a ſhaft at *Cronebane* on the N. ſide of the river, that proved far richer than the former.

BALLYNA, ſee *Ballina*.

BALLYNACARGY, ſit. in co. Cavan, prov. Ulſter; 131 miles from Dublin.—Alſo a place in co. Cork, prov. Munſter; otherwiſe called *Daw's-town*.

BALLYNACARNE-BRIDGE, ſit. over the river Inny, in bar. Raconrath and Moygeeſh, co. Weſtmeath, prov. Leinſter; it is ſometimes called *Ballynacarra*.

BALLYNACARRA, ſee *Ballynacarne*.

BALLYNACARROW, a fair town in co. Sligo, prov. Connaught. Fairs held 14 May, June, Oct. and Dec.

BALLYNACLASSEN, ſit. near Macroomp, in co. Cork, prov. Munſter: a deep boggy tract runs thro' this place till you come to *Dunmanaway*.

BALLYNACLUSH, ſit. in co. Carlow, prov. Leinſter; 2 miles from Rathdrum. Here was formerly one of the moſt conſiderable iron works in the kingdom, and there is ſtill a good foundery; but the ſcarcity of wood fuel which ſuch works muſt neceſſarily occaſion, has been the cauſe of the decline of this and other works of the ſame kind in different parts of Ireland.

BALLYNACOUR, a bar. with a ſmall village of ſame name in co. Wicklow, prov. Leinſter. Alſo village in bar. Delvin, co. Weſtmeath, prov. Leinſter.

BALLYNACOURTY, a rectory in dioc. of Ardfert, ſit. in bar. Corkaguinny, co. Kerry, prov. Munſter.

BALLYNACOURTY-POINT, a cape in bar. Decies without Drum, co. Waterford, prov. Munſter.

BALLYNACRAGGY, ſit. in bar. Moygeeſh, co. Weſtmeath, prov. Leinſter.

BALLYNAGANNY, ſit. in co. Meath, prov. Leinſter; 40 miles from Dublin. Here is a noted flour mill; and within about 2 miles are the ruins of a caſtle ſeated at the foot of a hill.

BALLYNAGAR, ſit. in bar. Geaſhil, King's co. prov. Leinſter; 41 miles from Dublin.—Within 3 miles of which are the ruins of a church.

BALLYNAGEERAH *mountains*, ſit. at the N. W. angle of co. Cavan, prov. Ulſter.

BALLYNAGORE, ſit. in bar. Moycaſhel, co. Weſtmeath, prov. Leinſter.

BALLYNAGORY, a fair town in co. Tyrone, prov. Ulſter. Fairs held 3 May, 5 July and 2 Nov.

BALLYNAHASSACK, a ſmall village on the N. ſide of the river Conbury, ſit. in co. Cork, prov. Munſter.

BALLYNAHINCH, a poſt town in bar. Kinclearty, co. Down, prov. Ulſter; near 76 miles from Dublin: it lies in the midſt of the great roads leading from Lurgan, Dromore, Liſburn, and Hilliborough to Downpatrick; and ſtands near the centre of the county on a little river: The country about it is extremely coarſe, full

of

J

of rocks and hills, from whence this place has been called *Magheredroll*, i. e. the field of difficulties. Here is the country refidence of the earl of Moira. Within 2 miles of this place, at the fkirts of Slieu-Crobb mountain, is an excellent chalybeate fulphurceous fpa. At Ballynahinch is a church, refidentiary houfe, Charter-fchool and Prefbyterian meeting-houfe. The fchool is endowed with 2 acres of land belonging to the fee of Dromore; and the late earl of Moira befides a fubfcription, granted 20 acres of land at 3*l* 5*s* per ann. in lieu of 10 acres formerly let by him to the incorporated fociety. *William Johnfton* late of Finglas bridge *efq.* bequeathed 100*l* to this fchool, the intereft whereof is appropriated towards the fupport of it. Fairs are held here on the 1 Jan. 12 Feb. 5 April, 10 July and 2 Oct.—There is alfo a bar. with a village in it of fame name in co. Galway, prov. Connaught; otherwife called *Ballinehinch*. The Northern parts of this bar. and of the bar. of Rofs are called *Joyce's* country, and inhabited chiefly by a clan of that name.

BALLYNAHOOGH, fit. in bar. Boyle, co. Rofcommon, prov. Connaught.

BALLYNAHOWN, a fair town in co. Weftmeath, prov. Leinfter; fairs held 1 July and 11 Sep.

BALLYNAKELLY, a fair town in co. Cork, prov. Munfter. Fairs held from 3 to 6 and from 18 to 21 Sep.—Alfo a rectory in dioc. of Tuam, fit. in bar. Killihan, co. Galway.—And a vicarage in dioc. of Elphin, fit. in bar. Tyraghrill, in fame co. both in prov. Connaught.

BALLYNAKILL, a borough, market, fair and poft town, in bar. Cullinagh, Queen's co. prov. Leinfter; 48 miles from Dublin.—Lat. 52 : 49, lon. 7 : 15. Fairs held on Thurfday after Whit. Monday, 12 Aug. and 16 Nov. It fends 2 members to parliament. Patron the *marquis of Drogheda*. Here are the ruins of a caftle deftroyed by Oliver Cromwell in 1642, when it bravely refifted his forces.—Alfo the name of a fmall village in co. Sligo, prov. Connaught.—and of a handfome feat in co. Carlow, prov. Leinfter. — Alfo a village in bar. Leitrim.—A fecond in bar. half Ballimoe.—And a third in bar. Ballinahinch, all in co. Galway, prov. Connaught. The firft of thefe is a rectory in dioc. of Clonfert; the fecond a vicarage in dioc. of Elphin; and the laft a rectory in dioc. of Tuam.—There is a vicarage of fame name in dioc. of Waterford, fit. in bar. Gualtiere, co. Waterford, prov. Munfter.—And a vicarage in dioc. of Kildare, fit. in bar. Coole'ftown, King's co. prov. Leinfter; the church of which is at *Clonbulloek*.

BALLYNALACK, a village fit. in bar Corkerry, co. Weftmeath, prov. Leinfter.

BALLYNAMARA, fit. in co. Kilkenny, prov. Leinfter; where fairs are held annually on the day after Trinity Sunday.

BALLYNAMONA, a village fit. in bar. Barretts, co. Cork, prov. Munfter; 137 miles from Dublin; otherwife called *Ballynemony*. Fairs held on Whit. Monday, 21 Aug. and 5 Dec. Near the church of this place are the ruins of the great preceptory of *Mourne*. Alfo a vicarage in dioc. of Emly; fit. in bar. Small county, co. Limerick, prov. Munfter.

BALLYNAMORE, or *Ballinamore*, fit. in co. Galway, prov. Connaught, above 74 miles from Dublin: Alfo a place in bar. Carrigallen, co. Leitrim, prov. Connaught; 71 miles from Dublin.

BALLYNAMULLY, fit. in bar. Athlone, co. Rofcommon, prov. Connaught.

BALLYNARD-CASTLE, fit about 4 miles beyond Mullinahone, co. Tipperary, prov. Munfter; alfo a vicarage in dioc. of Emly, fit. in bar. Small-county, co. Limerick, prov. Munfter.

BALLYNARIES, fit. in co. Down, prov. Ulfter.

BALLYNASKELIGS, a *village* and *bay* in bar. Iveragh, co. Kerry, prov. Munfter; where are to be feen the ruins of an antient abbey or friary, of the order of St. Auguftin canons. It was formerly removed hither from the ifland called *Great-Skelig*, where there was a monaftery confifting of feveral cells, dedicated to St. Michael the archangel, as mentioned by *Girald: Camb.* The time of its foundation is not known, but it muft have been of great antiquity; probably as early as the 6th century. The annals of Inisfallen in Lough-lane, fay, that *Flan M'Callagh*, abbot of Skelig, died in 885.—Lat 51 : 42, lon. 9 : 14.

BALLYNASLOE, fee *Ballinafloe*.

BALLYNASMALL, fit. in bar. Clonmorris, co. Mayo, prov. Connaught. One *Prendergaft* in the 13th century founded a friary here, dedicated to the Virgin-Mary, for Carmelites; it was an extenfive building, part of which may ftill be feen.

BALLYNASPEG, otherwife *Bifhop's-town*, fit. about 2 miles W. of Cork, in co. Cork, prov. where there is a neat houfe and chapel.

BALLYNASTOE, fit. in bar. Newcaftle, co. Wicklow, prov. Leinfter.

BALLYNATRAY, a handfome feat, fit. by the river Black-water, in co. Waterford, prov. Munfter: near it is a fmall ifland in this river called Dar Inis, or the ifland of St. Molanfide, now Molana, in which are the remains of an abbey of regular canons, founded in the 6th century by that Saint, who was the 1ft abbot. In this abbey *Raymond le grofs* the Englifh general, who with *Strongbow* contributed fo much to the reduction of Ireland, is faid to be buried. Somewhat lower than Molana are the ruins of the church and caftle of *Temple-Michael*, which feem to have been demolifhed by powder; as

does

does another building a little more to the S. fit. on a high point now called *Rhincrew*, but in some old M.S.S. *Kilcrew*, which place is faid by tradition to have been a houfe of the knights Templars.

BALLYNAVE, fit. in bar. Leitrim, co. Leitrim, prov. Connaught.

BALLYNCOLLY, a large caftle, 4 miles W. of Cork, in co. Cork, prov. Munfter.

BALLYNDOON, fit. in co. Sligo, prov. Connaught.

BALLYNDRIN, fit. in bar. Dunluce, co. Antrim, prov. Ulfter.

BALLYNEAGH, fit. between Monafterevan and Kildare, in co. Kildare, prov. Leinfter. On thefe lands is a ftrong calcareous fpring, which throws up great quantities of ftalaétitical matter, and even incruftates bodies immerfed in it.

BALLYNEALE, a village in bar. Ida, co. Kilkenny, prov. Leinfter.

BALLYNEBRAHER, fit. near *Lough-Gir*, in bar. Small-county, co. Limerick, prov. Munfter. A friary for conventual Francifcans was founded here by the family of Claugibbon, in the 13th century.

BALLYNECLOFFY, fit. near Athlone, in co. Weftmeath, prov. Leinfter; during the wars of 1641, two foot companies of Englifh forces were quartered here under the command of Capt. *Bertie*, brother to earl *Lindfay*, then lord Chamberlain. Having unfortunately plunder'd the nunnery of *St. Clare* at Bethlem near this place, and got themfelves intoxicated, they were on their return fuddenly attack'd by fome of the Irifh forces, and entirely cut off.

BALLYNEGALGA, fit. in co. Down, prov. Ulfter.

BALLYNEGALL, fit. near Kilmallock, in co. Limerick, prov. Munfter. It was built by the Englifh, and formerly a town of fome note; the family of *Roche* founded a monaftery here for Dominican friars in the 14th century, of which *Dònogh O'Dangane* was the laft prior: Q. Eliz. in the 39th year of her reign, granted it, with certain lands belonging thereto, to the univerfity of Dublin.

BALLYNEHINCH, fit. in a *barony* of fame name in co. Galway, prov. Connaught. A monaftery for Carmelites was founded here by *O'Flaherty* in 1356. It is otherwife written *Ballinahinch*.

BALLYNEKILL or *Ballinakill*, a parifh in co. Waterford, prov. Munfter, which begins about a mile E. of the city of Waterford; a pleafant road runs thro' it from the city towards *Paffage*, affording a traveller an agreeable profpeét of the city and veffels failing up and down the river. An ifland called the *little Ifland* in the Suir, belongs to this parifh; it is about a mile long, and as much in breadth, and a very pleafant fpot.

BALLYNEMONY, otherwife *Ballinamony*, or *Ballinemona*, fit. in co. Cork, prov. Munfter, 3 miles S. of Mallow. Here was a preceptory of Knights hofpitalers, founded in the reign of king John; it was ruinated in the reign of Edward IV.th. There is a church not far diftant; which was rebuilt A. D. 1717, at which time in the ruins of the old church, was found a large fpur, and the head of an antique fpear; probably belonging to one of the knights buried here in his martial habiliments. — Fairs held Whit. Monday, 21 Aug. and 5 Dec. Adjacent to the church is a charity-fchool-houfe, and about a mile to the S. is a fmall place named *Bòttle-hill*, remarkable for a ftout fkirmifh fought there between the Englifh and king James IId. forces, on 29 Apr. 1691.

BALLYNETTY, a village in bar. Clanwilliam, co. Limerick, prov. Munfter, 169 miles from Dublin; fometimes written *Ballyneety*.

BALLYNGUILE, a good feat with large orchards and plantations, lying eafterly on the river *Awbeg*, co. Cork, prov. Munfter. The houfe was built on the foundation of an antient caftle of the *Stapletons*, erected foon after the reign of king John.

BALLYNITTY, a vicarage in dioc. of Ferns, fit. in bar. Shelmaliere, co. Wexford, prov. Leinfter.

BALLYNOE, fit. in bar. Kilnataloon, co. Cork, prov. Munfter; there are large ruins of an antient building here, faid to have been a religious houfe.

BALLYNOWLART, fit. in King's co. prov. Leinfter, near *Rathangan* and about 28 miles from Dublin; here are the ruins of a church, which, tradition fays, had been converted into a ftable by fome of *Oliver Cromwell's* forces.

BALLYNTOBBER, a bar. in co. Rofcommon, prov. Connaught.—Alfo a place near *Kinfale*, in co. Cork, prov. Munfter.

BALLYNTOY, fit. in bar. Carie, co. Antrim, prov. Ulfter.

BALLYNUNNERY, fit. in bar. Forth, co. Carlow, prov. Leinfter.

BALLYNURE, a village in bar. Belfaft, co. Antrim, prov. Ulfter; it is a rectory in dioc of Down; above 90 miles from Dublin.—Alfo a village in bar. Cooleftown, King's co. prov. Leinfter.—Likewife a rectory in dioc. of Leighlin, fit. in bar. Talbot's-town, co. Wicklow, prov. Leinfter.—Alfo a rectory in dioc. of Cafhel, fit. in bar. Slewardagh, co. Tipperary, prov. Munfter.

BALLYNVRENEY, a fair town in co. Limerick, prov. Munfter: fairs held 21 Apr. 21 June, for yearlings; 31 Aug. and 19 Nov.

BALLYONAN, a fair town in co. Kildare, prov. Leinfter; fairs held 5 May and 28 Oét.

BALLY

BALLYYOUTERAGH, (or the town of braziers) so called from a remarkable copper manufactory, once carried on here; it is sit. near Castlemartyr, co. Cork, prov. Munster, in which was antiently a Leper-house. There is no copper ore near this place, but *iron-mine* almost every where round it.

BALLYOWEN, sit. in bar. Newcastle, co. Dublin, prov. Leinster.

BALLYPATRICK, a village in bar. Iffa and Offa, co. Tipperary, prov. Munster.

BALLYPHILLIP, a rectory in dioc. of Down, sit. in bar. Ardes, co. Down, prov. Ulster.

BALLYPOREEN, a fair town in co. Tipperary, prov. Munster, near 97 miles from Dublin; where is a handsome seat, with a fine wood; fairs held 12 May, 21 Aug. and 17 Dec.

BALLYQUILLANE, a rectory in dioc. of Leighlin, sit. in bar. Stradbally, Queen's co. prov. Leinster.

BALLYQUINTIN-POINT, a *cape* in bar. Ardes, co. Down, prov. Ulster

BALLYRAGGET, sit. in bar. Fassadinning, co. Kilkenny, prov. Leinster, near 50 miles from Dublin; here is a barrack; also a fine seat, with handsome improvements: fairs held 20 Feb. 20 Apr. 22 June, 4 Sept. 20 Oct. and 10 Dec.

BALLYRASHANE, a vicarage in dioc. of Connor, sit. in bar. Dunluce, co. Antrim, prov. Ulster.

BALLYROAN, a fair town in Queen's co. prov. Leinster, above 44 miles from Dublin, and within about 5 miles of Maryborough: fairs held 15 May, first Wednesday, O. S. in July and second Wednesday, O. S. in Nov.

BALLYRONEY-LAKE, sit. near Rathfryland, in co. Down, prov. Ulster.

BALLYSADERE, see *Ballysedere*.

BALLYSAX, a seat of the Annesley family, sit. near Kilcullen bridge, in bar. Ophaly, co. Kildare, prov. Leinster: within half a mile of it are the ruins of a castle.

BALLYSCADDEN, a rectory in dioc. of Emly, sit. in bar. Small county, co. Limerick, prov. Munster.

BALLYSCANDLAN, a fair town in co. Limerick, prov. Munster: fairs held 8 June, 12 Aug 29 Sept. and 16 Nov.

BALLYSCULLEN, a rectory in dioc. of Derry, sit. in bar. Loughinsholen, co. Londonderry, prov. Ulster.

BALLYSEDERE, or *Ballysadere*, a vicarage in dioc. Achonry, sit. in bar. Leney, co. Sligo, prov. Connaught.—Also a village in bar. Tyraghrill, in same co. in which are the ruins of *Ballysedere-abbey*, awfully magnificent; near it are the ruins of a church. Fairs held 4 Aug. 12 Nov. and 15 Dec. Hereabouts are very pretty waterfalls; the scenery is bold, and if the falls were thro' a dark wood, would be amongst the best views, perhaps, in the world. This place is sometimes written *Ballysedare*.

BALLYSEEDY, sit. 2 miles S. E. of Tralee, in co. Kerry, prov. Munster.

BALLYSHANNON, a borough, market and post-town, in bar. Tyrhugh, co. Donegal, prov. Ulster, 100 miles from Dublin; having a good harbour E. of Donegal bay: it has a bridge of 14 arches, over a river which runs out of Lough-Erne, and falls down a ridge of rocks, about 12 feet, and at low water forms a most beautiful and picturesque cascade; it is rendered singular by being the principal *salmon-leap* in Ireland. Lat. 54:25, lon. 8:30. It has a barrack for one company of foot, and returns two members to parliament; patron, Rt. Hon. Mr. Conolly. Fairs held 4 April, Tuesday before 11 June, 18 Sept. and Tuesday after 11 Nov. Near Ballyshannon are the remains of the abbey of *Ashrow*; some of the gilding in the vault of the cloister is still visible. Also a village of same name in bar. Ophaly, co. Kildare. prov. Leinster.

BALLYSODARE see *Ballysedere*.

BALLYSOMAHAN, sit. in bar. Tyraghrill, co. Sligo, prov. Connaught.

BALLYSONNON, a rectory in dioc. of Kildare, sit. in bar. Ophaly, co. Kildare, prov. Leinster.

BALLYSPELLAN, a village sit. near *Beggar's-inn*, in bar. Galmoy, co. Kilkenny, prov. Leinster; here is a famous Chalybeate spa, excellent for disorders of the stomach and eruptions of the skin.—Also a vicarage in dioc. of Cloyne, sit. in bar. Barrymore, co. Cork, prov. Munster.

BALLYTEAGUE, sit. in co. Kildare, prov. Leinster: here is a very extensive bog, thro' which the grand canal from Dublin to Monaster-evan is cut: on the banks of it stands the old castle of Ballyteague. This place is otherwise called *Ballinteague*.

BALLYTEIG-BAY, sit. in bar. Bargie, co. Wexford, prov. Leinster.

BALLYTENAVE, sit. in co. Roscommon, prov. Connaught: having a bridge over part of Lough Allen.

BALLYTORE, a beautiful village in co. Kildare, prov. Leinster; near 28 miles from Dublin; where is a colony of Quakers: it lies in a valley, a small distance from the high road to Carlow; the river *Griss* winds its streams very near the houses; and the buildings, orchards and gardens shew a kind of elegant simplicity peculiar to that people. This is a post-town. Fairs held 10 March, 15 Aug. and 30 Nov.

BALLYTRANE, sit. in bar. Idrone, co. Carlow, prov. Leinster.—There is a place of same name in co. Monaghan, prov. Ulster.

BALLYTRANT, sit. in bar. Forth; co. Wexford, prov. Leinster.

BALLY

BALLYTRISNA, a fair town in co. Kilkenny, prov. Leinfter. Fairs held 19 Sep.

BALLYTURRIN, fit. in co. Galway, prov. Connaught.

BALLYVACADANE, a ruined abbey founded in 1450, in the road from Cork to Bandon, prov. Munfter. It is fit. 4 miles from Cork ; part of the walls ftill remain ; and not far from it ftands a large caftle called *Ballincolly caftle*, built upon a rock, and flanked with towers at each angle.

BALLYVAGHAN-BAY, fit. in bar. Burrin, co. Clare, prov. Munfter.

BALLYVALDON, a vicarage in dioc. of Ferns, fit. in bar. Ballagheen, co. Wexford, prov. Leinfter.

BALLYVARY, a fair town in co. Mayo, prov. Connaught : fairs held 29 May, 17 Aug. and 14 Nov.

BALLYVASTON, a town land on the fea fhore, between Terela and Killough, in co. Down, prov. Ulfter ; on which a remarkable accident happened fome years ago ; a ftrong wind fetting in on the land, raifed the fandy foil about 10 feet from the bottom, and thereby overwhelmed and almoft deftroyed a rabbit borough, by which the veftiges of feveral cabbins were difcovered, and the hearth ftones and wooden chimney frames furrounding them appeared ; from thefe places it is manifeft that this place was formerly inhabited : by the prodigious quantity of fand thrown up at that time, a confiderable fpace of ground was reduced to the ftate of a defert, in which condition it ftill remains.

BALLYVELY, a fair town in co. Mayo, prov. Connaught ; fairs held 14 May and 2 Oct.

BALLYVENINE, fit. about 1 mile W. of Rofs, in co. Cork, prov. Munfter. Here ftand the ruins of a large houfe erected by *Sir Walter Coppinger*, who alfo defigned to build a market-town here, but was hinder'd by the rebellion of 1641, at which time this houfe was deftroyed.

BALLYVILLE, fit. in bar. Coftello, co. Mayo, prov. Connaught.

BALLYVOGY-HEAD, fit. near *Crook-haven*, in co. Cork, prov. Munfter : between this place and the oppofite cape called *Mizen-head*, is a great bay ; and another between that and *Three-caftle-head*, fo called from 3 fquare towers built on it.

BALLYVOLANE, fit. at cove of Cork, in co. Cork, prov. Munfter ; fairs held 20 Apr. and 15 Oct.

BALLYVONY-COVE, fit. in bar. Decies without Drum, in co. Waterford, prov. Munfter. At Ballivony are fome remains of a large building 150 feet in length and 90 in breadth ; thought by fome to have been a houfe belonging to the knights hofpitalers : there are ftill the remains of feveral large out-offices, and the ground plan much refembles that of a monaftic edifice.

BALLYVOURNEY, (i. e. the town of the beloved ;) a fmall village fit. 6 miles W. of Macroomp, in bar. Mulkerry, co. Cork, prov. Munfter. Here is a ruined church dedicated to *St. Gobnate*, who in the 6th century was made abbefs of a nunnery of regular canoneffes here by *St. Abban*. This church is 104 feet long by 24 broad : the 14 Feb. is the patron day of this faint. About 30 yards W. of the church is a fmall ftone crofs, where her rood or image is fet up on that day ; and near it is a well dedicated to her, the water of which is pure, foft and light. A little to the N. of this well is a circle of ftones about 2 feet high and about 9 feet in diameter, which feems to have been the foundation for one of the fmall round towers, we find frequently placed near churches. This place is a rectory in dioc. of Cloyne.

BALLYWALTER, a village in co. Down, prov. Ulfter ; noted only for a good flate quarry, and a prefbyterian meeting houfe. It is diftant above 89 miles from Dublin, and holds fairs 22 June, and 8 Nov.

BALLYWILLAN, a vicarage in dioc. of Connor, fit. in bar. Dunluce, co. Antrim, prov. Ulfter.

BALLY-WILLIAM-ROE, fit. in co. Carlow, prov. Leinfter ; here are the ruins of a fpacious building, erected by the Knights Templars, about the year 1300. This was their principal feat in Ireland, which they did not enjoy above 8 years before their diffolution.

BALLYWIRE, a curacy in dioc. of Armagh, fit. in bar. Ferns, co. Armagh, prov. Ulfter ; 58 miles from Dublin.

BALNABARA, a fair town in co. Weftmeath, prov. Leinfter. Fairs held 19 Mar. 15 May, 14 Aug. and 28 Nov.

BALNALACK, a fair town in co. Weftmeath, prov. Leinfter. Fairs held 15 Febr. 18 May, 2 Oct. and 20 Dec.

BALNEGLERA, a fair town in co. Armagh, prov Ulfter. Fairs held 5 Jan. 8 June, 12 Aug. 2 Oct. 8 Nov. and 11 Dec.

BALON, a fair town in co. Carlow, prov. Leinfter. Fairs held 28 Mar. and 12 Aug.

BALONESTEAR, fit. in bar. Shelmaliere, co. Wexford, prov. Leinfter.

BALRAIN, a rectory in dioc. of Kildare, fit. in bar. Ikeath, co. Kildare, prov. Leinfter.

BALRIGGAN-CASTLE, fee *Ballrigan*.

BALRODDAN, a rectory in dioc. of Meath, fit. in bar. Deece, co. Meath, prov. Leinfter.

BALRUDDERY, or *Balrothery* a bar. in co. Dublin, prov. Leinfter ; in which is a poft and fair town of fame name ; it is a vicarage in dioc. of Dublin ; and is a good thoroughfare to the N. fit. about 1 mile from the Irifh channel,

channel, nearly oppofite St. Patrick's Ifle, and above 14 miles from Dublin. Fairs held 6 May and 12 Aug. for the fale of cattle, and pedlar's goods. This place is a fifhing town.

BALSCADDAN, fit. in bar. Balruddery, co. Dublin, prov. Leinfter.

BALSOON, a rectory in dioc. of Meath, fit. in bar. Deece, co. Meath, prov. Leinfter; it lies near Trim, and oppofite Bective abbey, and was formerly the eftate and refidence of the celebrated primate Ufher.

BALTEAGH, a rectory in dioc. of Derry, fit. in bar. Kenoght, co. Londonderry, prov. Ulfter.

BALTIBOYS, fit. near Nans, co. Kildare, prov. Leinfter.

BALTIMORE, a borough town in bar. Carberry, co. Cork, prov. Munfter, 168 miles from Dublin, having a commodious harbour; it lies in the antient diftrict of Leam-Con in the W. of Carberry, on a headland that runs into the fea; 15 miles S. W. of Rofs, and 5 miles N. E. of the ifland of Cape-clear; lat. 51 : 15, long. 9 : 15. It was formerly called Dunafhad; the prefent name is a corruption of Beal-timore, or the great habitation of Beal, it having been a fanctuary for the Druids. 'Twas formerly a place of fome confequence, but on 20 June, 1631, being taken and plunder'd by the Algerines, the terror fpread thereby fubfifted fo long, and deterred people fo much from fettling there, that it has never fince recovered; and is now only a decayed fifhing town. Here are fome ruins of antient caftles, once efteemed proof againft the ftrongeft rocks. It fends two members to parliament, patronage in fir J. Freke, bart. The firft Englifh plantation made here, was by fir Thomas Creek, who took a leafe of this place from fir Fineen O'Drifcol. — Alfo a place in co. Longford, prov. Leinfter, which gives title of baron to the noble family of Calvert.

BALTINGLASS, a borough and market town fit. on the river Slaney, in bar. Talbot's-town, co. Wicklow, prov. Leinfter, 29 miles S. of Dublin, lat. 53 : 00, lon. 6 : 25. It is a rectory in dioc. of Leighlin, and fends two members to parliament; patron, the earl of Aldborough. Fairs held 2 Feb. 17 Mar. 12 May, 1 July, 12 Sept. and 8 Dec. It gives title of baron to the noble family of Stratford, now earl of Aldborough. Here are extenfive manufactures of linen, woolen and diaper; the name is derived from Beal-tinne-glas, or the fire of Beal's myfteries, the fires being lighted there by the Druids in honour of the fun, on 1 May and Aug. It was the grand Beal-tinne of the fouthern ftates of Leinfter; there are ftill remaining in it's neighbourhood, a number of Druidic altars, and other monuments of heathen fuperftition; a parliament was formerly held at this town, as

alfo the affizes; here is a venerable caftle, alfo a fine old abbey called St. Mary's; it was founded about the year 1148 of Ciftertian monks, by Dermot M'Murchad O'Cavanagh king of Leinfter, who is buried there.

BALTINORN, fit. near Clonard, co. Meath, prov. Leinfter.

BALTRACY, fit. in bar. Dundalk, co. Louth, prov. Leinfter.

BALTRASANA, fit. in bar. Balrudderry, co. Dublin, prov. Leinfter. —— Alfo a place near Ardee, in co. Louth, prov. Leinfter.

BALYNA, fit. near Clonard, co. Meath, prov. Leinfter.

BAN or Bann, a river famous for it's falmon and eel fifheries, it falls into Lough Neagh, and iffuing from the N. end of it, divides the countries Antrim and Londonderry, prov. Ulfter, and is loft in the fea a little N. W. of Colerain. It runs thro' the counties Down, Louth, Armagh, Antrim, Tyrone and Londonderry, and is adjacent to Carlingford, Newry, Tanderagee, Portadown, Charlemont, Dungannon, Lurgan, Glanevy, Antrim, Randal's-town, Caftledawfon, Kilreagh, Lifnagrot, Ballmoney and Colerain. —— Alfo a lough fo called, fit. in bar. Half-fore, co. Weftmeath, prov. Leinfter, and a river in bar. Scarawalfh, co. Wexford, prov. Leinfter.

BANADA, a fair town, in bar. Leney, co. Sligo, prov. Connaught. Fairs held 17 Jan. Whitfun Monday and 7 Aug.

BANAGHER, a borough, market and poft-town, in bar. Garrycaftle, King's co. prov. Leinfter, fit. on the river Shannon, about 15 miles S. of Athlone, and 66 from Dublin. Lat. 53 : 20, long. 4 : 15. It is a pretty large place, tolerably built, having two bridges over the Shannon, and a barrack for two companies of foot; and returns two members to parliament; patron, W. B. Ponfonby, efq; fairs held 1 May, 15 Sept. 28 Oct. and 8 Nov. —— Alfo a rectory in dioc. of Derry, fit. in bar. Kenoght, co. Londonderry, prov. Ulfter.

BANAGHER-CHURCH, fit. in co. Tyrone, prov. Ulfter, 101 miles from Dublin: four miles beyond it are the ruins of Straid church.

BANAGROTAY, a fair town in King's co. prov. Leinfter. Fairs held day before Afcenf. and 11 Aug.

BANAKERRY, fit. in bar. Upper Offory, Queen's co. prov. Leinfter: otherwife called Bannakerry.

BANBRIDGE, or Bannbridge, a village in bar. Upper Iveach, co. Down, prov. Ulfter; remarkable for its great fairs of linen cloth; 'tis fo called from a ftone bridge built there over the river Ban; it lies about 18 miles S. W. of Downpatrick, and 60 from Dublin. Fairs held

12 Jan. 15 Mar. 9 June, 26 Aug. and 16 Nov. This is a poſt town.

BANDON, a river in the liberties of Kinſale, co. Cork, prov. Munſter; it extends from Kinſale to Dunmanaway, W. 24 miles, runs thro' the co. Cork; and is adjacent to Kinſale, Inniſhannon, Bandon-bridge, Inniſkean, and Dunmanaway. Dr. Beauford's memoir places it (we preſume, by accident) in the co. *Londonderry*. The head of this river is about one mile S. of *Tagher-caſtle*.

BANDON-BRIDGE, or *Bandon*, a borough, market and poſt-town in bar. Kinalmeaky, co. Cork, prov. Munſter; it lies on a river which gives name to the town, and was built in 1610, by *Rich. Boyle*, the firſt earl of Cork, with walls, fortifications, two churches, two market houſes, &c. the Iriſh demoliſhed the walls in 1689. for which, by a ſtanding law of the corporation, no Roman catholic can dwell in the town. It has a barrack for two companies of foot, and gives title of viſc. to a branch of the Boyle family: 'tis ſit. about 12 miles S. W. of Cork, and 137 from Dublin. Lat. 51:36, lon. 8:35. It gives title of *Baron* to the family of Bernard, and ſends two members to parliament; patron, the earl of Shannon. Fairs held 6 May, 29 Oct. and 8 Nov. Not far from this place is the old caſtle of *Dundanere*; and near the town is a good chalybeate ſpring.

BANDUFF, now called *Caſtle-Salem*, it is a ſtrong romantic building, ſit. one mile N. E. of Roſs, in co. Cork, prov. Munſter.

BANGOR, a borough town, in bar. Ardes, co. Down, prov. Ulſter; 90 miles N. of Dublin. Lat. 54:44, lon. 6:13. It ſtands on the S. ſide of the bay of Carrickfergus, and near 4 miles E. N. E. of *Newtown*; it is a curacy in the dioc. of Down, and returns two members to parliament: patron, lord *Bangor*: it gives title of viſc. and baron to the family of *Ward*. Fairs held 12 Jan. 1 May and 22 Nov. Near it to the E. and part of the manor of Bangor, is the great bog of *Cotton* and *Granſhaw*; containing at leaſt, 1000 acres; which the owners began to reclaim and improve in 1743. The church of Bangor was firſt built within the precincts of the old abbey, about the year 1617, and was not finiſhed 'till 1623: the ſteeple was erected in 1693. This was one of the ſeats of the *Hamiltons*, lords *Clancbois*; a deſcendant of which family was afterwards created earl of *Clanbraſſil*. The abbey for which it was famous, was founded by St. *Congal*, about the year 555, it was an elegant building of lime and ſtone, and ſaid to have been the firſt of that ſort made in Ulſter. A ſmall part of the ruins of Malachy's building yet ſubſiſts, and the traces of the old foundation ſhew it to have been of great extent.

BAN-HARBOUR, ſee *Bann-Harbour*.

BANKAULE-CASTLE, ſit. in bar. Bunratty, co. Clare, prov. Munſter.

BANKMORE, a ſand bank, ſit. a mile S. of Portaferry harbour, in co. Down, prov. Ulſter.

BANKSTOWN, ſit. in bar. Ferrard, co. Louth, prov. Leinſter.

BANLAHAN, a fair town in co. Cork, prov. Munſter; fairs held on Aſcenſion day.

BANN, ſee *Ban*.

BANNBRIDGE, ſee *Banbridge*.

BANN-FOOT-FERRY, ſit. in bar. Oneilland, co. Armagh, prov. Ulſter.

BANN-HARBOUR, or *Ban-harbour*, ſit. in co. Londonderry, prov. Ulſter.

BANNOW, a ſmall borough town, in bar. Bargie, co. Wexford, prov. Leinſter; about 10 miles S. W. of Wexford. Lat. 52:5, lon. 6:50. It is a vicarage in dioc. of Ferns, and ſends two members to parliament; patron, lord Loftus. Near this place earl *Strongbow* landed, who reduced Ireland in the reign of king *Hen. 2d*.

BANNOW-BAY, ſit. in co. Wexford, prov. Leinſter.

BANSHAW, a rectory in dioc. of Caſhel, ſit. in bar. Clanwilliam, co. Tipperary, prov. Munſter.

BANTRY, a bar. in which is a poſt-town, har. and bay of ſame name, ſit. in co. Cork, prov. Munſter. The bar. is joined to that of Bear or Beer, and is uſually called *Beer and Bantry*; It was antiently called *Bentraighe*, and reckoned a part of Carberry; 'tis ſaid to have its name from *Beaunt-Mac-Favolla*, a perſon deſcended from the O'Donovans and Mahonys. The bar. is very large, but barren and deſolate. The bay however is one of the nobleſt in the world, and capable of containing all the ſhipping of Europe. The town is ſeated at the bottom of this extenſive bay, 30 miles W. of Cork and 164 from Dublin. Lat. 51:30, lon. 9:20. It was formerly called *Ballygobbin*, as alſo the *old-town*, to diſtinguiſh it from another ſettlement, more to the N. called *New-town*; where *Ireton*, in the time of Oliver Cromwell, had a fortification erected with 4 regular baſtions; which cauſed the inhabitants to build near it; but when this fort went to decay, they returned by degrees to the old town called Bantry. Near this ſtood a Franciſcan abbey, founded in 1460 by *Dermot O'Sullivan*, but now entirely demoliſhed. This place is memorable for the ſea fight in 1689 between admiral Herbert and the French fleet, in which the former proved victorious; and on the 7th May following brought the conquered veſſels into Plymouth. Fairs are held here 9 June, 21 Aug. 15 Oct. and 1 Dec.—There is alſo a bar. of ſame name in co. Wexford, prov. Leinſter.

BARANAGH, ſit. in bar. Erris, co. Mayo, prov. Connaught.

BARBER'S.

BARBER's-TOWN, fit. in co. Kildare, prov. Leinfter ; 23 miles from Dublin. Here is a caftle ; and near Barberftown are the church and round tower of *Teghadow*.

BARGIE, a bar. adjoining that of Forth, in co. Wexford, prov. Leinfter. The inhabitants fpeak a kind of Saxon language, and have feveral cuftoms peculiar to themfelves. This bar. as well as *Forth*, is of a light foil, producing large quantities of barley.

BARISHOOL, fit. in co. Mayo, prov. Connaught.

BARLEY-COVE, fit. near Mizen-head, in bar. Carberry, co. Cork, prov. Munfter.

BARMEATH, fit. in bar Ferrard, co. Louth, prov. Leinfter ; 29 miles from Dublin.

BARNACH-ISLAND, fit. in bar. Erris, co. Mayo, prov. Connaught.

BARNAHELY, a rectory in dioc. of Cork, fit. in bar. Kinalea, co. Cork, prov. Munfter.— Alfo a rectory in dioc. of Cafhel, fit. in bar. Eliogurty, co. Tipperary, prov. Munfter.

BARNASNE *mountains*, fit. in bar. Dunkerrin, co. Kerry, prov. Munfter.

BARNE *river*, fit. in co. Cavan, prov. Ulfter: it communicates with Lough *Ern* ; and the borough of *Belturbet* is feated on it.

BARNESMORE *mountains*, fit. in bar. Raphoe, co. Donegal, prov. Ulfter.

BARONRATH, fit. in co. Kildare, prov. Leinfter.—Here is the feat of William Wolf, efq. near the banks of the grand canal, leading to Monafterevan.

BARON's-COURT, the feat of lord Abercorn, fit. near Newtown-Stewart, co. Tyrone, prov. Ulfter. The houfe (exclufive of the offices) coft £20,000 ; it was erected by a Mr. Stewart an Englifh architect; and is thought to be one of the moft compleat models of a nobleman's houfe ; the grounds are fine and well wooded with oaks ; near them is a large lake with an ifland on which are the ruins of a caftle called *Mac Que*, where a chief of that name formerly refided.

BARONSTON, fee *Barran's-town*.

BARON's-TOWN, a rectory in dioc. of Armagh, fit. in bar. Dundalk, co. Louth, prov. Leinfter.

BARR *river*, fit. in bar. Raphoe, co. Donegal, prov. Ulfter.

BARRADORE, fit. in bar. Talbot's-town, co. Wicklow, prov. Leinfter.

BARRAGH, a vicarage in dioc. of Leighlin, fit. in bar. Forth, co. Carlow, prov. Leinfter.

BARRA-LOUGH, a *lake* fit. in bar. Kilmacrenan, co. Donegal, prov. Ulfter.

BARRAN's-TOWN or *Baronfton*, a feat of lord Sunderland, fit. in bar. Moygeeth, co. Weftmeath, prov. Leinfter.

BARRELS, *rocks* fit. in the coaft of the co. Wexford, in the bar. Forth, prov. Leinfter.—

There are others of fame name on the coaft of co. Cork, in bar. Barryroe, prov. Munfter.

BARRETTS, a bar. in co. Cork, prov. Munft.

BARROE, a *lough* fit. in bar. Cremourne, co. Monaghan, prov. Ulfter.

BARRON's-TOWN, fit. in bar. Talbot's-town, co. Wicklow, prov. Leinfter.

BARROW *River*, antiently called *Breba* and *Berva*, and in later ages obtained the name of *Barragh* or boundary river, being for fome centuries the boundary between the Englifh pale and the Irifh fepts ; it runs thro' the Queen's co. King's co. and co. Carlow, Kildare, Weftmeath, Kilkenny, Wexford, is joined by the *Noire* before it arrives at Rofs, and falls into the fea at *Waterford haven*. It is adjacent to the towns of Rofs, Graigenemanagh, Wells, Laughlinbridge, Caftledermot, Maryborough, Monafterevan, Kildare, Clonbullock, Philip's-town, Edenderry, Kinnegad and Mullingar, &c.—There is alfo a river called the leffer or little Barrow, which is fit. in bar. Tinehinch, Queen's co. prov. Leinfter.

BARROW-MOUNT, a fair town in co. Kilkenny, prov. Leinfter. Fairs held 13 April, 15 June, 1 Aug. and 15 Oct.—alfo a place fit. near *Gowran* in fame co.

BARRY, fit. in bar. Shroole, co. Longford, prov. Leinfter; above 54 miles from Dublin.

BARRY-CASTLE, fit. S. W. of Carigaline, in co. Cork, prov. Munfter ; it is built on a rock hanging over the fea,

BARRYMORE, a bar. in co. Cork, prov. Munfter : which gives title of earl to the antient and noble family of Barry, from whom it derives its name. This diftrict was antiently called *Aoibh-Liathain*, from whence its chiefs obtained the name of Hy Lehane or O'Lehane ; they were difpoffeffed by the Barrys, who came into Ireland under earl Strongbow, in the time of Henry IId.

BARRYMORE-ISLAND, fometimes called the great ifland, fit. on the fide of the river *Lea*, in co. Cork, prov. Munfter. It contains about 1600 Irifh acres, is nearly 2 miles long, and 1 broad, and diftant about 3 miles from the city of Cork.—There runs thro' this whole ifland a ftratum of lime ftone ; which is the more remakable, as there is not any thing like it to be found in any of the neighbouring quarries on the northern coaft ; which, however near, contain no more than red gritty ftone.

BARRY-POINT, a cape, fit. in bar. Kinalea, co. Cork, prov. Munfter.

BARRYROE, a bar. in co. Cork, prov. Munft.

BARRY's-COURT, fit. in co. Cork, prov. Munfter; here was a caftle now in ruins; it is fit. in the paffage into the great ifland, in the harbour of Cork.

BARSLFIRF, fit. in bar. Tyreragh, co. Sligo, prov. Connaught.

BARTHO-

BARTHOLOMEWELL, a fair town in co. Cork, prov. Munster; fairs held 4 Sept.

BARTRACH-ISLAND, sit. in bar. Tirawly, co. Mayo, prov. Connaught.

BASLICK, a vicarage in dioc. of Elphin, sit. in bar. Ballintober, co. Roscommon, prov. Connaught; where an abbey was formerly founded.

BATTAFFNEY, a village in bar. Half-fore, co. Meath, prov. Leinster.

BAUNBOY, see *Bawnboy*.

BAWN, a fair town in co. Kilkenny, prov. Leinster; fairs held on Ascension day and 29 Oct.—Also a place in bar. Moydoe, co. Longford, prov. Leinster.

BAWNBOY, a village sit. in bar. Fullaghah, co. Cavan, prov. Ulster; above 69 miles from Dublin.

BAYMORE, sit. near Drogheda, co. Louth, prov. Leinster.

BEAL, a fair town in co. Kerry, prov. Munster; fairs held 24 Sept.

BEALANENY, sit. in co. Roscommon, prov. Connaught; here was a friary for conventual franciscans.

BEALATHA, i. e. the place of Beal on the waters; now *Athenry*, in co. Galway, prov. Connaught; it was destroyed in 1133, by Conor O'Brien.

BEAL-CASTLE, a ruin near the mouth of the river *Shannon*, in co. Kerry, prov. Munster; 'tis in a fine situation, commanding a noble prospect of the Shannon, several miles up the country, which river is here 3 leagues broad. In the work called *Pacata Hibernia*, this place is named *Beau-lieu*, and is there noted for being the place of the murder of the brave *Maurice Stack*, who commanded a party of queen Eliz. forces, against the Irish. Near this castle is a fine warren, well stocked with rabbits; Patrick lord Kerry demolished the fortifications of this castle, anno 1600.

BEALINSTOWN, sit. in bar. Nethercross, co. Dublin, prov. Leinster.

BEALLA-FEARSAD, (from *Beallagh*, a town, and *Fearsad*, the mouth of a river or harbour.) The antient name of the harbour and town of Belfast. Beala is the fine rath at Drumboe, being 2526 feet in circumference, called the Giant's ring.

BEALNABRACH, or *Bealnabrack*, a village and river of same name, sit. in bar. Ross, co. Galway, prov. Connaught.

BEALTIMORE, see *Baltimore*.

BEALTINNEGLAS, see *Baltinglass*.

BEAMORE, sit. in bar. Duleek, co. Meath, prov. Leinster; here was a preceptory, which belonged to the priory of Kilmainham; a small part of which still remains.

BEANABEOLA *mountains*, sit. in bar. Ballynahinch, co. Galway, prov. Connaught.

BEAN-PARK, sit. in bar. Duleek, co. Meath, prov. Leinster.

BEAR and BANTRY, a bar. in co. Cork, prov. Munster; with a village of same name. Lat. 51:20, lon. 10:4. The antient proprietors of this district were the O'Sullivans.

BEARAGH, a fair town in co. Tyrone, prov. Ulster; fair days 1 Mar. 29 May, Aug. and Nov.

BEAR-HAVEN, a harbour in bar. Bear and Bantry, co. Cork, prov. Munster. It gave title of visc. to the family of *Berkley*, as it now does to that of *Chetwynd*. 'Tis 26 miles long, and in most places, above a league broad, and in the midst of it, are 40 fathom water: there are few strands round it; the coasts being all high stupendous rocks.

BEAR-ISLAND, sit. in Bantry bay, in bar. Bantry, co. Cork, prov. Munster.

BEATTA *Lough*, sit. in bar. Tirawly, co. Mayo, prov. Connaught.

BEAUFORT, a seat in co. Kerry, prov. Munster; within a mile of it is a large and fine edifice, called the *Castle of Pallis*.

BEAULIEU, a rectory in dioc. of Armagh, sit. near Drogheda, in bar. Ferrard, co. Louth, prov. Leinster.

BECTIVE, a rectory in dioc. of Meath, sit. in bar. Navan, co. Meath, prov. Leinster; having a bridge over the river Boyne: it gives title of earl to the family of *Taylor*; and holds fairs on 16 May and 1 Nov. Here are the ruins of Bective abbey.

BECTIVE-ABBEY, sit. at *Bective*, in bar. Navan, co. Meath, prov. Leinster; it is now in ruins, but was antiently a rich foundation, for Cistertian monks; established by Murchard O'Melaghlin, king of Meath, about 1146. The cloysters with a tower are nearly entire. Here was Bective castle, said to have been erected in 1014, and to be the oldest in Ireland.

BEECHWOOD, sit. near Birr, King's co. prov. Leinster.

BEELTAGH, a vicarage in dioc. of Cloyne, sit. in bar. Condons, co. Cork, prov. Munster.

BEENMORE, a fair town in co. Kerry, prov. Munster; fairs held 1 June and 10 Nov.

BEERHAVEN, see *Bear-haven*.

BEGERI, (or the little land in the water) an island on the coast of Wexford, prov. Leinster, where St. *Ibarus* had a monastery and school, A. D. 420, he died 23 April, A. D. 500. and was buried here.

BEGGAR's-BRIDGE, a village in bar. Fartullagh, co. Westmeath, prov. Leinster, 37 miles from Dublin; at half a mile's distance from which are the ruins of a castle.

BEGGAR's

passed thro' it; it is in a very pleasant country, with a variety of gentlemen's seats about it; and was rendered remarkable by the duke of Ormond's review in 1704. About a 1¼ from Bennet's-bridge are the ruins of *Aanmault castle*; and beyond that are the ruins of *Ennisnag castle*.

BENNEVANAGH *mountains*, sit. in bar. Kenought, co. Londonderry, prov. Ulster.

BENNY-HANLY, sit. in bar. Clare, co. Galway, prov. Connaught.

BENNYKENY, a seat in co. Carlow, prov. Leinster; built by *Vigors* bishop of Leighlin and Ferns; but since the death of that prelate, it has gone to decay.

BENVARDON, sit. in bar. Dunluce, co. Antrim, prov. Ulster.

BENVOLIBEN, a famous mountain in bar. Carbury, co. Sligo, prov. Connaught; near which the *Nagnata* of Ptolemy is supposed to be sit. It was formerly called *Bengolban*, i. e. the head of the woody country; and lies 4 miles N. of Sligo.

BERRY-ISLE, sit. in the Atlantic ocean, off the coast of the bar. Carbury, co. Sligo, prov. Connaught.

BERT-CHURCH, sit. in bar. Innishowen, co. Donegal, prov. Ulster.

BERVA *river*, the antient name of the river *Barrow*; it obtained in latter ages the name of Barragh or boundary river, being for some centuries the boundary between the English pale and the Irish septs.

BESSBOROUGH, a fine seat in co. Kilkenny, prov. Leinster; about 63 miles S. of Dublin: it gives title of earl to the noble family of *Ponsonby*.

BESSY-BELL *mountain*, sit. in bar. Strabane, co. Tyrone, prov. Ulster.

BETHLEM, sit. in co. Westmeath, prov. Leinster, 5 miles from Athlone; here was a nunnery so named of the order of St. *Clare*; the mother abbess whereof was a lady of good distinction, and daughter of sir *Ed. Tuite* of Tuite's-town. This place was burned in the war of 1641, and its destruction attended with very bad circumstances; for 2 foot companies of English forces quartered at *Ballinedeffy* near this place, under the command of capt. *Berin*, brother to earl Lindsay then lord chamberlain of England, unfortunately after their march to the nunnery, which they plunder'd; (whether with or without order is unknown) got themselves intoxicated, and on their return to their quarters, not apprehending any enemy near them, were suddenly attacked by the Irish forces and entirely cut off.

BEWLY, a fine old seat near the mouth of the river Boyne, within about 3 miles of *Drogheda*, prov. Leinster; it was built by sir Henry Tichbourne, afterwards lord Ferrard.—Also

a place 2 miles E. of Lismore, co. Waterford, prov. Munster; where are the remains of a monastic edifice, said to have belonged to the knts. of St. John of Jerusalem.

BEYLANE, sit. in bar. Scarawalsh, co. Wexford, prov. Leinster.

BHURRIN, see *Burrin*.

BIG-ISLAND, one of the *Copland islands*, sit. at the entrance into Carrickfergus bay, co. Down, prov. Ulster; it is distant 1½ N. of Donaghadee, and near 4 miles E. of Bangor; the sound between the island and the main land is very good, and has in depth from 7 to 8 fathom water; but the side next the main land is foul, and therefore must be avoided, especially the Northward.

BILBOA, a fair town in co. Limerick, prov. Munster; fairs held 12 May and Aug.

BILE *church*, or the church of Bile, sit. in *Magh-hill* in Innishowen on the N. W. of Lough Foyle, in co. Londonderry, prov. Ulster. This church was founded by St. Patrick, wherein, after ages, a monastery was erected.—Also a place in bar. Leney, co. Sligo, prov. Connaught; where an abbey was erected by St. *Fechin*.

BILL, a rectory in dioc. of Cashel, sit. in bar. Killnemana, co. Tipperary, prov. Munster.

BILLS, a rock on the coast of co. Mayo, in bar. Burrishoole, prov. Connaught.

BILLY, a vicarage in dioc. of Connor, sit. in bar. Dunluce, co. Antrim, prov. Ulster.

BINBURG, see *Benburb*.

BINGAN *mountains*, sit. in the half bar. of Mourne, co. Down, prov. Ulster; *Bin* or *Bien* in the Irish language, signifies a pinnacle and *Gan*, difficult, i. e. the pinnacle of difficult ascent.

BINWY-HEAD, a *cape* in bar. Erris, co. Mayo, prov. Connaught.

BIRCH-GROVE, a fair town in co. Wexford, prov. Leinster. Fair days 24 June, 29 Sep. *custom free*.

BIRD-ISLAND, sit. at the entrance of Dunmanus bay, co. Cork, prov. Munster.—Also in bar. Ardes, by the coast of co. Down, prov. Ulster.

BIRR, (otherwise called *Parson's-town*) sit. in bar. Ballibritt, King's co. prov. Leinster; it is a good market and post-town: also a rectory in dioc. of Killaloe; and distant near 64 miles from Dublin. Lat. 53: 2, lon. 8: 0. Fairs are held here on 11 Feb. 5 May, 25 Aug. and 12 Dec. Here is a castle erected by the family of *Parsons*, which was besieged by general Sarsfield and relieved by *Kirk*. In the midst of this town is a stone column of the Dorick order with the shaft about 25 feet high, on the top of which is placed a pedestrian statue of the late duke of Cumberland in a Roman habit, cast

in

in lead, and painted stone colour ; it was erected in 1747.

BIRTERBUY-BAY, sit. in bar. Ballinahinch, co. Galway, prov. Connaught.

BIRT'S-HALL, sit. in bar. Moycullen, co. Galway, prov. Connaught.

BISHOP'S-COURT, a handsome seat of George Ponsonby, esq. sit. near Cross Keys, co. Kildare, prov. Leinster; near which, on the summit of a hill, stand the ruined church and tower of Aughterard.—Also a parish in co. Waterford, prov. Munster.

BISHOP'S-HALL, the seat of Samuel Boyce, esq. near Waterford, in co. Waterford, prov. Munster.

BISHOP'S-ISLE, an island sit. near bar. Moyferta, coast of co. Clare, prov. Munster.

BLACK-ABBEY, sit. in parish St. Andrew, co. Down, prov. Ulster; formerly an abbey of Benedictine monks, founded by John de Courcy, before the year 1210.

BLACK-BANK, sit. in co. Armagh, prov. Ulster; 55 miles from Dublin: the mountain lands hereabout appear to have been formerly cultivated; vestiges of the plough are still visible there.

BLACK-BULL, sit. in co. Wicklow, prov. Leinster.

BLACK-BULL-INN, sit. in co. Meath, prov. Leinster; about 10 miles from Dublin.

BLACK-CASTLE, sit. in bar. Navan, co. Meath, prov. Leinster.—The like in bar. Corkerry, co. Westmeath, prov. Leinster.

BLACK-CAVE-HEAD, a cape in bar. Glenarm, co. Antrim, prov. Ulster.

BLACKHALL-HEAD, a cape in bar. Bear and Bantry, co. Cork, prov. Munster.

BLACK-HARBOUR, sit. in bar. Erris, co. Mayo, prov. Connaught, opposite the Atlantic ocean.

BLACK-HAVEN, sit. in bar. Glenarm, co. Antrim, prov. Ulster.

BLACK-HEAD. There are 3 capes so called. 1st in bar. Belfast, co. Antrim, prov. Ulster. 2d in bar. Courceys, co. Cork, prov. Munster. 3d in bar. Burrin, co. Clare, prov. Munster.

BLACK-LION, a village in bar. Skreen, co. Meath, prov. Leinster, 19 miles from Dublin.

BLACK-LION-INN, sit in co. Cavan, prov. Ulster, above 84 miles from Dublin; it is otherwise called *Largay*, and a mile beyond it are the ruins of a church.

BLACK-MILLS, sit. in co. Dublin, prov. Leinster, 2 miles beyond Chapelizod, and 4¼ from the castle of Dublin. They were the first erected in Ireland for the purpose of flattening iron.

BLACKMOOR-HILL, a mountain in bar. Talbot's-town, co. Wicklow, prov. Leinster.

BLACK-ROCK, a large and handsome village in bar. Half-Rathdown, co. Dublin, prov.

Leinster, 4 miles from the castle of Dublin. It is most agreeably seated on Dublin bay, and has a fine prospect, on one side of the numerous vessels that arrive in or go out of the harbour, and on the other of the adjacent country, terminated by the mountains of Wicklow. The pleasing situation of this place, purity of the air, and conveniency for bathing, induces persons of the first distinction to choose it for their summer residence. Near it is *Neptune* the elegant seat of lord *Clenmel*.—Also a country residence of lord Cloncurry.—Likewise the name of a rock sit. in the bay of Galway, prov. Connaught, lat. 53 : 55, lon. 10 : 47. — Another on coast of co. Sligo, prov. Connaught.—Also an island near bar. Forth, on coast of co. Wexford, prov. Leinster.

BLACK-ROCKS, rocks so called sit. on the coast of co. Mayo, and bar. Erris, prov. Connaught.

BLACKSOD-BAY, sit. in bar. Erris, co. Mayo, prov. Connaught.

BLACKSTAFF-RIVER, sit. in co. Down, prov. Ulster; called also *Annadorn river*, from an inconsiderable place of that name near which it rises, taking a S. W. course, and falls into the N. end of the inner bay of Dundrum.

BLACKSTAIRS *mountains*, sit. in co. Carlow, prov. Leinster.

BLACKSTONES *mountains*, sit. in bar. Dunkeron, co. Kerry, prov. Munster.

BLACKWATER-BRIDGE, sit. in co. Kildare, prov. Leinster, 22 miles from Dublin; one mile and half beyond which are *Rylough* ruins.

BLACKWATER-FOOT, sit. in co. Down, prov. Ulster, above 72 miles from Dublin; near which is a seat of the earl of *Charlemont*, in an island in Lough-Neagh, near Cooney island.

BLACKWATER-RIVER, a large river which rises in co. Kerry, prov. Munster, and having passed several towns in the co. Cork, falls into the sea at Youghal. — Also several other rivers of same name, viz. 1st that which runs thro' the co. Armagh, prov. Ulster, and falls into Lough Neagh. 2d in co. Meath, prov. Leinster, which falls into the Boyne at Navan. 3d in co. Longford, prov. Leinster, which falls into the Shannon N. of Lanesborough, and 4th in the co. Wexford, prov. Leinster, which is lost in the sea at Bannow bay.

BLACKWATER-TOWN, sit. in bar. Armagh, co. Armagh, prov. Ulster; above 66 miles from Dublin.—Also a village in co. Wexford, prov. Leinster, where fairs are held on 25 Mar.

BLACKWOOD, sit. in co. Down, prov. Ulster.

BLADHMA-SLIABH, (or *Slieub-bloom*) a range of mountains between the King and Queen's co. prov. Leinster, which in antient times was one of the boundaries of Munster on the Leinster side; there is still remaining in these mountains,

tains a large pyramid of white ſtones, the true ſimulacre of the ſun-fire among all the Celtic nations.

BLAN, ſit. near the river Barrow, in co. Wexford, prov. Leinſter.

BLANCHFIELD-TOWN, ſit. in bar. Gowran, co. Kilkenny, prov. Leinſter.

BLANEY-CASTLE, ſee *Blayney-caſtle*.

BLARNEY, a village in bar. Muſkerry, co. Cork, prov. Munſter; above 128 miles from Dublin. Here was a caſtle eſteemed one of the ſtrongeſt in that prov. it ſtands 3 miles W. of Cork upon a rock, cloſe to a ſmall river of ſame name, over which is a handſome bridge, and on the other ſide a lake of 30 acres extent. The caſtle was built by Cormac M'Carty, who came into the lordſhip in 1449; the earl of *Clancarty* was firſt ſummoned to parliament as baron of Blarney by Queen Eliz. and created viſc. Muſkerry and earl of Clancarty in 1658, the 10 Car. 2. the eſtate was forfeited by their adhering to king James IId. The walls of the caſtle are 18 feet thick; it ſtood out a formal ſiege againſt king William's forces, but a battery from a riſing ground, compelled them to give up the caſtle, after their commander had made his eſcape. The conquerors demoliſhed the fortifications, leaving nothing remaining but one large tower; but the apartments erected ſince are handſome and ſpacious, and the gardens adjoining it are well laid out. During the grand rebellion, this caſtle was alſo taken by Roger earl of *Orrery*, then lord *Broghill* in 1646. The lands about Blarney are moſtly under corn and paſture, and dairies occupy a great part of the adjacent country; the ſoil is a yellowiſh clay, which is manured moſtly with lime ſtone. At Blarney is a vein of lime-ſtone, from whence there is none to the N. nearer than *Blackwater river*. Fairs are held here on Eaſter Monday and Tueſday, 8 and 9 June, 18 Sep. and 11 Nov.

BLARNEY-RIVER. ſit. in bar. Muſkerry, co. Cork, prov. Munſter: it is a ſmall river, on which the village of Blarney ſtands; from whence it takes its name. Upon a rock cloſe to this river ſtands *Blarney caſtle*.

BLASKET'S, ſee *Blaſques*.

BLASQUES, (*Blaſkets* or *Blaſquet*) iſlands otherwiſe called *Ferreter's iſlands*, ſit. off the bay of Dingle, in bar. Corkaguinny, co. Kerry, prov. Munſter: between the large one and the main, is a deep ſound called the ſound of the Blaſquets, and a ſtrong tide. Lat 52 : 00, lon. 10 : 30. It lies directly thro' N. and S. There are 10 fathom water in it at the loweſt tides, which flow here E. N. E. and W. S. W.——Theſe iſlands are 12 in number, but 4 of them are only rocks; they formerly belonged to the earl of Deſmond, who gave them to the family

of *Ferreter*, from whence they got the name *Ferreter's iſlands*. Beſides that already mentioned, the moſt conſiderable are thoſe called *Inis Mac Kilane* or Mackilan's iſland, *Inis ni Broc* or quern iſland, Iniſtuſkard or *Iniſhuigh*, i. e. the Northern iſland, and *Beginis* the Small iſland. There is a ſmall bird ſaid to be peculiar to theſe iſlands, called by the Iriſh *Gourdet*; it is ſomewhat larger than a ſparrow, the feathers of the back are dark, and thoſe of the belly are white, the bill is ſtrait, ſhort and thick, and it is web-footed: when they are firſt taken, the country people affirm that they caſt up about a tea ſpoonful of a very fœtid oil out of their bills; they are almoſt one lump of fat; when roaſted they are of a moſt delicious taſte, and are reckon'd to exceed the *Ortolon*; for which reaſon the gentry hereabouts call them the *Iriſh Ortolon*.

BLAYNEY-CASTLE, (or *Blaney caſtle*) ſit. in bar. Cremourne, co. Monaghan, prov. Ulſter; here is the ſeat of lord Blayney. Lat. 54 : 7 lon. 7 : 13.

BLESKIN, ſit. in bar. Forth, co. Wexford, prov. Leinſter.

BLESSED ROCK, ſit. in bar. Talbot's-town, co. Wicklow, prov. Leinſter.

BLESSINGTON, a borough, poſt, market and fair town in bar. Talbot's-town, co. Wicklow, prov. Leinſter; pleaſantly ſit. on a riſing ground near the river Liffey, 14 miles S. W. of Dublin. Lat. 53 : 10, lon. 6 : 40. It gave title of viſc. to a branch of the *Boyle* family, as it afterwards did that of earl to the family of *Stewart*, then viſc. Mountjoy. Here is a neat church; and alſo a handſome ſeat with a chapel belonging to it, which was built by primate *Boyle*, who firſt erected this town. It returns 2 members to parliament; patron, the marquis of Downſhire. Fairs are held 12 May, 5 July and 12 Nov.

BLIND-HARBOUR, a *bay* ſit. in bar Carbery, co. Cork, prov. Munſter.

BLOGHNANE, ſit. in bar. Ballybritt, King's co. prov. Leinſter.

BLOODY-FARLAND-POINT, a *cape* ſo called, ſit. in bar. Kilmacrenan, co. Donegal, prov. Ulſter.

BOAHINSHI *rocks*, ſit. in bar. Carbury, co. Sligo, prov. Connaught.

BOAND, a name of the river *Boyne*, prov. Leinſter.

BOARD-TOWN, ſit. near Mullingar, in bar. Fertullagh, co. Weſtmeath, prov. Leinſter.

BOCKWORTH *mountains*, ſit. in bar. Erris, co. Mayo, prov. Connaught.

BODEN's-TOWN, a vicarage in dioc. of Kildare, ſit. near Sallins, in bar. Naas, co. Kildare, prov. Leinſter. Here is an antient burial place, and the ruins of a church.

BOFFIN

*Boffin *lough*, ſit. between the co. Weſtmeath, prov Leinſter, and co. Roſcommon, prov. Connaught.

Bog-of-Allen, an immenſe tract of bog (by much the largeſt in the kingdom) which extends a conſiderable diſtance, and runs thro' a part of the King's co. Queen's co. and co.'s Kildare, Meath, Weſtmeath, Longford, Roſcommon, Galway and Tipperary. A great part of it has of late years been reclaimed by burning and the ſowing of rape ſeed.

Bogra, an uncultivated mountainous tract, in bar. Duhallow, co. Cork, prov. Munſter; upwards of ten miles long, and in ſome parts 6 miles over: it bounds the bar. of Muſkerry on the N. and is common to the adjacent eſtates. In winter it is for the moſt part deep, marſhy and impaſſible; but in ſummer hard and firm, producing graſs and heath, and is then grazed by vaſt herds of cattle, which are removed to the lower lands when this ſeaſon is over; the whole place is covered with black fogs for the greateſt part of the year; and ſeveral conſiderable rivers, beſides an infinite number of brooks, flow from this wild country.

Bohea island, ſit. in Lough Erne, co. Fermanagh, prov. Ulſter.

Bohillane, a rectory in dioc. of Cloyne, ſit. in bar. Imokilly, co. Cork, prov. Munſter.

Bohoe, a rectory in dioc. of Clogher, ſit. in bar. Clonawly, co. Fermanagh, prov. Ulſter.

Boilean-clair, ſit. in dioc. of Tuam, co. Galway, prov. Connaught. A monaſtery for Franciſcans was founded here, A. D. 1291.

Boirce (or the magnificent place) the palace of the kings of Ullagh or Down; and probably the rath of Dunum or Downpatrick, in co. Down, prov. Ulſter.

Boithbolcain, a church near Connor, in co. Antrim, prov. Ulſter; founded by St. Bolcain, who was a diſciple of St. Patrick.

Bolton-inn, a village in bar. Gualtiere, co. Waterford, prov. Munſter.

Bolus-Head, a cape in bar. Iveragh, co. Kerry, prov. Munſter.

Boly, a rectory in dioc. of Caſhel, ſit. in bar. Eliogurty, co. Tipperary, prov. Munſter.

Bombrusna, a village in bar. Corkerry, co. Weſtmeath, prov. Leinſter.

Bonamargy, a ſmall monaſtery, founded in co. Antrim, prov. Ulſter; by *M'Donnell*, whoſe family ſettled in this country, in the 15th century, and were afterwards ennobled. The abbey became the burial place of the M'Donnells.

Bonlaghy, a fair town in co. Longford, prov. Leinſter; fair days 16 May, 26 July, 15 Oct. and 11 Dec.

Bonnet, a river in co. Leitrim, prov. Connaught.

Bonnogrow, ſit. in bar. Arklow, co Wicklow, prov. Leinſter.

Bonohan, a rectory in dioc. of Killaloe, bar. Lower Ormond, co. Tipperary, prov. Munſter.

Boom-hall, a handſome ſeat, within 2 miles of Londonderry, near the river *Foyle*, prov. Ulſter. So called, becauſe juſt under the houſe the boom was fixed, which the French and Iriſh armies threw acroſs the river Foyle; to prevent relief from coming up the river, when they beſieged the city of Londonderry, in 1689.

Booter's-town, a pleaſant village on the bay of Dublin, 3¼ miles from Dublin caſtle; and within ¼ a mile of the Black rock. Near it is *Seafield*, a very handſome ſeat, commanding a fine view of the mountains, and of Dublin bay and harbour.

Boranstown, ſit. in bar. Balruddery, co. Dublin, prov. Leinſter.

Bordwell, a rectory in dioc. of Oſſory, ſit. in bar. Upper Oſſory, Queen's co. prov. Leinſter.

Borr *river*, ſit. in bar. Bantry, co. Wexford, prov. Leinſter.

Boreum, a promontory in the N. of Ireland, mentioned by Ptolemy: *Boreum* ſignifies northern; whence *Boreum promontorium* is the northern promontory. It is now called the *North cape* or *Horn-head*, and is ſit. in the N. of co. Donegal, prov. Ulſter.

Borheen, ſit. in co. Limerick, prov. Munſter, 172 miles from Dublin.

Borrin-island, ſit. in the bay of Galway, co. Galway, prov. Connaught.

Borris, a fair town in co Carlow, prov. Leinſter; fairs held 1 May, 2 July, 15 Aug. and 14 Nov.

Borriscarra, ſit. in co. Mayo, prov. Connaught. The Carmelites or White-friars had a houſe here, which pope John gave to the Auguſtin Eremites, A. D. 1412.

Borris-in-Ossory, ſee *Burris-in-Oſſory*.

Borrisokeon, ſee *Burroſukean*.

Borrisoleagh, ſee *Burroſleigh*.

Bosa-river, now the river *Lagan*, ſit. in co. Down, prov. Ulſter.

Bothchonair, ſit. in bar. Iniſhowen, co. Donegal, prov. Ulſter. It was formerly a celebrated abbey, and there are ſtill preſerved in the hands of the religious in this neighbourhood, many books that formerly belonged to the abbey, written by the hand of St. *Mœliſa*, who was educated here, and died 16 Jan. 1086.

Bothon, a curacy in dioc. of Cloyne, ſit. in bar. Orrery, co. Cork, prov. Munſter: it is now called *Buttevant*.

Bottle-hill, ſit. midway between *Cork* and *Mallow*, co. Cork, prov. Munſter. It is
remarkable

remarkable for a battle fought there, between the English and king James IId. forces, on 29 April, 1691; in which the former proved victorious.

BOVAUGH-BRIDGE, fit. in co. Tyrone, prov. Ulster; about 104 miles from Dublin; near it is a feat of the marquis of Waterford: near this place also is *Bovaugh-cafile*, fit. on the banks of *Agivey-river*: and about 1¼ mile beyond Bovaugh, are the ruins of a church.

BOVEVAGH, a rectory in dioc. of Derry, fit. in bar. Kenoght, co. Londonderry, prov. Ulster.

BOWFINAN, fit. in bar. Tirawly, co. Mayo, prov. Connaught: here was a friary belonging to conventual Francifcans.

BOW-ISLAND, fit. in Lough Erne, co. Fermanagh, prov. Ulster.

BOYANE, fit. in co. Rofcommon, prov. Connaught.

BOYLAGH and BANNOGH, a bar. in co. Donegal, prov. Ulster.

BOYLE, a bar. in co. Rofcommon, prov. Connaught, in which is a borough, market and poft-town of fame name, fit. 20 miles N. of Rofcommon, 32 N. W. of Athlone, and 84 from Dublin. Lat. 53:56, lon. 8:32. It is a vicarage in dioc. of Elphin, and returns 2 members to parliament; patron, the earl of *Kingston*. Fairs are held 30 May, 25 July and 1 Oct. It has a barrack for a troop of horfe, and is regularly governed according to the fpirit of a charter granted by king James IId. It lies on the banks of the river *Buelle*, over which there are 2 ftone bridges; on one is a pedeftrian ftatue of king William IIId, well executed. On the N. fide of the river a little Eaftward of the town, ftands a ftately abbey of gothic architecture, built in 1152; at the fuppreffion of the monafteries it was difmantled, but ftill exhibits a piece of noble ruins; the arches are efteemed by the curious, for their noble elevation and grandeur, equal to any in Europe: and being built of ftone of a peculiarly firm texture, have withftood the fevereft affaults of time. From hence this place has been alfo called *Abbey-boyle*. The ftump of a round tower is ftill to be feen near the abbey, the ruins of which are now enclofed in the demefne of the earl of Kingston.

BOYLE-RIVER, rifes in a romantic fheet of water called *Lough Gara*, adjoining the bar. Boyle, co. Rofcommon, prov. Connaught; thence meandering thro' woods and dales, it enters Kingfton lake or Lough Kay; a beautiful piece of water, interfperfed with feveral iflands, fome of which are adorned with old caftles and ruins, others in the ftate of nature, wooded with lofty timber trees, and fome highly im-

proved without a tree to be feen; but the more pleafing profpect of perpetual verdure. The river again emerges out of the Eaftern fide of this lake, as it were by conftraint, and then glides on to pay its tribute to the Shannon.

BOYNE-RIVER, runs thro' the co.'s Louth, Meath, Weftmeath and Kildare, prov. Leinfter. It is adjacent to Drogheda, Slane, Navan, Trim, Longwood, Clonard, Edenderry, Kinnegad and Mullingar; and falls into the Irifh channel, a little below Drogheda. It is memorable for a battle fought upon its banks, 1 July 1690, between king James IId, and king William IIId, in which the latter was victorious. In remembrance of this victory, a handfome Obelifk, efteemed the grandeft modern one in Europe, was erected in 1736 on the banks of this river, about 2 miles from Drogheda: it ftands on a rock, and is of fquare ftone, 20 feet to each fide at the bafe, and about 150 feet high; the duke of *Dorfet* laid the firft ftone. This place gives title of vifc. to a branch of the noble family of *Hamilton*. The river Boyne is fuppofed to be the *Buvinda* or *Bubinda* of Ptolemy; the word Buvinda is faid to be derived from the Cimbric Britifh words *Bu-iien-daw*, i. e. the clear rapid water, whence by the Irifh *Boand* or Boüind, by corruption the *Boyne*.

BOYNE's-CROSS, this is a very old and curious crofs, erected in the church yard of Monafterboyce, about 3 miles from Drogheda, co. Louth, prov. Leinfter. It is about 18 feet high, on all fides full of fculpture; 'tis faid to be all of one ftone fent from Rome, and erected by order of a pope. On the centre of the crofs on one fide, is a figure reprefenting Chrift, and oppofite on the other, St. Patrick; at the bottom are the figures of Adam and Eve, &c. and oppofite on the other, that of St. *Boyne*. The whole feems to be a fort of hiftory from the creation, but as the figures are very old and imperfect, they are difficult to make out. Near the crofs are the ruins of an old church, and alfo an old tower 110 feet high, beautifully diminifhing from a bafe of 18 feet.

BOYSTOWN, a vicarage in dioc. of Dublin, fit. in bar. Talbot's-town, co Wicklow, prov. Leinfter.

BRACKEN, fit. in bar. Coftello, co. Mayo, prov. Connaught.

BRACKENAGH, fee *Brefcanagh*.

BRACKDENSTOWN, fee *Brackenftown*.

BRACKENSTOWN, fit. in co. Dublin, prov. Leinfter; within 6½ miles of the metropolis; half a mile from this place are the ruins of the old family feat of the *Boltons* of Brazil; here is alfo the country refidence of lord Molefworth. The proper name of this place is *Brackden's-town*.

BRACKLAN

BRACKLAN, fit. between the bar. Moycafhel, co. Weftmeath, and bar. Ballycowen, King's co. prov. Leinfter.—Alfo a village near Portarlington, fit. in Queen's co. prov. Leinfter.

BRACKLANAGH, fit. in bar. Leney, co. Sligo, prov. Connaught.

BRACKLOWN-INN, fit. in co. Kerry, prov. Munfter; 158 miles from Dublin. 3 miles beyond this, and about 1 mile to the left, are the ruins of *Minard-caftle*.

BRACONSTON, fit. in bar. Ophaly, co. Kildare, prov. Leinfter.

BRAGANSTOWN, fit. in co. Louth, prov. Leinfter, above 35 miles from Dublin.

BRAID, a *river* in bar. Antrim, co. Antrim, prov. Ulfter.

BRAKES-*of*-SCORNEY, a ridge of mountains fit. in bar. Upper crofs, co. Dublin, prov. Leinfter.

BRALAZON'S-PARK, fit. in bar. Dundalk, co. Louth, prov. Leinfter.

BRAMBLESTOWN, fit. near Gowran; in co. Kilkenny, prov. Leinfter.

BRAMHALL, a fair town in co. Meath, prov. Leinfter. Fairs held 1 June and Dec.

BRANDEN or BRANDON, fit. in co. Kerry, prov. Munfter; it gives title of baron to the family of Crofbie, (now vifc. Crofbie.)

BRANDON-BAY, fit. in bar. Corkaguinny, co. Kerry, prov. Munfter.

BRANDON HEAD, fit. in bar. Corkaguinny, co. Kerry, prov. Munfter.

BRANDON HILL, fit. in bar. Gowran, co. Kilkenny, prov. Leinfter.

BRANDON-MOUNTAINS, fit. in bar. Corkaguinny, co. Kerry, prov. Munfter. On one of thefe called *Brandon-hill*, which lies near the fea coaft 4 miles N of Dingle, is an oratory or chapel, dedicated to St. *Brandon*; and alfo a fine fpring of water near the fummit of the hill.

BRANNOCK'STOWN, fit. in co. Kildare, prov. Leinfter. In 1784, an antient tobacco pipe was found here, fticking between the teeth of a human fkull; on digging in an elevated field, near the banks of the river Liffey, the labourers found an intrenchment, filled with human bones; under the bones lay a number of ftone coffins formed of flag ftones without cement; in each coffin was a fkeleton. A battle was fought here, according to *Keating*, between the Irifh and Danes in the 10th century; the pipes moft probably belonged to the Danes.

BRAWNY, a bar. (or territory as it is called) in co. Weftmeath, prov. Leinfter.

BRAY, a rectory in dioc. of Dublin; it is alfo a port and fair town fit. in bar. Rath-down, co. Wicklow, prov. Leinfter; about 11 miles S. of Dublin. Lat. 53 : 12, lon; 6 : 16. Fairs held 1 May and 20 Sept, at which are fold large

quantities of frize and flannel, together with fome black cattle and fheep. The town is divided between the co.'s Wicklow and Dublin, by a river abounding with excellent trout. It is a defirable fituation during the fummer feafon for fea bathing. Here is an old caftle, a decent church, a new Romifh chapel, and a good barrack. The fee fimple of the town, (or at leaft the greateft part of it) is vefted in the earl of Meath.

BRAY-BANK, a *fandbank* on coaft of the co. Wicklow, in bar. Rathdown, prov. Leinfter.

BRAY-BRIDGE, fit. over the river Boyne, between the bar.'s of Slain and Duleek, in co. Meath, prov. Leinfter.

BRAY-HEAD, fit. in bar. Rathdown, co. Wicklow, prov. Leinfter. Lat. 51 : 47; lon. 10 : 30.

BRAZEEL or *Brazil*, the antient feat of the *Bolton* family; fit. in bar. Nethercrofs, co. Dublin, prov. Leinfter.

BREAFY, a rectory in dioc. of Tuam, fit. in bar. Carragh, co. Mayo, prov. Connaught.

BREA-HEAD, a cape in bar. Iveragh, co. Kerry, prov. Munfter.

BREBA, the Northern branch of the Abhan Breoghan, called alfo *Berva*; the antient name of the river Barrow: in latter ages it obtained the name of *Barragh* or boundary river; being for fome centuries the boundary between the Englifh pale and the Irifh fepts.

BREDACH, a parifh in the co. Down, prov. Ulfter; the church of which is perhaps one of the neateft of its kind in the kingdom: It was built at the fole expence of the vifc. Dowager Middleton; 'tis fit on an eminence, commanding a view of the bay and town of Carrickfergus, the town of Belfaft, and great part of the country round about; it is, exclufive of the chancel; 50 feet by 25 and 25 in height : from the middle of the church on each fide fprings a femicircle of 18 feet diameter, which befides enlarging the room, adds greatly to the beauty of the building; the fteeple with the fpire is finifhed with the greateft exactnefs to the moft perfect rules of architecture.—*Bredagh* or *Breda* is the name alfo of a fmall river that rifes in a mountain near Lough Foyle and Lough Swilly, in bar. Innifhowen, co. Donegal, prov. Ulfter; after a fhort S. E. courfe it falls into Lough Foyle. Near this place St. Patrick founded the church of *Domnach bile* in the middle of the 5th century.

BREFNEY or *Breghane*, (i. e. the country of little hills) called alfo *Hy Re Leigh* or the diftrict of the country of the king, the chiefs of which were the *O'Reily's*; the fubordinate diftricts of it were each governed by their refpective chiefs, viz. *O'Rourc*, *O'Brady*, *O'Corry*, *O'Sheridan*,

Sheridan, M'Kiernan and M'Gauroll; most of whom were in poffeffion of their eftates at the beginning of the laft century. *Brefney* is now called the co. of *Cavan*, in prov. Ulfter, tho' formerly it took in *Leitrim* and part of *Annaly*, and was divided into E. and W. Brefney.

BREGIA or *Bregmuin*, a plain extending round the royal palace of *Tarah*, called alfo *Magh Bregh*; it reached as far as Trim and Duleek, co. Meath, prov. Leinfter.

BREGMUIN, an antient territory of the *O'Brians*; fit. in co. Weftmeath, prov. Leinfter.

BREGOGE, a vicarage in dioc. of Cloyne, fit. in bar. Orrery, co. Cork, prov. Munfter.

BREMORE *caftle*, fit. ¼ mile W. of Balbriggen, co. Dublin, prov. Leinfter.

BRENAN'STOWN, fit. about 9 miles from Dublin, in co. Dublin, prov. Leinfter. In a glen adjoining it is a fuperb *Cromicach*, fuppofed to have been a druidical altar or tomb.

BREOGHAIN, an antient diftrict containing the entire co. of Waterford, in prov. Munfter; fo denominated from lying on the river Braghan or Brigus. The inhabitants of this diftrict were frequently called *Slioght Breaghan*, or the race dwelling on the forked river; and were the Brigantes of Ptolemy; their country was bounded on the E. by *Abhan Braghan*, on the N. by the *Suire*, on the W. by the *Blackwater*, and on the S. by the fea. Their moft antient chiefs were denominated *Hy Breaghan* and *O'Breaghan*, whence by corruption *O'Brain*, and made by the genealogifts of latter ages to defcend from the O'Briens of *Thomond*, whereby they have confounded one race with the other. The *Hy Breaghans* were difpoffeffed of the S. parts of their country by *Aongus*, at the head of the clan of the *Defii*, who had been expelled the co. of Meath by *Cormac Mac Art* in 278. From that time the Southern parts of this antient diftrict were in poffeffion of the chiefs of the *Defii*, but the Northern remained under the government of its antient princes, until the arrival of the Englifh, when the greater part of the country was divided among the *Boyles*, *Sherlocks*, *Poors*, *Aylwards*, *Daltons*, *Waddings*, &c. feudatory tenants of Henry IId. who, after the general diftribution of the kingdom amongft his followers, referved to himfelf all the country from Cork to Waterford. The antient princes however ftill retained a part, which they held by grant from the Englifh monarchs, and we find an *O'Brien* in the tenure of a confiderable landed property in this co. at the commencement of the laft century; but whether defcended from the *Hy Breaghans* or *O'Briens* of Thomond, is not certain. The *Slioght Breoghan* was alfo called by the antient writers *Slioght Luguch* or the race on the water, which feem to be the fame as the *Luceni* of Ptolemy: tho' others place the

Luceni or *Lucenii*, along Dingle bay in the co. Kerry, prov. Munfter.

BRESCANAGH or *Brackenagh*, a manor in the bar. Coole's-town, King's co. prov. Leinfter; in which are very extenfive flour mills erected by Mr. Montgomery, called *John's-ville mills*. Here is an antient burial place.

BRIAL-POINT, fit. in bar. Ardes, co. Down, prov. Ulfter; from this place the coaft bends in a little to the W. 'till you come to Green ifland, about a 1½ mile, which contains 2 acres always green, and to which, at low water, a man may walk dry. Here is a kind of harbour never frequented but by fhips in great diftrefs, by reafon of a dangerous entry, having on the S. the fatal *North rocks*, which are a long range, ftretching N. N. E. at leaft a league, of which many lie funk in the water; fo that 'tis hazardous to venture between them and the main land. On thefe rocks 18 failors were loft fome years ago, and all buried together in one common grave, in the neighbouring church yard of Slane. The N. rocks are otherwife called St. *Patrick's rocks*, from a feat of ftone among them, called St. *Patrick's chair*, from whence thefe rocks have taken this fecond name.

BRIAN's-FORD, a village fit. in bar. upper Iveach, co. Down, prov. Ulfter; within 2 miles W. of Newcaftle: near which, on the fkirts of *Slieu Neir* and *Slieu Snavan* mountains, are 2 deer parks, remarkable for excellent venifon; or rather 1 park divided into 2 (by a wall carried thro' the middle of it) finely wooded, cut into ridings and viftoes, and water'd by a river running thro' it in a channel of rocks and precipices, which paffes under a bridge of hewn ftone; from whence are beautiful profpects of the fea. This place is 65 miles diftant from Dublin: fairs held on afcenfion day and 3 June. Near it is *Tullamor*, a feat of lord *Clanbraffil*.

BRICKLEEUSE, fit. in bar. Corran, co. Sligo, prov. Connaught.

BRICK RIVER, fit. in bar. Clanmaurice, co. Kerry, prov. Munfter; it rifes about a mile E. of *Ardfert*, and running Eafterly, and then Northerly, paffes by *Lixnaw*, and joins the *Feal* and *Galey*.

BRICKY RIVER, fit. in bar. *Decies without*, in co. Waterford, prov. Munfter; it takes its rife near *Clonkardine*, and empties itfelf into the bay of *Dungarvan*, after a courfe of about 5 miles.

BRIDE-CHURCH, a vicarage in dioc. of Kildare, fit. in bar. great Connell, co. Kildare, prov. Leinfter.

BRIDE RIVER, rifes in bar. Barrymore, co. Cork, prov. Munfter, near a place called Glanprehan; takes its courfe Eafterly, and runs thro' the bog of Kilrea, and paffes thro' part of the co. Waterford, after a multiplicity of windings

windings for a courfe of about 14 miles, it at laft falls into the *Blackwater*. On the E. of this river are a vaft number of fubterraneous caverns, compofed of great pillars fupporting large arches of lime ftone rocks.

BRIDESWELL, fit. in bar. Athlone, co. Rof-common, prov. Connaught.

BRIDGETOWN, (called by the Irifh *Ballin-droghed*) a town fit. on the river Blackwater, in bar. Fermoy, co. Cork, prov. Munfter; about 1½ mile from which is the ruined church of *Monani-my*, with a large chancel. Adjacent to it is a caftle that in former times was a preceptory be-longing to the Knts. of St. John of Jerufalem; round the caftle are traces of very large build-ings; the whole being auguftly fit. on an high bank over the Blackwater: as there is no other mention of this houfe than in the quit rent books, the founder and time of the foundation is uncertain. On the oppofite fide of the river are large rocks of lime-ftone, wherein are feveral fubterraneous caverns. At Bridgetown a priory was founded in the reign of king John, to which the family of *Roche* gave large contributions; oppofite the high altar is the ruined tomb of the founder. We find that in 1375, king Edw. IIId. directed his writ to the bifhops and com-mons to elect chofen perfons who were to repair to England, to confult with his majefty and council, concerning the government of this kingdom, and fupport of the war in which he was engaged; and *Thomas*, a prior of Bridge-town, was one of the perfons appointed to that bufinefs.—Alfo a fair town of fame name, fit. in co. Clare, prov. Munfter; diftant above 90 miles from Dublin: where fairs are held on 10 June and 3 Nov.—Alfo a place near Wexford, in co. Wexford, prov. Leinfter.

BRIGGO, fit. in bar. Ardes, co. Down, prov. Ulfter.

BRIGOS, a range of black rocks in the bay of Carrickfergus, co. Down, prov. Ulfter; which runs from the N. fide of it into the fea, for 3 or 400 yards.

BRIGHT, a rectory in dioc. of Down, fit. in bar. Lecale, co. Down, prov. Ulfter.

BRIGH-THAIGH (or *Brigh-mac Thaidghe*, i. e. the habitation of *Mac Thiagh*;) fit. in co. Meath, prov. Leinfter; here *Geafius*, bifhop of Armagh, held a fynod in 1153.

BRIGOWNE, a fair town in bar. Condons, co. Cork, prov. Munfter; 1 mile E. of Mitchel's-town. Fair day 6 Dec. St. *Abban* founded this place, which was called *Brighgobban*, and ftiled a city; there yet remain here the walls of a church, built of large block of a very fine free-ftone, brought with much labour from the mountains; and the ruins of a round tower which fell in 1720: the church is fuppofed to have been erected by St. *Finchu*, whofe ftaff was

kept here as an holy relique; and the adjacent country people ufed to fwear upon it. His feftival is obferved on 25 Nov. Brigown is a rectory in dioc. of Kildare.

BRINNY, a rectory in dioc. of Cork; it is fit. in the Weftern extremity of the bar. Kinalea, co. Cork, prov. Munfter; where there is a handfome country feat, and a decent parifh church.

BRITWAY, a rectory in dioc. of Cloyne, fit. in bar. Barrymore, co. Cork, prov. Munfter.

BRIZE, a fair town in co. Mayo, prov. Connaught: fair held 11 Aug.

BROADFIELD, a pleafant village fit in bar. Newcaftle, co. Dublin, prov. Leinfter; 1½ mile beyond Rathcool, and near 9 miles from Dublin caftle. The air is extremely pure and falutary; and it is in every refpect a moft defire-able fituation for a country refidence.

BROADFORD, a fair town in bar. Tullagh, co. Clare, prov. Munfter; above 95 miles from Dublin: fair days 21 June and Nov:

BROADHAVEN, fit. in bar. Erris, co. Mayo, prov. Connaught: lat. 54:6, lon. 10:38.

BROADWAY, a fair town in bar. Forth, co. Wexford, prov. Leinfter. Fairs held on Thurf. after Trin. Sunday and 18 Oct.

BROCA, fit. in co. Mayo, prov. Connaught.

BROCKAGH, a village in bar. Dungannon, co. Tyrone, prov. Ulfter.

BRODAGH, a fair town in co. Clare, prov. Munfter; fairs held 20 May and 15 Aug.

BROGHILL, a feat, fit. on the Silver river, near Frankford, in King's co. prov. Leinfter.

BROGHILL-CASTLE, fit. about ½ a mile S. W. of Charleville, co. Cork, prov. Munfter; it formerly belonged to the *Fitzgeralds*.

BROOK'S-BOROUGH, a fair town in bar. Ma-gheraft, co. Fermanagh, prov. Ulfter; near 87 miles from Dublin. One mile beyond it, on the right, is *Aghavea church*. Fairs held 4 May, 31 July, 3 Nov. and 11 Dec.

BROOMFIELD, a feat of lord Mountcafhel, fit. near Ballymore Euftace, co. Dublin, prov. Leinfter.

BROSNA or *Brofney*, a fair town in bar. Clon-lifk, King's co. prov. Leinfter. Fairs held 8 May and 4 Aug.—Alfo a river in co. Weft-meath, prov. Leinfter, which rifes in Lough Foyle, paffes thro' Cullenmore, and thence to Mullingar. Its name fignifies a bundle of fticks. It takes its courfe thro' the King's co. and into the Shannon, at or near Bannagher.—Alfo a rectory in dioc. of Ardfert, fit. in bar. Truaghnacmy, co. Kerry, prov. Munfter.

BROUGHSHANE, a fair town in bar. Antrim, co. Antrim, prov. Ulfter: 95 miles diftant from Dublin, where fairs are held on 17 June and 1 Sept. Two miles beyond this place, on the fummit of a hill, are the ruins of *Skirry* church.

BROW-HEAD, a cape in bar. Carbery, co. Cork, prov. Munfter.

BROWNFLESK, a river in co. Kerry, prov. Munfter.

BROWNHALL, fit. in co. Donegal, prov. Ulfter; in the demefne of this feat is a curious fubterraneous river.

BROWN'S-BARN, fit. near Thomaftown, co. Kilkenny, prov. Leinfter.

BROWN'S-POINT, fit. between Magee ifland and the bar. Glenarm, co. Antrim, prov. Ulfter.

BROWN'S-TOWN, fit. in bar. Naas, co. Kildare, prov. Leinfter.—Alfo a curacy in dioc. of Meath, fit. in bar. Duleek, co. Meath, prov. Leinfter.

BROWN'S-TOWN-HEAD, fit. near Tramole bay, co. Waterford, prov. Munfter.

BRUCE-HILL, a mountain in bar. Tullaghonoho, co. Cavan, prov. Ulfter.

BRUFF, a fair town in bar. Cofhma, co. Limerick, prov. Munfter; 103 miles from Dublin: it is a rectory in dioc. of Limerick. Fairs held on the day before Afcenfion, 23 July, 18 Oct. and 28 Nov. ½ a mile beyond this are the ruins of a caftle.

BRUIGHEN-DA-DARO, the rath which contained the royal palace of Tarah, in co. Meath, prov. Leinfter; it was fit. in view of and not far from the hill of Tarah, whereon the antient Irifh ftates affembled. *Conar-mor* originally built the palace of Tarah, called the habitation or rath of the caves; from containing feveral caves under the platform. By fome accident the royal palace fit. on the rath, was burned to the ground in the firft year of its erection, but was immediately repaired and improved by Conar, who refided in it feveral years: this king having expelled *Ankle* one of his captains into the ifle of Man, the latter returned with an army, took Tarah by furprize, and fet fire to the palace, in the flames of which Conar perifhed: it was however in fome time rebuilt in great fplendor, and fo continued for a number of years, till finally deftroyed by *Brien Boromh* in 995, near 1000 years after its firft erection: the rath of this celebrated palace is yet remaining, under which, tradition fays there are a number of caves; the royal apartments, and other buildings fit. within the ramparts, were conftructed of wattles or wicker work, fupported by white pillars formed of the trunks of trees, and whofe walls were lined with mats made of fine rufhes: the number and dimenfions of the principal buildings compofing the palace of *Teamor* or *Tarah*, during the middle ages, have been given by the Irifh hiftorians; but it is faid they have in general con-

founded them with the *Noifteaghan* on the hill of Tarah, where the ftates affembled: the buildings of the palace confifted of the *Teach Miodh Cuharta*, or chief court, where the princes were entertained; and 4 other large houfes for the lodging of the nobles and the royal family, all fit. round the foot of the rampart, after the manner of the antient Greeks in the conftruction of their villas: according to *Keating* it was 300 feet long, 40 feet high and 60 broad. In the middle of the court was erected the throne whereon the monarch fat; the kings of Munfter with the provincial deputies on his left hand, thofe of Ulfter on the right, the king of Leinfter in front, and the king of Connaught behind; they being, after the manner of the Pagan times, feated circularly round the throne.

BRUIS, a rectory in dioc. of Emly, fit. in bar. Clanwilliam, co. Tipperary, prov. Munfter.

BRURY or *Bruree*, a fair town in bar. Conello, co. Limerick, prov. Munfter, 15 miles S. W. of Limerick; having a good bridge over the river *Meage* or *Meige*, which meanders thro' a moft fertile and beautiful country, until it empties itfelf into the river Shannon. Fairs held 9 May, 25 June, 14 Sep. and 25 Nov.— Here is a handfome feat. This town is a vicarage in dioc. of Limerick; and remarkable for the feffions held there every half year by the Irifh *bards*, which, according to Mr. O'Halloran, were continued down to the year 1746.— Its antient name was *Brughrigh* or the habitation of the king, it being the feat of the kings of *Caibre Aobhdha*, now called *Kenry*, in co. Limerick, and appears to be the *Regia altera* of Ptolemy. Here *Auliffe Mor O'Donaghue*, king of *Caibre Aobhdha*, was flain by *Murtagh O'Brien* in 1165.

BRYANS-FORD, fit. in co. Down, prov. Ulfter; about 65 miles from Dublin, a feat of lord *Clanbraffil*.

BRYANSTON, fit. in co. Dublin, prov. Leinfter, a few miles from the metropolis. Here is a Cromleich, by fome fuppofed to have been an altar, by others a grave of the Druids; it confifts of 6 ftones placed upright, and another laid on the top of them; this laft is 14 feet long 12 broad and from 2 to 5 feet thick; by the fpecific gravity of like folids, it is computed to weigh upwards of 26 tons.

BUAN-RATH, fit. near Limerick, in co. Limerick, prov. Munfter: 'tis the remains of an antient monaftic building, where is a princely hall and fpacious chambers; the fine ftucco in many of them is ftill vifible, tho' uninhabited for above a century.

BUCHLA, fit. in bar. Half-Fore, co Weftmeath, prov. Leinfter.

BUCHOLLA, fit. in bar. Gallen, co. Mayo, prov.

prov. Connaught. It is a vicarage in dioc. of Achonry.

BUCK-HOUSE-INN, fit. in co. Westmeath, prov. Leinster; 47 miles from Dublin. Here are the ruins of a church.

BUCKOYD, fit. in co. Leitrim, prov. Connaught.

BUCKS, fit. in bar. Shelburne, co. Wexford, prov. Leinster.

BUELY, a rectory in dioc. of Offory, fit. in bar. Iverk, co. Kilkenny, prov. Leinster.

BUINAHA-POINT, a cape in bar. Morisk, co. Mayo, prov. Connaught.

BUIOWNA, a rectory in dioc. of Tuam, fit. in bar. Downamore, co. Galway, prov. Connaught.

BULL island, fit. in bar. Bear and Bantry, on coast of co. Cork, prov. Munster.

BULL rock, fit. in bar. Cary, on coast of co Antrim, prov. Ulster.

BULLAN, fit. by Clew bay, co. Mayo, prov. Connaught.

BULLAN-BAY, fit. in bar. Erris, co. Mayo, prov. Connaught.

BULL cow and CALF, rocks fo called, fit. off Durfey ifle, near the bar. of Bear and Bantry, co. Cork, prov. Munster.

BULLDOYLE, fee Baldoyle.

BULL-HEAD, a cape fit. in bar. Corkaguinny, co. Kerry, prov. Munster.

BULLOCK, an antient village fit. within 6¼ miles of the city of Dublin, in co. Dublin, prov. Leinster; near which is a fine gothic castle, and a singular piece of druidical antiquity called a rocking stone. It is a curacy in dioc. of Dublin, and about 1¼ mile distant from Dalkey.

BUMLIN, a vicarage in dioc. of Elphin, fit. in bar. Roscommon, co. Roscommon, prov. Connaught.

BUNAMACK, fit. in bar. Tyreragh, co. Sligo, prov. Connaught.

BUNATRAHER-BAY, fit. in bar. Tirawly, co. Mayo, prov. Connaught.

BUNBRUSNY, fit. in bar. Corkerry, co. Westmeath, prov. Leinster.

BUNCLOADY, a fair town in bar. Scarawalsh, co. Wexford, prov. Leinster, bordering on the co. Carlow. Fairs held 29 Apr. 17 and 18 June for frize and linen, 20 Aug. 14 Sep. 4 and 30 Nov. It is a vicarage in dioc. of Ferns. This place is now called Newtown Barry, and belongs to lord Farnham. It is much improved and pleafantly fit. by the river Slaney, adjoining which is a large wood and elegant improvements, with an artificial cafcade. Here is a neat church and fome flour mills. Distant from Dublin above 47 miles.

BUNCRANA, a fair town in bar. Inishowen, co. Donegal, prov. Ulster. Fairs held 9 May and 27 July.—Also a place in co. Londonderry, prov. Ulster.

BUNDORAN, a village in bar. Tyrhugh, co. Donegal, prov. Ulster.

BUNDUFF, a village in bar. Carbury, co. Sligo, prov. Connaught.

BUNGLASS, fit. in bar. Dunluce, co. Antrim, prov. Ulster.

BUNLAHY, fit. in bar. Granard, co. Longford, prov. Leinster.

BUNNIDANE, a fair town in co. Sligo, prov. Connaught. Fairs held 20 May, 6 Aug. 9 Oct. and 27 Nov.

BUNOCK, fit. in bar. Bantry, co. Wexford, prov. Leinster.

BUNOWEN, a curacy in dioc. of Meath, fit. in bar. Kilkennyweft, co. Westmeath, prov. Leinster.—Also a village in bar. Ballinahinch, co. Galway, prov. Connaught.

BUNRATTY, a bar. in co. Clare, prov. Munster, having a village in it of fame name, fit. near Meelick, which is a rectory in dioc. of Killaloe. Here is Bunratty castle, which was the antient feat of the earls of Thomond; it lies near the fide of the river Shannon, and was built in 1277, and besieged, but not taken in 1305; the town of Bunratty, however, was burned to the ground in 1314.

BUNREE-RIVER, fit. in bar. Tyreragh, co. Sligo, prov. Connaught.

BUNROSS-RIVER, fit. in bar. Carbury, co. Sligo, prov. Connaught.

BUNSINGLASS, a fair town in co. Mayo, prov. Connaught; fairs held 20 May, 6 Aug. 9 Oct. and 27 Nov.

BUOLICK, a rectory in dioc. of Cafhel, fit. in bar. Slewardagh, co. Tipperary, prov. Munster.

BURDALE-RIVER, fit. in co. Donegal, prov. Ulster.

BURGAGE, a vicarage in dioc. of Dublin, fit. in bar. Talbotstown, co. Wicklow, prov. Leinster.

BURGESBEG, a rectory in dioc. of Killaloe, fit. in bar. Arra, co. Tipperary, prov. Munster.

BURISHOOLE or Burrishoole, a bar. in co. Mayo, prov. Connaught; it is mountainous, but there are fome fruitful grounds along the coaft and in the vallies. There is a village in it of fame name, fit. on the bay of Burrishoole, which is a rectory in dioc. of Tuam; at which place Richard de Bourke founded a monaftery for dominican friars; and a great patron is held on 4 Aug. being St. Dominick's day.

BURKE'S-HILL, fit. near Birr, in King's co. prov. Leinster.

BURK'S-TOWN, a village in bar. Shelburne, co. Wexford, prov. Leinster.

BURLYBRIDGE, fit. near Ardee, in co. Louth, prov. Leinster.

BURMOUNT, fit. near Ennifcorthy, co. Wexford, prov. Leinster.

BURNAR

BURNARGOR, fit. in bar. Forth, co. Wexford, prov. Leinfter.

BURNHAM-CASTLE, fit. on the S. W. fide of Dingle harbour, in co. Kerry, prov. Munfter; 'tis now a pleafant feat, and was formerly called *Ballingolin-caftle*, deftroyed in 1641, and belonged to the family of Rice.

BURNTCHURCH, a fair town in bar. Shellilogher, co. Kilkenny, prov. Leinfter; it is a vicarage in dioc. of Offory. Fairs held 25 July, and 18 Oct.

BURREN-CASTLE, fit. near *Rathclarin-church*, in co. Cork, prov. Munfter.

BURRIN or *Burren*, a bar. in co. Clare, prov. Munfter; it is exceedingly rocky, but fuch is the luxuriance of the pafture interfperfed among the rocks, that thefe feemingly barren hills fupport a great number of cattle and very large flocks of fheep. This place is remarkable for that fpecies of oyfter, called the Burrin-oyfter; and was formerly denominated *Hy-Lochlean*, or the diftrict on the waters of the fea, the chiefs whereof were called *O'Loghlin* or *O'Laghlin*; fome of whom remained in poffeffion at the commencement of the laft century. In this diftrict were the *Canganj* of Ptolemy. Burrin gives title of *baron* to the noble family of O'Brien, (now earl of Inchiquin.)

BURRIS, a fmall town in co Carlow, prov. Leinfter, 54 miles from Dublin; fit. on a branch of the Barrow, over which it has a decent bridge.—Alfo a place in bar. Maryborough, Queen's co. prov. Leinfter.—Another in bar. Scarawalfh, co. Wexford, prov. Leinfter; where are the remains of an old caftle.

BURRISAKANE, fee *Burrofakean*.

BURRISCARRA, a rectory in dioc. of Tuam, fit. in bar. Carra, co. Mayo, prov. Connaught.

BURRISHOOLE, fee *Burifhoole*.

BURROGHMORE, fit. in co. Leitrim, prov. Connaught.

BURROS, a rectory in dioc. of Leiglin, fit. in bar. Maryborough, Queen's co. prov. Leinfter.

BURROSAKEAN, or *Borrifakean*, a fair town in bar. lower Ormond, co. Tipperary, prov. Munfter; above 81 miles from Dublin. Fairs held 26 Apr. June and Sept. and 15 Dec. It is a rectory in dioc. of Killaloe.

BURROSILEAGH, or *Borrifileagh*, a fair town in bar. Ileagh, co. Tipperary, prov. Munfter; above 78 miles from Dublin. Fairs held 9 June, 6 Aug. and 27 Nov. Four miles beyond it are the ruins of *Latragh-caftles*.

BURROS-IN-OSSORY, or *Borris in-Offory*, a fair and poft town in bar. upper Offory, Queen's co. prov. Leinfter; above 53 miles from Dublin. Fairs held on third Tuefday O. S. in May, and firft Tuefday O. S. in Oct.

BURROSLEIGH, a rectory in dioc. of Cafhel, fit. in bar. Eliogurty, co. Tipperary, prov. Munfter.

BURROSNAFARNEY, a rectory in dioc. of Killaloe, fit. in bar. upper Ormond, co. Tipperary, prov. Munfter.

BURRY, a chapelry in dioc. of Meath, fit. in bar. Kells, co. Meath, prov. Leinfter.

BURTON, fit. in co. Cork, prov. Munfter; formerly a noble feat of the *Percival* family, burned down in the late wars by the fame party of King James's forces that burned Charleville; the walls of the houfe ftill remain, which fhew it to have been a large elegant building, moftly of hewn ftone; from Burton to the new parifh church, there is an avenue well planted. The manor of Burton is very large; the foil is exceedingly good in this neighbourhood, being a light loamy earth; confiderably deep, over a lime ftone bottom.

BURTON-HALL, a handfome feat in bar. Carlow, co. Carlow.—Alfo a place in co. Dublin, —and another in co. Wicklow, all in prov. Leinfter.

BURTOWN, fit. in bar. Kilkea and Moon, co. Kilkenny, prov. Leinfter.

BUSH-HEAD, fit. in co. Antrim, prov. Ulfter.

BUSH-MILLS, fit. in bar. Dunluce, co. Antrim, prov. Ulfter, 120 miles from Dublin. Fairs on 28 Mar. 24 June, 21 Oct. and 12 Dec. Above 3 miles beyond it are the ruins of a caftle.

BUSH-RIVER, fit, in bar. Dunluce, co. Antrim, prov. Ulfter.

BUTLER'S-BRIDGE, fit. in bar. Loughtee, co. Cavan, prov. Ulfter; 57 miles from Dublin. A mile and half beyond which, at the edge of a fmall lough, are the ruins of a church.

BUTLER'S-TOWN, fit. in bar. Balruddery, co. Dublin, prov. Leinfter.

BUTTEVANT, fit. in bar. Orrery, co. Cork, prov. Munfter; $73\frac{1}{4}$ miles from Dublin, on the new turnpike road from Cork to Limerick. It is called in the Ecclefiaftical books *Bethon*; by the Irifh and *Spencer*, Kilnemullagh; and was formerly an antient corporation, being once governed by a mayor and aldermen; but by the wars it has gone to decay: 'tis faid to have fuffered greatly in the laft plague in Ireland. There are ftill to be feen the remains of a wall that furrounded the town: in this place are the remains of the once fumptuous abbey of Buttevant, founded by *David de Barry*, (who lies buried therein) in the reign of Edw. Ift. He was lord juftice of Ireland, and his tomb remains in the choir, oppofite the great altar. The walls of the choir, with the nave of the church, and feveral other buildings remain entire; alfo the fteeple, which is

a high

a high square tower, erected on a large gothic arch. To the S. is St. Mary's chapel, in which are several tombs of antient Irish families; on the N. W. side of the abbey. stands a ruined tower, said to have been erected by an earl of *Desmond*, who retired here; 'tis called *Cullin*. On each side of the W. entrance of the abbey, are large piles of skulls, which some say were brought thither after the battle of *Knocknanoiss*; which was fought but five miles from hence. Near this abbey stands part of another ruin, said to have been a nunnery, dedicated to St. *Owen*, or according to others, to St. John Baptist. The name Buttevant, according to tradition, takes its rise from a word given in battle by David de Barry, who overthrew the *Macartys*, and cried out *Boutez en avant*, i. e. Push forward: which is the present motto of the *Barrymore* family, who take title of visc. from this place. To the E. of the town stands the church, which is a modern building; but the antient remains of two churches, one dedicated to St. Bridget, and the other to the virgin Mary, are still visible, both having stood in the same church yard, which is very uncommon. There are also the ruins of a chapel of ease at Spittle bridge, one mile E. of Buttevant; and about two miles from Buttevant on the right, are the ruins of *Kilcolman-castle*, famous for having been the residence of the celebrated poet *Spencer*, and where he compleated his beautiful poem, called the "*Fairy Queen*." This whole place seems to have been formerly an assemblage of churches and religious houses, which being dissolved, it consequently went with them to ruin. Near *Kilmaclenine*, two miles S. W. of Buttevant, there is a pit of good yellow ochre, used for painting. Buttevant holds fairs 27 Mar. and 14 Oct.

BUVINDA or *Bubinda*, the antient name of a river mentioned by Ptolemy, and thought to be the *Boyne*, in prov. Leinster.

C A

CABLE-ISLAND, sit. in bar. Imokilly, near the coast of co. Cork, prov. Munster.

CABINTEELY, a small village, in bar. Rathdown, co. Dublin. prov. Leinster; about 7 miles distant from Dublin castle.

CABRA, sit. near Rathfriland, co. Down, prov. Ulster.

CABRA-CASTLE, sit. near Kells, co. Meath, prov. Leinster.

CABRAGH, sit. within 2 miles of Dublin castle, in co. Dublin, prov. Leinster. It is the antient seat of the *Segrave* family. The name

Cabragh or *Cabaragh*, is of great antiquity, and said to be derived from the *Cabiri*, (in Irish *Cabhar*; i. e. aid or assistance,) or the gods which the *Corybantes* (who were the priests of the Irish as well as of the Greeks) invoked on sudden emergencies. Hence *Cabaragh* seems still to retain the name, from having been a seminary of these *Corybantes*.—There is also a place called Cabragh or *Cabra*, sit. near Rathfriland, co. Down, prov. Ulster.

CABRIDGE, sit. in bar. Kilmacrenan, co. Donegal, prov. Ulster.

CADAMSTOWN, sit. in bar. Ballybritt, King's co. prov. Leinster.

CAGHRYARIFF, sit. in co. Clare, prov. Munster; 125 miles from Dublin; within 2 miles of which are the ruins of a church.

CAHEROUGH, sit. in bar. Beer and Bantry, co. Cork, prov. Munster.

CAHIR or *Cahier*, sit. in bar. Iffa and Offa, co. Tipperary, prov. Munster; it is a vicarage in dioc. of Lismore, and gives title of baron to a branch of the noble family of *Butler*. 'Tis distant about 8 miles S. E. from Cashel, and above 85 S. W. from Dublin; 3 miles beyond it are the ruins of a castle. Fairs are held here 27 May, 20 July, 18 Sept. and 7 Dec. This is a small but neat town; and on the opposite banks of the river *Suir*, are the ruins of *Cahier-abbey*. On an island in the river is the castle of Cahier; it was taken by sir *Geo. Carey*, in the reign of queen Eliz. and afterwards by *Cromwell*. The castle and the abbey were erected before the year 1142, by *Conor*, king of Thomond and monarch of Ireland. And in the reign of king John, *Geoffry de Camville* founded a priory for Augustinians, some ruins of which are still to be seen.—*Cahier* is also the name of a rectory in dioc. of Ardfert, sit. N. E. of Valentia island, in bar. of Iveragh, co. Kerry, prov. Munster; its church is the only one in repair, in the same bar. Near it are the ruins of several small houses, built formerly by the neighbouring inhabitants, as places of sanctuary in time of war: about a mile S. E. is a castle called *Littur*, and opposite to Cahier stand the ruins of Ballycarberry.—There is also an *Island* of this name, on coast of the bar. Kilmain, co. Mayo, prov. Connaught.

CAHIRAGH, a rectory in dioc. of Cork, sit. in bar. Carberry, co. Cork, prov. Munster.

CAHIRCANAWAY, certain very high hills, in co. Kerry, prov. Munster; called *Drung* and *Cahircanaway*, thro' which a road runs from the other parts of Kerry, and hangs in a tremendous manner over that part of the sea that forms the bay of Castlemain; it is not unlike the mountain of *Penmenmaur*, in North Wales, except

except that the road here is more ftoney, and lefs fecure for a traveller.

CAHIRCON, fit. in bar. Clanderlaw, co. Clare, prov. Munfter.

CAHIRCONLISH, a fair town in bar. Clanwilliam, co. Limerick, prov. Munfter; above 100 miles from Dublin. It is a vicarage in dioc. of Emly. Fairs held 16 May, 20 Aug. 17 Oct. and 5 Dec.—Alfo a fair town in King's co. prov. Leinfter; fairs held on 20 Aug.

CAHIRCONRIGH or *Cahirconree*, (i. e. the fortrefs of *Con-righ* or king *Con*) a confiderable mountain in bar. Corkaguinny, co. Kerry, prov. Munfter: on the top of which is a circle of maffy ftones, laid one on the other, in the manner of a Danifh intrenchment. Several of them are from 8 to 10 cubical feet, but they are all very rude. From the fituation of this place, it refembles a *Beacon*, or place of guard to alarm the country; but from the prodigious fize of the ftones, it rather feems to be a monument of fome great action performed near this place; or perhaps a fepulchral trophy raifed over fome eminent perfon. The mountain is conical, and more than 700 yards above the level of the fea; forming a kind of peninfula between the bays of Caftlemain and Tralee.

CAHIRCORNEY, a vicarage in dioc. of Emly, fit. in bar. Small county, co. Kerry, prov. Munfter.

CAHIRDONEL, fit. in parifh of Kilcraghan, co. Kerry, prov. Munfter; where there is a circular fortification of large ftones, 7 feet high, and faid to be the work of the Danes.

CAHIRDOWGAN or *Cahirduggan caftle*, fit. about 3 miles N. of Mallow, in co. Cork, prov. Munfter. This place formerly belonged to the family of the *Roches*. The lands about here are but indifferent, notwithftanding they are all of a limeftone bottom.

CAHIRDRINY-CASTLE, fit. 1 mile S. of Michael's town, co. Cork, prov. Munfter; commanding a very extenfive profpect; it was built by the *Roches*, and may be feen from every part of the adjacent country. The name fignifies *Fort-profpect*.

CAHIRDUGGAN, a curacy in dioc. of Cloyne, fit. in bar. Fermoy, co. Cork, prov. Munfter.

CAHIRELLY-WEST, a vicarage in dioc. of Emly, fit. in bar. Clanwilliam, co. Limerick, prov. Munfter. Fairs held 14 May, 26 Aug. and 6 Nov.

CAHIRKEGAN, fit. in parifh of Clondrohid, in co. Cork, prov. Munfter. The foil here is cold, mountainous, rocky and boggy, and not fitted for tillage, without the greateft induftry, not only in manuring the land, but alfo of clearing it of ftones; otherwife it is impoffible to plough it. When the ftones are removed the foil is fufficiently deep: but this requires

great labour. Upon the larger rocks they kindle turf fires, and keep them burning 'till the rocks grow hot, after which they eafily fplit; and the readier if cold water be poured on them, before they cool. This labour is not unlike *Hannibal's* in paffing the *Alps*.

CAHIRLAG, a vicarage in dioc. of Cork, fit. in bar. Barrymore, co. Cork, prov. Munfter.

CAHIRMEE, fit. in co. Cork, prov. Munfter; above 114 miles from Dublin.

CAHIRMORRES, fit. in bar. Clare, co. Galway, prov. Connaught; 142 miles from Dublin; 3 miles beyond which is *Creg caftle*.

CAHIRNARY, a rectory in dioc. of Limerick, fit. in the liberties of the city of Limerick, prov. Munfter.

CAHIR-TRANT, the weftern point of Ventry harbour, in co. Kerry, prov. Munfter; where there is an old Danifh intrenchment.

CAHIRVALLY, a rectory in dioc. of Limerick, fit. in liberties of the city of Limerick, prov. Munfter.

CAHIRULTAN, a rectory in dioc. of Cloyne, fit. in bar. Imokilly, co. Cork, prov. Munfter.

CAILTREE ISLAND, fit. in Lough Derg, by the river Shannon, and bordering the co. Clare, prov. Munfter; here is one of the antient round towers.

CAIRBRE-AOBDHA, the prefent bar. of Kenry, in co. Limerick, prov. Munfter; the antient chiefs whereof were the *O'Donovans*.

CAIRN-HILL, fit. in co. Meath, prov. Leinfter; above 31 miles from Dublin.

CAIRN LOUGH, fit. in co. Antrim, prov. Ulfter; 143 miles from Dublin. Here is a fmall village, but agreeably fituated on the fea-fhore; commanding a full profpect of the bays of Cufhendal and Glenarin.

CALARY, a fair town in co. Wicklow, prov. Leinfter; where fairs are held on 12 Feb.

CALEDON, a village in bar. Dungannon, co. Tyrone, prov. Ulfter; 70 miles from Dublin. *James Alexander* was created baron Caledon of Caledon 1790. Fairs are held here 21 June and Aug. It is otherwife written *Callidon*. Near it is a fine feat of lord Belmore called *Aghinnas*.

CALDRON, fit. in bar. upper Dungannon, co. Tyrone, prov. Ulfter.

CALF, a *rock* fo called, fit. on the coaft of co. Cork, in bar. Bear and Bantry, prov. Munfter.

CALLA, fit. in bar. Kilconnel, co. Galway, prov. Connaught.

CALLABEG, a rectory in dioc. of Cafhel, fit. in bar. Eliogurty, co. Tipperary, prov. Munfter.

CALLAGHAN'S-MILLS, fit. in bar. Tullagh, co. Clare, prov. Munfter; about 98 miles from Dublin. Fairs held 8 May, 27 June and 15 Nov.

CALLAGHEN

CALLAGHENE, a fair town in co. Fermanagh, prov. Ulster ; fairs held on 2 Aug.

CALLAHILL, fit. in co. Fermanagh, prov. Ulster ; above 68 miles from Dublin. Near it are the ruins of a castle ; and 3 miles beyond it are the ruins of a church.

CALLAN, see *Callen*.

CALLAN-MOUNTAIN, (in Irish *Altoir na Griene* or altar of the sun) fit. about 8 miles W. of Ennis, co. Clare, prov. Munster. Here is a large stone or monument of granite, 11 feet 6 inches in length and 3 feet in breadth ; its greatest thickness one foot ; with an inscription in *Ogham* characters that runs thus,

Ⲫⲁⲛ ⲗⲓⲟ ⲁ ⲫⲉⲁ Ⲥⲟⲛⲁⲛ Ⲥⲟⳑⳅⲁⲇ Ⲥⲟⲣⲟⲃⲙⲟⲇ

which has been interpreted, " *Beneath this flag is interred Conan the turbulent and swift footed.*" It was discovered in 1785 by the Rt. Hon. W. B. Conyngham in company with Mr. O'Flannagan; the latter gentleman being sent from Dublin for that purpose by the Royal Irish Academy : it is placed upon a kind of Tumulus, and lies on an eminence above a small lake, facing the S. on a soft black quarry, and was erected to commemorate *Conan* one of the Connaught knts. who fell in battle. This stone has long been celebrated in the co. of Clare ; it is rude, the surface uneven, with natural wormlike irregularities. The lines on which the *Ogham* is inscribed are 9 feet long, the *Ogham* line is prolonged beyond the other two : this piece of antiquity, which is in itself curious, becomes also interesting by the degree of authenticity which it seems to stamp on the early Irish manuscripts. In an historical tale, written (as it is supposed) by *Ossian* about the year 296, is the following passage, " *But the intrepid hero Conan was not at this bloody battle : for going to the adoration of the Sun the preceding May, he was cut off by the Leinster troops, tho' he but a single knt. of Connaught ; and his body lies interred on the N. W. side of the dreary mountain of Callan, and over a flag is his name inscribed in the Ogham.*" The *Ogham* was a character sacred to the Druids, the alphabet of which is still preserved. On the S. side of this mountain is a very large druidical altar, about 12 feet by 4 ; this altar, the most regular of the kind now remaining, and of the highest antiquity, stands about ¼ mile distant from the high road leading from *Ennis* to *Ibrikan*, on the right hand.

CALLEN or *Callan*, a borough, post and fair town, fit. on a stream called *King's river*, in an agreeable situation, in bar. Kells, co. Kilkenny, prov. Leinster ; about 65 miles from Dublin. Lat. 52 : 25, lon. 7 : 46. Fairs held 10 July and 21 Aug. Within 1½ mile of it are the ruins of *Eve castle*. It is now a rectory in dioc. of Ossory, and returns 2 members to parliament ; patron, lord *Callan*. The Rt. Hon.

George *Agar* was created lord baron Callen 4 June 1790 ; and the family of *Fielding* was created visc. Fielding of Callan 22 Nov. 1622. This place seems to be in the same ruined state in which *Cromwell* left it, tho' it was formerly a town of some note, and has the remains of 3 castles. Here was an Augustinian friary founded in the 15th century, by James the father of Peter earl of Ormond, who died in April 1487, and was interr'd here. The friary was repaired in 1461 ; the tower and walls still remain, and it is probable that the bones of the founder were laid in the wall under 2 gothic arches, which yet stand near the E. window. In the parish church of Callen there were 2 chantries, dedicated to the holy Trinity and St. Catherine. The nave of the church remains in good preservation, the choir is now the parish church ; and the cemetery of the founder's family adjoins the choir, and is overgrown with moss and ivy. There is another place of this name fit. in co. Kerry, prov. Munster : here the *M'Carties* gained a complete victory over the *Fitzgeralds* Anno 1261. This defeat so reduced the *Fitzgeralds*, that none of that name durst put a plough into the ground for 12 years ; until dissentions arising amongst the Irish chiefs, they again recovered their former patrimony.

CALLEN MOUNTAIN, see *Callan mountain*.

CALLEN RIVER, fit. near Armagh, in co. Armagh, prov. Ulster ; in which *Nial*, one of the Irish kings, was unfortunately drowned : he was succeeded by Malachy the 1st.

CALLIAGH-CRUM, a *rock* in bar. Bear and Bantry, on coast of co. Cork, prov. Munster.

CALLIAGH TOWN, fit. in bar. Duleek, co. Meath, prov. Leinster : here was a cell dependent on the nunnery of St. Bridget of Odder ; it was supposed to stand near the well of Shallon, dedicated to St. Columb, to which great numbers resorted on the festival of that saint.

CALLIDON, see *Caledon*.

CALLOE. fit. in bar. Boyle, co. Roscommon, prov. Connaught.

CALLOW-HILL or *Callyhill*, a fair town in bar. Knockniny, co. Fermanagh, prov. Ulster : fair days 28 Mar. 2 Aug. and 11 Dec. It is a chapelry in dioc. of Kilmore.

CALLYHILL, see *Callow hill*.

CALMARO, fit. in bar. Loughlinsholin, co. Londonderry, prov. Ulster.

CALRAGHSTOWN, a curacy in dioc. of Dublin, fit. in bar. Newcastle, co. Dublin, prov. Leinster.

CALTLOUGH, a lake in bar. Leney, co. Sligo, prov. Connaught.

CALTRAGH, a fair town in bar. Kilconnel, co. Galway, prov. Connaught : 79 miles from Dublin. Fairs held 14 May, a Monday after 12 July, 21 Sept. and 14 Dec.

CALVER-

CALVERSTOWN, fit. in bar. Kilcullen, co. Kildare, prov. Leinfter. Fair days 1 May, 21 Sept. cuftom free.

CALVES, *rocks* fit. off Helvick-head, at the entrance of Dungarvan bay, co. Waterford, prov. Munfter.

CALVES-ISLANDS, fit. in co. Cork, prov. Munfter, midway N. W. between Cape clear and the main; they are 3 iflands: that called the *Weft-calf* contains about 44 acres, *Cartys-Ifland* lies between thefe and the fhore, and is larger than any of the *Calves-Iflands*.

CAMAWN, fee *Camowen*.

CAMBRICK-HILL, fit. in bar. Dundalk, co. Louth, prov. Leinfter.

CAMERON-RIVER, fit. in bar. Omagh, co. Tyrone, prov. Ulfter.

CAMLAGHT, a chapelry in dioc. of Armagh, bar. Orior, co. Armagh, prov. Ulfter.

CAMLIN, a vicarage in dioc. of Connor, fit. in bar. Maffareen, co. Antrim, prov. Ulfter.

CAMLIN-RIVER, fit. in co. Longford, prov. Leinfter.

CAMOLIN, a fair town in bar. Scarawalfh, co. Wexford, prov. Leinfter. Fairs held 9 June, Aug. and Nov. Here is a handfome feat belonging to Lord Valentia, and near it is *Slieu-Buoy*, a high, fertile and beautiful mountain.

CAMOWEN-RIVER, otherwife called *Camawn*, fit. in co. Tyrone, prov. Ulfter.

CAMUS, a rectory in dioc. of Derry, fit. in bar. Colerain, co. Londonderry, prov. Ulfter; here was a celebrated abbey, over which St. *Comgal* prefided A. D. 580.—There is another rectory of fame name in the fame dioc. fit. in bar. Strabane, co. Tyrone, prov. Ulfter.

CANAL, fee *Grand canal* and *Royal canal*.

CANCORA, a rath or caftle near Killaloe, in co. Clare, prov. Munfter; the palace of the antient kings of Thomond, built by *Brian Boromh*. It was deftroyed by *O'Neil*, and his Ultonians in 1101; the only remains now vifible of this antient royal palace, are the ramparts and foffe of the rath.

CANGANÆ-INSULE, mentioned by Richard of Cirencefter: they are the prefent South ifles of Arran, on coaft of the bar. Burrin, co. Clare, prov. Munfter. The *Cangany* of Ptolemy.

CANICE, fee *St. Canice*.

CANNAWAY, a rectory in dioc. of Cork, fit. in bar. Mulkerry, co. Cork, prov. Munfter.

CANNON-ROCK, fit. off the coaft of the bar. Ardes, co. Down, prov. Ulfter.

CANTUBRID, fit. in bar. Cremourne, co. Monaghan, prov. Ulfter.

CAPARD, fit. in bar. Finchinch, Queen's co. prov. Leinfter.

CAPE-CLEAR, fit. in bar. Carberry, co. Cork, prov. Munfter: lat. 51 : 19, lon. 9 : 46; it is deemed the moft Southern land in Ireland, contains 12 plough lands, and is a parifh of it-

felf. In the ecclefiaftical books it is called *Infula fancta Clara*; and in the old Irifh M. SS. *Inis Damhly*. The N. fide bears potatoes, barley and a little wheat, and the South is moftly a craggy rock; on the N. W. point ftands the ruin of a caftle, built on a rock in the fea, called *Dunanore*, i. e. the golden fort: there is a very narrow paffage about a yard broad and ten yards in length to this caftle. An ifland alfo called *Cape-clear-Ifland*, lies at a fmall diftance from Baltimore haven, in which there is a lough, the waters whereof having a deterfive and faponaceous quality, the inhabitants who are very poor, apply them to the wafhing and cleanfing their flax, of which they raife a confiderable quantity. The caftle and ifland formerly belonged to *O'Drifeol*, and were taken on 27 Mar. 1601 by capt. *Harvey*, who foon after obliged fir *Fineen O'Drifeol* to fubmit to Queen Eliz. A little to the E. of this caftle is a cave called *Ira Kieran* or St. Kieran's ftrand: and near it are the walls of a ruined church, dedicated to the fame St. On the S. W. fide of the ifland, is a creek on which a large veffel may be faved upon occafion; there is a fmaller creek on the N. fide oppofite to it, only fit for boats; in the S. cove there are from 7 fathom to 18 feet water. Many of the rocks of this ifland are compofed of an excellent white free ftone, refembling Portland ftone: they have alfo a black kind proper for flags and hearth-ftones, which are carried by fea to Cork.

CAPE-LEON, fee *Loop-head*.

CAPE-PLEASKIN, a curious cape, confifting of an eminence founded on a Bafaltic rock; it is fit. at Bengore promontory, in co. Antrim, prov. Ulfter.

CAPE-SYPEL, fit. in bar. Corkaguinny, co. Kerry, prov. Munfter.

CAPE-WHITE-HEAD, fit. on coaft of co. Antrim, prov. Ulfter.

CAPPA, fit. on the N. fide of the parifh of Whitechurch, in co. Waterford, prov. Munfter; near it are the remains of an antient building faid to have belonged to the knts. templars. Excellent marl has been found, lying deep in an adjacent bog; but the place being fubject to be filled with water on digging, makes it difficult to get any quantity of this manure.

CAPPAGH, fit. in bar. Ballinacour, co. Wicklow, prov. Leinfter.—Alfo a place in co. Waterford, prov. Munfter, 3½ miles W. of Dungarvan, where are the remains of an antient building, faid to have belonged to the knts. templars, and otherwife written *Cappa*.—Alfo a rectory in dioc. of Derry, fit. in bar. Strabane, co. Tyrone, prov. Ulfter.

CAPPATAGGEL, a fair town in co. Galway, prov. Connaught; fair day 13 May.

CAPPAH, a fair town in co. Tipperary, prov. Munfter:

Munster: fairs held 4 June, 27 July, 29 Sept. 16 Nov. and 21 Dec.

CAPPA HILL, fit. in bar. Ikeath, co Kildare, prov. Leinfter.

CAPPANACUSHY, the ruins of a *castle* fo called, fit. in the parifh of Templenoe, co. Kerry, prov. Munfter; it belonged to a younger branch of *O'Sullivan More's* family, and is faid to have been built by *Mac Crath*, brother to *O'Sullivan More*, from whom the *Mac-raths* of this place derive their name.

CAPPANESHY-CASTLE, fit. on the N. bank of Kenmare river, in co. Kerry, prov. Munfter.

CAPPAVARNA, fit. in bar. Kiltartan, co. Galway, prov. Connaught.

CAPPENDERRY, fit. in bar. Rofs, co. Galway, prov. Connaught.

CAPPERNANE, a fair town in co. Mayo, prov. Connaught. Fair days 27 June, 7 Sept. and 3 Dec.

CAPPOGE, a village in bar. Ikeath, co. Kildare, prov. Leinfter.—Alfo a rectory in dioc. of Armagh, fit. in bar. Ardee, co. Louth, prov. Leinfter.

CAPPOGE-BRIDGE, fit. in bar. Ardee, co. Louth, prov. Leinfter.

CAPPOGE-HILL, fit. 3 miles beyond Kilcock, co. Kildare, prov. Leinfter; from which is a very grand and extenfive profpect.

CAPPOQUIN, fit. in bar. Cofhmore, co. Waterford, prov. Munfter; near 98 miles from Dublin. Fairs held 17 March, 31 May, 5 July, 20 Sept. and 14 Oct. Here is a horfe barrack; and a bridge over the Blackwater. Near it is *Kilbree*, formerly belonging to the knts. templars. The *castle* of Cappoquin was built by the *Fitzgerald* family, but at what time is uncertain; it commands a very extenfive profpect of the country both to the W. and S. and alfo a great part of the plain between this and Dungarvan. In the time of the rebellion the castle was mostly in the hands of the Englifh, being garrifon'd for the earl of Cork, by one captain *Hugh Croker*. In 1642 lord *Broghill*, on his return from the relief of Knockmoan, with about 60 horfe and 140 foot, defeated a party of the rebels, ftrongly pofted near this place, and killed 200 men and one of their captains, with the lofs of only one Englifhman. It was taken in 1645 by lord *Caftlehaven*, after an obftinate refiftance.

CAR, a *lake* in bar. Orior, co. Armagh, prov. Ulfter.

CARA, a lough in co. Sligo, prov. Connaught.

CARAGHROE, fit. in bar. Omagh, co. Tyrone, prov. Ulfter.

CARBERY or *Carbury*, a large bar. in co. Cork, prov. Munfter; which gives title of baron to the family of *Evans*. The Weftern parts of it are poor and little improved; it was for-

merly called *Core-cael-luigh*, the antient chiefs of which were called *Mac-cor-teagh*, by corruption *Mac-Carty*; by which means they have been confounded with the Mac-Cartys of Kerry. The lefter districts of this country were under the dominion of their refpective chiefs, *O'Leary*, *O'Mahony* and *O'Dryfcol*, all dynafts or fubordinate chiefs to Mac Carty king of *Corcaluighe*, who in procefs of time became the fovereign of all the petty ftates in the prefent co. of Cork, and was therefore denominated *Macartyreagh* or Macarty the king; fome of whofe defcendants were in poffeffion at the commencement of the laft century, tho' the Englifh families of the *Courcies* and *Barrys* had eftates therein.— Some Irifh antiquarians allow but 8 families of royal extraction in Munfter, of whom they place 4 in Carbery, under the names of *Macarty*, *O'Mahon*, *O'Donovan* and *O'Dryfcol*: according to them there were 3 brothers, viz. 1. *Carbry Riada*, 2 *Curbry Mufe*, 3 *Gabry Bafcoin* who was brother to *Eana Aighnach* monarch of Munfter: from the 1ft of thefe this bar. is faid to take its name.—2d. Another bar. in co. Kildare, prov. Leinfter; which gives title of baron to the family of *Pomeroy*, now vifc. *Harberton*: and has a village in it of fame name, which is a vicarage in dioc. of Kildare.—3d. Alfo a bar. in co. Sligo, prov. Connaught; the two latter are frequently written *Carbury*.

CARBERY-ISLAND, a *rock* fit. in bar. Carbery, on coaft of co. Cork, prov. Munfter.

CARBURY, fee *Carbery*.

CARCEYLE, fit. in bar. Moyarta, co. Clare, prov. Munfter.

CARDANGAN, a vicarage in dioc. of Emly, fit. in bar. Clanwilliam, co. Tipperary, prov. Munfter.

CARDIFFSTOWN, a vicarage in dioc. of Kildare, fit. in bar. Naus, co. Kildare, prov. Leinfter.

CARDY ROCK, fit. off the coaft of bar. Balruddery, co. Dublin, prov. Leinfter.

CAREYSFORT or *Carysfort*, a borough town in co. Wicklow, prov. Leinfter; fit. about 7 miles S. W. of Wicklow. It gives title of baron to the family of *Proby*, and returns 2 members to parliament; patron, lord Carysfort. It is otherwife called *Macreddin*.

CAREYS-VILLE, a *feat* of the *Carey* family near Fermoy, in co. Cork, prov. Munfter. Here is the castle of *Ballymacpatrick*, built by the *Condons*, on a rifing ground above the river Black water. In Jan. 1642, this castle was taken by David earl of Barrymore, after an obftinate refiftance: the garrifon were all made prifoners, and afterwards put to death. The foil about this place is a lime ftone bottom and mellow clay, mixed with fand about 7 inches deep.

CARL

CARI-CASTLE, see *Garrycastle*.

CARICK, fit. in bar. Fertullagh, co. Weftmeath, prov. Leinfter.—Alfo a place in bar. Carbury, co. Kildare, prov. Leinfter.

CARICKABRICK, a caftle in co. Cork, prov. Munfter, lying E. of Fermoy, on the S. fide of the Black water, on the oppofite fide is another caftle called *Liclafh*.

CARICKAFOUKY, (called by fome *Carrickafouky*,) a caftle 2 miles W. of Macroomp, in co. Cork, prov. Munfter; it was built by the *Macartys* of Drifhane, in a wild and romantic fituation. The entrance to it is by a wild craggy rock, of dangerous and flippery footing, hanging frightfully over the river *Sullane*, which runs foaming at the foot of it. To the E. of the caftle is a large ftone placed upon a high rock, fecured by wedges of other ftones; and near it, the remains of a druidical altar, encompaffed with a circle of ftones, pitched end-ways.

CARICK-RUE, fit. in co. Wexford, prov. Leinfter.

CARIE, a bar. in co. Antrim, prov. Ulfter.

CARIGACUSHIN, a caftle of the *M'Auliffs*, fit. 1 mile N. E. of Newmarket, in co. Cork, prov. Munfter.

CARIGADROIIID, a caftle 3 miles E. of Macroomp, in co. Cork, prov. Munfter; built on a fteep rock, in the middle of the river *Lee*, by one of the *Macarty* family. It is faid this romantic fituation was the choice of the lady *O'Carrol*, wife to Macarty: yet others fay it was built by the *Learys*. This caftle and the bridge formed a noted pafs in the wars of 1641, and were often taken and retaken by the contending forces.

CARIGAHALY, fit. in bar. Moyarta, co. Clare, prov. Munfter.

CARIGAHOOLY *caftle*, fit. at the end of a nook or inlet in the bay of Newport, co. Mayo, prov. Connaught: the proper name is *Carrack a Uile*; it is a ftrong fquare tower about 50 feet high, divided into four ftories; at the N. and S. angles are two fmall projecting turrets: and the roof was raifed confiderably above the parapet wall that furrounds it, as may be perceived by the gable ends, in one of which was a window. This ferved as a banqueting room, as it has a chimney, the only remains of one to be feen. On the S. W. angle is a low round tower, which ferved for a guard room, this has two ftones and loop holes for the difcharge of mufquetry. In this caftle lived the famous *Grace O'Maly*, known among the Irifh by the name of *Grana Uile*: fhe was the daughter of *Owen O'Maly*, and widow of *O'Flaherty*, two Irifh chiefs in thofe parts. After the death of the laft, fhe married *fir Richard Bourke*, ftiled *Mac William Eighter*, who died in 1585, after having by her, three fons and one daughter.

Lord deputy *Sidney* writ to the council in England in 1576, that O'Maly was powerful in gallies and feamen. Grana who was a high fpirited lady, became fond, at an early age, of the watery element, and accompanied her father and his fept, in many naval expeditions. The coaft was plunder'd of cattle and other property, and many people were murdered in thefe excurfions. *Grana* was ever foremoft in danger; courage and conduct fecured her fuccefs, and the affrighted natives trembled at her name along the N. W. fhore of Ireland; her fame attracted many defperate and hardy mariners from diftant parts. Her larger veffels were moored in *Clare Ifland*, where fhe had a ftrong caftle: and her fmaller craft fhe kept at *Carigahooly*. A hole in the caftle wall is now fhewn, thro' which a cable was run from a veffel, and faftened to her bed, that fhe might be the eafier alarmed, and prevent furprife.

CARIGALINE, or *Carrigallen*, a bar. in co. Leitrim, prov. Connaught: having a village in it of fame name, which holds fairs 7 May, 9 Aug. 8 Oct. and laft Friday in Dec. it has a village in it of fame name, which is a vicarage in dioc. of Kilmore.—Alfo a fair town in bar. Kinilea, co. Cork, prov. Munfter, otherwife called *Beaver*: containing 4 plow lands. It holds fairs Eafter Monday, Whitf. Monday, 12 Aug. and 8 Nov. The caftle here was built by the *Cogans*, on a lime ftone rock, at the upper end of *Crofshaven*: but was many years after poffeffed by the Defmond family; in Q. Eliz. time it was called the impregnable caftle of Carigaline; but it is now quite demolifhed. The parifh church ftands a little way to the S. it is a rectory in dioc. of Cork.

CARIGANASS, a caftle which belonged to the O'Sullivans, built near the river *Oavane*, 4 miles from Bantry, in co. Cork, prov. Munfter. It was a high ftructure, with a fquare court, and flanked with four round towers. In it *Den. O'Sullivan* (furnamed *Caumb* i. e. crooked) kept garrifon in Queen Eliz. time; but on Tyrrell's flying the country, after the conqueft of Dunboy, this caftle was furrendered to the Queen's forces. Near this is a fine oak wood: one *Dennis Harley*, who lived to above 96 years, remembered the cutting this wood three different times, and at each cutting the trees were fit for beams, boat-timber, and moft other ufes.

CARIGANASSICK, a caftle now in ruins, fit. near the village of Dunderrow, in co. Cork, prov. Munfter.

CARIGANURE, a caftle built by the *Condons*; 1 mile W. of Mitchel's-town, co. Cork, prov. Munfter.

CARIGART, a village in bar. Kilmacrenan, co. Donegal, prov. Ulfter.

CARIG-

CARIGFOYLE, a caftle fit. near Rofheen, in co. Kerry, prov. Munfter; it was formerly a place of importance, and the antient feat of *O'Connor Kerry.* It lies in a fmall ifland, which ftands in a baftion formed by the river Shannon; it was defended on the land fide oppofite the ifland by double walls; the outermoft having fquare flankers, and the inward round baftions, built in the infancy of fortification; the ifland at the back of the caftle defended it from being batter'd by fhipping.

CARIGILIKY, fit. in parifh of *Miros,* co. Cork, prov. Munfter, where the foundation of extenfive ruins have been difcovered, together with a large cemetery with great quantities of human bones. It was probably the fite of the antient abbey *de fanEto Mauro,* which fome falfely place at *Abbeymahon* near Timoleague. The houfe of *Abbey Shrowry* was a cell to this; the parifh church ftands in ruins on the coaft; and oppofite to it, in a fmall ifland called *Arahas,* is a ruined chapel.

CARIGNACURRA, fit. in bar. Carbury, co. Cork, prov. Munfter.

CARIGOGONILL, fit. on river Shannon, 8 miles W. of Limerick, in co. Limerick, prov. Munfter; there was a houfe for knts. Templars in this village, which, in the year 1530, was the feat of *Donogh O'Brien* lord of *Poble O'Brien.* In 1691 it was a place of ftrength.

CARIGROHAN *caftle,* fit. at the Weftern limit of the liberties of Cork, in co. Cork, prov. Munfter; it is built on a high precipice over the river, and was much larger than at prefent, being ruined in 1641. At the entrance of the outward gate is a remarkably large fycamore tree, whofe branches form a circle of 90 feet in diameter, and the thicknefs of the body is proportionably great.

CARIGTOWHILL, a fair town fit. 8 miles E. of Cork, in co. Cork, prov. Munfter; it is feated on an arm of the fea, which, at high water flows under a bridge of 4 arches, and covers a large tract of land, making an excellent marfh for feeding cattle. Near this place to the N. E. is a large cavity running under a rock for a confiderable way in the earth. Fairs held 12 March and May, 26 Aug. 19 Sept. and 8 Nov.

CARIGUE ISLAND, fit. off the coaft of co. Kerry, in bar. Irraghticonnor, prov. Munfter.

CARINISH POINT, a cape in bar. Bear and Bantry, co. Cork, prov. Munfter.

CARLAN'STOWN, fit. in bar. Kells, co. Meath, prov. Leinfter; near 33 miles from Dublin. Here is a feat of earl Nugent, marquis of Buckingham.

CARLETON'S ISLAND, fit. in Lough Earn, co. Fermanagh, prov. Ulfter.

CARLINGFORD, a borough, fea-port and poft-town, fit. in bar. Dundalk, co. Louth, prov. Leinfter: near 52 miles from Dublin. Lat. 54 : 4, lon. 6 : 37. It is now a vicarage in dioc. of Armagh. Holds fairs on 10 Oct. and returns 2 members to parliament; patronage in the families of *Moor* and *Rofs.* This place is remarkable for a fine flavoured fpecies of oyfter. The harbour here is between 3 and 4 miles long and as many broad, fo that the largeft veffels may harbour there; the entrance is however full of rocks, and the place not much frequented but by fifhing boats. At Carlingford is an old caftle, called *King's caftle,* faid to have been built by order of king *John,* when he was in this kingdom about A. D. 1210: it muft formerly have been a fine building, the foundation is on a folid rock wafhed by the fea, and fome of the walls are 11 feet thick. At the oppofite end of the town to that caftle, there are ftill to be feen the ruinous remains of a fine monaftery, founded in 1305 for Dominican friars, by *Rich. de Burgh* earl of Ulfter: and not far from it, on the fummit of a neighbouring hill, a fpacious burying ground, and a little church or chapel adjoining to it. By reafon of the pofition of the neighbouring mountains, the inhabitants of this town lofe fight of the fun feveral hours before he fets in the horizon. Carlingford affords a ftrong pafs between the Northern and Southern co.'s by means of its bridge and narrow caufeway over a great and impaffible bog. This place gives title of vifc. to the family of *Carpenter,* now earl of *Tyrconnel.*

CARLISLE FORT, fit. near Cork harbour, co. Cork, prov. Munfter.

CARLON'STOWN BRIDGE, a fair town in co. Meath, prov. Leinfter. Fairs held 12 March, 1 May, 6 Aug. and 19 Nov.

CARLOW COUNTY, fit. in prov. Leinfter. It is joined by the co.'s Wicklow, Wexford, Kilkenny, Queen's co. and co. Kildare; it meafures 26 miles in length from N. to S. and 23 in the greateft breadth from E. to W. it contains 137,000 acres, or 214 fquare miles, and is divided into 5 baronies and 50 parifhes, which, with 13 churches, are all in the dioc. of Leighlin. The baronies are *Ravilly, Catherlough* (which was the antient name of this co.) *Idrone, Forth,* and *St. Mullins.* It returns 2 knts. of the fhire to parliament, and 4 other members for boroughs: and contains 8,763 houfes, and about 44,000 inhabitants. The river *Barrow,* which is navigable, runs thro' it from N. to S. the *Slaney* croffes it alfo in its courfe from Wicklow to Wexford. That part of co. Carlow, which lies on the W. of the Barrow, is covered with rough and high hills; another mountainous tract continues all along the bounds of *Wexford*

Wexford, beginning at the N. with the high and rocky *Mount Leinster*, and terminating in that which is called the *Black-stairs* in the S. The scenery in this co. is agreeable for the most part, and the champaign country is extremely rich and fertile, great part thereof being occupied by graziers. It comprehended the antient districts of *Hy Cabanagh* and *Hy Drone*, being the Northern part of the principality of Hy Kinselagh, and was made a co. by King John about A. D. 1210. It's most antient families are the *M'Morroughs, Cavanaghs, O'Rians, Bagnals, Carews* and *Cœks.*

CARLOW TOWN, a borough, post and fair town, sit. in bar. Catherlough, co. Carlow, prov. Leinster; being the assizes town for that co. and is a rectory in dioc. of Leighlin. Lat. 52:46, lon. 7:18. Distance from Dublin 39 miles. Fairs held 4 May, 22 June, 26 Aug. and 8 Nov. It returns 2 members to parliament; patron, *Wm. Burton*, esq. The town consists of a main street and another not of so large extent, that crosses it in the middle, together with a few back lanes: the church is but an ordinary structure, but the market-house is neat enough. The court-house is built over the goal, which you ascend by a flight of steps. Here is a horse barrack, and lately has been erected a handsome Roman catholic chapel, and a college for the youth of that profession. The river *Barrow* is navigable from this town to *Ross*, and also to *Athy*, where it forms a junction with the Grand canal. Some of the most beautiful and picturesque views in Ireland, are in the vicinity of Carlow, on the Barrow. On an eminence overhanging the river, is an old castle, of an oblong square area, with large round towers at each angle, which has a fine effect; it is said to have been erected by king *John*, to secure a pass over the Barrow; some writers say it was constructed by lord justice *Lacey*, in 1180, tho' *Cox* speaks of a castle erected here by *Isabel*, daughter of *Strongbow*; it was however always considered as a strong protection to the English pale in Leinster. In the 20th year of Rich. 2d. it was taken by one of the Cavanaghs, named *Donald Mac Art*, who stiled himself king of Leinster: in his possession it remained for some time. In 1577 Carlow sustained a long siege against *Roryoge O'More* or *Moor*, then in rebellion against Q. Eliz. but at last was obliged to surrender, when it was miserably plundered, and many of the inhabitants inhumanly put to the sword. It was once walled; but submitted to *Cromwell*, on his first approach. In 1642, four troops under sir *Pat. Wemys*, were sent from the earl of Ormond's army, to relieve Carlow; it was defended by 700 men, but on the approach of Wemys, they fled and burned the town; about 50 were slain in the pursuit, and 500 Englishmen delivered from imprisonment in the castle, where they were almost starved. In 1650, the castle was in the hands of the confederate catholics; but after a close siege, was surrendered into the hands of the parliamentary forces. This town was incorporated by king James 1st, at present it contains about 850 houses, and 5100 inhabitants: a considerable trade is carried on in coals, from the collieries of Doonane and Castlecomer, and here is a manufacture of the coarsest kind of woollen cloaths. There is also the ruin here of a very fine abbey, built about A. D. 634, whose founder was buried here, and gave name to the structure. Carlow gives title of visc. to the family of *Dawson*, as it did that of marquis to the duke of *Wharton.*

CARMEN, the capital of the antient *Coulan*, and the Naasteighan, where the states of the southern parts of Leinster met. It was sit. on a gently sloping hill, about 5 miles E. of Athy, in co. Kildare, prov. Leinster; now distinguished by the *moat of Mullamast*; i. e. the moat of decapitation, from the murder of a number of Irish gentlemen, by several English adventurers, in the 16th century. The hill of Carmen exactly resembles that of *Tarah*, in co. Meath; issuing originally from the bottom of a thick wood, of an oblate conical figure, about a mile in diameter at the base; from the summit, (which is nearly $\frac{3}{4}$ of a mile in height,) the several co.'s of S. Leinster may be seen. There are yet remaining on it, the *rath* and *laois* in which the chiefs encamped; also the labereigh or areopagus, consisting of 16 conical mounds of earth, in a circle of 68 feet in diameter, on which the chiefs sat in council. Near this place was fought the celebrated battle of Carmen, towards the close of the 3d century; between the people of S. Leinster, and *Carmar Cas*, king of Munster: the field where this battle was fought, is about 3 miles from *Carmen*, and 2 from Athy: at this day numbers of bodies of the slain, are frequently dug up, about a foot below the present surface, and in the several directions in which they fell.

CARMONEY, sit. in bar. Belfast, co. Antrim, prov. Ulster; 86 miles from Dublin; there is a parish church belonging to it, being a vicarage in dioc. of Connor.

CARMOYLE, see *Garmoyle.*

CARNAGH, a rectory in dioc. of Ferns, sit. in bar. Bantry, co. Wexford, prov. Leinster.

CARNALLOCK, a village in bar. Glenarm, co. Antrim, prov. Ulster.

CARNALWAY, a village in bar. Naas, co. Kildare, prov. Leinster; being a rectory in dioc. of Kildare.

Tutbury Castle

CARNAMART *river*, fit. in bar. Dunkellin, co. Galway, prov. Connaught.

CARNATHEN-HILL or *Scot's-hill*, a rifing ground, about ¼ of a mile S. of Donaghadee, in co. Down, prov. Ulfter.

CARNBANE, fit. in bar. lower Iveach, co. Down, prov. Ulfter.

CARN-CASTLE, fit. near Larne, in bar. Glenarm, co. Antrim, prov. Ulfter; about 100 miles from Dublin. Lat. 54:57, lon. 6:30. Near it is Carn-caftle church; it is a rectory in dioc. of Connor.

CARNDONAGH, a fair town in co. Donegal, prov. Ulfter; fairs held 21 Feb. May, Aug. and Nov.

CARNE, fit. in co. Weftmeath, prov. Leinfter; near Ballymore.—Alfo a place in bar. Erris, co. Mayo, prov. Connaught; and in co. Cavan, prov. Ulfter.—Alfo a rectory in dioc. of Kilfenora, fit. in bar. Burrin, co. Clare, prov. Munfter.—Alfo a village in bar. Inifhowen, co. Donegal, prov. Ulfter.—Alfo a rectory in dioc. of Kildare, fit. in bar. Ophaly, co. Kildare, prov. Leinfter.—Alfo a rectory in dioc. of Ferns, fit. in bar. Forth, co. Wexford, prov. Leinfter.

CARNE-CASTLE, fee *Carn-caftle*.

CARNEKILL, fit. in bar. Dunluce, co. Antrim, prov. Ulfter.

CARNEW, a fair town in bar. Shillelagh, co. Wicklow, prov. Leinfter; 44 miles from Dublin, where are the remains of a large caftle. This town tho' feemingly defpicable, has fome little trade. Fairs held on fecond Thurfday O. S. in Feb. 1 Apr. 15 May, 1 July and firft Thurfday O. S. in Aug. It is a rectory in dioc. of Ferns.

CARNI-CASTLE, fit. in bar. Dungannon, co. Tyrone, prov. Ulfter.

CARNSORE-POINT, fit. by St. George's channel, bar. Forth, co. Wexford, prov. Leinfter. Lat. 52:11, lon. 6:51. St. *Domangart* built a monaftery here at the foot of *Slieu Domangaird*, a mountain hanging over the fea, that immediately flows between England and Ireland. Here is a parifh church in the dioc. of Ferns.

CARNTEEL, fit. in co. Tyrone, prov. Ulfter; about 80 miles from Dublin. Fairs held 26 May and Aug. 29 Sept. and 26 Nov.

CARNTOGHER, fit. in bar. Loughlinfholen, co. Londonderry, prov. Ulfter. There are mountains of this name fit. in the co.'s Londonderry and Tyrone.

CAROBEGG, fit. in bar. Tyreragh, co. Sligo, prov. Connaught.

CAROLANS, fit. in bar. Fore, co. Weftmeath, prov. Leinfter.

CAROTOGHAR, fit. in bar. Boyle, co. Rofcommon, prov. Connaught.

CARRA-CASTLE, fit. in co. Mayo, prov. Connaught. Fairs held 13 Feb. 4 June and 2 Sept.

CARRAGH, a bar. in co. Mayo, prov. Connaught.

CARRAGH-LOUGH, (or *Carrah lough*) fit. in bar. Carragh, co. Mayo, prov. Connaught. In the flat country that borders this lake and Lough Mafk, are many miles of rocky ground, which at a diftance appears as one immenfe fheet of white ftone; but on nearer infpection of thefe fingular rocks, they are perceived to ftand in parallel lines, from 1 to 3 feet above the furface, like flag ftones, pitched in the ground on their edges: and however they may vary in fhape, fize and diftance, they are all calcareous, and have all the fame direction.

CARRAGH-ROE *mountains*, fit. in bar. Omagh, co. Tyrone, prov. Ulfter.

CARRANFEARAIDHE, now *Knockaine*, in co. Limerick, prov. Munfter. At or near this place, a bloody battle was fought between the princes of Connaught, and *Dioma* king of Munfter; in which the former were entirely defeated, and five chiefs and 4000 officers and foldiers left dead on the field.

CARRA-RIVER, fit. in bar. Dunkerron, co. Kerry, prov. Munfter, (in Irifh it fignifies ftony or rocky.) It rifes in the mountains of Dunkena, and paffing Northerly through Glencare, empties itfelf into the bay of Caftlemain.

CARRENDUFF, fit. in bar. Tyreragh, co. Sligo, prov. Connaught.

CARROGUNELL, fee *Carrickogonel*.

CARRICK, a rectory in dioc. of Ferns, fit. in bar. Shelmaliere, co. Wexford, prov. Leinfter.—Alfo a rectory in dioc. of Armagh, fit. in bar. Ferrard, co. Louth, prov. Leinfter.—Alfo a rectory in dioc. of Meath, fit. in bar. Fertullagh, co. Weftmeath, prov. Leinfter.

CARRICKAMFEL, a *rock* in bar. Ballinahinch, on coaft of co. Galway, prov. Connaught.

CARRICK-A-OWLY, fit. in bay of Newport, co. Mayo, prov. Connaught.

CARRICKAQUICY, a village in bar. Poblebrien, co. Limerick, prov. Munfter.

CARRICK-A-REDE, or *Carrick-a-ramhead*, i. e. the rock in the road,) fit. in bar. Carey, fomewhat E. of Ballintoy, on the coaft of co. Antrim, prov. Ulfter. It is connected to the continent or main land by a bridge of ropes 60 feet in length, over a chafm 84 feet in depth; over which extraordinary bridge and frightful precipice, the fifhermen inhabiting this part of the country, pafs and repafs.—Alfo a mountain in bar. Gallen, co. Mayo, prov. Connaught.

CARRICKASTICKEN, a fmall river in co. Louth, prov. Leinfter, fo called from a mountain of fame name from whence it defcends.

CARRICK-A-UILE, fee *Carigahooly*.

CARRICK-

CARRICKBEG, fit. in the parifh of Defert, co. Waterford, prov. Munfter; on the river *Suir*, oppofite to the town of *Carrick-on-Suir*, being feparated by a bridge from the co. Tipperary. This place was formerly called *Carrick-mac-griffin*; and here are the remains of an abbey of Francifcan friars, founded by James the firft earl of *Ormond* in 1336. A fteeple erected on the fide wall of the church, is accounted a great curiofity, it projecting about 2 feet over the wall from which it takes its rife, in a point at 20 feet from the ground.

CARRICKBRACK, fit. in bar. Innifhowen, co. Donegal, prov. Ulfter.

CARRICKCHAD *mountains*, fit. in bar. Leney, co. Sligo, prov. Connaught.

CARRICKDOWNAN, a rectory in dioc. of Cloyne, fit. in bar. Fermoy, co. Cork, prov. Munfter.

CARRICKDRUMMIN, a rock in bar. Carey, on coaft of co. Antrim, prov. Ulfter.

CARRICKDRUMRUSK, fee *Carrick-on-Shannon*.

CARRCIKDUNAMACE, fee *Dunamace*.

CARRICKEDMOND, fit. in co. Louth, prov. Leinfter, about 1 mile from *Balrichan*; and near the river *Carrickaflicken*. Here we fee the rude remains of a facred grove, or feat of the Druids ; and on digging near this place, feveral decayed human bones were found : and fome urns of baked clay, one of which was filled with burned bones and pieces of charcoal.

CARRICKENEDY, fit. in bar. Burrifhoole, co. Mayo, prov. Connaught.

CARRICKFERGUS, a fea port, and poft town in bar. Belfaft, co. Antrim, prov. Ulfter; 88 miles from Dublin. Lat. 54 : 45, lon. 6 : 10 it is a town and county in itfelf, and returns 2 members to parliament, of whom lord *Donegal* has the nomination. This place is fit. in a bay of its name in the Irifh channel, where is an excellent harbour, with a ftrong caftle on a high rock, built by fir *Henry Sidney*, and an antient palace now converted into a magazine for arms. It is a market and affizes town ; fortified, walled, and has fome modern outworks. The *bay* is fafe and fpacious, and memorable for the landing of duke *Schomberg*; who anchored in *Groom's-port-bay* near Bangor, on 13 Aug. 1689 with 10,000 men, fent by king William the IIId: the king himfelf followed the year after, and landed near Carrickfergus 14 June 1690. The French under *Thurot* made a defcent here in 1760, and laid the town under contributions. This bay is now called the *Lough* of *Belfaft*. Here is an old gothic church, with many family monuments. In 1232, a monaftery for Francifcans was erected here : at the fuppreffion of religious houfes it was granted to fir *Arthur Chichefter*, anceftor to the earl of Donegal, who erected a noble caftle (now in dec.y) on the

fcite of the monaftery, about the year 1610. The mayor of this town was formerly admiral of a confiderable extent of the coaft in the co.'s Down and Antrim, the corporation enjoying the cuftoms paid by all veffels within thefe bounds; the creeks of Belfaft and Bangor excepted. This grant was repurchafed, and the cuftom-houfe transfer'd to Belfaft.

CARRICKGEEN, a hill fit. near Dunamace in Queen's co. prov. Leinfter: at the foot of which is a fmall entrance into a fubterraneous paffage which runs a confiderable way under this hill.

CARRICKGLASS, fit. in bar. Ardagh, co. Longford, prov. Leinfter.

CARRICK-KELLY, fit. in bar. Louth, co. Louth, prov. Leinfter.

CARRICKLOGHER, fit. near Nenagh, in co. Tipperary, prov Munfter.

CARRICKMACRA, fit. in bar. Carbery, co. Cork, prov. Munfter.

CARRICKMACREILY *mountains*, fit. in bar. Newcaftle, co. Wicklow, prov. Leinfter.

CARRICKMACGRIFFIN, fee *Carrickbeg*.

CARRICKMACROSS, fit. in bar. Donaghmoine, co. Monaghan, prov. Ulfter; it is a poft and fair town above 42 miles from Dublin; fair days 27 May, 10 July, 27 Sept. 9 Nov. and 10 Dec.

CARRICKMAGRIFFIN, fit. in bar. Iffa and Offa, co. Tipperary, prov. Munfter. Lat. 52 : 15, lon. 7 : 44.

CARRICKMAKAN, fit. near Ennifcorthy, co. Wexford, prov. Leinfter.

CARRICKMAGUIGLY, a village in bar. Inifhowen, co. Donegal, prov. Ulfter.

CARRICKMINES, a village in co. Dublin, prov. Leinfter; diftant about 3 miles from *Stillorgan*, and 7 from the caftle of Dublin. It holds fairs on 14 and 15 Apr. and Oct.

CARRICKOGONEL, or *Carrigoginniol*, fit. in co. Limerick, prov. Munfter. Here is a caftle magnificently placed on the fummit of a lofty hill, within about 4 miles of Limerick city ; it muft have been a place of great ftrength, but was difmantled by Cromwell; the remains however are fufficient to fhew its former confequence. In 1211 *Donagh Cairbreach O'Brien* received from king *John*, patents for the eftate of *Carrigoginniol*, at the yearly rent of fixty marks. This place is fince called *Poble-Brien*.

CARRICK-ON-SHANNON, (fo called to diftinguifh it from another town called *Carrick-on-Suir*) fit. in bar. Leitrim, co. Leitrim, prov. Connaught, 77 miles from Dublin. It is otherwife called *Carrickdrumruffk*, and has a barrack for a company of foot. It holds fairs on 12 May, 11 Aug. and 21 Nov. 'Tis the fhire town of that co. and returns two members to parliament. Lat. 53 : 45, lon. 8 : 10. This town

town is feated on the river Shannon, whofe name it takes.

CARRICK-ON-SUIR, fit. in bar. Iffa and Offa, by the boundary of co. Tipperary, prov. Munfter; being joined to co. Waterford by a bridge over the river *Suir*. 'Tis diftant above 74 miles from Dublin. Lat. 52 : 12, lon. 7 : 10. It lies in a beautiful country; the caftle and large park adjoining, belong to the *Butler* family, but are now neglected; it was formerly a walled town, and part of the wall ftill remains; *William de Cantell* founded a priory here on the banks of the Suir, in honour of St. John the Evangelift: on the fcite of which Thomas Duff or *black Thomas* earl of Ormond, erected his caftle. The woollen manufacture is carried on here very extenfively, both of broad clooths and *ratteens*; it has a barrack for 2 troops of horfe, and gives title of earl to a branch of the *Butler* family, as it formerly did to the duke of Ormond. This is a market and poft town, and holds fairs on 15 Aug. Whit. Tuefday, and 1 Thurfday O. S. in Oct.

CARRICKPARSON, a vicarage in dioc. of Emly, fit. in bar. Clanwilliam, co. Limerick, prov. Munfter.

CARRICKRUAGH *mountains*, fit. in bar. Gorey, co. Wexford, prov. Leinfter.

CARRIG-ABBEY, fit. 1 mile E. of *Caftle-fcreen*, in co. Down, prov. Ulfter; at a place called *Erynagh*; it was founded by *Magnellus Mackentiff* one of the petty princes of Ulfter, on 8 Sept. 1127 for Benedictines; and was called *Carrig* from a rock on which it ftood. Here is alfo a famous well dedicated to St. Finian.

CARRIGACUSHIN *caftle*, fit. in bar. Duhallow, co. Cork, prov. Munfter.

CARRIGALLEN, fee *Carigaline*.

CARRIGANS, fit. in bar. Raphoe, co. Donegal, prov. Ulfter; 110 miles from Dublin.

CARRIGART, a fair town in bar. Kilmacrehan, co. Donegal, prov. Ulfter. Fairs held 21 June and 31 Oct.

CARRIGHAMLEARY, a village in bar. Fermoy, co. Cork, prov. Munfter. It is a vicarage in dioc. of Cloyne.

CARRIGIN, a rectory in dioc. of Tuam, fit. in bar. Clare, co. Galway, prov. Connaught.

CARRIGNENEELOGH, fit. in co. Cork, prov. Munfter; 147 miles from Dublin: the caftle here is in ruins, and diftant about 5 miles from Macroomp.

CARRIGROHANBEG, a rectory in dioc. of Cloyne, fit. in bar. Barrett's, co. Cork, prov. Munfter.

CARRIGROHANE, a rectory in dioc. of Cork, fit. in liberties of Cork, prov. Munfter.

CARRIOSLANEY, fit. in bar. Forth, co. Carlow, prov. Leinfter.

CARRINGOON, fit. near Mallow, in co. Cork, prov. Munfter: here there was a garrifon for king James the IId. in the late wars, the river Black-water being the boundary between the Englifh and Irifh quarters.

CARRINTEEL, a village in bar. Dungannon, co. Tyrone, prov. Ulfter. 'Tis is a rectory in dioc. of Armagh. Fairs held 26 May, 26 Aug. 19 Sept. and 26 Nov.

CARROGH, a vicarage in dioc. of Kildare, fit. in bar. Claine, co. Kildare, prov. Leinfter.

CARROONAKILLY, fit. in bar. Athenry, co. Galway, prov. Connaught.

CARROWBEG, fit. in bar. Athlone, co. Rofcommon, prov. Connaught.

CARROW CASTLE, fit. in bar. Inchiquin, co. Clare, prov. Munfter.

CARROWKILL, a village in bar. Bunratty, co. Clare, prov. Munfter.

CARROWMOGON, fit. in bar. Tirawly, co. Mayo, prov. Connaught.

CARRYCASTLE, fee *Garrycaftle*.

CARRYGLASS, fit. in bar. Kilnatalown, co. Cork, prov. Munfter.

CARSIOL, the antient name of Cafhel in co. Tipperary, prov. Munfter.

CARSTOWN, fit. in bar. Ferrard, co. Louth, prov. Leinfter.

CARTON, the elegant feat of his grace the duke of Leinfter; fit. in co. Kildare, prov. Leinfter; 2¼ miles beyond Leixlip and 10½ miles from the caftle of Dublin: there is however a nearer road than the high one, lately finifhed by his grace, which turns off to the right, a little below lord Carhampton's feat at Luttrel'ftown, and is extremely pleafant. The *park* at Carton ranks among the fineft in the kingdom; a large but gentle vale winds thro' the whole, in the bottom of which a fmall ftream has been enlarged into a fine river, which throws a chearfulnefs thro' moft of the fcenes: over it is a handfome ftone bridge. Here is a cottage, the views about which are uncommonly pleafing, and on one of the moft rifing grounds in the park is a tower, from the top of which the fcenery of the whole demefne is beheld.

CARTON'STOWN, fit. in bar. Ferrard, co. Louth, prov. Ulfter.

CARTRON-CASTLE, fit. about 2 miles beyond Athlone, in co. Rofcommon, prov. Connaught.

CARY, a bar. in co. Antrim, prov. Ulfter. Alfo the name of a *river* in that bar.

CARY CASTLE, now in ruins, fit. near Kilglafs, in co. Galway, prov. Connaught.

CARY RIVER, fit. in bar. Cary, co. Antrim, prov. Ulfter.

CARY'SFORT, fee *Carcy'sfort*.

CARY'SFORT *houfe*, fit. at Caryfort or *Carey'sfort*, in bar. Ballinacour, co. Wicklow, prov. Leinfter. 'Tis the feat of lord *Cary'sfort*.

CASCARRAIGN, fit. near *Carrick-on-Suir*, prov. Munfter.

CASH, fit. in co. Fermanagh, prov. Ulſter; 90 miles from Dublin: about ¼ mile from it, at the edge of Lough Erne, are the ruins of a caſtle.

CASHEL, a city and poſt-town in co. Tippe-rary, bar. Middlethird, and prov. of Munſter; about 76 miles S. W. of Dublin, and 16 N. W. of Clonmell. Lat. 52 : 23, lon. 8 : 13. It holds fairs on 26 Mar. the laſt Friday in July, 7 Aug 9 Sept. and 3 Nov. It is the ſee of an archbiſhop, and governed by a mayor, recorder and bailiffs, and ſends 2 members to parliament. Caſhel has been a very antient epiſcopal city, to which the biſhoprick of Emly is united: it was either founded or reſtored at the beginning of the 10th century: the ruins of the old cathe-dral, teſtify its having been an extenſive as well as handſome ſtructure, boldly towering on the celebrated *rock* of Caſhel. The old epiſcopal ſeat was at the W. end of the cathedral; but was battered by lord *Inchiquin* during the wars in king Char. Iſt. reign. Lord *Taffe* had placed a ſtrong garriſon here, but the former took it by ſtorm, and great ſlaughter was made of the garriſon and citizens, amongſt whom were above 20 prieſts or friars: adjoining the cathe-dra, are the ruins of Cormac's chapel, built in 901 by *Cormac mac Culinan*, at once king and arch-biſhop of Caſhel, who is alſo ſuppoſed to have erected the round tower which ſtands upon the top of the rock. This is ſuppoſed by ſome to have been the firſt ſtone building in Ireland, but we doubt if there are not yet earlier evidences of ma-ſonry in this kingdom; it ſeems to have been co-pied after the Grecian architecture, and long to have preceded that which is uſually called gothic. The tower is lofty, and defied the too ſucceſsful attempts of archbiſhop *Price*, who in the pre-ſent century, to his eternal diſgrace, unroofed and thereby demoliſhed the antient and vene-rable cathedral, which had been erected by St. Patrick. *Cormac mac Culinan* was deſcended from Enguſa Nafrack, the firſt ſon of the king of Caſhel, who was a chriſtian; Enguſa having been converted by St. Patrick, who came to Ireland in 431: hiſtory gives different accounts of the death of Cormac; but the beſt accounts of it, namely the annals of Ulſter and thoſe of Inniſfallen, ſay that he was killed in battle by the army of *Flan* king of Ulſter in 908; he was buried at this place, and eſteemed a learned man, having written that hiſtory of this king-dom, known by the name of the Pſalter of Caſhel. Donald O'Brien king of Limerick, built a new church from the ground in 1169, and en-dowed it: converting the old church of Coomac into a Chapel or chapter houſe on the S. ſide of the choir. *Richard O'Hedian* archbiſhop of Caſhel, in the reign of Henry V. repaired this church in 1421, it being then much decayed; he alſo

built a hall for the vicars choral, to whom he gave the lands called *Grange-connel* and *Thurlis-beg*. About the year 1495 the earl of Kildare being offended with *David Creagh*, archbiſhop of Caſhel, burned the cathedral, impiouſly in-tending (as he himſelf confeſſed) to deſtroy the archbiſhop, whom he ſuppoſed to have been in the cathedral at the time. In the choir are the monuments of *Myler Magrath*, archbiſhop of this ſee in the reign of Queen Eliz: and ſome other pieces of antiquity. Here are the ruins of an old monaſtery of Dominicans, and the walls of the old church which was dedicated to St. John *Baptiſt*. The city was originally ſur-rounded by a wall, which tho' now mouldering, ſeems to have been of better materials than the generality of ſuch incloſures; two gates are ſtill remaining of tolerable workmanſhip. On the aſcent to the cathedral, is a ſtone whereon according to tradition the kings here were crowned; for Caſhel was formerly the royal ſeat and metropolis of the kings of *Munſter*. There is alſo a ſeſſion-houſe here, a handſome market-houſe, charter-ſchool, and barrack for 2 compa-nies of foot. The charter-ſchool was opened in 1751, and the late archbiſhop *Price* ſubſcribed toward the ſupport of it 50l. per ann. during his life: and by his will bequeathed 300l. the inte-reſt whereof is applied to the maintenance of the children. The corporation of Caſhel granted 22 acres of land for 99 years, for which the maſter pays 22l. per ann. and the late Rich. Price eſq. of Ardmayle gave a rent charge of 30l. per ann. for ever. William Palliſer eſq. gave 600. to the incorporated ſociety, for the perpetual ſupport of five children in this ſchool. The city and ſuburbs were certainly once very large, ſince no leſs than 38 brewers were cited before a convention, for not paying dues to the church, of two flaggons of ale at each brewing. King Henry IId. in this city received the ho-mage of *Donald* king of *Limerick*, anno 1172; and here he held a ſynod. It appears from an inquiſition made 2 Henry IV. that the do-nation of certain lands to the church, founded here as before mentioned by Donald O'Brien, was confirmed by letters patent of king *John*. Donald was brother to Morough O'More, king of Munſter, A. D. 1086. This authentic re-cord is to be ſeen *Rot. Parl.* ii. T. i. 3 pt. D. *Cormac's Chapel* is computed to be two centuries older than the church. The antient name *Caſhel* was *Carfiol* or the habitation on the rock, being compounded of *Car* or *Carrie* and *fiol*. The rock was originally a *dun* or *caſtle* of the antient chiefs of *Eoganacht-Caiſil* or *Magh Fei-min*, called from their habitation on this inſu-lated rock, *Hy Dun-na-moi*, or " chief of the hill of the plain:" by corruption *O'Donahue*; in later ages they were diſtinguiſhed by the name

name of *Cartheigh*, or inhabitants of the rock; whence descended the *Macarthys*, hereditary chiefs of this district. There is also a place called *Casiol Irra* or West *Cashel*, 6 miles S. of Sligo, prov. Connaught; where a bishoprick was erected by St. *Bron*, in the beginning of 6th century.—There is also a vicarage of same name in dioc. of Ardagh, sit. in bar. Rath line, co. Longford, prov. Leinster.

CASHEL-MOUNTAINS, sit. in bar. Ballinahinch, co. Galway, prov. Connaught.

CASHEN *river*, sit. in co. Kerry, prov. Munster. It is formed by the union of the Feale and the Gale, and is navigable for 8 or 10 miles.

CASHENDAL, see *Cashendon-bay*.

CASHENDON-BAY and *harbour*, sit. in bar. Glenarm, co. Antrim, prov. Ulster. It is sometimes written *Cushindon* and *Cashendal*.

CASHLEH-BAY, sit. in bar. Moycullen, co. Galway, prov. Connaught.

CASIOL-IRRA or *W. Cashel*, sit. 6 miles S. of Sligo, prov. Connaught; where a bishopric was erected by St. *Bron* in the beginning of the 6th century.

CASTALL, sit. in bar. Ballinahinch, co. Galway, prov. Connaught.

CASTLE-ARCHDALE, sit. in bar. Lurge, co. Fermanagh prov. Ulster: Lat. 54 : 28, lon. 8 : 14.

CASTLE-AUDLEY, see *Audley-castle*.

CASTLE-AULIFF, sit. in bar. Duhallow, co. Cork, prov. Munster.

CASTLEBALDWIN, a fair town in co. Sligo, prov. Connaught; fair days 4 June, 29 July, 6 Sept. and 1 Nov.

CASTLE BALLINCARRIGY, sit. near *Iniskean*, by the river Bandon, in co. Cork, prov. Munster.

CASTLEBAR, an assizes and post-town in bar. Carragh, co. Mayo, prov. Connaught; being also a borough: it returns 2 members to parliament; patron, lord Lucan. Charles Bingham was created baron Lucan of Castlebar 1776.: It has a barrack for a troop of horse, and is sit. 114 miles from Dublin: lat. 53 : 50 N. lon. 9 : 0 W. Fair days 11 May, 9 July, 16 Sept. and 18 Nov. This town carries on a brisk trade, and is well inhabited. Here is a charter-school, and near it is the fine seat of lord Lucan.

CASTLE-BELLEW, sit. near Castleblakeney; prov. Connaught.

CASTLEBELLINGHAM, a very pleasant village in bar. Ardee, co. Louth, prov. Leinster, being also a post town, distant from Dublin 34 miles; it has fairs on Easter Tuesday and 10 Oct. There is one of the finest old, spreading elms here, that is to be seen in the kingdom.

CASTLE-BINE, sit. in bar. Kilconnel, co. Galway, prov. Connaught.

CASTLEBLAKENEY, sit. in bar. Kilconnel,

co. Galway, prov. Connaught, being a post and fair town; distant from Dublin 80 miles. Fair days 1 Jan. 17 Mar. Whitsun-Tuesday, 26 July, and 2 Oct.

CASTLEBLANEY, a fair and post town, in bar. Cremourne, co. Monaghan, prov. Ulster; sit. about 51 miles S. W. of Dublin. Fair days 13 May, 16 Aug. 8 Nov. and 6 Dec. Here is the handsome seat of lord *Blaney*. Lat. 54 : 7, lon. 7 : 13.

CASTLEBRACK; a fair town in bar Tinehinch, Queen's co. prov. Leinster. Fair day 12 Aug. It is a vicarage in dioc. of Kildare.

CASTLEBREY, the remains of an old building, about 1½ miles. W. of *Slane*, in co. Down, prov. Ulster; it is otherwise called *Johnstown*, and was once a preceptory of St. John's of Jerusalem. The family of the *Echlins* have several town lands in freehold, belonging to this place; which have a manor court also.

CASTLEBRIDGE, a fair town in bar. Shelmaliere, co. Wexford, prov. Leinster. Fair days 11 Apr. and 26 Dec.

CASTLEBRIGHT, sit. on the W side of the road leading from Killough to Downpatrick, in co. Down, prov. Ulster.

CASTLEBROWN, a handsome seat, sit. near Clain, co. Kildare, prov. Leinster.

CASTLE-BURKE, sit. near Tynagh, in co. Galway, prov. Connaught; the castle which is now in ruins was built by Tibot Burke, esq. ancestor of the present possessor.—There is also a place of same name, in bar. Corragh, co. Mayo, prov. Connaught.

CASTLE BUY, sit. near Lough Strangford, co. Down, prov. Ulster. *Hugh de Laccy*, in the 12th century, founded here the commandery of St. John the Baptist: it is now a great heap of ruins.

CASTLE-CALDWELL, the handsome seat of sir J. Caldwell, bart. sit. 5 miles beyond *Churchhill*, in co. Fermanagh, prov. Ulster. Nothing can be more beautiful than the approach to it; the promontories of thick wood which shoot into Lough Earn, on which Castle-caldwell is sit. under the shade of a great ridge of mountains, have the finest effect imaginable. This demesne forms a promontory 3 miles long, projecting into the lake, a beautiful assemblage of wood and lawn, one end a thick shade, the other grass, scattered with trees and finishing with a wood. The promontory in the front of the house is called *Ross-ugoul*, and commands a noble hanging wood on the banks of *Ross-moor*; and the woody necks that stretch from the land beyond the house, with several islands, give the greatest diversity to the scene. About a mile beyond Castle-caldwell, is *Lewrae*, another very beautiful seat.

CASTLE-

CASTLECARBERY, sit. on the verge of the Bog of Allen, in co. Kildare, prov. Leinster, near 26 miles from Dublin; here is a charter school, which was endowed by the late Mrs. Eliz. Colley and her sister, Mrs. Pomeroy, coheiresses of Castlecarbery, with 2 acres of land in perpetuity; they also granted 20 acres adjoining, at a moderate rate for 3 lives, and gave 20l. per Ann. as a rent charge for ever, towards the support of the school. Mrs. Eliz. and Mrs. Judith Colley, aunts to the said ladies, built the school at their own expence; and 100l. was bequeathed to it by the late Tho. Dallyel, esq. About ⅓ of a mile distance, are the ruins of a large castle, built about A. D. 1180, seated on a high peninsulated hill, rocky and steep on 3 sides, from which there is a very fine prospect. It was formerly the residence of the Cowley family. Fairs are held at Castlecarbery on 26 May and 2 Oct.

CASTLECAREY, sit. on the eastern coast of co. Antrim, prov. Ulster.

CASTLECARGAN, sit. in co. Leitrim, prov. Connaught, 84 miles from Dublin, otherwise called Cascarrigan; where fairs are held on 1 Jan. 24 June and 14 Aug. At this place are the ruins of a castle, and 2½ miles further, are the ruins of a church.

CASTLECARON, sit. in bar. Leney, co. Sligo, prov. Connaught.

CASTLECAULFIELD, a village sit. in bar. Dungannon, co. Tyrone, prov. Ulster, 75 miles from Dublin, it is now a complete ruin, and was demolished by the Irish in 1641, at which time the owner was murdered. Here are fairs on Shrove-tuesday, Whitsun-monday, 14 Aug. and 30 Nov. There was a charter school here, which was endowed with an acre of land by the late Rev. Mr. Vincent, who also granted a lease during incumbency, of 21 acres at 4s. 6d. per acre, tithe free.

CASTLECAVEN, sit. in bar. Newcastle, co. Wicklow, prov. Leinster.

CASTLECOM, a village in bar. Morgallion, co. Meath, prov. Leinster.

CASTLECOMER, a market and fair town, in bar. Fassadinning, co. Kilkenny, prov. Leinster, 45 miles from Dublin, celebrated for its coal pits, which produce the kind of coal, called Kilkenny coal, remarkable for not having any smoak. It gives title of visc. to the family of Wandesford, and lies about 8 miles N. of Kilkenny. The present lord, on whose estate the coal pits are, is said to clear by them yearly 10,000l. Fair days 3 May and 12 Aug. Castlecomer is a rectory in dioc. of Ossory.

CASTLECONNEL, sit. 6 miles N. of Limerick, on the E. side of the river Shannon, in bar. Clanwilliam, co. Limerick, prov. Munster; the castle here is very antient, and was the seat of the O'Briens, kings of Munster; the grandson of Brien Boromh was here treacherously murdered by the prince of Thomond. When the English landed in Ireland, it was granted to Richard de Burgo, earl of Ulster, known by the name of the red Knight. William de Burgo in the reign of queen Eliz. was created baron of Castle-connel. This family was afterwards attainted, but the estates restored on king James's accession to the throne. At the revolution of 1688, they were again attainted; the castle had a strong garrison of king James's forces, and general Ginkle sent 700 men from Limerick under the command of the prince of Hesse, when the garrison surrendered after a siege of two days. Ginkle considered it a strong hold, and ordered it to be dismantled and blown up; the explosion was so great, that it shook the houses in Limerick, and broke several windows. The castle was so spacious and the ascent by steps so easy, notwithstanding its being built on a very high rock, that a troop of horse has been drawn up in the hall. At Castleconnel is an excellent spa, which Dr. Rutty places in the same class with the German spa. The soil about it is of a calcareous nature, the water every where leaving an ochre coloured matter; the sediment of it is used successfully in curing ulcers and sores. An earth worm put into this water instantly dies; hence it has been found effectual for worms in children; it is a strong chalybeat, and seems to be peculiarly adapted to those complaints, where preparations of steel are ordered by the physician. Castleconnel is a rectory in dioc. of Killaloe.

CASTLECONNOR, sit. in bar. Tyreragh, co. Sligo, prov. Connaught; it is noted for a hill which has chambers made within of great stones, set archways. This place is a vicarage in dioc. of Killala. Lat. 54: 3, lon. 9: 38.

CASTLECONWAY, sit. in co. Kerry, prov. Munster, standing near the mouth of the river Lane; it is otherwise called Kilorglin, and holds fairs 19 and 20 May, 12 Aug. and 18 and 19 Nov.

CASTLECOOL, the seat of lord Belmore, sit. in co. Fermanagh, prov. Ulster; Armar Lowry Corry being created visc. Belmore, of Castle-cool, 1790.

CASTLECOOT, sit. in bar. Athlone, co. Roscommon, prov. Connaught. The family of Coot, (now earl Mountrath) was created visc. Coot of Castlecoot, in 1660. This place made a noble defence in 1642; in an assault made against it by the rebels, many of them were slain, who (as Borlase observes) were decently interred and not beheaded, as the Irish were accustomed to do; for this kindness the Irish commander sent capt. Coote a present of tobacco.

bacco, then very acceptable. Decapitation was an old Scythian practice, and introduced by the northern colonies into these Isles.

CASTLECOR, a rectory in dioc. Meath, sit. in bar. Half-fore, co. Meath, prov. Leinster.—Also a village in bar. Duhallow, co. Cork, prov. Munster; where an abbey was once erected.

CASTLECORITH, otherwise *Castlecor* in co. Cork, prov. Munster; here is a handsome house fronted with hewn stone and flanked at each angle with turrets: and near it is a pleasant park, where are the remains of a fortification, in the midst of which stood a castle; to the W. are the ruins of the parish church of *Kilbrin*.

CASTLECORRA, sit. in bar. Corrah, co. Mayo, prov. Connaught.

CASTLECORRY, sit. near Enniskillen, prov. Ulster.

CASTLECREAGH, sit. in bar. Moycarne, co. Roscommon, prov. Connaught.

CASTLECUFF, sit. in bar. Tinehinch, Queen's co. prov. Leinster. Fairs held 22 Nov.

CASTLEDAWSON, a fair town in co. Londonderry, prov. Ulster. Fair days 1 Jan. Wedn. after Easter day, 1 June and Aug.

CASTLE-DE-BURGO, sit. near Loughrea, co. Galway, prov. Connaught.

CASTLEDERG, a fair town in bar. Omagh, co. Tyrone, prov. Ulster; fairs held 1 Jan. 16 Feb. 26 May, 1 July, 3 Aug. 20 Oct. and 3 Dec.

CASTLEDERMOT, a fair and post town in bar. Kilkea and Moone, co. Kildare, prov. Leinster; sit. near 34 miles S. W. of Dublin: lat 52:53, lon. 6:55. It is a vicarage in dioc. of Dublin, and was once a large fortified town, and the residence of the kings who bore the name of Dermot. Here is one of the antient round towers, and the first charter school was erected in this town, which was endowed with 20 acres of land, rent free for ever, by the most noble James marquis of Kildare, whose father, earl of Kildare, gave 500*l.* in his life time, and bequeathed 500*l.* more, which was applied in building and enlarging the school, which was opened in 1734, for the reception of 40 children. Fairs held 24 Feb. Tuesday after Easter Tuesday, 24 May, 4 and 5 Aug. 29 Sept. and 19 Dec. This place was for some ages called Tristledermot: we are likewise told that St. *Diermit* about the year 500, founded a priory of regular canons here, from whence it was named *Disart Diarmuda*. In the 9th century it was plundered by the Danes; at which time there was a celebrated school here, in which *Cormac* bishop of Cashel was educated, who on his decease in 907 or 908, was interred in this priory. In this age or the

succeeding one, the round tower, old church and crosses which are here, are supposed by some to have been erected. Strongbow, earl of Pembroke, bestowed on the soldiers who followed him into Ireland, large possessions. To Walter de Riddlesford he gave the lands of Murthy and Imaile, in which Castledermot stands, being the antient patrimony of the O'Tohills or O'Tools. The 3rd lord Offaly marrying the daughter and heir of Riddlesford, became possessed of Castledermot and his other lands, and erected a castle in the town. In 1264 Rich. de Rupella, lord justice of Ireland, together with lord Theobald Butler and lord John Cogan, were taken prisoners by Maurice Fitz-Gerald and Maurice Fitz-Maurice, as was the red earl of Ulster. The Burkes and Geraldines quarrelled about some land in Connaught, and filled the whole kingdom with war and tumult: a meeting was appointed at Castledermot, when the foregoing outrage was committed, and the prisoners sent to Fitz-Gerald's castle of Ley. In 1302 Thomas lord Offaly founded a monastery for conventual franciscans in Castledermot, to which the family of Delahoide were great benefactors. In 1315 Roger Mortimer opposed Bruce the Scottish invader, a battle was fought at Kells in Meath, Bruce was victorious, over-ran the country and took Castledermot, and the next year spoiled the town: just before this the lord justice made a great slaughter of the rebels at this place, who had risen against the government while deeply engaged with Bruce: the latter after destroying the franciscan convent in Castledermot, and taking away the books, vestments, and all the ornaments of the church, with the most impious and sacrilegious violence, was entirely defeated by lord Edmund Botiller near the town. In 1328 Thomas the 2d earl of Kildare died; he built St. Mary's chapel in the convent, and was interred in it, together with his wife Joan, daughter of Richard earl of Ulster. In 1414 the Irish rebelled in Leinster; and Thomas Crawley archbishop of Dublin and lord justice, advanced as far as Castledermot with a small army to oppose them: he continued there with his clergy in prayer for their success; the event was answerable to their wishes, for the enemy were defeated with the loss of an 100 men at Kilkea. In 1499 on the 26 Aug. a parliament was held at Castledermot, which granted to the king an impost of 12*d.* per pound upon all merchandize imported to be sold, wine and oil excepted; orders were also made that the nobility should ride on saddles, according to the English fashion, and should wear their robes in parliament, and both clergy and laity gave the king a subsidy. In 1532 Gerald the 9th earl of Kildare rebelled, and after destroying the co. Kil-

kenny

kenny with fire and fword, plundered the people of Caftledermot on a fair day, and killed many of them. During the rebellion of 1641 Caftledermot was alternately in the hands of oppofite parties. In 1650 it was taken by colonels Reynolds and Hewfon : from that time its walls have mouldered to decay, fo that now not a veftige remains : the caftle and fome parts of the monafteries ftill exift. The number of houfes in 1793 was 163 ; 63 were of lime and ftone, and flated, the reft were cabins. It has no manufactures, and is principally fupported by the great poft road running thro' it from Dublin to Cork. The round tower is ufed as a belfry, the arch of it is femicircular, and feems to have been adorned with the chevron moulding. It is faid that a mint was eftablifhed to coin money in this town about 1377, and that the houfe in which the parliament then was holden here, has been fince converted into an inn.—There is alfo a place of this name in bar. Bantry, co. Cork, prov. Munfter.

CASTLE-DILLON, the magnificent feat of the Rt. Hon. fir Caple Molyneux, fit. near Rich-hill, in co. Armagh, prov. Ulfter. Here 2 confpicuous obelifks ftand in view ; one of them has been erected to commemorate the order of St. Patrick ; the other in honour of the volunteers of Ireland.

CASTLE-DOBBS, fit. near 3 miles from Carrickfergus, co. Antrim, prov. Ulfter.

CASTLE-DOD, fit. about 2 miles S. of *Charleville*, co. Cork, prov. Munfter ; it formerly belonged to the family of the Fitzgeralds, but is now only a modern built good houfe.

CASTLE-DRUM, fit. 3 miles W. of *Caftlemain*, co. Kerry, prov. Munfter ; this place was deftroyed in 1641. It was built by the *Moriarties*, or as others fay by an Englifh family called *Maurice*, by an heirefs of whom the anceftors of all the *Fitzgeralds* got their poffeffions in Kerry.

CASTLE DURROW, a poft town, fit. in co. Kilkenny, prov. Leinfter. Here is a handfome feat of lord Afhbrook.

CASTLE-ELLIS, or *Caftle-ellifh*, a curacy in dioc. of Ferns, fit. in bar. Ballaghkeen, co. Wexford, prov. Leinfter.

CASTLE-FIERY, fit. towards the banks of the river *Mang*, in co. Kerry, prov. Munfter ; it formerly belonged to the *Macarties*, and is on the eftate of lord Kenmare.

CASTLE-FIN, fit. in bar. Raphoe, co. Donegal, prov. Ulfter ; 107 miles from Dublin. Fairs held Eafter-monday, Whitfun-monday, 1 Monday before 10 Oct. 22 Nov. and Monday after Chriftmas.

CASTLE-FORBES, the feat of lord Granard, fit. near Longford, co. Longford, prov. Leinfter.

CASTLE-FORE, fit. in bar. Leitrim, co. Leitrim, prov. Connaught.

CASTLE-FREEMAN, fit. near *Oldcaftle*, prov. Leinfter.

CASTLE-FREKE, a pleafant feat, about 3 miles S. E. from Rofs, in co. Cork, prov. Munfter ; it commands an extenfive view of the ocean and coaft to the W. Adjacent to it is a large park, and alfo a fine frefh water lake, ftored with pike ; over which is an agreeable terrace.

CASTLE-GALLEA, fit. by the adjoining borders of the co. Leitrim and Sligo, prov. Connaught.

CASTLE-GAR, fit. near *Ballinafloe*, prov. Connaught.

CASTLE-GORE, fit. in bar. Omagh, co. Tipperary, prov. Munfter.

CASTLE-GRACE, fit. in bar. Offa, co. Tipperary, prov. Munfter.

CASTLE-GREGORY, in co. Kerry, prov. Munfter ; before the wars of 1641, it was poffeffed by *Walter Huffey*, efq. who was proprietor of the *Magheries* and *Ballybegan*, and having a confiderable party under his command, made a garrifon of his caftle ; where being long preffed by Cromwell's forces, he efcaped in the night with all his men, and got into *Minard* caftle, in which being foon befet by the colonels *Le' Hunt* and *Sadler*; after fome time fpent, the Englifh obferving that the befieged made ufe of pewter bullets, he and his men were blown up by powder, laid under the vaults of the caftle.

CASTLE-GUARD, at Ardee, co. Louth, prov. Leinfter ; it is a magnificent mount of an amazing magnitude, all artificial, and encompaffed with a double ditch and vallum ; 'tis now all planted with wood, and looks very romantic ; the perpendicular height of the mount from the bed of its foundation, is nearly 90 feet, and the depth of the main trench, between 30 and 40 ; the circumference at the top is not lefs than 140, and round the foundation upwards of 600 feet. There appears to have been from foundations yet remaining, two concentric octagonal buildings upon the fummit of it ; the one feems to have been a fort of town or caftle, and the other a kind of breaft work or gallery by way of parapet or battlement, probably an outward keep or guard. On one fide there is alfo a fally terras, which croffes the main ditch, and communicates with the outward works. This is manifeftly a work of great labour, and fome conclude it to be a fepulchral monument and burying place of fome of the Irifh kings ; others, that it was for affemblies of the people to debate on public affairs.

CASTLE-

CASTLE-HACKET, fit. in co. Galway, prov. Connaught; above 97 miles from Dublin; it has fairs on 2 Oct. near which at the foot of *Knocmac-hill* are the ruins of a castle.

CASTLE-HAVEN, a village with a small but neat harbour, fit. in bar. Carbury, co. Cork, prov. Munster: the entrance to it by the harbour is not half a mile over. Lat. 51:25, lon. 9:0. It gives title of earl to the family of *Touchet*, lord Audley, antient barons of England: and is a rectory in dioc. of Ross. The family of *Luttrell*, was also created visc. *Carhampton*, of *Castlehaven*, in 1781, and afterwards *earl Carhampton*. It was formerly called *Glanbarahane*, and by the Spaniards *Porto Castolo*; being famous for a sea fight between sir *Richard Levison* and *Don Pedro de Zuibar*, the Spanish Admiral, A. D. 1602. Near the entrance is an old castle, to command the harbour; but the hills adjoining command the castle. The parish church of *Castle-haven* is dedicated to St. *Barahane*, and near it is a deep rocky glen, called *Glanbarahane*. The eastern point, is called *Galleon point*; since *Adm. Levison* in queen Eliz. time sunk some galleons in it. Here are the remains of an intrenchment cast up by the Spaniards, and the ovens used by them, are also still to be seen; on one side are the ruins of *Rahine-castle*, which belonged to the O'*Donovans*. In the wall are several cannon balls, which were shot at it, from some vessels in the harbour. The channel here is bold and deep, gradually decreasing from 30 to 14 feet water at low tides; opposite *Castlehaven* which lies on the W. shore, there is good anchoring ground.

CASTLE-HIDE, a village in bar. Condons, co. Cork, prov. Munster.

CASTLE-HILL, fit. near *Annadorn*, in bar. *Kinelearty*, co. Down, prov. Ulster. This was the principal seat of the *Macartanes*. A neighbouring old church in *Loughin Island*, is thought to have been the place of their sepulture, and there is a chapel there, called *Mac-Cartane's* chapel.

CASTLE-HUMES, fit. in bar. Maghereboy, co. Fermanagh, prov. Ulster.

CASTLE-FANE, fit. near Tipperary, prov. Munster.

CASTLE-INCH, fit. in bar. Shellilogher, co. Kilkenny, prov. Leinster.

CASTLE-ING, fit. near Roscrea, prov. Munst.

CASTLE-ISHIN, fit. on the extremity of co. Cork, prov. Munster; was one of the seats of the *Fitzgeralds*.

CASTLE-ISLAND, fit. in bar. Truaghnacmy, co. Kerry, prov. Munster; above 133 miles from Dublin, about 8 miles E. of *Tralee*, and 30 N. W. of Cork; it holds fairs on 1 Aug. and Oct. Here is a decent parish church, a good parsonage house, a foot barrack, a session and market house, with a handsome assembly room for dancing, and some tolerable inns, tho' the town has been much decayed, owing, we are told, to some division of interest among the proprietors. In descending the mountains towards Castle Island, the country hath a vegetable agreeable aspect; the soil being mostly a fine limestone ground; and yet there are fewer improvements, and less tillage here, than in other places, where the land is not so proper for it; tho' much has lately been done by reclaiming bogs as well as by new roads. This place gave the title of baron to the family of *Herbert*; and now gives that of visc. to the family of *Gage*. The castle is said to have been erected by *Geoffry Maurice*, or *de Marscis*, lord justice of Ireland, anno 1226, during the reign of Henry IIIrd. the ruins of which castle still remain. Round the walls the river *Mang*, being here but an inconsiderable stream, flowed in a kind of ditch, over which were formerly drawbridges, &c. In antient times it was reckoned a place of strength, and was taken anno 1345, by sir *Ralph Ufford*, lord justice of Ireland, it being then held out for *Maurice FitzThomas Fitzgerald*, the first earl of Desmond, by sir *Eustace de la Poer*, sir *Wm. Grant*, and sir *John Cotterel*, who were all executed by *Ufford*. Near this place also Gerald IVth. earl of *Desmond*, commonly called the poet, is said to have been murdered in 1397. In Q. Eliz's grant of this seignory to the family of *Herbert*, it is stiled the manor and seignory of *Mount Eagle Loyal*. It extends about 12 Irish miles in length, and 10 in breadth, and contains 37,128 Irish plantation acres; of which only 14,211 are reckoned profitable, the remainder being mountain and bog. Castle Island is a rectory in dioc. of Ardfert; it has a charter-school, to which Rob. Fitzgerald, esq; in behalf of himself and the Rt. Hon. lord Branden, the Hon. Arthur Crosby, esq; John Blennerhasset, esq; Rich. Meredith, esq; Edw. Herbert, esq; granted about 26 acres of land: and the aforesaid gentlemen engaged to procure 200l. toward building the school, which was accordingly opened in 1762, for the reception of 40 children.

CASTLE-JORDAN. fit. according to Scale's *Hib. Atl.* in the most Eastern part of the bar. of *Lune*, but according to Dr. Beaufort it is in the bar. of *Moysenarth*, in co. Meath, prov. Leinster. It is a curacy in dioc. of Meath.

CASTLE-KEILY, fit. near the Leinster aqueduct of the grand canal, in co. Kildare, prov. Leinster; not far from the village of Sallins; here are the ruins of an antient church, with a burial ground still used.

CASTLE-KELLY, fit. near Athlone, prov. Connaught.

CASTLE-KIRK, fit. in bar. Ballinahinch, co. Galway; prov. Connaught.

CASTLEKNOCK, a bar. with a decayed village in it of fame name, fit. in co. Dublin, about 3 miles from Dublin, prov. Leinfter; here are the ruins of a caftle, formerly a place of great ftrength, built by the *Tyrrels*, in the reign of Hen. IId. It is otherwife written *Caftlenock*. Rich. Tyrrel founded an abbey here, dedicated to St. Brigid, for regular canons following the rule of St. Auguftin; it became in time a parifh church, and is now a vicarage in dioc. of Dublin.

CASTLE-LAGHAN, fit. in co. Mayo, prov. Connaught, 132 miles from Dublin.

CASTLE-LEHAN, fee *Caftle-Lyons*.

CASTLE-LESLIE, a handfome feat fit. at Glafslough, in co. Monaghan, prov. Ulfter. Here is a fine lake covering 120 acres; and a wood of 100 acres fpreading over a fine bold hill, and hanging down to the water in one deep fhade, the effect of which is remarkably beautiful.

CASTLE-LINY, fit. in bar. Ikerin, co. Tipperary, prov. Munfter.

CASTLE-LOST, a rectory in dioc. of Meath, fit. in bar. Fartullagh, co. Weftmeath, prov. Leinfter.

CASTLE-LOUGH, the ruins of this caftle, which was built on a rock, are fit. in co. Kerry, prov. Munfter, near *Killarney*: it was entirely demolifhed in the wars of 1641.

CASTLE-LUMNEY, fit. in bar. Ferrard, co. Louth, prov. Leinfter.

CASTLE-LYONS, a vicarage in dioc. of Cloyne, fit. in bar. Barrymore, co. Cork, prov. Munfter. This place was formerly called *Caftle Lehan*, from the *O'Lehans*, an antient Irifh fept; 'tis now called *Caftle-Lyons*, and fit. 111 miles from Dublin; a well built market town, pleafantly feated and well watered, in a rich fruitful foil, a fhort way from the river *Bride*. In this place *John de Barry* founded a monaftery for conventual francifcans, anno. 1307; upon the diffolution it was granted to the earl of *Cork*, who affigned it to his fon-in-law, David, the firft earl of *Barrymore*; or rather to his daughter, for in his will, he leaves this place to his "daughter Barrymore, to buy her gloves and pins." A confiderable part of this abbey ftill remains, particularly the choir, nave, and fteeple of the church. This town lies well for the linen manufacture, and is diftant 12 reputed miles from Cork. The lord Barrymore built an elegant houfe here, on the foundation of *O'Lehan's caftle*. In throwing down fome of the old walls of it, a chimney-piece was difcovered with this infcription, "*Lehan O'Cullene hoc fecit*, MCIII." which fhews that ftone buildings were much earlier in Ireland, than fome of our modern antiquarians

allow them to have been. This is a poft-town, and holds fairs on 1 Jan. Eafter Tuefd. Whir. Mond. 28 Aug. 29 Sept. and 16 Nov.—This is alfo the name of a feat near *Hazle-hatch*, by the borders of the co. Kildare and banks of the grand canal, prov. Leinfter, about 11 miles from Dublin. Here is a fuperb manfion houfe erected by Mr. Aylmer.

CASTLE-MACADAMS, fit. in bar. Arklow, co. Wicklow, prov. Leinfter. It is a rectory in dioc. of Dublin.

CASTLE-MAGARRET, fit. in bar. Clanmorris, co. Mayo, prov. Connaught.

CASTLEMAGNER or *Caftlemagnor*, fit. according to Dr. *Smyth*, in bar. Duhallow, co. Cork, prov. Munfter, about 2 miles to the N. of Clonmene, near the Blackwater; but Dr. Beaufort and others place it in the bar. of Orrery. It is a vicarage in dioc. of Cloyne. In the rebellion of 1641, this caftle belonged to *Richard Magner*, agent for the Irifh inhabitants of *Orrery* and *Kilmore*. When Cromwell was at *Clonmel*, he went to pay a vifit to him, but being reprefented as a very troublefome fellow, who had been active in the rebellion, Cromwell fent him with a letter to col. *Phare*, the governor of Cork, in which was an order to execute the bearer.—*Magner* who fufpected foul play, had fcarce left Clonmel when he opened the letter, read the contents, and fealing it up, inftead of proceeding towards Cork, turned off to *Mallow* and delivered it to the officer who commanded there, with directions as from Cromwell, for *him* to deliver it to col. *Phare*. This officer had often preyed upon *Magner's* land, for which he was refolved to be revenged. The officer fufpecting no deceit, went with the letter, which greatly amazed the governor, who knew him to be an honeft man, and immediately fent an exprefs to Cromwell for further directions, who being extremely chagrined to be fo ferv'd, fent orders to let the officer have his liberty, and to apprehend *Magner*, but the latter had taken care to get out of his reach.

CASTLEMAIN, a fair town, fit. in bar. Traghnacmy, co. Kerry, prov. Munfter, about 148 miles from Dublin; it gives title of vifc. to the family of *Child*. Lat. 52, N. lon. 9: 35, W. it lies about 4 miles S. of *Tralee*, and holds fairs 3 Sept. and 21 Nov. It takes its name from an antient caftle that was erected here, on a bridge over the river *Mang*, faid to have been built at the joint charge of *Macarty More*, and one of the earls of *Defmond*, as a place of defence between their refpective frontiers. Each of thefe great men was to have an equal claim to this fortrefs, and they agreed to give and receive poffeffion of it alternately; *Macarty* went firft into the caftle, and furrendered it to *Defmond*, who inftead of giving poffeffion of it in

his

his turn, ordered his followers to hold it, who shut the gates, and drove off *Macarty* and his people. This place continued in Desmond's family, until Queen Elizabeth's reign, when it was delivered up to *James* the *last earl*. During the troubles of 1641, the *Irish* kept a constant garrison therein, until it was taken and demolished by *Ludlow*; on the restoration it was kept in the hands of the crown, and a constable appointed to guard it, (tho' it has been a long time in ruins) the clerk of the crown for this county, was commonly appointed to this office, having a small piece of land annexed to it for his salary. It formerly gave title of visc. to the family of *Monson*, and afterwards the dignity of earl to *Roger Palmer*, esq. who was so created by king Char. IId. 1661, but the title in that family is now extinct. Castlemain is but an inconsiderable village, and hath nothing in it remarkable; the banks of the river *Mang*, which wind from hence in a serpentine manner to the sea, are composed of a rich clay, and the same soil lies at the bottom of the river, which is deep enough for vessels of 50 tons and upwards, to sail up to the bridge at high water, where they may lie in soft oozy ground to discharge; some vessels are unloaded here on the bank side, which serves as a wharf; they are generally freighted with *rock-salt* from England, considerable quantities of which are refined in this neighbourhood; and others are laden with iron ore, which is carried on horses to the iron foundery near *Mucruss*. 3 miles W. of *Castlemain*, are the ruins of *Castle-drum*; it was destroyed in 1641. The *Bay of Castlemain* is extremely wild and dangerous, nor is it advisable for any vessel to trust to her being saved by sailing up towards the *harbour* of Castlemain, which lies in the bottom of the bay; she ought therefore to endeavour as the wind may happen to blow, to sail either into *Valentia* or *Dingle*, which last lies on the N. side of the bay, in either of which places she will be secure from all winds. 1¼ mile N. W. of Castlemain, on the lands of *Farnass*, part of the estate of the college of *Dublin*, there is a strong chalybeat water, which at the well has a sulphureous smell, like the washing of a gun barrel; this water has been little used, and therefore nothing positive can be said of its virtues.

CASTLE-MARTIN, sit. in bar. Kilcullen, co. Kildare, prov. Leinster. Here are the ruins of a chapel, which was founded about A. D. 1200 by *Richard* lord of *Castlemartin*, and dependent on the church of Kilcullen; it was a mausoleum and chapel for his family, according to the custom of that age, and therefore very small, being only 20 feet by 16: in the centre was the tomb of the founder, now almost destroyed: what renders this chapel deserving of notice, is the singularity of the steeple, consisting of little more than 2 parallel walls: a door from the chapel conducts by 6 or 7 steps, to a narrow passage between the walls, about 3½ feet wide, from which opening into the chapel, is a door about 8 feet from the floor; and at the end of that passage, by an ascent of 4 more steps, is a similar door opening into the church-yard; these doors are just sufficient for a man to stand in, and were evidently intended as portals to the pulpit, from whence the priest exhorted the congregation. The chancel being small, none were admitted into it, except the family of the founder; the others, as tenants and strangers, remained in the open air. From one portal the priest preached to the congregation within, and from the other to those without. Several such pulpits are in the churches on the continent, but we do not know of any other in Ireland. In the arched ceiling of the pulpit, is a round hole thro' which evidently came the rope of a bell. The original height of the steeple, from the ruins cannot now be determined. The chapel, by its founder, was granted in 1212, to the priory of Christ-church Dublin, with 7 acres of land.

CASTLE-MARTYR, a borough, fair and post town, also a rectory in dioc. of Cloyne, sit. in bar. Imokilly, co. Cork, prov. Munster; distant 123 miles from Dublin, and about 12 S. E. of Cork. Lat. 31 : 48, lon. 8 : 0; it holds fairs on 2 May and Oct. and returns two members to parliament, patron the earl of *Shannon*. It gives title of baron to a branch of the noble family of *Boyle*, and has a charter-school which was opened in 1749 for forty children, which was endowed by the Rt. Hon. Henry earl of Shannon, with two English acres of land in perpetuity; he also gave a lease of lives renewable for ever, of 10 English acres of land at the yearly acknowledgment of 5 shillings during his life, and granted to it 10 English acres more, at the yearly acknowledgment of 4 shillings per acre for three lives. Here is a handsome church, alms-house, and spinning-school for the encouragement of the linen manufacture. This place was formerly called *Ballymartyr*, and was a seat of a branch of the *Fitzgeralds*, called Seneschals of *Imokilly*. In the year 1663, it was incorporated by the interest of the *first* E. of Orrery; and was also called *Leper's-town*, as it is said from a leper-house belonging to an adjacent place named *Ballyouteragh*, which is a village said to have been remarkable for a copper manufactory; *Ballyouteragh* literally signifying a town of braziers; yet there is no *copper ore* near this place, but *iron mine* almost every where round it. At Castlemartyr is a seat of the earl of Shannon; and a mile S. E. a river called the *Dowr* breaks out of a lime-stone rock, after taking a subterraneous course of
about

about a mile, having its rise near *Magerly*; not far off is the ruined castle of *Ballyrenone*, sit. near the E. end of the strand of *Ballyeetton*.

CASTLE-MARY, a handsome seat in co. Cork, prov. Munster; a small mile W. of Cloyne, and no great distance from the E. side of *Cork harbour*; having an agreeable prospect of it. It was formerly called *Cot's-rock*, from the remains of a Druid's altar still to be seen in an orchard on the demesne of this estate. This altar consists of a large stone 15 feet long and 8 broad, of a rough irregular figure, approaching to an oval form. The highest part of it is 9 feet from the ground: it is supported by three other great stones; adjoining to it is a large round flag or table which was probably used for cutting up the victims for the sacrifice. On these lands there is a white chalkey substance, which does not ferment with acids; it is tinged with a yellow ochre, and lies 7 or 8 feet from the surface; it is said to plaister well; and if tempered with proper liquids might make a good material for stucco; it burns red and will not make pipes; being laid on land, no corn came up where it was used.

CASTLE-MATRASS, sit. near Rathkeale, in bar. Connillo, co. Limerick, prov. Munster.

CASTLE-MITCHEL, sit. near Mullingar, prov. Leinster.

CASTLE-MOGHAN, the ruins of a castle so called; sit. near *Crook-haven*, co. Cork, prov. Munster.

CASTLE-MOORISK, sit. in bar. Moorisk, co. Mayo, prov. Connaught.

CASTLEMORE, sit. in the parish of Movily, co. Cork, prov. Munster; it was formerly built by the *Mac Swineys*, but afterwards belonged to the *Macartys*; being fortified by *Phelim Mc. Owen Carty*, in the rebellion of 1641. —Also a place in bar. Ballybritt, King's co. — and another in bar. Ravilly, co. Carlow, both in prov. Leinster; the latter is a chapelry in dioc. of Leighlin.—There is also a vicarage of same name in dioc. of Killala, sit. in bar. Costello, co. Mayo, prov. Connaught.

CASTLEMORRES, a fair town in co. Kilkenny, prov. Leinster; having fairs on 12 May, Aug. and Nov. The family of Morres was created visc. Mountmorres of *Castlemorres*, in 1763.

CASTLE-MOUNTJOY, sit. near Dungannon, prov. Ulster.

CASTLE-NOCK, see *Castleknock*.

CASTLE-OLIVER, sit. near *Mitchel's-town*, prov. Munster.

CASTLEOTWAY, a fair town in co. Tipperary, prov. Munster; having fairs 5 and 6 Apr. 18 and 19 Sept.—Also a fair town in co. Limerick, prov. Munster: having fairs on 5 Apr.

CASTLEOYNE, a seat of lord Shelburne, near Templemore, co. Tipperary, prov. Munster.

CASTLE-PALACE, a fine and large edifice, sit. near Dunloe castle, in co. Kerry, prov. Munster. Near it is *Beaufort*, a handsome seat.

CASTLEPLUNKET, a fair town in bar. Ballintobber, co. Roscommon, prov. Connaught; near 79 miles from Dublin. Having fairs on 1 Thursday O. S. May, 13 Aug. and 11 Oct. Within a few miles of which are the ruins of a church and an abbey.

CASTLEPOLLARD, a fair and post town, in bar. Half-fore, co. Westmeath, prov. Leinster; having fairs on 21 May, 1 and 2 Aug. 10 Oct. and Dec. distant about 49 miles from Dublin.

CASTLEPOOKY, sit. near Doneraile, in co. Cork, prov. Munster; at this place lived one Mr. *Richard Morgan*, who died 15 Oct. 1748, in the 107th year of his age; he had been clerk of the Crown and Peace for this co. in king James IId's time; he never eat salt with his meat, and died with no other complaint, than the mere effect of old age.

CASTLERAGHAN, or *Castleraghen*, a bar. with a village in it of same name, sit. in co. Cavan, prov. Ulster; the latter is a rectory in dioc. of Kilmore: lat. 53:48, lon. 7:42.

CASTLERATH, this is a very old castle, sit. a small distance from Ballymascanlan, in co. Louth, prov. Leinster; it appears to have been an antient dwelling of some person of distinction; and probably that of a bishop or abbot; if we may judge of the chapel adjoining it. It stands on the plain between the sea and the mountains of Carlingford; and near it are several old forts or raths, such as the first invaders, or prime planters of this island are supposed to have inhabited. A few roods from it are the remains of a tumulus or sepulchral mount: and about a mile farther, towards the sea, stands the tower or castle of *Ballug*.

CASTLEREA, a fair and post town in bar. Ballintobber, co. Roscommon, prov. Connaught; 84 miles from Dublin, and about 12 miles N. W. of Roscommon; it has fairs 23 May, 21 June, 23 Aug. and 7 Nov. Here is an elegant seat, built on the scite of the old castle, with beautiful improvements all round it. A mile from hence are the ruins of a church.

CASTLEREAGH, a bar. having a village or post town in it of same name, sit. in co. Down, prov. Ulster; 'tis so called from an antient castle, the ruins of which lie about 2 miles S. E. of Belfast bridge; it is seated on the top of a hill, and is one of those forts, the erection of which is usually ascribed to the Danes. This fort has a fosse which encompasses three-fourths of it, and once probably surrounded the whole: in the midst of the fort stood the castle, formerly the seat of *Con O'Neille*, proprietor of that large tract of country which was afterwards divided among the lords Claneboys, Ardes, and the ancestors of the present lord Hillsboro'. It was otherwise called *Castleclaneboy*, and also said to have been inhabited sometime by one of the *O'Neils* family called *Hugh Flain*, whose posterity enjoyed this barony, with other baronies in the co. Down and Antrim, 'till the beginning of the reign of king James Ist. Castlereagh is now the estate of lord Hillsborough, and tho' made up of a few scattered houses, yet it is the head of a manor, where his seneschal holds his courts. Fairs are held here 5 July, 27 Oct.—This is likewise the name of a place in bar. Castleraghan, co. Cavan, prov. Ulster.—And another in bar. Decies without Drum, co. Waterford, prov. Munster.

CASTLEREYNELL, sit. near *Mullingar*, prov. Leinster.

CASTLERICARD, a rectory in dioc. of Meath, sit. in bar. Moyfenrath, co. Meath, prov. Leinster.

CASTLERICHARD, sit. in bar. Coshmore, co. Waterford, prov. Munster.

CASTLEROACH, or *Castleroche*, (now in ruins) sit. about 4 miles from Dundalk, in bar. Dundalk, co. Louth, prov. Leinster.

CASTLEROCK, a place so called in bay of Carrickfergus, co. Antrim, prov. Ulster; it stands on a hill to the E. a little above *Carmoyle*.

CASTLEROE, sit. in bar. Colerain, co. Londonderry, prov. Ulster.

CASTLEROY, sit. in bar. Pobleobryan, co. Limerick, prov. Munster.

CASTLERUDDERY, sit. in bar. Talbots-town, co. Wicklow, prov. Leinster.

CASTLESAFFRON, sit. 1 mile E. of Doneraile, co. Cork, prov. Munster; so called from the large quantities of that plant formerly growing there; adjoining is a well built house, agreeably seated on the banks of the river, which forms several pleasant cascades in view of the house, which has a regular front of grey marble. The castle was boldly erected on the banks of the river Awbeg.

CASTLESALEM, now called *Banduff*; sit. 1 mile N. W. of *Rofs*, in co. Cork, prov. Munster; 'tis a strong romantic building.

CASTLESAMPSON, sit. in co. Roscommon, prov. Connaught; having fairs on 7 May, 6 Aug 19 Sept. and 6 Dec.

CASTLESCREEN, sit. on the W. side of the road leading from *Killough* to *Downpatrick*, in co. Down, prov. Ulster; it is now in ruins, and was built within a Danish rath, near which are many remains of heathen monuments.

CASTLESHANE, sit. in bar. Monaghan, co. Monaghan, prov. Ulster; 59 miles from Dublin, where fairs are held on 21 June and July, 12 Aug. and 15 Dec.

CASTLESHANNON, a handsome seat near the village of Ballyheigh, in co. Kerry, prov. Munster.

CASTLESTRANGFORD, see *Strangford*.

CASTLESTEWART, sit. in co. Tyrone, prov. Ulster; it gives title of visc. and baron to the family of *Stewart*.

CASTLESYBIL, a ruined castle so called by the Irish; which signifies *Elizabeth Castle*, it is sit. on the isthmus between the harbour of Smerewick and Ferriter's creek, in co. Kerry, prov. Munster.

CASTLETALBOT, sit. near Ennifcorthy, prov. Leinster.

CASTLETARMON, sit. in co. Donegal, prov. Ulster, 1 mile beyond *Pettigoe*. Here are the ruins of a castle; also the seat of the Rev. Mr. Tifdal.

CASTLETERRA, sit. in bar. Loughtee, co. Cavan, prov. Ulster.

CASTLETOWN, a fair town in bar. Bear and Bantry, co. Cork, prov. Munster, sit. 110 miles from Dublin; it has fairs on 1 Jan. Easter-tuesday, 12 May and 4 Sept. and lies opposite to the *Island of Beerhaven*, which is about 6 miles long, very coarse, mountainous and rugged. This place is also called *Castledermot*; S. E from which, stood the celebrated castle of *Dunboy*.—*Castletown* is also the name of a fair town in bar. Upper Ossory, Queen's co. prov. Leinster, 48 miles from Dublin, having fairs on 29 June and 18 Oct. 2 miles from which, are the ruins of the castle of *Rush-hall*. Here is a handsome moat, on which a stone building was formerly erected, but 'tis now destroyed.—Also a village of same name in bar. Slewmargy, Queen's co. prov. Leinster.—Another in bar. Moycashel, co. Westmeath, prov. Leinster.—Also a rectory in dioc. Killaloe, sit. in bar. Aria, co. Tipperary,—and a village in bar. Coonagh, co. Limerick; both in prov. Munster.—There is also a fair town of same name in co. *Louth*, prov. Leinster, where fairs are held on 5 July. *Castletown* is likewise the name of Mr. *Conolly's* superb house and demesne, 2 miles beyond *Leixlip*, co. Kildare, prov. Leinster, about 10 miles from Dublin. This house is generally considered as one of the finest in the kingdom, it is built entirely of hewn stone, and contains a range of 13 windows in each of the three stories. A colonade supported by 9 columns on each side, joins the house to the 2 wings, which are each 2 stories high, and 7 windows in breadth. The apartments are elegantly finished; the grand stair-case is very magnificent, and ornamented with brass ballustrades.

The

The demefnes and plantations about the houfe are extenfive and beautiful.

CASTLETOWNCASTLE, fit. about a mile W. of *Dundalk*, in co. Louth, prov. Leinfter. This caftle has feveral rooms in it very habitable, and lies on the N. fide of a hill, being obfervable for feveral miles along the great N. road; it commands a full view of the harbour and bay of Dundalk, *Sleive-gullion*, and the mountains of Carlingford. The fine old Danifh ftation and mountain, which borrows its name from the neighbourhood of this caftle, crowns the fame hill, and a little below, ftand the ruins of an an old church or chapel, now covered with ivy, and made ufe of by the country people as a burial place. The caftle was formerly defended by a ftrong wall, and other works of circumvallation, and not far from it, on the plain below, there has been formerly a very confiderable fort or camp, little inferior to that above it; being more advantageofly fit. near the river, which runs clofe by one fide of it. Caftletown was facked and deftroyed by *Edw. le Bruce*, brother to the king of *Scotland*, about the year 1318.

CASTLETOWN-DELVIN, fit. in bar. Delvin, co. Weftmeath, prov. Leinfter; above 35 miles from Dublin. Here is the fine feat of the earl of *Weftmeath*; this is a poft and fair town. Fairs held 1 Aug. and Dec. it is alfo a vicarage in dioc. of Meath.

CASTLETOWN-ELY, a rectory in dioc. of Kilaloe, fit. in bar. Clonlifk, King's co. prov. Leinfter.

CASTLETOWN-GEOGHAN, a fair town in co. Weftmeath, prov. Leinfter. Fairs held 29 Sept. and 10 Oct.

CASTLETOWNLANDS, a fair town in co. Mayo, prov. Connaught. Fair days 15 June, and 29 Sept.

CASTLETOWN-MACENERY, a fair town in co. Limerick, prov. Munfter. Fair days 11 Feb. 17 Apr. 3 Nov. 1 Dec. It was formerly the feat of *Mac Enery*. Here we find the ruins of a very large monaftery, and fome other fuch buildings, which evince the dignity and fplendor of that antient family.

CASTLETOWN-ROCHE, a fair and poft town, in bar. Fermoy, co. Cork, prov. Munfter; 115 miles from Dublin. Here are the ruins of a fine old caftle, feated on an eminence, once the feat of the *Reaches*, lords of *Fermoy*, which they forfeited. It lies over the river Awbeg, and is built on a rock, from whence there is a paffage cut down to the river. Oppofite to it is a field which they call the *camp-field*; from whence a battery was erected, by a party of the parliament's forces, anno 1649, againft the caftle; which was then defended by the lady of lord Roche for feveral days, in a very gallant manner: this lord refufed a compofition for his

eftate from Oliv. Cromwell. Here is a parifh church, which is a vicarage in dioc. of Cloyne. Fairs are held 25 May, 28 July, 29 Sept. 12 Dec. A mile from Caftletown-roche on the oppofite fide of the *Awbeg*, is the caftle of *Carrignaconny*: and at *Bridgetown*, which is alfo about a mile from Caftletown, where the *Awbeg* empties itfelf into the *Blackwater*, are the ruins of an abbey, built in 1314, oppofite the great altar of which are the remains of the tomb of the founder, *Alex. Fitz-hugh Roche*. It was moft pleafantly fit. at the very confluence of the two rivers, which glide thro' a deep rocky glen, oppofite to the building. Here was a bridge formerly over both the rivers.

CASTLE-TOWNSHEND, a village in bar. Carberry, co. Cork, prov. Munfter.

CASTLE-UPTON, the feat of lord Templetown, fit. in co. Antrim, prov. Ulfter.

CASTLE-WARD, fit. a mile W. of Strangford, co. Down, prov. Ulfter: and feated on a bay of the fame name; it is fo called from a caftle erected there when the family of the *Wards* firft fettled in Ireland, but the antient name of the place was *Carrick-ne-Sheannagh*, i. e. the Fox's rock. On the bay that opens to the gardens of this demefne, (which formerly was occupied by the late Mr. Juftice Ward) is a fingular contrivance for fupplying a mill with water. A dead wall is carried acrofs the gut, in which are the two arches, and in them two flood-gates fixed, the one to admit the tide, and the other to keep it in, or let it out as occafion ferves: by this means a corn-mill is perpetually fupplied with water, which can never fail as long as the tide flows here. Here is the feat of lord Bangor: *Robt. Ward* being created vifc. Bangor of Caftleward in 1781.

CASTLEWARDEN, fit. in bar. *Salt*, co. Kildare, prov. Leinfter.

CASTLEWELLAN, otherwife written *Caftlewellin* or *Caftlevellin*; a fair and poft town fit. in bar. upper Iveagh, co. Down, prov. Ulfter; 63 miles from Dublin. Fair days 1 Feb. May, June, Sept. and 13 Nov. and Tuefday before Chriftmas. It lies near 2 miles N. of *Briansford*; is the head of a manor, and formerly one of the feats of the family of *Magenis*. It is pleafantly fit. on the fide of a fmall lake, called after the name of the place. Here is a park and plantations of lord *Glerawly*. The family of Annefley (now *earl of Annefley*) was created baron Annefley of Caftlewellan 20 Sept. 1758.

CASTLEWRAY, fit. in bar. Kilmacrenan, co. Donegal, prov. Ulfter.

CASTRACORE, a rectory in dioc. of Cloyne, fit. in bar. Imokilly, co. Cork, prov. Munfter.

CASTROPETER, a rectory in dioc. of Kildare, fit. in bar. Coole'stown, King's co. prov. Leinfter.

CASTROVENTRY, a vicarage in dioc. of Rofs, fit. in bar. Carberry, co. Cork, prov. Munfter.

CAT, a rock on coaft of co. Cork, in bar. Bear and Bantry, prov. Munfter.

CATHAIGH-INNIS, or *Inis Cathay*, an Ifland fit. in the mouth of the river Shannon, between the co's Clare and Kerry, prov. Munfter. St. Patrick founded a monaftery here, and placed St. *Senan* over it; it became afterwards a bifhoprick, and was united to that of Limerick in 1188 or 1190. The monaftery was frequently plundered by the Danes. It is now called *Inis Scattery* or the Ifland of Scattery. Here is one the antient round towers.

CATHERINE's-GROVE, fit. in bar. Dundalk, co. Louth, prov. Leinfter.

CATHEMAINE, fit. in bar. Magunihy, co. Kerry, prov. Munfter.

CATHERLOGH, a bar. in co. Carlow, prov. Leinfter. It was alfo the antient name of that co.

CAT's-HOLE, a great cave under a hill in co. Weftmeath, prov. Leinfter; the firft paffage into it is very low, fo that you muft creep on all fours, if you would enter. When you have proceeded in this pofture, about 14 or 15 feet, you may rife and walk upright, for here the cave is 7 or 8 feet high; and if you bring light with you, you may behold a piece of nature's architecture, the vault being handfomely arched; the firft room that entertains you is pretty large, about 10 or 12 feet fquare; hence are divers narrow apartments, verging E. S. and W. two of thefe of the length of one perch or two, grow fo narrow and incommodious, that they give but little encouragement to a further fearch; the third towards the W. is larger, but grows at laft both uneven and narrow; the natives hereabout pretend that it ends at *Croach Patrick*, in Connaught. Towards the latter end of the wars of 1641, this cave was for fome time the lurking place of the chief of the *Weftmeath* rebels.

CAUM-CARIG, a hill fo called, fit. about 6 miles from *Macroomp*, in co. Cork, prov. Munfter; the name fignifies, the *crooked rocks*, it is a rugged hill, which you muft pafs over, before you come to the village of *Millftreet* in that co.

CAVAN, a co. in the prov. Ulfter, bounded by the co.'s Fermanagh, Monaghan, Meath, Longford and Leitrim; its length from E. to W. is 40 miles, and the breadth from N. to S. 22 miles; it contains 301,000 acres, 30 parifhes, 7 baronies, and fends 6 members to parliament: its baronies are Tullalagh, Loughtee, Tullagharvey, Clonehee, Caftleraghan, Clonmoghan, and Tullaghonoho; the number of houfes 16,314, and inhabitants 81,570. The principal antient families of this diftrict are the O'Reilys,

O'Sheridans, O'Currys, O'Bradys, M'Kiernans, Plunkets, and M'Tiernans. This co. is well inhabited, tho' rough, and is fprinkled with many pleafant lakes; it has much fenny pafture ground, and coarfe land in many places, yet in others is not void of a rich and fertile foil. The family of *Lambert* take title of earl from this co. The linen manufacture is carried on in it, tho' it does feem to improve here as much as in other of the Northern co.'s Its yearly trade in it has been averaged at £68,200. The bleach greens here are few and much fcattered. *Cavan* is alfo the name of the principal town in this co. which is fit. in bar. Loughtee, 54 miles N. W. of Dublin; it is a borough, poft and fair town, and returns 2 members to parliament, patronage in the families of *Nifbit* and *Clements*. It has a weekly market on Tuefdays; a barrack for a troop of horfe; and holds fairs on 1 Feb. 14 May, 14 Aug. 25 Sept. and 12 Nov. Lat. 54 : 2, lon. 7 : 23. Here was antiently a monaftery founded in the year 1300 by *O'Reilly*, dynaft of Breffany; *Owen O'Neil* the famous general of the Irifh army, dying by poifon (as fome fuppofe) on 16 Nov. 1649, was buried in this abbey, of which there are not now the leaft remains. 1¼ mile from Cavan is *Farnham-houfe*, the feat of lord Farnham.—There is alfo a place of this name fit. in bar. Boyle, co. Donegal, prov. Ulfter; the lat. of which is found to be 54 : 51' : 41" lon. 7 : 23. Mr. Mafon erected a temporary obfervatory here, by appointment of the royal fociety, in the year 1769, to obferve the tranfit of Venus.

CAVE-HILL, a mountain in bar. Belfaft, co. Antrim, prov. Ulfter.

CAVETOWN, fit. near Elphin, prov. Connaught.

CAUNGLASS-POINT, a *cape* in bar. Iveragh, co. Kerry, prov. Munfter.

CAUNERA-HEAD, a *cape* in bar. Corkaguinny, co. Kerry, prov. Munfter.

CECIL's-TOWN, a fair town in co. Cork, prov. Munfter; fair days 25 Apr. 14 May, 18 Oct. and 24 Nov.

CELBRIDGE, a very handfome village in bar. Salt, co. Kildare, prov. Leinfter, about 10 miles from Dublin. 'Tis fit. on the banks of the river *Liffey*, over which it has a fine ftone bridge. The church is a very neat ftructure, adorned with a very noble monument belonging to the *Conolly* family. In the nighbourhood are feveral handfome feats and fine improvements, among which the *Liffey* meanders in a beautiful manner. Here is a curious manufacture of *chip* hats; alfo an extenfive cotton manufacture. This place is a vicarage in dioc. of Dublin.

CHANTINEE or *Shentinagh*, a feat with neat improvements, belonging to *James Corry*, efq;

fit. near Carrickmacrofs, in co. Monaghan, prov. Ulfter.

CHAPEL, fit. in bar. Bantry, co. Wexford, prov. Leinfter.

CHAPEL-BAY, fit. in *Big-ifland* one of the *Copland iflands* off the N. E. coaft of the co. Down, prov. Ulfter; it is fo called from a church clofe to it, the ruins of which remain, and in the cemetry whereof the inhabitants of that ifland bury their dead.

CHAPELCARRON, a vicarage in dioc. of Ferns, fit. in bar. Shelmaliere, co. Wexford, prov. Leinfter.

CHAPEL-EYEN, (or chapel of *St. Eyen* or *Keyon*) fit. in co. Weftmeath, prov. Leinfter. This chapel is on a hill, and cut out of the natural rock, for all one fide of it appears to be the natural ftone inftead of a wall. It is much decayed, and has in it a curious purling brook of chryftal water, which iffuing out of the rock fide of the chapel, traverfes it and falls thro' the oppofite fide of the wall, into the waters below.

CHAPEL-IZOD, a village in bar. Newcaftle, co. Dublin, prov. Leinfter, fit. near 3 miles from Dublin, pleafantly feated on the banks of the Liffey, adjoining the Phœnix park; here is a church, and a barrack for the *Royal Irifh Artillery*. This place is remarkable for fupplying the capital with the fineft *Strawberries*; the beds of which extend for fome miles towards *Lucan*, in a fine fouthern afpect. It is a vicarage in dioc. of Dublin; and takes its name after *la Beale Ifoud*, the daughter of Anguifh or Aengus king of Ireland.—Alfo a feat a few miles from *Bennet's-bridge*, co. Kilkenny, prov. Leinfter.

CHAPEL-IN-THE-WOODS, a chapelry in dioc. of Armagh, fit. in bar. Loughlinfholen, co. Londonderry, prov. Ulfter.

CHAPELMIDWAY, a village fit. in bar. Caftle-knock, co. Dublin, prov. Leinfter, within 7 miles of the metropolis. It is a curacy in dioc. of Dublin.

CHAPEL-WARD, a curacy in dioc. of Dublin, fit. in bar. Caftleknock, co. Dublin, prov. Leinfter.

CHARLEMONT, a borough and fair town in bar. Armagh, co. Armagh, prov. Ulfter, about 68 miles N. W. of Dublin; it is governed by a portrieve, and is reckoned a garrifon, and has a military governor on the eftablifhment, with a barrack for 3 companies of foot. It gives title of earl to the noble family of *Caulfield*. It ftands on the river *Blackwater*; fair days, 12 May, 16 Aug. 12 Nov. It fends 2 members to parliament; patron, the earl of *Charlemont*. Lat. 54 : 26, lon. 7 : 14.

CHARLESFORT, a royal fortification within ¼ mile E. of Kinfale, in bar. Kinfale, co. Cork, prov. Munfter. So called in honour of king Charles IId. by the duke of *Ormond* in 1681; it was begun in the year 1670, the firft ftone being laid by the earl of *Orrery*, and was finifhed at the expence of £73,000. This fort is fo fit. that all fhips coming into the harbour of *Kinfale*, muft pafs within piftol fhot of the battery. It is diftant 108 miles from Dublin.—Alfo the name of a village in bar. Kells, co. Meath, prov. Leinfter.

CHARLESTOWN, a fair town in the King's co. prov. Leinfter: fair days 20 Apr. and Oct.—Alfo a vicarage in dioc. of Armagh, fit. in bar. Ardee, co. Louth, prov. Leinfter.

CHARLEVILLE, a borough, poft and fair town in co. Cork, prov. Munfter, in the bar. of *Orrery*; about 108 miles from Dublin. Fair days 10 Oct. and 14 Nov. It fends 2 members to parliament; patron, the earl of Shannon.—It was formerly called *Rathcogan*, and was erected into a corporation at the expence of the firft earl of Orrery, lord prefident of Munfter, where he kept his prefidential court, and adorned this town with a magnificent houfe built in 1661, which was burned down in 1690, by a party of king James's foldiers, under command of the duke of *Berwick*. Here is a charter-fchool, which was endowed by the Rt. Hon. the earl of Cork and Orrery, with 15 acres of land and in which 23 children are ufually kept: a decent parifh church; and a good horfe barrack. No turf bogs being contiguous fo this place, fuel is dear; the lands round Charleville, are moftly under ftock for butter and beef, with very little corn: the foil is a light brown earth, lying deep on a limeftone bottom. This place gave title of earl to the family of Moore. Lat. 52 : 13, lon. 9 : 2.—Alfo a place near *Burros-in-Offory*, prov. Leinfter.

CHERRYMOUNT, fit. in bar. Arklow, co. Wicklow, prov. Leinfter.

CHILCOMB, fit. near *Rofs*, prov. Connaught.

CHORE-ABBEY, fit. in the village called *Middletown*, co. Cork, prov. Munfter; about 122 miles from Dublin; this abbey is now in ruins. It was founded in 1180 by the Fitzgeralds, or according to fome, by the family of Barry; and was fupplied with monks of the Ciftertian order from the abbey of *Neney* in co. Limerick, and was called the abbey of St. Mary of Chore, or of the Chore of St. Benedict.

CHURCH-BAY, fit. in Rathlin Ifland, in bar. Antrim, co. Antrim, prov. Ulfter.

CHURCH-HILL, a fair and poft town in bar. Magheraboy, co. Fermanagh, prov. Ulfter. Fair days 14 May, 30 Aug. and Nov. Here is a church belonging to the dioc. of Clogher.—Alfo a fair town in bar. Kilmacrenan, co. Donegal, prov. Ulfter; fairs held, 14 May, 15 Aug. and 7 Nov.

CHURCH-ISLAND, otherwife *Innismore*, fit. in Loughgilly, bar. Carbury, co. Sligo, prov. Connaught. Here St. Loman founded an abbey, which was deſtroyed by an accidental fire in 1416; in which the valuable manuſcripts of *O'Curnin*, together with the ſhort book of that family, and many other curioſities periſhed. The church lies at the eaſt end of the iſland, and was the burial place of the pariſh of Calry. In a rock near the door of the church, is a cavity called " *our lady's bed*," which is viſited by women in pregnancy, as favourable to them if they go into it, and turn thrice round, ſaying certain prayers, &c. The church and rock are entirely covered with ivy.

CHURCH-LAND, a fair town in co. Kilkenny, prov. Leinſter; fair day 14 Aug.

CHURCH-TOWN, a fair town in bar. Rathconrath, co. Weſtmeath, prov. Leinſter; it is a rectory in dioc. of Meath. Fair day 29 Aug. Alſo a place of ſame name fit. in bar. Orrery, co. Cork, prov. Munſter; in which are the ruins of the old church called *Bruheny*. In the 9th. queen Ann; an act paſſed for removing the ſcite of this church. The new church is a good building in form of a croſs, the chancel is paved with black and white marble, the produce of this country; in the chancel is a vault, wherein ſeveral of the earl of Egmont's family are interred. This is a rectory in dioc. of Cloyne.—*Church-town* is alſo the name of a ſmall village, fit. 1 mile beyond *Miltown*, in co. Dublin, prov. Leinſter; about 3½ miles from the metropolis; it has an antient burial place, formerly much made uſe of.—There is alſo a place of ſame name, in co. Waterford, prov. Munſter.—There is alſo a fair town of this name, co. Derry, prov. Ulſter; fairs held on 12 Feb. 15 May, 24 Aug. and 1 Nov.—Alſo, a curacy in dioc. of Meath, fit. in bar. Navan, co. Meath, prov. Leinſter.—Likewiſe a curacy in dioc. of Dublin, fit. in bar. Narragh, co. Kildare, prov. Leinſter.

CIARUIDHE, the preſent bar. of Iraght, in co. Kerry, prov. Munſter, on the ſouthern banks of the Shannon, and from which is derived *Cerrigia*, or Kerry. The chiefs of this country were called *Hy-Cain-air-Ciaruidhe*, by contraction *O'Conor Kerry*; whoſe deſcendants were in poſſeſſion of their antient patrimony, in the beginning of the laſt century.

CIERRIENAOITEAGHAN, now corruptly called *Carrickaſiicken*, that is the rock or hill of the aſſembly of the elders; the maiſtean of the antient inhabitants of the co. Louth, the *voluntii* of Ptolemy. It is fit. near Dundalk, in co. Louth, prov. Leinſter. In ſeveral hills or mounds compoſing the Leaberagh or Areopagus, urns, containing the aſhes of the old chiefs, have been found; but the principal rath has been in part deſtroyed.

CILLAICE, i. e. the full grown wood; or it may be interpreted the ſtrong church; it was a place fit. in co. Meath, prov. Leinſter, and deſtroyed by Callaghan, a king of S. Munſter, in 939.

CILLY, a lake in co. Sligo; prov. Connaught.

CINEAL-EOGHEAN, pronounced *Connal Owen*, or the principal diviſion of the northern co. of the Oll or Bolga; an antient diſtrict in the prov. of Ulſter, comprehending originally, the preſent co.'s of Tyrone, Armagh, Donegal and part of the co. of Derry, being the antient diviſions of *Eirgall* and *Orgall*. It was the firſt ſettlement of the Bolga in the N. about 300 years before Chriſt, the chiefs of which were denominated Connel or Connar, until the 4th century, when one of the ſons of O'Nial, the great principal king of Hy Faillia, took poſſeſſion of the eaſtern part, or *Orgall*; whilſt the weſtern, or *Eirgall*, remained under the dominion of its native princes, which from them, was called in the latter ages, *Tir Connal*, or the country of Connal, comprehending the preſent co. of Donegal. *Cinel Eoghean* being thus confined to the co's of Derry, Tyrone and Armagh, continued under the dominion of the O'Nials, ſometime after the arrival of the Engliſh, but at length was reduced to the preſent co. of Tyrone, being called *Tir Owen*, or the land of Owen, from whence Tyrone is derived.

CINEALFEARMAIC, a country in the antient Thomond and co. of Clare, prov. Munſter: the chiefs thereof were the *O'Dea:*.

CINNEICH, or the chief place, the reſidence of *Dermod M'Carthy*, near Bandon, in co. Cork, prov. Munſter; it was deſtroyed by Mortogh O'Brien in 1150.

CLABOY, or *Clabby*, a fair town in co. Fermanagh, prov. Ulſter; fair days 10 July and 15 Oct.

CLADY, (uſually called *Cumber Clady*) a fair town in bar. Tyrekerin, co. Londonderry, prov. Ulſter; near 108 miles from Dublin; fair days 17 May and Nov. 1½ mile beyond this are the ruins of *O'Cane's* caſtle.—Alſo a fair town in bar. Strabane, co. Tyrone, prov. Ulſter; fit. half-way between Strabane and Caſtlefin. Fair days 1 Feb. 16 May, 1 Aug. and 16 Nov.

CLAGBALLYMORE, fit. in bar. Kiltartan, co. Galway, prov. Connaught.

CLAGGON-BAY, fit. in bar. Ballinahinch, co. Galway, prov. Connaught.

CLAGGON-POINT, a *cape* in bar. Ballinahinch, co. Galway, prov. Connaught.

CLAGHANS, a ridge of rocks ſo called by the *Scotch*, but by the Iriſh *Briggs*; they lie in the bay of Carrickfergus, co. Antrim, prov. Ulſter; running from the N. fide of it, about 300 yards into the ſea.

CLAHAMAN, ſee *Cloghamon*.　　　CLAIN,

CLAIN, see *Clane*.

CLAMINE, sit. in bar. Shelburne, co. Wexford, prov. Leinster : lat. 52 : 13. lon. 7 : 5.

CLANBRESSAIL, or *Clanbrassil*, an antient district in co. Armagh, prov. Ulster, the chiefs whereof were the M'Canes; it now gives title of earl to the family of *Hamilton*.

CLANDERLAGH, or *Clanderlaw*, a bar. with a village in it of same name, sit. in co. Clare, prov. Munster.

CLANDEVA, sit. in bar. Kilmacrenan, co. Donegal, prov. Ulster.

CLANE or *Clain*, a bar. having a fair town in it of same name, sit. in co. Kildare, prov. Leinster. The latter is distant about 15 miles from Dublin. Fair days 28 Apr. 25 July, and 15 Oct. This is a vicarage in dioc. of Dublin, and a small village on the river Liffey, with a neat church and the ruins of an abbey: the abbey here was founded for regular canons, by St. *Aile*, who made St. *Senchell* the elder, abbot of it. Senchell, afterwards removed to *Killachad Dromfoda*, where he died on 26 Mar. 548. A synod consisting of 26 bishops, with a great number of abbots, &c. was convened here in the year 1162, under *Gelasius*, archbp. of Armagh, who passed a decree, that no person should be admitted professor of divinity in any church in Ireland, who had not studied at *Armagh*. A Franciscan friary was also erected here about the year 1266, supposed to have so been by *Gerald Fitzmaurice*, lord *Offaly*: the effigies of the founder remained, about the beginning of the last century, on a marble monument, which was placed in the middle of the choir. The family of *O'Hogain* came afterward into the possession and patronage of the priory and its estate; two miles beyond *Clane*, are the ruins of a castle: and near Clane, is an antient mote or rath. The grand canal, which from Dublin passes thro' the co. Kildare, crosses the Liffey on an aqueduct bridge; and soon after branches off near Clane in a collateral cut to the river Shannon.

CLANEBOYS, an antient name of part of the bar. of Ardes, in co. Down, prov. Ulster; and extending from the *Dufferin* to *Carrickfergus bay*; this tract was called *South Claneboy* to distinguish it from the *Rout* or *Glynnes* in the co. Antrim, which was called *North Claneboy*; it gives title of baron to the family of Hamilton, now *earl Clanbrassill*. Both were possessed in the reign of Edward III. by the sept of *Hugh-boy-O'Neil*; in 11 queen Eliz. an act passed for investing the queen with all the lands of *Claneboy* and the *great Ardes* that belonged to *Shane O'Neill*, many of the sept of the *O'Neills*, who were joined in rebellion with the said *Shane*; which territories were granted by patent the same year to sir Thomas Smyth, the father,

and Thomas Smyth the son, on condition that they should expel all the rebels out of the said lands, and plant the same with faithful subjects, that they should maintain for every plough land of 120 acres one English foot soldier, armed after the English manner, and for every two plough lands one light horseman armed the same way; that they should attend for 40 days the lord deputy at all hostings in the earldom of Ulster, and at 15 days warning with the third part of all such horse and foot as they covenanted to maintain by the said tenures; that they should pay to the crown 20s. per ann. rent for every plough land. These covenants however being broke through, king James I. became seized in *Jure Coronæ*, of all the said manors and lands; and divided them between *Con O'Neil*, who then obtained his pardon, sir *Hugh Montgomery* and sir *James Hamilton*.

CLANECOLMAN, a district sit. near the river Inny, in co. Westmeath, prov. Leinster; the antient proprietors of which were the O'Melaghlins, by corruption M'Laughlins.

CLANECONNEL, otherwise called *Waringstown*, a neat village in co. Down, prov. Ulster; about 2 miles S. W. of *Magherelin*, and near 14 N. of *Newry*. In this place and neighbourhood, the linen manufacture has been carried on to great advantage. Here is a well finished church, roofed with Irish oak, and remarkable for the workmanship of it. *William Waring*, esq; who first settled here, gave the ground for this use, and obtained an act of parliament for changing the scite of the old parish church from *Donoghcloney* bridge; after which in the year 1681, he built this church at his own expence. This place was then thin of inhabitants, and much overgrown with woods: near it is a *Danish rath*, which was opened about the year 1684, and in it was found a large flat quarry-stone, placed upright like a door, which being removed, laid open an entrance into a narrow low passage about 10 feet long, and only wide enough to admit a man to creep in upon his hands and knees. This passage led into a small round vault, about 6 feet high and 8 feet wide, placed in the centre of the mount. In the middle of the vault, four long small stones were fixed in the ground, each about $2\frac{1}{2}$ feet high, standing upright as supporters to a flat quarry-stone $2\frac{1}{2}$ feet long, and 20 inches broad, placed on them in manner of a table; under which on the ground stood an handsome earthen urn, of a dark brownish colour, as if not thoroughly baked, about $\frac{1}{4}$ inch thick in its sides, containing broken pieces of burnt bones, mixed with ashes and fragments of burned wood.

CLANEHUGH, sit. in co. Longford, prov. Leinster; it gives title of baron to the family of *Forbes*, (now earl *Granard*.)

CLANFERGAIL, an antient diſtrict in co. Galway, prov. Connaught; the proprietors of which were the O'Hallorans.

CLANFROUGHT, a bar. in co. Kerry, prov. Munſter: otherwiſe written *Glanerought*.

CLANGIBBON, ſee *Clongibbon*.

CLANKONOW, an antient diſtrict in co. Galway, prov. Connaught; of which the *Bourkes* were the principal proprietors.

CLANMALIRE, ſee *Clanmalugra*.

CLANMALUGRA, or *Clanmaliere*, an antient diſtrict in the King's and Queen's co.'s, prov. Leinſter; the chiefs of which were the *O'Demp-ſeys*, formerly lords of Clanmaliere.

CLANMAURICE, an antient bar. in co. Kerry, prov. Munſter; it takes its name from *Maurice* the ſon of *Raymond le Groſs*, ſo named from the corpulency of his body. Raymond received a grant of this place from *Dermot M'Carty*, as a recompence for the aſſiſtance he had given him in recovering his poſſeſſions, of which he had been deprived by the cruelty of his own ſon *Cormac O'Lehanagh*. Raymond ſettled his ſon *Maurice* here, and hence the country was called *Clanmaurice*: its former name being *Lixnaw* from the antient *Lucenſii of Spain* who ſettled in it. *Thomas Fitzmaurice*, the lineal deſcendant of ſaid *Maurices*, was created viſc. Clanmaurice and earl of Kerry, 17 Jan. 1722.

CLANMORE, a village in bar. Ida, co. Kilkenny, prov. Leinſter.

CLANMORRIS, an antient diſtrict in co. Mayo, prov. Connaught; the proprietors of which were the *M'Morris's*.

CLANRICARD, an antient diſtrict in co. Galway, prov. Connaught: it was formerly called *Hy Fiacria Aidne*; the Rt. Hon. Henry Smyth de Burgh was created *marquis* Clanricard by letters patent 1789.

CLANROAD, a fair town in co. Clare, prov. Munſter. Fairs held 8 May, 1 Aug. 13 and 14 Oct. and 2 Dec.

CLANWILLIAM, a bar. in co. Limerick, prov. Munſter.—Alſo a bar. in co. Tipperary in ſame prov. which gives title of earl and viſc. to the family of *Meade*.

CLARA, a fair and poſt town in bar. Kilcourſy, King's co. prov. Leinſter; near 49 miles from Dublin. Fair days 1 Feb. 12 May, 25 July, 1 Nov. Within 1½ mile of *Clara* are the ruins of a caſtle.

CLARAGHMORE, ſit. in bar. Omagh, co. Tyrone, prov. Ulſter.

CLARAH, a vicarage in dioc. of Oſſory, ſit. in bar. Gowran, co. Kilkenny, prov. Leinſter.

CLARA-ISLAND, ſit. off Clew bay, in bar. Moriſk, co. Mayo, prov. Connaught; it belongs to the antient family of *Mallie* or *O'Mea-ly*; and contains about 2400 acres, worth on an average 200*l*. per ann. In 1224 a cell for

Carmelites was founded here, and afterwards annexed to the abbey of Knockmoy, in co. Galway, prov. Connaught. This is otherwiſe called *Clare-Iſland*.

CLARANBRIDGE, a fair town in bar. Dunkellin, co. Galway, prov. Connaught. Fairs on 1 Thurſday O. S. Feb. 1 Thurſday after 12 May, 1 Thurſday O. S. in Aug. and Nov.

CLARE, otherwiſe called *Thomond*, a co. in the prov. of Munſter. In the reign of queen Eliz. it was added to Connaught; but tho' it ſtill continues in the Connaught circuit, it has long been reſtored to the ſouthern province: it lies on the W. ſide of the river Shannon, by which it is bounded on the E. and S. as it is by Galway on the N. and the ocean on the W. It hath its preſent name from *Richard* and *Thomas de Clare*, ſons of the earl of Glouceſter, to whom king Edw. Iſt. granted this co. It is remarkable for breeding more horſes than any other co. in Ireland. Towards the N. part it is rocky coarſe, particulary in the bar. of *Burren*, where Oliver Cromwell's ſoldiers ſaid, there was neither water to drown a man, wood to hang him, or earth to bury him. *Thomond* gave title of earl to a branch of the noble family of *O'Brien*, deſcended from *Brien Boru*, the celebrated monarch of Ireland; and by a new creation in 1766, it gave the ſame title to *Percy Windham O'Brien*, eſq; heir to *Henry O'Brien*, the laſt earl of Thomond. It contains 476,200 plantation acres, 79 pariſhes, 9 bar.'s, and ſends 4 members to parliament; it extends from N. to S. 33 miles, and from E. to W. 52 miles. The bar.'s are, Corcomroe, Inchiquin, Ibrickan, Moyferta, Clanderlagh, Iſlands, Bunratty and Tullagh; theſe contain about 17,396 houſes and 96,000 inhabitants. Ennis is the co. and aſſizes town, which is large and populous, and has the advantage of a ſmall port at the *town* of Clare, which is a poſt town and is ſit. a few miles lower, on the river *Fergus*; the tide bringing up large boats from thence to *Ennis*. An abbey was founded here about 1195, for canons regular, following the ord r of St. Auguſtin; by *Donald O'Brien* the great, king of Limerick, who appointed Donatus abbot, and richly endowed the abbey. A great battle was fought here in 1278, by. *Donell*, ſon of *Tiegue Cauluiſhe O'Brien*, againſt Mahon O'Brien, who was defeated with a great ſlaughter. Lat. 52:42, lon. 9:22.—*Clare* is alſo the name of a bar. in co. Galway, prov. Connaught; in which is a village of ſame name, which is a vicarage in dioc. of Tuam.—There is alſo a river of that name in this bar. which unites with the Moyne, under ground, their waters alternately appearing and retiring from view in the *Turlachmore*; which in winter, forms a lake, and in ſummer, a beautiful and

X

found

found sheep walk, upwards of 6 miles in length and 2 in breadth.—Likewise the name of a fair town in bar. Orior, co. Armagh, prov. Ulster, near 65 miles from Dublin; fair day, 12 May: at which place is *Clare-castle.*—Also the name of a fair town in bar. Clanmorris, co. Mayo, prov. Connaught; 103 miles from Dublin, at which are fairs on 24 May, 22 June, 17 Aug. 27 Sept. and 23 Nov.—Likewise a fair town in King's co. prov. Leinster; fair day, 12 Nov.

CLARE-ABBEY, sit. in bar. Islands, co. Clare, prov. Munster; it was founded about 1195 for canons regular following the order of St. Augustin, by Donald O'Brien the great, king of Limerick, who appointed Donatus abbot, and richly endowed the abbey.

CLARE-CASTLE, sit. near *Ennis*, co. Clare, prov. Munster.

CLARE-GALWAY, sit. about 5 miles from the town of Galway, in co. Galway, prov. Connaught. Here are the ruins of an abbey, and opposite to it stands the antient castle of Clare-Galway. There is a weekly market for cattle here, on the 4 Thursdays next preceding Christmas. The abbey was built by *John de Cogan*, about 1290; the high tower in the middle of the church erected on arches is a curious work: and the chapel is now the Romish mass-house.

CLARE-HILL, a mountain in bar. Duhallow, co. Cork, prov. Munster.

CLARE-ISLAND, sit. in the bay of Baltimore, bar. Carbery, co. Cork, prov. Munster; it is a vicarage in dioc. of Ross.—Also an island sit. in bar. Morisk, on coast of co. Mayo, prov. Connaught, otherwise called *Clara-Island*; (*which see.*)

CLAREMORE, or *Clarmore*, a fair town in co. *Galway*, prov. Connaught; fair days 26 May, 9 Aug. 26 Sept. and 20 Dec.

CLARETOWN, a fair town in co. Clare, prov. Munster; fairs held Saturday before Whitsun Tuesday, and 11 Nov.

CLARE-TUAM, sit. in bar. Clare, co. Galway, prov. Connaught.

CLARISFORD, sit. in co. Clare, prov. Munster; near a mile beyond *Killaloe*. This was the old English name of this place, given it by the first settlers, in or about the time of *Thomas de Clare*, earl of Gloucester; and was so called from being the only ford over the *Shannon* into the co. Clare.

CLAREVILLE, sit. near Tullamore, King's co. prov. Leinster.

CLASHACROW, a rectory in dioc. of Ossory, sit. in bar. Crannagh, co. Kilkenny, prov. Leinster.

CLASHBAWN-BOG, a large tract of boggy ground, sit. near *Prosperus*, in co. Kildare, prov. Leinster.

CLASHMORE, a parish and village in bar. Decies within Drum, co. Waterford, prov. Munster; here was antiently an abbey of canons regular, founded in the 7th century, by St. *Cronan Mochua*, the lands whereof, on the dissolution, were granted to sir *Walter Raleigh*, in fee farm. Some say the abbey was founded by *Cuanchear*, at the command of *St. Mochua* or *Mochoemoc*, who had raised Cuanchear from the dead; that St. died 13 Mar. 655. This place is now a vicarage in dioc. of Lismore.

CLAY-CASTLE, sit. on *Youghal strand*, in co. Cork, prov. Munster. Here is a very bold sudden rising ground, or rather a small promontory of a loose sandy clay, which has been incroached on very considerably by the sea; this hill stands about a mile S. W. from the town of *Youghal*, and affords a very pleasing scene to the curious naturalist: for the pieces of the bank which break off and are washed down by the sea, are by degrees petrified into a very hard firm grit, as solid as any stone; the hill seems perfectly dry, nor is there any spring in which this petrifying quality can reside; but it seems to exist entirely in the clay.

CLAY-LOUGH, a lake in bar. Armagh, co. Armagh, prov. Ulster.

CLEAN-LOUGH, a lake in bar. Dromahaire, co. Leitrim, prov. Connaught.

CLEENISH, a rectory in dioc. of Clogher, sit. in bar. Clonawly, co. Fermanagh, prov. Ulster.

CLEER, sit. in bar. Omagh, co. Tyrone, prov. Ulster.

CLEGIN, sit. in bar. Erris, co. Mayo, prov. Connaught.

CLEGYROTTY, sit. in bar. Loughrea, co. Galway, prov. Connaught.

CLENCARRE, see *Glencarre*.

CLENDUFF, sit. in bar. Shroole, co. Longford, prov. Leinster.

CLENORE, a rectory in dioc. of Cloyne, sit. in bar. Fermoy, co. Cork, prov. Munster.

CLENTIBRET *church*, sit. in co. Monaghan, prov. Ulster, 57 miles from Dublin.

CLERMONT, sit. near Glasnevin, co. Dublin, prov. Leinster.—Also a place in co. Louth, prov. Leinster, which gives titles of earl, visc. and baron to the family of *Fortescue*. Here is the seat of lord Clermont.

CLEW-BAY, sit. in bar. Burrishoole, co. Mayo, prov. Connaught. This bay being sheltered on the N. and S. by the mountains of Burrishoole and Morisk, and defended from the Western storms by the high and rocky isle of Clare, affords a deep and safe anchorage among the innumerable islands which are scattered hereabouts.

CLEYDUFF, sit. in bar. Shroole, co. Longford, prov. Leinster.

CLIFDEN, fit. in co. Kilkenny, prov. Leinfter ; it gives title of vifc. and baron to the family of *Agar*. — Alfo a place fit. near Ennis,
prov. Munfter.

CLIFFONY, a fair town in co. Sligo, prov.
Connaught; fair days 18 May and June, 5 Oct.
6 Nov. and 15 Dec.

CLINISH-ISLAND, fit. in Lough Earn, co.
Fermanagh, prov. Ulfter. St. *Synell* prefided
over an abbey here, about the middle of the
6th. century.

CLINTON'STOWN, fit. in bar. Athardee, co.
Louth, prov. Leinfter.

CLOADY, a river in co. Wexford, prov.
Leinfter.

CLOAN-ROE, fit. in bar. Newcaftle, co. Wicklow, prov. Leinfter.

CLODAGH, a caftle now in ruins, fit. in the
parifh of Kilmurry, co. Cork, prov. Munfter ;
faid to have been built by the *Mac Swineys*, who
were antiently famous for Irifh hofpitality. On
the W. fide of the high road near *Dunufky*, there
was a ftone fet up, (which now lies in a ditch)
fignifying to all paffengers, to repair to the houfe
of Mr. *Edmond Mac Swiney* for entertainment.—
Clodagh is alfo the name of a river in bar. Balli-
cowen, King's co. prov. Leinfter.—And of another in bar. Clonawly, co. Fermanagh prov.
Ulfter.

CLODAN, fit. in bar. Tirawly, co. Mayo,
prov. Connaught.

CLODY, a village in bar. Loughlinfholen, co.
Londonderry, prov. Ulfter.—Alfo a *river* in
fame bar.

CLOGA, a fair town in co. Kilkenny, prov.
Leinfter ; fairs held Thurfday after Trin. Sund.

CLOGH, a fair town in bar. Kilconway, co.
Antrim, prov. Ulfter, 81 miles from Dublin ;
near which are the ruins of 2 caftles; fairs held
5 Aug. 8 Nov. and 9 Dec.—Alfo the name of
a fair town in co. Down, prov. Ulfter, 69 miles
from Dublin ; having fairs on 5 June, 5 July,
3 Friday in Oct. 22 Nov. and 24 Dec. Not far
from this place are the ruins of *Dundrum caftle* ;
and alfo a feat of lord Glerawly, called *Mount-
panther*. Near *Clogh* is a Danifh rath, furrounded by a broad deep foffe, and (which is fomething fingular) on the top of it, a plain ftrong
caftle of ftone.

CLOGH-A-MEATHER, fit. near *Johnfton's-fews*,
in co. Armagh, prov. Ulfter ; near which is to
be feen the trace of an encampment, upward of
a mile in circumference ; where it is faid, part
of the Englifh army under *Cromwell* were obliged to continue for a whole winter, having been
hemmed in by the Irifh on all fides.

CLOGHAMON, a fmall village fit. near the river *Cloady*, in co. Wexford, prov. Leinfter.—
Here is one of the caftles which formerly belong-

ed to the kings of Leinfter. Fairs held here on
11 June.

CLOGHAN, a fair town in bar. Garrycaftle,
King's co. prov. Leinfter, 62 miles from Dublin ; near which are the ruins of a church ; and
3 miles beyond Cloghan are thofe of a caftle,
on the fide of *Moyftown* road.—Alfo a place in
co. Donegal, prov. Ulfter, 118 miles from
Dublin.—Alfo a village in bar. Kilconway, co.
Antrim, prov. Ulfter.

CLOGHANBEG, a fair town in co. Donegal,
prov. Ulfter ; fair days 1 Feb. 19 May, 25 Aug.
and 19 Nov.

CLOGHAN-CASTLE, fit. near Kilglaffan, in
co. Galway, prov. Connaught.

CLOGHANE, a vicarage in dioc. of Ardfert,
fit. in bar. Corkaguinny, co. Kerry, prov.
Munfter.

CLOGHANES, fit. in bar. Athlone, co. Rofcommon, prov. Connaught.

CLOGHANLEA, fit. in bar. Boyle, co. Donegal, prov. Ulfter, 152 miles from Dublin. It is
now called *Dunglo*.

CLOGHANS, fit. in bar. Kilmane, co. Mayo,
prov. Connaught.

CLOGHARNEY *church*, fit. in co. Tyrone,
prov. Ulfter, near 92 miles from Dublin.

CLOGHBEMAN, fit. in bar. Scarawalfh, co.
Wexford, prov. Leinfter.

CLOGHCLAGH, fit. in bar. Idrone, co. Carlow,
prov. Leinfter.

CLOGHEA, fit. in bar. Condons, co. Cork,
prov. Munfter.

CLOGHEEN, a fmall poft town in bar. Iffa and
Offa, co. Tipperary, prov. Munfter, 91 miles
from Dublin, fit. on the great Munfter road ;
it has fairs on Whitfun Tuefday, 1 Aug. 28
Oct. and 12 Dec.

CLOGHE-MOUNTAINS, fit. in bar. Newcaftle,
co. Wicklow, prov. Leinfter.

CLOGHER, a bar. in which is a bifhoprick and
borough of fame name in co. Tyrone, prov.
Ulfter, fit. near 77 miles from Dublin ; the borough is a poft town, and has fairs on 6 May
and 26 July : lat 54 : 23, lon. 7 : 44. It fends
2 members to parliament ; patron, the bifhop of
Clogher. It is called *Regia* by Ptolemy, and in
a very early age an abbey of regular canons,
dedicated to the Virgin Mary, was founded here.
St. Patrick is faid to have prefided over the
church of Clogher ; and having appointed St.
Kertcen to be his fucceffor, he refigned this government and went to Armagh, where he founded his celebrated abbey. Tho' 'tis faid the monaftery and bifhoprick here was founded by St.
Macartin or *Kertcen*, by order of St. Patrick in
490. In 1041 the church of Clogher was rebuilt,
and dedicated to the memory of St. *Macartin*,
fince which time it received many alterations
and

and improvements, especially by *Mathew Mc. Catafaid*, who in 1295 rebuilt the cathedral, erected other buildings, and granted several valuable donations to it. On the 20 April 1396, a dreadful fire burnt to the ground the church, two chapels, the abbey, the court of the bishops, and 32 other buildings, with all the sacerdotal vestments, utensils, &c. belonging to the bishops, chapter and church. In the year 1610, on the 24 July, whilst George Montgomery was bishop of Clogher, king James annexed this abbey and its revenues to that see. Here was also sit. the royal seat of the antient kings of *Ergal*, which place comprehended the present co.'s of Fermanagh and Donegal. The see of *Louth* was united to this bishoprick about the middle of the 11th. century, together with the deanaries of Drogheda, Atherdee and Dundalk. *Clogher* signifies the place of the stone, and lies by the river *Launy*: during the times of paganism it was a Druidic sanctuary, in which was kept a stone of divination, called the golden stone, which some antiquaries have supposed to be the famous *Lee Fail*; but from its name it appears to have been a gem of a yellow colour, probably of that species which *Pliny* calls *Ananchites*; by which the Greeks, Romans, and all the aborigines of Europe divined, resembling the *Urim* and *Thummin* of the Hebrews. The see of Clogher comprises some portion of 5 co.'s viz. Donegal, Fermanagh, Tyrone, Monaghan and Louth. The cathedral, which is at the same time the parish church, is a plain handsome modern structure; the bishop's palace is large, with a fine park and demesne. — *Clogher* is also the name of a vicarage in dioc. of Cashel, sit. in bar. Killnemanagh, co. Tipperary, prov. Munster.—And a rectory in dioc. of Armagh, sit. in bar. Ferrard, co. Louth, prov. Leinster.

CLOGHERAN, see *Cloghran*.

CLOGHERBRIN, a rectory in dioc. of Ardfert, sit. in bar Truaghnaemy, co. Kerry. prov. Munster.

CLOGHER-HEAD, a promontory sit. in bar. Ferrard, co. Louth, prov. Leinster.

CLOGHRINTEMPLE, sit. in bar. Omagh, co. Tyrone, prov. Ulster.

CLOGHERNAGH, sit. in bar. Strabane, co. Tyrone, prov. Ulster.

CLOGHERNY, a rectory in dioc. of Armagh, sit. in bar. Omagh, co. Tyrone, prov. Ulster.

CLOGHGRENAN, a ruined seat of the *Butler's*, sit. near the river Barrow, in bar. Slewmargy, Queen's co. prov. Leinster; it is a very antient castle, almost covered with trees, and just hanging over the river, which makes the situation very elegant and picturesque; but it is now in so ruinous a state, that it must shortly be entirely lost.

CLOGHJORDAN, a fair town in co. Tipperary, prov. Munster; fairs held 12 May, Aug. and 1 Dec.

CLOGHLEAGH, a strong castle on the river Funcheon, co. Cork, prov. Munster; from whence there is a subterraneous passage to the river.

CLOGHLEMON, sit. in bar. Scarawalsh, co. Wexford, prov. Leinster.

CLOGHMANTAGH, a rectory in dioc. of Ossory, sit. in bar. Crannagh, co. Kilkenny, prov. Leinster.

CLOGHMESKEEN, sit. in bar. Gorey, co. Wexford, prov. Leinster.

CLOGHMILLS, a village in bar. Kilconway, co. Antrim, prov. Ulster.

CLOGHNAKELTY, see *Cloghnikelty*.

CLOGHNALLIS, a rectory in dioc. of Kildare, sit. in bar. Salt, co. Kildare, prov. Leinster.

CLOGHNIKELTY, or *Cloghnakilty*, and sometimes written *Cloghnakelty*, and *Clonakilty*, a borough, post and fair town, (antiently called *Clowncallow*) sit. in the bar. of Carberry, co. Cork, prov. Munster; 146 miles from Dublin: it is built in the form of a cross, and has a decent church on a rising ground. Here is a good market for linen yarn; also fairs held 6 Apr. 10 Oct. and 12 Nov. This place supplies Cork, Kinsale and the neighbouring parts with considerable quantities of turkeys, geese, &c. It was incorporated by the interest of the first earl of Cork, anno 2 Jac. Ist. a new charter was granted by king James IId. dated 12 July, 1688; but this charter has become void. This town flourished greatly before the wars of 1641, but being entirely burned down, it has since but slowly recovered. About a mile to the N. E. at *Temple Brien*, are the remains of an antient heathen temple. Here is a bay also called *Cloghnakilty bay*, but 'tis dangerous and sandy, and inconvenient for vessels. *Cloghnakilty* sends 2 members to parliament; patron, the earl of *Shannon*.

CLOGHOGALL, sit. in bar. Strabane, co. Tyrone, prov. Ulster.

CLOGHONAN, sit. in bar. upper Ormond, co. Tipperary, prov. Munster.

CLOGHPRIOR, a vicarage in dioc. of Killaloe, sit. in bar. lower Ormond, co. Tipperary, prov. Munster.

CLOGHRAN or *Clogheran*, sit. in bar. Coolock, co. Dublin, prov. Leinster; it is a rectory in dioc. of Dublin. The church of Cloghran stands by the direct road from Dublin to Swords, it is distant 1¼ mile from the latter, and 5¼ from the former: the ground about is high and rocky.

CLOGHROCA, sit. in bar. Doonkillen, co. Galway, prov. Connaught.

CLOGHROE, a village in co. Cork, prov. of Munster.

CLOGHY-

Cloghgrenan Castle.

CLOGHY-BAY, fit. in bar. Ardes, co. Down, prov. Ulfter.

CLOLUGH river, in bar. Upperthird, co. Waterford, prov. Munfter.

CLOMEDON, fit. in co. Dublin, prov. Leinfter.

CLOMINES, fee *Clonmines.*

CLOMOGH, fit. in bar. Leney, co. Sligo, prov. Connaught.

CLONABRENY, a rectory in dioc. of Meath, fit. in bar. Half-fowre, co. Meath, prov. Leinfter.

CLONAGAM, a fair town in co. Waterford, prov. Munfter. Fairs held 28 May and 26 Aug.

CLONAGH, a town-land, fit. in co. Kildare, prov. Leinfter: in which is a piece of ground containing 1 acre furrounded by a ditch. We are told that at the time of the general fuppreffion, there was a religious houfe or chapel here, dedicated to St. Finian; in the centre of the circle was a ftone crofs, and two yew trees, from one of which hung a bell. This was in being in 1396, but *John Lye* of Rathbride, being afterwards feized of this town-land, threw down and deftroyed the whole, and erected a tower or fmall caftle, with other buildings.

CLONGHEEN, fit. in bar. Maryborough, Queen's co. prov. Leinfter; it is a rectory in dioc. of Leighlin.

CLONABRENY, fit. near *Kells,* prov. Leinfter.

CLONAGANA, fit. near *Rofcrea,* prov. Munfter.

CLONAGOOSE, a vicarage in dioc. of Leighlin, fit. in bar. Idrone, co. Carlow, prov. Leinfter.

CLONAGOWN, a village in bar. Cooleftown, King's co. prov. Leinfter.

CLONAKENNY, fit. in co. Tipperary, prov. Munfter; 78 miles from Dublin, where are the ruins of a caftle.

CLONAKILTY, a village in bar. Carbery, co. Cork, prov. Munfter.

CLONALLEN, fit. near *Newry,* in bar. upper Iveagh, co. Down, prov. Ulfter; it is a rectory in dioc. of Dromore.

CLONALVY, a curacy in dioc. of Meath, fit. in bar. Duleek, co. Meath, prov. Leinfter.

CLONAMERY, a rectory in dioc. of Offory, fit. in bar. Ida, co. Kilkenny, prov. Leinfter.

CLONARD, a poft town, fit. near the river Boyne, in bar. Moyfenrath, co. Meath, prov. Leinfter, 25 miles from Dublin; it is a vicarage in dioc. of Meath. *Clonard* is the fame as *Cluainiraird,* i. e. the retirement on the weftern height, a religious houfe deftroyed by *Callaghan* in 939. Tho' now an inconfiderable place, it was formerly a bifhop's fee. In 506 or according to others 520, an abbey for regular canons was founded here by St. *Finian,* who was of noble extraction and an eminent philo-

fopher; he died of the plague, 12 Dec 548, before which he eftablifhed a fchool here, celebrated for producing feveral learned men. Some ruins of the abbey ftill remain; at a little diftance from the E. window in the burial ground, ftands a fmall chapel, in which there is a table monument, ornamented with the effigies of a man and woman in a praying pofture, and decorated with the ruff wore in Queen Eliz. days; the fides are adorned with many coats of arms, but that of the *Dillon* family is moft confpicuous. On the S. fide of the altar, fixed in the wall, is a fmall double arch, in the old Saxon manner, and divided by a pillar thro' which iron bars were fixed; this is fuppofed to have been the founder's tomb. There was alfo a nunnery for regular canoneffes founded here, and endowed before the arrival of the Englifh, by *O'Melaghlin,* king of Meath, it was dedicated to the Virgin Mary. The bifhoprick of Clonard, with thofe of Trim, Ardbraccan, Dunfhaghlin, Slane and Foure, were all confolidated before the year 1152; and united to that of Meath, about the beginning of the 13th century.

CLONARD-BRIDGE, fit. in bar. Moyfenrath, co. Meath, prov. Leinfter; 1½ mile beyond it, are the ruins of the caftle and abbey of *Tyrcroghan.*

CLONARNEY, a rectory in dioc. of Meath, fit. in bar. Delvin, co. Weftmeath, prov. Leinfter.

CLONASLEE, a fair town in the Queen's co. prov. Leinfter. Fair held 3 May.

CLONATTIN, fit. near *Gorey,* prov. Leinfter.

CLONAUL, fit. in co. Tipperary, prov. Munfter. Here was originally a foundation for the Knts. Templars, on whofe downfall it became a commandery, and was given to the Knts. Hofpitalers.

CLONAWLY, a bar. in co. Fermanagh, prov. Ulfter.

CLONBEG, a rectory in dioc. Emly, fit. in bar. Clanwilliam, co. Tipperary, prov. Munfter.

CLONBRAEN, a rectory in dioc. of Tuam, fit. in bar. Downamore, co. Galway, prov. Connaught.

CLONBROCK, fit. in co. Galway, prov. Connaught; it gives title of baron to the family of *Dillon,* being fo created in 1789.

CLONBRONEY, a vicarage in dioc. of Ardagh, fit. in bar. Granard, co. Longford, prov. Leinfter.

CLONBROOK, fit. in bar. Kilconnell, co. Galway, prov. Connaught.

CLONBULLOCK, otherwife called *Purefoy's-place,* a fair town in bar. Cooleftown, King's co. prov. Leinfter; above 40 miles from Dublin: fair day 10 July. Within 2 miles of *Clonbullock* is *Millgrove,* a very pleafant feat on the banks

banks of the *Violet River*. The church at Clonbullock, serves as a chapel of cafe to the parifh of Clonfaft, or Cloncaft, in the fame bar. the church of which is now in ruins.

CLONBULLOGE, a rectory in dioc. of Emly, fit. in bar. Clanwilliam, co. Tipperary, prov. Munfter.

CLONCAGH, a vicarage in dioc. of Limerick, fit. in bar. Connello, co. Limerick, prov. Munfter.—Alfo a rectory in dioc. of Derry, fit. in bar. Inifhowen, co. Donegal. prov. Ulfter.

CLONCAST, fit. in bar. Cooleftown, King's co. prov. Leinfter.

CLONCE, fit. in bar. Mofhill, co. Leitrim, prov. Connaught.

CLONCHANACK, fit. in bar. Geafhill, King's co. prov. Leinfter.

CLONCHEE, *Clonkee*, or *Clonchy*, a bar. in co. Cavan, prov. Ulfter.

CLONCHURCH, a chapelry in dioc. of Kildare, fit. in bar. Phillipftown, King's co. prov. Leinfter.

CLONCLARE, a vicarage in dioc. of Kilmore, fit. in bar. Dromahaire, co. Leitrim, prov. Connaught.

CLONCORAGH, a vicarage in dioc. of Limerick, fit. in bar. Connello, co. Limerick, prov. Munfter.

CLONCORIG, fit. near *Carrigaline*, in co. Leitrim, prov. Connaught.

CLONCRAFT, a rectory in dioc. of Elphin, fit. in bar. Rofcommon, co. Rofcommon, prov. Connaught.

CLONCURRY, fit. in co. Kildare, prov. Leinfter; about 19 miles from Dublin. A carmelite friary under the invocation of the Virgin Mary, was founded here by *John Roche*, A. D. 1347. Sir Nich. Lawlefs, bart. was created *baron* Cloncurry, in 1789.

CLONDALKIN, a village in bar. Newcaftle, co. Dublin, prov. Leinfter; near 5 miles from Dublin caftle, and fit. on the great road to Naas and Kildare. It is a rectory in the dioc. of Dublin. Here is a new built parifh church, and one of the antient round towers, of the origin of which there have been various conjectures. This tower is 84 feet in height, and built of ftones each about a foot fquare, forming a circle of 15 feet in diameter: the walls are upwards of a yard thick, and about 15 feet above the ground is a door without any fteps to afcend to it, nor are there any fteps on the infide, and whether there ever were any, admits a doubt. The bafe is folid; towards the top are 4 fmall oblong holes which admit the light, and it is terminated by a conic covering. In the church yard is a plain crofs, of a fpecies of white granite unpolifhed: it confifts of a fingle ftone, and is 9 feet in height. At Clondalkin are gun-powder mills, erected

by Wm. Caldbeck, efq; in the year 1783; great part of them were by fome unknown accident blown up in April 1787, but they have been fince renewed. Where the church ftands, was antiently an abbey, of which St. *Cronan Mochua* was the firft abbot; it was fpoiled and burnt in the years 832, 1071 and 1076. The palace of Clondalkin, belonging to *Amhlaibh*, king of the Danes, was fet on fire and deftroyed by *Ciaran*, fon of *Ronan*, A. D. 866. Here are fome remains of an old caftle.

CLONDEHORKY, a village in bar. Kilmacrenan, co. Donegal, prov. Ulfter; it is a rectory in dioc. of Raphoe.

CLONDERMOTT, a rectory in dioc. of Derry, fit. in the liberty of Derry, co. Londonderry, prov. Ulfter.

CLONDEVADDOCK, a rectory in dioc. of Raphoe, fit. in bar. Kilmacrenan, co. Donegal, prov. Ulfter.

CLONDRA, a rectory in dioc. Ardagh, fit. in bar. Longford, co. Longford, prov. Leinfter.

CLONDROHID, (fometimes written *Clondrohill*) fit. in bar. Mufkerry, co. Cork, prov. Munfter; it is a rectory in dioc. of Cloyne. Here is an old church, and near it are feveral old Danifh intrenchments, vaulted under ground. About a mile farther W. of *Clondrohid*, on the top of a hill called *Leffecrefig*, are the remains of a Pagan altar, compofed of 3 ftones, pitched clofe together, and a broad flat ftone lying near them.

CLONDUFF, a vicarage in dioc. Dromore, fit. in bar. upper Iveagh, co. Down, prov. Ulfter.

CLONDULLANE, a vicarage in dioc. of Cloyne, fit. in bar. Condons, co. Cork, prov. Munfter.

CLONE, fit. in bar. Galmoy, co. Kilkenny. prov. Leinfter.—Alfo a village near a river of fame name, in bar. Mohill, co. Leitrim, prov. Connaught; where an abbey was founded about A. D. 570, by St. *Fraech*; it is now a parifh church in the dioc. of Ardagh. Here are fairs on 12 Feb. 5 April, 26 May, 13 June, 10 July, 26 Aug. 29 Sept. 2 Nov. and 20 Dec.—Alfo a place on the river Camlin, 2 miles E. of Longford, in co. Longford, prov. Leinfter, where an abbey was alfo founded, A. D. 665.

CLONEA, a vicarage in dioc. Lifmore, fit. in bar. Decies without Drum, co. Waterford, prov. Munfter. The land in this parifh produces fome corn, but is moftly pafture. In cutting trenches for draining a bog here, fome cannon ball were difcovered, they probably lay there fince *Cromwell's* time, who might have made ufe of them againft an old caftle in the neighbourhood, which together with the ruins of a church, are the only remarkable buildings in the parifh; the caftle belonged to the lord of *Decies*, but is at prefent gone to decay. Here

is

is a village, and near it a *bay* of the same name.

Clonebirn, fit. in bar. Rofcommon, co. Galway, prov. Connaught.

Clonebreny, fit. in bar. Half-fore, co. Meath, prov. Leinfter.

Clonebrone, fit. in bar. Granard, co. Longford, prov. Leinfter. St. Patrick founded a nunnery here, and placed over it 2 fifters of St. *Guafaël*. It is faid that at the time of their receiving the veil from St. Patrick, they left the impreffion of their feet in the ftone on which they ftood. This abbey was deftroyed by fire, 2 Aug. A. D. 778.

Clonecan, fit. in bar. Ikerin, co. Tipperary, prov. Munfter.

Clonecoe, fit. in bar. Inifhowen, co. Donegal, prov. Ulfter.

Clonee, a village in bar. Dunboyne, co. Meath, prov. Leinfter; about 3¼ miles beyond Caftleknock, on the great road to Navan, Kells, Cavan, &c.

Cloneen, fit. in co. Tipperary, prov. Munfter; near 75 miles from Dublin, where is a caftle called *Cloneen caftle*.

Clonefad, fit. by the adjoining borders of the co.'s Meath and Weftmeath, in prov. Leinfter.

Clonegad, fit. in bar. Iflands, co. Clare, prov. Munfter; it is a rectory in dioc. of Killaloe.

Clonegal, a fair and poft town in co. Wexford, prov. Leinfter, above 47 miles from Dublin; 3¼ miles from which are the ruins of caftle *Ryland* and *Clohaman* caftle. There are alfo the ruins of another caftle 5¼ miles from *Clonegal*. Fairs held 30 May.—Alfo a fair town, fit. in bar. Forth, co. Carlow, prov. Leinfter; fairs held 1 Wednefday in Feb. March, Afcenfion day, 1 Wednefday in May, *frize*, 31 July, *cattle*, 12 and 22 Nov. *cattle*, 1 Wednefday, and 11 Dec. *cattle*.

Clonegan, a rectory in dioc. of Lifmore, fit. in bar. Upperthird, co. Waterford, prov. Munfter.

Clonegath, fit. near *Monafterevan*, prov. Leinfter.

Clonegonelly, fit. near *Cavan*, prov. Ulfter.

Clonegowan, a fair town in bar. Phillip's-town, King's co. prov. Leinfter, 40 miles from Dublin; fairs held on 22 July. Within 1½ mile of this place are the ruins of a caftle.

Cloneguin, fit. in bar. Rofcommon, co. Rofcommon, prov. Connaught.

Clonekilty, fee *Cloghnikelty*.

Clonelty, a vicarage in dioc. of Limerick, fit. in bar. Connello, co. Limerick, prov. Munfter.

Clonemore, fit. in bar. Ballybritt, King's co. prov. Leinfter. A monaftery was founded here by St. *Mochoemee*.—Alfo a place fit. near

the river Slaney, 2 miles S. W. of Ennifcorthy, co. Wexford, prov. Leinfter; where St. *Maidoc* founded a celebrated monaftery. St. *Finian* the leper was abbot of it for a feries of years; he died A. D. 680, and was interred here. This monaftery was feveral times burnt and pillaged by the Danes: here is now a parifh church in the dioc. of Ferns.

Clonenagh, a village in bar. Maryborough, Queen's co. prov. Leinfter: here was an abbey founded by St. *Fintan*; it was at different times plundered by the Danes, and is now a rectory in dioc. of Leighlin.

Clones, a poft and fair town in bar. Dartree, co. Monaghan, prov. Ulfter, 61½ miles N. W. of Dublin, and about 9 miles S. W. of Monaghan. 'Tis corruptly called *Clounifh* or *Clounes*; and is a rectory in dioc. of Clogher. Here are large ruins of an antient abbey founded by St. *Tigernach* for regular canons of the Auguftinian order, dedicated to St. Peter and St. Paul: This faint (who was of the blood royal) removed the epifcopal feat *from Clogher* to this place. The manor of this abbey is now called the manor of St. Tierny, which, at the fuppreffion of monafterys, was granted to fir Hen. Duke, and fince became the property of lord Dacre. There is ftill remaining here one of the antient round towers, and 2 Danifh raths. St. *Tigernach* (who in his old age loft his fight) died of the plague 4 Apr. 548, and was interred here. Fair days 15 Apr. laft Thurfday in May, June and July, 2 Sept. 1 Thurfday Oct. Nov. and Dec. Lat. 54: 18, lon. 7: 45.

Cloney, a *lake* in bar. Glanerought, co. Kerry, prov. Munfter.—Alfo a rectory in dioc. of Kilfenora, fit. in bar. Corcomroe, co. Clare, prov. Munfter.

Clonfad, fit. in bar. Ferbill, co. Weftmeath, prov. Leinfter; here was an antient abbey, and we find that St. *Ethchen*, who died in 577, was once bifhop of this place.

Clonfadforan, a rectory in dioc. of Meath, fit. in bar. Furtullagh, co. Weftmeath, prov. Leinfter.

Clonfeckle or *Clonfeakle*, fit. in bar. Dungannon, co. Tyrone, prov. Ulfter; it is a rectory in dioc of Armagh. The name fignifies the church of the tooth; it was fo called from a tooth of St. Patrick, faid to have been preferved here. 'Tis fit. about 5 miles from Armagh.

Clonfert, a bifhop's fee and fair town in bar. Longford, co. Galway, prov. Connaught: the latter is a vicarage in dioc. of Clonfert, diftant from Dublin about 65 miles. Lat. 53: 15, lon. 8; 32. The fee is faid by fome to have been founded in the beginning of the 7th. century; tho' we are told that an abbey, church, and bifhoprick was founded here in 558 by St. *Brendan*, who was interred in his own church in

May

May 577 : the name signifies " the holy retirement." During the middle ages, this church
was celebrated for its 7 altars; and the W. front
supposed to have been erected by John bishop
of Clonfert about 1270, is still beautiful. The
bishoprick of *Chilmacduagh* or *Kilmacduah* was
united to this see in 1602. Clonfert was often
burned and pillaged by the Danes. Fair days
are on 12 May, Aug. and 22 Nov. It lies about
65 miles S. W. of Dublin.—Also a vicarage in
dioc. of Ardfert, sit. in bar. Duhallow, co.
Cork, prov. Munster.

CLONFERTMULLOE, sit. in King's co. prov.
Leinster; a monastery was founded here in the
6th century by *St. Molua*; it is now a parish
church in the antient dioc. of *Roserea*, now united to Killaloe. St. Christan, St. Lonan, St.
Mellan, Sœrgalus and Mœnachus, all reverend
abbots of this house, were interred here.

CLONFINLOGH, a chapelry in dioc. of Cashel, sit. in bar. Clanwilliam, co. Tipperary, prov.
Munster.—Also a vicarage in dioc. of Elphin,
sit. in bar. Roscommon, co. Roscommon, prov.
Connaught.

CLONGEEN, a curacy in dioc. of Ferns, sit.
in bar. Shelmaliere, co. Wexford, prov. Leinster

CLONGERAH, sit. in bar. Bantry, co. Wexford, prov. Leinster.

CLONGUSH, a rectory in dioc. of Ardagh, sit.
in bar. Longford, co. Longford, prov. Leinster.

CLONGIBBON, a bar. joined with that of *Condons*, in co. Cork, prov. Munster; otherwise
written *Clangibbon*.

CLONGILL, a rectory in dioc. of Meath, sit.
in bar. Morgallion, co. Meath, prov. Leinster.

CLONIE, a vicarage in dioc. of Killaloe, sit.
in bar. Bunratty, co. Clare, prov. Munster.

CLONIN, a rectory in dioc. of Cathel, sit.
near *Fethard*, in bar. Middlethird, co. Tipperary, prov. Munster.

CLONINE, see *Clonin*.

CLONKEE, see *Clonchee*.

CLONKEEHAN, sit. in bar. Atherdee, co.
Louth, prov. Leinster.

CLONKEEM or *Clonkin*, a vicarage in dioc. of
Clonfert, sit. in bar. Tiaquin, co. Galway,
prov. Connaught: the parish church was once
converted into a monastery for friars of the 3d.
order of St. Francis, by *Thomas O'Kelly*, bishop
of Clonfert, about the year 1435.—Also a rectory in dioc. of Emly, sit. in bar. Clanwilliam,
co. Tipperary, prov. Munster.—Likewise a rectory in dioc. of Armagh, sit. about 36 miles
from Dublin, in bar. Ardee, co. Louth, prov.
Leinster.

CLONKELLY, a bar. in co. Fermanagh, prov.
Ulster.

CLONKINNY, a village in bar. Ikerin, co.
Tipperary, prov. Munster.

CLONLA, sit. in bar. Tirawly, co. Mayo,
prov. Connaught.

CLONLEA, an insignificant village in co.
Waterford, prov. Munster. — Also a vicarage
in dioc. of Killaloe, sit. in bar. Tullagh, co.
Clare, prov. Munster.

CLONLEAD, a rectory in dioc. of Cork, sit.
in the liberty of Kinsale, co. Cork, prov.
Munster.

CLONLEIGH, sit. on the river Foyle, two
miles N. of Lifford, in bar. Raphoe, co. Donegal, prov. Ulster. A church was founded
here by St. Columb: and we find St. *Carnach*
was abbot and bishop here, about A. D. 530;
it is now a rectory in dioc. of Derry.

CLONLISK, a bar. with a village in it of same
name, sit. in King's co. prov. Leinster.

CLONLOGHAN, a vicarage in dioc. of Killaloe, sit. in bar. Bunratty, co. Clare, prov.
Munster.

CLONLOGHER, a vicarage in dioc. of Kilmore, sit. in bar. Dromahaire, co. Leitrim,
prov. Connaught.

CLONLONAN, a bar. in co. Westmeath,
prov. Leinster: sometimes written *Clunlonan*.

CLONLOST, sit. in co. Westmeath, prov.
Leinster; near 45 miles from Dublin.

CLONLYON, sit. near Roscommon, prov.
Connaught.

CLONMACDUFF, a rectory in dioc. of Meath,
sit. in bar. Navan, co. Meath, prov. Leinster.

CLONMACKNOIS, or *Cluainmacnois*, i. e. the
retirement or resting place of the sons of the
chiefs; on account of its being the cemetary or
burying place of a number of the antient Irish
christian kings; it is sit. on a rising ground on
the E. bank of the Shannon, in bar. Garrycastle, King's co. prov. Leinster: and was antiently denominated *Druim Tipraid* or *Druim
Tipraic*, i. e. the church of the nobles, or the
church in the centre, it being supposed to stand
in the centre of Ireland. An abbey was founded here in 548, by St. *Kiaran*, which abbey
church was converted into a Cathedral, and to
which in procefs of time, 9 other churches
were added by the kings and petty princes of
the country, as places of sepulture; all erected
in one inclosure of about 2 Irish acres; since
which time the churches, episcopal palace and
other buildings have been suffered to decay,
being at present little better than a heap of
ruins, entombing a number of the sepulchres
of the nobility and bishops; it is however observable, that many pieces of cut stone are to
be found in the walls of the antient ruins, that
have been evidently used in former buildings.
The learned *Tigernach* was abbot of Clonmacnois and Roscommon, and died in 1088; several transcripts from his works are in Mr.
O'Connor's copy of the *annales quatuor magistra-
rum*.

rum. The abbey was frequently plunder'd by the Danes and others, and several times burn'd. In 1198 *Roderick O'Connor* king of Ireland was interr'd here, in the great church, on the N. side of the high altar. The landed property of the monastery was so great, and the numbers of the other religious places subject to it were so numerous, that almost half Ireland was said to have been within the bounds of Clonmacnois. This bishoprick was united to that of Meath by authority of parliament in 1568. In 1214 a castle was erected here by the English: here are two of the antient round towers, and many inscriptions of the *Greek, Latin, Hebrew and Irish* languages have been dug up here. Clonmacnois is now a vicarage in the dioc. of Meath.

CLONMACOWEN, or *Clonmacow*, a bar. in co. Galway, prov. Connaught.

CLONMAGEE, fit. in bar. Inishowen, co. Donegal, prov. Ulster.

CLONMAGORMACUM, a vicarage in dioc. of Elphin, fit. in bar. Half-ballimoe, co. Roscommon, prov. Connaught.

CLONMANIN, fit. in bar. Newcastle, co. Wicklow, prov. Leinster.

CLONMANY, fit. in bar. Inishowen, co. Donegal, prov. Ulster. St. Columb founded an abbey here, which was formerly very rich; this place is now a rectory in dioc. of Derry.

CLONMEL, a borough, post and market town, in bar. Iffa and Offa, co. Tipperary, prov. Munster, fit. on the river Suir, about 19 miles S. W. of Tipperary town, and 85 from Dublin. It has a barrack for 2 troops of horse, and holds fairs on 5 May and Nov. it sends 2 members to parliament; patron, lord Mountcashel. It is governed by a mayor, bailiffs and town-clerk: and a manufacture of woollens is carried on here, but not very considerable. The Rt. Hon. John Scott, chief justice of his majesty's court of King's bench in Ireland, was created earl of Clonmel in 1793. This town consists of four cross steets; it has a bridge of 20 arches over the *Suir*, which is navigable from hence to Carrick and Waterford. Here is a well built market house, and a charter-school for 40 children which was opened in 1748, towards the support of which the late *John Dawson esq.* bequeathed 500l. to purchase lands, and also gave an estate of 82l. per ann. for ever; the late sir *Charles Moore* bart. also granted 24 acres and a half of land at 12l. per ann. whereon the school is built, and gave 100l. towards building thereof. There is a spring here which issues out of a rising ground, and has been found very beneficial in scorbutic and chronic distempers. This town gave birth to the Rev. *Laur. Sterne*, the celebrated author of *Tristram Shandy*, &c. he was born 24 Nov. 1713.

A dominican friary was founded in 1269, and dedicated to St. *Dominick*. In the same year *Otho de Grandison* erected here a Franciscan friary, the church of which was esteemed one of the most magnificent in Ireland: in it was kept the image of St. *Francis*; the church of this friary is now the meeting house for dissenters. This town is very antient, having been built before the invasion of the Danes; it was formerly defended by a strong wall. Oliver Cromwell met with greater resistance here than in any other part of the kingdom; he demolished the castles and fortifications, of which now only the ruins remain. The gothic church here is still kept in good repair. Lat. 52 : 15, lon. 8 : 00. *Clonmel* is also the name of a vicarage in dioc. of Cloyne, fit. in co. Cork, prov. Munster.

CLONMELLAN, a fair town in bar. Delvin, co. Westmeath, prov. Leinster; above 32 miles from Dublin. Here is an elegant church, with a steeple and spire, lately built in the gothic taste; in the vicinity of Clonmellan is a small lough, nearly of an oval figure; also the ruins of a church and castle. Fair days 28 Jan. 2 May, 25 July and 29 Sept.

CLONMELLANE *castle*, now in ruins; fit. in the parish of Aglish, co. Kerry, prov. Munster, towards the banks of the river *Mang*; near it are the castles of *Mulahaff* and *castle Fiery*; they formerly belonged to the *M'Carties*, and are now the estate of lord *Kenmare*.

CLONMENE, a parish in co. Cork, prov. Munster; the castle of which was ruined in the wars of 1641. At *Clonmene*, was antiently (according to *Colgan*) a monastery of Augustinian friars founded by O'Callaghan. Not far from Clonmene is the hill called *Knocknolssy*, celebrated for a defeat given to *Donough*, then lord *Muskerry*, (who with 4000 Irish was marching to raise the siege of *Limerick*) by the lord *Broghill*, with 1000 English, in July 1651.

CLONMESS *Island*, fit. in bar. Kilmacrenan, by the coast of co. Donegal, prov. Ulster.

CLONMETHAN, a village in bar. Nethercross, co. Dublin, prov. Leinster; it is a rectory in dioc. of Dublin.

CLONMINES, a borough town in bar. Shelburne, co. Wexford, prov. Leinster; it is governed by a portrieve, and stands about 6 miles W. of Wexford town. Lat. 52 : 18, lon, 6 : 30. It sends 2 members to parliament, patron, earl of *Ely*. It is a curacy in dioc. of Ferns. The family of *Cavenagh* founded a monastery here for Eremites, following the rule of St. Augustin; it was enlarged and beautified in 1385; and the friars of the order of St. Dominic afterwards obtained possession of it.

CLONMOGHAN, a bar. in co. Cavan, prov. Ulster.

CLONMORE, a vicarage in dioc of Ferns, fit. in bar. Bantry, co. Wexford, prov. Leinster.—Also

Alfo a rectory in dioc. of Leighlin, fit. in bar. Ravilly, co. Carlow, prov. Leinfter.—Alfo a rectory in dioc. of Offory, fit. in bar. Iverk, co. Kilkenny, prov. Leinfter.—Alfo a rectory in dioc. of Cafhel, fit. in bar. Ikerin, co. Tipperary, prov. Munfter.—Likewife a rectory in dioc. of Armagh, fit. in bar. Ferrard, co. Louth, prov. Leinfter.

CLONMORE-CASTLE, fit. near *Hacket's-town*, in co. Carlow, prov. Leinfter.

CLONMORRIS, a bar. in co. Mayo, prov. Connaught; the ground here is arable and champaign, and tho' not yet arrived at a high degree of cultivation, produces corn and flax fufficient for home confumption; and fupples other parts with fat and ftore cattle.

CLONMOYLE, fit. in bar. Fertullagh, co. Weftmeath, prov. Leinfter.

CLONMULSH *church*, fit. in bar. Catherlough, co. Carlow, prov. Leinfter; 43 miles from Dublin.

CLONMULT, a rectory in dioc. of Cloyne, fit. in bar. Barrymore, co. Cork, prov. Munfter.

CLONNEGAD, a vicarage in dioc. of Killaloe, fit. in bar. Iflands, co. Clare, prov. Munfter.

CLONOE, a rectory in dioc. of Armagh, fit. in bar. Dungannon, co. Tyrone, prov. Ulfter.

CLONOGHILL, a rectory in dioc. of Achonry, fit. in bar. Corran, co. Sligo, prov. Connaught.

CLONOKINNY, a village in bar. Ikerin, co. Tipperary, prov. Munfter.

CLONONASLEE, fit. in the Queen's co. prov. Leinfter; 48 miles from Dublin, 2 miles from which are the ruins of *Caftlecuff*, pleafantly fit. in the midft of a fine plantation of trees, belonging to the earl of *Mountrath*.

CLONONY, a fair town in King's co. prov. Leinfter; fairs held 16 Aug.

CLONOULTY, a fair town in bar. Kilnemanagh, co. Tipperary, prov. Munfter; fair days 5 July and 12 Nov. It is a curacy in dioc. of Cafhel.

CLONPITT, a vicarage in dioc. of Emly, fit. in bar. Clanwilliam, co. Tipperary, prov. Munfter.

CLONPRIEST, a rectory in dioc. of Cloyne, fit. in bar. Imokilly, co. Cork, prov. Munfter.

CLONRAHAN, fit. in co. Rofcommon, prov. Connaught: *O'Connor Roe* built a monaftery here, in the reign of Hen. 7th; for Francifcans of the 3d order.

CLONROCH, fit. in co. Wexford, prov. Leinfter; 65 miles from Dublin; 5 miles beyond which is a fine feat called *Robin's-town*.

CLONRUSH, a vicarage in dioc. of Killaloe, fit. in bar. Leitrim, co. Galway, prov. Connaught.

CLONSAST, or *Cloneaft*, a parifh in King's co. prov. Leinfter, the church of which is in ruins; and is fit. about 1 mile beyond *Millgreve*.

CLONSHAMBO, a vicarage in dioc. of Kildare, fit. in bar. Ikeath, co. Kildare, prov. Leinfter.

CLONSHANVILL, fit. in bar. Boyle, co. Rofcommon, prov. Connaught; it is a fmall village, where an abbey was founded by St. Patrick. It was rebuilt and new founded by *M'Dermot Roe*, in 1385; the walls of the friary and church may yet be feen. On the fuppreffion, it was granted to lord *Dillon*.

CLONSHOUGH, a village 2¼ miles beyond *Artane*, and 4¼ from Dublin caftle, fit. in co. Dublin, prov. Leinfter.

CLONSILLAGH, fit. in bar. Caftleknock, co. Dublin, prov. Leinfter; it is a rectory in dioc. of Dublin.

CLONSINLAGH, fit. in bar. Rofcommon, co. Rofcommon, prov. Connaught.

CLONSKEERE, a rectory in dioc. of Limerick, fit. in bar. Connello, co. Limerick, prov. Munfter.

CLONTARF, fit. above 2 miles from Dublin, on the fea fide, in bar. Coolock, co. Dublin, prov. Leinfter. It is a rectory in dioc. of Dublin; and much reforted to for the purpofe of fea bathing. Here is the "*Royal Charter-fchool*," which was opened in 1749, for the reception of 100 boys. The late Mr. Phil. Ramfay bequeathed 200l. the intereft whereof he appropriated towards the maintainance of the children in this fchool: and his grace, the then lord primate, made a prefent of a clock to it. Here is alfo a caftle well preferved and elegantly improved, which is the refidence of the *Vernon* family. In April 1014, there was a long and bloody battle fought at Clontarf, between the Irifh and the Danes, which terminated in favour of the former; who foon after were enabled to expel their proud oppreffors. Near the caftle ftands Clontarf church. About ¼ of a mile from Clontarf, ftand the *Sheds of Clontarf*, fo called from feveral Sheds or pent-houfes, originally erected there for perfons employed in preferving fifh, of which great quantities were formerly cured here. A monaftery was founded at Clontarf, A. D. 550.

CLONTHUSKERT, fit. in bar. Clonmacowen, co. Galway, prov. Connaught, 6 miles N. W. of *Clonfert*. Here a monaftery for Auguftin canons was founded by *Bondan*, who died about 809.—Alfo a place in bar. Rofcommon, co. Rofcommon, prov. Connaught, where an abbey was founded in the earlier ages, by St. *Faithlee*.

CLONTIBRET, a vicarage in dioc. of Clogher, fit. in bar. Cremourne, co. Monaghan, prov. Ulfter.

CLONTUBRID, a vicarage in dioc. of Offory, fit. in bar. Crannagh, co. Kilkenny, prov. Leinfter.

CLONTURK

CLONTURK, a curacy in dioc. of Dublin, fit. in bar. Coolock, co. Dublin, prov. Leinfter; the church of which is at *Drumcondra*.

CLONTUSCART, a vicarage in dioc. of Clonfert, fit. in bar. Clonmacowen, co. Galway, prov. Connaught.—Alfo a vicarage in dioc. of Elphin, fit. in bar. Rofcommon, co. Rofcommon, prov. Connaught.

CLONYMEAGHAN, formerly a village of note, fit. in bar. Corran, co. Sligo, prov. Connaught. A monaftery was founded here by *Bernard M'Donogh*; the church was dedicated to St. Dominick; and fome ruins of it are ftill to be feen.

CLOOX, a fair town in bar. Mohill, co. Leitrim, prov. Connaught; fairs held 12 Feb. 5 Apr. 26 May, 13 June, 10 July, 26 Aug. 29 Sept. 2 Nov. and 20 Dec. It is a rectory in dioc. of Ardagh.

CLOONAGH, a rectory in dioc. of Limerick, fit. in bar. Connello, co. Limerick, prov. Munfter.

CLOONAKENNY, fit. in co. Limerick, prov. Munfter; 118 miles from Dublin.

CLOONCURRY, fee *Cloncurry*.

CLOONICK-COYLE, fit. in bar. Coftello, co. Mayo, prov. Connaught.

CLOPOKE, fee *Dun-cluin-poke*.

CLORNE, fit. in bar. Mohill, co. Leitrim, prov. Connaught. Lat. 53 : 46, lon. 8 : 18.

CLOUGH, a village in bar. Kinelearty, co. Down, prov. Ulfter. — Alfo another in bar. Bantry, co. Wexford, prov. Leinfter. — likewife a rectory in dioc. of Ferns, fit. in bar. Gorey, co. Wexford, prov. Leinfter.

CLOUGH-CASTLE, fee *Aglifh*.

CLOUGHE, fit. in bar. Talbot'stown, co. Wicklow, prov. Leinfter.

CLOUGH-MILLS, fit. in bar. Kilconway, co. Antrim, prov. Ulfter.

CLOVER-HILL, fit. in bar. Athlone, co. Rofcommon, prov. Connaught; 72 miles from Dublin; within ¼ mile of which are the ruins of a church.

CLOWN-CALLOW, fee *Cloghnikelty*.

CLOWNISH, fee *Clones*.

CLOYDON, a vicarage in dioc. of Leighlin, fit. in bar. Idrone, co. Carlow, prov. Leinfter.

CLOYNE, a fmall town in bar. Imokilly, co. Cork, prov. Munfter, fit. 125 miles S. W. of Dublin, 10 miles W. of Youghal, and about 12 miles E. of Cork, and one mile from the fea coaft. Lat. 51 : 43, lon. 8 : 19. It is a vicarage in dioc. of Cloyne, which is a bifhop's fee likewife, being fo erected, and a church built here by St. *Colman*, who died 4 Nov. 604. The bifhoprick of *Cluain-vamah* (the antient name of Cloyne, which fignifies " the fequeftered cave or habitation") was united to that of Cork in 1430, which union continued until 11 Nov. 1638, when *Geo. Synge* D. D. was confecrated

bifhop of Cloyne. From that time Cloyne has been governed by its own prelates. The cathedral is a decent gothic building; the nave is about 120 feet long, having lateral ayfles, befides the crofs ayfles, divided by gothic arches, 5 on each fide; in the choir there is an excellent organ; and at the entrance of it is a handfome portal of wood. The bifhop's palace, which was rebuilt at the beginning of the prefent century, is large and convenient. Near the cathedral is a Danifh rath, and a round tower 92 feet high, and 10 feet in diameter. The door faces the W. entrance of the church, and is about 13 feet from the ground. N. W. of Cloyne is a reputed holy well, dedicated to St. *Colman*, whofe patron day is 24 Nov. ¼ mile beyond Cloyne is Ballynaloe caftle.

CLUAINAINEACH, a church or monaftery in Queen's co. prov. Leinfter: it was deftroyed in 939 by *Callaghan*, king of S. Munfter.

CLUAINCAGH, fit. in co. Limerick, prov. Munfter; here a religious houfe was built by St. *Maidoc* of Ferns, who died A. D. 624. It is now a parifh church not far from Rathkeale.

CLUAINENACH, fit. in co. Donegal, prov. Ulfter; an abbey was founded here by St. *Columb*; it is now a chapel in bar. Inifhowen, fit. near *O'Cahane's caftle*, about 3 miles N. of Londonderry.

CLUAINFOIS, an abbey founded by St. *Iarlath*, in which there was a celebrated fchool in the year 540. It is now a chapel not far from Tuam, in co. Galway, prov. Connaught, and at prefent called ' *the high temple*'.

CLUAIN-VAMAH, fee *Cloyne*.

CLUGGIN, a fair town in co. Limerick, prov. Munfter; fairs held 13 May, and 24 Sept.

CLUNLONAN, fee *Clonlonan*.

CNAMHCHOILL, fee *Knawhill*.

COAGH, a village in bar. Dungannon, co. Tyrone, prov. Ulfter, about 81 miles from Dublin: here are the ruins of a church. — Alfo a place in co. Antrim, prov. Ulfter.

COAL-ISLAND, fit. in bar. Dungannon, co. Tyrone, prov. Ulfter, 74 miles from Dublin; where are coal works, and a canal from *Lough Neagh*, which paffes by this place towards *Dungannon*.

COALMINES, fit. in bar. Boyle, co. Rofcommon, prov. Connaught.

COALP, fit. near *Drogheda*, prov. Leinfter.

COAL-PIT-HILL, fit. in bar. Faffachdinning, co. Kilkenny, prov. Leinfter.

COALPITS, fit. in bar. Cary, co. Antrim, prov. Ulfter.—Alfo in bar. Duhallow, co. Cork, prov. Munfter.—Alfo in bar. Faffachdinning, co. Kilkenny, prov. Leinfter.

COALWORKS, fit. in bar. Dromahaire, co. Leitrim, prov. Connaught.

COCK-HILL, fit. in bar. O'Neiland, co. Armagh, prov. Ulfter.

COD's-HEAD *cape*, sit. at the Southern point of Quolagh bay, in bar. Bantry, co. Cork, prov. Munster. Dr. Beaufort's *memoir* places it in co. Leitrim.

CONNAMOCHT, sit. in bar. Connello, co. Limerick, prov. Munster.

COIGEA-LAGFAN, a name given antiently to the prov. of Leinster; the people of which were called *Lagenians* from the *Lagean*, an instrument like a broad edged launce or javelin, which was introduced amongst them by *Labra Longsech* after his return from his exile in Gaul, about 266 years before the birth of Christ.

COIL-BRIDGE, sit. in co. Down, prov. Ulster, being the passage from Downpatrick to the island of *Inch*. The bridge is composed of 6 arches, and has a gate-way over one end of it; perhaps it should be called *Coyne bridge*, as it affords a safe way over a branch of the lake antiently called *Lough Coyne*, and gives a short passage from *Downpatrick*, in the bar. of *Lecale*, into the bar.'s of *Dufferin* and *Castlereagh*. The quay for shipping to the port of *Downpatrick*, is a quarter of a mile below this bridge, and about 1 mile from the town.; ships of 50 tuns and upwards can come up to it, and there are good store houses erected at the quay.

COILOGH, a rectory in dioc. of Cashel, sit. in bar. Middlethird, co. Tipperary, prov. Munster.

COLEDI or *Colp*, see *Invercolpa*.

COLDCUTT, sit. in bar. Balruddery, co. Dublin, prov. Leinster.

COLEDAGH-HEAD, sit. in bar. Inishowen, co. Donegal, prov. Ulster

COLEDUFF, sit. in bar. Inishowen, co. Donegal, prov. Ulster.

COLEMAN, a rectory in dioc. of Cashel, sit. in bar. Middlethird, co. Tipperary, prov. Munster.

COLE-HILL, a post town, sit. in co. Longford, prov. Leinster; 50 miles from Dublin, 1¼ mile beyond which is *Tashiny* church.

COLERAIN, a bar. having in it a borough, fair and post town of same name, sit. 114 miles from Dublin, in co. Londonderry, prov. Ulster. Lat. 55 : 10, lon. 7 : 00. Fairs held on 12 May and 5 July. This town lies on the river *Ban*, 4 miles S. of the ocean, and about 23 N. E. of Londonderry: it is a rectory in dioc. of Connor, and is noted for its Salmon fishery; it returns 2 members to parliament; patron, the marquis of Waterford. Here is a barrack for three companies of foot. This town is of a tolerable size and very well built: it was once a place of great consideration, being the chief town of a co. erected by sir *John Perrot*, during his government of Ireland; but it is now only the head of the bar. it gives title of *baron* to the family of *Hanger*. The port is indifferent, occasioned by the rapidity of the river, which makes the coming up to the town difficult. St. *Carbreus* a disciple of St. *Finian* of Clonard, was the first bishop of *Coleraine*, and flourished about the year 540. He was succeeded by St. *Eonall*, who was bishop in the time of St. *Columb*, the famous founder of the abbey of *Derry*. *Ardmediæ* abbot of Colerain, was put to death by the Danes, in 930; *Manus M'Dunlave*, in 1171, plundered the church here, and several others. *Thomas M'Uchtry*, and the Galls of Ulster, built a castle here in 1213, for which purpose they raised all the pavements, and destroyed every part of the abbey, the church only excepted. A Dominican friary, which was also called the monastery of the *Bann*, was founded here in 1244, by the *O'Cahanes*, or by the *M'Evelins*; and was dedicated to the Virgin Mary. Sir Robert Savage of Ulster, Knt. an excellent soldier, who died in 1360, was buried here. Near Colerain is a small kearn or mount, easily distinguished from a *rath*, by not being surrounded by ditches or intrenchments: here a considerable linen manufacture is established. This is also the name of a village in King's co. prov. Leinster, about 48 miles from Dublin.

COLGAN-RIVER. This river which is very inconsiderable, collects other small streams, and runs from Galway, prov. Connaught, into the Grand Canal at Portumny, in a course of about 20 miles E. S. E. and is adjacent to Galway, Dunkellin, Kilcongan, Loughrea, Pallice, Leitrim and Woodford.

COLGAN's-TOWN, sit. in co. Dublin, prov. Leinster.

COLGOGH, sit. near *Kilcock*, prov. Leinster.

COLIN-MOUNTAIN, sit. in bar. Antrim, co. Antrim, prov. Leinster.

COLLIGAN, sit. in bar. Decies without Drum, co. Waterford, prov. Munster; it is a vicarage in dioc. of Lismore.

COLLIN's-TOWN, a village in bar. Half-fowre, co. Westmeath, prov. Leinster. It holds fairs 8 May and 30 Oct.

COLLON, a post and fair town in bar. Ferrard, co. Louth, prov. Leinster; 29 miles from Dublin. Fair days 3 June and 24 Nov; it is a vicarage in dioc. of Armagh. This is a neat, well built town, with a church and handsome spire, and here is the much improved seat of the Rt. Hon. John Foster, the present speaker of the house of Commons, who has established here an excellent stocking manufactory, and for the use of the company, has compleated an extensive bleach green. Three miles beyond Collon, is *Millextown*, where there is a church, which greatly attracts the attention of the public, on account of the extraordinary position of one of its gable-ends.

COLLOVILLE

COLLOVILLE, a fair town in co. Armagh, prov. Ulster. Fair days 27 Apr. and 26 Oct.

COLLUMKILL, fit. near Thomastown, in bar. Gowran, co. Kilkenny, prov. Leinster; it is a rectory in dioc. of Offory. — Also a vicarage in dioc. of Ardagh, fit. in bar. Granard, co. Longford, prov. Leinster.

COLMAN, an antient name of the present co. Westmeath, prov. Leinster.

COLMOLIN, a vicarage in dioc. of Meath, fit. in bar. Deece, co. Meath, prov. Leinster.

COLOONY, a fair town in bar. Tiraghrill, co. Sligo, prov. Connaught, near 99 miles from Dublin; having fairs on 3 May, 5 Sept. 21 Nov. and 16 Dec. There is a parish church to this place, and within 1¼ mile of it, is Mercrea, a very fine seat. The family of Coot, (now earl Bellamont) was created baron Coote of Coloony, 6 Sept. 1660.

COLP, see Invercolpa.

COLPE, a curacy in dioc. of Meath, fit. in bar. Duleek, co. Meath, prov. Leinster.

COLT, fit. in bar. Maryborough, Queen's co. prov. Leinster.

COLTIECH-TOWN, fit. in bar. Ferrard, co. Louth, prov. Leinster.

COLTRAIN, a village in bar. Magheraftephana, co. Fermanagh, prov. Ulster.

COLTRAIN CHURCH, fit. in co. Tyrone, prov. Ulster, near 85 miles from Dublin.

COMBER, or Cumber, a fair town in bar. Castlereagh, co. Down, prov. Ulster; fair days 1 Thursday O. S. Jan. 5 April, 28 June and 19 Oct. It is a curacy in dioc. of Down This is a post town, and distant 88 miles from Dublin It stands on a branch of the lake Strangford; at low water there is a pleasant strand of some thousands of acres, and near the town a horse-course of a noted fine sod, 2 miles in circuit. Here was formerly an abbey of Cistertian-monks, founded in 1199 by Brien Catha-Dun, i. e. Brien of the battle of Down, who was slain there by sir John de Courcy, about the year 1201. Of this Brien were descended the O'Neils of Upper and Lower Claneboys. The site and possessions of this house, were granted to James Hamilton, lord Claneboys, at the rent of 2l. 2s. 2d. Irish money, and from him came by assignment to the lord visc. Ardes. There is now in the town, a large meeting house, and a decent church with a parsonage house. Here also are the ruins of Mount Alexander castle, the antient seat of the earls of Mount Alexander.— There is also a place of same name in bar. Tyrkerrin, co. Londonderry, prov. Ulster, which is a rectory in dioc. of Down.

COMHOLA, a river in bar. Bear and Bantry, co. Cork, prov. Munster.

COMMERAGH mountains, fit. in bar. Decies without Drum, co. Waterford, prov. Munster.

COMMONT, fit. in bar. Tirawly, co. Mayo, prov. Connaught.

COMOLIN PARK, the elegant seat of the earl of Mountnorris, fit. near Gorey, in co. Wexford, prov. Leinster.—Near it is the village of Comolin, which is sometimes written Camolin.

COMPSY, a district joined with that of Stewarda, in co. Tipperary, prov. Munster; and forming the bar. of Stewarda and Compfy.

CONAGLOUR, otherwise called Oonaglour, and " the pigeon's hole;" fit. in the parish of White-church, co. Waterford, prov. Munster. It is a most stupendous cavern, above 150 feet in length, with a curious subterraneous rivulet. In the cave are different chambers, where the stallactical matter descending from the roof, presents a great variety of shapes and figures. A little to the Northward is a smaller cave, called Oonamort; and in this neighbourhood are several others.

CONCK, fit. in bar. Dunkerron, co. Kerry, prov. Munster.

CONDONS, a district joined to that of Clongibbon, and called the bar. of Condons and Clongibbon, in co. Cork, prov. Munster.

CONEVAL, a rectory in dioc. of Raphoe, fit. in bar. Kilmacrenan, co. Donegal, prov. Ulster.

CONEY-ISLAND, an island so called in Bantry bay, co. Cork, prov. Munster.—Also a small island in St. George's channel, near the coast of the co. Down, prov. Ulster.—And another in Lough Neagh, near the coast of co. Armagh, prov. Ulster.

CONFOY, a curacy in dioc. of Dublin, fit. in bar. Salt, co. Kildare, prov. Leinster.

CONG, once the chief city of the prov. Connaught, but now a small village in bar. Killmain, co. Mayo, prov. Connaught; it is a rectory in dioc. of Tuam; and fit. about 5 miles S. W. of Ballinrobe; on the edge of Lough Corrib; the views from it are the most picturesque that nature can form; the late bishop Pococke often declared, they exceeded any thing he had ever seen in his travels. Here is a handsome seat; also the ruins of a large abbey, erected by St. Fechan, in 664. Roderick O'Connor the last monarch of Ireland, died in it the 16 May 1150, in the 75th year of his age, and was interred at Clonmacnoise. Near it is a subterraneous cave, to which there is a descent by 63 steps; at the bottom runs a clear stream, where the trout may be seen sporting in the water. Cong was for some time the residence of the kings of Connaught, and the ruins of several churches may still be seen here. At the back of this village, a very broad river rushes at once from beneath a gently sloping bank, and after a rapid course of about a mile, loses itself in Lough Corrib. It is supposed to be the outlet of a subterraneous chan-

nel

eel, thro' which the superfluous waters of *Lough Mask* and *Lough Carrah* are discharged into *Corrib*.

CONGILL, sit. in bar. Morgallion, co. Meath, prov. Leinster.

CONMACNE, a district sit. on the Shannon, in co. Leitrim, prov. Connaught; the chiefs of which were corruptly called *Magrannals*, or *Macharnals*, some of whom were in the possession of the country in the beginning of the last century.

CONMACNE-CUILT-OLA, an antient district, which comprehended the present co. Mayo, prov. Connaught, the principal residence of the Olnegmachts. Also *Magh-nay*, the present co. of Roscommon, in same prov. The hereditary chiefs of this district were the *Genairs*, kings of all Connaught, and whose principal seat was at Croghan. From *Conmacne* is derived Connaught, or Conaught, the Western prov. of Ireland.

CONMACNE-DE-DUNMORE, a district which antiently comprehended the Northern and Eastern parts of the co. Galway, prov. Connaught; the chiefs of which were the *Hy Cellaghs* or *O'Kellys*; a number of whom were in possession of it, at the beginning of the last century; except a considerable part which was occupied by the English settlers, the *Birminghams*, *Burks* and others.

CONMACNEMARA, an antient district formerly called *Iar-connaught*, or West Connaught; it contained the present bar.'s of Moragh, Moycullin and Ballinahinch, in co. Galway, prov. Connaught; the chiefs of which were denominated *Hy Flagherty* or *O'Flagherty*.

CONN *Lake*, sit. in bar. Tirawley, co. Mayo, prov. Connaught.

CONNA, a fair town in co. Waterford, prov. Munster; fairs held 14 May.

CONNALUA, or lower Connal, in the co. Limerick, prov. Munster; it was also called *Thyhan*, or the N. country; the chiefs of which were the *Hy Thyhans*, or *O'Thyhans* called *Hy Cinealagh* or *O'Kinealy* and *O'Collins*: dispossessed by the *Fitzgeralds*.

CONNAMARA, sit. in bar. Ballinahinch, co. Galway, prov. Connaught. It is remarkable for a manufacture of coarse and very warm stockings, called *Connamaras*.

CONNAUGHT, the most Western prov. of Ireland, containing 5 counties, viz. Leitrim, Sligo, Mayo, Roscommon and Galway; they are subdivided into 42 bar.'s and 296 parishes. It is almost surrounded by the river *Shannon* and the Western ocean. It extends from 53, to 54: 20 N. lat. and from 8 : 4 to 10: 35 W. lon. including the co. *Clare*, which was once annexed to Connaught, but is now considered

as part of *Munster*. This country is said to increase in numbers, owing to the introducing the linen trade into the parts bordering on *Ulster*; tho' its capital is declining, and its most fertile parts like those of Munster, are verging to depopulation. Its chief town is *Galway*. There are many loughs in this province, and its most noted rivers are the *Moy*, *Duffy*, *Gora*, *Cara*, *Conn*, *Owenbwee* and *Allin*. Its antient name was *Olnegmacht*, or *Conmachtne*, being inhabited by several powerful tribes of the *Belgians*, viz. the *Olnegmacts*, *Galenians*, *Damnonians*, *Cathragians*, *Gamanradii*, &c. and their several countries were known by the names of *Tuatha-Taidan*, *Maonmoy*, *Breffny*, *Coran*, *Galeng*, *Errus*, *Murisg*, and *Moy Nay*: in this latter territory stood *Drum Druid*, famous for its great cave and Druidical rites; a place which long before *Ptolemy's* time, got the name of *Croghan*, where the states of *Connaught* assembled, and where *Eochy-Feylogh* erected a celebrated *rath* in the time of *Augustus Cæsar*.

CONNELL, or *Great Connell*, a bar. in co. Kildare, prov. Leinster; in which are the ruins of Great Connell abbey.

CONNELLO, or *Connillo*, a bar. in co. Limerick, prov. Munster; the antient chiefs of which were the *O'Kincalys*, *O'Collins's*, and *O'Thyans*, now called *Thayns*; who were dispossess'd by the *Fitzgeralds*.

CONNO, a village in bar. Kilnatalown, co. Cork, prov. Munster.

CONNOR, a bishop's see, and village of same name in bar. Antrim, co. Antrim, prov. Ulster. This village holds fairs 2 Aug. and 28 Oct. It is distant 89 miles from Dublin; Lat. 54 : 48 lon. 6 : 47. The bishoprick was (according to some writers,) founded by St. *Macnisius*, in the beginning of the *sixth* century, and united to that of Down in 1442 or 1454; but Dr. Beaufort in his memoir, states both sees to have been founded in the 5th century. The cathedral of Connor is now a ruin.

CONNOR-CASTLE, sit. near Ballina, in co. Mayo, prov Connaught.

CONNOR-VILLE, an inconsiderable village in co. Cork, prov. Munster, between *Dunmanway* and *Bandon*.

CONNORS *mountain*, sit. in the bar. Corkaguinny, co. Kerry, prov. Munster; otherwise called *the Connors*.

CONRY, a chapelry in dioc. of Meath, sit. in bar. Rathconrath, co. Westmeath, prov. Leinster.

CONVOY, a village in bar. *Boylagh* &c. co. Donegal, prov. Ulster. *Dr. Beaufort*: 'tis placed by others in bar. *Raphoe*. (Scale.)

CONWALL, sit. near the river Swilly, in bar. Kilmacrenan, co, Donegal, prov. Ulster; here was

was an abbey, over which St. *Fiachry* prefided, about the year 587 ; it is now a parifh church in dioc. of Raphoe.

COOK'SBOROUGH, fit. in bar. Magheredernon, co. Weftmeath, prov. Leinfter.

COOK'STOWN, a fair and poft town in bar. Dungannon, co. Tyrone, prov. Ulfter, 81 miles from Dublin ; lat. 54 : 38' : 20" lon. 6 : 40 ; fair days 2 Sat. in Feb. 28 Mar. 2 Sat. in May, 1 Tuefd. O. S. June, 2 Sat. in Aug. 4 Sept. 10 Oct. 2 Sat. Nov. and laft Sat. in Dec. Within 1 mile of this place is *Killymoone*, the very handfome feat of James Stewart, Efq.—Alfo a place of fame name in bar. Atherdee, co. Louth, prov. Leinfter.—Likewife a curacy in dioc. of Meath, fit. in bar. Ratoah, co. Meath, prov. Leinfter.

COOL, fit. in bar. Colerain, co. Londonderry, prov. Ulfter.

COOLACORKE, fit. in bar. Arklow, co. Wicklow, prov. Leinfter.

COOLAGHMORE, a rectory in dioc. of Offory, fit. in bar. Kells, co. Kilkenny, prov. Leinfter.

COOLAGURAGH, a fair town in co. Cork, prov. Munfter ; fairs held 13 July.

COOLANY, a *river* in bar. Leney, co. Sligo, prov. Connaught.

COOLASTIGUE-CASTLE, , fit. 2½ miles beyond *O'Brien's bridge*, in co. Clare, prov. Munfter.

COOLATIN, a fair town in co. Wicklow, prov. Leinfter ; fair days 26 Feb. May, Aug. and Nov.

COOLAVIN, a bar. in co. Sligo, prov. Connaught, the greater part of which is covered by the *Curlews* and other mountains.

COOLBOY, a fair town in bar. Shillelagh, co. Wicklow, prov. Leinfter ; fair days laft Wed. nefd. Jan. 1 Wednef. O. S. Mar. laft Wednef. April, 1 Wednef. O. S. June, laft Wednef. July, Sept. Oct. and Wednef. in Ember week.

COOLCASHIN, a vicarage in dioc. of Offory, fit. in bar. Gallmoy, co. Kilkenny, prov. Leinfter.

COOLCLIFFE, fit. near Rofs, prov. Munfter.

COOLCRAGHIN, a rectory in dioc. of Offory, fit. in bar. Faffadining, co. Kilkenny, prov. Leinfter.

COOLCULLEN, fit. in bar. Faffadining, co. Kilkenny, prov. Leinfter.

COOLDROMMIN, fit. in bar. Omagh, co. Tyrone, prov. Ulfter.

COOLE, a bar. in co. Fermanagh, prov. Ulfter.—Alfo a fair town in co. Weftmeath, prov. Leinfter ; fairs held 20 May and Nov.

COOLE'STOWN, a bar. in King's co. prov. Leinfter.

COOLFIN, fit. in bar. Leitrim, co. Galway, prov. Connaught.

COOLGRANY or *Coolgreny*, a village in bar. Gorey, co. Wexford, prov. Leinfter.

COOLINANTA, a fair town in co. Kilkenny, prov. Leinfter ; fairs held on Whitfun-Mond.

COOLINAY, a rectory in dioc. of Cloyne, fit. in bar. Barrymore, co. Cork, prov. Munfter.

COOLISTOWN, fit. near *Dunleer*, prov. Leinft.

COOLKENNO, a fair town in bar. Shillelagh, co. Wicklow, prov. Leinfter, about 28 miles from Dublin ; fairs held 1 Feb. May, Aug. and Nov. Here is a parifh church, and a handfome feat.

COOLKERRY, a rectory in dioc. of Offory, fit. in bar. upper Offory, Queen's co. prov. Leinfter.

COOLMAIN *caftle*, fit. in co. Cork, prov. Munfter ; oppofite to *Courtmacfherry* : it is now in decay.

COOLNAGOPOGE, fit. in bar. Corkaguinny, co. Kerry, prov. Munfter.

COOLNAHARGELL, fit. in bar. Iveragh, co. Kerry, prov. Munfter.

COOLNAKENNY, a village in bar. Connello, co. Limerick, prov. Munfter.

COOLNEHORN, fit. in bar. Scarawalfh, co. Wexford, prov. Leinfter.

COOLNEMUCKY, fit. in bar. Upperthird, co. Waterford, prov. Munfter.

COOLOCK, a bar. with a village in it of fame name, fit. in co. Dublin, prov. Leinfter : the latter is a vicarage in dioc. of Dublin, and lies 1 mile beyond *Donnycarney*, and 3 miles from the caftle of Dublin ; it has a fmall but neat church.

COOLRAHERY, fit. near *Kilkenny*, prov. Leinfter.

COOLSTUFFE, a rectory in dioc. of Ferns, fit. in bar. Shelmaliere, co. Wexford, prov. Leinfter.

COOLY, fit. in bar. Inifhowen, co. Donegal, prov. Ulfter.

COOLY-POINT, a cape in bar. Dundalk, co. Louth, prov. Leinfter.

COONAGH, a bar. in co. Limerick, prov. Munfter.

COOTE-HILL, a poft and fair town in bar. Tullagharvey, co. Cavan, prov. Ulfter, about 52 miles from Dublin ; the linen bufinefs is carried on here confiderably. Fairs are held 12 Mar. 9 June, 12 Sept. and 6 Dec.

COPLAND-ISLANDS, fit. in bar. Ardes, on coaft of co. Down, prov. Ulfter, at the S. entrance of *Carrickfergus bay* ; they are fo named from a family of the *Coplands*, who fettled there in the time of *John deCourcey* in the 12th century, of whom are fome remains in the adjacent tract called *Bally-copland*, on the continent. They are diftinguifhed by the names of the *Big*, *Crofs*, and *Mew ifland* ; in the fecond of which is a light-houfe. The *Big ifland* is inhabited by about half a dozen families, who are all *Diffenters*. Lat. 54 : 43, lon. 5 : 55.

COPPER-MINES, fit. near Wicklow, prov. Leinfter.

CORAN,

CORAN, an antient diſtrict, in which was the reſidence of the chiefs of Luigny, ſit. in co. Sligo, prov. Connaught.

CORANDULLA, ſit. in bar. Clare, co. Galway, prov. Connaught.

CORBALLIS, ſit. in bar. Nethercroſs, co. Dublin, prov. Leinſter. — Alſo a place near Kilkenny, prov. Leinſter.

CORBALLY, a rectory in dioc. of Emly, ſit. in bar. Clanwilliam, co. Tipperary, prov. Munſter.—Alſo a ſeat near Caſtletown and Celbridge, in co. Kildare, prov. Leinſter, belonging to Sam. Kuthrens, eſq; near which are the old church and tower of Teghadoc.—Alſo a rectory in dioc. of Waterford, ſit. in bar. Gualtiere, co. Waterford, prov. Munſter.—Alſo a vicarage in dioc. of Cork, ſit. in bar. Barretts, co. Cork, prov. Munſter.—Likewiſe a place 2 miles S. of Roſcrea, in bar. Ikerin, co. Tipperary, prov. Munſter; in which was an antient chapel appendant to Monaincha, in ſame co. — Alſo a place near Athy, prov. Leinſter.

CORBET'STOWN, ſit. in bar. Faſſadining, co. Kilkenny; prov. Leinſter.

CORCAGUINNY, ſee Corkaguinny.

CORCAHLANN, a diſtrict in co. Roſcommon, prov. Connaught; the antient proprietors of which were the O'Hanlys and O'Briens.

CORCALUIGHE, i. e. the woody morafs on the water; an antient diſtrict in the S. part of the co. Cork, prov. Munſter; containing the preſent bar. of Carberry, the antient chiefs of which were called Magh Cor Teagh, or the chief of the habitation of the morafs, by corruption Mac Carty, by which means they have been confounded with the Mac Cartys of Kerry. The leſſer diſtricts of this country were Hy Leareigh, Hy Maghoneigh, and Hy Driſcuil, under the dominion of their reſpective chiefs, O'Leary, O'Mahony, and O'Driſcol, all dynaſts and ſubordinate chiefs to Mac Carty, king of Corcaluighe, who in proceſs of time became the ſovereign of all the petty ſtates in the preſent co. of Cork, and was therefore denominated Mac Carty Reagh, or Mac Carty the king; ſome of whoſe deſcendants were in poſſeſſion at the commencement of the laſt century; tho' the Engliſh families of the Courcies and Barrys had eſtates therein.

CORCLONE, a rectory in dioc. of Leighlin, ſit. in bar. Stradbally, Queen's co. prov. Leinſter.

CORCOMOHIDF, a vicarage in dioc. of Limerick, ſit. in bar. Connello, co. Limerick; prov. Munſter.

CORCOMROE, or Corcumruadh, a bar. ſit. on the Weſtern coaſt of the co. of Clare, prov. Munſter; in which is the antient biſhoprick of Fineore or Kilfenora. In 1317, a battle was fought here, in which were ſlain Mortogh Garbh

and Tiegue O'Brien. The antient families of this diſtrict were the O'Connors and O'Laughlins. Alſo a village of ſame name, ſit. in bar. Burrin, in ſame co. where a very ſumptuous abbey was founded in 1194, by Donald king of Limerick; it was afterwards made ſubject to the celebrated abbey of Furnes in Lancaſhire. This is now a rectory in dioc. of Kilfenora.

CORCREAGH, ſit. in co. Louth, prov. Leinſter; near 42 miles from Dublin.

CORCUMRUADH, ſee Corcomroe.

CORDALLA, ſit. in bar. Clare, co. Galway, prov. Connaught.

CORDEN'STOWN, ſit. in bar. Balruddery, co. Dublin, prov. Leinſter.

CORDERCY, ſit. in bar. Louth, co. Louth, prov. Leinſter.

CORDRINY, a fair town in co. Cork, prov. Munſter; fairs held 5 Aug.

CORDROHY, a fair town in co. Cork, prov. Munſter; fairs held 20 Jan. May, 24 June, Aug. 29 Sept. and 18 Dec.

CORK, the largeſt co. in Ireland, ſit. in prov. Munſter, having a city in it of ſame name, which is a biſhop's ſee. This co. has the co. Limerick on the N. the ſea on the S. Kerry on the W. and Waterford on the E. and is ſaid to have more good and bad land in it, than any other co. in the kingdom. The lands-end of England bears S. E. from the harbour of Cork, at about 120 miles or 40 leagues diſtance. The greateſt length of the co. is about 110 Engliſh, or 93 Iriſh miles, and its greateſt breadth 56 Engliſh, or 44 Iriſh miles. It contains 269 pariſhes, in which are 105 churches, 16 bar.'s 12 boroughs, and returns 26 members to parliament. It gives title of earl to the elder branch of the illuſtrious family of Boyle. It abounds with excellent harbours well fitted for foreign trade, and with many fine rivers, as the Blackwater, Lee, Bandon, Ilen, &c. and being inhabited by an induſtrious people, is rich and populous, tho' tillage is too much neglected, the lands being chiefly under paſture, the caſe of many other co.'s of Ireland. It is plentifully ſtored with all kinds of game for fiſhing and fowling. The firing is generally turf, but the ſea-port towns uſe coal brought from England, tho' conſiderable quantities of this ſubſtance have been diſcovered in many parts of the country. Before the arrival of the Strongbonian conquerors, this co. was a kingdom in itſelf, the kings of which were the Mc. Cartys. In 1210 it was made ſhire ground by king John, who appointed ſheriffs and other officers. In this co. are the ſoft Mallow waters, whoſe degree of heat compared with thoſe of a neighbouring cold ſpring, and the Briſtol waters, is by Forenheit's thermometer as 68 to 50. Here are alſo many Daniſh mounts, with hollow chambers and winding

inlets

inlets; alfo fubterranean caves antiently dug in clay ground.

CORK-CITY, the principal town in co. Cork, prov. Munfter, diftant 124 miles from Dublin, and about 50 miles S. of Limerick. It is a poft, port and fair town ; having fairs on the day after Trin. Sund. and on 1 Oct. It fends two members to parliament. It is faid to have been founded by the Danes, and inclofed by them with walls about the middle of the 9th century. It is the fecond city in Ireland, and lies moftly on a marfhy ground furrounded by the river *Lee*, being defended only by the above-mentioned walls, and fome round towers. It was never a place of any confiderable ftrength, efpecially fince the modern method of befieging places was in ufe ; yet it made a refiftance of 5 days againft a regular army in Sept. 1690, when it was befieged by the earl of Marlborough, who took it from king *James's army*, at which time the duke of Grafton, who ferved as a volunteer, was flain in the attack. The garrifon confifting of 4,500 men, furrendered on *Michaelmas-day*, and were made prifoners of war. It contains upwards of 70,000 inhabitants, and has 12 companies of foot quartered in the barracks. Here is a fpacious harbour, where almoft any number of fhips may lie with eafe and fafety. The flaughtering feafon continues from the month of Aug. to the latter end of Jan. in which fpace it has been computed that they kill and cure feldom fewer than 100,000 head of black-cattle ; the reft of their exports confifts of butter, candles, hides *raw* and *tanned*, linen cloth, pork, calves, lambs and rabbit fkins, tallow, wool for England, linen and woollen yarn and worfted. The merchants of Cork carry on a very extenfive trade to almoft all parts of the world, fo that their commerce is annually increafing. The air of this city is indifferently clear and healthy : in it, befides the cathedral, are the churches of St. *Mary Shanden* and St. *Ann*, in the N. fuburb, *Chriftchurch*, St. *Peter's* and St. *Paul's*, within the city and on the S. fide, St. *Nicholas's-church*. The cathedral is dedicated to St. *Finbar*, and was founded by that Saint in the 7th century. In 1725 it was taken down and rebuilt about 10 years after. There were feveral abbeys founded here, and there are now many charitable inftitutions in it. The Cuftom-houfe is a large building and elegant, the old one having been taken down in 1724 ; the Exchange, which almoft divides the main ftreet of the city into 2 parts, N. and S. is an handfome regular ftructure of hewn ftone. Here are a co. Courthoufe, where the affizes are held, Goals, Markets, Hofpitals, Barracks, a Theatre, and a Bifhop's palace. The bifhoprick of *Rofs* was annexed to that of Cork, by Q. Eliz. in 1586.

Here was one of the antient round towers, but 'twas deftroyed about 60 years ago. The corporation confifts of a mayor, fheriffs, recorder, aldermen and burgeffes. 6 miles W. of *Cork*, upon the E. of the river *Bride*, are a vaft number of fubterranean caverns, compofed of great pillars, fupporting large arches of lime-ftone rocks. The firft entrance appears as if it was the work of art, but upon ferious confideration it is found to be all *natural* ; in fome places the entrance is very low, but the arch fuddenly rifes from 6 to 10 feet high ; the tops and fides of which are fmooth as if polifhed by the hands of workmen. The antient name of this city was *Corcag*, i. e. the W. plain, marfh or morafs, which name it took from *Corcabhaifcin*, or the morafs of the harbour or bay, the name given to an antient diftrict round the harbour of Cork. The Englifh families who fettled in this part of the country, were the *Boyles* and *Barrys*. At 5 miles diftance from the harbour of Cork lies *Great ifland*, on which are feveral villages ; and Wefterly are vaft fubterranean caves called the *Ovens*.

CORK, (*Harbour*) in co. Cork, prov. Munfter. Lat. 51 : 42, lon. 8 : 35. This harbour is large enough to contain the whole navy of Great Britain ; the entrance is free, open and bold ; there are the remains of an old fort on the right hand, as you enter between the 2 head-lands. On the W. fide of Cork harbour, within the mouth, is an high round land called *Corribiny-point*, on its fummit is one of the antient tumuli, raifed to the memory of fome eminent warrior. The mouth of the channel is narrow, and the cannon may reach from fhore to fhore ; where the ruins of the old fort ftand, the cape is very high, and the channel is not above an hundred yards from the fhore. *Dog's-nofe-point*, which is farther up the harbour, is another formidable fituation. When you are in, you come to anchor off a village called *Cove*; here you are land locked, and fecured from all danger. Here are 2 iflands called *Spike* and *Hawlhowling*, that ferve as bulwarks to protect veffels riding at anchor, from being damaged by the tide of ebb, or floods off the land. On the latter of thefe iflands, are the remains of an old fortification, erected about the end of queen Eliz.'s reign, and which commanded all veffels of burthen paffing up to Cork. One fide of Cork harbour is formed by the *Great Ifland*, formerly called *Barrymore Ifland*, from its belonging to that family; as a defence to this paffage, (the only one by which the ifland can be entered at low water) ftands *Belvelly-caftle*. The firft earl of *Orrery* in one of his letters obferves, that this ifland is very fertile, about 6 miles in circumference, and a pafs of fuch confequence,

2 B

that

that were he an enemy about to invade this kingdom, it is one of the firſt places he would ſecure, as being near equally diſtant from *Cork, Youghal* and *Kinſale*. This iſland is ſomething more than 4 miles long, and 2 broad; the land is every where high and ſteep, and all round it is great depth of water.

CORKAGUINNY, a bar. in co. Kerry, prov. Munſter; the name ſignifies a fertile country. This bar. is a peninſula of about 24 Iriſh miles in length and 8 in breadth, it is waſhed on the S. ſide by the bay of *Dingle*, or Caſtlemain, and on the N. by *Tralee* bay. It contains no leſs than 20 pariſhes, which ſhews that this bar. was formerly better inhabited than it is at preſent, each pariſh having had its reſpective church, moſt of which churches were very large, as appears by their ruins. *Corkaguinny* is generally ſub-divided into 2 parts or half bar.'s; they give that name to the Southern and Weſtern part of this peninſula; and the Northern ſide, which is very coarſe and mountainous, is called *Litteragh*. In the Southern diviſion, are alſo large tracts of mountain, which have been formerly cultivated up to the top; ſeveral of them which are now but poor barren rocks, have great numbers of old incloſures and marks of culture on their ſides, which are now neglected; the country people have an opinion that moſt of the old fences in theſe wild mountains, were the work of the antient *Danes*, and that they made a kind of beer of the heath which grows there; but theſe incloſures are more modern, than the time when that Northern nation inhabited Ireland; many of them were made to ſecure cattle from *wolves*, which animals were not entirely extirpated, until about the year 1710, as we find by preſentments for raiſing money for deſtroying them in ſome old grand-jury books. The feet of theſe mountains have ſeveral ſmall brooks flowing from them, into both bays, near which the induſtrious inhabitants have cultivated ſeveral large tracts of ground, that produce good crops of barley, oats and wheat; they are encouraged to purſue agriculture, becauſe of the convenience of ſea-ſand, which is an excellent manure, and this bar. is thereby eſteemed the granary of the whole county.

CORK-BEG, the name of a handſome ſeat, ſit. near to the mouth of Cork harbour to the S. W. It is built on a peninſula, to which is a narrow iſthmus from the main land; near it are the ruins of an old caſtle and a decayed church. This is alſo a rectory in dioc. of Cloyne, ſit. in bar. Imokilly, co. Cork, prov. Munſter.

CORK-KENNY, ſit. in bar. Bantry, co. Cork, prov. Munſter.

CORKERRY, a bar. in co. Weſtmeath, prov. Leinſter.

CORKMORE, ſit. in bar. Poble-O'Brien, co. Limerick, prov. Munſter.

CORNAGOUR, ſit. in bar. Arklow, co. Wicklow, prov. Leinſter.

CORNERSTOWN, ſit. in half-bar. Rathdown, co. Dublin, prov. Leinſter.

COROCK, ſit. in bar. Strabane, co. Tyrone, prov. Ulſter; here was a monaſtery erected in the 15th century, for Franciſcan friars of the 3d order. At the ſuppreſſion it was granted to ſir Hen. Piers, who aſſigned it to ſir Arth. Chicheſter: the ruins of it diſplay a ſingular neatneſs, and an elegant ſtile of architecture.

CORONERY, ſit. in co. Cavan, prov. Ulſter; near 48 miles from Dublin; within ¼ of a mile of which is *Knockbride-bridge*, ſit. on the banks of a ſmall lough; and 3 miles beyond *Coronery*, are the ruins of a church.

CORONODY, the name of a ſeat in co. Cork, prov. Munſter.

CORRAAN, a peninſula in bar. Burriſhoole, co. Mayo, prov. Connaught.

CORRAH. Mr. *Echard* places this as a bar. in co. Mayo, prov. Connaught; but it ſeems he miſtakes it for *Carragh*.

CORRAN, a bar. in co. Sligo, prov. Connaught.

CORRELLSTOWN, ſit. in bar. Farbill, co. Weſtmeath, prov. Leinſter.

CORREN, a *rock* ſo called, ſit. in co. Sligo, prov. Connaught; remarkable for its caves, ſometimes called *the giant's houſe*. A path is cut in the rock before the cave, 100 paces long; and after deſcending a ſteep, difficult paſſage, you enter very curious receſſes.

CORRIB-LOUGH, ſit. in bar. Clare, co. Galway, prov. Connaught. This lake ſomewhat reſembles *Lough Erne* in its form, and extends 20 miles in length, being 11 miles wide in the broadeſt part; in the middle it is contracted to a ſmall channel, which is croſſed by a ferry at *Knock*. A great number of concealed rocks render the navigation of this lake dangerous, to thoſe who are not well acquainted with it. There is a freſh-water muſcle in this lake, that produces pearls, of which *Dr. Beaufort* ſays, he has ſeen ſome very fine ſpecimens.

CORRIBINNY-POINT, ſit. by Cork harbour, co. Cork, prov. Munſter; on its ſummit is one of the antient tumuli, raiſed to the memory of ſome eminent warrior.

CORROFIN, ſit. in bar. Inchiquin, co. Clare, prov. Munſter; 109 miles from Dublin; 5 miles from which are the ruins of a church. Fairs are held here on the day before Aſcenſion day and 22 Nov.

CORROMANANE, ſit. in bar. Louth, co. Louth, prov. Leinſter.

CORRY-

CORRYHEEN, fit. in bar. Kerry, co. Limerick, prov. Munfter.

CORTANTY, fit. in bar. Clonlifk, King's co. prov. Leinfter.

CORVILLE, fit. near *Rofcrea*, prov. Munfter.

COSCRADIA, an antient territory in co. Waterford, prov. Munfter; it contained but a fmall narrow tract, the inhabitants of which made no great figure, and probably were early fwallowed up by the encroachments of their more powerful neighbours the Defii; for we read nothing of them after the 7th century.

COSHBRIDE, a bar. in co. Waterford, prov. Munfter; joined to that of *Cofhmore*, and commonly called the bar. of *Cofhmore* and *Cofhbride*; in the former divifion ftands *Lifmore*, a bifhop's fee and borough; and in the latter ftands the borough of *Tallow*. It is the moft Weftern bar. in that co. That part of it which lies to the N. of the *Black-water* is incumbered with mountains, being coarfe and rugged, except a narrow tract running along the river. This bar. contains the parifhes of *Lifmore*, *Mocollop*, *Tallow*, *Kilwatermoy*, *Kilkeckan* and *Temple-michael*.

COSHENNY, or *Cufhina*, fit. near Portarlington, in bar. of Portarlington, King's co. prov. Leinfter. The grounds hereabout are partly bog, and partly a light and very fandy foil.

COSHLEA, a bar. in co. Limerick, prov. Munfter.

COSHMA, a bar. in co. Limerick, prov. Munfter.

COSHMORE, a diftrict joined to that of *Cofhbride*, and together called the bar. of Cofhmore and Cofhbride, in co. Waterford, prov. Munfter.

COSTELLO, a bar. in co. Mayo, prov. Connaught; the Rt. Hon. *Charles Dillon Lee*, is by defcent vifc. Dillon of *Coftello-gallen*. The family of Dillon being fo created in 1622.1

COSTLET'S-BRIDGE, fit. in co. Down, prov. Ulfter; it is the entrance into the bar. of *Lower Iveach*, on the N. E. fide from the co. *Antrim* from *Lifburn*; over a fmall river called *Garrielogh* river, which rifes out of *Lough-heney*.

COTLAND'S-TOWN, a vicarage in dioc. of Dublin; fit. in bar. Naas, co. Kildare, prov. Leinfter.

COT'S-ROCK, now called *Caftlemary*, fit. in co. Cork, prov. Munfter. It obtained the former appellation, from the remains of a Druid's altar ftill to be feen here. This altar confifts of a large ftone 15 feet long, and 8 broad, of a rough irregular figure, approaching to an oval form: the higheft part of it is 9 feet from the ground, and it is fupported by three other great ftones. Adjoining to it is a large round flag or table, which was probably ufed for cutting up the victims for the facrifice.

COTTER'S-BOROUGH, a fair town in co. Cork, prov. Munfter. Fairs held 21 May and 15 Nov.

COTTON, a large tract of bog, commonly called the great bog of *Cotton* and *Granfhaw*, being part of the manor of Bangor, in co. Down, prov. Ulfter. This bog which contained at leaft one thoufand acres, the owners began to reclaim and improve in 1743.

COTTRELL'S-TOWN, fit. in bar. Balruddery, co. Dublin, prov. Leinfter.

COULYCLARE, fit. in co. Clare, prov. Munfter; 136 miles from Dublin: not far from which are the ruins of a caftle and a church.

COURCEYS, a bar. in co. Cork, prov. Munfter.

COURNELLANE, fit. near *Leighlin bridge*, prov. Leinfter.

COURT, fit. in bar. Leney, co. Sligo, prov. Connaught; 3 miles N. W. of Achonry: here a fmall monaftery was erected by *O'Hara*, for Francifcan friars of the third order; the fteeple and other fine ruins of this building yet remain.

COURT-AND-CORRAGHEEN, a fair town in co. Limerick, prov. Munfter. Fairs held 23 Apr. 10 June, 2 Sept. and 30 Nov.

COURTEL, fit. in bar. Bantry, co. Wexford, prov. Leinfter.

COURT-FERRY, fit. in co. Limerick, prov. Munfter; 100 miles from Dublin, and above 6 from *Limerick city*.

COURT-MAC-SHERRY, fit. in bar. Barryroe, co. Cork, prov. Munfter. Here is a bay which affords plenty of various kinds of fea-fifh; formerly *Pilchards* were taken in it, and on the fhore are feveral buildings, called *fifhpalaces*, for curing that fifh. *Plaice* are fo good here, that when in feafon, many prefer them to turbot, and fome are near as large. Confiderable draughts of falmon have been alfo taken in this bay: on both fides are prodigious high cliffs, towards the entrance of this bay, where eagles, hawks and herons build their nefts; on the oppofite fide of the river from *Court-mac-fherry*, is the decayed caftle of *Coolmain*.

COURTOWN, fit. in co. Wexford, prov. Leinfter; it gives title of earl and vifc. to the family of *Stopford*; here is a handfome feat of the Rt. Hon. the earl of Courtown.

COURTRA-LOUGH, or *Coutra-lough*, fit. in bar. Kiltartan, co. Galway, prov. Connaught. This lake is faid to poffefs all the beauties that hills, woods and iflands can impart to water; it lies near the borders of co. Clare.

COURTSTRAND, a village in bar. Carbury, co. Sligo, prov. Connaught.

COVE, a fmall village in co. Cork, prov. Munfter, fit. in an ifland called the *Great ifland* which

which forms one side of Cork harbour; it is about 7 miles distant from Cork city. This village is built under a high steep hill; opposite to which the largest vessels trading to Cork, generally anchor; upwards of 200 sail have been moored here often; with sufficient room for twice as many in the bay. Cove is inhabited by fishermen and a few custom-house officers; on the island are some good houses and a decent parish church. This place is a post town, and usually called the *Cove of Cork*. Near Cove are two islands called *Spike* and *Hawlebowlis*; on the latter are the remains of an old fortification, built about the end of Queen Eliz.'s reign, and which commanded all vessels of burden passing up to Cork,

COVIA-MOUNT, sit. in bar. St. Mullins, co. Carlow, prov. Leinster.

Cow and CALF, *rocks* sit. by the entrance of Dundrum bay, in bar. Lecale, co. Down, prov. Ulster. Lat. 51 : 26, lon. 10 : 22.

COYNE-BRIDGE, see *Coil bridge*.

CRAGANE-CASTLE, sit. about 3 miles from Kilmallock, co. Limerick, prov. Munster.

CRAGHWELL *bridge*, sit. in bar. Dunkellin, co. Galway, prov. Connaught, 94 miles from Dublin. It is otherwise written *Cragwell bridge*.

CRAIGAVADE, sit. in co. Down, prov. Ulster.

CRAIGBALLY, a fair town in co. Antrim, prov. Ulster. Fairs held 26 June and 21 Aug.

CRAIGTOWN, sit. in co. Tyrone, prov. Ulster; near 114 miles from Dublin, near which is the place called *Solomon's porch*, it was formerly a very fine cave, but the rock being limestone, is quarried down, and the cave greatly damaged.

CRANFIELD, a rectory in dioc. of Connor, sit. in bar. Toome, co. Antrim, prov. Ulster.

CRANFIELD-POINT, sit. Eastward of Carlingford bay, in bar. Mourne, co. Down, prov. Ulster.

CRANNA, a village in bar. Clonmorris, co. Mayo, prov. Connaught.

CRANNAGH, a bar. in co. Kilkenny, prov. Leinster.

CRANNY-BRIDGE, sit. in bar. Clanderlaw, co. Clare, prov. Munster.

CRATELAGH, or *Cratelow*, a fair town in bar. Bunratty, co. Clare, prov. Munster. Fairs held 5 July.

CRAWFORDSBOURN, a village in bar. Castlereagh, co. Down, prov. Ulster.

CRAYFORD, sit. near Bangor, co. Down, prov. Ulster.

CREAGH, a rectory in dioc. of Ross, sit. in bar. Carbury, co. Cork, prov. Munster.—Also a rectory in dioc. of Clonfert, sit. in bar. Moycarne, co. Roscommon, prov Connaught.—Also a rectory in dioc. of Dublin, sit. in bar. Newcastle, co. Dublin, prov. Leinster.

CRECORAH, a vicarage in dioc. of Limerick, sit. in bar. Poblebrien, co. Limerick, prov. Munster.

CREDAN-HEAD, a *cape* sit. about a league from the entrance into *Waterford harbour*, in bar. Gualtiere, co. Waterford, prov. Munster; it is pretty high, and runs elbowing out from the W. side of the harbour about a mile, forming a small bay on its S. side, which takes its name from the head. This bay is a good road in Northerly winds, and great freshes of the river, and in it, near the land, there are from 20 to 30 feet water; tho' the author of the *Atlas Maritimus* places a shoal here, where there is no such thing.

CREEK'STOWN, a rectory in dioc. of Meath, sit. in bar. Ratoath, co. Meath, prov. Leinster, 13 miles from Dublin; the church of which is in ruins.

CREELY, sit. in co. Tyrone, prov. Ulster, 108 miles from Dublin.

CREEPING-MOUNTAIN, a name given to *Slieve Snavan*, in co. Down, prov. Ulster.

CREEVE, sit. in bar. Kilmacrenan, co. Donegal, prov. Ulster.—Also a vicarage in dioc. of Elphin, sit. in bar. Boyle, co. Roscommon, prov. Connaught.

CREEVE-ROCKS, sit. within ¼ mile of *Newry*, in co. Down, prov. Ulster, where are the remains of an old chapel whose name is lost. On these rocks is found in great plenty, a mineral body, deserving the attention of the metallurgist; it is a compound metallick stone, which has somewhat the appearance of a spar, with a brownish matter, and certain small black shining bodies cemented together, and is very ponderous; it made no ebullition with acids crude or calcined; tho' in both states powdered, rubbed and mixed with syrup of violets, it acquired a greenness; upon calcination, the brownish coloured matter becomes reddish, and is strongly attracted by the *load-stone*, and the sparlike matter continues its whitish colour, but the dark shining bodies become of the colour of gold, and are divisible into very minute parts, by rubbing between the fingers; but on their being digested severally by *aquafortis*, and spirit of *sal armoniac*, and giving a blue tincture to this last, and a deep green one to the other, it is evident here is *copper* as well as *iron*.

CREEVLEA, sit. near Dromahaire, co. Leitrim, prov. Connaught; it is seated on the river *Boonid*, which falls into *Lough Gille*. A house was founded here for Franciscans of the strict observance, by *Margaret* daughter of lord *O'Brien* in 1508; she was wife to *Eugene*, lord *O'Rourke*, and was interred here, having died in 1512. This building however was never compleated; the walls of the abbey are still entire, and the altar is nearly so: there are
several

feveral curious figures inferted in the walls, and over fome graves of the *Murroghs,* the *Cornins* (a very antient family) the *O'Roirks,* &c. The great *O'Roirk* lies at full length on a tomb over the burial ground of his family. This building, tho' of the fame extent with the abbey of Sligo, is thought to be rather inferior in the execution.

CREGAN, a fair town in King's co. prov. Leinfter ; fair days 1 Apr. and 12 Dec.

CREG-CASTLE, fit. 3 miles from *Cahirmorris,* in co. Galway, prov. Connaught ; this is the *laft* caftle that was built in that co. having been erected by one of the anceftors of *Rich. Kerwan,* efq ; in 1648, who in *Cromwell's* time received the thanks of general *Ireton,* and a permiffion under his hand and feal, to carry arms, in confequence of the protection he afforded the Proteftants, during the rebellion of 1641.

CREGGAN, a rectory in dioc. of Armagh, fit. in bar. Fews, co. Armagh, prov. Ulfter. Here is a charter-fchool which was opened in 1737 for 30 children, and is endowed with 3 acres of land in perpetuity ; one by the late Rev. *Hugh Hill,* D. D. when incumbent of the parifh, who alfo fubfcribed 5*l.* annually ; another by *Francis Hall, efq,* and the third by the late *Thom. Ball, efq.*

CREGGS, a fair town in co. Galway, prov. Connaught ; fairs held 12 May, June, Aug. and 19 Dec.

CREHELP or *Crehelp,* fit. in bar. Talbot's-town, co. Wicklow, prov. Leinfter. It is a curacy in dioc. of Dublin.

CREMORGAN, a rectory in dioc. of Leighlin, fit. in bar. Cullinagh, Queen's co. prov. Leinfter ; Dr. Beaufort's *memoir* places it by miftake in co. *Wicklow.*

CREMOURNE, a bar. in co. Monaghan, prov. Ulfter.

CREVAGHBANE, fit. in co. Galway, prov. Connaught ; a friary for Carmelites was here erected by the earl of *Clanrickarde* in the 14th century.

CREVAGHMORE, fit. in bar. Shroole, co. Longford, prov. Leinfter.

CREVENIS, fit. in bar. Lurge, co. Fermanagh, prov. Ulfter.

CREWSTOWN, fit. in bar. Kells, co. Meath, prov. Leinfter.

CROAGH, fit. in bar. Connello, co. Limerick, prov. Munfter ; this was formerly a corporation town, where we find a very large church, which is faid to have been in former ages collegiate ; 'tis a rectory in dioc. of Limerick.

CROAGH-DURGESS, a fair town in co. Limerick, prov. Munfter ; fairs held 1 Mar. May, 3 Aug. and 1 Nov.

CROAGH-PATRICK, an high mountain in the bar. Morifk, co. Mayo, prov. Connaught ; from whence (as tradition fays) St. Patrick drove all venemous creatures, fuch as ferpents, &c. into the fea. Its antient name was *Cruachan Achuil,* or mount Eagle : it obtained its prefent name of *Croagh-Patrick,* from St. *Patrick's* fafting here during lent, in imitation of *Jefus Chrift.* This mountain may be feen at 60 miles diftance, and has the form of a fugar loaf, and an altar or Cairn ftands on its fummit. It is a place of pilgrimage, and has been much frequented by thofe of the Roman Catholic perfuafion. From *Croagh-Patrick* there runs a continued chain of lofty mountains between the Atlantic ocean and the Loughs, Curra, Mafk, and Corrib, to Galway bay. This is efteemed the higheft mountain in Ireland, and rifes 2,666 feet above the level of the fea.

CROAN, fit. in bar. Boyle, co. Rofcommon, prov. Connaught.—Alfo a place fit. near *Kilkenny,* prov. Leinfter.

CROBANE, the name of a feat 2 miles E. of *Newry,* in co. Down, prov. Ulfter.

CROFTY-HILL, fit. near Drogheda, about 21¼ miles from Dublin, in co. Dublin, prov. Leinfter.

CROGHAN, a fair town in bar. Boyle, co. Rofcommon, prov. Connaught ; fairs held Wednef. after Trin. Sund. and 28 Oct. This was a royal refidence, and the antient capital of that prov. It was anciently denominated *Atha, Cromchin, Drum-Druid,* and *Rath-Crayhan.* It is fit. near *Elphin.* The Irifh annals mention a *rath* or fort being erected here by *Eochy Feylogh,* in the time of *Auguftus Cæfar.* It took the name *Croghan* from its fit. near a hill, and *Cromchin* in confequence of a facred Druidic cave in the adjacent mountain dedicated to *fate* or *providence,* which in old Irifh was called *Crom.* The only remains of this famous antient city, where one *Cathmor* the friend of ftrangers exercifed his unbounded hofpitality, are the celebrated rath already mentioned, the *Naafteaghan* where the ftates of Connaught affembled, and the facred cave. Near *Croghan* ftands *Relig-na-Riagh,* or the refting place of the kings of *Commacne Cuilt Ola.* It confifts of a circular area of about 200 feet in diameter, furrounded with a ftone ditch greatly defaced. Several tranfverfe ditches are within the area ; alfo heaps of coarfe ftones piled upon each other, fpecifying the graves of the interred perfons. From the conftruction of this cemetary, it appears to have been erected in the latter ages of Paganifm, about the clofe of the firft century. *Dathias* the laft of the heathen kings, having died abroad, his corps was carried to this place from the foot of the *Alps,* in the year 429.—Alfo a rectory in dioc. of Kildare, fit. in bar. Philipftown, King's co. prov. Leinfter. — Likewife the name of a river, fit. in co. Cavan, prov. Ulfter.

CROGHAN-BOO, sit. in bar. Decies without Drum, co. Waterford, prov. Munster.

CROGHAN-HILL, sit. near *Tubberduly*, in bar. Philipstown, King's co. prov. Leinster: it is said there are some rich mines about this place.

CROHANE, a rectory in dioc. of Cashel, sit. in bar. Slewardagh, co. Tipperary, prov. Munster.

CROKANE *mountains*, sit. in bar. Decies without Drum, co. Waterford, prov. Munster.

CROM, an antient district in co. Kildare and part of the co. Dublin, prov. Leinster: being sit. in the bend of the river Liffey, from whence it was called *Ibh crom abh*, or the district on the crooked water, and the hereditary chiefs were denominated *Crom-abh-ibh*, corruptly written *Crom a bhoe*. In the early ages this district extended over the greater part of Hy Allain, and after the arrival of the English, fell to the share of *Hugh de Lacey* and *Gilbert de Borard*; but some time after came into the possession of the noble family of the *Fitzgeralds*, in whose hands it still remains. This family on obtaining the above property, obtained among the native inhabitants the original title of *Crom a bhoe*, or chiefs of the district on the crooked water; a title still retained as a motto to their arms, and in former ages was the *war-cry* of the sept, according to the custom of the old Irish clans. Hence the Irish Stat. 10 Hen. 7 ch. 22, recites and enacts as follows, viz.— " Forasmuch as there hath been great variances, malices, debates and comparisons, between divers lords and gentlemen of this land, which hath dayly increased, by seditious means of diverse false and illdisposed persons, utterly taking upon them to be servants to such lords and gentlemen, for that they would be borne in their said idleness, and their own unlawful demeaning, and nothing for any favour or entire good love and will that they bare unto such lords and gentlemen, *Therefore*, be it enacted, &c. that no person or persons, of whatsoever estate, condition or degree, he or they be of, take part with any lord or gentleman, or uphold any such variances or comparisons in word or deed; as in using these words, " *Cromabo, Butterabo*," or other words like, or otherwise contrary to the king's laws, his crown, dignity and peace, &c."

CROMARTIN, sit. near *Ardee*, prov. Leinster.

CROM-CASTLE, sit. about 14 miles W. of Limerick, prov. Munster; 'twas founded by the *O'Donovans*, but is said to have been for many years the residence of the *Fitzgeralds*.

CROMLA, or *Crommal*, a mountain or hill, sit. between Lough Foyle and Lough Swilly, in co. Donegal, prov. Ulster. From the Eastern side of this mountain proceeded the river Labur, called by the Irish *Bredagh*; and from the Western side proceeded the *Lavath*, near the source of which, on the declivity of the mountain, was the cave of *Cluna*, where resided *Ferad Artho*, and the bard *Condan*, after the murder of *Cormac Mac Art*, his nephew. In the neighbourhood of *Cromla*, stood the rath or fortress of *Tura*, called by the Irish writers *Ailich Neid*, celebrated by all the antient Irish histories, as the principal residence of the Northern kings of Ulster.

CROMLA SLIABH, the antient name of the present *Hill of Allen*, in co. Kildare, prov. Leinster.

CROMLIN, or *Crumlin*, i. e. the temple of *Crom*, where the Heathen Irish sacrificed to that Deity. A village in co. Dublin, prov. Leinster; near 3 miles from the metropolis, and almost the same distance from Tallagh; sit. in bar. Newcastle, co. Dublin, prov. Leinster. It is a curacy in dioc. of Dublin. It is pleasantly sit. in a very wholesome air, but is not nearly so much frequented by the citizens of Dublin, as it used to be. The church is a very old building. Tradition says, part of king William 3d's forces were encamped hereabout in 1690. This place is still a great thorough-fare, as it lies on the high road to Blessington, Baltinglass, &c. Here is a large extent of waste ground, called the *Commons of Crumlin*, on which horse races were formerly frequent. *Cromlin* was one of the 4 antient manors in this co. annexed to the crown; of which *Hollinshed* in his Chron. tells us, " *the* " *manor of Crumlin paieth a greater chief rent to the* " *prince, than any of the other three, which proceedeth* " *of this. The Seneschall being offended with the* " *tenants for their misdemeanor, took them up very* " *sharplie in the court, and with rough and mina-* " *torie speeches, began to menace them. The lobbish* " *and desperate clobberiousnesse, taking the matter* " *in dudgeon, made no more words, but knocke* " *their seneschal on the costard, and left him there* " *spralling on the ground for dead. For which* " *detestable murther, their rent was inhansed, and* " *they paie at this daie nine pence per acre, which* " *is double to any of the other three manors.*" The three other manors he mentions were, *Newcastell, Massagard* and *Eschire*.—*Crumlin* is also the name of a village, sit. in bar. Massareene, co. Antrim, prov. Ulster; 78 miles from Dublin; it holds fairs 23 July and 20 Nov. Near this place is a large flour mill.—Also the name of a parish in co. Down, prov. Ulster.

CROMOGE, sit. in bar. Maryborough, Queen's co. prov. Leinster.

CROMWELL'S FORT, sit. in Valentia Isle, off the bar. of Iveragh, co. Kerry, prov. Munster.

CRONAGH RIVER, sit. in bar. Athlone, co. Roscommon, prov. Connaught.

CRONEBANE, fit. near *Arklow*, in bar. Arklow, co. Wicklow, prov. Leinfter. This is an hill of 2 miles in circumference, and about 1000 feet in heigth. It is on all fides full of rich mines, the principal of which lie on the E. fide, about half-way up the hill, where are feveral fhafts funk from 50 to 70 fathoms deep. In finking thefe fhafts, the firft mineral met with, is an *iron ftone*; beneath this they arrive at a *lead ore*, which feems mixed with clay, yet yields a large quantity of lead and fome filver. Underneath this, lies a rich rocky filver ore, which fparkles brightly, and yields 75 ounces of pure filver out of one ton of ore, befides a great quantity of fine lead. Having pierced fome fathoms thro' this, they arrive at the *copper ore*, which is very rich and may be purfued to a great depth. In order to carry off the water from the mines, there are levels conducted a great way under ground to the lower part of the hill; out of thefe levels iffue large ftreams of water, moft ftrongly impregnated with copper.

CRONELUSK, fit. in bar. Arklow, co. Wicklow, prov. Leinfter.

CRON-ROW, a fair town in co. Wicklow, prov. Leinfter; fairs held 12 May and 2 Oct.

CROOBY-MOUNT, fit. in bar. upper Iveagh, co. Down, prov. Ulfter.

CROOK, fit. in bar. Gualtiere, co. Waterford, prov. Munfter, 4 miles E. of the city of Waterford; it is a rectory in dioc. of Waterford. Here is a ruined caftle, which belonged to the knts. of St. John of Jerufalem; and was erected in the 13th century, by the baron of *Curraghmore*.

CROOK-HAVEN, fit. 2 leagues N. W. from *Cape-clear*, in bar. Carbery, co. Cork, prov. Munfter. A fhip bound in there from the E. muft run in along by *Cape-clear*, fo far to the N. as you may fee the ocean through, between the cape and the main, as thro' a hole, and then fteer W. N. W. keeping the faid hole to the N. of *Cape-clear* open; then you fhall fall in right with *Crook-haven*, which lies W. S. W. and there you may anchor before the town, in 18 or 20 fathom water; it was formerly deeper, but has been filled up with ballaft; further out, there is deeper water and clean anchoring ground. Lat. 51 : 19, lon. 9 : 55.

CROOK's-TOWN, a fair town in co. Cork, prov. Munfter; fair days 14 May, 26 Aug. and 17 Nov. On the W. fide of the road from *Crook's-town* to *Bandon*, is a large ftone monument, of great length and breadth. Tradition fays it was erected to the memory of one of the *Nial's*, who is faid to have been flain in battle near this place.

CROO... a village in bar. Cofhma, co. Limerick, ... Munfter; it is a vicarage in dioc. of ...

CROSBIE-PARK, a highly improved farm, in co. Wicklow, prov. Leinfter, where is the feat of fir *Edw. Crofbie*, bart.

CROSS, a fair town in co. *Armagh*, prov. Ulfter. Fair days 30 May, 5 Aug. 4 Sept. and 27 Dec. — Alfo a fair town in co. *Cavan*, prov. Ulfter. Fairs held 17 Mar. — Alfo a village in bar. Tyrekerin, co. Londonderry, prov. Ulfter. Likewife a place in the *Muller*, (a peninfula, in bar. Erris, co. Mayo, prov. Connaught,) and oppofite Ennis Glory Ifland: in which we find the religious houfe of the *Holy crofs*, dedicated to the Virgin Mary, the ruins of which ftill remains.

CROSS-A-KEEL, a fair town in co. Meath, prov. Leinfter; above 54 miles from Dublin. Fairs held 9 May, 16 Aug. and 15 Dec.

CROSSBOYNE, fit. in bar. Clonmorris, co. Mayo, prov. Connaught; it is a rectory in dioc. of Tuam.

CROSSDONY, a fair town in bar. Clonmoghan, co. Cavan, prov. Ulfter; 56 miles from Dublin. Fair days 5 Apr. 27 May, 26 Aug. and 17 Nov.

CROSSDRUM, fit. near *Oldcaftle*, prov. Leinfter.

CROSSERLOGH, a vicarage in dioc. of Kilmore, fit. in bar. Clonmoghan, co. Cavan, prov. Ulfter.

CROSS-FERRY, fit. in co. Londonderry, prov. Ulfter; above 119 miles from Dublin.

CROSS-HAVEN, fit. in bar. Kinalea, co. Cork, prov. Munfter; it is a fafe creek, lieing on the W. fide after you enter Cork harbour, where a veffel may go in to ftop a tide occafionally; and here alfo you are land locked, and free from all winds. Sir *Francis Drake*, in 1559, having a fmall fquadron of five fhips of war, was chafed into Cork harbour, by a fuperior fleet of *Spaniards*, he run into *Crofs-haven*, and moored his fhips behind the fhelter of *Corribinyhill*, in a fafe bafon; the Spaniards failed up the harbour of Cork, and were furprifed not to fee the fhips they had juft before chafed into it. Thus having miffed their prey, they came out again without doing fir Francis the leaft harm.

CROSS-ISLAND, one of the *Copland-Ifles* fo called; fit. in the bay of Carrickfergus, near the coaft of the co. Down, prov. Ulfter; it contains about 30 acres; and on it ftands a light-houfe, (for which it is called by fome *Light-houfe Ifland*) built of lime-ftone, which the Ifland affords in abundance. It is of a fquare form, 70 feet high to the lanthorn, and the walls of it 7 feet thick. It confifts of 3 ftories, of which the lower and fecond are laid with beams, and boarded; but the third is arched and covered with large flag ftones 7 or 8 feet in length. In the middle of the houfe is erected a round tower, on which the grate is

fixed

fixed on a thick iron spindle. *Scotland* supplies it with coals, of which in a windy night it consumes a ton and a half, burning from evening to day-light, both winter and summer. It sheds its light to the S. E. to save ships from the N. and S. rocks, (about 3 leagues and half distance from it) and to the N. and W. to warn ships from the danger of the *Whillans* (rocks so called) that lie between the mouths of *Larne* and *Glenarm* bays, and are also called the *Maidens*, about 4 or 5 leagues distant from it. The light is plainly seen at *Port-patrick*, and the Mull of *Galloway*, which last place stands near 10 leagues distant from it.

CROSS-KEYS, sit. in co. *Kildare*, prov. Leinster; about 10 miles from Dublin, a mile beyond which, is Bishop's-court, a handsome seat, near which on the summit of the hill, stand the church and tower of *Oughterard*. There is also another place of same name in co. *Meath*, prov. Leinster; 37 miles from Dublin, within a mile of which, are good flour-mills.

CROSSMAGLIN, a village in bar. Fews, co. Armagh, prov. Ulster. Here is a *lake* also of same name. This place is otherwise written *Crossmeglan*.

CROSSMALINA, a rectory in dioc. of Killala, sit. in bar. Tirawly, co. Mayo, prov. Connaught; it is otherwise called *Crossmolyna* and *Crossmaling*: and has fairs 23 May, 12 Sept. and 17 Dec. Distance from Dublin about 134 miles. Here was an abbey dedicated to the Virgin Mary.

CROSSMALING, see *Crossmalina*.

CROSSMEGLAN-LOUGH, sit. in bar. Fews, co. Armagh, prov. Ulster, otherwise called *Crossmaglin-lough*.

CROSSMOLYNA, see *Crossmalina*.

CROSSPATRICK, a rectory in dioc. of Ferns, sit. in bar. Gorey, co. Wexford, prov. Leinster.

CROSS-ROADS, there are several places distinguished in the kingdom by this appellation, such as in co. *Carlow*, prov. Leinster; 54 miles from Dublin. In co. *Cavan*, prov. Ulster; 50 miles from Dublin.—The like in co. Cavan, near *Florence-court*.—The like in co. *Monaghan*, above 66 miles from Dublin;—and another in co. *Down*, prov. Ulster; 84 miles from Dublin.

CROSS-TOWN, a fair town in co. Wexford, prov. Leinster; having fairs on 12 May.

CROTTINTEGALL, sit. in bar. Slewmargy, Queen's co. prov. Leinster.

CROTTO, a seat in co. Kerry, prov. Munster; distant 138 miles from Dublin; a mile from which, is *Kilflin* church; between this seat and *Ardfert*, are the venerable ruins of the antient abbey of *Odorney*.

CROUGHNAMALLIN *mountains*, sit. in bar. Tirawly, co. Mayo, prov. Connaught.

CAOUTEN's-TOWN, sit. near the Curragh of Kildare, in co. Kildare, prov. Leinster. Here is a church belonging to it.

CROW-HEAD, a *cape* in bar. Bear and Bantry, co. Cork, prov. Munster.

CROWN-BRIDGE, sit. in co. Down, prov. Ulster, 1 mile E. of *Newry*; it is so called from a Danish rath, seated in the neighbourhood, which bears some resemblance to a crown. It is erected on the top of a hill of easy ascent, and surrounded by meadows, thro' which a river gently glides in two channels, forming an island, in which the *rath* or hill is sit. it is of a flat unequal form at top, being 63 feet one way, and only 27 another: surrounded by a deep fosse, 27 feet broad, out of which the rath has been thrown up; the compass of it, taken at the bottom of the fosse, is about 579 feet, and the conical height, near 110 feet; on the W. side of the rath, and separated from it only by the surrounding fosse, is a square artificial platform, taking up about 130 feet on each side, and hollowed in the middle, being of near 30 feet conical height at a medium, so that the rath overlooks it, and has a fosse encompassing it, about 15 feet broad; this platform (if we may credit tradition) was erected as an area, where two royal competitors in single combat, decided the possession of a crown; and the rath was raised to perpetuate the memory of the action. Southward of the mount on a little hill, at the N. end of a small lake called *Derike-lagh*, are the ruins of the chapel of *Temple Gaurin*, which in Irish signifies *Goat's church*.

CRUANACARRA, an *Island*, sit. by the coast of bar. Ballinahinch, co. Galway, prov. Connaught.

CRUCKFALLA *mountain*, sit. in bar. Kilmacrenan, co. Donegal, prov. Ulster.

CRUISETOWN, a rectory in dioc. of Meath, sit. in bar. Kells, co. Meath, prov. Leinster. Dr. *Beaufort.*—A village sit. in bar. Ferrard, co. Louth, prov. Leinster. *Scale.*

CRUIT-ISLAND, sit. off the bar. Boylagh, co. Donegal, prov. Ulster.

CRUMARAD *mountains*, sit. in bar. Boylagh, co. Donegal, prov. Ulster.

CRUM-CASTLE, the seat and handsome improvements of lord visc. *Erne*, sit. by the side of *Lough Erne*, in co. Fermanagh, prov. Ulster. Lat. 54:20, lon. 7:56.

CRUMLIN, see *Cromlin*.

CRUMLIN-WATER, a river in bar. Massareene, co. Antrim, prov. Ulster.

CRUMP-HALL, sit. in bar. Colerain, co. Londonderry, prov. Ulster.

CRUMP-ISLAND, sit. off the bar. Middlethird, co. Tipperary, prov. Munster.

CRUMP'STOWN, a rectory in dioc. of Cashel, sit. in bar. Middlethird, co. Tipperary, prov. Munster.

CRUSHEEN, sit. in bar. Bunratty, co. Clare, prov. Munster, near 106 miles from Dublin, a mile beyond which are the ruins of a castle, near the side of a lough which nearly surrounds them.

CRUSRATH, sit. near *Drogheda*, prov. Leinst.

CRYCRIM, a curacy in dioc. of Leighlin, sit. in bar. Ravilly, co. Carlow, prov. Leinster.

CUALGNEY, probably the town of *Dunleer*, in co. Louth, prov. Leinster.

CUCKOLDS-HILL, sit. in bar. O'Neiland, co. Armagh, prov. Ulster.

CULDAFF, a rectory in dioc. of Derry, sit. in bar. Inishowen, co. Donegal, prov. Ulster.

CULFAGHTRIN, a village in bar. Cary, co. Antrim, prov. Ulster; it is a vicarage in dioc. of Connor.

CULLEN, a fair town in co. Tipperary, prov. Munster; it holds fairs on 28 Oct. At the bog near this place was found a golden crown, weighing 6 ounces; many other antient curiosities have been discovered in it, particularly some gorgets of gold, and gold handled swords; for which reason it goes by the name of the *Golden bog.*—*Cullen* is also the name of a tower on the N. W. side of *Buttevant abbey*, in co. Cork, prov. Munster; it is now in ruins, and said to have been built by an earl of Desmond who retired here.—Also a rectory in dioc. of Cork, sit. in bar. Kinalea, co. Cork;—and another in dioc. of Ardfert, sit. in bar. Duhallow, in same co. both in prov. Munster.—Also a village in bar. Coonagh, co. Limerick, prov. Munster, which is a rectory in dioc. of Emly.—Also a place in bar. Ferrard, co. Louth, prov. Leinster;—and another in bar. Tyrhugh, co. Donegal, prov. Ulster; which gives title of visc. to the family of *Cockayne*.

CULLENAGH, sit. in bar. Decies without Drum, co. Waterford, prov. Munster.

CULLENBEGG, sit. in bar. Ferrard, co. Louth, prov. Leinster.

CULLEN'STOWN, sit. in bar. Bargie, co. Wexford, prov. Leinster.

CULLENWAINE, a rectory in dioc. of Killaloe, sit. in bar. Clonlisk, King's co. prov. Leinster. It is a fair town, fairs being held 20 Aug. and 11 Nov.

CULLEN's WOOD, sit. near the road to Miltown, in the suburbs of Dublin, co. Dublin, prov. Leinster; memorable for a slaughter of about 500 citizens, (being a colony from *Bristol*) who were here put to death by the Irish, as they assembled to divert themselves on *Easter monday* in 1209, whence that day was afterwards called *Black monday*.

CULLIHILL, a fair town in Queen's co. prov. Leinster; fair days 27 May, and 2 Oct.

CULLINAGH or *Cullenagh*, a bar. having a village in it of same name, sit. in Queen's co. prov. Leinster; the latter holds fairs on 8 May, and 18 Dec.

CULLINMORE, sit. in bar. Moyashill, co. Westmeath, prov. Leinster.

CULLINSTOWN, a curacy in dioc. of Meath, sit. in bar. Skryne, co. Meath, prov. Leinster.

CULLIVORE, a fair town in co. Longford, prov. Leinster; fairs held 24 June and 21 Sept.

CULLOVILLE, sit. in bar. Fews, co. Armagh, prov. Ulster, 49 miles from Dublin; about ¼ mile beyond which is *Ardkirk*, a seat of lord *Weymouth*.

CULLY, sit. in bar. Iverk, co. Kilkenny, prov. Leinster.

CULLYBACKY, a village in bar. Toome, co. Antrim, prov. Ulster.

CULLYHILL, sit. in bar. Ossory, Queen's co. prov. Leinster.

CULLYMORE, sit. in bar. Ballycowen, King's co. prov. Leinster.

CULMORE, a *fort* sit. at the bottom of the bay of *Loughfoile*, co. Londonderry, prov. Ulster; about 4 miles N. of that city.

CULMULLIN, a fair town in co. Meath, prov. Leinster; fairs held 21 Nov.

CULTRA, sit. in co. Down, prov. Ulster.

CUMBER, see *Comber*.

CUMEEN, sit. in bar. Clanfrought, co. Kerry, prov. Munster.

CUNY-ISLAND, sit. off the coast of bar. Carbury, co. Sligo, prov. Connaught.

CUOLAGH-BAY, sit. in bar. Bear and Bantry, co. Cork, prov. Munster.

CUOLAN or *Criocheuolan*, that narrow plain in co. Wicklow, prov. Leinster, contained between the mountains and the sea; the people of which were the *Evoleni* of Probus, the *Menapii* of Ptolemy. This country was under the dominion of the *Mac Mhthuils* or *O'Tools*, and has been sometimes confounded by antiquaries with *Coalan* or *Caëlan*, both countrys having been frequently governed by the same chief, that is, either the *O'Tools* or *Mac Kellys*, which probably occasioned the error.

CURAGHBRACK, sit. in bar. Omagh, co. Tyrone, prov. Ulster.

CURLAGH, sit. in bar. Ballimoe, co. Galway, prov. Connaught.

CURLEW *mountains*, sit. in co. Sligo and Roscommon, prov. Connaught.

CURRABANE, sit. near *Tuam*, prov. Connaught.

CURRAGH (of *Kildare*,) sit. in bar. Ophaly, co. Kildare, prov. Leinster, about 30 miles from Dublin; it is the race-ground of Kildare,

where

where all great matches are run ; it is the *New-market* of Ireland, and fportfmen fay that the turf is equal to any in England, and exceeds that at *Newmarket* in circumference. It is a fine fod for the diverfions, and if it has any fault, it is its evennefs. It is a moft delightful fpacious common and fheep-walk, and the land extremely good ; but this plain is gradually narrowing, by a few enclofures now and then creeping forward. Government gives annually two plates of 100*l*. each, to be run for. Thefe were originally granted upon the fuggeftion of *Sir William Temple*, who among other fchemes, for the improvement of Ireland, recommended this, with a view of improving the breed of Irifh horfes. As this fpot was remarkable for horfe-racing, long before king's plates were eftablifhed here, it is natural to fuppofe, that it took its name from its being a horfe-courfe, and that it was called *Curragh*, from the latin word *Curro*, to run. Races begin here on the laft week in Apr. 2 Mond. in June and Sept.

CURRAGHA, fit. in co. Meath, prov. Leinfter, near 14 miles from Dublin.

CURRAGHBEGLAND, a fair town in co. Cork, prov. Munfter ; having fairs on 17 Mar. Whit. Mond. 24 Aug. and 20 Dec.

CURRAGHMORE, fit. in co. Waterford, prov. Munfter, in the parifh of *Clonegam*, about 8 miles W. of Waterford, and 4 miles S. E. of Carrick, near a fmall river called *Clodagh*, which falls in the *Suir*, about 3 miles E. of this place. Here is the feat of lord *Tyrone*; the houfe ftands where an antient caftle belonging to the family was built, a part of which ftill remains ; the prefent houfe was erected, A. D. 1700. Sir *Richard le Poer* was created baron *le Poer* and *Curraghmore*, on 13 Sept. 1535, whofe defcendant *Richard le Poer*, was created vifc. *Decies*, and earl of *Tyrone*, 9 Oct. 1673. He was fucceeded by his fon John, who dying without iffue, in 1693, the honours of the family devolved on his brother James, by whofe death, on 19 Aug. 1704, without iffue male, they ceafed, and his only daughter, the lady *Catherine Poer*, being married to fir *Marcus Berefford*, bart. he was created vifc. Tyrone, by king George I. from whom is defcended the prefent *earl*. *Curraghmore* is 84 miles from Dublin.

CURRAGHROE *mountains*, fit. in bar. Omagh, co. Tyrone, prov. Ulfter.

CURRAHA, a village, fit. in bar. Ratoath, co. Meath, prov. Leinfter.

CURRAN, a fair town in bar. Loughlinfholen, co. Londonderry, prov. Ulfter ; fairs held 23 June and 22 Nov.

CURRAN-LOUGH, fit. in bar. Iveragh, co. Kerry, prov. Munfter.

CURRAN-ROE BRIDGE, a village in bar. Kiltartan, co. Galway, prov. Connaught.

CURRANS, a parifh and fair town in co. Kerry, prov. Munfter ; fairs held 6 May, 21 Aug. and 29 Oct. It is a rectory in dioc. of Ardfert. Here is a good feat, which ftands on a rifing ground, not far from the river *Mang*, 3 miles W. by S. from *Caftle Ifland*.

CURRAS-and-MAUN, a fair town in co. Cork, prov. Munfter; fair days 6 May, 16 July 14 Sept. and 5 Nov.

CURROHEEN, fit. near Cafhel, prov. Munft.

CURRYGLASS, a pleafant and well watered village in bar. Killnataloon, co. Cork, prov. Munfter, not far from *Knockmourne*. At this place is a fine *Cedar* tree, and the largeft *Holly* tree fuppofed in the kingdom.

CURRIKIPPANE, a village in liberties of Cork, co. Cork, prov. Munfter ; it is a rectory in dioc. of Cork.

CUSHEENY *river*, fit. in bar. Ophaly, co. Kildare, prov. Leinfter.

CUSHENDON-BAY, fit. in bar. Glenarm, co. Antrim, prov. Ulfter.

CUSHENDON *river*, fit. in bar. Glenarm, co. Antrim, prov. Ulfter.

CUSHER *river*, fit. in co. Down, prov. Ulfter, and falls into the Canal a little Northward of *Knockbridge*.

CUSHINA, fit. near *Portarlington*, co. Kildare, prov. Leinfter. Hereabout the foil is partly a light fand and partly bog. There is a high fandy hill here called *Cufhina-hill*.

CUSHINSTOWN, fit. in bar. Kilmane, co. Mayo, prov. Connaught.

D A

DAIBRE, called alfo *Iveragh*, the prefent bar. of *Iveragh*, co. Kerry, prov. Munft.

DAIRCALGATE, an antient diftrict comprehending the prefent town and co. of Londonderry, and part of Donegal, being feated on both fides of Lough Foyle, prov. Ulfter. It was the *Darnii* of Ptolemy, the antient chieftains of which were called *Hy Daherteagh*, by corruption *O'Dogherty* : they were difpoffeffed of the Southern part of their country, in an early period by the *O'Donalds* and *O'Connors*.

DAIRMACK, fee *Durrow*.

DALARADIA, or the diftrict of the E. country next the fea, an antient name for that diftrict, which comprehended the S. and S. E. parts of the co. Antrim, and all the co. Down, during the middle ages ; called alfo frequently *Magh Gemuifge*, or the diftrict of the bays, or heads of lakes ; having the bays of *Curlingford* and

Dundrum

Dundrum on the S. *Strangford* and *Carrickfergus* on the E. and Lough *Neagh* on the N. W. The perpetual chiefs of which were the *Mac Gennis*, fome of whom were in poffeffion of this country in the beginning of the laft century; but a branch of the *O'Neils* had taken poffeffion of the Northern parts of it in a very early period.

DALARIDA, now the *Ardes* or high lands in co. Down, prov. Ulfter, between the bay of *Strangford* and the fea; the antient chiefs of which were called *Magh Ardan*, by corruption *M'Artan*; they were difpoffeffed by the *Savages*; fome of them remained in poffeffion of the Weftern parts at the commencement of the laft century.

DALCAS, a diftrict which formerly contained the prefent co. Clare, prov. Munfter. A fon of *Olliol Olim*, about the beginning of the 3d. century, was elected chief of this diftrict, on which he took the name of *Cormac Cas*.

DALDICHU, an antient diftrict, fit. in the plain and peninfula between the bays of Dundrum and Strangford, co. Down, prov. Ulfter. The dynafts of this diftrict were called Daldichu or *Cathel*; it is remarkable from its chief Dichu, who was the firft convert St. Patrick made to the chriftian faith, in the N. of Ireland.

DALE, a *river* and *lake* in bar. Raphoe, co. Donegal, prov. Ulfter; the river is navigable by boats for a few miles from the river *Foyle* to the village of *Ballindrait*.

DALKEY, a fmall romantic village in co. Dublin, prov. Leinfter, about 7 miles from Dublin; it lies at the Northern bafe of a high mountain, commanding a beautiful view of the bay of Dublin. This village in the reign of Queen Eliz. and during a great part of the laft century, before the port of Dublin was improved, was the repofitory of the goods belonging to the merchants of Dublin. Here are the ruins of a few old caftles, places of defence againft the incurfions of the pirates, who at that period fwarmed on the Irifh coaft.

DALKEY-ISLAND, fit. near the village of Dalkey, off the coaft of the bar. of Half-Rathdown, co. Dublin, prov. Leinfter. It is fo called from *Dalki*, on account of the Pagan altar there. It is divided from the main land by a channel called the found of Dalkey, in which there is never lefs than 8 fathom water at the loweft tide, fhips of the greateft burthen may fafely lie at anchor perfectly fecure from the N. E. winds, unto which every other part of the bay is expofed. This *ifland* contains about 18 acres, having plenty of herbage and fome medicinal plants; the only building on it, is the ruin of an old church.

DALKEY-SOUND, fee *Dalkey ifland*.

DALMACHSCOER, a diftrict comprehending all the country on the Eaftern coaft of the co.'s Wicklow and Wexford, prov. Leinfter, between the mountains and the fea.

DALNARUIDHE, a diftrict containing the N. part of the co. Antrim, prov. Ulfter; the *Robogdij* of Ptolemy; it has been corruptly called *Dalriadia*, and fometimes *Ava*. During the latter ages it frequently went by the denomination of *Andruim* or *Eandruim*, i. e. the habitation on the waters; from whence the prefent name of *Antrim*: it was divided into feveral fubordinate divifions, whofe refpective chiefs were *Maghenillan*, *O'Hara*, *O'Donnal*, and *O'Sheil*, feveral of whom were in poffeffion of the country in the laft century. From this part feveral colonies tranfmigrated to Caledonia about the year 503; they were principally of the race of the Scots of *Hy Failgea*, who fettled in the Northern parts of this country, about the commencement of the 5th. century, under the conduct of *O'Neil the great*; in confequence of which they were denominated *Scots*, and have thereby communicated their name to the entire N. diftrict of Britain.

DALRIADIA, fee *Dalnaruidhe*.

DALUA *river*, fit. in co. Cork, prov. Munfter.

DALY'S-BRIDGE, fit. in bar. Clonmoghan, co. Cavan, prov. Ulfter, 46 miles from Dublin, about a mile from which is *Lough Sheaklin*, in which are fome fmall iflands, and the ruins of a caftle and a church. This lough is of confiderable magnitude, extending to *Finae*, where it communicates with Lough Inny.

DAMER'S COURT, a handfome feat of lord *Milton*, fit. in co. Tipperary, prov. Munfter.

DANESTOWN, a vicarage in dioc. of Meath, fit. in bar. Skryne, co. Meath, prov. Leinfter.

DANGAN, fit. in co. Meath, prov. Leinfter, here is the handfome feat of lord *Mornington*.

DANGANDARGAN, a rectory in dioc. of Cafhel, fit. in bar. Clanwilliam, co. Tipperary, prov. Munfter.

DANGIN, a feat near Lough Corib, in co. Galway, prov. Connaught: the fituation of which, with its contiguity to the lake, and the various beauties it unites, make it one of the moft delightful places of abode in the kingdom.

DANGON, a fair town in co. Cork, prov. Munfter; fairs held 5 Aug.

DANIEL'S-TOWN, a handfome feat in co. Cork, prov. Munfter, by the river *Awbeg*, near *Doneraile*.

DANYAN, a fair town in co. Rofcommon, prov. Connaught; fair days 25 May, 6 Aug. and Nov.

DARABONIS, a bay or river in the N. of Ireland, mentioned by *Rich. Cirenceft.* it is the prefent Lough Foyle in co. Donegal, prov. Ult.

DARDIS-

DARDIS-RATH, fit. in bar. Ferrard, co. Louth, prov. Leinfter.

DARDISTOWN BRIDGE, fit. over the river *Nanny*, in co. Meath, prov. Leinfter, 19 miles from Dublin.

DARGEL, or *Dargle*, a romantic fpot in co. Wicklow, prov. Leinfter. It is a narrow vale, formed by the fides of two oppofite mountains; the whole thickly fpread with oak at the bottom; it is narrowed to the mere channel of the river, which tumbles from rock to rock. The extent of wood that hangs to the eye in every direction is great, and the depth of the precipice immenfe, which with the roar of the water forms a fcene truly interefting. In lefs than a quarter of a mile, the road paffing through the wood, leads to another point of view to the right; it is the crown of a vaft projecting rock, from which you look down a precipice abfolutely perpendicular, and many hundred feet deep, upon the torrent, which finds its noify way over large fragments of rocks. The point of view is a great projection of the mountain on this fide, anfwered by a concave of the oppofite, fo that you command the *Glen*, both to the right and left; it exhibits immenfe tracts of foreft, that have a moft magnificent appearance. Beyond the wood to the right, are fome enclofures hanging on the fide of a hill, crowned by a mountain. The folemnity of fuch an extent of wood unbroken by any intervening objects, and the whole hanging over declivities, is alone great; but to this the addition of a conftant roar of falling water, either quite hid, or fo far below as to be feen but obfcurely, unite to make thofe impreffions ftronger. Many fimilar fcenes, pleafingly diverfified are to be met with here; awful, fublime, retired, gloomy; fpots fit for contemplation, and melancholy retreats.

DARIEN'S-BRIDGE, in co. Cavan, prov. Ulfter; 51 miles from Dublin.

DARINIS, otherwife called *Molana*, an Ifland at the mouth of the bay of Youghal, co. Cork, prov. Munfter. A monaftery was founded here by St. *Molanfid*, in the 6th century: in which was interr'd *Raymond le Grofs* the Englifh general, who contributed with *Strongbow* to the reduction of Ireland.—Alfo another ifland fit. near Wexford, co. Wexford, prov. Leinfter; where a monaftery was founded by St. *Nemamb*, about the middle of the 7th century.

DARTISHEN, fit. in bar. Ravilly, co. Carlow, prov. Leinfter.

DARTREE or *Dartry*, a bar. in co. Monaghan, prov. Ulfter.

DARTRY, fee *Dartree*.

DARVER, fit. in bar Louth, co. Louth, prov. Leinfter.

DAUGH-BRIDGE, fit. in bar. Antrim, co. Antrim, prov. Ulfter.

DAUGHTONS, fubterraneous caves fit. four miles N. W. of Enniikillen, co. Fermanagh, prov. Ulfter. They are the curious work of nature: the entrance is by a large arched cave 25 feet high; the roof is rock compofed of various pieces in regular order. This leads to another not quite fo high, and from that is continued by narrow paffages to a brook, which paffing thro' thefe unknown receffes, difcharges itfelf at the firft entrance.

DAUNCE-MOUNTAINS, thefe form the N. W. boundary of the bar. of *Carberry*, co. *Cork*, prov. Munfter, and run thro' the N. parts of *Bantry*, into Glanerought in Kerry. At the foot of one of thefe mountains called *Seefhy* is a lake ftored with a fpecies of red trout, which never rife at a fly.

DAVID'S-TOWN, fit. in bar. Narragh, co. Kildare, prov. Leinfter; it is a rectory in dioc. of Dublin.

DAVUGH-PHADRIG, fit. at *Bel-cou*, near Enniikillen, co. Fermanagh, prov. Ulfter; it is a celebrated well, and reputed the beft cold bath in the kingdom, having relieved numbers in paralytic and nervous diforders. It exhibits a large ftream, which turns two mills at 150 yards diftance from the head.

DAWNMOON, fit. in bar. Ballinahinch, co. Galway, prov. Connaught.

DAWSON'S-BRIDGE, fit. in bar. Loughlinfholen, co. Londonderry, prov. Ulfter, 90 miles from Dublin, near which is *Caftle Dawfon*, a handfome feat; it is a chapelry in dioc. of Derry.

DAWSON'S-COURT, the handfome feat of lord *Portarlington*, fit. near *Emo Inn*, Queen's co. prov. Leinfter.

DAWSON'S-GROVE, the feat of lord *Cremorne*, fit. in co. Monaghan, prov. Ulfter.

DAW'S-TOWN, a pretty feat, two miles from *Blarney*, co. Cork, prov. Munfter.

DEADMAN'S-BAY, fit. in bar. Moycullen, co. Galway, prov. Connaught.

DEALBHNA, the prefent bar. of *Delvin*, co. Weftmeath, prov. Leinfter. There were *feven* territories of this name in Ireland, viz. 1ft *Dealbhna Mor*, the country of the *O'Finlands*, afterwards the *Nugents*. 2d *Dealbhna Beg*, contiguous to the former; thefe two make the before mentioned bar. 3d *Dealbhna Eathra*, the bar. of Garrycaftle, King's co. prov. Leinfter; this was the country of the *Mc Coghlans*. 4th *Dealbhna Iarthar*, or O'Scoluigh's country, in the antient territory of Meath. 5th *Dealbhna Nuadhat*, the prefent bar.'s of Athlone and Moycarne, co. Rofcommon, prov. Connaught. 6th *Dealbhna de Cuilfebhair*, co. Galway, prov. Connaught. 7th *Dealbhna Feqdha*, the prefent

fent bar. of Moycullen, in the fame co. it was divided into two diftricts, viz. *Gno-more* and *Gno-beg*: the *O'Conrys* were chiefs of *Gno-beg*, until they were partly difpoffeffed and partly made tributaries by the *O'Flahertys*.

DEAN-RATH, fit. in bar. Ferrard, co. Louth, prov. Leinfter.

DEARING's-BRIDGE, fit. in bar. Clonmoghan, co. Cavan, prov. Ulfter.

DECIES, otherwife *Deaffies*, or Southern people, a territory containing the greater part of the co. of *Waterford*, prov. Munfter; it is at prefent divided into two bar.'s viz. *Decies* within, and *Decies* without Drum. The former is bounded on the S. and E. by the ocean, on the W. by the *Black-water*, and on the N. by *Decies* without *Drum*. The latter is bounded on the S. by *Decies within* Drum, on the S. E. by the ocean, on the W. by *Coſhmore* and *Coſhbride*, on the E. by *Upper-third* and *Middle-third*, and on the N. by *Upper-third* and *Glanchiry* bar.'s; according to fome Irifh chronicles, the *Decii* or *Deaffies* were a colony from a people of that name who inhabited the S. parts of the co. *Meath*, near the co. Dublin. A chief of this diftrict, about the year 278, having rebelled againft *Cormac Mac Art*, king of Meath, entered the royal palace at *Taragh*, and flew *Kellach* the king's fon; on which *Cormac* raifed an army, fuppreffed the rebellion, and drove moft of the *Decii* out of Meath, who thereupon fettled in the co. Waterford. The antient proprietors of this diftrict were the *O'Faos* now called *O'Fays*.

DECUREAGH, a *lake* in co. Weftmeath, prov. Leinfter.

DEE, a *river* in bar. Ardee, co. Louth, prov. Leinfter.

DEECE, a bar. in co. Meath, prov. Leinfter, otherwife called *Decies* or *Deſies*.

DEEL *river*, fit. in bar. Tirawly, co. Mayo, prov. Connaught.

DEEPS, fit. in bar. Shelmaliere, co. Wexford, prov. Leinfter.

DEER's-MEADOWS, a place fo called in the midft of the mountains of *Mourne*, co. Down, prov. Ulfter: by fome called *King's-meadow*, (becaufe people have their grazing here free) extending fome miles in breadth and length: to which great numbers of poor people refort in the fummer months to graze their cattle. They bring with them their wives, children, and little wretched furniture, erect huts, and live thereabout two months, and often cut their turf, to ferve for the next returning feafon; which done, they retire with their cattle to their former habitations.

DESERTERN, fit. in bar. Inifhowen, co. Donegal, prov. Ulfter.

DEGE, fit. in bar. Kilmacrenan, co. Down, prov. Ulfter.

DELEROCK, fit. in bar. Longford, co. Longford, prov. Leinfter.

DELGENY, *Delgany* or *Delgenny*, a fmall village, fit. near Newtown-mount-kennedy, 16 miles from Dublin, and 6 miles beyond Bray, in co. Wicklow, prov. Leinfter.

DELVIN, a bar. in co. Weftmeath, prov. Leinfter; it was the antient territory of the *O'Finnalans*, and afterwards poffeffed by the *Nugents*, now *earls of Weftmeath*, to whom it gives title of *baron*.

DELVIN-LODGE, the feat of the *earl of Weftmeath*, fit. in co. Meath, prov. Leinfter.

DEMKERNERY, a vicarage in dioc. of Offory, fit. in bar. Knocktopher, co. Kilkenny, prov. Leinfter.

DENN, fit. in bar. Loughtee, co. Cavan, prov. Ulfter; it is a vicarage in dioc. of Lifmore.

DEPATY *rock*, fit. by the coaft of the bar. Ardes, co. Down, prov. Ulfter.

DERACHY, fit. in bar. Maffareen, co. Antrim, prov. Ulfter.

DEREGRETH, a parifh within the deanery of *Ardfinane*, in co. Waterford, prov. Munfter.

DERG, or *Derg-abhan*, i. e. the river of the woody morafs; it rifes out of a lake of that name, in bar. *Tyrhugh*, co. Donegal, prov. Ulfter, from whence joining feveral other rivers, as the *Mourne*, and *Finney*, it falls into *Lough Foyle* at Derry. The lake from whence this river rifes, is famous for having in it, the ifland that contains St. *Patrick's Purgatory*; it is a narrow cell, hewn out of the folid rock, in which a man could fcarcely ftand upright. In this lake there are feveral iflands; on the largeft, called St. Fintan's, a priory of Auguftinians was founded by St. Auguftin, in which St. *Daobec* is faid to have been buried: it had a chapel with convenient houfes for the monks, the remains of which may yet be feen.—There is another lake of fame name, fit. between co. Galway, prov. Connaught, and co. Tipperary, prov. Munfter; in which is a very beautiful and fruitful ifland, having a fine anchoret tower, above 70 feet high; and the remains of 7 fmall churches. It was founded in the 6th century by St. *Commin*.

DERG BRIDGE, fit. by *Caſtlederg*, co. Tyrone, prov. Ulfter.

DERIG ISLAND, fit. near bar. Carbery, co. Sligo, prov. Connaught.

DERIG *lake*, fit. in bar. Granard, co. Longford, prov. Leinfter.

DERIKELAGH, a fmall lake in co. Down, prov. Ulfter: at the N. end of which, are the ruins of the chapel of *Temple Gaurin*, i. e. "Goat's church."

DERIM-

DERIMTOGHNY, fit. in bar. Athenry, co. Galway, prov. Connaught.

DERINA *lake*, fit. in bar. Iveragh, co. Kerry, prov. Munfter.

DERNOGE POINT, fit. in bar. Mourne, co. Down, prov. Ulfter.

DERREGONELLY, fit. in bar. Maghereboy, co. Fermanagh, prov. Ulfter.

DERRICAMMAGH, fit. near *Dunleer*, co. Louth, prov. Leinfter.

DERRILIN, a fair town in co. Fermanagh, prov. Ulfter. Fair days 27 May and 27 Oct.

DERRINGFORD, fit. in bar. Athlone, co. Rofcommon, prov. Connaught.

DERRY, a bifhoprick, conftituted in the year 1158, and extending into the co.'s Londonderry, Donegal, Tyrone and Antrim, in prov. Ulfter.

DERRY, *city and co*. fee Londonderry.

DERRYAGHY, a vicarage in dioc. of Connor, fit. in bar. Belfaft, co. Antrim, prov. Ulfter.

DERRYARD, fit. in bar. Kenought, co. Londonderry, prov. Ulfter.

DERRYBRYAN, fit. in bar. Leitrim, co. Galway, prov. Connaught; near 89 miles from Dublin.

DERRYCLONEY, fit. near Cafhel, co. Tipperary, prov. Munfter.

DERRYCREENY, fit. in bar. Dungannon, co. Tyrone, prov. Ulfter.

DERRYCURRY, fit. in bar. Clonawly, co. Fermanagh, prov. Ulfter.

DERRYDOWN, fit. in bar. Maffareen, co. Antrim, prov. Ulfter.

DERRYGALVIN, a rectory in dioc. of Limerick, fit. in the liberties of the city of Limerick, in prov. Munfter.

DERRYGLASS, fit. in bar. lower Ormond, co. Tipperary, prov. Munfter; about 76 miles from Dublin. Here are the remains of an antient monaftery, fit. near the river Shannon.

DERRYCONELLY, a fair town in co. Fermanagh, prov. Ulfter. Fairs held 10 July.

DERRYGRATH, a vicarage in dioc. of Lifmore, fit. in bar. Iffa and Offa, co. Tipperary, prov. Munfter.

DERRYGULANE, fit. in bar. Duhallow, co. Cork, prov. Munfter.

DERRYKEEGAN, or *Derrykeighan*, fit. in bar. Dunluce, co. Antrim, prov. Ulfter; it is a rectory in dioc. of Connor.

DERRYLORAN, a rectory in dioc. of Armagh, fit. in bar. Dungannon, co. Tyrone, prov. Ulfter.

DERRYLOSSORY, a vicarage in dioc. of Dublin, fit. in bar. Ballinacor, co. Wicklow, prov. Leinfter.

DERRYMORE, fit. in bar. Moycullen, co. Galway, prov. Connaught.

DERRYNEFLIN, a rectory in dioc. of Cafhel, fit. in bar. Slewardagh, co. Tipperary, prov. Munfter.

DERRYNOOSE, a rectory in dioc. of Armagh, fit. in bar. Armagh, co. Armagh, prov. Ulfter.

DERRYVILLANE, a vicarage in dioc. of Cloyne, fit. in bar. Fermoy, co. Cork, prov. Munfter.

DERRYVULLAN, a rectory in dioc. of Clogher, fit. in bar. Tyrefkenedy, co. Fermanagh, prov. Ulfter.

DERVER, a rectory in dioc. of Armagh, fit. in bar. Louth, co. Louth, prov. Leinfter.

DERVERAGH LOUGH, fit. in bar. Corkerry, co. Weftmeath, prov. Leinfter. It is otherwife called *Lough Derrivaragh*; near it is fuppofed to have been the plain *Ath Maighne*, noted for a bloody battle fought there in 1152, between *Turlogh O'Brien* king of Munfter, and *Turlogh O'Connor* king of Connaught, when the latter was defeated with the lofs of 9 chiefs and 900 common men. This plain is faid to lie a little N. of the lough, in the parifh of Maina.

DERVOCK, fit. in co. Antrim, prov. Ulfter, 120 miles from Dublin: near which are the feats of *Belleifle* and *Clover-hill*. It has fairs on 12 Jan. 23 Feb. 12 Aug. 27 Oct. *cuftom free*.

DERRYNEE, fit. in bar. Coftello, co. Mayo, prov. Connaught.

DESART, a feat in co. Kilkenny, prov. Leinfter, which gives title to the baron to the family of Cuff; fit. 2 miles from *Callan*, 4 S. W. from *Kilkenny*, and 64 S. W. from Dublin.

DESART *church*, fit. in co. Derry, prov. Ulfter; about 119 miles from Dublin; near which is a feat called *Mulletragh*. An abbey was founded here by St. *Columb*.

DESART-CREAT, or *Defert-creat*, fometimes written *Difert-creat*, fit. in in bar. Dungannon, co. Tyrone, prov. Ulfter; here is a church diftant about 78 miles from Dublin, which is a rectory in dioc. of Armagh.

DESART-MARTIN or *Defert-martin*, a fair town in bar. Loughlinfholen, co. Derry, prov. Ulfter, 88 miles from Dublin; fairs held 4 Feb. 8 May, 7 June, 28 July, 1 Oct. 8 Nov. and 27 Dec. It is a rectory in dioc. of Derry.

DESERT, a parifh and prebendary in co. Waterford, prov. Munfter; bounded on the N. by the *Suir*, on the S. by *Mothil*, on the E. by *Fenncagh*, and on the W. by *Glapatrick*. The moft remarkable place in this parifh is *Carrickbeg*, where there is a communication by a ftone bridge between the 2 co.'s of Waterford and Tipperary; and the remains of an abbey for Francifcan friars, founded by James the 1ft. earl of *Ormond*.

DESERT-CREAT, fee *Defart-creat*.

DISERT-

DESERT MARTIN, fee *Defart-martin.*

DESERTMORE, a rectory in dioc. of Cork, fit. in bar. Mufkerry, co. Cork, prov. Munfter.

DESERTOGHILL, a rectory in dioc. of Derry, fit. in bar. Colerain, co. Londonderry, prov. Ulfter.

DESERTSERGES, a vicarage in dioc. of Cork, fit. in bar. Carberry, co. Cork, prov. Munfter.

DESIES or *Decies,* a bar. in co. Waterford, prov. Munfter ; the antient proprietors of which were the *O'Faos,* now called *O'Fays.*

DESMOND, antiently *Deas Mumhan,* or S. Munfter ; formerly a co. in the prov. Munfter, but now a part of the co.'s *Kerry* and *Cork.* Its antient kings were the M'Carthys, heredi. tary chiefs of *Corcaluighe* or *Cork.* After the arrival of the Englifh it gave title of earl to a branch of the *Fitzgeralds,* who were afterwards attainted by Queen Eliz. Alfo to fir. *Rich. Prefton,* lord Dingwall in Scotland ; and at prefent it gives title to the family of *Fielding,* earl of Denbigh in England.

DESMOND'S-CHAPEL, fit. within about 5 miles of *Caftle-ifland,* in co. Kerry, prov. Munft.

DEVA, a river mentioned by *Rich. Ciren.* and feems to be the prefent bay of *Carlingford,* co. Louth, prov. Leinfter.

DEVENISH-ABBEY, fit. on Devenifh ifland in *Lough Erne,* co. Fermanagh, prov. Ulfter. It is faid to have been built in 1449, but the Ulfter annals ftate it to have been erected fo early as 1130.

DEVENISH-ISLAND, or *Divinifh ifland,* fit. in Lough Erne, in bar. Magheraboy, co. Fermanagh, prov. Ulfter, about 3 miles from Enniikillen ; where there is one of the moft perfect round towers in Ireland. It is exactly circular, 69 feet high to the conical covering at the top, which is 15 feet more ; it is 48 feet in circumference, and the walls are 3 feet 5 inches thick ; thus the infide is only 9 feet 2 inches in diameter ; befides the door which is elevated 9 feet above the ground, there are 7 fquare holes to admit the light. The whole tower is very neatly built with ftones of about 1 foot fquare, with fcarcely any cement or mortar, and the infide is almoft as fmooth as a gun-barrel. At the outfide bafe, a circle of ftone projects 5 inches. Near it are the vene- rable ruins of *Devenifh abbey,* faid to have been built in 1449, but the Ulfter annals ftate it to have been erected fo early as 1130. St. *Lafe- rian* is faid to have founded a monaftery here in 563 : he was otherwife named *Molaife,* and here are his reliques contained in a vaulted building of hewn ftone, called St. Molais's houfe. This place is a rectory in dioc. of Clogher.

DEVIL'S-BIT, fit. between the bar.'s of upper Ormond and Ikerin, co. Tipperary, prov. Munfter.

DEVIL'S-CASTLE, a high cliff, fo called by the country people ; it ftands to the N. of *Lick,* in the bar. of *Iraghticonnor,* co. Kerry, prov. Munfter ; it is inacceffible to any creature but fowls, and hath an *Eagle's* neft on its fummit. The whole fhore hereabouts has a great variety of romantic caves and caverns, formed by the dafhing of the waves : in fome places are high open arches, and in others impending rocks, ready to tumble down upon the firft ftorm.

DEVIL'S-GLEN, fit. near *Dunran,* in co. Wicklow, prov. Leinfter ; this place, and the beautiful roads now made about it, affording a variety of the moft pleafing profpects in na- ture, is well worth a traveller's attention.

DEVIL'S-PUNCH-BOWL, a large deep hole fo called, filled with water, on the W. fide of *Mangerton* mountain, in co. Kerry, prov. Munfter ; which overflows and makes an agreeable cafcade down the fide of the moun- tain, in the view of *Mucrufs houfe.* This water fupplies the mills for the iron works, and then falls into *Lough Lane,* or what is more properly termed the lake of *Killarney,* which forms one of the greateft natural beauties in the kingdom.

DEVINISH, fee *Devenifh abbey* and *ifland,*

DIAMOR, fit. in bar. Half-fore, co. Meath, prov. Leinfter. It is a vicarage in dioc. of Meath.

DILLON'S-GROVE, fit. near Rofcommon, prov. Connaught.

DILLON'S-LODGE, fit. in bar. Upper-crofs, co. Dublin, prov. Leinfter.

DILLON'STOWN, fit. in bar. Atherdee, co. Louth, prov. Leinfter.

DINGANDONOVAN, a rectory in dioc. of Cloyne, fit. in bar. Imokilly, co. Cork, prov. Munfter.

DINGLE or *Dingle-i-Couch,* a poft, port and borough town in bar. Corkaguinny, co. Kerry, prov. Munfter ; it has a harbour, and ftands in a bay of its own name, about 79 miles W. of Limerick, and 166 from Dublin, and is go- verned by a fovereign. It is the moft Wefterly town in Europe, and has a barrack for a com- pany of foot, and a tolerable good Saturday market. Here was a caftle built about 1580, the vaults of which are now ufed as the town goal. Several of the houfes are built in the Spanifh fafhion, with ranges of ftone balcony windows ; this place being formerly much fre- quented with fhips from that nation, who traded with the inhabitants, and came to fifh on this coaft ; many of the houfes have dates on them as old as Queen Eliz.'s time, and fome earlier ; but the modern edifice in this town belongs to the *knight* of *Kerry.* The parifh church dedi-

cated

cated to St. *James*, is said to have been formerly built at the charge of the Spaniards. It was
originally very large, but moſt of the old ſtructure is gone to ruin, a part only of which is
kept in repair for divine ſervice, and is called
St. *Mary's* chapel. There was formerly an antient monaſtery in this town. *Dingle* was incorporated by Queen Eliz. in 1585, who granted
to it the ſame privileges which Drogheda enjoyed, with a ſuperiority over the harbours of
Ventry and *Smerewick* ; and allowed 300*l.* to the
inhabitants to wall the place. King James Iſt.
renewed its privileges by charter, bearing date
at Weſtminſter, 2 Mar. in the 4th year of his
reign. The Iriſh formerly called it *Dangean in
Cuſhy*, i. e. the fortreſs or caſtle of *Huſſey*, an old
Engliſh family to whom one of the *Fitzgeralds*,
earl of Deſmond had formerly granted a conſiderable traċt of land from *Caſtle Duen* to
Dingle. This place ſends 2 members to parliament ; patronage in the *Townſhend* family. On
the lands of *Ballybeg*, 1 mile N. E. of Dingle, is
a vitriolic ſpa ; and about 1 mile S. W. is
Burnham, formerly called *Ballingollin caſtle* ;
deſtroyed in 1641. Dingle was once a town of
good commerce ; and tho' it bears at preſent
ſome evident marks- of decay, ſtill preſerves
ſome little trade, and exports beef, butter,
corn and even linen. It is a curacy in dioc. of
Ardfert. Near this town, in the caves on the
ſea-ſhore, there is an abundance of very clear
and hard chryſtals.

DINGLE-HARBOUR, ſit. in co. Kerry, prov.
Munſter ; towards the N. ſide of *Caſtlemain-bay*,
and near the harbour of *Ventry*, the laſt being
half a league W. of the other, and divided
from it by a narrow iſthmus ; between both
theſe harbours is a rock, about a mile from
the ſhore, called the *Crow*: within a mile of
which is *Dingle harbour*, being but a ½ mile broad
at the entrance ; the W. point is called *Binbeg*,
and the E. point *Binbane*; there are 30 feet at
low water in the entrance, and ſo gradually
to 18 and 12 feet, the channel is pretty ſtrait
and runs near the W. ſhore ; the harbour
grows wider when you are in : the E. ſhore is
ſhoal for a conſiderable way over, and therefore to be avoided ; you may anchor in any
part of the channel from 20 to 12 feet water,
where you are landlocked from all winds.
Lat. 51 : 55, lon. 10 : 36.

DINGLE-ICOUCH, ſee *Dingle*.

DINIS *river*, ſit. in bar. Faſſachdining, co.
Kilkenny, prov. Leinſter.

DINISH ISLAND, ſit. in the river *Kenmare*,
bar. Dunkerron, co. Kerry, prov. Munſter ;
this, with the iſland of *Scariff* near it, is farmed
from the earl of *Cork* and *Orrery*, by a family of the name of *Connell*.

DINROY, or rather *Dun-riogh*, i. e. the dun
or fort of the king ; by ſome placed near *New
Roſs*, in co. *Waterford*, but Mr. Beauford ſtates
it to be a royal reſidence of the chiefs of *Corcaluighe*, which was ſit. in co. Cork, near *Roſs-
Carbery*, prov. Munſter. See *Coll. Reb. Hib.*
No. 11.

DIRELEHAN, ſit. in bar. Leitrim, co. Galway, prov. Connaught.

DIRPATRICK, ſit. in bar. Deece, co. Meath,
prov. Leinſter.

DIRWAY, ſit. in bar. Kells, co. Meath,
prov. Leinſter.

DISERT. There are many places of this
name in Ireland, viz. 1ſt a fair town in bar.
Maryborough, Queen's co. prov. Leinſter,
which is a vicarage in dioc. of Leighlin, and
holds fairs on Whit. Mond. and 12 Nov.
Here one of the antient round towers has been
erected ; and to this place St. *Ængus* retired,
and founded an abbey here. It is ſit. about
2 miles S. E. of Maryborough. 2d A rectory
in dioc. of Cloyne, ſit. in bar. Barrymore, co.
Cork, prov. Munſter. 3d A vicarage in dioc.
of Roſs, ſit. in bar. Carbery, in ſame co. 4th
A curacy in dioc. of Oſſory, ſit. in bar. Faſſachdining, co. Kilkenny, prov. Leinſter. 5th
A vicarage in dioc. of Liſmore, ſit. in bar.
Upperthird, co. Waterford, prov. Munſter.
6th A rectory in dioc. of Meath, ſit. in bar.
Moyaſhel, co. Weſtmeath, prov. Leinſter.
7th a vicarage in dioc. of Killaloe, ſit. in bar.
Inchiquin, co. Clare, prov. Munſter. 8th A
vicarage in dioc. of Elphin, ſit. in bar. Athlone, co. Roſcommon, prov. Connaught. 9th
a rectory in dioc. of Limerick, ſit. in bar.
Coſhma, co. Limerick, prov. Munſter. 10th
a rectory in dioc. of Armagh, ſit. in bar. Ferrard, co. Louth, prov. Leinſter. 11th A vicarage in dioc. of Ardfert, ſit. in bar. Clonmaurice.—Alſo a rectory in ſame dioc. ſit. in bar.
Truaghnacmy, both in co. Kerry, prov.
Munſter.

DISERT-CREAGH, ſee *Deſartcreat*.

DISERT-LYN, a rectory in dioc. of Armagh,
ſit. in bar. Loughinſholen, co. Londonderry,
prov. Ulſter.

DISERTMORE, a vicarage in dioc. of Oſſory,
ſit. in bar. Ida, co. Kilkenny, prov. Leinſter.

DISNIE, a *river* in co. Kilkenny, prov.
Leinſter.

DISWELL'S-TOWN, ſit. near Caſtleknock, co.
Dublin, prov. Leinſter.

DIVIS *mountains*, ſit. in bar. Belfaſt, co. Antrim, prov. Ulſter.

DOAGH, a village ſit. in bar. Antrim, co.
Antrim, prov. Ulſter ; about 90 miles from
Dublin.

DOANE, ſit in bar. Iraghticonner, co. Kerry,
prov. Munſter.

DOGGER.

DOGGER-BANK, fit. at the mouth of Wexford bay, co. Wexford, prov. Leinster.

DOG'S-HEAD, a *cape* in bar. Ballinahinch, co. Galway, prov. Connaught. It is the most Western point of the co. and stretches out into the Atlantic ocean.

DOG'S-NOSE-POINT, a place so called, fit. in *Cork harbour*, co. Cork, prov. Munster.

DOG'S-TOWN, a rectory in dioc. of Cashel, fit. in bar. Middlethird, co. Tipperary, prov. Munster.

DOIREMELLE, fit. on the banks of Loughmelve, in lower Breffiny, co. Leitrim, prov. Connaught. Here a nunnery was erected by St. *Tigernach* for his mother St. Mella, who died before the year 787.

DOLLA, a rectory in dioc. of Killaloe, fit. in bar. lower Ormond, co. Tipperary, prov. Munster.

DOLLARD'S-TOWN, fit. in bar. Kilkea, co. Kildare, prov. Leinster; here is Leinster-lodge, a seat of his grace the duke of Leinster.

DOLLYBROOK, fit. near Ballibay, co. Monaghan, prov. Ulster.

DOMACASTEN, fit. in bar. Castleraghan, co. Cavan, prov. Ulster.

DOMCOMAGH, fit. near Tarboy-harbour, in bar. Erris, co. Mayo, prov. Connaught.

DOMLEAGH, the antient name of *Duleck*, in co. Meath, prov. Leinster.

DOMNACH-BILL, fee *Bill-church*.

DOMORTING, fit. in bar. Corkaguinny, co. Kerry, prov. Munster.

DONABATE, a vicarage in dioc. of Dublin, fit. in bar. Balruddery, co. Dublin, prov. Leinster.

DONABROOK, fee *Donnybrook*.

DONACOMPER, or *Donacumper*, fit. near St. *Woolstans*, in bar. Salt, co. Kildare, prov. Leinster; it is a curacy in dioc. of Dublin. Here are the ruins of a church; this place is sometimes written *Donacumber*.

DONADEA, fit. in bar. lkeath, co. Kildare, prov. Leinster. Here is a chapel which contains the family vault of the Aylmer family, with an antient monument, erected by Sir *Gerald Aylmer*, the first bart. of that branch, which settled at this place: who also built the *church* of Donadea, and added a new building to the old castle, in the then fashionable style. *Donadea-castle* was besieged by the Irish rebels in 1691, but bravely defended by Ellen daughter of Thomas visc. Thurles, fifter of James Ist duke of Ormond, and wife to fir *Andrew Aylmer*, the second bart. They however burnt the new houfe, which from that period lay in ruins, until it came into the poffeffion of fir *Fitzgerald Aylmer*, the prefent and 7th bart. by whom it was repaired in a good style and at a considerable expence. The family of Aylmer is antient,

and faid to be descended from *Aylmer* or *Æthelmare*, earl of Cornwall, in the time of king Ethelred: in memorandum of which they have constantly borne four Cornish choughs in their arms. They early fettled in Ireland, (fometime in the reign of King John,) at or near *Lyons* in the co. Kildare, which still remains to the elder branch of the family, and from which are defcended the barons Aylmer of *Balrath*, and the family of *Donadea* and feveral others. *Donadea* is a rectory in dioc. of Kildare, and otherwife written *Donedea*.

DONAGAR, fit. in bar. Antrim, co. Antrim, prov. Ulster.

DONAGH, a vicarage in dioc. of Clogher, fit. in bar. Trough, co. Monaghan, prov. Ulster. — Also a rectory in dioc. of Derry, fit. in bar. Inishowen, co. Donegal, prov. Ulster.

DONAGHADEE, a post, market and port town in bar. Ardes, co. Down, prov. Ulster; fit. 10 leagues due W. of *Port-Patrick* in Scotland, where the Scotish pacquets land. Its trade chiefly confifts in the exportation of horfes to Scotland. It stands 24 miles N. E. of *Downpatrick*, and 94 N. E. of Dublin; lat. 54 : 45 N. lon. 5 : 40 W. Within a mile of this place are the ruins of the church of *Templepatrick*. The quay of Donaghadee is made of large ftones in form of a crefcent, without any cement, and is 128 yards in length, and about 21 or 22 feet broad, befides a breaft wall of the fame kind of ftones about 6 feet broad. The town confifts of two principal ftreets (befides crofs lanes) one open and expofed to the fea, and the other at the back of it, which is well paved. The Diffenters have a large meeting-houfe here, and the conformifts a decent church, which tho' an old building is in good repair, and erected in form of a crofs with narrow gothic arched windows. The church ftands on an eminence at the N. W. end of the town, and may be feen in clear weather from *Portpatrick*. The rath at Donaghadee ftands on the N. E. fide of the town, on a natural hill which has been by art fhaped round, on the top of it a hollow is cut from E. to W. it is encompaffed by a large dry foffe: the circumference at bottom of the trench is 448 feet, but much more if meafured on the outfide; the circumference at the top is 219 feet, and the conical height on the N. 140 feet; you afcend the mount by feveral narrow paths which are carried about it fpirally, and appear to have been originally made with the mount, from the top of which the bearings of feveral parts of Scotland and the Ifle of Man appear very vifible in clear weather. It is probable there is an arched gallery within the body of the mount, which together with the town are commanded by a rifing ground; about a quar-

ter

ter of a mile to the S. called Carnathen-hill or Scot's-hill; and on the S. fide of the rath is an area, or level piece of fine green fod, on which 3000 men may be drawn up in rank and file. Here was a univerfity or fchool kept in the middle ages, but it was deftroyed by the Danes in 837. Donaghadee holds fairs on 6 June, 4 July, 16 Aug. 10 Oct. and 2 Wednefd. in Dec. This is a vicarage in dioc. of Down.

DONAGHCLONEY, fee *Donaghlony*.

DONAGHEAVY, a rectory in dioc. of Clogher, fit. in bar. Clogher, co. Tyrone, prov. Ulfter.

DONAGHEDY, or *Donagheady*, a rectory in dioc. of Derry, fit. in bar. Strabane, co. Tyrone, prov. Ulfter, 108 miles from Dublin; 1½ mile beyond it is a feat called *Ballykellaghan*.

DONAGH-HENRY, a rectory in dioc. of Armagh, fit. in bar. Dungannon, co. Tyrone, prov. Ulfter.

DONAGHLONY, or *Donaghcloney*, a rectory in dioc. of Dromore, fit. in bar. lower Iveagh, co. Down, prov. Ulfter; the fcite of the parifh church of which was changed in 1681, from Donaghlony-bridge to *Clanconnell*, otherwife *Warrinflown*, or *Warringstown*.

DONAGHMAIN, fee *Donaghmoyne*.

DONAGHMORE, there are feveral places of this name. 1ft. A parifh and fair town in bar. Mufkerry, co. Cork, prov. Munfter, which gives title of baron to the family of Hutchinfon, and is a rectory in dioc. of Cloyne: fairs held 12 May and 21 Nov.—2d. A fair town in bar. upper Offory, Queen's co. prov. Leinfter; fairs held 28 March, 12 and 13 June, 31 Aug. and 12 Dec. it is a rectory in dioc. of Offory.—3d. A prebendary in dioc. of Waterford, co. Waterford, prov. Munfter, united to *Killtigan*.—4th. A place in bar. Dungannon, co. Tyrone, prov. Ulfter, 2 miles beyond Dungannon; it is a rectory in dioc. of Armagh.—5th. Another in co. Armagh, prov. Ulfter, diftant about 75 miles from Dublin.—6th. In bar. Navan, co. Meath, prov. Leinfter, where there is an antient round tower; this place is a vicarage in dioc. of Meath. There is alfo a river of this name in fame co.—7th. The ruins of a church, fit. near Leixlip, co. Dublin, prov. Leinfter; near which ftands a handfome obelifk, erected by lady Ann Conolly.—9th. A rectory in dioc. of Derry, fit. in bar. Raphoe, co. Donegal, prov. Ulfter. 10th. A vicarage in dioc. of Dublin, fit. in bar. Talbot's-town, co. Wicklow, prov. Leinfter.—11th. A curacy in dioc. of Ferns, fit. in bar. Ballagheen, co. Wexford, prov. Leinfter.—12th. a vicarage in dioc. of Offory, fit. in bar. Faffachdinning, co. Kilkenny, prov. Leinfter.—13th. a rectory in dioc. of Lifmore, fit. in bar. Middlethird, co. Tipperary, prov. Munfter.—14th. A vicarage in dioc. of Lime-

rick, fit. in co. of the city of Limerick, prov. Munfter.—15th. a rectory in dioc. of Rofs, fit. in bar. Barryroe, co. Cork, prov. Munfter. 16th. A rectory in dioc. of Meath, fit. in bar. Ratoath, co. Meath, prov. Leinfter.

DONAGHNAGHTA, a vicarage in dioc. of Clonfert, fit. in bar. Longford, co. Galway, prov. Connaught.

DONAGHMOYNE, or *Donaghmain*, a bar. having a village in it of fame name, fit. in co. Monaghan, prov. Ulfter; the latter is a rectory in dioc. of Clogher.

DONAGHPATRICK, fit. in bar. Kells, co. Meath, prov. Leinfter; it is a vicarage in dioc. of Meath. An abbey was founded here by St. Patrick; it was pleafantly fit. near the river Blackwater, but fuffered much by fire, and was often plundered by the Danes.—Alfo a rectory in dioc. of Tuam, fit. in bar. Clare, co. Galway, prov. Connaught.

DONAGHY, a fair town in bar. Dungannon, co. Fermanagh, prov. Ulfter; fairs held 10 July and 26 Aug.

DONAMAGHAN, fit. in bar. Kells, co. Kilkenny, prov. Leinfter.

DONANY, a vicarage in dioc. of Kildare, fit. in bar. Ophaly, co. Kildare, prov. Leinfter.

DONARD, a fair town in bar. Talbot's-town, co. Wicklow, prov. Leinfter; fairs held 4 May and 12 Aug. This is a vicarage in dioc. of Dublin. *St. Silvefter* was interred here, but his reliques were tranflated to the monaftery of *St. Baithen*.—There is alfo a place of fame name near *Killcullen*, co. Kildare, prov. Leinfter.

DONARD'S-CHAPEL, fit. on the N. E. fide of Slieub Donard mountain, in co. Down, prov. Ulfter. *Sir Will. Petty's* map mentions it by the name of *Leniard's* chapel; but *Dr. Smith* in his hift. of that co. fays it fhould have been called *Donard's-chapel*.

DONASSE, a fair town in co. Clare, prov. Munfter; fair days 17 Mar. 21 Sept. and 30 Nov. *cuftom free*.

DONBEG, fit. in bar. Ibrickan, co. Clare, prov. Munfter.

DONBOY, a chapelry in dioc. of Dublin, fit. in bar. Talbot'stown, co. Wicklow, prov. Leinfter.

DONEDEA, fee *Donadea*.

DONEGAL, otherwife *Tyrconnel*, a co. in the prov. of Ulfter, bounded by the fea on the N. W. and the bay of *Donegal* and *Fermanagh* co. on the S. thofe of *Tyrone* and *Londonderry*, and part of *Fermanagh* co. on the E. It is a very large mountainous and coarfe country, abounding with good harbours. It gives title of earl to the family of Chichefter; contains about 679,550 acres, 42 parifhes, 5 bar.'s and 5 boroughs, and returns 12 members to parliament.

'Tis

'Tis about 57 miles long and 40 broad ; the co. town is *Lifford*. Its bar.'s are Inishowen, Kilmacrenan, Raphoe, Boylagh, Bannagh, and Tyrhugh ; number of houses 23,521, and inhabitants 140,000. No part of the kingdom is better calculated for Summer and Winter fisheries than this co. The linen trade carried on here is mostly ⅞ wides, from 9 to 12 hundreds, and averaged at about £15,000 yearly. The antient families of this co. were the *O'Gallaghers*, *O'Doghertys*, *O'Clerys*, *O'Donalds*, *M'Wards*, *M'Sweenys* and *O'Doyles*.

DONEGAL *(haven)*, a large bay in the co. Donegal, prov. Ulster ; it lies 9 or 10 miles to the E. of Killybegs, and in the entrance is much encumbered with shelves, sands and rocks ; so that great circumspection must be used in passing in or out of it with safety. Lat. 54 : 30, lon. 8 : 45.

DONEGAL *(town)* a borough, post and market town in bar. Tyrhugh, co. Donegal, prov. Ulster, sit. 111 miles from Dublin. Lat. 54 : 30, lon. 8 : 30. It has fairs on 5 and 29 May, 9 July, 4 Sept. 28 Oct. and Nov. In this town is a handsome old castle belonging to the earl of Arran. This borough returns 2 members to parliament ; patron, lord *Arran*. A monastery for Franciscan friars was founded here by *Odo Roe*, in 1474, the remains of which are to be seen at a small distance from the town. *Donegal* is a vicarage in dioc. of Raphoe.

DONEGOR, a vicarage in dioc. of Connor, sit. in bar. Antrim, co, Antrim, prov. Ulster.

DONENY, a vicarage in dioc. of Clonfert, sit. in bar. Leitrim, co. Galway, prov Connaught.

DONERAIL or *Donneraile*, a borough, market, fair and post town in co. Cork, prov. Munster, about 20 miles N. E. of Cork, and 113 S. W. of Dublin. It gives title of visc. to the family of *St. Ledger*. Lat. 52 : 5 N. lon. 8 : 25 W. Fair days 12 Aug. and Nov. This town is sit. on the river *Awbeg*, over which there is a good bridge. There is a neat church here, with a good steeple and spire ; and on the remains of the castle a barrack is erected for a troop of horse. Near this town are several quarries of beautiful variegated marble. *Donerail* is a curacy in dioc. of Cloyne ; it returns 2 members to parliament ; patron, lord Donerail, who has a country seat here.

DONFRENY, a vicarage in dioc. of Killala, sit. in bar. Tyrawly, co. Mayo, prov. Connau.

DONIEL, sit. in bar. Tyreragh, co. Sligo, prov. Connaught.

DONISLE BAY, sit. between the bar.'s Middlethird and Upperthird, co. Waterford, prov. Munster.

DONKILL, sit. in bar. Middlethird, co. Waterford, prov. Munster. It is a vicarage in dioc. of Lismore.

DONMACPHELBIN, sit. in bar. Burrishoole, co. Mayo, prov. Connaught.

DONMORE, a fair town in co. Galway, prov. Connaught ; fairs held 29 May, 9 July, 10 Oct. and 11 Dec.—Also a place of same name, sit. in the liberties of Kilkenny, prov. Leinster.

DONNAGURRAGH, sit. near Ennis, co. Clare, prov. Munster.

DONNARISK, sit. near Dungannon, co. Tyrone, prov. Ulster.

DONNERAILE, see *Donerail*.

DONNORLING-HARBOUR, sit. in co. Kerry, prov. Munster, opposite the Atlantic ocean.

DONNYBROOK, or *Donabrook*, a village and rectory in dioc. of Dublin, within 2 miles of the metropolis in co. Dublin, prov. Leinster. Fairs held 26 Aug. for horses and pedlars wares.

DONNYCARNEY, a village within 2 miles of Dublin, in co. Dublin, prov. Leinster. Here is *Marino* the elegant seat with fine improvements of the earl of *Charlemont*.

DONOHILL, a vicarage in dioc. of Cashel, sit. in bar. Clanwilliam, co. Tipperary, prov. Munster.

DONORE, a fair town in bar. Duleek, co. Meath, prov. Leinster ; fairs held 29 June. It is a rectory in dioc. of Meath.—Also a place in bar. Clain, co. Kildare, prov. Leinster.

DONOUGH, sit. in bar. Coole, co. Fermanagh, prov. Ulster, 67 miles from Dublin. Here are the ruins of a church near a small lake.

DONSEVERICK, sit. in bar. Caric, co. Antrim, prov. Ulster, near the *Giant's-causeway*.

DONURLING, a rectory in dioc. of Ardfert, sit. in bar. Corkaguinny, co. Kerry, prov. Munster.

DONYMANAGH, sit. in bar. Strabane, co. Tyrone, prov. Ulster.

DOOBALLY, a fair town in co. Cavan, prov. Ulster ; fairs held 15 Aug.

DOOLAGHS, see *Douloughs*.

DOON or *Doone*, a rectory in dioc. of Emly, sit. in bar. Coonagh, co. Limerick, prov. Munster.

DOONAS, a village in bar. Clanwilliam, co. Limerick, prov. Munster.

DOONAUN or *Dunane*, a village in bar. Slewmargy, Queen's co. prov. Leinster ; it is sometimes written *Doonun*. In this neighbourhood are extensive coal pits ; the ground is fertile, and the coal dips to 20 or 28 fathom, being from 20 inches to 3½ feet in thickness, running in a direction nearly parallel to the horizon : here at about 12 fathom beneath the surface, is found a rock of win-stone, resting on a stratum of columnar basaltes, perpendicular to the horizon : the columns are from 2 to 6 feet in length, the articulations from 3 to 6 inches, forming both convex and concave joints, of an irregular pentagonal figure, whose sides in different joints are plain, convex and concave :

these

thefe columns in feveral places reft on a light grey ferruginous rock or win-ftone, on a flatey rock, beneath which is a vein of rich Iron ore, parallel to the horizon, from one to three inches thick: under the iron is a ftratum of flate, and then the bed of coal: beneath the bed of coal, is a foft micaceous flate ftratum, 10 or 12 fathom deep, and under that a hard rock, thro' which no one has yet bored; the miners think that the great and principal bed of coal lies beneath this rock, at about 50 fathom from the furface.

DOONE, fee *Doon.*

DOONFIN, fit. in bar. Tyrawly, co. Mayo, prov. Connaught.

DOONKILLEN, fee *Dunkellin.*

DOON-POINT, fit. in ifland of Raghery, co. Antrim, prov. Ulfter; it is remarkable for its bafaltic rocks and pillars.

DOORE, a *river* in co. Donegal, prov. Ulfter.

DORRHA, a rectory in dioc. of Killaloe, fit. in bar. lower Ormond, co. Tipperary, prov. Munfter.

DOUDSTOWN, fit. in co. Meath, prov. Leinfter, about 23 miles from Dublin.

DOUGLAS, fit. in co. Cork, prov. Munfter, 126 miles from Dublin. In this place tho' a fmall village, is the largeft manufactory for *Sail-cloth* in the kingdom.

DOUGLAS-BRIDGE, fit. in bar. Strabane, co. Tyrone, prov. Ulfter, 97 miles from Dublin, 1 mile beyond which, fit. on the *Foyle*, are the ruins of a church.

DOULOUGHS, or *St. Douloughs*, fit. within 4¼ miles of Dublin, in co. Dublin, prov. Leinfter. In the neighbourhood of this place are fome handfome feats. *St. Doulough's church* is well worthy the attention of the antiquarian and the man of tafte. It is one of thofe few ftructures in this kingdom, erected from the beginning of the 8th to the clofe of the 11th century; and in different ftile of architecture from any at this day to be found, either in Britain or the Weftern parts of Europe, being evidently built in imitation of the original Chriftian churches in the Southern countries, taken from the antient heathen temples of the *Greeks* and *Romans*; and which probably were introduced into this ifland by the Greek and Roman clergy who retired from their native countries, on the arrival of the *Goths* and *Vandals* into the Roman empire. It is 48 feet long by 18 wide, and has a double ftone roof; the external which covers the building, and that which divides the lower from the upper ftory; you enter thro' a fmall door to the S. juft as you enter, the tomb of *St. Doulagh* or *Doulach* prefents itfelf. By ftooping you pafs a narrow way, and enter the

chapel, which is 22 feet by 12 and lighted by 3 windows, one at the E. and two at the S. the arches pointed, and gothic decorations, with the tower are faid to be later additions; the ftones which cover it are not large, but fo well beded with mortar, that after fo many centuries this roof admits neither light or water. The well near the church is dedicated to the Virgin Mary, and adjoins a place called *St. Catherine's pond*, it is an octangular inclofure, and was antiently the baptiftry; about it are fome emblematic frefco paintings. This place is fometimes written *Doolaghs*; and ftands 2¼ miles beyond *Donnycarney*, and ¼ mile beyond *Belchamp*.

DOUR, a river in co. Cork, prov. Munfter; which iffues from a limeftone rock, after a fubterraneous courfe of ¼ mile, having its rife at Moygeely; where it breaks out and forms a fmall lake, about a mile in circumference. In the proper feafon this lake is frequented by a variety of wild fowl.

DOUTH, fee *Dowth.*

DOVEA, a vicarage in dioc. of Cafhel, fit. in bar. Eliogurty, co. Tipperary, prov. Munfter.

DOVE-HILL, fit. in co. Dublin, prov. Leinft.

DOWESTOWN, a vicarage in dioc. of Meath, fit. in bar. Skryne, co. Meath, prov. Leinfter.

DOWKINALLY, fit. in Achill ifland, co. Mayo, prov. Connaught.

DOWLAHE, fit. in bar. Erris, co. Mayo, prov. Connaught.

DOWLAS-HEAD, fit. on the coaft of the co. Kerry, prov. Munfter, near *Cahir.* About this coaft are feveral large caves near this place, one of which has its entrance fo low, as hardly to admit of a boat with a man ftanding up in it, but farther in, the roof is as high as that of a gothic cathedral. In this cave there is a confufed echo, but when a perfon fpeaks, the voice is fo reverberated from fide to fide, as to feem louder than a fpeaking trumpet.

DOWN, a *bifhoprick*,—alfo a large rich and populous co. in prov. Ulfter. The bifhoprick of *Down* is united to that of *Connor*, fince 1454; and both fees were founded in the 5th century. The co. is noted for its great trade in the linen manufacture, which is averaged at 151,960*l.* yearly: it gives title of vifc. to the family of *Dawney*; and is bounded on the E. and S. by the fea, on the W. by *Armagh*, and on the N. by *Antrim* co.'s. Its length from N. to S. is 40 miles, the breadth from E. to W. 31, and the area 348,550 acres, having 8 bar.'s and the lordfhip of Newry, viz. upper and lower *Iveagh* or *Iveach*, *Kinelearty*, *Caftlereagh*, *Dufferin*, *Ardes*, *Lecale* and *Mourne*; in which are 60 parifhes, 55 churches, 36,636 houfes, and

and about 201500 inhabitants; it has 6 boroughs, and returns 14 members to parliament; chief town *Downpatrick*: moſt parts of this co. are fertile; in the rougher parts they breed a great number of horſes, with which the fairs of diſtant co.'s are ſupplied. It is ſaid that the antient name of this co. was *Ullad* or *Ullah*; which ſome ſay it received from *Ulagh* a *Norwegian*, who flouriſhed here long before the Chriſtian æra, from whom they alledge that ſhe whole prov. of Ulſter had its name; and they affirm that all Ireland being divided into 5 provinces, that which is now called Ulſter by the Engliſh, was formerly and ſtill is called by the Iriſh *Cuig Ullagh*, i. e. *Ullagh's fifth*; and further, that a family of good note in co. *Antrim*, and others of leſs account, have taken their names from this *Norwegian*, and are all called *Mac Ullagh* or *Macullagh*. Mr. *Beauford* in the 11th. number of the *Col. Reb. Hib.* derives the word *Ullad* from *Thmath all, adh*, that is " the Northern diviſion of the *Oll* or *Bolgæ*," pronounced *Ullagh*. The common opinion is that this country was reduced into ſhire ground, and divided into bar.'s in the reign of Queen Eliz. yet it is evident that two co.'s under the names of *Down* and *Newtown*, were ſo called much earlier; *John de Mandeville* being made ſheriff of Down and Newtown by patent, anno 1325. 20 Edw. IId. In this co. there are great numbers of bleach greens, particularly on the river *Bann*, where, in the courſe of 7 miles, paſſing by *Banbridge*, *Gilford* and *Moyallen* are 12 bleach greens, which on the whole finiſh 90,000 pieces annually. The river *Newry* which runs into *Carlingford bay*, divides the co. *Down* and *Armagh*. The antient families of this co. are the *O'Neils*, *Mc Gennis's*, *Macartanes* and *Whites*.—Down is alſo the name of a place ſit. near *Letterkenny*, co. Donegal, prov. Ulſter;—and another 6 miles N. of *Enniſcorthy*, in co. Wexford, prov. Leinſter, where an abbey for regular canons was founded, before the arrival of the Engliſh in this country.— Alſo a chapelry in dioc. of Dublin, ſit. in bar. Newcaſtle, co. Wicklow, prov. Leinſter.

DOWNAMORE, a bar. in co. Galway, prov. Connaught; it is ſometimes written *Dunamore*, or *Dunmore*.

DOWNAN *caſtle*, ſit. in co. Carlow, prov. Leinſter, about 1 mile from *Tullow* on the river *Slaney*. It was demoliſhed by Oliver Cromwell, who is ſaid to have had an engagement here, with the troops commanded by col. *Butler*, who were defeated by the former.

DOWNDERRY, a fair town in co. Cork, prov. Munſter; fairs held on Whitſun Monday.

DOWNEEN, ſit. in co. Cork, prov. Munſter, near *Roſs-carberry*; on theſe lands and on others contiguous, called *Tralong*, about 1 mile W. of *Roſs-carberry*, are two remarkable great holes in the ground 80 yards deep, and each about 300 yards from the cliffs, in both which the ſea flows by ſubterraneous paſſages; theſe holes are called E. and W. *Pouladuff*.

DOWNGATE-MOUNTAINS, ſit. in bar. Dungannon, co. Tyrone, prov. Ulſter.

DOWNGATE *rock*, ſit. in co. Tyrone, prov. Ulſter, 108 miles from Dublin.

DOWNHILLS, ſit. in co. Londonderry, prov. Ulſter, 117 miles from Dublin.

DOWNINGS, a rectory in dioc. of Kildare, ſit. in bar. Clain, co. Kildare, prov. Leinſter: here are the ruins of a church.

DOWNINGS-HILL, ſit. in co. Kildare, prov. Leinſter; a part of the *Grand Canal* has been cut thro' this hill, which is about 18 miles from Dublin; the ſoil of which is a loamy gravel. Over the canal is a ſmall bridge, called Downing's-bridge. Here the level of the canal is at the ſummit, which commences at this hill and extends to *Ballyteague*, which is 22 miles diſtant from Dublin.

DOWNONY, a curacy in dioc. of Ferns, ſit. in bar. Bantry, co. Wexford, prov. Leinſter.

DOWNPATRICK, ſit. in bar. Lecale, and is the chief town of the co. Down, prov. Ulſter, about 7 miles W. of *Strangford-bay*, and 72 N. E. of Dublin; it is a borough, poſt and fair town, and ſends 2 members to parliament, election by *Potwallopers*. It is a rectory in dioc. of *Down*, which biſhoprick was united to that of *Connor* in 1442, or according to others 1454. This town has long been celebrated as the burial place of St. *Patrick*; and has a barrack for a troop of horſe; fairs held 17 March, 22 June and 29 Oct. Lat. 54:23 N. lon. 5:50 W. 2 miles from hence, are the ruins of the monaſtery of *Saul*, ſaid to have been built by St. *Patrick*; and near it is the famous well, called after the ſame ſaint, and much frequented on account of its ſuppoſed virtues. Downpatrick has been eſteemed one of the moſt autient towns in the kingdom, being noted in hiſtory before the arrival of St. Patrick; its preſent name ſignifies the *mount of Patrick*, which has been given to it, from the rath which lies on the N. W. ſide of the town, the conical height of which is 60 feet, and the circumference 2100 feet; it is ſurrounded by 3 great ramparts, one of which is 30 feet broad, and the whole circuit of the works, is ¼ of a mile. This is ſuppoſed to have been formerly the place of the palace of the kings of *Ublagh* or *Down*. This town is now of a large compaſs, compoſed of 4 long ſtreets, centring near a point, interſected by lanes and ſmall ſtreets; it is diſtinguiſhed into ſeveral quarters, as the *Iriſh* quarter, *Engliſh* quarter, *Scotch* quarter, &c. It was made the ſeat of a biſhop by St. *Patrick*

Patrick; the cathedral ſtands near the town on the aſcent of a hill; over the E. window, are 3 handſome antient niches, in which the pedeſtals ſtill continue, whereon it is ſuppoſed the ſtatues of St. *Patrick*, St. *Bridget* and St. *Columb*, formerly ſtood; for tradition and hiſtory ſay, that theſe 3 ſaints were depoſited here; 2 ſquare columns adjoin the E. end of the cathedral; one of which is ſolid and the other hollow, and in it 20 winding ſteps remaining, which were ſuppoſed to have led up to the roof; on a ſtone over the E. window, is a very antient inſcription; there is at the W. end a very high pillar, that was repaired at the expence of dean *Daniel*; this church, &c. was deſtroyed by *Leonard* lord *Grey*, lord deputy of Ireland, A. D. 1538, the profanation thereof being one of the articles of impeachment laid to his charge; and he was beheaded 3 years after; ſome repairs however have been lately made to it. The dioceſan ſchool, market-houſe and preſbyterian meeting-houſe here, are handſome buildings, and the ſeſſions houſe is a large and elegant ſtructure; here are accommodations for 3 clergymen's widows, and an hoſpital erected by Mr. *Southwell*, for decayed tenants of the family, and other charitable purpoſes. No leſs than 5 religious houſes ſtood antiently in this town, viz. one of *Benedictines*, (being the old cathedral church juſt mentioned) which before *de Courceys* time, was a houſe of ſecular canons, and by him converted into a Benedictine ſeminary; one of crouched friars, called the *Engliſh Priory*, one of canons regular, called the *Iriſh Priory*, one of Ciſtertian nuns, and the 5th of obſervantine *Franciſcans*, founded in the 12th. century; the iſt. was enlarged and beautified by *de Courcey*, the 2d. was founded by him, the 3d. by *Malachy O'Morgair*, biſhop of *Down*, in 1138; and the laſt by *Hugh de Lacey*, earl of *Ulſter*. It is uncertain who founded the nunnery; beſides theſe religious houſes, there was an hoſpital for lepers, dedicated to St. Nicholas, and another of the ſame ſort at *Kilcliff*, in bar. of *Lecale*, under the invocation of St. *Peter*; the cuſtody of both which hoſpitals were by patent, dated 2 April, 1413, granted to *John Young*, *John Molyn* and *Walter Coby*, with all their lands, tenements and appurtenances, being then in the king's hands, for certain cauſes, to hold as long as they ſhould continue in the king's poſſeſſion. The preſent church of *Down*, being 90 feet by 40 in the clear, ſtands in another part of the town, and was rebuilt in 1735. Near the old abbey was a round tower, which ſtood about 40 feet from the cathedral, 66 feet high, the thickneſs of the walls 3 feet, and the diameter on the inſide 8 feet; this tower was lately taken down, in order to enlarge the W. end of the cathedral; and it is remarkable that under the foundation of this tower, were found the veſtiges of a more antient church, of exceeding good maſonry, and on a larger ſcale than the preſent old fabric, in the walls of which are many pieces of cut ſtone, that have evidently been uſed in ſome former building. On a riſing ground, at the entrance into this town, formerly ſtood a noble houſe of the lord *Cromwell*, burned down by the Iriſh, in 1641; about a mile S. of the town, is a noted horſe-courſe, where purſuant to a charter, granted by king *James* IId. plates given by the *corporation* of *horſe-breeders*, are run for.

Downſtown, ſit. near Drogheda, prov. Leinſter.

Dowrie, a rectory in dioc. of Killaloe, ſit. in bar. Bunratty, co. Clare, prov. Munſter.

Downs, a fair town in co. Wicklow, prov. Leinſter; fairs held 12 Jan. 4 May, 5 Aug. and 12 Nov.—Alſo a place in bar. Ferbill, co. Weſtmeath, prov. Leinſter.

Downs-glen, ſee *Glen of the Downs*.

Dowth, or *Douth*, a vicarage in dioc. of Meath, ſit. in bar. Slane, co. Meath, prov. Leinſter; this place gives title of viſe. to the family of *Netterville*, now viſe. *Netterville* of *Dowth*. Here is the *ſeat* of lord Netterville, which commands an extenſive view of a beautiful and well cultivated country; and near it are many druidical remains.

Drakestown, a rectory in dioc. of Meath, ſit. in bar. Morgallion, co. Meath, prov. Leinſt.

Drangan, a rectory in dioc. of Caſhel, ſit. in bar. Middlethird, co. Tipperary, prov. Munſter.

Draper's-hill, a favourite ſpot of the late celebrated dean *Swift's*, to which he gave that name; it is ſit. near *Market-hill*, co. Antrim, prov. Ulſter.

Dremoge, ſit. in bar. Dungannon, co. Tyrone, prov. Ulſter.

Drennenstown, ſit. by the banks of the Grand canal, in co. Kildare, prov. Leinſter: On one ſide of it are ruins of a caſtle, and on the other are ruins of a church at *Feighcullen*: diſtant 24 miles from Dublin.

Drew'stown, ſit. near Kells, co. Meath, prov. Leinſter.

Drihidtarsna, a rectory in dioc. of Limerick, ſit. in bar. Coſhma, co. Limerick, prov. Munſter.

Drimana-point, a cape in bar. Boylagh, co. Donegal, prov. Ulſter.

Drimbar, a fair town in co. Antrim, prov. Ulſter; fairs held 21 May.

Drimesen, a round church ſo called, ſit. about 6 miles W. of *Mount Leinſter*, prov. Leinſter. Near this place there were many habitations

habitations in the time of king James IId. but they have been deserted by the inhabitants. Many people have been brought from several miles distance to be interred here, pursuant to their desire; and on Easter-monday, a grand *Patron* is held here.

DRIMISKIN, sit. in bar. Louth, co. Louth, prov. Leinster; one of the antient round towers was erected here, part of which yet remains. This place is otherwise called *Dromiskin*, and is a rectory in dioc. of Ardfert.

DRIMNA, see *Drumna*.

DRIMOLEAGUE, a fair town in co. Cork, prov. Munster; fairs held 25 Sept.

DRINAGH, a vicarage in dioc. of Cork, sit. in bar. Carbury, co. Cork, prov. Munster.

DRINAUGH, a rectory in dioc. of Ferns, sit. in bar. Forth, co. Wexford, prov. Leinster.

DRINIDALY, sit. in bar. Navan, co. Meath, prov. Leinster.

DRIPSEY *river*, sit. in bar. Muskerry, co. Cork, prov. Munster.

DROGHEDA, otherwise called *Tredagh*, a post town sit. near 24 miles from Dublin: generally included in the co. Louth, prov. Leinster: but is also considered as a co. and town in itself, returning two members to parliament, elected by freemen and freeholders, it contains above 10,000 inhabitants. It is partly sit. in co. Meath, and lies on the river *Boyne*, about 5 miles W. of the Irish channel. It has a fine harbour; and is governed by a mayor and Sheriffs; it gives title of marquis, earl and visc. to the family of *Moore*; and has a barrack for 2 companies of foot. The town has been entirely walled in, but most of the gates and greater part of the walls much decayed; it was taken by storm by *Oliver Cromwell*, who put all the garrison to the sword; this is a place of good trade, large and well built: St. *Peter's* church, (a new building) is elegantly finished; that of St. *Mary's* on the other side of the river is gone to decay: near it in the church-yard are the remains of an old castle almost quite destroyed. One of these parishes is a vicarage in dioc. of Armagh, and the other a vicarage in dioc. of Meath. Here is a good tholsel, excellent fishmarket remarkable for the fine *Salmon* caught in the *Boyne*. Some fine ruins of abbeys are to be met with in or about this town; we find particularly recorded, the priory of St. *Lawrence*, that of canons regular; the hospital of St. *Mary*; a Dominican friary; Grey friary, Augustinian friary, and the house of St. James, which were all erected in this town: and on the co. Meath side of the river was a priory and hospital of St. John, and a Carmelite friary. About 2 miles up the river is an obelisk, erected in memory of the victory obtained there by king William the IIId, in 1690. At Grange near Drogheda is a vaulted cave in the form of a cross, with a gallery leading to it 80 feet long; and 3 miles beyond Drogheda are the ruins of the antient abbey of *Monaster-boice*; two chapels, a round tower; and the large stone cross, called St. *Boyne's cross*, deemed the most antient religious relique now in Ireland. Drogheda suffered much during the wars of 1641, at which time it was besieged, sir *Henry Tichbourne* being appointed with some forces to undertake its relief. On St. *Thomas's Eve*, the Irish made an assault on the town, but were repulsed by sir Henry; and on the 7th Jan. 1641, he forced the breast works of the enemy, entered their quarters and destroyed many of them, at which time *Art. Roe Mac Mahon*, one of their chief leaders was killed. The Irish then endeavoured to stop the channel, but on 11th Jan. the shipping came to the English army, from *Skerries* to the *quay of Drogheda* in one tide; a thing hardly known before. On 21 Feb. sir *Phelim O'Neal* attempted the town with scaling ladders, but proved unsuccessful; his party however maintained their ground a long time after many skirmishes, until the army under sir Henry Tichbourne, was from time to time increased by additional companies under lord *Moore* of Drogheda, sir *John Borlace*, lieut. col. *Byron*; lieut. col. *Philip Wenman* and others, of whom the three last, though they had been *officers of the field*, yet out of their zeal to the service, went on this occasion as private captains. The siege was at last raised; and the town walls bear evident marks of the contests during this time and that of *Cromwell*. Fairs held here on 12 May, 22 June, 26 Aug. and 29 Oct. Lat. 53 : 44, lon. 6 : 42.

DROM, a vicarage in dioc. of Cashel, sit. in bar. Eliogurty, co. Tipperary, prov. Munster.

DROMAGH, a fair town in bar. Duhallow, co. Cork, prov. Munster. Fair days 20 May, Aug. and Nov. The castle of Dromagh is about 3 miles S. W. of *Kanturk*, it was built by the *O'Keef's* and was their chief seat; it is well walled and flanked with four turrets. Near this place a vein of coal has been discovered, which make a lasting fire with little or no smoke. They have very good culm which covers the large coal, useful in forges and burning lime. The lands hereabout are coarse, and afford little tillage. W. of Dromagh is the parish of *Cullen*, and near the church are some ruins, said to have been an antient nunnery; but not mentioned in any record.—Also the name of a village in bar. upper Iveagh, co. Down, prov. Ulster.

DROMAHAIRE, see *Drumahare*.

DROMALEGUE, a small village in co. Cork, prov. Munster; W. by S. of *Dunmanway*, to
the

the N. of Dromalegue, about two miles is *caftle Donawan*.

DROMANA, a feat of the earl of *Grandifon*, fit. in co. Waterford, prov. Munfter; otherwife called *Drummana*.

DROMANAGH, fit. in bar. Duhallow, co. Cork, prov. Munfter; here is a colliery; and fome iron is raifed about this neighbourhood.

DROMANTINE, fit. near *Newry*, prov. Ulfter.

DROMARAGH, a parifh in bar. lower Iveagh, co. Down, prov. Ulfter; the old church of which about 3 miles S. S. W. of *Anahilt*, lay in ruins fince 1641, 'till fome years ago, when its walls which out-braved the injuries of time, were repaired and the place rendered fit for fervice; it is a vicarage in dioc. of Dromore. Near this church a good *Slate quarry* was found on the eftate of lord *Hillfborough*. In this parifh is an artificial cave, about 6 miles S. E. of Dromore, fit. on a rifing ground, fomething higher than the adjacent lands. The entrance is of a quadrilateral form, each fide meafuring about 3 feet in length, and defcending near the fame number of feet from the furface to the lower part of the aperture. This place cannot be entered but by creeping into it, but afterwards it is fo high that a man can ftand almoft erect in it; it runs in a direct line 32 yards from N. to S. is in moft places 6 feet broad: the floor is fandy and tolerably level, but covered with water, intenfely cold and exceeding limpid, for the fpace of 15 yards. In the cave on the W. fide from the entrance, a chamber branches off 8 yards long and 2 broad, the workmanfhip of which is more regular and better finifhed than that of the long entry.

DROMARD, a rectory in dioc. of Killala, fit. in bar. Tyreragh, co. Sligo, prov. Connaught. — Alfo a village in bar. Ikerin, co. Tipperary, prov. Munfter.

DROMCARR, fit. about 5 miles E. of Atherdee, co. Louth, prov. Leinfter. An abbey was erected here; 'tis now a parifh in dioc. of Armagh.

DROMCASHEL, a fair town in co. Louth, prov. Leinfter; Fairs held 19 May, 12 Oct. *cuftom free*.

DROMCLIFF, a vicarage in dioc. of Elphin, fit. in bar. Carbury, co. Sligo, prov. Connaught.—Alfo a vicarage in dioc. of Killaloe, fit. in bar. Iflands, co. Clare, prov. Munfter.

DROMCOLLUM, a vicarage in dioc. of Elphin, fit. in bar. Tyraghrill, co. Sligo, prov. Connaught.

DROMCULLIHER, a village in bar. Conillo, co. Limerick, prov. Munfter: it is a vicarage in dioc. of Limerick.

DROMDOWNY, a vicarage in dioc. of Clovne, fit. in bar. Duhallow, co. Cork, prov. Munfter.

DROMILLY, fit. in co. Armagh, prov. Ulfter, near 51 miles from Dublin.

DROMIN, a vicarage in dioc. of Limerick, fit. in bar. Cofhma, co. Limerick, prov. Munfter.

DROMINEER, or *Drominheer*, a rectory in dioc. of Killaloe, fit. in bar. lower Ormond, co. Tipperary, prov. Munfter.

DROMISKIN, fee *Drimifkin*.

DROMKEEN, a fair town in co. Kerry, prov. Munfter; fairs held 2 May, 16 July, 15 Nov. Alfo a rectory in dioc. of Emly, fit. in bar. Clanwilliam, co. Limerick, prov. Munfter.

DROMLINE, a rectory in dioc. of Killaloe, fit. in bar. Bunratty, co. Clare, prov. Munfter.

DROMMAGH, fit. in bar. lower Ormond, co. Tipperary, prov. Munfter.

DROMOD, a rectory in dioc. of Ardfert, fit. in bar. Iveragh, co. Kerry, prov. Munfter.

DROMON, a fair town in co. Limerick, prov. Munfter; fairs held Mond. and Tuefd. after Trinity, 18 Aug. 23 Sept. and 14 Dec.

DROMORE, a poft town fit. in bar. lower Iveagh, and is a rectory in dioc. of fame name, in co. Down, prov. Ulfter, 66 miles from Dublin; lat. 54 : 27, lon. 6 : 42. Dr. Smith fays it borrows its name like many other places in Ireland, from its fituation, being a clufter of houfes fpread on the fide of a hill; and derives its name from *Druim* a back, and *Mor* great, or the great back of a hill; Mr. Beauford, in Coll. Reb. Hib. No. 11. fays this place was antiently denominated *Dromaragh*, i. e. the church or habitation in the maritime country; others derive it from *Drubhmor*, i. e. the great houfe, on account of the antient caftle and rath that are here. The bifhoprick of Dromore was founded by St. *Colman* in the 6th century, in the antient diftrict called *Mockmarragh*, according to Mr Harris; this fee comprehends part of the co.'s Armagh, Down, and Antrim: its chapter was new modeled and eftablifhed with fome peculiar privileges, by patent of king James the Ift. Among other marks of royal favour, he diftinguifhes the bifhops of this fee by the ftile of " A. B. by divine providence bifhop of Dromore;" whereas all other bifhops in Ireland, except thofe of *Meath* and *Kildare*, are ftiled " by divine permiffion," &c. The cathedral of Dromore is very fmall, but the bifhop's houfe which was erected a few years ago by Dr. *Beresford*, the prefent bifhop of *Offory*, is a handfome and convenient refidence, near the town and not 20 miles diftant from any part of the dioc. This town is very antient, its church lay in ruins until it was rebuilt after the reftoration, by bifhop *Taylor*, and dedicated to " *Chrift our redeemer*." There are 4 prelates of this fee interred in one vault in the

the chancel, viz. *Taylor*, *Ruſt*, *Digby* and *Wiſeman*. An abbey was founded here for regular canons, by St. Colman; at the W. entrance of the town are two decent alms-houſes; a dioceſan ſchool, and on a hill at the S. E. ſide of the town are two meeting-houſes; in the ſquare is erected a market-houſe with ſtone arches; conſiderable quantities of linen cloth are ſold in the markets and fairs here. Fairs are held on 12 May, 28 July and 10 Oct. They have plenty of firing in the neighbouring turbaries, and marle in the adjoining lands; the river *Lagan* divides the town, there being a communication by a bridge of two arches. It was through this town king Wm. IIId marched to join his army on 24 June 1690. At the N. end of the town is a high Daniſh rath of great extent, conſpicuous to travellers and the adjacent-country; from the river *Lagan* to this antient fortification, is a covered way 260 feet long, 7 feet wide and 9 feet deep. In Dromore are the remains of a ſmall caſtle or tower, probably the antient reſidence of the biſhops. This biſhoprick was refounded by James Iſt who by his charters granted it very great and uncommon privileges; the firſt charter bears date the 7th year of his reign. At this place there is a mineral ſpring that riſes by the river ſide, covered by an arch: it is a chalybeate water, and has been drank with ſucceſs for gravelly complaints; and at ſome particular times eſpecially in dry ſeaſons, it is of a purgative quality. On the ſee lands of the biſhop of Dromore, were found in 1783 a pair of *Mooſe-deer* horns, that meaſured from tip to tip 14 feet 4 inches; and alſo almoſt the entire ſkeleton of the enormous animal which wore them, and was computed to have been about 20 hands high. At what period theſe creatures (called by the Iriſh *Damh-ailza*, or the *wild-ox*) were firſt known here, or how long they continued before their extinction is uncertain; but their remains are generally found in the ſtratum of marle that has been covered with bog.—Dromore is alſo the name of a fair town in bar. Inchiquin, co. Clare, prov. Munſter; fairs held 17 June, and 26 Sept.—Another fair town in co. Sligo, prov. Connaught; fairs held 1 Thurſd. in Jan. and 6 June.—Alſo another fair town in bar. Omagh, co. Tyrone, prov. Ulſter; fairs held 2 Feb. 1 May, 24 June, 1 Aug. 29 Sept. and 1 Nov. It is a rectory in dioc. of Connor.

DROMOTE, a village in bar. Mohill, co. Leitrim, prov. Connaught.

DROMY, ſit. E. of Macroomp, in co. Cork, prov. Munſter.

DROMYN, a rectory in dioc. of Armagh, ſit. in bar. Ardee, co. Louth, prov. Leinſter.

DROSS, a *river* in co. Clare, prov. Munſter.

DROUM-ALAGREE, a fair town in co. Cork, prov. Munſter; fairs held 20 May and 27 Oct. This place is otherwiſe named *Drumalagree*.

DRUE'STOWN, ſit. in bar. Kells, co. Meath; prov. Leinſter.

DRUIM-CLIABH. In this place St. Patrick founded a church and biſhoprick, tho' it is now only the antient name of the preſent village of *Drumclive*, ſit. about 3 miles N. of Sligo, in bar. Carbury, co. Sligo, prov. Connaught.

DRUIM-SAILEC, or *Drumſallagh*, the antient name of the cathedral of *Armagh*, in co. Armagh, prov. Ulſter, being as moſt of the primitive churches of Ireland were, conſtructed with wattles, or willows wrought in the manner of wicker-work; it ſeems derived from *Druim* a cave or cell, and *Saileog* a willow.

DRUM, a fair town in bar. Dartree, co. Monaghan, prov. Ulſter, near 54 miles from Dublin; on either ſide of which is a ſmall lough. Fair days 5 Apr. 20 June, 19 Sept. and 1 Mond. in Nov.—Alſo a fair town in co. Tipperary, prov. Munſter; fairs held 10 May and 20 Oct.—Alſo a town in bar. Caſtlereagh, co. Down, prov. Ulſter. Lat. 54 : 36, lon. 6 : 28.—And another in bar. Athlone, co. Roſcommon, prov. Connaught. Lat. 53 : 17, lon. 8 : 30. It is a rectory in dioc. of Tuam.—Alſo a range of *mountains* ſo called, ſit. in bar. Decies, co. Waterford, prov. Munſter.

DRUMACHOSE, a rectory in dioc. of Derry, ſit. in bar. Kenoght, co. Londonderry, prov. Ulſter.

DRUMACON, ſit. near Newtownlimavady, in co. Londonderry, prov. Ulſter.

DRUMACROE, a vicarage in dioc. of Kilmacduagh, ſit. in bar. Dunkellin, co. Galway, prov. Connaught.

DRUMADOON, a fair town in co. Antrim, prov. Ulſter; fairs held 9 June and 28 Nov.

DRUMAHARE or *Dromahaire*, a bar. having a fair town in it of ſame name, ſit. in co. Leitrim, prov. Connaught, diſtant about 102 miles from Dublin; fairs are held 1 Jan. 1 Tueſ. O. S. June, 21 July and 31 Oct. Near this are the ruins of an abbey and of Drumahare caſtle. A great part of the bar. of Drumahare is occupied by *Sliebh-an-Erin* and other mountainous groups; but theſe great hills are far from being unprofitable; they produce abundance of coarſe graſs, and annually pour forth conſiderable numbers of young cattle.

DRUMANA, a fair town in co. Waterford, prov. Munſter; having fairs on 5 June, 4 and 19 Sept. Here is a noble ſeat of the earl of Grandiſon.

DRUM-

DRUMANAGILLIBEG, a fair town in co. Cork, prov. Munster ; fairs held 20 Apr. and June and 15 Nov.

DRUMANE, fit. in bar. Glanarm, co. Antrim, prov. Ulster.

DRUMANEEN, a castle in the parish of Kilshanick, co. Cork, prov. Munster ; standing over the river *Black-water*. About the reign of king James Ist. a very stately house was erected on the foundation of the castle, which was ruined in the late wars : the castle bawn is large, and well inclosed with a high stone wall, flanked with round towers ; and the whole tho' in ruins, from the opposite side of the river, by its lofty situation, has still an august appearance.

DRUMARAN, fit. in bar. Tullagh, co. Clare, prov. Munster.

DRUMARESS, fit. in bar. Kenought, co. Londonderry, prov. Ulster.

DRUMARTE, fit. near Randalstown, co. Antrim, prov. Ulster.

DRUMASNAVE, fit. in co. Leitrim, prov. Connaught, 72 miles from Dublin.

DRUMAULE, a vicarage in dioc. of Connor, fit. in bar. Toome, co. Antrim, prov. Ulster.

DRUMBALLYRONEY, a vicarage in dioc. of Dromore, fit. in bar. upper Iveagh, co. Down, prov. Ulster.

DRUMBANAGHER, a chapelry in dioc. of Armagh, fit. in bar. Orior, co. Armagh, prov. Ulster.—Also a place fit. W. of Glasslough, in co. Monaghan, prov. Ulster ; being a remarkably high hill, on the summit of which was a fort, defended by a deep ditch filled with water. This place was taken possession of, in the rebellion of 1641, by a party of Protestants, headed by capt. *Anketell*, who was treacherously shot, whilst talking to a leader of the opposite party : the garrison being much exasperated at this, sallied forth and put the enemy to flight, many of whom were drowned in an adjacent bog.

DRUMBANE, a handsome seat fit. in co. Down, prov. Ulster ; near the edge of the co.

DRUMBEG, fit. in bar. Iraghticonnor, co. Kerry, prov. Munster.—Also a rectory in dioc. of Down, fit. in bar. Castlereagh, co. Down, prov. Ulster.

DRUMBOE, fit. in bar. Castlereagh, co. Down, prov. Ulster, 3 miles S. of *Belvoir*, where are the ruins of a church, 45 feet in length and 20 broad ; and at the N. W. corner of the church, 24 feet distant from it, stands an old round tower about 35 feet high, 47 in circumference, and 9 in diameter in the clear ; the entrance into which is on the E. 6 feet from the ground. It was antiently an abbey founded by St. Patrick ; and in 1130

was plundered by Connar, the son of Artgal M'Loghlin. It is now a rectory in dioc. of Down. It is the opinion of some, that there has been a small fortified town on the hill of *Drumboe*, and that the foundation of the wall is at this day easy to be seen ; and 'tis observed that the spot of ground whereon the town seems to have stood, is more fertile than any other round about it, which is imagined to have proceeded from the lime and rubbish of the houses. 2 miles N. of the tower of Drumboe, is *the Giant's ring*, an artificial rath regularly thrown up, encompassing 2526 feet circumference, but it has no advantage of height. The ground about it is often used as a race-course, and contains 842 paces. About the middle of this rath stands an antient Druidical monument ; contiguous to the rath there was a small mount, formerly dug thro' to get stones for building, in the middle of which great quantities of bones were found.— Also the name of a village fit. in bar. Raphoe, co. Donegal, prov. Ulster.

DRUMBOLE, fit. in bar. Donaghmain, co. Monaghan, prov. Ulster.

DRUMBOTE, a town in co. Monaghan, prov. Ulster, about 10 miles W. of *Dundalk*. Lat. 54 : 5 N. lon. 6 : 45 W.

DRUMBRIDGE, a fair town in co. Meath, prov. Leinster ; fairs held 12 Feb. — Also a place in bar. Castlereagh, co. Down, prov. Ulster ; — and another near *Lisburn*, co. Antrim, in same prov.

DRUMBROHAS, fit. in bar. Coole, co. Fermanagh, prov. Ulster.

DRUMCALLAGHER, a fair town in co. Cork, prov. Munster ; fairs held 3 Sept.

DRUMCANNON, a parish in bar. Middlethird, co. Waterford, prov. Munster ; the church of which is fit. 78 miles from Dublin. Fairs held 25 Sept. It is a rectory in dioc. of Waterford.

DRUMCAR, a vicarage in dioc. of Armagh, fit. in bar. Atherdee, co. Louth, prov. Leinst.

DRUMCASKELL, fit. in bar. Atherdee, co. Louth, prov. Leinster.

DRUMCLIEVE or *Drumcliffe*, a village fit. in bar. Carbury, co. Sligo, prov. Connaught, about 3 miles N. of the town of Sligo ; tho' now only a vicarage in dioc. of Elphin, it was once a bishoprick founded by St. Patrick, and afterwards united to that of Elphin. St. *Columba* founded a celebrated monastery here in 590 ; the parish church is built on the old foundation ; here are the ruins of a round tower. *Drumclieve* was antiently called *Druimcliabh*.—There is another place of same name fit. in bar. Islands, co. Clare, prov. Munster ; where there is another of the antient round towers.

towers: this latter place is a vicarage in dioc. of Killaloe.

DRUMCONDRA, sit. in co. Cavan, prov. Ulster, 80 miles from Dublin.—There is also a a village so called, sit. in bar. Coolock, co. Dublin, prov. Leinster, within about 2 miles of the metropolis. It is a curacy in dioc. of Dublin, and more properly called *Drumconrath*. Here is a neat church, with a beautiful monument erected to the memory of the late *Marmaduke Coghill*, L. L. D. In this neighbourhood are several handsome seats. There is also an *Union-school* founded here by the late *Geo. Purdon Drew*, esq. which admits children of every mode of religious persuasion; it has 15 boys and the same number of girls, who are cloathed and educated.

DRUMCONG, a seat in co. Galway, prov. Connaught, 113 miles from Dublin.

DRUMCONRATH, a village and rectory in dioc. of Meath, sit. in bar. Slane, co. Meath, prov. Leinster.

DRUMCOOLY, sit. in bar. Coole'stown, King's co. prov. Leinster.

DRUMCORK, sit. near Tynan, co. Armagh, prov. Ulster.

DRUMCREE, sit. in bar. O'Neiland, co. Armagh, prov. Ulster: there is a church belonging to it, which is a rectory in dioc. of Armagh. Also a place in bar. Delvin, co. Westmeath, prov. Leinster; in which there was an establishment for Eremites in the 9th century.

DRUMCREEHY, a rectory in dioc. of Kilfenora, sit. in bar. Burrin, co. Clare, prov. Munster.

DRUMCULLACHER, sit. in co. Limerick, prov. Munster, 133 miles from Dublin. A mile and ½ beyond which is *Springfield*, a very fine seat with handsome improvements of lord *Muskerry*.

DRUMCULLIN, a vicarage in dioc. of Meath, sit. in bar. Eglish, King's co. prov. Leinster.

DRUMDA, a village in bar. Boyle, co. Roscommon, prov. Connaught.

DRUMDALEAGUE, a rectory in dioc. of Cork, sit. in bar. Carbery, co. Cork, prov. Munster.

DRUMDEER, a fair town in co. Cork, prov. Munster, near Doneraile. Here is a red and grey marble quarry. Fairs held 12 and 13 June, 12 and 13 Oct.

DRUMDOWNE, a ruined castle in co. Cork, prov. Munster, within a few miles of Mallow; it belonged to the *Barrys*.

DRUMENAGH, sit. in bar. Maghereboy, co. Fermanagh, prov. Ulster.

DRUMFIN, a ruined *castle*, sit. about 6 miles from *Ballinafad*, co. Sligo, prov. Connaught.

DRUMFRY, a chapelry in dioc. of Leighlin, sit. in bar. Idrone, co. Carlow, prov. Leinster.

DRUMGATH, a vicarage in dioc. of Dromore, sit. in bar. upper Iveagh, co. Down, prov. Ulster.

DRUMGAWLY, sit. in bar. Strabane, co. Tyrone, prov. Ulster.

DRUMGLASSE, a rectory in dioc. of Armagh, sit. near Dungannon, in bar. Dungannon, co. Tyrone, prov. Ulster. Here, and in this part of the country at *Creenough* and *Coal-island*, some very extensive collieries have been established, the works of which are curiously constructed.

DRUMGOLAND or *Drumgoolan*, a rectory in dioc. of Dromore, sit. in bar. upper Iveagh, co. Down, prov. Ulster. In the town land of *Leganeny* in this parish, on a mountain called *Slieve-na-boiltrough*, (being a part of *Slieve Crob*) is a *Cromlech*, made of a huge gritty rock, in shape of a monstrous coffin, supported by 3 feet, and is 11 feet long, 5 feet over in its broadest part, and diminishing gradually from thence to each end in a point; it is 20 inches thick in most parts, in one but 18, and in other 2 feet. The 3 supporters of this great stone are proportionable to the upper one, and the cavity underneath is such, that a man of 6¼ feet high can stand upright in it. The parish church of *Drumgoolan* is about 3 miles N. W. of *Castle Vellin*; about 30 feet from the church door, is a *stone cross*, composed of one entire coarse gritty stone, fixed to a pedestal 3½ feet square and 4 feet above the surface. The shaft or cross part is 10 feet high, 1 foot thick, and 18 inches broad. The want of letters on it, and the coarseness of the work shew its antiquity. N. of *Drumgoolan* the country is coarse and mountainous, more employed in grazing than tillage, and more black cattle are to be seen hereabouts, than in any other part of the country.

DRUMGOOLE, sit. near *Killesandra*, co. Cavan, prov. Ulster.

DRUMGOON, a rectory in dioc. of Kilmore, sit. in bar. Tullagharvey, co. Cavan, prov. Ulster.

DRUMGOOTHER, sit. in bar. Ferrard, co. Louth, prov. Leinster.

DRUMHOLM or *Drumhome*, sit. in bar. Tyrhugh, co. Donegal, prov. Ulster; here was a celebrated monastery, in which Flahertach O'Maldory king of Tyrconnel, was buried A. D. 1197. It is now a vicarage in dioc. of Raphoe.

DRUMIN, sit. in bar. Atherdee, co. Louth, prov. Leinster.—Also a place in bar. Coshma, co. Limerick, prov. Munster.

DRUMIRORK, a fair town in co. Kerry, prov. Munster; fairs held 10 June, 17 and 18 Oct. 5 and 6 Dec.

DRUM.

DRUMKEIRN or *Drumkerrin*, a fair and poſt town in bar. Drumahair, co. Leitrim, prov. Connaught ; fairs held 2 Wedneſ. in Feb. 27 May, 18 July, 19 Oct. Wedneſ. before Chriſtmas.

DRUMKILEEVE, ſit. in bar. Iſlands, co. Clare, prov. Munſter.

DRUMKIN, a rectory in dioc. of Clogher, ſit. in bar. Coole, co. Fermanagh, prov. Ulſter.

DRUMLAGHDED-HILL, ſit. in co. Donegal, prov. Ulſter, 131 miles from Dublin.

DRUMLAINE or *Drumlane*, ſit. in bar. *Clonrhee*, co. Cavan, prov. Ulſter ; it is otherwiſe called *Drumlaghan*, and diſtant about 3 miles from *Belturbet* : here is one of the antient round towers. There was alſo a celebrated monaſtery founded here before the year 550, and dedicated to the Virgin Mary: the churchyard here has been for many years a famous burial-place. *Monaſt. Hib.* According to Dr. Beaufort's *memoir*, this place is in the bar. of *Loughtee* : it is a vicarage in dioc. of Liſmore.

DRUMLARGAN, a rectory in dioc. of Meath, ſit. in bar. Deece, co. Meath, prov. Leinſter.

DRUMLEASE, a vicarage in dioc. of Kilmore, ſit. in bar. Dromahaire, co. Leitrim, prov. Connaught.

DRUMLEGAGH-WOOD, this was a fine wood, and one of the largeſt in the kingdom ; but has been cut down. It was ſit. in co. Kerry, prov. Munſter ; the river *Feal* running thro' it.

DRUMLEY, ſit. in bar. Kiltartan, co. Galway, prov. Connaught.

DRUMLISH, a fair town in co. Longford, prov. Leinſter ; fairs held 14 May, 6 Aug. 19 Sept. and 2 Dec.

DRUMLOCH, a town-land in pariſh of Dromore, co. Down, prov. Munſter ; from which one of the heads of *Ballinchinch* river proceeds.

DRUMLUMMON, a vicarage in dioc. of Ardagh, ſit. in bar. Cloninoghan, co. Cavan, prov. Ulſter.

DRUMMINÆSH, ſit. in bar. Glenarm, co. Antrim, prov. Ulſter.

DRUMMORE *Church*, ſit. in co. Tyrone, prov. Ulſter, 94 miles from Dublin.

DRUMMOTE, ſit. in co. Leitrim, prov. Connaught, 67 miles from Dublin.

DRUMMULLY, a rectory in dioc. of Clogher, ſit. in bar. Coole, co. Fermanagh, prov. Ulſter.

DRUMMURGHILL, a curacy in dioc. of Kildare, ſit. in bar. Ikeath, co. Kildare, prov. Leinſter.

DRUMMURY, ſit. in bar. Louth, co. Louth, prov. Leinſter.

DRUMNA, or *Drimna*, ſit. near *Cromlin*, co. Dublin, prov. Leinſter, and about ¼ of a mile from the banks of the Grand Canal. On theſe lands ſtands an antient caſtle, in tolerable preſervation, and inhabited : it was a place of ſome ſtrength, and partly encompaſſed with a broad and deep foſſe ; ſome modern additions have been made to it, that have altered its original form.

DRUMNASNAVE, ſit. on the confines of the co.'s Leitrim and Roſcommon, prov. Connaught ; having a bridge over part of *Lough-Bofin*.

DRUMNOVER, ſit. near Fair-head, in co. Antrim, prov. Ulſter.

DRUMOD, or *Drumot*, a fair town in co. Leitrim, prov. Connaught ; fairs held 1 Jan. 28 March, 1ſt Saturd. O. S. May, 26 June, 1ſt Saturd. after 12 Aug. 10 Oct. and Sat. before 12 Dec.

DRUMOYLE, ſit. in bar. Ballybritt, King's co. prov. Leinſter.

DRUMOYLIN, ſit. in bar. Conillo, co. Limerick, prov. Munſter.

DRUMQUIN, a fair town in bar. Omagh, co. Tyrone, prov. Ulſter ; fairs held 9 June and 8 Nov.

DRUMRAGH, a rectory in dioc. of Derry, ſit. in bar. Omagh, co. Tyrone, prov. Ulſter.

DRUMRANY, otherwiſe called *Drumrath*, ſit. about 6 miles N. E. of Athlone, in bar. *Kilkenny-weſt*, co. Weſtmeath, prov. Leinſter. *Monaſt. Hib.* It is a vicarage in dioc. of Meath, and according to Dr. Beaufort's *Mem.* is in bar. *Brawny.* Here was a celebrated monaſtery, founded in 588, in honour of *St. Enan* ; it was burned to the ground with 150 perſons in it, by the *Oſtmen*, A. D. 946.

DRUMRASTILL, a ſeat ſit. on the river *Blackwater*, in co. Cork, prov. Munſter.

DRUMRAT, a vicarage in dioc. of Achonry, ſit. in bar. Corran, co. Sligo, prov. Connaught. A monaſtery was founded here by St. *Fechin*, about A. D. 645.

DRUMRATH, ſee *Drumrany*.

DRUMREILY, a rectory in dioc. of Kilmore, ſit. in bar. Carrigallen, co. Leitrim, prov. Connaught.

DRUMSALLAGH, or *Drum-Saillee*, i. e. the church built with willows ; the antient name of the cathedral of *Ardmagh*, being originally as moſt of the primitive churches of Ireland were, conſtructed with wattles or willows, wrought in the manner of wicker work.

DRUMSHALLEN, or *Drumſhallen*, ſit. in bar. Ferrard, co. Louth, prov. Leinſter ; here St. Patrick founded a noble monaſtery for canons regular ; it is now a curacy in dioc. of Armagh.

DRUMSHAMBO, or *Drumſhanbo*, a fair town in bar. Leitrim, co. Leitrim, prov. Connaught ; fairs held 12 Feb. May, 2 Frid. in June, 16 July, 6 Oct. and 16 Nov.

DRUMSHICANE, ſit. near the *Blackwater*, in co. Cork, prov. Munſter. Here is a good houſe, and was alſo a fortified caſtle of the *O'Keifs*,

O'Keifs, with turrets and an high square tower in the centre; but the whole is now demolished. The walls were built with flat stones or flags, exceedingly well cemented.

DRUMSKINBOE, sit. in bar. Dungannon, co. Tyrone, prov. Ulster.

DRUMSNA, a fair town in co. Leitrim, prov. Connaught; fairs held 20 May, 22 June, 25 Aug. 7 Oct. and 13 Dec.

DRUMSNAT, or *Drumsnut*, sit. in bar. *Monaghan*, co. Monaghan, prov. Ulster. Dr. *Beauford*. (according to *Scale*, in bar. *Dartree*.) It is a vicarage in dioc. of Clogher.

DRUMSNAW, a village in bar. Leitrim, co. Leitrim, prov. Connaught.

DRUMSWORDS, a village in bar. Dartree, co. Monaghan, prov. Ulster.

DRUMTARIFF, a vicarage in dioc. of Ardfert, sit. in bar. Duhallow, co. Cork, prov. Munster.

DRUMTEMPLE, a vicarage in dioc. of Elphin, sit. in bar. Ballimoe, co. Roscommon, prov. Connaught.

DRUMURRY, sit. in bar. Belfast, co. Antrim, prov. Ulster. (Dr. *Beauford*.)

DRUMURY, sit. in bar. Loughtee, co. Cavan, prov. Ulster. (*Scale*.)

DRUNG, a vicarage in dioc. of Kilmore, sit. in bar. Tullagharvey, co. Cavan, prov. Ulster.

DRUNG-HILLS, sit. in the parish of Glanbehy, co. Kerry, prov. Munster. The road over these hills hang in a tremendous manner over that part of the sea which forms the bay of Castlemain. There is a custom amongst the country people, to enjoin every one who passes here, to make some verses to the honour of the mountain, otherwise they affirm, that whoever attempts to pass it without versifying, must meet with some mischance: the original of which notion seems to be, that it will require a person's whole circumspection to preserve himself from falling off his horse.

DRUNMON, sit. in bar. Kiltartan, co. Galway, prov. Connaught.

DRY BRIDGE, sit. in bar. Ferrard, co. Louth, prov. Leinster.

DUAGH, a vicarage in dioc. of Ardfert, sit. in bar. Clonmaurice, co. Kerry, prov. Munst.

DUAGHMORE, an *island* sit. near Tramore bay, co. Waterford, prov. Munster.

DU ARAGIL, a ruined castle, built by the *O'Keifs*, in the parish of *Cullen*, co. Cork, prov. Munster.

DUBBER, sit. in bar. Coolock, co. Dublin, prov. Leinster.

DUBLIN CITY, the metropolis of Ireland, sit. in prov. Leinster, adjoining a co. of same name. This antient city now lies on either side the river *Liffey*, or Anna-Liffey, was called *Eblana Civitas* according to Ptolemy, who flou-

rished in the reign of Antoninus Pius, about the year of Christ, 140. It has been known by various names; the Irish called it *Drom-Choll Coil*, i. e. "The brow of a hazel wood." At this day they call it *Ath-cliath*, i. e. "The ford of hurdles;" and *Bally Ath-Cliath*, i. e. A town on the ford of hurdles," for before the river Liffey was embanked by quays, people had access to it by means of hurdles laid on the low and marshy parts of the town, adjoining the water. The inhabitants of Fingal, towards the N. of the city, call it *Divelin*; and the Welsh, *Dinas-dulin*, or "The city of Dublin." The *Blanii*, *Eblani*, or *Deblani*, the original inhabitants of this place, are said to have come from that part of Britain called Wales; on account of its proximity, the almost identity of languages, and the close conformity of antient religious rites and ceremonies of both people. Upon the submission of Ireland to Henry the IId of England, 1172, that king granted by charter, to his subjects of Bristol, the city of Dublin to inhabit, and to hold of him and his heirs for ever, with all the liberties and free customs, which his subjects of Bristol then enjoyed at Bristol, and through all England. This charter is the foundation of the liberties of the city of Dublin, which were afterwards enlarged and confirmed by king John and other succeeding monarchs, and by divers acts of parliament. It is generally admitted that the walls and fortifications about Dublin, were raised by the Ostmen, or Danes, in the 9th century; who made it the head or capital of their colonies in Leinster, from whence they issued out upon all occasion against their enemies. In the year 1000, the same people repaired and fortified the city with new works, and five years after, king Melaghlin marched to Dublin, and set fire to the suburbs, but the strength of the walls hindered him from making any impression on it. The walls of the city, including those of the castle, in the largest extent, did not take up an Irish mile; and it appears from the account given by Pembridge, that they were carried from Winetavern-gate, along the S. side of Cook-street, 'till they joined Owen's-arch, which was a portal to the city. And from thence were continued N. of Owen's church-yard, to a castle called Fagan's castle in Page's-court, where was another Portal, and from thence was extended to where Newgate formerly stood. These walls however are for the most part either destroyed or built on, whereby very little of them are to be seen at this day. W. on the walls of the city, at the end of Fishamble street, stood a castle, that in different ages bore two names, viz. *Proudfort's-castle* and *Fyan's-castle*, possibly from some families of both these names, who either built or in-

habited

habited it. Wm. Proutefort was a man of some figure in the reign of Edw. IIId. Three of the Fyans bore high offices in the city, in the 15th and 16th centuries; for John Fyan was mayor in 1472 and 1479. Thomas Fyan was one of the Sheriffs in 1540, and Richard Fyan was mayor in 1549 and 1564. In 1316, the mayor and citizens enlarged and built a new wall to the city from Newgate, (from thence fo called) to Ormond's-gate, which stood at the foot of king John's bridge. The buildings of the city of Dublin, like those through other parts of the kingdom, were antiently mean and contemptible, erected of wattles daubed over with clay to keep out the cold, and covered with sedge or straw. The Danes who fortified the city, applied their labours to make it defensible and not ornamental, nor could this latter circumstance (fays Mr. Harris,) be expected to be considered by a people, engaged in perpetual wars, undefended by laws, and in a flitting, shifting condition, ready to make room for the first powerful invader. It was of fuch rude materials, that king Hen. IId either out of necessity, or in compliance with the fashions of the place, erected in 1172, a royal palace with uncommon elegance, of smoothed wattles, in which his majesty, with the kings and princes of Ireland, folemnized the festival of Christmas. Many of the antient streets, lanes and alleys have been either totally annihilated, or loft or changed their names, but those of the streets, &c. now existing amount to about 600. Grangegorman, Stoney-batter and Glaffmanogue, now united to the town, were formerly villages at fome distance from it; in the latter of which places, the sheriffs of Dublin have been known to hold their courts in the times of the plague, and particularly in the year 1575, as being remote from the city. A village called Hogges, lay alfo withoutside the city walls, and E. of George's-lane, in which a nunnery, under the invocation of the B. V. Mary, was founded by Dermot M'Morough, king of Leinster, about A. D. 1146, before the arrival of the English in this kingdom. This village is mentioned in several very early charters, &c. the footsteps or traces of the name whereof, remain in a street called Hog-hill, and Hoggingreen, whereon St. Andrew's-church now stands. This was a large fpace of ground, and is often mentioned by the Irish historians, as the common place for the execution of criminals; amongst whom we have an instance in Adam Duff O'Toole, who in 1327 was burned there for herefy and blafphemy. Part of this green is now called College-green, from a college founded there by Queen Eliz. in the latter end of the 16th century, on the

fite of the monastery of All-faints. The bounds of the city and its liberties, have been ascertained and confirmed by divers charters; and agreeable to antient ufage, the Franchifes are perambulated every 3d year. The corporation of the city confifts of a lord mayor, two sheriffs, twenty-four aldermen, befides the common council and sheriff's peers. The city was formerly under the direction of provoft and bailiffs, then mayor and bailiffs, afterwards mayor and sheriffs, and next lord mayor and sheriffs, thus: In 1308, John le Decer was provoft; Rich. de St. Olave and John Stakebold, bailiffs. In 1409, Tho. Cufacks was mayor; Rich. Bove, and Tho. Shortall were bailiffs. In 1547, Thady Duffe was mayor; Jn. Ryan and T. Comin were sheriffs. In 1665, fir D. Bellingham was ld. mayor; C. Lovet and J. Quelfh were sheriffs. 1301, A great part of the city, together with St. Werburgh's church, was accidentally burned down on St. Columb's eve. The nature of buildings at that time will not admit of our being furprifed at the frequency of fires. At this time the common-pleas, and the pleas of the crown, were not held before judges appointed in the courts for that purpofe, but before the chief governor of Ireland, and fometimes when he was otherwife employed, by commiffioners appointed by him. In 1320, an univerfity was erected in St. Patrick's church, Dublin. In 1338, was an extraordinary hard frost, which held from 2 Dec. to 10 Feb. In 1343, St. Thomas-street was burned down on 13 Feb. by an accidental fire. In 1348 a pestilence raged through moft parts of the world, and among other places deftroyed vaft numbers in the city of Dublin. 1359, 'till this time there was only one judge to difpatch the bufinefs of the court of King's-bench, viz. John Rednefs, who was then called plainly, only juftice. But now the bufinefs being found too much for one man, the king upon the application of the fubject, appointed William Polit, a fecond juftice, under the name of an affociate to Rednefs; and allotted him an annual fee of 40l. and he had liberty to practice as a lawyer, notwithstanding his being appointed a judge. In 1362, on the 6 April, St. Patrick's church was burned down by the negligence of John the fexton: a few years after it was rebuilt, and the prefent steeple added to it by archbifhop Minot. In 1370, and 1383, the pestilence raged here and deftroyed many. In 1447, a plague and famine this year afflicted moft parts of this kingdom. In 1452, the river Liffey at Dublin was entirely dry for the fpace of two minutes. In 1452, a mint was opened in the castle of Dublin, where not only filver but brafs money was coined. In 1466 and 1477, the plague again wafted Dublin, as it did alfo again in 1484.

In

In 1489, the first muskets or fire arms, that perhaps were ever seen in Ireland, were brought to Dublin from Germany; and six of them as a great rarity were presented to Gerald earl of Kildare, then lord deputy, which he put into the hands of his guards as they stood centinels before his house in Thomas-court. In 1525, a plague: and 1528, a pestilential sickness, called the English-sweat. In 1559, large bibles printed in the English language, were placed in the middle of the choirs of St. Patrick's and Christ church, which caused great resort on purpose to read them. In 1560, queen Elizabeth caused the castle of Dublin to be repaired for her lieutenants or deputies to dwell in; at which time the castle clock and other public clocks were set up. In 1562, the roof and part of the body of Christ-church fell, by which the antient monument of Strongbow was broken. In 1571, Irish characters for printing, were first brought into Ireland by Nicholas Walsh, chancellor of St. Patrick's, Dublin. In 1575, a very great plague destroyed above 3000 persons, and the city was so depopulated, that grass grew in the streets. In 1604, 5 and 6, a plague in the city. In 1605, the customs of Tanistry and Gavelkind were abolished by judgment in the King's-bench. In 1627, July 24, a second examinator was first added to the court of Chancery. In 1701, the city of Dublin erected the statue of king William, on horseback, in brass, upon a marble pedestal in College-green, with the following inscription on the marble work.

Gulielmo Tertio,
Magnæ Britanniæ, Franciæ & Hiberniæ,
Regi.
Ob Religionem Conservatam.
Restitutas Leges.
Libertatem Assertam.
Cives Dublinienses hanc statuam posuere.

It was begun, A. D. 1700.
Sir Anth. Percy, Lord Mayor.
Charles Forrest, } Esqrs. Sheriffs.
James Barlow,

Finished, A. D. 1701.
Sir Mark Rainsford, Lord Mayor.
John Eccles } Esqrs. Sheriffs.
Ralph Gore,

And was opened with great solemnity on the 1 July, 1701, being the anniversary of the victory of the Boyne. There are 2 cathedrals, viz. St. Patrick's and Christ-church, and 18 parish churches, some of which are elegant structures, besides 2 chapels of ease, 6 private chapels, where the service of the established church is regularly attended; besides 3 churches for French and 1 for Dutch Protestants, 17 meeting-houses for Protestant dissenters, 2 for Quakers, 3 for Methodists, 1 for Anabaptists, 1 for Moravians, and 16 Roman-catholic chapels. The *Castle* within the walls of the city hath indeed lost its antient strength, but hath assumed a more graceful form; and is better fitted for the times of peace and tranquillity. It was erected, or at least begun by and in the government of Meiler Fitzhenry, about the year 1205, as appears by a patent granted to him for that purpose. It consisted of a regular fortification, draw-bridge, &c. with several towers, the strongest of which was Birmingham tower lately rebuilt; this tower was often used as a prison for state criminals, and afterwards for preserving the antient records of the kingdom. This building was not converted into the seat of government, 'till the reign of queen Eliz. before that period there does not appear to have been any fixed place for the reception of the chief governors, who sometimes held their courts at Thomas-court, (in which was a chamber of Presence called the King's chamber, wherein the lords of the council assembled) sometimes at the palace of the Archbishop of Dublin, at St. Sepulchre's, but oftener in the castle of Kilmainham. Near the castle, viz. in Great Ship-street, stood one of the antient round towers, but it was destroyed a few years ago. It may be observed that in the early ages of the English government, the courts of justice were ambulatory, and not fixed to any certain place. In the reign of Edw. IIId the Common-pleas and Exchequer were held at Carlow. In the 37th year of that reign (1363) the Common-pleas was by writ removed from Carlow back to Dublin. Parliaments also were unfixed and held in various places, but more frequently in Dublin, and sometimes in the castle itself, as was done 11th James Ist and 10th and 15th Charles. In the latter end of the reign of Queen Eliz. and the beginning of that of James Ist. both terms and parliaments were held at the castle: but now a sumptuous *Parliament house* hath been erected with all convenient chambers and offices for the dispatch of the business of the nation. This superb pile was begun in 1728, during the administration of John, lord Carteret, and finished in about 10 years, the expence amounting to near 40,000*l*. The structure deserves the greatest praise; and is even now undergoing farther improvements; it may be happily imitated, but has not as yet been exceeded, and is now justly accounted one of the foremost architectural beauties; affording perhaps the most stately senatorial hall in Europe. The *Four-courts*, containing
the

the Chancery, King's-bench, Common-pleas and Exchequer were fet apart in Chrift-church-lane for the bufinefs of the law, in the year 1695: but a new building for that purpofe is now begun at the Inn's-quay, the firft ftone being laid by the duke of *Rutland*, ld. lieutenant 1786: adjoining to which intended building are a new range of law offices, finifhed in a moft ftriking and elegant manner. The *Univerfity* in 1311, John Lech. archbp. of Dublin, procured a bull from Pope Clement Vth for the foundation of an Univerfity for fcholars at Dublin, but this projeâ fell by the death of the archbifhop about 2 years after. In 1320 his fuccefsor renewed this foundation, and procured a confirmation thereof from the then Pope, but for want of a fufficient fund to maintain the ftudents, the Univerfity in a fhort time dwindled to nothing. In 1585, fir J. Perrot, then lord lieutenant, reprefented to Queen Eliz. the neceffity of fuch an inftitution, and in confequence thereof that Queen caufed a Univerfity to be erected where it now ftands in College-green, then called All-hallows, by the name of the College of the Holy and Undivided Trinity, near Dublin, &c. which confifted of a Provoft, fenior and junior Fellows, Scholars of the houfe, Students, &c. The prefent building (the old one being almoft deftroyed) is without queftion the nobleft of the kind in Europe, carrying with it more the appearance of a royal manfion than a number of Collegiate cells; it extends in front above 300 feet, built of Portland ftone. The library is moft fuperb and curious. And the *Provoft's houfe* lately erected on the E. fide of Grafton-ftreet, near the College, may in point of architectural elegance be ranked in the firft clafs of ftructures in this kingdom. The *Barracks* is an extenfive building founded in 1706, at the expence of the crown, and lately much enlarged. It confifts of four courts, three of them open to the river Liffey, and the other fronts Oxmantown-green. It is pleafantly fit. on an eminence, in a healthful air, and is faid to be the largeft and completeft building of the kind in Europe. The *Cuftom houfe* formerly ftood on the S. fide of the river Liffey, near Effex bridge, and was at the time of its erection a handfome and convenient building, but being fince found too fmall for the great increafe of trade, &c. a moft fuperb ftructure has been erected in its ftead lower down the river, on the oppofite fide called the N. ftrand. The *Tholfel* was erected in Skinner-row at the charge of the city in 1683; great part of it however has been lately taken down, and the erection of a new one in a

convenient fituation is now in agitation. This building had its name from the old word, *Toll-ftall*, i. e. a ftall or feat where the toll-gatherers attended to receive the toll or cuftom, for fuch goods as were liable to a city impoft. Here the lord mayor, fheriffs and commons meet to tranfact city bufinefs, &c. The building is a large quadrangular pile of hewn ftone, fupported by arches and pillars; the front having a magnificent appearance. And it was formerly alfo the Stadthoufe or Exchange for merchants, but a new Exchange has lately been erected, called the *Royal Exchange*, near the caftle, and oppofite that elegant ftreet called Parliament-ftreet. This noble and expenfive ftructure, is allowed by all who have beheld it, to be the moft fuperb and beautiful building for the purpofe, of any perhaps in the world. The *Linen-hall* was erected at the public expence, and opened in 1728, for the reception of fuch linen cloths, as were brought to Dublin for fale. 'Tis a handfome and convenient building, and of late much enlarged, improved and beautified. St. *Stephen's-green*, is a moft extenfive and handfome fquare, one of the largeft in Europe, being an Englifh mile in circumference; fit. at the E. end of the city. It was levelled and laid out in walks for the recreation of the citizens in 1670. It is enclofed by a low wall with entrances from every quarter by gates and turnftiles at proper diftances. The outer walls are graveled and planted with trees on each fide; the interior walks are inclofed by thorn hedges on each fide, and divided from the other by a foffe. The infide is a fpacious lawn, at the centre of which is a curious equeftrian ftatue in brafs, of his majefty king George IId executed by Van Noft. The *city Bafen*, is the pleafanteft, moft elegant and fequeftered place of relaxation the citizens can boaft of; the refervoir which in part fupplies the city with water, is mounded and terraced all round, and planted with quick-fet-hedges, limes and elms, having beautiful green walks between. In a fituation which commands a moft fatisfactory profpect of a vaft extent of fine country to the S. The entrance is elegant by a lofty iron gate, and the water that fupplies it, is conveyed from the neighbouring mountains. The *charitable inftitutions* in Dublin are very numerous, and adapted to every fituation and every age of life, infomuch that no city can boaft of greater examples of humanity and public attention to all the objects of diftrefs. Amongft thefe the moft remarkable are the Blue-coat-hofpital; the Royal hofpital; the Work-houfe, the Houfe of Induftry, in Channel-row,

nel-row; the Charitable infirmary; the hofpital for incurables; Mercer's hofpital; Dr.
Steeven's hofpital; the Lying-in-hofpital; St.
Patrick's hofpital for lunatics; Simpfon's
hofpital; the Meath hofpital; and many
others we might add of inferior note.
The *Blue-coat-hofpital*, formerly fit. in Queen
ftreet, but now a new and moft elegant building in Oxmantown-green, was firft founded
in 1670, by king Charles IId for the educat-
ing, fupporting and apprenticing the fons of
reduced freemen of the city of Dublin.
This charity has been much enlarged and
improved as its revenues increafed, and the
building has been executed in the moft ftriking
manner at a very confiderable expence. The
Royal hofpital, of king Charles IId for the
fupport of old and decayed foldiers of the
army of Ireland, fit. near Kilmainham, is
pretty much after the manner of Chelfea-
college, and is a noble inftitution, and ftands in
a delightful part of the country. The total
expenditure in building, amounted to 23,559*l.*
16*s.* 11*d.* The approaches to this ftately
edifice are through feveral rows of tall trees;
with fields in the front, and a gradual afcent
from the river Liffey. The building being
quadrangular, forms a fpacious area, laid out
in grafs-plots and gravelled walks, with a pi-
azza about the whole, by which there is a
covered paffage from every quarter to the
chapel and hall, both which are curioufly
decorated; the ftucco and carving of the chapel is mafterly, and the hall enriched with
elegant whole length portraitures of feveral
kings, queens and other perfonages of diftinc-
tion. The *Foundling-hofpital*, for the reception of infant and other young but deftitute
children of both fexes, is an extenfive and
commodious building in St. James's-ftreet; it
has been regulated fince its original inftitution
by different acts of parliament, and hath remained under its prefent ftate fince 1730.
Dr. *Steeven's-hofpital* was built purfuant to the
will of an eminent phyfician in Dublin, and
lies between James's-ftreet and the Royal
Hofpital, for the relief and maintenance of
curable poor perfons. It is a fpacious ftructure, finifhed in 1734. St. *Patrick's-hofpital*,
for lunatics, fit. very near the former, was
founded in 1745, in confequence of a bequeft
of about 11,000*l.* devifed by Dr. Swift, the
celebrated dean of St. Patrick's. There are
two large areas for the patients to exercife;
the one on the E. fide for men, the other
on the W. for women; and they are kept
apart from each other, by a divifion in the
building. The *Lying-in-hofpital*, for poor women, fit. in Great Britain-ftreet, was founded
by Surgeon Mofs. It was the firft inftitution

of the kind attempted in any part of his majefty's dominions. The foundation ftone
of it was laid by the Rt. Hon. Tho. Taylor,
then lord mayor of the city of Dublin, 24
May, 1751. The whole forms a moft beautiful and elegant ftructure. Adjoining to it
are the gardens called the New-gardens, and
the Rotunda, where mufical concerts are occafionally performed for the fupport of this
laudable and truly ufeful charity. The Hofpital was opened for the reception of patients,
on the 8 Dec. 1757. The *Bridges* in Dublin
acrofs the Liffey are 6, of which 2 are finifhed
in a manner fimilar to that of Weftminfter;
viz. Effex-bridge and the Queen's-bridge. The
former of which was conftructed by the late
Mr. George Simple, and coft 20,661*l.* 11*s.* 4*d.*
Carlifle-bridge which is the neareft to the new
Cuftom-houfe, and newly erected, is alfo large
and handfome. The *Churches* in general are
large and elegant, and the 2 cathedrals which
are very antient, deferve particular attention.
St. *Patrick's cathedral* was erected in the S. fuburbs of the city, about the year 1190, by John
Comyn, then archbifhop of Dublin, on ground
where an old parochial church had before
ftood; tho' Henry Loundres his fucceffor
erected this church which was collegiate in
its firft conftitution, into a cathedral; Tho.
Minot, archbifhop of Dublin, rebuilt part of
the cathedral which had been deftroyed by
fire. He alfo built a high fteeple of fquared
ftone, about the year 1370; and by a legacy
bequeathed by the Rev. Dr. Sterne, late bifhop
of Clogher, a lofty fpire was erected on the
fteeple, in 1750. Whether we confider the
compafs, or the beauty and magnificence of
the ftructure, it is without fcruple to be pre-
ferred before all the cathedrals in Ireland. The
cathedral of *Chrift church*, or of the Bleffed
Trinity, was firft built by Sitricus the fon of
Amlave, king of the Oftmen of Dublin, and
Donat then bifhop of Dublin, in the middle
of the city, about the year 1038. This bifhop's
fucceffors from time to time enlarged and improved it. It is now very fpacious and ornamental, and the monuments in both this and
the other cathedral which are many, are moft
of them executed in a mafterly and fuperb
manner. The names of the parifh churches
in Dublin, are as follows, viz. St. Andrew's;
St. Ann's; St. Audeon's; St. Bridget's; St. Catherine's; St. James's; St. John's; St. Luke's;
St. Mark's; St. Mary's; St. Michael's; St.
Michan's; St. Nicholas within; St. Nicholas
without; St. Paul's; St. Peter's; St. Thomas's; St. Werburgh's; with 2 chapels of
eafe, viz. St. George's and St. Kevin's. After
this fhort defcription of Dublin, we may
fairly infer from its prefent ftate, that the
character

character of *Nobilissima Civitas*, given to it by king Edgar's charter in the 10th century, is now truly applicable to it. It is above 10 miles in circumference, and is the second city in his Majesty's dominions, and perhaps the fourth in Europe. Besides the many other improvements, is that of divers handsome fountains, for the convenience of the inhabitants, which are not less useful than ornamental, and dispersed throughout the different streets in a most judicious manner. The *Theatre* in Crow-street, (for which Mr. Daly is manager by a particular act of Parliament) is the only one now kept open in this city; and it is but justice to say the public are much indebted to that gentleman for his taste and abilities, and unlimited desire to give general satisfaction. Such is the present state of this city: with respect to former times; we find it abounded with religious houses, such as the following, viz. the priory of all-Saints, founded 1166, for *Augustinian* canons, of the order of *Aroacia*; St. Mary's-abbey, built by the Danes in 948 for Benedictine Monks; the priory of St. *Sepulchre's*; the nunnery of St. *Mary les Dames*, from whence Dame-street takes its name; the abbey of St. *Olave*, built by a colony from Bristol, for such of their countrymen as should embrace the order of St. Augustin; the *Monastery of Witsschau*, founded about 1268; the abbey of St. Thomas, founded by *Wm. Fitz-Andelm*, butler to Henry IIId. in 1172, for canons of St. Victor; the priory of St. *John Baptist*, erected by *Alured de Palmer* in 1188; on the N. side of Thomas-street, a Roman Catholic chapel, called St. John's chapel, is built on part of the site of this priory, of which there are now no other remains, but the ruins of the steeple; the priory of St. *Saviour*, founded for Cistertian friars about 1202, by *Wm. Marshal*, earl Pembroke; the monastery of St. *Francis*, built in 1235; the monastery of the Holy Trinity, founded in 1259, by the family of *Talbot*; another for Carmelites, built by sir *Robert Bagot*, chief justice of the King's-bench, about 1278; the parliament sat in this monastery in 1333; a priory for *Knight's Templars*, founded at Kilmainham, by *Strongbow* in 1174; the church of St. *Michael le Pole*, on the W. side of Great ship-street, where was one of the antient round towers, (the only one built in Dublin) and which continued in tolerable preservation 'till 1781. The lat. of Dublin is 53 : 21' : 2" its lon. corrected by astronomical observations (made by order of Trinity College, for their observatory at *Dunsink* near Dublin) is 6 : 15 W. of the meridian of *Greenwich*. This town

returns 2 members to parliament; electors, freemen and freeholders. Its University returns 2 more, being a borough in itself; election in the Fellows and Scholars. Dublin was erected into an *Archbishoprick* in 1152, and the see extends thro' the whole of the co. of Dublin, the greater part of co. Carlow, and part of the co.'s Kildare, Wicklow and Wexford.

DUBLIN-COUNTY, sit. in prov. Leinster; is bounded S. by Wicklow, N. by East Meath, W. by Kildare, and E. by the Irish sea; it is from N. to S. 24 miles, and from E. to W. 15; it contains 142,050 acres; and exclusive of the city and liberties of Dublin, comprises 6 bar.'s viz. *Balruddery*, *Nethercross*, *Coolock* and *Castleknock* on the N. side of the river Liffey, and *Newcastle* and *Half-Rathdown* on the S. side; these bar.'s with the city contain 107 parishes and 58 churches; and the co. is computed to contain about 54,000 souls. Along with the City and University of Dublin, it returns 10 members to parliament. Excepting a mountainous tract on the S. part of this co. it is very fertile, and exceeds any other part of the kingdom in populousness, culture, trade and wealth, as well as every species of elegance and improvement. The most antient families of this co. are the *Tristrams* or *St. Laurences*, *Wolverstons*, *Wallis's*, *Talbots*, *Sarsfields*, *Whites*, *Lutterells*, *Taylors* and *Deases*.

DUBLIN-HARBOUR, sit. in co. Dublin, prov. Leinster; lat. 53 : 20, lon. 6 : 43. This harbour is large and affords good anchorage; ships may be sheltered in it from the S. to the N. E. by E. winds. The best anchorage is from 5 to 7 fathoms water on the S. side; when the light-house on *Howth* bears N. E. or N. E. ¼ E. Ships of a large draft of water coming from the S. that can't get through *Bray-swash*, must be careful to avoid the N. ground, and the bank called *the Kish*; if low water, on the former there is not more than 10 feet; and the greatest depth between the N. end and the *Kish*, does not exceed 15 feet at low water; the S. end of the *Kish* is the shoalest; on it there is from 6 to 7 feet at low water; it bears E. S. E. ¼ E. from the high land of *Dalkey*, S. E. from the *new light-house* or *Caffoon* at the end of the piles, S. S. E. from the light house of Howth, E. N. E. from the big *Sugar-loaf hill*, and S. W. from *Lambay*. The height of the Shoal is about two cable lengths, and its breadth from E. to W. is about 20 fathoms: this bank stretches across the bay N. by E. When you sail so far Northward as to bring the end of the piles W. N. W. you have about 2¼ fathoms at low water; then *Ireland's eye* will be quite open with *Howth*; on

the

the S. end of the *Kish* you will have them open and shut. When you intend sailing without it, you must keep them a large ship's length open; it is not safe to come nearer to it than 7 fathoms either within or without; as soon as you are over this bank, you will find 14 fathoms water between it and the bay. On some parts between the N. end of this bank (which is broad) and the S. you'll find 4 fathoms at low water. The navigation is difficult from the *bay* to *Poolbeg*; there are two channels, one called the S. and the other the N. the former is best with the winds for E. by N. to W. N. W. and has the deepest water, viz. about 7 or 8 feet at low water. Sailing in by this channel with an Easterly swell, or little wind, you must be careful that the tide of flood does not draw you to the Westward of the piles. The best of the channel is about ¼ a cable's length from the S. buoy, fixt at the S. edge of the bank that separates the two channels. When the wind is between the N. and E. most ships come over the bar, or N. channel; there is a buoy fixt there on the S. end of the narrow spit, joining to the *N. bull*; which you are to keep on the starboard hand coming in; the best of this channel is a short cable's length to the Southward of the buoy, which lies about E. ¼ S. from the piles end, at about ⅜ of a mile. On the starboard hand coming into *Poolbeg*, there is another buoy fixt on the edge of the *N. bull*, abreast to the E. end of the piles. In *Poolbeg* you have from 9 to 13 feet water: the deepest water is at the E. end, a little above the *Light-house*. All ships in *Poolbeg*, moor athwart, with the Northmost anchor near the edge of the bull; as the deepest water is to the N. side. Ships that can endure the ground, run up as far as they have water, and moor on the S. side of the channel.

DUBRONA, an antient name of the river *Blackwater*, which falls into the bay of *Youghal*, in co. Cork, prov. Munster; and called by Ptolemy *Dabrona*.

DUCARIG, sit. in bar. Kilmacrenan, co. Donegal, prov. Ulster.

DUCK's-POOL, a seat within about 1½ mile of *Dungarvan*, co. Waterford, prov. Munster; near it are the remains of an antient and venerable abbey, founded by *Thomas Fitzgerald*, in the 13th century.

DUFF, sit. in bar. Clunlonan, co. Westmeath, prov. Leinster.

DUFFE, a *river* in co. Leitrim, prov. Conn.

DUFFERIN, a bar. in co. Down, prov. Ulster; the antient proprietors of which were the *Macartanes* and *Whites*.

DUFFREY-HALL, a handsome seat in co. Wexford, prov. Leinster, near 66 miles from Dublin.

DUFFS-FORT, sit. in bar. Raphoe, co. Donegal, prov. Ulster.

DUHALLOW, a bar. in co. Cork, prov. Munster. At *Dromagh* and *Dromanagh* in this bar. there are coal pits: iron is also raised hereabouts, and there are some furnaces.

DULAS, sit. in the *liberties* of Cork, prov. Munster.

DULEEK, a bar. in co. Meath, prov. Leinster, in which is a borough-town of same name, sit. about 4 miles S. of *Drogheda*, and near 21 from Dublin. In the reign of Edw. IIId it was the estate and manor of *Theobald de Vernon*, who in 1338, obtained the grant of holding a Friday market here, and a fair for 8 days; its antient name was *Domleagh*, i. e. the house of stone, and 'tis celebrated for having in it the first stone church in Ireland, built by St. *Kenau*, in the 4th century, and was the head of a bishoprick for several ages. It was frequently plundered by the Danes, especially in 830, 878, 1023, 1037, 1149, and 1171, and twice burned, that is, in 1050, and 1169. The bishoprick of *Domleagh*, was united to that of Meath, in the 13th century. Duleek sends 2 members to parliament; patron, col *Bruin*. Lat. 53:28, lon. 6:51. This place gave title of *baron* to the family of *Bellew*. A priory was also founded here for regular canons, long before the arrival of the English, by one of the family of *O'Kelly*, the possessions of which were on the suppression granted to sir *Gerald Moore*.

DULEENE, a chapelry in dioc. of Meath, sit. in bar. Kells, co. Meath, prov. Leinster.

DUMFEAGHNY, sit. in bar. Clanfrought, co. Kerry, prov. Munster.

DUMWIGAN-BRIDGE, sit. in bar. Dundalk, co. Louth, prov. Leinster.

DUNABATE, sit. in bar. Nethercross, co. Dublin, prov. Leinster.

DUNAGHY, a fair town in bar. Kilconway, co. Antrim, prov. Ulster, 78 miles from Dublin, at which place there is a celebrated spa; fairs held 1 and 13 Feb. 6 April and 3 Dec. It is a rectory in dioc. of Connor.

DUNAIN-CHURCH, sit. near *Moneyglass*, in co. Antrim, prov. Ulster.

DUN-ALMHAIN, the present *Hill of Allen*, sit. in co. Kildare, prov. Leinster.

DUNAMASE, or *Dun-na-maes*, i. e. the fort or dun of the plain: which refers to the plain or great heath of *Maryborough*, being a flat of considerable extent, to the N. E. of the *Dun*. It is an insulated rock, about 4 miles E. of Maryborough, in the Queen's co. prov. Leinster, originally the royal residence of *Laoisach Hy-Moradh*, or the honourable *O'More*. The property of *O'More* extended from *Abbey Leix*,
{where

(where it joined the *M'Gill Phadrick's* or *Fitz-patrick's*) to *Dunamase*, and from that to *Mul-lamast*. It is said to have been made a fortress by *Laigseach*, about the beginning of the 3d century, from which time it not only continued the paternal residence of the chiefs of this district, but on their connection with the *Mac-Morroghs*, chieftains of *Hy Morragh*, was esteemed one of the royal fortresses of *Hy Kin-selagh*, and frequently was one of the seats of the kings of *Leinster*. On the arrival of the English it was in possession of *Dermot Mac-Murrogh*, king of Leinster. This prince marrying his daughter *Eva* to *Strongbow*, earl of Pembroke, it fell into the possession of that nobleman, whose only daughter *Isabel*, espousing *Wm. Marshal*, earl of Pembroke, *Dunamase* with the adjacent territory, came into the possession of the said earl, who erected it into a county palatine and built on the *Dun*, about the year 1216, an elegant castle. In 1325, it was taken by *Lysach O'More*, the antient proprietor of this country; in 1329, it was recovered from the Irish, and was again seized by the *O'Mores* about 18 Edw. IIId, but they were dispossessed about 2 years after. At the beginning of the rebellion 1641, the insurgents secured this with other places, which were relieved by sir *C. Coote*; on the retreat of *Ormond*, it submitted to general Preston, but was retaken by the king's forces, in whose possession it continued 'till 1646, when it fell into the hands of *Owen Roe O'Neil*. In 1650, it surrendered to the colonels *Heufon* and *Re-nolds*, and was then blown up and effectually dismantled. The only remains of this antient castle and fortress, are some of the walls and gates, which are yet venerable in their ruins. The present possessor however, (sir *J. Parnell*, bart.) has lately began to rebuild a considerable part of it, after the antient model. The rock on which the castle stands, is an elliptical connoid, inaccessible on all sides except the E. which in its improved state was defended by the barbican. On each side of the barbican were ditches; and where they could not be continued for the rock, walls were erected. To the S. and S. E. were two towers, the latter protecting the barbican. From the barbican you advance to the gate of the lower ballium, it is 7 feet wide, and the walls 6 feet thick; it had a parapet, crenelles and embrasures. The lower ballium is 312 feet from N. to S. and 160 from W. to E. you then arrive at the gate of the upper ballium, which is placed in a tower; and from this begin the walls which divide the *upper* and *lower* ballium. On the highest part was the *keep*, and the apartments for the officers; there was a sally-port and a prison.

DUNAMON, a fine old castle and handsome seat, sit. by the river *Suck*, in co. Roscommon, prov. Connaught.—Also a vicarage in dioc. of Elphin, sit. in bar. Half-Ballimoe, co. Galway, prov. Connaught.

DUNAMONA, a fair town in co. Mayo, prov. Connaught; fairs held 26 May and 17 Oct.

DUNAMORE, sit. near Maryborough, Queen's co. prov. Leinster.—Also in co. Meath, prov. Leinster; the latter gives title of baron to the family of *Baker*, now lord Sheffield.

DUNANE, see *Doonaun*.

DUNANORE, i. e. the golden fort, the ruins of a castle built on a rock in the sea, at the N. W. point of *Cape-clear*, in co. Cork, prov. Munster.

DUNANY, sit. in bar. Ferrard, co. Louth, prov. Leinster; it is a vicarage in dioc. of Armagh.

DUNARD, sit. near Fair-head, co. Antrim; prov. Ulster.

DUNASHAD, the antient name of *Baltimore*, in co. Cork, prov. Munster.

DUNBAR, a handsome seat sit. 3 miles from Enniskillen, co. Fermanagh, prov. Ulster.

DUNBEACON, sit. in bar. Carbery, co. Cork, prov. Munster.

DUNBEG, a village sit. in bar. Ibricken, co. Clare, prov. Munster.

DUNBILL, sit. near *Gowran*, co. Kilkenny, prov. Leinster.

DUNBOE, a rectory in dioc. of Derry, sit. in bar. Colerain, co. Londonderry, prov. Ulster.

DUNBOY, sit. in co. Cork, prov. Munster, near *Castletown*; it was a celebrated castle, which in the year 1602, was taken by sir *George Carew*, after a most obstinate and vigorous defence

DUNBOYNE, a bar. in co. Meath, prov. Leinster, in which is a fair town of same name, sit. 8 miles from Dublin castle, and one mile beyond Clonee. Fairs held annually on 9 July: this place is a vicarage in dioc. of Meath, and gives title of *baron* to the family of *Grinston*, (now *visc.* Grinston.) Lord Dunboyne has here a handsome seat.

DUNBRO, sit. in bar. Coolock, co. Dublin, prov. Leinster.

DUNBRODY, sit. near *Porto bello*, in bar. Shelburne, co. Wexford, prov. Leinster. Here are extensive ruins of of *Dunbrody-abbey*; it is a curacy in dioc. of Ferns. The interior walls of the church are nearly entire, as also the chancel, on each side of which are three chapels vaulted and groined; the great aisle is divided into three parts, by a double row of arches supported by square piers: the inside of those arches have a molding which

springs

springs from beautiful confoles. The tower, rather low in proportion to the reft of the building, is fupported by a grand arch; the cloifters appear to have been fpacious, but their foundations alone remain: fome other ruinous walls indicate where the hall, refectory, dormitory &c. ftood. The W. window, of an uncommon form, is entire; and the door beneath it was very magnificent, being adorned with filligree open work, cut in ftone, and fo raifed as to allow a finger eafily under it; one precious fragment only of this curious work now remains.

DUNBULLOGE, a rectory in dioc. of Cork, fit. in bar. Barrymore, co. Cork, prov. Munfter.

DUNBYN, a rectory in dioc. of Armagh, fit. in bar. Dundalk, co. Louth, prev. Leinfter.

DUNCANELY, a village in bar. Boylagh and Bannagh, co. Donegal, prov. Ulfter.

DUNCANNON, a village with a fort which commands the harbour of Waterford; fit. in bar. Shelburne, co. Wexford, prov. Leinft. 92 miles from Dublin. Lat. 52 : 10, lon. 6 : 50. Here are upwards of 30 pieces of cannon in three ranges. Without the fort is a mean ftreet moftly confifting of poor cabbins. You enter the fort over a draw-bridge, which is drawn up at night. The governor's houfe and chapel are fmall but neat; the barracks are well built. Thefe buildings are furrounded with a ftrong wall built upon the flat of a high rock, that overlooks the fea. There is a perpetuity of land, granted by queen Eliz. to keep this fortrefs in repair; it was taken by king Wm.'s army in 1690, and from it king James IId fled into France. It gives title of vifc. to the family of Ponfonby, now earl of Befsborough.

DUN-CLUIN-POIC, or the Dun of Clopoke, as it is now called, fit. in the Queen's co. prov. Leinfter; about 4 miles S. of Stradbally. It was a fort or caftle of a branch of the family of O'Mores, antient chieftains of Leix. It confifts of an infolated rock, in which are fome natural caves; on the top is a plain, formerly furrounded by a wall, compofed of rock ftones without cement, with a grand entrance from the S. There doth not appear ever to have been any building of lime and ftone erected on this Dun, but the feveral edifices were conftructed entirely in the antient Irifh ftile. That it was an habitation fome years before the eftablifhment of chriftianity in this ifle, is extremely probable, as in an adjacent field is an antient tomb-ftone, with an infcription in druidic characters, fignifying, Hy Mordha the great king; near it is the church of Clopoke.

DUNCORMAC, a vicarage in dioc of Ferns, fit. in bar. Bargie, co. Wexford, prov. Lein-

fter, 82 miles from Dublin; within a mile of it are the ruins of a caftle.

DUN-CRUITHAN, or Dun-croichean, that is, the caftle of the diftrict of the water, the refidence of O'Gahan, chief of Hy-gahan, or the diftrict of the fea, containing the Northern part of the bar. of Colerain, in the co. Londonderry, prov. Ulfter. Here St. Patrick founded a church.

DUNDALEATHGLASS, a rath fit. near Bangor, in co. Down, prov. Ulfter; where during the middle ages a fchool or univerfity was kept, but it was deftroyed by the Danes in 837. The ruins of this univerfity are ftill vifible in the rath of Donaghadee.

DUNDALK, a bar. in co. Louth, prov. Leinfter, in which is a borough, market, poft and fair town of fame name, having an harbour on a bay of the Irifh channel, bearing its name; it lies above 18 miles N. of Drogheda, and 40 miles from Dublin. Lat. 53 : 57, lon. 6 : 42. Fairs held Mond. 8 days before Afh-Wednef. 17 May, 1 Mond. in July, laft Mond. in Aug. 2 Mond. O. S. in Oct. and 2 Mond. in Dec. It returns 2 members to parliament; the patronage of this borough has been in lord Clanbraffil, but fome attempts have lately been made to reftore its freedom. This place gave title of baron to the family of Georges. It is an affizes town, and has fome trade; it confifts of a wide ftreet near a mile long, and fome crofs lanes; has a very good market houfe, and carries on that fpecies of manufacture called Dundalk Cambricks. It has been fortified, (tho' now difmantled) as may be feen by the ruins of the walls, and a caftle deftroyed in 1641. In the reign of Edw. IId. it was a royal city, and is the laft we read of, where a monarch of Ireland was actually crowned and refided. Spencer relates that in this reign Robert le Bruce, king of Scotland, taking advantage of the then civil wars, with the barons of England, fent over his brother Edward with an army of Scots and others into Ireland, who gathering unto him all the outlaws of the North out of the woods and mountains, marched into the Englifh pale, and facked, burned and deftroyed all that came in his way, fpoiling all the cities and corporate towns he met with; and coming laftly to Dundalk, he there made himfelf king, and reigned the fpace of one year, until Edw. king of England, having fome quiet in his affairs at home, fent over lord Bermingham with the command of an army againft him, who encountering him near Dundalk, overthrew his forces and flew him. This town has formerly been in a manner entirely compofed of towers and fmall caftles, a great number

number of which were some time ago destroyed by order of the then lord *Limerick*, and other buildings raised on the old foundations. It is very advantageously sit. for an inland trade, and the port is very safe for shipping; the *bay* has good moorings at all times, in 4 to upwards of 8 fathom water, with very good land marks, either for bringing up, or making the harbour; and in crossing the bar at high water, in ordinary neap-tides, there is from 15 to 18 feet water; besides many other good qualities, the bay abounds with all kinds of fish customary in the channel. At Dundalk is a handsome seat of lord *Clanbrassil*. Here also is a charter school, which was opened in 1738 for 40 children, and was endowed with a house and garden by the late Rt. Hon. earl of Clanbrassil, and by the late Hon. Mrs. *Ann Hamilton* his lordship's mother, with lands at Killinchy in the co. Down, then set for 34*l.* 19*s.* 6*d.* per ann. which have since risen considerably. In the reign of Hen. IId. *Bertram de Vernon* founded a priory for Cross bearers, and on the E. side of the *town*, *John de Vernon* erected a grey friary, in the reign of Hen. IIId. the E. window of its church was singularly admired for its curious and elegant workmanship. A chapter of the order was held here in 1282. 2 miles beyond Dundalk are the ruins of *Balriggan castle*, and a mile farther those of *Castle Roach*; 1 mile W. of Dundalk is *Castletown castle.*—Dundalk is also the name of a village sit. in bar. Cremourne, co. Monaghan, prov. Ulster.

DUNDANEERE, a castle so called, sit. near *Bandon*, in co. Cork, prov. Munster.

DUNDARERK, a castle in co. Cork, prov. Munster, in the parish of *Clondrohid*; it is seated on a hill, and commands a vast extended view to the W. as far as the bounds of *Kerry*; the E. almost to *Cork*; and a great tract to S. It is a high square building, having 70 stone steps to the battlements: adjoining to it stood some modern buildings now in ruin; here were large gardens and orchards, now destroyed; a little to the N. is the ruined church of *Kilnamartery.*

DUNDEDE, a castle in a small island, at the extreme S. point of land, near the coast of the co. Cork, prov. Munster, to which there is a narrow passage from the main, being equally the work of nature and art; it is commonly by sailors called the *Galley-head*, and is sometimes fatally mistaken by them for the old head of *Kinsale*, when the light of the latter is not seen. This promontory, like that of *Kinsale*, stretches itself a good way into the ocean, and is also of a considerable height; there are several caverns formed at its base by the working of the waves.

DUNDERLEAGUE, sit. in bar. Coshlea, co. Limerick, prov. Munster.

DUNDERMOTT, sit. near Roscommon, prov. Connaught.

DUNDERROW, a small village within 2 miles of *Kinsale*, in co. Cork, prov. Munster; near which is a large Danish entrenchment; it is a rectory in dioc. of Cork.

DUNDERRY-BRIDGE, a village in bar. Navan, co. Meath, prov. Leinster.

DUNDONALD, a rectory in dioc. of Down, sit. in bar. Castlereagh, co. Down, prov. Ulster.

DUNDONNEL, a rectory in dioc. of Limerick, sit. in bar. Connello, co. Limerick, prov. Munster.

DUNDRUM, a fair town in bar. Lecale, co. Down, prov. Ulster, 68 miles from Dublin; fairs held 12 May and 10 Oct. This, tho' now a mean village, was formerly a place of some consequence, on account of a strong fortified castle, the ruins of which yet remain. It is boldly seated on a rock, and commands a view of the whole bay. 'Tis said to have been built by sir *John de Courcy*, for the Knts. Templars, who enjoyed it 'till their overthrow in 1313, and that it was afterwards granted to the prior of Down, who possessed it, and a small manor about it 'till the general dissolution of abbeys; after which it was granted by the crown to lord *Cromwell* of *Oakham*, whose son *Thomas*, lord *Cromwell* created visc. *Lecale*, disposed of it to sir *Francis Blundell*, whose descendant lord Blundell became possessed of it. In 1517, the earl of Kildare, then lord deputy, took it by storm, it being garrisoned at that time by the Irish, who had drove out the English some time before. It was again possessed and repaired by the *Magennis's*, and retaken by the lord deputy *Gray*, anno 1538. It afterwards got into the hands of *Phelim Mc. Ever Magennis*, who was obliged to yield it to the lord *Mountjoy*, in the year 1601. It met with another fate, during the progress of the war of 1641, when it was dismantled by the order of *Cromwell*, tho' then garrisoned by Protestants, and has ever since been suffered to run entirely to ruin. Its remains are of an irregular multangular form, with a fine round tower, which is about 35 feet in diameter in the inside. — *Dundrum* is likewise the name of a fair town in co. Tipperary, prov. Munster, 81 miles from Dublin; fair days Whit. Tuesd. and 1 Tuesd. O. S. in Oct. Here is the elegant seat of lord *de Montalt*. — There is also a village of this name, sit. in bar. Ballaghkeen, co. Wexford, prov. Leinster;—and another in co. Dublin, prov. Leinster, about 4 miles from the metropolis, and 1½ mile beyond *Miltown*; it is on the high road to Powerscourt,

and

and has a very old caftle, much decayed, tho' in part inhabited.

DUNDRUM-BAY, fit. in co. Down, prov. Ulfter; this is divided into the *inner* bay and the *outward* bay; the former is fmall and very fecure; but the latter one of the moft dangerous bays for fhipping in the kingdom, by reafon of fand banks, which fhift their ftations almoft in every ftorm: this *outward* bay is large, and formed by St. *John's point* to the E. and the point of *Bealach-a-neir* to the W. ftanding upwards of 2 leagues afunder, both which points are furrounded with rocks. It is mentioned as a fafe good haven by Dr. *Boat*, and the author of the *Atlas Maritimus*; yet it is fhallow and dangerous; only fmall veffels can ride in the middle of it, and that too at high water. The Northern and Southern tides meet off it, and break upon St. *John's point*, which occafion a greater eddy or fuction inwards, than in other places; fo that fhips have often found themfelves embayed here, when they were thought to be out in the channel; and if this once happens with an E. or S. E. wind, they have no tide to help them out, but are fuddenly forced among the breakers. The lofty mountains near Dundrum, are a good mark in a clear day; but in hazy weather they are of little ufe, being covered with clouds and hid from fight. Ships failing near this coaft, ought therefore to keep a good offing, efpecially in clouded weather. The earl of *Ardglafs* found the effects hereof to his coft, being wrecked on this ftrand.

DUNDURERK, fee *Dundarerk*.

DUNE, *(caftle)* fit. in the bar. of Iraghticonnor, co. Kerry, prov. Munfter; it was built on a high clift, ftanding perpendicularly over the ocean. Between this and another caftle called *Lich*, there was fome years ago, a kind of *volcano*, which burnt for fome time, as it was then termed by fome unfkilful naturalifts, who went to fee it. But this burning was by no means to be accounted among the number of thofe dreadful eruptions called *volcanoes*, in other places, but rather an accidental kindling of combuftible matter on the external furface of the clift, which became quite extinguifhed, when the pabulum or fuel was exhaufted, that fed the flame. A confiderable part of this clift is compofed of a ftone, called by naturalifts *Pyrites*; and there are alfo the marks both of *fulphur* and *iron ore* on the clift; many of the *pyritæ* will take fire upon wetting.

DUNEAN, a vicarage in dioc. of Connor, fit. in bar. Toome, co. Antrim, prov. Ulfter.

DUNEGAL, an ifland in the bay of Baltimore, co. Cork, prov. Munfter; it is a large and fruitful fpot.

DUNELONG, a fair town in co. Tyrone, prov. Ulfter; fairs held 12 Jan. 21 May, 12 Aug. and 16 Nov.—Alfo the name of a caftle fit. in the ifland of Inifhircan near cape Clear, co. Cork, prov. Munfter; near it are the remains of a barrack, and there are fome old pieces of iron ordnance ftill lying among the rocks.

DUNENOUR, fit. in bar. Carberry, co. Cork, prov. Munfter,

DUNFANAGHY, a fair town in bar. Kilmacrenan, co. Donegal, prov. Ulfter, 132 miles from Dublin. Fairs held Thurf. after Whitfun-fund. 5 Aug. 2 Oct. and 17 Nov. Within 2 miles of this place, at the foot of a lofty hill are the ruins of a caftle; and about ¼ mile from Dunfanaghy are the ruins of a church.

DUNFARNHY, fit. in bar. Kilmacrenan, co. Donegal, prov. Ulfter.

DUNFERT, fit. in bar. Carbury, co. Kildare, prov. Leinfter.—Alfo a vicarage in dioc. of Offory, fit. in bar. Shellilogher, co. Kilkenny, prov. Leinfter.

DUNGAMORE, fit. in bar. Ballaghkeen, co. Wexford, prov. Leinfter.

DUNGAN, fit. in bar. Clanderlaw, co. Clare, prov. Munfter.

DUNGANNON, a bar. in co. Tyrone, prov. Ulfter, having in it a borough, market, fair and poft town of fame name; fit. about 11 miles N. of Armagh, and 72 N. W. of Dublin. Lat. 54 : 28, lon. 7 : 18. It gives title of *vifc.* to the family of *Trevor*, and gave that of *baron* to lord vifc. *Vane*. It was formerly the chief feat of the *O'Neils*, kings of Ulfter. In 1498 it was the principal refidence of *Neil Mac Art O'Neil*, who had a ftrong caftle here, which was taken the fame year by Gerald, the 8th earl of Kildare. The caftle was foon recovered by its former poffeffor, but in 1517 was again furrendered to Gerald the 9th earl of Kildare, who burnt it. The caftle experienced the viciffitudes of turbulent ages, being alternately in the hands of contending parties, fometimes difmantled, and fometimes repaired. In the troubles of 1641, it was one of the firft feized by the Northern infurgents, but it fhared the fate of the other fortreffes, being demolifhed by the parliamentary forces. In the reign of Hen. VIIth. *Con O'Neil* built a fmall monaftery on the S. fide of this town for *Francifcan* friars of the third order; on the fuppreffion of monafteries, it was granted to Richard earl of *Weftmeath*, who affigned it to fir *Art. Chichefter*. Dungannon returns 2 members to parliament; patron, lord *Northland*, who has a handfome feat here. Fair days 1 Thurfd. Feb. 2 Thurfd. Apr. 2 Mond. May, 1 Thurfd. July, 3 Tuefd. Aug. 1 Mond. O. S. Oct. laft Tuefd. Nov. This town was made remarkable for the *Ulfter* delegation of Volunteers on the 15 Feb. 1782.   DUNGAN's

DUNGAN'STOWN, fit. near *Wicklow*, prov. Leinfter.

DUNGARVAN, a borough, poft and fair town in bar. Decies without Drum, co. Waterford, prov. Munfter, 100 miles from Dublin. This is one of the greateft fifhing towns in Ireland, and is feated on a bay of the fame name. It has a barrack for two companies of foot, and gives title of vifc. to the noble family of *Boyle*, earl of Cork. Lat. 51 : 57 N. lon. 7 : 55 W. Fairs are held here on 22 June and 8 Nov. It fends 2 members to parliament ; patron, the duke of *Devonfhire*. The parifh of Dungarvan is of great extent. The town was antiently called *Achad-Garbain* from St. *Garbain*, who founded an abbey of canons here in the 7th. century, of which there are now no remains. It is tolerably well built, and agreeably fit. the fea flowing up to the town walls; it has a good market and feffion houfe. The barrack is fit. within the walls of an antient caftle, built by king *John*, and afterwards repaired and poffeffed by the *Defmond* family ; it was vefted in the crown by act of parliament, in the reign of Hen. VIIIth. The town was incorporated about the year 1463, by act of parliament ; and king James Ift. for the fidelity of its inhabitants to the crown, during the rebellion in Queen Eliz.'s time, renewed their privileges, and changed the government of portrieve into that of a fovereign, recorder and 12 brethren, who are to be yearly chofen, 5 days after the feaft of St. *Peter*. The admiralty of the harbour was granted to the fovereign, with the fame extent of power as the mayor of Briftol had. This charter was renewed by *Rich. Cromwell* whilft protector, in Apr. 1659. King James IId in 1689, granted a new charter, and enlarged the former privileges, but it was not long enjoyed, for on the coming in of king Wm. IIId, the charters of king James, granted after his abdication, became ufelefs. *Thomas* lord *Offaly*, jufticiary of Ireland in 1295, erected an *Auguftinian* friary for Eremites, on the other fide of the water oppofite to this town ; it has been a neat, light, gothic building, as appears from the remaining walls of the church ; the fteeple is about 60 feet high. On the N. fide of the church, near the altar, is the tomb of *Donald Magrath*, who was interred there in 1400. Dungarvan has been much frequented in the fummer feafon, for the purpofe of fea-bathing. Great quantities of potatoes are cultivated about this place, which are fent up to Dublin in boats loaded likewife with birch-brooms, and this cargo is jocofely called " *fruit* and *timber*." An aqueduct has been conftructed here by parliamentary encouragement, for fupplying the place with frefh water, which is brought for fome miles from the river *Phynifk*.—Dun-

garvan is alfo the name of a vicarage in dioc. of Offory, fit. in bar. Gowran, co. Kilkenny, prov. Leinfter.

DUNGIVIN, a fair town in bar. Kenought, co. Londonderry, prov. Ulfter, 99 miles from Dublin. Near which are the ruins of a church. Fairs are held 25 May and Oct. *O'Cahane* prince of the country, founded a priory here, for canons regular of St. Auguftin ; it is now a vicarage in dioc. of Derry.

DUNGLO, fit. in bar. Boylagh, co. Donegal, prov. Ulfter, 152 miles from Dublin. It was 'till lately called *Cloghanlea*, and is but a fmall place. An arm of the fea extends to it in the centre of the diftrict called the *Roffes*. Here ftands the parifh church, the mill, &c. Near Dunglo are fome fmall but handfome lakes.

DUNGNEEN, fee *Dunqueen*.

DUNGOURNEY, a rectory in dioc. of Cloyne, fit. in bar. Barrymore, co. Cork, prov. Munfter.

DUNISKY, fit. in bar. Mufkerry, co. Cork, prov. Munfter ; it is a rectory in dioc. of Cork.

DUNKANALLY, a fair town in co. Donegal, prov. Ulfter ; fairs held 6 Feb. 1 July and 16 Oct.

DUNKERHAN, a village fit. in bar. Erris, co. Mayo, prov. Connaught.

DUNKELD, a vicarage in dioc. of Offory, fit. in bar. Ida, co. Kilkenny, prov. Leinfter.

DUNKELLIN, or *Doonkillin*, a bar. in co. Galway, prov. Connaught. The foil here covers a ftratum of limeftone rock, which in many places rifes fo thick above the furface, as to render thefe parts unfit for tillage, tho' they are excellent for pafture. This bar. gives title of *baron* to the noble family of *de Burgh*, (now marquis *Clanricarde*.)

DUN-KERMNA, or the Dun of the rock, a fortrefs of the antient chiefs of *Corcaluighe*, where *Kinfale* now ftands, in co. Cork, prov. Munfter.

DUNKERRIN, fit. in bar. Clonlifk, King's co. prov. Leinfter, near 64 miles from Dublin. Near 1½ mile from which are the ruins of *Rahanvegue* caftle. Here are fairs on 9 May, day before Whitfunday, 3 Nov. and 21 Dec. It is a rectory in dioc. of Killaloe.

DUNKERRON, a bar. in co. Kerry, prov. Munfter ; it has its name from an antient caftle, which was the chief feat of *O'Sullivan More*, ftanding near the bottom of the river *Kenmare*. According to *Cambden*, the caftle was antiently built by the *Carews* of England ; but this feems to be a miftake, as is likewife his faying that it was poffeffed by *Donald M'Carty More*,, for it was always accounted the principal refidence of the *O'Sullivans*, and probably erected by an anceftor of that houfe. Among the rough and high hills in this bar. fome pleafant vallies and improveable grounds

are

are interspersed. It gives title of *baron* to the family of *Petty*, (now earl *Shelburne*.)

DUNKITTLE, sit. within about 3¼ miles of Cork, in co. Cork, prov. Munster; here is a handsome seat commanding a delightful prospect.

DUNLADY, a handsome seat in co. Down, prov. Ulster; at the N. part of the bar. of *Castlereagh*; it is remarkable for a good slate quarry.

DUNLAVEN, a market town in bar. Talbot's-town, co. Wicklow, prov. Leinster, 22 miles from Dublin. It has been much improved by the late sir *J. Tynte*, bart. His grand-father the Rt. hon. *James Tynte*, formerly representative for *Youghall*, expended 1200*l*. in erecting an elegant market-house and stores, all of cut stone, with 4 porticoes, and columns of the Doric order supporting it. Here are fairs on 20 May, 1st Frid. O. S. in July, 21 Aug. 3d Tuesd. in Oct. It is a vicarage in dioc. of Dublin.

DUNLAVIN, sit. near *Kilcullen*, in co. Kildare, prov. Leinster.

DUNLEARY, a sea-port town, sit. in bar. Half Rathdown, co. Dublin, prov. Leinster, within 5 miles of the metropolis, and 1¼ mile from the *Black Rock*.

DUNLECKNEY, sit. in bar. Idrone, co. Carlow, prov. Leinster, 46 miles from Dublin. It is a vicarage in dioc. of Leighlin; and here is the antient seat of *Beauchamp Bagnel*, esq; about 2 miles from it are the ruins of a castle.

DUNLEER, a borough, post and fair town in bar. Ferrard, co. Louth, prov. Leinster, 30 miles from Dublin, and about 6 miles N. of Drogheda. It sends 2 members to parliament; patronage in the families of *Foster* and *Coddington*. Fairs held 14 May, 5 July, 19 Sept. and 11 Dec. This place is a rectory in dioc. of Armagh.

DUNLOST, a curacy in dioc. of Dublin, sit. in bar. Kilkea and Moon, co. Kildare, prov. Leinster.

DUNLOW, or *Dunloe*, a fair town in co. Galway, prov. Connaught; fair days 7 May and 13 to 18 July.—Also the name of a castle, sit. near *Killarney*, in co. Kerry, prov. Munster, boldly seated on an eminence over the river *Lane*; to the S. of it is a very craggy, deep and romantic chasm in the mountain.

DUNLUCE, a bar. having a fair town in it of same name, sit. in co. Antrim, prov. Ulster; fairs held 12 Nov. Here is the antient castle of Dunluce on the *Antrim* coast, beneath which there is a curious cave in the rock, well deserving the traveller's inspection. This village is a rectory in dioc. of Connor.

DUNMACREEN, sit. in co. Mayo, prov. Connaught, 96 miles from Dublin.

DUNMAHON, a ruined castle in co. Cork, prov. Munster.

DUNMANWAY, or *Dunmanaway*, a pleasant village, sit. in bar. Carbery, co. Cork, prov. Munster, 12 miles W. of Bandon, and 151 from Dublin; it is the first place in that prov. where the linen manufacture flourished. Here are fairs on 4 May, 1 Tuesday O. S. in July, 17 Sept. and 26 Nov. The linen manufacture here is owing to the encouragement of the late sir *Richard Cox*, who had his country seat at this place; the town is seated on the centre of a small valley, surrounded with hills to the W. N. and S. Within a mile of the town there is a perfect wall or mound of rocks, running a considerable way; a *yew* tree grows in a reclining manner out of the crevices of one of these rocks, the body of which is 17 feet in circumference. Near a mile beyond Dunmanway, are the ruins of *Kilbarry* church. Here is a charter school for 40 children: it was opened in 1741, and sir Rich. Cox before mentioned, gave for that purpose a lease to the incorporated society of 20 English acres of good land, well inclosed, for 990 years, at 2*l*. 5*s*. per ann. and was also at the expence of raising and drawing all the stones and slates, and paying day labourers for the building.

DUNMANUS-BAY, sit. in bar. Carbery, co. Cork, prov. Munster; it is a neat bay, on the S. W. coast of Ireland, and is sufficiently deep and safe for large vessels, tho' very seldom frequented; it is separated from that of *Bantry*, by a narrow point of land; it lies in lat. 51:28, lon. 10:2. It takes its name from a castle contiguous to it, called *Dunmanus-castle*, which was formerly fortified with walls and flankers, but is now in ruins.

DUMOGHDAIRNE, an antient fortress destroyed by *Conar O'Brien* in 1133; the word signifies the fortress of the pleasant plain; this place was sit. in co. Galway, prov. Connaught.

DUNMORE, sit. in bar. Downamore, co. Galway, prov. Connaught, about 91 miles from Dublin, it is a rectory in dioc. of Tuam. It was a royal seat of the *O'Kelly's*, and destroyed in 1133 by *Conar O'Brien*; it gives name to the bar. in which it stands, but which is generally written *Downamore*. Its antient name was *Dumoghdairne*. St. Patrick built a monastery here, upon the old scite of which, a friary for Augustin Eremites was afterwards founded by *Walter de Bermingham*, lord *Athenry*, in 1425; part of it was converted into a parish church, the rest being levelled, and now forms the market place. *Henry Mossop* the celebrated actor, was born in this town; his father was rector of Dunmore, and an eminent mathematician.—There is also a vicarage of this name

 in

in dioc. of Offory, fit. in the *liberties* of Kilkenny, prov. Leinfter.

DUNMORE-BAY, fit. in bar. Ibricken, co. Clare, prov. Munfter.

DUNMORE-CAVE, fit. in co. Kilkenny, prov. Leinfter, within 2 miles of the ruins of *Dunmore-houfe*, which houfe was formerly the habitation of the duke of Ormond. The paffage into it is down a fquare hole, or rather precipice upwards of 60 feet deep, by 12 wide; at the bottom whereof is the mouth of the cave, which is but low, arched with rocks, feemingly dropping on the head, where from a number of petrifactions like icicles, there falls a vaft quantity of drops of limpid water, which alfo petrify into clear cryftal lumps, upon the rocks whereon they fall. After proceeding about a quarter of a mile in this curious cavern, you are entertained with the murmurings of a fubterraneous river, but how far it or the cave extends, none have yet been bold enough to attempt difcovering. Many of the rocks on the roof and fides of the cave, are black marble, full of white fpots, of a fhell-like figure; and the whole neighbourhood is full of quarries of this beautiful ftone, which takes a fine polifh, and is much ufed both here and in England, for flabs, chimney-pieces, &c. In fome deep and wet parts of thefe quarries, this elegant foffil is in its firft ftage of formation: the fhells are real, but fo foftened by time and their moift fituation, as to be fufceptible of receiving the ftoney particles into their pores: by which cohefive quality they in time become thofe hard and white curls, that give value to the marble: and it is very remarkable, and a proof that thefe white fpots have been real fhells and thus formed, that the longer a chimney-piece or flab is ufed, the more of thefe fpots ripen into view.

DUNMORE-HEAD, a cape fit. in bar. Corcaguinny, co. Kerry, prov. Munfter; it is the moft *Weftern* point of Ireland, and confequently of Europe; the great *Blafquet Ifland*, oppofite to this place, is faid to have been formerly joined to the continent; the found between this ifland and the main land, is of a great depth, which caufes the currents, at both ebb and flood, to fet thro' it with prodigious rapidity. It was here, that on 10 Sept. 1588, a fhip of the Spanifh *Armada*, of 1000 tons burthen, fuffered fhip-wreck, one perfon only efcaping. *Ventry* or *Fintry bay* near this, is open and much expofed to *Southerly* winds; however there is a fufficient depth of water in any part of it, for veffels to anchor; nor is there any danger, but what is apparent in the entrance. There is another

bay called *Dunmore* or *Whitehoufe* bay in co. Waterford, prov. Munfter, which lies about 2 miles to the S. S. E. or without *Credan-head*; in its mouth there are but 18 feet water; this bay is only frequented by boats, the common charts exprefs it to be withinfide of *Credan-head*, but this error has been rectified by Mr. *Doyle*, in his chart of this harbour. From *Credan-head* to the oppofite fhore, it is fcarce 2 miles over.

DUNMORE-ROCKS, fit. near *Rathlin Ifland*, in the N. fea, off the coaft of co. Antrim, prov. Ulfter.

DUNMOW, a rectory in dioc. of Meath, fit. in bar. Morgallion, co. Meath, prov. Leinfter.

DUNMULL, a *mountain*, fit. between Colerain and the river Bufh, in co. Antrim, prov. Ulfter.

DUNMURRY, a rectory in dioc. of Kildare, fit. in bar. Ophaly, co. Kildare, prov. Leinfter, about 26 miles from Dublin. Here are the remains of an old church, and an antient burial ground. The name fignifies *Red hills*; *Dun Almhain* or the hill of *Allen*, being feparated from *Dunmurry* by a valley about a mile in breadth. The latter forms a kind of headland; towards the N. is fertile in corn and pafturage, and compofed of lime-ftone rock. The loofe ftones on its furface frequently appear as if calcined in the fire, and of a red purple colour, and fometimes tinctured with fulphur; whence thefe hills have from remote periods obtained the name of *Murach*, or reddifh purple. Tho' fuch ftones are certain indications of copper being contained in the internal parts, no fearch or difcovery was made refpecting the fact until about the year 1786, when fome of the neighbouring farmers opening a gravel pit on the N. declivity of Dunmurry, near the bafe, fomething like metallic ore was difcovered; which upon examination was found to be rich copper. This induced the proprietor of the foil, his grace the duke of Leinfter, in conjunction with James Spencer efq. and Richard Evans efq. and fome other gentlemen, to eftablifh a fmall fund in order to examine the hill. Miners were therefore employed, and fhafts funk, on different elevations of the declivity, in the folid rock, of the depths from 4 to 15 fathom. During thefe operations, quantities of yellow fulphureous copper ore were found, of near 40 per cent. purity, mixt with fulphur and calcar. Thus encouraged, levels were opened, from whence proceeds a ftrong vitriolic water, which indicates the mine to be copious and rich. The principal bed of the mine feems to lie deep within the hill, and even to dip under the valley which feparates *Dunmurry* from the hill of *Allen*. A branch of the Grand canal

runs

runs thro' the middle of the valley. The ftone contained in the rocks is calcareous; but in many places of a very fine grain, and would be both durable and ornamental in building. There is alfo found near the bafe of the hill, an alkaline argillaceous earth, of a white or light grey colour, which is found to have many qualities of fuller's earth. In the veins of the rocks and matrix of the ore, are found quantities of fine yellow ochre: great quantities of coak are alfo found, with much calcareous fpar; alfo a kind of foffil, in which there is fome filver, but not enough to be of any value.—There is alfo a place of this name fit. near *Belfaft*, prov. Ulfter.

DUNNA-CAEL, now the co. of *Donegal*, prov. Ulfter; otherwife called *Tirconal*.

DUNNAIN, fit. near *Randalftown*, in co. Antrim, prov. Ulfter.

DUNNAMANA, fee *Dunnemanagh*.

DUNNARD, fit. in bar. Talbot's-town, co. Wicklow, prov. Leinfter.

DUNNEMANAGH, a fair town in co. Tyrone, prov. Ulfter; fairs held 27 Feb. May, Aug. and Nov. 'Tis otherwife called *Dunymana*, and *Dunnamqna*, and is 107 miles diftant from Dublin, within half a mile of it are the ruins of a caftle.

DUN-OF-CLOPOKE, fee *Dun-cluin-paic*.

DUNORLING, a rectory in dioc. of Ardfert, fit. in bar. Corcaguinny, co. Kerry, prov. Munfter.

DUNQUIN, or *Dunqueen*, a parifh in bar. Corcaguinny, co. Kerry, prov. Munfter, Weftward of *Ventry*; the outward point of which is called *Dunmore-head*; it is a vicarage in dioc. of Ardfert.

DUNRAN, commonly called the *Glen of Dunran*; fit. in co. Wicklow, prov. Leinfter; in its neighbourhood the traveller may be gratified with the moft agreeable fcenes that art and nature can furnifh.

DUNRATH-CASTLE, fit. near the banks of the Grand canal, about 7 miles from Dublin, in co. Dublin, prov. Leinfter.

DUNSACHLIN, fit. in bar. Caftleknock, co. Dublin, prov. Leinfter.

DUNSANDLE, fit. in co. Galway, prov. Connaught; the moft magnificent and beautiful feat of the late *Denis Daly*, efq.

DUNSANY, fit. in bar. Skryne, co. Meath, prov. Leinfter; it is a rectory in dioc. of Meath. Here is *Dunfany-caftle*, the family feat of the *Plunkets*, who have from thence the title of *vifc. Dunfany*.

DUNSHAGHLIN, a poft and fair town, fit. in bar. Ratoath, co. Meath, prov. Leinfter, 14 miles from Dublin. Fairs held 11 June and 10 December. *St. Seachlin* who came into Ireland A. D. 439, founded the church here, which is now a vicarage in dioc. of Meath.

He died 27 Nov. 448 in his 75th year, and was here interred. In 1043 the abbey was burned. It was alfo plundered and fpoiled in 1152, by the fept of *Hy Brinn*.

DUNSINK, fit. in co. Dublin, prov. Leinfter, within about 3 miles of the metropolis; where on a rifing ground, and very eligible fituation, an aftronomical obfervatory has been erected by order, and for the ufe of *Trinity-College*.

DUNSKERRIN or *Dunfcerrin*, fit. in bar. Ikerrin, co. Tipperary, prov. Munfter.

DUNSOBARKY, or *Dunfobarchiegh*, i. e. the impregnable fortrefs, from *Dun*, a fortrefs, and *fobhar* ftrong or powerful; it is now called Knockfergus or *Carrickfergus*, i. e. the rock, hill or fort of the general, to which alfo its antient name may be tranflated, *fofar* or *obhar* fignifying *valiant*. It is fit. in co. Antrim, prov. Ulfter.

DUNSPORT or *Dunsfort*, a rectory in dioc. of Down, fit. near *Killough bay*, in bar. Lecale, co. Down, prov. Ulfter.

DUNTRILEAGUE, a rectory in dioc. of Emly, fit. in bar. Cofhlea, co. Limerick, prov. Munfter.

DUNUSKY, fit. in co. Cork, prov. Munfter; an inconfiderable place.

DUNWORLY *ftrand*, fit. in co. Cork, prov. Munfter; here is a fpring called St. *Ann's well*, vifited by the fuperftitious on her feftival. To the W. the coaft is all a bold high fhore, abounding with ftupendous cliffs, which aftonifh whilft they pleafe us.

DUNYMANAGH, fit. near *Strabane*, prov. Ulft.

DUR, a river or rather inlet, placed by *Ptolemy*, between the river *Kenmare* and the *Shannon*, which he calls *Oftia flumen Dur*, fuppofed by *Cambden* to be the rivulet which runs by *Tralee*; but Mr. *Smith* from its fituation in *Ptolemy's* map, thinks it fhould rather feem to be the deep bay of *Caftlemain*, which may as well be termed a river, as that of *Kenmare*, both of them being arms of the fea, that run up the country for feveral miles, in co. Kerry, prov. Munfter.

DURAS, a vicarage in dioc. of Killmacduagh, fit. in bar. Kiltartan, co. Galway, prov. Conn.

DURRON, fit. in bar. Ballycowen, King's co. prov. Leinfter.

DURROW, a fair and poft town, fit. in bar. Gallmoy, co. Kilkenny, prov. Leinfter. Fairs 2d Thurfd. O. S. in May, Aug. and Nov. It is diftant from Dublin near 52 miles; near it is *Caftle Durrow*, the magnificent feat of lord *Afhbrook*. 2¼ miles from *Durrow* are the ruins of *Mackin caftle*; and near a mile further, are the ruins of the ftrong caftle of *Cullyhill*, with an old church. *Durrow* was formerly part of the Queen's co. but on coming into the poffeffion of the *Butler* family, who were perpetually

tually harraffed by the powerful fept of the *Fitzpatricks*, the earl of *Ormond* procured an act of parliament, to make this eftate part and parcel of the co. of *Kilkenny*, altho' furrounded by the Queen's co. and the offending *Fitzpatricks* being taken, were tranfmitted immediately to Kilkenny, and there removed from their connections, they fuffered the penalties of the law.—There is alfo a village of fame name, fit. in bar. Ballycowen, King's co. prov. Leinfter, in which St. *Columb* founded a fumptuous monaftery, in 546; it was otherwife called *Dairmach*, and is now a curacy in dioc. of Meath.

DURRUS, a vicarage in dioc. of Cork, fit. in bar. Carbery, co. Cork, prov. Munfter.

DURSEY-ISLAND, fit. in bar. Bear and Bantry, off the coaft of the co. Cork, prov. Munfter; antiently called *Bea Infula*; this ifland is very ftrong by nature, becaufe of the difficulty of landing, which can be but by one narrow entrance, that might be defended by a few hands, and was formerly fortified by a caftle, miftaken by fome for the ruins of an abbey. It is impoffible to arrive at this fpot but in a dead calm, the leaft gale of wind raifing fuch billows as render it very dangerous for a boat to come near the fhore. This feemingly impregnable place was chofen as a retreat by the Irifh, who committed the cuftody of it to *Connor O'Drifcol*, who procured 3 pieces of Spanifh ordnance to be conveyed into it, with ftores, ammunition, and 60 men; but they were foon obliged to furrender to captain *Roftoick*, who demolifhed the forts, feized the garrifon and caufed the prifoners to be executed. This ifland is exceedingly rough and coarfe, and about 3 Irifh miles long.

DYON, fit. in bar. Dungannon, co. Tyrone, prov. Ulfter, 65 miles from Dublin.

DYNISH-ISLAND, fit. in bar. Moycullin, co. Galway, prov. Connaught.

DYSART, fit. in bar. Mullingar, co. Weftmeath, prov. Leinfter; where an abbey was founded by St. *Colman*.—Alfo a *caftle* now in ruins, fit. near *Corrofin*, in co. Clare, prov. Munfter; here is one of the antient round towers.

DYSERT, fit. in co. Limerick, prov. Munfter, where is one of the antient round towers; there is another of them at a place of fame name, which is a village in Queen's co. prov. Leinfter.

DYSERTAGNEY, a rectory in dioc. of Derry, fit. in bar. Inifhowen, co. Donegal, prov. Ulfter.

DYSERTGALLEN, a rectory in dioc. of Leighlin, fit. in bar. Cullinagh, Queen's co. prov. Leinfter.

EAGLE ISLANDS, 2 iflands in *Clew bay*, on the W. coaft of the co. Mayo, prov. Connaught, otherwife called *Achill Ifles*; they are not mentioned by *Ptolemy* or *Richard* of *Cirencefter*; and appear to have obtained their names from the great refort of eagles thither.

EAGLE'S-NEST, (otherwife *Aileach* or *Ailich Neid*), a rath or caftle of the *O'Neil's* in the bar. of *Inifowen*, 3 miles N. of Derry, prov. Ulfter. It was the royal palace of *Tyrconnel*; this rath, which is yet remaining, is afferted to have been erected by the great *Hy Faillia*, or *Hy Maillia*, antient chief of *Hy Faillia*, on his fettlement in the N. of Ireland, in the 4th century. This antient palace which probably obtained the appellation of Eagle's-neft, from the height of its ramparts, is of the fame conftruction as thofe monuments of antiquity, commonly called Danifh forts, and was laid by *Murtogh Mor O'Brien*, in 1101. There is alfo a particular fpot fo called, on one of the eminences adjoining the lake of *Killarney*, in co. Kerry, prov. Munfter.

EAMANIA, or *Eamhain*, derived from aem-huim-ui, i. e. the potent or noble place or city, an antient royal refidence, and capital of Ulfter, fit. near Armagh. It is faid to have been originally founded by one of the Scottifh chiefs, near 200 years before the Chriftian æra, and was deftroyed by *Caibre Liffechar*, a prince of Connaught, at the beginning of the 4th century. *Colgan* fays there were fome ruins of it remaining in his time, probably the rath in which the royal palace called *Crove-roigh* was erected. Mr. *O'Connor* places the building of it 353 years before Chrift.

EAMHAIN, fee *Eamania*.

EARL'S-TOWN, fit. near Kilkenny, in bar. Shelilogher, co. Kilkenny, prov. Leinfter. It is a rectory in dioc. of Offory.

EARNE, fee *Erne*.

EASK-LOUGH, a lake, fit. in bar. Boylagh, co. Donegal, prov. Ulfter.

EASTERSNEW, a vicarage in dioc. of Elphin, fit. in bar. Boyle, co. Rofcommon, prov. Connaught.

EAST-MEATH, a co. fo called to diftinguifh it from Weftmeath; but it is otherwife and generally called *Meath*, and fit. in prov. Leinfter.

ECHLIN'S-GROVE, a feat near *Donaghadee*, in co. Down, prov. Ulfter.

ECHLIN'S-VILLE, formerly called *Rheubane*, a feat 2 miles N. of *Ardchin*, in co. Down, prov. Ulfter. The fpirit of agriculture, fo

peculiarly

peculiarly neceſſary to the welfare of the nation, has here been carried on to ſingular advantage.

EDENBOROUGH, ſit. in bar. Kilconway, co. Antrim, prov. Ulſter.

EDEN-DERRY, a fair and poſt town in bar. Cooleſtown, King's co. prov. Leinſter, 29 miles from Dublin; fairs held Shrove-Tueſd. Thurſd. after Whitſun-Tueſd. and 4 Nov. Here, on the ſummit of the hill, are the ruins of a caſtle, formerly the ſeat of the *Blundel* family. This town has been much inhabited by the people called quakers; and carries on ſome trade.—There is alſo a place of ſame name ſit. near Belfaſt, in bar. Caſtlereagh, co. Down, prov. Ulſter.

EDENRUBBEN, ſit. in bar. Orior, co. Armagh, prov. Ulſter.

EDERMINE, ſit. in bar. Ballagheen, co. Wexford, prov. Leinſter; it is a rectory in dioc. of Ferns.

EDERNY-BRIDGE, a fair town in co. Fermanagh, prov. Ulſter; fairs held 6 Jan. 1 March, 15 May, 17 July, 6 Oct. and 28 Nov.

EDGEWORTH'S-TOWN, a poſt and fair town in bar. Ardagh, co. Longford, prov. Leinſter, 52 miles from Dublin; fairs held day before Shrove-Tueſd. 2 July, 12 Sept. and 3 Wedneſ day in Dec.

EDMOND-HILL, ſit. near *Roſtrevor*, co. Down, prov. Ulſter.

EFFIN, a rectory in dioc. of Limerick, ſit. in bar. Coſhma, co. Limerick, prov. Munſter.

EGLISH, a bar. in King's co. prov. Leinſter; it has a village in it of ſame name, which is a vicarage in dioc. of Meath, diſtant from Dublin about 60 miles. Here is the ſeat of Mr. Barry, near the church. The bar. of Egliſh is otherwiſe called *Fircal*.—There is a village of ſame name in bar. Dungannon, co. Tyrone, prov. Ulſter.—Alſo a curacy in dioc. of Armagh, ſit. in bar. Tyranny, co. Armagh, prov. Ulſter.

EGLISS, ſit. in bar. Armagh, co. Armagh, prov. Ulſter. *Scale.*

EGMONT, ſit. in bar. Oſſory, co. Cork, prov. Munſter, about 20 miles N. of *Cork*; it gives title of earl to the family of *Percival*; the country about it for ſome miles, is planted with aſh, elm, oak, and large quantities of fir; round *Egmont*, the ſoil is a grey clay, reſembling marle, but it does not ferment with acids, and yet the rocks are all good limeſtone. At *Burton* near Egmont, are the ruins of the family manſion of the *Percivals*, which was burned down by the forces of *James* IId.

EIGHT-MILE-BRIDGE, ſit. in bar. upper Iveagh, co. Down, prov. Ulſter, 55 miles from Dublin.

EILE UI BOGARTEAGH, or the level diſtrict of the race of the boggy country, comprehending the plain and moraſſes N. of Caſhel, the chiefs of which were called *Hy Bhogartegh*, by corruption O'Fogarty. The Engliſh families of *Butler*, *Purcel* and *Mathew*, were ſettled in this country before the beginning of the laſt century.

EILE UI CHEARBHUIL, ſit. S. of the King's co. and W. of *Sliab-bloom* mountains; whence it obtained the name of *Eile Ui Chearbhuil*, or the plain diſtrict near the rock; the chiefs of it were called *O'Carrol*, under whom was a ſubordinate Dynaſt, named *O'Delany*, preſiding over a diſtrict in the S. called *Dal Leagh n'ui*, or the diſtrict of the flat country.

EILE UI MORDHA, an antient diſtrict which comprehended the greater part of the preſent Queen's co. prov. Leinſter; and was diſtinguiſhed in the latter ages by the name of *Leix*; it was bounded on the N. and E. by the river Barrow, on the W. by *Slieve-bloom* mountains, and on the S. by the river *Nore* and *Slieve-marragagh* mountains. The hereditary chiefs were called *Hy Mordha* or *O'More*; they were frequently ſtiled kings of Leinſter; and remained in poſſeſſion of the greater part of their country, 'till the commencement of the laſt century; when being in rebellion, the lands were forfeited, and diſtributed amongſt the Engliſh adventurers.

EIRCAEL, or *Eargal*, a large diſtrict in the W. of the prov. Ulſter; comprehending the preſent co.'s of Fermanagh and Donegal.

EIRKE a rectory in dioc. of Oſſory, ſit. in bar. Gallmoy, co. Kilkenny, prov. Leinſter.

ELAGH, ſit. in bar. Gallen, co. Mayo, prov. Connaught.

ELAND, ſit. near *Kilkenny*, in co. Kilkenny, prov. Leinſter.

ELEN, a river ſo called, ſit. in co. Down, prov. Ulſter.

ELENBOROUGH, a town ſit. at the mouth of the river *Elen*, in co. Down, prov. Ulſter, where Mr. *Camden* ſays a beautiful altar of red ſtone, with an inſcription on it, was dug up, which the firſt cohort of the *Dalmatians*, who were garriſoned here, erected to the honour of their commander, G. *Cornelius Peregrinus*, with theſe words, " *Volantii vivas*," i. e. may you live at *Volantium*; the antient name given to this place.

ELFIN, ſee *Elphin*.

ELIOGURTY, or *Eliogarthy*, a bar. in co. Tipperary, prov. Munſter.

ELLEN-MONEY, or the wonderful bog, ſit. in co. Down, prov. Ulſter, between *Pointzpaſs* and *Teryhogan*; it is ſo called from the nature of a rivulet, the current of which immediately on its riſing, takes a Northerly and Southerly courſe, one branch running towards *Lough Neagh*, and the other towards *Newry*. Between theſe places lies the higheſt ground of the whole canal, where, by means of two locks, the water is forceably retained on a level, for near three miles; were it not for this contrivance, as the courſe of the waters incline N. and S. the intermediate ſpace would be left dry.

ELLISTRON, ſit. near *Ballinroab*, in bar. Kilmane, co. Mayo, prov. Connaught.

ELPHIN, a ſmall market, poſt and fair town, ſit. in bar. Roſcommon, co. Roſcommon, prov. Connaught, about 75 miles N. W. of Dublin. Lat. 53 : 46, lon. 8 : 20 It is a rectory in dioc. of ſame name, this being a biſhop's ſee, the church of which was founded by St. Patrick, who appointed St. *Aſſicus* biſhop thereof; by advice of the Saint, *Aſſicus* introduced here a celebrated college of monks, and preſided over them. In proceſs of time this became a pariſh church, and was dedicated to the original founder. *Elphin* was burned in the years 1167 and 1177; in the latter year it was deſtroyed by the Engliſh. The ſee comprises the greater part of the co. Roſcommon, and a great part of Sligo and Galway, with ſome of Mayo. Fairs held 3 May and 10 Dec.

EMATRAS, a rectory in dioc. of Clogher, ſit. in bar. Dartree, co. Monaghan, prov. Ulſter.

EMLAGHFADD, an antient town ſit. 1 mile from Ballymote, in bar. Corran, co Sligo, prov. Connaught; where *Richard* earl of *Ulſter* built a caſtle about the year 1300. An abbey was built here in a magnificent ſtile by *St. Columb*: it is now a vicarage in dioc. of Achonry, and otherwiſe written *Emlyfadd*.

EMLAGHRASH or *Emleghreſh*, a *peninſula* ſit. in bar. Erris, on coaſt of co. Mayo, prov. Connaught.

EMLY; a biſhop's ſee, having in it a village of ſame name, ſit. in bar. Clanwilliam, co. Tipperary, prov. Munſter, 14 miles W. of Caſhel; which is a vicarage in that dioc. Lat. 52 : 20, lon. 8 : 42. This church and biſhoprick are ſaid to have been founded by *St. Aibe* towards the cloſe of the 4th century, ſome years before the arrival of St. Patrick; on the arrival of St. Patrick, and the converſion of *Angus Mac Nafrick*, king of Caſhel, the church was declared the metropolitan church of Munſter, in which dignity it continued ſeveral centuries, until tranſlated to *Caſhel*, where it now remains. This city was plundered by robbers in 1123, and the mitre of St. *Aibe* burnt. It was alſo deſtroyed by fire in 1192, but was afterwards rebuilt, and continued a conſiderable town for ſeveral ages,

even to the time of Hen. VIIIth. in whoſe reign *Thomas Hurly*, biſhop of *Emly*, erected a college for ſecular prieſts; but the only remains at preſent of this antient, and perhaps firſt eccleſiaſtical city in Ireland, are the ruins of a church, ſome walls, a large unhewn ſtone croſs, and a holy well. The ſee of *Emly* was united to that of *Caſhel* in 1568: it compriſes a part of co. Tipperary, and a larger ſcope of Limerick

EMLYFADD, ſee *Emlaghfadd*.

EMLYGRENNAN, a rectory in dioc. of Limerick, ſit. in bar. Coſhlea, co. Limerick, prov. Munſter.

EMO, ſit. in Queen's co. prov. Leinſter, 34 miles from Dublin; adjoining is *Dawſon's-court*, the elegant ſeat of the earl of *Portarlington*.

EMPOR, a fair town in co. Weſtmeath, prov. Leinſter; fairs held 31 May.

EMY-VALE, a fair town in bar. Trough, co. Monaghan, prov. Ulſter, near 67 miles from Dublin; fairs held 1 Jan. 1 Mond. Feb. 1 Mond. O. S. in Apr. 2 Mond. May, 13 June, 1 Mond. Aug. 4 Sept. and 2 Mond. Nov.

ENACH-DUNE or *Eoghnach-dun*, an antient royal reſidence ſit. near Tuam, in co. Galway, prov. Connaught, and ſaid to be the ſame as *Dunmore*, which was a ſeat of the *O'Kelly's* and deſtroyed in 1133 by *Conor O'Brien*.

ENAGH, a fair town in co. Clare, prov. Munſter; fairs held 31 July and 17 Dec.

ENAGHBEACH, ſit. in bar. Dungannon, co. Tyrone, prov. Ulſter.

ENDOR, ſit. in bar. Erris, co. Mayo, prov. Connaught.

ENFIELD, ſit. near Roſcommon, co. Roſcommon, prov. Connaught.

ENISCRONE, a fair town in co. Sligo, prov. Connaught; fair days, day after Trinity-Sund. and 18 Sept. It is ſit. 132 miles from Dublin. Here is a pariſh church.

ENISHOWEN, ſee *Iniſhowen*.

ENISKEEN, a curacy in dioc. of Meath, ſit. in bar. Clonchee, co. Cavan, prov. Ulſter.— Alſo a village in co. Monaghan, prov. Ulſter, where is one of the antient round towers.

ENISKEON, a fair town in co. Cork, prov. Munſter; fairs held 5 Apr. 22 June, 12 Aug. and 2 Oct. It is otherwiſe called *Euniſkeane*.

ENISLAVEG, a *lake* in co. Londonderry, prov. Ulſter.

ENISTEAGUE, ſee *Iniſtioge*.

ENISTON-HEAD, a noted head land in co. Donegal, prov. Ulſter. Lat. 55 : 10, lon. 8 : 40.

ENKIMACOODY, a fair town in co. Kilkenny, prov. Leinſter; fairs held 10 Oct.

ENNEL-LOUGH, a lake ſit. in bar. Moyaſhel, co. Weſtmeath, prov. Leinſter.

ENNIS,

ENNIS, a borough, post and market town sit. in bar. Islands, co. Clare, prov. Munster; being the assizes town of that co. distant 112 miles S. W. from Dublin. Lat. 52 : 42, lon. 9 : 0. It returns 2 members to parliament; patron, sir *Lucius O'Brien* bart. Fairs are held here on Saturday in Easter week and 3 Sept. Here are the remains of one of the finest abbey churches in the kingdom, one of the aysles of which now serves for the parish church. It was built in 1240 by *Donagh Carbrac O'Brien*, for conventual Franciscans. Here is a fine school on the foundation of the late *Erasmus Smith's* charities.

ENNISBEG, one of the *Blasques* or Ferriter's islands, otherwise called *Inisbeg*, sit. off the coast of co. Kerry, prov. Munster.

ENNISBOFINE or *Inisbofin*, a small island in the Atlantic ocean, sit. S. of Achil head, and between the co.'s Galway and Mayo, prov. Connaught.

ENNISCOE, a village in bar. Tyrawly, co. Mayo, prov. Connaught.

ENNISCOFFEY, a rectory in dioc. of Meath, sit. in bar. Fartullagh, co. Westmeath, prov. Leinster.

ENNISCORTHY, a borough, market, fair and post town, in co. Wexford, prov. Leinster, formerly called *Corthæ*, being the capital of the *Coriandii*. It hath a barrack for 2 companies of foot, and is sit. about 60 miles almost S. of Dublin; lat. 52 : 25, lon. 6 : 30. Fair days 21 Feb 25 Apr. 5 July, 26 Aug. 19 Sept. 10 Oct. 15 Nov. and 21 Dec. It returns two members to parliament; patronage in the *Colclough* family. Here are the ruins of an old church, and a very considerable castle, built by the first English settlers. Here was also an abbey of regular canons, of which the patron *Gerald de Prendergrast*, made a grant to be a cell to the abbey of *St. Thomas* in Dublin. Also a Franciscan friary founded in 1460 by *Donald Cavanagh*.

ENNISCRONE, see *Eniscrone*.

ENNISDONY, an *island* sit. in Lough Erne, co. Fermanagh, prov. Ulster.

ENNISFALLEN-ISLAND, sit. in the lake of *Killarney*, co. Kerry, prov. Munster; this is generally the dining place of those who go to visit this place, there being a kind of hall fitted up there by lord *Kenmare*, out of one of the aysles belonging to an antient abbey, the ruins of which are still seen on this island. This island includes about 12 acres of most luxuriant soil; the trees are intermixed with little plots of such rich and luscious pasturage, that the fat of a beast in a week's feeding on it, will be converted into a species of very *marrow*, even too rich for the chandler's use, without a mixture of a grosser kind. This is otherwise called *Inis-fallen*.

ENNISGLORA, sit. near *Achill island*, co. Mayo, prov. Connaught.

ENNISGRANY, an island in *Lough Erne*, in co. Fermanagh, prov. Ulster.

ENNISHIBROE, one of the *Blasques* or Ferriter's islands, off the coast of co. Kerry, prov. Munster.

ENNISHMORE, sit. near Cavan, co. Cavan, prov. Ulster.

ENNISHOWEN, see *Inishowen*.

ENNISIUSH, sit. in bar. Loughlinsholen, co. Londonderry, prov. Ulster.

ENNISKEANE, see *Eniskeon*.

ENNISKEEL *church*, sit. in co. Donegal, prov. Ulster; 136 miles from Dublin.

ENNISKERRY, a village sit. in bar. Rathdown, co. Wicklow, prov. Leinster, near 10 miles from Dublin. It is pleasantly sit. at the foot of a hill near a river, and is of late much improved, and frequented by people for the recovery of their health.—This is also the name of 2 islands on the coast of the co. Clare, prov. Munster; sit. in the bay of *Kilmurry*, 2 leagues from the main land. Lat. 52 : 40, lon. 9 : 35. In one of them an abbey was built by St. *Senan* of *Iniscathy*.

ENNISKILLEN, otherwise called *Inniskillen*, a borough, market, fair and post town in co. Fermanagh, prov. Ulster, lying between 3 lakes. It is about 24 miles E. of Ballyshannon, and 79 N. W. of Dublin. Lat. 54 : 17, lon. 8 : 13. It sends two members to parliament; patron, lord *Enniskillen*, this place giving title of visc. to the family of *Cole*. Its inhabitants distinguished themselves in several considerable engagements in the wars of Ireland at the revolution, out of which a regiment of dragoons, bearing the title of the *Inniskilleners*, was mostly formed. It has a barrack for three companies of foot. Fair days 10 May, 12 Aug. and 1 Nov. Before you cross the bridge of Enniskillen, on a small height, are the remains of a redoubt, which was occupied by the people of this town when they defended themselves so successfully against the army of king *James* IId.

ENNIS-MAC-SAINT, an island sit. in *Lough Erne*, co. Fermanagh, prov. Ulster; an abbey was founded here by *St. Nenn*, who died about A. D. 523; his bell ornamented with gold and silver is yet preserved here as a precious relique.

ENNISMORE, an island in *Lough Erne*, co. Fermanagh, prov. Ulster.

ENNISMURRY or *Inismurry*, an island near the coast of the bar. of Carbery, co. Sligo, prov. Connaught.

ENNIS-

ENNISNAG, fit. within a few miles of Kilkenny, in bar. Gallmoy, co. Kilkenny, prov. Leinfter ; it is a rectory in dioc. of Offory.

ENNISRUSH, a chapelry in dioc. of Derry, fit. in bar. Loughlinfholen, co. Londonderry, prov. Ulfter.

ENNISTIMON, a poft town fit. in co. Clare, prov. Munfter.

ENNISTRAHUL, an ifland fit. off the coaft of co. Donegal, prov. Ulfter.

ENNISTUSK, a fmall ifland fit. near *Clew-bay*, co. Mayo, prov. Connaught.

ENOGH, fit. near *Tynan church*, in co. Armagh, prov. Ulfter.

ENORELLY, a vicarage in dioc. of Dublin, fit. in bar. Arklow, co. Wicklow, prov. Leinft.

EOGHNACHDUN, fee *Enachdune.*

EREW, a *peninfula* in co. Mayo, prov. Connaught ; which ftretches from the bar. Tirawly into Lough Conn ; at the extreme end of which ftood a friary, over which St. *Leogar* prefided. His feaft is held the 30 Sept.

ERIGILL, fee *Errigall.*

ERNE-LOUGH, a lake in co. Fermanagh, prov. Ulfter ; commonly called *Lough-Erne* or *Earne* : it gives title of *earl* to the family of *Creightou.* This lake extends 20 miles in length, joined by a narrow ftreight, on which ftands the town of *Ennifkillen*, the inhabitants whereof expreffed an uncommon bravery at the revolution in 1688. There are feveral iflands in this lake, on which different religious houfes were eftablifhed ; and it is remarkable for fine pike and eels, and a fifh nearly of the fhape of a herring, found only in the month of *May*, and called *Goafke. Lough Erne* is faid to cover 47,400 acres, and properly confifts of *two* lakes, in which there are above 400 iflands interfperfed ; on one of them is the moft compleat round tower in Ireland ; 'tis 69 feet high to the conical covering at the top, which is 15 feet more ; it is 48 feet in circumference, the walls 3 feet 5 inches thick, and the infide, which is as fmooth as poffible, is 9 feet 2 inches diameter : there are 7 fquare holes to admit the light, and the door is elevated 9 feet above the ground : at the outfide bafe, a circle of ftone projects 5 inches. Near it are the venerable ruins of an abbey, built in 1449.

ERNE-RIVER, fit. in prov. Ulfter ; this *river* extends from Ballyfhannon to Killifhandra, E. N. E. 45 miles ; runs thro' the co.'s Fermanagh and Cavan, and is adjacent to Killibeggs, Donegal, Ballyfhannon, Belleek, Pettigoe, Ennifkillen, Canauly, Cullahill, Lifnafkeugh, Newtownbutler, Belturbet, Cavan and Killifhandra.

ERRIGALL, a rectory in dioc. of Derry, fit. in bar. Colerain, co. Londonderry, prov. Ulfter. — Alfo a vicarage in dioc. of Clogher,

fit. in bar. Trough, co. Monaghan, prov. Ulfter ; the church of which is diftant 69 miles from Dublin.

ERRIGALKEEROGE, a rectory in dioc. of Armagh, fit. in bar. Clogher, co. Tyrone, prov. Ulfter.

ERRIS, a bar. in co. Mayo, prov. Connaught.

ERRY, a rectory in dioc. of Cafhel, fit. in bar. Middlethird, co. Tipperary, prov. Munft.

ERRY-CASTLE, fit. near Clara, King's co. prov. Leinfter.

ERYNACH, fit. in co. Down, prov. Ulfter ; about a mile E. of *Caftlefcreen* ; it is a famous well, dedicated to St. *Finan*, where *Magnellus Mackenleff*, one of the petty princes of Ulfter, on 8 Sept. 1127, founded a Benedictine abbey, and called it the abbey of *Carrig*, from a rock on which it ftood. It was converted into a garrifon, and did infinite mifchief to *John de Courcey* ; for which reafon he demolifhed it, and about the year 1188 or 1180, in recompence of that action, founded the abbey of *Inis-Curcey*, in an ifland of the lake *Strangford*, and endowed it with the lands of this abbey of *Carrig* ; or rather tranflated it from hence to that place, and filled it with Ciftertian monks out of the monaftery of *Furnes* in *Lancafhire.*

ESK, *(Lough)* fit. in co. Donegal, prov. Ulfter, about 112 miles from Dublin. This *Lough* abounds with a moft excellent kind of fifh, called *char*, it is about 9 inches in length, and in fome degree refembles a trout. Thefe fifh are not to be caught by bait, but feeding in deep water are taken only in nets. The adjacent mountains to *Lough Efk* abound with wild *red deer.*

ESKER, fit. in bar. Half Rathdown, co. Dublin, prov. Leinfter ; it is a vicarage in dioc. of Dublin. This was one of four antient manors in this co. that were annexed to the crown, and named the king's land.—There is a place of fame name fit. in bar. Garrycaftle, King's co. prov. Leinfter, near the borders of co. Weftmeath ; it has a caftle called *Efker-caftle.*

ESKY, a fair town in bar. Tyreragh, co. Sligo, prov. Connaught, 125 miles from Dublin. It is a vicarage in dioc. of Killala ; fairs held 3 June and 18 Nov. At *Efky-bridge* are the ruins of a caftle.

ESOKAGH-BRIDGE, fit. in bar. Tyreragh, co. Sligo, prov. Connaught.

ETHNEA, a branch of Lough Ru, formerly called *Ethnea river*, mentioned by Ptolemy, and runs between the co.'s Longford and Weftmeath, prov. Leinfter.

ETTAGH, a rectory in dioc. of Killaloe, fit. in bar. Ballibritt, King's co. prov. Leinfter.

EVAGH, a bar. in co. Down, prov. Ulfter, divided into *upper* and *lower* Evagh, otherwife

. called

called *Iveagh* or *Iveach*: in the former of these divisions is a ridge of mountains called *Evagh-mountains*.

EYRE-CASTLE, fit. near *Callen*, in co. Kilkenny, prov. Leinster.

EVEROG-BRIDGE, fit. in co. Down, prov. Ulster; 78 miles from Dublin.

EYNES, a priory in the bar. of Ardes, co. Down, prov. Ulster. The exact situation of this priory cannot now be ascertained; but that there was such a one in this bar. appears from a patent roll 13 Hen. IVth. On 1 May, 1412, a patent passed for granting the alien priory of *Eynes* in the *Ards*, in co. Down, to *Thomas Chenele*, being seized by the king as an alien priory, " *Ratione Guerræ inter nos et Adversarios nostros Franciæ motæ*" to hold as long as it should on that account remain in the king's hands.

EYRE-COURT, a fair and post town in bar. Longford, co. Galway, prov. Connaught, near 72 miles from Dublin. Here is the fine seat of lord Eyre; and also the ruins of a castle. Fairs held Mond. after Easter Mond. 9 July, 8 Sept. and 21 Dec.

EYREFIELD, fit. near Galway, in co. Galway, prov, Connaught.

F A

FABILL, see *Farbill*.

FABY, fit. near *Eyre-court*, co. Galway, prov. Connaught.

FAGHALSTOWN, a vicarage in dioc. of Meath, fit. in bar. Half-fowre, co. Westmeath, prov. Leinster.

FAGHY, a vicarage in dioc. of Clonfert, fit. in bar. Longford, co. Galway. prov. Conn.

FAGORT, fit. in bar. Donaghmoyne, co. Monaghan, prov. Ulster.

FAHAN, fit. in bar. Inishowen, co. Donegal, prov. Ulster, 6 miles N. W. of Londonderry; it is now a rectory in dioc. of Derry. Here St. *Columb* founded a church. The monastery of Fahan was richly endowed and dedicated to St. *Muran*; many monuments of antiquity were destroyed here after the reformation; amongst the few reliques that were preserved, was the book of the acts of St. *Columb*, written by St. *Muran* in Irish verse, some fragments of which yet remain: also a very large antient chronicle held in great repute. The pastoral staff of St. *Muran* richly ornamented with jewels and gilding is still preserved by the *O'Neils*, on which they used to swear in the decision of controversies. Here is a parish church.

FAIRFIELD, fit. near *Coothill*, prov. Ulster.

FAIRHEAD, the N. E. cape of Ireland, which forms the E. side of the bay of *Ballycastle*, in bar. Cary, co. Antrim, prov. Ulster; lat. 55 : 17 N. lon. 6 : 35 W. This promontory is the *Robogdium* of Ptolemy, and raises its lofty summit, more than 400 feet above the sea, presenting a rude mass of vast columnar stones, many of them near 150 feet long. A savage wildness characterises the place, and at its foot the ocean rages with uncommon fury: scarce a single mark of vegetation has yet crept over the hard rock, to diversify its colouring; but one uniform greyness clothes the scene all around. The Irish name of this place is *Ben-more* or the great promontory. At *Fair-head* is a passage between a heap of Basaltic pillars, called *Fhir-leith* or " the grey man's path;" well worth the traveller's attention.

FAIR-VIEW, fit. a ½ mile beyond Ballybough-bridge, and 1¼ mile from Dublin castle: it is on the road to Donnycarney, and near it stands the royal Charter-school at Clontarf.

FAIRY-ROCK, fit. about 5 miles from the head of *Kenmare-river*, in co. Kerry, prov. Munster; on this rock there appear the impressions of several human feet, of all sizes, from infancy to manhood; it is presumed this rock might have been once in a soft and impressible state, and afterwards became petrified, which may account for this circumstance.

FAITHLEG, or *Faithleag*, a fair town fit. in bar. Gualtiere, co. Waterford, prov. Munster; fairs held 20 May and June, 14 Aug. and 10 Oct. It lies near *Passage*; and is a rectory in dioc. of Waterford. Here are the ruins of a church, and from the top of *Faithleg-hill* is a charming and extensive prospect of both land and sea, with a view of the mountains of Waterford, Tipperary, Wicklow and Wexford: and part of the co.'s of Kilkenny, Carlow, King's co. and Queen's co. Under the hill is the market town of *Bolton*, formerly called *Check-point*; the estate of Mr. *Bolton* who has established a large cotton manufactory there, together with an hosiery. There is also a very large and commodious inn here, for the conveniency of passengers, coming or going in the Waterford pacquets to and from *Milford*, in Wales; as the pacquets which are very fine vessels, constantly lie opposite to the inn.

FALKLAND, fit. near *Tynan*, prov. Ulster.

FALLEN, a *river* in bar. Longford, co. Longford, prov. Ulster.

FANE, fit. in parish of Ventry, co. Kerry, prov. Munster; here is a small cell or hermitage, being an arch of stone, neatly put together, without any mortar or cement, which admits no rain through its roof; it is however now getting into a ruinous state.

FANZGARAGH, fit. in co. Donegal, prov. Ulfter: a fmall houfe for friars of the third order of St. *Francis* was built here by *M'Ruinfaig*.

FANLOBBISH, a vicarage in dioc. of Cork, fit. in bar. Carbery, co. Cork, prov. Munfter.

FARAHY, a rectory in dioc. of Cloyne, fit. in bar. Fermoy, co. Cork, prov. Munfter.

FARBILL, or *Fabill*, a bar. in co. Weftmeath, prov. Leinfter.

FARMOY, fee *Fermoy*.

FARNASS, fit. near *Caftlemaiu*, in co. Kerry, prov. Munfter; on thefe lands there is a good chalybeate fpa, it has a fulphureous fmell, like the wafhings of a gun-barrel, but which it lofes when carried to any confiderable diftance. Thefe lands are part of the eftate of *Trinity College*, Dublin.

FARNEY-BRIDGE, a village fit. in bar. Killnalongerty, co. Tipperary, prov. Munfter.

FARNHAM, fit. near Cavan, co. Cavan, prov. Ulfter: it gives title of earl to the *Maxwell* family. Here is *Farnham-houfe*, the handfome feat of lord Farnham.

FARNI-BRIDGE, fit. near *Cafhel*, prov. Munft.

FARNICARNEY, a fair town in co. Sligo, prov. Connaught. Fairs held 26 May, 21 Sept. and Dec.

FARNY-DONAGHMAIN, otherwife called *Donaghmain* or *Donaghmayne*, a bar. in co. Monaghan, prov. Ulfter.

FARRA, fit. in co. Weftmeath, prov. Leinfter; where is a charter-fchool for 40 children; it was opened in 1758, and the late Rev. *Wm. Wilfon*, in order to have this fchool erected here, bequeathed to the incorporated fociety, his moiety of the lands of *Forra*, and ordered by his will, that his eftate of *Shinglifs*, with fome other lands therein mentioned, fhould be fold, and after payment of his debts and legacies, the overplus to be paid to the fociety, towards building and maintaining the faid fchool.

FARRAHY, fit. in bar. Connillo, co. Limerick, prov. Munfter.

FARRANTEMPLE, a fair town in co. Kilkenny, prov. Leinfter; fairs held 2 May.

FARTAGH, fee *Fertagh*.

FARTIN *river*, rifes in parifh of *Killenaue*, co. Kerry, prov. Munfter, towards the S. end of the parifh, and is navigable a confiderable way up, from *Valentia harbour*. *Fearthain* in the old Irifh, fignifies rain; and this river is confiderably augmented in wet weather.

FARTREY, a *river*, fit. in bar. Newcaftle, co. Wicklow, prov. Leinfter.

FARTULLAGH, fee *Fertullagh*.

FASSAGHDINING, or *Faffaghdinning*, and fometimes *Faffadining*, a bar. in co. Kilkenny, prov. Leinfter.

FATHOM-MOUNTAINS, fit. in bar. Orior, co. Armagh, prov. Ulfter.

FAUGHAN, a *river*, fit. in bar. Tyrekerrin, co. Londonderry, prov. Ulfter.

FAUGHAN-VALE, fit. in bar. Tyrekerrin, co. Londonderry, prov. Ulfter; it is a rectory in dioc. of Derry.

FAUGHARD, or *Faugher*, fit. in co. Louth, prov. Leinfter, it is an artificial mount, upon the N. frontier of what is now called the *Englifh-pale*; it is compofed of ftones and terras, (with a deep trench round it) raifed to the height of 60 feet, in the form of a fruftum of a cone; there has been formerly fome fort of an octagonal building on the top of it; it ftands about 2 miles N. of *Dundalk*; and near it lord *Mountjoy*, in the reign of queen Eliz. at feveral times encamped, during the rebellion of *Tyrone*. Here was the birth place of St. *Brigid*, where St. *Monena* erected a nunnery in 638, and prefided over 150 virgins: a monaftery is faid to have been erected here and dedicated to St. *Brigid*; but it exifted only in the earlier ages, and in time became a parifh church.

FAUK's-COURT, fit. in bar. Gallmoy, co. Kilkenny, prov. Leinfter.

FEACLE, a village fit. in bar. Tullagh, co. Clare, prov. Munfter; it is a vicarage in dioc. of Killaloe.

FEADENS, fit. in bar. Upperthird, co. Waterford, prov. Munfter.

FEAL, a *river* which has its origin in the mountains, bounding the co.'s of *Kerry* and *Limerick*, in prov. Munfter, and after making fome progrefs in the latter co. runs thro' the town of *Abeyfeale*, and proceeds in a winding courfe Wefterly, towards Liftowel and other villages in that co. dividing the bar.'s of *Clanmaurice* and *Iraghticonnor*.

FEANAGH, a rectory in dioc. of Ardagh, fit. in bar. Leitrim, co. Leitrim, prov. Connaught.

FEARBANE, fee *Ferbane*.

FEARTAMORE, fit. in co. Galway, prov. Connaught, where one of the antient round towers was erected.

FEATHERD, a borough and poft town, fit. in bar. Shelburne, co. Wexford, prov. Leinfter, 81 miles from Dublin; it is fit. near the fea, and is governed by a *portrieve*. Lat. 52:10, lon. 6:42; it returns two members to parliament; patron, lord *Loftus*. It is a rectory in dioc. of Ferns. Here are the ruins of three caftles.

FEBALL-LAKE, a name given formerly to *Lough Foyle*, in co. Londonderry, prov. Ulfter.

FEDAMORE, or *Fedemore*, a fair town in bar. Small-county, co. Limerick, prov. Munfter; fairs held 5 May and 9 Oct. It is a vicarage in dioc. of Limerick.

FEDOM,

FEDOM, a castle in co. Down, prov. Ulster, within less than 1 mile of *Newry*, in which *sir Nicholas Bagnal* found *Shane O'Neil* living, on his arrival here, the latter suffering no subject to travel from *Dundalk* Northward; but after the buildings and fortifications made by *Bagnal*, all the passages were laid open, and much of the country adjacent reduced to civility.

FEDOMMET, sit. in bar. Monaghan, co. Monaghan, prov. Ulster.

FEIGHCULLEN, a rectory in dioc. of Kildare, sit. in bar. Ophaly, co. Kildare, prov. Leinster.

FELL's WELL, sit. in co. Kerry, prov. Munster; towards the W. end of *Knockanure* mountain, a mile E. of *Dun castle*, in bar. *Iraghticonnor*. It is a pure chalybeate water, and the well is called after the gentleman who first discovered it, and made a trial of its virtues in scorbutic cases, which it relieved; this water sparkles like *German spa* at the fountain head.

FELTRUM, a village in bar. Coolock, co. Dublin, prov. Leinster, near 2 miles on the right of *Swords*, 1¼ mile on the left of St. *Doolough's*, and 7 miles from Dublin castle; at the foot of *Feltrum-hill* is a pleasant seat belonging to sir *Annesley Stewart*, bart.

FENAGHT; see *Fenought*.

FENARD, a village sit. in bar. Tyrhugh, co. Donegal, prov. Ulster.

FENIT-ISLAND, sit. close to the shore, on the N. side of co. Kerry, prov. Munster, between which and the main, there is a small creek for ships, which must be entered from the N. but the passage is so narrow and foul, that it cannot be entered without a good pilot. Most of the maps of Ireland and sea charts, place *Fenit-Island*, which they call *Fenor*, in the middle of *Tralee-bay*, but that is erroneous. To the N. of *Fenit*, is the bay of *Ballyheige*, infamous for ship-wrecks. On *Fenit-Island*, there is an old castle in ruins.

FENIX, a *river*, sit. in bar. Imokilly, co. Cork, prov. Munster.

FENNAGH, see *Fenought*.

FENNOR, a rectory in dioc. of Cashel, sit. in bar. Slewardagh, co. Tipperary, prov. Munster.—Also a rectory in dioc. of Meath, sit. in bar. Duleek, co. Meath, prov. Leinster.

FENO, a *lake*, sit. in bar. Carrigallen, co. Leitrim, prov. Connaught.

FENOAGH, a rectory in dioc. of Lismore, sit. in bar. Upperthird, co. Waterford, prov. Munster; it was antiently called *Finwaghc*; the land in this parish is generally arable and pasture, with some unprofitable rock and mountain.—Also a vicarage in dioc. of Killa-

loe, sit. in bar. lower Ormond, co. Tipperary, prov. Munster.

FENOUGH, or *Fennagh*, and sometimes *Fenaght*, a rectory in dioc. of Leighlin, sit. in bar. Idrone, co. Carlow, prov. Leinster, 45 miles from Dublin. At *Fenough church* are the ruins of an old castle, which appears to have been well fortified by strong ramparts, and a double ditch; formerly the seat of one of the kings of *Leinster*.

FENWICK's-PASS, sit. in co. Down, prov. Ulster. Here are the remains of an old castle. Almost midway between *Fenwick's-pass* and *Scarvagh pass* there is a small lake called *Lough Shark*, from an abundance of pike found in it.

FEORUS, the antient name of the river *Nore*, which rises near the *Devil's-bit*, in co. Tipperary, and falls into the Barrow; Feorus is evidently derived from *Abham-n-Feoruis*, or the river of the rapid stream, whence it was frequently called *Abham-n Feor*, and by the English "*the Nore*;" this river in times of floods being exceedingly rapid.

FERBANE, or *Fearbane*, and sometimes *Firbane*, a fair town in bar. Garrycastle, King's co. prov. Leinster, 57 miles from Dublin; within 1½ mile of which, near the river *Brosna*, are the ruins of *Killcolgan-castle*, and a mile further, the ruins of *Cool-castle*; fairs held 1 Aug. and 20 Oct.

FERCALL, or *Fearcall*, a district in King's co. prov. Leinster, the antient proprietors of which were the *O'Molloys*. It is now a bar. and sometimes written *Fircal*.

FERGUS, a *river* in bar. Islands, co. Clare, prov. Munster.

FERMANAGH, a co. in the prov. Ulster, bounded by the co.'s *Donegal* and *Tyrone* on the N. by another part of *Tyrone* and *Monaghan* on the E. by *Cavan* and *Leitrim* on the S. and by another part of *Leitrim* and the *ocean* on the W. its principal town is *Inniskillen* or *Enniskillen*. It is navigable throughout its whole length, by means of *Lough Erne*. It is difficult for travellers to pass through, by reason of that lake, and also the mountain and boggy grounds it abounds with. It is about 34 miles long, and 26 broad, contains 283,400 acres, 18 parishes, 8 bar.'s, 1 borough, and sends 4 members to parliament, and gives title of vise. to the family of the E. of *Verney*. Its bar.'s are Lurge, Tyrskennedy, Magherastephana, Clonkelly and Coole, Magheraboy, Clonawly and Knockninny; number of houses about 11,969; inhabitants about 71,800. The surface of this co. is very uneven, but its mountains afford a coarse pasture to large herds of young cattle; and most of them are capable of great improvement. This country has been also called *Magh Guhuir*, or the plain of
the

the waters, and was made a co. in the reign of Queen Eliz. the antient chiefs of which were called *Magh Guhuir* or *Mac Guire*, who remained in the entire possession of their country, until the beginning of the last century. The linen manufacture forms the chief trade of this co. the sale of which is averaged at 4,100*l.* yearly. There are only 4 bleach-yards in it, and one linen market, but the country abounds with spinners and good flax.

FERMOY, a bar. in co. Cork, prov. Munster, otherwise called *Armoy*, containing a considerable tract, both for the quantity of the land and the goodness of the soil. It abounds with lime stone for manure, also with a lime stone gravel, which being laid out, dissolves in the air, and is an excellent cheap manure for *corn*, but will not answer so well for meadow grounds. The bar. of *Fermoy* was formerly the country of the *Gibbons*, *Condons* and *Roches*. It was also in antient times denominated *Glean na Mhain* or *Magh na Feine*, i. e. the sacred plain, or plain of the learned. About the year 254, *Fiach Muillethan* provincial king of Munster, bestowed the greatest part of this country on the druid *Mogruith*, from whom it obtained the name of *Dal Mogruith*. The druid on coming into possession of the country, converted it into a kind of sanctuary, and on the high land which bounds it, erected a number of altars and places of worship, several of which are remaining to this day. From this circumstance *Dal Mogruith* obtained the name of *Magh Feine* or the sacred plane, which before bore that of *Magh Neircv*. In the latter ages the inhabitants of *Magh Feine* were called *Fear-magh Feine*, or the man of the sacred plane, or *Fear Magh*, and by corruption *Fermoy*.—There is also a village of this name in same co. which tho' called Fermoy, is sit. in the bar. of Condons and Clangibbon; it is distant about 107 miles from Dublin, and is seated on the Blackwater, over which is a large stone bridge of 13 arches, built in 1689, and cost 7,500*l.* Near this place in 1690, there were some mineral purging waters discovered, found to be of the same nature as those of *Tunbridge* in *Kent*, and every way as useful; but the place is now stopt up. Here was an abbey for *Cistertian* monks, called our *Lady de Castro Dei*, founded in 1270. The spiritualities of this house were assigned by the lord treasurer of England, to sir *George Harvey*, for the use of the first earl of *Cork*, who purchased them and several lands in *Fermoy*, from sir *Bernard Grenville*. Near Fermoy are the ruins of *Carrickabrick* and *Liclash* castles. About ¼ a mile N. E. of Fermoy, is a fine bed of white freestone. Fair days 21 June, 20 Aug. and 7 Nov.—*Fermoy* is also the name

of a village sit. in bar. Rathline, co. Longford, prov. Leinster.—And of a place near *Roscommon*, prov. Connaught.

FERRARD, sit. in bar. Beer and Bantry, co. Cork, prov. Munster.

FERN-LOUGH, a *lake* in bar. Kilmacrenan, co. Donegal, prov. Ulster.

FERNS, a market, post and fair town, sit. in bar. Scarewalsh, co. Wexford, prov. Leinster, 54 miles from Dublin, and now a vicarage in dioc. of same name. A monastery and bishoprick was founded here by St. *Edan* about the year 598; and the church of Ferns was in the middle ages frequently esteemed the metropolitan church of Leinster; the cathedral which stands in the town, and serves as a parish church, is small and plain, being part of a more extensive building. The see of *Ferns* was united to that of *Leighlin* in 1600, and comprises the whole of the co. Wexford and a small part of the co. Wicklow. At this place the kings of Leinster for some time resided; and there are the remains of a large castle erected about A. D 1180. The patron of this town was St. *Moeg*, who was interred at the cathedral, and whose sepulchre is there shewn: near the church is a celebrated well dedicated to that saint. Fairs are held 11 Feb. 12 May, 4 Sept. and 29 Oct. Lat. 52 : 23, lon. 6 : 28.

FERNUS, an antient name of the present co. of Wexford, prov. Leinster; said to be derived from *Fear na xis*, or " men of the district on the water." It is more particulaly applied to *Ferns*, which was the principal residence of the antient chiefs of this district.

FERRARD, a bar. in co. Louth, prov Leinst.

FERRITER's-COVE, sit. in bar. Corkaguinny, co. Kerry, prov. Munster.

FERRITER's-ISLANDS, otherwise called *Blasques*, sit. near coast of bar. Clanmaurice, co. Kerry, prov. Munster.

FERRY-BANK, sit. in co. Londonderry, prov. Ulster, 114 miles from Dublin.—Also a place of same, in co. Kilkenny, prov. Leinster, 74 miles from Dublin.

FERRY-CARRICK, sit. in bar. Shelmaliere, co. Wexford, prov. Leinster. Here is a passage boat kept for the convenience of travellers, across the river *Slaney*, which is here very broad and empties itself into Waterford harbour. The ground is exceeding high and rocky at both sides, and on the top of one of the rocks are the remains of a strong though not very large castle, which commanded this part of the river.

FERRY POINT, a fair town in co. Waterford, prov. Munster; fairs held 8 May and 3 Oct.

FERTAG, see *Fertagh*.

FERTAMORE, fit. at the adjoining borders of the co.'s Galway and Mayo, in prov. Connaught.

FERTAGH or *Fortagh*, and sometimes written *Fertag*, fit. in bar. Gallmoy, co. Kilkenny, prov. Leinfter. It is a rectory in dioc. of Offory; diftant about 54 miles from Dublin. The name fignifies "*the cemetary*," and here was the burial place of the *Fitzpatricks*, or *Mac-gill-Padruicks*, chiefs of upper Offory for feveral ages. In the old church of Fertagh is an antient infcription on the tomb of one *Mac-gille-Patrick*, who died in May, 1525; it is much defaced, but may be thus interpreted, "*Here lieth at reft entombed the chief Mac-gille-Patrick, who died May 1525, and God have mercy on his foul*;" this is fuppofed to be the fame perfon who a few years before his death fent an exprefs meffenger to king *Henry* VIIIth. to complain of *Pierce Butler* earl of *Ormond*, otherwife called *red Peter*; which meffenger taking an opportunity to meet the king in going to chapel, delivered his embaffy in thefe words; "*Sta pedibus, domine rex, dominus meus Gilla Patricius me mifit ad te, et juffit dicere, quod fi non vis caftigare Petrum Rufum, ipfe faciet bellum contra te.*" Here is one of the antient round towers. This place is otherwife called *Beggar's inn*.

FERTULLAGH, a bar. in co. Weftmeath, prov. Leinfter; otherwife written *Fartullagh* and *Furtullagh*.

FETHARD, a borough and fair town in co. Tipperary, prov. Munfter, fit. 78 miles S. W. of Dublin; this was formerly a town of fome note, but is now in a decayed ftate; the walls of the town, and fome of the gates ftill remain, alfo the ruins of a fine abbey founded in 1306. Within ¼ mile of *Fethard* are the ruins of *Crump-caftle*. This place returns 2 members to parliament; patron, lord *Lifmore*. Fairs held 20 Apr. Frid. before Trinity Sund. 7 and 19 Sept. and 21 Nov.

FEWS, a bar. in co. Armagh, prov. Ulfter; in it there runs a ridge of mountains acrofs the co. which is called the *Fews mountains*: the antient proprietors of this diftrict were the *O'Neils*.—Alfo the name of a village fit. in this bar.—There is likewife a parifh of fame name in bar. Decies without Drum, co. Waterford. prov. Munfter: it is a vicarage in dioc. of Lifmore.

FIDDOWN, antiently called *Fedh-duin*, a fair town fit. in bar. Iverk, co. Kilkenny, prov. Leinfter. It is a rectory in dioc. of Offory. St. *Maidoc* or *Momoedoe* was abbot of this place. It is feated by the river *Suir*. Fairs held 25 Apr. 10 June, 29 Sept. and 30 Nov.

FIELDTOWN or *Field'stown*, fit. above 10 miles from Dublin, in bar. Nethercrofs, co. Dublin, prov. Leinfter; it holds fairs annually on Whitfun Mond.

FIGIVEE, a fair town in co. Londonderry, prov. Ulfter; fairs held 12 Nov.

FIN, a *river* in co. Donegal, prov. Ulfter.

FINA, a *river* in co. Monaghan, prov. Ulfter.

FINAE, a fair town fit. in bar. Half-fowre, co. Weftmeath, prov. Leinfter, near 48 miles from Dublin; it is a fmall but neat village, on a ftream that unites the two lakes of *Lough Shillen* and *Lough Inny*: over this ftream there is a bridge which feparates the co.'s of Weftmeath and Cavan. Within 2 miles of *Finae*, oppofite a race-courfe, are the ruins of a caftle. Fairs held Sat. before Whitfun-day, 27 July, 18 Aug. and Sept. and 15 Nov.

FINAN'S-WELL, fee *Erynagh*.

FIN-AWN, a river in co. Cork, prov. Munfter; which difcharges itfelf into the *Blackwater*.

FINGAL, a diftrict fit. to the N. of Dublin, and extending along the coaft of that part of co. Dublin, prov. Leinfter. It is inhabited by people ufually called *Fingallians*; they have a peculiar kind of dialect, in a broken Englifh, fhort, guttural, and difagreeable to a nice ear. This place gives title of *earl* to the family of *Plunket*.

FINGLAS, a village in bar. Nethercrofs, co. Dublin, prov. Leinfter; it is a vicarage in dioc. of Dublin, and holds an annual fair on 6 May for horfes and chapmen's wares: it is diftant 3 miles from Dublin caftle. The parifh church is of an old, plain but ftrong ftructure, and near it is a celebrated fpa, which was much frequented a few years paft, but is now difufed. An abbey was founded here in the early ages, of which St. *Kenicus* or *Kenny* was abbot; and there was preferved in the church of Finglas an old book containing the life of this Saint, as archbifhop *Ufher* was particularly informed by fir *Chrift. Plunket*. St. *Flann*, St. *Noe* and St. *Foelchu* were all interred in this church, which is dedicated to St. *Kenny*. Alfo a rectory in dioc. of Killaloe, fit. in bar. Clonlifk, King's co. prov. Leinfter.

FINGLAS-BRIDGE, fit. in bar. Nethercrofs, co. Dublin, prov. Leinfter, 2½ miles from Dublin caftle, and within ½ mile of Finglas. The bridge itfelf is inconfiderable, but there are a good many tolerable houfes near it, which makes it rank as a village.

FINNIBROGUE, a feat near *Lough Coyne*, in co. Down, prov. Ulfter.

FINNIS, a town land fo called, fit. in co. Down, prov. Ulfter; in parifh Dromaragh, about 3½ miles S. E. of Dromore, on which there is an antient *Cromleach* or ftone altar.

FINNISTOWN, fit. in bar. Newcaftle, co. Dublin, prov. Leinfter.

FINN-

Fixn-lough, a *lake* fit. in bar. Boylagh, co. Donegal, prov. Ulfter; from whence iffues a river of fame name, which croffes the co. from W. to E. It is otherwife written *Fin Lough*.

Finogh, a rectory in dioc. of Killaloe, fit. in bar. Bunratty, co. Clare, prov. Munfter.

Fintan's-island, fit. in *Lough Derg*, co. Donegal, prov. Ulfter; a priory for Auguftinians was founded here by St. *Auguftin*, in which St. *Daboec* is faid to have been buried; it had a fine chapel, with convenient houfes for the monks, the remains of which may ftill be feen; this place is otherwife called *St. Fintan's*.

Fintona, a fair town in bar. Clogher, co. Tyrone, prov. Ulfter, 93 miles from Dublin; fairs held 4 May, 22 June and 29 Oct.

Fin-town, fit. in bar. Boylagh, co. Donegal, prov. Ulfter, near 126 miles from Dublin. Within a mile of *Fintown* is a fmall lough that communicates with the river *Fin*; and within a ¼ mile of *Fintown* is another lough 2 miles long, but not very broad, called *Lough Fin*. Fairs held at *Fintown* on 16 May, 3 July, Sept. and Nov.

Fintra-bay, fit. in bar. Boylagh, co. Donegal, prov. Ulfter.

Finuge, a vicarage in dioc. of Ardfert, fit. in bar. Clanmaurice, co. Kerry, prov. Munfter.

Finvarra-point, a *cape* fit. in bar. Burrin, co. Clare, prov. Munfter.

Finvoy, a rectory in dioc. of Connor, fit. in bar. Kilconway, co. Antrim, prov. Ulfter.

Fiodh-aongusa, a diftrict in bar. Rathconrath, co. Weftmeath, prov. Leinfter. It was in the early ages called *Coen-druim*, or the diftrict of the hill or dome, from containing the *hill* of *Ufneach*, famous for being the place where the antient fynods and public affemblies were frequently held; efpecially that in 1112, or 1111, under *Celfus* archbifhop of *Armagh*.

Fircal, fee *Fercall*.

Firmount, a village with a handfome feat, fit. in bar. Granard, co. Longford, prov. Leinfter.

Firthuathal, an antient diftrict which comprehended the mountainous tract of country on the W. of the co. Wicklow, prov. Leinfter; the antient chiefs of which were called *Hy Tuathal*, by corruption *O'Tools*.

Fishing-bay, fit. in co. Antrim, prov. Ulfter; it is a part of *Lough Neagh* fo called, and remarkable for its healing quality. This bay is about ½ mile broad, and has a fine fandy bottom without a pebble in it, fo that one may fafely walk in it from the depth of the ancle to the chin, on an eafy declivity, at leaft 300 yards before you come to that depth.

Five-mile-bridge, fit. in co. Cork, prov. Munfter, on the river *Conbury*, being the mid-

way between *Cork* and *Kinfale*. Here is a chalybeate fpring, impregnated with fulphur, and it has a ftrong tafte of iron at the fountain head. Some years ago a fhaft of coals was funk here, but with little fuccefs; however, the black flate that was dug up, on examination was found to be full of fulphureous marcafite, and on being burnt produced both fulphur and iron. Fairs are held here 9 June and 10 Oct.

Five-mile-town, a fair town fit. in bar. Clogher, co. Tyrone, prov. Ulfter, above 81 miles from Dublin; fairs held 20 Jan. 2d Sat. O. S. March, Thurfd. before Whitfund. 3d Sat. Aug. and 22 Nov.

Flesk, there are two rivers of this name in co. Kerry, prov. Munfter; one of which empties itfelf into the river *Mang*, about a mile W. of *Teernigoofe*; the other rifes near the Eaftern bounds of Kerry, and runs Wefterly in a very winding courfe through *Glanflefk*, a mountainous country to which it gives its name; from whence it collects feveral ftreams in its paffage, and empties itfelf into the lake of *Killarney*, after paffing thro' a handfome ftone bridge.

Flurry-bridge, a poft town, diftant 46 miles from Dublin; fit. in bar. Dundalk, co. Louth, prov. Leinfter.

Foclut, an antient foreft in bar. Tirawly, co. Mayo, prov. Connaught, on the Weftern bank of the river *Mayo*; it is famous for being the fubject of the celebrated dream of St. Patrick, before he entered on his miffion to Ireland.

Fogart, a fair town in bar. Dundalk, co. Louth, prov. Leinfter; fairs held 12 Feb. It is otherwife written *Foghart*, and is a rectory in dioc. of Armagh.

Foghall's-town, fit. in bar. Half-fowre, co. Weftmeath, prov. Leinfter.

Foghart, fee *Fogart*.

Foghina, a vicarage in dioc. of Clonfert, fit. in bar. Killconnel, co. Galway, prov. Connaught.

Foherish, a river in co. Cork, prov. Munfter.

Fohy, fit. in bar. Tullagh, co. Clare, prov. Munfter.

Follistown, a rectory in dioc. of Meath, fit. in bar. Skryne, co. Meath, prov Leinfter.

Foly-island, fit. in bar. Barrymore, on coaft of co. Cork, prov. Munfter.

Fontstown, a rectory in dioc. of Dublin, fit. in bar. Narragh, co. Kildare, prov. Leinfter.—Alfo a rectory in dioc. of Leighlin, fit. in bar. Balliadams, Queen's co. prov. Leinfter.

Fook's-mill, fit. in bar. Shelmaliere, co. Wexford, prov. Leinfter, 75 miles from Dublin; a mile beyond which are the ruins of
Rathgowrey

Rathgowrey castle. Fairs are held here Easter Tuesday and 2 Nov.

FORE, a small borough town in bar. Half-fore, or Half-fowre, co. Westmeath, prov. Leinster; it is governed by a portrieve, and sends 2 members to parliament; patron, the earl of Westmeath; fairs are held here 30 Jan. and 24 Aug. This was an antient corporation, and it is said there was formerly an university here; its name in the Irish language, signifies the town of books; if this was not a town of learning, it certainly was of devotion, for here are the ruins of 3 parish churches, 1 monastery, the cell of an Anchorite, and other evidences of antient piety. This is a curacy in dioc. of Meath.

FOREST, sit. 5 miles from Dublin, and 2 miles beyond *Glasnevin*, in co. Dublin, prov. Leinster.

FORETALL, sit. in bar. Ballybritt, King's co. prov. Leinster.

FORGLINIO, sit. near Ballimore, co. Westmeath, prov. Leinster.

FORGNEY, a curacy in dioc. of Meath, sit. in bar. Shrowle, co. Longford, prov. Leinster.

FORKHILL, sit. in bar. Orior, co. Armagh, prov. Ulster, 45 miles from Dublin, 2 miles beyond which is *Slieve Gullen*, one of the highest mountains in the kingdom; here are fairs held on 29 Sept. It is a rectory in dioc. of Armagh.

FORT-CHESTER, sit. in co. Wicklow, prov. Leinster.

FORT-DEL-ORE, a fortress built by some Spaniards and Italians, who landed in 1581, at *Smerewick*, in co. Kerry, prov. Munster; it was taken by sir *Wm. Pelham*, and the earl of *Ormond*; it has its name from some treasure, which has been discovered near it, and also several corslets of pure gold, which were dug up on the lands of *Clonties*, near a small chapel which the *Spaniards* had erected about a mile from the fort.

FORTH, a bar. in co. Carlow,—also a bar. in co. Wexford, both in prov. Leinster: in the latter the inhabitants in general speak a dialect of the *Anglo-Saxon* tongue, free from any intermixture of the Irish; and have a variety of customs that distinguish them from their neighbours. They are a cleanly industrious people, and neat in their apparel.

FOUR-MILE-WATER, a small village in bar. Glanehiry, co. Waterford, prov. Munster; which takes its name from its distance from Clonmel, where over the river *Nier* there is a stone bridge.—Also a *river* in co. Cork, prov. Munster.

FOWRE, or *Fore*, and sometimes written *Foore*, a district divided into two bar.'s, one being in co. Meath, and the other in co. Westmeath,

prov. Leinster; each being called the bar. of *Half-fowre*.

FOX, sit. in bar. Newcastle, co. Dublin, prov. Leinster.

FOX-AND-GEESE, a village in bar. Upper-cross, co. Dublin, prov. Leinster; it is sit. between *Cromlin* and *Clondalkin*, and has a large tract of commonage, or waste ground, called the *commons of Fox-and-geese*.

FOXE's CASTLE, sit. in co. Waterford, prov. Munster; on the bank of the river *Bonmahon*, and within about 8 miles of *Dungarvan*.

FOXFORD, a market and fair town, sit. in bar. Gallen, co. Mayo, prov. Connaught, 112 miles N. W. of Dublin. It has a barrack for a company of foot, and lies about 8 miles N. of Castlebar. It is pleasantly sit. on the river *Moy*, which about 1 mile from this village unites with the river *Guisden*, and ¼ mile farther runs into *Lough Conn*. Fairs held here 15 May, 25 June, 3 Oct. and 10 Dec.

FOYLE-LOUGH, sit. between the co.'s Londonderry and Donegal, prov. Ulster. It is a bay, or arm of the sea 14 miles long, and 6 to 8 broad, into which the sea flows by a narrow channel, little more than a mile over. Three miles from the lake stands the city of *Londonderry*. Before the mouth of this lough is a great sand, called the *Touns*, which however does not obstruct the navigation, as there are at all times 14 and 15 fathom water in the channel, which is broad and deep. In the entrance of the lough there are very great sands on the left hand, from one end to the other, which are some miles broad off the land; and on the right hand, are little sands or shelves lying close to the land. Between these there is a broad channel, in most parts 3 and 4 fathoms deep; and in that arm whereon *Londonderry* stands, it is 10 or 12, and before the town 4 and 5, so that it is justly deemed as good and commodious a harbour as any in the kingdom.

FOYLE-RIVER, sit. in bar. Tyrekerin, co. Londonderry, prov. Ulster; over this river a wooden bridge was erected in 1791, of singular and excellent construction, completed in the short space of 15 months, by an American artist named *Lemuel Cuxe*; it is 1068 feet in length.

FOYNS-ISLAND, sit. in bar. Connello, near coast of co. Limerick, prov. Munster.

FOYRAN, a curacy in dioc. of Meath, sit. in bar. Half-fowre, co. Westmeath, prov. Leinster.

FRAILS-ROCKS, sit. in bar. Bargie, by the coast of co. Wexford, prov. Leinster.

FRANKFORD, a fair town in bar. Balliboy, King's co. prov. Leinster, above 55 miles from Dublin. Here is a charter-school which at present prefent contains above 40 children. The late *James Frank* efq. in order to have this fchool erected, granted to the incorporated fociety, with the confent of Francis Rollefton, efq; two acres of land for ever; and let by leafe for 31 years 20 acres of land at the yearly rent of 4*l.* 10*s.* He alfo gave 100*l.* towards building the fchool, which was opened in 1753. Fairs held 28 May and 8 Nov. *Frankford* was formerly known by the name of *Kilcormuck* and a monaftery for Carmelites was founded here by *Odo*, the fon of *Nellan*, head of the fept of the *Molloys*; it was dedicated to the Virgin Mary. *Nellan Molloy* died in 1454, and was buried before the high altar in this abbey. This houfe and its poffeffions were granted on the fuppreffion to *Robert Leicefter*.

FREATH-CASTLE, fit. in bar. Ibrickan, co. Clare, prov. Munfter. Lat. 52:43, lon. 9:51.

FREDERICK'S-TOWN. a fair town in co. Tyrone, prov. Ulfter. Fairs held 3 Jan. March, June and Oct.

FRENCHFURZE, a fair town in co. Kildare, prov. Leinfter. Fairs held 26 July.

FRENCH-PARK, fit. in co. Rofcommon, prov. Connaught; 83 miles from Dublin. It has fairs 21 May, 12 July and 21 Sept. There is a church belonging to it; and a handfome feat.

FRESHFORD, a poft and fair town in bar. Crannagh, co. Kilkenny, prov. Leinfter, 64 miles from Dublin. The church of *Frefhford* is very antient; it belonged to the abbey founded here by St. *Laftan*, who was himfelf the firft abbot, and died 19 March 622; it is now a parifh church in the dioc. of *Offory*, and called the prebend of *Aghour*, (or *Achadhur*, i. e. Waterfield.) Over the door of the church, is a curious infcription engraven on feveral ftones; it runs thus, " Aodos M'Roen, ocas cuce cneabdocum doimrac neibnifan cuirce. Acos dor eacleag amarc mearg ufe acos clar fni deorfoich en argis." In modern Irifh, " Aoda M'Roen agus coighe flath teampall talamh as dlightheach deaglais coirce agus dorais en cloch amairc fleas ufa agus e fearann dofhin devirfeach en archios." That is, " *The Prieft* M'Roen and chief, *gave to this church the glebe of arable land: and over the door placed this ftone, as a true token; and with this favour, the land, flaves and tribute.*" There being no date, the time of this gift cannot be determined. Fairs are held here 5 Aug. and 7 Sept. *cuftom free*, and 17 Dec. At lefs than two miles diftance from Frefhford, are the ruins of 4 feveral caftles.

FRETH-CASTLE, fee *Freath-caftle*.

FRIENDSTOWN, a curacy in dioc. of Dublin, fit. in bar. Talbot'ftown, co. Wicklow, prov. Leinfter.

FRODEEN, a village in bar. Boyle, co. Rofcommon, prov. Connaught.

FUERTY, a fair town in bar. Athlone, co. Rofcommon, prov. Connaught. Fairs held 1 Wed. O. S. May, 4 Aug. and 21 Nov. It is a curacy in dioc. of Elphin.

FUNCHEON-RIVER, fit. in bar. Condons, co. Cork, prov. Munfter.

FUNSHOG, a village fit. in bar. Ferrard, co. Louth, prov. Leinfter.

FUOGH-RIVER, fit. in bar. Moycullin, co. Galway, prov. Connaught.

FURNACE, fee *Furnefs*.

FURNAUGHTS, a curacy in dioc. of Kildare, fit. in bar. Salt, co. Kildare, prov. Leinfter; it is fometimes written *Furnie*, or *Furncy*.

FURNESS, or *Furnace*, the antient feat of the *Nevill* family, fit. 1 mile from Johnftown, and about 14 from Dublin caftle, in co. Kildare, prov. Leinfter. It is beautifully improved; and in a back lawn ftands a ruin of an old chapel, which has a window of painted glafs, of great antiquity, and not inferior in colour and beauty to any in Europe; it is kept in perfect repair.

FURNEY, fee *Furnaughts*.

FURREN-LOUGH, a *lake*, fit. in bar. Burrifhoole, co. Mayo, prov. Connaught.

FURRY-PARK, fit. in co. Dublin, prov. Leinfter; it lies oppofite to *Killcfter*, 1 mile from *Donnycarney*, and 3 from Dublin caftle: here is a handfome demefne, belonging to the earl of *Shannon*, which he purchafed from the late *Gorges Edmond Howard*, efq.

FURTULLAGH, fee *Fertullagh*.

FYANSTOWN, fit. in co. Meath, prov. Leinfter, 30 miles from Dublin. About 2 miles from this is *Headford*, the fuperb feat of the earl of *Bective*.

G A

GABHRA, faid to have been fit. in co. Meath, prov. Leinfter; where a battle was fought between the *Belgians* and *Fene-Fians*, or people of Finland, A. D. 296.

GABRIEL *mountain*, fit. in bar. Carbery, co. Cork, prov. Munfter.

GABRHAN, from *Gabh-re-au*, the high habitation of the king; the capital and royal refidence of the kings of Offory. The rath of this antient palace is yet remaining, fit. in *upper Offory*, in the Queen's co. prov. Leinfter.

GAFNEY, fit. near Drogheda, co. Louth, prov. Leinfter.

GALBALLY, fit. in the bar. of *Cofhlea*, co. Limerick, prov. Munfter, 24 miles from Limerick

rick. One of the *O'Brien* family founded a considerable monastery here for grey frairs; the ruins of which yet remaining with those of several other religious foundations, sufficiently shew the antient magnificence of this place. This monastery with certain lands was granted in *capite*, to John earl of *Desmond* for ever, 20 Jan. 35 Hen. VIIIth. Fairs held here 12 May and 15 Oct. This is now a rectory in dioc. of Emly.

GALE, a *river*, which takes its rise in co. Limerick, and runs into co. Kerry, prov. Munster; falling at last into the river *Feal*. It is otherwise written *Galey*, or *Gally*.

GALEN, see *Gallen*.

GALEY, a village sit. in bar. Iraghticonnor, co. Kerry, prov. Munster: it is a vicarage in dioc. of Ardfert.

GALGOM, a village sit. in bar. Toome, co. Antrim, prov. Ulster.

GALIAN, an antient district, comprehending the greater part of the co.'s Kildare, Carlow, and Queen's co. prov. Leinster: it was in the early ages almost one continued forest.

GALLEA-CLIFF CASTLE, sit. in bar. Carbury, co. Sligo, prov. Connaught. Lat. 54 : 16, lon. 8 : 58.

GALLEN, a. bar. in co. Mayo, prov. Connaught.—Also a vicarage in dioc. of Meath, sit. in bar. Garrycastle, King's co. prov. Leinster. Here St. *Canoc* erected a monastery, near the river *Brusna*, about the year 492. It was at different times plundered and spoiled, viz. in the years 949, 1003, 1519, and 1531. Some emigrants from Wales founded a celebrated school there, from whence it acquired its present name.

GALLEN-HILLS, sit. in co. Tyrone, prov. Ulster.

GALLEON-POINT, the Eastern point of the harbour of Castle-haven, in co. Cork, prov. Munster; it was so called since admiral *Leviston* in queen Eliz.'s time, sunk some Spanish galleons near it.

GALLERUS *castle*, sit. towards the bottom of *Smerwick harbour*, in co. Kerry, prov. Munster; near it is a large fresh water lake, frequented in some winters by considerable flocks of wild swans. This castle was built by the *Fitzgeralds*, knights of *Kerry*. Near Gallerus is one of the curious stone cells, intirely perfect. The door is 5 feet high, and about 2½ broad, at one end of the building, and at the other end is a small neat window, the sides and bottom of which consist only of one stone, extremely well cut, with hardly any mark of the tool upon it. The room is about 20 feet long, by 10 broad, and 20 feet high on the outside to the top of the arch, and the walls are about 4 feet thick. The whole is so neatly jointed

within side, that it would be very difficult to put the point of a knife between any of the stones, which are dove-tailed for the most part into each other, and placed without the least particle of any kind of mortar; the side walls incline together from the bottom to the top, forming a kind of parabolic curve.

GALLEY-HEAD, a promontory sit. in bar. Ibawne, co. Cork, prov. Munster; on the extremity of which is *Dundede* castle : this is sometimes fatally mistaken by sailors for the old head of *Kinsale*, when the light of the latter is not seen.

GALLMOY or *Galmoy*, a bar. in co. Kilkenny, prov. Leinster.

GALLOOM, a rectory in dioc. of Clogher, sit. in bar. Dartree, co. Monaghan, prov. Ulst.

GALLOW, a rectory in dioc. of Meath, sit. in bar. Deece, co. Meath, prov. Leinster.

GALLOWS-HILL, sit. in co. Mayo, prov. Connaught; where fairs are held on Whitsun Tuesd. 21 Aug. 7 Nov. and 20 Dec.

GALLSKILL, a rectory in dioc. of Ossory, sit. in bar. Ida, co. Kilkenny, prov. Leinster.

GALLY-HEAD, see *Galley-head*.

GALLY-MOUNTAINS, sit. in bar. Tullahaw, co. Cavan, prov. Ulster.

GALTIES or *Gaultirs*, a range of mountains so called, in co.'s Tipperary and Limerick, prov. Munster. The sides of these mountains are almost perpendicular, and form a most romantic tho' pleasing appearance : they are remarkable for their height. They are sometimes written *Galtees*.

GALTRIM, a vicarage in dioc. of Meath, sit. in bar. Deece, co. Meath, prov. Leinster. This district was an antient palatinate, and gave title to *Hussey*, baron of Galtrim.

GALWAY-BAY, a large bay in co. Galway, prov. Connaught, the N. side of which is foul, and very dangerous for vessels, but is more safe on the S. side ; small ships only can sail up to the town of Galway. In this bay are fisheries of herring, cod, hake and mackarel; there are between 2 and 3 thousand fishing boats belonging to the town.

GALWAY-COUNTY, sit. in prov. Connaught, and esteemed to be the second largest co. in the kingdom. It has Mayo and Roscommon on the N. the ocean on the W. Clare, Tipperary and Galway bay on the S. and part of Roscommon, the King's co. and Tipperary on the E. a great part of it is fertile, being a warm, limestone soil, which rewards both the industry of the husbandman and shepherd ; but is very coarse towards the N. and W. being in these parts rather thinly inhabited ; it extends about 43 miles from N. to S. and 76 from E. to W. chief city *Galway* ; and contains 989,950 acres, 116 parishes, 28 churches, 3 boroughs, and fends 8 members to parliament. Its bar.'s are thofe of Clare, Downamore, Half-Ballimoe, Killihan, Tiaquin, Athenry, Kilconnel, Clonmahow, Longford, Leitrim, Loughrea, Kiltartan and Dunkellin; the Weftern part of this co. is much indented with bogs, and bordered with green iflands and rugged rocks; and the whole co. is reckoned the leaft populous of perhaps any other co. in the kingdom. The principal Irifh and Englifh families in this co. at the commencement of the laft century, were the O'Hallorans, O'Kirwans, O'Dalys, O'Kellys, O'Maillys, O'Flaghertys, O'Maddens, O'Shagnefhys, Burkes, Blakes, Skerrets, Martins, Lynchs, Frenchs, Browns, and Birminghams. This co. is computed to contain 28,212 houfes, and 142,000 inhabitants; and it is remarkable that old caftles are more frequent in it, than in any other part of Ireland.

GALWAY, (town) fit. in bar. Moycullen, co. Galway, prov. Connaught, on *Galway bay* in the Weftern ocean, about 104 miles W. of Dublin; advantageoufly fit. for foreign trade. It is the chief town of that co. and governed by a mayor, fheriffs and recorder, and returns 2 members to parliament. It has but one parifh church, which is a large and beautiful gothic ftructure, and is a vicarage in dioc. of Tuam; an exchange, three nunneries, three monafteries, barracks for ten companies of foot, a charter-fchool and an hofpital. It is a poft town, and gives title of vifc. to the family of *Monkton*; and has fairs on 4 Sept. Lat, 53 : 16, lon. 9 : 12. This was one of the ftrongeft towns in the kingdom: it held out fome time againft general *Ginkle*, who invefted and took it after the battle of Aughrim. Its fortifications were then repaired; the walls are flanked by baftions, but are moftly gone to decay. The falmon and herring fifheries are carried on here with great fpirit, the quantity of kelp manufactured and exported is confiderable, and the growth of the linen manufacture, tho' of late introduction, is become very important. In 1296, fir *Wm. de Burgh* founded a monaftery here for *Francifcan* friars, on St. Stephen's ifland, fit. without the N. gate of the town. In 1381, there being two popes at Rome, and the people of Ireland being doubtful to which they fhould pay obedience, pope *Urban*, to fix them entirely to his intereft, empowered the guardian of this monaftery to excommunicate every perfon in the prov. of Connaught, who fhould adhere to *Clement* VIIth. who he affured them was Anti-pope. The tomb of the founder of this monaftery was difcovered in June 1779, upwards of 4 feet under ground, with his family arms, and a very long broad fword,

elegantly carved thereon; fome of the remains are ftill to be feen. Near the W. gate of the town without the walls, was the monaftery of St. *Mary of the hill*: on the nuns forfaking it, the fecular clergy entered into and kept poffeffion of it for a confiderable time; but on the petition of the inhabitants of the town to pope Innocent VIIIth. it was granted to the Dominican friars, by a bull, dated the 4 Dec. 1488; there are no remains of this foundation except the cemetery; the whole building having been demolifhed by the townfmen, in the year 1652, in order to prevent *Cromwell* from turning it into a fortification againft themfelves; there was alfo an Auguftinian friary, on a hill near this town, founded by Stephen Lynch, and Margaret his wife, in the year 1508, at the earneft follicitation of Rich. Nangle, a friar of the fame order, who afterwards became archbifhop of *Tuam*. Fairs held at E. gate, Galway, 31 May, 21 Sept. and 21 Oct.

GAMANRADII, or the government of the diftrict of the fea, comprehending the Northern part of the co. Mayo, between the river *May* and the fea, prov. Connaught.

GAP-OF-GLANDINE, this is a very difficult and narrow pafs, between the King's co. and Queen's co. prov. Leinfter. The high and fteep mountains of *Sliebh-bloem* form fo impracticable a barrier between thefe two co.'s, that in a range of 14 miles, they afford but this only and difagreeable entrance from the one into the other.

GARADISE, fit. in bar. Carrigallen, co. Leitrim, prov. Connaught.

GARAHINCH, or *Garryhinch*, the feat of *John Warburton* efq. fit. within a few miles of *Maryborough*, Queen's co. prov. Leinfter.

GARA-LOUGH, a *lake* fit. in bar. Coolavin, co. Sligo, prov. Connaught.

GARAN, fit. in bar. Decies within Drum, co. Waterford, prov. Munfter.

GARANCANTY, fit. near Cafhel, co. Tipperary, prov. Munfter.

GARBALLY, fit. in bar. Kilconnel, co. Galway, prov. Connaught.

GARDE, a *lake* in co. Sligo, prov. Connaught.

GARDEN-HILL, a chapelry in dioc. of Clogher, fit. in bar. Clonawly, co. Fermanagh, prov. Ulfter.

GARE, a vicarage in dioc. of Cafhel, fit. in bar. Slewardagh, co. Tipperary, prov. Munfter.

GARFINAGH, a vicarage in dioc. of Ardfert, fit. in bar. Corkaguinny, co. Kerry, prov. Munfter.

GARIANDSTOWN, fit. near *Caftlebellingham*, co. Louth, prov. Leinfter.

GARISON, fee *Garrifon*.

GARMAN,

GARMAN, or *Garmen*, i. e. the place or habitation of the fea; it was the principal place of Hy Morragh, the *Carioudii of Ptolemy*; it was either the prefent town of *Wexford* or *Enniscorthy*, tho' probably the former; in prov. Leinfter.

GARMAYLE-*pool*, or *Garmoyle-pool*, in co. Down, prov. Ulfter; it is ufed as the harbour for fhips, trading to *Belfaft*, on account of the fhallownefs of the water at Belfaft *bridge*. Here is a depth that 20 veffels may ride in a float at low water, tho' within cable's length, barks lie round them dry; and from thence fmall fhips fail up at high water to the quay of Belfaft; this pool lies a mile from the S. fhore, near *Hellywood*, about 5 miles S. W. of *Carrickfergus*; it is extremely full of weeds in the channel, but from thence to Belfaft are feveral poles erected as marks to direct the courfe, and thofe who are unacquainted may have pilots at *Carrickfergus*; there is a long fpit of fand runs out from the N. fhore, to avoid which, and come fafe into *Garmayle*, the failor muft run up into 4 fathom at low water, almoft oppofite to the *White-houfe*, bring *Caftle-rock* to bear upon a little village ftanding on the fhore, and then run two thirds over, which will bring him fair before *Garmayle*: the *Caftle rock* ftands on a hill to the E. a little above Garmayle.

GARNISH-*POINT*, fit. at the entrance of Ballydonagh-bay, in bar. Beer and Bantry, co. Cork, prov. Munfter.

GARRANMORRIS, a handfome feat in the parifh of *Kilbarmedan*, co. Waterford, prov. Munfter.

GARRETEVELIN, fit. in bar. Cremourne, co. Monaghan, prov. Ulfter.

GARRETSTOWN, a fair town in co. Meath, prov. Leinfter; fairs held 26 Aug. — Alfo a place near *Kinfale*, co. Cork, prov. Munfter.

GARRICLOUGH, a *river* in co. Waterford, prov. Munfter, which rifes out of Lough Honey; by croffing this river at *Coftet's bridge*, you enter the bar. of *lower Iveagh*.

GARRICLOYNE, a rectory in dioc. of Cloyne, fit. in bar. Mufkerry, co. Cork, prov. Munfter.

GARRILOUGH, a village in bar. Ballaghcen, co. Wexford, prov. Leinfter.

GARRINDINNY, a fair town in the Queen's co. prov. Leinfter; fairs held 2 Wed. O. S. in Nov.

GARRISON, or *Garifon*, fit. in bar. Magheraboy, co. Fermanagh, prov. Ulfter, 102 miles from Dublin; near it are the ruins of a barrack, and within a mile and a half of it are the ruins of a church; fairs are held here, 21 May, 19 July and Oct. and 21 Dec.

GARRISTOWN, a fair town in co. Dublin, prov. Leinfter; fairs held 5 May, 15 Aug. and 1 Nov.

GARRIVOE, a vicarage in dioc. of Cork, fit. in bar. Imokilly, co. Cork, prov. Munfter.

GARRY, an Irifh name which fignifies *the garden*, and has been given to the parifh of *Miros*, co. Cork, prov. Munfter, on account of its being better land than the reft of the furrounding bar. it lies on the W. of Glandore harbour; in this parifh was antiently an abbey called *Sancto Mauro*. At a place called *Carigiliky* in this parifh, the foundation of extenfive ruins were difcovered, together with a large cemetery, with great quantity of human bones; it was probably the fcite of that abbey which fome falfely place at *Abbey-Mahon*, near *Timoleague*; the houfe of *Abbey Shrowry* was a cell to this; the parifh church ftands in ruins on the coaft, and oppofite to it, in a fmall ifland called *Arahas*, is a ruined chapel.

GARRYCASTLE, a bar. having a *village* in it of fame name, fit. in King's co. prov. Leinfter; the latter lies near *Banagher*.

GARRYCLOUGH, fee *Garriclough*.

GARRYDUFF, fit. in bar. Kilnataloon, co. Cork, prov. Munfter.

GARRYHADDON, fit. in co. Carlow, prov. Leinfter; it is a ftately feat, belonging to an antient branch of the Ormond family; tho' now much neglected, it ftill keeps an appearance of its antient magnificence, particularly in a noble park, a fine wildernefs of lofty fir trees, and vaft canals, fifh-ponds, &c.

GARRYHASTY, a pleafant feat, fit. not 2 miles from *Kilcrea-abbey*, in co. Cork, prov. Munfter.

GARRYHIGGINS, fit. in bar. Crannagh, co. Kilkenny, prov. Leinfter.

GARRYHILL, a large ruin near the church of *Drimefen*, in co. Carlow, prov. Leinfter; it was antiently one of the caftles of the kings of Leinfter.

GARRYHINCH, fee *Garrahinch*.

GARTAN or *Garton*, a rectory in dioc. of Raphoe, fit. in bar. Kilmacrenan, co. Donegal, prov. Ulfter; the celebrated St. *Columb* was born here in 521, and educated under St. *Finian*, in the great fchool of *Clonard*. A monaftery was alfo founded here by St. *Columb*, which afterwards became the parifh church.

GARVAGH, a fair town in bar. Colerain, co. Londonderry, prov. Ulfter, 100 miles from Dublin; it is a fmall place, feated on the river *Agivey*, over which it has two bridges; near a mile from it are the ruins of a church; fairs held 23 May, 26 July and 5 Nov.

GARVAGHY, a parifh in co. Down, prov. Ulfter; the church of which, and vicarage houfe,

houfe, ftands on the edge of the bar. of *upper-Iveach*, about 3 miles E. of *Banbridge*. It is a vicarage in dioc. of Dromore.

GARVAGTO, fit. in bar. Colerain, co. Londonderry, prov. Ulfter.

GAULSTOWN, fit. in co. Weftmeath, prov. Leinfter; here was formerly the feat of lord chief-baron *Rochfort*; but fince purchafed from the late earl of *Belvedere* by fir *John Browne*, (now lord *Kilmaine*) who has erected a noble houfe here, on the fcite of the old one, which was fo often mentioned by dean *Swift*.

GAUL'STOWN-PARK, a feat of the *Rochfort* family, fit. in co. Weftmeath, prov. Leinfter.

GAVRA, fit. near *Tamar* or *Tarah* in co. Meath, prov. Leinfter; it was the theatre of a a bloody battle between *Cairbre* of the inchanted banner, king of Leinfter, and the troops of *Fienn* of Allen, father of *Uffin*, whofe fon *Ofcar*, with many kings, were flain in that engagement.

GAWNAGH-LOUGH, a *lake* fit. in bar. Granard, co. Longford, prov. Leinfter.

GEAL, a rectory in dioc. of Cafhel, fit. in bar. Middlethird, co. Tipperary, prov. Munft.

GAYBROOK, fit. near *Mullingar*, co. Weftmeath, prov. Leinfter.

GEASHILL, fee *Gefhil*.

GEEVACH *mountains*, fit. in the co.'s Leitrim, and Rofcommon, prov. Connaught.

GENEVA or *New-Geneva*, a village fit. in bar. Gualtiere, co. Waterford, prov. Munfter; it was elegantly and regularly built, and was erected by government a few years fince, for the reception of expatriated citizens of Geneva; but they having relinquifhed the defign of fettling in Ireland, this place remains ftill uninhabited.

GERARD'STOWN, fit. in co. Meath, prov. Leinfter, 3 miles beyond *Ratoath*. Near it is the old church of *Trevet*, at which place an Englifh colony was formerly fettled.

GERARSTOWN, fit. in bar. Balruddery, co. Dublin, prov. Leinfter.

GERMAN'STOWN, a place fo called, fit. on the borders of co. Meath, prov. Leinfter.

GERNAN'STOWN, a rectory in dioc. of Armagh, fit. in bar Ardee, co. Louth, prov. Leinfter.—Alfo a rectory in dioc. of Meath, fit. in bar. Slane, co. Meath, prov. Leinfter.

GERON-POINT, a *cape* fit. in bar. Glenarm, co. Antrim, prov. Ulfter.

GERRANEKENNIF, a rectory in dioc. of Cloyne, fit. in bar. Imokilly, co. Cork, prov. Munfter.

GERVAGHKERIN, fit. in co. Tyrone, prov. Ulfter; a monaftery for Francifcan friars of the third order was erected here in the 15th century, it was afterwards granted to fir *Henry Piers*.

GESHIL, a bar. in King's co. prov. Leinfter, having a village in it of fame name, which is a rectory in dioc. of Kildare, and diftant about 53 miles from Dublin. It is otherwife written *Geafhill*, and has been a place of fome antiquity, and exhibits the lofty ruins of a caftle; it takes its name from *Gael fiol*, or the habitation of the race of the wood, and was the antient refidence of the chiefs of *Hy Falgia*, fit. in the diftrict of the *O'Malloys*. At this place was a very great battle between *Hebar* and *Heremon*, the fons of *Milefius*, who had both reigned over the kingdom peaceably for one year, 'till the wife of the latter created a difpute between the two brothers, about the poffeffion of a certain valley, the difference was decided by an engagement at *Gefhil* or *Gefiol*, which left *Heremon* fole monarch of the kingdom. Fairs are held here 1 May, 6 Oct. and 26 Dec. This place gives title to the family of *Digby*, created baron Digby of *Geafhil*, 29 July, 1620.

GESSIGO-POINT, a *cape* fit. in bar. Carbery, co. Sligo, prov. Connaught.

GIANT'S-CAUSEWAY, a promontory in bar. Cary, co. Antrim, prov. Ulfter, fit. in lat. 55 : 20 N. lon. 6 : 50 W. It is efteemed one of the greateft natural curiofities in the world, and is diftant from Dublin 122 miles. The name of it may naturally convey to us the idea of fome ftupendous work of art; and as fuch it feems to have been confidered in the days of ignorance when the term was firft applied; modern philofophy however looks on it with a different eye. To conceive a proper idea of this extraordinary place, we may imagine an approach to it from the fea; its firft appearance is that of a bold rocky fhore, with extenfive ranges of fhelving, on which people may walk. The rocks inftead of being difpofed in laminæ or ftrata, form bafaltes or angular columns. The columns are generally pentagonal, or have five fides, and are fo clofely attached to each other, that tho' perfectly diftinct from top to bottom, fcarce any thing can be introduced between them. This extraordinary difpofition of the rocks, continues to the water's edge and under the fea; it alfo obtains in a fmall degree on the oppofite fhore of Scotland. It is obfervable that the chryftals of falts in the works of creation as well as under a chymical procefs, affume certain regular and determinate forms, as cubes, various forts of pyramids, parallelopipeds, &c. and we might imagine that this celebrated promontory, made up of thefe innumerable maffive columns of ftone, owing their origin to fome fimilar operation of nature, were not at all more wonderful than the chryftallization of falts, except their ftupendous fize imprefs us with amazement; but

the

the *caufey* is ftill more curious in the little than the great. The columns themfelves are not each of one folid ftone in an upright pofition, but compofed of feveral fhort lengths, exactly joined, not with flat furfaces as in works of art, but what is moft extraordinary, they are articulated into each other, as a ball in a focket, the one end of the joint having a cavity into which the convex end of the other is exactly fitted; this is not vifible but by disjointing the two ftones. The depth of the concavity or convexity is generally from 3 to 4 inches; and it is ftill farther remarkable of the joint, that the convexity and the correfponding concavity is not conformed to the external angular figure of the column, but exactly round, and as large as the fize of the column will admit. It is likewife remarkable that the articulations of thefe joints are frequently inverted. In fome the concavity is upwards, in others the reverfe. The lateft and moft philofophical conclufions on the formation of this natural curiofity appear to be, that the whole body of the rock was once in a ftate of fluidity, being no other than the lava of a burning mountain; that the predigious mafs of melted ftone, cracked in its cooling into the forms we now fee it in, (and in fome of the joints the ftone is not cracked quite through, but folid in the middle) that it may fince have been deranged and broken by earthquakes; that thefe have fwallowed up the volcano itfelf, and that the waters of the neighbouring ocean now roll over the place where it once ftood.

GIANT'S-GRAVE, a place fo called, fit. near Sligo town, in co. Sligo, prov. Connaught; it is otherwife called *Lugna Clogh*; here are feveral large ftones raifed upon the ends of others, which are pitched perpendicularly, not unlike thofe very remarkable ones at *Stonehenge* on Salifbury plain in England; they are the monuments of feveral famous perfons who have been buried there; as is evident from their bones, which have been found under thefe venerable pieces of antiquity.

GIANT'S-LOAD, this is a maffy ftone or *Cromlech* at *Ballrichan*, in co. Louth, prov. Leinfter. It meafures 12 feet one way, and 6 another, and muft from the fpecific gravity of like folids, weigh between 30 and 40 ton weight. It is fupported by 3 other irregular ftones fet upright. The Irifh fay the whole was brought all at once to this place from the neighbouring mountains, by a giant called *Parragh-bough-Mc. Shag-jean*; and who they fay was buried near this place; but there are many other works of like conftruction to be found in different parts of this kingdom.

GIANT'S-RING, an artificial rath in co. Down, prov. Ulfter; about 2 miles Northward of the tower of Drumboe, it is regularly thrown up, encompaffing many acres, but has no advantage of height, like other raths. The ground about it is often ufed as a race-courfe, round which the horfes run 6 times in each heat, which makes 2 miles, and it is confequently judged to be ¼ of a mile in circumference; but this conjectural manner of admeafurement is not fo certain as that the circuit of it takes up 842 paces. On the top of it is an antient pagan altar.

GIANT'S-STAIRS, a place fo called, near *Cove* in co. Cork, prov. Munfter; this appearance of fteps has been formed by nature, though moft of the people thereabouts, infift on their being the work of art.

GIBBAROW, a river in co. Donegal, prov. Ulfter, 146 miles from Dublin. It is fordable at low water.

GIBBON'S-GROVE, formerly called *Toonmore*; fit. 3 miles S. of *Charleville*, in co. Cork, prov. Munfter; this place has been famous for a celebrated cyder apple, called the *Toonmore-apple*. Some years ago there was difcovered near this place in the centre of a large ftone, the rowel of a fpur; which affords an evident proof of the growth of ftones.

GILBERTSTOWN, fit. in bar. Eliogurty, co. Tipperary, prov. Munfter.—Alfo a rectory in dioc. of Leighlin, fit. in bar. Forth, co. Carlow, prov. Leinfter.

GILCAGHE, a parifh in bar. *Upper-third*, co. Waterford, prov. Munfter; it is bounded on the E. by the bar. of *Middle-third*, on the N. by the parifh of Clonegam, on the W. by Mothil, and on the S. by Decies. The foil here is for the moft part tolerably good, but intermixed with fome unprofitable rock and mountain.

GILFORD, fit. in bar. lower Iveagh, co. Down, prov. Ulfter, 62 miles from Dublin, on the river *Ban*, about 3 miles S. W. of *Waringtown*. The meanders of the river, about this place (over which is a good ftone bridge of 22 arches) and the rifing grounds furrounding it, adorned with wood; and the bottoms variegated with bleach yards, afford altogether an agreeable profpect, efpecially in the bleaching feafon. The linen trade is carried on very extenfively here, and the cloth is as remarkable for the finenefs of its texture, as the river is for giving it an excellent bleach. At *Gilford* is a chalybeate fpa, of a very good quality. Fairs are held here on 21 June and Nov. *cuftom free*. This is a poft town, and gives title of *baron* to the family of *Meade*, (now *earl of Clanwilliam.*)

GILGORIN-

GILGORIN-CASTLE, (or *Gilgorn*) sit. in co. Antrim. prov. Ulster, not far from *Ballymena*; on a rising ground opposite to it, is a settlement of *Moravian* brethren, at a place called *Grace-hill*.

GILHALL, a handsome seat of lord *Clonwilliam*, sit. in co. Down, prov. Ulster, 1½ mile W. of *Dromore*, on the river *Lagan*, over which is a stone bridge near the house.

GILL-LOUGH, see *Gilly-lough*.

GILLING, sit. in bar. Ballycowen, King's co. prov. Leinster.

GILLSTOWN, sit. in bar. Lune, co. Meath, prov. Leinster.

GILLY-LOUGH, a *lake*, sit. in bar. Carbery, co. Sligo, prov. Connaught; a chain of hills extends from this lough to the bounds of the co.'s Leitrim and Roscommon. It is otherwise called *Lough-Gill*.

GILTOWN, a curacy in dioc. of Dublin, sit. in bar. Naas, co. Kildare, prov. Leinster.

GINNETTS, sit. in co. Meath, prov. Leinst.

GIRLY, a vicarage in dioc. of Meath, sit. in bar. Kells, co. Meath, prov. Leinster.

GLAN, sit. in bar. Erris, co. Mayo, prov. Connaught.

GLANARM, see *Glenarm*.

GLANAVAN, a *lough* sit. near Castlemain harbour, in co. Kerry, prov. Munster.

GLANBANE, a rectory in dioc. of Emly, sit. in bar. Clanwilliam, co. Tipperary, prov. Munster.

GLANBEG, a seat in co. Waterford, prov. Munster; adorned with good plantations of fruit and timber trees.

GLANBEHY, a parish in bar. Iveragh, co. Kerry, prov. Munster. It is a rectory in dioc. of Ardfert.

GLANBIG, sit. in bar. Barrymore, co. Cork, prov. Munster.

GLAN-CASTLE, sit. near *Broadhaven*, co. Mayo, prov. Connaught.

GLANCARTY, sit. in bar. Iveragh, co. Kerry, prov. Munster.

GLANCOLLINKITTLE, sit. in bar. Boylagh, co. Donegal, prov. Ulster.

GLANCREW, sit. in bar. Ballinahinch, co. Galway, prov. Connaught.

GLANDAGH, a *river* in co. Donegal, prov. Ulster.

GLANDELOUGH, see *Glendelogh*.

GLANDINE, sit. in bar. Corkaguinny, co. Kerry, prov. Munster.

GLANDORE, a village sit. near the harbour of same name, in co. Cork. prov. Munster; it gives title of *earl* to the family of *Crosbie*.

GLANDORE-HARBOUR, sit. in bar. Carbery, 2 leagues W. of the *Galley-head*. in co. Cork, prov. Munster; lat. 51 : 22 N. lon 8 : 56 W. Between this harbour and *Ross*, the coast continues high and bold, with only 2 small coves:

that to the E. called *Millcove*, and that to the W. *Cow-cove*. This harbour lies 3 miles W. of *Ross*, and tho' small, is an exceeding good one; near it is a castle of the same name, and on the upper end is a deep and dangerous glin, called the *Leap*.

GLANDUFF, sit. in bar. Connillo, co. Limerick, prov. Munster.

GLANE, sit. in bar. Barrymore, co. Cork, prov. Munster.

GLANEERAGH, a fair town in co. Kerry, prov. Munster; fairs held 28 Oct.

GLANEHIRY or *Glauncherry*, a bar. in co. Waterford, prov. Munster.

GLANEKILLY, sit. near *Nenagh*, co. Tipperary, prov. Munster.

GLANELAN, sit. in bar. Boylagh, co. Donegal, prov. Ulster.

GLANELY, a village in bar. Newcastle, co. Wicklow, prov. Leinster; it is a chapelry in dioc. of Dublin.

GLANEROUGHT, (by some written *Glancfrought*) a bar. in co. Kerry, prov. Munster; it is entirely covered with exceeding high and rugged hills, and separated from the co. Cork by an immense and almost impassible ridge of rocky mountain, over which there is but 1 pass, and that very difficult, called the *priest's leap*.

GLANEVY or *Glenavy*, a fair town in bar. Massareen, co. Antrim, prov. Ulster, 77 miles from Dublin; fairs held 14 May and 29 Oct. It is a vicarage in dioc. of Connor.

GLANFLESK, sit. in co. Kerry, prov. Munster; it has of late years been much improved and cultivated. It antiently belonged to *O'Donoghoe*, and is now mostly the estate of lord *Kenmare*.

GLANGARIFF-BAY, sit. in co. Cork, prov. Munster; in this bay and towards the N. W. part of *Bantry-bay*, they dredge up large quantities of a coral sand, found to be a most excellent manure, and lasts in the ground above 20 years.

GLANGOWRA, a fair town in co. Cork, prov. Munster; fairs held 1 Aug. and Nov.

GLANINAGH, a rectory in dioc. of Kilfenora, sit. in bar. Burrin, co. Clare, prov. Munst.

GLANINEY, sit. in bar. Burrin, co. Clare, prov. Munster.

GLANKEEN, a vicarage in dioc. of Cashel, sit. in bar. Ileagh, co. Tipperary, prov. Munst.

GLANLAHY, sit. in bar. Dunkerron, co. Kerry, prov. Munster.

GLANMIRE. There are 2 villages of this name, both sit. in bar. Barrymore, co. Cork, prov. Munster; they are distinguished respectively by *upper* and *lower Glanmire*. In the latter, which is an agreeable outlet near the city of Cork, there is a curious bolting mill, being the first of the kind erected in the kingdom: the road to Glanmire is decorated with

many

many handsome adjoining feats: here is a bridge by which you pass to *Ballyrochine*, called Glanmire bridge, over a river of the same name. At *Ballyrochine* is a mill for making rod iron, and a paper mill; all worked by the *river Glanmire*.

GLANMORE, fit. in bar. Ida, co. Kilkenny, prov. Leinfter, 76 miles from Dublin. At this place there is a very fteep glen, and within ½ mile of Glanmore are the ruins of a church. A little better than 1 mile beyond Glanmore are the ruins of a caftle.

GLANORE, fit. in bar. Fermoy, co. Cork, prov. Munfter; it is a rectory in dioc. of Cloyne: the name fignifies " *the golden glen* ;" and the church of this parifh is at *Glanworth*.

GLANORGRA, a fair town in co. Limerick, prov. Munfter; fairs held 31 May, and 28 Oct.

GLANPATRICK, fit. in bar. Upperthird, co. Waterford, prov. Munfter.

GLANSTEAD, fit. in bar. Burrin, co. Clare, prov. Munfter.

GLANTON, fit. in bar. Duhallow, co. Cork, prov. Munfter, 133 miles from Dublin: within 2 miles of which is a very handfome feat called *Newberry*.

GLANWORTH, a fair town in bar. Fermoy, co. Cork, prov. Munfter; the village here has gone to decay, tho' it was antiently a corporation. Here was an abbey of Dominicans, or friars preachers, founded by the *Roaches*, in the year 1227, of which the nave of the church with a low fteeple remain. Near this abbey, on the verge of the *Funcheon river*, is a fine fpring of limpid water, bubbling out of a limeftone rock, and dedicated to St. *Dominick*. Here are alfo the magnificent ruins of a fumptuous caftle, which confifted of feveral buildings, and a large high tower, all ftrongly erected on arched vaults, and built of very maffy ftones. The whole of this edifice is environed with a ftrong wall flanked with turrets; near it is a ftone bridge over the river *Funcheon*. Fairs are held here on 16 March, 13 May, 10 Aug. 24 Sept. and 30 Nov.

GLANYFREHANE, a fair town in co. Cork, prov. Munfter; fairs held 3 Nov.

GLASLOUGH, fit. in bar. Trough, co. Monaghan, prov. Ulfter. Here is a beautiful feat, with a fine fheet of water. Fairs held here on the laft Saturday in every month. Here is a church, and a caftle lately repaired; Lat. 54 : 18, lon. 7 : 26.

GLASS-LOUGH, a *lake* fit. in bar. Half-fowre, co. Weftmeath, prov. Leinfter.

GLASSCARRICK, fit. in bar. Ballagheen, co. Wexford, prov. Leinfter. Here a priory for Benedictine monks was founded by the families of *Condon*, *Barry*, *Bourke*, *Roch*, *Carrin* and *Fytte*: who joined in the grant of certain lands for that purpofe.

GLASSCARRICK-POINT, a *cape* in bar. Ballagheen, co. Wexford, prov. Leinfter.

GLASSDRUMMIN, fit. near Donagh, co. Fermanagh, prov. Ulfter.

GLASSDRUMMOND *caftle*, fit. in bar. Fews, co. Armagh, prov. Ulfter.

GLASSELLY, fit. in bar. Narragh, co. Kildare, prov. Leinfter.

GLASSMALLAGH, fit. in bar. Omagh, co. Tyrone, prov. Ulfter.

GLASSNEVIN, an agreeable village fit. on a rifing ground, in bar. Coolock, co. Dublin, prov. Leinfter, within 2 miles of the metropolis; having a parifh church belonging to it, which is a curacy in dioc. of Dublin. Here was the feat of dean *Delany*, the well known acquaintance of *Swift*. There are many handfome feats and villas in and near this place that merit a traveller's notice.

GLAWNWHIN, fit. in bar. Connillo, co. Limerick, prov. Munfter.

GLEANE, or *Glin*, fit. in bar. Garrycaftle, King's co. prov. Leinfter, on the river *Brufna* near *Firbane*. St. *Diermit* built an abbey here; it was plundered in the year 1041, and deftroyed by fire in 1077.

GLEMEE, fit. in bar. Raphoe, co. Donegal, prov. Ulfter.

GLENAA *mountains*, fit. in bar. Dunkerron, co. Kerry, prov. Munfter.

GLENANE, fit. in bar. Tirawly, co. Mayo, prov. Connaught.

GLENARM, or *Glanarm*, a bar. in co. Antrim, prov. Ulfter, having in it a bay and village of fame name, fit. 105 miles from Dublin; this is a poft town. Here is *Glenarmcaftle*, a handfome and magnificent building, the feat of the earl of *Antrim*; it is pleafantly fit. on the fea fhore near the *bay of Glenarm*. A monaftery of Francifcan friars of the third order, was built here in the year 1465, by *Robert Biffet*, a Scots-man; this monaftery, and the lands belonging thereto, were granted to *Alexander M'Donnell*, anceftor to the earls of *Antrim*; there are ftill fome remains of this building on the *bay of Glenarm*; fairs are held here 26 May and 29 Oct. Lat. 55 : 3, lon. 6 : 36.

GLENAVY, fee *Glancvy*.

GLENBESK, a *river* in co. Antrim, prov. Ulfter.

GLENCARRE, or *Glencarr*, the Weftern part of the parifh of *Knockane*, in co. Kerry, prov. Munfter; it gave title of earl to *Donald M'Carty More*. All or the greater part of the hills and mountains hereabouts, were formerly covered with trees, which have been deftroyed by the iron works, erected near the river *Carra*, at a place called *Blackftones*, by fir *Wm. Petty*: and carried on till fome years ago, the workmen were obliged to ftop fmelting for want of charcoal.   GLENCOLM-

GLENCOLMKILL, a rectory in dioc. of Raphoe, sit. in bar. Boylagh, co. Donegal, prov. Ulster.

GLENDALOGH, otherwise called " *the Seven Churches*," sit. 5 miles N. W. of *Rathdrum*, in bar. Balinacour, co. Wicklow, prov. Leinster; the name signifies the valley of the 2 lakes. In this valley surrounded by high and almost inaccessible mountains, St. *Cavan*, called also St. *Coemgene*, about the middle of the 6th century, founded a monastery, which in a short time from the sanctity of its founder, was much resorted to, and at length became a bishoprick and a religious city. St. *Kevin* or *Cavan*, was born, A. D. 498; he died 3 June, 618, aged 120; and on that day annually, numbers of persons flock to the *Seven Churches*, to celebrate the festival of that venerated saint. During the middle ages the city of *Glendalogh*, called by Hovedon, *Episcopatus Bistagniensis*, was held in great esteem, and received several valuable donations and privileges, its episcopal jurisdiction extending to the walls of Dublin. About the middle of the 12th century, on some account or other, it was much neglected by the clergy, and became instead of a holy city, a den of thieves, wherefore cardinal *Papiro*, in 1214, united it to the see of *Dublin*, which union was confirmed by king *John*. The *O'Tool's*, chiefs of *Firthuathal*, however by the assistance of the pope, continued long after this period, to elect bishops and abbots to *Glendalogh*, tho' they had neither revenues or authority, beyond the district of *Tuathal*, which was the Western part of the co. Wicklow, in consequence of which the city was suffered to decay, and became nearly a desart, in 1497, when *Dennis White*, the last titular bishop surrendered his right, in the cathedral church of St. *Patrick*, Dublin. From the ruins of this antient city still remaining, it appears to have been a place of consequence, and to have contained 7 churches and religious houses, small indeed, but built in a neat elegant stile, in imitation of the *Greek* architecture; the cathedral, the walls of which are yet standing, was dedicated to St. *Peter* and St. *Paul*. S. of the cathedral stands a small church roofed with stone, nearly entire; and in several parts of the valley are a number of stone crosses, some of which are curiously carved, but without any inscriptions. In the N. W. corner of the cemetery belonging to the cathedral, stands a round tower, 95 feet high, and 15 in diameter; and in the cemetery of a small church, on the S. side of the river, near the great *lake*, called the *Rhefeart* church, are some tombs, with Irish inscriptions, belonging to the *O'Tools*. Another round tower was erected here, but it is not now perfect.

In a perpendicular projecting rock on the S. side of the great lake, 30 yards above the surface of the water, is the celebrated *bed* of St. *Kevin*, hewn out of the rock, exceeding difficult of access, and terrible in prospect. Amongst the ruins have been discovered a number of stones, curiously carved, and containing inscriptions in the Latin, Greek and Irish languages. As this city was in a valley, surrounded on all sides, except the E. by high, barren and inaccessible mountains, the artificial roads leading thereto, are by no means the least curious part of the remains, the principal is that leading into the co. *Kildare*, thro' *Glendasou*. This road for near 2 miles is yet perfect, composed of stones placed on their edges, making a firm and durable pavement, about 10 feet broad. At a small distance from St. *Kevan's bed*, on the same side of the mountain, are to be seen the ruins of a small stone building, called St. *Kevan's cell*. *Glendalogh* is now a vicarage in dioc. of Dublin. It is otherwise written *Glandelough*. Fairs are held here annually on 20 Sept.

GLENEGAD-HEAD, a *cape* sit. in bar. Inishowen, co. Donegal, prov. Ulster.

GLENELY, a *river* in bar. Glenarm, co. Antrim, prov. Ulster.

GLENGARIFF *harbour*, sit. in bar. Bear and Bantry, co. Cork, prov. Munster.

GLEN-INN, sit. in co. Donegal, prov. Ulster, 124 miles from Dublin; 2 miles beyond which are some magnificent ruins of a castle.

GLEN-MOLAUR, sit. near the river *Avonmore*, co. Wicklow, prov. Leinster, about 3 miles from *Ballinaclash*. It was once the asylum and great fastness of *Teagh M'Hugh O'Bryn*, (celebrated by *Spencer*) when he kept the highest powers of this co. at bay, in the reign of queen *Eliz*. Near it is a lead mine, which is now working by a company, with considerable advantage.

GLENNY-BRIDGE, sit. in co. Down, prov. Ulster; over the river *Newry*.

GLENOE, a village sit. in bar. Belfast, co. Antrim, prov. Ulster.

GLENOGRA, a vicarage in dioc. of Limerick, sit. in bar. Small-county, co. Limerick, prov. Munster.

GLENRAVIL, sit. in co. Antrim, prov. Ulster.

GLENTIS, sit. in co. Donegal, prov. Ulster, 123 miles from Dublin. This village lies on the river *Amdrafs*; and there is one of the most considerable fairs held here for *black-cattle*, in the N. of Ireland.

GLENVILLE, sit. near *Newry*, co. Down, prov. Ulster.

GLENWHIRRY, a *river* sit. in bar. Antrim, co. Antrim, prov. Ulster.

GLESTER-

GLESTERBOY, fit. in bar. Ikerrin, co. Tipperary, prov. Munfter.

GLIDE *river*, fit. in co. Louth, prov. Leinft.

GLINDOY, fit. in bar. Dunkerrin, co. Kerry, prov. Munfter.

GLINFLESK, fit. in bar. Maguinny, co. Kerry, prov. Munfter.

GLINLOUGH, a *lake*, fit. in bar. Roffclogher, co. Leitrim, prov. Connaught.

GLINSK, a fair town in co. Galway, prov. Connaught; fairs held 18 Sept.

GLINVILLE, a fair town in co. Cork, prov. Munfter; fairs held 4 May and 3 Nov.

GLISSHARE, a rectory in dioc. of Offory, fit. in bar. Galmoy, co. Kilkenny, prov. Leinfter.

GLOCESTER, fit. near *Birr*, in King's co. prov. Leinfter.

GLYN, or *Glin*, a fair town in bar. Connello, co. Limerick, prov. Munfter, 121 miles from Dublin. Here is the *Glyn-houfe*, the pleafant feat of Mr. *Fitzgerald*, knt. of the *Glyn*. Fair days 1 Wed. O. S. in Sept. and 1 Dec.— Alfo a village in bar. Belfaft, co. Antrim, prov. Ulfter, which is a vicarage in dioc. of Connor.

GLYN-CAUM, i. e. " *the crooked Glyn*," it leads to *Macroom* or *Macroomp*, from other parts of the co. Cork, prov. Munfter; it is a deep gloomy hollow way. On either hand is a perfect wall of fteep craggy rocks, covered in fome places with oak, afh and birch. To the S. of this hollow way, ftands the high tower of *Magfhanaglafs*.

GLYN of AGERLOW, fit. in co. Cork, prov. Munfter; it is fenced by a long chain of hills which feem to difpute pre-eminence of altitude with *Mangerton*, in the co. *Kerry*.

GLYN *of the* DOWNS, fit. 4 miles beyond *Bray*, and 14 miles from Dublin caftle, in co. Wicklow, prov. Leinfter; it is a pafs between two vaft ridges of mountains covered with wood, which have a very noble effect; the vale is no wider than to admit the road, a fmall gurgling river almoft by its fide, and narrow flips of rocky and fhrubby ground which part them: in the front all efcape feems denied by an immenfe conical mountain which rifes out of the Glen, and feems to fill it up. The fcenery is of a moft magnificent character.

GLYN-WOOD, fit. in the parifh of Donoghmore, and bar. of *upper Iveach*, in co. Down, prov. Ulfter; it was an antient manor of the family of *Magenis*.

GOAT's-CHURCH, otherwife *Temple Gaurin*, the ruins of a chapel, at the N. end of a fmall lake called *Derikelagh*, in co. Down, prov. Ulfter.

GOAT's-POINT, fit. in bar. Bear and Bantry, co. Cork, prov. Munfter.

GOLA, adjoining *Lough-Erne*, 5 miles S. E. of *Ennifkillen*, and within 3 miles of *Macguire's-bridge*, in co. Fermanagh, prov. Ulfter. Here a monaftery for Dominican friars was founded by *M'Manus*, lord of the place; and dedicated to the Virgin Mary: fome remains of it are yet to be feen, where formerly ftood the *village of Gola*.

GOLANE, fit. in bar. Rofs, co. Galway, prov. Connaught.

GOLDEN, a village in bar. Clanwilliam, co. Tipperary, prov. Munfter, 80 miles from Dublin, fit. on the river *Suir*. A mile from which on one fide of the river, are the ruins of the extenfive and magnificent abbey of *Athaffel*. Fairs are held here 18 May, 26 Aug. and Oct. and 15 Dec. It is otherwife written *Goolden* and *Gouldin*.

GOLDEN-GARDEN, fit. near *Caffel*, co. Tipperary, prov. Munfter.

GOLDEN-GROVE, fit. near *Rofcrea*, co. Tipperary, prov. Munfter.

GOOSEBERRY-HILL, fit. in co. Cork, prov. Munfter; fairs are held here on 20 March, June, Sept. and Nov.

GOOSE-GREEN, a fmall village in co. Dublin, prov. Leinfter, ¼ a mile beyond *Drumcondra*, and above 2 miles from Dublin caftle.

GORE's-BRIDGE, a village fit. in bar. Gowran, co. Kilkenny, prov. Leinfter; 51 miles from Dublin. It lies on the river *Barrow*, and near it are the ruins of *Bally-ellan caftle*.

GOREY, a bar. in co. Wexford, prov. Leinfter, in which is a borough, fair and poft town of fame name, otherwife called *Newborough*: it is a rectory in dioc. of Ferns, fit. about 18 miles N. of *Wexford* town, and 45 miles from Dublin; lat. 52 : 40, lon. 6 : 30. It fends 2 members to parliament, patronage in the family of *Ram*. Fairs held 1 June, 10 July, 31 Aug. and 27 Oct.

GOREY *mountains*, fit. in bar. Raphoe, co. Donegal, prov. Ulfter.

GORMAN'sTOWN, a fair town in co. Tipperary, prov. Munfter; fairs held on Eafter Monday and 5 Aug.—Alfo a village in bar. Duleek, co. Meath, prov. Leinfter; where is the feat of lord Gorman's-town, fit. 3½ miles from Balruddery. The houfe is old, but has very noble and fplendid apartments, and by late improvements, promifes to become an elegant and beautiful manfion.

GORMONS-ISLAND, fit. off the bar. Moycullen, co. Galway, prov. Connaught.

GORT, a poft and fair town in bar. Kiltartan, co. Galway, prov. Connaught, 99 miles from Dublin. 2 miles W. of which is the antient

monaftery

monaftery with the church and chapels of *Kilmacduagh*, whence the dioc. receives its name. Thefe fine old buildings are moftly in ruins, except a fteeple, or rather an obelifk of a prodigious height, which is ftill entire. Fairs held here 10 May, 11 Aug. and 7 Nov.

GORTAHURK, fit. in co. Donegal, prov. Ulfter, 169 miles from Dublin.

GORTEEN, fit. in bar. Louth, co. Louth, prov. Leinfter.

GORTIN, a fair town in bar. Strabane, co. Tyrone, prov. Ulfter, 99 miles from Dublin. Fairs held on Eafter Monday.

GORTMORE, fit. in bar. Moycullen, co. Mayo, prov. Connaught.

GORTNAR-ABBEY, fit. by *Lough-Con*, in co. Mayo, prov. Connaught; oppofite to it near a church, are the ruins of a caftle.

GORTNATOBRID, fit. in bar. Connillo, co. Limerick, prov. Munfter.

GORTNEIGHRAHT, a fair town in co. Fermanagh, prov. Ulfter; fairs held 13 May, 13 July, 12 Sept. and 11 Nov.

GORTNICLEA, fit. in bar. upper Offory, Queen's co. prov. Leinfter.

GORTORMEVAN, fit. in bar. Innifowen, co. Donegal, prov. Ulfter.

GORTROE, a rectory in dioc. of Cloyne, fit. in bar. Barrymore, co. Cork, prov. Munfter.— There is another village of this name, fit. in bar. Carbury, in fame co.

GOSFORD-CASTLE, the beautiful feat of lord Gosford, fit. near *Market-hill*, in co. Antrim, prov. Ulfter.

GOUGANE BARRA, (the hermitage of St. *Finbar*) fit. near *Inchigeela*, in bar. Mufkerry, co. Cork, prov. Munfter; this retreat, the approach to which is exceeding difficult, is deemed one of the greateft curiofities in that country. Tradition fays, St. *Finbar* lived here a reclufe, before he founded the cathedral of Cork: it lies in the remoteft folitude imaginable, and is really a moft elegant and romantic fpot, fit. in a fmall ifland, furrounded by a fine deep and capacious lake of the fame name, almoft circular. In the ifland are the ruins of a chapel, with fome chambers and conveniencies erected by a reclufe (one *O'Mahony*) who lived an hermit on this fpot 28 years. Oppofite to this ifland on the main land, is his tomb placed in a low little houfe, on which is this infcription, " *Hoc fibi & fuccefforibus fuis in eadem vocatione, monumentum impofuit Dominus D. Dyonifius O'Mahony, Prefbyter licet indignus, A. D. 1700.*"

GOWRAN, a bar. in co. Kilkenny, prov. Leinfter, having in it a borough, fair and poft town of fame name, fit. above 8 miles E. of Kilkenny, and 52 from Dublin: it is a rectory in dioc. of Offory. Lat. 52 : 34,

lon. 7 : 0. It returns 2 members to parliament, patronage in the *Agar* family. Here is the handfome feat of the late lord *Clifden*; alfo the ruins of an old church. 3 miles beyond *Gowran* are the ruins of *Ballinabola caftle*. Fairs held at Gowran annually on 8 Dec. This place gives title of baron to the family of *Fitzpatrick*, now earl of upper Offory.

GRACE-DIEU, fit. in bar. Balruddery, co. Dublin, prov. Leinfter, 3 miles N. of *Swords*. About the year 1190, *John Comin*, archbifhop of Dublin, removed the nunnery from *Lufk* hither, and dedicated it to the Virgin Mary; he filled it with regular canoneffes of St. *Auguftin*, and granted to it the parifh church of St. *Audeon*, Dublin; inftead of which, *Henry de Londres* archbifhop of Dublin, afterwards granted to it the parifh church of *Ballymadon*: part of the ruins yet remain, in which is an head carved in ftone, by no means of bad workmanfhip. The antient road leading from this nunnery to *Swords* is ftill to be feen, paved with a reddifh ftone, whereon are feveral fmall bridges. — There is alfo a place of fame name, fit. near the river *Suir*, in co. Kilkenny, prov. Leinfter.

GRACE-HALL, fit. near *Lurgan*, co. Armagh, prov. Ulfter.

GRACE-HILL, fit. in bar. Toome, co. Antrim, prov. Ulfter; within 1½ mile of *Ballymena*, on a rifing ground oppofite *Gilgorin caftle*. Here is a fettlement of *Moravian brethren*; and near it is a feat of lord *Mountcafhel*.

GRAGE, fit. near *Neuagh*, co. Tipperary, prov. Munfter.

GRAIGBILLY, fit. in bar. Antrim, co. Antrim, prov. Ulfter.

GRAIGE or *Graig*, fit. near Wexford, co. Wexford, prov. Leinfter: it is a poft-town.

GRAIGENAMANAGH or *Graigeuemana*, a village and rectory in dioc. of Leighlin, fit. in bar. Gowran, co. Kilkenny, prov. Leinfter; 57 miles from Dublin; having a good bridge over the Barrow, where the tide flows up, notwithftanding it is about 20 miles from the fea. Here are the ruins of a fine abbey, the octagon tower of which fell down in 1744, an event to be regretted, becaufe it was one of the moft beautiful religious ftructures in the kingdom. The embellifhments of this abbey are curious, and the building was formerly of a large extent. Here are alfo the ruins of a caftle; and other ruins of the like kind 4 miles farther.

GRAIG'STOWN, fit. in co. Kilkenny, prov. Leinfter; fairs held 22 June, 13 July and 7 Dec.

GRALLAGH, fit. in bar. Eliogurty, co. Tipperary, prov. Munfter. — Alfo a vicarage in
dioc.

dioc. of Dublin, fit. in bar. Balruddery, co. Dublin, prov. Leinfter.

GRANARD or *Grenard*, a bar. in co. Longford, prov. Leinfter, in which is a borough, fair and poft town of fame name, fit. 52 miles from Dublin, and about 16 N. E. of *Longford*. Lat. 53 : 44, lon. 7 : 30. Here is a remarkable hill or mount, called the moat of Granard, thought to be artificial, and the fite of a Danifh caftle or fort; which commands from its fummit a moft extenfive profpect into 6 or 7 adjoining countries. In this town have lately been given annual prizes to the beft performers on the Irifh harp. *Granard* has a barrack for a company of foot; and returns 2 members to parliament; patronage in the families of *Macartney* and *Greville*. Fairs held 3 May and 1 Oct. This place takes its name from *Grian-ard*, or the height of the fun, and was formerly the refidence of the chiefs of *North Teffia*. It gives title of earl to the family of *Forbes*.

GRAND-CANAL. This branch of inland navigation commenced in 1756, under the direction of parliament, but after fome years unfavourable efforts, encouragement was given to private fubfcribers, who under the fanction of the legiflature, and a fubfcription of 100,000, profecuted that work, being incorporated by the name of the " *company of undertakers of the Grand canal.*" They began in 1772, and after combating a variety of difficulties, and enlarging their capital, compleated the line from *Dublin* to *Monafterevan* in 1786. This canal proceeds from the W. end of the metropolis, paffes thro' *Sallins*, *Robert'ftown* and *Rathangan*, to *Monafterevan*, and from thence to *Athy*. It croffes the river Liffey on an aqueduct bridge of 7 arches, called the *Leinfter aqueduct*, which is diftant 15 miles from Dublin, and fit. between *Callan's-bridge* and *Waterftown*: it is built in 5 feet water, fubject to violent floods that rife to 15 feet. The foundation is funk 7 feet thro' fand and gravel and large ftones, to ftrong blue clay: the whole river acrofs has the fame ftrata at equal depths. It was paffable for boats in 18 months from the day of laving the foundation, and coft 7,500l. It is 78 feet longer than the aqueduct *Pont de Ceffe*, the largeft canal of *Languedoc*. The Grand canal afterwards pierces the hill of *Downings* feveral hundred yards, runs thro' a great part of the bog of Allen, and alfo paffes over another aqueduct called the *Griffith aqueduct*, which lies over the *Miltown river*, about 23 miles from Dublin: this aqueduct is built with perforated cylinders, on piles and counterarches, in foft bog and marl. This canal joins the river *Barrow* at *Monafterevan*, and is navigated by boats from 30 to 50 tons burden; and fupplied with water from numerous ftreams and rivers particularly the *Great Morrel*, which is taken in at the 15 lock, about 12 miles from Dublin. Between Dublin and Monafterevan there are 26 locks, viz. 6 double and 20 fingle; the falls in which vary from 4 feet 3 inches to 19 feet 7 inches. The fummit level is 202 feet 4 inches above the *James's-ftreet harbour*; 82 feet 9 inches above the river *Barrow* at Monafterevan; and 265 feet above the tide in the *Liffey* at Dublin. The *Leinfter* and *Griffith* aqueducts, together with the entire line from *Downings* to *Monafterevan*, and the bringing to its prefent ftate of perfection, the whole of the *Grand-canal* is due to the abilities and indefatigable labours of *Rich. Evans*, efq; who was engineer to the company.

GRANEY, a fair town in co. Kilkenny, prov. Leinfter; fairs held 12 Apr. 14 May, 4 Sept. and 11 Dec.—Alfo a village in bar. Kilkea and Moone, co. Kildare, prov. Leinfter; which is a vicarage in dioc. of Dublin.—Likewife a village in bar. Newcaftle, co. Dublin, prov. Leinfter. — Another in half-bar. Rathdown, in fame co. — Another in bar. upper Offory, Queen's co. prov. Leinfter. — There is another in bar. Coonagh, co. Limerick, prov. Munfter; which was formerly a corporation town, and had a collegiate church. It is otherwife written *Greany*.

GRANGE, a fair town in co. Sligo, prov. Connaught; fairs held 1 and 2 May, 25 Aug. 28 Oct. and 10 and 11 Dec.—Alfo a fair town in co. Tyrone, prov. Ulfter, 106 miles from Dublin; having fairs 28 March and 12 Nov. This place is otherwife called *Mount-Hamilton*. —Alfo a place of fame name, in co. Antrim, prov. Ulfter, 93 miles from Dublin. — And another in co. Meath, prov. Leinfter; 18 miles from Dublin: otherwife called *New-Grange.*— Alfo a curacy in dioc. of Armagh, fit. in bar. Armagh, co. Armagh, prov. Ulfter.—Likewife a rectory in dioc. of Leighlin, fit. in bar. Catherlogh, co. Carlow, prov. Leinfter.

GRANGEBEGG, fit. in bar. Ophaly, co. Kildare, prov. Leinfter.

GRANGE-CAPPOGE, fit. in bar. Caftleknock, co. Dublin, prov. Leinfter.

GRANGE-CLEAR, fit. in that tract of land called the *ifland of Allen*, and near the *Grand canal*, in co. Kildare, prov. Leinfter, about 21 miles from Dublin; here are fome antient ruins.

GRANGE-FORTESCUE, fit. in co. Meath, prov. Leinfter, 27 miles from Dublin; within a mile of which are the ruins of a church.

GRANGE-GEETH, a rectory in dioc. of Meath, fit. in bar. Slane, co. Meath, prov. Leinfter.

GRANGE-MELLON, fit. in co. Kildare, prov. Leinfter, 23 miles from Dublin.

GRANGEMOCLER, otherwife called *Nine-mile houfe*, fit. in bar. Slewardagh, co. Tipperary, prov. Munfter; here are the ruins of a church. It is a vicarage in dioc. of Lifmore, and diftant about 70 miles from Dublin.

GRANGE-MORE, a fair town in co. Weftmeath, prov. Leinfter; fairs held 7 May and Nov. — Alfo a place in bar. Tyreragh, co. Sligo, prov. Connaught.

GRANGE *(new)* fit. in co. Meath, prov. Leinfter, near *Slane*. Here is a large mount, which has been found to be the cover of a noble Heathen temple; near the foot of the mount there is an aperture or entrance, which overhead is covered with a large flat ftone, a perfon who enters muft ftoop for a confiderable diftance, when the upper part rifes higher, until you enter the temple, which is formed in fhape like a bee-hive, rifing in height upwards of 20 feet, and in circumference 30 feet; the fides are made up of prodigious large ftones, with fome fculptures upon the ends and fides; there are two altar ftones, one on the right and the other on the left. Col. *Vallancy* thinks *Grange* is a corruption of *Grein-uagh*, i. e. the *uagh*, cave or den of *Grian*, i. e. *Mithras* or the fun.

GRANGENOLVEN, a vicarage in dioc. of Dublin, fit. in bar. Kilkea, co. Kildare, prov. Leinfter.

GRANGE *(old)*, fit. in co. Dublin, prov. Leinfter.

GRANGESILVIA, a rectory in dioc. of Leighlin, fit. in bar. Gowran, co. Kilkenny, prov. Leinfter.

GRANGY-BRIDGE, fit. in bar. Conillo, co. Limerick, prov. Munfter.

GRANSHAW, otherwife called *Grangee*, fit. in the bar. of *Ards*, co. Down, prov. Ulfter; here is an excellent *fpa*, which lies in a valley furrounded on all fides by hills of eafy afcent; it has an afpect to the E. and on the S. there is a large *bog*. This water has on proper trials been found not inferior in ftrength, to the beft Britifh chalybeats; fits eafy on the ftomach, and has been highly ferviceable in the gravel. —Alfo a fair town of fame name, in co. Kerry, prov. Munfter; fair days, 15 and 16 May, 1 and 2 Nov.

GRANSHOGH, fit. in bar. Caftlereagh, co. Down, prov. Ulfter.

GRANT'STOWN, fit. in bar. upper Offory, Queen's co. prov. Leinfter.

GRANY-FERRY, fit. in the co.'s *Waterford* and *Kilkenny*, 76 miles from Dublin.

GRAWLIN-HEAD, fit. in co. Galway, prov. Connaught.

GRAY-ABBEY, or *Grey-abbey*, now a curacy in dioc. of Down, fit. in bar. Ardes, co. Down, prov. Ulfter, 89 miles from Dublin. Here are the large remains of a fine gothic cathedral, a part of which is roofed and fitted up for church fervice; it was founded for Ciftertian monks, by *Africa*, the wife of *John de Courcey*, and daughter of *Godred* king of *Man*, A. D. 1193, who was buried in it, and whofe image made of grey free-ftone, in *alto relievo*, much defaced, with her hands clofed in a pofture of devotion, is yet to be feen fixed in an arch of the wall, on the left fide of the high altar; the E. window of the church is a noble piece of workmanfhip, compofed of three compartments, each 6 feet and more wide, and upwards of 20 feet high; on each fide of the altar, in the N. and S. walls, is alfo a ftately window of free-ftone, neatly hewn and carved; thefe are now grown over with ivy, which gives them an awful appearance. In the gardens of this abbey, is a large well of good water, over which is raifed a high vaulted arch, ornamented with heads and fome other fculpture in ftone, which feems to be the fame that ftood here when the abbey fubfifted. A bell metal pot, about 8 inches high, made in form of a jug, ftanding on three feet, with a fpout projecting out of the fide, like a tea pot, and a handle on the oppofite part, was found in 1722, 12 feet deep in a bog, near the abbey; and is now depofited among other pieces of antiquity, in the univerfity of Dublin. The old town of *Grey abbey* has been quite renewed, and fome handfome flate houfes erected for the habitation of manufacturers in the linen trade; the Diffenters have a meeting houfe here; fair days 28 Mar. 2 Tuef. O. S. June, 29 Oct.

GRAYSTONES, a noted fifhing place 4 miles beyond *Bray* and 14 from Dublin, fit. in co. Wicklow, prov. Leinfter. The herrings firft brought into Dublin are ufually taken by the fifhing boats of this place.

GRAYSTOWN, a rectory in dioc. of Cafhel, fit. in bar. Slewardagh, co. Tipperary, prov. Munfter; fairs are held here on 12 July and 6 Dec.

GREANY, fee *Graney*.

GREAT-CONNELL, a bar. with a village in it of fame name, fit. in co. Kildare, prov. Leinfter. It is remarkable for its famous abbey, once one of the moft magnificent buildings of the kind in Ireland: it is fit. near *Newbridge*, and contiguous to it is the feat of Mrs. *Poole Eyre*; and alfo *Old-Connell*, where there is a fine Danifh mount. This abbey was founded by *Meyler Fitzhenry* in 1202, who was buried here; it is now a curacy in dioc. of Kildare.

GREAT-HEATH, a common fit. about 2 miles N. of Maryborough, Queen's co. prov. Leinfter: otherwife called *Ratheen-common*, from a rath of that name fit. thereon. It is nearly a plain, interfperfed with gentle rifings and fmall vallies, being about 2 miles long, ¼ a mile broad, and containing an area of 600 acres. The foil is calcareous, and appears deep and fertile, on a limeftone gravel. Tho' no appearance indicates trees to have been produced on this foil, yet the bodies of large ones have frequently been dug up in the vallies, 4 or 5 feet beneath the furface; and what is very remarkable, on inclofing a part of this common where nothing had been produced for a number of ages except heath and grafs, without the leaft cultivation of any kind, the fecond fummer after the inclofing, an infinite number of young Scotch firs fprang up, tho' there was never known any of this fpecies in that part of the kingdom, except fuch bodies of them as have been difcovered from time to time at the bottom of the adjacent bogs. If this fpecies of pine was ever the produce of this diftrict, it muft have been in very antient periods, as the common has been for feveral centuries a fheep walk; and prior to that, appears to have been under agriculture, as the furrows of the plough are every where vifible. It was in former times part of the domain of the antient manor of *Dunamacs*, and was early brought under cultivation, and all wood that might have grown thereon, muft have been deftroyed foon after, if not prior to the arrival of the Englifh. From whence therefore thofe fhoots of *Scotch-fir* could proceed, is not eafy to divine; but all this common is fubject to the fame when protected from the browfing of the cattle; and being an elevated ground, feems to be formed on a large limeftone rock, under which are immenfe fubterraneous caverns full of water; fome of which communicate with the furface by means of gullies, or ducts, which draw off the rain and other waters that occafionally fall on the diftrict. One of thefe was difcovered fome years fince, at the bottom of a bog in one of the vallies, taking a perpendicular direction above 50 fathoms deep, before it came to the water. On the Eaftern confines of this common, is a range of hills compofed of calcareous rocks, in moft parts fertile and cultivated. The antient name of this heath was *Magh-riada*; and in it was fought a memorable battle between the people of Munfter and thofe of Leinfter, under the command of *Laoighois Cean Mordha*, about the middle of the 3d century: the bones of the flain being found at this day a few inches below the furface of the ground, on the borders of the heath.

GREAT-ISLAND, an ifland fo called, fit. in *Cork-harbour*, co. Cork, prov. Munfter.

GREAT-ISLE, fit. in bar. Shelburne, co. Wexford, prov. Leinfter. It lies in the river *Barrow*.

GREAT-MAN'S-BAY, fit. in bar. Moycullen, co. Galway, prov. Connaught.

GREAT-SKELIG ISLAND, an ifland fit. in the Weftern ocean, off the coaft of co. *Kerry*, prov. Munfter.

GREECE or *Grifs*, a river in co. Kildare, prov. Leinfter; it runs near the town of *Timolin*, and empties itfelf into the *Barrow*.

GREENAGH, a rectory in dioc. of Cloyne, fit. in bar. Barrymore, co. Cork, prov. Munft.

GREENAN, fit. in bar. Faffadinning, co. Kilkenny, prov. Leinfter.

GREENANSTOWN, fit. near the adjoining borders of the co.'s Meath and Weftmeath, prov. Leinfter.

GREENCASTLE, a village fit. in bar. Inifhowen, co. Donegal, prov. Ulfter: (*Beaufort*) fairs held 12 Jan. and 13 Aug.—Alfo an antient *caftle*, fit. (according to Dr. *Smith*) in bar. *Mourn*, in fame co. it ftands on a gut or inlet of the fea, and was reputed a ftrong caftle, fortified by the *Burghs*, earls of Ulfter, and lords of Connaught. It was remarkable for two eminent marriages, celebrated here in 1312, one between *Maurice Fitzthomas* and *Catherine*, daughter to the earl of Ulfter, on 5 Aug. and the other between *Thomas Fitz-John* and another daughter of the faid earl, on the 16 of fame month. It was deftroyed by the Irifh A. 1343, but foon after repaired and better fortified. Green caftle, and the caftle of *Carlingford*, appear by a record, 1 Hen. IVth to have been governed by one conftable, the better to fecure a communication between the *Englifh pale* of the co. *Louth*, and the fettlements of the Englifh in *Lecale* and thofe Northern parts, and *Stephen Gernon* was conftable of both, for which he had a falary of 20*l. per annum* for Green caftle, and 5*l. per annum* for Carlingford. In 1495 it was thought to be a place of fuch importance to the crown, that no perfon but of *Englifh birth*, was declared capable of being conftable of it: it was a garrifon in the rebellion of 1641, and helped to reftrain the Irifh in thofe then uncultivated parts.—There is alfo a place of fame name, on the borders of Lough Foyle, in bar. Inifhowen, co. Donegal, prov. Ulfter; along the fide of which Lough are 3 caftles, viz. *Green-caftle*, *Red-caftle* and *White-caftle*, all in fame bar. (*Scalé*)

GREENFIELD, a good feat on one fide of the river *Blackwater*, in co. Cork, prov. Munfter.

GREEN-

GREENHILLS, fit. near *Tallow*, co. Dublin, prov. Leinfter.—Alfo a feat near Drogheda, in co. Meath, prov. Leinfter. — Alfo a ridge of hills in bar. Great Connell, co. Kildare, prov. Leinfter.

GREEN-ISLAND, a fmall ifland containing only 2 acres, in the harbour of *Donaghadee*, co. Down, prov. Ulfter; it is always green, and at low water a perfon may walk dry to it. —There is another ifland of fame name, in the fame co. and prov. fit. in *Carlingford* bay, which is otherwife called *Guerno ifland*.

GREEN-MOUNT, fit. near *Caftlebellingham*, in co. Louth, prov. Leinfter; (known alfo by the name of *Gernard'stown* ;) here appears to have been formerly a very ftrong camp, in the fhape of an heart; 'tis fit. on the top of a fine green hill, and overlooks all that part of the country; the people who live near it have a tradition, that here was held the firft parliament in Ireland; but there are other accounts, and not without as good foundation, that make the firft meeting of an *Irifh* parliament in the adjacent co. of Meath. There is a *Tumulus* or Barrow in this camp, which probably is the fepulture of fome eminent warrior, fuch being commonly found in or near moft forts and camps of any confequence, and known to be a practice of the Danes.

GREENOUGE, a village fit. in bar. Ratoath, co. Meath, prov. Leinfter; it is a rectory in dioc. of Meath.

GREENOGUE-POINT, fit. in *Green-ifland*, in Carlingford bay, co. Down, prov. Ulfter.

GREENORE-BAY, fit. in bar. Forth, co. Wexford, prov. Leinfter.

GREENORE-POINT, the Eaftern point of *Greenore bay*, in co. Wexford, prov. Leinfter.

GREENVILLE, fit. near *Caftledermot*, in co. Kildare, prov. Leinfter.

GREGORY'S-ISLAND, one of the iflands of *Arran*, fit. in the Atlantic ocean, oppofite the co. Clare, prov. Munfter.

GREGORY'S-PASSAGE, fit. between 2 of the iflands of *Arran*, oppofite co. Clare, prov. Munfter.

GRENOGH, a fair town in co. Cork, prov. Munfter; fairs held 25 Apr. and 2 Nov.

GREY-ABBEY, fee *Gray-abbey*.

GRIB, fit. in bar. Dartree, co. Monaghan, prov. Ulfter; it it is otherwife called *Newtown*.

GRIFFIN'STOWN, fit. in co. Wicklow, prov. Leinfter, 25 miles from Dublin.

GRISS, fee *Greece*.

GROOMPORT, a village fit in bar. Ardes, co. Down, prov. Ulfter.

GROOM'S-PORT-BAY, fit. near *Bangor*, in co. Down, prov. Ulfter; at this place duke *Schomberg* anchored on 13 Aug. 1689, with 10,000 men, fent over by king William IIId.

The king himfelf followed the year after, and landed near *Carrickfergus*, 14 June, 1690.

GROSSBOROUGH, fit. in co. Monaghan, prov. Ulfter, 66 miles from Dublin.

GROSS-PATRICK, fit. in bar. Gorey, co. Wexford, prov. Leinfter.

GUALTIERE, a bar. in co. Waterford, prov. Leinfter.

GUIBARRA, a *river* fit. in bar. Boylagh, co. Donegal, prov. Ulfter.

GUIDORE, a *river* in bar. Kilmacrenan, co. Donegal, prov. Ulfter.

GUILCAGH, a vicarage in dioc. of Lifmore, fit. in bar. Upperthird, co. Waterford, prov. Munfter.

GUISHDEN, a *river* in bar. Gallen, co. Mayo, prov. Connaught.

GULE *(Lough)* fit. in co. Antrim, prov. Ulfter; here is *Liffanoure cafile*, the beautiful feat of lord *Macartney*, furrounded by the lough and a canal; this lough is diftant from Dublin 105 miles. It was antiently called *Longhecoleth*. In 710 the Britons of Cumberland invaded the principality of *Dalreida*; they were oppofed and defeated in a battle at this place by *Duncha*, chief of that diftrict.

GUR-LOUGH, a *lake* fit. in bar. Small-county, co. Limerick, prov. Munfter. Hereabouts are feveral Druidical monuments: near this lake on the road fide between *Limerick* and *Bruff* is a Druidical temple, confifting of 3 circles of ftones; the principal, which is about 150 feet in diameter, confifts of 40 ftones, of which the largeft is 13 feet long, 6 broad and 4 thick. At *Lough Gur*, a friary was founded for conventual Francifcans, in the 13th century, by the family of *Clangibbon*. On the 4 Feb. 35 Hen. VIIIth. this friary with 3 acres, and a flang of arable land in Ballynebrahar, was granted for ever, in capite, at the yearly rent of 12d. Irifh money, to Robert Brown; to whom alfo was granted a Dominican houfe, which ftood at Ballyniwellin, in the co. Limerick. James Gould died on 6 Sept. 1600, feized of the priory of *Loughgur*, and of one carucate of land, in free and common focage.

GURTEEN BAGH, a well improved feat on the N. fide of the river *Blackwater*, co. Cork, prov. Munfter.

GURTEEN-CASTLE, fit. within 2 miles of Mullinahone, co. Tipperary, prov. Munfter.

GURTNAMACKIN, a *river* in bar. Kiltartan, co. Galway, prov. Connaught.

GUYDORE *river*, fit. in co. Donegal, prov. Ulfter, 159 miles from Dublin; this river is fordable at low water.

GYLL *river*, fit. in co. Galway, prov. Connaught.

H A

HACKETSTOWN, a fair town fit. in bar. Ravilly, co. Carlow, prov. Leinfter, 44 miles from Dublin, 2½ miles beyond which, are the ruins of *Clonmore-caftle*; fairs held 1 Thurfd. Feb. 12 March, 4 May, Thurfd. after Trinity-fund. 21 Aug. 18 Sept. 3 Thurfd. Nov. 21 Dec. it is a rectory in dioc. of Leighlin.—Alfo a place of fame name in co. Waterford, prov. Munfter, the church of which was formerly a chapel of cafe to *Ardmore*, being in the fame parifh.

HACKLY, fit. in bar. Kilcullen, co. Kildare, prov. Leinfter.

HACERSTOWN, or *Haggardflown*, a curacy in dioc. of Armagh, fit. in bar. Dundalk, co. Louth, prov. Leinfter.

HAG's BED, fee *Labacally*.

HAG's-HEAD, a *cape* fit. in bar. Corcomroe, co. Clare, prov. Munfter.

HAG's-TOOTH *mountain*, fit. near Killenane, N. of *Cahir*, in co. Kerry, prov. Munfter; it is of a remarkable height, on the N. fide of which are fome romantic lakes, the mountains hereabouts are frequented by herds of fallow deer, that range about in perfect fecurity, no perfon difturbing them in thefe wild places.

HAINSTOWN, a curacy in dioc. of Kildare, fit. in bar. Salt, co. Kildare, prov. Leinfter.

HALF-FORE, or *Half-fowre*, a bar. in co. Meath, prov. Leinfter, the other part of the bar. of *Fore*, being annexed to co. Weftmeath, in fame prov.

HALF-WAY-HOUSE, a place fo called fit. in co. Sligo, prov. Connaught, 109 miles from Dublin.

HALL's-MILL, fit. in co. Down, prov. Ulfter, 63 miles from Dublin, near the banks of the river *Ban*; here is a bleach-yard of large extent, the *Banwater* being efteemed excellent for whitening linen.

HAMILTON's BAWN, this place which has been recorded in the poetical works of the celebrated *Swift*, is fit. in bar. Fews, co. Armagh, prov. Ulfter, 60 miles from Dublin; it is a large well built village, and has a good barrack; fairs held here 20 May and Nov.

HAMPSTEAD, a village in co. Dublin, prov. Leinfter, ½ a mile beyond *Glafnevin*, and about 2½ miles from Dublin caftle. It abounds in fine feats and villas; poffeffes a pure air with all the advantages of a dry foil and pleafant fituation.

HAMPTON-HALL, a handfome feat of the late baron *Hamilton*, fit. near Balbriggan, co. Dublin, prov. Leinfter.

HANALOCK *river*, fit. in co. Down, prov. Ulfter; it is formed by two ftreams which iffue from the N. fide of *Slieve Neir* in the bar. of *upper-Iveach*.

HANGMAN's-POINT, a *cape* fit. in the liberties of Kinfale, co. Cork, prov. Munfter.

HANMORE *ifland*, the largeft ifland in *Lough Derg*, between the co.'s Galway and Tipperary, it contains above 100 acres well cultivated and fertile.

HANNEL, a *lake* fit. in co. Weftmeath, prov. Leinfter.

HARE-ISLAND, fit. in Lough-Ree, and bordering on Kilkenny-W. in co. Weftmeath. prov. Leinfter, where an abbey was built by the family of *Dillon*.

HAROLD's-CROSS, a fuburb, or outlet of Dublin, about 1 mile from Dublin caftle; near it are the wiremills of Mr. *Cuppaidge*. Before thefe mills were erected, great fums of money were yearly fent out of the kingdom, to Holland and other parts, for the wire ufed in various manufactures: but all kinds and quantities can now be had here on as reafonable terms, and of equally good, if not fuperior qualities.

HARRIBROOK, fit. near Tanderagee, co. Armagh, prov. Ulfter.

HARRISTOWN, a fmall borough town in co. Kildare, prov. Leinfter, which now confifts only of a fingle houfe, fit. 23 miles S. W. of Dublin. It fends 2 members to parliament, patron, duke of *Leinfter*; and formerly gave title of baron to the *Euflace* family.—Alfo a place near Ardee, co. Louth, prov. Leinfter. And another near Rofcommon, co. Rofcommon, prov. Connaught.—Alfo a rectory in dioc. of Kildare, fit. in King's co. prov. Leinfter.

HARRYMOUNT, fit. near *Roftrevor*, co. Down, prov. Ulfter.

HARTSFORT, fit. near *Roftrevor*, co. Down, prov. Ulfter.

HARTSMOUNT, fit. in bar. Half-fore, co. Meath, prov. Leinfter.

HAULEBOWLING, an ifland or more properly a rock in the entrance of *Carlingford bay*, between the co.'s *Louth* and *Down*; it is covered before full fea, and lies about a mile on the W. fide, without the bar and block houfe; it is a dangerous rock, and the tide of flood fucks a fhip towards it.

HAWKSFORD, fit. in bar. Coftello, co. Mayo, prov. Connaught.

HAWKSROCK, fit. N. E. of Cork harbour, co. Cork, prov. Munfter.

HAWLE.

HAWLEBOWLIS, an *island* near Cove in Cork harbour, co. Cork, prov. Munster. It serves along with *Spike island*, as a bulwark to protect vessels riding at anchor from being damaged by the tide of ebb, or floods of the land. On it are the remains of an old fortification, built about the end of Queen Eliz.'s reign ; and which commanded all vessels of burden passing up to Cork.

HAZELHATCH, a village sit. about 8 miles from Dublin, in bar. Newcastle, co. Dublin, prov. Leinster. The *Grand-canal* from Dublin to Monasterevan, &c. passes thro' this place.

HAYES, sit. in bar. Dunluce, co. Meath, prov. Leinster.

HAYNESTOWN, or *Heynstown*, a rectory in dioc. of Armagh, sit. in bar. Dundalk, co. Louth, prov. Leinster.

HEADBOROUGH, sit. in co. Waterford, prov. Munster; it is a handsome seat near the *Black-water*, in the parish of *Killwater-mcy*.

HEADFORD, sit. in bar. Leitrim, co. Leitrim, prov. Connaught.—Also in co. Meath, prov. Leinster, which gives title to the eldest sons of the earls of *Bective*. Here is his lordship's seat, having a farm yard 280 feet square, totally surrounded with offices of various kinds.

HEADFORT, sit. in co. Galway, prov. Connaught, 103 miles from Dublin, a little better than 2 miles from this are the ruins of *Ross-abbey*; fairs are held here on 11 May and 14 Oct.

HEARTLAND, sit. in bar. Balruddery, co. Dublin, prov. Leinster.

HELVICK-HEAD, or *Helwick-head*, a cape sit. on the S. side of the entrance of Dungarvan bay, co. Waterford, prov. Munster.

HEN *and* CHICKENS, *mountains* sit. in bar. upper Iveach, co. Down, prov. Ulster.

HEREMON, the present prov. of *Leinster* ; the *Hermonii* were an antient people, inhabiting the Eastern and middle parts of Ireland ; they are said to have descended from *Heremon* a son of *Milesius* the Spaniard ; according to others they were *Belgians*, who arrived from Britain under the conduct of *Hugoni*, about the middle of the 4th century.

HERMITAGE, sit. near Newtownmountkennedy, co. Wicklow, prov. Leinster.

HERVEY'S-HILL, sit. in co. Londonderry, prov. Ulster, 117 miles from Dublin ; here are the curious improvements of the bishop of Derry, earl of *Bristol*.

HETTY-ROCKS, sit. in the Atlantic ocean, between the bar.'s of Ballynahinch and Moycullen, co. Galway, prov. Connaught.

HEYNSTOWN, see *Haynestown*.

HIGH-PARK, sit. in co. Wicklow, prov. Leinster, 33 miles from Dublin ; it is a handsome seat, lying under *Cadeen* mountain.

HILFOTHUIR, sit. in co. Donegal, prov. Ulster ; here an abbey was founded by *O'Dogharty*, in 1194, for monks of the Cistertian order.

HILL OF ALLEN, sit. in co. Kildare, prov. Leinster ; it was formerly called *Cromla Sliabh*, or the mountain in the district of Crom. It is a conical hill, standing opposite to that called *Dun-murry*, and is composed of calcareous rocks. From the surface there is every appearance of a copper mine : the loose stones, and even the points of rocks, in the external parts appear as if vitrified by fire, and numbers are richly impregnated with blue and green vitriol ; which strongly indicates the mine to be rich, and of no great depth. Among the rocks is also found a stone, which from its texture seems proper for mill-stones.

HILL OF ARDAGH, sit. near Drogheda, co. Louth, prov. Leinster.

HILLBROOK, sit. in bar. Shillelagh, co. Wicklow, prov. Leinster.

HILL-HALL *castle*, now a private seat, sit. near Drumboe, in co. Down, prov. Ulster ; it is a square fortification with 4 flankers.

HILLSBOROUGH, a borough, fair and post town in co. Down, prov. Ulster, 69 miles from Dublin ; here is a fine seat of the earl of *Hillsborough* ; the town is pleasantly sit. and almost new built, in view of *Lisburn, Belfast* and *Carrickfergus bay* ; the church is magnificent, having an elegant spire, as lofty as that of St. *Patrick's* in Dublin, and seven painted windows : it was built by lord Hillsborough, and cost him near 15,000l. Here is an excellent inn, and a thriving manufacture of *muslins*. There is also a small castle here, still in repair. It returns 2 members to parliament ; patron, the earl of *Hillsborough* ; this place giving title of earl to the family of *Hill*, now marquis Downshire. Lat. 54 : 30 N. lon. 6 : 20 W. Fairs held 3 Wednesd. Feb. May, Aug. and Nov.

HOATH, see *Howth*.

HOARTOWN, sit. in bar. Shelmaliere, co. Wexford, prov. Leinster, about 3 miles W. of *Taghmon*. In the 14th. century a monastery for Carmelites was founded here by one *Furlong* ; who endowed and dedicated it to the Virgin Mary : on the suppression it was granted to sir *John Davis*, who assigned it to *Fran. Talbot*. This place was called *little Horton*, and is a rectory in dioc. of Ferns.

HOG-HEAD, a *cape* sit. in bar. Dunkerron, co. Kerry, prov. Munster.

HOG-ISLAND, sit. in the bay of *Bantry*, co. Cork, prov. Munster ; this, and the other islands in this bay, fatten lean horses in the spring season to admiration.

HOLLY-

HOLLY-HILL, a handsome seat sit. near *Dunderrow*, in co. Cork, prov. Munster.

HOLLYMOUNT, a fair and post town in bar. Kilmain, co. Mayo, prov. Connaught, 105 miles from Dublin; fairs held 16 May and 11 Dec. 1 mile beyond it are the ruins of *Robin castle*.—Also a place so called in co. Down, prov. Ulster; being a handsome seat sit. on the W. arm of *Strangford-lake*.—There is also a place of same name sit. in co. Down, prov. Ulster, about 84 miles from Dublin.

HOLLYWOOD, a village in bar. Castlereagh, co. Down, prov. Ulster, 84 miles from Dublin; it is a curacy in dioc. of Down. The shores about here afford vast quantities of muscles, but not of the sort that breed pearls. The poor of the neighbourhood feed much on them, without feeling any inconvenience: they dress them when shelled, with butter, pepper and onions.—Also a fair town sit. in bar. Talbotstown, co. Wicklow, prov. Leinster; fairs held 1 Feb. 3 May, 1 Aug. and Nov. It is a rectory in dioc. of Dublin.—Also a vicarage in dioc. of Dublin, sit. in bar. Balruddery, co. Dublin, prov. Leinster. Lat. 54 : 42, lon. 6 : 23.—There is a place of same name sit. near Belfast, co. Antrim, prov. Ulster; otherwise called *Holywood*.

HOLMPATRICK, sit. near Skerries, in bar. Balruddery, co. Dublin, prov. Leinster; it is a curacy in dioc. of Dublin, and famous for having been the residence of the Irish apostle, St. *Patrick*; and here are still to be seen the venerable remains of a church, dedicated to that Saint.

HOLY CROSS, sit. in bar. Eliogurty, co. Tipperary, prov. Munster, above 69 miles from Dublin; fairs held 11 May, 24 Sept. and 18 Oct. It is a curacy in dioc. of Cashel. 7 miles from *Cashel*, on the river *Suir*, are the ruins of the famous abbey of *Holy cross*. *Murtough*, monarch of Ireland, and grandson of *Brien Boru*, having received from pope *Pascal* IId. in 1110, a gift of a piece of the cross, covered with gold, and ornamented with precious stones, determined to found a monastery, and dedicate it to the Holy Cross, which he began, but did not live to finish. *Donald O'Brien* compleated the church and abbey in 1169; he was king of N. Munster, and his monument is still to be seen near the high altar, of which, Mr. *O'Halloran* has given a view, as also the shryne in the S. Ayle, wherein some pieces of the cross were supposed to be deposited, both of which are more highly embellished than any other gothic remain to be seen in the kingdom.

HOLY-ISLAND, sit. in co. Clare, prov. Munster; fairs held Good-friday, and Whitsun-Monday.

HOLY-RIVER, a spa so called, sit 1¼ mile from *Blackwater-foot*, in co. Down, prov. Ulster.

HOLYWOOD, see *Hollywood*.

HOOK, a vicarage in dioc. of Ferns, sit. in bar. Shelburne, co. Wexford, prov. Leinster.

HOOK-TOWER, now a *Light-house* for shipping, sit. at the extreme Southern point of the bar. Shelburne, co Wexford, prov. Leinster: opposite to the Atlantic ocean.

HORE-ABBEY, sit. in bar. Middlethird, co. Tipperary, prov. Munster; it is a rectory in dioc. of Cashel.

HORN-CASTLE, see *Ardglass*.

HORN-HEAD, sit. in bar. Kilmacrenan, co. Donegal, prov. Ulster; it is a promontory mentioned by *Ptolemy*, under the name of *Boreum Promontorium*, or the Northern promontory, it is now called N. *cape* or Horn head; in some maps it is written *Hore-head*.—This is likewise the name of a handsome seat in this country, where there is a very great curiosity called *Mac Swine's gun*. It consists of a funnel perforated thro' a rock by the beating of the sea against it; by which means it has forced a passage, and rises in an enormous jet d'eau of 6 or 7 feet thickness, sometimes to the height of 30 or 40 feet. Its roaring is often heard 10 miles off, in calm weather. The stone which the rock is formed of, is a granite of greenish colour, spotted with black, like the *Ophytes* of the antients.

HORRIB, a *lake* in co. Galway, prov. Connaught; it is so called in some old maps; but is now written *Corrib*.

HORSE-ISLAND, sit. in the bay of Bantry, co. Cork, prov. Munster.

HORSE-LEAP, sit. in bar. Moycashel, co. Westmeath, prov. Leinster, 47 miles from Dublin. It was antiently called *Ardnorchor*, and the castle there was a very stately structure, founded if not finished by sir *Hugh de Lacey*, who was one of the first English adventurers, that fixed in Ireland in or very near the reign of Hen. IId. 2 miles beyond it are the ruins of another castle.

HORSE-PASS-BRIDGE, a village sit. in bar. Talbot'stown, co. Wicklow, prov. Leinster.

HORSE-SHOE, a bank or rock so called, sit. in the Irish sea, opposite the bar. Arklow, co. Wicklow, prov. Leinster.

HORTLAND, a fair town in co. Kildare, prov. Leinster; fairs held 2 May and 9 Dec.

HOSPITAL, a fair town in bar. Small-county, co. Limerick, prov. Munster; fair days 10 May, 9 July, 8 Sept. and 30 Oct. It is a vicarage in dioc. of Emly. In the records this is always called the Hospital of *Any*, tho' 'tis a full mile N. of that village. A commandery for Knts. Hospitalers was founded here in the reign of king *John*, by *Geoffry de Marischis*, who

who was governor of Ireland in 1215; it was dedicated to St. John the Baptift. Queen *Eliz.* granted this place to fir *Val. Brown,* who erected a magnificent caftle on the fcite of the fame, which caftle is now in ruins. The walls of the antient church yet remain; and in a nich on the N. fide of the high altar, is the tomb of a Knt. in alto relievo, which is faid to be that of the founder.

HOUGHTON-HALL, fit. near *Enniscorthy,* co. Wexford, prov. Leinfter.

HOWTH, *(Hoath* or *Houth)* a promontory which forms the N. entrance of Dublin bay, fit. in bar. Coolock, co. Dublin, prov. Leinfter. Lat. 53 : 22, lon. 6 : 41. Is generally called the *hill of Howth.* It gives title of earl to the family of *St. Lawrence;* and has on it a fmall village of fame name, fit. about 7¼ miles from Dublin caftle. The fhores off this hill are rocky and precipitous, affording however a few harbours for fmall craft. It was formerly called *Benhedar,* i. e. " *the Birds promontory,*" and celebrated for having *Dan Criomthan* or the rath or royal palace of *Criomthan* erected on it, he having been chief or king of that diftrict, and memorable for making feveral fuccefsful defcents on the coaft of *Britain,* againft the Romans, in the time of *Agricola. Howth,* tho' now ftript of trees, was formerly covered with venerable oaks, and was a feat of the Druids; one of their altars ftill remains in a fequeftered valley on the E. fide of the hill. The family of *St. Lawrence,* which was formerly called *Triftram,* but acquired the prefent name from a victory obtained by fir *Armoricus Triftram,* over the Danes, on *St. Lawrence's* day 1177; the fword with which he obtained that victory, ftill remains hung up in the hall of Howth caftle to perpetuate it: and this place has continued in poffeffion of that family above 600 years. This caftle or manfion houfe, being the feat of lord *Howth,* was probably erected by fir *Armoricus Triftram.* Near the houfe ftands the family chapel, and on the Weftern fhore are the ruins of St. *Mary's* church, with fome antient monuments of lord *Howth's* anceftors. Due W. of Howth houfe, are the ruins of St. *Fenton's* church. In 1575, the celebrated *Grace O'Maley,* better known by the name of *Granuweal,* brought 4 veffels of force before Howth caftle, and landed a number of men to befiege it. The caufe of offence was her meffenger being refufed entrance at dinner time: fhe carried her purpofe into effect, and the condition of peace was, that the gates of Howth caftle fhould never be fhut at dinner time; which is obferved to this day. The village of Howth is a curacy in dioc. of Dublin.

HOYLE-LOUGH, a lake fit. in bar. Corkerry, co. Weftmeath, prov. Leinfter; it is fingular that from this lake 2 rivers flow in oppofite directions: the *Brofna* takes a Southern courfe, while a fhort and rapid ftream runs Weftward into *Lough Iron,* which difcharges its waters by the Inny into the Shannon.

HUDDERSFIELD, a good feat fit. 1 mile W. of Crofhaven, in co. Cork, prov. Munfter; on a rifing ground near the houfe is a gazado, which commands a profpect of the harbour of Cork, the ocean, and a vaft tract of fea coaft.

HULIN-ROCKS, fit. in bar. Glenarm, co. Antrim, prov. Ulfter.

HUME-CASTLE, fit. in bar. Magheraboy, co. Fermanagh, prov. Ulfter. Lat. 54 : 18, lon. 8 : 17.

HUME-WOOD, a handfome feat fit. in co. Wicklow, prov. Leinfter; 31 miles from Dublin. — Alfo a place near Caftledermot, co. Kildare, prov. Leinfter.

HUNGRY-HILL, a mountain in co. Cork, prov. Munfter; of a vaft height, rocky and almoft perpendicular, at leaft 700 yards above the level of *Bantry-bay.* On its top is a large lake, formed by a collection of water from various fmall rivulets and fprings, which produces one of the fineft cataracts in the kingdom.

HUNTINGBROOK, fit. near *Gowran,* co. Kilkenny, prov. Leinfter.

HUNTINGTOWN, fit. between *Ballybrittas* and *Portarlington,* Queen's co. prov. Leinfter.

HUNTSTOWN, fit. in bar. Caftleknock, co. Dublin, prov. Leinfter.

HY CABHANAGH, a part of the antient diftrict of *Hymoragh,* in the prefent co. of Wexford, the chiefs of which were the *O'Cavanaghs.*

HY CONOIR, a diftrict of the *O'Connors,* formerly fit. between the rivers *Boyne* and *Liffey,* in co. Kildare, prov. Leinfter.

HY DA LEIGH, the diftrict of the *O'Daly's,* in the prov. of Leinfter; they were in poffeffion of their antient patrimony, at the commencement of the laft century.

HYDE-PARK, fit. near *Clonard,* co. Meath; — likewife near Arklow, co. Wicklow, both in prov. Leinfter.

HY DRISCOL, one of the antient diftricts in the S. part of the co. Cork, prov. Munfter, which belonged to the *O'Drifcols,* fubordinate chiefs to the *Mac Cartys.*

HY DUNGHUI, a diftrict of the *O'Donoghs,* fit. between the co.'s *Cork* and *Kerry,* in prov. Munfter.

HY FOGARTY, a diftrict fit. by *Thurles,* in co. Tipperary, prov. Munfter; the chiefs of which were the *O'Fogartys.*

HY GARMAN, a diftrict in the Southern part of the co. Clare, prov. Munfter; where was

was the antient patrimony of the *O'Gormans*.

HY KERIN, an antient diftrict fit. in the King's and Queen's co.'s prov. Leinfter, the antient proprietors of which were the *O'Meaghers*.

HY KINSELLAGH, a large antient diftrict, comprehending a great part of S. Leinfter; being an union of the fepts of Hy Moragh, Coulan, Hy Tuathal, Hy Broghan, Gabhran, Eli-ui-Mora, and fometimes Offory; the refpective chiefs being O'More, Coulan, O'Tool, O'Broghan, &c. This part contained the prefent co.'s of Wexford, Wicklow, Kilkenny, and the S. part of the Queen's co. the principal chief of which was generally O'Moragh, (or *O'More)* hereditary chief of *Hy Moragh*, and in confequence denominated *King of Leinfter*; tho' from the antient Irifh hiftory, it appears that the chiefs of *Eli-ui-Mora, Coulan* and *Tuathal*, according to the feniority, were elected chiefs of Kinfeagh, and kings of Leinfter. Hence the name of *O'Kinfhelagh.*

HY LOCHLEAN, or the diftrict on the waters of the fea; it was fince called Burrin, a bar. in co. Clare, the chiefs whereof were called *O'Loghlin* or *O'Laghlin*; fome of whom remained in poffeffion at the commencement of the laft century. In this diftrict were part of the *Canganij* of Ptolemy.

HY MAGHLONOGH, a diftrict of the *O'Malones*, in the King's co. and co. Weftmeath, prov. Leinfter; it formed a part of the *S. Hy Falia,* which was compofed of a union of the fepts of the O'Malones, O'Dalys, O'Molloys, O'Connors, O'Dempfys, Macloghlins, Mageoghegans, Macawleys and O'Faleys; and formerly comprehend E. and W. Meath, Dublin, part of Kildare, and the King's co.

HY MAGHUI, a diftrict antiently fit. in the Southern extremity, of the co. Cork, prov. Munfter.

HY MAINE, a diftrict in co. Galway, prov. Connaught, which antiently belonged to the *O'Dalys* and *O'Kellys.*

HY MALIA or *Umalia*, i. e. the diftrict near the watry plain; an antient divifion in the W. of the co. of Mayo, prov. Connaught; comprehending the prefent bar. of *Morifk*, and half the bar. of Rofs, in the co. Galway; being the S. of the antient Hy Murifg, the Auterij of Ptolemy. The hereditary chiefs of this diftrict were denominated *Hy Malia* or *O'Maly*, fome of whom were in poffeffion of the Southern parts at the beginning of the laft century. In this country St. *Patrick* founded the church of *Achad Fobhair*, afterwards a bifhoprick; now *Aghagower.*

HY MEITH, the diftrict of the *O'Hanlons,* which was fit. in co. Armagh, prov. Ulfter.

HYNE-LOUGH, a *bay* fit. in bar. Carbery, co. Cork, prov. Munfter.

HY NELLIA, the diftrict of the *O'Neils,* in co. Tyrone, prov. Ulfter.

HY REGAN, the antient diftrict of the *O'Regans,* fit. in Queen's co. prov. Leinfter.

HY VEACH, the antient territory of the *Mc. Gennis's,* fit. in co. Down, prov. Ulfter; now divided into the bar.'s of upper and lower *Iveach* or *Iveagh.*

I E

IARCONNAUGHT, an antient diftrict which contained the prefent bar.'s of Morogh, Moycullen and Ballinahinch, in co. Galway, prov. Connaught. It was called alfo *Conmacnemara, Conmacne-ira* and *Hy Jartagh;* the chiefs of which were denominated Hy Flaherty or O'Flaherty.

IARMUMHAN, or *W. Munfter,* comprehending the prefent co. of Kerry, in prov. Munfter.

JAMES'TOWN, a borough and fair town in bar. Dromahaire, co. Leitrim, prov. Connaught; fit. 5 miles N. W. of *Carrick on Shannon,* and 73 N. W. of Dublin. Lat. 53 : 44 N. lon. 8 : 15 W. It has a barrack for a company of foot, and returns 2 members to parliament; patronage in the family of *King.* Fairs held 28 May, 8 July and 20 Dec.—Alfo a place near Portarlington, Queen's co. prov. Leinfter.

JAMES'WELL, a fair town in co. Sligo, prov. Connaught; fairs held 5 Aug.

JASPER'S-POUND, fit. in co. Clare, prov. Munfter; where fairs are held on 19 May and 26 Nov.

IBAWNE, a bar. in co. Cork, prov. Munfter.

IBERCON, a bar. joined with *Ida* and *Igrin,* in co. Kilkenny, prov. Leinfter.

IBERIA, an antient diftrict mentioned by *Rich. Ciren.* fit. round *Beer-haven,* co. Cork, prov. Munfter; the chiefs of which were the O'Sullivans.

IBH-TORNA-EIGEAS, the prefent bar. of Clanmorris, in co. Kerry, prov. Munfter: it was in early ages diftinguifhed by the name of *Conal Eachluath.*

IBRICKIN or *Ibrickan,* a bar. in co. Clare, prov. Munfter.

IDA, a bar. joined with *Igrin* and *Iberkon,* co. Kilkenny, prov. Leinfter.

IDRONE, a bar. in co. Carlow, prov. Leinfter.

IERNUS, a river mentioned by *Ptolemy,* which appears to be the prefent river *Kenmare,* in co. Kerry, prov. Munfter.

JER-

JERPOINT, a vicarage in dioc. of Offory, fit. in bar. Gowran, co. Kilkenny, prov. Leinfter, 58 miles from Dublin.

JERPOINT-ABBEY, fit. in bar. Knocktopher, co. Kilkenny, prov. Leinfter; it is a vicarage in dioc. of Offory. The ruins of this once beautiful abbey are well worthy the attention of a traveller; it was founded by *Donogh O'Donoghoe*, king of Offory, in 1180 for Ciftertian monks, whom he removed hither from a diftant part of Offory; and it was dedicated to the Virgin Mary. He died in 1185, and was here interred. The abbot of Jerpoint was a lord of parliament.

JERVISTOWN, a fair town in co. Clare, prov. Munfter; fairs held 28 March and 2 Oct.

JEVERSTOWN, fit. near *Six-mile-bridge*, co. Clare, prov. Munfter.

IFFA, a bar. joined with that of *Offa*, and called the bar. of Iffa and Offa, fit. in co. Tipperary, prov. Munfter.

IGHTERMURAGH, a caftle fit. on the antient high road from *Cork* to *Youghal*, in co. Cork, prov. Munfter.

IGRIN, a bar. joined to *Ida* and *Iberkon*, in co. Kilkenny, prov. Leinfter.

JIGGIN'STOWN, fit. in co. Kildare, prov. Leinfter, about 16 miles from Dublin. Here are the ruins of a magnificent houfe, begun, but never finifhed, by Thomas Wentworth, earl of *Strafford*, when lord lieutenant of Ireland. It is entirely of brick, and of confiderable extent, with great vaultage under it; and ftands by the fide of the high-road beyond Naas.

IKEATH, a bar. joined to *Oughterany*, and called the bar. of Ikeath and Oughterany, fit. in co. Kildare, prov. Leinfter.

IKERIN, a bar. in co. Tipperary, prov. Munfter; it gives title of vifc. to the family of *Butler*, now earl of Carrick.

ILANMORE, an ifland fit. near the coaft of the bar. Burrifhoole, co. Mayo, prov. Connau.

ILEAGH, a bar. in co. Tipperary, prov. Munfter: fometimes written *Ifcagh*.

ILEN, a *river* fit. near *Baltimore*, co. Cork, prov. Munfter.

IMLACH, a rectory in dioc. of Meath, fit. in bar. Kells, co. Meath, prov. Leinfter.

IMLEACH-JOBHUIR, the antient name of the bifhoprick of *Emly* in co. Tipperary, prov. Munfter.

IMOKILLY, or *Imokelly*, a bar. in co. Cork, prov. Munfter.

IMPHRICK, a rectory in dioc. of Cloyne, fit. in bar. Fermoy, co. Cork, prov. Munfter.

INANE, fit. near Rofcrea, co. Tipperary, prov. Munfter.

INCH, a rectory in dioc. of Cloyne, fit. in bar. Imokilly, co. Cork, prov. Munfter.—Alfo

a rectory in dioc. of Down, fit. in bar. Lecale, co. Down, prov. Ulfter.—Alfo a vicarage in dioc. of Dublin, fit. in bar. Gorey, co. Wexford, prov. Leinfter.—Alfo a vicarage in dioc. of Ferns, fit. in bar. Shelmaliere, co. Wexford, prov. Leinfter.—Alfo a village fit. in bar. Crannagh, co. Kilkenny, prov. Leinfter. And a place near *Athy*, co. Kildare, in fame prov.

INCHBEG, fit. near Kilkenny, prov. Leinfter.

INCHIGEELAGH, fit. in bar. Mufkerry, co. Cork, prov. Munfter, 6 miles S. W. of Macroomp, and 148 from Dublin. It is a fmall village in the midft of mountains, having a barrack built in a ftone fort of 4 baftions, erected on the N. end of a bridge over the river *Lee*, which opens about a mile farther into a fine lake called *Lough Allua*, near which is another lake called *Gouganbarra*, remarkable for the hermitage of St. *Finbar*. Near *Inchigeelagh* many pieces of metalic fubftance have been found, in the form of cubes, as hard as iron, and glittering with fparks intermixed of a pale yellow, fhining like gold. Thefe cubes are wafhed out of the rocks on the banks of the river, by winter floods. They ftrike fire with fteel; will not ferment with *Aquafortis*; in the fire they emit a blue flame, and calcine to a fine florid red. Fairs held here on 31 May, Aug. and 3 Dec. This place is a rectory in dioc. of Cork.

INCHIHOLAHAN, a rectory in dioc of Offory, fit. in bar. Shellilogher, co. Kilkenny, prov. Leinfter.

INCHINABACKY, a rectory in dioc. of Cloyne, fit. in bar. Barrymore, co. Cork, prov. Munfter.

INCHINAMO, or *Inchinemeo*, a name given by *Cambrenfis*, to Monaincha in the co. Tipperary, prov. Munfter.

INCHIQUIN, or *Inchequin*, a bar. with a village in it of fame name, fit. in co. Clare, prov. Munfter. It has a *caftle* called the caftle of Inchiquin, which has not been inhabited for above a century paft: this place gives title of earl to the noble family of *O'Brien*, defcended from *Brien O'Boromh*, the famous monarch of Ireland.

INCHIQUIN-LAKE, fit. in bar. Inchiquin, co. Clare, prov. Munfter.

INCH-ISLAND, otherwife called *Inifcurrecy*, fit. in the Weftern branch of *Lough Con*, now called *Strangford lake*, in co. Down, prov. Ulfter, about 74 miles from Dublin. Here are the ruins of the abbey, and abbey church of *Inch*, built for Ciftertian monks by fir *John de Courcy* in 1180, who in his wars had demolifhed the abbey of *Erynach*. *Inch* or *Inis* fignifies *Ifland*, but this place is a peninfula, having a land paffage into it on the N. fide. The

church

church of this abbey was erected in the form of a crofs, part of which remains, and on the S. fide feems to have ftood a fteeple, fupported by an elegant arch, of which fome of the beads or ftrings are yet to be feen. At the E. end of the church are 3 large arched windows, upwards of 20 feet high; and on each fide, in the N. and S. walls, are 2 windows compofed of 2 arches, little inferior in height or elegance to the great window on the E. Thefe windows for light and ornament muft have had a grand effect, when the church was in its fplendor: in the S. wall yet remain 3 tops of ftalls. In this *ifland* (if it may be fo called) immediately after the entrance into it by a caufeway, is an old church, which perhaps was a chapel to the great abbey; over the S. door of which is a piece of fculpture reprefenting the image of *Chrift* on the crofs, and a perfon on his knees, with his hands elevated, praying to him. In the fame church lies buried fir *James Melville*, fuppofed to be a defcendant of fir James Melville, fecretary to *Mary* Queen of *Scots*, and author of the memoirs that pafs under his name. The firft mentioned of thefe Knts. has here a monument of free-ftone erected to his memory, and placed in an arch on the N. fide of the altar.— There is alfo an *ifland* of this name, fit. in Lough Swilly, in bar. Inifhowen, co. Donegal, prov. Ulfter; it is a chapelry in dioc. of Derry.

INCHKENNY, a rectory in dioc. of Cork, fit. in the liberties of Cork, prov. Munfter.

INCHMORE, fit. near Kilkenny, co. Kilkenny, prov. Leinfter.—Alfo an ifland in *Lough Rea*, in co. Clare, prov. Munfter, where St. *Senan* built a monaftery.

INCHNEMEA-ABBEY, fee *Moraincha*.

INCH-POINT, a *cape* fit. in bar. Corcaguinny, co. Kerry, prov. Munfter.

INCHY, fit. in bar. Stradbally, Queen's co. prov. Leinfter.

INCHYCRONANE, an ifland fit. in the river Shannon, in co. Clare, prov. Munfter: here *Donald O'Brien* king of Limerick founded an abbey for canons regular, about the year 1190.

INGARD-POINT, a *cape* fit. in bar. Shelburne, co. Wexford, prov. Leinfter.

INISBEG. There are 3 *iflands* of this name; viz. 1ft. fit. in bar. Kilmacrenan, co. Donegal, prov. Ulfter. — 2d in bar. Corcaguinny, co. Kerry, prov. Munfter.—3d in bar. Carbery, co. Cork, prov. Munfter.

INISBEGIL, an *ifland* fit. in bar. Erris, co. Mayo, prov. Connaught.

INISBOFIN or *Inifbofin*, an *ifland* fit. near *Newport bay*, which lies between the co.'s Mayo and Galway, prov. Connaught: it is a rectory in dioc. of Tuam. St. *Colman* bifhop

of Lindisfern, with a number of Scots and 30 Saxons, founded a monaftery here in 676, and refided there 9 years. It is otherwife written *Ennifbofin*, and is 3 leagues diftant from land. Lat. 53 : 31, lon. 10 : 25. The name fignifies the ifland of the white cow.—There is another ifland of fame name, fit. in *Lough Ree*, co. Longford, prov. Leinfter; where St. *Rioch*, nephew to St. Patrick, founded an abbey about the end of the 5th century: it was plundered by the Danes in 1089. — Alfo an ifland fit. in bar. Kilmacrenan, co. Donegal, prov. Ulfter.

INISCALTRA, an ifland fit. in the river Shannon, bar. Leitrim, co. Galway, prov. Connaught.

INISCARRA, fit. in bar. Barretts, co. Cork, prov. Munfter: it is a rectory in dioc. of Cloyne. Here St. *Senan* built an abbey. A charter-fchool was opened here for 20 female children in 1760, to which fir *John Conway Colthurft*, bart. granted 2 acres of land, rent free in perpetuity; and alfo fet for 3 lives or 31 years 20 acres more, at the yearly rent of 7s per acre. The rev. *Chriftopher Donnellan*, D. D. fometime incumbent of the parifh, bequeathed 184*l* 3*s* 1½*d* which was applied (according to his intention) towards building this fchool.

INISCATHY, an *ifland* fit. in the mouth of the river Shannon, between the co.'s Clare and Kerry, prov. Munfter; it was alfo called *Cathaigh-inis*, and fince named *Inifcatry*, or the ifland of *Scattry* or *Scattery*. St. Patrick founded a monaftery here, and placed St. *Senan* over it. It is faid to have been made an epifcopal fee at a very early period, from which time, 'till long after the reformation, no woman was permitted to fet her foot in it: it was united to the fee of Limerick about the year 1190. The monaftery was frequently plundered by the Danes. In the days of queen *Eliz.* this ifland contained 11 churches; the remains of 7 befides a round tower are yet to be feen. This is now a rectory in dioc. of Killaloe.

INISCATTERY, fee *Inifcathy*.

INISCLOGHRAN or the *ftoney ifland*, an ifland in Lough *Ree*, in the river *Shannon*, between the co.'s Weftmeath and Rofcommon; at which place a monaftery was founded by St. *Dermod*, about the beginning of the 6th century.

INISCRONAN, fit. in bar. Bunratty, co. Clare, prov. Munfter; it is a vicarage in dioc. of Killaloe.

INISCOURCEY or *Inifcurcy*, fee *Inch ifland*.

INISDRISNA, an *ifland* fit. in bar. Carbery, near coaft of co. Cork, prov. Munfter.

INIS-

INISDUFF, an *island* fit. in bar. Boylagh, co. Donegal, prov. Ulster.

INISFAIL, derived from *Inis Bheal*, that is the island of *Beal*, one of the antient names of Ireland, fo denominated from *Beal*, the principal object of adoration among the antient inhabitants of the British isles. *Inis-fail* has been erroneously tranflated the *island* of *Destiny*, as *Beal* was fometimes taken for *fate* or *providence*.

INISFALLEN, an island in the lake of Killarney, co. Kerry, prov. Munster; in it are the ruins of a very antient religious houfe, founded by St. *Finian*, the patron faint of thefe parts, and to him the cathredral of *Aghadoe* is alfo dedicated. The remains of this abbey are very extenfive, its fituation romantic and retired. Upon the diffolution of religious houfes, the poffeffions of this abbey were granted to capt. *Rob. Collam*. The island contains about 18 acres, is agreeably wooded, and has a number of fruit trees. St. *Finian* flourilhed about the middle of the 6th century, he was firnamed in Irifh *Lobhar*, his father's name was *Conail*, the fon of *Efchad*, defcended from *Kian* the fon of *Alild*, king of Munster. There was formerly a chronicle kept in this abbey, which is frequently cited by fir *J. Ware* and other antiquaries under the title of the *annals of Inis-fallen*: they contain a lketch of univerfal hiftory, from the creation of the world to the year 430 or thereabouts; but from thence the annalift has amply enough profecuted the affairs of Ireland down to his own times: he lived to the year 1215. Sir *J. Ware* had a copy of them, whereof there is an imperfect tranfcript among the MSS. of the library of *Trinity-college, Dublin*. They were continued by another hand to the year 1320. Bifhop *Nicholfon* in his Irifh hiftorical library, informs us that the duke of *Chandos* had a compleat copy of them down to 1320 in his poffeffion. Thefe annals tell us that in the year 1180, the abbey, which had at that time all the gold and filver, and richeft goods of the whole country depofited in it, as the place of greateft fecurity, was plundered by *Milawin* fon of *Daniel O'Donoghoe*, as was alfo the church of *Ardfert*, and many perfons were flain in the very cemetery by the *M'Cartys*; but God, as it is faid in this chronicle, punifhed this impiety by the untimely end of fome of the authors of it. In 1197 on the 19 Dec. died *Gilla Patrick O'Huidar*, in the 79th year of his age; he was archdeacon of *Faithlin*, fuperior of this convent, and founder of many religious houfes, a celebrated poet, and famous for his piety, charity and wifdom.

INISFREE, an island fit. in bar. Boylagh, co. Donegal, prov. Ulster.

INISFREE-BAY, a harbour fit. in bar. Boylagh, co. Donegal, prov. Ulster.

INISGLORA, an island fit. in bar. Erris, co. Mayo, prov. Connaught.

INISGOULA, an island fit. in bar. Burrifhoole, co. Mayo, prov. Connaught.

INISHAE, an island fit. in bar. Ballynahinch, co. Galway, prov. Connaught.

INISHARGY, an agreeable habitation in the centre of the bar. of *Ardes*, co. Down, prov. Ulster; having two frefh water lakes, one to the N. and the other to the S.

INISHANNON, or *Inifhonan*, a fair town in bar. Kinalea, co. Cork, prov. Munster; 134 miles from Dublin; fit. on the river *Bandon*, 6 miles from *Kinfale*. Here is a charter-fchool for 40 boys, it was opened in 1752, and the building completed by *Thomas Adderly* efq; for 420l. which was eftimated at 800l. He granted to it alfo two acres of land in perpetuity, and a leafe of 40 acres at 10l. per ann. with claufes of renewal. The linen manufacture has been much encouraged by the late Mr. Adderly. The river is navigable to *Collier's-quay*, about ¼ a mile below the place; on the W. fide of the town is a ftone bridge. This place is a rectory in dioc. of Cork, and was formerly walled, and of fome note, as appears by the foundations of feveral caftles and large buildings difcovered in it. The town of *Inifhannon*, together with its ferry, were granted to *Philip de Barry*, by *Hen.* Vth by letters patent, anno 1412. Fairs held 29 May and 3 Oct.

INISHARK, an island fit. in bar. Ballynahinch, co. Galway, prov. Connaught.

INISHARN, an island fit. in bar. Morilk, near the coaft of co. Mayo, prov. Connaught.

INISHEGIL, an island fit. in bar. Erris, by the coaft of co. Mayo, prov. Connaught.

INISHERE, an island fit. in Galway-bay, co. Galway, prov. Connaught.

INISHERKAN, or *Inifhirkan*, an island fit. between *Cape-clear Ifland* and *Baltimore-bay*, in co. Cork, prov. Munster; in this island ftood the caftle of *Dunelong*, poffeffed by the O'Drifcolls, which was furrendered after the defeat of the Spaniards to capt. *Hervey*, on 23 Feb. 1602. There was afterwards a regular fortification erected on part of the island which was garrifoned in queen Ann's time, but it has been for feveral years difmantled; about a mile to the S. are the remains of an antient abbey, founded in 1460, for Francifcans, by Florence O'Drifcoll. In 1537 the citizens of Waterford, deftroyed all the villages on this island, with the mill, caftle and friary. This island has very good land, and is vaftly preferable to that of *Cape-clear iflands*. To the N. W. of *Inifhirkan* island, lies *Hare* island,

a large

a large fruitful fpot, and near it are four fmall iflands called the *Schemes*; alfo along the coaft in the following order from E. to W. are *Horfe* ifland, containing 100 acres, *Caftle* ifland, containing 119 acres, *Long* ifland, containing 316 acres; and W. of all thefe, is a fmall fpot called *Goat ifland*; all thefe iflands, together with the adjacent coaft, produce large crops of fine Englifh barley.

INISHMURRY, an ifland fit. in bar. Clanderlogh, co. Clare, prov. Munfter.

INISHONAN, fee *Inifhannou.*

INISHOWEN, or *Inifowen*, and fometimes *Ennifhowen*; a bar. in co. Donegal, prov. Ulfter.

INISHRATER, an ifland in Lough Corrib, in bar. Clare, co. Galway, prov. Connaught.

INISHRUIN, a ifland fit. in bar. Ballinahinch, on coaft of co. Galway, prov. Conn.

INISHUGH, an ifland fit. by the coaft of bar. Burrifhoole, co. Mayo, prov. Connaught.

INISKEA, there are two iflands of this name diftinguifhed by *N.* and *S. Inifkea*, both fit. in bar. Erris, co. Mayo, prov. Connaught.

INISKEANE, fee *Inifkeen.*

INISKEEL, fit. in bar. Boylagh, co. Donegal, prov. Ulfter; it is a rectory in dioc. of Raphoe.

INISKEEN, or *Inifkeane*, a village fit. in bar. Carbery, co. Cork, prov. Munfter, 144 miles from Dublin, in the bar. of *Carbery*, 6 miles N. from *Cloghnikelty*; 'tis a fmall village, and has a good weekly market; according to tradition, it takes its name from *Kean Mac Moile More*, anceftor of the *Mahonys*. From *Inifkean* to the village of *Nuceftown*, the country is for the moft part mountainous and rocky, being covered over with heath, furze and fern. To the N. of *Iuifkean*, is the ruined church of *Kineigh*, with a remarkable round tower, above 70 feet high, and 124 feet from the W. end of the church. Contrary to all others of the kind, the firft ftory is in the form of an *Hexagon*, but the other five ftories above it are round. This place is fometimes written *Innifkean.*

INISKELLY, a feat within 4½ miles of Loughrea, co. Galway, prov. Connaught; where are the ruins of a church and of a caftle.

INISKERAGH, or *Inifkerach*, an ifland fit. in bar. Erris, co. Mayo, prov. Connaught.

INISKERRY, an ifland fit. on coaft of bar. Ibrickan, co. Clare, prov. Munfter.

INISLINY, fee *Innifliny.*

INISLIRE, an ifland on coaft of bar. Burrifhoole, co. Mayo, prov. Connaught.

INISLOUGH, a rectory in dioc. of Lifmore, fit. in bar. Iffa and Offa, co. Tipperary, prov. Munfter: it is otherwife written *Iniflounagh*, and ftands on the banks of the river *Snire*, 3½ miles W. of Clonmel. Here an abbey was founded by St. *Mochoemoe*, at which place *Maryan O'Bride*, archbifhop of Cafhel died

in 1238, and was there interred: it was a fingularly beautiful building; here is alfo a celebrated well.

INISLOUNAGH, fee *Iniflough.*

INISMACSAINT, an ifland fit. in Lough Erne, co. Fermanagh, prov. Ulfter.—Alfo a rectory in dioc. of Clogher, fit. in bar. Magheraboy, in fame co. and prov.

INISMAGRATH, a rectory in dioc. of Kilmore, fit in bar. Dromahaire, co. Leitrim, prov. Connaught.

INISMAIN, an ifland fit. in Galway-bay, co. Galway, prov. Connaught; it is a rectory in dioc. of Tuam.

INISMAKEERA, an ifland fit. in bar. Boylagh, co. Donegal, prov. Ulfter.

INISMANAN, an ifland fit. in bar. Kilmacrenan, co. Donegal, prov. Ulfter.

INISMOUTHY, a vicarage in dioc. of Meath, fit. in bar. Slane, co. Meath, prov. Leinfter.

INISMURRY, an ifland fit. off the coaft of bar. Carbery, co. Sligo, prov. Connaught. Here is the temple of the monument of *Muidhr*: the cells are covered with light earth, fo as to make them in a manner fubterraneous; fome cells are fallen in, others look horrid and gloomy, having a fmall hole at top and another in the fide, feemingly to give *air*, not *light*. They have been all vaulted with the fame rude ftones. The walls (built without mortar) are from 5 to 10 feet thick, and 10 feet high.

INISTEGILL, an ifland fit. in bar. Morifk, co. Mayo, prov. Connaught.

INISTIOGE, a poft and fair town in bar. Gowran, co. Kilkenny, prov. Leinfter, 63 miles from Dublin. It is alfo a borough, and returns 2 members to parliament; patronage in the family of *Tighe*. Fairs held 9 June, 13 and 14 Dec. This is a vicarage in dioc. of Offory.

INISTORRY, or *Inis-torre*, i. e. the *High ifland* an ifland 8 miles from the N. W. coaft of the co. Donegal, prov. Ulfter.

INISTUISKAR, fee *Iniftufker.*

INISTURC, an ifland contiguous to that of *Inis Claire*, at the entrance of *Clew bay*, on the coaft of the co. Mayo, prov. Connaught, where ftood a cell of the abbey of *Knockmoy*; this ifland is alfo adjacent to *Inifbofin ifland.*

INISTUSKER, or *Iniftuifkar*, an ifland fit. in bar. Corcaguinny, co. Kerry, prov. Munfter.

INISTYMON, or *Iniftymond*, a village fit. in bar. Corcomroe, co. Clare, prov. Munfter, 123 miles from Dublin; three miles beyond which are the ruins of *Moyvore* caftle. At *Iniftymond* is the *caftle*, now a handfome feat, the prefent poffeffor is now acknowledged the head of the *O'Brien* family, and would be earl of *Thomond*, were it not for the attainder

of

of the laft lord *Clare*, thro' whom he muft derive.

INNISKILLEN, fee *Enniſkillen*.

INNSLINY, fit. in bar. Corcomroe, co. Clare, prov. Munfter.

INNY, a *river* fit. in bar. Rathline, co. Longford, prov. Leinfter.—Alſo a river fit. in bar. Iveragh, co. Kerry, prov. Munfter.

INNY-BRIDGE, this bridge of which there is now but fmall appearance, was raiſed over the river *Inny*, in co. Kerry, prov. Munfter; it having fallen down fome years ago; it was 24 feet wide and but a yard thick, being only a foot path, which was aſcended and defcended by fteps, it was of a confiderable height over the river, and built almoft femi-circular, which gave it the name of the *Rainbow-bridge*: what feems very fingular is, that it did not ftand on any highway; from its narrownefs it had more the appearance of a triumphal arch than a bridge, and was erected over a very deep part of the river; but at what time or on what occaſion, there is not the leaft tradition in the country.

INOSH, an iſland in the river Shannon, fit. in bar. Bunratty, co. Clare, prov. Munfter.

INSHIANLY, a vicarage in dioc. of Caſhel, fit. in bar. Eliogurty, co. Tipperary, prov. Munfter.

INVER, a rectory in dioc. of Raphoe, fit. in bar. Boylagh, co. Donegal, prov. Ulfter, 117 miles from Dublin: a fmall monaftery was founded here in the 15th century for friars of the third order of St. Francis.—Alſo a rectory in dioc. of Connor, fit. in bar. Belfaft, co. Antrim, prov. Ulfter.—Alſo a village fit. in bar. Erris, co. Mayo, prov. Connaught. And a *river* fit. in bar. Boylagh, co. Donegal, prov. Ulfter.

INVERCOLPA, now called *Colp*, fit. at the mouth of the river Boyne, in co. Meath, prov. Leinfter. Here St. Patrick landed on his miſſion to the ftates of Ireland aſſembled at *Tarah*. In 1182 *Hugh de Lacey* founded a monaftery here for canons regular of St. Auguftin; the walls of the church, in ruins, are ftill to be feen, the arches of which are both in the Saxon and gothic ftile, and the E. window, which appears older than the reft, is fuppoſed to have made a part of the abbey. On the N. fide is a fmall chapel, and to the S. two other chapels; one of which is at prefent the burial place of the family of *Bellew*.

JONSTOWN, fit. in bar. Uppercrofs, co. Dublin, prov. Leinfter, about 2 miles from *Tallagh*.

JOHN's, *(Saint)* fit. in bar. Ballaghkeen, co. Wexford, prov. Leinfter. — Alſo in bar. Athlone, co. Rofcommon, prov. Connaught.— Alſo a *cape* fit. in co. Donegal, prov. Ulfter.

JOHNSTON'S-BRIDGE, a fair town in co. Armagh, prov. Ulfter; fairs held 25 May, July, Sept. and Nov.—Alſo a fair town in co. Donegal, prov. Ulfter, otherwife called *Saint Johnſton's bridge*. Fairs held here 3 Aug.

JOHNSTON'S-FEWS, fit. in co. *Armagh*, prov. Ulfter; a barrack was erected there in the time of the noted *Redmond O'Hanlon*, the Irifh rapparee, in which there is generally a company or two of infantry quartered. Diftance from Dublin 50 miles.

JOHNSTOWN, a village fit. in bar. Naas, co. Kildare, prov. Leinfter, within 2 miles of Naas, and about 13 from the caftle of Dublin. It is a vicarage in dioc. of Kildare.—Alſo a village fit. in bar. Gallmoy, co. Kilkenny, prov. Leinfter, 59 miles from Dublin.—Alſo a rectory in dioc. Cathel, fit. in bar. *Middlethird*, co. Tipperary, prov. Munfter. *(Dr. Beaufort.)*—Alſo a place fit. in bar. *Slewardagh*, in fame co. and prov. *(Scalè.)*

JOHN'STOWN-BRIDGE, fit. in bar. Carbery, co. Kildare, prov. Leinfter, 21 miles from Dublin; 1½ mile beyond which, is a fine feat called Kilmurry; fairs are held at *John'ſtown-bridge* on Eafter Tuefd. 8 Sept. and 21 Dec.

JOHN's-WELL, a place fo called, in co. Clare, prov. Munfter; having fairs on 5 July,

JONESBOROUGH, fit. in bar. Orior, co. Armagh, prov. Ulfter, 45 miles from Dublin; fairs held here on 4 June, 14 Aug. 21 Oct. and 3 Dec. It is a rectory in dioc. of Armagh.

JORDANSTOWN, fit. in bar. Balruddery, co. Dublin, prov. Leinfter.

JOYCE's-COUNTRY, a diftrict fit. according to the old maps in bar. *Morifk*, but which fhould have been placed in bar. *Ballinahinch*, co. Galway, prov. Connaught.

IRAGHTICONNOR, a bar. in the Northern part of the co. Kerry, prov. Munfter, on the banks of the *Shannon*. The chiefs of this country were called *Hy Cain câ Ciarnidhe*, and by contraction, *O'Conor Kerry*, whofe defcendants were in poſſeſſion of their antient patrimony, in the beginning of the laft century.

IRALAGH-ABBEY, now in ruins, was fit. near *Killarney*, co. Kerry, prov. Munfter; it was founded by *Donald* fon of *Thady M'Carthy* in 1440, and re-edified by the roman catholics in 1602. The remains of this building are worth attention.

IRELAND's EYE, a fmall iſland on the coaft of the co. Dublin, prov. Leinfter, one mile N. of *Howth*. It belongs to the bar. of Coolock, and was antiently called *Adros*; by Ptolemy, *Adri-deſerta*, by Pliny *Andros*, and by *Rich. Ciren.* Edria. It is compoſed of a high rock on the N. fide; and what is called the *Stags* on the E. the latter being very dangerous to fhipping : the ifland produces many curious medicinal plants, which in the months of May and June, yield a ftrong odoriferous effluvia ; it was formerly joined to the hill of Howth ; and on the S. W. fide are the ruins of a fmall but very antient chapel. St. *Neffan* founded an abbey here about the year 570 ; and here was preferved the book of the four gofpels, called the ' *Garland of Howth.*'

IRISHTOWN, a decayed village fit. in bar. Half-Rathdown, on the fea fhore, in co. Dublin; prov. Leinfter, about 1½ mile from the metropolis. It is a chapelry in dioc. of Dublin.—Alfo a borough town joining the city of Kilkenny, prov. Leinfter, otherwife called St. *Canice* : it is a place of antiquity, and enjoyed peculiar privileges, and ftill returns 2 members to parliament ;. patronage in the bifhop of Offory. Here is one of the antient round towers.

IRON-LOUGH; a *lake* fit. in bar. Moygoifh, co. Weftmeath, prov. Leinfter.

IRRIGIL, fit. in bar. Trough, co. Monaghan, prov. Ulfter.

ISERKELLY, a vicarage in dioc. of Kilmacduagh, fit. in bar. Loughrea, co. Galway, prov. Connaught.

ISERTKERRIN, a rectory in dioc. of Cafhel, fit. in bar. Slewardagh, co. Tipperary, prov. Munfter.

ISERTLAWRENCE, a vicarage in dioc. of Emly, fit. in bar. Clanwilliam, co. Limerick, prov. Munfter.

ISHARTMON, a curacy in dioc. of Ferns, fit. in bar. Forth, co. Wexford, prov. Leinfter.

ISLANDAKEAN, a rectory in dioc. of Waterford, fit. in bar. Middlethird, co. Waterford, prov. Munfter.

ISLAND-BRIDGE, fit. in co. Dublin, prov. Leinfter, about 1½ mile from Dublin caftle. Here is a well dedicated to St. John of Jerufalem ; and an antient burial place, adjoining the lands belonging to the Royal-hofpital. A bridge was erected here over the river Liffey, in the year 1577, in the reign of queen Eliz. whofe armorial bearings carved in ftone, were affixed to the wall on one fide of the bridge. The bridge going to decay, was lately taken down, and a new one erected, called *Sarah's-bridge*, which is large and beautiful, confifting of only one extenfive arch which croffes the river : it was built under the particular care and direction of the Rt. Hon. fir *John Blaquiere*, K. B.

ISLANDINE, a vicarage in dioc. of Tuam; fit. in bar. Burrifhoole, co. Mayo, prov. Connaught.

ISLAND-MAGEE, a *peninfula* fit. in bar. Belfaft, co. Antrim, prov. Ulfter : it is a rectory in dioc. of Connor.

ISLANDS, 2 bar. in co. Clare, prov. Munfter.

ISLEAGH, fee *Ikagh.*

ISEALONG, fee *Annalong.*

ISLE of ALLEN, or *Hy-al-Lain*, i. e. the diftrict of the great plain country, containing the Eaftern part of the *Magh Leana*, at prefent diftinguifhed under the denomination of the *ifle* of *Allen*, being furrounded by a Log, and is fit. in co. Kildare, prov. Leinfter ; in which ftands the *hill* of *Allen*, the *mount Cremla* of the antient bards ; the chiefs of this diftrict were denominated *Hy Allain*.

ISLE-OF-ALL-SAINTS, fit. in *Lough Rie*, co. Longford, prov. Leinfter. Here St. *Kieran* built a noble monaftery in the year 544. *Auguftin Al'Graidin*; who died in 1405, was interred here ;. he wrote the lives of the faints of Ireland, and continued the annals of this abbey down to his own time ; which work is ftill preferved in the Bodleian library at Oxford.

ISLES OF-ICANE, fit. off the coaft of co. Waterford, prov. Munfter.

ISSERKELLY, a fair town in co. Galway, prov. Connaught ; fairs held 22 June and 25 Aug.

ITERMURROUGH, a rectory in dioc. of Cloyne, fit. in bar. Imokilly, co. Cork, prov. Munfter.

IVEAGH or *Iveach*. There are 2 bar.'s of this name in co. *Down*, prov. Ulfter ; they are diftinguifhed into *upper* and *lower Iveagh* ; the former is by much the largeft bar. in that co. The name of *Iveagh* or *Hy Veach* is faid to be taken from *Achaius*, in Irifh called *Eachach*, grandfather to king *Coelopaig*, as much as to fay the territory of *Eachach* ; for *Hy* in the Irifh language, is a common adjective, denoting not only the heads and founders of families, but alfo the territories poffeffed by them. *Iveagh* (including both bar.'s) was otherwife called the *Magennifes* country, and in queen Eliz.'s time was governed by fir *Hugh Magennis*, efteemed to have been one of the moft polite of all the natives in thofe parts, who was brought by fir *Richard Bagnal*, from paying the tribute called *Bonaught* to the *O'Neils*, and took his lands by letters patent from the crown, to be held by *Englifh* tenure to him and his heirs male. We are told that he wore *Englifh* garments amongft his own followers every feftival day, and was able to bring into the field 60 horfemen and near 80 foot. This family continued powerful until the rebellion of 1641, the confequences of which put a final period to their greatnefs. Thro' part of this bar. runs a chain of mountains confiderably high, known by the name of *Iveach* mountains.

IVERAGH, a bar. in co. Kerry, prov. Munfter ; it contains 7 parifhes, 1 *Cahir*, 2 *Glanbehy*, *hy*, 3 *Killenane*, 4 *Valentia*, 5 *Prior*, 6 *Kellemly*, 7 *Drummod*.

IVERK, a bar. in co. Kilkenny, prov. Leinst.

IVERNIS, an antient city and capital of the Irish *Scots*, as mentioned by *Rich.* of *Cirencest.* who asserts that it was sit. on the Eastern banks of the *Shannon*, but where is not very certain; though most probably it was the present town of *Banagher*, in the King's co. prov. Leinster; as *Banagher* has the same signification with *Ivernis*, viz. the Western habitation on the water; and is sit. in the antient *Coitiduzarian*, the *Scotii* of Richard.

JULIAN'STOWN, sit. in bar. Duleek, co. Meath, prov. Leinster, 20 miles from Dublin. It is a vicarage in dioc. of Meath.

K A

KADDY-CARNE, a long ledge of rocks, on one of the *Copland islands*, called *Big-island*, in co. Down, prov. Ulster; they take their name from a small *Karne* or heap of stones placed near them on the island.

KAHIRNABREDAGH, sit in bar. Carbury, co. Cork, prov. Munster.

KANBO-CASTLE, now in ruins, sit. on the side of a lough about 4 miles from Elphin, co. Roscommon, prov. Connaught.

KANEBANE, sit. on the coast of co. Antrim, prov. Ulster.

KANTURK, sometimes called *Kancturk* and *Kinturk*, a fair town in bar. Duhallow, co. Cork, prov. Munster; 3 miles W. of *Castle-magner*, the name was antiently written *Keanturk*. i. e. a Boar's head, probably from one of those animals having been slain here by some Irish chief in former times. It belonged to a branch of the *Macartys* called *Mac Donough*, who forfeited his estate in 1641. In queen Eliz.'s time they erected a most magnificent pile near this place, the walls of which remain entire; it was a parallelogram 120 feet in length by 80 in breadth, flanked with 4 square buildings. But being represented to the council as a place which might be made dangerous to government, the building was put a stop to, tho' far from being capable to be made any use of to that purpose. All the window frames, coigns, beltings and battlements were of hewn stone, and the whole made a most grand and regular appearance. This castle with the town and manor of *Kanturk*, gave title of visc. to the family of *Perceval*, now earl of Egmont. In the town is a neat market-house, and the worsted manufacture is that chiefly carried on there. At *Curragh*, a little to the N. of *Kanturk*, was a castle of the *Macartys*, and near

it is a most excellent chalybeate water. *Dromagh castle* stands about 3 miles S. W. of *Kanturk*; it was built by the *O'Keefs*, and was their chief seat; it is well walled, and flanked with 4 turrets; near this place a vein of coal was discovered somewhat similar to that at *Kilkenny*. Fair days 4 May, July, 3 Nov. and 11 Dec.

KARNBANE, a place so called, from a large *Kairn* or heap of stones placed there. It lies in co. Armagh, prov. Ulster; by the edge of the co. Down near Newry. This *Kairn* is 180 yards in circumference, and 10 yards in conical height.

KARN-GUAR, the " *Goat's mount*," a hill sit. 2 miles N. of *Scraba*, in co. Down. prov. Ulst.

KARRICK CASTLE, or *Carrick Castle*, sit. 2 miles from the town of Wexford, co. Wexford, prov. Leinster. It is built on a high rock, overlooking the sea; there is a ferry-boat kept here for the convenience of passengers, from which circumstance this place is also called *Ferry-carrick*; the castle was built by *Robert Fitzstephens*, and fortified; but the people of Wexford got him into their power by stratagem, and confined him and most of his followers in prison, till the arrival of *Hen.* IId when they delivered him to that monarch; and were the first who submitted as subjects to England.

KATE'S-HOLE, a deep hole sit. in a field S. of Liscarrol, in co. Cork, prov. Munster; which is generally supposed not to be fathomed; a stone thrown into it, may be heard distinctly for about 15 seconds before it reaches the water.

KEADY, sit. in bar. Armagh, co. Armagh, prov. Ulster, 58 miles from Dublin. About this place and along the banks of the river *Callon* to *Armagh*, are many considerable bleach-mills, the linen manufacture being carried on there very extensively. Fairs held 4 April, 14 Aug. and 14 Oct. This place is a rectory in dioc. of Armagh.

KEAMORE, sit. in co. Cork, prov. Munster; from this there is a very extensive prospect of a great part of the sea coast, with the harbours of Glandore and Castlehaven.

KEANY, a fair town in co. Westmeath, prov. Leinster; fairs held 20 Sept.

KEARN, sit. in bar. Burrin, co. Clare, prov. Munster.

KEARNEYVILLE, sit. near *Ross*, co. Cork, prov. Munster.

KEENAGH, a fair town in co. Longford, prov. Leinster; fairs held 10 Oct.

KEEPER, or *the Keeper*, a mountain sit. in bar. Arra, co. Tipperary, prov. Munster.

KELLS, a bar. in co. Meath, prov. Leinster, having in it a borough, fair and post town of fame name, fit. 31 miles from Dublin: it returns 2 members to parliament; patron, the earl of *Bective*. This place gives title of vifc. to the family of *Cholmondeley*. Lat. 53 : 45, N. lon. 7 : 20 W. Near it is *Headfort*, the magnificent feat of lord *Bective*. This town is pleafantly fit. on the river *Blackwater*: it was antiently called *Kenanue*, and afterwards *Keniis*. In former ages it was reckoned one of the moft famous cities in the kingdom; and on the arrival of the English, was walled and fortified with towers. In 1178, a caftle was erected. where the market houfe is now; and oppofite the caftle was a crofs of an entire ftone, ornamented with bas relief figures, and many curious infcriptions in the antient Irifh character. Within a fmall diftance was the church of St. *Senan*; and on the S. of the church yard is a round tower, which meafures 99 feet from the ground, the roof ending in a point, and near the top were 4 windows oppofite the cardinal points. There was a celebrated monaftery founded here about anno 510 for regular canons, dedicated to the Virgin Mary. It owed its origin to St. *Columb*, called alfo St. *Columb Kill*, to whom the fite of the abbey was granted by *Dermod Mac Carval*, or *Dermod* the fon of *Kervail*, king of Ireland. An epifcopal fee was afterwards erected here, which in the 13th century was united to that of Meath. A priory or hofpital was alfo erected by *Walter de Lacie*, lord of Meath, in the reign of Rich. Ift for Crofs-bearers or crouched friars, following the order of *St. Auguftin*. There was likewife a perpetual chantry of 3 priefts or chaplains, in the parifh church of St. *Columb* in Kells, to celebrate mafs daily; 1 in the Rood chapel, another in St. Mary's chapel, and a 3 in the chapel of St. Catherine the Virgin. Fair days Thurfd. before Shrove Tuefd. day before Afcenfion, 9 Sept. and 16 Oct. This place is a vicarage in dioc. of Meath.—Alfo the name of a bar. in co. Kilkenny, prov. Leinfter, which has alfo a village in it of fame name, being a poft and fair town, diftant from Dublin 64 miles. It is an antient place, fit. on *King's river*, and was noted for a priory of *Auguftines*, built, and richly endowed by *Geoffry Fitz-Roberts*, who came into this kingdom with *Strongbow*. The prior of this place had the title of lord fpiritual, and as fuch fat in the houfe of peers before the reformation: the ruins only of this abbey now remain: a fynod was held in it A. 1152, when *John Paparo*, legate from Rome, made one of the number of bifhops that were convened there at that time to fettle the affairs of the church. The prefent church is built in the gothic manner. It is a rectory in dioc. of Offory. Fairs held 13 July.—There is a third place of this name, fit.

in bar. Antrim, co. Antrim, prov. Ulfter, 89 miles from Dublin; near which are the ruins of a church; and here *Kellach* an anchorite died in 828, on the fcite of whofe cell, a priory was erected by *O'Brian Carrog*, before the arrival of the Englifh. This place is but a fmall village, feated on a river of fame name, over which it has a bridge. Lat. 52 : 27, lon. 3 : 6.—Alfo the name of a place in bar. Iveragh, co. Kerry, prov. Munfter.

KELLYMOUNT, fit. in bar. Gowran, co. Kilkenny, prov. Leinfter; this place is otherwife called *Ballymaelaghna*, and is remarkable for a banditti who ufed formerly to commit their depredations in very large bodies, and made a little inn near this place, their houfe of rendezvous. Near Kellymount is a *ford*, that parts the co.'s of Kilkenny and Carlow; within this ford the fheriffs of both co.'s meet, and deliver and receive the judges in their circuits; formerly there was a battle fought near it, between the inhabitants of both co.'s, concerning their limits, which are now amicably fixed at the middle of the ford.

KELLY'STOWN, fit. in bar. Catherlough, co. Carlow, prov. Leinfter, on the E. fide of the river *Barrow*; here is a large ruined church dedicated to St. *Patrick*, and faid to have been built by him. It formerly belonged to the antient family of *Cummins*, a name ftill furviving, and numerous in this part of the country. There are feveral of that name interred in the church, whofe vaults are ftill remaining, tho' there is but one whofe infcription is intelligible; it is as follows, " *Hoc jacet fub lapide Hugo Mac Cummins*, 1603." This is a rectory in dioc. of Leighlin.

KELVIN, a *river* fit. in bar. Kenoght, co. Londonderry, prov. Ulfter.

KENADUS, from *Cean-au-uis*, i. e. the principal country of the water; an antient diftrict in co. Weftmeath, prov. Leinfter: fit. near the *lakes* in that country.

KENAGH, fit. in bar. Moydoe, co. Longford, prov. Leinfter, 56 miles from Dublin; 2 miles from which are the ruins of a church and caftle. Here is alfo a *river* of fame name.

KENARD, fit. in bar. Moygeefh, co. Weftmeath, prov. Leinfter; an antient nunnery was erected here.

KENE, a rectory in dioc. of Armagh, fit. in bar. Dundalk, co. Louth, prov. Leinfter.

KENELLY, fit. near Rofcommon, prov. Connaught.

KENITH, fit. near *Iniffcan*, co. Cork, prov. Munfter.

KENMARE *river*, fit. in co. Kerry, prov. Munfter; the entrance to which lies between the *Skeligs* to the N. W. lat. 51 : 35 N. and lon. 11 W. from London, and the *Bull, Cow* and

and *Calf*, the *Bull* lieing in lat. 51 : 20 N. and lon. 10 : 40 W. This river is about 14 leagues in length, and in breath from the *Skeligs* to the *Bull*, *Cow* and *Calf*, 5 leagues and half; and from *Scariff island* on the N. side to the *Dursey island*, on the S. side it is about 3 leagues or 8 Irish miles. The entrance of this river is deep, fair and navigable up to its head, having nothing of danger all the way but what appears; and that only on the coast at both sides, until you are 8 leagues up to the river, and a-breast with *Ardea* castle on the S. side, where there is a funk rock called *the maiden*.

KENMARE *town*, fit. in bar. Glancrought, co. Kerry, prov. Munster; 155 miles from Dublin. This place gives title of vise. to the family of *Brown*; and is a rectory in dioc. of Ardfert; near it, is the celebrated and beautiful *lake* of *Killarney*. The town is but small, yet remarkable for its *bay*; which is 30 miles in length, and from 3 to 9 in breadth, in which are several good harbours.

KENOGHT, or *Kenought*, a bar. in co. Londonderry, prov. Ulster.

KENRY, a bar. in co. Limerick, prov. Munster; antiently called *Carbre Aobhdha*, the kings of which had their seat at *Brury* in this co. at which latter place *Auliff-Mor-O'Donaghue* king of Kenry, was slain by *Murtogh O'Brien* in 1165.

KENTSTOWN, fit. in bar. Duleek, co. Meath, prov. Leinster; it is a rectory in dioc. of Meath.

KERRY, a co. in the prov. of Munster; antiently called *Corrigia*, or the rocky country, from *Cerrig* or *Carric* a rock. It is bounded by the *Shannon*, which river divides it from *Clare* on the N. by *Limerick* and *Cork* on the E. by another part of Cork on the S. and by the *Atlantic ocean* on the W. The best town in it is *Dingle*, fit. in a *bay* of the same name. It comprehends a great part of the territory formerly called *Desmond*, and consists of very different kinds of soil. The S. parts are plain and fertile, but the N. full of high mountains, which though remarkably wild, produce a great number of natural curiosities. It contains 647,650 acres, 83 parishes, 8 bar.'s, 3 boroughs, returns 8 members to parliament; and gives title of earl to the family of *Fitzmaurice*. It is 53 miles from N. to S. and in the broadest part from E. W. 41, and lies within lat. 51 : 30 and 52 : 24 N. the lon. at mouth of *Kenmare river*, being 10 : 35 W. or 42 m. 20 s. difference of time with *London*. Its bar.'s are Iraghticonnor, Clanmaurice, Truaghnacmy, Corcaguinny, Magunihy, Glancrought, Dunkerron and Iveragh: containing about 19,395 houses, and 107,000 inhabitants. It is the fourth co. as to extent in Ireland,

and the second in this prov. but in respect to inhabitants and culture doth not equal many smaller co.'s In it there are two episcopal sees, which have been annexed to the bishoprick of *Limerick*, since the year 1663. viz. *Ardfert* and *Aghadoe*. The fee of *Ardfert* was antiently called the dioc. of *Kerry*, and its bishops were named bishops of *Kerry*. Few mountains in Ireland can vie with those in this co. for height; during the greater part of the year their sides are obscured by fogs, and it must be a very serene day when their tops appear. *Iron ore* is to be had in great plenty in most of the Southern bar.'s. The principal rivers are the *Black-water*, *Feal*, *Gale* and *Brick*, *Cashin*, *Mang*, *Lea*, *Flesk*, *Lanne*, *Carrin*, *Fartin*, *Inny* and *Roughty*, and the principal lake is *Killarney*. There are some good medicinal waters discovered in this co. particularly *Killarney water*, *Iveragh spa*, *Fell's-well*, *Dingle*, *Castlemain*, and *Tralee spas*, as also a saline spring at Maheribeg. Some rare and useful plants grow in Kerry, of which *Dr. Smyth* gives a particular account in his history of that county. Amongst the antient Irish and English families of this co. we find those of Fitzgerald, M'Carty, M'Gillicuddy, O'Sullivan, O'Conor, Fitzmaurice, Desmond, Crosby, Blenerhasset, Denny, Trant and Brown.

KERRY-CURRY, or *Kerrycurrighy*, a bar. joined with *Kinalea*, in co. Cork, prov. Munster.

KERRY-HEAD, a *cape* fit, in bar. Clanmaurice, co. Kerry, prov. Munster, 10 miles from Ardfert, between Tralee bay and the Shannon mouth. Here are found great quantities of Amethysts, commonly called *Kerry-stones*; they are of a chrystalliform figure, and found adhering by their bases to stoney matter, crusting over the perpendicular fissures, in rocks of ferruginous stones. Their colours are various degrees of shades of purple: some approach to a violet, and others are of a pale rose colour. Some parts of different specimens of these gems, are often found as colourless as chrystal.

KERRY-POINT, a cape fit. in bar. Ardes, co. Down, prov. Ulster.

KESH, a village fit. in bar. Clonawly, co. Fermanagh, prov. Ulster.

KEY-LOUGH, a *lake* fit. in bar. Boyle, co. Roscommon, prov. Connaught.

KID, an *island* fit. in bar. Erris, near the coast of co. Mayo, prov. Connaught.

KIERRIGIA, a district fit. in co. Mayo, prov. Connaught; the antient proprietors of which were the M'Costellos.

KIERRIGIA-LUACRA, a district in co. Kerry, prov. Munster, that antiently belonged to the Desmonds and O'Connors.

KILABINY, fit. near Ardfert, co. Kerry, prov. Munster. KILLA-

KILABRAHAR, i. e. the church of the bro-therhood: this place which stands between *Churchtown* and *Liscarol*, in co. Cork, prov. Munster, had formerly a monastery, now in ruins, but of what order is uncertain.

KILARD, sit. in bar. Ibrickan, co. Clare, prov. Munster; it is a vicarage in dioc. of Kil-laloe; otherwise called *Killard*; and gives title of baron to the family of *Arundel* now visc. Galway.

KILDALLYBOYNE, sit. near *Loop-head*, co. Clare, prov. Munster.

KILBARON, sit. on the bay of Donegal, in bar. Tyrhugh, co. Donegal, prov. Ulster. It is a vicarage in dioc. of Raphoe. St. *Columb* founded a church here. *Barrind*, who flou-rished about the year 590, gave his name to this church, and was bishop of it.

KILBARRY, sit. in co. of the city of Water-ford, prov. Munster; it is a curacy in dioc. of Waterford. A house was founded here in the 12th century for knights templars; and given afterwards to the knights of St. John of Jerusa-lem. Besides the grand priory of *Kilmainham* near Dublin, we find but 8 houses or preceptories of this order in Ireland; 3 of which, viz. *Kil-barry*, *Crook* and *Killure*, were in the co. Wa-terford. Kilbarry with its demesnes, were granted to *Thomas* earl of *Ormond*, in fee-farm, and assigned to *Thomas Wadding.*—Also the name of a seat, sit. 3 miles S. of Macroom, co. Cork, prov. Munster.

KILBEGGAN, a borough, fair and post town, sit. in bar. Moyashel, co. Westmeath, prov. Leinster, 44 miles from Dublin; it returns 2 members to parliament; patronage in the *Lam-bert* family. It is seated on the river *Brosna*, over which there is a bridge; there was here a monastery founded in 1200, and dedicated to the Virgin Mary; it was inhabited by monks from the Cistertian abbey of *Melefont*; 1½ mile beyond this village, are the ruins of *Moycashill* castle; an abbey at *Kilbeggan* was founded by St. *Beaan*, son of *Murchade* of the blood royal of Munster, in a very early age. Fairs held here 16 June and 28 Oct: This place is a curacy in dioc. of Meath; lat. 53 : 18, lon. 7 : 57.

KILBEGS, or *Kilbeg*, a rectory in dioc. of Meath, sit. in bar. Kells, co. Meath, prov. Leinster. Lat. 53 : 46, lon. 7 : 20.—Also a place sit. 4 miles N. W. of *Naas*, co. Kildare, prov. Leinster: 'tis said the knts. Templars had a commandery here.

KILBERRY, sit. in bar. Narragh, co. Kildare, prov. Leinster, 35 miles from Dublin. It is now but a small village, tho' formerly a place of greater note; there was an abbey erected here in an early age, of the ruins of which there are still some remains to be seen; be-tween 3 and 4 miles from this, are the ruins

of *Kildangan* castle. Kilberry is a vicarage in dioc. of Dublin.—Also a village sit. in bar. Morgallion, co. Meath, prov. Leinster, which is a rectory in dioc. of Meath: it lies 4 miles N. of *Navan*, where a perpetual chantry of 2 priests or chaplains was formerly established in the church of Kilberry.

KILBIXY, sit. in bar. Moygoish, co. West-meath, prov. Leinster; it was the chief seat of Sir *Geoffry Constantine*, one of the English settlers, *temp. Hen.* IId. and of old, a town of great note, having (as 'tis said) had 12 burgesses in their scarlet gowns, a mayor and sovereign, with other suitable officers; how-ever of all this state, the remains are now so small, that we may justly apply to it what *L. Florus* says of the Veii in Italy; Laborat anna-lium fides, ut, Veios fuisse credamus." This is a curacy in dioc. of Meath : and here a castle was erected by *Hugh de Lacey* in 1192; and an hospital for lepers, which was called the leper house of St. *Brigid.*

KILBOLANE, a parish in bar. Orrery, co. Cork, prov. Munster; here is a castle called *Kilbolane castle*, about 4 miles S. W. of *Broghill*; it belonged to the earls of *Desmond*, but is said to have been built soon after the coming over of *Stronghow* by the *Cogans*; it is now a good house and improvement: not far from it is the parish church of *Kilbolane*. It is a curacy in dioc. of Cloyne.

KILBOY, sit. near *Silvermines*, co. Tipperary, prov. Munster.

KILBRENIN, now called *Straw-hall*, sit. in co. Cork, prov. Munster; it was an abbey founded in the 8th century, part of whose ruins are remaining on a rising ground.—Also a place of same name, where a monastery was founded, sit. in co. Galway, prov. Connaught.

KILBRIDE, sit. in co. Carlow, prov. Leinster, 42 miles from Dublin, a pleasant seat, lately occupied by *Arthur Baillie*, esq; deceased.——There is also a place of same name in bar. Arklow, co. Wicklow, prov. Leinster, 29 miles from Dublin. It is a curacy in dioc. of Dublin.—Also a rectory in dioc. of Meath, sit. in bar. Fartullagh, co. Westmeath, prov. Lein-ster.—Also a vicarage in dioc. of Connor, sit. in bar. Antrim, co. Antrim, prov. Ulster.—Also a vicarage in dioc. of Ferns, sit. in bar. Shelmaliere, co. Wexford, prov. Leinster. —Also a vicarage in dioc. of Ossory, sit. in bar. Ida, &c. in co. Kilkenny, prov. Leinster.—Also a rectory in dioc. of Waterford, sit. in bar. Middlethird, co. Waterford, prov. Munster.—Also a vicarage in dioc. of Elphin, sit. in bar. Roscommon, co. Roscommon, prov. Conna.—Also a chapelry in dioc. of Meath, sit. in bar. Dunboyne, co. Meath, prov. Leinster.—Also a chapelry in dioc. of Meath, sit. in bar:

bar. Geſhil, King's co. prov. Leinſter. — Alſo the ruins of a church called *Kilbride church*, ſit. in co. Dublin, prov. Leinſter, within about 8 miles of the metropolis.

KILBRIDE-PASS, a village ſit. in bar. Fartullagh, co. Weſtmeath, prov. Leinſter, 33 miles from Dublin ; near it are the ruins of a church, and 2 caſtles at different diſtances.

KILBRIDGE, ſit. near *Gorey*, co. Wexford, prov. Leinſter.

KILBRIN, a pariſh church now in ruins, ſit. near *Caſtle-Cor*, in bar. Orrery, co. Cork, prov. Munſter : it is a vicarage in dioc. of Cloyne.

KILBRITTON, a fair town in bar. Carbery, co. Cork, prov. Munſter : the cantred of *Kilbritton* antiently belonged to the bar. of *Courceys* in this co. The caſtle was formerly a ſeat of the lords *Courcey*, and afterwards of *Mac Carty Reagh* : when ſtanding it was a ſtately building, environed with a large bawn, fortified with 6 turrets on the walls ; but it was ſome years ago taken down, and a handſome dwelling houſe erected in its ſtead : to this caſtle belongs a privilege of fairs and markets, granted by ſeveral patents ; fairs held 22 Nov. This is a rectory in dioc. of Cork.

KILBRONEY, ſit. near *Roſe-Trevor*, in bar. upper Iveagh, co. Down, prov. Ulſter ; where are the ruins of the old pariſh church. It is a rectory in dioc. of Dromore.—Alſo a vicarage in dioc. of Cloyne, ſit. in bar. Fermoy, co. Cork, prov. Munſter.

KILCARN, ſit. near *Navan*, co. Meath, prov. Leinſter.

KILCAROON, ſit. in bar. Offa, co. Tipperary, prov. Munſter.

KILCASH, a handſome ſeat of the *Butler* family, from thence called the *Butler's of Kilcaſh*, ſit. in bar. Iffa, &c. co. Tipperary, prov. Munſter, near a ſmall village of ſame name, where fairs are held on 5 Aug. The latter is a vicarage in dioc. of Liſmore.

KILCHAIRPRE, ſit. in the territory of Tirfiachra, which adjoins the river Moy, in co. Sligo, prov. Connaught ; at which place a church was founded by St. *Carpreus* about the year 500.

KILCLARAN, a fair town in co. Clare, prov. Munſter ; fairs held 31 May and 2 Dec.

KILCLEEHEEN, ſit. in co. Kilkenny, prov. Leinſter, on the river *Suir*, oppoſite Waterford. Here a nunnery was founded in 1151 by *Dermod* ſon of *Murchard* king of Leinſter : it was endowed by *John* earl of *Moreton*, lord of Ireland, and afterwards king of England, and by *David Fitzmilo* : the whole was granted to the corporation of Waterford, 20 Nov. 26th queen *Eliz.*

KILCLIEF, a caſtle with lands belonging to it, ſit. in co. Down, prov. Ulſter ; 'tis ſeated (as alſo the church of that name) on the entrance into the bay of *Strangford*, in bar. Lecale : this caſtle and lands were an antient ſee, houſe and manor belonging to the biſhops of *Down*, and is now a rectory in dioc. of Down : it was there that *John Cely*, biſhop of that ſee, publicly cohabited with *Lettice Thombe* a married woman, for which ſcandal, *Swain*, archbiſhop of *Armagh*, had him ſerved with a monitory proceſs in his caſtle of *Kilclief*. There was a chamber in the caſtle called the *Hawk's chamber*, where 'tis ſaid the biſhop's falconer and hawks were kept ; yet poſſibly this tradition may have been taken up from the figure of a fowl reſembling a *hawk*, carved on a ſtone chimney piece, in a room on the ſecond floor, on which alſo is cut in bas-relief a croſs patee ; the caſtle has been preſerved, but covered with thatch ; it is a large building, and the firſt floor of it vaulted ; has two front wings, in one of which is a ſtair-caſe, and in the other a ſtack of cloſets ; the lands ſurrounding the caſtle are a fine demeſne, and ſome of the beſt land in the bar. on which there is a water mill. An hoſpital for lepers was founded here under the patronage of St. *Peter* ; there was alſo an abbey for regular canons, over which St. *Eugene* and St. *Niall* preſided.

KILCLOGHAN, ſit. in bar. Shelburne, co. Wexford, prov. Leinſter : here a preceptory for Knts. Templars was founded by *O'More* ; a leaſe of which was granted 30th queen *Eliz.* to ſir *Henry Harrington*, knt.

KILCOCK, a fair and poſt town ſit. in bar. Ikeath, co. Kildare, prov. Leinſter, 14 miles from Dublin, ſit. on a branch of the *river Liffey* ; fairs held 25 Mar. 11 May, Aug. and 29 Sept. This place ſtands on the great road from Mullingar to Longford : an antient monaſtery was erected here, dedicated to St. *Colcha*, who was honoured here annually on 6 June.

KILCOE, ſit. in bar. Carbery, co. Cork, prov. Munſter ; an inconſiderable village, but it is a vicarage in dioc. of Roſs.—Alſo a rectory in dioc. of Down, ſit. in bar. upper Iveagh, co. Down, prov. Ulſter.

KILCOGNY, a fair town in co. Cavan, prov. Ulſter ; fairs held 25 May and 3 Aug.

KILCOLEMAN, a ruined caſtle of the earls of *Deſmond*, 2 miles N. W. of *Doneraile*, in bar. Barretts, co. Cork, prov. Munſter ; celebrated for having been the reſidence of the immortal *Spencer*, where he compoſed his excellent poem called " *the Fairy Queen* :" the caſtle is now almoſt level with the ground, and was ſit. on the N. ſide of a fine lake, in the midſt of a vaſt plain, terminated to the E. by the co. Waterford mountains, Ballyhoura-hills to the N. (or as *Spencer* terms them, the *mountains of Mole*) Nagle mountains to the S. and Kerry mountains

mountains to the W. It commanded a view of above half the breadth of Ireland, and mult have been, when the adjacent uplands were wooded, a moft pleafant and romantic fituation ; from whence no doubt, *Spencer* drew feveral parts of the fcenery of his poem. Here is a parifh of this name, which is a rectory in dioc. of Cloyne. — Alfo a vicarage in dioc. of Killaloe, fit. in bar. Ballibritt, King's co. prov. Leinfter. — Alfo a rectory in dioc. of Limerick, fit. in bar. Connello, co. Limerick, prov. Munfter. — Alfo a rectory in dioc. of Tuam, fit. in bar. Clanmorris, co. Mayo, prov. Connaught.—Alfo a vicarage in dioc. of Achonry, fit. in bar. Coftello, in fame co. and prov.—Alfo a curacy in dioc. of Ardfert, fit. in bar. Truaghnacmy, co. Kerry, prov. Munfter.

KILCOLGAN, fit. in bar. Dunkellin, co. Galway, prov. Connaught ; it is a vicarage in dioc. of Kilmacduagh. Here was an abbey, over which St. *Colgan* was abbot in 580. There was alfo another abbey of fame name in this co. founded by St. *Columb-Kill*. — Alfo a place in King's co. prov. Leinfter, where another abbey was founded by St. *Colgan* before mentioned.

KILCOMKAY, fit. in bar. Upperthird, co. Waterford, prov. Munfter.

KILCOMMON, fit. near *Birr*, King's co. prov. Leinfter.

KILCOMODON-HILL, fit. near *Aughrim*, in co. Galway, prov. Connaught : at this place was fought the famous battle of Aughrim, on 12 July, 1691, between the Englifh and Irifh forces, in which St. *Ruth* who commanded the latter, loft his life, and the former obtained a complete victory.

KILCONERY, fit. in bar. Bunratty, co. Clare, prov. Munfter.

KILCONNEL, a bar. with a village in it of fame name, fit. in co. Galway, prov. Connaught, 78 miles from Dublin ; here are the magnificent ruins of an antient abbey ; this place is a vicarage in dioc. of Clonfert. Fair days 9 May 4 Aug. and 11 Nov. A monaftery for Francifcan friars was founded here in 1400, by *Wm. O'Kelly*.—Alfo a rectory in dioc. of Cafhel, fit. in bar. Middlethird, co. Tipperary, prov. Munfter.

KILCONWAY, a bar. in co. Antrim, prov. Ulft.

KILCOO, a village fit. in bar. upper Iveagh, co. Down, prov. Ulfter ; it is a vicarage in dioc. of Down.

KILCOOL, fit. in bar. Newcaftle, co. Wicklow, prov. Leinfter, 16 miles from Dublin ; here are the ruins of a church and a fmall inn : between Kilcool and the fea, is the celebrated falt marfh of *Cooldrofs*, remarkably efficacious in curing furfeited horfes. Kilcool is a vicarage in dioc. of Dublin, and holds fairs on Whit. Mond. and 4 Sept.

KILCOOLY, a fair town in bar. Slewardagh, co. Tipperary, prov. Munfter ; fairs held 6 April and 10 Oct. It is a rectory in dioc. of Cafhel. *Donagh Carbragh O'Brien* founded an abbey here for Ciftertian monks about the year 1200.—Alfo a rectory in dioc. of Elphin, fit. in bar. Rofcommon, co. Rofcommon, prov. Connaught, where an abbey was founded by St. *Olchan*. — Alfo a curacy in dioc. of Meath, fit. in bar. Navan, co. Meath, prov. Leinfter.—Alfo a vicarage in dioc. of Clonfert, fit. in bar. Leitrim, co. Galway, prov. Connaught.

KILCOONAGH, a rectory in dioc. of Tuam, fit. in bar. Clare, co. Galway, prov. Connaug.

KILCORBAN, a fair town in co. Galway, prov. Connaught ; fairs held 18 Sept. Here are the ruins of a chapel, now under the invocation of the Virgin Mary, but originally dedicated to St. *Corban*, who died in 732. *Thomas Burgh*, bifhop of Clonfert, in 1446 granted this chapel with fome land adjoining thereto, to the friars of the third order of St. Dominick, at the earneft requeft of *John Fitz Rery* vicar general of that order, and his brethren. This donation was confirmed by the bull of pope Eugene IVth. dated 15 March 1446. The ftatue of the Virgin Mary, which was worfhipped in that chapel, is ftill preferved by the family of the *Burghs* of Palluis, and many miracles ufed to be afcribed to it.

KILCORKEY, a fair town in bar. Ballintobar, co. Rofcommon, prov. Connaught. Fairs held 17 March, 1 Thurfd. May, 3 Aug. and 29 Sept. It is a vicarage in dioc. of Elphin.

KILCOURSEY, fee *Killcourfey*.

KILCOW, a feat near *Caftle ifland*, in co. Kerry, prov. Munfter.

KILCREA, a large tract in the co. Cork, prov. Munfter, formerly Bog-land, but now much reclaimed and improved, it was once the eftate of the earl of *Clancarty* ;—alfo the name of a caftle in the parifh of *Killonane* in faid co. it is a ftrong building, having an excellent ftair-cafe of a dark marble, from bottom to top, about 70 feet high : it ftands a little S. of the river *Bride* ; the Barbicans platforms and ditch ftill remain. Near this caftle are fome quarries of a fine cloudy grey marble, which takes a good polifh ; about 2 fields E. of this caftle, are the ruins of the *abbey* of *Kilcrea*, founded by *Cormac*, furnamed *Laidar*, lord *Mufkerry*, for *Francifcans* ; he alfo built the before-mentioned caftle, and was buried in this abbey 1494 ; it was dedicated to St. *Bridget*, and began (according to *Ware*) in 1465, but the *Ulfter* annals place it in 1478 ; the number of bones and human fculls ftrewed about

about this place, shew it to have been once a very great cemetery; a great part of this building still remains, amongst which is the nave and choir of the church; on the S. side of the former, is a handsome arcade of three gothic arches, supported by marble columns thicker than those of the *Tuscan* order. This arcade continues to form one side of a chapel, being a cross ayle; in the choir are some old tombs, several of the lords *Clancarty* being here interred, as were the *Barrets*, and other principal persons of the country, who always opposed the entire demolishing of this pile; the steeple is a light building, about 80 feet high, placed between the nave and the choir, it is still entire, and supported by gothic arches; from the gateway of this abbey to the road, there are high banks on either side, formed entirely of human bones and skulls, cemented together with moss; at the end of a lane leading to this ruin, stands a large wooden cross, which has remained there ever since the demolition of the abbey; and this entrance to the abbey, is by an avenue of venerable oak.

KILCREDAN, a vicarage in dioc. of Cloyne, sit. in bar. Imokilly, about 3 miles E. of *Castlemartyr*, co. Cork, prov. Munster; in it are 2 antient monuments. That on the S. side of the altar, has the following inscription. " *Hic jacet corpus Roberti Tynte Militis Aureti, hujus provinciæ Regis consiliis, Filii Edmund Tynte de Wrexhall comitatu somersetensi in Anglia Armigeri, qui honorem suum gladio acquisivit. Hanc Ecclesiam atque monumentum fieri fecit, Dei Omnipotentis Providentia. An. Dom.* 1663.

KILCREUNTA, sit. in co. Galway, prov. Connaught, it is called also the *nunnery of the chaste wood*: it was founded about the year 1200 by *Cathal O'Conor Croaderg*, for nuns of the Benedictine order.

KILCRIST, sit. in co. Galway, prov. Connaught, 89 miles from Dublin; about 2 miles beyond which are the ruins of a church.

KILCROHAN, a large parish, being a rectory in dioc. of Ardfert, sit. in bar. Dunkerron, co. Kerry, prov. Munster; reaching from a river called *Blackwater* in this co. to the bay of Ballinskeligs, being about 14 Irish miles in length, and 5 or 6 miles up the country towards the mountains. In this parish about a mile from the church, is a curious hermitage or cell, hewn out of the solid rock, sit. on the top of a hill, by some antiquarians said to have been the residence of St. *Kieran*, when he composed his rule for monks. It is sometimes written *Kilcroghan*. At Aghamore towards the Western extremity of this parish are the remains of a small abbey for canons regular of St. Augustin, which was founded by the monks of St. *Finbar* in the 7th century.

There is also in this parish at *Cahirdoncl*, a circular fortification of large stones, 7 feet high, said to be the work of the Danes.—Also a vicarage in dioc. of Cork, sit. in bar. Carbery, co Cork, prov. Munster.

KILCULLEN, a bar. having a village in it of same name, sit. in co. Kildare, prov. Leinster; 'tis a fair and post town, 21 miles from Dublin. Here is a pretty church, on a hill, with a round tower, about half its original height. This town gave title of baron to a branch of the *Eustace* family, and tho' mean and low, was formerly very large, and surrounded by a wall; for you enter thro' an arch at the turn-pike. A monastery was founded here in a very early age. St. *Iserin* was bishop of it, who died in 469. The town and abbey were plundered in the years 936. 944 and 1037. A bridge was built over the river Liffey about a mile to the N. W. of the town, in 1319, by *Maurice Jakis*, canon of the church of Kildare; where another town soon after sprang up, called *Kilcullen-bridge*, and from that time we may date the fall of *old Kilcullen*. A little beyond the 23d mile stone, in a field on the left, is an antient obelisk of a single rude stone, sit. on a rising ground. A mile beyond *old Kilcullen* is *Castlesish*, the seat of *Curtis Crofton*, esq. Fairs held 2 Feb. 25 March, 14 and 22 June, 8 Sept. 2 Oct. and 8 Dec. Kilcullen is a curacy in dioc. of Dublin.

KILCULLEN-BRIDGE, see *Kilcullen.*

KILCUMIN, a vicarage in dioc. of Killalla, sit. in bar. *Tirawly*, co. Mayo, prov. Connaught. (Dr. *Beaufort*) According to Mr. *Seale*, it is sit. in bar. *Erris*.

KILCUMMER, a fair town in co. Cork, prov. Munster; fairs held 24 Apr. July, Sept. and Dec.

KILCUMMIN, a fair town in King's co. prov. Leinster; fairs held 4 May, 5 July and 18 Oct. Also a vicarage in dioc. of Ardfert, sit. in bar. Magunihy, co. Kerry, prov. Munster: it lies 13½ miles from Thurles. Here a priory was founded by Philip of Worcester, who was chief governor of Ireland, A. D. 1184, which he dedicated to St. *Philip*, St. *James* and St. *Cumin*; he filled it with benedictine monks from the abbey of *Glastonbury* in Somersetshire, and appointed *James*, one of the brethren, to be the first prior.

KILCUNIHINE-BAY, sit. near Beerhaven, co. Cork, prov. Munster.

KILDALKEY, a curacy in dioc. of Meath, sit. in bar. Lune, co. Meath, prov. Leinster.

KILDALTON, the antient name of Bessborough, the superb seat of the earl of Bessborough, sit. in bar. Iverk, co. Kilkenny, prov. Leinster. This place was forfeited in the rebellion

Anth.Hib
Pl. I.
Apr. 1794
W.B.delin.
Clayton sculp
Kildare

lion of 1641, and granted to fir *John Ponfoby,* an officer in the parliament army, the direct anceftor of the prefent noble proprietor.

KILDANGON, a. fair town in bar. Ophaly, co. Kildare, prov. Leinfter; fairs held 1 May; 20 July and 29 Sept. It is a rectory in dioc. of Kildare,: here are the remains of an antient caftle..

KILDARE-COUNTY, fit. in the prov. Leinfter, it is bounded by E. Meath on the N. by Dublin and Wicklow on the E. by Carlow on the S. and by W. Meath and King's and Queen's co. on the W. It is a fine arable country, well watered by the *Barrow, Liffey,* and other rivers, and well inhabited and cultivated, containing 236,750 acres, 113 parifhes, 10 bar.'s, 4 boroughs, and returns 10 members to parliament. It is about 32 miles from N. to S. and 21 from E. to W. chief town *Kildare,* and gives title of earl to the noble family of *Fitzgerald.* Its bar.'s are Carbery or Carbury, Ikeath and Oughterancy, Claine, Salt, Naas, Great Connel, Ophaly, Kilcullen, Narragh and Rheban, Kilkea and Moon, number of houfes about 11,205, and inhabitants about 56,000. It was antiently called *Chille-dair,* i. e. (according to fome) the wood of oaks, from a large foreft which comprehended the middle part of this co. in the centre of this wood was a large plain, facred to heathen fuperftition, and at prefent called the *Curragh of Kildare;* at the extremity of this plain, about the commencement of the 6th century, St. *Brigid* one of the heathen veftals, on her converfion to the chriftian faith, founded with the affiftance of St. *Conlœth,* a church and monaftery near which after the manner of the Pagans, St. *Brigid* kept the facred fire in a cell, the ruins of which are ftill vifible. The principal antient families of this co. are the Fitzgeralds, Euftaces, Allens and Wogans.

KILDARE *town,* a borough, poft and fair town, being the principal town in co. Kildare, prov. Leinfter, fit. in bar. Ophaly, 24 miles S. W. of Dublin. Lat. 53: 8, lon. 7: 24. It returns 2 members to parliament; patron, the duke of *Leinfter.* The church of Kildare is faid to have been founded by St. *Coulœth,* in the latter end of the 5th or beginning of the 6th century: it feems to have been one of the primitive churches of Ireland, and what is termed a mother church, numbers of which were deemed in fubfequent periods, bifhopricks, tho' few, prior to the 10th century, were other than convents of regular canons, who refided in or near their churches with their families and pupils or difciples, where they inftructed youth in the principles of learning and religion. Under this circumftance Kildare was one of the antient fchools or academies of Ireland,

during the middle ages. Of the original church and city of Kildare, there are at prefent no remains; both the church and other buildings being frequently plundered and deftroyed by the Danes. This church however was very early erected into a cathedral, with epifcopal jurifdiction, which dignity it retains to this day; and to it is annexed the deanery of *Chrift's-church* in Dublin. This fee is rated in the king's books at 52*l.* 3*s.* 6*d.* but is worth 2,600*l.* per ann. The cathedral now ferves for the parifh church, which is a rectory in dioc. of Kildare; near it is a round tower in good prefervation; it is 130 feet in height, built of white granite, to about 12 feet above the ground, and the reft of common blue ftone; the door is 14 feet from the foundation: the pedeftal of an old crofs is to be feen here, and the upper part of a crofs lies near it on the ground. According to fome accounts St. *Brigid,* an illegitimate daughter of an Irifh chieftain, was the original founder of the church and convent of Kildare about the year 484, which afterwards came into the poffeffion of the regular canons of St. Auguftin. 'Tis faid St. *Brigid* died 1 Feb. 523, and was here interred, but that her remains were afterwards removed to the cathedral church of Down. From other authorities it appears that St. *Brigid* was not a native of Ireland, but of Nerica in Sweden; that neither fhe or her nuns were known before the year 1360; that their rule was nearly the fame as that of St. Auguftin, and both nuns and monks refided in the fame monaftery, that is, in one part the women, and in the other the men, and both under the government of the abbefs, and her fuffragan the abbot; fo that we fhould conclude from hence, that all early accounts of Brigidines in Ireland are unfounded. It feems likewife that the regular order of St. *Auguftin,* was not founded before 1139 by pope *Innocent* IId. The church however of Kildare, and its fchool flourifhed for fome years; but about the year 770, the town and abbey were unfortunately deftroyed by fire. It was however foon rebuilt, and nearly regained its priftine fplendour. In the year 638 *Aod Dubh* or *Black Hugh,* king of Leinfter, abdicated his throne, and took on him (it is faid) the Auguftinian habit in this abbey; he was afterwards chofen abbot and bifhop of Kildare, and died on the 10th May. In 756, *Eiglitigin* the abbot, who was alfo bifhop of Kildare, was killed by a prieft, as he was celebrating mafs at the altar of St. *Brigid;* fince which time no prieft whatfoever was allowed to celebrate mafs in that church in the prefence of a bifhop. In 830, *Ceallach M'Brann,* an Irifh chieftain of the Eaftern parts of the co. Kildare, plundered both the town and abbey, during

ing which a number of the clergy were slain: about 5 years after, Farannan, abbot of Armagh, attended by a number of his clergy, visited this place, probably to repair and re-establish the monastery, but was seized by Fethlemid, son of Crimthan, and made captive. In 836, the Danes burnt the town and monastery of Kildare, and are said to have carried away the shrine of St. Conlæth. In 843, the Danes made another attack on Kildare, and slew Cudinasgh the prior with several others. So attached were the clergy or monks to their antient dwellings, that they constantly repaired them, and suffered the same depredations from these plunderers in 882; when M'Duff Davorean with his family, and 280 of the clergy and students were carried into captivity. In 887, 889, 895 and 920 the Danes also plundered this town. In 907, Cormac the king and archbishop of Cashel, gave his horse, one ounce of gold, and an embroidered vestment to this abbey; but which with other rich articles, were taken by the Danes of Dublin and Waterford in 924, 926 and 927. In 962, the town was almost entirely destroyed by the Danes, and the greater part of the inhabitants captured. Notwithstanding these frequent losses, the collegiate school of Kildare still continued, and professors constantly resided here. The number of people who frequented this seat of learning, made it constantly an object to the Danish plunderers, for in 965, 992, 998 and 1012 they plundered this town, and in the last mentioned year destroyed it by fire; and in 1016 the Danes of Dublin, under the command of Sitric Mac Amhlaf, laid waste the town. The buildings, which after the frequent depredations were rebuilt, consisted of wattled cottages, and were therefore easily destroyed either by premeditated or accidental fire. Whence in 1018 the whole town except one house was destroyed by lightning: it was also destroyed by fire in 1038, 1040, 1071, 1098 and 1099. During these periods flourished the professors or teachers Cosgrach, Diermit O'Lachan, M'Dougal, and several others. In 1096 a council was held in Ireland by Moriertach O'Brien, amongst other subjects to consider of the repair of churches, when it is probable the church of Kildare was erected of stone. In 1143 and 1155 the town and all its edifices were destroyed by fire. In 1220, Hen. de Loundres, archbishop of Dublin, extinguished the fire called inextinguishable, which was kept here for superstitious purposes, in a small cell or house near the church, 20 feet square, some ruins of which are still visible, and called the fire house. This fire was however relighted, and continued to burn 'till the total suppression of monasteries. Soon after the arrival of the English, the town and

church came into their possession, and a castle was erected for the security thereof by the de Vescies, to whom the town and district were granted. In 1229, the cathedral, if not rebuilt, was repaired and beautified at great expence by the bishop, Ralph de Bristol. In 1260, William de Vescy, then earl of Kildare, began a monastery for friars of the Francifcan order on the S. side of the town, but it was compleated by Gerald Fitz-Maurice, lord Offaly, in 1271, the ruins of which are still visible. About the year 1291, John Fitz-Thomas, lord Offaly, having a quarrel with William de Vescy earl of Kildare and lord justice of Ireland, when de Vescy refused to decide the contest by single combat, according to the custom of the times, the king granted the town and manor of Kildare, with most of the de Vescy's other property to the said lord Offaly, who became the first earl of Kildare of the Geraldines in 1316. In 1294 Calbhach O'Connor having taken arms against the English, took the castle of Kildare, and burnt the rolls and tallies belonging to the manor, and wasted the adjacent country, but was defeated in 1307 by the lord Offaly, and obliged to return to Hy Falia, his own district in the King's co. In 1309 a parliament was held in this town, but we have no account of the business transacted by it. About the year 1486, bishop Lane founded a college in the co. of Kildare, in which the Dean and Chapter might live in a collegiate manner, but of which there are now no remains. David O'Buge, who was born in this town, celebrated for his found erudition, and in the highest estimation at Oxford and Treves, having written many learned works, flourished about the year 1320, and died in the Carmelite monastery founded here by Wm. de Vescy in 1290. The ruins of this Carmelite monastery or White friars, are seen a little to the W. of the present town, but of no great extent, and was granted at the dissolution to Anth. Deeringe, in 1585. In the reign of queen Eliz. this town suffered severely; bishop Daly was three times turned out of his house almost naked, and plunder'd by the rebels; so that in 1600, all the houses were in ruins, and without a single inhabitant. This with the almost total alienation of the church lands, by the bishops Craik and Pilfworth, from 1560 to 1604, prevented the town of Kildare from rising again to distinction. In 1643 a garrison was established in the castle by the earl of Castlehaven, which in some measure re-assembled the inhabitants, but the cathedral which had gone much to decay in the time of Hen. VIIth. and was repaired by bishop Lane, was nearly destroyed in 1641, and the steeple beat down by cannon. In 1647 colonel Jones took the

town

town upon quarter, but it was foon after retaken by the Irifh, who held it 'till the beginning of June 1649, when it was repoffeffed by the lord lieutenant. The prefent town which feems to be fit. Eaftward of the antient, ftands boldly on a rifing ground, and confifts of the church, part of the caftle ftill inhabited, the co. infirmary, the parifh fchool adjoining the church, a roman catholic chapel, a market houfe; and about 180 houfes, moft of which however are wretched cabbins. In the reign of *James* the Ift it was inftituted a borough, governed by a fovereign, recorder, and two portrieves. Here are no manufactures, except a fmall one of felt-hats, and the general fcarcity of water muft in a great meafure prevent any being eftablifhed. It has four fairs yearly, held on 12 Feb. 26 April, 12 May and 19 Sept. There appeared here a fubject of natural hiftory worthy of notice, which came to the poffeffion of Mr. *Daniel Bagot*, furgeon of the co. infirmary. It was taken from the head of a woman fome years fince, and in every refpect refembles a ram's horn, containing feveral volutes, forming a fcroll about 2 inches diameter. There were two growing on the fame head, but this was the largeft and moft perfect.

KILDAVAN, or *Kildavin*, a fmall village fit. in bar. Forth, co. Carlow, prov. Leinfter.— Alfo a rectory in dioc. of Ferns, fit. in bar. Forth, co. Wexford, prov. Leinfter.

KILDIMMA, fit. near *Adaire*, co. Limerick, prov. Munfter; a monaftery was founded here by one *Dimma* a prieft, before the arrival of St. Patrick in Munfter; and at this day retains its antient name.

KILDORERY, a fair town in bar. Condons, co. Cork, prov. Munfter, 107 miles from Dublin. Here are the ruins of *Ballynamana* caftle. Fairs held 1 May, 27 June, 3 Sept. and 27 Nov. It is a vicarage in dioc. of Cloyne.

KILDROGHILL, a fair town in co. Kildare, prov. Leinfter; fairs held laft Tuefd. in April, 8 Sept. and 7 Nov.

KILDYSART, a fair town in bar. Clanderlogh, co. Clare, prov. Munfter, 122 miles from Dublin. Here are the ruins of *Kildyfart caftle*. Fairs held 22 May and 27 Aug. This is a vicarage in dioc. of Killala; it is otherwife written *Kildifart*.

KILEBBANE, fit. in bar. *Ballyadams*, Queen's co. prov. Leinfter, about 4 miles S. W. of Athy. St. *Abban* built a fumptuous monaftery here, about A. D. 650; it is now a rectory in dioc. of Leighlin. *(Archd. Monaft.)* According to Dr. *Beaufort's* memoir, it is in bar. *Slewmargy*.

KILEDELLIG, fit. in bar. upper Offory, Queen's co. prov. Leinfter, 2 miles S. W. of Aghaboe. Here a monaftery was founded, which afterwards became a parifh church, but is gone to ruin. St. *Cuanan* of Kiledellig died A. D. 721.

KILEMLY, or *Killemlagh*, a rectory in dioc. of Ardfert, fit. in bar. Iveragh, co. Kerry, prov. Munfter: it has fome very good land near the church, which is in ruins, and was dedicated to St. *Finian*. It ftands at the bottom of a long bay formed by *Puffin-ifland* to the N. and by *Bolus-head* to the S. in which there is generally a prodigious rolling fea, from the great Weftern ocean; it hath only one fmall creek towards the North part, where a boat can poffibly land. From this bay, the iflands of *Skeligs* range in a direct line, W. S. W.

KILENHA, fit. in bar. Magunihy, co. Kerry, prov. Munfter.

KILEVALLY, a fair town in co. Weftmeath, prov. Leinfter; fairs held 12 June and 23 Oct.

KILFADOW, fit. in bar. Clanderlaw, co. Clare, prov. Munfter.

KILFANE, a rectory in dioc. of Offory, fit. in bar. Gowran, co. Kilkenny, prov. Leinfter: it lies about 7 miles from Kilkenny. Here St. *Fian* erected an abbey.

KILFARGUS, fit. in bar. Connillo, co. Limerick, prov. Munfter: it is a vicarage in dioc. of Limerick, and otherwife called *Kilfergus*.

KILFEARMAGH, fee *Killfiernagh*.

KILFENORA, a village fit. in bar. Corcomroe, co. Clare, prov. Munfter, 125 miles from Dublin. It is a vicarage in the dioc. of fame name, Kilfenora having been eftablifhed as a bifhoprick about the 12th century: it was united to *Killaloe* in 1752. This bifhoprick extends only 18 miles by 9, and is confined to the bar.'s of Burrin and Corcomroe. It is otherwife called *Tenabore*. The cathedral is very antient but in good repair; the nave is full of old family ornaments, and in the choir is that of St. *Fechnan*, its original founder, having the effigies of the St. carved at full length. Here are alfo feven croffes, each of which is formed of a fingle ftone; and ornamented with very antient fculpture. The annals of Munfter tell us that *Murogh O'Brien* burnt the abbey of Kilfenora, and flew many people therein, A. D. 1055. Fairs held here Wednefd. before Whit. Sund. and 9 Oct. Lat. 52 : 45 N. lon. 9 : 10 W.

KILFENY, fit. in bar. Connillo, co. Limerick, prov. Munfter.

KILFENY-COMMON, fit. in co. Limerick, prov. Munfter; where fairs are held on 15 May, 14 July, 12 Sept. and 22 Dec.

KILFER-

KILFERGUS, fee *Kilfurgus*.

KILFIACLE, a fair town in co. Tipperary, prov. Munfter; fairs held 10 July.

KILFIN, a fair town in co. Kerry, prov. Munfter, 138 miles from Dublin. Within 2½ miles of which are the ruins of a church. Fairs held 11 and 12 May, 7 and 8 July, Oct. and 5 Nov.

KILFINANE, a fair town in bar. Cofhlea, co. Limerick, prov. Munfter; where there is a charter fchool for 20 children: it was built at the expence of *Robert Oliver*, efq; fairs held 19 May, 9 Aug. and 25 Oct. This is a vicarage in dioc. of Limerick.—Alfo a place in bar. Corragh, co. Mayo, prov. Connaught; where an abbey was founded by St. *Finan*, but it was only of fhort duration.

KILFREE, a vicarage in dioc. of Achonry, fit. in bar. Coolavin, co. Sligo, prov. Connau.

KILGARVAN, fit. in bar. Glanerought, co. Kerry, prov. Munfter, 162 miles from Dublin. This is a fmall mean place, in a very mountainous country; it is a vicarage in dioc. of Ardfert. The river *Roughy* hath its rife in this parifh, and runs into that of *Kenmare*, which is the beft land in the bar. one fide of the vale thro' which this river glides being a fine lime-ftone foil, and well improved and planted.—Alfo a rectory in dioc. of Cloyne, fit. in bar. Great-ifland, co. Cork, prov. Munfter.—Alfo a rectory in dioc. of Ferns, fit. in bar. Shelmaliere, co. Wexford, prov. Leinfter.—Alfo a fair town in co. Weftmeath, prov. Leinfter; fairs held 26 Aug.—Likewife a place near *Burris-o-kean*, co. Tipperary, prov. Munfter.

KILGLASSAN, fit. in bar. Kilmain, co. Mayo, prov. Connaught; 102 miles from Dublin. Within 2 miles of which are the ruins of a caftle; near it is *Cloghan caftle* and *Turin caftle*, two good feats: alfo the ruins of *Cary caftle*, and of an old church.

KILGLASSE, a vicarage in dioc. of Elphin, fit. in bar. Rofcommon, co. Rofcommon, prov. Connaught.—Alfo a vicarage in dioc. of Killala, fit. in bar. Tyreragh, co. Sligo, prov. Connaught.

KILGOBBIN, a fmall village fit. in bar. Half-Rathdown, co. Dublin, prov. Leinfter, 4 miles beyond *Miltown*, and 6 from Dublin. It is a curacy in dioc. of Dublin, and lies in the direct road to *Powerfcourt*, from which it is diftant about 4 miles. Here are the ruins of an antient caftle and church.

KILGOBNET, a parifh and fair town in bar. Decies without, co. Waterford, prov. Munfter; fairs held 22 Feb. 3 May. 11 June, 1 Nov. and 27 Dec. It is a vicarage in dioc. of Lifmore.

KILGOLA, a fair town in co. Cavan, prov.

Ulfter; fairs held 17 Jan. March, 26 Apr. and Nov.

KILGOLBAN-CASTLE, fit. near *Bandon*, co. Cork, prov. Munfter.

KILGORMAN, a vicarage in dioc. of Dublin, fit. in bar. Gorey, co. Wexford, prov. Leinfter. St. *Mogorman* nephew of St. Patrick, was bifhop of this place, but it is now only parochial.

KILGOWEN, fit. on the road to Timolin, near *Kilcullen*, in co. Kildare, prov. Leinfter. Here is an antient pillar, ftone, or monument, which ftands upon a hill, and is about 9 feet above the ground, and 3½ feet thick, it flopes confiderably, and on the S. fide has a rude mark of a crofs in creux. Thefe fpecies of antient monuments fo frequently difcovered in all the Northern nations of Europe, were denominated in Irifh *Gobhian* or *Gobhain* pronounced *Gowen*, and with the tumuli, cromlechs, &c. were the fepulchres of the chiefs and heroes of former times. On the introduction of the chriftian religion, the miffionaries obferving the attachment the people had to their old fepulchres and antient fanes, preached and propagated the principles and tenets of chriftianity at thofe places; on the tumuli, raths, &c. they erected ftone and wooden croffes, and the pillar ftones were converted into croffes by cutting on them the figure in creux. At thefe croffes, baptifm and moft other rites of the chriftian religion were made, and from hence they promulgated the truths of the gofpel.

KILHILL, fit. in bar. Salt, co. Kildare, prov. Leinfter, 6 miles E. of *Naas*. A commandery for knts. hofpitalers was founded here by *Maurice Fitzgerald* in the 13th century. At the fuppreffion of monafteries this commandery was granted to *John Allen*.

KILKEA, a bar. fit. in co. Kildare, prov. Leinfter; it is joined to *Moon*, and commonly called the bar. of *Kilkea and Moon*: it has a village in it of fame name, which is a vicarage in dioc. of Dublin.

KILKEADY, a rectory in dioc. of Killaloe, fit. in bar. Inchiquin, co. Clare, prov. Munfter.—Alfo a rectory in dioc. of Limerick, fit. in bar. Poblebrien, co. Limerick, prov. Munfter.

KILKEARY, a rectory in dioc. of Killaloe, fit. in bar. upper Ormond, co. Tipperary, prov. Munfter.

KILKEEL, a village fit. in bar. Mourne, co. Down, prov. Ulfter; it is a rectory in dioc. of Down, and diftant 65 miles from Dublin.

KILKELLY, a village fit. in bar. Coftello, co. Mayo, prov. Connaught, 2 miles from which is a very beautiful glen, at the bottom of which runs a rivulet, the declivity on each fide being ornamented with different trees and ever-greens.

ever-greens. About the middle of it, there is an echo which repeats a found 7 times, loudly and diftinctly.—Alfo a place fit. near *Virginia*, co. Cavan, prov. Ulfter.

KILKENNY *county*, fit. in prov. Leinfter, bounded by the Queen's co. on the N. Wexford on the E. Waterford on the S. and Tipperary on the W. The foil is rich and fertile, being proper for tillage; it produces plenty of corn, wool, coal and marble; and the country abounds with fine plantations, and is from the purity of the air efteemed extremely healthful. It contains 300,350 acres, 127 parifhes, 9 bar.'s, exclufive of the *co. of the city* of Kilkenny, and the *liberties* of the town of *Callen*, 7 boroughs; and returns 16 members to parliament; it is about 35 miles from N. to S. and 19 from E. to W. and contains about 100,000 inhabitants; chief town *Kilkenny*. Its bar.'s are, Faffachdinning, Gallmoy, Crannagh, Gowran, Shellilogher, Kells, Knocktopher, Iverk and Ida, Igrin and Ibercon. Gilbert Clare, earl of *Gloucefter* and *Hereford*, marrying *Ifabella*, one of the daughters and co-heirefles of William earl Marfhal, received as her dowry the co. of Kilkenny. Amongft the moft antient families of this co. we find that of the *Butlers*.

KILKENNY *town*, fit. in co. Kilkenny, prov. Leinfter, on the river *Nore*, 57 miles S. W. of Dublin: it is a poft town, and one of the moft elegant cities in the kingdom, and the feat of the bifhops of *Offory*; lat. 53 : 24, lon. 8 : 18. It is governed by a mayor, recorder and aldermen. It comprizes two towns, viz. *Kilkenny* fo called, and *Irifh-town*, each of which fends two members to parliament, and together are computed to contain about 20,000 inhabitants. This city was once of great confequence, as may be feen by the venerable ruins yet remaining of churches, monafteries and abbeys; which even now in their delapidated ftate exhibit fuch fpecimens of exquifite tafte in architecture, as may vie with any modern improvements; the remains of its gates, towers and walls, fhew it to have been a place of great ftrength; here too at different times parliaments were held, in which fome remarkable ftatutes were paffed; it has 2 churches, and feveral catholic chapels; barracks for a troop of horfe, and 4 companies of foot; a noble caftle belonging to the *Butler* family; and a celebrated free fchool or college, lately rebuilt on a large fcale: it was founded by Pierce or Peter Butler earl of Ormond and Offory, and by his wife the countefle of Ormond, the lady Margaret Fitzgerald, fifter to Gerald then earl of Kildare. This town is faid to have taken its name from a holy and learned abbot called *Kanicus*, who Holinfhed

tells us was born in the co. Kilkenny, and in his infancy fuckled with the milk of a cow, tho' others fay he was a native of Connaught. A market is held on Wednefdays and Saturdays, and fairs on 5 and 28 March, Thurfd. after Trin. Sunday, 17 Aug. 12 Sept. 11 Oct. and 9 Nov. a charter fchool was opened here in 1745 for 40 boys; to which the Rev. Dr. *Moffom* late dean of Offory, bequeathed 50*l*. Mrs. *Scaak* bequeathed 10*l*. and Mr. *Rich. Dean* 50*l*. the intereft of all which fums is appropriated to the ufe of the fchool; which is likewife endowed by the corporation of Kilkenny with 20 acres of good land, and an annuity of 30*l*. for ever. *Irifh-town* is more properly called the borough of St. *Kanicus* or *Canice*, vulgarly *Kenny*; the patronage of which is in the bifhop of *Offory*. The cathedral ftands in a fequeftered fituation, is a venerable gothic ftile, built above 500 years; clofe to it is one of thofe remarkable round towers, which have fo much engaged the attention of travellers: the bifhop's palace is a handfome building, and communicates by a covered paffage with the church. The caftle was firft built in 1195, on the fcite of one deftroyed by the Irifh in 1173, the fituation in a military view was moft eligible; the ground was originally a conoid, the eliptical fide abrupt and precipitous, with the river running rapidly at its bafe; there the natural rampart was faced with a wall of folid mafonry, 40 feet high, the other parts were defended by baftions, courtins, towers and outworks, and on the fummit the caftle was erected. This place, as it now ftands, was built by the anceftors of the dukes of Ormond, and is now in poffeffion of their defcendant the prefent earl of Ormond; the tholfel and market-houfe are both good buildings; over the latter are a fuit of rooms, in which during the winter, and at races and affizes times, affemblies are held. There are two very fine bridges of cut marble over the *Nore*; *John's bridge* particularly is light and elegant. Here are the ruins of three old monafteries, called St. *John's* St. *Francis's* and the *Black-abbey*, all faid to have been erected by the *Marefchals*, earls of Pembroke: belonging to the latter, are the remains of feveral old monuments, almoft buried in the ruins; the court of St. *Francis-abbey* is converted into the horfe-barrack, and that of St. John's into a foot barrack. In the year 1400 *Robert Talbot* inclofed with walls the better part of the town; this gentleman died in 1415. In the choir of the friars preachers, was buried *Wm. Marfhal* earl Pembroke, who died 12th April 1234; he was intombed with his brother, over whom was placed this epitaph; "*Hic comes eft pofitus Richardus vulnere foffus, Cujus*
fub

fub foffa Kilkenia continet offa." The manufactures chiefly carried on here, are coarfe woollen cloths, blankets of extraordinary fine quality, and confiderable quantities of ftarch; in the neighbourhood alfo, are made very beautiful chimney pieces of that fpecies of ftone called *Kilkenny marble*; they are cut and polifhed by water, a mill for that purpofe (the only one of its kind perhaps in Europe) being invented by the late Mr. *Colles.* The Kilkenny *coal-pits* are within 9 miles of the town; they yield a coal poffeffing many peculiar properties; it is of a bright black, very hard, burns freely, and is found to be admirably adapted for malting, and various purpofes of manufacture. This city came by marriage into the antient family of *Le Defpenceer.* It was incorporated by charter from king James Ift in 1609. On 23 March 1650, *Cromwell* came before it, and fummoned it to furrender, but fir *Walter Butler* as abfolutely refufed, in confequence of which in a few days it was obliged to capitulate. Sir *Walter Butler* and the officers when they marched out, were complimented by *Cromwell,* who faid they were gallant fellows, and that he fhould have gone without the town had it not been for the treachery of the town's men. The *market-crofs* of Kilkenny continued an ornament to the city until 1771, when it was taken down; the date on it was MCCC. Sir *J. Ware* mentions bifhop Cantwell's rebuilding the great bridge of Kilkenny, thrown down by an inundation about the year 1447. It appears alfo that St. *John's* bridge fell down by a great flood in 1564; and on 2 Oct. 1763, by another like circumftance, *Green's bridge* near the cathedral fell, but happily no lives were loft by this latter accident. The borough of St. *Canice* or *Irifhtown* alway enjoyed very antient prefcriptive rights. A clofe roll of 5th Edw. IIId A. D. 1376, forbids the magiftrates of *Kilkenny* to obftruct the fale of victuals in the market of *Irifh-town,* or within the crofs, under the pretence of cuftom for murage: and leaft the ample grants made to Kilkenny might be interpreted fo as to *include Irifh-town,* the corporation of the latter fecured their antient rights by letters patent 15th Edw. IVth A. D. 1474. Thefe renew their former privileges, and appoint a *portrieve* to be chofen every 21 Sept. and fworn into office on the 11 Oct. The portrieve's prifon was at *Troy-gate.* Whenever the mayor of Kilkenny came within *Water-gate,* he dropt down the point of the city fword, to fhew he claimed no pre-eminence within the *borough.* A caftle was erected in this town by *Ranulph* earl of Chefter. In 1793 the Rt. Hon. *Edm. Butler* was created *earl* of Kilkenny.— *Kilkenny* is alfo the name of a rectory in dioc.

of Kilfenora, fit. in bar. Burrin, co. Clare, prov. Munfter.

KILKENNY-WEST, a bar. having a village in it of fame name, fit. in co. Weftmeath, prov. Leinfter; 'tis fo called to diftinguifh it from the city of that name in co. Kilkenny. It lies about 5 miles from *Athlone.* Here are to be feen fome ruins of an abbey or monaftery that belonged to the Knts. Templars. An abbey was founded here in a very early age, the abbot of which (St. *Scainnail)* died in 773. A priory or hofpital was afterwards erected in this town for *Crofs-bearers* (as fir *Js. Ware* thinks) or crouched friars, dedicated to St. *John* the *Baptift.* Some writers erroneoufly attribute the foundation to the family of *Tyrrel;* but from the beft authority it feems that friar *Thomas,* a prieft, and grandfon of fir *Thomas Dillon,* who came into Ireland in 1185, was the founder of this houfe. There was a holy well in this town, dedicated to the *Virgin Mary.*

KILKERRAN, a *bay* fit. in bar. Moycullin, co. Galway, prov. Connaught.

KILKERRANMORE, fit. in bar. Ibawne, co. Cork, prov. Munfter; it is a vicarage in dioc. of Rofs.

KILKERRIL, a vicarage in dioc. of Offory, fit. in bar. Knocktopher, co. Kilkenny, prov. Leinfter.

KILKERRIN, fit. in bar. Tiaquin, co. Galway, prov. Connaught, 83 miles from Dublin; about 3 miles from which are the ruins of a caftle and fome other buildings. At *Kilkerrin houfe* is a frefh water lake of 52 acres extent, ftored with fifh. Kilkerrin is a rectory in dioc. of Tuam.

KILKERRY, fee *Kilkeary.*

KILKEVAN, a rectory in dioc. of Ferns, fit. in bar. Gorey, co. Wexford, prov. Leinfter.—Alfo a vicarage in dioc. of Elphin, fit. in bar. Ballintobar, co. Rofcommon, prov. Connaught.—Alfo a village fit. in bar. Shillela, co. Wicklow, prov. Leinfter.

KILKILVERY, a rectory in dioc. of Tuam, fit. in bar. Clare, co. Galway, prov. Connaug.

KILKYRAN, a vicarage in dioc. of Offory, fit. in bar. Gowran, co. Kilkenny, prov. Leinfter.

KILL, fit. in bar. Half-Rathdown, co. Dublin, prov. Leinfter, 5 miles from the metropolis; not far from which are the ruins of an old church; it is a curacy in dioc. of Dublin.—Alfo a vicarage in dioc. of Kildare, fit. in bar. Salt, co. Kildare, prov. Leinfter, 12 miles from Dublin, having a parifh church belonging to it.—Alfo a feat in the King's co. prov. Leinfter, belonging to John Clarke, efq; diftant 2¼ miles from *Rathangan,* and about 31 miles from Dublin.

KILLACALRA, fit. in bar. Ibercon, co. Kilkenny, prov. Leinfter.

KILLACHAD, fit. in co. Cavan, prov. Ulfter. An abbey was founded here by St. *Tigernach*, (but not the faint of *Clunes*.)

KILLACHILL, fit. near Rofcrea, co. Galway, prov. Connaught.

KILLACOUNTY, a fair town in co. Cork, prov. Munfter; fairs held 5 Aug.

KILLADOON, the feat of lord *Leitrim*, fit. about 1 mile beyond *Celbridge*, in co. Kildare, prov. Leinfter.

KILLADREENY, a chapelry in dioc. of Dublin, fit. in bar. Newcaftle, co. Wicklow, prov. Leinfter.

KILLAFAIN, fit. in bar. Gowran, co. Kilkenny, prov. Leinfter.

KILLAFONA, fit. near Granard, co. Longford, prov. Leinfter.

KILLAG, a rectory in dioc. of Ferns, fit. in bar. Bargie, co. Wexford, prov. Leinfter.

KILLAGAN, a rectory in dioc. of Connor, fit. in bar. Kilconway, co. Antrim, prov. Ulft.

KILLAGH or *Killagha*, a vicarage in dioc. of Clonfert, fit. in bar. Magunihy, co. Kerry, prov. Munfter; in which are the ruins of the abbey of *Killagh*, near the church. It was of the order of canons regular, and called the priory of St. *Mary*, founded by *Geoffry de Maurifcis* in the reign of king Henry IIId. The walls of the church are of a great length and very ftrong, thefe with a noble window of gothic architecture at the E. end ftill remain entire. They are built of lime-ftone, or rather of a dark marble, as are fome other curious window frames, that have hitherto refifted the injuries of time. The manner of building, befide the materials, befpake this ftructure to be much more modern, than the foundation of the abbey. This houfe had very large poffeffions in feveral parts of this country: the adjacent lands are a rich lime-ftone foil, and good pafture ground, fit. on the fide of the river *Mang*: confiderable quantities of wild hops grow near the abbey, which were probably planted here by the monks. The poffeffions and fite of this religious houfe, were on the diffolution of abbeys, granted to capt. *Thomas Spring*, with the patronage of all the parifhes belonging thereto, which he forfeited after the wars of 1641. — Alfo a rectory in dioc. of Meath, fit. in bar. Delvin, co. Weftmeath, prov. Leinfter.

KILLAGHA or *Killaha*, fee *Killagh*.

KILLAGHIN, a rectory in dioc. of Ardfert, fit. in bar. Clanmaurice, co. Kerry, prov. Munfter.

KILLAGHINTOBBER, fit. in bar. Garrycaftle, King's co. prov. Leinfter.

KILLAGHTAN, a vicarage in dioc. of Ardfert, fit. in bar. Clonmacowen, co. Galway, prov. Connaught.

KILLAGHTEE, a rectory in dioc. of Raphoe, fit. in bar. Boylagh, co. Donegal, prov. Ulfter.

KILLAGHY, fit. in bar. Crannagh, co. Kilkenny, prov. Leinfter. St. *Sinchell* the elder, who died 26 Mar. 548, aged 130, was buried in this abbey. It is now deftroyed; and at prefent Killaghy is an appropriate rectory. *(Arch. Monaft.)*

KILLAHA or *Killagha*, fee *Killagh*.

KILLAHALLIEHAN, fit. in bar. Conillo, co. Limerick, prov. Munfter.

KILLAHINY, a curacy in dioc. of Clonfert, fit. in bar. Iraghticonnor, co. Kerry, prov. Munfter.

KILLAHURLER, fit. in bar. Arklow, co. Wicklow, prov. Leinfter: it is a vicarage in dioc. of Dublin.

KILLAHY, a vicarage in dioc. of Offory, fit. in bar. Knocktopher, co. Kilkenny, prov. Leinfter. — Alfo a vicarage in dioc. of Meath, fit. in bar. Balliboy, King's co. prov. Leinfter.

KILLALIATHAN. There are 2 vicarages of this name in dioc. of Limerick, 1 fit. in bar. Poblebrien and the other in bar. Conello, both in co. Limerick, prov. Munfter.

KILLALA, a market, fair and poft-town, in bar. Tirawly, co. Mayo, prov. Connaught, 127 miles N. W. of Dublin. It is a rectory in dioc. of fame name. Here is one of the antient round towers, and the bifhop's houfe. This fee is united to that of *Achonry* in the fame co. It was founded about the fame time as Elphin, and in the following century the fee of *Achonry* was eftablifhed. Killala is rated in the king's books at 23*l* 6*s* 8*d*, and Achonry at 10*l*. but united they are worth 2,000*l* per ann. Fairs held 6 May, 17 Aug. and 8 Nov. Lat. 54 : 7 lon. 9 : 44. This is alfo the name of a village fit. in bar. Farbill, co. Weftmeath, prov. Leinfter.

KILLALAN, a rectory in dioc. of Meath, fit. in bar. Half-Fowre, co. Meath, prov. Leinfter.

KILLALOE, a poft town fit. in bar. Tullagh, co. Clare, prov. Munfter, 86 miles from Dublin. It is otherwife called *Loania*, and was antiently written *Kill-da-lua*, i. e. the church of *Lua* or *Molua*, who founded an abbey near this place: it is a rectory in the dioc. of the fame name. The dioc. of Killaloe was founded early in the 5th century. In the 12th century it was incorporated with the antient bifhoprick of *Rofcrea* founded in 620; and in 1752 the fee of Kilfenora was united to it. It is rated in the king's books at 20*l*. but is worth 2,300*l* per ann. The fee thus united extends thro' part of the co.'s
Clare,

Clare, Tipperary, King's co. Queen's co. Galway and Limerick. St. *Molua* appears to have derived his name from *Loania*, the place of his refidence, as was cuftomary amongft the antient Irifh. On the death of St. *Molua*, St. *Flannan* his difciple, and fon of the chief of the diftrict, was confecrated bifhop of this place at Rome, about the year 639, and the church endowed with confiderable eftates by his father *Theodorick*. At Killaloe is a bridge over the Shannon of 19 arches, below it is a ledge of rocks, which prevents the navigation of this river up to *Lough Derg*; here is a confiderable falmon and eel fifhery, but there is nothing beautiful in the town. except the fituation; the river is navigable to *Carrick-on-Shannon*; there are many antient buildings in and about this town; the cathedral is a gothic edifice in form of a crofs, with the fteeple in the centre, fupported by four arches; it is about 200 feet in length, the fpan of the roof 30 in the clear; the E. window is large and fine; it was built by *Donald*, king of Limerick in 1160, there is a building near it, once the oratory of St. *Molua*, there is another of the fame kind in an *ifland* on the Shannon, having marks of ftill higher antiquity; the fee houfe of the bifhop is at *Clarisford*, near *Killaloe*; Clarisford was the old Englifh name given by the firft fettlers, in or about the time of *Thomas de Clare*, earl of Gloucefter, and was fo called from being the only ford over the *Shannon* into the co. of *Cork*. At Killaloe adjoining the cathedral, are faid to be yet fome relicts of the maufoleum of *Brien Boru*: at the Weftern end was the entrance, now clofed up, but the arch is vifible, fupported by two pillars, which tho' low, are covered with capitals of the *Ionic* order; which is a convincing proof of the elegance of the building, in fo early a time. Lat. 52 : 32, lon. 8 : 51.—Killaloe is alfo the name of a rectory in dioc. of Offory, fit. in bar. Shellilogher, co. Kilkenny, prov. Leinfter.

KILLALONE, fit. in bar. Half-fowre, co. Meath, prov. Leinfter.—Alfo a vicarage in dioc. of Lifmore, fit. in bar. Iffa and Offa, co. Tipperary, prov. Munfter.

KILLALOUGH, fit. in bar. Belfaft, co. Antrim, prov. Ulfter.

KILLAMERY, fit. in bar. *Kells*, co. Kilkenny, prov. Leinfter, about 5 miles S. of Callan. (*Arch. Monaft.*) It is a rectory in dioc. of Offory; (according to Dr. *Beaufort* in bar. *Gowran*) and we are told St. *Gobban*) of which name it feems there were no lefs than *feven* faints) prefided here over 1000 monks.

KILLAMEEN, a vicarage in dioc. of Tuam, fit. in bar. Moycullen, co. Galway, prov. Connaught,

KILLAN, a village fit. in bar. Omagh, co. Tyrone, prov. Ulfter.—Alfo a rectory in dioc. of Kilmore, fit. in bar. Clonchee, co. Cavan, prov. Ulfter.—Alfo a rectory in dioc. of Ferns, fit. in bar. Bantry, co. Wexford, prov. Leinft.

KILLANCOMY, fit. in bar. Ballagheen, co. Wexford, prov. Leinfter.

KILLANCOOLY, a curacy in dioc. of Ferns, fit. in bar. Ballagheen, co. Wexford, prov. Leinfter.

KILLANE, a rectory in dioc. of Offory, fit. in bar. Gowran, co. Kilkenny, prov. Leinfter. Alfo a vicarage in dioc. of Clonfert, fit. in bar. Kilconnel, co. Galway, prov. Connaught.

KILLANULLY, a rectory in dioc. of Cork, fit. in bar. Kinalea, co. Cork, prov. Munfter.

KILLANY, fit. in bar. Louth, co. Louth, prov. Leinfter. — Alfo a rectory in dioc. of Clogher, fit. in bar. Donaghmoyne, co. Monaghan, prov. Ulfter.—Alfo a vicarage in dioc. of Down, fit. in bar. Caftlereagh, co. Down, prov. Ulfter.

KILLANY-BAY, fit. in *Arranmore ifland*, co. Galway, prov. Connaught.

KILLARAGHT, fit. in co. Rofcommon, prov. Connaught, where a nunnery was founded by St. Patrick for the virgin of St. *Ath-atta*. There is another place of fame name in co. Sligo, prov. Connaught, where a like houfe was eftablifhed by the fame faint.

KILLARD, a vicarage in dioc. of Killaloe, fit. in bar. Ibrickin, co. Clare, prov. Munfter; it gave title of *baron* to the family of *Allington*.

KILLARD-POINT, a *cape* fit. near Strangfordbay, in bar. Lecale, co. Down, prov. Ulfter.

KILLARDY, a rectory in dioc. of Cafhel, fit. in bar. Clanwilliam, co. Tipperary, prov. Munfter.

KILLARE, fit. in bar. Rathconrath, co. Weftmeath, prov. Leinfter. It is a rectory in dioc. of Meath. Here we find *three* antient churches: one dedicated to St. *Aid*, another called *Temple Brigid*, and a third the *court* of St. *Brigid*. St. *Aid* was bifhop of this place in 588, in which year he died on 10th Nov. Here were alfo three celebrated wells.

KILLARGY, a vicarage in dioc. of Clogher, fit. in bar. Dromahaire, co. Leitrim, prov. Connaught.

KILLARNEY, a poft and fair town in bar. Magunihy, co. Kerry, prov. Munfter, feated near a fine lake called *Lough Lean* or Lake of *Killarney*, fit. N. W. of Cork, and 143 miles from Dublin; lat. 51 : 52 N. lon. 9 : 30 W. within 1½ mile of this place, are the ruins of *Aghadoe*, an antient bifhoprick united to *Ardfert*, and likewife the ruins of a round tower; within 4 miles of Killarney are the ruins of *Aglifh* church; at this town is the feat and

gardens

gardens of lord *Kenmare*. Fairs are held 4 July and 11 Nov. This is a vicarage in dioc. of Ardfert.

KILLARNEY *Lake*, this beautiful place is fit. near the town of fame name in co. Kerry, prov. Munfter; it is divided properly into 3 parts, called the lower, middle, and upper lake; the Northern or lower lake is 6 miles in length, and from 3 to 4 in breadth; the town of Killarney is fit. on its Northern fhore, the country on this and the Eaftern boundary is rather of a tame character, but is here and there diverfified with gentle fwells, many of which afford delightful profpects of the *lake*, the *iflands*, and furrounding fcenery; the Southern fhore is compofed of immenfe mountains, rifing abruptly from the water and covered with woods of the fineft timber; from the centre of the lake the view of this range is aftonifhingly fublime, prefenting the eye with an extent of foreft 6 miles in length, and from $\frac{1}{4}$ a mile to $1\frac{1}{2}$ mile in breadth, hanging in a robe of rich luxuriance on the fides of two mountains, whofe bare tops rifing above the whole, form a perfect contraft to the verdure of the lower region; on the fide of one of thefe mountains is *O'Sullivan's cafcade*, which falls into the lake with a roar, that ftrikes the timid with awe on approaching it; the view of this fheet of water is uncommonly fine, appearing as if it were defcending from an arch of wood, which over-hangs it above 70 feet in height from the point of view; coafting along this fhore, affords an almoft endlefs entertainment, every change of pofition prefenting a new fcene; the rocks hollowed and worn into a variety of forms by the waves, and the trees and fhrubs burfting from the pores of the faplefs ftone, forced to affume the moft uncouth fhapes, to adapt themfelves to their fantaftic fituations; the *iflands* are not fo numerous in this as in the *upper* lake, but there is one of uncommon beauty, viz. the *ifle of Innisfallen*, nearly oppofite O'Sullivan's cafcade; it contains 18 Irifh acres; the coaft is formed into a variety of bays and promontories, fkirted and crowned with arbutus, holly, and other fhrubs and trees; the interior parts are diverfified with hills and dales, and gentle declivities, on which every tree and fhrub appears to advantage; the foil is rich even to exuberance, and trees of the largeft fize incline acrofs the vales, forming natural arches, with ivy entwining in the branches, and hanging in feftoons of foliage. The promontory of *Mucrufs*, which divides the upper from the lower lake, is a perfect land of inchantment; there is a road carried through the centre of the promontory, which unfolds all the interior beauties of the

place; amongft the diftant mountains *Turk* appears an object of magnificence, and *Mangerton's* loftier, tho' lefs interefting, fummit rears itfelf above the whole. The paffage to the *upper* lake is round the extremity of *Mucrufs*, which confines it on one fide, and the approaching mountains on the other; here is the celebrated rock called the *Eagle's neft*, this rock produces wonderful echoes, a french-horn founded here raifes a concert fuperior to a hundred inftruments, and the report of a fingle cannon is anfwered by a fucceffion of peals, refembling the loudeft thunder, which feems to travel the furrounding fcenery, and die away among the diftant mountains. The *upper lake* is 4 miles in length, and 2 or 3 in breadth, it is almoft furrounded by mountains, from which defcend a number of beautiful cafcades; the iflands in this lake are numerous, and afford an amazing variety of picturefque views. The *centre lake* communicates with the *upper*, it is but fmall in comparifon with the other two, and cannot boaft of equal variety, yet 'tis not deftitute of natural advantages; the fhores are in many places indented with beautiful bays, furrounded with dark groves of trees, fome of which have a moft picturefque appearance when viewed from the water; the *Eaftern* boundary is formed by the bafe of *Mangerton*, down the fteep fide of which defcends a cafcade, vifible for 150 yards; this fall of water is fupplied by a circular lake, near the fummit of the mountain, called the *Devil's punch bowl*, which on account of its immenfe depth, and the continual over-flow of water, is confidered as one of the greateft curiofities in *Killarney*. Dr. *Smith* feems to think that one of the beft profpects this admired lake affords, is from a rifing ground near the ruined cathedral of *Aghadoe*. The *Lake of Killarney* is otherwife called *Lough Lane* or *Loch-lean*, from its being furrounded by high mountains. *Nennius* fays that thefe lakes were encompaffed by four circles of mines, the firft of *tin*, the fecond of *lead*, the third of *iron*, and the fourth of *copper*. In the feveral mountains adjacent to the lakes, are ftill to be feen the veftiges of the antient mines of iron, lead and copper, but *tin* has not as yet been difcovered here; *filver* and *gold* are faid by the Irifh antiquaries to have been found in the early ages, but this is fomewhat doubtful, efpecially in any confiderable quantity; tho' fome filver probably was extracted from the lead ore, and fmall quantities of gold might have been obtained from the yellow *copper* ore of *Mucrufs*. However in the neighbourhood of thefe lakes, were found in the early ages, as well as at prefent, *pebbles* of feveral colours, which taking a beautiful polifh, the antient

Irifh

Irifh wore in their ears, girdles and different articles of their drefs and furniture.

KILLARY, a vicarage in dioc. of Meath, fit. in bar. Slane, co. Meath, prov. Leinfter.

KILLASHEE, fit. in bar. Moydoe, co. Longford, prov. Leinfter, 61 miles from Dublin. It is a rectory in dioc. of Ardagh: 2½ miles beyond which is *Aghnagoe*, and near it the ruins of a church, and near Killafhee are the ruins of a caftle. Fairs are held here 2 Mond. in March, 24 May, 29 Sept. and 1 Wednef. in Dec.

KILLASNET, a vicarage in dioc. of Clogher, fit. in bar. Rofsclogher, co. Leitrim, prov. Connaught.

KILLASPUGBRONE, a rectory in dioc. of Elphin, fit. in bar. Carbury, co. Sligo, prov. Connaught.

KILLASPUGMULLEN, a vicarage in dioc. of Kilfenora, fit. in bar. Corcomroe, co. Clare, prov. Munfter. — Alfo a rectory in dioc. of Cork, fit. in bar. Barrymore, co. Cork, prov. Munfter; otherwife called *Killafpugmullane*.

KILLASSER, a vicarage in dioc. of Achonry, fit. in bar. Gallen, co. Mayo, prov. Connaught.

KILLATHY, a vicarage in dioc. of Cloyne, fit. in bar. Fermoy, co. Cork, prov. Munfter.

KILLAYS, a parifh in co. Leitrim, prov. Connaught, the church of which is diftant 9½ miles from Dublin.

KILLBALLIDUFF, fit. in bar. upper Offory, Queen's co. prov. Leinfter.

KILLBALLYHONE, a vicarage in dioc. of Killaloe, fit. in bar. Moyferta, co. Clare, prov. Munfter.

KILLBALLYMORE, fit. in bar. Clonkelly, co. Fermanagh, prov. Ulfter.

KILLBARMEDAN, a parifh in bar. Upperthird, co. Waterford, prov. Munfter; it is for the moft part arable and pafture, but intermixed with fome bog, rocks and fandy-banks. The lands belong to the fee of Waterford. This is a vicarage in dioc. of Lifmore, and otherwife written *Killbarrymeadon*.

KILLBARRACK or *Kilbarrick*, a village in bar. Coolock, co. Dublin, prov. Leinfter, within 5½ miles of the metropolis. Here are the ruinous remains of a church; and a 1½ mile beyond them is the hill of *Howth*. This is a curacy in dioc of Dublin.

KILLBARRAN, a vicarage in dioc. of Killaloe, fit. in bar. lower Ormond, co. Tipperary, prov. Munfter.

KILLBARRYMEADON, fee *Kilbarmedan*.

KILLBEACON, a vicarage in dioc. of Offory, fit. in bar. Knocktopher, co. Kilkenny, prov. Leinfter.

KILLEFAGH, a vicarage in dioc. of Achonry, fit. in bar. Coftello, co. Mayo, prov. Connau.

KILLBEGG, a rectory in dioc. of Meath, fit. in bar. Kells, co. Meath, prov. Leinfter.

KILLBEGGAN, fee *Kilbeggan*.

KILLBEGNET, a vicarage in dioc. of Elphin, fit. in bar. Half-ballimoe, co. Galway, prov. Connaught.

KILLBEHENNY, a rectory in dioc. of Emly, fit. in bar. Cofhlea, co. Limerick, prov. Munft.

KILLBELFAD, a vicarage in dioc. of Killala, fit. in bar. Tirawly, co. Mayo, prov. Connaug.

KILLBENNAN, a vicarage in dioc. of Tuam, fit. in bar. Downamore, co. Galway, prov. Connaught.

KILLBONANE, a vicarage in dioc. of Ardfert, fit. in bar. Magunihy, co. Kerry, prov. Munfter.—Alfo a vicarage in dioc. of Cork, fit. in bar. Mufkerry, co. Cork, prov. Munfter.

KILLBRACKAN, a vicarage in dioc. of Kildare, fit. in bar. King's co. prov. Leinfter.

KILLBREE, fit. in co. Waterford, prov. Munfter, between *Lifmore* and *Cappoquin*. A caftle here, long fince ruined, is faid to have been built by king *John*; and a houfe has been erected on its foundation. This place appears to have belonged to the Knts. Templars.

KILLBREEDY, a vicarage in dioc. of Killala, fit. in bar. Tirawly, co. Mayo, prov. Connau.

KILLBREEDY-MAJOR, a rectory in dioc. of Limerick, fit. in bar. Cofhma, co. Limerick, prov. Munfter.

KILLBREEDY-MINOR, a rectory in dioc. of Limerick, fit. in bar. Cofhma, co. Limerick, prov. Munfter.

KILLBREW, a rectory in dioc. of Meath, fit. in bar. Ratoath, co. Meath, prov. Leinfter.

KILLBRICKLAN-BRIDGE, fit. in bar. Maryborough, Queen's co. prov. Leinfter.

KILLBRIDETANGAN, a chapelry in dioc. of Meath, fit. in bar. Killcourfey, King's co. prov. Leinfter.

KILLBRIDEVASTY, a vicarage in dioc. of Meath, fit. in bar. Fartullagh, co. Weftmeath, prov. Leinfter.

KILLBRINE, a vicarage in dioc. of Elphin, fit. in bar. Boyle, co. Rofcommon, prov. Connaught.

KILLBRODERAN, a rectory in dioc. of Limerick, fit. in bar. Connello, co. Limerick, prov. Munfter.

KILLBROGAN, a rectory in dioc. of Cork, fit. in bar. Kinalmeaky, co. Cork, prov. Munfter.

KILLBRUE, fee *Killbrew*.

KILLBURNE, a parifh in co. Waterford, prov. Munfter; it is of but fmall extent.

KILLCADDON, fit. near *Killygordon*, in co. Donegal, prov. Ulfter; near it are the ruins of a caftle, feated on a very lofty hill.

KILL-

KILLCALERIN, fit. in bar. Beer and Bantry, co. Cork, prov. Munfter.

KILLCARAGH, fit. in bar. Gualtiere, co. Waterford, prov. Munfter; this parifh joined to Bifhop's-court, is but of fmall extent; there are fome ruins at *Bifhops-court*, probably they were built as a country retreat for the bifhops of Waterford. It is a rectory in dioc. of Waterford.—Alfo a vicarage in dioc. of Ardfert, fit. in bar. Clanmaurice, co. Kerry, prov. Munfter.

KILLCARN, a curacy in dioc. of Meath, fit. in bar. Skryne, co. Meath, prov. Leinfter.

KILLCARN-BRIDGE, fit. over the river *Boyne*, near *Navan*, in co. Meath, prov. Leinft.

KILLCARR, a rectory in dioc. of Raphoe, fit. in bar. Boylagh, co. Donegal, prov. Ulfter.

KILLCARRICK, a village fit. in bar. Idrone, co. Carlow, prov. Leinfter.

KILLCASH, a rectory in co. Waterford, prov. Munfter; the church of which is in ruins.

KILLCASKIN, a vicarage in dioc. of Rofs, fit. in bar. Bear and Bantry, co. Cork, prov. Munfter.

KILLCATERAN, a rectory in dioc. of Rofs, fit. in bar. Bear and Bantry, co. Cork, prov. Munfter.

KILLCASY, a vicarage in dioc. of Offory, fit. in bar. Knocktopher, co. Kilkenny, prov. Leinfter.

KILLCAVAN, a village fit. in bar. *Gorey*, co. Wexford, prov. Leinfter. *(Scale)* A rectory in dioc. of Ferns, fit. in bar. *Bargie*, co. Wexford, prov. Leinfter. *(Dr. Beaufort)*

KILLCHRIST, a village fit. in bar. Dunkellin, co. Galway, prov. Connaught, which is a vicarage in dioc. of Kilmacduagh.—Alfo a vicarage in dioc. of Killaloe, fit. in bar. Clanderlagh, co. Clare, prov. Munfter.

KILLCLEAGH, a vicarage in dioc. of Meath, fit. in bar. Clonlonan, co. Weftmeath, prov. Leinfter.

KILLCLONE, a vicarage in dioc. of Meath, fit. in bar. Deece, co. Meath, prov. Leinfter.

KILLCLONEY, a rectory in dioc. of Armagh, fit. in bar. Fews, co. Armagh, prov. Ulfter.—Alfo a rectory in dioc. of Cafhel, fit. in bar. Eliogurty, co. Tipperary, prov. Munfter.

KILLCLONFERT, a vicarage in dioc. of Kildare, fit. in bar. Phillipftown, King's co. prov. Leinfter.

KILLCLUNEY, a vicarage in dioc. of Clonfert, fit. in bar. Clonmacow, co. Galway, prov. Connaught.

KILLCOAN, a rectory in dioc. of Cork, fit. in bar. Barrymore, co. Cork, prov. Munft.

KILLCOCK, fee *Kilcock*.

KILLCOCKAN, a parifh in co. Waterford, prov. Munfter; the *Black-water* being here of a confiderable breadth, makes a beautiful appearance; its banks on both fides are fcarce any other than lofty hills, fhaded with woods, which in fummer afford very entertaining landfcapes.

KILLCOLA, a vicarage in dioc. of Elphin, fit. in bar. Boyle, co. Rofcommon, prov. Connaught,

KILLCOLEMAN, fee *Kilcoleman*.

KILLCOLEMANBANE, a rectory in dioc. of Leighlin, fit. in bar. Maryborough, Queen's co. prov. Leinfter.

KILLCOLM, a vicarage in dioc. of Offory, fit. in bar. Ida, co. Kilkenny, prov. Leinfter.

KILLCOMACK, a rectory in dioc. of Ardagh, fit. in bar. Rathline, co. Longford, prov. Leinfter.

KILLCOMB, a rectory in dioc. of Ferns, fit. in bar. Gorey, co. Wexford, prov. Leinfter.

KILLCOMEN, fit. in bar. Kilmane, co. Mayo, prov. Connaught.

KILLCOMENA, a vicarage in dioc. of Rofs, fit. in bar. Bear and Bantry, co. Cork, prov. Munfter.

KILLCOMENTY, a rectory in dioc. of Emly, fit. in bar. Arra, co. Tipperary, prov. Munfter.

KILLCOMIN, a rectory in dioc. of Killaloe, fit. in bar. Clonlifk, King's co. prov. Leinfter.

KILLCOMMON, a vicarage in dioc. of Killala, fit. in bar. Erris, co. Mayo, prov. Connaught.—Alfo a vicarage in dioc. of Dublin, fit. in bar. Newcaftle, co. Wicklow, prov. Leinfter.—Alfo a rectory in dioc. of Ferns, fit. in bar. Bantry, co. Wexford, prov. Leinfter.—Alfo a vicarage in dioc. of Tuam, fit. in bar. Moycullin, co. Galway, prov. Connaught.—Alfo a vicarage in dioc. of Tuam, fit. in bar. Kilmain, co. Mayo, prov. Connaug.

KILLCOONDUFF, a vicarage in dioc. of Achonry, fit. in bar. Gallen, co. Mayo, prov. Connaught.

KILLCONENAGH, a rectory in dioc. of Rofs, fit. in bar. Bear and Bantry, co. Cork, prov. Munfter.

KILLCONEY, a rectory in dioc. of Cork, fit. in bar. Courceys, co. Cork, prov. Munfter.

KILLCONICKNY, a vicarage in dioc. of Clonfert, fit. in bar. Loughrea, co. Galway, prov. Connaught.

KILLCONIRAN, a vicarage in dioc. of Clonfert, fit. in bar. Dunkellin, co. Galway, prov. Connaught.

KILLCONLA, a vicarage in dioc. of Tuam, fit. in bar. Downamore, co. Galway, prov. Connaught.

KILLCONLY. There are 2 parifhes of this name, the one fit. in bar. *Iraghticonnor*, the other in bar. *Iveragh*, co. Kerry, prov. Munfter: each is a rectory in dioc. of Ardfert.

KILLCONNEL, fee *Kilconnel*.

KILLCONRY,

KILLCONRY, a vicarage in dioc. of Killa-loe, fit. in bar. Bunratty, co. Clare, prov. Munfter.

KILLCOP, a rectory in bar. Gualtiere, co. Waterford, prov. Munfter; united to that of *Crook*.

KILLCORMUCK, a rectory in dioc. of Ferns, fit. in bar. Ballagheen, co. Wexford, prov. Leinfter.

KILLCORNAN, a rectory in dioc. of Emly, fit. in bar. Clanwilliam, co. Tipperary, prov. Munfter.—Alfo a rectory in dioc. of Limerick, fit. in bar. Kenry, co. Limerick, prov. Munfter.

KILLCORNEY, a rectory in dioc. of Cloyne, fit. in bar. Mufkerry, prov. Munfter.—Alfo a vicarage in dioc. of Kilfenora, fit. in bar. Burrin, co. Clare, prov. Munfter.

KILLCOURSEY, a bar. in King's co. prov. Leinfter: otherwife written *Kilcourfey*, or *Kilcourfie*; it gives title of vifc. to the family of *Lambart*, now *earl of Cavan*.

KILLCROGHAN, a vicarage in dioc. of Lifmore, fit. in bar. Cofhbride, co. Waterford, prov. Munfter.

KILLCRONAGHAN, a rectory in dioc. of Derry, fit. in bar. Loughlinfholen, co. Londonderry, prov. Ulfter.

KILLCRUMPER, a vicarage in dioc. of Cloyne, fit. in bar. Condons, co. Cork, prov. Munfter.

KILLCULLEN, fee *Kilcullen*.

KILLCULLIHEAN, a vicarage in dioc. of Offory, fit. in bar. Idu, co. Kilkenny, prov. Leinfter.

KILLCULLY, a rectory in dioc. of Cork, fit. in the liberties of Cork, prov. Munfter.

KILLCUMNER, a rectory in dioc. of Cloyne, fit. in bar. Fermoy, co. Cork, prov. Munfter.

KILLCUMNEY, a vicarage in dioc. of Meath, fit. in bar. Delvin, co. Weftmeath, prov. Leinfter.

KILLCUMRIRAGH, a chapelry in dioc. of Meath, fit. in bar. Moycafhel, co. Weftmeath, prov. Leinfter.

KILLCURFINN, a vicarage in dioc. of Cloyne, fit. in bar. Barrymore, co. Cork, prov. Munfter.

KILLCURTY, fit. in bar. Dundalk, co. Louth, prov. Leinfter.

KILLDACOMOGE, a rectory in dioc. of Tuam, fit. in bar. Carragh, co. Mayo, prov. Conn.

KILLDALLEN, a rectory in dioc. of Kilmore, fit. in bar. Tullaghonoho, co. Cavan, prov. Ulfter.

KILLDALLOCK, a rectory in dioc. of Connor, fit. in the liberties of Coleraiu, co. Londonderry, prov. Ulfter.

KILLDALLY, fit. near *Killifhandra*, co. Cavan, prov. Ulfter.

KILLDANGAN, fee *Kildangan*.

KILLDEEMO, a village fit. in bar. Kenry, co. Limerick, prov. Munfter: it is a vicarage in dioc. of Limerick.

KILLDELIG, a rectory in dioc. of Offory, fit. in bar. upper Offory, Queen's co. prov. Leinfter.

KILLDEMOCK, a vicarage in dioc. of Armagh, fit. in bar. Ardee, co. Louth, prov. Leinfter.

KILLDERRY, a rectory in dioc. of Offory, fit. in bar. Gowran, co. Kilkenny, prov. Leinfter.

KILLDOWEN, a curacy in dioc. of Dublin, fit. in bar. Salt, co. Kildare, prov. Leinfter.

KILLDRESS, a rectory in dioc. of Armagh, fit. in bar. Dungannon, co. Tyrone, prov. Ulfter.

KILLDRUM, a vicarage in dioc. of Ardfert, fit. in bar. Corcaguinny, co. Kerry, prov. Munfter.

KILLEA, a parifh in bar. Gualtiere, co Waterford, prov. Munfter; towards the extremity of which is *Leper's-town*, formerly bequeathed to the poor of Waterford, and by the Down-furvey, contained 419 acres. It is a vicarage in dioc. of Waterford.—Alfo a rectory in dioc. of Raphoe, fit. in bar. Raphoe, co. Donegal, prov. Ulfter. — Alfo a rectory in dioc. of Cafhel, fit. in bar. Ikerin, co. Tipperary, prov. Munfter.

KILLEAD, a vicarage in dioc. of Connor, fit. in bar. Maffareen, co. Antrim, prov. Ulfter.

KILLEAGH, a fmall village in bar. Imokilly, co. Cork, prov. Munfter, 112 miles from Dublin, and 4 from Youghal, in which is a decent church; it is a rectory in dioc. of Cloyne. At this place was an antient nunnery of Canonefies, founded by St. *Abban* in the 6th century, where he placed St. *Conchere* as priorefs. The rivulet that runs by it is remarkable for its ferpentine courfe, and is accounted good for whitening cloth; it difcharges itfelf into *Youghal bay*. Fairs are held here on 13 June and 12 Nov.

KILLEAK, a curacy in dioc. of Dublin, fit. in bar. Coolock, co. Dublin, prov. Leinfter.

KILLEAN, fit. in bar. Forth, co. Wexford, prov. Leinfter.

KILLEANY, fit. in bar. Delvin, co. Weftmeath, prov. Leinfter.

KILLEAR, a fair town in co. Weftmeath, prov. Leinfter; fairs held 1 Feb.

KILLEARY, fit. in bar. Slane, co. Meath, prov. Leinfter.

KILLEAVY, a rectory in dioc. of Armagh, fit. in bar. Orior, co. Armagh, prov. Ulfter.

KILLEBAN or *Killebane*, a rectory in dioc. of Leighlin, fit. in bar. *Slewmargy*, Queen's co.

co. prov. Leinster. *(Dr. Beaufort)* fit. in bar. *Ballyadams.* *(Scale)*

KILLEDAN, fit. on the river Moy, in bar. Gallen, co. Mayo, prov. Connaught: it is a vicarage in dioc. of Achonry. Here was a friary for conventual Francifcans.

KILL-EDMUND, a fmall town in co. Carlow, prov. Leinfter; within a few miles of *Tullow*, in which is a neat church, built by the late Mr. *Bagnall* of *Dunlakey.* This place is traverfed by a fmall but rapid river, which defcending from *Mount Leinfter*, empties itfelf into the *Barrow* near *Borris*, after a courfe of about 6 miles.

KILLEEDY, a vicarage in dioc. of Limerick, fit. in bar. *Pohlebrien*, co. Limerick, prov. Munfter.—Alfo a rectory in dioc. of Limerick, fit. in bar. *Conillo*, in fame co.

KILLEEN, fit. in bar. Skryne, co. Meath, prov. Leinfter: it is a vicarage in dioc. of Meath. Here is a caftle, the property of lord *Fingal*, adjoining the old church of Killeen: not far from it is *Dunfany caftle*, the feat of lord *Dunfany*: the caftle was built by Hugh de Lacie in 1180; the church was dedicated to St. Mary, and built in the gothic ftyle, beautifully carved: the E. window was of confiderable height; and W. of the church were 2 towers. The ruins of many antient tombs, and feveral figures in the epifcopal habit and mitred, may be feen here. This place is 2 miles S. of *Tarah*. *Chriftopher Plunket* (a perfon of great valour and wifdom, as *Camden* tells us, and who was deputy to Richard duke of York, viceroy in Hen. VIth's time) was raifed to the dignity of *baron* Killeen, which came to him by his wife, whom he married in 1403, and who was daughter and fole heirefs to fir *Lucas Cufack*, lord of Killeen, Dunfany and Gerardftown in co. Meath. Inquifition taken at Trim 13 Apr. 1618, finds that Chriftopher Plunket, baron of Killeen, was feized in fee of the manor of Killeen, in the co. Meath, and of the town and lands of Killeen, containing 380 acres of arable land with the appurtenances, and a mill and watercourfe; 15 acres, part of the faid manor called *Bacon's lands*; the town and lands of *Clowanfton*, 113 acres; the town and lands of *Smith'ftown*, 50 acres; in *Cawleftown* 40 acres; 25s chief rent out of the lands of *Smitefield*; all in the manor of Killeen.

KILLEENY, a curacy in dioc. of Dublin, fit. in bar. Half-Rathdown, co. Dublin, prov. Leinfter.

KILLEEVY, fit. in bar. Orior, co. Armagh, prov. Ulfter.

KILLEGALLY, a vicarage in dioc. of Meath, fit. in bar. Garrycaftle, King's co. prov. Leinfter.

KILLEGAN, a curacy in dioc. of Leighlin, fit. in bar. Talbot'ftown, co. Wicklow, prov. Leinfter.

KILLEGLAN, a rectory in dioc. of Meath, fit. in bar. Ratoath, co. Meath, prov. Leinfter.

KILLEIGH, a fair town in bar. Gethill, King's co. prov. Leinfter, above 46 miles from Dublin; near the church of which, at the foot of a hill, are the ruins of an abbey. This place is only remarkable for the religious houfes founded there at former diftant periods, viz. in 540, a priory for Auguftine canons of the holy crofs of St. *Sincheal*, who was himfelf the firft abbot: a few years after the arrival of the Englifh, a nunnery founded by the family of *Warren* for nuns of the order of St. *Auguftin*; and in the reign of Edw. IIt a houfe for grey friars erected by *O'Connor. Donald O'Brien* guardian of this monaftery was made bifhop of Clonmacnoife in 1303; at the general fuppreffion, this monaftery was granted to *John Allec.* Fairs held 1 June and 16 Oct.—Alfo a fmall village fit. 4 miles from *Youghal*, in bar. Imokilly, co. Cork, prov. Munfter. An abbey was built there by St. *Alban*, who died A. D. 650.

KILLEILAGH, a vicarage in dioc. of Kilfenora, fit. in bar. Corcomroe, co. Clare, prov. Munfter.

KILLEINY, a rectory in dioc. of Ardfert, fit. in bar. Corkaguinny, co. Kerry, prov. Munfter.

KILLELAGH, a village in bar. Armagh, co. Armagh, prov. Ulfter.—Alfo in bar. Clanlonan, co. Weftmeath, prov. Leinfter.

KILLELLY, a rectory in dioc. of Limerick, fit. in bar. Bunratty, co. Clare, prov. Munfter.—Alfo a curacy in dioc. of Ferns, fit. in bar. Ballagheen, co. Wicklow, prov. Leinfter.

KILLEMLAGH, fee *Kilemly*.

KILLEN, a fair town in co. Tyrone, prov. Ulfter; fairs held 4 Dec.—Alfo a fair town in co. Tipperary, prov. Munfter; fairs held 29 May. — Alfo a place in bar. Tinehinch, Queen's co. prov. Leinfter.

KILLENA, fit. in bar. *Gorey*, co. Wexford, prov. Leinfter. *(Scale)*

KILLENAGH, a curacy in dioc. of Ferns, fit. in bar. Ballagheen, co. Wexford, prov. Leinfter. *(Dr. Beaufort)*

KILLENAN, a vicarage in dioc. of Clonfert, fit. in bar. Longford, co. Galway, prov. Conn.

KILLENANE, fit. to the N. of *Cahir*, in co. Kerry, prov. Munfter; this parifh has many mountains towards the fea, which are profitable only during the fummer months; one of them called the *Hag's tooth*, is of a remarkable height, on the N. fide of which are fome romantic

mantic lakes; the N. fides of thefe mountains are wafhed by the fea, which forms one or two creeks; that called *Kells* is capable of fecuring a fmall veffel, as is another more to the W. called *L. Key.*

KILLENAULE, a fair town in bar. Slewardagh, co. Tipperary, prov. Munfter; 'tis a vicarage in dioc. of Cafhel, and fit. mid-way between *Callen* and *Cafhel.* Nothing can be more charming than the country around; but it bears upon the face of it an evident and fufficient caufe for the infurgency of the *Whiteboys,* if infurgency it may be called, where every houfe-keeper difclaims all connections with the poor wretches who were concerned in it. Fairs are held on 1 Thurfd. O. S. May and Oct. Within 2 miles of Killenaule are the ruins of *Grey'ftown* caftle, and ¾ of a mile further the ruins of another caftle.

KILLENEER, fit. in bar. Ferrard, co. Louth, prov. Leinfter.

KILLENEY, a vicarage in dioc. of Kilmacduagh, fit. in bar. Kiltartan, co. Galway, prov. Connaught.

KILLENORE, a curacy in dioc. of Ferns, fit. in bar. Gorey, co. Wexford, prov. Leinfter.

KILLENTERNA, a rectory in dioc. of Ardfert, fit. in bar. Truaghnacmy, co. Kerry, prov. Munfter.

KILLENUMERY, a vicarage in dioc. of Ardagh, fit. in bar. Dromahaire, co. Leitrim, prov. Connaught.

KILLENVOY, a vicarage in dioc. of Elphin, fit. in bar. Athlone, co. Rofcommon, prov. Connaught.

KILLENY, a village fit. in co. Dublin, prov. Leinfter, within 8 miles of the metropolis. The parifh of *Killeny* is united to that of *Monkstown* and *Dalkey;* the church being at Monkstown. At this place there are fome remarkable remains of Druidic antiquities.—Alfo a vicarage in dioc. of Offory, fit. in bar. upper Offory, Queen's co. prov. Leinfter.—Alfo a rectory in dioc. Tuam, fit. in bar. Clare, co. Galway, prov. Connaught.

KILLERAGHT, a vicarage in dioc. of Achonry, fit. in bar. Coolavin, co. Sligo, prov. Connaught.

KILLERVAHAM, fit. in bar. Loughlinfholen, co. Londonderry, prov. Ulfter.

KILLERICK, fit. in bar. Carlow, co. Carlow, prov. Leinfter.

KILLERIN, a rectory in dioc. of Tuam, fit. in bar. Clare, co. Galway, prov. Connaug.

KILLERIES *harbour,* fit. in bar. Ballinahinch, co. Galway, prov. Connaught.

KILLERIG, a vicarage in dioc. of Leighlin, fit. in bar. Catherlogh, co. Carlow, prov. Leinfter.

KILLERMOGH, fit. in bar. upper Offory, Queen's co. prov. Leinfter; it is a vicarage in dioc. of Offory, 2 miles S. of *Durrow.* St. *Columb* founded an abbey here A. D. 558, which is now in ruins.

KILLEROAN, a vicarage in dioc. of Elphin, fit. in bar. *Half-Ballimoe,* co. Galway, prov. Connaught.

KILLERORAN, a vicarage in dioc. of Elphin, fit. in bar. Killihan, co. Galway, prov. Connaught.

KILLERSHERDINY, a vicarage in dioc. of Kilmore, fit. in bar. Tullaharvey, co. Cavan, prov. Ulfter.

KILLERY, a vicarage in dioc. of Ardagh, fit. in bar. Tiraghrill, co. Sligo, prov. Connau.

KILLESHELL, a rectory in dioc. of Armagh, fit. in bar. Dungannon, co. Tyrone, prov. Ulfter.

KILLESHER, a rectory in dioc. of Kilmore, fit. in bar. Clonawly, co. Fermanagh, prov. Ulfter.

KILLESHANDRA, a poft town fit. in bar. Tullaghonoho, co. Cavan, prov. Ulfter, 60 miles from Dublin. Fairs are held here on 28 March, 22 June, 2 Wednefd. O. S. in Aug. and 8 Nov. It is a rectory in dioc. of Kilmore.

KILLESHILL, fit. in bar. Slewmargy, Queen's co. prov. Leinfter.

KILLESK, a curacy in dioc. of Ferns, fit. in bar. Ballagheen, co. Wexford, prov. Leinft.

KILLESKIN, a rectory in dioc. of Leighlin, fit. in bar. Slewmargy, Queen's co. prov. Leinfter.

KILLESOLAN, a vicarage in dioc. of Elphin, fit. in bar. Kilconnel, co. Galway, prov. Connaught.

KILLESTER, an agreeable village fit. 1 mile beyond Donnycarney, and three miles from Dublin, in bar. Coolock, co. Dublin, prov. Leinfter. Here is a handfome feat of Sir *Wm. Gleadow Newcomen,* bart. This place is a curacy in dioc. of Dublin.

KILLETTER, a fair town in co. Tyrone, prov. Ulfter. Fairs held 12 July, 26 Oct. and 19 Nov.

KILLEVAN, a rectory in dioc. of Clogher, fit. in bar. Dartree, co. Monaghan, prov. Ulfter.

KILLEVY, a rectory in dioc. of Armagh, fit. in bar. Orior, co. Armagh, prov. Ulfter.

KILLEYMER, a vicarage in dioc. of Killaloe, fit. in bar. Clanderlagh, co. Clare, prov. Munfter.

KILLFADA, fit. in bar. lower Ormond, co. Tipperary, prov. Munfter.

KILLFARBOY, a vicarage in dioc. of Killaloe, fit. in bar. Ibrickin, co. Clare, prov. Munfter.

KILLFA-

KILLFAUGHNAGHBEG, a vicarage in dioc. of Rofs, fit. in bar. Carbery, co. Cork, prov. Munfter.

KILLFEACLE, a rectory in dioc. of Emly, fit. in bar. Clanwilliam, co. Tipperary, prov. Munfter.

KILLFEDANE, a rectory in dioc. of Killaloe, fit. in bar. Clanderlagh, co. Clare, prov. Munfter.

KILLFEIGHNEY, a vicarage in dioc. of Ardfert, fit. in bar. Clanmaurice, co. Kerry, prov. Munfter.

KILLFENORA, fee *Kilfenora*.

KILLFERA, a curacy in dioc. of Offory, fit. in bar. Shellilogher, co. Kilkenny, prov. Leinfter.

KILLFIAN, a rectory in dioc. of Killala, fit. in bar. Tirawly, co. Mayo, prov. Connaug.

KILLFIERNAGH, (fometimes written *Kil-fearmagh*) a rectory in dioc. of Killaloe, fit. in bar. Moyferta, co. Clare, prov. Munfter.

KILLFINAGHTY, a vicarage in dioc. of Killaloe, fit. in bar. Tullagh, co. Clare, prov. Munfter.

KILLFINTINAN, a vicarage in dioc. of Limerick, fit. in bar. Bunratty, co. Clare, prov. Munfter.

KILLFITHMONE, a rectory in dioc. of Emly, fit. in bar. Eliogurty, co. Tipperary, prov. Munfter.

KILLFLIN, a village in bar. Clanmaurice, co. Kerry, prov. Munfter; it is a vicarage in dioc. of Ardfert.

KILLFRUSH, a vicarage in dioc. of Emly, fit. in bar. Small-county, co. Limerick, prov. Munfter.

KILLGALLY, fit. in bar. Donaghmoyne, co. Monaghan, prov. Ulfter.

KILLGARVEY, a vicarage in dioc. of Achonry, fit. in bar. Gallen, co. Mayo, prov. Conn.

KILLGARUFF, a vicarage in dioc. of Rofs, fit. in bar. Carbery, co. Cork, prov. Munfter.

KILLGARYLANDER, a rectory in dioc. of Ardfert, fit. in bar. Truaghnacmy, co. Kerry, prov. Munfter.

KILLGEFFIN, a vicarage in dioc. of Elphin, fit. in bar. Rofcommon, co. Rofcommon, prov. Connaught.

KILLGERRIE, a vicarage in dioc. of Clonfert, fit. in bar. Clonmacow, co. Galway, prov. Connaught.

KILLGIVOUR, a vicarage in dioc. of Tuam, fit. in bar. Morifk, co. Mayo, prov. Connau.

KILLGLASS, a rectory in dioc. of Ardagh, fit. in bar. Ardagh, co. Longford, prov. Leinft.

KILLGOBANE, a rectory in dioc. of Cork, fit. in bar. Carbery, co. Cork, prov. Munfter.

KILLGOBBAN, a rectory in dioc. of Ardfert, fit. in bar. Corcaguinny, co. Kerry, prov. Munfter.

KILLGRANT, a vicarage in dioc. of Lifmore, fit. in bar. Iffa and Offa, co. Tipperary, prov. Munfter.

KILLGULLANE, a rectory in dioc. of Cloyne, fit. in bar. Condons, co. Cork, prov. Munfter.

KILLIAN, a curacy in dioc. of Ferns, fit. in bar. Forth, co. Wexford, prov. Leinfter.—Alfo a vicarage in dioc. of Elphin, fit. in bar. Killihan, co. Galway, prov. Connaught.

KILLIBEGS, fee *Killybegs*.

KILLIBOY, a fair town in co. Kilkenny, prov. Leinfter; fairs held 10 July.

KILLICONIGAN, a curacy in dioc. of Meath, fit. in bar. Lune, co. Meath, prov. Leinfter.

KILLIGARVAN, a rectory in dioc. of Raphoe, fit. in bar. Kilmacrenan, co. Donegal, prov. Ulfter.

KILLIGNY, a vicarage in dioc. of Kildare, fit. in bar. Coole'ftown, King's co. prov. Leinfter.

KILLIGORDON, fee *Killygordon*.

KILLIHAN, a bar. in co. Galway, prov. Connaught.

KILLIKINEEN, a vicarage in dioc. of Kilmaeduagh, fit. in bar. Dunkellin, co. Galway, prov. Connaught.

KILLILEAGH, a borough and fair town in bar. Duffrin, co. Down, prov. Ulfter, 77 miles from Dublin; otherwife written *Killyleagh*. It is the principal town in the bar. of *Duffrin*, and feated on an arm of the lake of *Strangford*, from which it is fupplied with a great variety of fifh. The family of the *Hamiltons*, created firft lords *Clanebois*, and afterwards earls of *Clanbraffil*, had their feat and refidence here, in a caftle ftanding at the upper end of the great ftreet; at the lower end of the ftreet is a little fafe *bay*, where fhips lie fheltered from all winds; in the town are fome good houfes, a decent market-houfe, a horfe-barrack, and a Prefbyterian meeting-houfe. On an eminence a fmall diftance from the town is a handfome church built in the form of a crofs. This place fuffered much in the calamitous year 1641. It is now thriving, and the linen manufacture carried on in it, and fine thread made, for which it has a great demand. It returns 2 members to parliament; patronage in the *Blackwood* family. Fairs held 10 April, Mond. after Trin. 11 Oct. and 11 Dec. lat. 54 : 27, lon. 6 : 13. The celebrated naturalift and eminent phyfician fir *Hans Sloan* was born here 16 April 1660; his father *Alex. Sloan*, was at the head of that colony of Scots, which king James Ift fettled in this town, This town was incorporated by that king at the inftance of the firft earl of *Clanebois*. It is a rectory in dioc. of Down.—Alfo a rectory in dioc. of Derry, fit. in bar. Loughlinfholen, co.

co. Londonderry, prov. Ulster.—Alfo a place in bar. Armagh, co. Armagh, prov. Ulster.

KILLILIE, fit. in bar. Ballagheen, co. Wexford, prov. Leinfter.

KILLILY, a vicarage in dioc. of Kilmacduagh, fit. in bar. Dunkellin, co. Galway, prov. Connaught.

KILLIMERBULLOGE, a vicarage in dioc. of Clonfert, fit. in bar. Longford, co. Galway, prov. Connaught.

KILLIMERDALY, a vicarage in dioc. of Clonfert, fit. in bar. Killconnel, co. Galway, prov. Connaught.

KILLIMORE, a fair town in co. Galway, prov. Connaught; fairs held 22 Nov.

KILLINACARRICK, a fmall village fit. 3½ miles beyond Bray, and 13 from the caftle of Dublin: in co. Wicklow, prov. Leinfter.

KILLINAGH, a vicarage in dioc. of Kilmore, fit. in bar. Tullagharvey, co. Cavan, prov. Ulster.

KILLINAN, a vicarage in dioc. of Kilmacduagh, fit. in bar. Loughrea, co. Galway, prov. Connaught.

KILLINANE, a rectory in dioc. of Ardfert, fit. in bar. Iveragh, co. Kerry, prov. Munfter.

KILLINCHY, fit. in bar. Duffrin, co. Down, prov. Ulster, 84 miles from Dublin; having a parifh church; it is a rectory in dioc. of Down. Fairs held 1 Wednefd. Feb. May, and Auguft.

KILLINCOOL, fee Killingcool.

KILLINCUR, a chapelry in dioc. of Kildare, fit. in bar. Gefhill, King's co. prov. Leinfter.

KILLINE-BONAINA, fit. in co. Galway, prov Connaught. A friary for Francifcans of the third order was built here, A. D. 1428, which afterwards became one of the moft confiderable houfes of that order.

KILLINEEDY, a vicarage in dioc. of Limerick, fit. in bar. Connello, co. Limerick, prov. Munfter.

KILLINGCOOL, or Killincool, fit. in bar. Louth, co. Louth, prov. Leinfter; here is a fmall but fine old caftle upon an eminence, half way between Dundalk and Atherdee, full in view of all the country round about it. Underneath this caftle are many vaults and caves of 9 or 10 and 12 feet fquare, running into each other, and faid to communicate by a long fubterraneous paffage, with Caftlederver, diftant about 6 furlongs, from whence 'tis imagined in cafe of furprize, one caftle affifted the other. This parifh is a rectory in dioc. of Armagh.

KILLINICK, a fair town in bar. Forth, co. Wexford, prov. Leinfter; fairs held Whitfun Tuefd. Eafter Mond. 21 Sept. and 30 Nov. This is a rectory in dioc. of Ferns.

KILLINKERE, a vicarage in dioc. of Kilmore, fit. in bar. Caftleraghan, co. Cavan, prov. Ulster.

KILLINSERE, a village fit. in the liberties of Drogheda, co. Louth, prov. Leinfter.

KILLINURE, fit. near Ballymore, co. Weftmeath, prov. Leinfter.

KILLINVARRA, a vicarage in dioc. of Kilmacduagh, fit. in bar. Dunkellin, co. Galway, prov. Connaught.

KLLIISHEE, fee Killifhy.

KILLISHELL, fit. in bar. Dungannon, co. Tyrone, prov. Ulster; otherwife called Killyfhiel; it is about three miles diftant from Caftlecaulfield.

KILLISHY, or Killifhee, a rectory in dioc. of Kildare, fit. in bar. Naas, co. Kildare, prov. Leinfter.

KILLKELLANE, a vicarage in dioc. of Emly, fit. in bar. Small-county, co. Limerick, prov. Munfter.

KILLKIRE, fit. in bar. Kells, co. Meath, prov. Leinfter.

KILLMACABEA, a parifh in bar. Carbery, co. Cork, prov. Munfter, where is a lake called Loughdrine, which the country people believe to be miraculous, and fay, that on a certain day of the year, all the iflands in it change places, and fhift from one fide to the other; in fame parifh is another called Ballinlough, ftored with fine large red trout; on a hill to the E. of which is an antient Danifh intrenchment, faid to have a fubterraneous paffage down to the lake. This is a vicarage in dioc. of Rofs.

KILLMACAHILL, fee Kilmacahill.

KILLMACALLEN, a vicarage in dioc. of Elphin, fit. in bar. Tiraghrill, co. Sligo, prov. Connaught.

KILLMACALOGE, a village fit. in bar. Glanerought, co. Kerry, prov. Munfter.

KILLMACDUAGH, fee Kilmacduagh.

KILLMACDUANE, a vicarage in dioc. of Killaloe, fit. in bar. Moyferta, co. Clare, prov. Munfter.

KILLMACDONOUGH, a vicarage in dioc. of Cloyne, fit. in bar. Imokilly, co. Cork, prov Munfter.

KILLMACKENVOGE, a vicarage in dioc. of Dublin, fit. in bar. Ruthdown, co. Wicklow, prov. Leinfter.

KILLMACLASSAN, a vicarage in dioc. of Tuam, fit. in bar. Morifk, co. Mayo, prov. Connaught.

KILLMACLEAGUE, fee Killmaclege.

KILLMACLEGE, a parifh in bar. Gualtiere, co. Waterford, prov. Munfter, bounded on the N. by the parifh of Ballygunne; on the W. with Middle third barony; one the E. with
Killmacombe,

Kilmacombe, and on the S. with the sea. It is a vicarage in dioc. of Waterford.

KILLMACLENY, a rectory in dioc. of Cloyne, sit. in bar. Orrery, co. Cork, prov. Munster.

KILLMACNEVIN, a curacy in dioc. of Meath, sit. in bar. Moygoish, co. Westmeath, prov. Leinster.

KILLMACOE, see *Killmacow.*

KILLMACOMBE, a parish in bar. Gualtiere, co. Waterford, prov. Munster, bounded on the N. by *Crook* and *Kill St. Nicholas*, on the W. by *Ballygunner* and *Killmeeleague*, on the E. with Waterford *harbour*, and on the S. with Killear. It is a vicarage in dioc. of Waterford.

KILLMACOMMOGE, a vicarage in dioc. of Cork, sit. in bar. Bear and Bantry, co. Cork, prov. Munster.

KILLMACOW, or *Killmacoe*, a village sit. in bar. Iverk, co. Kilkenny, prov. Leinster; it is a rectory in dioc. of Ossory.—Also a vicarage in dioc. of Dublin, sit. in bar. Arklow, co. Wicklow, prov. Leinster.

KILLMACOWEN, a rectory in dioc. of Elphin, sit. in bar. Carbury, co. Sligo. prov. Connaught.

KILLMACREDA, a village sit. in bar. Boylagh, co. Donegal, prov. Ulster.

KILLMACREE, a curacy in dioc. of Ferns, sit. in bar. Forth, co. Wexford, prov. Leinster.

KILLMACRENAN, see *Kilmacrenan.*

KILLMACSHALGAN, a vicarage in dioc. of Killala, sit. in bar. Tyreragh, co. Sligo, prov. Connaught.

KILLMACTEIGHE, a rectory in dioc. of Achonry, sit. in bar. Leney, co. Sligo, prov. Connaught. It is otherwise called *Kilmacteague*, and is distant 112 miles from Dublin: within a few miles of it are the ruins of several churches.

KILLMACTHOMAS, a post town in bar Upperthird, co. Waterford, prov. Munster, 86 miles from Dublin, where there is an antient castle, built formerly by the *Powers* of that country; there is also a small barrack for 20 men: the castle was taken in 1643, by sir Charles Vavasor, who at that time reduced other castles in the Eastern parts of this co. Fairs held 12 May and Aug. and 6 Dec.

KILLMACTRANY, a vicarage in dioc. of Elphin, sit. in bar. Tyraghrill, co. Sligo, prov. Connaught.

KILLMACTULLY *bridge*, sit. in bar. Owen and Arra, co. Tipperary, prov. Munster.

KILLMACUMPSY, a vicarage in dioc. of Elphin, sit. in bar. Boyle, co. Roscommon, prov. Connaught.

KILLMADEMOGE, a rectory in dioc. of Ossory, sit. in bar. Fassachdinning, co. Kilkenny, prov. Leinster.

KILLMAGANNY, see *Kilmaganny.*

KILLMAHON, a rectory in dioc. of Cloyne, sit. in bar. Imokilly, co. Cork, prov. Munster.

KILLMAIN, see *Kilmain.*

KILLMAINBEG, a rectory in dioc. of Tuam, sit. in bar. Kilmain, co. Mayo, prov. Connaug.

KILLMAINHAM, see *Kilmainham.*

KILLMAINHAM-WOOD, see *Kilmainham-wood.*

KILLMAINMORE, a village sit. in bar. Kilmain, co. Galway, prov. Connaught: it is a rectory in dioc. of Tuam.

KILLMAKEA, a rectory in dioc. of Ferns, sit. in bar. Shelburne, co. Wexford, prov. Leinster.

KILLMALEERE, a vicarage in dioc. of Killaloe, sit. in bar. Bunratty, co. Clare, prov. Munster.

KILLMALLOCK, see *Kilmallock.*

KILLMALODA, a rectory in dioc. of Ross, sit. in bar. Carbery, co. Cork, prov. Munster.

KILLMALOG, a vicarage in dioc. of Ferns, sit. in bar. Ballagheen, co. Wexford, prov. Leinster.

KILLMALY, a vicarage in dioc. of Killaloe, sit. in bar. Islands. co. Clare, prov. Munster.

KILLMANA. or *Killmanagh*, a rectory in dioc. of Ossory, sit. in bar. Crannagh, co. Kilkenny, prov. Leinster. An abbey was founded here by St. *Natalis*, who died A. D. 563.

KILLMANAGHAN, a chapelry in dioc. of Meath, sit. in bar. Kilcoursey, King's co. prov. Leinster.

KILLMANAGHT, a rectory in dioc. of Ross, sit. in bar. Bear and Bantry, co. Cork, prov. Munster.

KILLMANAHEEN, a vicarage in dioc. of Kilfenora, sit. in bar. Corcomroe, co. Clare, prov. Munster.

KILLMANAN, a rectory in dioc. of Ferns, sit. in bar. Bargie, co. Wexford, prov. Leinster.

KILLMANBRANE, sit. in bar. Maryborough, Queen's co. prov. Leinster.

KILLMANIVOGE, a vicarage in dioc. of Ossory, sit. in bar. Ida, co. Kilkenny, prov. Leinster.

KILLMANYAN, sit. in bar. Tinchinch, Queen's co. prov. Leinster.

KILLMAOGE, see *Kilmeague.*

KILLMASTULLA, a rectory in dioc. of Emly, sit. in bar. Arra, co. Tipperary, prov. Munster.

KILLMCON, sit. in bar. Gallen, co. Mayo, prov. Connaught.

KILLMEADONE, see *Kilmeaden.*

KILLMEEDY, a vicarage in dioc. of Limerick, sit. in bar. Connello, co. Limerick, prov. Munster. KILL-

3 E

KILLMEEN, a vicarage in dioc. of Tuam, fit. in bar. Leitrim, co. Galway, prov. Connaught.—Alfo a vicarage in dioc. of Ardfert, fit. in bar. Duhallow, co. Cork, prov. Munft.

KILLMEGAN, a rectory in dioc. of Down, fit. in bar. upper Iveagh, co. Down, prov. Ulfter.

KILLMELCHEDOR, fee *Kilmelchedor*.

KILLMENAN, a rectory in dioc. of Offory, fit. in bar. Faffachdinning, co. Kilkenny, prov. Leinfter.

KILLMESSAN, a vicarage in dioc. of Meath, fit. in bar. Deece, co. Meath, prov. Leinfter.

KILLMICHAEL, a rectory in dioc. of Cork, fit. in bar. Mufkerry, co. Cork, prov. Munfter.

KILLMICHAEL-POINT, a *cape*, fit. in bar. Gorey, co. Wexford, prov. Leinfter.

KILLMIHILL, fee *Kilmighill*.

KILLMILCON, a rectory in dioc. of Emily, fit. in bar. Owney, co. Tipperary, prov. Munft.

KILLMINA, a vicarage in dioc. of Tuam, fit. in bar. Burrifhoole, co. Mayo, prov. Connaug.

KILLMINE, a rectory in dioc. of Rofs, fit. in bar. Carbery, co. Cork, prov. Munfter.

KILLMINEY, fit. in bar. Maryborough, Queen's co. prov. Leinfter.

KILLMO, fit. in bar. Kilmaine, co. Mayo, prov. Connaught.

KILLMOC, fit. near *Mizen-head*, co. Cork, prov. Munfter.

KILLMOCAR, a vicarage in dioc. of Offory, fit. in bar. Faffachdinning, co. Kilkenny, prov. Leinfter.

KILLMOCRISH, a curacy in dioc. of Ferns, fit. in bar. Ballagheen, co. Wexford, prov. Leinfter.

KILLMODEEN, a vicarage in dioc. of Offory, fit. in bar. Faffachdinning, co. Kilkenny, prov. Leinfter.

KILLMOE, a rectory in dioc. of Cork, fit. in bar. Carbery, co. Cork, prov. Munfter.

KILLMOILAN, a rectory in dioc. of Tuam, fit. in bar. Clare, co. Galway, prov. Connaug.

KILLMOILY, a vicarage in dioc. of Ardfert, fit. in bar. Clanmaurice, co. Kerry, prov. Munfter.

KILLMOLARA, a rectory in dioc. of Tuam, fit. in bar. Kilmain, co. Mayo, prov. Connaug.

KILLMOLASH, a parifh in bar. Decies without, co. Waterford, prov. Munfter, the foil of which is partly mountain, but towards the W. tolerably fertile; at a place called *Bewly* (a corruption of *Sea-lieu)* in this parifh, are the remains of a monaftic building, but to what order it belonged is uncertain; tradition will have it to be one of the *Templar's* houfes. This is a vicarage in dioc. of Lifmore.

KILLMOLERAN, a vicarage in dioc. of Lifmore, fit. in bar. Upperthird, co. Waterford, prov. Munfter.

KILLMOLINOGE, a rectory in dioc. of Clonfert, fit. in bar. Longford, co. Galway, prov. Connaught.

KILLMONEY, a rectory in dioc. of Cork, fit. in bar. Kinalea, co. Cork, prov. Munfter.

KILLMONOGE, a rectory in dioc. of Cork, fit. in bar. Kinalea, co. Cork, prov. Munfter.

KILLMOON, fee *Kilmoon*.

KILLMORE, fee *Kilmore*.

KILLMORE-ERRIS, a vicarage in dioc. of Killalla, fit. in bar. Erris, co. Mayo, prov. Connaught.

KILLMOREMOY, a vicarage in dioc. of Killalla, fit. in bar. Tyreragh, co. Sligo, prov. Con.

KILLMOREY, fee *Kilmurry*.

KILLMORGAN, a vicarage in dioc. of Killala, fit. in bar. Corran, co. Sligo, prov. Connaught.

KILLMOSAMOG, formerly a parifh and church which lay S. W. of Dublin, in co. Dublin, prov. Leinfter; at which place the Norman invaders *Ivor* and *Sithric* were attacked by *Niall*, then monarch of Ireland, but he unfortunately failed in the attempt.

KILLMOVEE, a vicarage in dioc. of Achonry, fit. in bar. Coftello, co. Mayo, prov. Connaug.

KILLMOYLAN, fee *Kilmoylan*.

KILLMUCRIDGE, fit. in bar. Ballagheen, co. Wexford, prov. Leinfter.

KILLMUD, a vicarage in dioc. of Down, fit. in bar. Caftlereagh, co. Down, prov. Ulfter.

KILLMURRY, fee *Kilmurry*.

KILLMURRY-ELY, a rectory in dioc. of Killaloe, fit. in bar. Clonlifk, King's co. prov. Leinfter.

KILLMURRYNEGAUL, a vicarage in dioc. of Killaloe, fit. in bar. Tullagh, co. Clare, prov. Munfter.

KILLNADEEMA, a vicarage in dioc. of Clonfert, fit. in bar. Loughrea, co. Galway, prov. Connaught.

KILLNAGARUFF, a vicarage in dioc. of Killaloe, fit. in bar. Clanwilliam, co. Limerick, prov. Munfter.

KILLNAGHTIN, a vicarage in dioc. of Ardfert, fit. in bar. Iraghticonner, co. Kerry, prov. Munfter.

KILLNAGLORY, a rectory in dioc. of Cork, fit. in bar. Barretts, co. Cork, prov. Munfter.

KILLNAGROSS, a rectory in dioc. of Rofs, fit. in bar. Carbery, co. Cork, prov. Munfter.

KILLNAHUE, a rectory in dioc. of Ferns, fit. in bar. Gorey, co. Wexford, prov. Leinfter.

KILLNALONGURTY, otherwife *Kilnagurty*, a bar. in co. Tipperary, prov. Munfter.

KILLNAMAN, a vicarage in dioc. of Kildare, fit. in bar. Tinehinch, Queen's co. prov. Leinfter.

KILLNAMANA, a vicarage in dioc. of Elphin, fit. in bar. Boyle, co. Rofcommon, prov. Connaught.

Connaught.—Alſo a rectory in dioc. of Ferns, ſit. in bar. Ballagheen, co. Wexford. prov. Leinſter.

KILLNAMANNA, a bar. in co. Tipperary, prov. Munſter.

KILLNAMARTORY, ſee *Kilnamartery*.

KILLNAMONA, a vicarage in dioc. of Killaloe, ſit. in bar. Inchiquin, co. Clare, prov. Munſter.

KILLNANEAVE, a rectory in dioc. of Killaloe, ſit. in bar. upper Ormond, co. Tipperary, prov. Munſter.

KILLNATALOON, a bar. in co. Cork, prov. Munſter.

KILLNEADY, a rectory in dioc. of Oſſory, ſit. in bar. Knocktopher, co. Kilkenny, prov. Leinſter.

KILLNEBOY, a vicarage in dioc. of Killaloe, ſit. in bar. Inchiquin, co. Clare, prov. Munſter.

KILLNEHAIRE, ſit. in bar. Drumahaire, co. Leitrim, prov. Connaught.

KILLNELAGH, ſit. in bar. lower Ormond, co. Tipperary, prov. Munſter.

KILLNEMANA, ſit. in bar. Gorey, co. Wexford, prov. Leinſter.—Alſo an antient abbey, founded by St. Fechin, ſit. in co. Sligo, prov. Connaught.

KILLNERATH, a vicarage in dioc. of Emly, ſit. in bar. Owney, co. Tipperary, prov. Munſt.

KILLNESOLLOGH, a rectory in dioc. of Killaloe, ſit. in bar. Bunratty, co. Clare, prov. Munſter.

KILLNOE, a vicarage in dioc. of Killaloe, ſit. in bar. Tullagh, co. Clare, prov. Munſter.

KILLNUNINE, ſit. in bar. Drumahaire, co. Leitrim, prov. Connaught.

KILLODIERNAN, a rectory in dioc. of Killaloe, ſit. in bar. lower Ormond, co. Tipperary, prov. Munſter.

KILLOEN, or *Killone*, a rectory in dioc. of Killaloe, ſit. in bar. Iſlands, co. Clare, prov. Munſter. *Donald O'Brien*, king of Limerick, founded an abbey here, about A. D. 1190, for nuns following the rule of St. Auguſtin.

KILLOFIN, a vicarage in dioc. of Killaloe, ſit. in bar. Clanderlagh, co. Clare, prov. Munſter.

KILLOGENEDY, a vicarage in dioc. of Killaloe, ſit. in bar. Tullagh, co. Clare, prov. Munſter.

KILLOGES, a fair town, ſit. in co. Mayo, prov. Connaught; fairs held 6 Sept.

KILLOGILLIN, a vicarage in dioc. of Kilmacduagh, ſit. in bar. Dunkellin, co. Galway, prov. Connaught.

KILLONE, ſit. in bar. Stradbally, Queen's co. prov. Leinſter.

KILLONE-HILL, ſit. in Queen's co. prov. Leinſter. This is a conical hill, near the ver-tex of which has lately been diſcovered the mouth of a cavern, ſloping towards the centre of the hill. This cavern at the entrance is narrow, but after a deſcent of ſome fathoms, opens near the baſe into a large ſaloon, 20 or 30 feet high, and ſomewhat more in diameter; on one ſide is a dark and dreadful precipice, not leſs from the ſound of ſtones thrown down into it than between 50 and 60 fathom deep, having at the bottom a ſubterraneous lake which moſt probably communicates with thoſe under the great Heath of Maryborough. The cavern when lighted only by a few candles or torches appears dark and diſmal, ſtudded with projecting and pendant rocks, which threaten the ſpectator with inſtant deſtruction; but on being fully illuminated, theſe horrors vaniſh, and give place to the moſt brilliant ſcene ever exhibited by nature, or deſcribed in fairy tale; the ſides, roof and every pointed rock, are inſtantly covered with feſtoons and bouquets of pearls, diamonds, rubies, and every other precious ſtone, in full oriental ſplendour; cauſed by the drops of water iſſuing from calcareous rocks, tho' there are no incruſtations to be ſeen. In the neighbourhood of this hill, towards *Stradbally*, is a quarry and extenſive bed of an excellent calcareous ſtone, of a fine light-grey colour and delicate texture, ſurpaſſing in beauty, and equal, if not ſuperior, in every other quality, to the beſt *Portland* ſtone.

KILLONGARON, ſit. in bar. Gallen, co. Mayo, prov. Connaught.

KILLONOGHAN, a vicarage in dioc. of Kilfenora, ſit. in bar. Burrin, co. Clare, prov. Munſter.

KILLOOMONE, ſit. in bar. Bantry, co. Wexford, prov. Leinſter.

KILLORA, a vicarage in dioc. of Kilmacduagh, ſit. in bar. Dunkellin, co. Galway, prov. Connaught.

KILLORAN, a vicarage in dioc. of Clonfert, ſit. in bar. Longford, co. Galway, prov. Connaught. — Alſo a vicarage in dioc. of Achonry, ſit. in bar. Leney, co. Sligo, prov. Connaught.

KILLORGLIN, ſee *Kilorglin*.

KILLOSCOBE, a vicarage in dioc. of Tuam, ſit. in bar. Tiaquin, co. Galway, prov. Conna.

KILLOSCULLY, a vicarage in dioc. of Emly, ſit. in bar. Arra, co. Tipperary, prov. Munſter.

KILLOSKEHAN, a rectory in dioc. of Cathel, ſit. in bar. Elliogurty, co. Tipperary, prov. Munſter.

KILLOSSORY, a curacy in dioc. of Dublin, ſit. in bar. Coolock, co. Dublin, prov. Leinſt.

KILLOSSY, now a pariſh church in dioc. of Kildare, co. Kildare, prov. Leinſter. St. Patrick

trick founded an abbey here for his nephew St. *Auxil*, who died 27th Aug. 454. At this place there are some subterraneous passages.

KILLOTERAN, fit. in co. of the city of Waterford, prov. Munster; in this parish there is a charter school, which is endowed by the corporation of Waterford, with 26 acres of land, for 999 years, at a pepper-corn per ann it was opened in 1744. This is a rectory in dioc. of Waterford.

KILLOUGH, a village fit. in bar. Lecale, co. Down, prov. Ulster, 76 miles from Dublin. It lies N. of St. John's point, and has a good quay, where ships lie very fafe; the town is agreeably fit. the fea flowing all along the backs of the houses, where ships ride in full view of the inhabitants. There is here a decent church and a horfe barrack. They have good fishing in the bay; but the principal trade of the place consists in the exportation of barley, and the importation of such commodities as are confumed in the adjacent country.——A manufacture of falt is also carried on here with great advantage. At a fmall diftance from the town is a charter working fchool, for the reception of 20 children. It was fet on foot by the late Mr. Juftice *Ward*. There is a remarkable well here called St. *Scordin's well*: it is highly efteemed for the extraordinary lightnefs of its water. It gushes out of a high rocky bank, clofe upon the fhore, and is obferved never to diminifh its quantity in the drieft feafon. There is also a mineral fpring near the fchool, the waters of which the inhabitants affirm to be both purgative and emetic. At a fmall diftance from the town near the fea is a rock in which there is an oblong hole, from whence at the ebbing and flowing of the tide, a ftrange noife is heard, fomewhat refembling the found of a huntfman's horn; at the coming in of the tide whilft the waters are beating up under the rock, a cold air burfts from it with a mixture of fpray; but as the waters retire during the ebb, there is a ftrong fuction like that of an air-pump. In an open field about a ¼ of a mile from the town, towards St. *John's point* there is a very curious cave, which has a winding paffage two feet and an half broad, with three doors in it befides the entrance, and leading to a circular chamber, 3 yards in diameter, where there is a fine cool limpid well. The cave is about 27 yards long. Fairs held here on 1 Frid. O. S. Feb. 9 June, 17 Aug. and 12 Nov.—Alfo a rectory in dioc of Meath, fit. in bar. Half-fowre, co. Meath, prov. Leinft.

KILLOUGH *harbour*, fit. in co. Down, prov. Ulfter; it is tolerably fafe and commodious, a fmall degree of caution however is neceffary in failing into it, for a rock ftands in the middle of the entrance, covered at half flood, commonly called the *water rock*. Either to the E. or W. of this rock is a fecure paffage, the inlet lying S. by E. and N. by W. On the W. fide of the rock open to *Coney-ifland*, is a ftrong quay, and a bafon for fhips, where they are defended from all winds, within which the harbour on both fides affords good anchorage for veffels of 150 tons. At the end of the quay the channel is 400 yards wide. The bay of *Killough* is formed by *Rin-fad* at the *Long-point* to the E. and St. *John's point* to the W. as the inner harbour is by a peninfula called *Coney-ifle*, from the number of rabbits thereon, and not *Canc-ifle* as Sir *Wm. Petty* has it. An impetuous fea runs on all this coaft in ftorms and fpring tides.

KILLOUGHTER, a chapelry in dioc. of Dublin, fit. in bar. Newcaftle, co. Wicklow, prov. Leinfter.

KILLOWEN, a fair town in co. Londonderry, prov. Ulfter; fairs held 12 May and 5 July. It is a rectory in dioc. of Derry.—Alfo a vicarage in dioc. of Ferns, fit. in bar. Bargie, co. Wexford, prov. Leinfter.

KILL-OWEN-POINT, an excellent natural harbour, about 2 miles S. of *Roftrevor* in co. Down, prov. Ulfter. It lies about a mile W. N. W. of *Point-Barry*, in the bay of *Carlingford*.

KILLOWER, a rectory in dioc. of Tuam, fit. in bar. Clare, co. Galway, prov. Connaught.

KILLPATRICK, a curacy in dioc. of Ferns, fit. in bar. *Shelmaliere*, co. Wexford, prov. Leinfter. (*Dr. Beaufort*) In bar. *Gorey* (*Scale*)—Alfo a rectory in dioc. of Cafhel. fit. in bar. Kilnamanna, co. Tipperary, prov. Munfter. — Alfo a curacy in dioc. of Cork, fit. in bar. Kinalea, co. Cork, prov. Munfter.— Alfo a rectory in dioc. of Meath, fit. in bar. Morgallion, co. Meath, prov. Leinfter.—Alfo a curacy in dioc. of Meath, fit. in bar. Half-fowre, co. Weftmeath, prov. Leinfter.

KILLPEACON, a vicarage in dioc. of Limerick, fit. in bar. Small-county, co. Limerick, prov. Munfter.

KILLPHELAN, a rectory in dioc. of Cloyne, fit. in bar. Condons, co. Cork, prov. Munfter.

KILLPIPE, a curacy in dioc. of Ferns, fit. in bar. Ballinacor, co. Wicklow, prov. Leinft.

KILLPOOLE, a vicarage in dioc. of Dublin, fit. in bar. Arklow, co. Wicklow, prov. Leinft.

KILLQUANE, a rectory in dioc. of Limerick, fit. in bar. Bunratty, co. Clare, prov. Munfter. Alfo a vicarage in dioc. of Clonfert, fit. in bar. Longford, co. Galway, prov. Connaught.— Alfo a rectory in dioc. of Ardfert, fit. in bar. Corcaguinny, co. Kerry, prov. Munfter.

KILLRAGHTIS, a vicarage in dioc. of Killaloe, fit. in bar. Bunratty, co. Clare, prov. Munfter.—Alfo a vicarage in dioc. of Connor, fit.

fit. in bar. Dunluce, co. Antrim, prov. Ulfter.

KILLRANE, a vicarage in dioc. of Ferns, fit. in bar. Shelburne, co. Wexford, prov. Leinfter.

KILLREA, fee *Kilrea*.

KILLREENY, a vicarage in dioc. of Kildare, fit. in bar. Carbury, co. Kildare, prov. Leinfter.

KILLRICKILL, a vicarage in dioc. of Clonfert, fit. in bar. Athenry, co. Galway, prov. Connaught.

KILLRIEDOON, a vicarage in dioc. of Elphin, fit. in bar. Tyraghrill, co. Sligo, prov. Connaught.

KILLROAN, a rectory in dioc. of Cork, fit. in bar. Barrymore, co. Cork, prov. Munfter.—Alfo a curacy in dioc. of Cork, fit. in bar. Courceys, co. Cork, prov. Munfter.

KILLRONAN, a rectory in dioc. of Waterford, fit. in bar. Middlethird, co. Waterford, prov. Munfter.—Alfo a vicarage in dioc. of Lifmore, fit. in bar. Glanchiry, co. Waterford, prov. Munfter.—Alfo a vicarage in dioc. of Ardagh, fit. in bar. Boyle, co. Rofcommon, prov. Connaught.—Alfo a name given to one of the S. iflands of Arran, otherwife called St. Gregory's ifland, fit. near co. Clare, prov. Munfter.

KILLROOT, a vicarage in dioc. of Connor, fit. in bar. Belfaft, co. Antrim, prov. Ulfter.

KILLROSS, a vicarage in dioc. of Elphin, fit. in bar. Tyraghrill, co. Sligo, prov. Conna.

KILLROSSANTY, a vicarage in dioc. of Lifmore, fit. in bar. Decies without, co. Waterford, prov. Munfter.

KILLRUSH, fee *Kilrufh*.

KILLRUTH, fit. in bar. Delvin, co. Weftmeath, prov. Leinfter.

KILL-SAINT-LAWRENCE, a rectory in dioc. of Waterford, fit. in bar. Gualtiere, co. Waterford, prov. Munfter.

KILL-SAINT-NICHOLAS, a parifh in co. Waterford, prov. Munfter, in which the little town of *Paffage* is fituated, being the only fpot between it and the *city* of Waterford, where a town could be fituated, both fides being hemmed in, by a continued chain of rocky hills.

KILLSARAN, a rectory in dioc. of Armagh, fit. in bar. Ardee, co. Louth, prov. Leinfter. A commandery was founded here in the 12th century by *Maud de Lacie*, for Knts. Templars. This place is otherwife called *Killforran*.

KILLSCANLAN, a curacy in dioc. of Ferns, fit. in bar. Bantry, co. Wexford, prov. Leinft.

KILLSCANNEL, a rectory in dioc. of Limerick, fit. in bar. Conello, co. Limerick, prov. Munfter.

KILLSCOMAN, fit. in bar. Forth, co. Wexford, prov. Leinfter.

KILLSCORAN, a rectory in dioc. of Ferns, fit. in bar. Forth, co. Wexford, prov. Leinfter.

KILLSEILY, a vicarage in dioc. of Killaloe, fit. in bar. Tullagh, co. Clare, prov. Munfter.

KILLSHALVEY, a vicarage in dioc. of Achonry, fit. in bar. Corran, co. Sligo, prov. Conna.

KILLSHANICK, a rectory in dioc. of Cloyne, fit. in bar. Duhallow, co. Cork, prov. Munfter.

KILLSHANNY, a rectory in dioc. of Kilfenora, fit. in bar. Corcomroe, co. Clare, prov. Munfter.

KILLSHARVAN, a vicarage in dioc. of Meath, fit. in bar. Duleek, co. Meath. prov. Leinfter.

KILLSHILAN, a vicarage in dioc. of Lifmore, fit. in bar. Iffa and Offa, co. Tipperary, prov. Munfter.

KILLSHINANE, a vicarage in dioc. of Ardfert, fit. in bar. Clanmaurice, co. Kerry, prov. Munfter.

KILLSHINNEY, a vicarage in dioc. of Meath, fit. in bar. Morgallion, co. Meath, prov. Leinft.

KILLSILAGH, a rectory in dioc. of Rofs, fit. in bar. Barriroe, co. Cork, prov. Munfter.

KILLSKERY, a rectory in dioc. of Clogher, fit. in bar. Omagh, co. Tyrone, prov. Ulfter.

KILLSLADE, fit. in bar. Clanwilliam, co. Tipperary, prov. Munfter.

KILLSOLOGHAN, a village in bar. Nethercrofs, co. Dublin, prov. Leinfter; it is a vicarage in dioc. of Dublin.

KILLSORRAN, fee *Killfaran*.

KILLTALE, a rectory in dioc. of Meath, fit. in bar. Deece, co. Meath, prov. Leinfter.

KILLTALLA, fee *Kiltallagh*.

KILLTARTAN, fee *Kiltarton*.

KILLTEAL, a vicarage in dioc. of Leighlin, fit. in bar. Maryborough, Queen's co. prov. Leinfter.

KILLTEEL, fee *Kilteel*.

KILLTEEN, fit. near Tarboy harbour, in bar. Erris, co. Mayo, prov. Connaught. Here is a falmon fifhery.

KILLTEEVAGH, a rectory in dioc. of Raphoe, fit. in bar. Raphoe, co. Donegal, prov. Ulfter.

KILLTEVAN, a vicarage in dioc. of Elphin, fit. in bar. Rofcommon, co. Rofcommon, prov. Connaught.

KILLTENANLEA, a rectory in dioc. of Killaloe, fit. in bar. Tullagh, co. Clare, prov. Connaught.

KILLTENNELL, fee *Kiltennel*.

KILLTERAGHT, a vicarage in dioc. of Kilfenora, fit. in bar. Corcomroe, co. Clare, prov. Munfter.

KILLTERNAN, fit. in bar. *Newcaftle*, co. Wicklow, prov. Leinfter. *(Scale)*

KILLTESKIN, a vicarage in dioc. of Clonfert, fit. in bar. Leitrim, co. Galway, prov. Con.

KILL-

KILLTHOMAS, a rectory in dioc. of Kilmacduagh, fit. in bar. Loughrea, co. Galway,
prov. Connaught.

KILLTIGAN, a vicarage in dioc. of Lifmore,
fit. in bar. Iffa, co. Tipperary, prov. Munfter.
Alfo a curacy in dioc. of Dublin, fit. in bar.
Talbot'ftown, co. Wicklow, prov. Leinfter.

KILLTINAN, a rectory in dioc. of Cafhel,
fit. in bar. Middlethird, co. Tipperary, prov.
Munfter.

KILLTOGHARD, a rectory in dioc. of Ardagh, fit. in bar. Leitrim, co. Leitrim, prov.
Connaught.

KILLTORA, a vicarage in dioc. of Achonry,
fit. in bar. Corran, co. Sligo, prov. Connaught.

KILLTORMER, a vicarage in dioc. of Clonfert, fit. in bar. Longford, co. Galway, prov.
Connaught.

KILLTOOM, a vicarage in dioc. of Elphin,
fit. in bar. Athlone, co. Rofcommon, prov.
Connaught.

KILLTOOMY, a vicarage in dioc. of Ardfert,
fit. in bar. Clanmaurice, co. Kerry, prov.
Munfter.

KILLTRISK, a rectory in dioc. of Ferns, fit.
in bar. Gorey, co. Wexford, prov. Leinfter.

KILLTRUSTAN, a rectory in dioc. of Elphin, fit. in bar. Rofcommon, co. Rofcommon,
prov. Connaught.

KILLTUBRID, a rectory in dioc. of Ardagh,
fit. in bar. Leitrim, co. Leitrim, prov. Conna.

KILLTULLAGH, a vicarage in dioc. of Clonfert, fit. in bar. Athenry, co. Galway, prov.
Connaught.—Alfo a rectory in dioc. of Tuam,
fit. in bar. Ballintobar, co. Rofcommon, prov.
Connaught.

KILLTURK, a vicarage in dioc. of Ferns,
fit. in bar. Bargie, co. Wexford, prov. Leinfter.

KILLUAGH, a vicarage in dioc. of Meath,
fit. in bar. Delvin, co. Weftmeath, prov.
Leinfter.

KILLUCAN, or *Killuken*, a fair town 5½ miles
E. of Mullingar, fit. in bar. Farbill, co. Weftmeath, prov. Leinfter; fairs held 27 March
and 28 Nov. Here St. *Luican* built an abbey,
his feftival is obferved here on 7th July: this
is a rectory in dioc. of Meath.—Alfo a rectory
in dioc. of Elphin, fit. in bar. Boyle, co.
Rofcommon, prov. Connaught.—Alfo a vicarage in dioc. of Elphin, fit. in bar Rofcommon, co. Rofcommon, prov. Connaught.

KILLUCQUIN, a fair town in co. Weftmeath,
prov. Leinfter; fairs held 27 March and 28
November.

KILLUKEN, fee *Killucan*.

KILLUMOD, a vicarage in dioc. of Elphin,
fit. in bar. Boyle, co. Rofcommon, prov.
Connaught.

KILLUNKART, fit. in co. Waterford, prov.
Munfter; here are the remains of an old building faid to have been a houfe of the Knts.
Templars; tho' it feems to have been only
one of their manor houfes, many of which
they had difperfed throughout the kingdom.

KILLURAN, fee *Kilurane*.

KILLURE, a parifh in co. Waterford, prov.
Munfter; in which was a preceptory of the
Knts. Templars, founded in the 12th century.
The lands were after the diffolution granted
to *Francis Felton*, in *fee farm*, at a rent of
13*l*. 6*s*. 8*d*. and affigned to Lawrence lord
Efmond.

KILLURIN, fee *Kilvrane*.

KILLURSA, a rectory in dioc. of Tuam,
fit. in bar. Clare, co. Galway, prov. Connaug.

KILLURY, a rectory in dioc. of Ardfert, fit.
in bar. Clanmaurice, co. Kerry, prov. Munfter.

KILLVARNET, a vicarage in dioc. of Achonry, fit. in bar. Leney, co. Sligo, prov. Connaug.

KILLVECONTY, a rectory in dioc. of Kilmacduagh, fit. in bar. Killtartan, co. Galway,
prov. Connaught.

KILLVELLANE, a vicarage in dioc. of Emly,
fit. in bar. Arra, co. Tipperary, prov. Munfter.

KILLVEMNON, a rectory in dioc. of Cafhel,
fit. in bar. Slewardagh, co. Tipperary, prov.
Munfter.

KILLVILLIN, fit. in bar. Drumahaire, co.
Leitrim, prov. Connaught.

KILLVINE, a rectory in dioc. of Tuam, fit.
in bar. Clonmorris, co. Mayo, prov. Connaug.

KILLVOLAGH, fit. in bar. Delvin, co. Weftmeath, prov. Leinfter.

KILLWAGHTER, fee *Kilwater*.

KILLWATERMOY, a vicarage in dioc. of Lifmore, fit. in bar. Cofhbride, co. Waterford,
prov. Munfter.

KILLWEILAGH, a vicarage in dioc. of Meath,
fit. in bar. Delvin, co. Weftmeath, prov.
Leinfter.

KILLWORTH, fee *Kilworth*.

KILLYAN, fee *Killihan*.

KILLYBEGS, a borough, fair and poft town
in bar. Boylagh, co. Donegal, prov. Ulfter;
123 miles from Dublin. 'Tis fit. on the N.
fide of Donegal bay, a place of no great trade,
but it has a harbour fpacious enough to contain a large fleet: it has a bold and ample
opening to the fea on the S. and is fecured within
by the fhelter of high lands furrounding it; fo
that veffels may enter in at any time of the tide,
there being from 5 to 8 fathom water. The
herring fifhery is the moft confiderable of any
carried on here; but the town is likely to
encreafe in trade and confequence. A fmall
houfe was built here for friars of the 3d order of St. Francis, by *Mac Sweeny Banig*.
It returns 2 members to parliament, patronage
in the *Conyngham* family. Fair days Eafter-
Monday and 12 Nov. This is a rectory in
dioc.

dioc. of Raphoe; lat. 54 : 33, lon. 8 : 58.—
Alfo a rectory in dioc. of Kildare, fit. in bar.
Claine, co. Kirldae, prov. Leinfter; other-
wife written *Killibegs*.

KILLYCLOIN, a pleafant feat in co. Cork,
prov. Munfter; near the fmall village of
Carrigtohill.

KILLYFADDY, fit. within 1 mile of Magherafelt; in co. Londonderry, prov. Ulfter.

KILLYGLASS, fit. in bar. Tyreragh, co.
Sligo, prov. Connaught. Lat. 54 : 8, lon. 2 : 33.

KILLYGORDON, fit. in bar. Raphoe, co.
Donegal, prov. Ulfter, 110 miles from Dublin. About 1½ mile from which, at the foot of
a very lofty hill are the ruins of a caftle. This
is fometimes written *Killiordin*.

KILLYLASTRA, fit. in bar. Ardagh, co.
Longford, prov. Leinfter.

KILLYLEAGH, fee *Killileagh*.

KILLYMAN, a parifh in bar. Dungannon,
co. Tyrone, prov. Ulfter, 71 miles from Dublin. It was antiently fpelt *Kil-Eamain*, and is
fuppofed to have been the old *Eamania*, once
the feat of the kings of *Ulfter*; it is a rectory
in dioc. of Armagh.

KILLYMARD, a rectory in dioc. of Raphoe;
fit. in bar. Boylagh, co. Donegal, prov. Ulfter.

KILLYMOON, fit. in bar. Dungannon, co.
Tyrone, prov. Ulfter.

KILLYMURE-BRIDGE, fit. over the river *Kil-
lymure*, in co. Galway, prov. Connaught; near
which are the ruins of a church: 3 miles beyond it are the ruins of a caftle.

KILLYNAULE, fee *Killenaule*.

KILLYOCK, fit. in co. Donegal, prov. Ulfter,
129 miles from Dublin, having a church belonging to it.

KILLYON, a fair town in King's co. prov.
Leinfter; fairs held Whit. Monday and 10
Oct. Alfo a curacy in dioc. of Meath, fit.
in bar. Moyfenrath, co. Meath, prov. Leinfter.

KILLYSHIEL, fee *Killifhell*.

KILMACAHILL, (or *Kilmac Cahal*) fit. in co.
Weftmeath, prov. Leinfter, on the N. fide of
the river *Inny*; here are the ruins of a diffolved
monaftery or friary of *Francifcans*; it was founded by the family of *Petyt*. 3 or 4 miles farther
Northwards on the lands of *Clonmore*, ftood the
nunnery of *Kenard*.—Alfo a vicarage in dioc. of
Leighlin, fit. in bar. Gowran, co. Kilkenny,
prov. Leinfter; otherwife written *Killmacahill*.

KILMACALOGE *harbour*, fit. in co. Kerry,
prov. Munfter, on the N. fide of *Kenmare river*.
When you are in the mouth of this harbour
you may run boldly up, keeping a S. E. by E.
courfe, which carries you clear of a funk rock,
which is known by the fea breaking over it;
facing a point about ¼ a mile diftant, and
oppofite the church of Kilmacaloge, otherwife
called *Kilmakeloge*.

KILMACDUAGH, fit. in bar. Kiltartan, co.
Galway, prov. Connaught; 2 miles W. of
Gort. Here is the antient monaftery, church
and chapels of *Kilmacduagh*, now moftly in
ruins. This is a rectory in dioc. of fame
name. Its antient name is Cill-Mac-Duagh,
or the church of *Mc. Duagh*, and was a bifhoprick founded in the middle of the 6th century by St. *Colman* fon of *Duagh*, defcended
from the antient chiefs of *Fir-malgaid*. The
bifhoprick of *Kilmacduagh* was united to that
of *Clonfert* in 1602. It is rated in the king's
book's at 10*l*. but the two fees are worth
2,400*l*. per ann. The church, tho' fmall, was
a very neat building: the pillars and arches
from the entrance to the altar part, and thofe
of the E. window were finifhed in an elegant
ftyle; and the angles at the E. end worked
in pillars. To the S. of the church is a fa-
crifty, and adjoining it a room where were probably depofited the valuable effects belonging to the church; and which being arched
is called the jail. On the S. of thefe is a
chapel and refectory. From the whole of
thefe we may infer that the canons and monks
dwelt in feparate houfes. To the N. about
2 feet from the church, is an old wall, which
according to tradition, was a place of penance:
there is alfo a holy well here, with a circular
inclofure. Here is a round tower which leans
17½ feet from its perpendicular: the celebrated tower at *Pifa* in Italy leans but 13 feet.
At the general fuppreffion, this monaftery was
granted to *Richard* earl of *Clanricard*.

KILMACLENON, a fair town in co. Cork,
prov. Munfter; fairs held 6 April, 21 June
and 2 Oct.

KILMACOW, a caftle about 1 mile W. of
Tallow in co. Cork, prov. Munfter; it was
built by *John Fitzgerald*, defcended from the
houfe of *Macollop*; this caftle with one plow-
land adjoining to it, being demifed to *Richard
Joke*, 1 July, 1586, was by him affigned to
Richard Crifhall, 30 Jan. 1593, and by him to
Sir *Richard Boyle*, 7 Jan. 1604; the caftle is
not very long fallen down. At this place the
firft earl of *Cork* had very large iron-works;
by the accounts in the caftle of *Lifmore*, there
were made here for his lordfhip in 7 years,
21,000 tons of bar-iron, which at 18*l*. the ton,
as it was then fold, was worth 378.000*l*. the
moft of the mine was dug at *Ballyrogan* in
that co. the bar-iron did not ftand his lordfhip
in more than 3*l*. per ton, wood being very
plenty.

KILMACRENAN, fit. in the bar. of fame
name, co. Donegal, prov. Ulfter, 118 miles
from Dublin; here are the ruins of a church;
and between this and *Glen-inn*, is *Lough-Salt*,
fit. on the top of a lofty mountain, encom-
passed

paſſed with clifts of rock; this, tho' a ſmall village, gives name to the bar. St. *Columb* founded an abbey here, which was richly endowed; and *O'Donnel* founded a ſmall houſe, on the ſcite of the antient abbey, for friars of the order of St. Francis; the preſent church is ſuppoſed to have been a part of this friary; over the door is a mitred head in relievo; and near the church are the ruins of a caſtle. Near *Kilmacrenan* is a rock on which the *O'Donnels*, princes of *Tyrconnel*, were always inaugurated. This is a rectory in dioc. of Raphoe. Lat. 54 : 56, lon. 8 : 22.

KILMACTHOMAS, ſee *Killmacthomas.*

KILMACUDD, a pleaſant village ſit. ¼ of a mile from Stillorgan, and 4 miles from Dublin caſtle, in co. Dublin, prov. Leinſter. It ſtands on a riſing ground, and has a pure and wholeſome air.

KILMAGANNY, ſit. in bar. Kells, co. Kilkenny, prov. Leinſter, 67 miles from Dublin; fairs held Eaſter Tueſd. and 4 Sept. It is a vicarage in dioc. of Oſſory.

KILMAIN, ſit. in bar. Roſcommon, co. Mayo, prov. Connaught, 104 miles from Dublin; here are the ruins of a church: half a mile beyond it are the ruins of a caſtle. Fairs held 12 July and 28 Oct. It is a vicarage in dioc. of Elphin.

KILMAINHAM, ſit. in co Dublin, prov. Leinſter, about ½ a mile from the metropolis. Here is a ſeſſion's-houſe and handſome goal, which tho' not long built, being however conſidered as not ſufficiently ſecure, a new one is began at a ſmall diſtance from it on a riſing ground, by the road from this to *Inchicore.* At this place the quarter ſeſſions are held for the co. Dublin, and Knts. of the ſhire elected for that co. This place was ſometimes the ſeat of government, before *Dublin caſtle* was converted to that purpoſe, and tho' now much decayed, it gives title of baron to the family of *Wenman;* Sir *Richard Wenman* bart. being by letters patent, dated at *Canterbury,* 30 July 1628, created *baron* Wenman of *Kilmainham,* and *viſe.* Wenman of *Tuam;* Hen. *Wenman,* eſq; grandfather of the ſaid Rich. was created a baronet, 5 April 1554. An antient priory was founded here, and a houſe for Knts. Hoſpitalers of St. *John* of *Jeruſalem,* upon the ſcite of an antient abbey, by *Strongbow* earl of *Pembroke,* about A. D. 1174. Here is an antient burial ground; and alſo a reputed holy well, dedicated to St. *John.* Near it ſtands the *Royal Hoſpital* founded by king *Charles* IId for the ſupport of invalid ſoldiers of the army in Ireland; on a plan ſimilar to that of Chelſea in England. The building was compleated in 1683, and coſt upwards of 23,500*l.* It is ſit. on a riſing ground near the S. ſide of the

river Liffey, from whence there is an eaſy aſcent to it through ſeveral rows of tall elms. This edifice is of a quadrangular form, encloſing a ſpacious area, handſomely laid out in graſs plots and gravelled walks: an arcade is carried along the lower ſtory in each ſquare, to the entrance of the hall and chapel, which are both curiouſly decorated; in the former are ſeveral whole-length portraits of royal perſonages and other diſtinguiſhed characters.

KILMAINHAM-WOOD, ſit. in bar. Kells, co. Meath, prov. Leinſter; it is a rectory in dioc. of Meath. A commandery for Knts. Hoſpitalers was founded here in the 13th century, by the family of *Preſton;* the ruins of a ſmall old church are ſtill to be ſeen here.

KILMALLOCK, a borough and fair town in bar. Coſhma, co. Limerick, prov. Munſter, 16 miles from the city of Limerick, and 107 from Dublin; it is a rectory in dioc. of Limerick. This town makes a conſpicuous figure in the military hiſtory of Ireland. In the 16th century it was a populous place; the remains of the wall which entirely ſurrounded the town, and of ſeveral large houſes, are ſtill to be ſeen. *Edward* VIth granted a charter to it, with many privileges, as did queen *Elizabeth* another, dated 24 April 1584. In 1598, it was inveſted by the Iriſh forces, when the earl of *Ormond* haſtened to its relief, and arrived in time to raiſe the ſiege; here was alſo ſome conteſt during the grand rebellion in 1641, and 1642. By an inquiſition 11 Aug. 29th *Elizabeth,* it appears that there had been an abbey or religious houſe in Kilmallock, called *Flaciſpaghe,* on which a ſtone houſe was erected. In the cathedral church here, are the remains of a monument erected over the *Verdon* family, one of whom repreſented this town in parliament, in 1613; here is one of the antient round towers. Kilmallock returns 2 members to parliament; patron, *Silver Oliver,* eſq. This place once gave title of viſe. to one of the *Sarsfield* family. Sir *James Ware* informs us, that an abbey of Dominicans or Black friars, was built here in the 13th century by the ſovereign, brethren and commonalty; from the many ruins here of caſtles and antient buildings it has acquired the name of the *Iriſh Balbeck;* the pariſh church was formerly an abbey for regular canons founded by St. *Mochoallog,* who died between the years 639 and 656; and ſome writers ſay that the Dominican abbey juſt mentioned was founded in 1291 by *Gilbert,* the ſecond ſon of John of *Calleen.* Within 2¼ miles of Kilmallock are the ruins of a caſtle. Fairs are held at this town on Whit. Tueſd. A charter ſchool for 20 children was opened here in 1783. The houſe was built at the ſole expence rence of *Robert Oliver*, esq.

KILMASHOGUE, a small village sit. in co. Dublin, prov. Leinster, 4½ miles beyond *Rath-farnham*, and 7½ from Dublin castle. Mr. *Latouche's* beautiful seat, *Marlay*, is between this place and Rathfarnham.

KILMATAGUE, see *Killmacteighe*.

KILMAYMOGE, sit. in bar. Upperthird, co. Waterford, prov. Munster.

KILMAYNHAM, see *Kilmainham*.

KILMEADEN, or *Killmeadone*, a vicarage in dioc. of Waterford, sit. in bar. Middlethird, co. Waterford, prov. Munster; it gives title of baron to the family of *St. Ledger* (now visc. *Doneraile*) by patent dated 28 Jan. 1703. *Kil-meaden-house* is built on the foundation of an antient castle, which was boldly erected on the bank of the river *Suir*, which is here of a considerable breadth, and deep enough for vessels of a large burden. At this place is a famous spa, which breaks out in the highway between 2 rising grounds, with such force, that in crossing the road it becomes a little brook; it is a light chalybeate water, very diuretick, and has been drank some years ago with great success; but in order to experience its virtues, it must be taken on the spot.

KILMEAGUE, sit. in bar. Great Connel, co. Kildare, prov. Leinster, 22 miles from Dublin; a mile beyond *Kilmeague* church is the village called *Allen*, which gives name to the famous bog, which in many parts may be seen from the tops of *Allen* and *Kildare hills*, and which extends thro' several co.'s. This place is a rectory in dioc. of Kildare, and otherwise written *Kilmaoge*; here are some antient ruins. Fairs held here 25 May, and 29 June.

KILMEASHILL, a fair town in co. Wexford, prov. Leinster; fairs held 13 April, 18 July, and 8 Sept. for *cattle*.

KILMEDY, a small castle now in ruins, near which was a redoubt for half a foot company. 'Tis sit. 1 mile from *Millstreet*, co. Cork, prov. Munster.

KILMELCHEDOR, i. e. *Milchedor's church*, a parish in bar. Corcaguinny, co. Kerry, prov. Munster. The church here is said to have been built by the *Spaniards*, who formerly erected many other churches hereabouts. Several Spanish merchants resided at *Dingle*, before Q. *Eliz.'s* time, who traded with the natives for fish and other kinds of provision; as appears by a tract written by *John Dee*, called the *British Monarchy*, in 1576; who complains much of the intrusion of foreigners upon our sea coasts, for the benefit of fishing, which he says they frequented with as much security, as if they were within their own king's peculiar limits. This is a rectory in dioc. of Ardfert.

KILMIDDY, a fair town in co. Limerick, prov. Munster; fairs held 7 Nov. and 31 Dec.

KILMIGHILL or *Killmihill*, a vicarage in dioc. of Killaloe, sit. in bar Clanderlagh, co. Clare, prov. Munster.

KILMITCHEL, a fair town in co. Clare, prov. Munster; fairs held 19 May, and 9 Oct.

KILMOON, sit. in bar. Duleek, co. Meath, prov. Leinster, the church of which is 15 miles distant from Dublin. It is a rectory in dioc. of Meath. About a mile from it are the ruins of *Macetown* castle, formerly of great importance; and about a mile further, the ruins of *Crossmacale church*.—Also a vicarage in dioc. of Kilfenora, sit. in bar. Burrin, co. Clare, prov. Munster.

KILMORE, a village sit. in bar. Loughtee, co. Cavan, prov. Ulster, called in former ages. *Clunes* or *Cluain*, i. e. the sequestered place; (*Collect*. No. 11.) It lies near *Lough Erne*, and is a rectory in dioc. of same name. In the 6th century an abbey was built here by St. *Columb*: it was created a bishoprick by St. *Fedlimid*, and afterwards removed to an obscure village called *Triburna*, where it continued until the year 1454, when *Andrew Mac Brady*, bishop of *Tri-burna*, erected a church on the site of that founded by St. *Fedlimid*, to whose memory it was dedicated, and denominated *Kilmore* or the great church. 'Tis said to have been also called *Brefny*, and changed its name to that of *Kilmore* in the 15th century. (*Beauf. mem.*) At present there are neither cathedral, chapter nor canons belonging to this see. The small parish church contiguous to the episcopal house, serving for the purpose of a cathedral. — Also a fair town sit. in bar. Castlereagh, co. Down, prov. Ulster: it is a rectory in dioc. of Down: fairs held 14 Mar. 1 May, 3 June, 5 Aug. 29 Sept. and 5 Nov.—Also a rectory in dioc. of Armagh, sit. in bar. Oneilland, co. Armagh, prov. Ulster, where a church was founded by St. *Mochtee*.—Also a rectory in dioc. of Clogher, sit. in bar. Monaghan, co. Monaghan, prov. Ulster.—Also a vicarage in dioc. of Meath, sit. in bar. Deece, co. Meath, prov. Leinster. — Also a vicarage in dioc. of Ferns, sit. in bar. Bargie, co. Wexford, prov. Leinster. — Also a vicarage in dioc. of Killaloe, sit. 4 miles S. of *Nenagh*, in bar. upper Ormond, co. Tipperary, prov. Munster, where an abbey was founded in 540.—Also a chapelry in dioc. of Cashel, sit. in bar. Kilnamanna, co. Tipperary, prov. Munster.—Also a vicarage in dioc. of Elphin, sit. in bar. Boyle, co. Roscommon, prov. Connaught; it is a village on the banks of Lough Rec, 6 miles N. W. of *Athlone*, where are the remains of a priory and an abbey; the latter was built by St. *Patrick*. — Also a place in bar.

Grenard,

Granard, co. Longford, prov. Leinster,—and another in bar. Dunluce, co. Antrim, prov. Ulster.

KILMOYLAN, sit. in bar. Connillo, co. Limerick, prov. Munster. It is a vicarage in dioc. of Limerick.

KILMURE-BRIDGE, sit. in co. Galway, prov. Connaught, 78 miles from Dublin.

KILMUCKRIDGE, a fair town in co. Wexford, prov. Leinster; fairs held 1 Jan. Easter Mond. 24 June and 29 Sept.

KILMURRAGHAN, a fair town in co. Cork, prov. Munster; fairs held 10 July.

KILMURRY or *Kilmorey*, sit. in bar. Muskerry, co. Cork, prov. Munster, 142 miles from Dublin. Here are the ruins of a castle. Also fairs held 1 May, 8 Sept. 1 Nov. and 21 Dec. It is a rectory in dioc. of Cork.—There is also a ruined church of that name in co. Kerry, prov. Munster, sit. between *Blackwater bridge* and *Killarney*. Near this place are also 3 ruined castles of the *Fitzgeralds*, said to have been possessed by three brothers of that name, who bore so great an enmity to each other, that no one of them would suffer the other to pass peaceably through his land.—There is also a village and church of same name in bar. Clanderlagh, co. Clare, prov. Munster, 129 miles from Dublin; sit. on the sea coast, which village gives title of visc. to the family of *Needham*. It is a vicarage in dioc. of Killaloe. Lat. 52 : 40 N. lon. 9 : 30 W. Within 2 miles of it at the foot of a hill, are the ruins of a castle.—Also a fair town in co. Kilkenny, prov. Leinster; fairs held 1 Jan. 5 Apr. 9 May, 26 July, 6 Aug. 10 Sept. 2 Oct. and 10 Dec.—Also a rectory in dioc. of Killaloe, sit. in bar. Ibrickin, co. Clare, prov. Munster.—Also a rectory in dioc. of Lismore, sit. in bar. Iffa and Offa, co. Tipperary, prov. Munster.—Also a rectory in dioc. of Limerick, sit. in co. of the city of Limerick, prov. Munster.—Also a place in bar. Talbot'stown, co. Wicklow, prov. Leinster.

KILMURRYIBRICKAN, a fair town in co. Clare, prov. Munster, 128 miles from Dublin. Near which are some handsome waterfalls; fairs held 17 May and 25 Aug.

KILMURRYMACMAHON, sit. in co. Clare, prov. Munster, having fairs on 24 May.

KILNAGRAICY, sit. by the river *Bride*, in bar. Cosh bride, co. Waterford, prov. Munster.

KILNAGURTY, see *Killnalongurty*.

KILNALECK, a fair town in co. Cavan, prov. Ulster; fairs held 2 Feb. 13 May, 10 Aug. and 1 Nov.

KILNAMARTERY, a ruined church, sit. in bar. Muskerry, co. Cork, prov. Munster. The country about it, to the N. and W. as far as the eye can see, is intermixed with large white rocks and green spots; at first sight, a stranger

at a distance might take them for the ruins of a vast city, the white crags resembling so many ruined castles, palaces, towers and churches. 1 mile W. stands the high castle of *Curickafouky*. This is a rectory in dioc. of Cloyne.

KILNEFREHAN, sit. near Dungarvan, co. Waterford, prov. Munster.

KILNELAGHIR, sit. in bar. *Decies Drum*, co. Waterford, prov. Munster.

KILNELOGURTY, see *Killnalongurty*.

KILNEMANA, see *Killnamanna*.

KILNEMANAGH, sit. in co. Sligo, prov. Connaught; where a monastery was founded by St. Fechin, early in the 7th century.

KILNEMULLAGH, a name given by *Spencer* to the town of *Buttevant*, in co. Cork, prov. Munster.

KILNENA, a fair town in co. Clare, prov. Munster; fairs held 11 June.

KILNENER, a fair town in co. Wexford, prov. Leinster; fairs held 8 September.

KILNOCKIN, a fair town in co. Tipperary, prov. Munster: fairs held 24 April, 22 June, and 24 Oct.

KILONAGHAN, sit. in bar. Burrin, co. Clare, prov. Munster.

KILORGLIN, sit. in bar. Truaghnacmy, co. Kerry, prov. Munster; this place is otherwise called Castle-Conway. It is a rectory in dioc. of Ardfert. It consists of several houses and by its neighbourhood to the sea, is well sit. for trade, if the harbour of *Castlemain* was better known and frequented. The lands hereabouts were granted by Q. Eliz. to the family of *Conway*, and afterwards descended by heirs female to that of *Blennerhasset*. Some time ago an odd accident happened, to the S. W. of this place occasioned by the sudden shifting of a large quantity of sand, in a violent storm, that spread it all over an adjacent bog, which became soon after a good meadow; and not far from the bog, a small lough was filled up by the sand, which also became good ground; something similar to this is said to have happened at *Suffolk* in *England*, and mentioned in *Philosoph. Transact*. No. 37. Fairs are held here on 19 and 20 May, 30 June and 1 July, 12 Aug. 18 and 19 Nov.

KILPENKAN or *Kilpencau*, sit. in bar. Small-county, co. Limerick, prov. Munster.

KILRANELAGH, a parish in co. Wicklow, prov. Leinster. An urn was found here some few years ago of great antiquity, 6 feet below the surface of the earth, in an inclosure of 8 flat stones, 6 of which formed the sides, and 2 the top and bottom: the urn was of a conical form, about 14 inches high, and 12 in diameter at the top, and $3\frac{1}{2}$ at the bottom: it contained a considerable quantity of ashes, and
calcined

calcined human bones. Fairs are held here annually on 1 Feb.

KILREA, fit. in bar. Loughlinfholen, co. Londonderry, prov. Ulfter, 103 miles from Dublin; fairs are held here 10 Oct. It is a rectory in dioc. of Derry.—Alfo a rectory in dioc. of Offory, fit. in bar. Kells, co. Kilkenny, prov. Leinfter. Here is one of the antient round towers.

KILREE, fee *Kilrea*.

KILRENELA, fee *Kilranelagh*.

KILRICKILL, fit. near *Loughrea*, prov. Conn

KILRUDDERY, the antient feat of the earls of *Meath*, fit. 1 mile beyond *Bray*, in co. Wicklow, prov. Leinfter.

KILRUE, fit. in bar. Ratoath, co. Meath, prov. Leinfter.

KILRUSH, a fair and poft town in bar. Moyferta, co. Clare, prov. Münfter, 142 miles from Dublin; fairs held 10 May and 12 Oct. Here is the feat of *Crofton Vandeleur*, efq. This is a vicarage in dioc. of Killaloe.—Alfo a rectory in dioc. of Ferns, fit. in bar. Searewalfh, co. Wexford, prov. Leinfter: the church of which was lately reftored, and is now in repair.—Alfo a rectory in dioc. of Offory, fit. in bar. Crannagh, co. Kilkenny, prov. Leinft. Alfo a rectory in dioc. of Waterford, fit. in bar. *Decies without*, co. Waterford, prov. Münfter.—Alfo a chapelry in dioc. of Dublin, fit. in bar. Balruddery, co. Dublin, prov. Leinfter. Here are the remains of a once very handfome caftle, about 9 miles from the metropolis.—Alfo a rectory in dioc. of Kildare, fit. in bar. Ophaly, co. Kildare, prov. Leinfter, about 3½ miles W. of old Kilcullen; an abbey was founded here about the beginning of the 13th century, for canons regular of St. Auguftin, by *William Marfhal* or *Marefchal* earl of *Pembroke*. It was granted with its appurtenances to the earl of *Ormond*.

KILSAGHLAN, fee *Kilfallaghan*.

KILSALLAGHAN, fit. in co. Dublin, prov. Leinfter, 8½ miles from the metropolis, and about 5 miles beyond Finglafs; here is a caftle which once was of importance, but now is in ruins, and a mile farther is the caftle of Greenoge; fairs held Afcenfion day, and 8 Sept. for horfes and pedlar's wares. An antient monaftery was founded here.

KILSELLKED, fit. near *Ventry*, co. Kerry, prov. Münfter.

KILSHALLAGH, fit. in bar. Clanwilliam, co. Tipperary, prov. Münfter.

KILSHANE, fit. in co. Limerick, prov. Münfter; here was a Francifcan friary erected by *Fitzgerald* lord of Clenlis. Alfo a Ciftertian abbey founded in 1198.

KILSHANICK, a parifh in co. Cork, prov.

Münfter, fit. on the S. fide of the river *Blackwater*. In this parifh there are feveral good feats.

KILSHOGAN, fit. in co. Dublin, prov. Leinfter, about 7 miles from the metropolis.

KILSIACLE, fit. in bar. Clanwilliam, co. Tipperary, prov. Münfter.

KILSKIRE or *Kilfkyre*, fit. in bar. Kells, co. Meath, prov. Leinfter: an abbey was founded here and dedicated to St. *Schiria* the virgin: fhe lived towards the end of the 6th century. It was pillaged by the Danes in 949. This is a rectory in dioc. of Meath.

KILSLIEVE, fit. in co. Armagh, prov. Ulfter; where was the antient chapel of *Monepua*. Concubran about A. D. 630, tells us it was built according to the Irifh fafhion, of wattles or fmoothed wood.

KILTALLAGH, a parifh in co. Kerry, prov. Münfter, having a decent church, frequented by the inhabitants of *Ballycrifpin* village, and alfo a good parfonage houfe.—Alfo a village fit. in bar. Ballintobbar, co. Rofcommon, prov. Connaught.

KILTALLAN, a feat in co. Clare, prov. Münfter, near which is a fubterraneous river that is efteemed a great natural curiofity.

KILTARTON or *Kiltartan*, a bar. in co. Galway, prov. Connaught. There is a fair town in it of fame name, which is a rectory in dioc. of Kilmacduagh. Fairs held 11 May, 3 Sept. and 21 Nov.

KILTEEL, a fair town in bar. Salt, co. Kildare, prov. Leinfter; fairs held 1 May, 24 June, 29 Sept. and 1 Nov. It is a vicarage in dioc. of Dublin.—Alfo a vicarage in dioc. of Emly, fit. in bar. Coonagh, co. Limerick, prov. Münfter; a church was erected here on an eminence that formerly belonged to the Knts. Templars.—Alfo a village fit. near *Dunamace*, in Queen's co. prov. Leinfter, where there is an antient burial place, and a church in ruins.

KILTEELY, a fair town in co. Limerick, prov. Münfter; fairs held 1 Feb. June, and 25 Oct.

KILTEEN *caftle*, fit. in co. Dublin, prov. Leinfter, about 3 miles beyond *Rathcool*: it is in tolerable repair, pretty large, and partly inhabited.

KILTENNELL, a rectory in dioc. of Ferns, fit. in bar. Gorey, co. Wexford, prov. Leinfter. The church here was erected principally at the expence of lord *Courtcwn*, who alfo built the tower here, and has the patronage of this living.—Alfo a vicarage in dioc. of Leighlin, fit. in bar. Idrone, co. Carlow, prov. Leinfter.

KILTERNAN, fit. in bar. Half-Rathdown, co. Dublin, prov. Leinfter, near 7 miles from the metropolis; a mile beyond this is a very remarkable.

remarkable chafm in the ridge of a mountain, called the Scalp. This is otherwife written *Kilternon*, and is a vicarage in dioc. of Dublin. It lies about 4½ miles beyond *Miltown*, and within 4 miles of *Powerfcourt*.

KILTOLLA, fit. in co. Galway, prov. Connaught, about 5 miles from *New-inn*, on the Loughrea road. Near it is another feat called *Carrow-roe*. The many ruins of churches and caftles hereabouts, arreft the attention of the traveller; and imprefs the beholder with a high idea of the population and piety of early ages.

KILTUHAWN, fit. near 28 miles from Dublin, by the banks of the grand Canal, in co. Kildare, prov. Leinfter: near it are the ruins of a church.

KILTURLY, fit. in bar. Iveragh, co. Kerry, prov. Munfter.

KILUA, fee *Killuagh*.

KILUNKART, fit. near *Dungarvan*, co. Waterford, prov. Munfter.

KILUPER, fit. in bar. Uppercrofs, co. Dublin, prov. Leinfter.

KILURANE, a fair town in bar. Shelmaliere, co. Wexford, prov. Leinfter; fairs held 21 Aug. It is a vicarage in dioc. of Ferns, and fometimes written *Killurin*. — Alfo a rectory in dioc. of Killaloe, fit. in bar. Tullagh, co. Clare, prov. Munfter.

KILWARLIN, an antient territory in the bar. of lower Iveach, in co. Down, prov. Ulfter, which gives title of *lord* by courtefey to the eldeft fon of the earls of *Hillfborough*. The chieftain of this territory, in the reign of queen Eliz. was by fir-name *Mc. Swine Mc. Rory*, who fubmitted to the queen, but before yielded part of his territories to the *O'Neals* of Claneboy. He was able to bring into the field 12 horfe and 80 foot foldiers.

KILWATER, fit. in bar. Glenarm, co. Antrim, prov. Ulfter, 95 miles from Dublin; and not far from it, on the road fide from *Ballymure*, is *Tubbermore well*, a remarkable fpring of fine water, the ftream of which turns 2 mills at a fmall diftance from the well. This is a rectory in dioc. of Connor, and otherwife written *Killwoaghter* or *Kilwoaghter*.

KILWOAGHTER, fee *Kilwater*.

KILWORTH, a poft town fit. in bar. Condons, co. Cork, prov. Munfter, 104 miles from Dublin, and 3 miles S. of *Mitchel'ftown*; it is a thriving place with a decent church, at the foot of a large ridge of mountains, called Kilworth mountains, through which a good turnpike road is carried from Dublin to Cork; below the town runs the river *Funcheon*, being well ftored with falmon and trout; and difcharges itfelf a mile S. of this into the Blackwater; near *Kilworth* is a good glebe and vicarage houfe: at this place is *Moorpark*, the fuperb

feat of lord *Mountcafhel*; adjoining his lordfhip's improvements ftands the caftle of *Cloughleagh*, boldly fit. on the river *Funcheon*, which has ftood feveral fieges. Fairs are held here on 25 Jan. Eafter Tuefd. Thurfd. after Trinity Sund. 11 Sept. 21 Nov. and 10 Dec. This is a vicarage in dioc. of Cloyne.

KIMMAGE, a pleafant village fit. in co. Dublin, prov. Leinfter, about 2 miles from Dublin caftle, and ¼ mile from *Templeoge*. Lord chief baron *Yelverton* has lately built a very elegant houfe here, and is making confiderable improvements. Near it are the feats of Mr. *Wilkinfon* and Mr. *Waller*.

KINALARTY, fee *Kinelearty*.

KINALEA, a bar. in co. Cork, prov. Munfter; 'tis joined to *Kerricurrihy*, and called the bar. of Kinalea and Kerricurrihy.

KINALEKIN, fit. in co. Galway, prov. Connaught. A commandery for Knts. Hofpitalers was founded here in the 13th century, by *O'Flagherty*.

KINALMEAKY, fee *Kinelmeaky*.

KINARD, fit. near *Dingle*, co. Kerry, prov. Munfter.—Alfo a place in co. Tyrone, prov. Ulfter; otherwife called *Galledgu*.

KINAWLEY, a rectory in dioc. of Kilmore, fit. in bar. Tullaghagh, co. Cavan, prov. Ulfter.

KINBANE, fit. near Fairhead, co. Antrim, prov. Ulfter.

KINDSTOWN, fit. in bar. Balruddery, co. Dublin, prov. Leinfter.

KINEAGH, a vicarage in dioc. of Dublin, fit. in bar. Kilkea, co. Kildare, prov. Leinfter.

KINEIGH, fit. near *Innifkean*, in bar. Carbery, co. Cork, prov. Munfter; here is a remarkable round tower, above 70 feet high, and 124 feet from the W. end of the church; it is faid to have been built about the year 1015, contrary to all others of the kind, the firft ftory is in the form of a hexagon, but the other 5 ftories above it are round. This place is otherwife written *Kineth*; it is a vicarage in dioc. of Cork.

KINEL-CONEL, an antient diftrict in co. Donegal, prov. Ulfter, formerly belonging to the *O'Donnels*.

KINELEARTY, or *Kinalarty*, a bar. fit. in co. Down, prov. Ulfter.

KINEL-ENDA, an antient diftrict of the *O'Brennans*, fit. in co. Weftmeath, prov. Leinft.

KINELMEAKY, or *Kinalmeaky*, a bar. fit. in co. Cork, prov. Munfter. On 28 Feb. 1627, in the reign of James I. the Hon. *Lewis Boyle*, 4th fon of Richard the 1ft earl of *Cork*, was created baron of *Bandon bridge*, and vifc. *Kinelmeaky*; he being then only *eight* years of age; he was killed in his 15th year, at the battle of *Lifcarrol*, on 3 Sept. 1642, this is the *only* inftance

ftance of any child being created a peer of this realm.

KINETH, fee *Kineigh*.

KINFUAD, fit. near *Timolin*, in co. Kildare, prov. Leinfter. A battle was fought here, in which *Sitric* the Norman commander obtained a compleat victory over the Irifh provincialifts.

KING's-COUNTY, fit. in prov. Leinfter. It was antiently called *Offaly* or *Ophaly*; and is bounded by Weftmeath on the N. by Kildare and the Queen's co. on the E. Tipperary co. on the S. and by the river *Shannon*, which feparates it from the prov. of Connaught, on the W. It is a fine fruitful country, and, except the mountains of *Slieb-bloom*, tolerably level; it contains 282,200 acres, 52 parifhes, 11 bar.'s, 2 boroughs, and returns 6 members to parliament. Its length from N. to S. is 34 miles, and the breadth from E. to W. in its broadeft part 32, and it is computed to contain above 74,000 inhabitants. The antient families of this diftrict are the O'Connors, O'Dempfeys, O'Carrols, O'Molloys, M'Coghlans and Fitzfimmons's. Its bar.'s are called Warrenftown, Cooleftown, Phillipftown, Ballycowen, Kilcourfey, Garryveaftle, Geathel, Balliboy, Eglifh or Fircal, Ballybrit, and Clonlifk. The *bog* of *Allen* covers a great part of this co. Its chief town is *Phillipftown*.

KING's COURT, a fair town in bar. Clonchee, co. Cavan, prov. Ulfter, 38 miles from Dublin, 3 miles beyond which is a fmall lake, called *Droughlone*, fit. at the foot of a hill; and a mile further, clofe to the road, on the fame fide, is another lake fomewhat fmaller; fairs held 23 May, 18 June, 19 Sept. 8 Nov. 4 and 24 Dec.

KING's RIVER, fit. in co. Kilkenny, prov. Leinfter; it is fo called from the following circumftance: *Nial*, a king of the race of *Heremon*, came with a great retinue of horfe to the border of this river, in order to ford to the other fide; the waters being rapid by means of a late flood, the firft man who rode in to try the paffage, was hurried down the ftream with fuch violence, that he was given over for loft; which the king feeing, ordered fome of his attendants that were beft horfed, to plunge in to fecure him, but all fhuddering at the danger of the ftream, were afraid to venture; the good natured monarch obferving this, went himfelf to feek for fome convenient place to plunge in with his horfe, and finding one, as he thought, to his purpofe, was preparing to jump in, when the bank being undermined by the violence of the torrent broke down, and the poor prince loft his life in his pious endeavour to fave one of his fubjects; this fatal accident happened in the year 859.—There is

also a *river* of this name, in bar. Talbotftown, co. Wicklow, prov. Leinfter.

KINGSTON, a place fo called in co. Wicklow, prov. Leinfter, 29 miles from Dublin. There is another in co. Rofcommon, prov. Connaught.

KINGSTON-HALL, fit. 1 mile beyond Ardkarna church, co. Rofcommon, prov. Connaught. Here is a moft magnificent and beautiful edifice, with extenfive and delightful parks and demefnes, the feat of the *earl of Kingston*; who has alfo a country refidence at *Boyle*, in the fame co.

KINGSTON-LODGE, a refidence of lord *Kingfton's*, fit. near *Boyle*, co. Rofcommon, prov. Connaught.

KINITTY, fee *Kinnitty*.

KINLOUGH, a village fit. in bar. *Roffclogher*, co. Leitrim, prov. Connaught.

KINMEAGH, fit. in bar. Ravilly, co. Carlow, prov. Leinfter.

KINNAFAD, fit. on the borders of the co. Kildare and King's co. prov. Leinfter.

KINNARD, a rectory in dioc. of Ardfert, fit. in bar. Corcaguinny, co. Kerry, prov. Munfter.

KINNEGAD, a poft town fit. in bar. Farbill, co. Weftmeath, prov. Leinfter, above 29 miles from Dublin, within a mile of which on the fummit of a hill, are the ruins of *Ardmullen* caftle, and 2 miles beyond Kinnegad, are the ruins of a church; fairs held 9 May. This is a curacy in dioc. of Meath.

KINNEIGH, fee *Kineigh*.

KINNERY, fit. in King's co. prov. Leinfter; fairs held 2 Oct.

KINNITTY, fit. in bar. Ballybritt, King's co. prov. Leinfter; it is a rectory in dioc. of Killaloe, 5 miles E. of *Birr*. An abbey was founded here in 557; it was deftroyed by the Danes in 839. The abbot *Colga M'Connazan* died here in 871, who was efteemed the beft and moft elegant poet, then in the kingdom, and was alfo the principal hiftorian.

KINSALE, a poft and borough town in co. Cork, prov. Munfter, 135 miles from Dublin: lat. 51 : 31, lon. 8 : 47. It is built under *Compafs-hill*, and extends about an Englifh mile; it is feated on the river *Bandon*, and governed by a fovereign and recorder; it returns 2 members to parliament, patronage in the *Southwell* family. This place is defended by a ftrong fort, built by king Charles IId, called *Charles fort*: on the oppofite fhore there are two well built villages called *Cove* and *Scilly*. In this *town* and *liberties* are 6 parifhes, 30 plough-lands, and therein 6,846 acres. The church here called *Multos* or *Multoria*, is faid to have been founded by the faint of that name in the 14th century.

cent. In this town was a foundation for White-friars, and also a priory of regular canons. The barracks here hold 12 companies of foot, besides a regiment at *Charlesfort*. The *Spaniards* made themselves masters of the town in 1600, but they were driven out of it the same year by the lord deputy *Mountjoy*, who obliged *Don John de Aquilla*, the Spanish commander, with 5000 Spaniards, to surrender the place. *Charlesfort*, tho' a place of great strength, was taken by the earl of *Marlborough*, from king James IId's forces in 1690. When *Cromwell* was preparing to invest *Kinsale* in 1649, the mayor of the town delivered up the keys to him, which instead of returning (as customary) to the magistrate, he handed to colonel *Stubber*, the governor: it was whispered to *Cromwell*, that *Stubber* was not strict in any religion; " *may be not*" replied Cromwell, " *but as he is a soldier he has honour, and therefore we will let his* religion *alone at this time.* In time of war, *Kinsale* is a place of much business, being then frequented by rich homeward bound fleets, and ships of war ; for which reason most of the houses are then let at double rents. It gives title of baron to the antient family of *de Courcy*, lineally descended from *John de Courcy*, earl of *Ulster*, who from him have the privilege to be covered in the presence of the king of England. Kinsale *harbour* is very commodious, and perfectly secure, so large that the English and Dutch *Smyrna* fleets have anchored therein at the same time : there is a dock and yard for repairing ships of war, and a crane and gun-wharf for landing and shipping heavy artillery ; ships may sail into or out of this harbour, keeping in the middle of the channel with the utmost safety : within the haven on the W. side lies a great shelf, which shoots a great way off from the land, but leaves an ample passage by the side of it, in which, as in all the rest of the harbour, it is many fathoms deep : this haven for some miles goes in N. N. E. but afterwards turns Westward 'till it reaches the key of Kinsale, where ships may ride in 8 or 9 fathom water, being perfectly secure from all winds. Lat. 51 : 35, lon. 8 : 46. In the centre of the town is a good market house, and near it a strong built prison ; here are the ruins of several monasteries and religious houses scattered up and down. This is a vicarage in dioc. of Cork. Fairs are held here on 4 May and Sept. and 21 Nov.

KINSALEBEG, a parish in bar. *Decies within*, co. Waterford, prov. Munster, the church of which stands almost opposite the town of *Youghal*. It is a vicarage in dioc. of Lismore.

KINTARK, sit. near *Castlebar*, co. Mayo, prov. Connaught.

KINURE, sit. in bar. Balruddery, co. Dublin, prov. Leinster.—Also a rectory in dioc. Cork, sit. in bar. Kinalea, co. Cork, prov. Munster.

KINVARRA, a fair town in bar. Kiltartan, co. Galway, prov. Connaught ; fairs held 18 May and 17 Oct. It is a vicarage in dioc. of Kilmacduagh.

KIPPURE *mountains*, sit. in the co.'s Wicklow and Dublin, prov. Leinster.

KIRCUBBIN, sit. in bar. Ardes, co. Down, prov. Ulster, 86 miles from Ulster ; fairs held here 28 Apr. May, Aug. and Nov.

KIRKEEL, a village sit. in co. Down, 4 miles E. of *Green castle*, between the fort of the mountains of *Mourne* and the sea ; the soil about which is generally good, and the country well inhabited ; here is a church and a dissenting meeting house.

KIRK-HILL, sit. in bar. Ardes, co. Down, prov. Ulster.

KIRKISTOWN or *Kirk'stown*, sit. in co. Down, prov. Ulster, the castle of which lies near 4 miles N. E. of *Portaferry* ; this castle and that of *Ballygalget* in this co. were built since the accession of James Ist by *Rowland Savage* of *Archin*.

KIRKSTOWN, see *Kirkistown*.

KISH, a *sand-bank* sit. in Dublin harbour, off the bar. *Half-Rathdown*, co. Dublin, prov. Leinster ; the S. end of it is the shoalest, and bears E. S. E. ¼ E. from the high land of Dalkey, S. E. from the new Light-house or *Caffoon* at the end of the piles, S. S. E. from the Light-house of Howth, E. N. E. from the big *sugar-loaf-hill*, and S. W. from Lambay. The height of the shoal is about 2 cables lengths, and its breadth from E. to W. is about 20 fathoms : this bank stretches across the bay N. by E.

KISHCARRIGIN, a village sit. in bar. Leitrim, co. Leitrim, prov. Connaught.

KISHCORRAN or *Kishkorran*, a range of mountains, sit. in bar. Corran, co. Sligo, prov. Connaught. On the summits of most of these mountains there are very large *Cairns*.

KITSHYNALL, sit. in bar. Idrone, co. Carlow, prov. Leinster.

KITTEMAN, sit. in bar. Boyle, co. Roscommon, prov. Connaught.

KLONKEEN, sit. in bar. Upper Ossory, Queen's co. prov. Leinster.

KNAPPAGH, sit. in bar. Morisk, co. Mayo, prov. Connaught.

KNAPTON, the seat of col. *Pigot*, sit. near *Durrow*, co. Kilkenny, prov. Leinster. It gives title of *baron* to the family of *Vesey*, now visc. *de Vesey*.

KNAVESTOWN, sit. in bar. Ophaly, co. Kildare, prov. Leinster : it is a vicarage in dioc. of Kildare.

KNAW-

KNAW-HILL, fit. between Cafhel and Sulchoid, in co. Tipperary, prov. Munfter: its
antient name was *Cnamhchoill*, or the *eminent
wood*; and it was celebrated on account of a
victory obtained there over the Danes in 968.

KNIGH, a rectory in dioc. of Killaloe, fit.
in bar. lower Ormond; co. Tipperary, prov.
Munfter.

KNIGHT's-BRIDGE, fit, in co. Cork, prov.
Munfter, 151 miles from Dublin, near which
is the nunnery of *Ballyvourney*.

KNOCK, fit. in bar. Morgallion, co. *Meath*,
prov. Leinfter. (Dr. *Beaufort*) It is a rectory
in dioc. of Meath. 'Tis placed by others in
co. *Louth*, prov. Leinfter. *Donchad Hua Kervail*, prince of the country, and *Edan Coellaid-
he* bifhop of Clogher, founded a priory here for
regular canons, under the rule of St. Augustin,
in the year 1148, which was dedicated to the
faints, *Peter* and *Paul*.

KNOCKADERRY, a fair town in co. Limerick,
prov. Munfter; fairs held Afcenfion day, 9
Sept. 29 Oct. and 19 Dec.

KNOCKANCHERRY, fit. in bar. Clanmorris,
co. Kerry, prov. Munfter.

KNOCKANE, a rectory in dioc. of Ardfert,
fit. in bar. Dunkerron, co. Kerry, prov. Munft.
Alfo a place near Toomavara, in King's co.
prov. Leinfter; where are the ruins of a caftle.

KNOCKANURE, a vicarage in dioc. of Ardfert, fit. in bar. Iraghticonnor, co. Kerry, prov.
Munfter.

KNOCKANY, fit. in co. Limerick, prov. Munfter; fairs held 11 Aug. 2 Oct. and 11 Nov.
At or near this place, a bloody battle was
fought between the princes of Connaught and
Dioma, king of Munfter, in which the former
were entirely defeated, and 5 chiefs and 4,000
officers and foldiers left dead on the field.

KNOCKARDING, a fair town in co. Tipperary, prov. Munfter; fairs held 7 Nov.

KNOCKAVILLY, a village fit. in bar. Kinalmeaky, co. Cork, prov. Munfter. — Alfo a
rectory in dioc. of Cork, fit. in bar. Mufkerry,
co. Cork, prov. Munfter.

KNOCKBOY, fit. in co. Monaghan, prov.
Ulfter; fairs held 1 June and 2 Dec.

KNOCKBRACK *mountains*, fit. in bar. Barretts,
co. Cork, prov. Munfter.

KNOCKBRANDON, fit. in bar. Corcaguinny,
co. Kerry, prov. Munfter.

KNOCKBREDA, a rectory in dioc. of Down,
fit. in bar. Caftlereagh, co. Down, prov. Ulfter.

KNOCKBRIDE, a rectory in dioc. of Kilmore,
fit. in bar. Clonchee, co. Cavan, prov. Ulfter.

KNOCKBRIDGE, fit in bar. Louth, co. Louth,
prov. Leinfter.

KNOCKBROOK-HILL, fit. in bar. Balruddery,
co. Dublin, prov. Leinfter.

KNOCK-CASTLE, now in ruins, fit. in co.
Down, prov. Ulfter, 82 miles from Dublin.

KNOCKCLOOHAN *mountains*, fit. in bar. Lough-
lintholen, co. Londonderry, prov. Ulfter.

KNOCKCOMMON, a rectory in dioc. of Meath,
fit. in bar. Duleck, co. Meath, prov. Leinfter.

KNOCKDRUMCALLY, a vicarage in dioc. of
Tuam, fit. in bar. Coftello, co. Mayo, prov.
Connaught.

KNOCKDUACH *mountains*, fit. in bar. Moycullin, co. Galway, prov. Connaught.

KNOCKFALY, fit. in bar. Ballinahinch, co.
Galway, prov. Connaught.

KNOCKENURE, fit. in bar. Iraghticonnor, co.
Kerry, prov. Munfter.

KNOCKEROGHERY, a fair town in co. Rofcommon, prov. Connaught; fairs held 21 Aug.
25 and 26 Oct.

KNOCKEYEN-HILL, fit. in bar. Half-fowre,
co. Weftmeath, prov. Leinfter.

KNOCKFAINE, fit. in bar. Conillo, co. Limerick, prov. Munfter.

KNOCKFERGUS, an antient name for *Carrickfergus*, in co. Antrim, prov. Ulfter.

KNOCKFERRY, fit. at *Lough Corrib*, co. Galway, prov. Connaught.

KNOCKGRAFFON, a rectory in dioc. of Cafhel,
fit. near *Cahier*, in bar. Middlethird, co. Tipperary, prov. Munfter; here are fome antient
ruins.

KNOCKINA, fit. in bar. Clunlonan, co.
Weftmeath, prov. Leinfter.

KNOCKLADE, fit. near *Ballycaftle*, in co. *Antrim*, prov. Ulfter. In May, 1788, an irrup-
tion took place here, which was announced by
a noife refembling a continual crafh of thunder,
with a column of fire and fmoke, which afcended about 60 yards into the air; after a fhower
of afhes and ftones, which extended ¼ of a
mile round the hill; in 46 minutes after the
firft fhock, a ftream of *lava* was poured out,
and rufhed in a fheet of liquid fire, about 60
yards in breadth down the fields, until it entered
adjoining the village of *Ballyowen*, where it
involved the houfes, and their unfortunate inhabitants, in one conflagrate ruin, none having efcaped but one man, his wife and two
children; it continued running 39 hours, and
then totally ceafed.

KNOCKLADE-MOUNTAIN, fit. in bar. Cary,
co. Antrim, prov. Ulfter.

KNOCKLOFTY, fit. in co. Tipperary, prov.
Munfter, on the banks of the *Suir*, 3 miles
from *Clonmel*, here is a feat of the prefent provoft of Trinity College, Dublin; 2 miles from
it are the ruins of *Ballindinny-caftle*; 2 miles
further, are the ruins of 2 other caftles, and a
mile beyond thefe is the ruin of *Ladies Abbey*.
The Rt. Hon. *Richard Hely Hutchinfon*, took his
feat

feat as lord baron *Donoughmore* of *Knocklofty*, 6 Feb. 1789; he succeeded his mother, who was a peeress in her own right.

KNOCKLONG, sit. in co. Limerick, prov. Munster, 97 miles from Dublin.

KNOCKLAVE *hill*, sit. in bar. Carbury, co. Sligo, prov. Connaught.

KNOCKLAYD, see *Knocklade*.

KNOCKMACE, sit. in bar. Ballybrit, King's co. prov. Leinster.

KNOCKMARK, a rectory in dioc. of Meath, sit. in bar. Deece, co. Meath, prov. Leinster.

KNOCKMAY-HILL, sit. in bar. Clare, co. Galway, prov. Connaught.

KNOCKMELEDOWN, a mountain in bar. Offa, co. Waterford, being one of that ridge of mountains, which divides the N. W. point of this co. from that of Tipperary, prov. Munster; its perpendicular height is 900 yards. On the top of this mountain *Henry Eeles*, an inhabitant of Lismore, was buried, agreeably to his own desire; he was an ingenious man, and published several tracts on the subject of electricity.

KNOCKMILL, a fair town in co. Carlow, prov. Leinster; fairs held 4 Sept. and 30 Nov.

KNOCKMOANE, a castle in co. Waterford, prov. Munster, said to have been built by a woman, whose tomb-stone is shewn here, being very large; but without any inscription or sculpture, except a kind of cross, circumscribed in a circle in relievo, of very rude workmanship, which shews its antiquity; near the castle are the ruins of a little chapel, where sir *Rich. Osborne* was buried in the last century.

KNOCKMOILE *hill*, sit. in bar. Tirawly, co. Mayo, prov. Connaught.

KNOCKMORE, sit. in bar. Tyrerill, co. Sligo, prov. Connaught. A friary was erected here in the 14th century, by *O'Gara*. Here is a ruined castle of the *O'Conners*.

KNOCKMOURNE, a village sit. in bar. Killnatalloon, co. Cork, prov. Munster; it is a vicarage in dioc. of Cloyne; near the decayed church of which are the ruins of a large building, and also a chalybeate spring.

KNOCKMOY, a rectory in dioc. of Tuam, sit. in bar. Tiaquin, co. Galway, prov. Connaught. (*Dr. Beaufort.*) It is placed by others in bar. Downamore. Here was a monastery founded in 1189, by *Cathal O'Connor*, monarch of Ireland, in remembrance of a victory obtained there by him, over *Almericus de St. Laurence*; the place was called in Irish, *Knockmoy*, i. e. the hill of the plain; and the abbey was called *Monasterium de colle victoriae*, from Cathal's success. The tomb of *O'Connor* here, is adorned with paintings in fresco; some of them relate to an historical fact. Six kings are represented, three deceased and three living. Of the latter, one in the middle is *Roderick O'Con-*nor, monarch of Ireland, at the English invasion; he holds in his hand the leaf of some plant, to denote his being lord proprietor of the whole kingdom. The princes on each side are his vassals. One with a hawk on his hand, is his grand falconer; the other with a sword, his grand marshal: these held their lands by grand serjeanty. Below them sits a Brehon with his roll of laws, having pronounced sentence of death on *Dermod M'Morough's* son, for the crime of his father in joining the English. The boy is tied to a tree, and two archers are executing the sentence, his body being transfixed with arrows. The workmanship, it is apprehended, can scarcely be so old as the 12th century.

KNOCKMOYLE, see *Knockmoile*.

KNOCKMUILAN, see *Knockmyland*.

KNOCKMUILDOWN, see *Knockmeledown*.

KNOCKMYLAND or Knockmuilan, a village sit. in bar. Knocktopher, co. Kilkenny, prov. Leinster. It holds fairs yearly on 5 Aug.

KNOCKNACRIOTH, sit. contiguous to the nunnery of *Grany*, in bar. Kilkea, co. Kildare, prov. Leinster. Here was a religious house, and some marks of its ruins still remain.

KNOCKNAGAUL, a vicarage in dioc. of Limerick, sit. in the liberties of Limerick, prov. Munster.

KNOCKNAGREE, a fair town in co. Cork, prov. Munster; fairs held 28 Apr. 25 July, 20 Oct. and 20 Dec.

KNOCKNAGYLAGH, sit. near *Red-hills*, in bar. Ophaly, co. Kildare, prov. Leinster; near it are the ruins of a church; also a well dedicated to St. *Brigid*.

KNOCKNAOA, sit. in bar. Idrone, co. Carlow, prov. Leinster.

KNOCKNAREA or *Knocknaree*, a *promontory* sit. in bar. Carbury, co. Sligo, prov. Connaug.

KNOCKNASHEE *mountains*, sit. in bar. Leney, co. Sligo. prov. Connaught: the river *Moy* rises in this place, and after receiving the waters of *Lough Calt* and *Lough Conn*, flows in a broad stream to the bay of Killalla.

KNOCKNEGULLAGH, see *Knocknagylagh*.

KNOCKNEMARIFF, a fair town in co. Cork, prov. Munster; fairs held 3 May, Aug. 20 Oct. and Dec.

KNOCKNICLASHY, sit. near *Clonmene*, in co. Cork, prov. Munster: this hill is celebrated for a defeat given to *Donough*, then lord *Muskerry*, who, with 4000 Irish, was marching to raise the siege of *Limerick*, by the lord *Broghill*, with 1000 English, in July 1651.

KNOCKNIMACE, sit. in bar. Ballybrit, King's co. prov. Leinster.

KNOCKNINOSS, sit. in co. Cork, prov. Munster; this place is remarkable for the defeat of the

the Irish in Nov. 1647, whereon the fate of this prov. depended.

KNOCKNINY, a bar. in co. Fermanagh, prov. Ulster, having a village in it of same name.

KNOCKOLIVER, sit. in bar. Conillo, co. Limerick, prov. Munster.

KNOCKOWNE, a hill in co. Cork, prov. Munster, near *Lough-Hyne*, remarkable for a very fine echo : a little to the W. of it is the castle of *Ardagh*.

KNOCK-PATRICK, a mountain sit. in co. Limerick, prov. Munster.

KNOCKRAMMER, sit. near *Lurgan*, co. Armagh, prov. Ulster.

KNOCKREA, sit. in bar. Ballinacour, co. Wicklow, prov. Leinster.

KNOCKROE, sit. near *Strabane*, co. Tyrone, prov. Ulster.

KNOCKSEDAN, a village sit. in co. Dublin, prov. Leinster, 4½ miles beyond *Glasnevin*, and 7 miles from Dublin castle. There is a remarkable mount here, in a pleasant field, from which is an extensive prospect of a beautiful and well improved country.

KNOCKTEMPLE, a rectory in dioc. of Cloyne, sit. in bar. Duhallow, co. Cork, prov. Munster.

KNOCKTOPHER, a bar. in co. Kilkenny, prov. Leinster. It has in it a borough, post and market town of same name, distant 63 miles from Dublin; which returns two members to parliament; patronage in the families of *Langrishe* and *Ponsonby*. It is a rectory in dioc. of Ossory. Lat. 52 : 24, long. 7 : 36. In 1356, James, the 2d *earl* of *Ormond*, founded a friary here for Carmelites or Whitefriars, under the invocation of the Virgin Mary. This friary and its possessions were granted 24 Oct. 34th *Hen.* VIIIth to *Patrick Barnwell* for ever, in capite, at the annual rent of 4s Irish money.

KNOCKTORY, sit. in bar. Scarawalsh, co. Wexford, prov. Leinster.

KNOCKVICAR, sit. in bar. Boyle, co. Roscommon, prov. Connaught. On the summit of this hill a monastery was erected for Franciscans of the 3d order; a lease of it was afterwards granted to *Rich. Kendlemarch*.

KNORDOE, sit. about 8 miles from Galway, co. Galway, prov. Connaught : it is famous for a battle fought there between the Irish and the Danes.

KORMESHTY *mountains*, sit. in bar. Erris, co. Mayo, prov. Connaught.

KUNAGURUFF, sit. in bar. Owneybeg, co. Limerick, prov. Munster.

KYLE, a village in bar. Ballagheen, co. Wexford, prov. Leinster, 56 miles from Dublin.— Also a rectory in dioc. of Killaloe, sit. in bar. upper Ossory, Queen's co. prov. Leinster.

Also a place in bar. Gallmoy, co. Kilkenny, prov. Leinster; in the neighbourhood of which stand the ruins of 4 old castles, all within the distance of one mile.

KYLE-HILL, sit. in bar. upper Ossory, Queen's co. prov. Leinster; here is one of the antient judgment seats of the Brehons; it is very near the top of the hill on its E. side, and formed from the solid rock; the common people call it *the fairy chair* : here the Brehon of the *Fitzpatricks* held his court.

KYNALYAGH, an antient district of the *Mc Geoghans*, sit. in co. Meath, prov. Leinster.

KYNNETHIN, sit. in co. Limerick, prov. Munster. In Michaelmas term 1300, a writ issued to the sheriff to distrain the abbot of this place, at the suit of *Robert de Bland*, for 13 marks, an arrear of rent. We find no other mention of this abbey.

L A

LABACALLY, (otherwise called *Hag's bed*) an antique sepulchral monument, sit. in co. Cork, prov. Munster; about mid-way between *Glenworth* and *Kilworth*, which places are about 3 miles distant. This monument by its size seems to have been designed for some eminent person of antiquity; but for whom or when erected, the least traces are not to be found, either in history or from tradition. It consists of several broad flag stones, supported by others which are pitched in the ground. One of these stones is of an enormous size, being not less than 17 feet long and 9 feet broad, and in the middle 3 feet thick, from whence it slopes away to the edges, like the roof of a house. But as if this huge stone was not a sufficient cover to the tomb, there are two others, one 11 by 7 feet, and the other 7 feet square. There was a fourth huge flag, which lies at the W. end, and covered that part. On each side are several broad flags, pitched in the ground in two ranges, on which the upper stones rest, as a tomb stone on the side walls. Some of those pillar stones are 6 feet high and 4 broad. The whole of this vast tomb, it being hollow underneath, is 40 feet on the outside, and 14 broad. The whole was inclosed within a circle of flag stones, pitched in the ground, at about 14 feet from the centre of the tomb. The bringing and erecting these stones hither must have been a work of immense labour, as there are none of the kind nearer than the mountains 5 or 6 miles distant. It is placed E. and W. and conjectured to have been erected since the ages of christianity.

LABERUS,

LABERUS, an antient city, mentioned by *Ptolemy: Richard* of *Cirencefter* makes it the capital of the *Voluntii*. *Laberus* is evidently derived from *Lhavar*, whence *Labhereigh* a fpeaking place, or figuratively a place of parliament where the ftates affembled. The *Laberus* of *Ptolemy* was the hill of *Tarah*, celebrated in the Irifh annals for being the place where fat the convention of *Tarah* during the pagan times. This celebrated convention is thought by fome to have been originally inftituted by the Heremonian Belgians, on their firft fettlement in Ireland, about 350 years before the Chriftian Æra. During the contefts between the feveral Belgian and Caledonian fettlers, the ftates feldom had the opportunity of affembling at ftated periods, until about the beginning of the firft century, when *Connar-mor*, called by feveral of the Irifh antiquaries, *Concohar Mac Neffan*, by the advice of the Arch-Druid *Cathbad*, (called by fome of the antient poems *Ollam Fodla)* revived the inftitution: from which period the monarchs of Ireland were conftantly inaugurated on the ftone of deftiny, erected on the hill near the *Labhereigh*; until the time of *Dermod M'Keruail*, in 560, when the chriftian clergy anathematized the place. From that time the ftates affembled in the court of the palace of *Tarah*, until the final deftruction of that fortrefs by *Brien Boromh*, in 995. The *Naafteighan* and *Labhereigh*, where the ftates affembled, are ftill vifible on the *hill of Tarah*.

LABIUS, a name given by *Rich. Cirenc.* to the prefent river Liffey, prov. Leinfter.

LACFODERY *mountains*, fit. in bar. Truaghnacmy, co. Kerry, prov. Munfter.

LACKAGH, a rectory in dioc. of Kildare, fit. in bar. Ophaly, co. Kildare, prov. Leinfter. Here is an antient burial ground, with the ruins of a church and caftle. The latter according to tradition, was built by a woman of the family of *Fitzgerald*; it was much injured by the affaults of Cromwell, and afterwards fuffered by fire. Near it is a mote or rath, which appears to have been furrounded by a ditch. Here is the burial place of the family of *Rice*, whofe antient feat of *Mountrice*, (once an elegant fituation) lies at a fmall diftance from thefe ruins. This place gives title of baron to the family of *Fielding*, now earl of *Defmond*.

LACKAH, a *river*, fit. in bar. Kilmacrenan, co. Donegal, prov. Ulfter.—Alfo a vicarage in dioc. of Tuam, fit. in bar. Clare, co. Galway, prov. Connaught.

LACKAN, a vicarage in dioc. of Killala, fit. in bar. Tirawly, co. Mayo, prov. Connaught.

LACKEEN, a rectory in dioc. of Cloyne, fit. in bar. Orrery, co. Cork, prov. Munfter.

LACKIN, a curacy in dioc. of Meath, fit. in bar. Corkerry, co. Weftmeath, prov. Leinfter.

LADIE's-TOWN, fit. in bar. Mullingar, co. Weftmeath, prov. Leinfter.

LADY-ISLAND, fit. in bar. Forth, co. Wexford, prov. Leinfter; where fairs are held on 15 Aug. and 19 Sept. This is a curacy in dioc. of Ferns.

LADYTOWN, fit. near *Naas*, in bar. Great Connel, co. Kildare, prov. Leinfter: it is a curacy in dioc. of Kildare.

LAGAN *river*, otherwife called *Locha* river, fit. in co. Down, prov. Ulfter; this, or rather the mouth of it, which is the bay of *Carrickfergus*, is called by *Ptolemy* the *Vinderius*; this river is mentioned under the name *Locha*, in the life of St. *Colman*, the firft bifhop and founder of the church of *Dromore*, who flourifhed in the 6th century, and is faid to have " founded a noble monaftery on the N. fide of the river *Locha*." It rifes in two fmall ftreams out of the mountains called *Slieve Croob*, in the bar. of *upper Iveach*, which unite into a river about 2 miles S. E. of *Dromore*, which at laft empties itfelf into *Carrickfergus bay*, after meandering a courfe of about 30 miles through this co.

LAGANSTOWN, fit. in bar. Middlethird, co. Tipperary, prov. Munfter.

LAGGAN-BRIDGE, fit. in co. Monaghan, prov. Ulfter, 38 miles from Dublin.

LAGHY, fit. in bar. Tyrhugh, co. Donegal, prov. Ulfter, 108 miles from Dublin.

LAMBAY, an ifland on the Eaftern coaft of this kingdom, in co. Dublin, prov. Leinfter, mentioned by *Ptolemy*, and called by *Pliny*, Limnus, a corruption from the antient Britifh (as Mr. *Beauford* thinks) *Lan-n'-iii*, or *intirely in the water*; being at fome diftance from the coaft; it lies about 12 miles from Dublin; lat. 53:30 N. lon. 6:12 W. It is remarkable for vaft quantities of rabbits and fea-fowl, and has a curious well and fine fpring of water, dedicated to the Holy Trinity. There is great plenty of crabs, lobfters, oyfters, &c. about this ifland, and abundance of kelp is made in it. In the reign of queen *Eliz.* a grant of the ifland of Lamoay was made to fir *William Ufher* and his heirs for ever, on condition of his paying 6*l.* per ann. to the fee of Dublin. There is a very curious old building on Lambay; it is a polygon, and appears to have been conftructed for the purpofe of defending the place, as its battlements and fpikeholes command the ifland in every direction round. This ifland is about 3 miles long and 1½ mile broad, nearly of an oval form. It is about 5 miles diftance from *Malahide*, and nearly the fame from *Rufh*.

LAMBEG,

LAMBEG, a village fit. near *Lifburn*, in bar. Belfaft, co. Antrim, prov. Ulfter. It is a curacy in dioc. of Connor. Here *M'Donnell* built a monaftery in the 15th century, for Francifcans of the 3d order.

LAMBSGROVE, fit. near Kilkenny, co. Kilkenny, prov. Leinfter.

LAMBSTOWN, fit. in bar. Shelburne, co. Wexford, prov. Leinfter.

LANDENSTOWN, fit. not far from *Sallins*, in bar. Clane, co. Kildare, prov. Leinfter. It is a very pleafant feat, belonging to Mr. *Digby*; and the Grand Canal from Dublin, which paffes thro' it, has contributed confiderably to its beauty.

LANE-LAKE, fee *Killarney Lake*.

LANE *river*, otherwife called *Laun*, fit. in bar. Magunihy, co. Kerry, prov. Munfter. Dr. Smyth obferves, that many of the antient Irifh names of our rivers and mountains, are the fame with others in *Great-Britain*; thus the river *Laune*, is the fame name with the *Lune*, which runs by *Lancafter*; he gives other examples, and from thence infers, that the firft and moft antient inhabitants of *Britain* and *Ireland*, fpoke one and the fame language.

LANESBOROUGH, a borough and fair town, fit. in bar. Rathline, co. Longford, prov. Leinfter, it is a borough and returns 2 members to parliament; patron, lord Conbrock: diftance from Dublin 62 miles. Fairs held on 12 Feb. This place is fit. on the river *Shannon*, and has a barrack for a troop of horfe. It gave title of vifc. to the family of *Lane*, and now gives title of earl to that of *Butler*. 2 miles beyond it are the ruins of a church. There is a bridge over the *Shannon* at *Lanefborough*, into the co. *Rofcommon*. Lat. 53 : 40 N. lon. 8 : 6 W.

LARABRYAN *church*, now in ruins, fit. 1½ mile beyond *Maynooth*, co. Kildare, prov. Leinfter.

LARAGH, fee *Lerha*.

LARAH, a vicarage in dioc. of Kilmore, fit. in bar. Tullagharvey, co. Cavan, prov. Ulfter.

LARCHFIELD, fit. in bar. Caftlereagh, co. Down, prov. Ulfter.

LARGAY, fee *Largy*.

LARGY, or *Largay*, fit. in bar. Tullaghagh, co. Cavan, prov. Ulfter, 84 miles from Dublin. A mile beyond it are the ruins of a church; and about a quarter of a mile from *Largay* is *Belcoo-bridge*. Fairs are held here 22 May, July, Sept. and 19 Nov.

LARNE, a fair and poft town in bar. Glenarm, co. Antrim, prov. Ulfter, 97 miles from Dublin. Fairs held 31 July and Dec. Near it are the ruins of a caftle.

LARNE-HARBOUR, fit. near Magee ifland, in co. Antrim, prov. Ulfter. Lat. 54 : 53, lon. 6 : 14.

LAROTAGH, a church-yard, or rather a burial place, for there is neither church or inclofure to it; fit. on the fide. of the public road, about 2 miles from *Kelly'ftown* in co. Carlow, prov. Leinfter. It is noted for the interment of one of the antient kings of Ireland.

LARRACOR, a vicarage in dioc. of Meath, fit. in bar. Moyfenrath, co. Meath, prov. Leinf.

LARRAGH, or *Larrow*, an antient abbey fit. near *Derryglafs* in bar. lower Ormond, co. Tipperary, prov. Munfter.

LARROW, fee *Larragh*.

LATTERAGH, a village fit. 6 miles S. E. of *Nenagh*, in bar. upper Ormond, co. Tipperary, prov. Munfter. It is a rectory in dioc. of Killaloe. St. *Odran* prefided over an abbey here; he died of the plague 2d Oct. 548, and 'tis faid had 3000 fcholars, remarkable for piety and learning.

LATTIN, a rectory in dioc. of Emly, fit. in bar. Clanwilliam; co. Tipperary, prov. Munft.

LAUDE-DEI, now called *Ballybogan*, fit. on the river Boyne, 3 miles S. of Clonard in co. Meath, prov. Leinfter. Here a priory was founded by *Jordan Comin* in the 12th century, for regular canons of St. Auguftin; and called the priory of *Laude-dei*.

LAUNDESTOWN *caftle*, fit. near *Turvey*, 8 miles from Dublin, in co. Dublin, prov. Leinfter.

LAUGHLINSTOWN, fee *Leighlin'ftown*.

LAUNE-RIVER, fee *Lane river*.

LAVATH, a *river* which iffues from the Weftern declivity of Mount Crommal, falls into Lough Swilly, prov. Ulfter.

LAXNA, fit. in bar. Clanmorris, co. Kerry, prov. Munfter.

LAYDE, a rectory in dioc. of Connor, fit. in bar. *Glenarm*, co. Antrim, prov. Ulfter. (Dr. *Beaufort*) It is placed by Mr. *Scalè* in bar. *Carie*.

LEA, fee *Ley*.

LEACARRO, fit. in bar. Rofcommon, co. Rofcommon, prov. Connaught.

LEA-CASTLE, fee *Ley-caftle*.

LEADSTOWN, fit. near Naas, prov. Leinfter.

LEAM *mountain*, fit. in bar. Moycullin, co. Galway, prov. Connaught.

LEAMCHUILL, fit. near *Lay*, in Queen's co. prov. Leinfter. Here St *Fintan-chorach* was abbot about the clofe of the 6th century: he is faid by fome to have been interred here, but others fay the place of his fepulture was at *Clonfert-Brendan*.

LEAN-CAPE, fit. in bar. Moyferta, co. Clare, prov. Munfter.

LEAP, a fair town in co. Cork, prov. Munfter; fairs held 24 May and 20 Oct. 'Tis fometimes written *Lepp*.—Alfo a village of fame name,

name, fit. in bar. Ballibritt, King's co. prov. Leinfter, 59 miles from Dublin. Here is a beautiful feat, with extenfive demefnes and plantations.

LEAP-GLYN, a deep and dangerous glen, fit. at the upper end of *Glandore* harbour, in co. Cork, prov. Munfter, on both fides of which is the high-road from *Rofs* to the other parts of *W. Carberry*: the road croffes this glen, which at that part is as fteep as a flight of ftairs, fo that few horfes, but fuch as are well ufed to it, attempt it with courage. To the W. of this precipice is a handfome feat called *Brede*, with large plantations.

LEA-RIVER, a fmall rivulet in co. Kerry, prov. Munfter, which rifes a few miles to the E. of *Tralee*, and being fupplied by feveral mountain ftreams, is pretty confiderable in time of great floods. It difcharges itfelf into *Tralee-bay*, and is navigable for boats up to that town, at time of high water. *Camden* will have this river to be the *Dur* of *Ptolemy*, but it is too inconfiderable a ftream to be noticed by that geographer, and therefore Dr. *Smith* places the *Dur* of that writer in the *bay of Caftlemain*.

LE-BERGERIE, fit. near *Portarlington*, prov. Leinfter.

LECAGHE, fee *Lackagh*.

LECAHILL, now the bar. of *Lecale*, in co. Down: it is faid by fome to have been an antient territory of the Savages, and was a part of the *Englifh pale*.

LECALE, antiently *Lethcathel*, from *Lea Caël*, i. e. the wood of the plain, a bar. in co. Down, prov. Ulfter: it was heretofore a part of the *Englifh pale*, and contains the towns of *Down-patrick*, *Dundrum* and *Strangford*. The chiefs or dynafts of this diftrict were called *Dal-dichu* or *Cathel*, and fubject to the *Magh Genuifge*; the *Magiunefs's* having the principal command over this place, tho' many fortreffes hereabouts were built by the *Savages*, and it appears by record, that 31 May, 28 Hen. VIIIth an indenture was made between *Leonard Grej*, lord deputy, and *Raymund Savage*, antient chief of his clan, by which it was covenanted, that " *Raymund* fhould have the chieftainfhip of his fept, in the territory of the *Savages*, otherwife called *Lecale*, as principal chieftain thereof, and that *Raymund* fhould give to the deputy, for acquiring his favour and friendfhip, 100 fat able cows, and a horfe, or 15 marks, *Irifh* money, in lieu thereof, at the pleafure of the deputy." But it feems this place belonged originally to the Magenifs's, and that the *Savages* were rather intruders; for there is a tradition that when the *Savages* had formed a ftrong body of men, in order to opprefs the Magenifs's and other Irifh families in *Lecale*, the latter were obliged to call for the affiftance of the earl of

Kildare, and promifed him one or two townlands, according to the extent of their territories, and that by thefe means that noble family got *Ardglafs* and other lands hereabouts. When the earl had marched as far as *Ballykinler*, the *Savages* fubmitted, and fo the quarrel ended. This country is remarkable from the Irifh chief *Dichu* being the firft convert St. *Patrick* made to the Chriftian faith, in the *N.* of Ireland.

LECK, a rectory in dioc. of Raphoe, fit. in bar. Raphoe, co. Donegal, prov. Ulfter.

LECKCARROW, a fair town in co. Rofcommon, prov. Connaught; fairs held 17 March, 27 June and Sept. and 20 Dec.

LECKIN, now a parifh church near *Bunbraf-ny*, on the river Inny, in bar. Corkerry, co. Weftmeath, prov. Leinfter. St. *Crumin* was formerly bifhop of this place in the time of St. *Fechin*, who died A. D. 664.

LECKPATRICK, a rectory in dioc. of Derry, fit. in bar. Strabane, co. Tyrone, prov. Ulfter.

LEDWICKSTOWN, fit. in bar. Mullingar, co. Weftmeath, prov. Leinfter.

LEE, a river in co. Cork, prov. Munfter, the head of which rifes in that romantic fpot, the lake of *Gougane Barra*; this river is the *Luvius* of *Ptolemy*.—Alfo a river in bar. Truaghnacmy, co. Kerry, prov. Munft.

LEEK, fit. in bar. Raphoe, co. Donegal, prov. Ulfter.

LEESTON *river*, fit. in co. Down, prov. Ulft. This river, like fome others in this co. fuddenly rifes with a little rain, and as fuddenly decreafes by the return of fair weather.

LEGACURRY, a fair town in co. Armagh, prov. Ulfter; fairs held Shrove Tuefd. 26 July and 15 Oct.

LEGAGOWEN, fit. in bar. Caftlereagh, co. Down, prov. Ulfter.

LEGANENEY, a town-land in the parifh of *Drumgoolan*, co. Down, prov. Ulfter, in which there is an antient *Crom-liagh* or altar ftone, on the mountain called *Slieve-naboil-trogh*, being a part of *Sleeve Croob*, near a fmall lake lying in the valley underneath it; it is a huge gritty ftone, in fhape of a monftrous coffin, fupported by three feet compofed of other ftones, and forming a cavity underneath, where a man $6\frac{1}{2}$ feet high may ftand upright.

LEGH-CON or *Leath Cuinn*, one of the antient grand divifions of Ireland, made towards the clofe of the fecond century, between *Eogan More*, furnamed *Mogh Nuagad*, king of Munft. and *Con* furnamed *Ceadchathach*, king of Tarah, dividing the ifland into two parts, by a line drawn from *Clavin's-bridge* near Galway, to the ridge of mountains, denominated *Eifgir Riada*, on which *Clonmacnois* and *Cionard* are
fit.

fit. and from thence to *Dublin*. The Northern division was called *Leagh Cuin*, or *Conn's part*; and the Southern, *Leagh Mogh*, or *Mogh's part*. The entire kingdom by this division was separated into two governments, which by the continual contentions of the several chiefs, subsisted only 15 years, tho' the names were retained for several ages after; the Southern part of Ireland being frequently called *Legh Mogh*, and the Northern *Legh Conn*, down to the 14th century.

LEGHINCH, fit. in bar. Kilmayn, co. Mayo, prov. Connaught.

LEGHINCH-BRIDGE, fit. in bar. Lower Ormond, co. Tipperary, prov. Munster.

LEGH-MOGH, fee *Legh Con*.

LEIGH, another name for *Gray abbey*, in co. Down, prov. Ulster.

LEIGHLIN,' (or *old Leighlin*) fit. in bar. Idrone, co. Carlow, prov. Leinster, about 43 miles from Dublin, near the river *Barrow*: It is a borough, and returns 2 members to parliament; patronage in the bishop of the dioc. this being a bishoprick united to *Ferns*. The town was incorporated in 1216, and the extent of its liberties were marked by large stones, inscribed, " *Terminus Burgens. Lechlinen. hic lapis eft.*" One of these stands near *Leighlin-bridge*, another near *Wells*, and a third in the mountains. At the E. end of the church of *Old-Leighlin*, is a famous well covered with great ash trees, and dedicated to St. *Lafarien*: within 2 miles of *Leighlin* are the ruins of a church. This place was formerly a city, tho' now a very mean village: the cathedral has been kept in good repair; fronting the entrance is a tomb, wherein it is said bishop *Cavanagh* was interred in 1587. It was a sole bishoprick, founded in 632, and joined to *Ferns* in 1600. It is also reported, that *Gurmundus*, a *Danish* prince, was buried in this church. The last bishop of *Leighlin*, before its union with *Ferns*, was the Right Rev. *Robert Grave*, who coming by sea to be installed, suffered shipwreck in the harbour of Dublin, and perished in the waves. This cathedral was burnt to the ground, it is said, by lightning, A. D. 1060; and afterwards rebuilt in 1232, or according to others, between 1158 and 1185, by bishop *Donat*, and dedicated to St. *Laufarien* or *Lazarinus*. Since the fees were joined, it has been used as a parish church, this being a rectory in dioc. of Leighlin. That part mostly in ruins, is the remains of *Donat's* fabrick. This town was plundered by the people of *Offory* in 916 and 978, and by the *Danes* in 982. *Burchard*, a Norwegian, built the priory of St. *Stephen* here, and was buried in the cathedral under a marble monument, whereon were his effigie and this inscription; " *Hic jacet humatus dux fundator Lenia en Germondi Burchar-*

dus, vir gratus ecclefiæ." St. *Gobban* founded also a celebrated abbey here, for regular canons, in which a famous assembly of the clergy was held A. D. 630, to debate on the proper time for the celebration of Easter. During the English and Irish wars, the town was laid waste in 1389, but revived so much in 1400, as to have 86 burgage tenements, a bishop's palace, deanery house and monastery, none of which now remain. *Maurice Jakis* in 1320, constructed the bridge of Leighlin over the *Barrow*, which gave the great Southern road a new direction, and *Old Leighlin* went rapidly to decay. Lat. 52:38, lon. 7:18.

LEIGHLIN-BRIDGE, fit. about 45 miles from Dublin and 2 miles from *Old Leighlin*, co. Carlow, prov. Leinster. About the end of the reign of *Hen*. IIId a monastery was founded here for Carmelites or Whitefriars, by one of the *Carews*, near the *Black-castle*, on the E. bank of the river Barrow: it was dedicated to the Virgin Mary. The bridge here was built in 1320, by *Maurice Jakis*, a canon of the cathedral of Kildare, who also built the bridge of *Kilcullen*. Here are still the remains of a castle built by the *Lacies*, and of an old abbey. This is a post town, and holds fairs on 14 May, 25 Sept. and 6 Oct. It was destroyed by the Irish in 1577.

LEIGHLIN'STOWN or *Laughlin'flown*, fit. in co. Dublin, prov. Leinster. A small village about 7 miles from the metropolis, on the road to *Bray*, which is only about 3 miles beyond it.

LEIGHMONEY, a rectory in dioc. of Cork, fit. in bar. Kinalea, co. Cork, prov. Munster.

LEIM-CON, a handsome feat in co. Cork, prov. Munster; fit. near a good harbour, between *Long-island* and the peninsula. It is also a name given to *Mizzen-head*, the Southern extremity of Ireland in that co.

LEIM-CUCULLAN, an antient name of *Loop-head*, or *Cape-lean*, at the mouth of the river *Shannon*.

LEINSTER, the Eastern prov. of Ireland, bounded by Ulster on the N. *St. George's*, or the *Irish Channel* on the E. and S. and by the prov.'s of *Connaught* and *Munster* on the W. The capital city of this prov. and of the kingdom is *Dublin*. It contains 12 co,'s, viz. Carlow, Dublin, Kildare, Kilkenny, King's-co. Longford, Louth, Meath, Queen's-co. Westmeath, Wexford and Wicklow. It is the most level and best cultivated prov. in the kingdom; containing 2,792,450 acres, 992 parishes, 97 har.'s, and 53 boroughs; it is about 124 miles long and 74 broad. *Dermod* king of Leinster marrying his daughter *Eva* to *Strongbow*, earl of *Pembroke*, on his decease made him his universal heir; whereby the earl inherited the prov. of Leinster, and was afterwards enfeoffed

of

of it by Hen. IId. He died in 1176, and left an only daughter Ifabel, efpoufed to *Wm. Marfhal,* earl of Pembroke, by her he had 5 fons, who fucceeded to his great eftates in Leinfter. This prov. gives title of duke to the antient and noble family of *Fitzgerald.* In the early ages, this diftrict was almoft one continued foreft, and was principally the feat of the *Kinfelaghs.* The chief refidence of its kings was at *Carman.* Mr O'Connor obferves that this prov. was originally called *Galian,* from its Galenian inhabitants of the *Belgic* race; but that about 270 years before Chrift, it took the name of *Lagean,* which it ftill retains, from *Labea Longfeach,* after his return from Gaul, who introduced the ufe of the *Lagean,* a fort of broadedged launce or javelin. This prov. was antiently divided among the *Brigantes,* inhabiting the co.'s Kilkenny, Carlow, King's co. and Queen's co. the *Menapii,* in and about Wexford; the *Caucii,* in and about Wicklow; and the *Blanii,* or *Eblanii,* in Dublin, Eaftmeath, and Weftmeath.

LEITRIM *county,* fit. in prov. Connaught, bounded on the N. by the bay of *Donegal,* and part of *Fermanagh;* on the S. and W. by *Sligo* and *Rofcommon;* and on the E. by *Fermanagh* and *Cavan.* It is a fruitful co. and tho' mountainous, produces great herds of black cattle; but has few places of note. It contains 255,950 acres, 17 parifhes, 5 bar.'s and 2 boroughs, and fends 6 members to parliament; it is about 41 miles long, and 16 broad. Chief town *Leitrim.* In this co. we find the antient families of *O'Rure,* or *Rourk,* and *M'Ranall.* Its bar.'s are Mohill, Leitrim, Carigallen, Dromahair, and Rofclogher. Number of houfes about 10,026, and inhabitants about 50,000.

LEITRIM *town,* fit. in the bar. and co. Leitrim, prov. Connaught. It is the fhire town of the co. and diftant about 80 miles from Dublin. Lat. 53:46 N. lon. 8:9 W. It is pleafantly fit. on the banks of the river *Shannon;* and appears to have been formerly a place of fome note. St. *M'Liegus* fon of *Cernac,* was bifhop here; and his feftival is obferved on the 8 of Feb. Fairs are held here on 22 Jan. 5 May, 16 June, 23 July, 3 Sept. and 1 Dec. This place gives title of vifc. to the family of *Clements.*

LEITRIM-RIVER, fit. in co. Wicklow, prov. Leinfter. The town of Wicklow has a narrow haven at the mouth of this river, fit only for fmall veffels, which carry provifions to Dublin.

LEIX, fee *Ley.*

LEIXLIP, a poft and fair town, pleafantly fit. in bar. Salt, co. Kildare, prov. Leinfter, about 8 miles from Dublin. Near it are the ruins of the church and caftle of *Confy.* The caftle of Leixlip, is beautifully feated on the banks of the river Liffey; it is a fine edifice with large and pleafant gardens, at one fide of which is a fine waterfall, called the *Salmon-leap,* there being plenty of that fpecies of fifh hereabouts. Near Leixlip a monaftery was erected, which was dedicated to the Virgin Mary. A mile from this is *Caftletown,* the magnificent feat of Mr. *Conolly.* Fairs held here 3 May, 11 July and 9 Oct. This is a vicarage in dioc. of Dublin.

LEMANAGHAN, a vicarage in dioc. of Meath, fit. in bar. Garrycaftle, King's co. prov. Leinfter; here was a monaftery, the ruins of which may yet be feen at a diftance, being now furrounded by an impaffible bog.

LEMNA, fit. near *Carrickfergus,* prov. Ulfter. In 697 a noted battle was fought here, between *Aodh* chief of the *Dalriadians,* and the Britifh *Picts,* who had invaded his territory; in this battle *Aodh* loft his life, as did alfo *Conquar Mac Echa Mac Maldwin,* chief of the Picts.

LEMON *ifland,* one of the *Skelig-iflands,* fo called; fit. off the coaft of the co. Kerry, prov. Munfter; it is rather a round rock, always above water, and therefore no way dangerous to fhips. An incredible number of *Gannets* and other birds, breed here; and it is remarkable that the *Gannet* neftles no where on the *Southern* coaft of Ireland, but on this rock, tho' many of them are feen on all parts of our coafts on the wing. There is another rock on the *Northern* coaft of Ireland, remarkable for the fame circumftance.

LENE-LOUGH, a *lake,* fit. in bar. Half-fowre, co. Weftmeath, prov. Leinfter.

LENEY, a bar. in co. Sligo, prov. Connaught; it contains a great many defolate hills, and a large fcope of bog.

LENNADERG, fit. near Gilford, prov. Ulfter.

LENY, fit. in bar. Corkerry, co. Weftmeath, prov. Leinfter, 44 miles from Dublin. Near it on a pretty high hill, is a *Charter-fchool.* This is a curacy in dioc. of Meath.

LEOGHMACKIVOGE, a chapelry in dioc. of Cafhel, fit. in bar. Eliogurty, co. Tipperary, prov. Munfter.

LEPERS-TOWN, fit. towards the extremity of the parifh of *Killea,* in co. Waterford, prov. Munfter; this place was formerly bequeathed to the poor of Waterford, and by the Downfurvey, contained 419 acres.

LERHA, or *Laragh,* fit. in bar. Granard, co. Longford, prov. Leinfter; it is a vicarage in dioc. of Ardagh, and otherwife called *Abbeylerha,* or *Abbey-laragh,* from a monaftery which was founded here by St. Patrick, and dedicated to the B. V. Mary.

LESECRESIG, a hill fit. in co. Cork, prov. Munfter, about 2 miles from *Macroomp;* on

the

the top of which are the remains of a pagan altar, compofed of 3 ftones pitched clofe together, and a broad flat ftone lieing near them; near this is a large circular intrenchment of ftone, made in the fame manner as thofe of earth; thefe kind of ftone intrenchments the Irifh call *Cairns* or *Caherns.*

LETHMORE, fit. in the diftrict of Ely, in the King's co. prov. Leinfter. Here St. *Pulcherius* founded a monaftery, and died A. D. 655. He was buried here.

LETRIM, (fometimes written *Leitrim)* a bar. in co. Galway, prov. Connaught; having a village in it of fame name, which is a vicarage in dioc. of Clonfert.—Alfo a vicarage in dioc. of Cloyne, fit. in bar. Condons, co. Cork, prov. Munfter.

LETTERKENNY, a poft and fair town in bar. Kilmacrenan, co. Donegal, prov. Ulfter, 113 miles from Dublin. It is fit. on the river *Swilly,* over which it has a bridge. Fairs held 1 Frid. in Jan. 12 May, 10 July, 3 Frid. in Aug. 8 Nov. Lat. 54: 45, lon. 8: 0.

LETTERMACWARD, a village fit. in bar. Boylagh, co. Donegal, prov. Ulfter; it is a rectory in dioc. of Raphoe.

LETTIKEEN, a village fit. in bar. Burrifhoole, co. Mayo, prov. Connaught.

LEUNE, a *river,* extending from Caftlemain harbour to Rofs-caftle, E. S. F. 14 miles; it runs thro' part of co. Kerry, prov. Munfter, and is adjacent to Kilorglan, Rofs-caftle and Killarney.

LEURAN-FIELD, fit. near *Galway,* prov. Connaught.

LEXARTOWN, fit. in bar. Erris, co. Mayo, prov. Connaught.

LEY, or *Lea,* a vicarage in dioc. of Kildare, fit. in bar. Portnehinch, Queen's co. prov. Leinfter.

LEYBEG, fit. in bar. Ballimoe, co. Rofcommon, prov. Connaught.

LEY-CASTLE, or *Lea-caftle,* fit. in bar. Portnehinch, Queen's co. prov. Leinfter, not far from *Portarlington.* This was the refidence of the famous Irifh chief *O'Morethic,* or *O'More,* and erected on a high, or gently rifing ground. Its length externally 60 feet, its breadth 46; the walls 8 feet thick, and in fome places 10. The arches are all circular, except 1 pointed, leading from the caufeway into the bawn. On the N. ran the river *Barrow,* the other fides were fecured by a ditch 25 feet broad, and could occafionally be filled with water from the river. Within the ditch was a wall, the foundation of which only remains. The approach to this caftle was by a caufeway 100 feet in length: the outer ballium from E. to W. is 410 feet, and from N. to S. including the bawn, 350 in diameter. The inner balli-

um from N. to S. 140, and from E. to W. 130 feet. The bawn was a large area furrounded with ditches and ramparts, within which cattle were driven, and protected from the enemy. About 1176, Hen. IId. beftowed on *Maurice Fitzgerald,* the bar. in which *Ley* is fit. The latter was the patrimony of the *O'Dempfies.* In 1284, the *O'Dempfies, O'Dunns* and *O'Carrols* united, and furprized and burnt the caftle of Ley. *Verdun* attempted to revenge the injury and to recover the fortrefs, but loft both his men and his horfes; however, the Irifh were foon difpoffeffed. In 1292, *John Fitzthomas Fitzgerald,* having fallen into contention with many of the nobility, and amongft others with *Rich. de Burgo,* the red earl; he took the latter prifoner, and detained him in the caftle of Ley, which was then in his poffeffion. On the eve of the tranflation of St. *Thomas à Becket* in 1307, the Irifh fepts before mentioned, burnt the town of *Ley,* and befieged the caftle, but they were foon defeated by *John Fitzthomas* and *Edmond Botiller.* In 1390, *O'Dempfy* took this caftle, but the next year it was furrendered to fir *John Darcy.* Near this caftle is a remarkable large afh tree, once of confiderable magnitude.

LEY-RIVER, or *Lee-river,* extends from Cork to Macroom, W. 20 miles; runs thro' part of co. Cork, and is adjacent to Cork, Carrickdrohid, Crookftown and Macroom.

LICANE, fit. in bar. Tireragh, co. Sligo, prov. Connaught.

LICARNIE, fit. in bar. Corkaguinny, co. Kerry, prov. Munfter.

LICILASH, a caftle feated on the banks of the Blackwater, in co. Cork, prov. Munfter; oppofite the caftle of *Carickabrick.*

LICKBLAH, a vicarage in dioc. of Meath, fit. in bar. Half-fowre, co. Weftmeath, prov. Leinfter.

LICKFLINN, a village fit. in bar. Slewardagh, co. Tipperary, prov. Munfter. It is a rectory in dioc. of Cathel.

LICKMOLASKY, a vicarage in dioc. of Clonfert, fit. in bar. Longford, co. Galway, prov. Connaught.

LICKRIG, a vicarage in dioc. of Clonfert, fit. in bar. Dunkellin, co. Galway, prov. Connaught.

LICKY *river,* fit. in bar. *Decies within,* co. Waterford, prov. Munfter.

LIFFEY, fee *Anna-Liffey.*

LIFFORD, a borough town in co. Donegal, prov. Ulfter, 102 miles from Dublin. It returns 2 members to parliament; patron, lord *Ennifkillen;* and gives title of vifc. to the family of *Hewitt.* It is fit. on the river *Foyle,* and has a barrack for a troop of horfe. Lat. 54: 7, lon. 8: 5.

LIGHT-

LIGHT-HOUSE. There are feveral *Light-houfes* thro' the different parts of Ireland, for the convenience of fhipping: fuch as, 1ft. At *Copland-ifle*, bar. Ardes, co. Down, prov. Ulfter.—2d. At *Balbriggen*, bar. Balruddery, co. Dublin, prov. Leinfter.—3d. At *Hoath-hill*, bar. Coolock, co. Dublin, prov. Leinfter.—4th. At the *S. wall*, in the liberties of city of Dublin, prov. Leinfter.—5th. Two at *Wicklow-head*, bar. Arklow, co. Wicklow, prov. Leinfter.—6th. At *Hook-tower*, bar. Shelburn, co. Wexford, prov. Leinfter.—7th. At *Duncannon-fort*, bar. Shelburn. co. Wexford, prov. Leinfter.—8th. At *Charlesfort*, bar. Kinfale, co. Cork, prov. Munfter.—9th. At the *old head* of Kinfale, bar. Courfeys, co. Cork, prov. Munfter.—10th. At *Loophead*, bar. Moyferta, co. Clare, prov. Munfter.

LIGHT-HOUSE-ISLAND, fee *Crofs-ifland*.

LIMBRICK, a village fit. in bar. Gorey, co. Wexford. prov. Leinfter; it holds fairs on 5 April, Whit-Mond. 21 Aug. and 12 Nov.

LIMERICK *county*, fit. in prov. Munfter. It has the river Shannon on the N. Tipperary on the N. E. Kerry on the W. and Cork on the S. It is a fruitful and populous tract, the foil requiring little or no manure in moft places. Befides rich grazing ground, it has a light limeftone for fheep and cows, and produces rich crops of all kinds of corn and rape, with fome hemp. It gave title of earl to the family of *Dongan*. It ftretches from E. to W. 40 miles, and from N. to S. 25, and contains 386,750 acres, 9 bar.'s, 125 parifhes, 2 boroughs, and returns 8 members to parliament, including the city of Limerick. The number of houfes are eftimated at 28,748, and inhabitants at upwards of 170,000. Chief town, *Limerick*. Here are fome clays, furze, fern and mountain lands, and it is famous for good *cyder*; it has much benefited by the *Palatines*, who fettled there, and increafed tillage; they are a laborious independant people, moftly employed in their own farms. This country is well watered by large and fmall rivers; the *Shannon* runs at the N. fide of the co. and fertilizes its banks. The firing of the inhabitants is chiefly turf, and the bogs are conveniently fit. At *Laghill* in the W. of the co. there is a mine of coal or culm, but 'tis more ufed in kilns, than in houfes. There are few lakes except *Lough Gur*, and the principal hills are *Knockgreuy*, *Knockany*, *Knockfiring* and *Toryhill*: the mountains lie Weftward, the higheft being *Knockpatrick*, or St. *Patrick's hill*. The bar's of this co. are Owneybeg, Clanwilliam, Coonagh, Smallcounty. Cofhlea, Cofhma, Poblebryan, Kenry and Conello, which laft is almoft, if not full as large the other 8. Amongft the antient families of this co. are the *O'Briens*.

LIMERICK *city*, the chief town in the co. of that name, prov. Munfter; it is a poft town fit. on the river *Shannon*, 94 miles S. W. by W. from Dublin. Lat. 52 : 35. lon. 8 : 30. The town is 3 miles in circumference, having weekly markets on Wednefd. and Saturd. and fairs on Eafter Tuefd. 4 July, 4 Aug. and 12 Dec. There is a privilege annexed to the fair held on 4 Aug. that, during 15 days, no perfon can be arrefted in the city or liberties, on any procefs iffuing out of the *Tholfel* court of Limerick. *Hollingfhead* tells us that this place was built by *Tuorus*, about the year 155, and that its Irifh name is *Loumneagh*, which he fays it acquired from the following circumftance, viz. that the town was planted in an ifland, which before the building of the city, produced abundance of grafs; during which time, one of the Irifh potentates raifing war againft another of his peers, incamped in that ifle, and had fo great a troop of horfemen, that the grafs was eaten up in 24 hours, from whence it was called *Loum-ne-augh*, or *Horfe bare*, i. e. a place made bare or eaten up by horfes. This was the ftrongeft fortrefs in the kingdom, and was taken by the *Englifh* in 1174. During the firft ages it was much frequented by foreign merchants, and after the arrival of the Danes, was a place of confiderable commerce, until the 12th century. It was plundered by *Mahon*, brother of *Brien Boromh*, after the battle of *Sulchoid*, in 970, and *Brien* in a future period exacted from the Danes of this city, 365 tons of wine as a tribute, which fhews the extenfive traffic carried on by thofe people in that article. About the middle of the 6th century, St. *Munchin* erected a church, and founded a bifhoprick here, which however was deftroyed by the Danes, on their taking poffeffion of this port in 853, and remained in ruins until their converfion to the Chriftian faith in the 10th century, at which period the church of St. *Munchin* was built, and the bifhoprick eftablifhed. *Donald O'Brien*, about the time of the arrival of the Englifh, founded a houfe for nuns of the order of St. Auguftin; he alfo endowed the cathedral; and Donat O'Brien, bifhop of Limerick, in the 13th century, contributed much to the opulence of the fee. Edw. IIId. by writ dated at Limerick 25 July, 1374, granted to the priorefs of the before mentioned houfe, his fpecial protection during his royal pleafure. About the clofe of the 12th century, the bifhoprick of *Inis-Cathay* was united to that of Limerick, and in 1663, Limerick was united to *Ardfert* and *Aghadoe*. In the reign of king *John*. a priory of regular canons was founded by *Simon Minor*, a citizen of Limerick. A Dominican friary was founded by *Donogh Carbreach O'Brien*, king of Thomond, who died in 1241, and according to *Ware*, was interred here, in a tomb with his ſtatue placed over it. Here was alſo a grey friary founded by *O'Brien*, a lineal deſcendant of the kings of Limerick and Thomond, in the reign of *Hen. IIId.* Likewiſe an Auguſtinian friary founded by the ſame. Part of the Dominican friary is now converted into a tan yard, and a large barrack has been erected on the other part; ſome ſmall remains of the church, walls, &c. may yet be ſeen. The grey friary ſtood without the town wall, where the co. court houſe is now erected: the old church has been ſince converted into the co. hoſpital. A trace of the Auguſtinian friary is not now to be found. The Knts. Templars, 'tis ſaid, had a houſe near the latter, but of which the ſmalleſt remains are not now diſcoverable. This city was beſieged in 1642, and a ſecond time in 1690, when it compelled king William IIId to raiſe the ſiege. The Engliſh and Dutch forces under general *Ginkle* inveſted it on 21 Sept. 1691, and loſt a great number of men before it; when the town capitulated on 13 Oct. following; the garriſon obtained very honourable terms under the conditions entitled, *the articles of Limerick*, being allowed to retire whenever they pleaſed, and tolerated in the free exerciſe of their religion. To perpetuate the memory of its ſurrender, a medal was ſtruck, whereon were the profiles of king Wm. and queen Mary: around the medal was this inſcription, " *Non hæc ſine numine Divum.*" on the exergue, " *Limarica capta, Hibernia ſubacta, Octobris 1691.*" Within a century this place was reckoned the ſecond city in Ireland; at preſent it has loſt its rank, not becauſe *it thrives leſs*, but becauſe *Cork thrives more*. It is compoſed of the *Iriſh* and *Engliſh town*; the latter ſtands on the King's-iſland, formed by the river *Shannon*. A charter was granted to this city by king *John*, and confirmed in ſucceeding reigns. Dr. *Campbell* obſerves, that as you approach *Limerick*, the grounds grow rich and exquiſitely beautiful; the only diſagreeable matter is, that the ſituation renders the air moiſt, and conſequently rather unwholeſome to ſtrangers. The town was formerly entirely walled in, and in 1760, there were 17 of the city gates ſtanding, but to the great improvement of the place they are now all demoliſhed, except the *water-gate of king John's caſtle.* The linen, woollen and paper manufactures are carried on here to great extent, and the export of proviſions is very conſiderable. Here are many charitable hoſpitals and handſome public buildings, beſides the cathedral and other churches. This city returns 2 members to parliament; and gives title of Viſc. to the family of *Hamilton.* It is governed by a mayor, ſheriffs, recorder, alder-

men and burgeſſes; there is alſo a barrack, and a military governor and town-major; it had ſome time ago the privilege of *coinage*, and different parliaments have been held there. It appears that Limerick obtained the privilege of having mayors, 10 years before that right was allowed to the citizens of *London.* It was before governed by provoſts, of which the firſt was *John Spafford*, in 1195 and 1197; during the provoſtſhip of *Henry Troy*, a charter was granted, 9 Rich. III. whereby the citizens were allowed to chooſe mayors and bailiffs, *Adam Servant*, in 1198, being the firſt mayor; he was ſucceeded by others, and in 1210, by *Roger Maij*; 1211, *John Cumbitor*; 1212, *Walter Crop*; 1213, *Robert White*; 1214, *Seward Minutor*; 1215, *Seward de Ferendona*; 1216, *John Ruſſell* alias *Creagh*, and 1217, *John Banbury.* The city continued thus governed by *mayors* and *bailiffs*, until the office of *bailiff* was changed into that of *ſheriff* in 1609, when *David White* and *William Reagh* were appointed to that dignity. About 6 miles from this is the famous *Caſtle-connel ſpa.* Limerick is 50 miles from Cork, 50 from Galway, and 73 from Waterford. Adjoining to it is *Newtown-Perry.*

LINESTREAM, ſit. in bar. lower Iveagh, co. Down, prov. Ulſter.

LINGAN *river*, ſit. in bar. Tipperary, co. Limerick, prov. Munſter.

LISADILL, a village ſit. in bar. Carbury, co. Sligo, prov. Connaught.

LISANE, a fair town in bar. Loughlinſholen, co. Londonderry, prov. Ulſter; fairs held 1 Jan. 12 May, Aug. and 26 Nov. It is a rectory in dioc. of Armagh, and otherwiſe written *Liſſan.*

LISANOURE-CASTLE, a ſeat of lord Macartney, ſit. in co. Antrim, prov. Ulſter; near it is Lough-Gule church.

LISBARNET, ſit. in bar. Caſtlereagh, co. Down, prov. Ulſter.

LISBELLAW, a fair town in bar. Tyroſkennedy, co. Fermanagh, prov. Ulſter, 75 miles from Dublin. Fairs held 11 May, 20 June, 10 Nov. and 23 Dec. It is a pariſh in dioc. of Clogher.

LISBIGNY, ſit. in bar. Cullinagh, Queen's co. prov. Leinſter.

LISBUNNY, a vicarage in dioc. of Killaloe, ſit. in bar. upper Ormond, co. Tipperary, prov. Munſter.

LISBURN, a borough, market, fair and poſt town, in bar. Maſſareen, co. Antrim, prov. Ulſter, 73 miles from Dublin, ſit. by the river *Lagan.* This town was burned in 1717, but it is rebuilt in a neat and very handſome manner. It has a large manufactory for linen cloth. It gives title of earl to the family of *Vaughan.* 2 miles beyond it are the ruins of *Drumbee* church.

church. It returns 2 members to parliament; one half of the patronage of this borough is in the earl of *Hertfort*. Fairs held 21 July and 5 Oct. This is a rectory in dioc. of Connor, and was formerly called *Lisnagarry*. Lat. 54 : 43, lon. 6 : 36.

LISCAHELOCK, fit. in bar. Kenoght, co. Londonderry, prov. Ulster.

LISCANOR, fit. in bar. Corcomroe, co. Clare, prov. Munster.

LISCARROL, fit. in bar. Orrery, co. Cork, prov. Munster, 127 miles from Dublin, and 5 miles W. of *Buttevant*. Near which, on the 3 Sept. 1642, was fought a battle between the English, commanded by the lord *Inchiquin*, and the Irish, under lord *Mountgarret* and other generals; where was slain the valiant *Lewis*, lord visc. *Kinelmeaky*, governor of *Bandon*, and son to the first earl of *Cork*. But victory fell to the English, with the slaughter of 1500 of their enemies. This battle was fought to the W. of the castle, in which sir *Philip Percival* kept a garrison for several years at his own expence, and raised many out-works about it, in the modern stile of fortification. In August, 1642, it was besieged by a regular army consisting of 7000 Irish, and obliged to furrender. The day following, lord *Inchiquin* coming up with the English army, defeated the Irish; who again besieged it, in 1646, with an army of 5000 foot, and 500 horse, commanded by the earl of *Castlehaven*, who then took most of the strong holds in this country; lord *Inchiquin* for want of supplies, being then obliged to stand upon the defensive. The news of *Castlehaven's* success had such an effect, that this castle which had been before so well defended, surrendered without firing a shot, tho' then in the best posture of defence, and commanded by the same officer, one capt. *Raymond*, who had defended it so gallantly during the former siege, and who for his cowardice and treachery, was condemned to be shot, together with a steward of sir *Philip Percival's*, but by his indulgence they were pardoned. This castle is a parallelogram, of 120 by 140 feet; it was flanked by 6 great towers, (2 square, and 4 round;) the gate-way which faced the S. was defended by a strong castle, from which on either hand were the apartments; the walls were 30 feet high. This castle is said to have been built by king *John*. It was recovered from the Irish in 1650, a breach made at that time is still visible, near the S. E. tower, and it has ever since remained in a ruinous condition. Near it are several subterraneous passages, and to the S. is *Kate's-hole*, a prodigious deep hole, said to be unfathomable. The lands hereabouts are all pasture, the soil is a yellow clay, intermixed with a grey earth; in some places deeper than in

others. Fairs are held here on 1 and 31 May, 31 Aug. and 29 Nov. This is a vicarage in dioc. of Cloyne.

LISCARTAN, a rectory in dioc. of Meath, fit. near *Ardbraccan*, in bar. Navan, co. Meath, prov. Leinster. The *castle* here, was the birth place of the first lord *Cadogan*, to which family it belongs.

LISCLEARY, a rectory in dioc. of Cork, fit. in bar. Kinalea, co. Cork, prov. Munster.

LISCOLEMAN, a curacy in dioc. of Leighlin, fit. in bar. Shillelagh, co. Wicklow, prov. Leinster.

LISCORMUCK, a rectory in dioc. of Emly, fit. in bar. Coonagh, co. Limerick, prov. Munster.

LISELTIN, a vicarage in dioc. of Ardfert, fit. in bar. Iraghticonnor, co. Kerry, prov. Munster.

LISFIN-CASTLE, fit. near *Tullagh*, co. Clare, prov. Munster.

LISFINNY, a castle in co. Waterford, prov. Munster; fit. W. of Tallow-bridge. It formerly belonged to the earl of *Desmond*, whose castles in this co. were very numerous.

LISGENAN, a vicarage in dioc. of Lismore, fit. in bar. *Decies within*, co. Waterford, prov. Munster.

LISGOLD, a fair town, fit. in bar. Barrymore, co. Cork, prov. Munster; fairs held 1 May, 23 June, 1 Nov. and 21 Dec. This is a vicarage in dioc. of Cloyne.

LISGOOL, fit. on the W. bank of the river Earn, near Enniskillen, in co. Fermanagh, prov. Ulster. A monastery was founded here, in the early ages of Christianity.

LISGRIFFEN, fit. in co. Cork, prov. Munster, 2 miles W. of Buttevant, on the estate of the earl of *Egmont*. At this place several chrystals have been found, of the *Kerry-stone* kind.

LISINISKY, a fair town in co. Tipperary, prov. Munster; fairs held 14 Oct.

LISIZE, a neat and well improved seat in co. Down, prov. Ulster, a mile N. E. of *Ballyroney*, and near the verge of a lake called *Ballyroney* lake.

LISKEERY, a vicarage in dioc. of Tuam, fit. in bar. Downamore, co. Galway, prov. Connaught.

LISKINFERE, a rectory in dioc. of Ferns, fit. in bar. Gorey, co. Wexford, prov. Leinster.

LISLAHAN or *Lislaghtin*, a ruined friary in co. Kerry, prov. Munster; near *Slattery island*. It was founded by *O'Conchovar* or *O'Connar*, prince of Kerry, in 1464, (others say by *John O'Connor* in 1478) for minorites, who were observantine Franciscans of the strict order. The parish church was dedicated to St. *Laghtin*, who died in 622. The friary was granted in fee to *James Scolls*, at the yearly crown rent of 3*l.* 16*s.*

Ed.

8*d*. who affigned his intereft in the fame to *Thomas Law*; but they neglecting to pay the rent, the premifes were feized by the crown, being 12 acres of land; and the collector of the co. not being able to let the land for the yearly value of the faid rent, the premifes became greatly in arrear, and were fet up to auction, and fold for 40*s*. per ann. which leafe being expired, *Henry Rofe*, formerly of *Dublin*, efq; having lands contiguous, propofed to give 4*l*. per year for it, and had a leafe for 99 years of it, at that rent. The fteeple, choir, and feveral other parts of this abbey ftill remain.

L'ISLE, or *little ifle*, an ifland in the river *Len*, co. Cork, prov. Munfter; it bears this denomination to diftinguifh it from *Barrymore* or the *great ifland*. It contains about 1600 Irifh acres, and is 3 miles long and 1 broad; there are 3 or 4 good houfes built on it, with convenient offices; it is part of the eftate of the prefent lord *L'ifle*. This is a vicarage in dioc. of Rofs.

LISLEA-CASTLE, fit. in bar. Dartree, co. Monaghan, prov. Ulfter. Lat. 54:7, lon. 7:39.

LISMALIN, or *Lifmaline*, a rectory in dioc. of Cafhel, fit. in bar. Slewardagh, co. Tipperary, prov. Munfter; it lies about 4 miles from *Killenaule*. Here are the ruins of a caftle.

LISMORE, a borough, market, fair and poft town in bar. Cofhmore, co. Waterford, prov. Munfter, 100 miles from Dublin. Lat. 52:5 N. lon. 7:50 W. Antiently called *Leffmore* or *Lios-mor*, i. e. the great inclofure, or habitation; it is now a bifhoprick and very antient city, formerly an univerfity. St. *Carthagh* or *Mechuda*, in the beginning of the 7th century, founded an *abbey* and *fchool* in this place, which in a fhort time was much reforted to, not only by the natives, but alfo by the *Britons* and *Saxons*, during the middle ages. According to an antient writer of the life of St. *Carthagh*, Lifmore was in general inhabited by monks, half of it being an afylum into which no woman dare enter; confifting intirely of cells and monafteries, the ruins of which, with 7 churches, are yet vifible; a caftle was built here by king John. The fite of *Lifmore* was in early ages denominated *Magh Sgiath*, or the *chofen field*; being the fituation of a *dun*, or fort of the antient chieftains of the *Decies*, one of whom granted it to St. *Carthagh*, on his expulfion from the abbey of *Ratheny* in Weftmeath. On becoming a univerfity, *Magh Sgiath* obtained the name of *Dunfginne*, or the fort of the Saxons, from the number of Saxons which reforted thereto; but foon after 'twas called *Lios-mor* or *Lefmore*, and now *Lifmore*; the bifhoprick of which was united to that of *Waterford* in 1536, being 730 years after its foundation. The dioc. of Lifmore includes a great

part of Waterford co. and a confiderable portion of co. Tipperary. The public road to *Cork* was formerly thro' this place, and at that time it had a better face of bufinefs. St. *Carthagh*, who retired to this place with fome of his religious, in 636, to avoid the fury of the then Irifh monarch, tied his difciples to a moft ftrict rule of life; they never were allowed the ufe of flefh, fifh or fowl; only the vegetables that the ground produced at the expence of their own labour. Father *Daniel*, in his *Hiftoire Monaftique*, mentions one on the fame foundation in *France*. The *caftle* here, which as we mentioned, was built by king *John*, was erected in 1195, on the ruins of the abbey of St. *Carthagh*; it belonged to the duke of *Devonfhire*, and gave birth to the great philofopher, *Robert Boyle*. In 1189, it was demolifhed by the Irifh, who took it by furprize. Being afterwards re-edified, it was for many years an epifcopal refidence, 'till *Myler Magrath*, abp. of Cafhel, and bifhop of this fee, granted the manor of Lifmore to that noted fcholar and foldier, fir *Walter Raleigh*, in the reign of queen Eliz. at the yearly rent of 13*l* 6*s* 8*d*, but that eftate was lopped off with his head, in the reign of king James Ift. after which it fell into the hands of fir *Rich. Boyle*, who purchafed all fir *Walter's* lands; he beautified the whole, and added many buildings to it, moft of which were burned down in the Irifh rebellion; at the breaking out of which it was clofely befieged by 5,000 Irifh, commanded by fir *Richard Beling*, and was well defended by the young lord *Broghill*, third fon of the earl of *Cork*, who obliged them to raife the fiege. The caftle is boldly feated on the verge of a rocky hill, rifing almoft perpendicularly to a confiderable height over the river *Blackwater*: the entrance is by an antient and venerable avenue of trees; over the gate are the venerable arms of the firft earl of *Cork*: oppofite to the entrance is a modern portico of barh ftone, of the *Doric* order, defigned by *Inigo Jones*. Moft of the buildings have remained in ruins fince the æra of the rebellion; but the feveral offices that make up two fides of the fquare are kept in repair. At each angle is a tower, the chief remains of its former magnificence. In Oct. 1785, the late duke of *Rutland*, then lord lieutenant of Ireland, whilft on a tour in Munfter, held a council in, and iffued proclamations from this caftle. The cathedral is ftill pretty well kept in repair. Here was an hofpital for lepers dedicated to St. *Brigid*; alfo an anchorite cell, which was endowed with the lands of *Ballyhaufy* or anchoret's town, a burgage in Lifmore, and 6 ftangs of land, a field, and 2 fmall gardens; all of the annual value of 10*l*. Here is a fine bridge over the river *Blackwater*

erected

erected at a very great expence by the duke of *Devonshire*: this bridge is remarkable for the extent of its principal arch, the span of it being 90 feet. Below the town is a rich fishery for *Salmon*, which is the greatest branch of trade here. Tho' this place is at present much reduced, yet *Cambrensis* informs us, not many years after the conquest this was a very rich city, and held out some time against the English, who took it at last by storm, and gained rich plunder here, enough to load 16 fail of ships. It returns 2 members to parliament; patron, the duke of *Devonshire*, but the electors are called *potwollopers*. Fairs held on 25 May, Sept. and 12 Nov. Lismore is a rectory in the dioc of same name.—Also the name of a town in bar. Clonmoghan, co. Cavan, prov. Ulster; lat. 53 : 55, lon. 7 : 55.

LISMULLANE, a fair town in co. Limerick, prov. Munster; fairs held 10 Oct.

LISMULLIN, a chapelry in dioc. of Meath, fit. in bar. Skryne, co. Meath, prov. Leinster. Here is a feat of lord Dillon, fit. near Tarah hill. A nunnery was established at this place in 1240, by *Alicia*, fifter to *Richard de la Corner* bishop of Meath. *Maria Cufake* the last priorefs furrendered it, on 10th June, 31ft Hen. VIIIth.

LISMULLAW, fit. in bar. Tyrefkennedy, co. Fermanagh, prov. Ulster.

LISMYNY, fit. in King's co. prov. Leinster, 46 miles from Dublin.

LISNACON, a fair town in co. Cork, prov. Munster; fairs held 15 May, 16 June and 14 November.

LISNADILL, a curacy in dioc. of Armagh, fit. in bar. Fews, co. Armagh, prov. Ulster, within 5 miles of Armagh town. The church here was erected by lord *Rokeby*, the present archbishop of Armagh; near it is an elegant glebe house. The church and house are both finished in a stile truly characteristic of their noble founder.

LISNAGAN, fit. in bar. Leitrim, co. Leitrim, prov. Connaught.

LISNAGARRY, fee *Lifburn*.

LISNAKILL, fee *Lifnekill*.

LISNARICK, a fair town, in bar. Lurge, co. Fermanagh, prov. Ulster; fairs held 12 Jan. 5 Apr. 9 May, 22 June and 15 Oct.

LISNAKEA, a poft and fair town, fit. in bar. Magheraftephana, co. Fermanagh, prov. Ulster, 70 miles from Dublin; lat. 54 : 14 N. lon. 7 : 40 W. Near it is *Belfour-caftle*, a handfome feat. Fairs held Mond. before Eafter Sund. Mond. after Afcenfion and 10 Oct.

LISNEGAR, a fine feat in co. Cork, prov. Munster, with a handfome *canal*, and other improvements, adjoining the village of *Rathcormuck*, 110 miles from Dublin.

LISNEGROT, fit. in bar. Loughlinfholen, co. Londonderry, prov. Ulster.

LISNEKILL, alias *Liftine*, a parifh in bar. Middlethird, co. Waterford, prov. Munster; it is bounded on the N. by the *Suir*; on the E. with the parifhes of *Killoteran*, *Killronan* and *Killbride*; on the S. with the parifh of *Reifk*; and on the W. with *Killmeaden*. This is a rectory in dioc. of Waterford, and otherwise written *Lifnakill*.

LISNINNY, a village fit. in bar. Moycafhel, co. Weftmeath, prov. Leinster.

LISNOVER, a village in co. Cavan, prov. Ulster, fit. near *Killefhandra*.

LISNUSKY, fit. in bar. Conillo, co. Limerick, prov. Munster.

LISONUFFY, a vicarage in dioc. of Elphin, fit. in bar. Rofcommon, co. Rofcommon, prov. Connaught.

LISPOLE, fit. in bar. Corcaguinny, co. Kerry, prov. Munster, 162 miles from Dublin.

LISRA, fit. in bar. Omagh, co. Tyrone, prov. Ulster.

LISRABBIN, fit. in bar. Duhallow, co. Cork, prov. Munster.

LISRONAGH, a parifh fo called, in co. Waterford, prov. Munster.

LISRONAN, a vicarage in dioc. of Lifmore, fit. in bar. Iffa and Offa, co. Tipperary, prov. Munster.

LISSAN, fee *Lifane*.

LISSANOUR *caftle*, fee *Lifanoure caftle*.

LISSDORNAN, fit. in bar. Duleck, co. Meath, prov. Leinster.

LISSIN or *Lifhin*, a feat of lord *Clanwilliam*, fit. in co. Tipperary, prov. Munster.

LISSIN-HALL, fit. in bar. Nethercrofs, co. Dublin, prov. Leinster.

LISTERLING, a rectory in dioc. of Offory, fit. in bar. Ida, co. Kilkenny, prov. Leinster.

LISTOADER, fit. in bar. Caftlereagh, co. Down, prov. Ulster.

LISTOWEL, a parifh, alfo a poft and fair town in bar. Iraghticonnor, co. Kerry, prov. Munster, 131 miles from Dublin; antiently *Lis Tuathal*, i. e. the fort of *Tuathal*, who was exiled in the 1ft century, but returned, and his life forms a brilliant æra in Irifh hiftory. Near this are the ruins of a caftle, pleafantly fit. on the river *Feale*; it was taken in Nov. 1600, by fir *Charles Wilmot*, being then held out for the lord *Kerry*, againft queen Eliz. 5 miles beyond *Liftowel* are the ruins of a church. Fairs held on 13 May, 25 July and 28 Oct. This is a vicarage in dioc. of Ardfert, and fometimes written *Liftowhill*.

LISTOWHILL, fee *Liftowel*.

LITTER, a rectory in dioc. of Cloyne, fit. in bar. Fermoy, co. Cork, prov. Munster.

LITTER-

LITTERGARAVE, fit. in bar. Dunkerron, co. Kerry, prov. Munfter.

LITTERLCASK, fit. in bar. Tirawly, co. Mayo, prov. Connaught.

LITTERMORE-ISLAND, fit. on coaft of bar. Moycullin, co. Galway, prov. Connaught.

LITTERTINLIS, a caftle fit. near *Skibbereen*, in co. Cork, prov. Munfter.

LITTLE-CASTLE, fit. in bar. Forth, co. Wexford, prov. Leinfter.

LITTLE-CORK, a village fit. within ½ mile of *Bray*, and near 10 miles from Dublin, in co. Dublin, prov. Leinfter; in its neighbourhood are feveral handfome feats.

LITTLE-ENGLAND, a name given to *Lurgan*, in co. Armagh, prov. Ulfter.

LITTLE-IRELAND, otherwife *Begery*, an ifland quite to the N. of Wexford harbour, prov. Leinfter. St. *Ibar* built a celebrated monaftery here, where he founded a fchool, over which he prefided fo early as 420. He died 23d April, A. D. 500, and was interred here.

LITTLE-ISLAND, fit. in the river *Suire*, bar. Gualtiere, co. Waterford, prov. Munfter.—Alfo in Cork harbour, bar. Barrymore, co. Cork, prov. Munfter: the latter is a rectory in dioc. of Cork.

LITTLE-LIMERICK, fit. near Gorey, prov. Leinfter.

LITTUR, a handfome feat in bar. Iraghticonnor, co. Kerry, prov. Munfter, which commands a fine view of the river *Shannon*.—Alfo a place in bar. Iveragh, fame co.—Likewife a village in bar. Ballibritt, King's co. prov. Leinfter.

LITTURAGH, a name given to the Northern fide of the bar. of *Corcaguinny*, in co. Kerry, prov. Munfter, which is very coarfe and mountainous.

LITTUR-CASTLE, fit. in the parifh of *Cahir*, co. Kerry, prov. Munfter; it was erected by the *O'Sullivans*, and in later times poffeffed by a branch of that family, called *Macrehan*. The univerfity of Dublin hath a large eftate hereabout, a great part of which is *bog*, but very reclaimable, and might be converted into fine meadow and pafture land; but the expence is too great for any private individual, nor can it be attempted on the terms of a fhort college leafe, and the fame may be obferved of other large tracts, belonging to that univerfity in this co.

LIXNAW, a bar. now called *Clanmaurice*, in co. Kerry, prov. Munfter, which gives title of baron to the earls of *Kerry*; the village here of this name being their antient feat; where the *caftle* was erected. This feat ftands agreeably on the river *Brick*, which is here cut into feveral pleafant canals, that adorn its plantations and gardens; the improvements are extenfive,

moft of the viftoes and avenues terminating by different buildings, feats and farm-houfes. The tide flows up to the gardens, whereby boats of a confiderable burden, may bring up goods to the bridge near the houfe; here are two ftone bridges over the *Brick*, the oldeft of which was built by *Nicholas* the 3d baron *Lixnaw*, who was the firft perfon that made caufeways to this place, the land being naturally wet and marfhy. Lat. 52 : 15, lon. 9 : 15.

LOANIA, the antient name of *Killaloe*, co. Clare, prov. Munfter. St. *Molua* founded an abbey here about the beginning of the 6th century. On his death his difciple St. *Flannan* was confecrated bifhop of *Kill-da-lua*, or Killaloe, at Rome about the year 639. Towards the clofe of the 12th century, the antient fee of *Rofcrea* was united to Killaloe.

LOCH CUAN, the prefent *lake Strangford*, in co. Down, prov. Ulfter.

LOCH FEBAIL, now *lough Foil*, prov. Ulfter.

LOCH-LONT, fit. in co. Clare, prov. Munfter.

LOCHRUSBEG *bay*, fit. in bar. Boylagh, co. Donegal, prov. Ulfter.

LOCHRUSMORE *bay*, fit. in bar. Boylagh, co. Donigal, prov. Ulfter.

LOCH SUIDY, now *lough Swilly*, in co Donegal, prov. Ulfter.

LOCH-UAR, antiently fit. near *Mullingar*, co. Weftmeath, prov. Leinfter; at which place *Turges*, the Norman leader was defeated and feized by king *Malachy*, who put him to death.

LOCKEEN, a vicarage in dioc. of Killaloe, fit. in bar. lower Ormond, co. Tipperary, prov. Munfter.

LODGE-PARK, fit. in co. Kildare, prov. Leinfter.

LOFTUS-HALL, fit. in bar. Shelburne, co. Wexford, prov. Leinfter.

LOGACURREEN, fit. in bar. Stradbally, Queen's co. prov. Leinfter; near it is the *Dun* of *Clopoke*.

LOGHART, a caftle fit. within a few miles of Mallow, in co. Cork, prov. Munfter. It was built in King John's reign, but remained for many years a melancholy proof of the devaftation of the civil wars. It was not long fince repaired by the earl of *Egmont*: it is 80 feet high, the walls are 10 feet thick, and moated round with a deep trench, which is paffed by a draw bridge.

LOGHCREW, a vicarage in dioc. of Meath, fit. in bar. Half-fowre, co. Meath, prov. Leinft.

LOGHGALL, fit. in bar. Oneiland, co. Armagh, prov. Ulfter. Lat. 54 : 25, lon. 7 : 11.

LOGHGILLY, a rectory in dioc. of Armagh, fit. in bar. Orior, co. Armagh, prov. Ulfter.

LOGHILL, fit. in bar. Connello, co. Limerick, prov. Munfter, 117 miles from Dublin, within a ¼ of a mile of which, are the ruins of a caftle. This is a rectory in dioc. of Limerick.

LOGH-

LOGHLIN, fee *Leighlin*.

LOGHLINSHOLEN, fee *Loughlinſholen*.

LOGHMORE, fit. in bar. Trough, co. Monaghan, prov. Ulſter.

LONDONDERRY *county*, otherwiſe called *Derry*, the latter name being given it, on account of its having become the property of the 12 trades or corporations of *London*; it is a county in the prov. of *Ulſter*, which has *Donegal* on the W. the ſea on the N. *Antrim* on the E. and *Tyrone* on the S. It is a pleaſant and fruitful country, well planted with Engliſh families, by the citizens of London, in the reign of king James Iſt. who granted the greater part of it to them on condition of ſettling it with Engliſh; being eſcheated to the crown by the attainder of *O'Neile*. They were incorporated by tho name of " the ſociety of the governors and aſſiſtants of London, of the new plantations of Ulſter, in the realm of Ireland." This co. contains 518,500 acres, 31 pariſhes, 4 bar.'s and three boroughs, and returns 8 members to parliament. It extends 32 miles from N. to S. and about the ſame from E. to W. The number of houſes are computed at 25,007, and may contain 125,000 inhabitants. Its bar.'s are Tyrekerin, Kenoght, Colerain, and Loughlinſholen; chief town, Londonderry. This co. is not much incumbered with mountains; it was a part of the antient *Dair-calgaic*, which diſtrict comprehended the preſent town and co. of *Derry*, and part of the co. *Donegal*; the antient chieftains of it being called *Hy Daher-teagh*, now by corruption *O'Dogherty*. The linen manufacture is much carried on here, its yearly trade therein, averaged at £16,720l. The bleach greens are principally ſit. in the neighbourhood of *Newtown-Limavady*, *Colerain*, *Moneymore* and *Cumberbridge*. The linens ſold in *Dungiven*, *Derry*, *Newtown-Limavady* and *Colerain*, are of that ſpecies, called *Colerains*, when bleached; and the market principally attended by drapers from *Derry* and *Donegal*. The principal families of this co. at the commencement of the 17th century, were the O'Cahans, O'Conors and O'Donalds.

LONDONDERRY *town*, the principal town in the co. of that name, prov. Ulſter, 115 miles from Dublin, ſit. on the river *Foyle*, near its mouth, about 3 miles S. of the lake or bay of *Lough Foyle*, and 50 W. of *Carrickfergus*. It is remarkable for the long ſiege it ſuſtained under the command of Mr. *Walker*, a clergyman, againſt the forces of King James IId in 1689. It is a city and co. of itſelf, and was built by the citizens of *London*, in the reign of James Iſt. It is the ſee of a biſhop, having been ſo conſtituted in 1158; the ſee extends into part of four counties, viz. Londonderry, Donegal, Tyrone and Antrim: it is rated in the king's books at 250l. but is worth above 7,000l. per ann. This town is governed by a mayor, aldermen, recorder and ſheriffs, and returns 2 members to parliament. It has a military governor, who is commander of *Culmore Fort*. The family of Pitt take title of earl from this city; it is a poſt and fair town; fair days 17 June 4 Sept. and 17 Oct. Lat 55: 0, lon. 7: 55. This town conſiſts chiefly of 2 ſtreets, which croſs each other, and an exchange is built in the centre; there is a good market place, and handſome church with a lofty ſpire; the walls of the town are in good repair, tho' built in 1614, but the quay and great part of the city are not within the walls. Theſe walls are built in the modern ſtyle of fortification, conſiſting of a thick rampart of earth, faced with ſtone, and flanked with baſtions, capable of containing the proper force for defence; the platform on the top of the rampart being covered by parapets. Beſides the ſiege before mentioned, *Londonderry* is remarkable for the noble defence it made at the *revolution*, during 105 days, under the ſevereſt famine, againſt a numerous army. *George Farquhar*, a celebrated dramatic writer, was born here in 1678. In the year 546, an abbey for regular canons, under the rule of St. *Auguſtin*, was founded here by St. *Columb*, and in aftertimes, was dedicated to the St. himſelf. Here was alſo an abbey for nuns of the *Ciſtertian* order, founded in 1218, by *Turlogh Leinigh O'Neill*, of Strabane; and likewiſe a Dominican friary, in 1274, by *O'Donnel* the younger, prince of *Tyrconnel*, at the requeſt of St. *Dominick*. This latter building was ſit. on the N. ſide of the city, but there are now no remains of it; there was alſo a *Franciſcan* friary here. The cathedral is pretty good, and the biſhop's palace (which was erected by Dr. *Barnard*, when biſhop of this ſee) is large and handſome. This town contains about 10,000 inhabitants, and carries on a good trade with *America* and the *Weſt-Indies*. Londonderry gives title of *baron* to the family of *Stewart*.

LONG, a vicarage in dioc. of Emly. ſit. in bar. Coſhlea, co. Limerick, prov. Munſter.

LONGFIELD, a fair town in co. Leitrim, prov. Connaught; fairs held 17 May, 10 Oct. and laſt Mond. in Dec.—Alſo a rectory in dioc. of Derry, ſit. in bar. Omagh, co. Tyrone, prov. Ulſter.

LONGFIELD *mountains*, ſit. in bar. Omagh, co. Tyrone, prov. Ulſter.

LONGFORD, *county*, in the prov. of *Leinſter*, bounded by the co. of *Leitrim* and *Cavan* on the N. Weſtmeath on the E. and S. and Roſcommon on the W. It extends in length from N. to S. 20 miles, and in breadth from E. to W. 19 miles. It contains 134,152 acres, 23 pariſhes, rifhes, 6 bar.'s and 4 boroughs, and returns 10 members to parliament. It is fmall and much encumbered with bog, intermixed with a tolerable good foil, and is computed to contain 10,026 houfes, and above 50,100 inhabitants; chief town *Longford*. 'Tho' by far the greateft part of this co. is flat, and in fome places fubject to be overflowed, yet the farmers are able to fend large cargoes of oats to the port of Drogheda. Many hands are employed in fpinning and weaving: much linen is made in this co. and great quantities of yarn are fent to more diftant markets. The *Shannon* forms the Weftern boundary of this co. The *Inny* flows at the S. *Lough Gawnagh* expands its waters over many miles in the N. and the *Camlin* and *Fallen*, with other fmaller rivers, fupply the heart of it. In this co. we find the antient proprietors in the families of *O'Feral*, *Tuite*, and *Delamar*: its bar.'s are Longford, Granard, Ardagh, Moydoe, Rathline, and Shrowle. This co. was part of the antient diftrict of *Angalia* or *Annaly*, which belonged to the O'Ferrals, who were in poffeffion of the N. W. and S. parts of the co. Longford, on the commencement of the laft century, but were difpoffeffed of the Eaftern parts of it by the English fettlers, the *Tuites* and *Delamares*.

LONGFORD *town*, fit. on the river *Camlin*, in the bar. of Longford, co. Longford, prov. Leinfter, 58 miles from Dublin; which river falls a few miles below this place into the *Shannon*. It is a borough, poft, market and fair town, and returns 2 members to parliament; patron, lord *Longford*; it gave title of earl to the family of *Aungier*; of vifc. to the family of *Micklethwaite*; and now gives that of *baron* to the family of *Packenham*. Lat. 53 : 42 N. lon. 8 : 0 W. Within 4 miles of *Longford* are the ruins of a *church*, and a mile nearer thofe of a *caftle*. Within 1¼ mile of the town is a *Charter-fchool* for 80 children; it was opened in 1753, and the Rt. Hon. lord Longford granted to it 2 acres of land for ever, and let a leafe of 33 acres, at the yearly rent of 18l 2s 7d for 31 years; he alfo endowed the fchool with a rent charge on his eftate of 20l per annum for ever, and gave 172l towards the building. *Payton Fox*, efq; of Portmaon in co. Longford, bequeathed to it 100l the intereft of which was appropriated to the fupport of the fchool. This place has a barrack for a troop of horfe; it is large and well built. In a very early age an abbey was founded here, of which St. *Idus*, one of St. *Patrick's* difciples, was abbot. In the year 1400, a fine monaftery was founded to the honour of the Virgin Mary, for Dominican friars, by *O'Ferral*, prince of *Annaly*; this monaftery being deftroyed by fire, pope *Martin* Vth by a bull, in the year 1429, granted an

indulgence to all who fhould contribute to the re-building of it: in 1433, pope *Eugene* IVth granted a bull to the like purpofe, and in 1438, he granted another to the fame effect; the church of this friary, now the parifh church, is in the dioc. of *Ardagh*. On 29 Jan. 1615, king *James* Ift granted this monaftery to *Francis*, vifc. *Valentia*. Fairs held 10 June, 19 and 20 Aug. and 22 Oct. Longford is alfo the name of a bar. and village in co. Galway, prov. Connaught. In this bar. a houfe for Francifcan friars was founded by *O'Madden*, about the beginning of the 16th century; it was called *Clonchincantualaig*: this bar. was the original country of the *O'Maddens*.—Alfo a village fit. in bar. Tyreragh, co. Sligo, prov. Connaught.

LONGFORD *pafs*, fit. in co. Tipperary, prov. Munfter, 63 miles from Dublin, where are the ruins of an old barrack, and 2 miles farther the ruins of the church of *Leigh*; near which is a handfome new built church and fpire.

LONG-GRANGE, fit. near Rofs, prov. Munft.

LONG-ISLAND, an *ifland* fit. in bar. Carbery, near coaft of co. Cork, prov. Munfter.

LONG-ROCK, fit. in the harbour of *Donaghadee*, in co. Down, prov. Ulfter: this is a ridge of rocks which ftretch a good way into the fea, and are often fatal to failors.

LONG-WOOD, a fair town in bar. Moyfenrath, co. Meath, prov. Leinfter; fairs held 1 Feb. Whitfun Tuefd. 12 July and 11 Dec.

LOOP-HEAD, fit. in bar. Moyferta, co. Clare, prov. Munfter, at the mouth of the river *Shannon*; otherwife called *Cape-lean*, antiently called *Leim-euchulan*, or *Leim-na-con*, i. e. the harbour of the cape. Lat. 52 : 20, lon. 9 : 58.

LORRAH, a village fit. in bar. lower Ormond, co. Tipperary, prov. Munfter. Here an abbey of regular canons was founded by St. *Ruadan*, who died A. D. 584. It was twice deftroyed by accidental fire, viz. in 1154, and 1157. This is a rectory in dioc. of Killaloe, and is otherwife written *Lorrha*, or *Lorhoe*.

LORUM, a vicarage in dioc. of Leighlin, fit. in bar. Idrone, co. Carlow, prov. Leinfter.

LOUGH-AGHREE, fit. in the bar. of *lower Iveach*, and parifh of Dromore, co. Down, prov. Ulfter, near 4 miles E. S. E. of Dromore; it is in length near an English mile, and about a quarter broad, ftored with excellent trouts and eels.

LOUGH-ALLEN, fit. in co. Leitrim, prov. Connaught; it is encompaffed by high mountains, and more than 30 miles in circuit; bringing the *land* and *lake* under one view; a more picturefque landfcape cannot be found. This diftrict abounds with coal and iron mines. Meffrs. *O'Reilly* of Dublin, have lately eftablifhed in the vicinity of *Lough Allen*, an iron manufac-

manufactory. Were the canals opened from the capital and other parts, communicating with the river here, they would, in a few years, render the cutting of bogs unnecessary, save large sums now annually sent for foreign coals, and establish manufactures on different parts of these lines, of the greatest value and extent. From the great collection of water here, swelled by the accession of numberless rivulets from the mountains, the lake, as if surcharged, vomits forth the *Shannon* at Bellatnava ; which increasing as it flows thro' several counties, forms the largest river in the three kingdoms, and considering the shortness of its course to the ocean, the largest in Europe.

LOUGH-ALLUA, sit. in co. Cork, prov. Munster, within 1 mile of *Inchigeela* ; 'tis otherwise called *Gougane Barra*, and remarkable for the hermitage of St. *Finbar*, sit. on an island in this lake.

LOUGH-ARROW, see *Arrow Lough*.

LOUGH-ARROW, sit. in co. Sligo, prov. Connaught, 2 miles beyond *Ballinafad* ; it has in it a number of islands, most romantically sit. and well planted.

LOUGH BALLYDOWGAN, sit. in bar. *Lecale*, co. Down, prov. Ulster ; it covers about 30 acres, and is stored with trouts, eels and roach.

LOUGH BALLYKILBEG, sit. in bar. *Lecale*, co. Down, prov. Ulster.

LOUGH BALLYKINLER, sit. in bar. *Lecale*, co. Down, prov. Ulster ; it covers about 60 acres, and contains trout, pike and roach.

LOUGH BALLYNAHINCH, sit. in bar. Kinelearty, co. Down, prov. Ulster, it contains pike and eels.

LOUGH-BEG, a small lake which touches upon Lough Neagh, co. Antrim, prov. Ulster.

LOUGHFRACCAN, a curacy in dioc. of Meath, sit. in bar. Slane, co, Meath, prov. Leinster.

LOUGHBRICKLAND, a fair and post town, sit. in bar. upper Iveagh, co. Down, prov. Ulster, 58 miles from Dublin. The name signifies the lake of the *speckled trout*, and it was so called from a lake near it, which abounds with that particular species of fish. It consists of one broad street, at the end of which is the parish church, said to have been rebuilt by Dr. *Taylor* when bishop of *Dromore*, soon after the restoration. The linen manufacture is carried on here very extensively ; and the town is a great thorough fare, the turnpike road from *Dublin* to *Belfast* passing through a red bog near it. Fairs held 1st Tuesd. in Feb. 28 March, 10 July, 3d Tuesd. Sept. and 12 Nov. The body of *English* forces which were quartered in this part of the N. of Ireland, *anno* 1690, had their first rendezvous at this place under king Wm. IIId. who encamped within a mile of the town, his majesty and prince *George* of *Denmark* lay in the camp, extended in two lines, the horse in one, and the foot in the other, as far as *Scarvagh* and *Pointz's* passes. This town was antiently called *Brechachluan*: the *Ulster* annals inform us that the Danes and Norwegians, having filled the sea between Ireland and Scotland with their piracies from the year 792 to 810, they invaded Ulster, and in 827 ravaged the principalities of the Dalnarians in the co. Antrim, but were opposed by *M'Lonich*, and defeated at the battle of *Brech-achluan* in co.Down.

LOUGH-CLEAN, sit. in bar. Drumahaire, co. Leitrim, prov. Connaught.

LOUGH-CONE, *(Coyne* or *Cuan)* the present lake Strangford, in co. Down, prov. Ulster.

LOUGH-CONN, sit. in co. Mayo, prov. Connaught, on the edge of which is a handsome seat called *Moneymore*. St. *Leogar* presided over an abbey which was erected here, at the extreme end of the peninsula called *Errew*, which stretches from the bar. of Tirawly into this lake.

LOUGH-CORRIB, sit. in co. Galway, prov. Connaught ; this lake is upwards of 20 miles long, having many very fine islands in it. It is remarkable for the *Gillaroe trout*, a very delicate fish, which weighs from 12 to 18 pounds ; this trout is remarkable for having an extraordinary *gizzard*, resembling that of a large fowl ; it is there common to dress the gizzards only, which is esteemed a very favourite dish. In the river which runs from Lough Corrib to Galway, there is near that town a considerable salmon fishery.

LOUGH-CREW, sit. in bar. Half-fowre, co. Meath, prov. Leinster.

LOUGH-CURRANE, the present *Lough-Lee* near the bay of Ballinaskeligs, co. Cork, prov. Munster.

LOUGH-DERG, see *Derg*.

LOUGH-DERRIVARAGH, see *Derveragh-Lough*.

LOUGH DIAN, a small lough, sit. in co. Down, prov. Ulster.

LOUGH-DORN, sit. in co. Down, prov. Ulst.

LOUGH-DRINE, sit. in co. Cork, prov. Munster ; the islands on which, the country people lay, change places on a certain day of the year.

LOUGH-ENNELL, sit. in the bar.'s of Mullingar and Fertullagh, co. Westmeath, prov. Leinster.

LOUGH-ERIN, sit. in co. Down, prov. Ulster, in the parish of *Anahilt* ; it is of so prodigious a depth, that a line of 16 fathom has proved insufficient to reach the bottom of it in some places. It is remarkable for breeding pikes, trouts and eels of a very great size.

LOUGH-ERNE, see *Erne-Lough*.

LOUGH-

Lough-Esk, fit. in co. Donegal, prov. Ulſter; it produces plenty of that delicate fiſh called *char*; which are not to be caught by *bait*, but feeding in deep water, are taken only in *nets*. The mountains adjacent to Lough-Eſk, abound with red deer.

Lough-Falcon; fit. in co. Down, prov. Ulſter.

Lough-Foyle, ſee *Foyle-lough*.

Lough-Gall, a village fit. in bar. O'Neiland, co. Armagh, prov Ulſter; it is a rectory in dioc. of Armagh. Fairs are held here Frid. before old Chriſtmas, Afcenſion-day, 8 July and 4 Sept.

Lough-Gara, fit. in co. Sligo, prov. Connaught; the river *Boyle* rifes from this lake.

Lough-Gill, fit. in co. Sligo, prov. Connaught; cloſe to it is *Hazlewood*, a very handſome feat. This is alſo the name of a fair town in co. Antrim, prov. Ulſter; fairs held 19 June and Nov.

Lough-Glinn, a village fit. in bar. Boyle, co. Roſcommon, prov. Connaught; here is a feat of lord *Dillon*, fit. near *Caſtlereagh*.

Lough-Gur, ſee *Gur-lough*.

Lough-Gule, fit. in bar. Dunluce, co. Antrim, prov. Ulſter; here is Liſſanour caſtle, the handſome feat of lord *Macartney*, 105 miles from Dublin. This is a vicarage in dioc. of Connor. The Britons of Cumberland having invaded the principality of Dalrieda in 710, *Duncha* the ſucceſſor of Aodh, chief of that diſtrict, oppoſed and defeated them, at a battle in this place, which was formerly called *Loughecoleth*.

Lough-Hanch; fit. between the confines of the King's co. and Queen's co. prov. Leinſter.

Lough-Henney, fit. in co. Down, prov. Ulſter; the ſmall river called *Garriclogh* rifes out of this lake.

Loughill, fit. in bar. Carrigallen, co. Leitrim, prov. Connaught.—Alſo in bar. Conillo, co. Limerick, prov. Munſter.

Loughin *iſland*, fit. in bar. Kinelearty, co. Down, prov. Ulſter; it is a rectory in dioc. of Down.

Lough-Hine, fit. in co. Cork, prov. Munſter; it is about 2 miles in circumference; and in the midſt of it is a ſmall iſland on which ſtands an old caſtle, now in ruins, built by the O'Drifcolls. This lake abounds with ſalmon, white-trout, lobſters, crabs, efcalops, and ſmall deep oyſters.

Lough-Hoyle, ſee *Hoyle-lough*.

Lough-Inchiquin, ſee *Inchiquin-lakr*.

Lough-Inny, fit. in co. Weſtmeath, prov. Leinſter; it is united to Lough-*Shillen*, by a ſtream on which the ſmall but pleaſant village of *Finaé* is fit.

Loughinsholen, (or *Loughlinſholen*) a bar. in co. Londonderry, prov. Ulſter.

Lough-Kay, fit. in co. Leitrim, prov. Connaught; this is otherwiſe called *Kingston-lake*, it is a beautiful piece of water, interſperſed with ſeveral iſlands, ſome of which are adorned with old caſtles and ruins, others in the ſtate of nature, wooded with lofty timber trees, and ſome highly improved without a tree to be ſeen, but the more pleaſing proſpect of everlaſting verdure.

Lough-Kent, fit. within a few miles of *Caſhel*, co. Tipperary, prov. Munſter; here is a ruined church and caſtle.

Lough-Kernan, fit. in co. Down, prov. Ulſter; it lies about half a mile S. of *Tullelifh* church, on the edge of the bar. of *lower Iveach*, and about 1½ mile E. of the new *canal* in this co.

Lough-Lane, fit. in co. Weſtmeath, prov. Leinſter; the name ſignifies the *Lake of Learning*; there is an *iſland* in this lake which bears the ſame name, and is reported to have been the retiring place of the learned who taught there.

Lough-Lean, the preſent Lake of *Killarney*, co. Kerry, prov. Munſter.

Lough-Lee, otherwiſe *Lough Currane*, fit. near the bay of *Ballinaſkeligs*, in co. Cork, prov. Munſter; it is of an oval form, 3 miles in length, and about half as broad: it abounds with excellent white trout and ſalmon; it is bounded on the S. by mountains partly covered with woods; there are 3 ſmall iſlands in it, on one of which are the remains of a church and cell, and ſome other veſtigia of ruined buildings.

Lough-Lheighs, or the *healing lough*, a lake ſo called in co. Cavan, prov. Ulſter, the waters of which are ſaid to poſſeſs a very healing quality.

Loughlin, fit. in co. Roſcommon, prov. Connaught, 93 miles from Dublin; fairs held 25 May, 29 July, 12 Sept. and 14 Oct.

Loughlinsholen, ſee *Loughinſholen*.

Loughlinstown, ſee *Leighlinſtown*.

Lough-Lynam, fit. in bar. Kells, co. Weſtmeath, prov. Leinſter.

Lough-Macnean, fit. in bar. Clonawly, co. Cavan, prov. Ulſter; in which are 3 well cultivated iſlands. It is improperly called in ſome maps, *Lough Cane*.

Lough-Maghan, fit. in co. Down, prov. Ulſter, in the bar. of *Kinelearty*; it covers about 23 acres, and is filled with *pike*, *eels*, *roach* and *bream*.

Lough-Mask, fit. in co. Galway and co. Mayo, prov. Connaught; fairs are held here 20 Sept.

Lough-Melve, fit. in bar. Roſclogher, co. Leitrim, prov. Connaught.

Lough-

Loughmoe, a vicarage in dioc. of Cashel, sit. in bar. Eliogurty, co. Tipperary, prov. Munster.

Lough-More, sit. in co. Limerick, prov. Munster, 97 miles from Dublin. Not far from this are the ruins of *Mungret-abbey*.

Lough-Neagh, sit. in the co.'s *Armagh*, *Down*, *Derry* and *Antrim*, in prov. of Ulster; it is the largest in *Europe*, those of *Ladoga* and *Onega* in Russia, and that of *Geneva* in Switzerland excepted; being 20 miles long, and 15 broad. The area of this lake is computed to be 100,000 acres, it gives title of baron to the family of *Skeffington*. It is fed by 6 considerable rivers, and 4 of less note; and having but 1 narrow outlet that affords not a sufficient vent, it frequently overflows the low grounds on its coasts. It abounds with great variety and plenty of fish; and one sort called the *Dolochan*, (a species of large trout) is said to be peculiar to it. 'Tis remarkable for a healing virtue; and likewise for petrifying wood, which is not only found in the water but in the adjacent soil at a considerable depth. On its shores several beautiful gems have been discovered. Its antient name was *Loch-eacha* or *Loch Neach*, from *Loch* a lake, and *Neach* wonderful, divine or eminent. Its petrifying powers are not instantaneous, as several of the antients have supposed, but require a long series of ages to bring them to perfection, and appear to be occasioned by a fine mud or sand, which insinuates itself into the pores of the wood, and which in process of time becomes hard like stone. On the borders of this lake is *Shane's-castle*, the elegant seat of the Rt. Hon. lord *O'Neil*. It may perhaps be thought a piece of needless vanity to point out from our antient historians, the time of the fabulous original of this lake: but they tell us, that it first burst out in the reign of *Lugaid Rhiabderg*, who mounted the throne of Ireland, A. D. 65. Dr. *Smyth* seems to doubt whether the healing quality in this lake is not to be confined to one side of it called the *fishing-bank*, and he informs us, that this virtue was discovered in the reign of *Charles* IId in the instance of the son of one Mr. *Cunningham*, who had an *evil* which run on him in 8 or 10 places, and notwithstanding the *Royal touch*, and other applications, seemed incurable; at length he was perfectly healed after bathing in this lough about 8 days. Hence that writer gives us another derivation of the name *Loughneagh*, which he says seems to hint at this quality; *Neasg* or *Neas*, in Irish signifying a sore or ulcer, which might not improbably be corrupted into *Neagh*: hence he apprehends this lake was remarked at a much earlier period for its healing property.

As to its petrifying power, 'tis mentioned by *Nennius*, a writer of the 9th century, who says, " Est aliud stagnum quod facit ligna durescere in lapides. Homines autem findunt ligna, et postquam formaverunt, projiciunt in stagnum, et manent in eo usq. ad caput anni, et in capite anni lapis invenitur, et vocatur stagnum *Luch Echach*.

Lough-Oughter, sit. in bar. Loughtee, co. Cavan, prov. Ulster, where an abbey was founded in 1237. *Cathal O'Reilly* made a grant of the ground, and the abbey was dedicated to the holy Trinity. In one very small bare island in this lake, stands the ruin of a castle, in which the good bishop *Bedell* was confined by the insurgents in the last century.

Lough-Pallas or *Pallis*, a lake sit. in bar. Balliboy, King's co. prov. Leinster.

Lough-Ramor, sit. in bar. Castleraghan, co. Cavan, prov. Ulster, near *Virginia*, about 40 miles from Dublin; in which are several islands, where there are ruins of some castles.

Loughrea, a bar. having in it a post and fair town of same name, sit. in co. Galway, prov. Connaught, distant 86 miles from Dublin. It is an agreeable well built place, and has a barrack for one troop of horse. It derives its name from a fine *lake* near the town, more than a mile in length, and nearly one in breadth. A castle was erected here by the *De Burghs*, and many ruined castles are to be seen in this neighbourhood. There was a chapel or house for lepers here, and about the year 1300, *Rich. de Burgh*, earl of Ulster, founded a monastery here for Carmelites or Whitefriars, dedicated to the Virgin Mary: this was granted to *Rich.* earl of *Clanrickarde*. In 1741, a Charter-school was opened here for 60 children: the earl of Clanrickard gave an acre of land whereon the school-house is built, and granted 40 acres more for 31 years, at 6l per annum. Fairs are held here 11 Feb. 20 May, 20 Aug. and 5 Dec.

Lough-Ree, sit. between the co. Longford and Roscommon, and between the prov.'s Leinster and Connaught. It is a handsome spacious lake, on which are several small islands.

Lough-Salt, sit. in co. Donegal, prov. Ulster, between *Kilmacrenan* and *Glenn-inn*, on the top of a lofty mountain.

Lough-Scudy, sit. in co. Westmeath, prov. Leinster, on which the village of *Baltimore* is seated; near it is the old dissolved monastery of *Plary*, where there was antiently both a friary and nunnery of the *Cistertian* order.

Lough-Scur, sit. in bar. Leitrim, co. Leitrim, prov. Connaught.

Lough-Shark, sit. in co. Down, prov. Ulster,

Ulster, in the bar. of *upper Iveach*; it covers about 80 acres.

LOUGH-SHEAKLIN, sit. about 1 mile from *Daly's-bridge*, co. Cavan, prov. Ulster, and otherwise called *Lough-Shellin*.

LOUGH-SHELLIN, otherwise called *Lough Sheaklin*, sit. within a mile of *Daly's-bridge*. In it are some small islands, where are the ruins of a castle and a church. This lough is of considerable magnitude extending to *Finae*, where it communicates with *Lough Inny*. Between the loughs is a bridge which separates the co.'s of *Westmeath* and *Cavan*. On an island in this lough, and near the co. West-meath, the ruins of a large friary are yet to be seen, which was built at an early but uncertain period: it still continues to be a burial place of note.

LOUGH-SHINNY, a small village sit. 2 miles beyond *Rush*, and 15 from Dublin castle, in bar. Balruddery, co. Dublin, prov. Leinster. There is a fine harbour here with a large pier, which deserves attention, and may be of great utility in affording shelter for shipping from violent storms.

LOUGH-SHY, sit. near *Ballinrobe*, in co. Mayo, prov. Connaught. On the banks of which, there is a *charter-school*. At *Ballinrobe* are the ruins of a once celebrated abbey.

LOUGH STRANGFORD, sit. in bar. Ardes, co. Down, prov. Ulster. It takes its present name from a small port town called *Strangford*, seated on the W. side of the narrow entrance into the sea. It was formerly known by the name of *Lough Cone*, or *Lough Coyne*; and our antient historians relate, that it had its beginning from the sea bursting into, and overwhelming this flat tract, *Anno Mundi* 1995; in the time of *Partholanus*, 339 years after the universal deluge, according to the *Hebrew* calculation. It is a deep bay or inlet of the sea, about 17 miles long, and 4 or 5 broad, it goes W. as far as Downpatrick, and N. as far as Comber and Newtown, and by computation covers 25,775 acres, Irish plantation measure. It abounds with excellent fish, particularly *smelts*; and off the bar, there is a periodical *herring fishery*, in or about *August*. The bar or entrance into this lough, is about three miles below Strangford. There is a long rock at the entrance in the middle of the passage, dangerous to strangers on account of the current; yet there is a broad passage on either side, and deep water. The current here is very strong and rapid, running at the rate of 6 or 7 miles an hour. There are but few vessels that go higher up than *Strangford*. A good many vessels, bound up the channel put in here, if the wind is unfavourable to their passage. The *islands* in this lake are numerous; Dr. *Boat*

enumerates them at 260. But from an actual survey made at the time Dr. *Smyth* wrote his history of that co. it appears there are 54 islands small and great, known by particular names, and many others nameless; the contents of these 54 islands added together, amount to 954½ acres. The great and profitable manufacture carried on in these islands, and the flat stoney coasts surrounding the lake, is the burning of sea-weed into kelp, which employs a number of hands, and has been computed to produce to the several proprietors, a neat profit of 1000*l* per ann. and upwards. 4 of the islands here are called *Swan-islands*, from the number of *Swans* that frequent them.

LOUGH-SWILLY, sit. in co. Louth, prov. Leinster.

LOUGHTEE, a bar. in co. Cavan, prov. Ulst.

LOUGHTOWN, sit. in bar. Newcastle, co. Dublin, prov. Leinster.

LOUGH-UVA, sit. in co. Fermanagh, prov. Ulster. An abbey was founded here in the year 500.

LOUTH *county*, sit. in prov. Leinster. This is the smallest co. in Ireland: it is bounded by Monaghan and Armagh on the N. by the Irish channel on the E. by Meath on the S. and by Cavan on the W. Its chief towns are *Dundalk* and *Carlingford*, unless we include *Drogheda*, a part whereof is in this co. It is 21 miles long from N. to S. and 14 broad from E. to W. containing 110,750 acres, 61 parishes in the dioc. of Armagh, and part of 2 parishes in the dioc. of Clogher; 4 bar.'s, viz. Dundalk, Louth, Ardee and Ferrard; 4 boroughs, and returns (if we include *Drogheda)* 12 members to parliament. Its houses are computed at 11,545, and inhabitants at about 57,750 souls. Its principal families at the commencement of the last century, were the Taffes, Flemings, Bellews, Dowdals and Gernons. This co. tho' small, is very fertile and pleasant, and abounding with many remains of antiquities, of which Mr. *Wright*, in his *Louthiana*, has given a very ample description. It may justly be called the heart of the old *English pale*, which originally extended from the town of *Wicklow* in the S. to the point of *Dunluce*, in the N. of Ireland; this co. is therefore filled with a variety of objects, all bearing evident marks both of grandeur and great antiquity.—*Louth* is also the name of a village sit. in bar. Louth, in this co. It is a rectory in dioc. of Armagh; and holds fairs on 28 March. Lat. 53 : 57, lon. 7 : 5. Here St. *Patrick* founded an abbey for St Moetcus, a Briton, who died 19 Aug. 534. *M'Geoghegan* tells us this saint lived to the amazing age of 300 years and 3 days. 100 bishops, and 300 presbyters were educated in this school, all famous for piety and learning.

Louth

Louth was confumed by fire in 1152, 1160 and 1166. Edan *O'Cellaidhe*, bifhop of Clogher, was interred here in 1182. In 1242, a chapter was held here by the archbifhop of Armagh, at which were prefent all the abbots and priors of the regular canons in this kingdom. The prior of Louth fat in parliament. In 1488, the prior of this houfe (having been concerned in the rebellion of *Lambert Symnel*) this year received the king's pardon for the fame. The poffeffions of this houfe, were, on the general fuppreffion, granted to fir *Oliver Plunket*.

LOUTHERSTOWS, fee *Lowtherftown*.

LOUTH-HALL, fit. in bar. Atherdee, co. Louth, prov. Leinfter.

LOWER-IVEACH or *Iveagh*, a bar. in co. Down, prov. Ulfter.

LOWER-ORMOND, a bar. in co. Tipperary, prov. Munfter.

LOWEY, a vicarage in dioc. of Kilmore, fit. in bar. Loughtee, co. Cavan, prov. Ulfter.

LOW-GRANGE, a handfome feat in co. Kilkenny, prov. Leinfter, within 1 mile of *Gowran*; the building is of a modern and elegant tafte, fronted with marble; the fpouts that throw off the water are of the fame materials, and fo contrived, as to appear an additional beauty to the building. Part of this noble dwelling was formerly the tower of an old caftle, but now it wears a modern face.

LOWRAN, fit. near *Leighlin-bridge*, in co. Carlow, prov. Leinfter, and within 1 mile of *Ballylaughan* caftle; it is but a poor place, with as poor a church; however the 18 of April being a patron day, St. *Lazarianus* is highly celebrated, who was one of the firft founders of the cathedral of *old Leighlin*, and was buried here.

LOWTHERLODGE, fit. near Balbriggen, co. Dublin, prov. Leinfter.

LOWTHERSTOWN or *Louthcrftown*, a fair town fit. in bar. Lurge, co. Fermanagh, prov. Ulfter; fairs held 12 May, 10 July, 26 Aug. and 11 Dec.

LUCAN, a pleafant village, fit. in bar. Newcaftle, co. Dublin, prov. Leinfter, within 6½ miles of the metropolis. It is much frequented on account of its medicinal fpring, difcovered in 1758; the waters of which are of great efficacy in many diforders. Here is the handfome feat of Mr. *Vefey*. This place is a vicarage in dioc. of Dublin. *Lucan* was the antient patrimony of the *Sarsfields*. The family of *Bingham* have alfo a peerage by the title of baron *Lucan* of *Cafilebar*, in co. Mayo, prov. Connaught.

LUDDENBEG, a vicarage in dioc. of Emly, fit. in bar. Clanwilliam, co. Limerick, prov. Munfter.

LUGGACURRIN, fee *Logacurreen*.

LUGNA-CLOGH, fit. near Sligo, co. Sligo, prov. Connaught, otherwife called the *Giant's-grave*; where feveral large ftones are raifed upon the ends of others, which are pitched perpendicularly, not much unlike thofe of *Stonehenge*, on Salifbury plain. They were the monuments of feveral famous perfons that have been buried here; as appears from the remains of their bones, which have been found under thofe venerable pieces of antiquity.

LUGNAQUILLA *mountains*, fit. in bar. Talbot'ftown, co. Wicklow, prov. Leinfter.

LULLIAMORE, a rectory in dioc. of Kildare, fit. in bar. Carbury, co. Kildare, prov. Leinfter.

LUMNEACH, the moft antient name of the prefent city of Limerick, prov. Munfter: the word is derived from *Luam* or *Liem*, a ftrand or port, and *Neach* eminent; whence *Lumneach*, by corruption *Limerick*, the eminent port: Ptolemy calls it *Macolicum*, which on the Cimbric dialect of the Celtic tongue, has much the fame fignification as *Lumneach*. However *Hollingfhead* gives it another derivation, and calls it *Loum-ne-avgh*, or *Horfe bare*, i. e. a place made bare or eaten up by horfes.

LUMNI, the prefent ifland of *Lambay*, fit. on coaft of co. Dublin, prov. Leinfter.

LUNE, a bar. in co. Meath, prov. Leinfter.

LUNEA, fit. in bar. Monaghan, co. Monaghan, prov. Ulfter.

LURAGH, fit. in bar. Caftleraghan, co. Cavan, prov. Ulfter.

LURGAN, a poft and fair town in bar. O'Neiland, co. Armagh, prov. Ulfter, 67 miles from Dublin; it is a flourifhing town, agreeably fit. in the midft of a much improved country; the inhabitants are extenfively engaged in the linen manufacture. It ftands on a gentle eminence, about 2 miles from *Lough Neagh*, of which it commands a moft beautiful and extenfive profpect. Fairs held 5 Aug. 22 and 23 Nov. Lat. 54 : 35, lon. 6 : 31. Here is the beautiful feat of the Rt. Hon. *Wm. Brownlow*.—Alfo a rectory in dioc. of Kilmore, fit. in bar. Caftleraghan, co. Cavan, prov. Ulfter.

LURGANBUY, a fair town in bar. Dromahair, co. Leitrim, prov. Connaught; fairs held 21 June and Aug. and 23 Oct.

LURGAN-GREEN, a poft and fair town in bar. Louth, co. Louth, prov. Leinfter, 37 miles from Dublin, a mile beyond which is a handfome feat of the earl of *Charlemont*. Fairs held 21 May, 25 July and 11 Nov.

LURGE, a bar. in co. Fermanagh, prov. Ulft.

LUSK, a village in bar. Nethercrofs, co. Dublin, prov. Leinfter, 11 miles from the metropolis, having a parifh church, and fmall common belonging to it. It is a vicarage in dioc. of Dublin. The church is very old, part only

only of it being ufed at prefent for divine fervice ; and near it is one of the noted *round-towers*. An abbey was founded here in the firft ages of Chriftianity, and a fynod was held there in 695, at which were prefent all the principal prelates of the kingdom. In 825 the abbey was pillaged, and in 854 the abbey and whole town was confumed by fire. The like happened in 1135, by *Donel M'Murogh O'Melaghlin*, in revenge for the murder of his brother *Conor*. Fairs are held here on 4 May, 13 July and 25 Nov. Near Lufk are the ruins of *White'ftown church*.

LUSMAGH, a vicarage in dioc. of Clonfert, fit. in bar. Garrycaftle, King's co. prov. Leinft.

LUTHERSTOWN, fit in bar. Omagh, co. Tyrone, prov. Ulfter.

LUTTERELL'STOWN, a fmall but pleafant village, fit. 2 miles beyond Chapelizod, and 5¼ miles from Dublin caftle, in co. Dublin, prov. Leinfter; it holds fairs for horfes and pedlary wares on 28 Mar. and 4 Sept. Here is the elegant feat of lord *Carhampton*, which is beautifully diverfified with wood and water, valleys and precipices.

LYNALLY, a vicarage in dioc. of Meath, fit. in bar. Ballycowen, King's co. prov. Leinfter. An abbey was founded here by St. *Colman Elo*, who was born in the prov. of Meath in 516, and died in 610.

LYNN, a rectory in dioc. of Meath, fit. in bar. *Fartullagh* (Dr. Beaufort) or bar. *Delvin*, (Archd. Monaft.) co. Weftmeath, prov. Leinfter. An abbey was built here in a very early age ; it fuffered by fire in the years 968, 1002, 1050, and 1148.

LYONS, a rectory in dioc. of Kildare, fit. in bar. Salt, co. Kildare, prov. Leinfter.

LYRE *river*, fit. in co. Cork, prov. Munfter.

LYSARDION, fit. in bar. Fews, co. Armagh, prov. Ulfter.

LYSDUFF, fit. in bar. Rofcommon, co. Rofcommon, prov. Connaught. Here we find a priory was eftablifhed, which was a cell and dependant on the abbey of *Cong*. By inquifition taken in the reign of queen *Eliz.* it was found to be feized of 4 quarters of land of various kinds, with the tythes and appurtenances thereof ; and the vicarage of *Lyfduff*: which poffeffions were granted to the provoft and fellows of Trinity college, Dublin.

M A

MAC-CAMON-ROCKS, fit. near the coaft of bar. Ardes, co. Down, prov. Ulfter.

MACETOWN, a curacy in dioc. of Meath, fit. in bar. Skryne, co. Meath, prov. Leinfter. Here is an antient caftle, diftant about 16 miles from Dublin.

MAC-GILLY-CUDDY'S-REECKS, a range of high mountains in bar. Dunkerron, co. Kerry, prov. Munfter, in the parifh of *Knockane*. They may be viewed from the *Lake of Killarney*, and are 1185 yards above the level of the fea ; taking their rife from *Ghirmeen*, a lofty mountain, which forms a right angle with the long range, and bounds the lake to the N. W. which terminates the view from the upper lake and fixes the boundary of the river *Kenmare*. Thefe mountains encircle a valley of pretty large compafs to the W. of the lake, and form an extenfive amphitheatre. They are the moft ftupendous of any hereabout, and very numerous, and broken into the moft irregular fantaftic fhapes, but concur to form a bold and rude contraft to the fofter parts of the landfcape. The family of *Mac-Gilly-Cuddy* has for fome centuries refided in thefe parts, and retained a confiderable eftate here.

MACHERA, fit. in bar. Loughlinfholen, co. Londonderry, prov. Ulfter.

MAC IDA'S CHAPEL, a fmall old chapel, fit. in co. Kerry, prov. Munfter, near *Ballyheigh* ; it is dedicated to an Irifh faint called *Mac Ida*, where an image of the faint is kept, which is held in great veneration by an old *Irifh* family, named *Corridon*, who fettled here fome centuries ago, from the co. *Clare*, and brought their tutelary faint with them.

MACKEEN, a *lake* fit. in co. Fermanagh, prov. Ulfter, otherwife called *Macnean*.

MACLONEIGH or *Maclony*, a rectory in dioc. of Cork, fit. in bar. Mufkerry, co. Cork, prov. Munfter.

MACLONY, fee *Macloneigh*.

MACNEAN, fee *Lough-Macnean*.

MACOLLOP, a rectory in dioc. of Lifmore, fit. in bar. Cofhmore, co. Waterford, prov. Munfter.

MACOSQUY, a chapelry in dioc. of Derry, fit. in bar. Colerain, co. Londonderry, prov. Ulfter.

MAC-QUE'S-CASTLE, is fit. in an ifland in a large lake near *Baron's-court*, co. Tyrone, prov. Ulfter, in which a chief of the name of *Mac Que* formerly refided.

MACREDDIN, a fair town in co. Wicklow, prov. Leinfter ; fairs held Whitfun Mond. and 12 Nov. It is otherwife called *Carty'sfort*, and is a borough, returning 2 members to parliament ; patron, lord Carysfort.

MACROMP (or *Macroomp*, and fometimes *Macroom*) a village fit. in bar. Mufkerry, co. Cork, prov. Munfter, 142 miles from Dublin ; it is fit. amongft hills, in a dry, gravelly, limeftone-foil. This place is faid to take its name from an old *crooked oak*, (fo called in Irifh) which formerly grew here : the *caftle* of *Macroomp* is very antient, being firft built in king

         John's

John's time, foon after the Englifh conqueft, (according to fir *Rich. Cox)* by the *Carews*; but others attribute it to the *Daltons*: it was repaired and beautified by *Tiegue Macarty*, who died in it *anno* 1565, and was father to the celebrated fir *Cormac Mac Tiegue*, mentioned by *Cambden* and other writers, as an active perfon in queen *Eliz.'s* time. The late earls of *Clancarty* altered this caftle into a more modern ftructure, it being burned down in the wars of 1641. It now confifts of 2 ftrong towers, about 60 feet high, with a large modern building between them: it is fit. on the E. fide of the river *Sullane*, over which there is a handfome bridge at the foot of the caftle. Dean *Swift*, in his progrefs through this country, was much pleafed with the fituation of this building, which is alfo noted for being the birth place of the famous admiral, fir *William Penn*. Oppofite to the bridge is the parifh church, dedicated to St. *Colman* of *Cloyne*. It is a rectory in dioc. of Cloyne. Here is a barrack for a foot company, a market-houfe and handfome Roman Catholic chapel. A confiderable number of perfons have been employed in this town in combing wool and fpinning yarn, and fome *falt-works* have been erected here: within 2 miles of it are the ruins of *Mafkanglafs-caftle*, and ¼ a mile from *Macroomp* is a fpa, that rifes on the very brink of a bog; its waters are a mild chalybeate, and have done great fervice in hypocondriacal cafes, and in cutaneous eruptions. Fairs are held here on 12 May, July, Sept. and Nov. Four miles N. W. of Macroomp, are the remains of a Danifh intrenchment, of an oval form; the greater diameter is 60 yards, and the fmaller 40: it is furrounded by a broad deep ditch, whofe fides are nearly perpendicular, and it has only one narrow path leading to it from the E. Near the road fide are 5 very large ftones, pitched end-ways, and forming an equilateral triangle, the area of which may contain a dozen perfons.

Macroom, fee *Macromp*.

Mac-Swine's-bay, fit. in bar. Boylagh, co. Donegal, prov. Ulfter.

Mac-Swine's-gun. This great curiofity is fit. on the demefne of *Horn-head*, within about 2 or 3 miles of *Dunfanaghy*, co. Donegal, prov. Ulfter. It confifts of a funnel perforated thro' a rock, by the beating of the fea againft it, by which means it has at laft forced a paffage, and rifes in an enormous jet d'eau of 6 or 7 feet in thicknefs, fometimes to the height of 40 or 50 feet. Its roaring is often heard 10 miles off in calm weather. The ftone the rock is formed of, is a granite of greenifh colour, fpotted with black, like the ophites of the antients.

Mac-Tegart's cross, fit. near *Dungannon*, co. Tyrone, prov. Ulfter.

Maddan-church, fit. 2 miles from *Keady*, co. Armagh, prov. Ulfter.

Madden'stown, fit. in bar. Ophaly, co. Kildare, prov. Leinfter.

Maddenton, fit. near *Clones*, prov. Ulfter.

Magawnah, a vicarage in dioc. of Killala, fit. in bar. Tirawly, co. Mayo, prov. Connaug.

Magee, commonly called an *ifland*, fit. on the N. E. coaft of co. Antrim, prov. Ulfter, on the N. fide of *Carrickfergus-bay*: it is however properly a peninfula, (tho' otherwife reprefented in the old maps) about 6 miles long, with an ifthmus about a mile in breadth. Lat. 54: 50 lon. 6: 0. It is a rectory in dioc. of Connor. At this place, *Moyfes Hill* (anceftor of the Irifh branch of the *Hill* family) faved his life about the year 1598, by hiding in a cave, when purfued by the *Mc. Donnels*, who had flain fir *John Chichefter* He came to this country under the earl of *Effex* in 1573, who was fent here to fubdue what was called *O'Neille's* rebellion.

Maghadhair, a place in co. Clare, prov. Munfter, where the kings of N. Munfter were antiently inaugurated.

Magharee *iflands*, fit. near the coaft of bar. Corcaguinny, co. Kerry, prov. Munfter.

Maghbreg, a plain fit. round Tarah-hill, co. Meath, prov. Leinfter, in which was contained the raths or palaces of the monarchs of Ireland, and of feveral of the princes and chiefs; it was alfo called *Bregia*, and extended as far as *Trim* and *Duleck*.

Magh Ceirtagh, fit. in co. Kerry, prov. Munfter; the proprietors of which were the *Mac-Cartys*.

Magh Colieghan, fit. in the Northern part of the King's co. prov. Leinfter; a diftrict of the *M'Coghlans*.

Magh-cru, a place fit. in the prov. of Connaught; the name fignifies *the field of murder*, which it obtained from the following caufe: towards the clofe of the early ages, the antient Irifh nobility diftinguifhed under the name of *Milefians*, by the flattery of the bards and other circumftances, carried themfelves with great haughtinefs towards the plebeians, not confidering them of the fame race, violating the chaftity of their wives and daughters with impunity, and triumphing over their lives and properties according to their wills. The people had long groaned under this tyranny of their chiefs, without the power of redrefs, as the arms were entirely lodged in the hands of the Milefians, the lower orders not being allowed to bear any other weapons than flings and ftaves. However about the beginning of the firft century, *Caibre* (called by hiftorians *Cin Coll*, or chief of the Scots,) a herdfman in Connaught, having attained fome authority among his brethren, from the quantity of his poffeffions;

poffeffions, was determined to attempt the deliverance of the people; but as force could not be employed, recourfe was had to ftratagem. For this purpofe, *Caibre* invited the principal chiefs to a grand entertainment at *Mugh-cru*, on condition they came unarmed; this term being affented to, the plebeians during the feftival, fell upon the defencelefs nobles and put them to death, fparing neither age or fex. Such a maffacre fpread univerfal confternation throughout the ifland, and numbers of the *Milefians* fled to Britain and Gaul, whilft others took refuge in unfrequented woods, leaving their raths or caftles to the infurgents, who ufurped the governments of the feveral diftricts, for near 50 years, but at length by the mediation of the Druids, who were in the intereft of the *Milefian race*, an accommodation took place on condition of the plebeian order receiving feveral privileges; and a fecurity being given for their lives and poffeffions, and thofe who had obtained any confiderable property in herds, were entitled in fome meafure to the rank of Milefians. So that from this period we may date the commencement of the emancipation of the old Irifh plebeian race.

MAGH EAN, or the plain on the water, a plain between the river Erne and bay of Donegal, prov. Ulfter.

MAGH EOGAN, or the diftrict of the *Mac Egans*, fit. in the Northern part of Munfter, adjoining *Lough Derg*.

MAGHERA, fit. in bar. Loughlinfholen, co. Londonderry, prov. Ulfter, 92 miles from Dublin, where are fairs on 12 Jan. 13 June, 16 Aug. 12 Oct. and 15 Nov. It is a rectory in dioc. of Derry.—Alfo a fair town of fame name, in bar. upper Iveagh, co. Down, prov. Ulfter; fairs held 26 Apr. Here are the ruins of an old church, where is a noted burial place. It is a vicarage in dioc. of Down; and near it formerly ftood a high tower, which, about the year 1714, was overturned by a violent ftorm, and lay at length, and entire on the ground, like a huge gun, without breaking to pieces, fo wonderfully hard and binding was the cement in this work.

MAGHERABOY or *Maghereboy*, a bar. in co. Fermanagh, prov. Ulfter.

MAGHERACLOGEE, fit. in bar. Kilmacrenan, co. Donegal, prov. Ulfter.

MAGHERACLONY, a vicarage in dioc. of Clogher, fit. in bar. Donaghmoyne, co. Monaghan, prov. Ulfter.

MAGHERACREEGAN or *Magheracrigan*, a fair town fit. in bar. Strabane, co. Tyrone, prov. Ulfter; Fairs held 6 May, 1ft Thurfd. before June, 2d Thurfd. Aug. 3d Thurfd. Oct. 24 Nov. and 3d Thurfd. Dec.

MAGHERACRIGAN, fee *Magheracreegan*.

MACHERACROSS, a rectory in dioc. of Clogher, fit. in bar. Tyrefkennedy, co. Fermanagh, prov. Ulfter.

MAGHERACULMONY, a rectory in dioc. of Clogher, fit. in bar. Lurge, co. Fermanagh, prov. Ulfter.

MAGHERADERNON, fee *Magheredernon*.

MACHERADROLL, fee *Magheredroll*.

MAGHERAFELT, a fair and poft town in bar. Loughlinfholen, co. Londonderry, prov. Ulfter; 87 miles from Dublin. Fairs held 25 May, Aug. and 29 Oct. It is a rectory in dioc. of Armagh.

MAGHERAGALL, a village fit. in bar. Maffareen, co. Antrim, prov. Ulfter. It is a vicarage in dioc. of Connor.

MAGHERALIN, a village fit. in bar. lower Iveagh, co. Down, prov. Ulfter; it is pleafantly feated on the river *Lagan*, 4½ miles N. W. of Dromore and 67 from Dublin. It is a rectory in dioc. of Dromore, and has a handfome church. *Tobias Pullein*, bifhop of Dromore in 1695, built an epifcopal houfe here, which was afterwards enlarged by one of his fucceffors; but is now abandoned, and the epifcopal refidence is reftored to Dromore. St. *Colman* founded a monaftery here, and died in 669. This town carries on the linen manufacture extenfively. Part of the lands here, as well as thofe leading to the co. *Antrim*, abounds with a white flinty lime-ftone, mixed with chalk, which renders the fprings iffuing from the higher grounds extremely foft, well tafted, and particularly noted for wafhing and whitening linen. This lime-ftone might prove an excellent manure for wheat grounds, and the grafs and herbage growing on the banks where it appears, is remarkably fweet. Marble pits have been opened in this neighbourhood; and near it are feveral manufactures and bleach-yards, there being fcarce a farmer hereabouts, who does not carry on fome branch of the linen bufinefs.

MAGHERALLY, a vicarage in dioc. of Lifmore, fit. in bar. lower Iveagh, co. Down, prov. Ulfter.

MAGHERAMISK or *Magheremufk*, a vicarage in dioc. of Connor, fit. in bar. Maffareen, co. Antrim, prov. Ulfter.

MAGHERASTEPHANA, a bar. in co. Fermanagh, prov. Ulfter.

MAGHERAVEELY or *Magherevaly*, a fair town fit. in bar. Clonkelly, co. Fermanagh, prov. Ulfter; fairs held 29 May and 2 Oct.

MAGHEREBOY, fee *Magheraboy*.

MAGHEREDERNON or *Magheradernon*, a diftrict joined to Moyafhel, and called the bar. of Moyafhel and Magheradernon, co. Weftmeath, prov. Leinfter.

MAGHEREDROLL, a name given to the country about *Ballinehinch*, in bar. Kinelearty, co. Down,

Down, prov. Ulster ; which being full of rocks and hills, renders all recefs to that place troublefome and unpleafant ; and from the terrible condition of the roads, has obtained the name of *Magheredroll*, which imports, " *the field of difficulties.*" This is a vicarage in dioc. of Dromore, and otherwife called *Magheradroll*.

MAGHEREGALL, fee *Magheragall*.

MAGHEREHOHIL, fit. in bar. Toome, co. Antrim, prov. Ulster.

MAGHEREINCH, a feat in co. Down, prov. Ulster, which ftands on an eminence, and has a beautiful profpect of wood, and the meanders of the river *Lagan*.

MAGHERELAVE, fit. near Lifburn, co. Antrim, prov. Ulster.

MAGHERELIN, fee *Magheralin*.

MAGHEREMUSK, fee *Magheramifk*.

MAGHERENTERMIN, fit. in bar. Boylagh, co. Donegal, prov. Ulster.

MAGHERESHERKAN, fit. in bar. Kilconway, co. Antrim, prov. Ulster.

MAGHERESTAPHANA, fee *Magherafephana*.

MAGHEREVOLY, fee *Magheraveely*.

MAGHERHEALY, fit. in bar. Inifhowen, co. Donegal, prov. Ulster.

MAGHERIBEG, fit. near Donegal, prov. Ulster : the word fignifies the little plain. Here a monaftery was founded by *O'Donnell*, about the middle of the fifteenth century, for friars of the third order of St. *Francis*.

MAGHERIES-BAY, fit. in co. Kerry, prov. Munfter ; between *Brandon-head* and the iflands called the *Magheries*. It is extremely dangerous, being full of funken rocks befides the frequent fqualls from the mountains, prevent any veffel from entering therein. Thefe iflands lie at the mouth of this dangerous bay, tho' in general they have not been hitherto noticed in the maps or charts.

MAGHEROSS, a vicarage in dioc. of Clogher, fit. in bar. Donoghmoyne, co. Monaghan, prov. Ulster.

MAGHERY, a fair town in co. Armagh, prov. Ulster ; fairs held 30 Apr. 24 June and 31 Oct.

MAGHERYBEG, fit. in bar. Corcaguinny, co. Kerry, prov. Munfter ; where is a fpring which rifes out of a clean white fand. Dr. *Rutty* calls it a *Salinonitrous fpring :* when properly applied, it proves antifcorbutic ; and is a purgative of confiderable ftrength.

MAGHINIS, a diftrict in co. Down, prov. Ulster, which antiently belonged to the family of *Savage*.

MAGLEANA, an antient diftrict comprehending the greateft part of the King's co. prov. Leinfter.

MACH NAMARA, fit. in the Eaftern part of the co. Clare, prov. Munfter ; the chieftains of which, were the *Mac-na-maras*.

MAGH-NAY, the prefent co. Rofcommon, prov. Connaught ; in which ftood the royal city of *Croghon*.

MAGH-OLL-LEIGH, a diftrict antiently belonging to the *Mac Culloghs*, fit. between the King's co. and co. Weftmeath, prov. Leinfter.

MAGHOONAGH, fit. in bar. Conillo, co. Limerick, prov. Munfter.

MAGHRAHOCHAL, fit. near *Balijmena*, prov. Ulster.

MAGHREMORE, a fair town in co. Donegal, prov. Ulster ; fairs held 2 June.

MAGHREMORE *bay*, fit. in bar. Arklow, co. Wicklow, prov. Leinfter.

MAGHRE-TIBOT, or the field of Theobald ; it is a large, even field, in co. Weftmeath, prov. Leinfter ; fit. on the road to *Athlone*, near the old monaftery of *Plurey*, fo called from the defeat of Sir *Theobald Verdon*, who here fought a battle in king Henry VIIIth's days, againft a party of the Irifh and was flain in the field.

MAGHRIADA, the prefent heath of Maryborough in Queen's co. prov. Leinfter : it was the original demefne of the *O'Mores*, chiefs of *Leix* : in which was fought a memorable battle between the people of Munfter and thofe of Leinfter, under the command of *Laoighois Cean Mordha*, about the middle of the 3d century. The bones of the flain are frequently found a few inches below the furface of the ground, on the borders of the heath.

MAGH-SLEUGHT, a place fit. near Fenagh, in the bar. of Mohil, and co. Leitrim, prov. Connaught ; celebrated in the antient Irifh poems for being the place where *Tigernmas* firft introduced the worfhip of *Crom* or *Fate* ; the principal deity of the *Cambric-Britons*, which fome years before the birth of Chrift, was by their Druids introduced into Ireland. This circumftance however fo difpleafed the Hibernian Druids, the worfhippers of *Beal*, that *Tigernmas* and his followers are faid to have been deftroyed by lightning.

MAGH-TUREY. There were 2 places of this name, the Northern and Southern. The Southern Maghturey was in the co. Galway, prov. Connaught, not far from *Lough-Mafk* ; and is celebrated in the Irifh poems for being the fcene of action between the Belgian and Danan or Caledonian fepts, about 80 or 100 years before the Chriftian Æra, in which the former were entirely defeated. The N. *Maghturey*, was fit. near *Lougharow*, in co. Rofcommon, prov. Connaught ; and is celebrated for an engagement there, between the *Belgians* and *Fomorians* on one fide, and the *Danans* on the other, fome few years before the birth of Chrift ; in which the *Belgians* were again defeated.

MAGH

MACH UIRE, the *Maguires* or *Magwires* country, fit. at *Lough Earne,* in prov. Ulster.

MAGHULLIN, an antient diftrict of the *O'Flahertys,* fit. in co. Galway, prov. Connaug.

MAGILLA, a fair town in co. Cork, prov. Munfter; fairs held 21 Aug.

MAGILLIGAN-POINT, a *cape* fit. in bar. Kenoght, co. Londonderry, prov. Ulfter; 118 miles from Dublin. Between this point and *Magilligan-church,* is the greateft Rabbit-warren in the kingdom, it is the property of the bifhop of Derry, and faid to be worth from 1500*l.* to 1800*l.* annually, having been computed to produce 3 or 4 thoufand dozen of fkins yearly. St. *Columb* erected a monaftery at the village of *Magilligan.* In this parifh Mr. Innis difcovered a curious variety of medicinal plants; infomuch that he calls it the phyfic garden of the kingdom.

MAGILLYCUDDY'S-REEKS, fee *Macgillycuddy's-reeks.*

MAGLASS, a vicarage in dioc. of Ferns, fit. in bar. Forth, co. Wexford, prov. Leinfter.

MAGOURNEY, a rectory in dioc. of Cloyne, fit. in bar. Mufkerry, co. Cork, prov. Munfter.

MAGOWREY, a rectory in dioc. of Cafhel, fit. in bar. Middletkird, co. Tipperary, prov. Munfter.

MAGUIRE'S-BRIDGE, a village fit. in bar. Tyrefkennedy, co. Fermanagh, prov. Ulfter, 72 miles from Dublin. Fairs are held here on 17 Jan. Wed. after Whitfunday, 5 July, 2 Oct. 1 Wednefd. after 12 Nov. Near 3 miles from it is *Bellifle,* an ifland in Lough *Erne,* the beautiful feat of the earl of *Rofs.*

MAGUNIHY, a bar. in co. Kerry, prov. Munfter.

MAHALLAGH, fit. 5 miles E. of Macroomp, in co. Cork, prov. Munfter; pleafantly feated on the S. bank of the river Lee.

MAHON-RIVER, fit. in bar. Upperthird, co. Waterford, prov. Munfter; it rifes out of *Cummeragh* mountain, and in its defcent forms an agreeable cafcade. It empties itfelf after a courfe of 7 or 8 miles into the ocean, at a place called *Bunmahon-bay.*

MAHOUNAGH, a rectory in dioc. of Limerick, fit. in bar. Connello, co. Limerick, prov. Munfter.

MAIDESS, or *Whillans,* rocks fo called, which lie between the mouths of *Larne* and *Glenarm* bays, in co. Down, prov. Ulfter; lat. 54 : 58, lon. 6 : 12.

MAIG-RIVER, fit. in bar. Kenry, co. Limerick, prov. Munfter.

MAIGEVILLE, called alfo *Moville,* a monaftery of Auguftin canons founded by St. *Finian,* about the year 550. It ftood near an Englifh mile E. N. E. of Newtown, on the road to Donaghadee in co. Down, prov. Ulfter. This

houfe fubfifted 'till the general diffolution of abbeys, in the reign of Henry VIIIth. as appears by an inquifition taken anno 1 Jac. 1. and was then feized of the fpiritualties and temporalties of feven town lands, and of the fpiritualties of 16 town lands and an half, and other poffeffions which were granted by the laft mentioned monarch, to James, vifc. *Claneboys,* in fee-farm, at the rent of 3*l.* 3*s.* 4*d.* Irifh money; and from him came by affignment to *Hugh* vifc. *Ardes.* Part of the ruins of the abbey church yet remain, and the veftiges of large foundations appear within fide of the cemetary, which is ufed as fuch to the parifh of Newtown. There are no infcriptions in this place that are antient, or any way fingular.

MAINE, a *river* fit. in co. Antrim, prov. Ulfter.

MAINHAM, a vicarage in dioc. of Kildare; fit. in bar. Ikeath, co. Kildare, prov. Leinfter.

MAIO, fee *Mayo.*

MAISTEAN, or the place of the affembly of the elders. It was fit. on a gentle floping hill, about 5 miles E. of Athy, in co. Kildare, prov. Leinfter; now diftinguifhed by the *Moat* of *Mullamaft,* or the moat of Decapitation; from the murder of a number of Irifh gentlemen by feveral Englifh adventurers in the 16th century. This hill exactly refembled that of *Tara,* in the co. *Meath,* and was alfo called *Carmen,* or the inclofed place, having been the capital of the antient *Coulan,* and the *Naufleighan,* where the ftates of the Southern part of Leinfter met: there are yet remaining on it, the rath and *Laios* in which the chiefs encamped; alfo the Labereigh or Areopagus, confifting of 16 conical mounds of earth, in a circle of 68 feet in diameter, on which the chiefs fat in council. Near this place was fought the celebrated battle of *Carmen,* the people of Munfter, and thofe of Leinfter, under the command of *Laoigheis Caen More,* chief of Leix, in the Queen's co. about the middle of the 3d century. *Lavigheis,* according to *Keating,* defeated the Munfter army from the top of *Maifeen* to *Athy,* in the co. Kildare, and purfued them to *Leix,* when the battle was renewed on the plains of *Magh-riada,* now the heath of Maryborough, where *Laoigheis* obtained a fecond victory, and drove the fugitives into their native country. The field where this battle was fought is about 2 miles from Athy; and at this day numbers of bodies of the flain, are frequently dug up, about a foot below the furface, and in the feveral directions in which they fell.

MAKCOAN, fit. in bar. Bantry, co. Wexford, prov. Leinfter.

MALAHIDE, fit. in bar. Coolock, co. Dublin, prov. Leinfter, 6¼ miles from the metropolis.

polis. It is pleafantly feated on the banks of a branch of the Irifh channel; but being without fhelter, and in an open country, is much expofed to the winds: the air is however very pure, tho' keen; the houfes are but low and meanly built in general. In the middle of the town is a well dedicated to the Virgin Mary and inclofed by a good ftone building: the water of this fpring is very clear, and wholefome. Near it is the *caftle*, or as it is ufu-ally ftiled, the *Court of Malahide*, the feat of the *Talbot* family; the building is large, irregular, and unequal in its height; it is nearly fquare, and has an area or court within. The fituati-on is lofty, and commands a fine view of the *town* and *bay* of *Malahide*. The hall is large and has an antient appearance, correfponding with the outfide. There are ten rooms on a floor; one of which (a parlour) is wainfcotted with carved oak, in a very curious antique man-ner. The lower ftory, confifting of fervant's offices, &c. is vaulted; and the whole is founded on a lime-ftone rock. This place is a curacy in dioc. of Dublin: it is a manor, and its royalties reach a confiderable way along the fea fhore. A cotton manufacture was efta-blifhed here, by the late col. Talbot, who erected a large mill, where cotton is fpun by water.

MALAHIDERT, fit. in co. Dublin, prov. Leinfter, about 6 miles from the metropolis, and 3 miles beyond *Caftleknock*; the church of which, formerly a large and beautiful fabrick, is now in ruins; the church yard is much ufed as a burial place. Near it is a very handfome well, fupplied with a remarkable fine fpring of water, and dedicated to the Virgin Mary: whofe ftatue in miniature is fet up in a niche of the building, which is made in form of a fmall houfe round the well.

MALBAY *bay*, fit. in bar. Ibrickin, co. Clare, prov. Munfter.

MALBY, or *Mount-malby*, a name given to Slieb Donard mountain, in co. Down, prov. Ulfter.

MALBOROUGH, fit. near *Downpatrick*, co. Down, prov. Ulfter.

MALIN, a fair town in bar. *Boylagh*, co. Do-negal, prov. Ulfter; fairs held Eafter Tuefd. 24 June, 1 Aug. 31 Oct. Here is a very anti-ent ecclefiaftical building, faid to have been a monaftery.—There is alfo another village of fame name; in bar. Inifhowen, in fame co.

MALIN-HEAD, a *cape*, fit. in bar. Inifhowen, co. Donegal, prov. Ulfter. Lat. 55:23.

MALKO, a *lake* in co. Mayo, prov. Connaug.

MALLARDSTOWN, fit. near Kilkenny, prov. Leinfter.

MAL AHIDERT *fee Malahidert*.

MALLONE, or *Malone*, a village fit. in bar. Belfaft, co. Antrim, prov. Ulfter.

MALLOW, a manor, and alfo a borough town in bar. Fermoy, co. Cork, prov. Munfter, 121 miles from Dublin; it returns two mem-bers to parliament; patronage in the *Jephfon* family. Lat. 51:58, lon. 8:54. Dr. *Smith* fays this manor lies next adjacent to the bar. of *Duhallow*, and was a diftinct feniory which formerly belonged to the earl of *Defmond*; and on his attainder, was granted by queen *Eliz.* to fir *John Norris*, who fettled the crown of *Por-tugal* on the houfe of *Braganza*, and was lord prefident of Munfter; fir *John Jephfon*, knt. marrying the heirefs of Norris, became pof-feffed of this eftate, and obtained new letters patent for the fame. Here were formerly two caftles, one on the N. fide of the town of *Mal-low*, called the *Short Caftle*, and the other on the S. end, being a noble pile of building, erected by the earls of *Defmond*, which was ruined in the rebellion of 1641; this town alfo partook of the contefts of the year 1690, after the battle of the *Boyne*. It was once reckoned the beft village in Ireland, and was incorporated by charter, in 1688; it is pleafantly fit. on the N. bank of the *Blackwater*, over which there is an excellent ftone bridge. Here is alfo a good church, a market houfe, and barrack for a troop of horfe; not far from the caftle is a fine fpring, of a moderately tepid water, difcovered in 1724, which burfts out of the bottom of a fine limeftone rock, and approach-es the neareft in all its qualities, to the hot-well waters of *Briftol*, of any that has been yet dif-covered in this kingdom, which brings a refort of good company there, frequently in the fum-mer months, and has caufed it to be called the *Irifh Bath*. Fairs are held here on 1 Jan. day before Shrove-tuefday, 11 May, 25 July, and 28 Oct. *Mallow* is a poft town, and a rectory in dioc. of Cloyne.

MALONE, fee *Mallone*.

MALTON, fit. in bar. Ballinacour, co. Wick-low, prov. Leinfter.

MAMARAGHTY *mountains*, fit. in bar. Burri-fhoole, co. Mayo, prov. Connaught.

MAMTRASNA *mountains*, fit. in bar. Rofs, co. Galway, prov. Connaught.

MANG, a *river*, fit. in bar. Truaghnacmy, co. Kerry, prov. Munfter; it rifes near *Caftle Ifland*, and is joined by the *Brown Flefk*, and after paffing thro' the bridge of *Caftlemain*, glides gently in a meandering courfe to the fea; it is navigable up to that bridge.

MANGERFORD, fit. near *Baltinglafs*, in bar. Talbotftown, co. Wicklow, prov. Leinfter.

MANGERTON-MOUNTAIN, fit. in bar. Ma-gunihy, co. Kerry, prov. Munfter, near Lough Lean, or the lake of *Killarney*; it is efteemed

the

the higheſt mountain in Ireland, being 2,500 feet above the ſea; but it is doubtful if *Magilly-cuddy's-reeks*, in that neighbourhood, do not exceed it in altitude.

MANILLA, a village in bar. Clonmorris, co. Mayo, prov. Connaught, 110 miles from Dublin.

MANNANSTOWN, ſit. near *Drogheda*, prov. Leinſter.

MANNINBAY, a *harbour* in bar. Ballinahinch, co. Galway, prov. Connaught.

MAN-OF-WAR, a village, ſit. in bar. Balrud-dery, co. Dublin, prov. Leinſter, above 12 miles from Dublin.

MANOOTH, ſee *Maynooth*.

MANOR-CUNNINGHAM, ſit. in bar. Ra-phoe, co. Donegal, prov. Ulſter, 126 miles from Dublin; fairs held 7 July and 6 Nov.

MANOR-GORE, ſit. in co. Donegal, prov. Ulſter; it gives title of baron to the family of *Gore*, now earl of Roſs.

MANOR-HAMILTON, ſit. in bar. Dromahaire, co. Leitrim, prov. Connaught, 94 miles from Dublin. Fairs held 8 May, 1 July, 7 Oct. and 1ſt Thurſd. O. S. in Nov.

MANORWATER-HOUSE, ſit. near *Liſneſkea*, prov. Ulſter.

MANSELLSTOWN, ſit. near *Thurles*, co. Tip-perary, prov. Munſter.

MANSFIELDSTOWN, a village ſit. in bar. Louth, co. Louth, prov. Leinſter; it is a rec-tory in dioc. of Armagh.

MAPLESTOWN, or *Mapuſtown*, ſit. in bar. Ardee, co. Louth, prov. Leinſter; it is a vi-carage in dioc. of Armagh.

MAPUSTOWN, ſee *Mapleſtown*.

MAQUASQUIN *church*, ſit. within 2 miles of *Colerain*, co. Londonderry, prov. Ulſter.

MARAGHAGH *mountains*, ſit. in the Southern part of the Queen's co. prov. Leinſter; other-wiſe called *Marghie* or *Maraghie* mountains. They lie E. of the co. Kilkenny, and comprehend the antient diſtricts of *Dunan, Clogh, Sean, Ogh-ragh, Maragheigh* and *Brenan*; they are rather hills than mountains, having no great eleva-tion, but form three diſtinct ridges, encloſing on the Northern extremities a kind of plain, conſiderably below the vertex of the hills, but much above the level parts of the adjacent countries. The Northern ridge, antiently call-ed *Shean Oghragh*, ſeems to be compoſed of cal-careous ſtone towards the vertex, on which is a mooriſh ſoil producing ruſhes and turf. Some-what lower towards the S. the ſoil changes to a vegetable earth, fruitful in graſs, meadow and corn, intermixed with watery bog, producing ruſhes, but no great quantity of good turf. On this part ſtood an antient foreſt called *Choille Oghragh*, now no more, and diſtinguiſhed only by its ruins: between the ſcite of this foreſt

and the moory land called *Carragh*, appears a kind of ſlate ſtratum, indicating coals at no great depth; the coal ſtratum being actually found about 6 feet beneath the ſurface, running in the direction of the declivity of the hill, about 16 inches deep, but not of good quality. Beyond the ſcite of the wood, the ſlates diſap-pear, and the ſtratum of coals dips from ſix feet to 5 and 8 fathom, and is in thickneſs from 12 to 20 inches, covered with the following ſtrata, that is, ſoil, argillaceous earth, a kind of argillaceous rock-ſtone, black ſlate, earth, &c. On entering the lands of *Clogh* and *Doo-nan*, the ground is fertile, and the coal dips from 20 to 28 fathom; being from 20 inches to 3½ feet in thickneſs, running in a direction nearly parallel to the horizon. Here, at about 12 fathom beneath the ſurface, is found a rock of win-ſtone, reſting on a ſtratum of columnar baſaltes, perpendicular to the horizon: the co-lumns are from 2 to 6 feet in length, the arti-culations from 3 to 6 inches, forming both con-vex and concave joints, of an irregular penta-gonal figure, whoſe ſides, in different joints, are plain, convex and concave. Theſe columns in ſeveral parts reſt on a light-grey ferruginous rock, or win-ſtone on a ſlatey rock, beneath which is a vein of rich iron ore, parallel to the horizon, from 1 to 3 inches thick. Under the iron is a ſtratum of ſlate, and then the bed of coal. Beneath the bed of coal is a ſoft micace-ous ſlate ſtratum, 10 or 12 fathom deep, and under that a hard rock, through which no one has yet bored: the miners think that the great and principal bed of coal lies beneath this rock, at about 50 fathom from the ſurface. In the Eaſtern ridge called *Brennan*, run a number of rich copious iron mines. From the remains of various ſhafts, it is evident theſe mines have been wrought in ſome, perhaps remote, period, as no tradition is now remaining of their hav-ing ever been opened. On the Eaſtern declivity of this ridge, are a number of coal mines, from 27 feet, to 12 fathom below the ſurface, and covered by argillaceous and yellow ferruginous rock, on a bed of black micaceous ſlate. In the Southern ridge from *Doonan*, no coals have yet been diſcovered; but on the Weſtern, or *Ma-raghie* ridge, belonging to the lordſhip of *Caſtle-comer*, coals are found from 6 feet to 4 fathom. From what has at preſent been diſcovered of theſe hills, they ſeem to be compoſed of moory ſoil, argillaceous earth, argillaceous and ferru-ginous ſtone, ſlate, baſaltes, iron ore, and coals in different ſtrata, at various depths, in irregular and broken maſſes; the whole reſting on a hard rocky baſe, not improbably granite. From the depth of the pits on the lands of *Doonan* and *Clogh*, great quantities of water are collect-ed in them, from whence it is diſcharged by

means

means of the improved ſtream engine. This, tho' originally conſtructed by *Bolton* and *Watts*, is ſtill more improved by that ingenious engineer, Mr. *Fenton*, whereby the power has not only been conſiderably augmented, but the quantity of fire much reduced, ſaving above ⅓ of the coals neceſſary to thoſe engines of the original patentees. The engine at *Doonàn* works 19 ſtrokes in a minute, raiſing a quantity of water equal to 16 hogſheads in an hour, or 96 tuns in 24 hours, from a depth of 54 yards. In this neighbourhood lives a Mr. *Farram*, a native of the place, who, tho' perfectly blind, has, by the effort of genius only, obtained a perfect knowledge of the French, Latin and Greek languages, Mathematics and natural philoſophy; and is an able performer on the Violin, which he plays with great accuracy.

MARALIN, ſee *Maghcrelin*.

MARDYKE, ſit. near Bandon, prov. Munſter. Alſo near *Roſcrea*, in ſame prov.

MARE BRENDANICUM, a name given by *Camden* to that part of the Weſtern ocean, into which the river *Shannon* diſcharges itſelf.

MARGHIE, ſee *Maraghagh*.

MARHIR, a vicarage in dioc. of Ardfert, ſit. in bar. Coreaguinny, co. Kerry, prov. Munſter.

MARINO, an elegant ſeat of the earl of *Charlemont*, ſit. near *Donnycarney*, about 1½ mile from Dublin, in co. Dublin, prov. Leinſter. The demeſne ſurrounding the houſe, conſiſts of about 200 acres, laid out and improved with ſingular taſte and elegance. The houſe makes an elegant appearance, is built of Portland ſtone, and the gardens are extenſive and beautiful. About ¼ mile from the manſion-houſe, pleaſantly ſit. in the park, ſtands the *Caſino*, a ſuperb temple, after a deſign of the celebrated ſir *William Chambers*.

MARKET-HILL, ſit. in bar. Fews, co. Armagh, prov. Ulſter, 58 miles from Dublin. Fairs held 6 May, 22 June and 29 Oct. This place is taken notice of by the celebrated dean *Swift* in his writings; who choſe a favourite ſpot not far from it, to which he gave the name of *Draper's-hill*. Near it is *Gosford caſtle*, the handſome ſeat of lord *Gosford*.

MARLAY, the handſome ſeat of the Rt. Hon. *David Latouche*, ſit. 1¼ mile beyond *Rathfarnham*, in co. Dublin, prov. Leinſter, and about 4 miles from Dublin caſtle. The approach to this place is romantically beautiful. A winding ſtream to the right, and a church-yard with its ivy'd ruins, ſit. on a ſmall eminence beyond the demeſne, form a ſcene truly pleaſing to the eye of contemplation. The farm and pleaſure grounds, which are highly dreſſed and richly planted, are agreeably broken by ſeveral pieces of water, falling in beautiful ſucceſſion, and have been conveyed from the neighbouring

ſtreams with great art, at a conſiderable expence.

MARLINSTOWN, a vicarage in dioc. of Armagh, ſit. in bar. Ferrard, co. Louth, prov. Leinſter.

MARLY, ſit. in bar. Ferrard, co. Louth, prov. Leinſter.

MARMULLANE, a curacy in dioc. of Cork, ſit. in bar. Kinalea, co. Cork, prov. Munſter.

MARSHAL'STOWN, a vicarage in dioc. of Cloyne, ſit. in bar. Condons, co. Cork, prov. Munſter.

MARSHBROOK, ſit. in King's co. prov. Leinſter, 56 miles from Dublin.

MARTRY, a vicarage in dioc. of Meath, ſit. in bar. Navan, co. Meath, prov. Leinſter.

MARYBOROUGH, a *barony* in Queen's co. prov. Leinſter, having in it a borough, market, fair and poſt town of ſame name. They were ſo called in honour of *Mary*, queen of England, who reduced this part of the country to ſhire-ground, by act of parliament, 6th and 7th *Phil.* and *Mary*. The *town* has a barrack for a troop of horſe. It returns 2 members to parliament; patronage in the families of *Parnell* and *Coote*. 'Tis diſtant from Dublin 40 miles; lat. 53 : 0, lon. 7 : 20. Fairs held 24 Feb. 12 May, 5 July, 4 Sept. and Dec. This place lies on the river *Barrow*. It has an antient caſtle, ſaid to have been built by *Bellingham*: and is the aſſizes town for the *Queen's co*. Between *Maryborough* and *Mountrath*, may be ſeen on the ſide of a hill, *Ballyfin*, the elegant ſeat of the Hon. *Welſeley Pole*, adorned with great variety of ground and beautiful woods, ſurrounding a conſiderable and very handſome lake. The *heath* of *Maryborough*, was the original demeſne of the *O'Mores*, chiefs of *Laoighois* or *Leix*; in it was fought a memorable battle, between the people of Munſter and thoſe of Leinſter, about the middle of the 6th century.

MARYBROOK, an agreeable ſeat in co. Down, prov. Ulſter, ſit. on a riſing ground near a lake, two miles S.S.E. of *Ballynahinch*.

MARY-GERANE'S-HOUSE, a name given to *Dunmore-head*, in the pariſh of *Dunqueen*, co. Kerry, prov. Munſter; it is the moſt Weſtern point of all *Europe*; the Iriſh call it *Ty Vorney Gecrane*: tis a point, as much celebrated by them, as *John* of *Groot's-houſe*, which is the utmoſt extremity of N. Britain.

MARY-GREY *mountain*, ſit. in bar. Strabane, co. Tyrone, prov. Ulſter: this mountain, and that called *Beſſy Bell*, in the ſame bar. are remarkably high.

MARYMONT, ſit. near *Belfaſt*, prov. Ulſter.

MARYVILLE, ſit. near *Sheepbridge*, co. Down, prov. Ulſter.

MASHANAGLASS, a high tower, S. of *Glin-Eaum*, leading to *Macroom*, in co. Cork, prov. Munſter.   MASK-

MASK-LOUGH, fee *Lough-mafk.*

MASLASCANLANE, a fair town in co. Cork, prov. Munfter; fairs held 2 Feb. Saturd. before Whitfunday, 15 Aug. and 8 Dec.

MASSAREEN, or *Mazareen*, a bar. in co. Antrim, prov. Ulfter. It has a village of fame name, where a fmall monaftery was founded by *O'Neil*, in the 15th century, for Francifcan friars of the 3d order. This place gives title of earl to the family of *Skeffington*; it is fometimes written *Maffereue.*

MASSYTOWN, a fair town in co. Cork, prov. Munfter; fairs held 14 and 15 June, 12 Aug. and Oct. 14 and 15 Dec.

MASTENSTOWN, fit. in bar. Middlethird, co. Tipperary, prov. Munfter.

MATTEHY, a rectory in dioc. of Cloyne, fit. in bar. Barrets, co. Cork, prov. Munfter.

MAUDLIN, a rectory in dioc. of Ferns, fit. in the liberties of *Wexford* town, prov. Leinft.

MAWHAN, fit. in co. Armagh, prov. Ulfter, 56 miles from Dublin.

MAYCOMB, a rectory in dioc. of Ferns, fit. in bar. Scarewalfh, co. Wexford, prov. Leinft.

MAYFIELD, fit. near *Tuam*, prov. Connaug.

MAYNE, a *river* in bar. Toome, co. Antrim, prov. Ulfter;—Alfo a rectory in dioc. of Offory, fit. in bar. Faffachdinning, co. Kilkenny, prov. Leinfter.—Alfo a rectory in dioc. of Armagh, fit. in bar. Ferrard, co. Louth, prov. Leinfter. — Likewife a vicarage in dioc. of Meath, fit. in bar. Half-foure, co. Weftmeath, prov. Leinfter.

MAYNOOTH, or *Manooth*, fit. in bar. Salt, co. Kildare, prov. Leinfter, 11 miles from Dublin; it is a poft town, and has fairs on 4 May, and 19 Sept. Within a mile of it, is *Carton-houfe*, the fuperb feat of the duke of *Leinfter*. Maynooth, tho' not very large, is regularly laid out, and confifts of good houfes. Here is a charter-fchool, which was opened 27 July 1750, for 40 boys, towards the building of which the late Rt. Hon. *Robert*, earl of *Kildare*, left 500*l.* and the marquis gave 14 acres of land, rent free, for ever. *Gerald* earl of Kildare, founded a college adjoining this town in which he placed a provoft, vice-provoft, and five priefts or fellows, two clerks and three boys, to pray for his foul and the foul of his wife: he died in Oct. 1513, and was interred in *Chrift-church*, Dublin. This is a vicarage in dioc. of Dublin.

MAYO *county*, fit. in prov. Connaught. It has Sligo and the fea on the N. Galway on the S. Rofcommon on the E. and the Atlantic ocean on the W. It extends from N. to S. 49 miles, and from E. to W. 45. It is exceeded in dimenfions by Cork and Galway only; it contains 790,600 acres, 9 bar.'s, 68 parifhes, about 27,970 houfes, and 140,000 inhabitants.

It has but one borough, and returns only 4 members to parliament. It gives title of earl to the family of *Bourke*. This county takes its name from an antient city, built in 664, in which was a monaftery and nunnery. St. *Segretia*, who prefided for fome time over the latter, died of the plague in 664, as did alfo 100 other virgins: the ruins of the cathedral, and fome traces of the ftone walls which encompaffed the city, yet remain on the plains of Mayo. It was a univerfity, founded for the education of fuch of the *Saxon* youths as were converted to the Chriftian faith: it was fit. a little to the S. of *Lough Conn*, lat. 54 : 7, lon. 9 : 40, and is to this day frequently called *Mayo* of the *Saxons*, being celebrated for giving education to *Ofwald*, and to *Aifred* the great, king of England. As this town has gone to decay, *Ballinrobe* is reckoned the chief town, tho' *Caftlebar* is the affizes town. The co. by the fea, is mountainous, but in-land has good paftures, lakes and rivers; its bar.'s are, Tyrawly, Gallen, Coftello, Clanmorris, Kilmain, Morifk, Carragh, Burrifhoole and Erris. The antient inhabitants of this co. are the *O'Mailleys*, *Burkes*, *Barretts*, *McWilliams*, *Browns*, *Lynotts*, *Binghams*, *Fitzmaurices* and *Joyces.*

MAYPOLE, fit. in co. Weftmeath, prov. Leinfter, 47 miles from Dublin, within a mile of which is *Kilpatrick* church.

MAYRE-CASTLE, fit. in bar. Orior, co. Armagh, prov. Ulfter. lat. 54 : 5, lon. 6 : 51.

MAZAREEN, fee *Maffareen.*

MAZE, a village fit. in bar. Maffareen, co. Antrim, prov. Ulfter.

MAZE-COURSE, fit. about 1 mile from Hillfborough, in co. Down, prov. Ulfter; it is a place fet apart for the public diverfions of horfe-racing, near the banks of the river *Lagan*; a rifing hill in the middle of the courfe, about 2 miles in circumference, gives the fpectators a full view of the whole field; and on the top of the hill a wooden tower is erected, open on all fides for fpectators to fit in, and view the courfe.

MEAD'STOWN, fit. in co. Meath, prov. Leinfter, above 32 miles from Dublin; near it are the ruins of a church.

MEARS-COURT, fit. in co. Weftmeath, prov. Leinfter.

MEATH, commonly fo called, or otherwife *Eaft* Meath, to diftinguifh it from the co. called *Weftmeath*; 'tis a co. in the prov. of Leinfter, bounded by the co.'s of Cavan and Louth on the N. the Irifh channel on the E. Kildare and Dublin on the S. and Weftmeath on the W. It is a fine champaign country abounding with corn, and well inhabited. It returns 14 members to parliament; and gives title of earl to the family of *Brabazon*. It has 12

bar.'s,

bar.'s, viz. Slane, Morgallion, Kells, *Half-Fowre*, Lune, Navan, Duleek, Skryne, Ratoath, Dunboyne, Deece, and Moyfenrath. Thefe contain 147 parifhes, about 22,468 houfes, and 112,400 fouls. The co. extends from N. to S. 29 miles, and from E. to W. 35, including an area of 327,900 acres. *Meath* contains 6 boroughs; its antient families are the *Nugents, Barnewells, Biotaghs*, or *Betaghs, Laceys* and *Cruces.* Much coarfe linen is made in this co. but its principal fources of wealth are derived from the flocks and herds that are fattened, and the abundance of corn that is raifed on its fruitful plains. Meath is alfo a *bifhopric* formed from feveral fmaller ones, which gradually coalefced into one fee; it has not however any *cathedral;* and the epifcopal refidence is at *Ardbraccan*; it is a new and elegant manfion erected by the prefent bifhop. *Trim* is the chief and affizes town of this co. This antient diftrict was the fettlement of the *Belgians* in Ireland, and in confequence of which, the inhabitants were efteemed the eldeft and moft honourable tribe: from which feniority their chieftains were elected monarchs of all the Belgæ; a dignity that was continued in the *Hy-n-Faillian* line without intermiffion, until the arrival of the Caledonian colonies, under the name of *Tuath de Danan*, when *Conor Mor* chieftain of thefe people, obtained or rather ufurped the monarchial throne, obliged *Eochy Failloch*, with feveral of his people to crofs the *Shannon*, and eftablifh themfelves in the prefent co. of Rofcommon, where *Crothar* founded the palace of *Atha* or *Croghan:* a circumftance which brought on a long and bloody war between the *Belgian* and *Caledonian* races, which was not finally terminated until the clofe of the 4th century, when the Belgian line was reftored in the perfon of *O'Nial* the great, and continued until *Brian Boromh* ufurped the monarchial dignity by depofing *Malachy O'Malachlin*, about the year 1001. *Tuathal Tetethomar*, by a decree of the Tarah affembly, feparated certain large tracts of land from each of the 4 prov.'s, where the borders joined together; whence under the notion of adopting this fpot for demefne lands to fupport the royal houfehold, he formed the co. or kingdom of *Meath*, which afterwards became the peculiar inheritance of the monarchs of Ireland. In each of the portions thus feparated from the 4 prov.'s, Tuathal caufed palaces to be erected, which might adorn them, and commemorate the name in which they had been added to the royal domain. In the tract taken out of Munfter, he built the palace called *Flachtaga*, where the facred fire, called by that name, was kindled, and where all the priefts and druids, annually met on the laft

day of Oct. on the evening of which day, it was enacted, that no other fire fhould be ufed throughout the kingdom, in order that all the fires might be derived from this, which being lighted up as a fire of facrifice, their fuperftition led them to believe would render all the reft propitious and holy; and for this privilege, every family was to pay three pence, by way of acknowledgement to the king of *Munfter*. The fecond royal palace was erected in the proportion taken out of *Connaught*, and was built for the affembly called the convocation of *Vifneach*, at which all the inhabitants were fummoned to appear on the 1 day of May, to offer facrifice to *Beal* or *Bel*, the god of fire, in whofe honour two large fires being kindled, the natives ufed to drive their cattle between them, which was fuppofed to be a prefervative for them againft accidents and diftempers, and this was called *Beal-tinne* or *Beal-tine*, or the feftival of the God of fire. The king of Connaught at this meeting, claimed a horfe and arms from every lord of a manor or chieftain, as an acknowledgement for the lands taken from that prov. to add to the territory of *Meath*. The third was, that *Tailtean* erected in the part taken from *Ulfter*; where the fair of that name was held, which was remarkable for this particular circumftance, that the inhabitants brought their children thither, males and females, and contracted them in marriage, where the parents having agreed upon articles, the young people were joined accordingly; every couple contracted at this meeting, paid the king of *Ulfter* an ounce of filver by way of acknowledgement. The royal manfion of *Tarah*, (formerly deftroyed by fire) being rebuilt by *Tuathal*, on the lands originally belonging to the king of *Leinfter*, was reckoned as the fourth of thefe palaces, but as a fabric of that name had ftood there before, we do not find that any acknowledgement was made for it to the king of *Leinfter*.

MEDIOLANUM, an antient city or diftrict in co. Meath, prov. Leinfter: and thought to be either *Trim* or *Kells*.

MEDY-HILL, fit. in bar. Scarewalfh, co. Wexford, prov. Leinfter.

MEELICK, fit. in bar. Bunratty, co. Clare, prov. Munfter, 97 miles from Dublin. It is a chapelry in dioc. of Killaloe. About a mile from it are the ruins of a church. From the heights beyond *Meelick*, may be feen *Bunratty-caftle*, the antient feat of the earls of *Thomond*, fit. near the fide of the Shannon. It was built in 1277, and befieged but not taken, in 1305. The town of *Bunratty*, however, in 1314, was burnt to the ground.—There is alfo a fair town of this name, in bar. Longford, co. Galway, prov.

prov. Connaught, where are the remains of an old monastery near the river *Shannon*; fairs held 1 Oct. It is a vicarage in dioc. of Clonfert. The monastery was founded by *O'Madden*, dynast of *Silanchia*, for conventual Franciscans: the situation was delightful, and the building itself spacious and beautiful. In 1203, *Wm. De Burgh* marched at the head of an army into Connaught, and so to *Meelick*, and did there profanely convert the church into a stable, round which he erected a *castle* of a circular form. This monastery was granted to sir *John King*, who assigned it to the earl of *Clanrickarde*.

MELCHESTOWN, sit. in bar. Moygeesh, co. Westmeath, prov. Leinster.

MELCOMBE REGIS, otherwise *Carraghreagh*, sit. in co. Mayo, bar. *Carragh*, prov. Connaught; fairs held 19 and 20 May, 29 and 30 June, 1 Aug. and 1 Dec.

MELEFONT, formerly a famous monastery, in bar. Ferrard, co. Louth, prov. Leinster, and in queen *Eliz.'s* time, said to have contained 140 monks. It was founded in the year 1142, by *O'Carrol*, prince of *Orgiel*, for the canons regular of St. Augustine. It has been said, that in 1152, cardinal *Papiro* here held the famous synod, in which he distributed palliums to the 4 archbishops of Ireland: it is certain that in 1157, a synod was held here, at which the monarch, the king of *Ulloa*, the prince of *Breffui*, and the prince of *Orgiel* assisted; when the great church was consecrated, and amongst other offerings, 180 oz. of gold, and a gold chalice were presented. This place, sometime since, was one of the seats of the earl of Drogheda, but now mostly demolished. It is a curacy in dioc. of Armagh; and there still remains in tolerable preservation, a beautiful little chapel, built of a yellowish freestone mixed with red; the entrance is thro' a superb gothic arch; the E. window is truly elegant. Here was a profusion of gilding, and painting in various colours. Near the chapel was a beautiful octagonal bath, or more likely a baptistry, but it has been since destroyed. This place is distant about 5 miles from *Drogheda*, and 1½ mile from the river *Boyne*.

MELICK, a vicarage in dioc. of Achonry, sit. in bar. Gallen, co. Mayo, prov. Connaught. Here is one of the antient round towers.

MELL, sit. in bar. Ferrard, co. Louth, prov. Leinster.

MELLIFONT, see *Melefont*.

MELOGH *river*, sit. in co. Down, prov. Ulster. It is an inconsiderable river, which increases and decreases suddenly by the effects of rain.

MELVIE-LOUGH, see *Melvin-Lough*.

MELVIN-LOUGH, (sometimes written *Melvie-Lough*) a lake sit. in bar. Magheraboy, co. Fermanagh, prov. Ulster.

MENAPII, an antient district on the Eastern coasts of Ireland, mentioned by *Ptolemy*; comprehending that part of the present co. Wicklow, prov. Leinster, between the mountains and the sea, called by the Irish, *Coulan*, or the narrow inclosed country.

MENLOUGH, sit. in bar. Tiaquin, co. Galway, prov. Connaught, above 83 miles from Dublin; about a mile from it are the ruins of a castle.

MERVILLE, sit. in co. Dublin, prov. Leinster, 1 mile beyond *Donnybrook*, and 3 miles from Dublin castle. It is a handsome seat.

MEVAGH, a rectory in dioc. of Raphoe, sit. in bar. Kilmacrenan, co. Donegal, prov. Ulst.

MEW-ISLAND, one of the *Copland-islands*, sit. at the S. entrance of *Carrickfergus-bay*, bar. Ardes, co. Down, prov. Ulster.

MIADHANACH, the present co. Meath, prov. Leinster.

MIDDLEMOUNT, sit. near *Athy*, prov. Leinst.

MIDDLETOWN, sit. in bar. Ballagheen, co. Wexford, prov. Leinster.

MIDDLE-DOWN, a sand bank in the Irish channel, which is visible even at high water.

MIDDLETHIRD, a bar. in co. *Tipperary*, and another in co. *Waterford*, prov. Munster.

MIDDLETON, a fair town in bar. Tyranny, co. Armagh, prov. Ulster, 63 miles from Dublin. Fairs held 5 Feb. 4 May, 8 Aug. 11 Sept. 3 and 28 Nov.—Also a borough and post town, in bar. Barrymore, co. Cork, prov. Munster, 122 miles from Dublin. It gives title of visc. to the family of *Broderick*, and returns 2 members to parliament; patron, lord *Middleton*. Lat. 51 : 40 N. lon. 8 : 15 W. It is pleasantly sit. on the N. W. angle of Cork harbour: not far from the water side are the remains of an antient building, supposed to have been a leper house: contiguous to the town there is a subterraneous river, and near it is a large romantic cave. An abbey was founded here in 1180, by the Fitzgeralds, and supplied with monks of the Cistertian order, from the abbey of *Nenay* or *Magio*, in the co. Limerick; it was called the abbey of St. *Mary of Chore*, or of the chore of St. *Benedict*. In 1476, Gerald, bishop of Cloyne, appropriated several vicarages to this abbey. This place is called *Middleton* from its situation, being mid-way between *Cork* and *Youghal*. Fairs held 14 May, 5 July, 10 Oct. and 22 Nov. This is a rectory in dioc. of Cloyne.

MIDPACE *river*, sit. in co. Down, prov. Ulst.

MILE-WATER, sit. between *Belfast* and *Carrickfergus*, co. Antrim, prov. Ulster.

MILFORD,

MILFORD, a fair town in co. Cork, prov. Munfter; fairs held 25 March, 20 May, 24 Aug. and 20 Nov.—Alfo a place in bar. Bally-moe, co. Galway, prov. Connaught.

MILICK, fee *Meelick*.

MILK-COVE, a *creek* fit. in bar. Ibawne, co. Cork, prov. Munfter.

MILK-HAVEN, a *bay* fit. in bar. Carbury, co. Sligo, prov. Connaught.

MILLAXTOWN, fit. near *Ardee*, co. Louth, prov. Leinfter, where are the ruins of a church, much reforted to on account of the furprifing pofition of the gable-end, which is confidently reported to have been blown away from its foundation in a violent ftorm, and placed up-right at a few feet diftance, where it now re-mains erect; this ftrange accident, tho' greatly enquired into, has no way yet been accounted for, in any fatisfactory manner.

MILLECENT, a pleafant feat belonging to *H. Griffith*, efq; fit. on the banks of the river *Liffey*, between *Clain* and *Sallins*, in co. Kil-dare, prov. Leinfter. Near it is the *Grand canal*, with a handfome aqueduct over the Liffey, con-ftructed by *R. Evans*, efq; formerly engineer to the Grand canal company.

MILLEFONT, fit. in co. Louth, prov. Lein-fter. It gives title of baron to the family of *Moore*, now marquefs of *Drogheda*.

MILLEXTOWN, fee *Millaxtown*.

MILLIMOUNT, fit. near Banbridge, prov. Ulfter.

MILL-ISLES, a group of rocks about 2 miles S. of *Donaghadee*, co. Down, prov. Ulfter; called by fome the *plow*, they are no way dan-gerous, becaufe well known, and feen above water at half tide; befides they ftand near the fhore, and are embayed on both fides.—Alfo a *village* fit. in bar. *Ardes*, in fame co.

MILL-OF-LOUTH, a village fit. in bar Louth, co. Louth, prov. Leinfter, about 40 miles from Dublin.

MILLSTREET, fit. in bar. Mufkerry, co. Cork, prov. Munfter, 136 miles from Dublin: it is a fmall village, and has a barrack for 2 companies of foot: fome manufactures of linen cloth have been introduced here. It is a poft town, and has fairs on 1 March, June, Sept. and Dec. At a little diftance from this place, the river *Blackwater* divides the co.'s *Kerry* and *Cork*.

MILTOWN, a poft town, fit. in bar. Truagh-nacmy, co. Kerry, prov. Munfter, 173 miles from Dublin. Fairs held 26 and 27 Apr. 24 June and Aug. 15 and 16 Dec.—Alfo a fair town in bar. Half fowre, co *Weftmeath*, prov. Leinfter; fairs held day after Trinity Sund. and 2 Oct. It gives title of vifc. to the family of *Fitzwilliam*, now earl *Fitzwilliam*.—Alfo a village of fame name, in bar. Newcaftle, co.

Dublin, prov. Leinfter, about 2½ miles from the metropolis. On the left of the bridge here, is one of the forts or raths, commonly afcribed to the *Danes*, but fo little of its primi-tive form remains, that few perfons would know by its prefent appearance, what it origi-nally was. This place gives title of earl to the family of *Leefon*.—There is alfo a place of fame name, in bar. Louth, co. Louth, prov. Leinfter.—Alfo a chapelry in dioc. of Meath, fit. in bar. Ratoath, co. Meath, prov. Leinfter. Alfo a place in bar. Coonagh, co. Limerick, prov. Munfter, in which a monaftery was erect-ed for Carmelite friars, by *Nellan O'Molloy*.

MILTOWN *caftle*, fit. in co. Louth, prov. Leinfter: it is 45 feet high, and ftands in the midft of a fine inclofed country, about 4 miles S. of *Dundalk*; it appears to be one of the old-eft fort of habitations now remaining in that county, and the manner of building it is faid to be borrowed from the *Spaniards*, who were early vifitors of this ifland; 2 or 3 furlongs from this dwelling, on the top of a rifing ground, an arched fubterraneous vault has been difcovered, running many roods under ground, and fuppofed to communicate with the caftle, as a fally-way for retiring in time of danger.

MILTOWN-DODWELL, fit. in bar. Athlone, co. Rofcommon, prov. Connaught.

MILTOWN-MALBAY, fit. in co. Clare, prov. Munfter; fairs held 1 Feb. 20 June, and 18 Oct.

MILTOWN-PASS, fit. in bar. Athlone, co. Rofcommon, prov. Connaught; fairs held 1 May, 22 July and Sept, and 20 Dec.—Alfo a place in bar. Fertullagh, co. Weftmeath, prov. Leinfter.

MINARD, a village fit. in bar. Corcaguin-ny, co. Kerry, prov. Munfter. It is a vicarage in dioc. of Ardfert.

MINARD *caftle*, fit. in co. Kerry, prov. Mun-fter, mid-way between the ifthmus called *Inch-ifland*, and *Dingle*, on the fea coaft: it was built by the Knts. of *Kerry*. To this place, *Walter Huffey*, efq; and his party, made their efcape in the night, being hard preffed by *Crom-well's* forces, but he was quickly befet by the colonels, *Lehunt* and *Sadier*; after fome time fpent, the *Englifh* obferving that the befieged made ufe of pewter bullets, *Huffey* and his men were blown up by powder, laid under the vaults of the caftle; there is a good quarry of freeftone at no great diftance from this caftle, of which the coin-ftones of feveral of the old buildings in this co. are compofed.

MINEGAHANE, fit. in co. Kerry, prov. Munfter, on the fea coaft; the moft remark-able curiofity of this place, is a prodigious noife made at certain feafons, by the fea, fome-what

what like the firing of cannon, which may be heard at a great diftance: this generally precedes a change of wind and weather, and frequently happens towards the approach of a ftorm.

MINE-HEAD, a *cape*, fit. in bar. *Decies within*, co. Waterford, prov. Munfter.

MININISH-ISLAND, fit. on coaft of bar. Ballinahinch, co. Galway, prov. Connaught.

MINOLA, fit. in bar. Carragh, co. Mayo, prov. Connaught, 109 miles from Dublin; fairs held 3 June and Nov. This is a rectory in dioc. of Tuam; a charter fchool was opened here in 1735, for 24 children; it was endowed by the late fir *John Brown*, bart. with 10 acres of land in perpetuity, and 20 acres more, rented at 5*l.* 2*s.* 6*d.* per ann.

MIROS, an antient parifh in co. Cork, prov. Munfter, called in Irifh, *Garry*, or the garden, as it is efteemed the beft land in that neighbourhood; it lies on the W. of Glandore harbour. At a place called *Garrigiliky* in this parifh, the foundation of extenfive ruins were difcovered, together with a large cemetery, with great quantity of human bones.

MISSEN-HEAD, fee *Mizen-head*.

MIS-SLIEBH, fee *Slicbh-mifh*.

MITCHEL'SFORT, fit. in co. Cork, prov. Munfter; fairs held 28 April and Oct.

MITCHEL'STOWN, a poft and fair town in co. Cork, prov. Munfter, 102 miles from Dublin. Here is a college for the fupport of 12 decayed gentlemen, and 12 decayed gentlewomen, who have 40*l.* yearly, and handfome apartments, and a chaplain at 100*l.* per year, with a houfe; divine fervice is daily performed in a neat chapel, belonging to the college; the whole was founded by the late earl of *Kingfton*; here is alfo a moft magnificent feat of lord *Kingfborough*; and about 1½ mile from this town, are the ruins of *Cahirdriny* caftle. Fairs held 30 July and 12 Nov. In fome old maps this place is written *Michelftown*, and fometimes *Michaelftown*.—There is alfo a place of fame name in bar. Ferrard, co. Louth, prov. Leinfter.—Alfo a rectory in dioc. of Meath, fit. in bar. Slane, co. Meath, prov. Leinfter.

MIZEN-HEAD, or *Miffen-head*, a *cape* in bar. Carbery, co. Cork, prov. Munfter; here is a large bay. Lat. 51:14, lon. 9:35. It is the moft S. point of Ireland, and the fame with the *Notium* of *Ptolemy*.—Alfo a *cape* in bar. Arklow, co. Wicklow, prov. Leinfter.

MOATE, or *Mote*, a handfome feat of fir *Edw. Crofton*, bart. fit. near Rofcommon, co. Rofcommon, prov. Connaught.—Alfo a place in bar. Clanmorris, co. Galway, prov. Connaught.—Alfo a place in co. Sligo, in fame prov.

MOATE-ARDSCOL, fit. about 3 miles from Athy, in co. Kildare, prov. Leinfter, antiently called, *Rath-aois Caël*, now corruptly *Rathafcul*, or *Moat of Afkul*; it was the principal refidence of the chiefs of the antient diftrict of Caëlan, called Hy Caëlan, or *O'Kelly*: this family of the O'Kellys, is now extinct, or at leaft reduced to a very low condition, being in an early period difpoffeffed of their property by the *Fitzgeralds*, *Fitzhenrys* and *Keatings*.

MOATE-GRENOGUE, a fair and poft town fit. in bar. Clonlonan, co. Weftmeath, prov. Leinfter: 52 miles from Dublin; about 2 miles beyond it are the ruins of 2 caftles. Fairs held 25 April, 22 June, 2 Oct. and 15 Dec.

MOATE-MULLAMAST, fee *Maiftean*.

MOCCORRY, fee *Mocurry*.

MOCKLERSTOWN-CASTLE, fit. about 6 miles from Clonmel, co. Tipperary, prov. Munfter.

MOCOLLOP, a parifh in co. Waterford, prov. Munfter.

MOCURRY, a fair town in co. Wexford, prov. Leinfter; fairs held Thurfd. after Trinity Sunday, 26 Oct. and 7 Nov. It is fometimes written *Moccorry*.

MODELIGO, a vicarage in dioc. of Lifmore, fit. in bar. *Decies without*, co. Waterford, prov. Munfter. In this parifh are the remains of fome antient caftles, belonging to the family of the *Magraths*, who had formerly a large eftate in this part of the country. *Mountaincaftle*, called alfo *Fernane*, was one of thefe, of which only the foundation now remains; the caftle of *Sledy* or *Curragh-na-Sledy*, is another, which was built in 1628, as appears from a date on a chimney piece, with the words, *Phillipus Mac Grath*. It is faid the occafion of building this caftle, was on a difpute between *Magrath* and his *wife*, who would not be reconciled to him, 'till he had built her a caftle on her own jointure; to do which, he received fuch large contributions from his vaffals, that when it was finifhed, he was much richer than when he began his work. A great quantity of fine oak was employed in this building, which is not much more than 130 years erected. Fairs are held at *Modeligo* on 26 Aug.

MODEREENY, a village fit. in bar. lower Ormond, co. Tipperary, prov. Munfter. It is a rectory in dioc. of Killaloe.

MODERSHILL, fit. in bar. Middlethird, co. Tipperary, prov. Munfter.

MODESHIL, a village fit. in bar. Slewardagh, co. Tipperary, prov. Munfter. It is a rectory in dioc. of Cafhel.

MODORN *river*, the prefent river *Mourne*, in prov. Ulfter, which has its head at *Lough Feil*.

MODRENY, see *Modereeny*.

MOGEALY, see *Mogeely*.

MOGEELY, a river sit in bar. Kilnataloon, co. Cork, prov. Munster, from whence the river *Dour* takes its rise; this river breaks out of a limestone rock, about a mile S. E. of *Castlemartyr*, after taking a subterraneous course of about a mile.—There is also a rectory of this name in dioc. of Cloyne, sit. in same bar. and co.

MOGESAGH, a rectory in dioc. of Cloyne, sit. in bar. Barrymore, co. Cork, prov. Munster.

MOGOLY, sit. in bar. Imokilly, co. Cork, prov. Munster.

MOGORBAN, a rectory in dioc. of Cashel, sit. in bar. Middlethird, co. Tipperary, prov. Munster.

MOHAN, a village sit. in bar. Fews, co. Armagh, prov. Ulster.

MOHANAGH, a seat in co. Cork, prov. Munster, it has 2 loughs on the S. and a wood to the N. It is observable, that in these loughs are a large kind of *trout*, that feed on the spawn of *eels*.

MOHILL, a bar. in co. Leitrim, prov. Connaught; it has a village in it of same name, which is a vicarage in dioc. of Ardagh, and holds fairs on first Thursday in Jan. 25 Feb. 8 May, first Thursd. in June, 31 July, second Thursd. in Sept. 19 Oct. and first Thursd. in Dec. St. *Manchan* built an abbey here for canons regular, in the year 652.—There is also a place of same name sit. near Longford, prov. Leinster.—Also a handsome seat in co. Carlow, prov. Leinster, otherwise called *Moyle*.

MOILENA, sit. in the district of Inishowen, near *Lough Foyle*, co. Londonderry, prov. Ulster.

MOILOGH, a village sit. in bar. Tiaquin, co. Galway, prov. Connaught; it is a rectory in dioc. of Tuam.—Also a rectory in dioc. of Meath, sit. in bar. Half-fowre, co. Meath, prov. Leinster.

MOINAINSEIGH, see *Monaincha*.

MOIN-MOR, (or the *great bog*) all that marshy ground, near the present city of Cork, being part of the antient *Corcaluighe*, prov. Munster: celebrated from being the field of battle between *Murtogh O'Brien* king of Thomond, and *Dermot M'Carthy* king of Desmond, in 1151; when the former was slain, with a considerable number of Dalcassian nobility.

MOINTAGLIS, a vicarage in dioc. of Dromore, sit. in bar. Oneilland, co. Armagh, prov. Ulster.

MOIRA, (sometimes written *Moyra*) sit. in bar. lower Iveagh, co. Down, prov. Ulster, 69 miles from Dublin; it is noted for its linen manufacture, is a post town, and has a monthly market for vending the same. It gives title of earl to the family of *Rawdon*: lord *Moira* has here a very beautiful seat; here is a handsome church, a charity school, and two dissenting meeting-houses. The church and school were erected by the late sir *John Rawdon*: it is a rectory in dioc. of Dromore. In this parish there are many quarries of white lime-stone. The antient name of this place was *Moirath*, and here was fought a famous battle between the exiled *Congal Claon*, and *Donald* king of Ireland, A. D. 637. It continued with various success for six whole days, 'till at length *Congal* was defeated.

MOIRUS, a rectory in dioc. of Tuam, sit. in bar. Ballinahinch, co. Galway, prov. Connau.

MOIVORE, a village sit. in bar. Rathconrath, co. Westmeath, prov. Leinster; it is a rectory in dioc. of Meath.

MOLAHIFFE, a vicarage in dioc. of Ardfert, sit. in bar. Magunihy, co. Kerry, prov. Munster.

MOLANA, a small *island*, sit. in the river Blackwater, co. Waterford, prov. Munster, 2½ miles N. W. of *Youghal*. St. *Molanside* founded an abbey here in the 6th century, for canons regular, and was the first abbot. *Raymond le Grofs*, who so highly contributed to the reduction of Ireland, is said to have been interred in this abbey, the nave and choir of which remain entire; adjoining are several ruinous walls, and the building (which is in the gothic style) appears to be very antient. On the suppression, queen *Eliz.* granted this abbey and its possessions to sir *Walter Raleigh*, who assigned it to the earl of Cork. This place was antiently called the *island of St Molanside*, and also *Darinis*.

MOLAUR, a *glen* so called, sit. in co. Wicklow, prov. Leinster; otherwise called *Glenmolaur*.

MOLINGAR, see *Mullingar*.

MONACOGLAN, sit. in the parish of *Aghaboe*, in Queen's co. prov. Leinster. Here is a high rath or mote, surrounded by entrenchments, and defended by outworks; it was the seat of a toparch, subordinate to the *M'Gille Padricks*, or *Fitzpatricks*.

MONAGHAN *county*, sit. in prov. Ulster. It has on the E. Armagh, on the W. Fermanagh, on the N. Tyrone, on the S. Cavan, and S. E. Louth and part of Meath. It extends 30 miles from N. to S. and 19 from E. to W. containing 179,600 acres, 5 bar.'s, viz. Trough, Monaghan, Dartree, Cremourne, and Donaghmoyne; 19 parishes, 1 borough, and returns 4 members to parliament. Chief town, *Monaghan*. It is computed to contain 21,523 houses and about 118,000 inhabitants. This co. is rather boggy and mountainous, but in some places well improved; its linen trade has been

averaged

averaged at 104,000*l.* yearly. This was the antient country of the *M'Mahons.*

MONAGHAN *town*, a poft, fair and market town, and the principal in the bar. and co of that name, **prov.** Ulfter, diftant 62 miles from Dublin; it is a borough, and returns 2 members to parliament, patron, lord *Clermont*; it gives title of baron to the family of *Blayney.* Lat. 54:15 N. lon. 7:10 W. Fairs held Eafter-tuefday, 28 May, 12 July, 18 Aug. 1 Tuefd. Oct. and 21 Nov. It was antiently called *Muineehan*: an abbey was founded here in a very early age, of which *Moelodius* the fon of *Aedh*, was abbot. In 1462, a monaftery for conventual Francifcans was erected on the fite of this abbey, which was granted on the general fuppreffion of monafteries, to *Edw. Withe*, and a caftle has been fince erected on the fite, by *Edw.* lord *Blayney.* This monaftery was founded by *Phelim M'Brien, M'Ardgal, M'Eda, M'Mahoune.* This town is a rectory in dioc. of Clogher.

MONAINCHA, (otherwife written *Moinainftigh*) called by Cambrenfis *Inchinemeo*; fit. in bar. Ikerin, co. Tipperary, prov. Munfter; almoft in the centre of the great bog of Molena, and about 3 miles S. E. of *Rofcrea.* It is remarkable for its antiquities, and the origin of the Irifh *Culdees*, a famous religious order, founded by St. *Columb Cell*, who erected here a Culdean abbey; to the E. of which ftands an oratory, and near them a fmall chapel. This abbey is 33 feet in length and 18 in breadth. The nave is lighted by 2 windows to the S. and the chancel by 1 at its E. end. The former are contracted arches, the latter is fallen down; the arch of this and that of the choir, are femicircular. Nothing can be more rich than the fculpture and mouldings; the ftones are of a foft whitifh grit, brought from the neighbouring hills of Ball ghmore, except the columns of the choir, which are of a harder texture, and were quarried at the S. W. fide of the bog; they are a fpecies of *lapidum fchiftarum*, fplitting into laminæ 6 feet long, with which moft of the abbey is cafed without. Adjoining the abbey on the N. fide, was the prior's chamber, which communicated with the church by a door with a gothic arch.; there was not long fince a good garden and orchard here. Many heaps of ftones and fome croffes are difperfed hereabouts. The antiquity of this monaftery is indifputable; for it is mentioned by *Girald. Cambrenfis*, who came into Ireland in 1185, as preceptor and fecretary to king *John*, the earl of *Morton.* Superftition eftablifhed an opinion fo early as the age of *Giraldus*, that no perfon could ever die in this ifle, and hence it acquired the appellation of *Infula viventium*, or the ifland of the living; however the fupernatural power of the ifle was not fo great, as

to prevent the emigration of its religious inhabitants to the main land. They found the vapours of the furrounding fwamps highly prejudicial to their conftitutions, and therefore fixed their refidence at *Corbally*; where there is at this day in good prefervation, a fmall neat chapel, of a cruciform fhape, with narrow flits for windows, and many other particulars, indicating a refpectable antiquity. Queen *Eliz.* granted this abbey to fir *Lucas Dillon.*

MONALLEN, fit. in co. Down, prov. Ulfter; at Shanmore, near this place, in cutting a channel for the *new canal* in that co. fome years ago, a fubterraneous foreft, or multitude of fallen trees, of *oak, afh, alder*, &c. was difcovered, lying for near a mile in length, under a covering of earth, in fome places fix, in others eight feet deep; many of them of large bulk, tumbled down, one over another, fome lying in ftrait lines, and others in an oblique or tranfverfe pofition.

MONAMULTINA, a fair town in co. Wexford, prov. Leinfter; fairs held 28 June.

MONANIMY, a rectory in dioc. of Cloyne, fit. in bar. Fermoy, co. Cork, prov. Munfter. Here is a ruined church with a large chancel, and in it is a modern tomb of the Nagles; adjacent to it, is a caftle, that in former times was a preceptory belonging to the Knts. of St. John of *Jerufalem*: round the caftle are traces of very large buildings, the whole auguftly fit. on a high bank over the *Blackwater*; as there is no other mention of this houfe, than in the king's quit-rent books, the founder, and time of the foundation is uncertain. On the oppofite fide of the river, are large rocks of limeftone, wherein are feveral fubterraneous caverns.

MONASTERBOYCE, fit. in bar. Ferrard, co. Louth, prov. Leinfter, 3 miles from *Drogheda*; here is a round tower, and the ruins of an antient abbey, founded by St. *Boetius*, who died 7 Dec. 521; the remains of 2 chapels are ftill to be feen here; the tower is 110 feet high, its circumference 17 yards, and it diminifhes gradually from the bafe, like a Tufcan pillar: the walls are 3 feet 6 inches thick, the door is 5 feet 6 inches in height, 22 inches in width, and 6 feet from the prefent level of the ground: it is arched, and built of freeftone, as are alfo the windows of the chapels; the diameter of the tower on the infide, is 9 feet, and above the door it is divided into 5 ftories by rings of ftone flightly projecting; there are two large ftone croffes at the S. fide of the church, the principal of which, called St. *Boyne's* crofs, is the moft antient religious relique now in Ireland; among other rude fculptures, there is an infcription on it in Irifh characters, in which

is

is ftill plainly legible, the name of *Muredach*, who was for fome time king of Ireland, and died in 534, about 100 years after the arrival of St. Patrick. This place is a rectory in dioc. of Armagh.

MONASTEREVAN, a poft town fit. in bar. Ophaly, co. Kildare, prov. Leinfter, 30 miles from Dublin; here is *Moore-abbey*, the elegant feat of the marquis of *Drogheda*; this town according to the monkifh annals, takes its name from a magnificent abbey which was founded here, in which St. *Evan*, in the beginning of the 7th century, placed a number of Monks from S. Munfter; it had the privilege of being a fanctuary. St. *Evan's* feftival is held on 22d Dec. The confecrated bell, which belonged to this St. was on folemn trials, fworn upon by the whole tribe of the *Eoganachts*, and was always committed to the care of the M'Egans, hereditary chief juftices of Munfter; the abbot of this houfe, fat as a baron in parliament; at the general fuppreffion of monafteries, this abbey was granted to *George*, lord *Audley*, who affigned it to *Adam Loftus*, vifc. *Ely*; it afterwards came into the families of *Moor*, marquifes of *Drogheda*, and has been beautifully repaired by the prefent lord Drogheda, ftill wearing the venerable appearance of an abbey. There is a nurfery at *Monafterevan*, for the charter-fchools of the prov. of Leinfter; and the *Grand canal* has been carried up to this town from Dublin, fince which, it has been much improved and enlarged, with feveral new buildings, this is a market town, and alfo holds fairs on 28 March, 29 May, 31 July, and 6 Dec. It is a curacy in dioc. of Kildare. Notwithftanding what has been mentioned of St. *Evan*, it appears that the grant of the land to this abbey by the charter of *O'Dimefey*, was witneffed by *Nehemiah* bifhop of *Kildare*, and muft have been executed between the years 1177 and 1185. The former derivation of the name of this place, is therefore rejected by others, upon ftrong grounds; and this place is faid to take its name from the river *Abhau* (now called *Barrow*) on which it ftands. The abbey appears to have been founded for Ciftertians in 1177 or 1185, and dedicated to St. Mary, by *Dermit O'Dimefey*, king of Offaly, by and with the confent of *Muredach O'Connor*, at a place called *Rofs-mac-trion*, or the wet field on the water, *Rofs-glafs*, or the wet green, and *De Rofea Balle*, or the habitation in the wet meadow. Being fit. in a woody and wild country, this place became in fome meafure an afylum for felons, plunderers and robbers, on which account, in 1297 the abbot was accufed of receiving fuch people into his houfe; but he proved that he never knowingly received either felons or robbers; nor had he

power to refift or detain them: the jury however fined him half a mark, for not endeavouring to raife the hue and cry, when any offences were committed in his neighbourhood. This town might be confiderably more improved than it is; mills for the manufacture of flour might be eftablifhed here, and alfo a linen and hempen manufacture, the adjacent lands being well calculated for the production of flax and hemp. The road from hence to Kildare lies thro' a bog, which was in former times an extenfive foreft. This bog refts on a bed of calcareous gravel and limeftone rock, and feems to be a branch of that extenfive morafs, the bog of *Allen*, and is every where furrounded with ftrong calcareous foils. There is alfo a place of fame name, in bar. Rofcommon, co. Rofcommon, prov. Connaught; where a monaftery was founded, as appears by an inquifition taken 28th queen *Elizabeth*.

MONASTERNAMONA, fee *Mourne-abbey*.

MONASTERNENAGH, a vicarage in dioc. of Limerick, fit. in bar. *Poblebrien*, co. Limerick, prov. Munfter. Here an abbey was founded by *O'Brien*, in 1148 or 1151, dedicated to the Virgin Mary. Near this monaftery, marfhal *Malby* in 1579 at the head of 100 horfe and 600 foot foldiers, defeated 2000 of the Irifh, tho' they fought valiantly at firft, yet were 260 of them flain, amongft whom was Dr. *Allen*, the famous legate from the fee of Rome. The abbot of this place fat as a baron in parliament. On the fuppreffion it was granted to fir *Henry Wallop*, knt. This place is fometimes written *Monafterrionagh*.

MONASTERNICALLIAGH, fit. near *Lough-gir*, in bar. Small-county, co. Limerick, prov. Munfter; here was formerly a nunnery for Canoneffes of the order of St. Auguftin; dedicated to St. Catherine.

MONASTER-NI-ORIEL, i. e. the *Abbey of Oriel*, fit. in parifh of *Kilgurvan*, co. Kerry, prov. Munfter, not far from a feat called *Ardtully*; here are the veftigia of an antient building, which by tradition was a religious houfe, called *Monafter-ni-Oriel*: fir *James Ware* does not mention it.

MONASTERORAS, fit. near *Edenderry*, in bar. Cooleftown, King's co. prov. Leinfter. fir *Jn. de Bermingham*, earl of *Louth*, founded a monaftery here in 1325 for conventual Francifcans; this place was formerly called *Totmoy* or *Thetmoy*, but after him was called in the Irifh tongue *Monafterfeoris*, or the monaftery of *Mac Feoris*. In the year 1511, *Cahir O'Connor*, lord of Ophaly, was flain near this place by his own countrymen. It was once a place of ftrength, and held out a confiderable time in the year 1521, againft the earl of *Surrey*, then

lord

lord lieutenant. who at last took poffeffion of it. On the general fuppreffion it was granted to *Nicholas Herbert.*

MONASTERRIONAGH, fee *Monafternenagh.*

MONEA, a fair town in bar. Magheraboy, co. Fermanagh, prov. Ulfter; fairs held Whitfun-monday, 26 Aug. and 12 Nov. It is a chapelry in dioc. of Clogher.

MONEDURLACK, fit. in bar. Scarewalfh, co. Wexford, prov. Leinfter.

MONEGAY, a rectory in dioc. of Limerick, fit. in bar. Connello, co. Limerick, prov. Munfter.

MONEMINTER, or *Monemoynter*, a rectory in dioc. of Waterford, fit. in bar. Gualtiere, co. Waterford, prov. Munfter.

MONETUAGH, fit. near Elphin, co. Rofcommon, prov. Connaught.

MONETY-BOG, fit. in co. Tipperary, prov. Munfter.

MONEY, fit. in bar. Shillelagh, co. Wicklow, prov. Leinfter.

MONEYGALL, fit. in bar. Clonlifk, King's co. prov. Leinfter, 66 miles from Dublin.— Alfo a place near *Roferea*, co. Tipperary, prov. Munfter.

MONEYGLASS, fit. in bar. Toome, co. Antrim, prov. Ulfter.

MONEYHORE, a fair town in co. Wexford, prov. Leinfter; fairs held 24 Feb. 26 May, 18 July, 2 Oct. and 6 Dec.

MONEYMORE, fit. in bar. Loughlinfholen, co. Londonderry, prov. Ulfter, 83 miles from Dublin; it is a poft and fair town; near it is *Spring-hill*, a very handfome feat; fairs held 4 Jan. and 8 May.

MONGARRET, fit. in bar. Bantry, co. Wexford, prov. Leinfter.

MONISEED, fee *Monyfeed.*

MONIVEA, fit. in bar. Athenry, co. Galway, prov. Connaught, 89 miles from Dublin; this place was built, and the linen manufacture eftablifhed in it. and the neighbourhood about it, by the late *Robert French*, efq; who in confideration of the incorporated fociety paying him 300l. built the charter fchool here for 40 children, provided furniture for the fame, and engaged to maintain and clouth them during his life, and provide them with all neceffaries, the fociety only paying the mafter's falary. He alfo granted 2 acres of land in fee, whereon the fchool is erected, and let 15 acres of arable land for 31 years at the yearly rent of 5 fhill. and 5 pence per acre. The profit of the land and labour of the children being applied to their maintenance and the fupport of the fchool. This is a chapelry in dioc. of Tuam. Fairs held 12 May and Oct.

MONIVERALAGH, fit. near *Granard*, prov. Leinfter.

MONKNEWTOWN, a rectory in dioc. of Meath, fit. in bar. Slane, co. Meath, prov. Leinfter.

MONKSGRANGE, a curacy in dioc. of Leighlin, fit. in bar. Ballyadams, Queen's co. prov. Leinfter.

MONKSTOWN, a village in bar. Kinalea, co. Cork, prov. Munfter, in which is an old caftle which was built by the family of *Archdeacon*, anno 1638; it is large and in ruins, and was flanked by four fquare turrets.—Alfo a place in bar. Belfaft, co. Antrim, prov. Ulfter.— Alfo a rectory in dioc: of Meath, fit. in bar. Skryne, co. Meath, prov. Leinfter.—Alfo a curacy in dioc. of Dublin, fit. in bar. Half-Rathdown, co. Dublin, prov. Leinfter, about 5 miles from Dublin, and 1 mile beyond *Black-Rock*: it is faid to have been fo called from an antient convent of Monks. Here is the country refidence of lord *Ranelagh*, with other handfome feats.

MONMAKEMOCK, a rectory in dioc. of Dublin, fit. in bar. Kilkea, co. Kildare, prov. Leinfter.

MONOMOLING, a rectory in dioc. of Ferns, fit. in bar. Ballagheen, co. Wexford, prov. Leinfter.

MONROE'S-GROVE, fit. in co. Down, prov. Ulfter, near *Gilford*, and on the banks of the river *Bann*; it is a gloomy plantation of fir trees. which gives a traveller no unpleafing variety; the profpect however is foon changed into an open, tho' hilly country, moftly under corn.

MONSEA, a vicarage in dioc. of Killaloe, fit. in bar. lower Ormond, co. Tipperary, prov. Munfter.

MONTAGH, fit. near *Elphin*, prov. Connaug.

MONTALTO, a feat of lord *Moira*, fit. near Ballinahinch, co. Down, prov. Ulfter.

MONTANAGEE, a fair town in co. Kerry, prov. Munfter; fairs held 19 July, 22 Sept. and 1 Dec.

MONTERBANY-HILLS, fit. in bar. Strabane, co. Tyrone, prov. Ulfter.

MONTPELIERE, fit. near *Mount-venus*, in bar. Upper Crofs, co. Dublin, prov. Leinfter, above 5 miles from Dublin caftle; here is a very large ftone houfe, the property of the Rt. Hon. *Tho. Conolly*, which however has long remained uninhabited.

MONTRATH, fee *Mountrath.*

MONYGLANE, fit. near *Rathfryland*, co. Down, prov. Ulfter.

MONYLANE, fit. in bar. Upper Iveach, co. Down, prov. Ulfter.

MONYSEED, a village fit. in bar. Gorey, co. Wexford, prov. Leinfter; otherwife written *Monifeed.*

MOON,

Moon, or *Moun*, a fair town in bar. Kilkea and Moon, co. Kildare, prov. Leinster, where is a large church, formerly a Franciscan monastery, and near it one of the large mounts or raths, where a gentleman was by his particular desire, interred not many years ago, on the very summit, which his heirs caused to be railed round and planted with trees; this village is sit. within 3 miles of *Castledermot*; fairs held 12 Aug. and 28 Oct. It is a vicarage in dioc. of Dublin.

Moor, a rectory in dioc. of Tuam, sit. in bar. Moycarne, co. Roscommon, prov. Conn.

Moor-abbey, the seat of the Rt. Hon. the marquis of *Drogheda*, sit. at Monasterevan, co. Kildare, prov. Leinster. It was originally an abbey of Cistertians, dedicated to St. Mary, and founded in 1177, or 1185, by *Dermit O'Dimesey*, king of Offaley, by and with the consent of *Muredach O'Connor*, at a place called *Rossmagh-trion*, or the wet field on the water; *Rossglass*, or the wet green, and *De Rosea Bulle*, or the habitation in the wet meadow. Tradition, or rather the monkish annals, relate, that in the 7th century, St. Abhan, St. Emin, or St. Evin, founded a sumptuous abbey here; and granted to it the privilege of a sanctuary; from whence it was denominated *Monasterevin*. It has however been asserted by some late writers, that St. *Emin*, or *Abhan*, is only the river *Barrow*, antiently called *Abhan*, (on whose banks the monastery stood) canonized and converted into a saint, as many such things were; and that *Monasterevan*, or *Monasterabhan*, signifies only the monastery on the river *Abhan*. At the general suppression, this abbey was granted to *George* lord *Audley*; who by assignment made it over to *Adam Loftus*, visc. *Ely*; who held the court of Chancery, during the rebellion in 1641, in the great hall of the monastery, yet in being, and lined with fine Irish oak. The lord chancellor's daughter *Alice*, marrying *Charles* the 2d visc. *Drogheda*, Monasterevan and the greater part of the *Ely* estate, came into the *Moor* family. In 1767, the present marquis of Drogheda, beautifully repaired the antient abbey, by enlarging the windows, placing a new roof, and recompartitioning the whole; preserving however, the external walls and original form, except somewhat lengthening the Eastern front. The great hall, and the antient door of the Southern front, still retain their pristine state; and the whole has the venerable appearance of the original gothic structure. His lordship also pulled down the old church, which stood near the monastery, on the right of the E. front; and rebuilt it, in a neat gothic stile, at the other end of the town. He also walled in the demesne, with a high wall, except on the side next the river. This

demesne contains near 1000 acres; nearly in the centre of which rises a large conical hill, well planted, and commanding an extensive and beautiful view of the country. Near the Deer-park, on the N. side of the hill, are some remains of the antient wood, in former times the retreat of felons, plunderers and robbers; and last occupied (towards the close of the last, and commencement of the present century) by one *James O'Dempsey*, commonly called *Jamus a Coppuil*, from his dexterity in horse stealing.

Moore-bay, sit. in bar. Moyferta, co. Clare, prov. Munster.

Moore-church, a vicarage in dioc. of Meath, sit. in bar. Duleek, co. Meath, prov. Leinster.

Moorfield, sit. near *Rostrevor*, prov. Ulster.

Moor-park, a seat of lord *Mountcashel*, sit. near Cork, prov. Munster.—Also a seat near *Rostrevor*, prov. Ulster.

Moortown, antiently called *Glassmore*, sit. about one mile from *Swords*, in co. Dublin, prov. Leinster. Here was an antient abbey, at which St. *Cronan*, with all his monks were inhumanly murdered by a party of Danish pirates.

Mora, a rectory in dioc. of Lismore, sit. in bar. Middlethird, co. Tipperary, prov. Munster. (Dr. *Beaufort*.)—A parish in co. *Waterford*, prov. Munster. (Dr. *Smith*.)

Moragh, a rectory in dioc. of Cork, sit. in bar. Kinalmeaky, co. Cork, prov. Munster.

Moregaga, a rectory in dioc. of Tuam, sit. in bar. Kilmain, co. Mayo, prov. Connau.

Morgallion or *Morgalyon*, a *barony* in co. Meath, prov. Leinster.

Morgans, a vicarage in dioc. of Limerick, sit. in bar. Connello, co. Limerick, prov. Munster.

Morisk, a bar. in co. Mayo, prov. Connaught. There is a village in it of same name, where the *O'Mallies*, lords of this district founded a friary for Eremites, following the rule of St. Augustin: large ruins of this building may still be seen.

Morit-castle, sit. about 1 mile from *Emo*, in Queen's co. prov. Leinster. It was a large and strong building, whose venerable ruins are now almost entirely clad in ivy. Near this is the elegant seat of lord *Portarlington*.

Mornanstown, a curacy in dioc. of Meath, sit. in bar. Duleek, co. Meath, prov. Leinster.

Morning, sit. in bar. Moydoe, co. Longford, prov. Leinster.

Mornington, sit. in co. Meath, prov. Leinster, it gives title of earl to the family of *Cooley*.

Morristown, a rectory in dioc. of Kildare, sit. in bar. great Connel, co. Kildare, prov. Leinster; here are some antient ruins. This place

place is also called *Morristown Biller*, to distinguish it from another place in same co. a few miles distant from it, called *Morristown Lattin*.

MORTLESTOWN, a rectory in dioc. of Lismore, sit. in bar. Middlethird, co. Tipperary, prov. Munster.

MOSGROVE, sit. in co. Cork, prov. Munster; fairs held 17 March, Thursday after Trinity-Sunday, 21 Sept. and 8 Dec.

MOSS-SIDE, sit. in co. *Antrim*, prov. Ulster, 123 miles from Dublin; fairs held 21 May, 21 July and 23 Nov.

MOSSTOWN, a vicarage in dioc. of Armagh, sit. in bar. Ardee, co. Louth, prov. Leinster.

MOSTRIM, a vicarage in dioc. of Ardagh, sit. in bar. Ardagh, co. Longford, prov. Leinst.

MOTHEL, a rectory in dioc. of Ossory, sit. in bar. Fassachdining, co. Kilkenny, prov. Leinster.—Also a vicarage in dioc. of Lismore, sit. in bar. Upperthird, co. Waterford, prov. Munster, sometimes written *Mothill*. It lies about 2 miles S. of Carrick; here was formerly an abbey of Canons regular of St. *Augustine*, or according to some, of Cistertian monks, founded by St. *Brogan* in the 6th century; and at the dissolution granted to sir *Walter Raleigh* in fee-farm: there are some remains of this abbey near the parish church.

MOUNTAIN-CASTLE, sit. in co. Waterford, prov. Munster; fairs held 1 May, 24 June, 29 Sept. and 30 Nov. Here is an antient castle, which belonged to the *Magraths*.

MOUNTAINSTOWN, sit. near *Navan*, prov. Leinster.

MOUNT-ALBANI, otherwise called *Moat albani*, is a small fort in co. Louth, prov. Leinster, with a double ditch round it, by the side of a river called *Carrickasticken*, about half a mile distant from *Ballirickan castle*; there appears to have been an outward camp adjoining to it, upon the banks of that river, capable of containing about 500 men. It is said to have been the station of a colony of Scotchmen or *Albanians*, from whence it has its name; and under the *tumulus*, or little mount, within the area, 'tis supposed the chief, or some eminent warrior was buried.

MOUNT ALEXANDER, a seat in co. Down, prov. Ulster, near *Comber* or *Cumber*; which gave title of earl to the family of Montgomery.

MOUNT-BAGNAL, sit. in bar. Dundalk, co. Louth, prov. Leinster.

MOUNTBELLEW, a village sit. in bar. Tiaquin, co. Galway, prov. Connaught.

MOUNT-BELLEW-BRIDGE, sit. in co. Galway, prov. Connaught, 80 miles from Dublin; here are good flour-mills; and about 2 miles from this place are the ruins of a castle.

MOUNT-BOLUS, sit. in King's co. prov. Leinster, 53 miles from Dublin; in the vicinity of this place, are the ruins of a church and some castles.

MOUNTCASHEL, sit. near Gowran, prov. Leinster: it gives title of *earl* to the family of *Moore*.

MOUNT-CHARLES, sit. in bar. Boylagh, co. Donegal, prov. Ulster, 114 miles from Dublin; fairs held 17 March, 9 June, 22 Sept. and 18 Nov.—Also a place sit. near *Ennifcorthy*, prov. Leinster.

MOUNTDILLON, sit. in bar. Half-rathdown, co. Dublin, prov. Leinster.—Also near Roscommon, prov. Connaught.

MOUNTDRUID, a seat near Killeny hill, in co. Dublin, prov. Leinster. Here is a Druid's-temple, or place of worship, a piece of curious antiquity: there is also a banquetting room erected in the gothic stile, which is often mistaken for an old castle; near it are the ruins of Killeny church, and also a very beautiful bay.

MOUNTEAGLE, a village sit. in bar. Corcaguinny, co. Kerry, prov. Munster.—Also a name given to a high mountain in bar. *Morisk*, co. Mayo, prov. Connaught, otherwise called *Croagh Patrick*. It gives title of *baron* to the family of *Brown*, now earl of *Altamont*.

MOUNT-EAGLE LOYAL, a manor or segniory, in co. Kerry, prov. Munster, otherwise *Castle-island*.

MOUNTEATON, sit. in bar. Gowran, co. Kilkenny, prov. Leinster.

MOUNTERCONAGHT, see *Munster-conagh*.

MOUNTEVANS, sit. within 2 miles of *Turvey*, co. Dublin, prov. Leinster.

MOUNTFIN, a handsome seat in bar. Scarawalsh, co. Wexford, prov. Leinster.

MOUNT-GABRIEL, a high conical hill, near the village called *Skull*, in co. Cork, prov. Munster; on the top of it is a remarkable deep lough, which is but a few yards over; it has been founded from the N. E. with a hundred fathom line, and yet the hole was deeper; the water oozes out of the mountain to the N. W. and this cone is above 300 yards higher than the level of the sea; from it is a prospect of a vast extent, over a rude uncultivated country, from the *mizen-head* to *Rofs*, with an infinite number of islands, bays, creeks and harbours.

MOUNTGARRET, a village in co. Wexford, prov. Leinster, which gives title of visc. to a branch of the family of *Butler*.

MOUNTGARRET-FERRY, sit. in co. Kilkenny, prov. Leinster, 65 miles from Dublin.

MOUNT-HALL, sit. in co. Down, prov. Ulster; where there is a pleasant seat.

MOUNT-HAMILTON, sit. in co. Tyrone, prov. Ulster, 106 miles from Dublin, otherwise called *Grange*; fairs held 4 Jan. 3 Mar. 4 June and Oct., not far from it are the ruins of a church.

MOUNT-

MOUNTHEATON, fit. near *Rofcrea*, prov. Munfter.

MOUNT-HILL, fit. in co. Antrim, prov. Ulfter; where fairs are held 1 July and Oct.

MOUNT-ICY, fit. in bar. Dungannon, co. Tyrone, prov. Ulfter.

MOUNT-IEVERS, fit. near *Six-mile-bridge*, co. Clare, prov. Munfter.

MOUNTJESSOP, fit. near *Longford*, prov. Leinft.

MOUNTJOY, fit. in bar. Dungannon, co. Tyrone, prov. Ulfter; it gives title of *baron* to the family of *Gardiner*. Lat. 54:53, lon. 7:11.

MOUNTJULIET, fit. near *Thomaftown*, prov. Leinfter.

MOUNTKENNEDY, fit. near *Newtown-mount-kennedy*, in co. Wicklow, prov. Leinfter.

MOUNT-LEADER, a handfome feat at the foot of a hill, called *Clara-hill*, fit. in co. Cork, prov. Munfter.

MOUNT-LEINSTER, fit. in co. Carlow, prov. Leinfter; on the top of it is plenty of groufe, hares, and foxes; and a well, faid to be unfathomable, the water of which is ufed as an antidote againft fcorbutic and fcrophulous humours; and faid to be ferviceable in healing the *King's evil*.

MOUNT-LOFTUS, fit. near *Gowran*, prov. Leinfter.

MOUNT-LONG, a handfome caftle of the *Longs*, on the E. fide of *Oyfter-haven*, in co. Cork, prov. Munfter; not far from which is *Bellgooly*, where the Irifh had their camp, for the firft years of the wars of 1641.

MOUNT-MALBY, a name given to *Slieu Donard* mountain, in co. Down, prov. Ulfter.

MOUNT-MELLICK, a poft town, fit. in bar. Tinehinch, Queen's co. prov. Leinfter, 41 miles S. W. of Dublin; it is much inhabited by the people called Quakers, and has fairs on 17 Mar. Thurfday after Trinity-funday, 26 Aug. 29 Sept. 1 Nov. and 11 Dec.

MOUNT-MERRION, a feat of lord *Fitzwilliam*; it is diftant 4 miles from Dublin caftle, and within ½ a mile of Stilorgan, in co. Dublin, prov. Leinfter; 'tis finely fit. on a rifing ground, the houfe is a large and handfome edifice, and the demefne adjoining is well improved.

MOUNT-NEBO, fit. near *Gorey*, prov. Leinfter.

MOUNT-NORTH, a handfome feat of lord *Lifle*, fit. within 3 miles of *Mallow*, in co. Cork, prov. Munfter; N. E. of which is *Drumdowne*, a ruined caftle of the *Barrys*.

MOUNT-NUGENT, fit. in co. Cavan, prov. Ulfter; where fairs are held on 1 June and 21 October.

MOUNT-ODELL, a handfome feat in co. Waterford, prov. Munfter, about ¼ a mile E. of *Knockmoan caftle*; near it a parcel of human bones, half burned, were difcovered in heaps

of ftones, called *kearns*: here is a vein of black marble, without the leaft intermixture of white.

MOUNT-PANTHER, a pleafant feat of lord *Glerawly*, fit. a little N. of *Dundrum*, in co. Down, prov. Ulfter; oppofite to which on the fea-fhore, is the fmall village of *Terela*.

MOUNT-PELIER, a fair town in co. Limerick, prov. Munfter; fairs held 8 May, 10 June, 8 July, 7 Sept. 19 Oct. and 8 Dec.

MOUNT-PLEASANT, fit. in bar. Dundalk, co. Louth, prov. Leinfter.—Alfo in bar. Uppercrofs, co. Dublin, prov. Leinfter.

MOUNT-PROSPECT, fit. near *Rofcommon*, prov. Connaught.

MOUNTRATH, fit. in Queen's co. prov. Leinfter, 46 miles from Dublin; it is a poft and fair town, and gives title of earl to the family of *Coote*. It lies a few miles S. W. of Maryborough, between which places may be feen *Ballyfin*, the magnificent feat of the Hon. *Welefley Pole*. Fairs held 17 Feb. 2 Thurfday in May, 29 Sept. Thurfday before 12 Nov.

MOUNT-RIVERS, a handfome feat in co. Cork, parifh of *Donaghmore*, prov. Munfter, about a mile S. of *Donaghmore caftle*; it commands an extenfive profpect to the S. near it a large human fkull was dug up, which was almoft double the common fize.

MOUNT-SHANNON, a feat of lord *Fitzgibbon*, fit. near *Limerick*, prov. Munfter.—Alfo a village in bar. Leitrim, co. Galway, prov. Conn.

MOUNT-SILK, a feat in co. Galway, prov. Connaught.

MOUNT-SION, fit. near Limerick, prov. Munft.

MOUNT-STEWART, the feat of lord *Londonderry*, fit. near *Down*, prov. Ulfter.

MOUNT-STILLARY, fit. in bar. *Duhallow*, co. Cork, prov. Munfter.

MOUNT-TALBOT, fit. in bar. Athlone, co. Rofcommon, prov. Connaught; where are fairs on 8 May, 14 June, 1 Nov. and 21 Dec.

MOUNT-TARRAN, fit. in bar. Shillelagh, co. Wicklow, prov. Leinfter.

MOUNT-TEMPLE, a village fit. in bar. Clonlonan, co. Weftmeath, prov. Leinfter —Alfo a feat in co. Sligo, prov. Connaught, which gives title of baron to the family of *Temple*, now vifc. *Palmerfton*.

MOUNT-TISDAL, fit. in bar. Kells, co. Meath, prov. Leinfter.

MOUNT-TOWN, fit. in bar. Skreen, co. Meath, prov. Leinfter.

MOUNT-UNIACK, a feat in the parifh of *Killeigh*, co. Cork, prov. Munfter; in the gardens of it are orange, plantane and cyprus trees; about 3 miles S. W. is the caftle of *Inchiquin*, near which are fome plantations of *witch elms*, which bear feed; this place is diftant from Dublin 109 miles.

MOUNT-

MOUNT-USHER, fit. in bar. Newcaftle, co. Dublin, prov. Leinfter.

MOUNT-VENUS, a fmall village 2¼ miles beyond *Rathfarnham*, and 5 miles from Dublin caftle, in co. Dublin, prov. Leinfter. It is greatly expofed to the air, which tho' fharp, is pure; and the general opinion of its falubrity is fuch, that this place is much reforted to, for the prefervation or recovery of health.

MOUNT-WOGAN, fit. near *Clain*, in co. Kildare, prov. Leinfter; here are good flour-mills, and an antient mote or rath.

MOURNE, a bar. in co. Down, prov. Ulfter, in which St. *Jarlath*, the fecond bifhop of *Armagh*, was born; it takes its name from a ridge of high mountains, called the mountains of *Mourne*, from the Irifh *Moor Kinn*, i. e. the great ridge; thefe mountains are remarkable for having been the birth-place of feveral men of very large ftature; infomuch that the " *men of Mourne*," became a proverbial faying: in this bar. is the lofty mountain called Slieb-Donard which is faid to be 3150 feet above the level of the fea.—Alfo the name of a *lake* and a *river* fit. in bar. Raphoe, co. Donegal, prov. Ulfter.

MOURNE-ABBEY, fit. in bar. Barretts, co. Cork, prov. Munfter; it is now a rectory in, dioc. of Cloyne. Here was a preceptory of Knts. Hofpitalers, or Knts. of St. John of Jerufalem; it was founded in the reign of king John, under the invocation of St. John the *Baptift*, by an Englifh gentleman, called *Alex. de Sancta Helena*; the Irifh call it *Monafter-namona*; it had feveral great poffeffions, particularly a large domain on the fpot, five plowlands in the parifh of *Temple Michael* in Mufkerry, befides a great number of parifh tythes; they were granted to *Tiegue Mac Carty*, whofe defcendants forfeited them in 1641. The body of the ruined church which ftill remains, was 180 feet long: in the church are fome graveftones of the Barretts, Quinlans, and other antient Irifh families; a fhort way from this ruin is *Ballynamona* church, rebuilt in 1717; near this church is a charity fchool.

MOVILL-*upper*, a rectory in dioc. of Derry, fit. on Lough Foyle, in bar. Inifhowen, co. Donegal, prov. Ulfter. A monaftery was founded here by St. Patrick.

MOVILL-*lower*, a rectory in dioc. of Derry, fit. in bar. Inifhowen, co. Donegal, prov. Ulfter.—There is alfo a place called *Movill*, fit. in bar. Ardes, co. Down, prov. Ulfter, where an abbey was erected; part of the ruins of the church ftill remain, and the veftiges of fome large foundations appear in the cemetery.

MOWNY, a rectory in dioc. of Cafhel, fit. in bar. Slewardagh, co. Tipperary, prov. Munfter.

MOY, fit. in bar. Dungannon, co. Tyrone, prov. Ulfter; where are fairs on 12 March, July, and 22 Nov.—Alfo a *river* which rifes at the foot of a mountain called *Knockneſhee*, in co. Sligo, prov. Connaught, and after meandering thro' a fertile country, about 45 miles, (accounting for its fituations) difcharges itfelf in the Atlantic ocean, under the port of Killela: on the banks of this river are 3 of the antient round towers, and feveral abbeys; it divides the co.'s *Mayo* and *Sligo*; on this river is one of the moft confiderable falmon fifheries in the kingdom.—Alfo a *river*, fit. in bar. Clare, co. Galway, prov. Connaught.

MOYAGH, fit. in bar. Strabane, co. Tyrone, prov. Ulfter.

MOYAGHER, a rectory in dioc. of Meath, fit. in bar. Lune, co. Meath, prov. Leinfter: it is in fome places written *Moyangher*.

MOYALBE, fit. near Leighlin, co. Carlow, prov. Leinfter. At this place *Cormac* king of Cafhel, fell in battle A. D. 908.

MOYALLEN, fit. near *Portadown*, in co. Down, prov. Ulfter, 63 miles from Dublin.

MOYALLIFFE, a rectory in dioc. of Cafhel, fit. in bar. Kilnamanna, co. Tipperary, prov. Munfter.

MOYANGHER, fee *Moyagher*.

MOYARD, fit. in bar. Ballinahinch, co. Galway, prov. Connaught.

MOYASHEL, a bar. joined with *Magheradernon*, in co. Weftmeath, prov. Leinfter.

MOYATTA *river*, fit. in bar. Bear and Bantry, co. Cork, prov. Munfter.

MOYBOLOGUE, a rectory in dioc. of Kilmore, fit. in bar. Clonchee, co. Cavan, prov. Ulfter.

MOYCARNE, a bar. in co. Rofcommon, prov. Connaught.

MOYCASHEL, a bar. in co. Weftmeath, prov. Leinfter, in which is a village and antient caftle of fame name.

MOYCOOL, fit. in bar. Gorey, co. Wexford, prov. Leinfter.

MOYCOSQUIN, fit. near *Colerain*, co. Londonderry, prov. Ulfter. In 1172, an abbey was founded here for Ciftertian monks.

MOYCULLIN, an antient bar. in co. Galway, prov. Connaught, in which is a village of fame name, which is a vicarage in dioc. of Tuam.

MOYDOW, a bar. in co. Longford, prov. Leinfter: in it is a village of fame name, which is a rectory in dioc. of Ardagh; here was a very antient abbey.

MOYDRUM, fit. in bar. Clunlonan, co. Weftmeath, prov. Leinfter.

Moy-

MOYFENRATH, a bar. in co. Meath, prov. Leinster.

MOYFERTA, a bar. in co. Clare, prov. Munster, in which is a village of same name, which is a vicarage in dioc. of Killaloe.

MOYGEESH, see *Moygoish*.

MOYGLARE, a vicarage in dioc. of Meath, sit. in bar. Deece, co. Meath, prov. Leinster.

MOYGOISH, or *Moygeesh*, a bar. in co. Westmeath, prov. Leinster.

MOYHENNY, sit. in co. Mayo, prov. Conna.

MOYINNIS, an antient city mentioned by Ptolemy, and sit. near the spot where the present town of Belfast now stands, in co. Antrim, prov. Ulster.

MOYKARKY, a rectory in dioc. of Cashel, sit. in bar. Eliogurty, co. Tipperary, prov. Munster.

MOYKETNEY, antiently sit. near the present bar. of Lurge, in co. Fermanagh, prov. Ulster.

MOYLAGH, sit. in bar. Half-towre, co. Meath, prov. Leinster.—Also in bar. Offa, co. Tipperary, prov. Munster, where an antient abbey was founded.

MOYLARY, a rectory in dioc. of Armagh, sit. in bar. Ferrard, co. Louth, prov. Leinster.

MOYLE *river*, sit. in bar. Strabane, co. Tyrone, prov. Ulster.

MOYLENA, sit. in co. Meath, prov. Leinster. In 906, *Cormac*, king of Cashel, was suddenly attacked by *Flan*, king of Meath, and *Carubhal*, king of Leinster, who plundered his country; but in 907, he defeated those enemies on the plains of Moylena. *Cormac* was again invaded in the year following, and fell in battle, on the plains of *Moyalbe*, not far from *Leighlin*.

MOYLISCAR, a parish in co. Westmeath, prov. Leinster.

MOYLURG, an antient district of the *M'Dermots*, in co. Roscommon, prov. Connaught.

MOYLUSK, a rectory in dioc. of Connor, sit. in bar. Belfast, co. Antrim, prov. Ulster.

MOYMET, a rectory in dioc. of Meath, sit. in bar. Navan, co. Meath, prov. Leinster.

MOYMURTEMNY, a district formerly adjoining the bay of Carlingford, in co. Down, prov. Ulster.

MOYNALTY, sit. in bar. Kells, co. Meath, prov. Leinster, 35 miles from Dublin; 3 miles beyond which are the ruins of a castle, and 2 miles farther those of a church. This village is a rectory in dioc. of Meath.

MOYNART, sit. in bar. Scarewalsh, co. Wexford, prov. Leinster.

MOYNE, a *river*, (sometimes called *Moy*) sit. in bar. Clare, co. Galway, prov. Connaught.— Also a rectory in dioc. of Cashel, sit. in bar. Eliogurty, co. Tipperary, prov. Munster— Also a place in bar. Moyarta, co. Clare, prov. Munster.—Also a fair town, sit. in bar. Ty-

rawly, co. Mayo, prov. Connaught; fairs held 25 July and 14 Oct. Here are the large remains of *Moyne-abbey*, once a beautiful and extensive building, sit. on the Western side of the river *Moy*, and about ¼ of a mile from the great road leading from *Ballina* to *Killala*. Its situation is beautiful, tho' lonely and sequestered; the grounds around it fall gently on every side, 'till they form a flat of four or five acres, partly surrounded by the river, but chiefly by a wall, which is still entire, and surrounds the precincts of the abbey on every side, 'till it meets the water, which is at this place very deep, and its banks rocky and shelving. One side of the abbey is shrouded with some old ash and oak trees; the abbey itself is almost perfect, except the roof and some buildings on the N. side, which were taken down about 40 or 50 years ago, by the proprietor, to furnish materials for a dwelling-house. This abbey was founded in 1460, by *M'William Burke*, for the strict order of Franciscan friars, by the advice of *Nehemiah O'Donoghue*, who introduced into Ireland the last reformation of the said order, which previous to the middle of the 15th century, had become much relaxed in their discipline and morals. Some however affirm, that *Thomas Bourk M'William Oughter* was the founder, and that father Nehemiah took possession of the house agreeable to the licence of pope Nicholas 5th. Provincial chapters of the order were held here in the years, 1464, 1498, 1512, 1541 and 1550. In the month of June 37th queen *Eliz.* a grant was made to *Edmund Barrett* of this friary and its possessions, at the yearly rent of 5 shill's. It has a remarkable square tower in high preservation, which you ascend by a helix of 101 steps, on one side of which there is a confessionary of hewn stone for two priests to sit in, with a hole on each side for the persons confessing to speak through. The cloisters are still entire and of exquisite workmanship; most of the beautiful ramified stone work of the windows is still preserved; the inside of the abbey has been long used as a burial place, and the chancel, with all the niches round the church, are filled with human bones. The only entrance is thro' a low arched door in the S. side. The river *Moy* is navigable for sloops and other small craft for about 40 yards above the abbey, where it begins to grow very shallow and rocky.

MOYNOE, a rectory in dioc. of Killaloe, sit. in bar. Tullagh, co. Clare, prov. Munster.

MOYNOY, antiently sit. near *Croghan*, in co. Roscommon, prov. Connaught.

MOYOWLA *river*, sit. in bar. Loughlinsholen, co. Londonderry, prov. Ulster.

MOYRA, see *Moira*.

Moyne Abbey

MOYSLECHT, an antient diſtrict, ſit. near *Fenagh*, in bar. Mohill, co. Leitrim, prov. Connaught: celebrated in the antient Iriſh poems, for being the place where *Tigernmas* firſt introduced the worſhip of *Crom* or Fate; for which he and his followers are ſaid to have been deſtroyed there by lightning.

MOYSTOWN, ſit. by the river *Bruſna*, in bar. Garrycaſtle, King's co. prov. Leinſter.

MOY-TURLY. There were two places under this name. 1ſt, the *Southern Moyturey*, ſit. not far from *Lough Maſk*, in co. Galway, prov. Connaught; celebrated for being the ſcene of action between the *Belgian* and *Danan*, or Caledonian ſepts, about 80 or 100 years before the Chriſtian æra.—2nd, the *Northern* Maghturey, ſit. near *Lough Arrow*, in co. Roſcommon, prov. Connaught; celebrated for an engagement there between the *Belgians* and *Fomorians* on one ſide, and the *Danans* on the other, ſome few years before the birth of Chriſt; in which the *Belgians* were again defeated.

MOYVALLY, ſit. in bar. *Kilkennyweſt*, co. Weſtmeath, prov. Leinſter.—Alſo in bar. Carbury, co. Kildare, prov. Leinſter.

MOYVIDDY, a rectory in dioc. of Cork, ſit. in bar. Muſkerry, co. Cork, prov. Munſter.

MOYVORE, ſit. in co. Weſtmeath, prov. Leinſter, 48 miles from Dublin; 2½ miles beyond which, is *Forgny church*; fairs held 4 May, 20 Aug. and 5 Dec.

MOYVORE-CASTLE, now in ruins, ſit. 3 miles beyond *Iniſtimond*, co. Clare, prov. Munſter.

MUAD RIVER, now the river *Moy*, ſit. in co. Sligo, prov. Connaught.

MUCHALLY, ſit. in bar. Faſſachdining, co. Kilkenny, prov. Leinſter.

MUCK, an *iſland*, ſit. on coaſt of the bar. Belfaſt, co. Antrim, prov. Ulſter.

MUCKISH *mountains*, ſit. in bar. Kilmacrenan, co. Donegal, prov. Ulſter.

MUCKNO, a rectory in dioc. of Clogher, ſit. in bar. Cremourne, co. Monaghan, prov. Ulſter.

MUCKRIS-POINT, a *cape*, ſit. in bar. Boylagh, co. Donegal, prov. Ulſter.

MUCKULLY. There are two vicarages of this name in dioc. of Oſſory, one ſit. in bar. Knocktopher,—the other in bar. Faſſachdining, both in co. Kilkenny, prov. Leinſter.

MUCRUSS, ſit. in co. Kerry, prov. Munſter, 146 miles from Dublin, it is a handſome ſeat, near the lake of *Killarney*; here is alſo a lake called *Mucruſs lake*; the natural appearance of this place, before it was adorned by any improvement, was that of a luxuriant garden; where a great variety of trees and ſhrubs, the produce only of a more favourable clime, flouriſhed ſpontaneouſly; as the *Arbutus, Juniper, Yew, Buckthorn, Service* and others, found growing among the crevices of marble rocks; the

ſeeds and original plantation of which, Dr. *Smith* ſuſpects to have been laid here many centuries ago, by the monks of the adjacent abbeys, where meeting with a ſoil and climate favourable to their propagation, they have wonderfully flouriſhed ever ſince, without requiring any aſſiſtance from art. An abbey was founded here in 1440, for mendicants of the order of St. Francis; it is ſit. on an eminence riſing over the *lake*, and is in tolerable preſervation; it ſerves as a burial place to the inhabitants of the neighbourhood, where according to tradition, many Iriſh kings and chiefs lie buried. In the centre of the building is a curious *yew* tree, the trunk of which is between 7 and 8 feet in circumference, and its boughs form a complete covering to the cloiſter, which is a ſquare of 12 yards.

MUCULLAGH *rocks*, ſit. in bar. Corcaguinny, co. Kerry, prov. Munſter.

MUDHORN, now the bar. of *Mourne*, in the S. of co. Down, prov. Ulſter; in which St. *Jarlath*, the 2d biſhop of Armagh, was born.

MUFF, ſit. in bar. Clonchee, co. Cavan, prov. Ulſter, 72 miles from Dublin; cloſe by the road ſide are the ruins of a caſtle; fairs are held on 12 Aug.—Alſo a place of ſame name in bar. Tyrſkerin, co. Londonderry, prov. Ulſter, 120 miles from Dublin; where are fairs on 1ſt Thurſd. in Feb. May, Aug. and Nov.—Likewiſe a fair town in bar. Iniſhowen, co. Donegal, prov. Ulſter; fair days 4 May, 5 Aug. 25 Oct. and 11 Dec.

MUGGORT'S-BAY, ſit. in bar. Decies within Drum, co. Waterford, prov. Munſter.

MUGHERINY, ſit. in bar. Omagh, co. Tyrone, prov. Ulſter.

MUGLINS *rocks*, ſit. near *Dalkey iſland*, co. Dublin, prov. Leinſter.

MULAGHCREW, ſit. near Ardee, co. Louth, prov. Leinſter; fairs held 2 Feb. 17 Mar. Eaſter-Monday and Tueſday, 1 May, 17 June, 26 July, 15 Aug. 18 Sept. 18 Oct. 16 Nov. and 21 Dec. This place is ſometimes called *Mulleghgrew*.

MULAHISH, ſit. in co. Kerry, prov. Munſter; fairs held 26 May, 17 Aug. and 20 Sept.

MULAHUFF, or *Mullahaff*, a fair town in co. Kerry, prov. Munſter; here is a ruined caſtle near the banks of the river *Mang*, called *Mulahuff caſtle*; fairs are held here 26 and 27 May, 21 Aug. and 18 Sept.

MULHUSSY-CASTLE, ſit. in co. Meath, prov. Leinſter.

MULKAN, ſit. in bar. Roſclogher, co. Leitrim, prov. Connaught.

MULLABRACK, a rectory in dioc. of Armagh, ſit. in bar. *Fews*, co. Armagh, prov. Ulſter. (Dr. *Beaufort.*) It is placed by *Scalè* in bar. *Orior.*

MULLAGH,

Mullagh, a vicarage in dioc. of Kilmore, fit. in bar. Caftleraghan, co. Cavan, prov. Ulfter.—Alfo a place fit. near *Longford*, co. Longford, prov. Leinfter.

Mullaghan, fit. in bar. Dungannon, co. Tyrone, prov. Ulfter.

Mullaghearn *mountains*, fit. in bar. Strabane, co. Tyrone, prov. Ulfter.

Mullaha *mountains*, fit. in bar. Dromahaire, co. Leitrim, prov. Connaught.

Mullahaff, fee *Mulahuff*.

Mullahithart, a village fit. in bar. Caftleknock, co. Dublin, prov. Leinfter; it is a curacy in dioc. of Dublin; here are the ruins of a church and antient burial place.

Mullahoo, fit. in bar. Balruddery, co. Dublin, prov. Leinfter.

Mullamore, fit. in bar. Dunluce, co. Antrim, prov. Ulfter.

Mullanstown, fit. near *Ardee*, co. Louth, prov. Leinfter.

Mullavilly *church*, fit. in bar. Orior, co. Armagh, prov. Ulfter; it is a chapelry in dioc. of Armagh.

Mullechgrew, fee *Mulaghcrew*.

Mullet, a *peninfula*, fit. in bar. Erris, co. Mayo, prov. Connaught.

Mullinabro, fit. in bar. Ibercon, co. Kilkenny, prov. Leinfter.

Mullinacuff, a curacy in dioc. of Leighlin, fit. in bar. *Shilelagh*, co. Wicklow, prov. Leinfter. (Dr. *Beaufort*.) It is placed by *Scalé*, in bar. *Ballinacour*.

Mullinahone, fit. in co. Tipperary, prov. Munfter, 70 miles from Dublin; fairs held 1 May, 1 Thurfd. July, 14 Sept. and 1 Thurfd. Dec. Two miles beyond it, is *Gurteen cafle*; 1¼ mile farther, is *Cloneen cafle*; and a mile beyond that, is *Ballynard cafle*.

Mullinahow, fit. in co. Kilkenny, prov. Leinfter; fairs held 25 Sept.

Mullinakill, fit. in bar. Oneiland, co. Armagh, prov. Ulfter.—Alfo near *Balruddery*, in co. Dublin, prov. Leinfter; the name is fometimes written *Mullynakill*.

Mullinavat, fit. in bar. Knocktopher, co. Kilkenny, prov. Leinfter, 68 miles from Dublin; fairs held Eafter-tuefday and 3 Oct. 'Tis fometimes written *Mulnavat*, and *Mullincvat*.

Mullincross, fit. in bar. Atherdee, co. Louth, prov. Leinfter.

Mullinderry, fit. in bar. Shelmaliere, co. Wexford, prov. Leinfter.

Mullingar, a borough and poft town, fit. in bar. Moyafhel, co. Weftmeath, prov. Leinfter. It is a vicarage in dioc. of Meath; diftant 38 miles from Dublin. Lat. 53 : 30, lon. 7 : 50. This is the affizes and fhire-town for the co. Weftmeath, it has a barrack for 2 troops of horfe, and returns 2 members to parliament;

patron, the earl of *Granard*. This place was an antient palatinate, and gave title of baron to the family of *Petit*. Within a few miles of it are the ruins of a *church*, and alfo thofe of a *cafle*; this town is fit. on the river *Foyle*; it holds a great *wool* fair, and is a place of good trade. In 1227, the priory of St. *Mary*, formerly known by the name of " *the houfe of God of Mullingar*," was founded here by *Ralph de Petyt*, bifhop of *Meath*, for regular canons of the order of St. Auguftin. A Dominican friary was alfo founded here in 1237, by the family of *Nugent*, fome ruins of which ftill remain. In 1622, the friars of *Multifarnham* began to erect a houfe here for friars of the order of St. *Francis*, but it was never compleated. Fairs held 6 April, 4 and 5 July, 29 Aug. and 11 Nov. 3 miles from this town is the feat of the Rt. Hon. the earl of *Belvedere*.

Mullits, or *Mullets*, a clufter of iflands, fit. on the N. W. point of the co. Mayo, prov. Connaught; the largeft being about 10 miles in length, in which was a barrack for a foot company.

Mullogh, a fair town in co. Tipperary, prov. Munfter; fairs held 12 Feb.

Mulloghanee Bridge, fit. in co. Armagh, prov. Ulfter, 51 miles from Dublin.

Mullogher, fit. in bar. Louth, co. Louth, prov. Leinfter.

Mullogheross, fit. in bar. Omagh, co. Tyrone, prov. Ulfter.

Mullone, a village fit. in bar. Belfaft, co. Antrim, prov. Ulfter.

Mullrankin, a rectory in dioc. of Ferns, fit. in bar. Bargie, co. Wexford, prov. Leinfter.

Mullrea *mountains*, fit. in bar. Morifk, co. Mayo, prov. Connaught.

Mullyglass *church*, fit. in bar. Orior, co. Armagh, prov. Ulfter.

Mulphedder, a fair town in co. Meath, prov. Leinfter; fairs held 23 May and 13 Nov.

Mulroy-bay, fit. in bar. Kilmacrenan, co. Donegal, prov. Ulfter.

Multifernon, or *Multifarnham*, a village fit. on the river *Gaine*, in bar. Corkerry, co. Weftmeath, prov. Leinfter. Fairs held 4 Mar. 13 May and 1 Sept. It is a rectory in dioc. of Meath. A monaftery was founded here for conventual Francifcans, in 1236, by *William Delamar*; and in 1460, we find it reformed by the friars of the ftrict obfervance. The rank of this houfe was fo high, that a provincial chapter of the order was held here in 1529. The Francifcans continued in open and peaceable poffeffion of this place 'till 1641, and 'tis faid the grand rebellion of that year was preconcerted and contrived in this friary. The building was rather neat than fumptuous; between the body of the church and the chancel, eel was a narrow but handsome steeple, 60 feet high; the whole was set on fire by the *Rochfort* family; some ruins which remain shew its extent and workmanship: the building was of a blackish stone, and the E. window, totally devoid of ornament, is still entire.

MUMHAN, the most antient name of the prov. of Munster, derived from the old Celtic *Mamman*, or the country of the great mother. All the Celtic tribes in general, denominated themselves, not from their chieftain as commonly supposed, but either from their situation or object of religion. The principal objects of adoration among them, were first, Fate or Providence, under the names of *Crom*, *Crim* or *Crum*; secondly, the sun or elementary fire, considered as the active principle of nature, under the names *Baal*, *Beal* and *Bol*, or *Heul*, *Ull* and *Oll*; thirdly, the earth or universal nature, considered as the passive principle or great mother; under the several names of *Mamman*, *Ama*, *Anum*, *Anagh*, *Aonagh*, *Ops* and *Sibhol*. Those who considered *fate* as their object of adoration, denominated themselves *Crombrii* or *Crimbrii*, as those who inhabited the Western coast of Belgium; and those, as the aboriginal Britons, who considered the *sun* as the principle, denominated themselves *Bolgæ*, *Bealadh* and *Ulladh*, whilst those who thought the earth the most worthy of esteem, denominated themselves *Mamanagh*, or Mamonii, i. e. the children of the earth or great mother. The most antient inhabitants of the S. of Ireland, derived their origin from the antient *Silures*, who inhabited the Southern coasts of Britain, and tho' of the *Belgian faith*, principally adored *Maman* or the great mother, when they in particular distinguished themselves by the name of *Momonii*, and on their arrival in Ireland, gave their division the name of *Moma* or *Mumhan*, a name which is still retained in the present name of Munster, comprehending the co.'s of Waterford, Cork, Limerick, Tipperary, Kerry and Clare. We have given this account from Mr. *Beauford's* tract on the antient topography of Ireland, contained in *Col. reb. Hiber.* No. 11. Mr. *O'Connor* in his *Dissert.* and other writers, derive the name Munster from *Eochy Mumha*, who was king of Ireland, several ages before the christian æra; they tell us that in this early period, *Degad*, of the race of *Oliol Aron*, transplanted also a considerable colony of the *Ernai* into Munster, where he was elected king, and his followers became a very considerable people for several ages, under the name of the *Degades*, or *Munster Ernai*.

MUNDREHID, sit. between *Borris* and *Anatrim*, in bar. Ossory, Queen's co. prov. Leinster. An abbey was founded here, over which St. *Lasarien* was abbot about the year 600.

MUNGRET, a village near Limerick, prov. Munster; it is a vicarage in dioc. of Limerick. Here are the remains of *Mungret abbey*, sit. near *Loughmore*; it is said to have been erected in the 4th century, before the arrival of St. *Patrick* in Munster; it is however indubitable that St. *Patrick* placed St. *Nessan* here, who died in 551; the *Psalter* of *Cashel* gives an account of this abbey, that it had within its walls six churches, which contained (exclusive of scholars) 1500 religious; 500 of whom were learned preachers, 500 psalmists, and the remaining 500 wholly applied themselves to spiritual exercises; the ruins of this abbey may still be seen, consisting of the walls of a church, which do not indeed bespeak either its antiquity, or former splendor: the E. end is 47 feet long by 16 broad, with a plain narrow window; the centre or nave, is 33 feet by 28½, and the communication from this with the E. end, is by a small arch; on the N. side of the nave, is a small porch or entrance; the W. end is 12 feet by 22; on the N. side whereof, is a small square tower, with ruined battlements; there are no tombs to be found here, but at a small distance N. E. are some old walls, which probably made a part of the abbey. In the year 908, *Cormac Mac Culnenan*, archbishop of Cashel, and king of Munster, by his last will, bequeathed to this abbey 3 ounces of gold, an embroidered vest, and *his blessing*.

MUNLEAGH, sit. near *Dundrum*, co. Down, prov. Ulster.

MUNRY river, sit. in bar. Erris, co. Mayo, prov. Connaught.

MUNSHEER-HILL, sit. in bar. Talbot'stown, co. Wicklow, prov. Leinster.

MUNSTER, a large, and the most Southern prov. of Ireland; a rich and pleasant country, bounded on the N. by Leinster and Connaught, and on the E. W. and S. by the ocean, it contains the co.'s Cork, Clare, Kerry, Limerick, Tipperary and Waterford, in which are 59 bar.'s, 816 parishes, and 3,377,150 acres, its principal town is Cork; its antient name was *Mumhan*, and in latter ages it was divided into *Desmond*, or S. Munster, *Ormond*, or E. Munster, and *Thomond*, or N. Munster; it lies between lat. 51: 15 and 53: 00, and lon. 7: 10 and 10: 40.

MUNSTER-CONOGH, sit. in bar. Castleraghen, co. Cavan, prov. Ulster: there was an endowed hospital here; king *James* granted a lease of it for the term of 21 years, to sir *Edw. Moore*, at the yearly rent of 1s. 4d. This place is sometimes written *Munterconnaught*, and is a rectory in dioc. of Kilmore.

MUNSTER-

MUSTERLONEY *mountains*, fit. in bar. Strabane, co. Tyrone, prov. Ulfter.

MURDERING-GLEN, a place fo called in co. Cork, prov. Munfter, within 3 miles of *Bantry*; it is a valley, in which are vaft quantities of rocks and ftones thrown together in a kind of fportive confufion, as if they were fhot out of the mouth of a prodigious large volcano, and the adjacent hill on the top, being hollow, with a ftony edge round it, looks not unlike the mouth of one.

MURHIR, a vicarage in dioc. of Ardfert, fit. in bar. Iraghticonner, co. Kerry, prov. Munfter.

MURLAGH, fit. near *Dundrum*, co. Down, prov. Ulfter.

MURRAGH, a village fit. in bar. Carbery, co. Cork, prov. Munfter.

MURVAGH, fit. in bar. Tyrhugh, co. Donegal, prov. Ulfter.

MUSCRIAGE-THIRE, an antient diftrict of the *O'Kennedys*, fit. in co. Tipperary, prov. Munfter.

MUSGRY, fee *Mufkerry*.

MUSKERRY, a bar. in co. Cork, prov. Munfter, antiently called *Mufgruidhe*, or *Mufgry*; it gives title of baron to fir *Rob. Tilfon Deane*, bart. who was created baron Mufkerry in 1780. Here are a chain of mountains to the W. of the *Boggra*, called Mufkerry, and fometimes *Mufhry*, or *Muffiry* mountains, fit. near *Macroomp*; on one of which *Mahon*, the brother of *Brien Boromh*, was flain, at the place called *Leaght Mhaghthamhna*, or Mahon's grave, about the year 976. Thefe mountains are diftinguifhed into *Mufkerrymore* and *Beg*, i. e. the larger and leffer mountains; thefe range partly N. and S. are high at both extremes, and hollow in the middle, the upper part is covered with fedgy grafs and bog, the rocks, with *London-pride*; the torrents have worn feveral deep furrows in their fides, which difplay no other foil but flaty pebbles, of a red, white, and dark colour; but nothing of any metallic fubftance. *Mufkerry* was the antient diftrict of the *Barrys*.

MUTHEL CHURCH, fit. in co. Waterford, prov. Munfter, 77 miles from Dublin; near 2 miles from it are the ruins of *Clonea caftle*.

MUTTOCK-BRIDGE, fit. in bar. Slane, co. Meath, prov. Leinfter.

MYRA-CASTLE, fit. in co. Louth, prov. Leinfter, about 44 miles from Dublin; it is now in ruins.

MYROS, a rectory in dioc. of Rofs, fit. in bar. Carbery, co. Cork, prov. Munfter.

MYRTLE-GROVE, fit. near *Roferea*, prov. Mun.

MYSHALL, fit. in bar. Forth, co. Carlow, prov. Leinfter, 47 miles from Dublin. It is a rectory in dioc. of Leighlin. Here are the ruins of a church.

NAAS, a bar. in co. Kildare, prov. Leinfter, having in it a borough and poft town of fame name, fit. on a branch of the river Liffey, about 15 miles S. W. of Dublin. Lat. 53:10, lon. 6:50. Fairs held 17 March, Afcenfion day, Whit.-monday, 10 Aug. and 22 Nov. It fends two members to parliament, patron, the earl of *Mayo*. This place gives title of vifc. to the family of *Burke*. Naas was a place of fome note, as appears by feveral ruins yet remaining; near the town is a Danifh mount or rath. This place was antiently the refidence of the kings of Leinfter; the name fignifies *the place of the elders*, for here the ftates of that prov. affembled, during the 6th, 7th and 8th centuries, after the *Naafteighan* of *Carmen*, had been anathematized by the Chriftian clergy. On the arrival of the *Englifh* it was fortified; many caftles were erected, the ruins of which are partly vifible; and parliaments were held there. At the foot of the mount or rath are the ruins of a houfe founded in 1484, for Eremites of the order of St. Auguftin. In the 12th century, the baron of Naas founded a priory dedicated to St. John the Baptift, for Auguftinian regular canons. In the centre of this town the family of *Euftace*, erected a monaftery for Dominican friars, dedicated to St. *Euftachius*; and it appears that their poffeffions in *Naas*, were granted them in the year 1355. A public inn is now erected on part of the antient foundation. Within half a mile of *Naas*, are the ruins of *Jiggins-town* houfe, began (but never finifhed) by lord *Strafford*, when lord lieutenant of Ireland, in the reign of king Cha. Ift. *Naas* is a vicarage in dioc. of Kildare.

NADRID, a fair town in co. Cork, prov. Munfter; fairs held 1 Jan. and 10 Oct.

NAFFOY LOUGH, a *lake*, fit. in bar. Rofs, co. Galway, prov. Connaught.

NAGLE-MOUNTAINS, fit. in bar. Fermoy, towards the S. of the co. Cork, prov. Munfter.

NAGNATÆ, fee *Naguatæ*.

NAGUATÆ, an antient diftrict in the W. of Ireland, mentioned by Ptolemy, and in fome copies corruptly written *Nagnatæ*; it was called by the old Irifh, *Slioght Gae*, and is the fame with the prefent co. *Sligo*, prov. Connaught.

NAIRN, fee *Narne*.

NALLENROE-LOUGH, a *lake*, fit. in bar. Erris, co. Mayo, prov. Connaught.

NANNY-WATER, a fmall river fit. in bar. Duleek, co. Meath, prov. Leinfter.

NANTENANE, a fair town in bar. Connello, co. Limerick, prov. Munfter; fairs held 10 July,

July, 5 Aug. and 12 Nov. It is a rectory in dioc. of Limerick, and otherwise written *Nantinan*.

NARNE, or *Naren*, or *Nairn*, fit. in co. Donegal, prov. Ulster, about 137 miles from Dublin ; it is a post town.

NARRAGH, a bar. joined with *Reban*, fit. in co. Kildare, prov. Leinster, and called the bar. of *Narragh and Reban*.

NARRAGHMORE, a fair town, fit. in bar. *Narragh*, co. Kildare, prov. Leinster ; fairs held 28 March. It is a rectory in dioc. of Dublin. Here is a handsome feat of *M. Keatinge*, esq.

NARROW-WATER, a village fit. in bar. upper Iveagh, co. Down, prov. Ulster, about 54 miles from Dublin ; fairs held 17 Jan. 4 May, and 2 Oct. It takes its name from the river *Newry*, which is also called *Narrow-water*, and from hence all the coals that come down the *Newry* canal, must be shipped off, for Dublin. On this part of the river stands the castle of *Narrow-water*, built on a rock, (which straitens the channel) where two ferry boats maintain a communication between this co. and that of Louth. Near it some salt works have been erected. At this place is three fathom water ; and from this point to the town of *Newry*, are two small leagues, but no depth of water except for small craft.

NASH, a fair town in co. Wexford, prov. Leinster ; fairs held 24 June and 20 Nov.

NATENENE, a fair town in co. Kerry, prov. Munster ; fairs held Whit.-tuefd. and Wednesd.

NAVAN, a bar. in co. Meath, prov. Leinster, in which is a borough, post and fair town of fame name, fit. on the river *Boyne*, about 23 miles N. W. of Dublin. Lat. 53 : 40, lon. 7 : 10. It is a rectory in dioc. of Meath ; and returns 2 members to parliament ; patronage in the *Preston* family. Fairs held Easter-mond. day after Trinity-fund. 2 Mond. in Sept. and 1 Mond. in Dec. The town confifts of 2 chief streets, which interfect each other at right-angles. The tholfel or town houfe, is a handsome stone building. This place was formerly in great repute ; and walled in by *Hugh de Lacey*, It was an antient palatinate, and gave title of baron to the family of *Nangle*. An abbey for regular canons dedicated to the Virgin Mary, was erected here ; but whether antecedent to the end of the 12th century is not certain : about that period however, it was either founded or re-edified by *Joceline de Angulo* or *Nangle*. In the burial ground are the remains of many antient tombs, with figures in alto relievo ; and the present barrack for one troop of horfe, is built on the fite of the abbey. Within a mile of Navan are the ruins of *Donaghmore* church. In the church-yard stands a round tow-

er, about 70 feet high, and 12 in diameter ; the door is 10 feet from the ground. This is an opulent town, and faid to contain about 4,000 inhabitants, most of them industriously occupied in different branches of trade.

NAUL, fit. in bar. Balruddery, co. Dublin, prov. Leinster, 14 miles from Dublin, and within 8 miles of *Drogheda*. It is a vicarage in dioc. of Dublin. At this place is a romantic glen, overhung with rocks, wherein are many caves ; the old *castle* of *Naul*, stands boldly fit. over this romantic glen, thro' which a small stream winds its course, dividing the co.'s of Dublin and Meath ; and a small distance lower down, it forms a fine waterfall, called *the Roches*. A little beyond *Naul*, are the ruins of Snowton *castle*.

NEAGH-LOUGH, fee *Lough Neagh*.

NEAL, fit. in bar. Kilmain, co. Mayo, prov. Connaught ; fairs held 5 Feb. 6 May, 4 Aug. and 5 Nov. It is ufually called " *the Neal* ;" here is the feat of lord *Kilmain* ; diftant from Dublin about 106 miles.

NEDDANS, a vicarage in dioc. of Lifmore, fit. in bar. Iffa and Offa, co. Tipperary, prov. Munster.

NEDEEN, or *Needen*, a fair town in bar. Glanerought, co. Kerry, prov. Munster ; fairs held 22 May, 1 July, 26 Sept. and 20 Nov.

NEIR, or *Sleeve Neir*, a mountain fo called, fit. in the bar. of *upper Iveach*, co. Down, prov. Ulster.

NENAGH, a post and fair town in bar. lower Ormond, co. Tipperary, prov. Munster, 75 miles from Dublin. It is fit. on a branch of the river *Shannon* that runs into *Lough Derg*. Here stand the ruins of an old castle, called *Nenagh-round*. Also thofe of an hospital founded in the year 1200, for canons following the rule of St. Augustin. It was dedicated to St. John the Baptift, and was ufually called *Teachon*, or St. John's houfe. In the reign of Hen. III. a friary for conventual Francifcans, was also founded here, and efteemed the richeft foundation of that order in the kingdom. Here is a barrack for 2 troops of horfe. Near this town *Brien*, fon of *Mahon Menevy O'Brien*, in 1370, obtained a complete victory over his uncle *Turlogh*, affifted by the English forces, under the command of the earl of Defmond. From which battle, he obtained the furname of *Brien Catha an Aonaig*, or " Brien of the battle of Nenagh." This town was burnt on St. Stephen's-day, 1348, by the Irifh. Fairs are held here on 29 May, 4 July and Sept. and 10 Oct. This is a vicarage in dioc. of Killaloe. Within 2 miles of it are the ruins of *Knockalton castle*.

NEPHIN *mountain*, one of the most remarkable mountains in Ireland, fit. about 8 miles beyond

beyond *Caftlebar*, in bar. Tirawly, co. Mayo, prov. Connaught.

NEPTUNE, a handfome feat of the late lord *Tratton*, and now belonging to lord *Clonmel*, fit. near the *Black-rock*, co. Dublin, prov. Leinfter, 4¼ miles from Dublin caftle.

NETHERCROSS, a bar. in co. Dublin, prov. Leinfter.

NETHLASH, a rectory in dioc. of Cloyne, fit. in bar. Condons, co. Cork, prov. Munfter.

NEURAGH-BRIDGE, fit. near *Newcaftle*, co. Wicklow, prov. Leinfter.

NEVIL-COURT, fit. near *Gorey*, prov. Leinfter.

NEVINSTOWN, fit. in bar. Ophaly, co. Kildare, prov. Leinfter; here is an antient burial place, and the ruin of an old church; near it is the feat of Mr. *Fitzgerald*.

NEW-ABBEY, fit. near *Kilcullen*, co. Kildare, prov. Leinfter. It was founded in 1460, by *Rowland Euftace*, of a great and antient family in this co. the tower is ftill ftanding, and fome part of the abbey, the ruins of the reft have contributed to build feveral dwellings near it. In the infide *Rowland Euftace* and his lady lie buried, their monument remained in prefervation 'till the year 1786, when it was deftroyed with other parts of the building, in order to erect a Roman catholic chapel with the ftones. On the tomb in alto relievo, was the effigies of fir Rowland, baron of *Portlefter*, and his lady, *Margaret Jenico*. Sir Rowland appeared cloathed in armour, according to the cuftom of the times. Lady Euftace was in the fafhionable Englifh drefs of her age. Round the figures on the outer edge of the tomb, was engraven in relief, in that fpecies of gothic characters, called church text, the following infcription. "*Orate pro anima Rolandi Fitz Euftace de Portlefter, qui hoc mo. conftruxit et fundavit, et qui cb. die Decemb. 19 A. D. 1496, etiam pro anima Margaretæ uxoris fuæ.*" The fteeple fell to the ground about the year 1764. This Rowland was fon to fir *Edw. Euftace* of *Harriftown*, lord baron of *Portlefter*; and many years chancellor and treafurer of Ireland; he built a chapel in St. *Audeon's* church, Dublin, to the honour of the Virgin Mary, and erected a monument therein, with this infcription, viz. "*Orate pro anima Rolandi Fitz Euftace de Portlefter, qui hunc locum five capellam dedit in honorem Beatæ Mariæ Virginis; etiam pro anima Margaretæ uxoris fuæ, et pro animis omnium fidelium defunctorum. Anno Dom. 1455.*" Lady *Elizabeth Zouch*, firft wife to *Gerald*, the 9th earl of Kildare, died 11 Oct. 1517, and was interred in this abbey, near to her mother *Alifon*, and to the earl her hufband. In Aug. 1582, a leafe of the abbey was granted to *Edmund Spencer*. Near this place is a handfome feat of the *Carter* family, on the oppofite fide of the river *Liffey*.

NEWBLISS, a fair town in co. Monaghan, prov. Ulfter; fairs held Sat. before Eafter-day, 30 May, 1ft Sat. July, and 30 Nov.

NEWBOROUGH, fit. in co. Galway, prov. Connaught, about 98 miles from Dublin.—Alfo a name given to the borough of *Gorey*, in co. Wexford, prov. Leinfter.

NEWBRIDGE, fit. in bar. Great Connel, co. Kildare, prov. Leinfter, near 21 miles from Dublin. Near it are the ruins of *Great Connel* abbey, formerly one of the moft magnificent buildings of that kind in this kingdom. At *old Connel* is a fine Danifh mount. Fairs are held at *Newbridge* 3 May and 15 Aug.—This is alfo the name of a place in bar. Duhallow, co. Cork, prov. Munfter, 126 miles from Dublin.—Alfo a place in bar. Connello, co. Limerick, prov. Munfter, 109 miles from Dublin.—Likewife a place in co. Wicklow, prov. Leinfter, 29 miles from Dublin.—Alfo a place fit. in bar. Nethercrofs, co. Dublin, prov. Leinft.

NEWBRIDGE-INN, fit. in co. Kildare, prov. Leinfter, 21½ miles from Dublin; between this and *Newbridge*, is the ruin of *Great Connel* abbey.

NEWBROOK, fit. near *Tuam*, prov. Connaught;—alfo in co. Mayo, fame prov. about 109 miles from Dublin.

NEWBUILDINGS, fit. in the liberties of Derry, co. Londonderry, prov. Ulfter, 110 miles from Dublin.

NEWCASTLE, a bar. in co. Dublin, prov. Leinfter, in which is a borough and fair town of fame name, fit. 2 miles from *Clondalkin*, and 7 from Dublin; it is a poor and reduced place, which returns 2 members to parliament, patronage in the *Latouche* family; fairs held 9 May and 8 Oct. This is a vicarage in dioc. of Dublin. Lat. 53 : 17, lon. 6 : 59.—Alfo a place in co. Down, prov. Ulfter, 75 miles from Dublin. At one fide of which is *Slieve Donard*, the higheft of the mountains of *Mourne*; the caftle here was built by *Felix Magennis*, in the year 1588. There is a handfome feat here; and in this co. is another caftle of fame name, ftanding boldly over the fea, on a neck of land 3 miles E. of Portaferry.—Alfo a place in bar. Connello, co. Limerick, prov. Munfter, on the high road to Kerry, 114 miles from Dublin, it is a handfome town, where was a religious houfe, poffeffed by the Knights Templars. It is faid they ufed fome barbarous cuftoms which greatly difgufted the Irifh, who watching a favourable opportunity, attacked a number of knights riding out together, and put them to death; the place is ftill remembered where their remains were interred. This order was fuppreffed in the famous council of *Vienna*, 22 March, 1312.. *Newcaftle* confifts of a large fquare, where markets and fairs are held; on

the

the Northern fide ftands a market-houfe, with an affembly room; on the S. fide the church, which is the neateft in the co. and is a rectory in dioc. of Limerick; it was finifhed in 1777, at the fole expence of lord *Courtenay*. It ftands clofe to the walls and fortifications of the Knts. Templars, of which one of the caftles is fitted up for lord *Courtenay's* agent. Fairs are held here on 3 May, 20 Aug. and 1 Oct.—Alfo a place in bar. Slane, co. Meath, prov. Leinfter, 36 miles from Dublin, about 2 miles from it is *Innifheene church*.—Alfo a bar. in co. Wicklow, prov. Leinfter, in which is a fair town of fame name, which is a rectory in dioc. of Dublin. Fairs held 1 April, 10 July, 1 Sept. and 6 Dec.—Alfo a vicarage in dioc. of Lifmore, fit. in bar. Middlethird, co. Waterford, prov. Munfter.—Alfo a place in co. Mayo, prov. Connaught, at which one of the antient round towers was erected.—Alfo a village fit. in bar. Shrowle, co. Longford, prov. Leinfter. Alfo a vicarage in dioc. of Lifmore, fit. in bar. Iffa and Offa, co. Tipperary, prov. Munfter.

NEWCESTOWN, a fair town in co. Cork, prov. Munfter; fairs held 8 Jan. Whit-tuefday, 15 Oct. and 14 Dec. 3 miles from this, is *Strawhill*, formerly called *Kilbrenin*, where an abbey was founded in the 8th century: part of the ruins thereof are ftill remaining on a rifing ground.

NEWCHAPEL, a rectory in dioc. of Cafhel, fit. in bar. Iffa and Offa, co. Tipperary, prov. Munfter.

NEWCHURCH, a village fit. in bar. Portnehinch, Queen's co. prov. Leinfter.

NEW-FERRY, fit. in co. Londonderry, prov. Ulfter, 113 miles from Dublin. Here is a handfome feat of the *Courtnay* family.

NEW-FORGE, fit. near Magherelin-bridge, in co. Down, prov. Ulfter. It is fo called from an *iron-forge* formerly erected there, on the river *Lagan*. On the 9 Aug. 1707, a ftorm of thunder and lightning happened here, which produced moft extraordinary effects, and is defcribed at large in Dr. *Smith's* hiftory of this co.

NEW-FORREST, fit. near *Rofcrea*, prov. Munft.

NEW-GRANGE, fee *Grange (new.)*

NEW-GROVE, fit. near *Kells*, prov. Leinfter.

NEW-HAVEN, fit. near *Balbriggan*, prov. Leinfter.

NEW-INN, fit. in bar. Killconnel, co. Galway, prov. Connaught, 82 miles from Dublin. On the *Loughrea road*, about a mile from this, are the ruins of a caftle; and a little farther thofe of a church.—There is alfo a place of fame name in co. Tipperary, prov. Munfter, 81 miles from Dublin. 1½ mile beyond which are the ruins of the church of Oughtra; and at like diftance on the other fide of this place,

ftands the caftle and mount of *Knockgraffon*, on the river *Suir*.—*New-inn* is likewife the name of a place, otherwife called *Nineteen-mile-houfe*, in bar. Moyfenrath, co. Meath, prov. Leinfter, diftant above 19 miles from Dublin.

NEWLAND, fit. near *Kilkenny*, prov. Leinfter.

NEWMARKET, a village and poft town, fit. in bar. Duhallow, co. Cork, prov. Munfter. 142 miles from Dublin, and 5 Englifh miles W. of *Kantirk*, in the N. W. part of the co. It confifts of one regular ftreet, and is a confiderable thorough-fare into the co. Kerry. Here is a decent parifh church. To the W. of this place, on the fide of the road, towards *Blackwater-bridge*, ftands *Caftle-Mac-Awliff*, formerly the chief feat of that fept. There is alfo another of their caftles at *Carigacufhin*, a mile N. E. of Newmarket; fairs are held here 8 June and Sept. 10 Oct. and 21 Nov.—Alfo a fair town in bar. Bunratty, co. Clare, prov. Munfter; fair days Eafter-monday, 25 Aug. and 31 Dec.—Alfo a fair town in co. Rofcommon, prov. Connaught; fairs held 2 May, 26 June, 5 Oct. and 28 Dec.—Alfo a village fit. in bar. Knocktopher, co. Kilkenny, prov. Leinfter, 65 miles from Dublin. A mile beyond which is *Caftle Morres*, the handfome feat of lord vifc. *Mountmorres*.

NEW-MILL, a fair town in co. Cork, prov. Munfter; fairs held 4 June.

NEW-MILLS, fit. in bar. Dungannon, co. Tyrone, prov. Ulfter, 75 miles from Dublin.

NEW-PARK, fit. near *Athlone*, prov. Connaught.—Alfo in co. Longford, prov. Leinfter, about 59 miles from Dublin.

NEW-PASS, fit. in co. Weftmeath, prov. Leinfter, 49 miles from Dublin.

NEW-PIER, a village fit. in bar. Corcomroe, co. Clare, prov. Munfter.

NEWPORT, a poft and fair town in bar. Owney, co. Tipperary, prov. Munfter, 86 miles from Dublin. Which gives title of *baron* to the family of *Jocelyn*. Here is a charter-fchool for a great number of boys, which was opened in 1751, to the building and fupport of which, the late lord *Jocelyn* contributed largely. Within 3 miles of this place is *Caftle-Connel* fpa, in co. Limerick; fairs held 23 Oct. Alfo a place fit. near *Ennifkillen*, prov. Ulfter.

NEWPORT-PRATT, a poft and fair town, fit. in bar. Burrifhool, co. Mayo, prov. Connaught, 128 miles from Dublin. Fairs held 8 June and 11 Nov.

NEWRAH-BRIDGE, a village fit. in bar. Newcaftle, co. Wicklow, prov. Leinfter.

NEWRATH, fit. in bar. Louth, co. Louth, prov. Leinfter.

NEWRE *river*, fee *Nore*.

NEW-ROSS, a borough town in bar. Bantry, co. Wexford, prov. Leinfter, 67 miles from Dublin.

Dublin. It returns 2 members to parliament; patron, lord *Loftus*. This town was formerly walled, and some of the gates still remain. It lies on the river *Barrow*, which is here very deep, and ships of burden can come up to the quay, even when the tide is out. Near this place the rivers *Nore* and *Barrow* unite themselves. The church is large, but the custom-house and quay are both small, and sometimes over flooded many feet. It is one of the staple ports for exporting *wool*, yet its trade is but inconsiderable; *beef* and *butter* are the principal articles exported. Here is a barrack for a troop of horse, and a good ferry into the co. Kilkenny. Near this town is a charter school, which was opened in 1741, for 20 boys. This is also a post town, and gives title of *earl* to the family of *Gore*. It was formerly adorned with many religious houses, among which was a crouched friary, built on the summit of a hill in the town; but one of the friars having killed a principal inhabitant, the whole body of the people arose, put the friars to death, and totally destroyed the friary; on the site of which the monastery of St. *Saviour*, for conventual Franciscans, was afterwards erected by sir *John Devereux*; and the E. end of this last building is now the parish church. A friary for *Eremites*, following the rule of St. *Augustin*, was also founded here in the reign of Edw. III. This town is a vicarage in dioc. of Ferns.

NEWRY, a borough, post and fair town in co. Down, prov. Ulster, above 50 miles N. of Dublin. Lat. 54: 12, lon. 6: 30. It is sit. on the *Newry-water*, which was made navigable by act of parliament; it is the most considerable for trade of any place in this co. tho' not the shire-town to it; and is almost surrounded by mountains and rocky hills, except to the N. and N. W. where a prospect opens into a good country, thro' which a canal is now carried. At the bottom of it runs the *Newry-water*, over which are two stone bridges, one to the *Dublin* road, of 6 arches, and the other in the way to *Armagh* of 10. It has the benefit of a large weekly market on every Thursday, a good market-house, and holds fairs on Mond. after Easter-week, and 29 Oct. As a town of any consequence it owes its rise to sir *Nicholas Bagnal*, knt. who was marshal of *Ireland*, and did many memorable exploits here. He re-edified the town, and erected a church in 1578, about which time he built a strong castle for the defence of the town. Here an abbey of Cistertian monks was founded in 1157, by *Maurice Mac Loughlin*, king of Ireland, and placed under the invocation of St. *Mary*, St. *Patrick*, and St. *Benedict*; the endowments of which were confirmed by *Hugh de Lacey*, earl of Ulster, A. D. 1237. It was called the abbey of *Newry*, in Latin *Nevoracense Monasterium*, and in the foundation charter *Ibar Cyn tracta*, i. e. the flourishing head of a *Yew-tree*; and that the place took its name from *yew* trees, is confirmed by a current tradition of the natives, who say that two large yew trees formerly grew within the precincts of this abbey; and from whence it was called in the barbarous Latin of that age, *Monasterium de viridi ligno*, and in Irish *Na Fur*, "of the yew-trees." And in antient writings the appellation of it for the most part plurally, viz. *the Newrys*. It is recorded that in 1162, the abbey library, all its effects, and a yew tree planted by the hands of St. *Patrick*, were destroyed by fire. In 1688, some *English* soldiers, in burying their dead, discovered in the S. E. quarter of the abbey, the stumps of some trees of fine wood, and without regard to the place, rooted up and converted them to several domestic utensils, the wood being red, and bearing a fine polish. A mitred abbot formerly possessed the lordships of *Newry* and *Mourne*, and exerted therein episcopal jurisdiction, which after the dissolution of the abbey was done by the temporal proprietor; these lordships now claim exemption from episcopal jurisdiction, and the proprietor (Mr. *Needham*) exercises the jurisdiction in his peculiar court, granting marriage licences, probates to wills, &c. under the old monkish seal. Some remains of the chapel of this abbey were standing about 50 years ago. The abbey was converted into a collegiate church for secular priests, by Hen. VIII. A. D. 1543, but a few years after it was dissolved, and granted by Edw. VI. to said marshal *Bagnal*, who made it his dwelling house, and soon after added many castles to the town, some of which still remain. From him is descended Mr. *Needham*, who exercises episcopal jurisdiction as before mentioned, the seal of his court is a mitred abbot in his albe, sitting in a chair supported by two yew trees, with this inscription, " *Sigillum exemptæ jurisdictionis de viridi ligno, alias* Newry *et* Mourne." The church is seated on an eminence at one end of the town. It is a vicarage in dioc. of Dromore. It was ruined in the rebellion of 1641, yet not so, but the steeple and walls remained entire; after the restoration it was in part covered in, and about 1720, the remainder was repaired. In 1729, it was raised 6 feet higher, to make room for a gallery, which the former height would not admit. It was originally built by sir *Nich. Bagnal*, who lies here interred. Not far from the church there is a Presbyterian meeting-house; and also a Roman Catholic chapel. In 1689, the duke of *Berwick* burnt this town, to secure his retreat to Dundalk from the English forces under duke *Schomberg*. *Newry* returns 2 members

bers to parliament, the electors being *potwollopers*. A mile E. of Newry, at a place called
Crown-bridge, is a Danish rath, beautifully sit.
near a pleasing river.

NEWRY-MOUNT, sit. near *Dundalk*, prov. Lein.

NEWSTONE, sit. in bar. Slane, co. Meath,
prov. Leinster.

NEWSTOWN, sit. near *Carlow*, prov. Leinster.

NEWTOWN, sit. in co. Cork, prov. Munster;
where are fairs on 13 May and 25 Sept.—Also
a fair town in co. Leitrim, prov. Connaught;
fairs held 25 Feb. May, Aug. and Nov.—Likewise a fair town in co. Sligo, prov. Connaught;
fair days 13 May and 5 Dec.—Also a fair town
in co. Waterford, prov. Munster; (at *Silver-
mines*) fairs held 1 May and 11 Nov.—Likewise
a post and fair town in co. Wicklow, prov.
Leinster; fairs held Easter-tuesday and 29 Oct.
Also a village sit. in bar. Erris, co. Mayo, prov.
Connaught.—Also a curacy in dioc. of Armagh,
sit. in bar. Ferrard, co. Louth, prov. Leinster.—
Also a chapelry in dioc. of Dublin, sit. in bar.
Newcastle, co. Dublin, prov. Leinster.—Also
a place in bar. Ophaly, co. Kildare, prov. Leinster.—Also a vicarage in dioc. of Meath, sit.
in bar. Kells, co. Meath, prov. Leinster; on
the N. bank of the river Boyne, at this
place, about ¼ a mile below *Trim*, a priory for
regular canons of the congregation of St. *Victor*,
was founded by *Simon de Rochfort*, bishop of
Meath, about the year 1206; he also erected
the church into a cathedral, dedicated to St.
Peter and St. *Paul*. In 1482 *William Shirwood*,
bishop of Meath, was interred here before the
high altar. The remains of the large old
church are still in being, where is also to be
seen an antient tomb, said to have been placed
there for a daughter of king *John*. Here was
also a priory or hospital erected in the 13th
century, for cross bearers, or crouched friars,
and the bishops of Meath were either the
founders, or great benefactors to this house.
The priory stands on the S. side of the river,
a little below the abbey and contiguous to the
bridge; the ruins are extensive, though by no
means remarkable for regularity of stile, nor
have they much appearance of a religious foundation. A square castle adjoins the bridge,
from whence a regular range of building along
the water's-edge, extends to another castle at
the E. end, near which stands the E. window
of a small chapel, of a light triple form, and
on the road side near the castle is a very neat
turret, built in an octagon form. This priory
and its possessions were granted to *Robert Dillon*.

NEWTOWN-ARDES, a borough, post and fair
town in bar. Ardes, co. Down, prov. Ulster,
87 miles from Dublin. Lat. 54: 38. lon. 6: 15.
It is agreeably sit. on the Northern point of

the lake of *Strangford*, which at low water
affords a fine level strand for many miles. It
was erected into a borough town, and incorporated under the name of a *provost*, 12 *burgesses
and commonality*, by patent 11 *Jac.* 1st and the
provost has power to hold plea of any sum not
exceeding 5 marks. The lake *Strangford* is
navigable, and the tide flows up as far as this
town; yet the principal and most beneficial
trade of it, is the linen manufacture, and it
is in repute for the sale of fine *diaper linen*. The
quakers established a factory in it; and the
presbyterians have 2 meeting houses, one of
the *new* and the other of the *old-light*. A convent of Dominican friars was settled here, as
'tis said by the *Savages*, others say by *Walter
de Burgh*, earl of Ulster, in 1244; in which
chapters of the order were held in 1298 and
1312. At the suppression of abbeys it was
granted by king James Ist, with 3 town-lands
belonging to it, to *James* visc. *Clanehoys*, at the
rent of 13s. 4d. They afterwards came by
assignment to *Montgomery*, visc. *Ardes*. The old
church is a large building, divided into aisles,
by 4 handsome stone arches of the *Dorick* order.
It was finished, or at least repaired, in 1632,
as appears by an inscription on the pulpit; the
steeple was finished in 1636. This church is
out of repair, and service performed in a chapel
adjoining to it, built by sir *Robert Colville*, since
the revolution. The entrance into it is by a
large stone door-case, curiously adorned with
sculpture. Within side, it is the neatest piece
of building to be met with in that prov. This
town returns 2 members to parliament; patron,
lord *Caledon*: it is a curacy in dioc. of Down;
and holds fairs on 23 Jan. 14 May, and 23 Sept.

NEWTOWN-BARRY, see *Buncloady*.

NEWTOWN-BELLEW, sit. in bar. Tiaquin, co.
Galway, prov. Connaught, 82 miles from
Dublin. Here are very good flour-mills, and
noted fairs for cattle. Within a mile of it are
the ruins of *Castle-Bellew*, and 6 miles beyond
this town are the ruins of a castle, on a small
lake. Fairs held 28 May, 11 Oct. and Nov.

NEWTOWN-BREDA, a village sit. in bar. Castlereagh, co. Down, prov. Ulster, 94 miles
from Dublin. The church here is remarkably
neat and elegant; it measures 50 feet by 25,
exclusive of the chancel, and is 25 feet in
height. From the middle of the church, on
each side, springs a semicircle of 18 feet diameter, which besides enlarging the room, adds
greatly to the beauty of the building. The steeple with the spire, built according to the exact
proportions of architecture, attracts the eyes
of all travellers. This church was erected under the direction of Mr. *Castell*, at the sole
expence of lady viscountess dowager *Middleton*.

Not

Not far from this place is *Belvoir*, a fine feat of lord *Dungannon*.

NEWTOWN-BUTLER, a fair town fit. in bar. Coole, co. Fermanagh, prov. Ulfter, 65 miles from Dublin. It gives title of *baron* to the earl of *Lanefborough*. Fairs held 12 May, 5 Aug. 7 Nov. and 5 Dec.

NEWTOWN-CORRY, fit. in co. Monaghan, prov. Ulfter. A charter fchool was opened here in 1740, for the reception of 40 children.

NEWTOWN-CUNNINGHAM, fit. in bar. Raphoe, co. Donegal, prov. Ulfter, 122 miles from Dublin. Near 2 miles from which are the ruins of a caftle. Fairs held 29 Oct. It is otherwife written *Newtown-conyngham*.

NEWTOWN-EYRE, fit. in co. Galway, prov. Connaught. A charter fchool was opened here in 1740, for the reception of 40 boys.

NEWTOWN-FARTULLAGH, a rectory in dioc. of Meath, fit. in bar. Moycafhel, co. Weftmeath, prov. Leinfter.

NEWTOWN-FORBES, fit. in bar. Longford, co. Longford, prov. Leinfter; fairs held Eafter-Tuefday, 4 Sept. and 31 Oct. It is diftant 61 miles from Dublin.

NEWTOWN-FORTESCUE, a village fit. in bar. Slane, co. Meath, prov. Leinfter.

NEWTOWN-GLENS, fit. in bar. Glenarm, co. Antrim, prov. Ulfter, 109 miles from Dublin. 1 mile from which are the ruins of *Red-caftle*. 3 miles beyond it are the ruins of a church.

NEWTOWN-GORE, fit. in co. Leitrim, prov. Connaught; fairs held 26 June and 15 Oct.

NEWTOWN-HAMILTON, fit. in bar. Fews, co. Armagh, prov. Ulfter, 53 miles from Dublin; 3 miles from it are the ruins of a barrack, built when the adjacent mountains were infefted with robbers. Near this place, the antient Irifh have recorded, that a battle was fought between *O'Neill* of Ulfter, called the *Blackbeard*, and one of the princes of *Louth*, in which many were flain on both fides, and where *O'Neill* alfo fell: the quarrel is faid to have originated at a feaft given on the fpot, by the prince of Louth's fetting fire to O'Neill's beard. This village is a rectory in dioc. of Armagh.

NEWTOWN-LENAN, a rectory in dioc. of Lifmore, fit. in bar. Iffa and Offa, co. Tipperary, prov. Munfter.

NEWTOWN-LIMAVADY, a borough and poft town in bar. Kenoght, co. Londonderry, prov. Ulfter, 106 miles from Dublin; fairs held 28 March, 13 June, 12 July and 29 Oct. It returns 2 members to parliament, patron, Mr. *Connolly*.

NEWTOWN-MOUNTKENNEDY, a village and poft town, fit. in bar. Newcaftle, co. Wicklow, prov. Leinfter, 17 miles from Dublin. In its neighbourhood are the beautiful feats and im-

provements of general *Conyngham* and Mr. *Tottenham*.

NEWTOWN-PERY, adjoining to, and may be confidered as part of the city of *Limerick*, prov. Munfter; the ftreets of it were marked out by the proprietor, *Edm. Sexton Pery*, now lord *Pery*, in 1769, fince which it has advanced rapidly in improvement, and forms an avenue to the city of Limerick, not to be excelled any where in the kingdom. This place was called *S. Prior's land*, and belonged to one of the religious houfes in *Limerick*; they were fupprefled in 1537, and the land was granted to lord *Pery's* anceftor, in 1543: St. *George's church* here, was opened firft for divine fervice on 14 June, 1789, it was fo called in honour of his prefent majefty; the church is light and elegant, of an oblong form; the Eaftern window is a beautiful antique of the 13th century, preferved and fent there by lady *Hartftonge*, from the church of the old Francifcan convent, in St. Francis's abbey.

NEWTOWN-SAVILLE, fit. in bar. Clogher, co. Tyrone, prov. Ulfter; fairs held 1 May and Nov.

NEWTOWN-STEWART, fit. in bar. Strabane, co. Tyrone, prov. Ulfter, 94 miles from Dublin. 2 miles W. of which is *Baron's-court*, a noble feat of the earl of *Abercorn*. Fairs held 28 March, 2 June, 10 Oct. and 10 Dec.

NICHOLASTOWN, a vicarage in dioc. of Dublin, fit. in bar. Kilkea, co. Kildare, prov. Leinfter.

NIER *river*, fit. in bar. Glanehiry, co. Waterford, prov. Munfter.

NINCH, fit. at the mouth of the river *Nanny*, and oppofite to *Ballygart*, in co. Meath, prov. Leinfter.

NINE-MILE-HOUSE, fit. in bar. Slewardagh, co. Tipperary, prov. Munfter, 71 miles from Dublin.—Alfo a place of fame name in co. Tyrone, prov. Ulfter, 78 miles from Dublin; half-way between Dungannon and Omagh. Within a mile of which are the ruins of a church.—Alfo a place fit. near Kilkenny, prov. Leinfter.

NINETEEN-MILE-HOUSE, fit. in co. Kildare, prov. Leinfter, near 20 miles from Dublin.

NIXON-HALL, fit. near *Ennifkillen*, prov. Ulft.

NIXON-LODGE, fit. near *Belturbet*, prov. Ulft.

NOBBER, a village in bar. Morgallion, co. Meath, prov. Leinfter, 33 miles from Dublin. Remarkable for being the birth place of *Turlogh O'Carrolan*, the famous *Irifh bard*; who was born there, in the year 1670. He died in March, 1738, in the 68th year of his age, at *Alderford*, a feat in the co. Rofcommon, prov. Connaught; and was interred in the parifh church of *Kilronan*, in the dioc. of *Ardagh*. Fairs held here 25 April and May, 20 June, 15 Aug.

15 Aug. 13 Oct. and 14 Nov. This is a curacy in dioc. of Meath.

NOGHAVAL, a rectory in dioc. of Cork, fit. in bar. Kinalea, co. Cork, prov. Munfter; the church of which ftands on the verge of this co. near which is the ftump of a round tower, which with the church, are dedicated to St. *Finian*, whofe feftival is here celebrated on the 13 Dec.

NOGHEVAL, a curacy in dioc. of Meath, fit. in bar. Kilkennyweft, co. Weftmeath, prov. Leinfter.

NOGHVALE, a vicarage in dioc. of Kilfenora, fit. in bar. Burrin, co. Clare, prov. Munfter.

NOHOVAL, a rectory in dioc. of Ardfert, fit. in bar. Truaghnacmy, co. Kerry, prov. Munfter.

NOHOVALDALY, a vicarage in dioc. of Ardfert, fit. in bar. Duhallow, co. Cork, prov. Munfter.

NONANE, a rectory in dioc. of Cloyne, fit. in bar. Condons, co. Cork, prov. Munfter.

NORE, a large river in co. Kilkenny, prov. Leinfter, which joins the river *Barrow* near *New-Rofs*, and they both difcharge themfelves into the bay of *Waterford*.

NORMAN'S-GROVE, fit. in co. Meath, prov. Leinfter, within a few miles of Dublin.

NORRIS, a fair town in co. Armagh, prov. Ulfter; fairs held 12 Feb. 14 May and 10 Oct.

NORTH-CAPE, fit. in co. Donegal, prov. Ulfter.

NORTH-DOWN, *fands* fo called, which lie a little way off the fhore of co. Wicklow, prov. Leinfter.

NORTH-ISLAND, otherwife called *Innis Tufkart*, one of the *Blafquet* iflands, fo called; fit. in co. Kerry, prov. Munfter. See *Blafques*.

NORTH-ROCKS, (otherwife called St. *Patrick's* rocks, from a feat of ftone amongft them called St. *Patrick's* chair, from whence the rocks have taken this fecond name) fit. in the harbour of Donaghadee, co. Down, prov. Ulfter. From N. to S. they are about ⅝ of a league, between which is clean good ground. But care muft be taken of the S. rock, on which many fhips have perifhed; for it is overflowed by every tide, and no crew can fave their lives if the wind blows high; this rock ftands a full mile from the fhore.

NOTIUM-PROMONTORIUM; the antient name of a promontory in the S. of Ireland, mentioned by *Ptolemy*, and thought by *Cambden* to be *Beer-head*; but moft probably it was *Miffen-head*, at the entrance of Dunmanus bay, in co. Cork, prov. Munfter. Lat. 51 : 14, lon. 9 : 35.

NUCK'STOWN, fee *Newceftown*.

NURNEY, a rectory in dioc. of Kildare, fit. in bar. Ophaly, co. Kildare, prov. Leinfter.— Alfo a rectory in dioc. of Leighlin, fit. in bar. Idrone, co. Carlow, prov. Leinfter.

NYMPH-BANK, fit. about 10 leagues off the coaft of the co. Waterford, prov. Munfter; it is a great fifhing place, and 11 leagues S. S. E. from the high head of *Dungarvan*. It abounds with cod, ling, fkate, bream, whiting, and other fifh; which was difcovered by Mr. *Doyle*, who on 15 July, 1736, failed to it, in company with 7 men, on board the *Nymph*, a fmall veffel of about 12 guns. This place is well adapted for a fifhing company, the great public advantages of which muft be very evident.

NYMPH-FIELD, fit. near *Boyle*, prov. Conna.

NYMPH-HALL, a handfome feat, fit. in the parifh of Killmacombe, co. Waterford, prov. Munfter.

NYNCH, a feat, fit. near *Julianftown*, co. Meath, prov. Leinfter.

O A

OAK-PARK, fit. near *Carlow*, prov. Leinfter.

OAK-PORT, fit. near *Boyle*, prov. Connaught.

OAT-FIELD, fit. near *Ballinafloe*, prov. Connaught.

OAT-LANDS, fit. near *Balbriggan*, prov. Leinfter.—Alfo near *Roftrevor*, prov. Ulfter.

OBERY'S-MILL, fit. in bar. Oneiland, co. Armagh, prov. Ulfter.

OBOCA, the antient name of a river or bay in the E. of Ireland, mentioned by *Ptolemy*, and thought by *Camden* and *Rich. Cirenc.* to be Arklow river; but was moft probably the bay of Dublin, as the foreign merchants, from whom *Ptolemy* received his account of thefe iflands, feldom vifited fuch obfcure rivers as that of *Arklow*.

OBRENNAN, a rectory in dioc. of Ardfert, fit. in bar. Truaghnacmy, co. Kerry, prov. Munfter.

O'BRIEN'S-BRIDGE, fit. in bar. Tullagh, co. Clare, prov. Munfter, 87 miles from Dublin. Where are fairs on 25 July and 7 Nov. At this place is *Mountpelier*, which has an excellent fulphureous fpring, famous for curing feveral diforders. 2¼ miles beyond *O'Brien's-bridge*, are the ruins of *Coolaftigue caftle*. 1 mile farther are the ruins of *Rhinrow caftle*; and about 1½ mile beyond them, are the ruins of *Caftle Troy*.

ODDER, a chapelry in dioc. of Meath, fit. 2 miles S. of *Tarah*, in bar. Skryne, co. Meath, prov. Leinfter. The family of *Barnwall* founded a nunnery here in honour of St. *Brigid*, for regular canoneffes of the order of St. Auguftin; to whom in the year 1195, pope *Celeftine* the 3d, granted a confirmation of their poffeffions. Several cells of nuns in Meath, were annexed to this houfe, and the prior of the Virgin Mary of Louth, had the first voice in electing the abbefs of it by letters patent, dated in 1418. *Margaret Silk*, the last abbefs, furrendered this nunnery, &c. anno 31ft *Hen.* 8th.

ODOGH, a vicarage in dioc. of Offory, fit. in bar. Faffachdining, co. Kilkenny, prov. Leinfter.

ODORNEY, the ruins of an antient abbey, a venerable remain of antiquity; fit. not far from *Ardfert*, and near the river *Brick*, in bar. Clanmaurice, co. Kerry, prov. Munfter. It was founded in 1154, under the invocation of the Virgin Mary, and otherwife called *Kirie Eleyfon*; and fupplied with monks from the Ciftertian abbey of *Mogis*, in co. Limerick. The abbot was a lord of parliament. This being a very rich abbey, *Edmund* lord *Kerry*, was in 1537, created baron of *Odorney* and vifc. *Kilmaule*; in the fame year a grant was made him of feveral religious houfes, among which was this abbey, to him and his iffue male, but in default thereof, they were reverted to the crown. 28 June, 39 queen *Eliz.* a part of the poffeffions of this abbey, was granted to the provoft and fellows of Trin. coll. Dublin. This building is now a fhapelefs ruin, nothing but the old walls are to be feen, which refemble thofe of an antient church without a fteeple.

OFFA and IFFA, a bar. in co. Tipperary, prov. Munfter.

OFFALY, fee *Ophaly*.

OFFERILLAN, a vicarage in dioc. of Offory, fit. in bar. Upper Offory, Queen's co. prov. Leinfter.

OGHAVAL, a vicarage in dioc. of Tuam, fit. in bar. Morifk, co. Mayo, prov. Connaught.

OGONILLOE, a vicarage in dioc. of Killaloe, fit. in bar. Tullagh, co Clare, prov. Munfter.

OGRAM-LOUGH, a *lake*, fit. in bar. Tullagh, co. Clare, prov. Munfter.

OGULLA, a rectory in dioc. of Elphin, fit. in bar. Rofcommon, co. Rofcommon, prov. Connaught.

OIGHMAGH, now *Omagh*, in co. Tyrone, prov. Ulfter, where was one of the antient raths or caftles of the old chiefs of that country.

OILEACH, a rath or palace of the *O'Neals*, fit. 3 miles from *Derry*, in prov. Ulfter.

OIRTHER, a diftrict in the S. part of the co. Armagh, prov. Ulfter; the hereditary chiefs of which were the *O'Hanlons*, fome of whom were in poffeffion of their antient patrimony, at the commencement of the laft century.

OLAVES *(St.)* a parifh in the city of Waterford, prov. Munfter; the church of which is fit. near the cathedral. It was rebuilt in 1734, and confecrated that year on 29 July, by *Tho. Milles*, bifhop of Waterford and Lifmore. The feats are fo difpofed, that the whole congregation can only face to the E.

OLD-ABBEY, fit. in co. Cork, prov. Munfter, where fairs are held on 8 days before Afcenfion-day, and 3 Nov.

OLD-BAWN, a fmall village, fit. in co. Dublin, prov. Leinfter, ⅜ of a mile on the left of *Tallagh*, and 4¼ miles from Dublin. Here was a handfome feat of the late fir *James Tynte*, bart. This place enjoys a pure air, and is fit. in the midft of fine meadow fields.

OLD-BRIDGE, fit. 2 miles from *Drogheda*, in co. Louth, prov. Leinfter; at this place an *obelifk* is erected on the banks of the river *Boyne*, to commemorate the victory gained by king William III. over the forces of James II. It is feated on a rock, and efteemed the handfomeft of the kind in Europe. It was erected in 1736, and is an elegant pillar, 150 feet high and 20 wide. At this place the main body of king William's army croffed the *Boyne*, under the command of duke *Schomberg*, who was unfortunately killed in the river, by a piftol fhot.

OLD-BURT, fit. in bar. Carbery, co. Kildare, prov. Leinfter.

OLD-CASTLE, a poft and fair town in bar. Half fowre, co. Meath, prov. Leinfter, 41 miles from Dublin. Fairs held laft Monday in Jan. 2 Monday in June, July, 20 Aug. laft Monday in Sept. 2 Monday in Dec It is a vicarage in dioc. of Meath.—Alfo a place in co. Cork, prov. Munfter; where are fairs on 1 May and 4 Sept.

OLD-CONNAUGHT, a village fit in bar. Half-Rathdown, co. Dublin prov. Leinfter, within 1¼ mile of *Bray*, and about 8½ miles from Dublin. Near it are fome handfome feats. It is a vicarage in dioc. of Dublin.

OLD-CONNEL, a vicarage in dioc. of Kildare, fit. in bar. Great Connel, co. Kildare, prov. Leinfter: here is a fine antient rath.

OLD-COURT, fit. near *Skibbereen*, co. Cork, prov. Munfter.—Alfo near *Bray*, prov. Leinfter.

OLD-DORICK, fit. in bar. Slewmurgy, Queen's co prov. Leinfter.

OLD-FLEET, a harbour in co. Antrim, prov. Ulfter.

OLD-GRANGE, fee *Grange (old.)*

OLD-HEAD, fit. in co. Cork, prov. Munfter, 4 miles S. of Kinfale, in the bar. of *Courcies*: it is a promontory, running far into the fea, on which is a light-houfe, for the convenience of fhipping. A mile from its extremity, is an antient caftle of the lords of *Kinfale*, built from one fide of the ifthmus to the other, which defended all the lands towards the head; this place was formerly called *Duncearma*, and was the old feat of the Irifh kings: the ifthmus by the working of the fea, was quite penetrated through, fo as to form a ftupendous arch, under which boats might pafs from one bay to the other; among the rocks of this coaft, there

are

are aviaries of good *hawks*, alfo the *fea-eagle* or *ofprey*, build their nefts and breed in them.

OLD-KILCULLEN, fee *Kilcullen*.

OLD-LEIGHLIN, fee *Leighlin*.

OLD-MERRION, fit. in co. Dublin, prov. Leinfter, about 2¼ miles from the metropolis; here is *Merrion caftle*, and the remains of an old church.

OLD-MILL-STREET, fit. in co. Cork, prov. Munfter; fairs held 12 June, Sept. and Dec.

OLD-ROSS, a village fit. in bar. Bantry, co. Wexford, prov. Leinfter, about 15 miles from Wexford-town, and 63 from Dublin. It is a vicarage in dioc. of Ferns.

OLD-STONE, fit. in co. Antrim, prov. Ulfter, fairs held 13 June and 22 Oct.

OLD-TOWN, fit. in co. Donegal, prov. Ulfter; fairs held 4 May, 8 June, 31 July and 8 Oct.— Alfo a place in co. Dublin, prov. Leinfter;— and another near *Naas*, in co. Kildare, prov. Leinfter.

OLECH NEID, antiently fit. in the bar. of Innis-Owen, in co. Donegal, prov. Ulfter.

OLER'STOWN, fit. in bar. Louth, co. Louth, prov. Leinfter.

OLNEMACT, the antient name of Connaught; this prov. probably obtained this denomination on the retreat of the Bolgæ from the *Tuath de Danans*, or Caledonian tribes, on their arrival in Ulfter, about the commencement of the 1ft century, prior to the Chriftian æra; it was alfo called *Coumaene*: the government of the Olne-machts was founded by *Eochy Fealogh* or *Crothar*, on his fettlement at *Croghan*, about the time of *Auguftus Cæfar*.

OMAGH, a bar. in co. Tyrone, prov. Ulfter, in which is a poft and fair town of fame name, diftant about 87 miles from Dublin. This is the affizes town of that co. Lat. 54 : 30, lon. 7 : 40. Its antient name is *Oigh-magh*, i. e. the refidence of the chief, it being formerly one of the antient raths or caftles of the old chief of that country. It was burnt down in 1743, but has fince been rebuilt. There are two dif-fenting meeting-houfes, and one church; at the N. end of the town, are the ruins of a caf-tle; and 4 miles from it are the ruins of a church. Fairs held 12 Jan. 2 Thurfd. O. S. Feb. 5 April, 2 Thurfd. O. S. May, laft Thurfd. June, 5 Aug. 2 Thurfd. O. S. Aug. 2 Oct. 3 Nov. and 3 Thurfd. Nov. An abbey was founded here fo early as the year 792, and in the 15th century, a monaftery for Francifcan friars of the third order was erected here. In fome old books we find this place called *Drum-maragh*.

OMERO, fit. to the E. of *Macroomp*, in co. Cork, prov. Munfter.

OMEY-ISLAND, fit. off the coaft of bar. Bal-linabinch, co. Galway, prov. Connaught.

ONEILLAND, a bar. in co. Armagh, prov. Ulfter; it is fometimes improperly written *Oneland*.

ONREAGH *river*, fit. in bar. Omagh, co. Tyrone, prov. Ulfter.

OON-A-GLOUR, a confiderable cavern, near the river *Phynifk*, co. Waterford, prov. Mun-ftery it is formed in a lime-ftone rock, and is tolerably dry; being about 100 feet fquare, but has its roof compofed of a great number of loofe ftones, which feem ready to tumble on one's head; there are feveral inward clofets, and fmall chambers on the left hand, and in moft places there diftils a limpid, infipid matter, the quantity of which increafes, the farther you enter into thefe fubterraneous paffages.

OON-A-MORT, a fmall cave, in co. Water-ford, prov. Munfter; not far from, and fimi-lar to that called *Oon-a-glour*.

OONBURY *river*, fit. in co. Cork. prov. Munft.

OPHALY, or *Offaly*, a bar. in co. Kildare, prov. Leinfter.

ORAN, a rectory in dioc. of Elphin, fit. in bar. Half-Ballimoe, co. Rofcommon, prov. Connaught. St. *Patrick* founded a church here, of which St. *Cethecus* was bifhop, who lies here interred. This place continues remarkable for the many pilgrimages made thereto. Near the church, is one of the antient round towers.

ORANAGH, fit. in bar. Upper Offory, Queen's co. prov. Leinfter.

ORANGE-FIELD, an improved feat in the bar. of *Caftlereagh*, co. Down, prov. Ulfter.

ORANMORE, fit. in bar. Dunkellin, co. Gal-way, prov. Connaught, 103 miles from Dublin. Between it and *Galway*, are the ruins of feveral caftles. It is a fmall village, fit. at the mouth of Galway bay, and has a bridge over a fmall ftream; and near it is a feat of the *Blake* family. Fairs held 23 May and 20 Oct. This is a vicar-age in dioc. of Tuam.

ORBSEN-LOUGH, an antient name of Lough *Coribb*, in prov. Connaught.

ORCHARD, fit. in co. Carlow, prov. Lein-fter; fairs held Whit-tuefday and 2 Oct.

OREGAN, a vicarage in dioc. of Kildare, fit. in bar. Tinehinch, Queen's co. prov. Leinfter.

ORGIEL, an antient extenfive diftrict, com-prehending the prefent co.'s of Louth, Mo-naghan and Armagh, which was governed by its proper king; fubject however, in fome ref-pects, to the fupreme monarch of Ireland. The fovereignty of this diftrict, was generally invefted in the family of the *O'Carrols*.

ORIEL ABBEY, fit. in co. Kerry, prov. Mun-fter; the ruins of which remain about a mile S. of *Fairy-Rock*.

ORIOR, an antient bar. in co. Armagh, prov. Ulfter; formerly the territorial diftrict of the *O'Hanlons*.

ORISTOWN,

ORISTOWN, fit. in co. Meath, prov. Leinfter; fairs held 13 May, and 11 Oct.

ORITOR, a fair town in bar. Dungannon, co. Tyrone, prov. Ulfter; fairs held 2 Wednefd. July, 3 Aug. 10 Oct. and 3 Wednefd. Nov.

ORLARE, or *Urlare*, fit. in bar. Coftello, co. Mayo, prov. Connaught. One of the family of *Nangle* founded a monaftery here for Dominican friars, and dedicated it to St. *Thomas.* This family afterwards took the name of *Coftello*, and became lords of the bar. This was eftablifhed in 1430, and pope *Eugene* 4th, granted licence to it by a bull, bearing date 18 March, 1434. It lay in a retired fituation, and was therefore appointed for the general reception of novices, throughout the prov. of Connaught. We are told that in antient times there was a town here, but at prefent there is no veftige of one to be feen; and the ruins of the abbey alone, preferves this place from total oblivion. On the diffolution of monafteries, this friary was granted to lord *Dillon.*

ORMOND. There are 2 bar.'s of this name, fit. in co. Tipperary, prov. Munfter, diftinguifhed into *upper Ormond* and *lower Ormond.* The antient title of *duke of Ormond*, belonged to the *Butler* family, to whom it now gives title of *earl.*

ORNAMORE *ifland*, fit. near *Dog's-head-point*, co. Galway, prov. Connaught.

ORRERY, a bar. in co. Cork, prov. Munfter; which gives title of earl to a branch of the *Boyle* family. This and *Kilmore* forms but one bar. formerly named *Orriria Barria*, the *Barrys* having had poffeffion of the greateft part of this country. *Orrery* and *Kilmore* contain 11 parifhes.

OSBERSTOWN, fit. near *Sallins*, in bar. Naas, co. Kildare, prov. Leinfter; here is an antient burial place and the ruins of a church.

OSRAIGH, the prefent bar. of *Offory*, in Queen's co. prov. Leinfter. The diftrict originally extended through the whole country, between the rivers *Nore* and *Suir*; being bounded on the N. and E. by the *Nore*, and W. and S. by the *Suir*, the hereditary chiefs of which were denominated *Giola Padruic*, or *Mac Gilla Padruic*: thefe princes make a confiderable figure in the antient Irifh hiftory; and one in particular diftinguifhed himfelf in the fervice of his country againft the Englifh, on their firft invafion. In an early period they were diffpoffeffed of part of their patrimony, by the kings of Cafhel; and the Southern parts were occupied by the *Butlers*, and other Englifh adventurers; but the Northern parts remained to the original proprietors, who on their connection with the Englifh, took or changed their name to *Fitzpatrick*; whofe defcendants to this day, enjoy a large landed property in the dominion of their anceftors, with the title of *earl* of *upper Offory.*

OSSORY, an antient bifhoprick, in prov. Leinfter, which was originally eftablifhed at *Saigar*, and afterwards at *Aghavoe*, and was founded very early in the 5th century. It includes almoft the whole of co. Kilkenny, a good part of the Queen's co. and part of the King's co. extending 36 miles in length, from N. to S. and 23 in breadth. The cathedral is a large handfome building, dedicated to St. *Canice*, whence the borough of *Irifhtown*, in which it ftands (adjoining to the city of *Kilkenny)* derives its name. The bifhop has a good houfe clofe to the cathedral, which is fit. about 30 miles from the fartheft part of the dioc. This fee is rated in the king's books at 66*l.* 13*s.* 4*d.* but is worth 2,600*l.* per ann.

OSSORY-UPPER, a bar. in Queen's co. prov. Leinfter; its antient name was *Ofraigii*, and it was a part of the diftrict of the *Mac Gill Padruics*, now *Fitzpatricks*, to whom it gives title of *earl* of *upper Offory.*

OUCHTERARD, fee *Oughterard.*

OUGHTERAGH, a parifh in co. Waterford, prov. Munfter.

OUGHTERARD, or *Ouchterard*, a poft town in bar. Moycullin, co. Galway, prov. Connaught, 119 miles from Dublin; within 2 miles of which are the ruins of a church, and a caftle.—Alfo a rectory in dioc. of Kildare, fit. near *Bifhop's-court*, in bar. Salt, co. Kildare, prov. Leinfter. Here, on the fummit of a hill, ftand the old church and round tower of *Oughterard.* By inquifition, 23 Feb. 33 queen *Eliz.* it was found that 12 acres of land, to the S. of the antient town of *Clonæaglifh*, were granted to this chantry contrary to the ftatute.

OUGHTER-LOUGH, fee *Lough Outer.*

OUGHTNANNA, a rectory in dioc. of Kilfenora, fit. in bar. Burrin, co. Clare, prov. Munfter.

OURRED-HILL, a *mountain*, fit. in bar. Moycullin, co. Galway, prov. Connaught.

OUTERAGH, a rectory in dioc. of Lifmore, fit. in bar. Middlethird, co. Tipperary, prov. Munfter.

OUTLAR, fit. in co. Wexford, prov. Leinfter; fairs held 6 Jan. and Shrove-tuefday.

OUTRAGH, a rectory in dioc. of Offory, fit. in bar. Shellilogher, co. Kilkenny, prov. Leinfter.—Alfo a vicarage in dioc. of Kilmore, fit. in bar. Carrigallen, co. Leitrim, prov. Connau.

OUVANE *river*, fit. in co. Cork, prov. Munft.

OVENS, a remarkable cave, with other fmaller ones, fit. in co. Cork, prov. Munfter, about 130 miles from Dublin. The whole form a perfect labyrinth under ground.

OVOCA *river*, fit. in bar. Arklow, co. Wicklow, prov. Leinfter; on which the town of *Arklow* ftands.

OWEN-

OWEN-NASSA, a river fit. in Queen's co. prov. Leinster.

OWENS, a village fit. in bar. Muskerry, co. Cork, prov. Munster.

OWEY, an *Island* fit. near the coast of bar. Boylagh, co. Donegal, prov. Ulster.

OWNALLO *river*, fit. in bar. Duhallow, co. Cork, prov. Munster.

OWNDALLOW, a *river* in co. Cork, prov. Munster.

OWNEY, a bar. in co. Tipperary, prov. Munster.

OWNEYBEG, or *Owynbeg*, a bar. in co. Limerick, prov. Munster.

OXMANTOWN, formerly an outlet of the city of Dublin, but now included in it; its antient name was *Ostmantown*, which it took from the *Ostmen*; it is now almost entirely built on, tho' formerly it was an open plain. *Holinshed* tells us that in the further end of this field there was a hole or cave, commonly termed *Scaldbrother's hole*, a labyrinth reaching two large miles under the earth. This hole was in old time (says he) frequented by a notorious thief named *Scaldbrother*, wherein he would hide all the plunder he could make, and who was so swift footed as to escape all his pursuers, but being at last overtaken, he was executed for his offences. The same writer tells us, that in 1189 there were three robbers and outlaws in England, two of whom were named *Robert Hood* and *little John*, the latter fled to Ireland, where the citizens of Dublin finding him to be an excellent archer, requested him to exhibit a specimen of his skill; upon which he stood on Dublin bridge, and shot his arrow into Oxmantown-green, as far as a little hillock, which from thence (says Holinshed) received the name of *little John's shot*. This place gives title of *baron* to the family of *Parsons*.

OXMOUNTAIN, mountains fit. in bar. Tyreragh, co. Sligo, prov. Connaught.

OYSTER-HAVEN, fit. in bar. Kinalea, co. Cork, prov. Munster, (so called from its being famous for *Oysters*.) 'Tis seldom frequented by vessels; the entrance is narrow, but sufficiently deep. Off this haven are high rocks, called the *Sovereigns*, never covered, and therefore not dangerous. About a mile S. W. of Oyster-haven, is *Hangman-point*, and about ½ a mile more N. W. by W. is *Prehan-point*, being the E. point of *Kinsale* harbour, from which a little to the S. E. lie three small rocks called the *Bullman*; they are very foul, but between them and the main, is a safe passage of 4 fathom water.

OYSTER *Island*, fit. off the bar. Carbury, co. Sligo, prov. Connaught.

PACKENHAM-HALL, a seat of lord *Longford*, fit. near *Castlepollard*, co. Westmeath, prov. Leinster.

PAINESTOWN, a rectory in dioc. of Leighlin, fit. in bar. Catherlogh, co. Carlow, prov. Leinster.—Also a rectory in dioc. of Meath, fit. in bar. Duleek, co Meath, prov. Leinster.

PALACE-ANN, a pleasant seat fit. a little E. of *Inisheen*, in co. Cork, prov. Munster.

PALATINE-TOWN, fit. in bar. Catherlogh, co. Carlow, prov. Leinster; fairs held 26 March, 23 April, 17 June and 6 Nov. This place is so called from a colony of industrious people, who were driven from their native country, by the persecuting arms of Lewis XIVth. of France.

PALICEGREAN, a village fit. in bar. Coonagh, co. Limerick, prov. Munster. It is a rectory in dioc. of Emly.

PALLAS-INN, fit. in King's co. prov. Leinster; 51 miles from Dublin. About ¼ of a mile beyond which are the ruins of a castle; there are the ruins of 4 other castles, between this place and Frankford.

PALLICE, fit. about 11 miles N. W. of *Portumna*, co. Galway, prov. Connaught. A friary dedicated to the Virgin Mary for Carmelite friars, was founded here in the 14th century by *Bermingham*, baron of *Athenry*.—Also a place in bar. Duhallow, co. Cork, prov. Munster.

PALLIS, fit. in co. Limerick, prov. Munster, 106 miles from Dublin. Here is a church and a very fine mount.—Also a fair town in co. Tipperary, prov. Munster; fairs are held on 28 October.

PALLIS-LOUGH, see *Lough Pallas*.

PALLISMORE, fit. in bar. Owney and Arra, co. Tipperary, prov. Munster.

PALMERSTOWN, a pleasant village fit. above 3 miles from Dublin, in bar. Newcastle, co. Dublin, prov. Leinster. It is a curacy in dioc. of Dublin, and stands on very high ground, enjoying a serene air; and is much frequented by travellers on account of its being in the great road to *Lucan*, *Leixlip*, *Mullingar* and *Longford*. Here are the ruins of a church. There is a great horse fair held here annually on 21 August. This place gives title of visc. to the family of *Temple*. It appears that a leper house or hospital was antiently erected here; the custody of which was granted in 1427 by *Hen.* VIth. to *John Wale.*—There is also a village of same name fit. in bar. *Balruddery, rudd·ry*, co. Dublin, prov. Leinfter, which is likewife a curacy in dioc. of Dublin.—-Alfo a feat fit. near Killala, in co. Mayo, prov. Connaught, oppofite to which are the ruins of an abbey.

PAPS, *mountains* fit. in bar. Magunihy, co. Kerry, prov. Munfter.

PARK, fit. near *Rofcrea*, prov. Munfter.

PARKGALE, a village fit. in bar. Toome, co. Antrim, prov. Ulfter.

PARKHILL, fit. in bar. Tyrhugh, co. Donegal, prov. Ulfter.

PARK-HOUSE, fit. in bar. Ballinacour, co. Wicklow, prov. Leinfter.

PARK-PHŒNIX, fee *Phœnix-park*.

PARKSTOWN, fit. in bar. Lune, co. Meath, prov. Leinfter.—Alfo in bar. Igrin, co. Kilkenny, prov. Leinfter.

PARSONSTOWN, a vicarage in dioc. of Armagh, fit. in bar. Ferrard, co. Louth, prov. Leinfter.—Alfo a name given to *Birr*, in bar. Ballibritt, King's co. prov. Leinfter.

PARTEEN, fit. in bar. Bunratty, co. Clare, prov. Munfter; 93 miles from Dublin. It is pleafantly feated by the fide of the river *Shannon*.

PARTREE, fit. in co. Mayo, prov. Connaught, 101 miles from Dublin; within 1½ mile of which, are the ruins of a caftle, and near *Partree*, are the ruins of a church.

PASSAGE, a place fit. in bar. Kinalea, co. Cork, prov. Munfter, 130 miles from Dublin. It is a fmall village, feparated from the *great Ifland*, on which the town of *Cove* is feated. Here all fhips of burden unload, and their cargoes are carried up to *Cork*, either on fmall cars drawn by one horfe, or in veffels of fmall fize, the channel higher up admitting only thofe of 150 tons burden, tho' the harbour ftretches above a mile from fhore to fhore. There are but few houfes at this place, but fairs are held here on 1 May and 25 July.—There is alfo a place of fame name in bar. Gualtiere, co. Waterford, prov. Munfter, above 129 miles from Dublin. It is fit. under a hill fo fteep, that few perfons (except the inhabitants) care to ride it up or down. On the top the church is erected, to which it is not a very eafy walk, and as the hill overhangs them confiderably and lies N. and S. they have but little of the fun after mid-day, efpecially in winter; here is an excellent road, where 500 fail of fhips may ride fafely. Where the *Pier* now ftands, was formerly a block-houfe, mounted with feveral great guns, then under the command of the governor of *Duncannon fort*, which is about a league diftance on the co. *Wexford* fide. In 1649, *Cromwell* fent 6 troops of Dragoons, and 4 of horfe, to take this place, which after fome difpute,

was effected. On 20 Feb. 1663, the duke of *Ormond* was made governor of the port and town of *Paffage* for life. Fairs are held here on 6 May, 12 June, 8 Sept. and 12 Nov.

PASS-*if*-YOU-CAN, a place fo called fit. in co. Dublin, prov. Leinfter, within 5 miles of the metropolis, it lies about 2 miles beyond *Finglafs*; here is *Plunket's caftle*, feated in the midft of a plantation of trees.—There is alfo a place of this name in bar. Moyafhel, co. *Weftmeath*, prov. Leinfter, 41 miles from Dublin; two miles from which are the ruins of a church.

PASS-*of*-KILBRIDE, fit. in co. Weftmeath, prov. Leinfter, 33 miles from Dublin; ¼ a mile beyond which are the ruins of a church, and about a mile farther, are the ruins of a church and caftle.

PATRICK, or *Knockpatrick*, a mountain in co. Limerick, prov. Munfter.

PATRICK's-ISLE, fit. in co. Dublin, prov. Leinfter, nearly oppofite *Balruddery* town; here are the ruins of a church dedicated to St. *Patrick*. It is faid this ifland was the firft fpot on which that faint landed, after his arrival in Ireland; and that the church likewife was built under his own immediate direction, at which time the *ifland* was parted from the main land, by only a fmall ftream of water at fpring tides, at other times acceffable on foot, but the interval is now impaffable at the loweft ebb of the tide, and on that account the facred pile has been fuffered to fall to ruins; on the fhore near this ifland, ftands the fifhing town of *Skerries*, to whofe inhabitants the faid church originally ferved as a place of worfhip, to fupply which, another church has been erected, which they call St. *Patrick's New church*.

PATRICK's-PURGATORY, fit. in an ifland in *Lough Derg*, co. Donegal, prov. Ulfter. It was firft fixed in the ifland called St. *Fintans*, but it being near to the fhore, and a bridge from the main land giving the people a free and eafy accefs to it, the cave was clofed up, and another opened in a leffer ifland, about ¼ a mile from the fhore. Some people have given the invention of this purgatory to the great. St. *Patrick*, but others with more probability afcribe it to *Patrick* who was prior here about the year 850. This purgatory or place of penance and pilgrimage, continued a long time in high repute both at home and abroad; we find in our records feveral fafe conducts granted by the Kings of England, to foreigners defirous to vifit it; and particularly in the year 1358, one to *Maletefta Ungarus* knt. Another bearing the fame date, to *Nicholas de Beccario*, a nobleman of Ferraria; and in 1397, one to *Raymond*, vifc. *de Perilleaux*

Perilleaux and knt of *Rhodes*, with a train of 20 men and 30 horses. But this place muft have fallen afterwards into difrepute, for by authority of pope *Alexander* 6th. who confidered it as an impofition, it was demolifhed on St. Patrick's day, in the year 1497, by the father guardian of the Francifcans of Donegal, and fome other perfons of the deanery of *Lough Ern*, who were deputed for this purpofe by the bifhop. A Canon of the priory of St. *Daboee* or St. *Fintan*, refided on the ifland for the fervice of the church and pilgrims. The cave of the purgatory is built of freeftone, covered with broad flags and green turf laid over them ; in length within the walls it meafures 16½ feet, and in breadth about 2 feet ; when the door is fhut, no light can be difcovered, but what enters at a fmall window in the corner. In 1630 the government of Ireland prudently thought fit to have it finally fuppreffed, and the place was dug up accordingly.

PATRICK's-WELL, fit. in co. Limerick, prov. Munfter, 99 miles from Dublin ; near which is *Athyflin*, and alfo *Ballybunage*, two agreeable feats.

PAULVILLE, a handfome feat in co. Carlow, prov. Leinfter, above 56 miles from Dublin.

PAWNSTOWN, fit. in bar. Atherdee, co. Louth, prov. Leinfter.

PEAK, fit. in co. Cork, prov. Munfter, near *Aghabollogue*. At this place a great number of fubterraneous rooms, or caverns, were difcovered in 1755, fome of which contained confiderable quantities of human fkeletons. To the S. is the caftle of *Carignamuck*, and near it a ftone bridge of 8 arches over the river *Dripfey*.

PEARSONBROOK, fit. near *Athlone*, prov. Connaught.

PENMORE, fit. in bar. Tullaghagh, co Cavan, prov. Ulfter.

PENNYCOMEQUICK, a village fit. near Arklow, in bar. Arklow, co. Wicklow, prov. Leinfter.

PEPERSTOWN, fit. in bar. Atherdee, co. Louth, prov. Leinfter.

PEPPARDSTOWN, a rectory in dioc. of Cafhel, fit. in bar. Middlethird, co. Tipperary, prov. Munfter.

PERSONSTOWN, fit. in bar. Ferrard, co. Louth, prov. Leinfter.

PETERBOROUGH, fit. in co. Monaghan, prov. Ulfter, above 45 miles from Dublin.

PETERSVILLE, fit. near *Kells*, prov. Leinfter.

PETERSFIELD, fit. near *Nenagh*, prov. Munft.

PETTIGOE, fit. in bar. Tyrhugh, co. Donegal, prov. Ulfter, 94 miles from Dublin ; ½ a mile beyond which, is *Caftle Termen*. Fairs held 25 July.

PHARAHY, fit. in co. Cork, prov. Munfter, 3 miles N. W. of *Glanworth*. Where there is a decent church and fteeple, an Englifh proteftant fchool, a glebe and parfonage houfe, belonging to the deans of *Cloyne*, who as fuch are incumbents of this parifh. The country adjacent is open, dry, and healthy, with good fheep-walks, and it is fit for fporting. Excellent quarries of lime-ftone fhew themfelves hereabouts.

PHEAL, an agreeable feat in co. Cork, prov. Munfter ; near *Inifkeen*.

PHILIPSBURGH, a pleafant village fit. ¼ of a mile beyond *Ballybough-bridge*, and 1¼ mile from Dublin caftle, prov. Leinfter. It is convenient to the fea and much frequented as a fummer refidence.

PHILLIPSTOWN, a bar. in King's co. prov. Leinfter, in which is a borough, poft and fair town of fame name, fit. 38 miles S. W. from Dublin. Lat. 53 : 18, lon. 7 : 20. It is a vicarage in dioc. of Kildare, and the fhire town of the King's co. It was fo named from king *Phillip* of *Spain*, hufband to *Mary*, queen of *England*, who made this part of the country fhire-ground in 1557. It gives title of *baron* to the family of *Molefworth*. It had formerly a garrifon, but there is now a barrack there for a company of foot. Here are the ruins of a caftle built by the *Bellinghams*, fit. on the very brink of the river. *Phillipftown* returns 2 members to parliament, patron, the earl of *Belvedere*. Fairs held 28 March, 22 June and 3 Dec.--Alfo a curacy in dioc. of Armagh, fit. in bar. *Dundalk*, co. Louth, prov. Leinfter. Likewife a rectory in dioc. of Armagh, fit. in bar. *Ardee*, in fame co.

PHINISK *river*, rifes near the N. W. bounds of the co. Waterford, prov. Munfter, and after a courfe of 6 or 7 miles, empties itfelf into the *Blackwater* to the N. of *Drumana*.

PHIPPSBOROUGH, a pleafant village newly built on the road to *Finglafs*, and about 1¼ mile from Dublin, in co. Dublin, prov. Leinft.

PHŒNIX-PARK, fit. in bar. Caftleknock, in the fuburbs of the city of Dublin, prov. Leinfter. This beautiful park is about 7 miles in circumference, and contains feveral handfome feats or villas, a magazine of powder, and a battery of 22 cannon. It was part of the lands belonging to the monaftery of St. *John* of *Jerufalem*, on the fcite of which the royal hofpital of Kilmainham now ftands. The park is finely diverfified with wood-land, champaign and rifing grounds ; and well ftocked with deer. In the middle of the park, and centre of a well grown wood, the late earl of *Chefterfield*, when lord lieutenant of Ireland, erected a large fluted Corinthian pillar 40 feet high, on the top of which is the figure of a

Phœnix

Phœnix burning in her neft, from whence this park obtained the name of the Phœnix-park. In it is an elegant lodge for the viceroy, and another for his fecretary, with feveral handfome feats; alfo a charitable inftitution called the "*Hibernian Military fchool*," for the maintenance and inftruction of the fons and daughters of foldiers: the building is of Portland-ftone, finifhed in a very handfome and commodious manner, and in 1773 an elegant chapel was erected near the fchool, built of hewn-ftone, with a fteeple adorned with a beautiful cupola.

PICKERSTOWN, fit. about 2½ miles beyond *Hampftead*, and above 5 from Dublin, in co. Dublin, prov. Leinfter.

PIERCEFIELD, fit. in bar. Corkerry, co. Weftmeath, prov. Leinfter.

PIERCETOWN, a rectory in dioc. of Meath, antiently called *Leckno*, fit. in bar. Rathconrath, co. Weftmeath, prov. Leinfter; it appears that an abbey was founded here in 750.

PIERCETOWN-LANDY, a vicarage in dioc. of Meath, fit. in bar. Duleek, co. Meath, prov. Leinfter.

PIGEONS-HOLE, otherwife called *Cou-a-glour*; it is a moft ftupendous cavern, fit. in the parifh of Whitechurch, co. Waterford, prov. Munfter. The entrance which faces to the S. E. is confiderably large, fo that a perfon may eafily defcend a fmall declivity of about 50 feet in length. Oppofite the entrance after paffing over fome rugged rocks, you enter in a fmall chamber, where the light begins to fail, but by the help of candles, and a murmuring found, a fmall fubterraneous rivulet is feen, running in a natural aqueduct through the folid rock. This river finks under ground at *Ballynacourty*, and proceeding through this cave, rifes again at a place called *Knockane*, about a mile from the place where it hides itfelf. Both to the right and left of the mouth of this cave, there are large chambers into which a perfon may enter by fuch narrow paffages, that he is forced however to creep thro' them for a confiderable way; and from fome of thefe chambers are paffages leading into others. In thefe chambers the ftalactical matter defcending from the roof prefents a variety of forms, which fancy will readily image into numberlefs different figures.

PILLTOWN, fit. in the parifh of *Kinfalebeg*, in bar. Decies *within Drum*, co. Waterford, prov. Munfter. At this place lived judge *Walfh*, the fuppofed author of the forged commiffion in favour of the Irifh rebels in king *Charles* Ift time; the particulars of which affair were not difcovered till after the reftoration; when lord *Mufkerry* confeffed the whole to lord *Orrery*, at the duke of *Ormond's* caftle of *Kilkenny*.

Alfo a village fit. in bar. Iverk, co. Kilkenny, prov. Leinfter.

PIMSDALE, fit. near *Maryborough*, prov. Leinfter.

PIPPARD-CASTLE, fit. about 3 miles from *Donamore*, co. Wexford, prov. Leinfter.

PITCHESTOWN, fit. in bar. St. Mullen, co. Carlow, prov. Leinfter.

PITCHFORD, a handfome feat in co. Kildare, prov. Leinfter.

PITCHFORDSTOWN, fit. in bar. Ikeath, co. Kildare, prov. Leinfter.

PLARY, an old. diffolved monaftery in co. Weftmeath, prov. Leinfter. Here was formerly both a friary and a nunnery in feparated buildings; both of the *Ciftertian* order, (or as fome fay of the order of *Gilbertines*) founded by the *Laceys*. King Hen. VIIIth converted its church into the cathedral of the diocefe of *Meath*; but 'tis uncertain how long it continued fo.

PLATTEN, a handfome feat 2 miles beyond *Duleek*, in co. Meath, prov. Leinfter. The houfe ftands on the fcite of a caftle, built by the *Darceys*, which was one of the greateft buildings of the kind in the kingdom.

PLYBBERSTOWN, fit. near *Iniftioge*, prov. Leinfter.

PLUCK, a village fit. in bar. Raphoe, co. Donegal, prov. Ulfter.

PLUNKET-CASTLE, fit. about 2 miles from *Finglafs*, and 5 from Dublin, in co. Dublin, prov. Leinfter.

POBLEBRIEN, or *Pobalbrien*, and fometimes written *Peble O'Brien*, a bar. in co. Limerick, prov. Munfter, otherwife called Carrigoginniol. *Donagh Carbreach O'Brien* in 1211, received from king *John*, patents for the eftate of Carrigoginniol, in co. Limerick, at the yearly rent of fixty marks. The earls of *Defmond* afterwards became lords of this diftrict.

POBLE-O'CALLAGHAN, an antient diftrict of the *O'Callaghans*, in co. Limerick, prov. Munfter.

POE, a *river*, fit. in bar. Omagh, co. Tyrone, prov. Ulfter.

POE-BRIDGE, fit. in bar. Strabane, co. Tyrone, prov. Ulfter.

POINTZPASS, a village fit. in bar. Upper Iveagh, co. Down, prov. Ulfter. At this place and at *Scarvagh-pafs* in fame co. was the firft affembly of the Englifh army in 1688.

POL-A-PHUCA, or *Poul-a-phouka*, fit. near *Rufsborough*, co. Wicklow, prov. Leinfter. The name fignifies the *Dæmon's-hole*, it being an immenfe whirlpool, whofe depth has never yet been afcertained; it is formed by the ponderous and rapid defcent of the whole body of the river *Liffey*, which is drawn by a fuction, whofe power nothing can refift, to the fummit of of a craggy precipice, divided into several distinct falls, in the manner of a stair-case. The fall of so great a mass of water over a declivity of this kind, is an amazing object; and the hoarse roaring of the cataract may be heard at the distance of some miles. The abyss into which the water is precipitated from the height of 154 feet, exhibits the appearance of a frightful vortex; into which all bodies that come down the stream, however bulky, are attracted with astonishing force and velocity. The perpetual agitation of the water in this whirlpool, which is circular, forms an eddy not unlike the phænomenon on the coast of *Norway*, called " the Navel of the sea," to which no vessel dare approach, lest the irresistable indraft should bury the unfortunate navigators in an unfathomable abyss. This place lies on the left hand of the great road from *Blessington* to *Ballymore-eustace*; and is about ¼ a mile to the S. of the magnificent seat of the earl of *Miltown*.

POLEKERRY, sit. by the river *Suir*, in bar. Iffa and Offa, co. Tipperary, prov. Munster.

POLERAN, a vicarage in dioc. of Ossory, sit. in bar. Iverk, co. Kilkenny, prov. Leinster.

POLES, a village sit. in bar. Kells, co. Meath, prov. Leinster.

POLLARDSTOWN, a rectory in dioc. of Kildare, sit. in bar. Ophaly, co. Kildare, prov. Leinster; here are the antient ruins of a church.

POMEROY, sit. in bar Dungannon, co. Tyrone, prov. Ulster, 80 miles from Dublin; fairs held 1 June and 11 Nov. It is a rectory in dioc. of Armagh.

POOLAHONY, sit. in bar. Arklow, co. Wicklow, prov. Leinster.

POOR HEAD, sit. near *Kinsale harbour*, in co. Cork, prov. Munster, whence there is a prospect of Kinsale-head to the W. and a considerable tract of the sea coast to the E. this cape is bold and lofty.

PORT, or *The Port*, sit. in co. Donegal, prov. Ulster, 118 miles from Dublin; 2 miles from which is *Duncanely church*, and 1 mile from it the ruin of a castle; fairs held 12 May, 26 Aug. 5 Nov. and 15 Dec.—Also a village sit. in bar. Ferrard, co. Louth, prov. Leinster; it is a rectory in dioc of Armagh.

PORTACHLOE, a village sit. in bar. Erris, co. Mayo, prov. Connaught.

PORTADOWN, sit. in bar. Oneilland, co. Armagh, prov. Ulster, 65 miles from Dublin; it is pleasantly sit. on the river *Bann*, over which it has a stone bridge; the canal from *Newry* falls into the *Bann*, within a mile of this place. *Portadown* is noted for its extensive business in the linen manufacture; fairs held here on Easter-monday, Whitsun-monday, and 13 Nov.

PORTAFERRY, a fair and post town in bar. Ardes, co. Down, prov. Ulster, 78 miles from Dublin; fairs held 31 July and 12 Dec. It is the first town in the bar. of *Ardes*, after passing over the rapid ferry of *Strangford*, on the other side of which it lies; for here a ferry boat maintains a constant communication between the bar.'s of *Lecale* and *Ardes*. Heretofore a pretty brisk trade was carried on in this place, and between 30 and 40 ships belonged to its port; but this trade is now lost. The castle of *Portaferry*, was the antient seat of the *Savages*; considerable additions were made to it, and finished in 1636. From the high lands about *Portaferry*, are fine prospects, extended over the whole lake of *Strangford*, the bar. of *Ardes*, *Lecale*, the sea and the *Isle of Man*; and the castle together with the town, from the opposite side makes a most beautiful landscape. Near the church of *Portaferry*, stands an antient chapel; a coarse building, of an odd contrivance; it is a room 37 feet in length, 16 broad and 20 high, covered with a coved arch of stone, so close and firmly cemented, that it does not appear to admit any water. Adjoining, is a similar building, divided into two apartments.

PORTARLINGTON, a borough, post and fair town, handsomely sit. on each side of the river *Barrow*, which divides the town, between the *King's co.* and *Queen's co.* prov. Leinster, distant above 35 miles from Dublin. Lat. 53° : 9' : 30", lon. 7 : 39. The greater part of it lies in the Queen's co. It is inhabited by very genteel families, and has a number of excellent schools; particularly for children under 12 years old. It gives title of earl to the family of *Dawson*, and within a few miles of it, is *Dawson's-grove*, the elegant seat of lord *Portarlington*. This place returns 2 members to parliament; patron, lord *Portarlington*. Fairs held Easter-Mond. 22 May, 12 Oct. and 23 Nov.

PORTAVOE, a seat in the neighbourhood of *Donaghadee*, co. Down, prov. Ulster.

PORT DANDY, sit. in one of the *Copland-islands*, co. Down, prov. Ulster.

PORTERIN, a vicarage in dioc. of Elphin, sit. in bar. Athlone, co. Roscommon, prov. Connaught.

PORT-GLENONE, sit. in bar. Toome, co. Antrim, prov. Ulster, 97 miles from Dublin. It is pleasantly sit. on the river *Bann*, over which there is a bridge at the end of the town, which divides the co.'s of *Antrim* and *Londonderry*. Fairs held 2 Tuesday in May, O. S. Also a fair town in co. Londonderry, prov. Ulster; fairs held 2 Tuesd. O. S. in May, and 12 August.

PORTLA-

4 A

PORTLAMAN, fit. in bar. Corkerry, co. Weftmeath, prov. Leinfter.

PORT-LARGY, a name corruptly given to the prefent city of Waterford, prov. Munfter; it was alfo called *Cuanleargi*, or the port on the fea ; and was the *Brigantia* of *Rd. Cirenceft*.

PORTLAW, fit. in bar. Upperthird, co. Waterford, prov. Munfter.

PORTLEMON, a rectory in dioc. of Meath, fit. in bar. Corkerry, co. Weftmeath, prov. Leinfter.

PORT-LESTER, fit. in bar. Lune, co. Meath, prov. Leinfter.

PORT-MAGEE, fit. by *Bray-head*, co. Kerry, prov. Munfter. On the Southward lie the *Skelig-rocks*; this place forms an entrance between the main land and *Valentia ifland*.

PORTMARNOCK, a curacy in dioc. of Dublin, fit. in bar. Coolock, co. Dublin, prov. Leinfter.

PORTMORE-CASTLE, fit. near *Ballinderry*, co. Antrim, prov. Ulfter.

PORTMUCK, fit. in *Magee-ifland*, off the coaft of co. Antrim, prov. Ulfter.

PORTNEHINCH, a bar. in Queen's co. prov. Leinfter, in which is a village of fame name.

PORTNESCULLY, a vicarage in dioc. of Offory, fit. in bar. Iverk, co. Kilkenny, prov. Leinfter.

PORT-NINIAN, fit. in one of the *Copland-ifles*, co. Down, prov. Ulfter.

PORT-NORRIS, a village fit. in bar. Orior, co. Armagh, prov. Ulfter.

PORTNURE, fit. near *Lough-ree*, in bar. Rathline, co. Longford, prov. Leinfter.

PORT-RAMAN, fit. in one of the *Copland-ifles*, co. Down, prov. Ulfter.

PORTRAHAN, a curacy in dioc. of Dublin, fit. in bar. Balruddery, co. Dublin, prov. Leinft.

PORTRANE, fit. in bar. Nethercrofs, co. Dublin, prov. Leinfter.

PORT-RENARD, fit. in co. Limerick, prov. Munfter; fairs held 2 May, 18 July, 13 Oct. and 15 Dec.

PORT-RUSH, a village fit. in bar. Dunluce, co. Antrim, prov. Ulfter. Lat. 55 : 15, lon. 7 : 0, diftant from Dublin 114 miles.

PORT-SAINT-ANN, formerly called *Killough*, fit. 7 miles E. S. E. of *Dundrum*, and almoft 5 S. of *Down-Patrick*, in co. Down, prov. Ulfter.

PORT-SAINT-MARY, fit. on the river *Barrow*, in bar. Shelburne, co. Wexford, prov. Leinfter, 4 miles S. of *Rofs*. An abbey was erected here for Ciftertian monks by one *Harvey*, who in 1179, entered into the monaftery of the holy Trinity in *Canterbury*. Herlewin, bifhop of Leighlin, was interred in the abbey-church in 1216, which he had himfelf caufed to be erected. In 1380 it was enacted that no mere

Irifhman fhould be fuffered to profefs himfelf in this abbey ; the abbot of which fat as a baron in parliament. The ruins of this very extenfive abbey exhibit an awful and picturefque fcene, the interior walls of the church are neat and entire, as is the chancel, on each fide of which (in the wings of the church) are three chapels, vaulted and groined : the great aifle is divided into three parts, by a double row of arches fupported by fquare piers; the infide of thofe arches have a molding which fprings from beautiful confoles. The tower (rather low in proportion to the reft of the building) is fupported by a grand arch. The cloifters appear to have been fpacious, but their foundations alone remain : fome other ruinous walls indicate where the hall, refectory, dormitory, &c. ftood. The E. window, of an uncommon form, is entire, and the door immediately beneath it was very magnificent, being adorned with filligree open work, cut in ftone, and fo raifed as to allow a finger eafily under it. This abbey is called *Dunbredy-abbey*.

PORTSHANE-CASTLE, fit. in bar. Leitrim, co. Leitrim, prov. Connaught.

PORTSHANGAN, a rectory in dioc. of Meath, fit. in bar. Corkerry, co. Weftmeath, prov. Leinfter.

PORT-SLATY, fit. in one of the *Copland-ifles*, co. Down, prov. Ulfter.

PORTUMNA, fit. in bar. Longford, co. Galway, prov. Connaught, 74 miles from Dublin. Lat. 52 : 59, lon. 7 : 43 Here is the caftle of *Portumna*, the feat of the marquis of *Clanricarde*; and near it are the ruins of an antient caftle, which was erected by the *De Burghos*, about A. D. 1180. There was formerly a wooden bridge at Portumna, but being broke down in time of war, it hath never been rebuilt. Here is a garrifon for a troop of horfe, and 2 companies of foot. This town is feated on the river *Shannon*, where it falls into *Lough Derg*. The monks of the Ciftertian abbey of *Dunbrody*, in the co. Wexford, had for a long time a chapel here, dedicated to St. *Peter* and St. *Paul*; but having at length forfaken it, *O'Madden*, dynaft of the country, gave it to the Dominican friars, who with the approbation of the monks of *Dunbrody*, erected a friary here, and a church, which they dedicated to the Bleffed Virgin, and the original patron faints; at the fame time they built a fteeple, and all other neceffary offices. Pope Martin V. granted a bull to confirm their poffeffions, dated 8 Oct. 1426, and on the 23 Nov. following, he granted indulgences to all who had contributed to the building. The walls are ftill nearly entire, and fhew that the monaftery of *Portumna* was by no means an ignoble ftructure.

The

The antient choir is now the parish church. Fairs held 15 Feb. May, Aug. and Nov.

POSSERTOWN, fit. near *Ardee*, prov. Leinfter.

POTALY, fit. in bar. Truaghnacmy, co. Kerry, prov. Munfter.

POULADUFF, two remarkable great holes in the ground, about a mile W. of *Rofs*, in co. Cork, prov. Munfter, 80 yards deep, in which the fea flows by fubterraneous paffages; they are called E. and W. *Pouladuff*, one is on the lands of *Downeen* and the other on *Tralong*.

POULAPHOUKA, fee *Pol-a-phuca*.

POULNE-LONG-CASTLE, now a pleafant feat, fit. in co. Cork, prov. Munfter.

POWERSCOURT, fit. in bar. Rathdown, co. Wicklow, prov. Leinfter, 10 miles from Dublin; it gives title of vifc. to the family of *Wingfield*; the prefent lord has an elegant feat here, near it are the celebrated *Dargle* and *Waterfall*; the park is prodigioufly fine, and the rocky precipices on all fides, as you approach the cataract, with the lofty trees growing thereout, form a delightful and contemplative fcene. *Powerfcourt* is a vicarage in dioc. of Dublin.

POWERSTOWN, a fair town fit. in bar. Gowran, co. Kilkenny, prov. Leinfter; fairs held 31 May. This is a rectory in dioc. of Leighlin.

PRIEST-HOUSE, a fmall village, fit. ¼ a mile beyond *Donnybrook*, and 2¼ miles from Dublin, in co. Dublin, prov. Leinfter.

PRIEST'S-LEAP, a well known place in co. Cork. prov. Munfter. From the S. part of *Bantry* bay to the N. there are but two paffages, by which a perfon can go into the co. *Kerry*; that on the N. end is a moft rugged and dangerous one, and is called *Prieft's-leap*, from whence the road leads over the mountain *Mangerton*, juftly efteemed one of the higheft in Ireland; among thefe wild tracts, are here and there fome *yew* trees remaining, of a very large fize, they were formerly in greater plenty, as was alfo the *Arbutus* or ftrawberry tree, which is remarkable for flourifhing in fuch foils; there were plenty of red deer in this country, but they are now very rare.

PRITCHARDSTOWN, fit. in co. Kildare, prov. Leinfter, about 16 miles from Dublin.

PROSPECT, fit. in co. Wexford, prov. Leinft.

PROSPECT-HALL, fit. in co. Waterford, prov. Munfter, in the parifh of *Kinfale-beg*; it is a handfome feat with good improvements, near the ferry point of *Youghal*.—Alfo another feat of fame name, in co. Kerry, prov. Munfter, having a good profpect of part of the lake of *Killarney*.

PROSPEROUS, a village in bar. Claine, co. Kildare, prov. Leinfter, about 15 miles from Dublin. A cotton manufactory of various ar-

ticles was eftablifhed here, by capt. *Brook*, under parliamentary encouragement, in 1780.

PUFFIN-ISLAND, fit. off the fhore of the co. Kerry, prov. Munfter; it is much frequented by the fowl called *puffins*; and is alfo well ftocked with rabbits; it is fteep and craggy, and has a remarkable open, or gap in its higheft part.

PULLEENS, caverns fo called, having in them a fubterraneous river; they are fit. in the demefne of *Brownhall*, co. Donegal. prov. Ulfter.

PURCEL'S-INCH, fit. near *Kilkenny*, prov. Leinfter.

PURDYSBURN, an agreeable feat, fit. in co. Down, prov. Ulfter.

Q U

QUANSBURY, fit. near *Eyrecourt*, prov. Connaught.

QUARRYMOUNT, fit. about 4 miles from Rofenallis, in Queen's co. prov. Leinfter.

QUEHWILL, an abbey mentioned to have exifted in co. Cork, prov. Munfter, in the year 1355, but there appears no particular account of it.

QUEENSBOROUGH, a feat of the earl of *Louth*, fit. within about 3 miles of Eyrecourt, co. Galway, prov. Connaught.

QUEEN'S-COUNTY, fit. in prov. Leinfter. It is bounded by the King's co. and the co.'s Kildare, Carlow, Kilkenny and Tipperary. Its antient name was *Leix*: it is 25 miles in length and as many in breadth; contains 235,300 acres and above 82,000 inhabitants, 8 baronies, 3 boroughs, and returns 8 members to parliament. Chief town, *Maryborough*; which with the co. was named in honour of *Mary*, queen of England. Its bar.'s are Portnehinch, Tinehinch, Upper Offory, Maryborough, Stradbally, Ballyadams, Cullinagh, and Slewmargy. This co. was formerly full of bogs, but is now a fruitful and pleafant country. The principal proprietors of this diftrict at the commencement of the laft century, were the families of *O'More*, *Fitzpatrick*, *O'Dou*, *O'Brenan*, *Wandesford* and *Delany*.

QUEEN'STOWN, the prefent town of *Maryborough*, in Queen's co. prov. Leinfter. Lat. 53:0. lon. 7:20.

QUERIN, a village fit. near the river Shannon, in co. Clare, prov. Munfter.

QUERN-ISLAND, fo called from its round form; it is one of the *Blafket Iflands*, fit. off the coaft of the co. Kerry, prov. Munfter; and otherwife called *Inis-ni-broe*.

QUIN, a fair town, fit. in bar. Bunratty, co. Clare, prov. Munfter; fairs held 7 July and

31 Oct. It is a rectory in dioc. of Killaloe. Here is an antient abbey, about 5 miles E. of *Ennis*; it was erected by *M'Namara*, and is one of the finest and most entire buildings of the kind in Ireland, and seated on a fine stream. There is an ascent of several steps to the church. At the entrance you have a view of the high altar entire, and an altar on each side of the arch of the chancel. To the S. is a chapel with three or four altars in it, and a very gothic figure in relief, of some saint. On the N. side of the chancel is a fine monument of the family of the *M'Namara's* of *Rance*, erected by the founder. On a stone by the high altar, the name of *Kennedye* appears in large letters: in the middle, between the body and the chancel, is a fine tower, built on the two gable ends. The cloister is in the usual form, with couplets of pillars; but is particular in having buttresses round it, by way of ornament; there are apartments on three sides of it; the refectory, dormitory, and another grand room to the N. of the chancel; with a vaulted room under them all. To the N. of the large room, is a closet, which leads thro' a private way to a very strong round-tower, the walls of which are near 10 feet thick. In the front of the monastery is a building, which seems to have been an apartment for strangers; and to the S. W. are two other buildings. Near it are also the ruins of a church, and of a castle.

QUINCE-ISLAND, sit. in bar. Carbery, co. Cork, prov. Munster.

QUIN'SBURY, sit. in bar. Ophaly, co. Kildare, prov Leinster.

QUINTIN-BAY, otherwise called *Tara bay*, from an inconsiderable place near it, sit. near *Donaghadee* harbour, in co. Down, prov. Ulster.

QUINTIN-CASTLE, sit. 2 miles S. of *Portaferry*, in co. Down, prov. Ulster.

QUOLAGH-BAY, sit. in bar. Beer and Bantry, co. Cork, prov. Munster.

R A

RABBIT-ISLAND, sit. to the W. of *Innisfallen*, in co. Kerry, prov. Munster, it is chiefly remarkable for its quarries of good limestone, which the neighbouring inhabitants dig and burn, in order to manure their ground.

RABEEN, sit. in bar. Ravilly, co. Carlow, prov. Leinster.

RACAHILL, a fair town, sit. in co. Limerick, prov. Munster; fairs held 26 Aug.

RACHLIN, see *Raghlin*.

RACAVAN, a rectory in dioc. of Connor, sit. in bar. Antrim, co. Antrim, prov. Ulster.

RACKIBIRN, an *island*, sit. off the coast of co. Donegal, prov. Ulster.

RACKWALLACE-CHURCH, sit. near *Castleshane*, co. Monaghan, prov. Ulster: 'tis now in ruins.

RACOFFY, see *Rathcoffy*.

RACONRATH, see *Rathconrath*.

RACOOLE, see *Rathcoole*.

RACOOLE-RIVER, sit. in co. Cork, prov. Munster.

RACROSS *church*, an old edifice sit. about 1 mile E. of *Tralee*, co. Kerry, prov. Munster.

RADDENSTOWN, see *Raddinstown*.

RADDINSTOWN, or *Raddenstown*, sit. in co. Meath, prov. Leinster, above 14 miles from Dublin. Here is a neat church; and a handsome seat of the *Tew* family.

RAFESTON, sit. near *Phillipstown*, prov. Leinster.

RAFORD, sit. near *Loughrea*, prov. Connau.

RAFRAN, see *Rathbran*.

RAGHAN, a vicarage in dioc. of Cloyne, sit. in bar. Fermoy, co. Cork, prov. Munster.— Also a village in bar. Ballycowan, King's co. prov. Leinster; it is a vicarage in dioc. of Meath, and otherwise written *Rahan*.

RAGHERA, a village sit. in bar. Garrycastle, King's co. prov. Leinster.

RAGHERY, see *Raghlin*.

RAGHLIN, an *island*, sit. opposite *Ballycastlebay*, between 6 and 7 miles off the N. coast of co. Antrim, prov. Ulster. Its being so much exposed to the Northern ocean, and the turbulence of its irregular tides, have thrown such difficulties in the way of landsmen, that few have visited it, but from necessity. It is called *Ricnia* by Pliny, *Ricinia* by Ptolemy, *Riduna* by Antonius, and *Recarn* or *Recrain* by the Irish historians; *Raelinda* by Buchanan, *Rachri* by Makenzie, *Raghlin* by Ware, and *Rathlin* by the modern map makers. Mr. Hamilton thinks its etymology might possibly be found in *Ragh-erin*, or " the fort of Erin," as its situation commanding the Irish coast, might make it, not unaptly, be stiled the fortress of Ireland. Lat. 54 : 36, lon. 9 : 15. It abounds with some curious arrangements of columnar basaltes; and is near 5 miles in length, and about 3¼ in breadth, toward the middle: it contains about 1200 inhabitants, and where cultivated, produces excellent barley. The rocks here afford a considerable quantity of sea-weed, for the manufacture of kelp. *Raghlin* has formerly been, as it were, a stepping stone between the Irish and Scottish coasts, which the natives of each country alternately used in their various expeditions, and for which they frequently fought. A number of small tumuli were, not long since, discovered in a little plane, about the middle of the island; brazen swords and spears were also found there,

and

and a large fibula in one of the tumuli, which is depofited in the mufeum of Trin. col. Dublin. During the difturbances in Scotland between *Baliol* and *Rob. Bruce*, the latter was obliged to take fhelter here, with a friend of his ; the remains of a fortrefs are yet vifible in the N. angle of the ifland, celebrated for the defence which this hero made in it, and is known by the name of *Bruce's caftle*; its antiquity therefore, is near 500 years. It is obfervable that the lime with which it was built, has been burned with fea-coal, the cinders of which are ftill vifible in it. About the middle of the 6th century, a religious eftablifhment was founded here by *Columbus*, the celebrated miffionary of the N. In 790, a fleet of Danifh pirates ravaged this ifland, with fire and fword ; the fhrines and holy altars perifhed in the general deftruction ; and in 973, they put to death St. *Feradach*, the abbot of this place. In 1558, the earl of *Suffex*, lord deputy, attacked the Scots here, who had got poffeffion of the ifland, and drove them out with great flaughter. *Raghlin* is now a rectory in the dioc. of Connor.

RAGHMFON, fit. in bar. Ballimoe, co. Rofcommon, prov. Connaught.

RAGHRA, fit. in bar. Garycaftle, King's co. prov. Leinfter.

RAGOREY, a fair town, fit. in co. Wexford, prov. Leinfter ; fairs held Afcenfion-day and 28 Oct.

RAHAN, fee *Raghan*.

RAHANNE, the ruins of an antient caftle, fit. to the W. of *Ardfert*, near the fea, in co. Kerry, prov. Munfter ; it was formerly the refidence of the bifhops of *Ardfert*.

RAHARROW, a vicarage in dioc. of Elphin, fit. in bar. Athlone, co. Rofcommon, prov. Connaught.

RAHENY, a village fit. in bar. Coolock, co. Dublin, prov. Leinfter, about 4 miles from Dublin ; about half a mile from it, is a pleafant ftrand by the fea-fide, where there is another village called Raheny *on the ftrand*, to diftinguifh it from the former, which is called Raheny *in the country*. Raheny is a rectory in dioc. of Dublin ; the church is a plain neat ftructure, ftanding on a rifing ground, in an agreeable fituation.

RAHILL, a curacy in dioc. of Leighlin, fit. in bar. Ravilly, co. Carlow, prov. Leinfter.

RAHIN, fit. near *Athy*, in bar. Ballyadams, Queen's co. prov. Leinfter.

RAHINE *caftle*, fit. on the Eaftern bank, at the head of *Caftlehaven* bay, co Cork, prov. Munfter ; in the walls are feveral cannon balls, which were fhot at it from fome veffels in the harbour.

RAHOLP, fit. in co. Down, prov. Ulfter, 77 miles from Dublin.

RAINBOW-BRIDGE, fit. over the river *Inny*, in co. Kerry, prov. Munfter. This bridge, the greater part of which fell down fome years ago, was 24 feet wide, and but a yard thick, being only a foot path, which was afcended and defcended by fteps ; it was of a confiderable height over the river, and built almoft femicircular, from whence it derived this name. What feems very fingular is, that it did not ftand on any high way ; from its narrownefs it had more the appearance of a triumphal arch, than of a bridge ; and it was erected over a very deep part of the river, but on what occafion, or when, there is not the leaft tradition in the country.

RAINILOUGH, fee *Ranelagh*.

RAKEMAN, fit. in bar. Ballimoe, co. Rofcommon, prov. Connaught.

RALLIHANE, a fair town, in King's co. prov. Leinfter ; fairs held 14 May.

RALOO, a rectory in dioc. of Connor, fit. in bar. Belfaft, co. Antrim, prov. Ulfter.

RALPHSDALE, fit. near *Caftletown-delvin*, prov. Leinfter.

RAMICAEL, a fair town in co. Dublin, prov. Leinfter ; fairs held 10 Oct.

RAM-ISLAND, fit. in *Lough-Neagh*, off the coaft of co. Antrim, prov. Ulfter : here is one of the antient round towers.

RAMOAN, a vicarage in dioc. of Connor, fit. in bar. Cary, co. Antrim, prov. Ulfter.

RAMORAN, fit. in bar. Clonkelly, co. Fermanagh, prov. Ulfter.

RAMOR-LOUGH, fee *Lough Ramor*.

RAMSFORT, fit. near *Gorey*, co. Wexford, prov. Leinfter.

RAMSGRANGE, a village fit. in bar. Shelburne, co. Wexford, prov. Leinfter.

RAMHEAD, a *cape*, fit. in bar. Decies within Drum, co. Waterford, prov. Munfter.

RAMULLIN, fit. in bar. Kilmacrennan, co. Donegal, prov. Ulfter ; fairs held 21 Aug. and Nov. It is fometimes written *Rathmullin*.

RANDALSTOWN, a borough in co. Antrim, prov. Ulfter, 88 miles from Dublin ; 2 miles beyond which is *Shane's caftle*, the elegant feat of the Rt. Hon. lord *O'Neil*; this place returns 2 members to parliament, patronage in the *O'Neil* family ; fairs held 16 July and 1 Nov. In the middle of this town is a handfome market houfe, with a large affembly room over it. A very great linen market is held here the firft Wednefday in every month ; the night before which, an affembly is held for the linen drapers who come to the market ; on which occafion, they dance in their boots and fpurs, to the detriment of the ladies aprons ; but as the deftruction of the aprons increafes the demand for fine linen, the patriotic ladies do not complain.

RANDOWN,

RANDOWN, fit. on *Lough-ree*, in bar. Athlone, co. Roscommon, prov. Connaught, about 7 miles N. of Athlone. A priory was founded here for Knights Hospitalers, or for cross bearers, in the reign of king *John*, and (as some writers say) by his express command. *Philip Nangle* was a great benefactor to this house, in the time of king Hen. IIId. In 1226, the English strongly fortified the *castle* of *Randown*, and in 1237, the town was plundered and pillaged by *Phelim O'Connor*. It appears that *John de Funtains* was constable of the castle in 1334, with the annual fee of 40*l.* sterl. but very little now remains either of the town or castle. *Clarus*, archdeacon of Elphin, founded a church here, dedicated to the holy Trinity.

RANELAGH, a territory in co. Wicklow, prov. Leinster, which gives title of visc. to the family of *Jones*, and gave that of baron to the family of *Cole*. It was antiently written *Rainilough*, and was the district of the *O'Birnes*.—Also a village in the vicinity of Dublin, fit. in co. Dublin, prov. Leinster; here was formerly the rural and beautiful seat of a bishop of Derry, which was afterwards converted into a place of public entertainment, and since, into that of a nunnery.

RANEW, fit. near Wicklow, in co. Wicklow, prov. Leinster.

RANTING WHEEL, a rock so called, fit. in *Strangford* bay, co. Down, prov. Ulster; it occasions an eddy tide at the entrance of the bay, and is for the most part under water, lying near *Quintin point*, and very dangerous for boats, as it causes a kind of whirlpool.

RAPHARN-LOUGH, a *lake*, fit. in bar. Burrishoole, co. Mayo, prov. Connaught.

RAPHOE, a bar. in co. Donegal, prov. Ulster, having in it a post and fair town of same name, fit. 107 miles from Dublin. Lat. 54:48, lon. 8:13. Fairs held 1 May, 22 June, 27 Aug. and 4 Nov.—It is also an antient bishoprick, said to have been founded by St. *Eunan* about the middle of the 6th century, and a cathedral was erected on the ruins of the church of St. *Eunan*, in the 11th. *Patrick Magonaile*, bishop of Raphoe, built 3 episcopal houses, in 1360; and bishop *Pooley* by will, bequeathed 200*l.* for repairing the cathedral, which money was applied by his successor: they shew still the bed of St. *Eunan*, and within these few years a round tower was standing on a hill, in which the bishops of *Raphoe* kept their studies; a celebrated cross, famous for the performance of miracles, stood in the cathedral, but was about the year 1438, removed to *Armagh*, by bishop *O'Galcher*. This bishoprick is rated in the king's books at 200*l.* per ann. but is worth 2,500*l.* At Raphoe is the mansion house of the bishop; it is properly a *castle*, built for defence,

at the expence of government, in the reign of *Charles* I. It stood a siege in the rebellion of 1641; it was beautified and repaired by bishop *Oswald*, and is now a handsome dwelling. *Raphoe* is a rectory in the dioc. of same name; its antient name was *Rath-both*.

RASHADOE, a village fit. in bar. Raphoe, co. Donegal, prov. Ulster.

RASHARKAN, fit. in bar. Kilconway, co. Antrim, prov. Ulster, 102 miles from Dublin; it is a rectory in dioc. of Connor. 2 miles from which, seated on a rising ground, is the village of *Kilrea*.

RASHEE, fit. in bar. Antrim, co. Antrim, prov. Ulster; it is a rectory in dioc. of Connor.

RATANE, a vicarage in dioc. of Meath, fit. in bar. Navan, co. Meath, prov. Leinster.

RATASS, the ruin of an old church, fit. about 1 mile E. of *Tralee*, in bar. Clanmaurice, co. Kerry, prov. Munster; it was built of *free-stone*, brought at a great distance from the mountains, altho' there were fine quarries of lime-stone, to be had on the spot. This is a rectory in dioc. of Ardfert.

RATH, a rectory in dioc. of Leighlin, fit. in bar. Ravilly, co. Carlow, prov. Leinster.—Also a vicarage in dioc. of Killaloe, fit. in bar. Inchiquin, co. Clare, prov. Munster.

RATHANGAN, fit. in bar. Ophaly, co. Kildare, prov. Leinster. It is a handsome thriving village, 28 miles from Dublin; having a neat church, seated on an eminence at one end of the town. It is a rectory in dioc. of Kildare. The *grand Canal* from Dublin passes by this place. Here is a handsome seat of Mr. *Spencer*; and 2 miles from it is *Kill*, in King's co. the seat of Mr. *Clarke*; ¼ a mile beyond which, are the ruins of *Ballynowlan church*. At *Rathangan* are good flour mills. Fairs held Whit-tuesday, 26 Aug. and 12 Nov.—Also a place in bar. Bargie, co. Wexford, prov. Leinster.

RATHASPICK, a rectory in dioc. of Ferns, fit. in bar. Forth, co. Wexford, prov. Leinster. Also a rectory in dioc. of Leighlin, fit. in bar. Slewmargy, Queen's co. prov. Leinster.—Also a curacy in dioc. of Ardagh, fit. in bar. Moygoish, co. Westmeath, prov. Leinster.

RATHBARRY, a vicarage in dioc. of Ross, in which is an antient castle of the *Barrys*, now called *Castle Freke*; fit. in co. Cork, prov. Munster, near *Ross-Carbery*. Here is a pleasant seat, commanding an extensive view of the ocean and coast to the W.

RATHBEAGH, fit. in co. Kilkenny, prov. Leinster; it is supposed to be the antient *Argiodross*; where was a copper mine in the mountains, near the river *Nore*, from whence silver was extracted, and according to antiquaries, money was first coined in Ireland by *Enius Ruber*. 'Tis fit. in lower *Ossory*, within 5 miles of Kilkenny.

kenny, and 3 of Ballyragget. Fairs held 1 May, 11 June, 1 Nov. and 6 Dec.

RATHREAL, fit. in bar. Nethercrofs, co. Dublin, prov. Leinfter.

RATHREG, fit. in bar. Clonlifk, King's co. prov. Leinfter, 3 miles S. E. of *Birr*. St. *Abban* founded a monaftery here; and died A. D. 650.

RATHBEGGAN, a vicarage in dioc. of Meath, fit. in bar. Ratoath, co. Meath, prov. Leinfter.

RATHBOTH, fee *Raphoe*.

RATHBOURNEY, a rectory in dioc. of Kilfenora, fit. in bar. Burrin, co. Clare, prov. Munfter.

RATHBOYNE, a chapelry in dioc. of Meath, fit. in bar. Kells, co. Meath, prov. Leinfter.

RATHBRACKEN, fit. in bar. Ballagheen, co. Wexford, prov. Leinfter.

RATHBRAN, (fometimes pronounced *Rafran*) fit. near the fea, in bar. Tirawly, co. Mayo, prov. Connaught, about 5 miles N. of Killala. The family of *Dexter*, who afterwards took the name of *M'Jordan*, founded a monaftery here for Dominican friars, in 1274; tho' fome writers give this foundation to fir *Wm. Burgh*, furnamed, "the grey headed," who was for fome time, lord juftice of Ireland. *Edmund Bourke*, of Cattlebar, was murdered in this monaftery, on the 2 Feb. 1513, by the fons of his brother *Walter*.—There is a fmall village here, confifting of a few wretched cabbins; and the walls of the monaftery, with its facred edifices, ftill remain.

RATHBRAND, fit in co. Wicklow, prov. Leinfter, 26 miles from Dublin.

RATHBRIDE, fit. in bar. Ophaly. co. Kildare, prov. Leinfter, 26 miles from Dublin. Here is a handfome feat; and fairs are held on 5 July.

RATHCLARE, fit. in co. Cork, prov. Munfter, above 126 miles from Dublin. Fairs held 26 April, 1 July and Nov. and 17 Dec.

RATHCLARIN, fit. in bar. Carbery, co. Cork, prov. Munfter; where is a church, fit. near a caftle called *Burren-caftle*, on the fide of the river *Arigideen*. It is a rectory in dioc. of Cork.

RATHCLINE, fee *Rathline*.

RATHCOFFY, commonly called *Racoffy*, an antient feat, fit. near Maynooth, in bar. Ikeath, co. Kildare, prov. Leinfter: lately in poffeffion of *Archibald Hamilton Rowan*, efq.

RATHCONNEL, fit. in co. Kildare, prov. Leinfter, 30 miles from Dublin. A mile beyond which is a feat called *Ardillas*.—Alfo a place fit. in bar. Moyafhel, co. Weftmeath, prov. Leinfter.

RATHCONRATH, a bar. in co. Weftmeath, prov. Leinfter, in which is a village of fame name, which is a rectory in dioc. of Meath. It was alfo called *Fiodh-Aongufa*, and in early ages, *Coen-druim*, from containing the hill of

U*fnach*, famous for being the place where the antient fynods and public affemblies were frequently held; efpecially that in 1112, under *Celfus*, archbifhop of Armagh.

RATHCOOL, (commonly called *Racool*) fit. in bar. Newcaftle, co. Dublin, prov. Leinfter, about 7 miles from Dublin; it is a vicarage in dioc. of Dublin, and gives title of vifc. to the family of *Tracey*. There are 3 fairs in the year for cattle and pedlar's wares, viz. 23 April, 18 June and 9 Oct.—Alfo a vicarage in dioc. of Offory, fit. in bar. Gowran, co. Kilkenny, prov. Leinfter.—Alfo a rectory in dioc. of Cafhel, fit. in bar. Middlethird, co. Tipperary, prov. Munfter.

RATHCORE, a vicarage in dioc. of Meath, fit. in bar. Moyfenrath, co. Meath, prov. Leinfter.

RATHCORMUCK, fit. in co. Cork, prov. Munfter, 111 miles from Dublin. It is a borough, poft and fair town, 11¼ Irifh meafured miles from *Cork*; fit. near the river *Bride*, and adorned with a handfome parifh church and fteeple, and a court-houfe. It returns 2 members to parliament; patronage in the *Tonfon* family. Fairs held 12 Aug. and 29 Oct. It is a rectory in dioc. of Cloyne.—Alfo a vicarage in dioc. of Lifmore, fit. in bar. Upperthird, co. Waterford, prov. Munfter.

RATH-CRAYHAN, otherwife called *Atha*, fit. near *Elphin*, in co. Rofcommon, prov. Connaught; it was alfo denominated *Cromchan*, and *Croghan*, and antiently *Drum Druid*. The Irifh annals mention a rath or fort, being erected here by *Eochy Feylogh*, in the time of *Auguftus Cæfar*. The only remains of this famous city, where once *Cathmor*, the friend of ftrangers, exercifed his unbounded hofpitality, are, the *rath*, the *cave*, and the *Naafteoghan*, where the ftates of Connaught affembled.

RATHDONNEL, a feat of lord *Newhaven*, fit. in co. Carlow, prov. Leinfter.

RATHDOWN, otherwife called "*the grounds*." They are fhelves of fand, fit. along the coaft in the Irifh channel, and appear dry, even at high water, yet between them and the fhore, the water is 7 fathom deep.—Alfo a diftrict which forms 2 bar.'s, one in co. Dublin, the other in co. Wicklow, diftinguifhed each by the name of *Half-Rathdown*, both in prov. Leinfter.

RATHDOWNEY, fit. in bar. Upper Offory, Queen's co. prov. Leinfter, 44 miles from Dublin. Fairs held 6 May, 10 July, 12 Sept. and 15 Dec. It is a vicarage in dioc. of Offory.

RATHDOWTAN, a rectory in dioc. of Cork, fit. in bar. Carbery, co. Cork, prov. Munfter.

RATHDRUM, a poft and fair town, fit. in bar. Ballinacor, co. Wicklow, prov. Leinfter, above 25 miles from Dublin. Near it was
Dunum,

Dunum, a city and capital of the *Menapii*, mentioned by *Ptolemy*; it was the feat of the chiefs of *Coulan*, and called by the Irish, *Rathdruim*, from whence the name *Rathdrum*. Fairs held 1 Thurſd. O. S. Feb. 5 April and July, 10 Oct. and 11 Dec. alſo on firſt Mond. in each month for *flannels*, except *July*, when it is held on the 2 of that month. 2 miles from *Rathdrum* is *Whaley-abbey*, a handſome feat. *Rathdrum* is a vicarage in dioc. of Dublin.

RATHDRUMMIN, a rectory in dioc. of Armagh, fit. in bar. Ferrard, co. Louth, prov. Leinſter.

RATHEEN, fit. in bar. Lune, co. Meath, prov. Leinſter.

RATHEEN-COMMON, now the *great-heath* of *Maryborough*, fit. in Queen's co. prov. Leinſter.

RATHENE, a church in dioc. of Raphoe, co. Donegal, prov. Ulſter, commonly called *Rathnanepſcóp*. St. *Aid Glaſs* fixed his reſidence here, where his feſtival is obſerved on 16 Feb. and the feaſt of St. *Fidmunius*, of Rathene, (his brother) who flouriſhed, A. D. 750, is obſerved here on 16 May.

RATHERNON, a rectory in dioc. of Kildare, fit. in bar. Great-connel, co. Kildare, prov. Leinſter.

RATHFARNE, a village, fit. in bar. Farbill, co. Weſtmeath, prov. Leinſter.

RATHFARNHAM, fit. in bar. Newcaſtle, co. Dublin, prov. Leinſter, near 3 miles from the metropolis. Here are the extenſive improvements and caſtle of the late earl of *Ely*, and preſent lord *Loftus*. Within 1½ mile of Rathfarnham, is *Marlay*, a beautiful feat of the Rt. Hon. *Dav. Latouche*. Fairs held at Rathfarnham, 10 July. This is a curacy in dioc. of Dublin.

RATHFEIGH, a rectory in dioc. of Meath, fit. in bar. Skryne, co. Meath, prov. Leinſter.

RATHFRAN, fit. in co. Mayo, prov. Connaught; fairs held 25 Aug. and 11 Nov.

RATHFRILAND, a poſt and fair town, fit. in bar. Upper Iveagh, co. Down, prov. Ulſter, 57 miles from Dublin. It is feated on a riſing ground, having 4 large ſtraight roads leading up to it, and centering in the town. It is built on a free-ſtone rock of a firm cloſe grit; and has a decent church, a meeting-houſe for *Diſſenters*, and a ſmall horſe-courſe. On the ſummit of the hill are the ruins of an old caſtle, antiently one of the manſion houſes of the *Magennis's*, lords *Iveach*, whom the *O'Neils* after the example of the more powerful Iriſh ſepts, cruelly oppreſſed by an exaction impoſed at pleaſure, called *Bonaght*. This caſtle was a much larger building than what it now appears to be, having been pulled down by Mr. *Hawkins*, the firſt Proteſtant proprietor of it, after the rebellion of 1641; with the materials

whereof, he built the *inn*, and other houſes in the town. About half a mile from Rathfriland is *Liſſize*, the feat of the earl of *Clanwilliam*. 2 miles N. E. of this town is a celebrated ſpa, called *Tierkelly* well. The water is a very ſtrong chalybeate, yet exceedingly light, and free from any conſiderable proportion of heterogeneous mixture; it hath been found very efficacious in ſcorbutic caſes, when uſed externally and internally. Fairs held here 2 Wedn. O. S. April, Wedn. after Trinity, 2 Wedn. O. S. Sept. 2 Wedn. in Dec.

RATHGOGGIN, a vicarage in dioc. of Cloyne, fit. in bar. Orrery, co. Cork, prov. Munſter.

RATHINBHER, a caſtle of the *O'Tools*, chiefs of *Croich Coulan*, fit. at the mouth of *Bray-river*, in co. Wicklow, prov. Leinſter. Here St. Patrick was refuſed admiſſion by the pagan inhabitants, on his arrival to convert them to the Chriſtian faith.

RATHJORDAN, a vicarage in dioc. of Emly, fit. in bar. Clanwilliam, co. Limerick, prov. Munſter.

RATHISCAR-LODGE, fit. near *Dunleer*, prov. Leinſter.

RATHKEAL, a poſt, market and fair town in bar. Connello, co. Limerick, prov. Munſter, 108 miles from Dublin; fit. on the river *Deel*. It was formerly a corporation town, and of much more conſequence than at preſent. Here are ſtill remaining the ruins of a priory, founded in a very early age by a perſon of the name of *Harvey*, and dedicated to the Virgin Mary, for Auguſtinian canons of the order of *Aroacia*. It takes its name from *rath* a fort, and *ciel* a wood, being formerly a place of conſiderable ſtrength; and ſuſtained an attack of the Engliſh army, in the reign of queen Eliz. Fairs held here 4 April, 1 June, 25 Aug. 18 Sept. and Nov. *horſes*. This is a rectory in dioc. of Limerick; within 2 miles of it, are the ruins of a caſtle.

RATH-KELTAIR, the antient caſtle, and principal reſidence of the chiefs of the *Ulidii*, and was fit. near Downpatrick, in bar. Lecale, co. Down, in the antient diſtrict of *Dal-Dichu*. The ditches and ramparts of this antient fortreſs are remaining to this day, and occupy near 2 acres of ground. It was probably erected by the chiefs of the *Ulleigh*, on their firſt eſtabliſhment in this country, ſome few years before the birth of Chriſt. On the arrival of St. *Patrick*, this rath was inhabited by *Keltair ma Duach*, chieftain of this diſtrict, who granted a place for the building of a church on a hill called *Dun*; and from which *Down* has obtained its preſent name. The church of *Down* was made a biſhoprick by St. Cailan, about 499.

RATHKELTY, a vicarage in dioc. of Caſhel, fit. in bar. Eliogurty, co. Tipperary, prov. Munſt.

RATHKENNY,

from the metropolis; here is an old moat or rath, with an entrenchment round it.

RATH-MOR-MUIGHE-LINE, the royal feat of the kings of *Dalnaruidhe*, in co. Antrim, prov. Ulster; fit. on the river Ban: it was probably the Rhobogdiu of *Rich. Cirenc.* and the prefent *Coleraine*.

RATHMOYLAN, a parish in bar. Gualtiere, co. Waterford, prov. Munster, in which on the coast towards the fea, there are feveral caves and fubterraneous paffages. It is a vicarage in dioc. of Waterford.

RATHMUIGHE, fit. on the fea-fhore near *Dunluce*, in co. Antrim, prov. Ulster. Here was a monastery over which St. *Olean* prefided; it was destroyed by fire in 612; and afterwards plundered in the years 831 and 960.

RATHMULLEN, a village fit. in bar. Kilmacrenan, co. Donegal, prov. Ulster; where a houfe was built for Carmelites or white friars, and dedicated to the Virgin Mary, by *Mac Swine Fannagh.*—Alfo in bar. Corran, co. Sligo, prov. Connaught.—Alfo a vicarage in dioc. of Down, fit. in bar. Lecale, co. Down, prov. Ulster.

RATHMULLER, fit. in bar. Lecale, co. Down, prov. Ulster.

RATHNAGANE, fit. in bar. lower Ormond, co. Tipperary, prov. Munster.

RATHNALLY-MILLS, fit. near *Trim*, prov. Leinster.

RATH-NA-NURLAN, a castle of a dynast, on the plains of Cafhel, co. Tipperary, prov. Munster; where *Lorcan* halted on his vifit to *Cormac*, king and archbifhop of Cafhel.

RATHNEW, a chapelry in dioc. of Dublin, fit. in bar. Newcastle, co. Wicklow, prov. Leinst.

RATHOSKER, fit. in bar. Atherdee, co. Louth, prov. Leinster.

RATH-OWEN, fit. in co. Weftmeath, prov. Leinster; fairs held 15 May and 2 Tuefd. Dec.

RATHPATRICK, a vicarage in dioc. of Offory, fit. in bar. Ida, co. Kilkenny, prov. Leinst.

RATHREA, a vicarage in dioc. of Ardagh, fit. in bar. Ardagh, co. Longford, prov. Leinst.

RATHREE, a vicarage in dioc. of Killala, fit. in bar. Tirawly, co. Mayo, prov. Connaught.

RATHREGAN, a rectory in dioc. of Meath, fit. in bar. Ratoath, co. Meath, prov. Leinster.

RATHRONAN, a parish in co. Waterford, prov. Munster.—Alfo a rectory in dioc. of Limerick, fit. in bar. Connello, co. Limerick, prov. Munster.—Alfo a vicarage in dioc. of Lifmore, fit. in bar. Iffa and Offa, co. Tipperary, prov. Munster.

RATHRUDDY CASTLE, fit. near *Loughrea*, co. Galway, prov. Connaught.

RATHSALLAGH, a curacy in dioc. of Dublin, fit. in bar. Talbot'ftown, co. Wicklow, prov. Leinster, 24 miles from Dublin. Fairs held 4 Sept.

RATHSARRAN, a rectory in dioc. of Offory, fit. in bar. upper Offory, Queen's co. prov. Leinster.

RATHSHERKIN, fit. in co. Antrim, prov. Ulster; fairs held 16 Nov.

RATHTOOLE, a vicarage in dioc. of Dublin, fit. in co. Dublin, prov. Leinster.

RATHTOY, fee *Rattoo*.

RATHTRUN, fit. in bar. Tirawly, co. Mayo, prov. Connaught.

RATHUE, a chapelry in dioc. of Meath, fit. in bar. Moycafhel, co. Weftmeath, prov. Leinst.

RATHVILLY, fee *Ravilly*.

RATHWERE, a village fit. in bar. Farbill, co. Weftmeath, prov. Leinster.

RATHYNE, fit. in bar. Fertullagh, co. Weftmeath, prov. Leinster. St. *Carthag*, alias *Mochuda*, erected a famous monastery here; where he prefided 40 years over 867 monks; who fupported themfelves and the neighbouring poor by labour. There was alfo a celebrated academy under the direction of this faint; but in Easter, 630, he and his monks were driven out of the abbey by king *Blathmac*, who was incenfed against them by the monks of a neighbouring abbey. St. Carthag took refuge at *Lifmore*, co. Waterford, where he died 14 May, 636.

RATOATH, a bar. in co. Meath, prov. Leinster, in which is a borough and fair town of fame name, fit. near 13 miles from Dublin; it is but a very poor village; the church is built on the ruins of an abbey; and near it is a very fine and confpicuous mount; this place returns two members to parliament, patronage in the family of *Lowther*; fairs held day before Whit-Sunday. It is a vicarage in dioc. of Meath. Lat. 53:28, lon. 6:54. Its antient name was *Rath Aodh*; here *Malachy* the Ift. held his third convention of the ftates of the kingdom. The abbey was under the invocation of St. *Mary Magdalene*, and exifted in 1450; fome old walls and the W. window of the abbey still remain.

RATORP, a village fit. in bar. Kiltartan, co. Galway, prov. Connaught.

RATTAN-CASTLE, fit. in co. Weftmeath, prov. Leinster; according to fir *William Petyt*, it had formerly 500 rooms in it; there is now but one tower left, which contains near 20 apartments.

RATTASS, a rectory in dioc. of Ardfert, fit. in bar. Truaghnacmy, co. Kerry, prov. Munst.

RATTOO, a village fit. in bar. Clanmaurice, co. Kerry, prov. Munster. It is a rectory in dioc. of Ardfert: here is now a handfome feat. Several tracts of land near this place, go by the name of the *Burgefs* land; from whence

it

it is thought that *Rattoo* had been formerly a corporation; in some old records, it is called *Rathtoy*, and in it stood an abbey of canons regular, of St. *Austine*; which had been originally a preceptory belonging to the Knights Hospitalers of St. John of Jerusalem, founded by one friar *William*, and confirmed by *Miler Fitz Miler*, in the reign of king *John*; it was again changed into *Arosian* canons, and dedicated to St. *Peter* and St. *Paul*. In Nov. 1600, it was burned down by the Irish, upon the approach of sir *Charles Wilmot's* forces to this part of the country. It is said that there were formerly 7 churches in the place, and some old MSS. mention it to have been a bishoprick, which notion the high antient round tower, standing in the church yard, seems to countenance.

RAVEN-POINT, a *headland*, sit. at the N. side of the entrance of Wexford bay, in bar. Shelmaliere, co. Wexford, prov. Leinster.

RAVENSDALE, sit. in co. Louth, prov. Leinster; fairs held Friday after Good Friday, 2 Friday July, 1 Friday Oct. and 2 Friday Nov.—Also a place near Leixlip, prov. Leinster

RAVENSDALE-PARK, sit. near *Flurry-bridge*, prov. Leinster.

RAVILL-WATER, a river so called, sit. in bar. Antrim, co. Antrim, prov. Ulster.

RAVILLY, (or *Rathvilly*) a bar. in co. Carlow, prov. Leinster; having in it a village of same name, distant about 25 miles from Dublin; which is a rectory in dioc. of Leighlin. 1 mile from this place is *Mount Neil*, the handsome seat of the hon. *John Stratford*. At Ravilly is one of the antient raths. Fairs held 1 Jan. 25 March, 24 June, 1 Aug. and 12 Nov.

RAY, a village in bar. Raphoe, co. Donegal, prov. Ulster, where there is a charter school for above 30 children; it was opened in 1740, and endowed with 2 acres of land in perpetuity, by *John Leslie*, esq; and 20 acres more for three lives, at 6*l.* per ann. The right Rev. Dr. *Forster*, late lord bishop of Raphoe, gave several sums towards erecting the building, and providing furniture for the school; also 400*l.* the interest of which his lordship appropriated towards maintaining the children. *Ray* is a rectory in dioc. of Raphoe.

RAYLESTOWN, a rectory in dioc. of Cashel, sit. in bar. Middlethird, co. Tipperary, prov. Munster.

RAYMUNTERDONY, a rectory in dioc. of Raphoe, sit. in bar. Kilmacrenan, co. Donegal, prov. Ulster.

REAGH, sit. near Killala, co. Mayo, prov. Connaught.

REA-LOUGH, a *lake*, sit. in bar. Loughrea, co. Galway, prov. Connaught.

REBAN, see *Rheban*

RED-BAY, sit. in bar. Glenarm, co. Antrim, prov. Ulster. Here is a castle called *Red-bay-castle*. Lat. 55:7, lon. 6:45.

RED-CASTLE, sit. near Lough Foyle, in bar. Innisowen, co. Donegal, prov. Ulster.

RED-CITY, a rectory in dioc. of Cashel, sit. in bar. Middlethird, co. Tipperary, prov. Munster.

RED-CROSS, sit. in bar. Arklow, co. Wicklow, prov. Leinster, 31 miles from Dublin. Near it is the turn to the copper mines of *Cronebawn*, *Kilmacoe* and *Connery*. Fairs held 6 May and 5 Aug.

RED-GATE, sit. in co. Clare, prov. Munster, 118 miles from Dublin. Near Red-gate inn are the ruins of a castle, and a little farther, those of a church.

RED-HALL, sit. near Carrickfergus, prov. Ulst.

RED-HILLS, sit. in co. Cavan, prov. Ulster; fairs held 1 Jan. 24 May, July and Oct.—Also in co. Kildare, prov. Leinster: these latter are sit. between 2 and 4 miles N. W. of Kildare, in a direction nearly N. and S. they consist of 3 elevations, the 2 Northern of which are denominated *Dun Murach*, or *Dun Murry*, i. e. the *Red hills*; the Southern *Dun Almhain*, or the *hill of Allen*; which is separated from *Dun Murry* by a valley about a mile in breadth. Dun Murry forms a kind of head-land towards the N. is fertile in corn and pasturage, and composed of limestone rock. The loose stones on its surface frequently appear as if calcined in the fire, of a red purple colour, and sometimes tinctured with sulphur; whence these hills have from remote periods, obtained the name of *Murach*, or reddish purple. Though such stones are certain indications of copper being contained in the internal parts, no search or discovery was made respecting the fact until about the year 1786, when some of the neighbouring farmers opening a gravel pit, on the N. declivity of Dun Murry, near the base, something like metallic ore was discovered; which upon examination was found to be rich copper. The principal bed of the mine seems to lie deep within the hill, and even to dip under the valley which separates Dun Murry from the hill of Allen. This valley is not only fertile and pleasant, but being well supplied with water, is rendered extremely convenient for the establishment of manufactures of most kinds. 2 flour mills have already been erected, and there is every convenience for cotton and linen manufactures.

RED-HOUSE, sit. near *Ardee*, prov. Leinster.

RED-LION, sit. in co. Kildare, prov. Leinster; fairs held 25 March and 8 Sept.

RED-WOOD, sit. in bar. Ballycowan, King's co. prov. Leinster.

REEK-PATRICK CHURCH, sit. near Ballymagarry, co. Tyrone, prov. Ulster.

REE-LOUGH, fee *Lough Ree*.

REGIA, an antient city in the N. of Ireland, mentioned by *Ptolemy*; it is the fame with the prefent *Clogher*, in co. Tyrone, prov. Ulfter; where was the rath or palace of the antient kings of *Ergall*, before which St. Patrick directed *Macartane* to build a monaftery, which afterwards became a bifhoprick.

REISK, a vicarage in dioc. of Waterford, fit. in bar. Middlethird, co. Waterford, prov. Leinfter.

RELIGMURRY, a rectory in dioc. of Cafhel, fit. in bar. Clanwilliam, co. Tipperary, prov. Munfter.

RELIG-NA-RIOGH, the fepulchral place of fome of the antient Irifh kings and chieftains, fit. near *Croghan*, in co. Rofcommon, prov. Connaught. It confifts of a circular area of about 200 feet in diameter, furrounded with a ftone ditch greatly defaced. Several tranfverfe ditches are within the area; alfo heaps of coarfe ftones piled upon each other, fpecifying the graves of the interred perfons. From the conftruction of this cemetary, it appears to have been erected in the latter ages of paganifm, about the clofe of the firft century.

REYNAGH, a vicarage in dioc. of Meath, fit. in bar. Garrycaftle, King's co. prov. Leinfter.

REYNOLD'STOWN, fit. in bar. Louth, co. Louth, prov. Leinfter.

RHEBA, an antient city mentioned by *Ptolemy*; fit. according to *Rich. Cirenc.* S. of Lough Erne. It was the rath of the *Magh Guires*, antient chieftains of the co. Fermanagh, prov. Ulfter.

RHEBAN, (or *Reban*) a diftrict joined to that of Narragh. and forming with it the *bar.* of *Narragh and Rheban*, in co. Kildare, prov. Leinfter. In it was the antient city of Rheban, fit. on the Weftern banks of the river Barrow, about 2 miles N. of *Athy*. The only remains of it is a deep quadrangular intrenchment, on the Weftern extremity of which is a high conical mount. It feems to have been a fort, commanding a pafs over the river, and fit. among antient woods, now no more. It belonged to the antient principality of *Hy Lavighfeagh*, or *Leix*; and was one of the outpofts on the confines of that diftrict, until the limits were enlarged in fubfequent periods. Being placed on a branch of the Southern road, it continued a place of importance until the arrival of the Englifh, when Dunnamafe and its feveral appurtenances, being erected into a bar. under *Marfhal*, earl of *Pembroke*, lord palatinate of Leinfter, Rheban was by him granted in fee to *Richard de St. Michael*, created baron of Rheban, who in the reign of king John, erected a caftle on the N. E. of the old fort, the ruins of which are ftill remaining. It was

for a long time a frontier caftle, and feat of the proprietors, when in 1325, on the abfence of moft of the Englifh fettlers, Dunnamafe, with all its fubordinate caftles, was taken by Lyfagh, or Lavifeagh O'More, the antient proprietor of the country; among which was the caftle of Rheban, and by him and his defcendants retained many ages. In 1315, *Robert Bruce* took Rheban, and almoft all the contiguous caftles in the co. Kildare. About 1424, Tho. Fitzgerald, lord of Offaly, and afterwards the 7th earl of Kildare, married Dorothea, daughter of Anthony O'More, and received in dower, the manors of *Rheban* and *Woodftock*, which continued for fome time, and in part remain ftill in that family. The caftle from the ruins, does not appear to have been very ftrong, tho' the outworks feem to have been extenfive; and in one part are evident remains of a baftion, after the modern method of fortification. No remains of the antient city are vifible, except fome ftone foundations near the rath; notwithftanding, Rheban exifted as a village with a caftle towards the clofe of the 16th century. In 1642, a detachment of the army under the marquis of *Ormond*, took the caftle; and in 1648, *Owen Roe O'Neil* feized this and other fortreffes; but being defeated by lord Inchiquin and col. Prefton, he made an overture to col. Jones, by his vicar general, *O'Reilly*, that he would furrender Athy, Maryborough and Rheban, provided he and the confederate catholics might have the privileges they enjoyed in the time of king James. Tradition afferts that there was a fair held here on St. Michael's day, fince removed to Athy, and there held on that day O. S. being 10 Oct. N. S.

RHEUBANE, a pleafant feat fit. 2 miles N. of *Ardchin*, in co. Down, prov. Ulfter; now called *Echlin's-ville*.

RHINCREW, fit. in bar. Cofhbride, co. Waterford, prov. Munfter; the abbey lands of which were granted to fir *Walter Raleigh*, in fee farm; and afterwards, with the reft of his eftate were purchafed by the earl of *Cork*. This is a vicarage in dioc. of Lifmore, and otherwife written *Rincrew*. The caftle here is faid to have belonged to the knights of St. *John* of *Jerufalem*.

RHOBOGDÆ-PROMONTORIUM, fo called by *Ptolemy*, it is the fame with the prefent *Fairhead*, in co. Antrim, prov. Ulfter.

RICHARDSTOWN, a fmall village near Caftledermot, in co. Kildare, prov. Leinfter. Here are the ruins of a very large caftle, and other antiquities.—Alfo a vicarage in dioc. of Armagh, fit. in bar. Ardee, co. Louth, prov. Leinfter.

RICHFIELD, fit. near Wexford, prov. Leinft.

RICH-

Rhéban

RICH-HILL, fit. in bar. Oneilland, co. Armagh, prov. Ulfter, 62 miles from Dublin.

RICHMOND, a handfome little village adjoining that of Ballybough, about 1¼ mile from the caftle of Dublin, in co. Dublin, prov. Leinfter.

RICH-MOUNT, fit. in bar. Oneilland, co. Armagh, prov. Ulfter.

RICKENHORE, fit. in bar. Nethercrofs, co. Dublin, prov. Leinfter.

RIGSDALE, fit. near Cork, co. Cork, prov. Munfter.

RIN, fit. in bar. Mohill, co. Mayo, prov. Connaught.

RINABELLY, fit. in co. Cork, prov. Munfter, about 3 miles S. of *Carrigaline*. There is here a dangerous fandy bay, fometimes fatally miftaken by mariners for the mouth of Cork harbour; a hard fand obftructs the entrance. The mouth of this bay opens due Weft, whereas that of Cork harbour lies in North.

RINBANE-CASTLE, fit. in bar. Carie, co. Antrim, prov. Ulfter. Lat. 55 : 15, lon. 7 : 00.

RINCOLISKY, (now called *Whitehall*) fit. about a mile S. of *Affadown*, in co. Cork, prov. Munfter. It is a caftle which belonged to the *Coppingers*: but it was originally built by the *O'Drifcols*.

RINCORAN, a rectory in dioc. of Cork, fit. in liberties of Kinfale, co. Cork, prov. Munft.

RINCREW, see *Rhincrew*.

RINDISART, (or *Rinedizart*) formerly a feat or caftle of the *O'Sullivans*, fit. near *Bantry*, in co. Cork, prov. Munfter. It was demolifhed by a fhip of war in *Oliver Cromwell's* time.

RINEOGONAGH, see *Ringonagh*.

RINFAD, a promontory which forms the Eaft of *Killough* bay, in co. Down, prov. Ulfter.

RINGDUFFERIN, or *Dufferin*, a barony in co. Down, prov. Ulfter; it was inhabited by an antient fept of the *Mac Cartanes*; they were neighbours to the *Maginnes's*, and defcended from the fame head, viz. from *Conall* the fon of *Coalbhaig*, who is faid to have been the 132d. king of Ireland, about the year of Chrift 357. This barony was formerly much incumbered with woods and faftnefles, and after the firft Englifh invafion was poffeffed by the *Mandevilles*, and in the reign of queen Eliz. by the *Whites*.

RINGFORT, an agreeable feat about a mile S. W. from *Charleville*, co. Cork, prov. Munft.

RINGHADDY, fit. N. of *Killeleagh*, on the fide of *Strangford lake*, in co. Down, prov. Ulfter; it is now noted for its oyfters, but formerly was remarkable for its caftle, which together with another erected not far from it, on the *Ifle* of *Seaterick*, formed two places for defence for thofe parts.

RINGONAGH, a vicarage in dioc of Lifmore, fit. in bar Decies without Drum, co. Waterford, prov. Munfter. This parifh is well cultivated, particularly that part of it which lies contiguous to the harbour of Dungarvan. In it is a refpected holy well, dedicated to St. Nicholas. This place is otherwife written *Rincogonagh*.

RING-ROAN, an antient caftle and fmall village in bar. Courceys, co. Cork, prov. Munfter, which gives title of baron to the lords of Kinfale. This manor had antiently 30 Knights fees: and was of a much greater extent than at prefent; it is a rectory in dioc. of Cork.

RINGS-END, a village fit. 1¼ mile from Dublin caftle, in bar. Half-Rathdown, co. Dublin, prov. Leinfter; it lies by the fea-fide, and is convenient for bathing; but not much frequented; adjoining it is the fmall village of *Irifhtown*, which has a church belonging to it. The proper name of this place is *Rin-ann*, i. e. *the point of the tide*, a term very applicable to it's fituation, but now corrupted into *Rings-end*.

RINNY-CASTLE, fit. in co. Cork, prov. Munfter; it was heretofore a part of the poet *Spenfer's* eftate.

RINVEEL-POINT, a *cape* fit. in bar. Ballynahinch, co. Galway, prov. Connaught.

RIVER ANNACLOY, fit. in co. Down, prov. Ulfter, between *Strangford lake* and the village of *Annacloy*; that part of it which runs by *Ballinahinch*, is called *Ballinahinch river*.

RIVERSTOWN, fit. in co. Galway, prov. Connaught, 92 miles from Dublin; a mile and a half beyond it, is a bridge over the river *Carnamart*; within a mile of which are the ruins of 6 caftles.—Alfo a village fit. in bar. Barrymore, co. Cork, prov. Munfter. Here is a handfome feat, the elegant gardens of which are watered by the river *Glanmire*.—Alfo a feat near *Monaftercvan*, in co. Kildare, prov. Leinfter.

ROACH, a curacy in dioc. of Armagh, fit. in bar. Dundalk, co Louth, prov. Leinfter.

ROAD, a village fit. in bar. Warrenftown, King's co. prov. Leinfter.

ROARING-WATER BAY, fit. in bar. Carbery, co. Cork, prov. Munfter.

ROBE, a *river* fit. in bar. Kilmain, co. Mayo, prov. Connaught.

ROBEEN, a vicarage in dioc. of Tuam, fit. in bar. Kilmain, co. Mayo, prov. Connaught.

ROBERTSOWN, a rectory in dioc. of Meath, fit. in bar. Kells, co. Meath, prov. Leinfter.

ROBERT'STOWN, fit. in co. Kildare, prov. Leinfter, 21 miles from Dublin: by which the *Grand Canal* paffes from Dublin to Monafterevan; there is alfo a caftle of this name, fit. in co. Cork, prov. Munfter; it is a high fquare tower,

tower, and lies to the E. of a small town called *Castle-lyons*.

ROBIN-CASTLE, fit. 1 mile from *Hollymount*, co. Mayo, prov. Connaught.

ROBIN'STOWN, fit. near Mullingar, prov. Leinfter.

ROBSWALL'S-CASTLE, fit. in bar. Coolock, co. Dublin, prov. Leinfter.

ROCHCONNEL, fit. in co. Weftmeath, prov. Leinfter, 2 miles E. of *Mullingar*, in the road to Dublin; the name fignifies O'Connel's rout or defeat; here general *Prefton* took his poft in a famous battle, between the Englifh and Irifh, in the wars of 1641, in which the former almoft miraculoufly came off victorious.

ROCHDALE, fit. in co. Louth, prov. Leinfter, near 46 miles from Dublin; fairs held 20 June and Oct.

ROCHESTOWN, fit. in co. Dublin, prov. Leinfter, 7 miles from the metropolis, and about 3 from the *Black-rock*. The air here is temperate and wholefome, and the place is much frequented by perfons who wifh to have the benefit of Goat's whey. Near it is a very beautiful obelifk on a rifing ground, which may be feen at a great diftance, and ferves as a land mark.—Alfo a rectory in dioc. of Lifmore, fit. in bar. Iffa and Offa, co. Tipperary, prov. Munfter.—Alfo a vicarage in dioc. of Emly, fit. in bar. Clanwilliam, co. Limerick, prov. Munfter.

ROCKFORD'STOWN, a pleafant feat in co. Cork, prov. Munfter, a few miles from the town of *Cork*.

ROCHFORT, fit. in bar. Fertullagh, co. Weftmeath, prov. Leinfter.

ROCKBELLEW, a feat of lord *Ludlow*, fit. near Julian'ftown-bridge, co. Dublin, prov. Leinfter.

ROCKBROOK, a fmall village fit. 2¼ miles from *Temple-oge*, and 5½ from Dublin, in co. Dublin, prov. Leinfter. It is pleafantly feated at the foot of the mountains, and enjoys a remarkably pure and wholefome air.

ROCK-CORRY, fit. in co. Monaghan, prov. Ulfter, 55 miles from Dublin; fairs held laft Wedn. Jan. Feb. 28 March, 2 Wedn. O. S. in Nov.

ROCKFIELD, fit. in co. Rofcommon, prov. Connaught; fairs held firft Monday O. S. in May and 28 Sept.—Alfo a pleafant feat in co. Cork, prov. Munfter, not far from *Knockninofs*. Alfo a place near *Flurrybridge*, prov. Leinfter. And another near Roftrevor, co. Down, prov. Ulfter.

ROCKHILL, fit. in co. Cork, prov. Munfter; fairs held 21 May, 19 June, 26 Aug. and 26 Oct.—Alfo a place near Rofcommon, prov. Connaught.

ROCKINGHAM, fit. in co. Rofcommon, prov. Connaught. It gives title of baron Kingfton of Rockingham, to the family of *King*, now earl of *Kingfton*.

ROCK-MOOR, fit. in bar. Dundalk, co. Louth, prov. Leinfter.

ROCK-SAVAGE, a feat of the family of *Cavanagh*, fit. between *Borris* and *Tullow*, in co. Carlow, prov. Leinfter. — Alfo a place near *Rofcommon*, prov. Connaught.

ROCK'SBOROUGH, fit. in bar. Ferrard, co. Louth, prov. Leinfter. — Alfo a place near *Loughrea*, prov. Connaught.

ROCKVIEW, fit. in co. Wexford, prov. Leinft.

ROCKVILLE, a village fit. in bar. Decies within Drum, co. Waterford, prov. Munfter. Alfo a place near *Elphin*, prov. Connaught.

ROCKWOOD, a feat in co. Kerry, prov. Munfter. having a fair profpect of *Killarney* lake and the adjacent iflands.

ROE, an *ifland* fit. off the coaft of bar. Burrifhoole, co. Mayo, prov. Connaught.—Alfo a *river* fit. in bar. Kenoght, co. Londonderry, prov. Ulfter.

ROEBUCK, fit. near *Old-caftle*, prov. Leinfter.

ROE-CASTLE, fit. in bar. Colerain, co. Londonderry, prov. Ulfter; lat. 55:2, lon. 7:14.

ROE'SBOROUGH, fit. in co. Cork, prov. Munfter.

ROES-GREEN, fit. in co. Tipperary, prov. Munfter; fairs held 2 Aug. and 3 Thurfday in Oct.

ROES-MOUNT, fit. near *Belfaft*, prov. Ulfter.

ROE-WATER, fit. in co. Londonderry, prov. Ulfter, on which the town of *Newtown-Limavady* is feated.

ROGANSTOWN, fit. in bar. Nethercrofs, co. Dublin, prov. Leinfter.

ROGER'STOWN, fit. near *Drogheda*, prov. Leinfter.—Alfo a fea-port in co. Dublin, prov. Leinfter, the channel of which affords good fhelter, and of eafy accefs. To go over the Bar, bring the fteeple of *Lufk* into a valley of the two Northernmoft hills, bearing N. W. ¼ N. which is your courfe to fteer. There is 10 feet water on the Bar, when *Lampfoon* head is juft covered; it flows in fpring tides about 15 feet, and there is about 5 feet difference in Highwater fprings, and Neap tides.

ROLL'S-CASTLE, fit. near *Birr*, prov. Leinfter.

RONANE'S-GROVE, formerly called *Hednet's wood*, fit. in co. Cork, prov. Munfter, not far W. from the caftle of *Belvelly*; here are fome good improvements, formerly in poffeffion of *Phill. Ronayne*, efq; who diftinguifhed himfelf by his mathematical knowledge, and his treatife on *Algebra*; he invented a *cube* perforated in fuch a manner, that a fecond *cube* of the fame dimenfions exactly in all refpects, might pafs
through

through it; the poffibility of which he demon-
ftrated both algebraically and geometrically,
and which was actually put in practife, by the
late ingenious Mr. *Daniel Vofter*, of Cork.

ROO-WATER, fee *Roe-water*.

RORY-RIVER, fit. in co. Cork, prov. Munfter;
it runs 1 mile W. of *Rofs*.

ROSAPEN, fit. near *Sheephaven*, co. Donegal,
prov. Ulfter.

ROSBERKIN, fit. in bar. Ida, co. Kilkenny,
prov. Leinfter; fairs held Eafter-monday, 3
May, Whit-monday, 10. Aug. 5 and 18 Oct.
It is a vicarage in dioc. of Offory; and fometimes written *Rofbercon*, and *Roffibercan*; It lies
oppofite to *Rofs* on the river Barrow. The
families of *Grace* and *Walfh*, are faid to have
founded a monaftery here, dedicated to the
affumption of the Virgin Mary, where friars
preachers were firft introduced, 19 Sept. 1267.
From the ruins it appears, that this monaftery
was by no means an ignoble ftructure.

ROSCAN, fit. near *Galway*, co. Galway, prov.
Connaught.

ROSCLOGHER, a bar. having a village in it of
fame name, fit. in co. Leitrim, prov. Connaught; it is otherwife written *Roffclogher*.

ROSCOM, a rectory in dioc. of Tuam, fit. in
bar. Dunkellin, co. Galway, prov. Connaught.

ROSCOMMON, a bar. fit. in the co. of fame
name, prov. Connaught.

ROSCOMMON (*county,*) fit. in prov. Connaught;
it is bounded by Sligo and Leitrim on the N.
Longford and Weftmeath on the E. Galway
on the S. and another part of Galway and Mayo
on the W. This is a long narrow co. and the
foil in moft places plain and fertile. It contains
346,650 acres, 56 parifhes, 6 bar.'s, and 3 boroughs, and returns 8 members to parliament;
it gives title of earl to the family of *Dillon*;
its length from N. to S. is 47 miles, the breadth
varies confiderably, and in the broadeft part,
about the middle of the co. is 29 miles; chief
town Rofcommon. The bar.'s are Boyle, Ballintobber, Half-Ballinoe, Rofcommon, Athlone and Moycarne. Number of houfes 17,137,
and inhabitants about 86,000, it being the beft
peopled of any county Weft of the Shannon.
The principal families of this co. at the commencement of the laft century, were thofe of
O'Connor Dun, O'Flanegan, O'Hanly, O'Do-
nallan, Crofton and Bermingham.

ROSCOMMON (*town.*) the fhire town of the
co. Rofcommon, prov. Connaught; it is a borough, market and poft-town, in the barony
of fame name, and has a barrack for a troop
of horfe: it is 69 miles from Dublin; lat.
53:31 N. lon. 8:20 W. It returns 2 members to parliament; patronage in the *Sandford*
family. This place is fortified with a caftle,
erected here in an early age, and re-edified in

1268 by fir *Rob. de Ufford*, jufticiary of Ireland. It is the affizes town for the co. Rofcommon, and near it are the remains of a monaftery of friars preachers, where a monument was
erected in fine Irifh marble, to *Feidlim O'Connor*, king of Connaught, who died in 1253;
he was reprefented furrounded by his body
guards, in their antient dreffes; this monument was, with more than favage brutality,
confiderably defaced fome years ago, by a parcel of drunken dragoons. Fairs held at Rofcommon, Whit-mond. and 5 Dec. Here is a
linen market on the firft Thurfd. in every
month. We find feveral religious foundations
formerly eftablifhed in this town, viz. an abbey of regular canons founded by St. *Colman*.
A Dominican friary founded by the before-
mentioned *O'Connor*, and a friary for conventual Francifcans founded in 1269, but totally
deftroyed by fire the year following.

ROSCONNEL, or *Roffconnel*, a rectory in dioc.
of Offory, fit. in bar. Faffachdining, co. Kilkenny, prov. Leinfter. Over the door of the
old church of Rofconnel, is the following infcription in old characters, viz. " *Hæc ecclefia
pia cura H. Wilfon, reftaurata eft 19 Aug. Anno
Do: 1646.*" The rev. *Hugh Wilfon* here mentioned was rector of this parifh about the year
1640, and married *Margaret* daughter of *James
Whyte* efq; efcheater general in 1637. Here
was an antient caftle and village of the *O'Mares*,
on the confines of the co. Kilkenny, and
Queen's co. but no remains are now vifible,
but the ruins of an old church.

ROSCREA, a poft and fair town in co. Tipperary, prov. Munfter, 59 miles from Dublin;
it is a neat thriving town; the church has a
curious gothic frontifpiece at the W. end;
near it ftands one of the largeft round towers
in the kingdom, all built with fquare ftone,
which is unufual in thefe edifices. It is 80 feet
high and 15 feet in diameter, with two fteps
round about it at the bottom. At 15 feet from
the ground is a window with a regular arch, and
at an equal height is another window with a
pointed arch. If this latter is not a more re-
cent addition, it certainly reduces the date of
this tower to the 12th century: which is rather
earlier than the time generally allowed for the
ufe of this arch. Rofcrea is now a vicarage in
dioc. of Killaloe; it was once a bifhoprick,
but was united to *Killaloe* in the 12th century;
in the town is a large old caftle, built by the
Ormond family; here is a barrack for a company of foot. In 1213, king *John* erected a
caftle in this town, and an abbey of regular
canons was founded here by St. *Cronan*, who
died 10th May, in the beginning of the 7th
century. The church is very old, the front
confifts of a door and two flat nitches on either
fide,

fide, of Saxon architecture, with a mezzo relievo of the patron faint, much defaced by time. At a little diftance is a crofs in a circle, with a crucifix on one fide, adjoining which is a ftone carved in various figures, and on each end a mezzo relievo of a faint, which is called the fhrine of St. Cronan; a *Francifcan* friary was alfo founded here in 1490, at the N. W. part of the town, by *Mulrony O'Carrol* king of Munfter; its remains are ftill in good prefervation. Fairs held 7 May, 21 June, 8 Aug. 9 Oct. and 29 Nov. *Keating* tells us the *Danes* came with a numerous and well difciplined army from Limerick and Connaught, under the command of *Alfin*; with a defign to furprize the natives, who were then affembled from all parts of the country at the fair of Rofcrea, that was then annually kept on the feaft of St. Peter and St. Paul; but the Irifh knowing the treachery of the Danes, brought arms with them, and an engagement enfued, in which the Danes were entirely routed, 4000 of them flain, amongft whom was *Alfin* their commander; and thus a compleat victory was obtained by the Irifh.

ROSDAREAGH, fit. in bar. upper Offory, Queen's co. prov. Leinfter.

ROSEGARLAND, fit. near *Rofs*, prov. Leinft.

ROSEMOUNT, fit. near *Newtownnards*, prov. Ulfter.

ROSENALLIS, (or *Rofenellis*) a village fit. in bar. Tinehinch, Queen's co. prov. Leinfter, about 44 miles from Dublin: 3 miles beyond which are the ruins of a caftle.

ROSERK-ABBEY, fit. on the river Moy, two miles S. E. of Killala, co. Mayo, prov. Connaught. It was founded by one *Joyce* for Francifcans of the 3d order. Here is a tower built on the fame plan with that of *Moyne*, but exactly on the middle of the gable-end. It is remarkable that in each of thefe monafteries, there is a clofet of hewn-ftone for two confeffors to fit in, with a hole on each fide for the perfons who confefs, to fpeak thro'; where this ftands is a village of fame name.

ROSLARE, fee *Rofsclare*.

ROSLEE, fee *Rofslee*.

ROSNIVER, fee *Rofsinver*.

ROSMANAHER, fit. in co. Clare, prov. Munfter; Fairs held 10 May, 15 June, 12 Sept. and 16 Oct.

ROSMEAD, fit. near *Caftletown-delvin*, co. Weftmeath, prov. Leinfter. Here is the feat of *Hans Wood*, efq.

Ross, or *Rofs-carberry*, fit. in bar. Carbery, co. Cork, prov. Munfter, 152 miles from Dublin; it is a fmall town, and together with Cork forms the fee of a bifhop; the cathedral is a fmall neat gothic ftructure, the choir of which is more modern; the ftalls are newly

erected, and neatly difpofed; in the S. wing is a handfome chapter room; the church-yard is wafhed by an arm of the fea, that flows up to the town; the harbour (according to *Camden*) was formerly navigable for fhips, but it was in his time quite choaked up with fand, and is now fo fhallow, that no veffel can come up to the town; here is a good foot barrack and a fmall market-houfe. Some few years fince, feveral fubterraneous paffages were difcovered near the cathedral; lat. 51:20 N. lon. 8:55 W. Fairs held 19 Sept. and 8 Dec. The foundation of the bifhoprick of Cork is placed by fome in the 7th. century: that of *Rofs* is unknown; they were united by queen *Eliz.* in 1586, are both contained in the co. of Cork, and are partly intermixed: they are reckoned to be worth 2,700l. per ann. *Hanmer* fays this town was walled about, but by the wars of the Irifh fepts, the foundations could fcarce be traced; he adds, there was in it antiently a famous univerfity, whereto reforted all the S. W. part of Ireland to be 'educated. In this fchool St. *Brenan* was reader; the cathedral is fuppofed to have been founded by St. *Feachan*, named *Fachan Mongach*, or the *Hairy*, who flourifhed in the beginning of the 6th century; he alfo founded an abbey here of regular canons, the ruins of which ftill remain. This town is now a vicarage in dioc. of Cork.—*Rofs* is alfo the name of a barony in co. Galway, prov. Connaught, in which is a village of fame name; which is a rectory in dioc. of Tuam.—Alfo a village in bar. Carbery, co. *Sligo*, prov. Conn.

Ross, *(new)* fee *New-Rofs*.

Ross, *(old)* fee *Old-Rofs*.

ROSSAGOUL, fee *Caftle-Caldwell*.

ROSSANA, fit. near Wicklow, prov. Leinfter, about 22 miles from Dublin.

ROSSBEGG, fit. near Lough Erne, in bar. Lurge, co. Fermanagh, prov. Ulfter.

ROSS-BRIN, a caftle erected on a rock, which hangs over the ocean, on the peninfula of *Ivaugh*, in co. Cork, prov. Munfter.

ROSS-CARBERRY, fee *Rofs*.

ROSS-CASTLE, fit. in co. Kerry, prov. Munfter, on an Ifthmus in the celebrated Lough Lean, or lake of Killarney. It was formerly a ftrong place, and was befieged and taken in the wars of 1641, by general *Ludlow*. It is now converted into a barrack for 2 companies of foot, and has a governor on the eftablifhment. It was the laft place that held out in Munfter againft the Englifh parliament, during the rebellion.

ROSSCLOGHER, fee *Rofclogher*.

ROSSCONNEL, fee *Rofconnel*.

ROSSCOMROE, a vicarage in dioc. of Killaloe, fit. in bar. Ballibritt, King's co. prov. Leinfter.

ROSSDAGH, a rectory in dioc. of Cloyne, fit. in bar. Fermoy, co. Cork, prov. Munfter.

ROSSDROIT,

ROSSDROIT, a rectory in dioc. of Ferns, fit. in bar. Bantry, co. Wexford, prov. Leinster.

ROSS-DUFF, a parish in co. Waterford, prov. Munster.

ROSSELLA, fit. in bar. Talbot'stown, co. Wicklow, prov. Leinster.

ROSSERELLY, fit. on the river Ross, in bar. Clare, co. Galway, prov. Connaught. Lord *Granard* founded a monastery here for Franciscans of the strict observance in 1498. A chapter of the Franciscan order was held here in 1509. The Roman Catholics repaired this monastery in 1604; and the ruins which yet remain shew it to have been a very extensive building.

ROSSES, (or "*the Rosses*") fit. in bar. Boylagh, co. Donegal, prov. Ulster. Here is a considerable herring fishery.

ROSSESTOWN, fit. near Thurles, co. Tipperary, prov. Munster.

ROSS-IBARCAN, a place in co. Kilkenny, prov. Leinster; it lies opposite to New Ross in co. of Wexford, between which there is a ferry over the river *Barrow*; it confists but of a few cabbins, which are covered by several high trees, that give a pleafing profpect to the eye.

ROSSINVER, or *Rofniver*, a vicarage in dioc. of Kilmore, fit. in bar. Rofclogher, co. Leitrim, prov. Connaught.

ROSS-ISLAND, fit. in the lake of Killarney, co. Kerry, prov. Munster; on it ftands an antient caftle, formerly the feat of *O'Donaghoe Rofs*; this place was made a military garrifon, and fome old guns mounted there, gave it fomewhat the air of a fortification; this ifland contains about 80 or 100 acres.—Alfo an ifland fit. in Lough Erne, co. Fermanagh, prov. Ulfter.

ROSSKEEN, a vicarage in dioc. of Cloyne, fit. in bar. Duhallow, co. Cork, prov. Munfter.

ROSSKILLARY, fit. in bar. Ballinahinch, co. Galway, prov. Connaught.

ROSSLEE, (or *Roflee*) a rectory in dioc. of Tuam, fit. in bar. Carragh, co. Mayo, prov. Connaught. Fairs held 28 Oct.

ROSS-MAC-OWEN, fit. in co. Cork, prov. Munfter, within 14 miles of *Bantry*; here is one of the largeft and higheft waterfalls in the kingdom, which is collected from various fmall rivulets and fprings, forming a large lake on the top of a high, rocky, and almoft perpendicular mountain, called *Hungry Hill*, which is at leaft 700 yards above the level of *Bantry Bay*.

ROSSMERE, a vicarage in dioc. of Lifmore, fit. in bar. Decies without Drum, co. Waterford, prov. Munfter.

ROSSMENOGUE, a rectory in dioc. of Ferns, fit. in bar. Scarewalfh, co. Wexford, prov. Leinfter.

ROSSMORE, a pleafant feat in co. Cork, prov. Munfter.—Alfo an *ifland*, fit. off the bar. Dunkerron, co. Kerry, prov. Munfter.

ROSSORY, a rectory in dioc. of Clogher, fit. in bar. Magheraboy, co. Fermanagh, prov. Ulfter.

ROSS-RYAL, fit. in bar. Clare, co. Galway, prov. Connaught.

ROSTELLAN, fit. in bar. Imokilly, co. Cork, prov. Munfter; here are the magnificent improvements and demefnes of the earl of *Inchiquin*. Fairs held 25 March and 15 Aug. This is a rectory in dioc. of Cloyne.

ROSTREVOR, (or *Rofe-trevor)* fit. in bar. Upper Iveagh, co. Down, prov. Ulfter; it is a poft and fair town, 52 miles from Dublin. This village is feated on *Carlingford bay*, and well defended from the feverity of the winds and open fea; at the lower end of it is a fmall quay for fhips, which ride at anchor within a few yards of the fhore; here is alfo a falt work, and a pottery for white earthen ware.—Alfo a handfome feat. Near a mile from it, are the ruins of *Kilbreny church.* Fairs held Shrove-monday, Eafter-tuefday, Whit-tuefday, 1 Aug. 19 Sept. 1 Nov. 11 Dec. This place took its name from an heirefs, whofe name was *Rofe*, that married into the family of the *Trevors*; and was the feat of the *Trevors*, vifcounts *Dungannon*.

ROSTUEHAN-POINT, fit. in bar. Kenmare, co. Kerry, prov. Munfter.

ROSYPARK, fit. in bar. Louth, co. Louth, prov. Leinfter.

ROUGHTY-BRIDGE, fit. in bar. Glanerought, co. Kerry, prov. Munfter; fairs held 29 Oct.

ROUGHTY-RIVER, fit. in bar. Glanerought, co. Kerry, prov. Munfter; it has its rife in the parifh of *Kilgarvan*, and runs into the river *Kenmare*.

ROUNDSTONE-BAY, a harbour fit. in bar. Ballinahinch, co. Galway, prov. Connaught.

ROUNDWOOD, fit. near Newtown-mount-kennedy, prov. Leinfter.

ROUSLEY, fit. in bar. Slane, co. Meath, prov. Leinfter.

ROWER, a rectory in dioc. of Offory, fit. in bar. Ida, co. Kilkenny, prov. Leinfter.

ROYAL CANAL. This work is carried on by fubfcription. The fubfcribers were incorporated by charter, and farther powers lately granted by act of parliament, for carrying on a Canal from Dublin to the river Shannon, near *Tarmonbury*. One branch takes its rife from *Glaffmanogue*, co. Dublin; and the other from the river Liffey at *the Lots*. The two branches unite near *Profpect*, on Glafnevin road, pafs near Lucan, Leixlip, Carton, Kilcock, Kinegad, Mullingar, &c. with off branches towards Trim, Kells, Athboy, and Caftletown-delvin. One

One third of the expence being 66,000*l.* to be defrayed by parliament.

ROYAL OAK, fit. in co. Carlow, prov. Leinfter, 47 miles from Dublin.

RUGGED-ISLE, an *ifland*, fit. off bar. Carbery, co. Cork, prov. Munfter.

RUGGSBOROUGH, fit. in co. Cork, prov. Munfter; fairs held 4 Sept.

RUNNIMEDE, a feat in co. Rofcommon, prov. Connaught; near it are the ruins of a caftle.

RUSCAR-CHURCH, fit. in bar. Magheraboy, co. Fermanagh, prov. Ulfter. It is a chapelry in dioc. of Cloyne.

RUSH, fit. in bar. Balruddery, co. Dublin, prov. Leinfter, 13 miles from the metropolis. It is a pretty large fifhing town, and well fituated for carrying on its bufinefs to advantage. The ling cured here, and which is exported in great quantities to foreign countries, has long been celebrated for its fuperior flavour. Fairs held 1 May and 29 Sept. for horfes and chapmen's goods. This place is fix miles beyond *Swords*, and feated on the fea coaft, between *Mallahide* and *Skerries*, having the *ifland* of *Lambay* in full view, from which it is about 5 miles diftant. Rufh harbour admits only fmall craft; the paffage to it is very narrow. To make to it, you muft give the rocks to the Eaftward a good birth, until you bring the Pier head on the tavern; then fail to the quay, keeping thofe marks, and you keep in the beft water.—Alfo the name of a *fandbank*, fit. in bar. Ballagheen, co. Wexford, prov. Leinfter, commonly called " *the Rufh.*"

RUSHALL, fit. in bar. Upper Offory, Queen's co. prov. Leinfter.

RUSHEEN, fit. in co. Kerry, prov. Munfter. It is a handfome feat, which ftands in a kind of ifthmus, formed by the river *Shannon*, and a creek which runs up from *Carigfoyle* to the abbey of *Liflaghtin*, which laft place was founded by *John O'Connor*, in 1478, for Minorites, who were obfervantine Francifcans of the ftrict order. The parifh church was dedicated to an *Irifh* faint, called St. Laghtin, who died in 622.

RUSKY, fit. near *Longford*, prov. Leinfter.

RUSKY-BRIDGE, a village fit. in co. Leitrim, prov. Connaught, about 66 miles from Dublin.

RUSSAGH, a vicarage in dioc. of Ardagh, fit. in bar. Moygoifh, co. Weftmeath, prov. Leinfter.

RUSSBOROUGH, the elegant feat of earl *Miltown*, fit. in co. Wicklow, prov. Leinfter. The houfe is efteemed one of the moft fuperb in the kingdom, being done after a defign of the celebrated Mr. *Caffels*. The front of the houfe and offices form an extenfive facade of hewn-ftone; the colonade ornamented with pilafters of the Corinthian and Ionic orders,

between which are feveral white marble ftatues. The whole range extends near 700 feet. All the apartments are fpacious and elegantly furnifhed; particularly with a moft valuable collection of paintings by the moft celebrated mafters; amongft which are two very famous pictures, viz. Benjamin and the cup, by *Pouffin*; and an antique Venus by *P. Battoni*.

RUSSELWOOD, fit. in co. Kildare, prov. Leinfter; fairs held 26 Aug.

RUTLAND, a village fit. in bar. Catherlogh, co. Carlow, prov. Leinfter. It is called by the Irifh *Rutlo*.—Alfo an ifland having a village in it of fame name, fit. off the bar. Boylagh, co. Donegal, prov. Ulfter. This village was built by the public fpirited exertions of the Rt. Hon. Mr. *Conyngham*, and was called after the late *duke* of *Rutland*, when lord lieutenant of Ireland. It is diftant about 138 miles from Dublin. Upwards of 400 veffels annually refort here to the fifhery, and lie in perfect fecurity in three fathoms water. The place is laid out perfectly regular, with ftreets from 40 to 50 feet wide, and fo difpofed that the quays and ftores lie to the rere of the houfes. Several ftore-houfes &c. are already built, and a moft compleat dock-yard is eftablifhed.

RYE-WATER, a river fit. in bar. Salt, co. Kildare, prov. Leinfter.

RYLAND-CASTLE, fit. 1½ mile beyond Newtownbarry, in co. Wexford, prov. Leinfter.

RYVES-CASTLE, fit. near Tipperary town, prov. Munfter.

S A

SACRUM PROMONTORIUM, a *cape* in the S. of Ireland, mentioned by Ptolemy; at prefent denominated *Carnfore-point*, in co. Wexford, prov. Leinfter.

SADAIR-BAY, fit. in co. Sligo, prov. Connaught, oppofite the Atlantic ocean.

SADDLEHEAD, a *cape* fit in bar. Erris, co. Mayo, prov. Connaught.

SAGGARD, fit. in bar. Newcaftle, co. Dublin, prov. Leinfter; fairs held Thurfd. after Trinity-fund. 10 Oct. and 8 Nov. This place ftands in a pleafant fituation, and enjoys a fine air; it is diftant about 6 miles from Dublin, and lies near *Rathcoole*: 'twas anticntly called *Taffagard*. The parifh church (now in ruins) was founded by St. *Mofacre*, who flourifhed before the middle of the 7th century. It is a curacy in dioc. of Dublin.

SAINT ANDREWS, a vicarage in dioc. of Down, fit. near *Newtownards*, in bar. Ardes, co. Down, prov. Ulfter.

SAINT

Saint Canice, (or *Kennis*,) a borough town adjoining to, and in some measure forming a part of the town of Kilkenny, in co. Kilkenny, prov. Leinster. It is a vicarage in dioc. of Ossory, and otherwise called *Irishtown*, and holds fairs on 22 Oct. This place enjoys particular privileges by charter: and returns two members to parliament: patronage in the *bishop of Ossory*; lat. 52 : 36, lon. 7 : 42.

Saint Catharine, a curacy in dioc. of Dublin, sit. near *Lucan* and the river Liffey, in bar. Newcastle, co. Dublin, prov. Leinster. Here was antiently a priory of the congregation of St. *Victor*, to which *Warrisius de Perch*, about the year 1220, granted large donations.

Saint Cunning, a rectory in dioc. of Connor, sit. in bar. Glenarm, co. Antrim, prov. Ulster.

Saint-Dolough, a curacy in dioc. of Dublin, sit. in bar. Coolock, co. Dublin, prov. Leinster, above 4 miles N. E. from the metropolis. It has been long noted for a well dedicated to the Virgin Mary, adjoining to which is a small place called St. Catharine's pond. The church here is worth attention. It is one of those few structures in this kingdom, erected from the beginning of the 8th to the close of the 11th century; and in a different stile of architecture from any at this day to be found, either in Britain or the Western parts of Europe; being evidently built in imitation of the original Christian churches in the Southern countries, taken from the antient Heathen temples of the Greeks and Romans; and which probably were introduced into this island by the Greek and Roman clergy, who retired from their native countries on the arrival of the *Goths* and *Vandals* into the Roman empire. These churches now remaining in Ireland are all remarkably small, seldom exceeding 40 feet in length, and 20 in breadth, being covered with circular stone arches, under stone pediment roofs; and the walls and arches frequently ornamented with columns and pilasters in rude imitation of the Corinthian and Doric orders. They are however in respect to taste, far superior to any erected during the beginning of the latter ages, when the *Gothic* method of building was introduced from *Britain*.

Saintfield, (otherwise called *Tullaghnaneve*) sit. in bar. Castlereagh, co. Down, prov. Ulster, 78 miles from Dublin, and 6 miles S. W. of *Cumber*. It was made a town by the late general *Price*, who began to improve here. It has a barrack, a decent parish church; and the linen manufacture has been much encouraged in it. Here is also a Presbyterian meeting-house. Fairs held 26 Jan. 2 Thursd. O. S. Feb. March, 3 Thursd. O. S. April, May, 26

June, 30 July, 26 Aug. 3 day, and 3 Thursd. Sept. 26 Oct. 3 Thursd. O. S. Nov. Thursd. after Christmas. It is a vicarage in dioc. of Down.

Saint Finian's-bay, a harbour in bar. Iveragh, co. Kerry, prov. Munster.

Saint Helen, a vicarage in dioc. of Ferns, sit. in bar. Forth, co. Wexford, prov. Leinster.

Saint Iberius, a curacy in dioc. of Ferns, sit. in bar. Forth, co. Wexford, prov. Leinster.

Saint John, a rectory in dioc of Ferns, sit. in bar. Bantry, co. Wexford, prov. Leinst.

Saint John's, sit. in bar. Athlone, co. Roscommon, prov. Connaught; fairs held 5 July. It is a vicarage in dioc. of Elphin.

Saint John's-grange, a rectory in dioc. of Lismore, sit. in bar. Middlethird, co. Tipperary, prov. Munster.

Saint John's-point, a *cape* sit. in bar. Lecale, co. Down, prov. Ulster, standing 1½ mile from *Killough* to the S. and is denominated by sea-faring men, *St. John's Fore-land*; it is the *Isamnium* of *Ptolemy*, called so, as *Cambden* conjectures from *Isa* or *Isel*, a British word, which signifies *low*; or perhaps from *Isheal*, an Irish word of the same import, from its flat or low appearance.—Also a *cape* sit. in bar. Boylagh, co. Donegal, prov. Ulster.

Saint Johnstown, a borough town sit. in bar. Granard, co. Longford, prov. Leinster. otherwise called *Ballnaree*; it is distant about 65 miles from Dublin: and returns 2 members to parliament, patron, the earl of *Granard*. Fairs held 11 May, 21 Nov. and 29 Dec. There was formerly, in or near this place, a Grey friary dedicated to St. John the Baptist; but no remains of it are now to be seen. There is also a borough of same name in bar. Raphoe, co. Donegal, prov. Ulster, above 108 miles from Dublin: and which returns 2 members to parliament, patronage in the family of *Forward*. Fairs held 7 April, 13 Oct. and 25 Nov. It is sit. on the river *Foyle*, which at this place is of a considerable breadth, and divides the counties of *Tyrone* and *Donegal*.

Saint Kennis, see *Saint Canice*.

Saint Kyron, sit. in bar. Ballibritt, King's co. prov. Leinster.

Saint Lasarien's well, sit. at the E. end of the church of *Old Leighlin*, in co. Carlow, prov. Leinster; it is covered with great ash trees, and much frequented by the Irish, who come to it from all parts of the kingdom.

Saint Lucy, sit. in co. Westmeath, prov. Leinster, 32 miles from Dublin. Here is the seat of sir *Ben. Chapman*, bart. and near it are the ruins of a church.

Saint Margaret's, sit. in bar. Castleknock, co. Dublin, prov. Leinster, near 6 miles from the metropolis, and 2¼ beyond *Finglass*. Here is an old church, and a few miles from it ſtands the caſtle of Kilfallaghan, in ruins. Fairs held 30 July. · It is a curacy in dioc. of Dublin.—Alſo a curacy in dioc. of Ferns, ſit. in bar. Forth, co. Wexford, prov. Leinſter.—Alſo a curacy in dioc. of Ferns, ſit. in bar. Shelmaliere, co. Wexford, prov. Leinſter.

SAINT MARTIN, a vicarage in dioc. of Oſſory, ſit. in bar. Gowran, co. Kilkenny, prov. Leinſter.

SAINT MICHAEL, a curacy in dioc. of Ferns, ſit. in bar. Forth, co. Wexford, prov. Leinſter. Alſo a rectory in dioc. of Limerick, ſit. in the co. of the city of Limerick, prov. Munſter.—Alſo a rectory in dioc. of Cork, ſit. in bar. Barrymore, co. Cork, prov. Munſter.

SAINT MICHAEL'S MOUNT, otherwiſe called Ballynaſcalligs, ſit. in bar. Iveragh, co. Kerry, prov. Munſter. There is a well here conſecrated to St. Michael, and viſited generally on 29 Sept. Here was alſo an abbey for regular canons of the order of St. *Auguſtin*.

SAINT MULLEN, a bar. in co. Carlow, prov. Leinſter, in which is a village of ſame name, that is a vicarage in dioc. of Leighlin ; it holds fairs on 17 June, 25 July, 8 Sept. and 1 Nov. This place lies on the river *Barrow*, and was otherwiſe called *Teghmolin*. An abbey was founded here about the year 634, by St. *Molin* or *Mullin*, who was biſhop of Ferns, and gave name to this place , he died 17 June, 697, and was here interred. This abbey was plundered in 951, and deſtroyed by fire in 1138. It was the burial place of the *Cavanaghs*, the antient kings of Leinſter ; and is ſtill ſo of their deſcendants. Near it is a ſmall proteſtant church.

SAINT MUNCHIN, a rectory in the dioc. of Limerick, ſit. in co. of the city of Limerick, prov. Munſter.

SAINT NICHOLAS, a curacy in dioc. of Ferns, ſit. in bar. Ballagheen, co. Wexford, prov. Leinſter.—Alſo a rectory in dioc. of Limerick, ſit. in co. of the city of Limerick, prov. Munſt.

SAINT OLAN'S CAP, a remarkable ſtone in the church-yard of the pariſh church of *Aghabolloge*, in co. Cork, prov. Munſter, on which the common people were accuſtomed to ſwear, and which they ſay, if carried from thence, would return again to its former ſituation. .

SAINT PATRICK'S-BRIDGE, a ridge of *rocks* ſo called, ſit. off the bar. Bargie, co. Wexford, prov. Leinſter.

SAINT PATRICK'S PURGATORY, ſee *Patrick's purgatory*.

SAINT PATRICK'S WELL, a village ſo called, ſit. in bar. Poblebrien, co. Limerick, prov. Munſter.

SAINT PETER, a curacy in dioc. of Elphin, ſit. in bar. Athlone, co. Roſcommon, prov. Connaught.

SAINT WOOLSTAN'S, ſit. on the river Liffey, about 2 miles S. W. of *Leixlip*, in bar. Salt, co. Kildare, prov. Leinſter. A priory was founded here in 1202 for canons of the order of St. *Victor*, by *Adam de Hereford* ; in honour of St. *Wolſtan* biſhop of *Worceſter*, then newly canonized ; it was of conſiderable extent, but now there only remains two towers, and two large gateways arched.

SALEEN-LOUGH, a *lake* ſit. in bar. Carragh, co. Mayo, prov Connaught.

SALLANS, a ſmall, but neat and new built town on the banks of the *Grand canal*, between Dublin and Monaſterevan ; it is 14 miles from Dublin, and ſit. in the co. Kildare, prov. Leinſter. Near it is *Millicent*, the handſome ſeat of Mr. Griffith. At *Sallans*, are very extenſive ſtore-houſes, and a large and elegant inn, erected at the expence of the *Grand Canal Company*.

SALMON-LEAP. There are ſeveral places which go by this name in Ireland. The moſt conſiderable are, firſt, one within a mile of Coleraiñ, co. Londonderry, prov. Ulſter, where there is a famous caſcade. —— Another at *Leixlip*, co. Dublin, prov. Leinſter, and a third at *Ballyſhannon*, co. Donegal, prov. Ulſter. The latter is ſaid to let at 400*l.* per ann. In order to explain this term, it is neceſſary to relate a few particulars concerning the ſalmon. Almoſt all the rivers, lakes and brooks, in this iſland, afford great plenty of theſe fiſh ; ſome during the whole year, and ſome only during certain ſeaſons ; they generally go down to the ſea about Auguſt and September, and up again in the ſpring months. It is ſaid that the females work beds in the ſandy ſhallows of rivers, and there depoſit her eggs, on which the male ſheds its feed ; afterwards they both join in covering the eggs with ſand. Theſe in time become vivified, and take their courſe to the ſea, being then about the ſize of a finger. After ſix weeks or two months ſtay, they return up the ſame rivers, the ſalt water having in that ſhort time cauſed them to attain nearly to half their full growth. They are then caught in *weirs*, which are formed by damming up the river, except a ſpace of 3 or 4 feet in the midd'e, which the ſalmon having paſſed, are caught in a ſmall encloſure, formed by ſtakes of wood ; the entrance is wide, and gradually leſſens, ſo as barely to admit a ſingle ſalmon at a time. Every morning during the fiſhery they are taken out, by means of a ſtaff, with a ſtrong barbed iron hook, which is ſtruck into them. But at Ballyſhannon, by far the greater number is caught in nets below the fall. The time of the fiſhery is limited ; and after it is elapſed, the encloſure is removed, the nets are laid
aſide,

aſide, and the fiſh are at liberty to ſtock the rivers with ſpawn. Were theſe fiſheries interrupted for a year or two, the fiſh would conſiderably increaſe both in number and ſize; for by over-fiſhing a ſufficient number cannot eſcape to ſtock the rivers. It is the ſame with lands, which requires a certain time to lie fallow, and to recover ſtrength. After the intermiſſion of fiſhing during the wars in 1641, ſalmon have been caught near Londonderry of ſix feet long, and were then ſold upon an average at ſix-pence a piece. The ſalmon in coming from the ſea are neceſſarily obliged to leap up the caſcade at Ballyſhannon, which (with the others we have noticed,) acquired from thence the name of the *Salmon-leap*. And it is hardly credible, but to thoſe who have been eye-witneſſes, that theſe fiſh ſhould be able to dart themſelves near 14 feet perpendicular out of the water; and allowing for the curvature, they leap at leaſt twenty; they do not always ſucceed at the firſt leap; ſometimes they bound almoſt to the ſummit, but the falling water daſhes them down again; at other times they dart head-foremoſt, and ſidelong upon a rock, remain ſtunned for a few moments, and then ſtraggle into the water again; when they are ſo lucky as to reach the top, they ſwim out of ſight in a moment. They do not bound from the ſurface of the water, and it cannot be known from what depth they take their leap; it is probably performed by a forcible ſpring with their tail bent; for the chief ſtrength of moſt fiſh lies in the tail. They have often been ſhot, or caught with ſtrong barbed hooks fixed to a pole, during their flight, as it may be termed, and inſtances have been known of women catching them in their aprons. At high water the fall is hardly 3 feet, and then the fiſh ſwim up that eaſy acclivity without leaping.

SALT, a bar. in co. Kildare, prov. Leinſter.

SALTEES, three iſlands on the coaſt of the bar. Bargie, co. Wexford, prov. Leinſter, ſit. about a league from the ſhore. Lat. 52 : 10, lon. 6 : 30.

SALTER'STOWN, ſit. in bar Loughlinſholen, co. Londonderry, prov. Ulſter.—Alſo a curacy in dioc. of Armagh, ſit. in bar. Ferrard, co. Louth, prov. Leinſter.

SALTIBRIDGE, ſit. in co. Waterford, prov. Munſter: between *Cappoquin* and *Liſmore*. It is only remarkable for ſome iron works, formerly ſupported there by the firſt earl of *Cork*; and the pits from which the ore was dug, remain ſtill open. His lordſhip had ſeveral of theſe works in different parts of that county, of which he made a conſiderable advantage.

SALT-WORKS, ſit. near *Roſtrevor*, prov. Ulſt.

SAMER, an antient name of the river *Erne*, which falls into the bay of Donegal, prov. Ulſter, otherwiſe called *Samor-abhan*, or the great river.

SAMOR-ABHAN, ſee *Samer*.

SAMORE-HILL, a *mountain* ſit. in bar. Carbury, co. Sligo, prov. Connaught.

SANBROKE-PARK, ſit. near Carlow, prov. Leinſter.

SANDFIELD, a village ſit. in bar. Athlone, co. Roſcommon, prov. Connaught.

SANDHOLES, a place ſit. in co. Tyrone, prov. Ulſter, 73 miles from Dublin. 1¼ mile from which, is *Dunaghy*, where there is a celebrated ſpa.

SANDY-MOUNT, a very pleaſant village ſit. in co. Dublin, prov. Leinſter, ¾ of a mile to the right of King's-end, and 2 miles from the caſtle of Dublin. There are many elegant villas and ſweet retreats at this place, chiefly belonging to the citizens of Dublin.

SANTRY, a village ſit. in bar. Coolock, co. Dublin, prov. Leinſter, about 2 miles beyond *Drumcondra*, and 3½ miles from Dublin caſtle. Here is the ſeat of *Charles Domvile*, eſq; which once belonged to the unfortunate lord *Santry*. This place is a vicarage in dioc. Dublin, and has a pariſh church, near the *demeſne* of Santry. A charter ſchool was opened here in 1744 for 60 girls, employed in ſpinning worſted, &c. It was endowed with 50l. per ann. by the bounty of the lord mayor, aldermen and commons of the city of Dublin. The late Rt. Hon. *Luke Gardiner* gave one acre of land rent free in perpetuity, and ſet 30 acres more at £.1 3 per acre, for the term of 999 years. The late lord primate *Boulter*, expended above 400l. towards the building of this ſchool.

SARGALAGH, ſit. in bar. Erris, co. Mayo, prov. Connaught.

SARGALTAGH, ſit. in bar. Erris, co. Mayo, prov. Connaught.

SARSFIELD, ſit. near *Drogheda*, prov. Leinſt.

SARSFIELD-COURT, a handſome ſeat in co. Cork, prov. Munſter, 3 miles N. of Cork city. From a terrace in the garden of this place, is one of the fineſt proſpects in all that co.

SAUL, a rectory in dioc. of Down, ſit. in bar. Lecale, co. Down, prov. Ulſter; here are the venerable ruins of a once famous abbey.

SAUL-ABBEY, ſit. in bar. Lecale, co. Down, prov. Ulſter. It was perhaps one of the firſt founded monaſteries in this kingdom, being erected by St. *Patrick*, in the year 432, it was erected for regular canons, and St. *Duny* was created abbot of it. The church was not built in the uſual manner E. and W. but N. and S. Large ruins remain of this abbey, with two ſmall vaulted rooms of ſtone, yet entire, about 7 feet.

7 feet high, 6 long, and 2 broad; one of them is now ufed as a tomb, the church yard being a great burial place. At fome diftance from the church, on the S. W. fide, ftands a battlemented caftle, but there are no ftairs leading to the top of it, as ufual in fuch buildings; it is probable there were ftairs of timber in the body of the building, which may have been deftroyed.

SAUNDERS-COURT, fit. near *Ennifcorthy*, prov. Leinfter.

SAUNDERS-GROVE, fit. in co. Wicklow, prov. Leinfter, 28 miles from Dublin, by the river *Slancy*. It is a handfome feat, remarkable for its woods, parks and waterfalls, and enjoys every advantage of fituation.

SAUNDERS-VILLE, a fmall village fit. near Saunders-grove, in co. Wicklow, prov. Leinfter; belonging to *Morley Saunders*, efq; it ftands near a rivulet called *Kyle*, which there runs into the *Slancy*; diftant about 27 miles from Dublin.

SCABRA, fee *Scraba*.

SCALMARTIN ROCKS, fit. in Donaghadee harbour, co. Down, prov. Ulfter. This is a dangerous fpot, being overflowed by the tide, yet it is likewife fo fmooth and flat, that few veffels fuffer by it. Upwards of half a league S. of *Scalmartin*, lies a fhoal, which muft not be approached nearer than 8 fathom.

SCALP, a curious chafm, where is a road cut thro' a rock, on the top of a very high mountain, about 6 miles from Dublin, in co. Wicklow, prov. Leinfter. This place confifts of heaps of ftone of enormous fizes, piled curioufly on each other, and forming one of the moft ftriking natural objects in the kingdom. The fides of the chafm are not perpendicular, but flope from the top confiderably. It is fit. about one mile beyond *Kilternan*.

SCAR, fit. in bar. Shelburne, co. Wexford, prov. Leinfter; fairs held 23 April, 11 June, 3 Aug. and 5 Nov.

SCARE, (or "*the Scare*") a *bay* fit. in bar. Shelburne, co. Wexford, prov. Leinfter.

SCAREWALSH, or *Scarawalfh*, a bar. fit. in co. Wexford, prov. Leinfter.

SCAREWALSH-BRIDGE, a village fit. in bar. Scarewalfh, co. Wexford, prov. Leinfter; fairs held 16 Aug.

SCARIFF, a village fit. in bar. Tullagh, co. Clare, prov. Munfter.—Alfo an *ifland* fit. in bar. Dunkerron, off the coaft of co. Kerry, prov. Munfter.

SCARIFF-BAY, fit. in co. Clare, prov. Munfter. There is a beautiful ifland in this bay, fit. on *Lough Derg*, in which are a fine tower 70 feet high, and the remains of 7 fmall churches. It was founded in the 6th century by St. *Commin*.

SCARIFF-BRIDGE, fit. over the river Boyne, in co. Meath, prov. Leinfter.

SCARVA, a fmall neat village, pleafantly fit. on the Newry canal, in bar. Upper Iveagh, co. Down, prov. Ulfter, 60 miles from Dublin. The canal at this place divides the co.'s of *Armagh* and *Down*. There is a large falt work carried on here; and near it is a fmall lake called *Lough Shark*.

SCARVAGH-PASS, fit. in bar. Upper Iveagh, co. Down, prov. Ulfter; hereabouts were fome caftles, built by col. *Monk*, afterwards duke of *Albemarle*, partly with ftones, and partly with earthen ramparts. The great bog about *Scarvagh*, thro' which this pafs runs, was antiently called *Glan Flufh*. Fairs held 21 March, 10 June, 5 Sept. and 14 Nov.

SCATERNA, fit. in bar. Arklow, co. Wicklow, prov. Leinfter.

SCATRICK, an ifland fit. in *Strangford lake*, co. Down, prov. Ulfter, on which a caftle is erected, this with *Ringhaddy*, formed two places of defence for thofe parts.

SCATTERY, fee *Inifcathy*.

SCAWLHILL, a *mountain*, fit. in bar. Glenarm, co. Antrim, prov. Ulfter.

SCILLY, a fmall village, in co. Cork, prov. Munfter, near *Kinfale*. It is inhabited by fifhermen, who have feveral fifhing veffels, and yearly take great quantities of fifh, which they falt for foreign markets, and home confumption. Thefe fifhermen were an Englifh colony, who fettled here after the defeat of the *Spaniards*, in queen *Eliz*. time; they feldom marry out of the village, fo that they are moftly all related to each other.

SCORDIN'S-WELL, (or *St. Scordin's*) fit. at *Killough*, co. Down, prov. Ulfter, it is highly efteemed for its water, and the application of it to all manner of ufes; it iffues out of a high rocky bank, clofe upon the fhore, never diminifhes in the drieft feafons, and produces 124 hogfheads in 24 hours; there is alfo a mineral well, near the charter-fchool of *Killough*, both purgative and emetic.

SCORNEY, fee *Brakes of Scorney*.

SCOT'SHOUSE, a village fit. in bar. Dartree, co. Monaghan, prov. Ulfter, near 58 miles from Dublin, about 2 miles from which, is a feat called *Maddenftown*.

SCOTSTOWN, fit. in co. Monaghan, prov. Ulfter; fairs held 17 May, June, Aug. and Nov.

SCOURLOGHSTOWN, fit. in bar. Deece, co. Meath, prov. Leinfter; it is a curacy in dioc. of Meath. Here are the ruins of a caftle.

SCRABA, (or *Scraby*.) a village fit. in bar. Tullaghanoho, co. Cavan, prov. Ulfter; fairs held on Afcenfion day and 11 Dec.—Alfo a hill fo called, fit. in co. Down, prov. Ulfter. It begins to rife about ¼ a mile S. of *Newtown*, and from its top, affords a vaft extended profpect.

pect. It is a fruitful hill, and the plowmen's furrows are carried up very near the summit of it, where was a fine spring well, but since filled up by idle persons. Hereabouts are good free-stone quarries.—About 2 miles N. of *Scraba*, is another hill much higher, tho' in appearance lower, because it rises more gradually, called *Karn-Gaur*, or *the Goat's mount*. Under the hill of *Scraba*, is a large and noted *salt-marsh*.

SCRABY, see *Scraba*.

SCREEB, a village sit. in bar. Moycullen, co. Galway, prov. Connaught.

SCREEN, a village sit. in bar. Tyreragh, co. Sligo, prov. Connaught: the church of which stands at the foot of a high hill, on the top of which is a curious circular stone-fort.

SCRIPLESTOWN, sit. about 3 miles from Dublin, co. Dublin, prov. Leinster.

SCROTAGLINY, sit. in co. Kerry, prov. Munster; fairs held 17 and 18 May, 18 Aug. 19 and 20 Oct. 16 and 17 Dec.

SCURLOGH'STOWN, see *Scourlogh'stown*.

SCURMORE, sit. in bar. Tyreragh, co. Sligo, prov. Connaught.

SEA-BANK, sit. in bar. Louth, co. Louth, prov. Leinster.

SEA-FIELD, sit. near *Rostrevor*, prov. Ulster. Also a seat near *Swords*, in co. Dublin, prov. Leinster.

SEAFORD, sit. in bar. Kinelearty, co. Down, prov. Ulster, 70 miles from Dublin. It was antiently called *Neoghen*, and has a parish church. A mile S. of this place, is the village called *Clough*, near which is a rath, surrounded by a broad deep fosse, and on the top of it (which is something singular) a plain strong castle of stone; this work is ascribed to the Danes. Fairs held at Seaford, 7 March, 9 June, 4 Sept. and 6 Dec.

SEAL, an *island* sit. off bar. Inishowen, co. Donegal, prov. Ulster.

SEA-MOUNT, sit. in bar. Balruddery, co. Dublin, prov. Leinster.

SEAPATRICK, sit. in bar. Lower Iveagh, co. Down, prov. Ulster, a little N. of *Banbridge*; it has a parish church and vicarage house, belonging to the dioc. of Dromore.

SEASLE, sit. near *Inver-castle*, in bar. Moycullen, co. Galway, prov. Connaught.

SEATOWN, a village sit. by the sea-side, and adjoining the town of *Dundalk*, in co. Louth, prov. Leinster.

SEESHY *mountain*, sit. in bar. Carbery, co. Cork, prov. Munster. At the foot of this mountain is a lake, stored with a species of red trout, which never rise at a fly.

SEGOE, a vicarage in dioc. of Dromore, sit. in bar. Oneilland, co. Armagh, prov. Ulster.

SEIKYRAN, or *Scirkeran*, a vicarage in dioc. of Offory, sit. in bar. Ballibritt, King's co.

prov. Leinster, 4 miles E. of *Birr*. A monastery was founded here and dedicated to St. *Kieran*.

SEIN-CULBIN, the bay in which the Fir-Bolgæ landed, under the conduct of *Larthon*. It is not certain where this bay is, tho' probably on the Southern coast of Ireland.

SENA, or the *bay*; a bay or river mentioned by *Ptolemy*, and thought to be the river *Shannon*, called by the Irish *Seinnon*, or *the place of bays*.

SEPHIN, a mountain so called, sit. in co. Down, prov. Ulster.

SESKINAN, a parish in bar. Decies without Drum, co. Waterford, prov. Munster; it is for the most part a mountainous and boggy tract, with little in it remarkable; at *Ballynamult* in this parish, is a redoubt for about 20 men; this is a vicarage in dioc. of Lismore.

SEVEN-CHURCHES, a name given to the ruins of *Clonmacnois*, in King's co. prov. Leinster. Fairs held 20 Sept.—Also to *Glendalough*, in co. Wicklow, prov. Leinster.

SEVEN-HEADS, *rocks* sit. in bar. Barryroe, off the coast of co. Cork, prov. Munster.

SEVILLE, sit. near *Dungannon*, prov. Ulster.

SHALLAGHAN BRIDGE, sit. in co. Donegal, prov. Ulster, 144 miles from Dublin.

SHALLEE, sit. in co. Tipperary, prov. Munster, near 79 miles from Dublin.

SHANAGOLDEN, see *Shangolden*.

SHANBALLYMORE, sit. in co. Cork, prov. Munster; fairs held 4 Feb. and May, 16 Sept. and 13 Dec.

SHANBOUGH, a vicarage in dioc. of Ossory, sit. in bar. Ida, co. Kilkenny, prov. Leinster.

SHANCOE, a vicarage in dioc. of Elphin, sit. in bar. Tyraghrill, co. Sligo, prov. Conn. Also a village sit. in bar. Glenarm, co. Antrim, prov. Ulster.

SHANDANGON, a pleasant seat near Macroomp, in co. Cork, prov. Munster.

SHANDON, a seat in co. Waterford, prov. Munster; it belonged to the family of *Hore*, but is now in a state of decay.

SHANDRUM, see *Shanedrum*.

SHANE-CASTLE, sit. in co. Antrim, prov. Ulster, 85 miles from Dublin. Here is the elegant seat of the Rt. Hon. lord *O'Neill*. Fairs held 3 July and 8 Oct.—There is also a place of same name, otherwise called *Shean's-castle*, being a manor, which was dependent on *Dunamase*, in the Queen's co. prov. Leinster. In a record of 20 Rich. IId. A. D. 1397, it is called *Sion*. The castle is sit. on one of those high conical hills, which are so common in its vicinity; tho' not remarkable for its magnitude, it was a place of considerable strength, the declivities round it being steep and easily defended. It appears that sir *Robert Preston*, in 1397, held

by

by the law of England, the inheritance of *Margaret* his late wife, the manor of *Sion* in *Leix*, of *Roger Mortimer*, as of his manor of Dunmalke *(Dunamafe.)* It fhared the revolutions of the latter, in the fubfequent periods of hiftory; but being neither fo ftrong or tenable it efcaped demolition, and continued for centuries in its priftine ftate, until it came into the poffeffion of the Rev. Dr. *Charles Coote*, dean of *Kilfenora*, who at a vaft expence embellifhed its fituation, and converted it into a delightful country refidence.

SHANEDRUM, or *Shandrum*, fit. in bar. Orrery, co. Cork, prov. Munfter; fairs held 25 May, and 20 Auguft. It is a rectory in dioc. of Cloyne.

SHANE-INN, fit. in co. Kerry, prov. Munfter; above 139 miles from Dublin.

SHANGAN, a village fit. in bar. Imokilly, co. Cork, prov. Munfter,

SHANGANA, fit. in bar. Ballyadams, Queen's co. prov. Leinfter.

SHANGENAGH, fit. in co. Dublin, prov. Leinfter, 9 miles from the metropolis. Here is an old caftle; and at a fmall diftance are the ruins of a church.

SHANGOLDEN, a village fit. in bar. Connello, co. Limerick, prov. Munfter, 114 miles from Dublin. About 3 miles from which, near *Loghill* are the ruins of a caftle. Fairs held Wedn. after Trinity-fun. and 4 Sept. This is a vicarage in dioc. of Limerick; and otherwife written *Shanagolden*, and *Shanegolden*.

SHANINAGH, fit. in bar. Rathdown, co. Dublin, prov. Leinfter.

SHANKILL, a rectory in dioc. of Leighlin, fit. in bar. Gowran, co. Kilkenny, prov. Leinfter; here is a feat of the *Aylward* family.—Alfo a vicarage in dioc. of Elphin, fit. in bar. Rofcommon, co. Rofcommon, prov. Connaught.—Alfo a rectory in dioc. of Dromore, fit. in bar. Oneilland, co. Armagh, prov. Ulfter.—Alfo a vicarage in dioc. of Connor, fit. in bar. Belfaft, co. Antrim, prov. Ulfter.

SHANKOE, fee *Shancoe*.

SHANMORE, fit. in co. Down, prov. Ulfter. In cutting a channel for the *New Canal* in that co. fome years ago, a fubterraneous foreft, or multitude of fallen trees, of oak, afh, alder, &c. was difcovered here, lying for near a mile in length, under a covering of earth, in fome places 6, in others 8 feet deep.

SHANNON-BRIDGE, fit. in co. Galway, prov. Connaught, 65 miles from Dublin.—Alfo a place in the King's co. prov. Leinfter, where fairs are held on 6 May, 24 June, 29 Sept. and 21 Dec.

SHANNON-GROVE, fit. in co. Limerick, prov. Munfter; here is a charter-fchool for above 80 children. It was opened in 1735, and endowed with two acres of land for ever, by *Will. Bury*, efq; who gave a leafe of 26 acres more for 3 lives or 31 years, at the rent of 4*l.* per ann.

SHANNON-PARK, fit. in co. Cork, prov. Munfter, near *Crofshaven*; it was formerly called *Ballinrea*, but is now entirely gone to ruin. From *Shannon-park*, a rivulet empties itfelf into a creek, a little to the S. of Monk's-town.

SHANNON-RIVER. This is by far the moft confiderable river in Ireland, or perhaps in any known ifland, not only on account of its rolling 200 miles, but alfo of its great depth in moft places, and the gentlenefs of its current, by which it might be made exceedingly ferviceable to the improvement of the country, the communication of its inhabitants, and confequently the promoting inland trade, through the greateft part of its long courfe, being navigable to a confiderable diftance, with a few interruptions only of rocks and fhallows, to avoid which there are in general fmall canals cut, to preferve and continue the navigation. This river might be navigable throughout, but for a ledge of rocks, near *Killaloe*, which crofs it. But the peculiar prerogative of the *Shannon*, is its fituation, running from N. to S. and feparating the prov. of *Connaught* from *Leinfter* and *Munfter*; and of confequence dividing the greateft part of Ireland, into what lies on the E. and that on the *W.* of the river. Toward the E. fide it has the co.'s *Leitrim*, *Longford*, *Weftmeath*, *King's* co. *Tipperary*, *Limerick* and *Kerry*; and on its W. the co.'s *Rofcommon*, *Galway*, and *Clare*; paffing by the towns of *Carrick-on-Shannon*, *Jameftown*, *Lanefborough*, *Athlone*, *Banagher*, *Killaloe* and *Limerick*. This river has its fource near *Manor-hamilton*, in co. Leitrim, prov. Connaught; and in its courfe expands itfelf into fix different *lakes*, feveral miles long, and from two to fix broad; the chief of which are called *Lough Ree*, and *Lough Derg*. Having continued this extenfive courfe, it at laft burfts its contracted bounds, and difcharges itfelf into the fea between *Cape-Lean* or *Loophead*, in the co. Clare on the N. and *Kerryhead* in the co. of Kerry on the S. two promontories of very bold and high cliffs, forming perhaps the nobleft mouth to any river in Europe, being 8 miles over. The rocks of the coaft are in the boldeft ftyle, hollowed into immenfe caverns, where the waves of the furious *Atlantic*, rolling with a prodigious fwell, and breaking on the rocks with fuch violence, as to raife an immenfe foam, roar with impetuous noife, and give an idea of all the grandeur and horrors of a ftorm. This river gives title of *earl* to the family of *Boyle*.

SHANRAHAN, a vicarage in dioc. of Lifmore, fit. in bar. Iffa, co. Tipperary, prov. Munfter.

Munſter. It is united to *Templetenny* in co. Waterford, and otherwiſe written *Shanraghan*.

SHAW's-BRIDGE, ſit. in bar. Caſtlereagh, co. Down, prov. Ulſter.

SHEAN's-CASTLE, ſee *Shane-caſtle*.

SHEAP, a river ſo called, ſit. in co. Down, prov. Ulſter.

SHEE-LOUGH, ſit. in bar. Kilmain, co. Mayo, prov. Connaught.

SHEEP-BRIDGE, ſit. in co. Down, prov. Ulſter, 53 miles from Dublin: the river *Newry* paſſes thro' it. Fairs held 1 Friday in Feb. May and Auguſt.

SHEEP-HAVEN, a *bay* ſit. in bar. Kilmacrenan, co. Donegal, prov. Ulſter.

SHEEP-HEADS, ſit. in bar. Belfaſt, co. Antrim, prov. Ulſter.

SHEEP-HILL, ſit. near *Dunſink*, co. Dublin, prov. Leinſter.

SHEEP-ISLAND, an iſland ſit. off the coaſt of bar. Cary, co. Antrim, prov. Ulſter.

SHEEP-LAND, ſit. near *Gun's-iſland*, in *Strangford-bay*, co. Down, prov. Ulſter; here is a little rocky creek, fit only for the reception of ſmall fiſhing boats.

SHEEP's-HEAD-POINT, ſit. in bar. Carbery, co. Cork, prov. Munſter; it forms the South entrance of *Bantry-bay*, the N. W. ſide being formed by the mountains of *Beerhaven*. It is otherwiſe called *Three-caſtle-head*. Lat. 51 : 24 Lon. 10 : 2.

SHEESHY, ſee *Shehy*.

SHEHAN-LOUGH, a *lake* ſit. in bar. Clonmoghan, co. Cavan. prov. Ulſter.

SHEHY or *Sheeſhy*, mountains ſit. in bar. Carbery, co. Cork, prov. Munſter.

SHELBURNE, a barony in co. Wexford, prov. Leinſter; which gives title of earl to the family of *Petty*.

SHELLILOGHER, a barony in co. Kilkenny, prov. Leinſter.

SHELMALIERE, a barony in co. Wexford, prov. Leinſter.

SHELTON, ſit. near *Arklow*, prov. Leinſter.

SHENEX, a rocky *iſland* in the Iriſh ſea, ſit. off the coaſt of co. Dublin, bar. Balruddery, prov. Leinſter.

SHENLIS, a vicarage in dioc. of Armagh, ſit. in bar. Ardee, co. Louth, prov. Leinſter.

SHENTINAGH, ſit. in co. Monaghan, prov. Ulſter.

SHERCOCK, ſee *Shircock*.

SHERKIN-ISLAND, ſit. in co. Cork, prov. Munſter. It lies S. W. of *Baltimore-bay*.

SHERLOCKSTOWN, a curacy in dioc. of Kildare, ſit. in bar. Naas, co. Kildare, prov. Leinſt.

SHERWOOD, ſit. in co. Carlow, prov. Leinſt. Fairs held 20 May and Auguſt.

SHIAN-CASTLE, ſit. about 3 miles from Liſmore, in co. Waterford, prov. Munſter; by

whom it was built is uncertain; but anno 28 Eliz. Maurice Mc. Gerrot M'en Eorla of *Shian*, was attainted, being concerned in the *Deſmond* rebellion.

SHILELAGH, a barony in co. Wicklow, prov. Leinſter, in which is a village of ſame name, diſtant about 30 miles from Dublin. Here are the poor remains of a foreſt, once the moſt celebrated in Ireland for the excellence of its oak, which was exported to Britain and different parts of Europe; and is ſtill ſhewn in the roof of *Weſtminſter-hall*, and of ſome antient buildings on the continent, even at this day.

SHILROW, ſit. near *Birr*, prov. Leinſter.

SHINACOURT, a village ſit. in bar. Leney, co. Sligo, prov. Connaught.

SHINDOLAGH-LOUGH, a *lake* ſit. in bar. Moycullin, co. Galway, prov. Connaught.

SHINRONE, ſit. in bar. Clonliſk, King's-co. prov. Leinſter. Fairs held 9 July and 21 Nov. It is a rectory in dioc. of Killaloe.

SHIP-POOL, a caſtle near *Iniſhannon*, in co. Cork, prov. Munſter, otherwiſe called *Poulnelong*. It was built by the *Roaches*, as appears from their arms over a chimney-piece. This caſtle was taken by the Bandonians (or people of *Bandon)* in 1642, whereby they gained a correſpondence to and from *Kinſale*. It is now a pleaſant ſeat, with good improvements.

SHIP-TEMPLE, a remarkable piece of Heathen antiquity, ſit. near *Dundalk*, in co. Louth, prov. Leinſter. The rev. Mr. *Ledwich* has given ſome curious and uſeful obſervations on it, which are annexed to the 11th number of the *Coll. de reb. Hib.*

SHIRCOCK, ſit. in bar. Clonchee, co. Cavan, prov. Ulſter, above 44 miles from Dublin; where is a handſome ſeat, and near it two ſmall loughs, and a larger lake called *Lough-Swillan*. Fairs held on Whit-mond. This is a rectory in dioc. of Kilmore, and otherwiſe written *Shercock*.

SHORT-CASTLE, ſit. on the N. ſide of the town of *Mallow*, in co. Cork, prov. Munſter.

SHRADUFF, otherwiſe called *Temple-diſert*, ſit. in co. Clare, prov. Munſter.

SHRAHEEN *mountain*, ſit. in bar. Tirawly, co. Mayo, prov. Connaught.

SHRONE-HILL, ſit. near Tipperary town, in co. Tipperary, prov. Munſter. Here is a large unfiniſhed houſe of lord *Milton's*; but the country round about it, is not much cultivated, except for paſturage, nor is the appearance pleaſant.

SHRONELL, a rectory in dioc. of Emly, ſit. in bar. Clanwilliam, co. Tipperary, prov. Munſter.

SHROOL, ſee *Shrowle*.

SHROWLE, a bar. in co. Longford, prov. Leinſter: otherwiſe written *Shrool*.

SHRULE,

SHRULE, fit. in bar. Kilmain, co. Mayo, prov. Connaught, 92 miles from Dublin. Near it are the ruins of a *castle*, and also those of the superb *abbey* of *Shrule*. Fairs held Easter-mond. 26 July, and 11 Nov. This village is a vicarage in dioc. of Tuam.—Also a vicarage in dioc. of Ardagh, fit. in bar. Rathline, co. Longford, prov. Leinfter.—Also a rectory in dioc. of Leighlin, fit. in bar. Slewmargy, Queen's co. prov. Leinfter.—Also the name of a *river*, fit. in bar. Strabane, co. Tyrone, prov. Ulfter.

SILANCHIA, or *Sillanchia*, an antient diftrict of the *O'Maddens*, fit. towards the W. of *Lough Ree*, in co. Galway, prov. Connaught.

SILVERMINES, fit. in bar. Upper Ormond, co. Tipperary, prov. Munfter, 77 miles from Dublin. Here are fome lead-mines, which (with thofe lately found on the eftate of Sir Wm. Godfrey, at Miltown, in co. Kerry, near the harbour of Caftlemain) are the only ones of that kind wrought in this kingdom to any confiderable extent: fome virgin filver has been found among the ore. ¼ a mile beyond *Silver-mines*, are the ruins of *Dunalty caftle*. Fairs held at Silvermines, 1 May, 8 June, 12 Sept. and 25 Oct.

SILVER-RIVER, fit. in bar. Balliboy, King's co. prov. Leinfter.

SINGLAND, fit. in co. of the city of Lime-rick, prov. Munfter; fairs held Eafter-tuefday, and 11 Dec. It is a rectory in dioc. of Lifmore.

SINUS-AUSOBA, the prefent *bay of Galway*, prov. Connaught.

SINUS-MAGNUS, the prefent *bay of Donegal*, prov. Ulfter.

SIOL-MUIRIDH, the Eaftern part of Con-naught, on the river *Shannon*. It was deftroyed in 1095, by *Murtogh Mor O'Brien*.

SION, fee *Shane's-caftle*.

SIR ALBERT'S BRIDGE, fit. in co. Donegal, prov. Ulfter, 120 miles from Dublin. Within about a mile of this, is a well called *Sir Albert's well*.

SIRMOUNT, a feat fit. on the river *Lee*, in co. Cork, prov. Munfter.

SIX-MILE-BRIDGE, a poft town, fit. in bar. Bunratty, co. Clare, prov. Munfter, above 102 miles from Dublin: near which is a fine feat called *Mount-Ievers*. Lat. 52 : 40, lon. 8 : 40. Fairs held 6 May and 5 Dec. This town was called in Irifh *Abhuin O'Gearna*, from the river *Gearna* which runs from thence to the *Shannon*. There was a chapel or vicarial houfe near it, which belonged to the Dominicans of Lime-rick, but of this there are no remains. The ruins of the famous caftle of *Bunratty*, are only 2 miles from this place.—Likewife a place of fame name in bar. Smallcounty, co. Limerick, prov. Munfter, 102 miles from Dublin; a mile

beyond which are the ruins of *Scule* caftle, and about a mile farther fit. on a hill, are the large ruins of Rockftown caftle.

SIX-MILE-CROSS, fit. in bar. Omagh, co. Tyrone, prov. Ulfter, 87 miles from Dublin, fairs held 19 June.

SIX-MILE-WATER, a *river* fit in co. Antrim, prov. Ulfter; the town of Antrim being feated on it, over which it has a bridge.—Also a vil-lage of fame name in co. Cork, prov. Munfter; where are fairs on 6 May.

SKEA *church*, fit. in bar. Clonawly, co. Fer-managh, prov. Ulfter. It is a chapelry in dioc. of Clogher.

SKEBREEN, fee *Skibbereen*.

SKEHEWRINKY, fit. in co. Cork, prov. Mun-fter; at this place there is a cave between *Mitchelftown* and *Cahier*, the opening to which is a cleft of rock in a lime-ftone hill, fo narrow that 'tis difficult to get into it; you defcend by a ladder about 20 fteps, and are then in a vault of 120 feet long, and 50 or 60 feet high. In fome places the cavity in the rock is fo large, that when lighted up with candles, it takes the appearance of a vaulted cathedral, fupported by maffy columns. The fpar in all this cave is very brilliant, and almoft equal to *Briftol-ftone*. For feveral hundred yards in the larger divifion of this cave, there is deep water at the bottom of the declivity to the right, which the common people call the *river*. A part of the way is over a kind of potter's clay, which is of a brown colour, and may be mould-ed into any form; a very different foil from any in the neighbouring country.

SKELLIGS, *iflands* fit. off the coaft of bar. Iveragh, co. Kerry, prov. Munfter; there are 3 of them, the largeft is called the *Great*, and the fmalleft the *Little Skellig*; the former is 3 leagues from the main, the others are but rocks of marble; it is remarkable that the *Ganet* never neftles on any place in the *South* coaft of Ireland, but on one of thefe iflands; lat. 51:35, lon. 10:30. There is a rock on the *North* coaft of the kingdom, which has the fame peculiarity. On the *Great Skellig* was an abbey, which the Danes plunder'd and def-troy'd in 812, and they kept the Monks in clofe confinement 'till they perifhed thro' hun-ger. The fituation of this abbey being found extremely bleak, and all accefs to it hazardous, it was removed to *Ballynafkeiligs*, a village in the fame county.

SKENER *ifland*, fit. off the coaft of bar. Bal-ruddery, co. Dublin, prov. Leinfter.

SKERRIES, a village fit. in bar. Balruddery, co. Dublin, prov. Leinfter, 3½ miles beyond *Rufh*, within 3½ of *Balbriggen*, and about 17 miles from Dublin. It is a pretty confiderable fifhing town, having a number of boats belonging

longing to it, that are the caufe of what little bufinefs it has. The town itfelf is ill-built, but enjoys a good air: and there are feveral very elegant feats and villas near it. The *Skerries rocks* are at about 2 miles diftance from the town; they are 3 in number, and remarkable for producing great quantities of fea weed, from which kelp is made; that called *Holm Patrick*, is famous for having been the refidence of the Irifh Apoftle, St. *Patrick*, where are ftill to be feen, the venerable remains of a church, dedicated to that Saint. To make the *harbour* of Skerries, failors muft keep clear of the *crofs*; give the ifland a good birth, until they bring the northernmoft houfe in Skerries in a line with a houfe that ftands on the *hill* of Skerries; when they bring thefe marks to bear, they are at the Northward of the *Crofs*. When they have all the town clear of the quay, they will have 4 and 5 fathoms of water in the road, which is very fafe except it comes to blow hard at E. or N. E.

SKERRIES-ISLANDS, fit. in the N. fea, off the bar. Dunluce, co. Antrim, prov. Ulfter.

SKIBBEREEN, a poft and fair town in bar. Carbery, co. Cork, prov. Munfter, above 161 miles from Dublin; it was antiently called *Staple'ftown*, and is fit. by the river *Ilen*, within about 5 miles of Baltimore: it was formerly a part of the domain of the caftle of *Gortnaclough*, which belonged to *Mac Carty Reagh*: this caftle has been fometime entirely deftroyed. Skibbereen is a fmall market town, where the revenue officers of the port of *Baltimore* refide. On the W. fide of the river *Ilen* is a church, and in the town a decent market-houfe, with a ftone bridge over the river: the cloathing trade and fome of the linen manufacture has been brought forward here: the lands near it are all cultivated; they manure with fea fand, the foil being a grey clay, and in fome parts red, with a flaty bottom: they have no limeftone nearer than *Mufkerry*. W. of *Skibbereen* is *Abbey Shrowry*, formerly a religious houfe, but now the ruins of a parifh church: there are feveral old tombs here, particularly a large one of the *Roaches*. Fairs held 14 May, 10 July, 2 Auguft, 12 Oct. 11 and 23 Dec. Lat. 51 : 22, Lon. 9 : 10.

SKIDDY'S-CASTLE, an old tower near the N. gate of Cork city, in prov. Munfter, the remains of a larger building, fit. by the river *Lea*; it is now converted into a magazine for powder, where is kept a conftant guard.

SKIDOW, fit. in bar. Nethercrofs, co. Dublin, prov. Leinfter.

SKIRK, fit. in bar. upper Offory, Queen's co. prov. Leinfter, near 50 miles from Dublin; ½ a mile from the church of which are the ruins of a caftle. This is a vicarage in dioc of Offory. Here is a Pagan fane, fit. on a lofty hill;

its area is furrounded with a deep intrenchment, and within it is a pyramidical ftone 6 feet high, with the ftumps of others which made the temple. Towards the E. is a cromleach, and towards the N. a high keep or exploratory fort, and contiguous is the parochial church.

SKIRRY, fit. in bar. Antrim, co. Antrim, prov. Ulfter.

SKREEN, a rectory in dioc. of Killaloe, fit. in bar. Tyreragh, co. Sligo, prov. Connaught. The church ftands at the foot of a high hill. This place is otherwife written *Screen*.

SKREGGS, fit. in bar. Athlone, co. Rofcommon, prov. Connaught.

SKRYNE, a bar. in co. Meath, prov. Leinfter, in which is a village of fame name, diftant about 20 miles from Dublin. It is a vicarage in dioc. of Meath: and holds fairs 20 June and 10 Oct. lat. 53 : 34, lon. 7 : 7. The roads hereabouts afford fome very extenfive and beautiful profpects of the country. This place gave title of *baron* to the family of *Marwood*.—Alfo a curacy in dioc. of Ferns, fit. in bar. Ballagheen, co. Wexford, prov. Leinft.

SKULL, an infignificant village in bar. Carbery, co. Cork, prov. Munfter, not far from *Skibbereen*; it has few buildings befides the church and a parfonage houfe. It is a rectory in dioc. of Cork.

SKULL-HARBOUR, fit. in co. Cork, prov. Munfter, near the E. point of which are the ruins of *Ardintenant caftle*.

SLADE-BAY, fit. about a mile N. E. of *Hook tower*, in the harbour of *Waterford*, prov. Munfter; it is foul ground, and the beft anchoring place in it, is found by bringing the *Pier-head* and *Caftle* in one, oppofite to a ftone wall extended to the fhore, then there is, in about five fathom water, clear fandy ground.

SLADESTOWN, fit. in bar. Shelburne, co. Wexford, prov. Leinfter.

SLANE, a bar. in co. Meath, prov. Leinfter, in which is a village of fame name, which is a rectory in dioc. of Meath, diftant about 24 miles from Dublin, fit. near the river *Boyne*. Lat. 53 : 42, lon. 7 : 4. It holds fairs on 2 April, 2 June, 2 Sept. and 8 Nov. This diftrict was the original fettlement of the *Firbolgæ* or Belgians, who tranfmigrated from Britain about 350 years before Chrift, under the conduct of *Learmon* or *Slaing*; they are afferted by the antient bards to have tranfmigrated from the bay of *Cluba* in Inis Ona, now the bay of Cardigan in Wales, called by Ptolemy *Canganii Sinus*: and to have landed at Inbher Colpa, or the bay of Culbin, now the bay of *Drogheda*, from whence they in procefs of time eftablifhed colonies throughout the prefent province of Leinfter. In this diftrict are ftill remaining the tombs of the original chiefs of

this

this race, at present known by the mounts or tumuli of *New-Grange*, and which in after ages became places of druidic sacrifice, in honour of *Tlacht*, or the earth. Though now a small village, *Slane* in the time of *Hugh de Laccy*, was a place of some note, being one of the boroughs in his palatinate of Meath; the hermitage of *Eirc*, which lies S. of the town near the river, takes its name from St. *Eirc*, the first bishop of *Slane*, who was consecrated by St. Patrick, and died Nov. 20th, A. D. 514, in the 90th year of his age; an abbey for canons regular, was founded here in a very early age, on the hill at some distance from the hermitage, and was remarkable for being many years the residence of a royal prince; for in 653, *Dagobert*, king of *Austrasia* (part of France) when only 7 years old, was taken by *Grimvald*, mayor of the palace, and by his direction was shorn as a monk, rendered unfit to hold the reins of government, and banished into Ireland. He was received into this abbey, where he obtained an education proper for the enjoyment of a throne; he continued here 20 years, when he was recalled into France and replaced in his government. A large castle was erected here by the family of *lord Slane*, who being afterwards engaged in the rebellion of 1641; the estate vested in the crown, and the castle has at length come into the possession of the Rt Hon. *William Conyngham*, who has made great improvements in this place. At Slane, St. Patrick pitched his tent before his arrival at the court of *Tarah*: and lighted up that fire early in the morning, which gave so much astonishment to the Druids and assembly of the states. On the right of the town of Slane, are the flour mills of Mr. *Jebb*, which deserve the attention of the curious. They are large and excellently well built; they were begun in 1763, and finished in 1766. The water from the Boyne is conveyed to them by a weir, 650 feet long, 24 feet in base, and 8 feet high, of solid masonry; and the flood gates are constructed with great ingenuity. The canal is 800 feet long and 64 feet wide: on one side is a wharf completely formed and walled against the river, whereon are offices of several kinds, and a dry dock for building lighters. The mill is 138 feet long, the breadth 54, and the height to the cornice 42 feet. The corn upon being unloaded, is hoisted thro' the doors to the upper story of the building, by a very simple contrivance, being worked by the water wheel, and discharged into spacious granaries which hold 5000 barrels; thence it is conveyed during seven months in the year, to the kilns for drying; the mill containing two, which will dry 80 barrels in 24 hours,; from the

kiln it is hoisted again to the upper story: thence to a fanning machine for re-dressing, to get out dirt, soil, &c. and thence by a small sifting machine, into the hoppers to be ground: and is again hoisted into the bolting mills to be dressed into different sorts of pollard and bran. In all this progress, the machinery is contrived to do the business with the least labour possible. The mill will grind with great ease 120 barrels, of 20 stone each, every day. Near Slane are the ruins of *Fiunar church*: and about 3 miles one side of Slane, is *Stackallen*, the handsome seat of lord visc. *Boyne*.

SLANE-CHURCH, an antient building sit. in co. Down, prov. Ulster, a little W.N.W. of *Kirkistown*; about half a mile W. of which, stand the remains of an old building, called *Castlebuy* or *Johnston*, once a preceptory of St. *John's* of *Jerusalem*: in the beginning of the present century, 18 sailors were buried at one time, in the old church of Slane; they were the crew of a ship that was wrecked on the rocks in the neighbourhood, called the North rocks.

SLANEY-RIVER, a considerable river in prov. Leinster, having the town of Wexford at its mouth; it runs thro' *Wexford, Carlow, Wicklow*, and part of *Dublin* counties.

SLATY, see *Sletty*.

SLATY-PORT, so called from a slate quarry which joins it; it is a little port belonging to *Carrickfergus* bay, co. Down, prov. Ulster.

SLEAGUFF, a vicarage in dioc. of Leighlin, sit. in bar. Idrone, co. Carlow, prov. Leinster.

SLEAMORE-POINT, a *cape* in bar. Carbery, co. Cork, prov. Munster.

SLEDY-CASTLE, sit. in the parish of *Modeligo*, co. Waterford, prov. Munster: otherwise called *Curragh-na-Sledy*. It belonged to the *Magraths*, and was built in 1628, as appears from a date on a chimney piece, with the words *Phillipus Mac Grath*. It is said the occasion of building this castle, was from a dispute between *Magrath* and his *wife*; who would not be reconciled to him, 'till he had built her a castle on her own jointure lands: to do which, he received such large contributions from his vassals, that when it was finished, he was much richer than when he began the work.

SLENISH *mountains*, sit. in bar. Antrim, co. Antrim, prov. Ulster.

SLETTY, or *Slaty*, a rectory in dioc. of Leighlin, sit. in bar. Slewmargy, Queen's co. prov. Leinster. Here was an abbey over which St. *Aid* presided, who died in 698. his festival is held here on 12 Oct. This place was antiently called *Slieb-teagh*: and is not far distant from the town of *Carlow*.

SLEW-

SLEWARDAGH, a diftrict joined to that of *Compfey*, and forming with it the *barony of Slewardagh* and *Compfey*, in co. Tipperary, prov. Munfter.

SLEWDUFF, fit. in bar. Tyreragh, co. Sligo, prov. Connaught.

SLEWMARGY, a bar. in Queen's co. prov. Leinfter.

SLIDERY, a *river* in co. Down, prov. Ulfter, which runs into the inner bay of *Dundrum*.

SLIDERY-FORD, fit. in co. Down, prov. Ulfter; near it is an antient *Cromlech*.

SLIEBH-AN-ERIN, *mountains* fit. in bar. Dromahaire, co. Leitrim, prov. Connaught.

SLIEBH-AN-EWR, *mountains* fit. in bar. Rofsclogher, co. Leitrim, prov. Connaught.

SLIEBH-BAUGH, *mountains* fit. in bar. Trough, co. Monaghan, prov. Ulfter.

SLIEBH-BAUGHTA, *mountains* fit. between the co.'s Clare and Galway.

SLIEBH-BEARNA, *mountains* fit. in bar. Mourne, co. Down, prov. Ulfter.

SLIEBH-BINGAN, a mountain fit. in bar. Mourne, co. Down, prov. Ulfter.

SLIEBH-BLOOM, a range of mountains between the King and Queen's co.'s, prov. Leinfter: and which in antient times was one of the boundaries of Munfter, on the Leinfter fide; they are otherwife called Sliebh-Bladhma. *Bladhma* (fays Mr. *Beauford*) is corrupted from *Beal-di-mai*, whence *Slíebh Beal-di-mai*, is the mountain of the worfhip or necromancy of *Beal's-day*. There is ftill remaining in thefe mountains, a large pyramid of white ftones, the true fimulacre of the fun-fire among all the Celtic nations. Thefe mountains are alfo named *Ard-na-erin*, which in the Irifh language fignifies *in the height of Ireland*: and they form fo impracticable a barrier between the two co.'s, that in a range of 14 miles, they afford but one, and that a very difficult and narrow pafs into the King's co. called the *Gap of Glandine*. In this great ridge are the fources of the *Barrow* and the *Nore*.

SLIEBH-BONN, *mountains* fit. in bar. Rofcommon, co. Rofcommon, prov. Connaught.

SLIEBH-BUY, a very high, fertile and handfome mountain, commanding a moft extenfive and beautiful profpect; it is fit. near the old town of *Bolenrufh*, in bar. Scarewalfh, co. Wexford, prov. Leinfter.

SLIEBH-CARMEN, a name given to the mountains of the co. Wicklow, prov. Leinfter; called alfo *Slieve Coulan*, or the diftrict of *Coulan*; this antient diftrict was likewife named *Hy Tuathal*, or the gloomy region, being compofed of barren mountains and dark vallies. The antient chiefs were called *Hy Tuathal* and *Mac Mhthuil*, by corruption O'*Toole*, they were alfo hereditary chiefs of *Coulan*, during the middle

ages, and often brought under their fubjection the chiefs of *Caölan* or *Galen*. This rocky diftrict was alfo denominated *Ciarmen*, or *Cicrmen*, that is, the place or country of rocks, corruptly written *Carmen*, whence the mountains next the bay of Dublin, are in the Irifh writings frequently called *Slíebh Ciermen* or the *Rocky mountains*. As the O'*Tools* were either by defcent, or marriage of the fame family with the *Mac Moroghs*, O'*Moras* and O'*Kellys* of *Caëlan*; they were frequently denominated kings of *Leinfter*, according to their feniority.

SLIEBH-CONN, or principal mountain, now called *Sliabh Riach*, between the bar. of *Fermoy*, and co. *Limerick*; faid by the annals of *Innisfallen* to be the place where *Maolmuadh* and his brothers waited for *Mahon*, king of *Munfter*, and brother of *Brien Boromh*, to put him to death. He was flain at the place called *Leacht Mhaghthamhna*, or *Mahon's Grave*, about the year 976.

SLIEBH-CROOBE *mountain*, fit. in bar. Upper Iveagh, co. Down, prov. Ulfter. On the fkirts of this mountain is an excellent fpa for all fcrophulous cafes, tho' not much frequented.

SLIEBH-CUALANN, a name given to the mountains of Wicklow, prov. Leinfter; which are faid by fome to have been fo called from *Cuala*, one of the leaders of the *Milefian* colony from Spain.

SLIEBH-DHAM, *mountains* fit. in bar. Leney and Tyreragh, co. Sligo, prov. Connaught.

SLIEBH-DONARD, fit. in bar. Mourne, co. Down, prov. Ulfter: faid to be 3150 feet high above the level of the fea. It was antiently called *Sliebh-Slang*, from *Slaing* the fon of *Partholanus*, who is faid to have been murdered here, *Anno Mundi* 1982. St. *Domangard*, (corruptly written *Donard*) a difciple of St. *Patrick*, fpent the life of a hermit on this mountain: he built a cell or oratory on the top of it, towards the clofe of the 5th century; on the fummit of this mountain, are two rude edifices (if they may be fo termed) one being a huge heap of ftones piled in a pyramidical figure, in which are formed feveral cavities, and in the centre of this heap, is a cave formed by broad flat ftones, fo difpofed as to fupport each other without the help of cement. The other edifice, is compofed of many ftones fo difpofed in rude walls and partitions, called *Chapels*, and perhaps was the oratory and cell of the Saint, as before-mentioned. This mountain is indifputably the higheft of that whole range, which extends from *Roftrevor* to *Newcaftle*.

SLIEBH-EAN, *mountains* fit. in bar. Glenarm, co. Antrim, prov. Ulfter.

SLIEBH-

SLIEBH-GALLAN *mountain*, fit. in bar. Lough-linfholen, co. Londonderry, prov. Ulster.

SLIEBH-GULLEN *mountain*, fit. in bar. Orior, co. Armagh, prov. Ulster.

SLIEBH-LEAGUE, *mountains* fit. in bar. Boy-lagh, co. Donegal, prov. Ulster.

SLIEBH-LOGHER *mountain*, fit. in bar. Tru-aghnacmy, co. Kerry, prov. Munster.

SLIEBH-MISH, or *Mis-Sliebh* ; there are two ranges of mountains under this denomination. The first is fit. in bar. Truaghnacmy, co. Ker-ry, prov. Munster, between the bays of Caf-tlemain and Tralee, and which divides thefe arms of the fea. They are of a great height ; the higheft peak of thefe mountains meafured by a good inftrument, by means of two stati-ons taken on the level ftrand of *Tralee* bay, was 750 yards perpendicular above the fea ; the other mountains that run Wefterly, go by various Irish names ; a remarkable one of thefe is called *Cahir-Conrigh*, or *Cahir-Conrigh*. On the top of this mountain is a circle of maffy ftones, laid one on the other, in the manner of a Danifh intrenchment, feveral of them are from 8 to 10 cubical feet, but they are all very rude. According to *Keating*, a king of Munfter called *Eadna-derg*, lies buried on the top of one of thefe mountains ; he died of the plague a fhort time after he had erected the firft mint here for the coinage of money, at *Argoid-Rofs*.—The fecond range of mountains of this name, are in the diftrict of *Dalaradia*, in co. Antrim, prov. Ulster ; on which St. *Patrick*, we are told kept the fwine of his maf-ter *Milco*. A battle was fought here in 775, between the Dalriadian fepts, in which *Nial M'Donnel* of the Hibernians were flain.

SLIEBH-MORE, *mountains* fit. in bar. Burri-fhoole, co. Mayo, prov. Connaught.

SLIEBH-MOURN, or the mountains of *Mourn*, fit. in co. Down, prov. Ulster. The Irish have three names by which they diftinguifh rifing grounds ; viz. *Knock*, *Beinn* and *Sliebh* or *Slieve* ; the firft fignfies a low hill ; the fecond, a high mountain ending in a precipice ; the third, a high craggy mountain continued in ridges.

SLIEBH-NA-BOILTRA, fome high mountains fit. in co. Down, prov. Ulster ; on one of which is an antient Cromlech,

SLIEBH-NA-COILTRA, *mountains* fit. in bar.'s of Bantry and Shelburne, co. Wexford, prov. Leinster.

SLIEBH-NA-GRIDEAL, i. e. the mountain of the *Griddel*, from the refemblance it bears to that utenfil. It is a druidical Cromlech on the top of a hill, and compofed of a huge flat unhewn rock, of the *Lapis molaris*, or grit kind, interfperfed with a mixture of red and white flint, in fhape fomething like a *Lozenge* in heraldry, 11 feet 2 inches long, from point to point, 8 feet and a half broad in the great ft dimenfion, and a foot and a half thick in moft places, tho' in fome not more than a foot. It is raifed upon two rude fupporters of the fame kind of ftone, placed edge-ways, one of which is 8 feet long, 3 feet broad, and a foot thick ; the other is not above 3 feet long, and feems to be a natural rock, ftanding in its original pofition : but by the advantage of the ground, the upper or table-ftone, ftands pretty nearly on a level, tho' with a fmall inclination. The cavity underneath is fuch, that a middle fized perfon, by ftooping a little can pafs thro' it ; and the ftratum upon which the fupporting ftones ftand, is a folid rock. This is fit. in the co. Down, prov. Ulster. There is another of this kind of monuments at *Slidery-ford*, near *Dundrum*, in that county.

SLIEBH-NA-MAN, *mountains* fit. in bar. Mid-dlethird, co. Tipperary, prov. Munfter.

SLIEBH-NEIR *mountain*, fit. in co. Down, prov. Ulster.

SLIEBH-RUSSEL, a large mountain fit. be-tween the co.'s Cavan and Fermanagh, prov. Ulster.

SLIEBH-SEPHIN, fee *Sliebh-fnavan.*

SLIEBH-SLANG, the antient name of *Sliebh-Donard* mountain, in co. Down, prov. Ulster.

SLIEBH-SNAGHT *mountain*, fit. in bar. Inifh-owen, co. Donegal, prov. Ulster.

SLIEBH-SNAVAN, a *mountain* fit. near *Brian's-ford*, in co. Down, prov. Ulster ; on the fkirts of this and Slieve Neir, are two Deer parks, remarkable for excellent venifon ; or rather one park divided into two, by a wall carried thro' the middle of it ; it is finely wooded, cut into ridings and viftoes, and watered by a river running thro' it, in a channel of rocks and precipices, which paffes under a bridge of hewn ftone, from whence are beautiful profpects of the fea.

SLIEVE-TEAGH, or *Sliebteagh*, an antient church and bifhoprick, founded by St. *Fiech* in the 5th century, and afterwards tranflated to *Leighlin* ; the only remains of this antient bifhoprick, are the ruins of a fmall church and two ftone croffes, apparently of the 9th. century ; it is now called *Sletty*, and is fit. in the Queen's co. on the river *Barrow*, above 1 mile N. of Carlow, prov. Leinster. St. *Aid* prefided over the abbey here, who died in 698.

SLIGO, *(county)* fit. in prov. Connaught. It lies on the W. of the co. Leitrim, and on the N. of co. Rofcommon : its greateft length is 31 miles, and the greateft breadth 29. It contains 247,150 acres, 39 parifhes, 6 baronies, about 60,000 inhabitants, and (with the *town* of *Sligo)* returns *four* members to parliament. Its boroughs are *Carbury* or *Carbery*, *Tyreragh*, *Leney*, *Corran*, *Coolavin* and *Tyraghrill*. The

principal

O'CONOR'S TOMB *in the* ABBEY *of* SLIGO.

principal proprietors of this diftrict at the commencement of the laft century, were the families of *O'Connor*, *M'Dermotroe*, *O'Hara*, *O'Bean*, *O'Birn*, *M'Donagh*, *M'Forbes*, *O'Dowda*, *Jordan*, *Dillon* and *Nangle*. This country contains fome very good land, but is intermixed with large tracts of coarfe and unprofitable ground. It is otherwife called *Slego*, and was named by the Irifh, *Sliogh Gac:* it is the *Naguatæ* of *Ptolemy*.

SLIGO *(town,)* fit. in co. Sligo, prov. Connaught, 105 miles from Dublin; it is a borough, poft and fair town; lat. 54:12, lon. 8:40. It is a town of confiderable trade, has a barrack for two companies of foot, and a charter fchool, which was opened in 1755, for 80 children. The governors of the fchools founded by the late *Erafmus Smith*, efq; in order to have a charter fchool here, paid to the incorporated-fociety, 500*l.* towards the building, and refolved to give 250*l.* annually towards the fupport of it. And the late *Owen Wynne*, efq; of *Hazelwood*, co. Sligo, granted to it four acres of land for ever, at 1 fhilling yearly. This town returns 2 members to parliament, patronage in the *Wynne* family. The abbey of Sligo owes its origin to *Maurice Fitzgerald*, lord juftice of Ireland, who in 1252, founded here a monaftery for Dominicans, under the invocation of the holy crofs. 10 years before, he had erected a ftrong caftle in the town; which, while it gave fecurity to the place, attracted a number of inhabitants to it; and thus, with the advantage of a good harbour, Sligo rofe to fome importance. *Thomas de Clare*, fon-in-law of Fitzgerald, having in 1277, flain *O'Brien Roe*, king of Thomond, then in rebellion, the Irifh deftroyed moft of Fitzgerald's caftles, and among the reft, that of Sligo; but *Richard*, the red earl of Ulfter, rebuilt it in 1310. The town was frequently deftroyed by barbarous contending factions; nor did the abbey efcape pillage. In 1414, there were but 20 friars refident in it, and the next year, the whole fabrick was confumed by fire; in confequence of which, pope *John* 23d. iffued his apoftolic letters dated at Conftance, 16 Feb. 1415, whereby he relaxed 10 years of penance to all who, at the feafts of the affumption of the *B. V. M.* and St. *Patrick*, fhould devoutly vifit that place and contribute to its reparation. Among the principal benefactors were *O'Conor*, lord of Sligo, and *Pierce O'Timony*, a man of confiderable wealth and property, whofe ftatue was placed in the cloyfter. At the fuppreffion of monafteries, this abbey and its poffeffions were granted to fir *Wm. Taafe*, anceftor to the firft lord *Taafe*, of Corren. The ruins of this once fpacious and beautiful monaftery, evince its former fplendour; 3 fides of the cloyfter ftill remain, covered with an arched

roof, the arches and pillars are of extraordinary workmanfhip, and a few of the latter are adorned with fculpture; the great E. window is beautiful and the high altar ornamented with relievo's in the Gothic ftile, but now fo overwhelmed with bones and fkulls, as to prevent a minute defcription; the *nave* is fpacious, with a paffage round it, in the nature of a gallery, and fupported by ftone pillars, about 4 feet diftant from each other; in the corner to the right, as you look towards the altar, is the tomb of *O'Connor*, with a reprefentation of himfelf and his lady, and an infcription now almoft defaced; no one has determined the date of this monument, or the perfon to whom it properly belongs. It cannot be coeval with the rebuilding of the church in 1415, for there is no tradition or record to that purpofe; but we know that, *Eleanor*, daughter of *Edmund*, lord *Dunboyne*, married *O'Connor*, of Sligo, and died in 1656. She directed a chapel to be built near the abbey of St. Dominick in Sligo, towards the erecting of which, and a monument therein, fhe bequeathed 300*l.* Here are alfo feveral vaults and cells, and the tower in the centre is pretty entire, except the battlements. This great and curious monument of antiquity, befides fuffering from the ravages of time, is faid to have alfo received fome injury from *Cromwell*. Here were alfo two of the antient round towers, of which there are now no remains. *Sligo* is the fhire town of the co. and the affizes are held there; it holds fairs on 27 Mar. 4 July, 11 Aug. and 9 Oct. Near Sligo is a place called *Lugna Clogh* or the Giant's grave, where feveral large ftones are raifed upon the ends of others, which are pitched perpendicularly, not unlike thofe very remarkable ones at *Stonehenge*, on Salifbury plain in England. They are the monuments of feveral famous perfons, who have been buried there, as is evident from their bones, which have been found under thefe venerable pieces of antiquity. Within about 3 miles of Sligo are other ruins of an abbey.

SLIGUFF, fit. in co. Carlow, prov. Leinfter; fairs held 12 Feb. and 1 Nov.

SLISHCARROW *mountain*, fit. in bar. Tiraghrill, co. Sligo, prov. Connaught.

SLUMCARTY, a village fit. in bar. Kells, co. Kilkenny, prov. Leinfter.

SLYMEHEAD, a *cape*, fit. in bar. Ballinahinch, co. Galway, prov. Connaught; it ftretches into the Atlantic ocean.

SMALLCOUNTY, a bar. in co. Limerick, prov. Munfter.

SMALLS, or *the Smalls*, iflands fo called, fit. between *Wales* and the co. Wexford.

SMERLAGH-RIVER, rifes near *Stack's-mountains*, in co. Kerry, prov. Munfter, and at laft falls into the river *Feal*.

SMERMORE,

SMERMORE, a vicarage in dioc. of Armagh, fit. in bar. Ardee, co. Louth, prov. Leinfter.

SMERWICK, a village fit. in bar. Corcaguinny, co. Kerry, prov. Munfter.

SMERWICK-HARBOUR, fit. in co. Kerry, prov. Munfter; it lies up from N. to S. and is expofed to N. and W. winds; the whole is deep and good holding ground, the bottom being actually a turf bog, which fhews that it was once dry land. There is no danger in failing into this place; towards the E. point is a rock, called *Black Rock*, always above water, and has clean ground near it. Lat. 52:5, lon. 10:28.

SMITH'SBOROUGH, fit. in bar. Monaghan, co. Monaghan, prov. Ulfter; above 67 miles from Dublin. Fairs held 2 April, Whit-monday, 2 Mond. in Aug. and Nov.

SNEEM-HARBOUR, fit. in co. Kerry, prov. Munfter; you may fafely fail along the S. fide of *Skerky-ifland* 'till you enter this harbour, and then give the E. point of the ifland a birth; you may run up to any reafonable diftance, and anchor in 10 or 12 fathom water, where you may wait conveniently for a flood.

SNUB, fit. in bar. Lecale, co. Down, prov. Ulfter.

SNUGBOROUGH, a pleafant feat with good plantations, fit. near the river *Bride*, in co. Cork, prov. Munfter.—Alfo a feat in co. Clare, prov. Munfter; near the ruins of Quin abbey.— Alfo a place near *Drogheda*, prov. Leinfter.

SOHO, fit. near *Caftlebar*, co. Mayo, prov. Connaught.

SOLDIERSTOWN, a vicarage in dioc. of Dromore, fit. in bar. Maffareen, co. Antrim, prov. Ulfter.

SOLLOGHODBEG, a rectory in dioc. of Emly, fit. in bar. Clanwilliam, co. Tipperary, prov. Munfter.

SOLLOGHODMORE, a rectory in dioc. of Emly, fit. in bar. Clanwilliam, co. Tipperary, prov. Munfter.

SOLOMON'S-PORCH, fit. in co. Tyrone, prov. Ulfter, near *Craigtown-ftrand*; it was formerly a very fine cave, but the rock being lime-ftone, is quarried down, and the cave greatly damaged.

SOLSBOROUGH, fit. near *Ennifcorthy*, co. Wexford, prov. Leinfter.

SOMMERVILLE, a neat lodge, fit. on the river *Blackwater*, in co. Cork, prov. Munfter.

SOUTH-BUSH-CASTLE, (now in ruins) fit. about 7 miles from *Belfaft*, co. Antrim, prov. Ulfter.

SOUTHPARK, a handfome feat in co. Rofcommon, prov. Connaught; fit. within a few miles of *Caftleplunket*; about a mile from it are the ruins of a church; and a little farther, thofe of an abbey.

SOUTHVILLE, fit. near *Athy*, co. Kildare, prov. Leinfter.

SOUTHWELL'S-GLEN, a beautiful feat, fit. 2 miles beyond *Rathfarnham*, and 5 miles from Dublin, in co. Dublin, prov. Leinfter. It is delightfully fit. on an eminence that commands a moft ample profpect of the adjacent country. The glen contiguous to the houfe, has been juftly admired by every perfon who has a tafte for the beauties of nature and the works of art. Here both are united, and fill the mind with the moft agreeable fenfations. Near this glen is a Druidical altar, and a judgment chair, in a very perfect ftate; thefe venerable antiquities are worthy the attention of the curious.

SPA. Under this title we fhall mention a few of the moft remarkable medicinal fprings in this country; viz. 1. An excellent water lately difcovered near Leixlip, co. Kildare, prov. Leinfter, on the eftate of the Rt. Hon. Mr. *Conolly*. It is of fingular benefit in fcrophulous and other diforders, and goes by the name of the *New-fpa*; it was firft found in confequence of the ground being cut through, in forming a branch of the New Canal, on the lands of *Croaghmouther*. From experiment made at the elaboratory of apothecaries-hall, Dublin; a wine gallon of this water, appeared to contain

	Grains
Of muriated mineral alkali, dried in the temperature of 200° of Farenheit's thermometer,	30,37
Of Muriated vegetable alkali - - -	2,07
Vitriolated vegetable alkali - -	0,07
Muriated lime - - - -	8,73
Vitriolated lime - - - -	1
Aerated lime - - - -	13,44
Muriated magnefia - - -	0,97
Argil, or clay - - - -	0,50
Silex, or earth of flints - -	0,25
Bituminous matter - - -	0,14

It was alfo found to yield in the temperature of 212° barometer 29,25, thermometer 70°

Of fixable air - - 1,50 cubic inches.

Atmofpheric air - 2,15

2d, At *Lucan*, in co. Dublin, prov. Leinfter, on the demefne of Mr. *Vefey*, is a noted medicinal fpring. The well is fheltered in a deep niche, neatly executed in hewn ftone; there is a rural thatched feat for the water drinkers, and fpace allowed for walking about.—3d, At *Caftleconnel*, co. Limerick, prov. Munfter, is a chalybeate, of the fame nature with the *German fpa*, and not much lefs pungent and fparkling; thefe waters have had great fuccefs in bilious cafes, and obftructions of the liver; near the fpa, are the ruins of an old caftle, which was a ftrong fortification in 1690, but blown up by the order of the prince of *Heffe*, who commanded the garrifon of Limerick.—4th, Another of thefe waters is at *Swanlinbar*, co. Cavan, prov. Ulfter; it is excellent for the fcurvy, nerves, low fpirits

and

and bad appetite; and is to be drank as the stomach can bear it, preparing first with gentle physic.—5th, At *Mallow*, co. Cork, prov. Munster. This place is noted for its hot wells; there is a small canal with walks on each side, leading to the spring, under cover of some very noble poplars; these waters are drunk with great success, where secretions are redundant; they are very serviceable in emaciated constitutions, after long fevers; cure ulcers in the bladder, and disorders in the urinary passages.—6th, At *Ballyspellan*, co. Kilkenny, prov. Leinster; this water has done great service in disorders of the stomach, in hypochondriac maladies, cholics, and stubborn eruptions of the skin.—7th, At *Starbog*, co. Tyrone, prov. Ulster.—8th, At *Clonmell*, co. Tipperary, prov. Munster. The cures performed by drinking this water in the scurvy, and several chronic distempers, formerly drew a great resort of people here; but fashion has brought other waters of late into higher credit.—9th, A mineral spring at the town of *Wexford*, co. Wexford, prov. Leinster: it is preserved in an enclosure of stone, and found efficacious in many cases.—10th, At *Dromore*, co. Down, prov. Ulster: it is a chalybeate, and has been drank with success for gravelly complaints; and at some particular times, especially in dry seasons, it is of a purgative quality.—11th, At *Dunaghy*, co. Tyrone, prov. Ulster.—12th, At *Granshaw*, co. Down, prov. Ulster: it lies in a little valley, surrounded on all sides by hills of easy ascent, and is found not inferior in strength to the best British chalybeates.—13th, At *Holy-river*, co. Down, prov. Ulster.—14th, At *Kilmeaden*, co. Waterford, prov. Munster: it is sit. near the church, and breaks out in the high way, between two rising grounds, with such force, that in crossing the road it becomes a little brook: it was drank about fifty years ago with great success, as a diuretic; but in order to experience its virtues it must be drank on the spot.—15th, At *Macroom*, co. Cork, prov. Munster—16th, At *Slieve-croob*, co. Down, prov. Ulster: it it sit. at the skirts of the mountain, is an excellent chalybeo-sulphureous spa, but not much frequented.—17th, At *Tierkelly*, co. Down, prov. Ulster, sit. about 2 miles N. E. of *Rathfryland*: it is a very strong chalybeate, yet exceedingly light, and free from any considerable proportion of heterogeneous mixture.—18th, At *Tralee*, co. Kerry, prov. Munster: it is sit. by the sea side, near a seat called *lower Cannon*.

SPA-HILL, sit. near *Leighlinbridge*, prov. Lein.

SPA-LODGE, sit. near *Ballinahinch*, prov. Ulst.

SPANCEL-HILL, see *Spanse-hill*.

SPANISH-COVE, a *creek* sit. in bar. Carbery, co. Cork, prov. Munster.

SPANISH-ISLAND, sit. in the bay of Baltimore, co. Cork, prov. Munster.

SPANSE-HILL, or *Spancel-hill*, sit. in co. Clare, prov. Munster, 107 miles from Dublin. Here are the ruins of a castle, and a few miles from which are the ruins of Quin abbey, the most perfect of its kind in Ireland, having a complete quadrangular building, with piazzas, supported by a number of pillars of the Corinthian order. Fairs held at Spanse-hill 23 and 24 June, and 20 August.

SPAW-HILL, see *Spa-hill*.

SPENCE'S-RIVER, an inconsiderable river sit. in co. Down, prov. Ulster.

SPIKE-ISLAND, sit. near Cork-harbour, in prov. Munster.

SPRINGFIELD, sit. in co. Cork, prov. Munst.—Also in co. Down, prov. Ulster.—And in co. Kildare, prov. Leinster.

SPRING-HILL, sit. near *Burros*, in Queen's co. prov. Leinster, the seat of the late *Francis Short* esq.—Also a village in bar. Loughlinsholen, co. Londonderry, prov. Ulster.

SPRINGVALE, otherwise called *Ballymagown*, a well improved seat in co. Down, prov. Ulst.

SPRUCES-HAYS, a village sit. in bar. Kells, co. Kilkenny, prov. Leinster.

SPURREBOY, sit. in co. Limerick, prov. Munster. Fairs held 11 Oct.

SQUINCE-ISLAND, sit. near *Glandore harbour*, in co. Cork, prov. Munster; it produces a wonderful sort of herbage, which fattens diseased horses to admiration.

STABANNON, a vicarage in dioc. of Armagh, sit. in bar. Ardee, co. Louth, prov. Leinster.

STACKALLEN, a rectory in dioc. of Meath, sit. in bar. Slane, co. Meath, prov. Leinster. Here is the seat of lord *Boyne*.—Also a place in bar. Ardee, co. Louth, prov. Leinster.

STACK'S-MOUNTAINS, sit. in co. Kerry, prov. Munster, in the bar. of *Clanmaurice*.

STACUMNEY, a curacy in dioc. of Dublin, sit. in bar. Salt, co. Kildare, prov. Leinster.

STAGS, *rocks* sit. in bar. Imokilly, co. Cork, prov. Munster.

STAGS of BROADHAVEN, *rocks* on coast of bar. Erris, co. Mayo, prov. Connaught.

STAGS of CASTLEHAVEN, *rocks* sit. near the coast of bar. Carbery, co. Cork, prov. Munst.

STAHALMUCK, a vicarage in dioc. of Meath, sit. in bar. Kells, co. Meath, prov. Leinster.

STALEEN, sit. near *Drogheda*, prov. Leinster.

STAMCARTHY, a vicarage in dioc. of Ossory, sit. in bar. Shellilogher, co Kilkenny, prov. Leinster.

STAMULLEN, a vicarage in dioc. of Meath, sit. in bar Duleck, co. Meath, prov. Leinster.

STAPLESTOWN, sit. about 2 miles S. E. of Carlow, in co. Carlow, prov. Leinster. Here is the handsome seat of Mr. *Bagnel*; it is a sweet situation, where nature has contributed greatly to assist art; the house is built on an eminence, that

that with a gentle declivity, leads you down to a pretty river called the *Burren*, which is croſſed by a bridge of ſeven arches. The houſe and gardens might ſerve an Italian prince, who need not be aſhamed of his reſidence. Tho' this place is called Stapleſtown, there are but few houſes in it. Fairs are held here on 1 May and 7 Nov.—*Stapleſtown* was alſo a name given formerly to the town of *Skibbereen*, co. Cork, prov. Munſter.

STARBOG-SPA, ſit. within about 4 miles of *Ballygawly*, co. Tyrone, prov. Ulſter.

STEBANNON, ſit. in bar. Atherdee, co. Louth, prov. Leinſter.

STEDALT, ſit. near *Balbriggen*, prov. Leinſt.

STEPHENON *mountain*, ſit. in bar. Talbot's-town, co. Wicklow, prov. Leinſter.

STEWART-HALL, the elegant ſeat of lord *Caſtleſtewart*, ſit. within 2 miles of Stewart'ſtown, co. Tyrone, prov. Ulſter.

STEWART'STOWN, ſit. in bar. Dungannon, co. Tyrone, prov. Ulſter, 77 miles from Dublin; within 2 miles of it is *Stewart's-hall*, a moſt ſuperb edifice, with extenſive and beautiful parks and demeſnes, the ſeat of lord *Caſtleſtewart*. Three miles from *Stewart'ſtown*, on a riſing ground, is *Ardtreagh church*. Fairs held at Stewart'ſtown 1 May, Nov. and 30 Dec.

STICKILLEN, a vicarage in dioc. of Armagh, ſit. in bar. Ardee, co. Louth, prov. Leinſter.

STILLORGAN, ſit. in bar. Half-Rathdown, co. Dublin, prov. Leinſter, within about four miles of the metropolis; it is a handſome ſeat, has a view of the ſea on one ſide, and the co. Wicklow on the other: near it there is a good pheaſantry. Here is an obeliſk very lofty and elegant; it is upwards of 100 feet in height, placed on a ruſtic baſe, to each ſide of which is a double ſtair-caſe, leading to a platform which encompaſſes the obeliſk, and from whence is a fine view of the bay of Dublin and Iriſh channel; from hence the hill of *Heath*, on the oppoſite ſhore, appears like the rock of *Gibraltar*. This is a curacy in dioc. of Dublin.

STOHOLMUCK, ſee *Stahalmuck*.

STONEHALL, ſit. in co. Limerick, prov. Munſter. 106 miles from Dublin; fairs held 14 May, and 25 Sept.—Alſo a rectory in dioc. of Meath, ſit. in bar. Corkerry, co. Weſtmeath, prov. Lein.

STONEHOUSE, ſit. at the foot of a hill, about 4 miles from Drogheda, co. Louth, prov. Leinſter; it was the ſeat of *Samuel Owens*, eſq; and is now the reſidence of *J. T. Foſter*, eſq.

STONEYFORD, ſit. in co. *Antrim*, prov. Ulſt. 77 miles from Dublin.—Likewiſe a place of ſame name in co. *Meath*, prov. Leinſter. thirty miles from Dublin.

STORMANSTOWN, ſit. in bar. Ardee, county Louth, prov. Leinſter.—Alſo a village in bar. Coolock, co. Dublin, prov. Leinſter.

STRABANE. a barony in co. Tyrone, prov. Ulſter, in which is a borough, poſt and fair town of ſame name, ſit. about 101 miles N.W. of Dublin. Lat. 54 : 46, lon. 8 : 4. It gives title of viſcount to a branch of the family of *Hamilton*. It is large, populous and well built, ſituated on the river *Mourne*, having a beautiful proſpect of *Lifford-bridge*, and is deemed as elegant a ſituation as any in Ireland. It returns 2 members to parliament; patron, the earl of *Abercorn*; fairs held 12 May and Nov.

STRABOE, a vicarage in dioc. of Leighlin, ſit. in bar. Ravilly, co. Carlow, prov. Leinſt.—Alſo a vicarage in the ſame dioc. ſit. in bar. Maryborough, Queen's co. prov. Leinſter.

STRABRAGY-BAY, ſit. in bar. Iniſhowen, co. Donegal, prov. Ulſter.

STRADBALLY, a barony in Queen's co. prov. Leinſter, in which is a poſt town of ſame name, ſit. about 38 miles from Dublin. Tho' ſmall, it is clean and neat; has a church, market-houſe and charter ſchool: the latter was opened in 1738, for 40 children, and owes its riſe to *Pole Coſby*, eſq; who expended 300*l*. in the building, gave an acre of land in perpetuity, and granted 30 acres for 31 years, at 11*l*. per ann. In the 12th century lord *O'Mora* founded a monaſtery here for conventual Franciſcans. Near *Stradbally* is *Stradbally-hall*, an elegant ſeat of Mr. *Coſby*, and within ¼ a mile of the town is *Brockley-park*, the ſuperb ſeat of the earl of *Roden*. Fairs are held at Stradbally on 6 May, 10 July, 21 Aug. and Nov. This is a vicarage in dioc. of Leighlin.—Alſo a rectory in dioc. of Ardfert, ſit. in bar. Corcaguinny, co. Kerry, prov. Munſt. —Alſo a vicarage in dioc. of Kilmacduagh, ſit. in bar. Dunkellin, co. Galway, prov. Conn.— Alſo a vicarage in dioc. of Liſmore, ſit. in bar. Decies without Drum, co. Waterford, prov. Munſter.

STRADE, or *Straid*, a village ſit. in bar. Belfaſt, co. Antrim, prov. Ulſter, 89 miles from Dublin: here are the ruins of a church.—— Alſo a fair town in bar. Gallen, co. Mayo, prov. Connaught. It is a vicarage in dioc. of Achonry. Fairs held 31 May, 30 July, 23 October and 27 Novem. This place is ſeated by the river *Moy*; the ſept of *M'Jordan* founded a houſe here, under the invocation of the holy croſs, for friars of the order of St. Francis; but it was given to the Dominicans in 1252. A very ſmall part of this friary ſtill remains, but the walls of the church, which was ſingularly beautiful, are ſtill entire; and the high altar is adorned with gothic ornaments. In the centre of the altar is an image of our Saviour when an infant, in the virgin's lap, and a perſon in relievo, within a compartment at each ſide: here is alſo a tomb adorned with curious relievos of 4 kings, in different compartments, one

one of whom is kneeling before a mitred person; near to it is another relievo of the saints *Peter* and *Paul*.

STRADONE, fit. in bar. Tullagharvey, co. Cavan, prov. Ulster, 49 miles from Dublin; fairs held 28 March, 24 June, 16 Aug. 10 Oct. and 18 Dec.

STRAFFAN, a vicarage in dioc. of Dublin, fit. in bar. Salt, co. Kildare, prov. Leinster. Here is a handsome seat belonging to *Joseph Henery*, esq;

STRAGONA, fit. in co. Fermanagh, prov. Ulster; fairs held 1 June, 21 Aug. and Tuesd. before Christmas.

STRAID, see *Strade*.

STRAMORE-INN, fit. in co. Tyrone, prov. Ulster, 91 miles from Dublin.

STRANCALLY, a castle fit. in the parish of Killcockan, in co. Waterford, prov. Munster, 2 miles below *Headborough*; it is built on a rock, directly over the *Black-water*. From the castle thro' the rock to the river a passage was cut, of considerable length and breadth, and pretty deep. This kind of cave (as tradition tells us) was formerly used by the tyrannical earls of *Desmond*, as a prison for such persons who had fortunes in this part of the country, whom they frequently invited to the castle to make merry, and afterwards confined to this dungeon, where they suffered them to perish; there is a hole cut thro' the rock, in the manner of a port-cullis, down which the dead bodies were cast into the river. One person by good fortune escaped out of this dungeon, who gave the government information of these horrid practises; and both the cave and castle, were by their orders soon afterwards demolished. The cave is entirely laid open, and half of the castle blown up, the powder having split it from top to bottom, and large pieces of the wall were thrown at a considerable distance from the rest by the force of the blast.

STRAND, fit. in co. Donegal, prov. Ulster, 138 miles from Dublin.

STRAND-HOUSE-INN, fit. in co. Sligo, prov. Connaught, 107 miles from Dublin; 2 miles beyond which are the ruins of a castle.

STRANDTOWN, a village fit. in bar. Castlereagh, co. Down, prov. Ulster.

STRANGFORD, a small but antient market and post town in bar. Ardes, co. Down, prov. Ulster, fit. on a river of the same name, 78 miles from Dublin; it gives title of visc. to the family of *Smythe*. A charter school was opened here in 1748, for 20 boys and 20 girls; for the erecting of which, the Rt. Hon. Robert, late earl of Kildare, bequeathed 500*l.* and the countess dowager gave 2 acres of land in perpetuity, and granted 20 acres more for 31 years, at less than half their value. Fairs are held on 12

Aug. and 8 Nov. Lat. 54 : 24, lon. 6 : 14. In the time of queen *Eliz.* there was a castle maintained here, for securing the quiet of this co. here is a church and presbyterian meeting-house; the former was built, and the bell given to it by *Valentine Pain*, and *Elizabeth*, his wife, in the year 1629, as appears by an inscription on the bell. It is said this *Val. Pain* was agent in these parts to the then earl of *Kildare*.

STRANGFORD-BAY, fit. in co. Down, prov. Ulster. This place takes its proper name, *Strongford*, from the rapidity with which the sea runs in the channel to Strangford *lake*, the current there being reckoned one of the strongest in *Europe*, insomuch that boats passing from *Portaferry* on the *Ardes* side, to *Strangford* on the *Lecale* side, are carried up and down the gulph with great force; nor can they make the opposite shore in a strait line, but are forced up and down the stream, oftentimes at a great distance from where they set off: when the tides and currents are strongest, ships in this bay are forced a-stern, tho' failing with a brisk gale. Lat. 54 : 17, lon. 6 : 15.

STRANGFORD-LOUGH, see *Lough-Strangford*.

STRANMORE, fit. near *Monallen*, co. Down, prov. Ulster.

STRANOCUM, fit. in co. Antrim, prov. Ulster, 108 miles from Dublin. Fairs held 20 April and 29 December.

STRANORLANE, fit. in bar. Raphoe, co. Donegal. prov. Ulster, 112 miles from Dublin. fairs held 29 March, 6 July, 12 August, 10 October and 9 December. It is a rectory in dioc. of Raphoe.

STRANYGORE, fit. in co. Down, prov. Ulster. There is a great tide which runs off from the E. of *Mew-island* in this co. to the N. E. and the *Mull* of *Galloway*, which is commonly called the tide of *Stranygore*, and occasioned by the flood tide coming in from the north, and meeting with an intercepting tide from the bay of *Carrickfergus*, which runs tide and quarter tide.

STRATFORD, or *Stratford* upon *Slaney*, fit. in bar. Talbot'stown, co. Wicklow, prov. Leinst, on the river *Slaney*, 26 miles from Dublin: it is a manufacturing town, built within these few years by the present earl of *Aldborough*. It consists of 4 squares and 12 streets, regularly laid out; the squares from 300 to 150 feet across, and streets from 60 to 40: there is a large reservoir of water in the centre of the town, constantly supplied from different springs; there is a church, and many improvements are intended to be added; but the design of the noble proprietor has not proved as successful as could be wished. Fairs are held here 21 Apr. and 7 Sep.

STRATFORD-LODGE, fit. near *Castledermot*, prov. Leinster.

STRAW-HALL, fit. within 3 miles of *Nucef-town*, in bar. Mufkerry, co. Cork, prov. Munfter: it was formerly called *Kilbrenin*. Here a monaftery was founded by *Aedh*, fon of *Breic*, who died 10 Nov. 588. *(Archd. monaft.)* According to fome it was an abbey founded in the 8th century.—Alfo a place in bar. Balruddery, co. Dublin, prov. Leinfter.

STREAMSTOWN, fit. in bar. Moyafhill, co. Weftmeath, prov. Leinfter. Lat. 53 : 22, lon. 8 : 2.—Alfo in bar. Clonmorris, co. Mayo, prov. Connaught.

STREET, a vicarage in dioc. of Ardagh, fit. in bar. Moygoifh, co. Weftmeath, prov. Leinft.

STROKESTOWN, fit. in bar. Rofcommon, co. Rofcommon, prov. Connaught, 70 miles from Dublin. Fairs held 1 Tuefd. O. S. May, June, Oct. and Nov. Near 4 miles beyond it are the ruins of a church; and 2 miles from Strokef-town, is *Kilthrufton church*, fit. on the fide of a hill, near the ruins of a caftle; this is a poft town.

STRUEL-WELLS, fit. in co. Down, prov. Ulfter; they are diftant 1 mile from *Downpatrick*, and called likewife St. *Patrick's wells*; they are 4 in number, each covered with a vault of ftone, and the water is conveyed by fubterraneous aqueducts from one to the other; but the largeft of them is the moft celebrated, being in dimenfion 16½ feet by 11. All thefe vaults feem to be very antient, and near one of them, are the ruins of a fmall chapel, dedicated to St. *Patrick*.

STRUVE-POINT, a *cape*, fit. in bar. Inifhowen, co. Donegal, prov. Ulfter.

SUBULTER, a rectory in dioc. of Cloyne, fit. in bar. Duhallow, co. Cork, prov. Munfter.

SUCCA river, fee *Suck*.

SUCK, a river, fit. between *Lough Derg* and *Lough Ree*, prov. Connaught.

SUDDAN, fit. in bar. Slane, co. Meath, prov. Leinfter.

SUGAR-LOAF-HILLS, 2 high, conical hills, diftinguifhed into great Sugar-loaf-hill, and little Sugar-loaf-hill, fit. within a few miles of the metropolis, in bar. Rathdown, co. Wicklow, prov. Leinfter.

SUIR, (otherwife *Suire*, *Shower*, *Shuir*, or *Sewer*) a large river, rifing out of the fame mountains as the river *Nore* and *Barrow*, and after a courfe of 70 miles, meets them again in the haven of Waterford, prov. Munfter, where they fall into the fea together.

SULCHOID, (from *Sulchath*, or the place of battle) fit. not far from *Limerick*, in co. Limerick, prov. Munfter, being a plain nearly furrounded by mountains, and frequently mentioned in different periods of Irifh hiftory, as a noted poft for the encampment of armies; in particular celebrated for a victory obtained over the *Danes* in 968.

SULLANE *river*, fit. in bar. Mufkerry, co. Cork, prov. Munfter.

SUMMER-HILL, a poft and fair town in bar. Moyfenrath, co. Meath, prov. Leinfter, 20 miles from Dublin; here is the beautiful feat of the Rt. Hon. lord *Langford*. This place gives title of *baron* to the family of *Rowley*, now vifc. *Langford*. Fairs held 30 Apr. *dry cows*, 9 June, 22 Sept. *fheep* and *calves*, and 25 Nov. *cattle*.—Alfo a feat near *Killala*, co. Mayo, prov. Connaught; contiguous to it are the ruins of *Rathbran abbey*.

SURGOWNY, fit. in co. Armagh, prov. Ulfter; fairs held 12 Jan. and 14 May.

SWAINSTOWN, fit. near *Trim*, prov. Leinfter.

SWAN-ISLAND, (fo called from the great number of *fwans* which frequent it,) fit. near *Downpatrick*, in *Strangford lake*, co. Down, prov. Ulfter.

SWANLINBAR, a village, fit. in bar. Tullaghagh, co. Cavan, prov. Ulfter, 74 miles from Dublin; within a mile of which are the ruins of a church; and 4 miles beyond it is *Florence-court*, the fuperb feat of lord vifc. *Enniskillen*; about half a mile from Swanlinbar is the celebrated fpa, the water of which is excellent for the fcurvy, nerves, lownefs of fpirits, or bad appetite; it is to be drank as the ftomach can bear it, preparing firft with gentle phyfic. The poft comes in here, and goes out three times in the week. Fairs held 18 May, 27 July and Nov.

SWATTERAGH, fit. in bar. Loughlinfholen, co. Londonderry, prov. Ulfter, above 96 miles from Dublin; fairs held 3 Mar. 17 May, July, and 3 Dec.

SWELLY *river*, fit. in bar. Raphoe, co. Donegal, prov. Ulfter.

SWILLY-LOUGH, fit. in bar. Kilmacrenan, co. Donegal, prov. Ulfter.

SWILLY *river*, fit. in bar. Kilmacrenan, co. Donegal, prov. Ulfter.

SWINFORD, or *Swineford*, fit. in bar. Gallen, co. Mayo, prov. Connaught, 103 miles from Dublin; 3 miles beyond which, is a very fine round tower, almoft perfect, and not far from it the ruins of *Melick* church. Fairs held 20 May, 2 July, 18 Aug. and Dec.

SWINZADO-CASTLE, fit. in bar. Boylagh, co. Donegal, prov. Ulfter. Lat. 54 : 52, lon. 8 : 56.

SWORDS, a borough, fair and poft town, in bar. Nethercrofs, co. Dublin, prov. Leinfter, above 7 miles from the metropolis; it fends 2 members to parliament, the electors are *potwollopers*; here is one of our round towers in a perfect ftate; it is 73 feet high, and 50 or 60 feet diftant from the church, of a plain fimple ftructure. Fairs held on 11 May, for horfes and pedlars wares. Lat. 53 : 28, lon. 6 : 43. At Swords are the ruined walls of fome old buildings,

buildings, covered with ivy, and forming a venerable appearance. A monastery was founded here by St. *Columb*, in 512. This town was confumed by fire, in 1012, 1016, 1069, 1130, 1138, 1150 and 1166. Here are fome ruins of a palace which formerly belonged to the arch-bifhops of Dublin; this is a vicarage in dioc. of Dublin.

SYBILHEAD, a *cape*, fit. in bar. Corcaguinny, co. Kerry, prov. Munfter.

SYDAN, a village in bar. Slane, co. Meath, prov. Leinfter; it is a vicarage in dioc. of Meath.

SYLVAN-PARK, fit. near *Kells*, prov. Leinfter.

SYMOND'S-COURT, a pleafant little village, fit. half a mile to the left of *Donnybrook*, and 2½ miles from Dublin, in co. Dublin, prov. Leinfter.

SYNGFIELD, fit. near *Birr*, prov. Leinfter.

T A

TA, (or *lough Ta*) a *lake*, fit. in bar. Forth, co. Wexford, prov. Leinfter: it receives into it two or three fmart rivulets, but having no outlet, the waters accumulate and gradually overflow the adjacent grounds; 'till the peafan-try once in three or four years let them off, by making a cut thro' the high fand-bank that parts the lake from the fea, which very foon fills up again.

TABLEMOUNTAIN, *mountains*, fit. in bar. Tal-botftown, co. Wicklow, prov. Leinfter.

TABONE, an antient name for the bor. of *St. Johnftown*, co. Donegal, prov. Ulfter.

TACUMSHIN, a rectory in dioc. of Ferns, fit. in bar. Forth, co. Wexford, pro. Leinfter.

TAGHADOE, a curacy in dioc. of Dublin, fit. in bar. Salt, co. Kildare, prov. Leinfter; here is a church and round tower.

TAGHBOY, a vicarage in dioc. of Elphin, fit. in bar. Athlone, co. Rofcommon, prov. Conn.

TAGHKEEN, a vicarage in dioc. of Tuam. fit. in bar. Kilmain, co. Mayo, prov. Connaught.

TAGHMACONNEL, a rectory in dioc. of Clon-fert, fit. in bar. Athlone, co. Rofcommon, prov. Connaught.

TAGHMON, a bor. poft and fair town, fit. in bar. Shelmaliere, co. Wexford, prov. Leinfter, above 70 miles from Dublin; it returns two members to parliament; patronage in the *Hore* family. Lat. 52 : 17 long. 6 : 58. Fairs held 1 Feb. and 21 Oct. This is a rectory in dioc. of Ferns, and diftant about 5 miles W. of Wex-ford. Saint *Munnu* founded an abbey here; he died 25th Oct. 634. Alfo a rectory in dioc. of Meath, fit. in bar. Corkerry, co. Weftmeath, prov. Leinfter.

TAGHSINNOD, a rectory in dioc. Ardagh, fit. in bar. Moydoe, co. Longford, prov. Leinfter.

TAGHSINNY, a village, fit. in bar. Shrowle, co. Longford, prov. Leinfter: it is a rectory in dioc. of Ardagh.

TAILTEAN, *fee Tilletehan*.

TALBOTSTOWN, a bar. in co. Wicklow, prov. Leinfter; having a village in it of fame name: Lat. 52 : 54. long. 6 : 59.

TALENSBRIDGE, fit. in bar. Ardee, co. Louth, prov. Leinfter.

TALLAGH, (or *Tallaght*) a large village, fit. in bar. Newcaftle, co. Dublin, prov. Leinfter; about 5 miles from Dublin, and 2½ miles be-yond *Cromlin*. It lies in a fine open country, enjoys a good air, and is a vicarage in dioc. of Dublin. Here is the antient refidence of the archbifhops of Dublin, and an old church, in which divine fervice is performed. An abbey was founded here in an early age, by St. *Mæl-ruan*. Fairs held 1 Tuefday in March, 7 July, 16 Sept. and 9 Nov. Near this latter place, is a high hill call'd *Tallagh-hill*, reckon'd 3 ms. over, it affords a moft beautiful profpect; to the one fide you view a fine well-improved country, with variety of old caftles, and new feats; be-fore you the fine city of *Dublin*; farther, a large harbour covered with fhipping, beyond that a-gain, a profpect of the open fea; and forward to the left, a neck of land or ifthmus, termina-ted by the *hill of Hoath*.

TALLANSTOWN, (or *Tullanftown*) a vicarage in dioc. of Armagh, fit. in bar. Ardee, co. Louth, prov. Leinfter, about 39 miles from Dublin; a mile beyond it are the ruins of a church.

TALLOW, (fometimes written *Tallagh*) a bor-ough, poft and fair town, in bar. Cofhbridge, co. Waterford, prov. Munfter, 104 miles from Dublin; it was erected into a borough at the re-queft of the firft earl of Cork, its charter bears date 10 James 1. by which the liberties of the borough were extended one mile and an half beyond the church every way; the jurifdiction of the fovereign and burgeffes is gone into dif-ufe, but the town returns two members to par-liament, the electors are deemed potwollopers, but the duke of Devonfhire has a principal in-fluence.—This town was never encompaffed with a wall, nor was it a place of any defence; but in the rebllion of 1641, an intrenchment was caft up round it, having four gates or en-trances, all made at the expence of the faid Earl, who maintained in it a garrifon of 100 foot foldiers.—Fairs held 1 Mar. day after Tri-nity Sunday, 10 Oct. and 8 Dec. Here is a barrack; and near Tallow are the ruins of *Lif-finic Caftle*. This is a vicarage in dioc. of Lif-more. Lat. 51 : 56. long. 8 : 16.

TALLOW-

TALLOWBRIDGE, a village fit. in bar. Cofh-bridge, co. Waterford, prov. Munfter.

TALLWATER, a *river*, fit. in bar. Oneilland, co. Armagh, prov. Ulfter.

TALLYHOF, fitu. near Loughbrickland, co. Down, prov. Ulfter.

TAMLAGCHURCH, fit. in bar. Loughlinfholen, co. Londonderry, prov. Ulfter, 103 miles from Dublin. It is a rectory in dioc. of Armagh.

TAMLAGHTARA, a rectory in dioc. of Derry, fit. in bar. Kenoght, co. Londonderry, prov. Ulfter.

TAMLAGHTFINLAGAN, a rectory in dioc. of Derry, fit. in bar. Kenoght, co. Londonderry, prov. Ulfter.

TAMLAGHTOCRELY, a rectory in dioc. of Derry, fit in bar. Loughlinfholen, co. Londonderry, prov. Ulfter.

TAMORA, fit. about 5 miles from Dublin, in co. Dublin, prov. Leinfter.

TANDERAGEE, a poft and fair town, in bar. Orior, co. Armagh, prov. Ulfter. 61 miles from Dublin ; it is well ftocked with manufactures in the linen branch ; the *Newry Canal* is brought within a mile of this place, and contributes greatly to its convenince. Fairs held 5 July and Nov. It is a rectory in dioc. of Armagh.

TANKARDSTOWN, a rectory in dioc. of Limerick, fit. in bar. Cofhma, co. Limerick, prov. Munfter. Alfo a feat, fit. 2 miles beyond *Ardbraccan*, in co. Meath, prov. Leinfter : near it are the ruins of a caftle, and alfo the church of *Donough-patrick*.

TANRAGOES, a river, fit. in co. Armagh, prov. Ulfter.

TANSYFORT, fit. near *Boyle*, co. Rofcommon, prov. Connaught.

TAPTOE, fit. in co. Dublin, prov. Leinfter; here are the remains of an antient round tower.

TARA, an inconfiderable place, fit. in co. Down, prov. Ulfter. Alfo a mountain, called *Tara-hill*, fit. in bar Gorey, co. Wexf. pro. Lein.

TARA-BAY, fee *Quintin-bay*.

TARAGH, a village in bar. Skryne, co. Meath, prov. Leinfter, it is a vicaiage in dioc. of Meath ; about 19 miles from Dublin. Here is the celebrated *Hill* of Taragh, where it is fuppofed there was antiently a magnificent royal palace, the refidence of the kings of Ireland, where triennial parliaments were held, in which all the nobility, gentry, and priefts, &c. affembled, and here laws were enacted or repealed, and the general advantage of the nation was confulted. It it certain fome writers have difputed that any building of lime and ftone was ever erected on this fpot, at the time we fpeak of ; but the fact is as pofitively infifted on by many others. This place is otherwife called *Teamor* from *Teagh-mor*, or the great houfe ; or *Teagh-mer-regh*, the great houfe of the king,

and much celebrated in the antient Irifh hiftory ; certain it is, that this hill was the *Naafteighan* whereon the ftates affembled, for feveral ages ; that is from the beginning of the firft to the middle of the 6th century ; from which period we hear no more of the general convention of the ftates, but each province was governed by their own local ordinances. About 2 miles beyond Taragh hill are the ruins of the old church of *Dendflown*.

TARBERT, fit. in bar Iraghticonnor, co. Kerry. prov. Munfter, 124 miles from Dublin : it is a poft, market and fair town, where there is a handfome feat, oppofite the demefne houfe of which, is a fmall ifland, within which is a fafe and commodious road and harbour for fhips, either bound up the *Shannon* for *Limerick*, or where they may wait for wind and weather to convey them to fea. This village has a *charter-fchool*, towards building of which the late Right Revd. Dr. *James Leflie*, bifhop of Limerick gave 200l. together with a certain quantity of land. Towards the end of lord *Chichefter*'s government in this kingdom, and during the reign of king *James* I. the fegniory of *Tarbert*, was granted to *Patrick Crofbie*, Efq; on condition of his keeping in it feveral *Irifh* families, who were tranfplanted hither from the king's co. Mr. *Crofbie*'s fon *Pierce*, fold this eftate to Alderman *Dominick Roche* of *Limerick*, from whofe family it was purchafed by Lord *Clare*, who forfeited it by his attachment to king *James* II. and upon the revolution it came to the family of *Lefley*.— Fairs held Eafter-monday, 22 June, 12 Auguft. and 11 Dec.

TARBERT-HOUSE, the handfome feat of Mr. *Lefley*, fit. in co. Kerry, prov. Munfter.

TARBERT-ISLAND, fit near the bar. Ballinahinch, off the coaft of co. Galway, prov. Connaught. This ifland, or point, forms a deep harbour, where a number of fhips generally lie, it being confidered the beft anchorage thereabouts.

TARMANCARRA, fee *Tarmoncarra*.

TARMONBARRY, a rectory in dioc. of Elphin, fit. in bar. Rofcommon, co. Rofcommon, prov. Connaught.

TARMONBARRY-BRIDGE, a village, fit. in co. Rofcommon, prov. Connaught, 64 miles from Dublin.

TARMONCARRA, fit. in the peninfula of the Mallet and Half-bar. Erris, co. Mayo, prov. of Connaught. Some old walls of a church appear here, nearly buried in the fands ; they are faid to have belonged to a nunnery, of which we can learn no account.

TARMON-CASTLE, fit. in bar. Lurge, co. Fermannagh, prov. Ulfter. Lat. 54 : 27. lon. 8 : 21.

TARMON-HILL, *mountains*, fit. in bar. Erris, co. Mayo, prov. Connaught.

TARTARAGHAN, a rectory in dioc. of Armagh,

fit. in bar. Oneilland, co. Armagh, prov. Ulſter.

TASCOFFIN, a rectory in dioc. of Oſſory, fit. in bar. Gowran, co. Kilkenny, prov. Leinſter.

TASHINY, fit. in co. Longford, prov. Leinſter ; fairs held 27 Mar. 28 May, 9 July and 26 Sept.

TASSAGARD, ſee *Saggard.*

TAUGHBOYNE, a rectory in dioc. of Raphoe, fit. in bar. Raphoe, co. Donegal, prov. Ulſter. The church was originally founded by St. *Baithen.*

TAUNAGH, a vicarage in dioc. of Elphin, fit. in bar. Tiraghrill, co. Sligo, prov. Connaught.

TAWNEY, a curacy in dioc. of Dublin. fit. in bar. Half-Rathdown, co. Dublin, prov. Leinſter ; it is fituated 1 mile beyond Miltown, and commonly called *Church-town.*

TAY *river,* fit. in bar. Decies without Drum, co. Waterford, prov. Munſter.

TEACH-SAXON, ſee *Templegale.*

TEACH-SCHOTIN, a *mountain,* fitu. in bar. Slewmargy, Queen's co. prov. Leinſter ; near which was a monaſtery built by St. *Schotin,* in the 6th century, whoſe feaſt is obſerved on the 2d of Jan.

TECROGHAN, ſee *Tyrcroghan-Caſtle.*

TEAMOR, ſee *Taragh.*

TEDOUNT, fit. in co. Monaghan, prov. Ulſter ; fairs held 2 Mon. *o. ſ.* Jan. Mond. before *Shrove-tueſ.* 31 Mar. 24 June, and 28 Sept.

TEFFIA, a diſtrict fit. to the N. of the co. Longford, prov. Leinſter, called *North Teffia,* the chiefs of which were formerly denominated *Hy Ferghaël,* or the prince of the men of *Ghaël,* by corruption *O'Feral.* The deſcendants of this antient family were in poſſeſſion of the N. W. and S. parts of the co. Longford, on the commencement of the laſt century, but were diſpoſſeſſed of the eaſtern parts by the Engliſh ſettlers, the *Tuites* and *Delameres.*

TEGHADOW, ſee *Taghadoe.*

TEGHMOLIN, ſee *St. Mullan.*

TEHALLAN, fit. in bar. Monaghan, co. Monaghan, prov. Ulſter, 4 miles S. of Glaſlough. St. *Killian* was biſhop of this place, which was deſtroyed by fire in 671.

TEINAGH, a village, fit. in bar. Leitriin, co. Galway, prov. Connaught. It is a rectory in dioc. Clonfert.

TELEN-HARBOUR, fit. about 6 miles from *Killybegs,* co. Donegal, prov. Ulſter. A conſiderable white fiſhery is carried on here during the ſummer months.

TELEN-HEAD, called alſo *Cape-Horn,* a noted promontory, in the co. Donegal, prov. Ulſter. Lat. 55 : 00 N. long. 8 : 35 W.

TELTOWN, (antiently called *Teachtelle)* a rectory in dioc. of Meath, fit. in bar. Kells, co. Meath, prov. Leinſter. The church here was founded by St. *Teallan.*

TEMPLEBODANE, a rectory in dioc. Cloyne, fit. in bar. Barrymore, co. Cork, prov. Munſter.

TEMPLEBOY, a vicarage in dioc. of Killala, fit. in bar. Tyreragh, co. Sligo, prov. Connaught.

TEMPLEBREDIN, a vicarage in dioc. of Emly, fit. in bar. Coonagh, co. Limerick, prov. Munſt.

TEMPLEBREEDY, a vicarage in dioc. of Cork, fit. in bar. Kinalea, co. Cork, prov. Munſter.

TEMPLEBRIAN, a rectory in dioc. of Roſs, fit. in bar. Carbery, co. Cork, prov. Munſter.—Here is a ſeat about 1 mile N. of Cloghnakilty, on the lands of which are the remains of an antient heathen temple. Not far from the church of Templebrian, is a ſtone circle with a central pyramidal pillar, and not far from it are two other pyramids.

TEMPLECAIRNE, a rectory in dioc. of Clogher, fit. in bar. Tyrhugh, co. Donegal, prov. of Ulſter.

TEMPLECORRAN, a vicarage in dioc. of Connor, fit. in bar. Belfaſt, co. Antrim, prov. of Ulſter.

TEMPLECROAN, a rectory in dioc. of Raphoe, fit. in bar. Boylagh, co. Donegal, prov. Ulſter.

TEMPLEDERRY, a vicarage in dioc. of Killaloe, fit. in bar. Upper-Ormond, co. Tipperary, prov. Munſter.

TEMPLEDISERT, ſee *Shraduff.*

TEMPLE-ERRY, a rectory in dioc. of Caſhel, fit in bar. Skerrin, co. Tipperary, prov. Munſt.

TEMPLEGALE, (otherwiſe called *Teach-Saxon)* fit. 2 miles W. of Athenry, co. Galway, prov. Connaught. The antient church of this place was burnt by lightning in 1177. A friary of ſmall extent was founded here in the reign of king Henry 7th. by one of the family of *Burgh,* for franciſcans of the 3d order. It was afterwards granted to the corporation of Athenry.

TEMPLE-GAURIN, the ruins of a chapel, fit. on a little hill, at the N. end of a ſmall lake, called *Derickelagh,* near Newry, co. Down, prov. Ulſter.

TEMPLEHARRY, a rectory in dioc. Killaloe, fit. in bar. Clonliſk, King's co. prov. Leinſter.

TEMPLEHAY, a vicarage in dioc. of Liſmore, fit. in bar. Iſſa and Offa, co. Tipperary, prov. Munſter.

TEMPLE-HOUSE, fit. in co. Sligo, prov. Connaught ; fairs held 24 May, 30 July, and 7 Nov.

TEMPLEICALLY *Church,* now in ruins, fit. near Killaloe, co. Clare, prov. Munſter.

TEMPLEJEHALLY, a vicarage in dioc. of Emly, fit. in bar. Arra, co. Tipperary, prov. Munſter.

TEMPLEMALY, a vicarage in dioc. of Killaloe, fit. in bar. Bunratty, co. Clare, prov Munſter.

TEMPLE-MARTIN, fit. in co. Kilkenny, prov. Leinſter ; fairs held 29 Sept. 9 and 22 Nov.—Alſo a rectory in dioc. of Cork, fit. in bar. Kinnalmeaky, co. Cork, prov. Munſter.

TEMPLE-

TEMPLE-MICHAEL, a parifh in co. Waterford, prov. Munfter, in which are the ruins of a church and a caftle, which feems to have been demolifhed by powder, as does another building. a little more to the S. fituated on a high point now called *Rhincrew*, but in fome old MSS. *Kilcrew* ; which place is faid by tradition, to have been a houfe of the *Knights Templars*. Alfo a rectory in dioc. of Ardagh, fit. in bar. Longford, co. Longford, prov. Leinfter. Alfo a rectory in dioc. of Cork, fit. in bar. Kinalea, co. Cork, prov. Munfter. Alfo a rectory in dioc. of Lifmore, fit. in bar. Slewardagh, co. Tipperary, prov. Munfter. Alfo a curacy in dioc. of Dublin, fit. in bar. Arklow, co. Wicklow, prov. Leinfter.

TEMPLEMORE. a poft town, fit. in bar. Eliogurty, co. Tipperary, prov. Munfter, 93 miles from Dublin. It is a vicarage in dioc of Cafhel. Here is a handfome feat of Sir John Craven Carden, Bart. A mile and an half beyond Templemore, are the ruins of a caftle. Fairs held 17 May, 28 June, 3 Sep. 21 Oct. and 7 Dec. Alfo, *for Wool*, on 11th, 12th, 13th, 29th, 30th and 31ft July. Alfo a rectory in dioc. of Derry, fit. in bar. Inifhowen, co. Donegal, prov. Ulfter.

TEMPLEMURRY, a vicarage in dioc. of Killala, fit. in bar. Tirawly, co Mayo, prov. Connought.

TEMPLENECARRIGY, a rectory in dioc. of Cloyne, fit. in bar Barrymore, co. Cork, prov. Munfter.

TEMPLENEILAN, a vicarage in dioc. of Elphin, fit. in bar. Rofcommon, co. Rofcommon, prov. Connaught.

TEMPLENOE, a parifh, fit. in bar. Dunkerron, co. Kerry, prov. Munfter, the church of which (now in ruins) is faid to have been built by the *O'Sullivans*, who have a tradition of their coming into thefe parts feveral centuries ago, from a place called *Knockgraffin*, in the co. Tipperary : This parifh is about 6 miles in length, extending along the river *Kenmare*, and runs a great way in breadth up the mountains. It is a rectory in dioc. of Ardfert.—Alfo a rectory in dioc. of Emly, fit. in bar. Clanwilliam, co. Tipperary, prov. Munfter.

TEMPLEOGE, an agreeable little village, fit. 3 miles from Dublin, in co. Dublin, prov. of Leinfter. Here is a handfome feat of Mr. *Domville*, and the ruins of an old church, and antient burial place.

TEMPLEOMALIS, a rectory in dioc. of Rofs, fit. in bar. Barryroe, co. Cork, prov. Munfter.

TEMPLEORAN, a curacy in dioc. of Meath, fit. in bar. Moygoifh, co. Weftm. prov. Leinfter.

TEMPLEOUTRAGH, a vicarage in dioc. of Cafhel, fit. in bar. Kilnalongurty, co. Tipperary, prov. Munfter.

TEMPLE-PATRICK, fit. in bar. Belfaft, co. Antrim, prov. Ulfter, 87 miles from Dublin; near it is *Cafleupton*, the handfome feat of Lord *Templeton*. Fairs held 10 July, 3 Tuefday O. S. in Oct. It is a rectory in dioc. of Connor. There is alfo a place called *Templepatrick*, fit. in co. Down, pro. Ulfter, about one mile S. of Donaghadee, remarkable for a fpring well of very limpid water, frequented by people afflicted with *head-achs*.— This latter place is otherwife called *Cragutboy*. Here are ruins of a church.

TEMPLEPETER, a vicarage in dioc. of Leighlin, fit. in bar. Forth, co. Carlow, prov. Leinft.

TEMPLEPORT, a rectory in dioc. of Kilmore, fit. in bar. Tullaghagh, co. Cavan, prov. Ulfter.

TEMPLEQUINLAN, a vicarage in dioc. of Rofs, fit. in bar. Carbery, co. Cork, prov. Munfter.

TEMPLEROBIN, a rectory in dioc. of Cloyne, fit. in *Great-ifland*, co. Cork, prov. Munfter.

TEMPLERONE, a rectory in dioc. of Cloyne, fit. in bar. Fermoy, co. Cork, prov. Munfter.

TEMPLE-ROW, an antient ruin, fit. a few miles beyond *Swineford*, co. Mayo, prov. Connaught. About a mile beyond it are the ruins of Ballylaghlan-caftle.

TEMPLESCOBBIN, a rectory in dioc. of Ferns, fit. in bar. Bantry, co. Wexford, prov. Leinfter.

TEMPLESHANBOUGH, a rectory in dioc. of Ferns, fit. in bar. Scarewalfh, co. Wexford, prov. Leinfter.

TEMPLESHANNON, a rectory in dioc. of Ferns, fit. in bar. Ballagheen, co. Wexford, pro. Lein.

TEMPLE-THIRTY, a parifh in co. Waterford, prov. Munfter.

TEMPLETOGHER, a vicarage in dioc. of Tuam, fit. in bar. Half-Ballimoe, co. Galway, prov. Connaught.

TEMPLETOHY, a rectory in dioc. of Cafhel, fit. in bar. Ikerin, co. Tipperary, prov. Munfter.

TEMPLE-TOWN, fit. in co. Wicklow, prov. Leinfter : Fairs held 2 Thurfday O. S. May, 26 July, 19 Sept. and 8 Nov. A charter-fchool was opened here, in 1737, for 40 children ; towards the building of which, the late *Tho. Acton*, Efq; gave 100l. It was alfo endowed with 40 acres of land, rent free, for ever, by the late Hon. *John Temple*.—Alfo a vicarage in dioc. of Ferns, fit. in bar. Shelburne, co. Wexford, pro. Leinfter.—Alfo a village in bar. Dundalk, co. Louth, prov. Leinfter.

TEMPLETRINE, a rectory in dioc. of Cork, fit. in bar. Bantry, co. Cork, prov. Munfter.

TEMPLEUDIGAN, a rectory in dioc. of Cork, fit. in bar. Bantry, co. Cork, prov. Munfter.

TEMPLEUSQUE, a rectory in dioc. of Cork, fit. in bar. Barrymore, co. Cork, prov. Munfter.

TEMPO, fit. in bar. Tyrefkenedy, co. Fermanagh, prov. of Ulfter, 85 miles from Dublin. Fairs held 29 Jan. 28 May, and 6 Nov.

TENELICK,

TENELICK, the feat of Lord *Annaly*, fit. near Colehill, co. Longford, prov. Leinfter.

TEN-MILE-BUSH, fit. in co. Meath, prov. Leinfter; near 12 miles from Dublin.

TEN-MILE-HOUSE, a place fo called, fit. in co. Wicklow, prov. Leinfter, above 11 miles from Dublin.

TERELA, a fmall village on the fide of Dundrum bay, in bar. Lecale, co. Down, prov. Ulfter; the lands about which are fo rich and fertile, by the manure of marle and fea-fhells, of which there is great plenty in the neighbourhood, that they fet from 15 to 20 fhillings per acre. The fhells lie within two feet of the furface of the earth, and ought to remain fpread on the land for 3 years before they are plowed in, and then it will produce all forts of grain for 10 years at leaft, after which it yields the fineft grafs. On the fhores here, and near the low-water mark, are found a great quantity of beautiful fhells. This is a rectory in dioc. of Down.

TERFECKAN, fee *Termonfeckin*.

TERMONAMONGAN, a rectory in dioc. of Derry, fit. in bar. Omagh, co. Tyrone, prov. Ulfter.

TERMONANY, a rectory in dioc. of Derry, fit. in bar. Loughlinfholen, co. Londonderry, prov. Ulfter.

TERMONFECKIN, (otherwife written *Terfeckan*) a rectory in dioc. of Armagh, fit. in bar. Ferrard, co. Louth, prov. Leinfter, three miles and an half from Drogheda. This village is feated on a fmall but pleafant river near the fea.— Here was formerly the refidence of the great primate *Ufher*. A monaftery was founded here in 665: alfo an abbey for regular canoneffes, under the invocation of the B. V. Mary; the remains of the Primate's palace was a few years ago totally deftroyed. There are the ruins of feveral fmall caftles in this neighbourhood: thofe of *Glaffpiftol* ftand about 2 miles diftant; and a little farther eaftward is a fine fifhery, the charter of which, 'tis faid, was held by the fifhermen waiting with their fifh in the town of *Termonfeckin*, till the lord of the caftle was ferved.

TERMONMAGUIRK, a rectory in dioc. of Armagh, fit. in bar. Omagh, co. Tyrone, prov. of Ulfter.

TERRENURE, an agreeable feat, fit. 2 miles from Dublin, and within half a mile of Rathfarnham, in co. Dublin, prov. Leinfter.

TERRILL'S-CASTLE, fit. near *Cellbridge*, co. Kildare, prov. Leinfter; near it on the river Liffey, are mills called *Terrill's-mills*.

TERRILL'S-MILLS, fee *Terrill's-caftle*.

TERRILL'S-PASS, fit. in bar. Moyenfhel, co. Weftmeath, prov. Leinfter, 40 miles from Dublin: here are the ruins of a caftle. Fairs held 17 May and Dec.

TERRYGLASS, a vicarage in dioc. of Killaloe. fit. in bar. Low. Ormond, co. Tipperary, pro. Mun.

TERRYHOGAN, fit. in co. Down, prov. Ulft.

TESSARARAGH, a vicarage in dioc. of Elphin, fit. in bar. Athlone, co. Rofcommon, prov. Conn.

TESSAURAN, a vicarage in dioc. of Meath, fit. in bar. Garrycaftle, King's co. prov. Leinft.

THE BREAKS *of* SCORNEY, a ridge of mountains, fit. in co. Dublin, prov. Leinfter.

THE COW, a *rock*, fit. off *Magee-ifland*, co. Antrim, prov. Ulfter.

THE DAUGHTONS, fee *Daughtons*.

THE DOWNS, fit. in bar. Half-Rathdown, co. Wicklow, prov. Leinfter.

THE HEAD, fit. in bar. Balruddery, co. Dublin, prov. Leinfter.

THE KISH, a bank, fit. at the mouth of Dublin bay, prov. Leinfter.

THE ROSSES, iflands fo called, fit. off the Weftern coaft of the co. Donegal, prov. Ulfter, where a confiderable *herring* fifhery is carried on every year; they lie oppofite to *Dunglo*, and near the north ifle of *Arran*.

THE TOUCH, fit. in bar. Caftleknock, co. Dublin, prov. Leinfter.

THE TOUNS, a great fand-bank, fit. before the mouth of Lough-Foyle, near Londonderry, prov. Ulfter, which however does not obftruct navigation, as there are at all times 14 or 15 fathoms of water in the channel, which is broad and deep. In the entrance of the Lough, there are very great fands on the left-hand, from one end to the other, which are fome miles broad off the land; and on the right-hand are little fands or fhelves lying clofe to the land; between thefe there is a broad channel, in moft parts 3 and 4 fathoms deep; and in that arm whereon *Londonderry* ftands, it is 10 or 12, and before the town 4 and 5; fo that this is juftly efteemed as good and commodious a harbour as any in the kingdom.

THOMAS-STREET, fit. in bar. Athlone, co. Rofcommon, prov. Connaught, 69 miles from Dublin; within a mile and half of which, are the ruins of a church.

THOMASTOWN, a borough, poft, and fair town, fit. in bar. Gowran, co. Kilkenny, prov. Leinfter, about 58 miles from Dublin; it is otherwife called in Irifh, *Bally-mac-Andan*, i. e. the town of Anthony: near it are the ruins of *Jerpoint-Abbey*, where a fynod was held in the year 1152, when *John Papero*, the Pope's legate, made one of the number of bifhops that were convened there, at that time, to fettle the affairs of the church. About the year 1180, a caftle was erected here by *Thomas Fitzanthony*. The church is part of an old abbey, in the ruins of which is a monftrous tomb-ftone, which they fay, covers the body of a giant; and tradition will have it, that one of the Irifh kings lay buried here, feveral ages before this kingdom fub-

mitted.

mitted to the English. There is a very fine bridge here over the river Newre, and from hence to Waterford the ſtream is navigable for ſmall veſſels. This is a rectory in dioc. of Oſſory. Fairs are held annually on 25 May. Lat. 52 : 26. Long. 7 : 28. It returns 2 members to parliament, patron, Lord *Clifden*.—There is alſo a place of ſame name in co. Tipperary, prov. Munſter, near 82 miles from Dublin, where is an antient but handſome edifice, with good improvements, the ſeat of Lord *Landaff*: it was once eſteemed the fineſt ſeat in this kingdom. Alſo a rectory in dioc. Kildare, fit. in bar. Ophaly, co. Kildare, prov. Leinſter. Alſo a place in bar. Louth, co. Louth, prov. Leinſter.

THOMOND, an antient diſtrict, containing the preſent co. Clare, prov. Munſter ; the principal chiefs of which, were called *Mc.Cas*, or *Magh Gaes*; a ſon of *Olliol Olum*, or *Olim*, about the beginning of the third century, was elected chief of this diſtrict, on which he took the name of *Cormac Cas*, and greatly diſtinguiſhed himſelf by his military abilities. From him the ſucceeding chiefs of *Dal-Cas* (another name for this place) endeavoured to derive their origin. However this may be, it appears from the Iriſh annals, that the chiefs of the ſubordinate diſtricts, were frequently choſen kings of *Dalcas*, until the ſovereignty came into the hands of *Brien Boromh*, hereditary chief of *Hy Loch-Lean*, now *Burrin*, whoſe deſcendants enjoyed that dignity, until the arrival of the Engliſh, when the *De-Clares* obtained a grant of the entire county, which from them has ſince obtained the denomination of *Clare*. *Dalcas* was originally inhabited by a colony, of the ſecond migration of the *Fir Bolgæ*, called *Momonii*, whence it obtained the name of *Tuath Mumham*, or North Munſter, by corruption, *Thomond*.

THORNHILL, fit. in co. Antrim, prov. Ulſter.

THORNSTOWN, fit. in bar. Caſtleknock, co. Dublin, prov. Leinſter.

THORNYHILL, fit. in co. Down, prov. Ulſter.

THREE CASTLE HEAD, fit. off the S. coaſt of co. Cork, prov. Munſter ; ſo called from three ſquare caſtles on it. It lies near *Mizen-head*, which is the extreme point of that county, and is otherwiſe called *Sheep's-head-point*.

THREE CASTLES, fit. near Kilkenny, co. Kilkenny, prov. Leinſter.

THREE-MILE WATER, fit. in Carrickfergus bay, co. Down, prov. Ulſter.

THREE-SISTERS, three remarkable hills, ſo called by ſailors, they are fit. on the iſthmus between *Smerewick* and *Ferritor's-creek*, in co. Kerry, prov. Munſter.

THURLES, a poſt town fit. in bar. Eliogurty, co. Tipperary, prov. Munſter, 70 miles from Dublin. It has a great market, the 1ſt. Tueſ-

day in each month, and gave title of Earl to the *Ormond* family. It is fit. on the river *Suir*, which divides the town nearly into two equal parts. A monaſtery was founded here by the *Butler* family, in A. D. 1300, for Carmelites or White-friars : a tower is ſtill remaining on the S. ſide of the river, and a part of the croſs ayſle leading to the N. There was alſo a caſtle erected here belonging to the Knights Templars, or Knights of St. *John* of Jeruſalem. Fairs held on Eaſter-monday, 21 Aug. and Dec. This is a rectory in dioc. of Caſhel ; Lat. 52 : 55. long. 8 : 9. About 5 miles beyond Thurles, are the ruins of *Ballybeg-Caſtle* ; and within 3 miles of Thurles are the large ruins of the famous abbey of *Holy-Croſs*.

TIAQUIN, a barony in co. Galway, prov. Connaught.

TIBRACH, fit. on the N. ſide of the river *Suir*, in co. Kilkenny, prov. Leinſter, about 2 miles E. of *Carrick-mac-girfith*. In antient times this town was well inhabited, and in high repute, particularly on the arrival of the Engliſh. A great ſtone is now ſtanding there, which is a boundary between the co. Kilkenny and Tipperary.

TICKMACREVAN, a vicarage in dioc. of Connor, fit. in bar. Glenarm, co. Antrim, prov. Ulſter.

TIDAVNET, a rectory in dioc. of Clogher, fit. in bar. Monaghan, co. Monaghan, prov. Ulſt.

TIDENSTOWN, fit. near Iniſtioge, co. Kilkenny, prov. Leinſter.

TIELLEN-HEAD, a cape, fit. in bar. Boylagh, co. Donegal, prov. Ulſter.

TIERHOGER, fit. near *Lea Caſtle*, in Queen's co. prov. Leinſter ; here is an antient burial-place, and the ruins of a church.

TIERKELLY, fit. 2 miles N. E. of *Rathfryland*, in co. Down, prov. Ulſter, where there is a very good chalybeate ſpring.

TIERNIGOOSE, a ſeat in co. Kerry, prov. Munſter, near the river *Fleſk*.

TIFFERNAN, a curacy in dioc. of Meath, fit. in bar. Corkerry, co. Weſtmeath, prov. Leinſter.

TIHALLEN, a rectory in dioc. of Clogher, fit. in bar. Monaghan, co. Monaghan, prov. Ulſter.

TIKILLEN, a vicarage in dioc. of Ferns, fit. in bar. Shelmaliere, co. Wexford, prov. Leinſter.

TILLETEAGHAN, (or *Tailtean*) a place in co. Meath, prov. Leinſter, where the Druids ſacrificed in honour of the marriage of the *Sun* and *Moon*, and *Heaven* and *Earth*, on the 1ſt of Aug. being the fifth revolution of the Moon from the vernal equinox. At this time the ſtates aſſembled, and young people were given in marraige according to the cuſtom of the Eaſtern nations.— Games were alſo inſtituted, reſembling the olympic games of the Greeks, and held 15 days before

Timohoe.

before and 15 days after the 1st of Aug. This festival was frequently denominated *Lughaid Naoistean*, or the matrimonial assembly.

TIMAHOE, or *Teach Mochoe*, sit. in bar. Cullinagh, Queen's co. prov. Leinster; above 42 miles from Dublin: It is a curacy in dioc. of Leighlin. Within a mile of this place, are 3 old forts. At Timahoe are the ruins of a very old church, built by St. *Mochoe*, and a fine round tower. The antient abbey of Timahoe, was burnt in 1142. It was granted by Queen Elizabeth, to Sir Robert Loftus. In 1642 *Monk* defeated the Irish rebels near this place. Fairs held 5 April, 2 July, and 18 Oct. Also a rectory in dioc. of Dublin, sit. in bar. Claine, co. Kildare, prov. Leinster.

TIMMIN, sit. in co. Dublin, prov. Leinster; it lies between Cromlin and Tallagh; on these lands stand the remains of an antient castle, sit. on a rising ground.

TIMOGE. a rectory in dioc. of Leighlin, sit. in bar. Stradbally, Queen's co. prov. Leinster.

TIMOLEAGUE, sit. in bar. Barryroe, co. Cork, prov. Munster; 4 miles East of Cloghnakilty. Lat. 51 : 27. Long. 8 : 57. 'Tis otherwise called *Tee Mologa*, i. e. the residence of St. Molaga; and lies on an arm of the ocean. From Courtmacsherry (the harbour's mouth) to Timoleague is 2 miles. This harbour formerly navigable, is now quite obstructed with sand. A small river discharges itself here, called the *Arigideen*; it runs at the foot of an hill covered with an oak wood, for a mile before it reaches the town, in a serpentine form. At its entrance into the town, it washes the walls of an antient castle, built by the *O'Shaghnessys*; next it washes the verge of the church-yard, and then glides by the walls of an antient abbey of Franciscans, founded by the *Macartys*, in the beginning of the 14th century, temp. Edw. II. In this abbey Edmund de Courcey, bp. of Ross was buried, in March 1518, who was a great favourite of king Henry VII. Timoleague was formerly a place of some note, being much resorted to by the Spaniards, who imported large quantities of wine here; and it is said there were formerly no less than 14 taverns that sold sack in the town. It is sit. between the castle and the abbey, under an hill which shelters it from W. and Northerly winds. This castle was built by the *Barretts*. Here is a regular street, one side of which was new built by the late Lord *Barrymore*, for the accommodation of linen-weavers, but the design happened to fail. Here is a market-house and bleach-yard, but no regular market. Near it is a well dedicated to the V. M. much frequented on the 8 Sept. The festival day of St. *Molaga*, (according to *Colgan*) is on the 20 Jan. he being the antient patron of this place. Fairs held 28 Mar. 5 July, 21 Aug. and 7 Dec. This is a rectory in dioc. of Ross.

TIMOLIN, sit. in bar. Narragh, co. Kildare, prov. Leinster; near 30 miles from Dublin.—Near it are the ruins of an old castle and church. Fairs held Easter-mond. and 28 June. It is a vicarage in dioc. of Dublin. A monastery for regular canons was founded here in a very early age: also a nunnery of the order of *Aroacia*.

TIMONY, sit. near Roscrea, co. Tipperary, prov. Munster.

TIMOOLE, a vicarage in dioc. of Meath, sit. in bar. Skryne, co. Meath, prov. Leinster.

TINEHALY, a post and fair town, in bar. Ballynacor, co. Wicklow, prov. Leinster, 38 miles from Dublin. Fairs held 1st Wed. Jan. 7 Feb. 2 Wed. O. S. March, 8 May, last Wed. June, 7 Aug. and 7 Nov.

TINEHINCH, a bar. in Queen's co. prov. Leinster, in which is a village of same name, where fairs are held 29 Oct. Also a place in co. Carlow, prov. of Leinster; fairs held 1 May and 29 Sept.

TINNECROSS, sit. near *Tullamore*, in King's co. prov. Leinster.

TINTERN, sit. in bar. Shelburn, co. Wexford, prov. Leinster; 85 miles from Dublin. It is a curacy in dioc. of Ferns. Here was an antient abbey, founded in the year 1200, by *William Marescal*, or Marshal Earl of *Pembroke*, on occasion of a vow he had made when in danger of being shipwrecked. It was built on the sea shore, endowed and supplied with monks of the Cistertian order, from *Tintern*, in Monmouthshire in Wales. Here is a seat of the *Colclough* family. Fairs held 24 Mar. 12 May and 21 Sept.

TIPPERAGHNY, a rectory in dioc. of Ossory, sit. in bar. Iverk, co. Kilkenny, prov. Leinster.

TIPPERARY, a *county*, in the prov. of Munster; bounded by the King's co. on the N. the Queen's co. and Kilkenny on the E. Waterford on the S. and Galway, Clare and Limerick on the W. It is one of the finest counties in Ireland; but is occupied chiefly in feeding sheep, and rather thinly inhabited. It was a palatinate under the jurisdiction of the Duke of Ormond, which was suppressed in the reign of King George I. after that nobleman's attainder. It is furnished with the greatest and best flocks of any co. in the kingdom. It stretches northward 52 miles, and measures from E. to W. 31 miles, and contains 554,950 acres, comprehending 12 baronies, viz. Iffa and Offa, Clanwilliam, Middlethird, Slewardagh and Compsey, Kilnemanna, Killnalongurty, Eliogurty, Ikerin, Ileagh, Owney and Arra, upper Ormond and lower Ormond, and it returns 8 members to parliament. This county contains about 169,000 inhabitants. Among the antient families of this co. are the Mc. Egans, O'Kennedys, O'Briens, O'Dwyers, Butlers, Purcells and Mathews.— Part of Tipperary was called Holy-crofs, and the

the Northern part, which is mountainous, was called Ormond. In it lie 12 mountains in an heap, called *Phelenge Modena*. Chief town, *Clonmel*.

TIPPERARY *town*, fit. in bar. Clanwilliam, co. Tipperary, prov. Munfter; near 87 miles from Dublin. Fairs held 5 April, July, 10 Oct. and Dec. A monaftery was founded here in the reign of King Henry III. for Eremites, following the rule of St. *Auguftin*. This town was burnt by *Breyn O'Breyn*, in the firft week of Aug. 1329. This is a rectory in dioc. of Emly, and a poft town.

TIRAGHRILL, a bar. in co. Sligo, prov. Connaught.

TIRAWLY, a bar. in co. Mayo, prov. Connaught; in this diftrict the wood *Foclut* ftood, celebrated for being the fcene of the vifion of St. *Patrick*, before he undertook the miffion of Ireland. It was antiently called *Hy-Firmalgaid*, and contained the N. part of the antient *Hy-Moruifg*, the *Auterij* of *Ptolemy*.

TIRCONAL, i. e. the land or wood of *Connal*, the word literally fignifies the country of the chief tribe, and comprehended the prefent county of *Donegal*.

TIRDAGLASS, fit. in bar. lower Ormond, co. Tipperary, prov. Munfter. Here St. *Colman* founded an abbey, which was twice deftroyed, viz. in 1112 and 1162. The town was alfo burned in 1140.

TIRENASCRAGH, a vicarage in dioc. of Clonfert, fit in bar. Longford, co. Galway, prov. Connaught.

TIRMALGAID, an antient diftrict, comprehending the barony of Tirawly, co. Mayo, prov. Connaught.

TISSASSON, a rectory in dioc. of Cork, fit. in the liberties of Kinfale, co. Cork, prov. Munft.

TITESKIN, a rectory in dioc. of Cloyne, fit. in bar. Imokilly, co. Cork, prov. Munfter.

TIVOHINE, a rectory in dioc. of Elphin, fit. in bar. Boyle, co Rofcommon, prov. Connaught.

TI-VOURNEY-GERAAN, fee *Tyvourney-gerran*.

TLACHGO, a place in co. Meath, prov. Leinfter, where the Druids in time of paganifm, facrificed on tombs of their antient heroes to the Earth or univerfal Nature, on the eve of the 1ft. of Nov.—the fanctuary here fpoken of, is ftill remaining, being the Tumulus at *New-Grange*, near Drogheda.

TLACHGO-BAN, or *Cairn ban*, that is the white cairn, or temple of Vefta, fituated near Newry, co. Down, prov. Ulfter; being 180 yards in circumference, and 10 in altitude. Another on the fummit of *Sliabh Croabh*, on the top of which are 22 fmaller Cairns from 5, 4, and 3 feet high. Alfo one at Warring's-town, in fame co. which was opened in 1614, difcovering a dome in the centre of which, under a tabernacle was placed a handfome urn of a brown

colour, containing burnt bones.

TOBARBUNNY, or *Toberbunny*, fit. in co. Dublin, prov. Leinfter, within a few miles of the metropolis.

TOBARCORRY, or *Tobbercorry*, and fometimes written *Tubbercorr*; a village fit. in bar. Leney, co. Sligo, prov. Connaught, diftant 103 miles from Dublin; within a mile of which are the ruins of a church and a caftle. Fairs held 22d. of May, 27 June, 4 Oct. and 29 Nov.

TOBARCURÆN, fee *Tubbercorker*.

TOBARDONY, or *Tubberdonny*, and fometimes *Tubberidany*, a village fit. in bar. Kiltartan, co. Galway, prov. Connaught, 102 miles from Dublin; three miles from which, at the foot of a hill, are the ruins of a caftle.— Near Tobardony are the ruins of the antient abbey of Kilmacdough, which formerly gave title to a bifhop. Fairs held 12 July and 20 Sept.

TOBARFUDDER, a village fit. in bar. Loughrea, co. Galway, prov. Connaught.

TOBARMORE, or *Tubbermore*, fituate in bar. Loughlinfholen, co. Londonderry, prov. Ulfter, above 90 miles from Dublin. Fairs held 17 Jan. 13 Feb. 28 Mar. 31 May, 5 July and 20 Oct.

TOBARSCANNOVAN, a village, fit. in bar. Tiraghrill, co. Sligo, prov. Connaught.

TOBER, fit. in co. Clare, prov. Munfter.— Fairs held 18 Sept.

TOBERCORMAC, or the *well of Cormac*, a place in co. Meath, prov. Leinfter, where a monaftery was founded in 1488.

TOBERDALY, fit. near Philipftown, King's co. prov. Leinfter.

TOE-HEAD, a high promontory in bar. Carbery, co. Cork, prov. Munfter, ftanding a little to the W. of Caftlehaven : Due S. of which in the ocean are the high fteep rocks, called the *Stags*, which however being always to be feen, are eafily avoided.

TOEM, a rectory in dioc. of Cafhel, fit. in bar. Kilnamanna, co. Tipperary, prov. Munfter.

TOEMONIA, called in Irifh *Touathmona*, fit. near Tulfk, in co. Rofcommon, prov. Connaught. A monaftery for Dominican friars was founded here by *O'Connor*.—No veftige of a village remains here, nor is there any appearance of other erections, fave only the walls of a very antient caftle that did belong to O'Connor.

TOGHER, a village fit. in bar. Ballinacor, co. Wicklow, prov. Leinfter. Alfo in bar. Ferrard, co. Louth, prov. Leinfter.

TOGHER CASTLE, fit. in co. Cork, prov. Munfter; in a wild tract, one mile farther S. of which, is the head of the river *Bandon*.

TOLLOGHORTON, a parifh in the dioc. of Lifmore, co. Waterford, prov. Munfter.

TOLLYNADELLY, fit. in co. Galway, prov. Connaught; Fairs held 1 Wed. aft. Trinity, and 21 Nov.

TOMAGH,

TOMAGH, fit. in bar. Clonlifk, King's co. prov. Leinfter.

TOMB, a rectory in dioc. of Ferns, fit. in bar. Gorey, co. Wexford, prov. Leinfter.

TOMBEOLA, fit. at the head of Round-ftone bay, in bar. Ballinahinch, co. Galway, prov. Connaught. A monaftery for Dominican friars was founded here about the year 1427, by the *O'Flahertys*, dynafts of *Eir Conaught*, in which elevated ftation they continued 'till the arrival of *Oliver Cromwell*. In the beginning of queen Eliz.'s reign this building was wholly demolifhed, and even the ftones (thofe of the church walls not excepted) were made ufe of to build a caftle in the neighbourhood. The few ruinous remains are fcarcely vifible, and very imperfectly mark the traces of this antient village.

TOMDEELY, a vicarage in dioc. of Limerick, fit. in bar. Connello, co. Limerick, prov. Munft.

TOMES, fit. in co. Kerry, prov. Munfter; to the W. end of *Killarney-lake*. It was the feat of *O'Sullivan More*,

TOMFINLOUGH, a vicarage in dioc. of Killaloe, fit. in bar. Bunratty, co. Clare, pro. Mun.

TOMGRANY, or *Toomgrany*, a village fit. in bar. Tullagh, co. Clare, prov. Munfter. It is a rectory in dioc. of Killaloe. Fairs held Thu. of Trinity and 10 Oct. An abbey was founded here in an early age.

TOMHAGGARD, fit. in bar. Bargie, co. Wexford, prov. Leinfter. Fairs held 26 July. It is a rectory in dioc. of Ferns.

TOMREGAN, a rectory in dioc. of Kilmore, fit. in bar. Tullaghagh, co. Cavan, prov. Ulft.

TONTINE-COVE, fit. in bar. Bear and Bantry, co. Cork, prov. Munfter.

TOOMAVARA, fit. in bar. upper Ormond, co. Tipperary, prov. Munfter, 69 miles from Dublin. Fairs held on Whit-monday and 4 Nov. Within a ¼ mile of this place are the ruins of *Knockane-caftle*, and on the oppofite fide are thofe of *Blanc-caftle*, at the foot of a high hill. At *Toomavara* are the ruins of a preceptory of the Knights Templars. This is a rectory in dioc. of Killaloe, and otherwife written *Toomevara*; but fhould properly be called *Twamywharra*, i. e. the burial place of *O'Mara*; and tho' but a fmall village, yet fhews by the veftiges of antient buildings, that it was formerly a place of fome confequence.

TOOMBS, a range of rocks, fo called by the Irifh, but by the Scotch " *the Cloghan.*" They are fit. in the bay of Carrickfergus, co. Down, prov. Ulfter; they run out into the fea for about 3 or 400 yards from the N. fide of it, and are covered at high water. They appear at low water like a parcel of cabbins.

TOOME, a bar. in co. Antrim, prov. Ulfter.— Alfo a place in bar. Kilnemanna, co. Tipperary,

prov. Munfter; where was a priory of canons regular.

TOOMEBRIDGE, a village fit. in bar. Toome, co. Antrim, prov. Ulfter. Fairs held 28 Mar. and 4 Dec.

TOOMEVARA, fee *Toomavara*.

TOOMGRANEY, fee *Tomgrany*.

TOOMISH *mountain*, fit. in bar. Dunkerron, co. Kerry, prov. Munfter.

TOONE *river*, fit. in bar. Mufkerry, co. Cork, prov. Munfter.

TOONMORE, fee *Gibbon's-grove*.

TOOREEN, a feat in co. Waterford, prov. Munfter; where was a caftle, the proprietors of which were the *Roaches*; but they forfeited it in the rebellion of 1641. The houfe is fit. on the W. of *Lifmore-river*, leading to which is a long and beautiful avenue of large elms; and here alfo are large tracts of orcharding, which afford confiderable quantities of cyder. The *Red-ftreak* of Herefordfhire thrives exceedingly well in the foil hereabouts. It is faid that the firft *cyder* made in this country was at *Affane*, by one *Greatrakes*, who came over upon the fettlement of Munfter.

TORC *mountain*, or *Turk-mountain*, fit. in bar. Mufkerry, co. Kerry, prov. Munfter.

TORFECKAN, fee *Termonfeckin*.

TORRE-ISLAND, fee *Tory-ifland*.

TORY-ISLAND, fit. off the coaft of bar. Kilmacrenan, co. Donegal, prov. Ulfter. It is fometimes written *Torre-ifland*, and is extremely fertile. It lies about 8 miles from the main-land. There was an abbey here over which *St. Ernan* prefided in 650.

TOUGH, a rectory in dioc. of Emly, fit. in bar. Owneybeg, co. Limerick, prov. Munfter.

TOUGHCLUGGIN, a vicarage in dioc. of Emly, fit. in bar. Coonagh, co. Limerick, prov. Mun.

TOWNAVILLY, fit. in co. Donegal, prov. Ulfter, above 114 miles from Dublin. Within a mile of which is *Lough Efk*, where there is a very handfome feat.

TOWNLY-HALL, fit. in bar. Ferrard, co. Louth, prov. Leinfter.

TOWN-MICHEL, fit. in co. Cork, pro. Munfter; here are the ruins of the fpacious abbey of Mourne, in a valley; and of a fmall caftle on the brow of a hill. There are fome venerable oaks, which ftretch their long arms acrofs the road, and from thence wind down a romantic glen, in view of a good houfe.

TRABOLGAN, an antient feat fit. to the S. of Cork harbour, in co. Cork, prov. Munft.

TRACTON, a curacy in dioc. of Cork, fit. in bar. Kinalea, co. Cork, prov. Munfter.

TRACTON-ABBEY, fit. in bar. Kinalea, co. Cork, prov. Munfter, 2 miles S. of Carigaline. It was founded anno 1224, for Ciftertian monks,

by

by the *Mac Cartys*. This foundation was confirmed by Edw. IIId. The abbots of it formerly fat in parliament. This abbey was granted by queen Eliz. to *Henry Guilford*, gent. and Sir *James Craig*, 20 March, 1568, on their paying beforehand the fum of 7l. 15s. Sir *James Craig* affigned it to the earl of *Cork*, who paffed a patent for this abbey 23 March, 7th Jas. Ift. and was by him given to his fon *Francis*, lord *Shannon*. It is now quite demolifhed, and a handfome feat made there. It gave title of *baron* to the late *James Dennis*, chief baron of the exchequer in Ireland. The monks who inhabited this abbey came from Wales, and the houfe was called "*de Alba Tractu*." Fairs held 5 Aug.

TRA-KIERAN-COVE, fit. in co. Cork, prov. Munfter.

TRALEE, a borough, poft and fair town in bar. Truaghnacmy, co. Kerry, prov. Munfter, 144 miles from Dublin. It was antiently written *Traleigh*, i. e. the ftrand of the river *Leigh*, which is a fmall rivulet that empties itfelf at the bottom of *Tralee-bay*, on the bank of which river this town is fituated. It is the fhire town of the co. Kerry, ever fince the attainder of *Gerald*, earl of *Defmond*, and was, during the exiftence of that earl's palatinate, the place where he chiefly refided and exercifed his jurifdiction. It was incorporated in 1612, by letters patent of king James Ift. and is governed by a provoft, burgeffes, common-council, a town-clerk, &c. The provoft is clerk of the market, juftice of the peace and quorum throughout the whole co. during his year, with power to hold a tholfel-court every thurfday, and a court of pied-powder. In the midft of the town is a fquare, environed on the N. fide with the co. court-houfe and the goal, and on the other fide with houfes and fhops. Thro' the middle of the town runs a rivulet, over which are fome fmall ftone bridges. There were in it formerly 4 caftles, all which, except one, have been taken down; the remaining caftle was the chief feat of the earls of *Defmond*, and afterwards was granted with a large eftate, by queen Eliz. to Sir *Edw. Denny*. In this caftle was committed the inhuman murder of Sir *Henry D'Anvers*, with the juftices *Meade* and *Chartres*, who were flain with all their fervants, while they were afleep in their beds, by Sir *John of Defmond*, the earl's brother, in the year 1579; which piece of barbarity paved the way for the deftruction of the Defmond family foon after: the pretence for this cruelty was, Sir *Henry D'Anvers* holding feffion of goal delivery in Defmond's palatinate. Adjacent to the caftle are good gardens, and a bowling-green. A monaftery for Dominican friars was founded here, under the invocation of the holy crofs, in 1260, or according to fome in 1243, by *John*, fon of *Thomas Fitzgerald*, who, with his fon

Maurice, was flain at *Callen* by *MacCarty More*: they are both interred in the N. part of this friary, which had formerly a good fteeple, but nothing now remains except fome of the vaults. The parifh church is well built, with good feats and handfome galleries. This town is fit. above a mile from the fea, to which diftance a veffel of 50 or 60 tons may come, and at high-water fmall boats row up to it; but it has little intercourfe with other places by fea, the bay being open, fhallow, and unfafe for fhipping. In this bay confiderable quantities of herrings are taken. There is a chalybeate fpa about 2 miles from Tralee, fit. on the N. fide of the bay, of an excellent quality, and in a fine air. This place fends two members to parliament, patronage in the *Denny* family. The town was deftroyed in the wars of 1641, and again in the time of James IId. It held out a long fiege againft the Irifh in 1642. Fairs held 4 and 5 Aug. 9 and 10 Oct. 7 and 8 Nov. Lat. 52 : 10, N. lon. 9 : 40, W.

TRALEE-BAY, fit. in bar. Truaghnacmy, co. Kerry, prov. Munfter: you enter it by giving the *Hogs-iflands* a birth, and failing E. by N. It is not much frequented by fhips, being dry at low water; however fmall veffels lie fafe aground in it. The channel is towards the middle of the bay: the entrance is between two fmall iflands, called the *Sampier-ifles*. Almoft all the maps of Ireland, and fea-charts, place *Fenit-ifland*, which they call *Fenor*, in the middle of this bay, whereas it lies clofe to the fhore on the N. fide, between which and the main there is a fmall creek for fhips, which muft be entered from the North; but the paffage is fo narrow and foul, that it cannot be entered without a good pilot. On one fide of this bay, near a delightful ftrand, very commodious for air and exercife, there is an excellent chalybeate fpring. The foil about it is gravelly, and fomewhat inclining to turf on the E. fide. The well is near a foot deep, and about 3 feet in diameter, flowing out of a fmall bank of yellow clay, mixed with gravel.

TRALONG, fit. about one mile W. of *Rofs*, in co. Cork, prov. Munfter: on thefe lands are one of thofe fubterraneous paffages, which are diftinguifhed by the names of Eaft and Weft *Pouladuff*.

TRAMORE, fit. in bar. Middlethird, co. Waterford, prov. Munfter; fairs held 3 May, 25 July, 1 Oct. and Nov. This place ftands in a broad, open and dangerous bay of St. George's channel, which is often taken for Waterford harbour, to the lofs of many; as the wind blowing hard from S.S.W. or S.E. tumbles in a great rolling fea, which renders it almoft impoffible for imbaying fhips to weather the heads, and the ground being generally foul and rocky, cables are frequently cut: in this extremity fuch as cannot make *Rineshark-harbour*, (for which the Eastern shore of the bay is to be kept close on board) ought, if possible, run on shore to the N. W. in the bottom of the bay, where, on a loose stoney beach, the water flows to a great height, by which means men and goods have been saved. *Tramore* is much frequented as a very pleasant summer bathing place, and is considered as the Baiæ of the Eastern coast of Ireland. It has been much improved by its present proprietor, *Barth. Rivers*, esq; who has erected a handsome market-house and assembly-room there.

TRANSTOWN, sit. in co. Cork, prov. Munst. Fairs held 3 April and 25 Sept.

TREMONT, sit. in co. Down, prov. Ulster.

TREVET, sit. about 3 miles E. of *Taragh*, in bar. Skryne, co. Meath, prov. Leinster. This antient town was rebuilt by *Hugh de Lacey*, who planted a colony here of his English followers. It became a place of considerable note, but is since fallen to decay. Here was a considerable monastery, which, in 1145, was destroyed by fire. The English erected a large church here, in honor of St. *Patrick*: it is now in ruins, but many fragments of beautiful tombs and monuments still remain. This place is a vicarage in dioc. of Meath.

TRIENAGH-BAY, sit. in bar. Boylagh, co. Donegal, prov. Ulster.

TRIERTY-LOUGH, a *lake* sit. in bar. Tyrhugh, co. Donegal, prov. Ulster.

TRIESTY-MOUNTAINS, sit. in bar. Erris, co. Mayo, prov. Connaught.

TRILLIC, sit. in co. Tyrone, prov. Ulster, 88 miles from Dublin: about 3 miles from it are the ruins of a church. Fairs held 14 May, 4 Sept. 1 Tuesd. Oct. and 14 Nov.

TRIM, a borough, post and fair town in bar. Navan, co. Meath, prov. Leinster, above 22 miles from Dublin. It is the shire town of the co. seated on the river *Boyne*, and is noted for several parliaments having been held therein, and also for a large antient castle, now in ruins, built by *W. Peppard*, and said to have been the residence of king *John*. Here are also the ruins of a church. The assizes are held here for the co. Meath, and the goal is a strong, good building. A fine row of trees, on both sides of the road, reaches from this town to the seat of lord *Trimlestown*, which is about 1½ mile distant. At Trim is a barrack for a troop of horse, and a charter-school for 40 children, endowed by the late earl of *Mornington*. This town is governed by a sovereign, recorder and town-clerk, and returns two members to parliament; patron, the earl of *Mornington*. It was a place of strength and consequence, surrounded by walls, and had many religious foundations in it. Mr. Beauford calls it *Brughna Boyne*, and says it was a cemetery of the antient kings of Ireland. In 432, St.

Patrick founded here an abbey for canons regular, dedicated to the Virgin Mary, and built on a piece of ground given by *Fethlemid*, son of *Laoghaire*, and grandson of *Niall*. St. Patrick made his nephew, St. *Loman*, bishop here, whose festival is held on 17 Feb. In 1538, an image of the Virgin Mary, which had been preserved for many centuries in this abbey, was publicly burned. The steeple of the abbey, called the yellow steeple, was a lofty, handsome square tower; one half of it was demolished by *Cromwell*, against whom it held out a considerable time as a garrison. The Grey friary here was dedicated to St. *Bonaventure*, and generally called the observantine friary of Trim. It was, according to some authors, founded by king *John*, but others say by the family of *Plunket*. The Dominican friary, sit. near the gate leading to Athboy, was founded in honor of the Virgin Mary, by *Geoffry de Geneville*, lord of *Meath*. The priory of cross-bearers was dedicated to St. John the *Baptist*: one of the bishops of Meath was said to have been the founder, and his successors in that see were great benefactors to this priory, which was a truly magnificent building; and it is probable that the parliaments of Trim were held in the great hall of this house. The church here is called the *Greek-church*. It is a vicarage in dioc. of Meath. Fairs held at Trim 27 March, 8 May, Wedn. after Trinity-sund. 1 Oct. and 16 Nov. Lat. 53 : 32, lon. 7 : 0

TRIMLESTOWN, a chapelry in dioc. of Meath, sit. in bar. Navan, co. Meath, prov. Leinster. Here is the handsome seat of lord *Trimlestown*, about 2 miles distant from Trim.

TRINITY-PARISH, sit. in co. Waterford, pro. Munster, it is part of the corps of the deanery.

TRISTERNAGH, a handsome seat within about 2 miles of Ballinalack, co. Westmeath, prov. Leinster, over lower *lough Erne*. Near it are the ruins of a monastery, which was built in the form of a cross, having in the centre a tower or steeple, raised on the four innermost corners of the cross. This abbey was founded, as Sir *H. Piers* tells us, by Sir *Geoffry Constantine*, about the time of *Henry* IId.

TRORY, a rectory in dioc. of Clogher, sit. in bar. Tyrskennedy, co. Fermanagh, prov. Ulst.

TROUGH, a barony in co. Monaghan, prov. Ulster.—Also a village sit. between four and five miles from Limerick, in co. Limerick, prov. Munster; where are the ruins of a church and castle.

TRUBLY, a rectory in dioc. of Meath, sit. in bar. Deece, co. Meath, prov. Leinster.

TRUAGHNACMY, a bar. containing 19 parishes, sit. in co. Kerry, prov Munster.

TRYADD, sit. in co. Londonderry, prov. Ulster; fairs held 5 July.

TRYVET, see *Trevet*.

T U A M

TUAM, a borough, poft and fair town in bar. Downamore co. Galway, prov. Connaught, 93 miles W. of Dublin. It is the feat of the Abps. of Tuam, and is a vicarage within their diocefe. In the year 487, an abbey was founded here, dedicated to the Virgin Mary, which, in the beginning of the 6th century, was made a cathedral by St. *Jarlath*; and a city was afterwards built here in honor of this exemplary bilhop, whofe remains were preferved in a chapel called *Temple-na-ferin*, or the church of the fhrine. After the death of this faint, we find exprefs mention made of three perfons who were abbots of Tuam, viz. *Cellach*, fon of *Ecchad*, who died in the year 808; *Nuadet-Hua-Bolchain*, abbot and anchorite, who died 3 Oct. 877, and *Conagh*, fon of *Kieran*, abbot of *Tuam* and prior of *Clonfert*, who died in 879. The priory of St. *John* the *Baptift* was founded here about the year 1140, by *Tirdelave O'Connor*, king of Ireland. It is not certain to what order this houfe belonged, but it was granted to *Richard*, earl of *Clanricarde*. The abbey of the holy Trinity was founded here either in the reign of king *John*, or of *Hen. IIId.* for premonftre canons. Tuam and all its churches were deftroyed by fire in the year 1244. Something better than a mile beyond *Tuam* is a round tower, and half a mile from it the ruins of a church. Within 1¼ mile of this town is *Bermingham*, a feat of the earl of *Louth*; and 4¼ miles beyond Tuam are the ruins of a caftle. *Tuam* gives title of vifcount to the family of *Wenman*; Sir *Richard Wenman*, bart. being created *Vifcount Wenman* of *Tuam*, by letters patent dated at *Canterbury*, 30 July, 1628, the 3d of *Charles Ift.* This town returns two members to parliament; patronage in the *Bingham* family. Fairs held 4 July and 15 Dec. The bifhoprick of Tuam is confiderably the largeft in the kingdom: it was rated in the king's books at 50*l.* per annum, but is worth 4000*l.* With this fee the bifhoprick of *Ardagh* is held in commendam.

TUBBER, a curacy in dioc. of Dublin, fit. in bar. Talbot'ftown, co. Wicklow, prov. Leinft.

TUBBER-COR, fee *Tobarcorry*.

TUBBERCORKER, fit. near *Lackagh*, in bar. Ophaly, co. Kildare, prov. Leinfter. Here is a reputed holy well, and fome remains of an old church in ruins. It is otherwife written *Tobbercurcan*.

TUBBERDALY, a feat within about 2 miles of *Croghan-hill*, in King's co. prov. Leinfter.

TUBBERDONNY, or *Tubberidony*, fit. in co. Galway, prov. Connaught, 102 miles from Dublin; 3 miles from which on the foot of a hill, are the ruins of a caftle. Near Tubberdonny are the ruins of the antient abbey of *Kilmadough*, which formerly gave title to a bilhop. Fairs held 12 July and 20 Sept.

TUBBERHANY, fit. in co. Tipperary, prov. Munfter; fairs held 2 Oct.

TUBBERMORE, fee *Toburmore*.

TUBBERMURRY, fit. in co. Limerick, prov. Munfter; fairs held 4 Apr. 26 Aug. and 19 Sep.

TUBBERPADDER, fit. in co. Galway, prov. Connaught; fairs held 9 July and 10 Oct.

TUBBERPOUND, fit. in King's co. prov. Leinfter, 51 miles from Dublin.

TUBBERSEANAVAN, fit. in co. Sligo, prov. Connaught; fairs held 17 May, 30 June, 18 Sep. and 31 Oct.

TUBERBRACKIN, fit. in co. Galway, prov. Connaught; fairs held Whit-mond. & 23 Oct.

TUBRID, an improved feat in co. Kerry, pro. Munfter, one mile E. of *Ardfert*. This place takes its name from a celebrated well which is near it.—Alfo a rectory in dioc. of Offory, fit. in bar. Iverk, co. Kilkenny, prov. Leinfter.—Likewife a vicarage in dioc. of Lifmore, fit. in bar. Iffu and Offa, co. Tipperary, prov. Munft.

TUBRIDBRITTAIN, a vicarage in dioc. of Offory, fit. in bar. Crannagh, co. Kilkenny, pro. Lein.

TUITSTOWN, fit. in bar. Fore, co. Weftmeath, prov. Leinfter.

TULLADONNELL, fit. in co. Louth, prov. Leinfter.

TULLAGH, a bar. in co. Clare, prov. Munfter.—Alfo a rectory in dioc. of Rofs, fit. in bar. Carbery, co. Cork, prov. Munfter.

TULLAGHAGH, or *Tullahow*, a bar. in co. Cavan, prov. Ulfter.

TULLAGHAN-BAY, fit. in bar. Erris, co. Mayo, prov. Connaught.

TULLAGHENOGUE, a curacy in dioc. of Meath, fit. in bar. Navan, co. Meath, prov. Leinfter.

TULLAGHLEASH, a vicarage in dioc. of Cloyne, fit. in bar. Duhallow, co. Cork, prov. Munfter.

TULLAGHMAIN, a rectory in dioc. of Offory, fit. in bar. Shellilogher, co. Kilkenny, prov. Leinfter.—Alfo a rectory in dioc. of Cafhel, fit. in bar. Middlethird, co. Tipperary, prov. Mun.

TULLAGHNANEEVE, fee *Saintfield*.

TULLAGHNISKIN, a rectory in dioc. of Armagh, fit. in bar. Dungannon, co. Tyrone, prov. Ulfter.

TULLAGHOBIGLY, a rectory in dioc. of Raphoe, fit. in bar. Kilmacrenan, co. Donegal, prov. Ulfter.

TULLAGHONOHO, a barony in co. Cavan, prov. Ulfter.

TULLAGHORTON, a vicarage in dioc. of Lifmore, fit. in bar. Iffu and Offa, co. Tipperary, prov. Munfter.

TULLAHANE, fit. in co. Leitrim, prov. Connaught; fairs held Whitfun-mond. 4 Auguft, and Thurfday before 12 Nov.

TULLAHAW, fee *Tullaghagh*.

TULLAMORE, a market and poft town in bar. Ballycowen, King's co. prov. Leinfter, 46 miles

from

from Dublin. It is but a small place, yet gives title of baron to a branch of the family of *Moore*, and is a chapelry in dioc. of Meath. The river *Tullamore* divides the town into two nearly equal parts. Here is a barrack, and near a mile beyond the town are the ruins of a castle; a mile farther is *Charleville*, formerly the seat of the earl of *Charleville*; opposite to it is *Merryfield*, the seat of Mr. *Crofton*, sit. on the banks of a small but fine river. Fairs held 10 May, July, and 21 Oct.—There is also a place of same name in co. *Antrim*, prov. Ulster. Fairs held 17 Nov.—And another in co. *Down*, prov. Ulster, otherwise called *Bryansford*, sit. above two miles N. W. of *New-castle*; a mile E. of which, in the road to *Dundrum*, are the ruins of an old church, at a place called *Mahera*, near which formerly stood a high round tower.

TULLANSTOWN, sit. in co. Louth, prov. Leinster, 39 miles from Dublin, otherwise called *Tallanstown*.

TULLIGARRON, sit. in co. Kerry, prov. Munster, about 3 miles N. E. of *Tralee*; near which place *Saunders*, the pope's nuncio, who was sent over in the year 1579, to forward an opposition to queen *Eliz.'s* government, died miserably of an ague and flux, brought on him by want and famine, in the wood of *Cloulish*, in 1582.

TULLIHALLEN, sit. in bar. Ferrard, co. Louth, prov. Leinster.

TULLILEASE, sit. in co. Cork, prov. Munst. Fairs held 1 March, 29 Apr. June, and 24 Oct.

TULLINALLY, sit. in bar. Foro, co. Westmeath, prov. Leinster.

TULLIVIN, sit. in co. Cavan, prov. Ulster; fairs held 7 Mar. 4 May, 5 July, 26 August and 11 Dec.

TULLO, sit. in bar. Tullogh, co. Clare, prov. Munster, 102 miles from Dublin; ¼ a mile on one side of which stands the castle of *Lisfin*. This place is sometimes written *Tulla*, and likewise *Tullagh*; fairs held 13 May, 4 Sept. and 1 Oct. This is a rectory in dioc. of Killaloe.

TULLOGHALLEN, a curacy in dioc. of Armagh, sit. in bar. Ferrard, co. Louth, prov. Leinster.

TULLOGHMELAN, a rectory in dioc. of Lismore, sit. in bar. Iffa and Offa, co. Tipperary, prov. Munster.

TULLOHERRIN, see *Tullowherin*.

TULLOW, a post town in bar. Ravilly, co. Carlow, prov. Leinster, 38 miles from Dublin, sit. on the river Slaney. Here is a small church, which is a rectory in dioc. of Leighlin, and a pretty market house. Over the river is a bridge of 6 arches, at the foot of which are the ruins of an Augustine monastery, which was granted, in the reign of queen Eliz. to *Thomas*, earl of *Ormond*. This place is remarkable for making the best *garters*. The castle is converted into a

barrack: it was a strong place in the time of *Cromwell*, who took it with a great slaughter of the Irish. Fairs held 21 April, 10 July, 29 Oct. and 21 Nov.—There is a place of same name in co. *Limerick*, prov. Munster; fairs held 27 and 28 April, 16 and 17 July, 13 Septem. and 5 Nov.

TULLOWBEG, a chapelry in dioc. of Leighlin, sit. in bar. Ravilly, co. Carlow, prov. Leinster.

TULLOWCRYN, a rectory in dioc. of Leighlin, sit. in bar. Idrone, co. Carlow, prov. Leinster.

TULLOWHERIN, or *Tulloherrin*, a rectory in dioc. of Ossory, sit. in bar. Gowran, co. Kilkenny, prov. Leinster. Here is one of the antient round towers.

TULLOWMAGRIMAH, a rectory in dioc. of Leighlin, sit. in bar. Catherlogh, co. Carlow, prov. Leinster.

TULLOWMOY, a rectory in dioc. of Leighlin, sit. in bar. Ballyadams, Queen's co. prov. Lein.

TULLOWROAN, a rectory in dioc. of Ossory, sit. in bar. Crannagh, co. Kilkenny, prov. Lein.

TULLY, sit. in bar. Ophaly, co. Kildare, prov. Leinster; fairs held 27 July and 21 Dec. It is a curacy in dioc. of Kildare.—Also a rectory in dioc. of Raphoe, sit. in bar. Kilmacrenan, co. Donegal, prov. Ulster.—Also a curacy in dioc. of Dublin, sit. in bar. Half-Rathdown, co. Dublin, prov. Leinster.—Also a village in bar. Kilcoursy, King's co. prov. Leinster.

TULLYBRACKY, a rectory in dioc. of Limerick, sit. in bar. Coshma, co. Limerick, prov. Munster.

TULLYCARBET, see *Tullycorbet*.

TULLYCLEA, a *river* sit. in bar. Tyreskennedy, co. Fermanagh, prov. Ulster.

TULLYCORBET, or *Tullycarbet*, a rectory in dioc. of Clogher, sit. in bar. Monaghan, co. Monaghan, prov. Ulster. Here is a parish church, distant about 56 miles from Dublin.

TULLYHOG, a village sit. in bar. Dungannon, co. Tyrone, prov. Ulster.

TULLYLISH, a vicarage in dioc. of Dromore, sit. in bar. lower Iveagh, co. Down, prov. Ulst.

TULLYMORE-PARK, a fine sequestered seat near *Bryansford*, co. Down, prov. Ulster; surrounded by most extensive plantations, particularly some of the finest groves of larch trees in the kingdom, planted by lord *Clanbrassil*: here is also a most romantic river, exhibiting a succession of the most picturesque cascades.

TULLYNAKILL, a vicarage in dioc. of Down, sit. in bar. Castlereagh, co. Down, prov. Ulster.

TULLYODONALD, sit. in co. Donegal, prov. Ulster; Fairs held 1 Feb. 17 May, 21 June, 1 Aug. 3 Nov. and 2 Dec.

TULLYQUIOLLY, sit. about 6 miles from Newry, co. Down, prov. Ulster.

TULLYRUSK, a vicarage in dioc. of Connor, sit. in bar. Massareen, co. Antrim, prov. Ulster.

TULLYVALLEN,

TULLYVALLEN, fit. in co. Armagh, prov. Ulfter ; fairs held 7 May and 6 Nov.

TULRAHAN, fit. in co. Mayo, prov. Conn. Fairs held 31 Jan. 15 May, 18 Oct. and Dec.

TULSK, a borough and market town in bar. Rofcommon, co. Rofcommon, prov. Connaught, 75 miles from Dublin. It fends 2 members to parliament, tho' it contains but about a dozen thatched cabbins. A mile beyond it are the ruins of a once beautiful church, and from one to two miles from it are the ruins of 3 caftles. O'Connor erected a caftle at *Tulfk*, in 1406, and a monaftery for Dominican friars is faid to have been built here in the 15th century, by *Mc. Duil* or *O'Dowell* ; but it is more probable that the founder was *Phelim*, fon of *Phelim Cleary O'Connor*, who, in 1448, was flain by the wound of a fpear in *Kilcula*, and interred in this friary, the very fame year in which he had given a quarter of land to erect the monaftery, which, tho' in ruins, is ftill pretty entire. Near this town are numbers of ruined edifices : caftles and churches, forts and towers lie in a promifcuous heap, levelled to the duft. The patronage of this borough is in the *Caulfield* family. Fairs held Eafter-monday, Friday before Whit-funday, 20 Aug. and 1 Monday O. S. Nov. Lat 53 : 44 lon. 8 : 42.

TUMNA, a vicarage in dioc. of Elphin, fit. in bar. Boyle, co. Rofcommon, prov. Connaught.

TUMORE, a vicarage in dioc. of Achonry, fit. in bar. Gallen, co. Mayo, prov. Conn.— Alfo a vicarage in dioc. of Achonry, fit. in bar. Corran, co. Sligo, prov. Connaught.

TUNS, *rocks* fo called, fit. off the coaft of bar. Bargie, co. Wexford, prov. Leinfter.

TUNYQUIN, fit. in co. Rofcommon, prov. Connaught, 77 miles from Dublin : it is pleafantly feated on a rivulet that divides it in the middle.

TUOSITA, a rectory in dioc. of Ardfert, fit. in bar. Glanerough, co. Kerry, prov. Munfter.

TURK-MOUNTAIN, fee *Tork-mountain*.

TURLACHMORE, fee *Turloughmore*.

TURLAMORE, fit. in co. Clare, prov. Munfter, where races are held 8 June, and fairs 29 Sept. and 12 Dec.

TURLOGH, fit. in bar. Carragh, co. Mayo, prov. Connaught : it is a feat of the *Fitzgerald* family : here is a round tower of a very great height, not above 9 or at moft 10 feet diameter on the infide ; the entrance within is about 4 feet from the ground, which is very uncommon, and yet the foil about it has not apparently gained any acceffion of elevation ; there is no veftige of an afcent, either on the infide or outfide. Fairs held 9 May, 13 June, 24 Auguft, and 8 Dec. There is a quarry here of beautiful marble, as black as jet, and free from any mixture of white or grey, but as yet very little

worked. *Turlogh* is a rectory in dioc. of Tuam.

TURLOUGHMORE, fit. in bar. Clare, co. Galway, prov. Connaught, fairs held 1 Aug. and 18 Sept. It is otherwife written *Turlachmore*. Here the rivers *Clare* and *Moyne* unite their waters under ground, alternately appearing and retiring from view. In winter they form a lake here, which, in fummer, becomes a beautiful and found fheep-walk, upwards of 6 miles in length and two in breadth.

TURVEY, a handfome feat in co. Dublin, prov. Leinfter, 9 miles from the metropolis.

TUSCAN-PASS, a pafs between the co.'s Down and Armagh, in prov. Ulfter ; otherwife called *Tufkin's-pafs*. Fairs held Eafter-monday and 8 Nov. Formerly there were three encumbered paffes thro' bogs, woods and moraffy grounds, affording a bad and dangerous communication between thefe counties ; they were called *Scarvagh-pafs, Pointz's, alias Fenwick's-pafs, and Lamb's, or Tufcan-pafs*, in Irifh, *Pafs Turrifhane*. The firft of thefe paffes is Northward of *Fenwick's-pafs*, upwards of 2½ miles, and Northwards of *Newry*, 8. The fecond is Northward of *Tufcan's-pafs*, about 2½ miles, and the third is Northward of *Newry*, upwards of three miles. A caftle was formerly erected on each of thefe paffes, and the ftumps of thofe of *Pointz's* and *Tufcan's-pafs* ftill remain, but that at *Scarvagh-pafs* is utterly deftroyed. Almoft midway between *Scarvagh-pafs* and *Fenwick's-pafs*, is a fmall lake called *Lough Shark*, from an abundance of pike, often known by the name of *Shark*, found in it, and another called *Lough Dian*, of fmaller dimenfions than the former, both of which lie near the bank of the new Newry canal.

TUSKAR-ISLAND, fit. near bar. Forth, off the coaft of co. Wexford, prov. Leinfter.

TUSKER-ROCKS, fit. in St. George's-channel, near the coaft of co. Wexford, prov. Leinfter. Lat. 52 : 11, lon. 6 : 45.

TWELVE-PINS, *mountains*, fit. in bar. Ballinahinch, co. Galway, prov. Connaught.

TWIGH, fit. in bar. Clunlonan, co. Weftmeath, prov. Leinfter.

TWO-MILE-BRIDGE, fit. in co. Waterford, prov. Munfter ; fairs held 25 July, and 18 Oct. —Alfo a village fit. in bar. Iffa and Offa, co. Tipperary, prov. Munfter.

TWO-MILE-WATER, fit. in co. Wicklow, prov. Leinfter, 26 miles from Dublin.

TWO-POT-HOUSE, fit. in co. Cork, prov. Munfter, 117 miles from Dublin.

TYBRACK-CASTLE, fit. within 2 miles of *Carrick-on-Suir*, prov. Munfter. It was built by king *John*, about the year 1180, and is fometimes written *Tybroghny*.

TYBROGHNY-CASTLE, fee *Tybrack caftle*.

TYLAGH, fee *Tallagh*.

TYNAGH,

TYNAGH, fituat. in co. Galway, prov. Connaught, 78 miles from Dublin ; within a mile of which are the ruins of *Palace-caftle*, feated in the midft of a fine grove of trees. Fairs held Afcenfion-day, 2 days; 31 Aug. and 11 and 12 Dec. About a mile from Tynagh is *Caftle de Burgho* or *Caftle Burke* ; the caftle, which is now in ruins, was built by *Tibot Burke*, efq; anceftor to the prefent proprietor.

TYNAN, fit. in bar. Armagh, co. Armagh, prov. Ulfter, about 65 miles from Dublin ; within a mile of which are the ruins of a caftle, amidft a good plantation of trees. Tynan is a rectory in dioc. of Armagh, and a poft-town.

TYONE, fit. in co. Tipperary, prov. Munfter ; fairs held 1 Aug. and 9 Sept.

TYRANNY, a bar. in co. Armagh, prov. Ulft.

TYRAWLY, a bar. in co. Mayo, prov. Connaught, which gave title of baron to the family of *O'Hara*.

TYRCONNEL, the antient name of the co. Donegal, prov. Ulfter. It gave title of *vifcount* to the family of *Brownlow*.

TYRCROGHAN-CASTLE, fit. in co. Meath, prov. Leinfter. It was formerly in the poffeffion of the *Fitzgeralds* of *Tyrcroughan*. This building was confiderably larger a few years fince : it is faid that it has been deftroyed to apply the ftones to the repair of the turnpike-roads, tho' there is a quarry near the place. It is furrounded by a rampart and baftion of earth, and a very deep dyke. It ftands 1½ mile beyond *Clonard-bridge*. Here are alfo the ruins of an abbey.

TYRELL's-PASS, fit. in bar. Fertullagh, co. Weftmeath, prov. Leinfter, otherwife called *Killevally*. Fairs held 12 June and 23 Oct.

TYRERAGH, a barony in co. Sligo, prov. Connaught. This barony, tho' level along the coaft, is interfected by large bogs, and the Southern part of it is bounded by the *Ox-mountain*, *Slicbh Dham*, and a great range of defolate hills, that extend a good way into the bar. of *Leney*, in which alfo there is a great fcope of bog.

TYRESKENEDY, a barony in co. Fermanagh, prov. Ulfter.

TYRHUGH, a bar. in co. Donegal, prov. Ulft.

TYRONE, a county in the prov. of Ulfter ; bounded on the N. by Londonderry, on the S. by the co. of Monaghan, on the E. by Lough Neagh and part of Armagh, and on the W. and S. W. by Donegal and part of Fermanagh. Immediately S. of Londonderry it extends 33 miles from N. to S. and 43 from E. to W. It contains 35 parifhes, 4 baronies, 467,700 acres, 4 boroughs, and returns ten members to parliament. Chief town, *Omagh*. Its baronies are *Dungannon*, *Strabane*, *Omagh* and *Clogher* ; the latter is otherwife called *upper Dungannon*. The antient families of this co. are thofe of *O'Neill*, *O'Hagan*, *Caulfield*, *Hamilton* and *Chichefter*. In this co. is *Lough Neagh*, the largeft lake in Ireland, overfpreading near 100,000 acres of land ; and tho' not diverfified and adorned with iflands and woods like *Lough Earne*, yet is much fuperior when confidered as a fheet of water. It communicates its benefits to five feveral co.'s, viz. Armagh, Tyrone, Londonderry, Antrim and Down. This co. formerly gave title of earl to the family of *O'Neil*, after whofe attainder the family of *Power* had that title ; the heirefs of that family being married into that of *Berefford*, they now enjoy the fame. It is a large co. and tho' a great part of it be rough and mountainous, yet for richnefs of foil and good pafture, it is not inferior to many counties in the kingdom. The bleach-greens in it are principally fituated in the neighbourhood of Dungannon, Cookftown and Stewartftown : from Caftlecaulfield to Strabane, in the N. W. part of the county, there are but few bleach-greens. The linen manufacture here is eftimated at 257,444*l.* yearly, the principal part of which confifts of feven-eight wides, of the denomination formerly of *Moncymores*, but may now be called coarfe and fine *Tyrones*, of an inferior quality to the feven-eight wides called *Coleraines*. About the beginning of the 5th century, a colony from the diftrict of *HyFalgia*, in the King's-co. prov. Leinfter, diftinguifhed afterwards by the name of the kingdom of *Offaly*, fettled in the N. of Ireland, where, for feveral ages, it was diftinguifhed by the name of *Hy-Faillia*, and *Tir-hy-n-Fail*, by corruption *Tironel* and *Tirone*, i. e. the land of the diftrict of *Fail* ; a circumftance that gave rife to the N. and S. *Hy-Falia*, fo much fpoken of by the Irifh hiftorians of the middle ages. In this county are fome very fine collieries, but the want of a more perfect inland water-carriage contracts the operation of the many benefits which the fituation of thefe collieries prefents.

TYVOURNEY-GERRAN, a village fit. in bar. Corcaguinny, co. Kerry, prov. Munfter. It is otherwife called *Mary Gerrane's-houfe*, and is the moft Weftern point of all Europe, whence it is of as much celebrity in the W. of Ireland, as *John-a-Groots-houfe* in the N. of Scotland.

V A

VALE of ANGELS, a name antiently given to the town of *Bangor*, in co. Down, prov. Ulfter.

VALENTIA, a large ifland in bar. Iveragh, on the S. W. coaft of the co. Kerry, prov. Munfter ; it is about 5 miles long, the fea running between it and the main like a river, which is, in moft places, about half a mile broad, and of a fufficient depth for veffels to fail thro' at any time of the tide. *Cromwell* had forts erected at
both

both ends of this island, which were since neglected. Vessels may enter the harbour at either end, and fail quite round the island. It was, in queen *Ann's* wars, much frequented by *French* privateers, who, by keeping a watch on the island, lay very secure ; for if any ship of war came to this place, the centinel gave notice to what end of the harbour she directed her course, and then the privateer failed directly out at the other, and thereby escaped. From *Valentia*, on the opposite shore, nearly the middle of the harbour, there is a good chalybeate spring. This island is a fertile tract, and esteemed, the granary of the country: it belonged mostly to the family of *Annesley*, to whom it gave title of viscount, sir *Francis Annesley* being created visc. *Valentia*, 11 March, 1621-2, the 19 of James Ist. in reversion after the decease of sir *Henry Power* of *Bersham* in Denbighshire, constable of the castle of Maryborough, knight marshal of Ireland, governor of *Leix*, and privy counsellor, who was created visc. *Valentia* in 1620, of whom some account may be seen in *Moryson's* history of *Ireland*. It gave also title of visc. to *Donald Mac Carty More*. Lat. 51 : 40, N. lon. 10 : 30, W. This is a rectory in dioc. of Ardfert. The name of this place seems to be of Spanish original, many of that people having formerly had settlements about this part of the kingdom.

VALENTIA-HARBOUR, fit. in co. Kerry, prov. Munster, now called *Port Magee*, the W. entrance to which is about a league to the N. of *Puffin-island* : there is another entrance to the N. E. the mouth of which is called *Beginnis*, from a small island so called, between which and *Valentia island*, is the channel, the other passage between *Beginnis* and the N. E. shore, being foul ground and full of sunk rocks. In this sound is another small island, but of no importance to navigators, called *Lamb-island* : what is of more consequence to them is a sunk rock, lying midway between *Beginnis* and *Valentia*, on account of which the Western shore is to be kept on board by such ships as enter the harbour on this side. Having passed the inward point of *Valentia*, the river runs up S. W. thro' which a vessel of a considerable burden may fail, or anchor in deep water and good holding ground ; but the best place to moor in is opposite to a red clift that is on the S. side. This harbour is justly esteemed the best in these parts, and almost the only one besides *Dingle*, of tolerable safety, after a ship has passed the river Kenmare.

VASTINA, a rectory in diocese of Meath, fit. in bar. Moycashel, co. Westmeath, prov. Leinster.

VELVET'S-TOWN, situated in co. Cork, prov. Munster, 113 miles from Dublin.

VENDERIUS, a river or bay mentioned by *Ptolemy*, and thought by *Camden* to be the bay of *Carrickfergus*, in co. Down, prov. Ulster ; but *Rich. Cirenc.* calls it *Viderius*, and thinks it to be the bay of *Strangford*, in said co. The name seems to be derived from *Uind e Riii*, or head of the river.

VENISNIA-INSULA, an island near the N. cape, mentioned by *Rich. Cirencest.* and made by him to be *Tory-isle* ; but it was more probably the N. isle of *Arran*, being opposite to the cape Vennicnium of Ptolemy.

VENNICNIUM-PROMONTORIUM, a cape mentioned by Ptolemy, and fit. in the N. W. of Ireland, at the entrance of Donegal bay, in co. Donegal, prov. Ulster.

VENTRY, a village fit. in bar. Corcaguinny, co. Kerry, prov. Munster. It is a rectory in dioc. of Ardfert.

VENTRY-HARBOUR, fit. in co. Kerry, prov. Munster. It is quite open, and exposed to the S W. winds, but tolerably defended from the N. and E. It is divided from that of *Dingle* by a narrow isthmus : the Western point is called *Cahier Trant*, where there is an old Danish intrenchment, and another at *Rathanane*, a ruined castle belonging to the knight of Kerry. The Irish have a tradition that this isthmus was the last ground in Ireland that was possessed by the Danes. Mr. *Smyth* thinks it is not improbable that this tradition may have been founded on the account of a great battle fought at *Ventry*, between the *Irish* and the *Danes*, as related by *Hanmer* in his chronicle, p. 24, 25, for which he cites the book of *Houth* ; this harbour is little frequented by shipping ; however there is a sufficient depth of water in any part of it for vessels to anchor in : nor is there any danger in the entrance, there being neither rock nor shoal but what is visible.

VERGIVIUM-MARE, that part of the *Atlantic-ocean*, which washes the Southern coast of Ireland.

VERSAILLES, fee *Bagnel's-town*.

VILLE, fit. in bar. Dundalk, co. Louth, prov. Leinster.

VILLIERSTOWN, a chapelry in dioc. of Lismore, fit. in bar. *Decies without*, co. Wexford, prov. Leinster.

VIRGINIA, fit. in bar. Castleraghan, co. Cavan, prov. Ulster ; it is a post and fair town, distant from Dublin above 40 miles, on one side of which is a pretty large lake called *Lough Ramor*, in which are several islands, where there are the ruins of some castles. 2½ miles beyond *Virginia* is *Lurgan church*. Fairs held 9 July and 21 Nov.

VODIE, an antient district mentioned by Ptolemy, containing the present bar. of Carbury, in co. Cork, prov. Munster.

VOW-FERRY, a village fit. in bar. Colerain, co. Londonderry, prov. Ulster.

ULLAD, the antient name of the prov. of Ulster. *Ullad* or *Ullagh* originally comprehended all the present prov. of Ulster, but was afterwards confined to the present co. of Down: however it is to this day retained in the name of *Ulster*, or the Northern country; whence we find in the antient poems and chronicles, the inhabitants of this diftrict denominated *Tuath de Danans*, or northern people.

ULLARD, a rectory in dioc. of Leighlin, fit. in bar. Gowran, co. Kilkenny, prov. Leinster.

ULLOE, a vicarage in dioc. of Emly, fit. in bar. Coonagh, co. Limerick, prov. Munfter. Here are the ruins of the church and caftle of Ulloe.

ULSTER, the moft northerly *province* in Ireland: It is bounded by the *Deucaledonian fea* on the N. on the W. by the *Atlantic-ocean*; on the E. by St. *George's-channel* and the *Irifh-fea*; and on the S. and S. W. by the province of *Leinfter* and *Connaught*. Its greateft length is 68 miles, and in breadth from *Malinbay* to the point at the entrance of *Strangford-bay*, is 98 miles. The circumference, including the windings and turnings, about 460 miles, and the area or fuperficial content 3,143,000 acres. *Ulfter* abounds in lakes and rivers, which fupply it with a great variety of fine fifh, befides what it has from the fea, by which a great part of it is bounded: the Southern parts are rich, fertile, well cultivated and inclofed; but the greater part of the Northern is open and mountainous. The *farm-houfes* here are the neateft and beft built in the kingdom: this prov. alfo includes within itfelf the whole, or by far the greater part of the *linen* manufactory, the beft branch of trade in the kingdom. It contains the counties Donegal, Londonderry, Antrim, Tyrone, Fermanagh, Cavan, Armagh, Monaghan and Down, 54 baronies, 332 parifhes, 58 market towns, 29 boroughs, 1 Archbifhopric and 5 bifhoprics, and gives title of *earl* to his royal highnefs *prince Frederick*, fon to his prefent majefty, Geo. IIId.

UMALIA, a diftrict which comprehended the prefent bar. of Morifk, in the co. Mayo, and half the bar. of Rofs, in the co. Galway, prov. Connaught, the chiefs of which were the *O'Malies* or *O'Ma'ys*, fome of whom are ftill in poffeffion of part of their antient patrimony.

UMMURUS, a large tract of boggy ground, fit. in co. Kildare, prov. Leinfter, thro' which the *Grand-canal* paffes, having a bridge here called *Ummurus-bridge*, about 29 miles diftant from Dublin.

UMOND, a rectory in dioc. of Tuam, fit. in bar. Ballinahinch, co. Galway, prov. Connau.

UPPER-CONELLO, fit. in the S. part of the co. Limerick, prov. Munfter; the chiefs of which

diftrict were the *Mac Encirys*, who were difpoffeffed of their country by the earls of Defmond.

UPPERCROSS, a barony in co. Dublin, prov. Leinfter.

UPPERTHIRD, a barony in co. Waterford, prov. Munfter.

UREGARE, a vicarage in dioc. of Limerick, fit. in bar. Cofhma, co Limerick, prov. Munft.

UROLIN, a rectory in dioc. of Leighlin, fit. in bar. Catherlough, co. Carlow, prov. Leinft.

URLINGFORD, fit. in bar. Gallmoy, co. Kilkenny, prov. Leinfter, above 61 miles from Dublin; a mile beyond which are the ruins of the *church* and *caftle of Fennor*, between which and *Urlingford* a fmall ftream runs thro' the centre of a bog, dividing the counties of *Kilkenny* and *Tipperary*, and the provinces of *Leinfter* and *Munfter*. Fairs held 12 May, 15 Aug. and 12 Oct. This is a rectory in dioc. of Offory.

URNEY, a vicarage in dioc. of Kilmore, fit. in bar. Loughtee, co. Cavan, prov. Ulfter.—Alfo a rectory in dioc. of Derry, fit. in bar. Strabane, co. Tyrone, prov. Ulfter.

URRIN, a *river* in bar. Scarewalfh, co. Wexford, prov. Leinfter.

URRISBEG *mountain*, fit. in bar. Ballinahinch, co. Galway, prov. Connaught.

URRISHEAD, a *cape* fituate in bar. Erris, co. Mayo, prov. Connaught.

USHET, the Eaftern part of the ifland of *Raghery*, co. Antrim, prov. Ulfter.

USK, fit. in bar. Narragh, co. Kildare, prov. Leinfter. Fairs held Thurfday before 12 May, 1 Thurf. and Frid. in Oct. It is a rectory in dioc. of Dublin.

USKEAN, a vicarage in dioc. of Killaloe, fit. in bar. Lower Ormond, co. Tipperary, prov. Munfter.

USNEAGH, a mountain in bar. Rathconrath, co. Weftmeath, prov. Leinfter, on which fires were kindled by the Druids on 1 *May*, in honour of *Beal* or the *Sun*. This was the grand Bealtinne of the Northern parts of Leinfter, where the ftates affembled and held judgment on all criminals worthy of death, and fuch as were found guilty were burnt between two fires of *beal*: children and cattle alfo were purified on this day, by paffing them between the fires.

UVERNI, an antient city mentioned by Ptolemy; it is not certain where it was fituated, but appears to have been either the prefent town of Bantry or Kenmare, prov. Munfter.

W A

WADDISTOWN, a rectory in dioc. of Cafhel, fit. in bar. Middlethird, co. Tipperary, prov. Munfter.

WALCHES-

WALCHESTOWN, fit. in bar. Ferrard, co. Louth, prov. Leinfter.

WALKINSTOWN, fit. near *Crumlin*, in co. Dublin, prov. Leinfter. Near it is *Drumna* or *Drumfna-caftle*.

WALLSTOWN, a rectory in dioc. of Cloyne, fit. in bar. Fermoy, co. Cork, prov. Munfter; here is a large building, fit. near the river *Awbeg*.

WALSHS'CASTLE, fit. near lake *Strangford*, in co. Down, prov. Ulfter; near it is another caftle called *Caftle-Audley*.

WALSHS'TOWN, fit. 1 mile N. E. of Burton, in co Cork, prov. Munfter; here was formerly a caftle built by the *Barrys*, feveral centuries ago. In the wars of 1641 it was fortified and garrifoned, but was taken by the Irifh in 1645, together with other caftles which belonged to them.

WALTERSTOWN, fit. in bar. Kilkenny-weft, co. Weftmeath, prov. Leinfter.—Alfo a rectory in dioc. of Kildare, fit. in bar. Ophaly, co. Kildare, prov. Leinfter.

WARD, a village fit. in bar. Caftleknock, co. Dublin, prov. Leinfter.

WARENSTOWN, fee *Warrenftown*.

WARINGSFORD, fit. on a branch of the river *Lagan*, in co. Down, prov. Ulfter.

WARINGS-POINT, fit. about 1 mile N. W. of *Roftrevor*, in bar. Upper Iveagh, co. Down, prov. Ulfter. It is looked upon as the entrance into the river of *Newry*, called alfo the *Narrow-water*, where all coals that come down the canal muft be fhipped off for Dublin. On this narrow part of the river ftands the caftle of *Narrow-water*, built on a rock (which ftraitens the channel) where two ferry-boats maintain a communication between this county and that of *Louth*; near it a *Salt-work* has been erected. At this place is 3 fathom water; and from this point the town of Newry are two fmall leagues, but no depth of water except for fmall craft.

WARINGSTOWN, fit. in the bar. of *Lower Iveach*, co. Down, prov. Ulfter; 'tis otherwife called *Clanconnel* about 2 miles S. W. of *Magheralin*, and near 14 N. of *Newry*. In this town and the neighbourhood of it, the linen manufacture is carried on to great advantage: having been introduced and cherifhed here by the late *Sam. Waring*, efq; whofe family have here an elegant feat. In this place and neighbourhood, the linen manufacture has been carried on to great advantage. Here is a well finifhed church, roofed with Irifh oak, and remarkable for the workmanfhip of it. *William Waring*, efq; who firft fettled here, gave the ground for this ufe, and obtained an act of parliament for changing the fcite of the old parifh church from *Donaghcloney* bridge; after

which in the year 1681, he built this church at his own expence. This place was then thin of inhabitants, and much overgrown with woods: near it is a *Danifh rath*, which was opened about the year 1684, and in it was found a large flat quarry-ftone, placed upright like a door, which being removed, laid open an entrance into a narrow low paffage, about 10 feet long, and only wide enough to admit a man to creep in upon his hands and knees. This paffage led into a fmall round vault, about 6 feet high and 8 feet wide, placed in the centre of the mount. In the middle of the vault, 4 long fmall ftones were fixed in the ground, each about 2½ feet high, ftanding upright as fupporters to a flat quarry-ftone 2½ feet long, and 20 inches broad, placed on them in manner of a table; under which on the ground ftood a handfome earthen urn, of a dark brownifh colour, as if not thoroughly baked, about ¼ inch thick in its fides, containing broken pieces of burnt bones, mixed with afhes and fragments of burned wood.

WARRENSBROOK, a pleafant feat, fit. to the W. of *Innifkeen*, on the S. fide of *Bandon-river*, co. Cork, prov. Munfter.

WARRENSTOWN, fit. in co. Meath, prov. Leinfter; fairs held 1 Jan. 26 April, 22 June and 2 Sept.—Alfo a barony in King's co. prov. Leinfter.—Likewife a village fit. in bar. Atherdee, co. Louth, prov. Leinfter.

WATERFORD *county*, fit. in prov. Munfter; it is bounded on the W. by the co. Cork, S. by the ocean, and on the N. by the river *Suir*, which parts it from the co.'s of Tipperary and Kilkenny, and on the E. by its own haven, which feparates it from the co. Wexford. It extends from E. to W. 40 miles, and from N. to S. 23 miles, contains about 262,800 acres, 7 baronies, viz. Cofhmore and Cofhbride, Decies within Drum, Decies without Drum, Glanehiry, Upper-third, Middlethird and Gualtiere; it has 74 parifhes, and at leaft 110,000 inhabitants, and returns 10 members to parliament; chief town *Waterford*. Its antient families are thofe of O'Feolan, M'Thomas, Boyle, Walfh, Aylward, Poer, Wyfe, Dalton and Sherlock. A people called the *Menapii*, inhabited the co.'s of Waterford and Wexford in the time of *Ptolemy*, the geographer, who flourifhed about A.D. 140. After which Waterford was peopled by the *Defii*, a very powerful clan, originally planted in Meath, from whom the bar. of *Decies* is denominated. St. *Declan*, one of the precurfors of St. *Patrick*, was defcended from the family of thefe Defii, was the firft who preached to them the Chriftian religion, and converted numbers of them in the year 402, thirty years before St. Patrick came to Ireland on the fame miffion. This is a maritime county, well inhabited, but moftly rough and mountainous.

WATERFORD *city*, fit. in co. Waterford, prov. Munfter; it is a poft, market, fair and fhire-town, diftant 74 miles S.S.W. from Dublin. It has been alfo called (but corruptly) *Port-Largy*. It ftands on the S. fide of the river *Suir*; a broad and rapid river without any bridge, and about 4½ miles from its junétion with the *Nore* and *Barrow*, all which united form the harbour. This city is diftant about 8 miles from the fea, and is a moft convenient port for foreign traffic; the harbour runs almoft 12 miles up the country, nearly in a ftraight line, all the way deep and clear. Waterford was originally built in 879, but deftroyed in 981; it was confiderably enlarged by *Strongbow* in 1171, and ftill further in the reign of *Hen.* VIIth. who granted confiderable privileges to the citizens. *Rich.* IId. landed and was crowned here in 1399. In 1690 *James* IId. embarked from hence for *France*, after the battle of the *Boyne*; and king Wm. IIId. refided here twice, and confirmed its privileges. This city is governed by a mayor, and other magiftrates, and fends 2 members to parliament; eleétors *Freemen* and *Freeholders*. It is the fee of a bifhop, who has here a fine palace, built of hewn-ftone with two fronts. To this bifhoprick that of *Lifmore* was united in 1363; the cathedral is extenfive and elegant, befides which there are three churches, (one of which is extremely beautiful and fpacious) four Roman Catholic chapels, and places of worfhip for *French* Proteftants, Prefbyterians, Quakers and Anabaptifts. The Court-houfe, Exchange, Cuftom-houfe and barracks, are handfome buildings; and the new Theatre and Affembly-rooms are fitted up in a very fine tafte. There are feveral charity-fchools and humane foundations well fupported; the private dwellings are generally modern, and with the other improvements of the city, keep pace with the increafe of its trade. The *White glafs*, and other manufaétures of *Waterford* are in a flourifhing ftate; and its export of Beef, Butter, Hides, Tallow, Pork, Corn, &c. is confiderable; to which the extenfive inland navigation it has by means of the *Nore*, *Suir* and *Barrow* greatly contributes; as they alfo do to the import trade, from the demand for foreign commodities in the feveral rich countries and flourifhing towns thro' which thefe rivers flow. The trade it carries on with *Newfoundland*, and of which it enjoys the principal fhare, is of the utmoft importance, as upwards of 70 fail of fhipping are employed in the fupply of the banks with provifions, &c. and return from thence and the *Weft-Indies* with *fifh*, *rum*, *fugar*

and *cotton*, &c. Some idea of the provifion trade here may be formed by the vaft number of large hogs killed, which amounts to upwards of 3000 per week, for many weeks together; and of butter there have been exported from hence, from 60 to 80,000 cafks per year. The lat. of Waterford is 52 : 10, and its lon. 7 : 25. The antient name given to this city by the Irifh, was *Cuan-na-Grioth*, i. e. *the harbour of the Sun*; a fecond name it was known by was *Gleann-na-Gleodh*, i. e. *the valley of lamentation*; from a bloody battle between the Irifh and the Danes, in which the former gained a complete viétory, and burned the city to the ground. Several towers and caftles have been ereéted here; of which *Reginald's tower* ftill remains: the founder of which is faid to have been fon to *Ivorus*, king of the *Danes*. Strongbow made ufe of it as a prifon for the chiefs of the Irifh and Danes. It came at laft into the poffeffion of the ftore-keeper of the fort of *Duncannon*, and fince 1663, was applied to the keeping of the king's ftores. Where the barracks now ftand, was antiently a fquare fort, mounted with great guns, and partly encompaffed by a moat. The cathedral commonly called *Chrift-church*, and dedicated to the bleffed Trinity, was at firft founded by the *Oftmen* or *Danes*, who built this city, and by *Malchus* the firft bifhop of this fee, after his return from his confecration out of England. St. *Saviour's* friary was founded here by the citizens for Dominicans, in 1235. St. *Catharine's* priory, founded by the Danes, and endowed by *Elias Ironfide*, about 1210. The priory of St. *John*, alias St. *Leonard's*, founded by *John* earl of *Moreton*, Peter de Fonte benefaétor, in the 12th century, for *Benediétines*; and the Holy Ghoft friary, founded by fir *Hugh Purcell*, in 1240, for Francifcan friars. The quay of this city, which is above ½ a mile in length, and of confiderable breadth, is not inferior to, but rather exceeds the moft celebrated in *Europe*. To it the largeft veffels may conveniently come up, both to load and unload, and at a fmall diftance oppofite to it, may lie conftantly a-float. There is a communication by a ferry-boat, from this city to the co. Kilkenny. Alfo packet-boats are eftablifhed between this port and *Milford-haven* in Wales, for the convenience of the S. of Ireland. This city is computed to contain 35.000 inhabitants. The fee of Waterford is rated in the king's books at 72*l*. 8*s*. 1*d*. but is worth 2.500*l*. per ann. Fairs are held at Waterford 4 May, 24 June and 25 Oét. This city gives title of earl to the family of *Talbot*, that of vifcount to the family of *Lumley*, and that of marquis to the earl of *Tyrone*. It is a vicarage in dioc. of Waterford. Oppofite Reginald's-
tower

tower (before mentioned) on the N. fide of the river, is *Cromwell's-fort*, fo called from having been his ftation when he laid fiege to and took poffeffion of this city. At the other extremity of the quay are vaft quarries rifing perpendicularly from the river, and called *Bilberry-rock*, and on the oppofite fide of the river is *Granny-caftle*.

WATER-PARK, fit. in co. Cork, prov. Munfter: it is a well improved feat.

WATER-GRASS-HILL, fit. in bar. Barrymore, co. Cork, prov. Munfter, 117 miles from Dub.

WATTLE-BRIDGE, fituate in bar. Coole, co. Fermanagh, prov. Ulfter, 62 miles from Dubl. Here are the ruins of an antient temple of the Druids, fit. on the edge of the river *Fin*; and at one fide of *Wattle-bridge* is St. *Mary's-church*.

WELLS, fit. in co. *Wexford*, prov. Leinfter, 54 miles from Dublin.—Alfo the name of a fair town in bar. Idrone, co. *Carlow*, prov. Leinfter; fairs held Afcenfion-day and 11 Dec. It is a rectory in dioc. of Leighlin.

WELLSTOWN, a fmall village fit. on the river *Fin*, about 3 miles from *Ballybofey*, in co. Donegal, prov. Ulfter.

WEST-CASHEL, (otherwife called *Caffel-irra*) fit. 6 miles S. of Sligo, in co. Sligo, prov. Connaught. A bifhoprick was erected here by St. Bren in the 6th century.

WESTMEATH *county*, fit. in prov. Leinfter: it is bounded on the N. by the co. of *Cavan*, on the E. by the co. of *Meath*, otherwife called *Eaft Meath*, on the W. by the co. *Longford* and *Lough Ree*, which feparates it from the co. *Rofcommon*. It is divided into 12 baronies, viz. Fore (a half bar.) Moygeefh, Corkerry, Moyafhill and Magheredernon, Delvin, Farbill, Rathconrath, Kilkenny-weft, Brawny, Clunlonan, Moycafhel and Fertullagh; containing about 231,538 acres, and 69,000 inhabitants: it extends from E. to W. 33 miles, and from N. to S. 27; has 62 parifhes, 3 boroughs, befides the manor of Mullingar, and returns ten members to parliament. Its antient families are thofe of O'Melaghlin, O'Malone, Macawly, Mageoghan, Dalton, Petit, Tyrel, Dillon and Fox. It gives title of earl to the family of *Nugent*. Befide the principal river, which is the Shannon, this county is watered with a number of agreeable lakes, viz. Lough-Leign, Lough-Derrivaragh, Lough-Iron, Lough-Ennell, Lough-Drin, having trouts in it of an emetic quality, and Lough-Banean-Annagh. Weftmeath is much intermixed with bogs; chief town, *Mullingar*, which is the affizes and fhire town for this county, and the fecond great fair in the kingdom for *wool*.

WESTPHALSTOWN, a curacy in diocefe of Dublin, fituate in bar. *Balruddery*, co. Dublin, prov. Leinfter. *Beaufort.*—Mr *Seale* places it in bar. *Newcaftle*.

WESTPORT, a poft and fair town in bar. Morifk, co. Mayo, prov. Connaught; fairs held 1 Jan. 25 May, 6 Aug. and 1 Dec. It is diftant about 123 miles from Dublin: within 3 miles of it is *Mount Brown*, a handfome feat; and near Weftport, beautifully fituated on a gently rifing ground, near the river which runs between the town and the fea, is a feat of the earl of *Altamont's*, commanding a fine view of the bay, with its numerous iflands, great and projecting promontories, and rich and hanging woods.

WESTOWN, fit. in bar. Balruddery, co. Dublin, prov. Leinfter.

WEXFORD *county*, fituated in prov. Leinfter; bounded by *Wicklow* on the N. St. *George's-channel* on the S. and W. and part of the counties of *Carlow* and *Kilkenny* on the E. It is in length from N. to S. 44 miles, and in breadth from E. to W. 25 miles, containing 342,900 acres, and about 115,000 inhabitants: it has 8 baronies, viz. Gorey, Scarewalfh, Ballaghkeen, Bantry, Shelmaliere, Shelburne, Bargic and Forth, 142 parifhes, 8 boroughs, and fends 18 members to parliament. The foil is various, in fome places it is coarfe and poor, in others fruitful both in corn and grafs: the chief town is *Wexford*. The bar. of *Forth* joins this town, where are the remains of an antient *Britifh colony*, planted there by Hen. IId. Thefe people retain their native language, manners, and many fingular cuftoms to this day: they intermarry amongft themfelves, and have intermixed little or none with the natives. Here, it is probable, the antient Britifh or *Celtic* language hath been preferved with lefs corruption than even in *Britain*, where the *Danifh*, *Saxon* and *French* languages have been interwoven with it; be that as it may, the inhabitants are remarkably induftrious, cleanly to an extreme, and poffeffed of great fimplicity of manners. In this co. is *Duncannon-fort*, which commands the harbour of *Waterford*, in co. Waterford, prov. *Munfter*.

WEXFORD-HAVEN, fit. in co. Wexford, prov. Leinfter: it runs in W. and by N. with its innermoft part wholly Northward: juft before the haven lie two great fhelves by the fide of each other, of which that on the S. fide is called *Hanman's-path*, and the other the *North grounds*: there is a channel between Hanman's-path, and the land on the S. fide of the haven, and another between the N. fide and the North grounds; but this laft has only 6 feet of water at full flood, and the other 8 feet at the ufual tides, and 10 feet at fpring-tides. The chief channel is between the two fands, being 4 and 5 fathoms deep. Befides thefe fands, there is another fhelf in the mouth of the harbour, which kind of fandy banks lying acrofs the

mouths

mouths of harbours and rivers, are ufually called *bars*, and the havens which have them, *barred havens.* With a high flood there are about 16 feet of water ; being paffed the *bar*, there are 3 fathoms of water, 3¼, and 4, but afterwards for a great way, but 10 feet and 10½, with a high flood ; tho' under the caftle, where the veffels come to an anchor, there are 4 fathoms, and before the *town*, 3: on account, however, of the fhallows before noticed, no veffels can go to *Wexford*, that draw above 10 feet water, but muft lade and unlade in a creek near the mouth of the haven, on the S. fide, about 3 miles from the *town*, where there is a fufficiency of water, but no fhelter from the S. W. winds : at the extremity of each of the two narrow necks of land which defend the entrance of this haven, there is a fort, that towards *Dublin* is called *Fort Marget*, the other *Fort Rofelair*. Lat. 52 : 21, lon. 6 : 52.

WEXFORD *town*, the capital of the co. of that name, prov. Leinfter ; nearly 67 miles S. from Dublin. It is the fhire and affizes town for that county ; alfo a market, poft and fair town ; fit. near the fea, upon the river *Slaney*, which empties itfelf into the ocean here. It is governed by a mayor, and other magiftrates, and fends 2 members to parliament. The *haven* is very large, and the entrance is defended by two narrow necks of land, each forming an ifthmus that ftretch forward to meet each other, leaving an opening of about ¼ a mile. It was called by the *Danes* who built it, *Wefsford*, and was alfo called *Carman*, and was formerly a place of more ftrength and trade than at prefent. The firft forces from *England* that attempted the conqueft of this kingdom landed here, (encouraged by king *Dermot)* a year before the earl of *Pembroke*. They were led by *Robert Fitzftephens* and *Maurice Fitzgerald :* the former built a caftle 2 miles from the town, called *Carrick*, which he fortified with the utmoft art of thofe times ; but the people of *Wexford* not brooking fuch a neighbour, got him into their power by a ftratagem, then confined him and moft of his followers in prifon, 'till the arrival of king *Hen.* IId, when the inhabitants brought *Fitzftephens* to Waterford, where they delivered him to that monarch, and were the firft who fubmitted as fubjects of England. *Fitzftephens* was appointed governor of the town, and the diftrict round it, which in a few years increafed fo much with Englifh inhabitants daily arriving here, that in fome time they fpread all over the country, where they ftill remain, and are famed for the beft improvements in the kingdom. From this town king *Henry* embarked for *England*, after receiving homage from moft of the kings and princes of this nation. Here was the ceremony of the firft Englifh marriage per-

formed, between *Raymond* (afterwards viceroy of Ireland) and the lady *Bafil*, fifter to *Strengbow*, earl of Pembroke ; and this was the fecond town which *Cromwell* befieged, or that had the courage to oppofe him. It is feated in a bottom, tho' where the caftle ftands is a rocky high hill, which overlooks the fea, and commands the port and town. There are feveral parts of the walls ftanding, which are very thick. The gates yet remain, and it contains fome handfome buildings. Near one of the gates is a fmall ftructure that covers a mineral well, which they call a *fpa* ; but the appearance of the water is not very inviting, as it is covered with an oily fcum, but it has many virtues attributed to it, and is frequented by individuals, but not as much as formerly ; at the end of the town are good barracks for foldiers, which have a fine profpect of the harbour ; moft of the old buildings are made of ftone of a reddifh colour : the church is in the main ftreet, of a modern tafte, tho' partly built on the old foundation. The town confifts of one long ftreet, with fome lanes on each fide ; there are feveral ruins of antient abbeys and religious houfes interfperfed ; the church, market-houfe, and cuftom-houfe, are handfome modern ftructures, the quay, like their trade, is not very extenfive : their chief export is *corn*, particularly *barley* and *malt*, of which they export pretty large quantities ; provifions of all kinds are plentiful and cheap here, and there is very fine wild-fowl to be had from the month of November to May. Fairs held 17 March, 1 May, 29 June, 2 Auguft and 1 November. Lat. 52 : 15, lon. 6 : 25. *Wexford* gives title of earl, as does *Waterford* alfo, to the family of *Talbot*, earl of *Shrewfbury* in *Great Britain*. It returns two members to parliament ; patronage in the families of *Neville* and *Le Hunte*. This town is a rectory in dioc. of Ferns ; in 1788 the number of houfes in it amounted to 1412.

WHALEY-ABBEY, fit. near *Rathdrum*, co. Wicklow, prov. Leinfter ; now the feat of Mr. Whaley ; it was erected on the antient feite of an abbey founded by a brother of St. *Kevin*, probably St. *Dangan*.

WHIDDY-ISLAND, antiently called *Fucida Infula*, fit. in bar. Bear and Bantry, co. Cork, prov. Munfter ; it lies oppofite to Bantry, and is a pleafant fpot of a triangular form, having a good deer-park and excellent foil ; here are plenty of rabbits, and fome good orchards.

WHILLANS-ROCKS, thefe *rocks* lie between the mouths of Larne and Glenarm bays, in one of the Copland iflands called Crofs ifland, off the coaft of co. Down, prov. Ulfter.

WHITE-CHURCH, a rectory in dioc. of Cloyne, fit. in the liberties of *Cork*, prov. Munfter.

ter.—Also a rectory in dioc. of Dublin, sit. in bar. Half-Rathdown, co. Dublin, prov. Leinster.—Also a rectory in dioc. of Ossory, sit. in bar. Iverk, co. Kilkenny, prov. Leinster. Also a vicarage in dioc. of Lismore, sit. in bar. Iffa and Offa, co. Tipperary, prov. Munster.— Also a vicarage in dioc. of Lismore, sit. in bar. Decies *without*, co. Waterford, prov. Munster; this parish is of considerable extent, and gave title to the family of *Maule*, the hon. *Wm. Maule*, being created *baron* Maule of *Whitechurch*, and earl of Penmure of Forth, in the co. Wexford, by patent dated 2 May, 1743. Some years ago the rib of an elephant was dug up within a mile of Whitechurch. It is well known this creature is a native of the warmer climates, far remote from this country. It is pretty certain the Romans never had any footing here: and it is doubtful whether they ever brought any of these animals even into *Britain*; the only author that hints at their being brought thither, is *Dion Cassius*, but *Suetonius*, who also wrote the life of the emperor *Claudius*, mentions nothing of the matter, nor does *Dion* say that he *brought* them with him, but that he gathered them together in order to do it. Yet *Cambden* thinks that the monstrous bones and teeth, which he takes notice to have been dug up in *England*, must have been the remains of *Elephants*, brought over by the emperor *Claudius*, as Dion reports. *Mat. Paris* says the first elephant seen on this side the *Alps*, was one sent as a present by *Lewis* 9th of France, to our king Hen. IIId. A. D. 1255, and perhaps, a few more since might have been brought over for shew or curiosity; we have no other method of accounting for these bones being found in this kingdom or in England. In *Whitechurch* parish, about a mile E. of the church, is a most stupendous cavern, called *Oon-a-glour* or the *Pigeons hole*; a little to the Northward is a smaller cave, called *Oon-a-mort*, and in this neighbourhood are several others. *Whitechurch* is distant from Dublin, 95 miles; fairs held 5 Aug.

WHITE-CHURCH *of Glynn*, a rectory in dioc. of Ferns, sit. in bar. Bantry, co. Wexford, prov. Leinster.

WHITE-HEAD CAPE, sit. in bar. Decies within, co. Waterford, prov. Munster.

WHITE-HOUSE, a seat in co. Down, prov. Ulster, joining the bay of *Carrickfergus*, at which spot king *William* IIId. landed. It is about 3½ miles distant from *Belfast*.

WHITESTOWN, sit. in bar. Balruddery, co. Dublin, prov. Leinster.

WHITEWOOD, a seat of lord *Gormanstown*, sit. near *Nobber*, co. Meath, prov. Leinster.

WICKLOW *county*, sit. in prov. *Leinster*: it is bounded by *Wexford* on the S. that of *Dublin*

and part of *Kildare* on the N. St. *George's channel* on the E. and by *Kildare* and *Carlow* co.'s on the W. It extends from N. to S. 32 miles, from E. to W. 26 miles; contains 311,600 acres, 58 parishes, about 58,000 inhabitants, has 4 boroughs, and returns 10 members to parliament. This co. is divided into the six baronies following, viz. *Rathdown*, (a half barony) Newcastle, Arklow, Ballynacour, Talbot'stown and Shillalev. Its antient families are those of O'Toole, O'Brien, MacMorogh, Cavanagh and Murphies. It is partly a fine arable county, and partly encumbered with mountains, but its lower lands and rich bottoms are found to be a good soil. In some places rich veins of copper and other minerals have been discovered. In the *Wicklow mountains* are some of those deep, dark valleys, called *glins*, extremely beautiful and picturesque, together with some astonishing waterfalls: that of *Powerscourt* is perhaps one of the most beautiful in the world, both for its prodigious height and pleasing appearance. Chief town, *Wicklow*.

WICKLOW *harbour*, sit. in co. Wicklow, prov. Leinster. This harbour at present admits of nothing but small craft, the bar having no more than 7 or 8 feet at high-water, spring-tides. In making for the bar, you must give the rock at the Black-castle a good birth.

WICKLOW *town*, sit. in bar. Newcastle, co. Wicklow, prov. Leinster, 24 miles from Dublin: it is a market, post and fair town, and the shire and assizes town for that co. It is seated on the sea side, and has a narrow haven at the mouth of the river *Leitrim*, fit only for small vessels which carry provisions to the capital, and that indeed is its chief trade: here is a rock, by some taken for the remains of a castle, surrounded by a strong wall. There are but few buildings, yet it has a barrack, and is remarkable for the best *ale* in the kingdom: about a mile and an half on the E. is a point of land called *Wicklow-head*. This place is a vicarage in dioc. of Dublin, and gives title of visc. to the family of *Howard*, and was antiently called *Wykenlooe*. Fairs held 28 Mar. Ascension-day, 12 Aug. and 25 Nov. Wicklow returns 2 members to parliament, patronage in the *Tighe* family. Lat. 52: 7, lon. 6: 30.

WILLBROOK, sit. near *Athlone*, in co. Westmeath, prov. Leinster.

WILLIAMSTOWN, a seat within about 2 miles of *Edenderry*, in King's co. prov. Leinster.

WILTOWN, sit. in bar. Clonchee, co. Cavan, prov. Ulster.

WINDGAP, sit. in co. Waterford, province Munster; fairs held 21 June and Aug.

WINDGATES, a small fishing village sit. 3½ miles beyond *Bray*, and 13½ from Dublin castle, in co. Wicklow, prov. Leinster.

WITTER, a rectory in dioc. of Down, sit. in bar. Ardes, co. Down, prov. Ulster.

WOODFIELD,

WOODFIELD, fit. near *Birr*, King's co. prov. Leinfter.

WOODFORD, fit. in bar. Leitrim, co. Galway, prov. Connaught, above 97 miles from Dublin; fairs held 12 and 13 May, 2 and 3 Oct.

WOODFORT, fit. near *Mallow*, in co. Cork, prov. Munfter; here is a handfome houfe, with elegant plantations and confiderably large orchards. To the S. of the houfe is a circular hill, covered over with trees, except fome viftoes that are cut thro' them; on the top of this mount is a turret, whence the eye may be feafted with a luxurious profpect of a great tract of country, with the adjacent town of Mallow, and the high mountains of Waterford, Limerick and Kerry. Near the foot of this mount runs the river *Clydagh*, in delightful meanders, thro' groves of ever-greens, and foon lofes itfelf in the *Black-water*, near *Kilbolady*, where are confiderable plantations of cyder-fruit, firs, and other foreft trees.

WOOD-LAWN, fit. in co. Galway, prov. Connaught, about 81 miles from Dublin.

WOODSTOCK-CASTLE, fit. near *Athy*, co. Kildare, prov. Leinfter: it was built by *Richard St. Michael*, lord of *Rheban*, as an appendage to the palatinate of *Dunnamacs*, granted to the earl of *Pembroke*. About the year 1424, *Thomas*, the 7th earl of *Kildare*, then lord *Offaly*, married *Dorothea*, daughter of *Anthony More* of *Leix*, and with her obtained the manors of *Rheban* and *Woodftock*, and in them erected a court-baron and court-leet, which are ftill held.

WYANSTOWN, fit. in bar. Deece, co. Meath, prov. Leinfter.

Y O

YAGOE, a vicarage in dioc. of Dublin, fit. in bar. Naas, co. Kildare, prov. Leinfter.

YELLOW-RIVER, fit. in bar. Warrenftown, King's co. prov. Leinfter.

YOUGHAL, fit. in co. Cork, prov. Munfter, 108 miles S. W. of *Dublin*, 20 miles N. E. of *Cork*, and 32 S. W. of *Waterford*; it is a borough, market, fair and poft town, pretty large, and fit. under a high hill, clofe to the water's edge, on the river *Black-water*, near the mouth of the bay. It is governed by a mayor and other magiftrates, being an antient corporation; the original inhabitants were a colony from Briftol, who ftill retain much of the old Englifh dialect. This place had formerly more trade than at prefent; it has a barrack, and returns 2 members to parliament: patron, the earl of *Shannon*. Lat. 51 : 50 N. lon. 7 : 50 W. Here is a manufacture of earthen ware, which is in a thriving ftate; there is a bar at the entrance of the port which makes

it troublefome, and often dangerous, but fhips when they are once in, lie very fafely, and it is equally convenient and capacious; fome time ago the ftrand here was efteemed proper for a horfe-race, but now the fea has worn fo many deep holes in it, that it is utterly fpoiled of that diverfion. The town confifts chiefly of one large ftreet, with a few outlets; the cuftom-houfe is pretty enough; this place held out for the crown againft the *Defmond* rebellion, in the reign of queen Eliz. the earl befieged it, and for want of promifed affiftance, the town yielded, but the mayor was hanged by order of this victorious male-content, in the year 1579. Youghall fubmitted to *Cromwell*, notwithftanding, in the year 1648, the corporation had proclaimed *Charles* IId. king of England, &c. At this port *Cromwell* embarked for England, after his incredible fucceffes in this kingdom; the inhabitants feem to have worn the badge of loyalty, more efpecially fince the proteftant fucceffion; and at the year 1678, an order appears on their records, that no *Roman Catholic* fhould *buy* or *barter* any thing at their public markets; and in the year 1704, there was but one popifh prieft in the town of *Youghal* and its precincts. Here are the ruins of two abbeys, one at the N. and the other at the S. end of the town, and fome remains of the college or abbey which was dedicated to St. *Mary*, fome of the apartments are kept in repair: they are the remains of a fpacious building; here are alfo the ruins of a Francifcan houfe, built by an earl of Kildare, in 1232. It was Cromwell's head quarters for fome time; there are feveral monuments belonging to fome branches of the *Boyles*, particularly *Roger Boyle*, famous for his art of war and fome dramatic pieces. In the gardens of *Youghal*, the *potatoe* it is faid, was firft planted in this kingdom, being firft introduced, as it is faid, by fir *Walter Raleigh*, which is not improbable, fince this was part of his eftate, which he fold to the earl of Cork. Fairs are held here Afcenfion-day, and 18 Oct. The collegiate church of Youghal is now united to the diocefe of *Cloyne*, the bifhop of which is obliged to keep 2 curates to perform divine fervice there: it is now more properly a parifh church; and faid to be one of the largeft parifh churches in Ireland. It is a very antient ftructure, built in the Gothic tafte, the nave is 135 feet long, and 66 broad, adorned with 6 Gothic arches at each fide. The E. window of the chancel is very fine, in the Gothic ftile; on the N. fide of the church, ftands a fquare tower about 30 feet high; there are 2 ruined chapels on each fide of the chancel, and another W. of the church: in thefe are feveral antient tombs and infcriptions.

APPENDIX

APPENDIX.

A P P E N D I X.

No. 1.

TABLE of additional *Places* and *Remarks*, &c.

*Thus marked * have been already mentioned in the foregoing Work.*

A

ABLERIAGH, fit. about 5 miles from *Caf-tleblaney*, co. Monaghan, prov. Ulfter.

AGHAREA *church*, fit. about 5 miles from *Donough*, co. Fermanagh, prov. Ulfter.

AMIGAN *caftle*, (in ruins) fit. near 5 miles from *Adair*, co. Limerick, prov. Munfter.

ARDMULLEN *caftle*, (in ruins) fit. about 2 miles beyond *Clonard-bridge*, co. Weftmeath, prov. Leinfter.

ARGONNEL *caftle*, (now in ruins) fit. about 3 miles from *Caftleshane*, co. Monaghan, prov. Ulfter.

ATHCARNE *caftle*, (in ruins) fit. near 4 miles from Kilmoon, co. Meath, prov. Leinfter.

AUCHADOWAY *church*, fit. near 3 miles from *Garvagh*, co. Londonderry, prov. Ulfter.

AUGHALEE *church*, (in ruins) fit. about 4½ miles from *Lurgan*, co. Armagh, prov. Ulfter; near it are fome flour-mills.

B

* BALERIGGEN (*harbour*.) In making this harbour, and coming from the Northward by night, you muft keep in 8 or 9 fathoms water, to keep clear of the *Carjee*, a half-tide rock, which lies about a mile N.N.E.¼E. from the pier. When you bring the pier to bear S. W. you may make bold for it: and as this harbour is all clear ground, and a foft fand, a veffel in a ftorm from E. without anchor or cable, may venture to run herfelf aground within it. The tide flows here until 11. o'clock full and change.

BALFOUR-CASTLE, a feat near *Lifneskea*, co. Fermanagh, prov. Ulfter.

BALLAGH-BUY *mountain*, fit. 1½ mile beyond *Boyle*, co. Rofcommon, prov. Connaught.

BALLI-GRIANAN, (i. e. the *Summertown*) now called Grenanftown, a feat about 1½ mile from *Toomavara*, co. Tipperary, prov. Munfter.

BALLYALENAN *caftle*, (in ruins) fit. 2 miles beyond *Rathkeale*, co. Limerick, prov. Munfter.

BALLYCARTHY *caftle*, (in ruins) fit about 1 mile beyond *Arbella*, and 6 miles beyond *Caftle-ifland*, co. Kerry, prov. Munfter.

BALLYENGLAND *caftle*, (in ruins) fit. near *Afkeyton*, co. Limerick, prov. Munfter.

BALLYGLASHIN *caftle*, (in ruins) fit. about 2 miles beyond the village of Ballypatrick, in co. Kilkenny, prov. Leinfter.

BALLYLAGHAN *caftle*, fit. about 6 miles beyond

yond *Swineford,* co. Mayo, prov. Connaught.

BALLYNABOLA *castle,* (in ruins) fit. about 3 miles from *Gowran,* co. Kilkenny, prov. Leinft.

BARAGH *castle,* (in ruins) fit. on the fide of the river Ban, about 4 miles from *Banbridge,* co. Down, prov. Ulfter.

BLACK-BANK *castle,* (in ruins) fit. near 2 miles beyond *Newtownhamilton,* co. Armagh, prov. Ulfter.

BLACKHALL *castle,* (in ruins) fit. about 4 miles beyond *Old Kilcullen,* co. Kildare, prov Leinft.

BLANF-CASTLE, (in ruins) fit. at the foot of a high hill near Toomavara, co. Tipperary, prov. Munfter.

BONHO-HALL, a fmall village fit. beyond *Timolin,* co. Kildare, prov. Leinfter.

BROGHILL *castle,* fit. 1 mile beyond *Frankfort,* King's co. prov. Leinfter.

BURROS *castle,* (in ruins) fit. about 5 miles beyond *Urlingford,* Queen's co. prov. Leinfter.

C

CAPPOGE *castle,* (in ruins) fit. near *Dunsink,* co. Dublin, prov. Leinfter.

CARRICKAFOIL *castle,* (in ruins) the antient manfion of *O'Connor Kerry;* fit. near Ballylongford, co. Limerick, prov. Munfter. It was once a place of great ftrength and importance.

CARRICKLEE, a feat near the S. fide of the river Fin, about 1½ mile beyond *Lifford,* co. Donegal, prov. Ulfter.

CARRIGANEURA *castle,* (in ruins) fit. 2 miles beyond *Mitchelstown,* co. Cork, prov. Munfter.

CARRIGNACONNY *castle,* fit. by the river *Blackwater,* about 1 mile from *Castletown-roach,* co. Cork, prov. Munfter.

CARTRON *castle,* (in ruins) fit. on the banks of Cronaugh river, 2½ miles from *Athlone,* co. Rofcommon, prov. Connaught.

CASTLE-BANGAN, (in ruins) fit. on the fide of a hill about 3 miles from *Knocktopher,* co. Kilkenny, prov. Leinfter.

CASTLE-GARDEN *castle,* (in ruins) fit. about 4 miles from *Gowran,* co. Kilkenny, prov. Leinft.

CASTLE-MAC-GARRET, (ufually called *Magarfet,*) a handfome feat, 1½ mile beyond *Ballindaggin,* co. Mayo, prov. Connaught.

CASTLE-SAUNDERSON, a feat near *Wattlebridge,* co. Fermanagh, prov. Ulfter; oppofite to it on the very edge of the river *Fin,* are the ruins of an antient temple of the Druids.

CASTLE-TROY, (ruins) fit. by the river Shannon, about 5 miles from *O'Brien's-bridge,* co. Clare, prov. Munfter.

CAUSWAYSTOWN *castle,* fit. about 8 miles from *Trim,* co. Meath, prov. Leinfter.

CLARE-CASTLE, a handfome feat near the river Cufhen, about 10 miles from *Newry,* prov. Ulfter.

CLINTONSTOWN *castle,* fit. about 1½ mile from *Dunleer,* on the N. bank of the river *Dee,* co. Louth, prov. Leinfter.

CLOGHAN-CASTLE, fit. about 8 miles from *Tuam,* co. Galway, prov. Connaught.

CLOGHANEELY *church,* fit. 3½ miles from *Dunfanaghy,* co. Donegal, prov. Ulfter.

CLONENAGH *church,* fit. 5 miles beyond *Maryborough,* Queen's co. prov. Leinfter.

CLONMORE *castle,* (in ruins) fit. 2½ miles beyond *Hacketstown,* co. Carlow, prov. Leinfter.

CONFY *castle,* fit. near *Leixlip,* co. Kildare, prov. Leinfter, it is in ruins, and fo is *Confy-church* contiguous to it.

CONNOR-CASTLE, (in ruins) fit. on the bank of the river Moy, about 3 miles beyond *Ballina,* co. Mayo, prov. Connaught; it commanded a fine view of *Killala-bay.*

CONNOUGH *castle,* (in ruins) fit. near *Tallow,* co. Waterford, prov. Munfter.

COOL-CASTLE, (in ruins) fit. on the banks of the river *Brofna,* about 5 miles beyond *Ballycumber,* King's co. prov. Leinfter.

CRUMPS-CASTLE, fit. within ½ a mile of *Fethard,* co. Tipperary, prov. Munfter.

CURRAGHA *church,* (in ruins) fit. about 3 miles from *Grenouge,* co. Meath, prov. Leinfter.

CURVAGH *church,* (in ruins) fit. on the edge of Lough Allen, 3 miles from *Ballintra,* co. Leitrim, prov. Connaught.

D

DERRY-CASTLE, fit. about 8 miles from *Nenagh,* co. Tipperary, prov. Munfter.

DERRYLIAGH *castle,* fit. near *Newport,* co. Tipperary, prov. Munfter.

DERRYLORN *church,* fit. about 8 miles from *Dungannon,* co. Tyrone, prov. Ulfter.

DONAGHMORE *church,* (in ruins) fit. within 1 mile of *Navan,* co. Meath, prov. Leinfter; in the church-yard ftands a tower about 70 feet high and 12 in diameter, the door of which is 10 feet from the ground.

DROUGHLONE, a fmall *lake* fit. about 3 miles from *King's-court,* co. Cavan, prov. Ulfter.

DRUMCUMET, fit. near *Dungiven,* co. Londonderry, prov. Ulfter.

DRUMMARA *church,* fit. about 3 miles from *Dromore,* co. Down, prov. Ulfter.

DUNALY *castle,* (in ruins) fit. about ½ a mile from *Silver-mines,* co. Tipperary, prov. Munft.

DUNDRUM *castle,* (in ruins) fit. a little beyond *Churchtown,* co. Dublin, prov. Leinfter.

DUNLEARY (harbour.) The harbour of Dunleary is formed with a new pier, it lies S. W. by W. from the light-houfe of Howth, and S. by W. ¼ W. from the light-houfe on the piles, diftance 1 league. In making for the harbour, you muft take care not to go too

far

far to the Weftward, to avoid the *Chickens*, rocks which are covered at ½ flood ; they bear from the end of the pier, N.W. by W. one-eighth of a mile. This harbour affords good fhelter from all winds but Northerly.

DUNNYMAYNE *church*, fit. near 5 miles from the *Mill of Louth*, co. Louth, prov. Leinfter.

E

EMYSCORE-GLEN, fit. near *Stramore-inn*, co. Londonderry, prov. Ulfter.

ERRY-CASTLE, (in ruins) fit. a little beyond *Clara*, in King's co. prov. Leinfter.

EVE-CASTLE, (in ruins) fit. within one mile of *Callen*, co. Kilkenny, prov. Leinfter.

F

FINLOY *church*, fit. about 3 miles from *Rath-fharkan*, co. Antrim, prov. Ulfter.

FIRMAR *church*, (in ruins) fit. near *Slane*, co. Meath, prov. Leinfter.

FLEET-CASTLE, (in ruins) fit. on a fmall *peninfula*, commanding the entrance into *Lough-Larne*, in co. Antrim, prov. Ulfter.

FORGNEY *church*, fit. 2½ miles beyond *Moy-fore*, co. Weftmeath, prov. Leinfter.

G

GARY-CASTLE, (in ruins) fit. near *Athlone*, co. Weftmeath, prov. Leinfter.

GARRYLOUGH *caftle*, (in ruins) fit. about 5 miles beyond *Olart*, in co. Wexford, prov. Leinfter.

GRAANEBUIE *caftle*, (in ruins) fit. 2 miles beyond *Adair*, co. Limerick, prov. Munfter.

GRANGE *church*, (in ruins) fit. near 5 miles from *Strabane*, co. Tyrone, prov. Ulfter.

H

HAGGARDSTOWN *caftle*, fit. about 4 miles from *Caftlebellingham*, co. Louth, prov. Leinfter ; 'tis now in ruins.

I

IRISHTOWN *caftle*, (in ruins) fit. about 1 mile beyond *Palmerftown*, co. Dublin, prov. Leinft.

K

KILBARRY *church*, (in ruins) fit. about ½ a mile beyond *Dunmanway*, co. Cork, prov. Munfter.

KILCOLGAN *caftle*, (in ruins) fit. about 4 miles from Ballycumber, King's co. prov. Leinfter.

KILDALLEN *church*, fit. about 3 miles from *Killefandra*, co. Cavan, prov. Ulfter.

KILKEA-CASTLE, fit. on the river Greece, in bar. Kilkea, co. Kildare, prov. Leinfter. This caftle was built about 1420 by John the 6th. earl of Kildare, but repaired and enlarged by Gerald the 11th. earl in 1573, as appears by infcription on the chimney piece in the dining room. On a ftone near the large gate-way is a curious fculpture, reprefenting two perfons wreftling, the one with the head of a fox, and the other of an ape : near them is another figure with the head of a dog. This fculpture feems to allude to the union of Gerald the 5th. earl, with Patrick Fox and Walter Fitzgerald, in the government of the co.'s Cork, Limerick and Kerry, in 1400. In 1513 Gerald the 8th. earl of Kildare, was fhot near this caftle as he was watering his horfe at the river, by one of the *O'Mores* of Leix, and died of the wound at Kildare on the 16th Oct. in that year.

KILLEGLAND *church*, (in ruins) fit. about 2½ miles from Grenogue, co. Meath, prov. Leinft.

KILMACURREL *church*, (in ruins) fit. about 7 miles from *Largay*, co. Cavan, prov. Ulfter.

KILTEEVAGH *church*, fit. about 4 miles from Ballybofey, co. Donegal, prov. Ulfter.

KIRKARD, *ruins* fit. between Strandhoufe-inn, and Efky-bridge, co. Sligo, prov. Conn.

KNOCKALTON *caftle*, (in ruins) fit. within 2 miles of Nenagh, co. Tipperary, prov. Munft.

KNOCKANE *caftle*, (in ruins) fit. near *Tooma-vara*, co. Tipperary, prov. Munfter.

L

LEMANAGH *caftle*, fit. about 3 miles from Inchiquin, co. Clare, prov. Munfter.

LEMANAGHAN *church*, (in ruins) fit. near 3 miles from Ballycumber, King's co. prov. Leinft.

LISMULLIN *caftle*, (in ruins) fit. about 4 miles from Killynaule, co. Tipperary, prov. Munfter.

M

MAGARSET, fee *Caftle-mac-garret*.

MAGHERALLY *church*, fit. about 2 miles from Banbridge, co. Down, prov. Ulfter.

MASHANGLASS *caftle*, (in ruins) fit. on a hill, within 2½ miles of Macroomp, co. Cork, prov. Munfter.

MODESHEL *church*, (in ruins) fit. within 4 miles of Callen, co. Kilkenny, prov. Leinfter.

MORINSTOWN *church*, fit. 2 miles beyond Racondra, co. Weftmeath, prov. Leinfter.

MOYCASHILL *caftle*, (in ruins) fit. about a mile beyond Kilbeggan-bridge, co. Weftmeath, prov. Leinfter.

4 R   MOY-

MOYLAGH *caftle*, (in ruins) fit. about ½ a mile from *Newtownbellew*, co. Galway, prov. Connaught.

MUCKAMORE *caftle*, (in ruins) fit. within a few miles of Lough Neagh, co. Antrim, prov. Ulfter.

MULLIBRACK *church*, fit. 1½ mile from Market-hill, co. Armagh, prov. Ulfter.

MULLINHONE *caftle*, (in ruins) fit. near the village of Killaghy, co. Tipperary, prov. Munft.

MYTERSTOWN *tower*, fit. about 4 miles from New-inn, co. Meath, prov. Leinfter.

N

NAUL-CASTLE, this old building is boldly fit. over a romantic glen, through which a fmall ftream winds its courfe, and divides the co.'s Dublin and Meath, in prov. Leinfter; at a fmall diftance lower down a fine water-fall is formed, called the *Roches*.

NEWTOWN-ABBEY, fituate near Trim, co. Meath, prov. Leinfter.

NIE-CASTLE, (in ruins) fit. 3 miles from Nenagh, co. Tipperary, prov. Munfter.

O

O'CANE'S-CASTLE, (in ruins) fit. 1½ mile beyond Clady, co. Londonderry, prov. Ulfter.

P

PORT-CASTLE, (in ruins) fit. 2 miles from Carrick, in co. Leitrim, prov. Connaught.

PURT *caftle*, (in ruins) fit. 1 mile beyond Abbeyfeal, co. Limerick, prov. Munfter.

R

RATHANVEGUE *caftle*, (in ruins) fit. about 4 miles beyond Rofcrea, co. Tipperary, prov. Munfter.

RATHGOWREY *caftle*, (in ruins) fit. 1 mile beyond *Fookfmill*, co. Wexford, prov. Leinfter.

RATHRUDDY *caftle*, fituate 1 mile from Loughrea, co. Galway, prov. Connaught,

REEK-PATRICK *church*, fit. near 3 miles from Strabane, co. Tyrone, prov. Ulfter.

RHINROW-CASTLE, (in ruins) fit. 3½ miles beyond *O'Brien's-bridge*, co. Clare, prov. Munft.

ROEBUCK *caftle*, fit. about 3 miles S. E. of Dublin, co. Dublin, prov. Leinfter; it was built at a very remote period and ftrongly fortified. About 1534 it was the refidence of lord *Tremleftown*, then chancellor of Ireland; it was occupied by king *James* IId. and the duke of *Berwick*, when they had their camp in its neighbourhood. The prefent lord' Tremleftown repaired it a few years ago, and intended it for his country refidence. There is a remarkable tree adjoining the caftle which grew out of an old wall, and has carried in its trunk a large ftone, which is now to be feen, upwards of 4 feet from the ground.

ROSHEEN-ABBEY, (in ruins) fit. within ½ a mile of *Ballylongford*, co. Limerick, prov. Munft.

ROSLINGAN *caftle*, (in ruins) fit. near Donegal-bay, in co. Donegal, prov. Ulfter.

ROUGHAN *caftle*, (in ruins) fit. about 1 mile from *Coal-ifland*, co. Tyrone, prov. Ulfter.

S

SKIRRY *church*, (in ruins) fit. on the fummit of a hill, about 2 miles beyond Broughfhane, co. Antrim, prov. Ulfter.

SNOWTON-CASTLE, (in ruins) fit. a little beyond *Naul*, in co. Dublin, prov. Leinfter.

SOLDIERSTOWN *church*, fit. about 1 mile beyond Moira, co. Down, prov. Ulfter.

T

TEMPLE-PATRICK *church*, (in ruins) fituate within a mile of Donaghadee, co. Down, prov. Ulfter.

TREVET-CHURCH, fit. about 3 miles beyond Ratoath, co. Meath, prov. Leinfter. It is an antient building. An Englifh colony was once fettled at this place.

TROUGH-CASTLE, (in ruins) fit. above 4 miles from Limerick, co. Limerick, prov. Munfter. Near it is *Trough-church*, alfo in ruins.

A P P E N D I X.

No. 2.

Antient *Septs* and *Colonies* inhabiting different diſtricts of *Ireland* in the early Ages.

AUTERII, a people of antient Ireland, mentioned by Ptolemy, and ſuppoſed to have inhabited parts of the co.'s Galway, Mayo and Roſcommon, prov. Connaught.

BOLGÆ, ſee *Fir Bolgæ.*

CAELANI, ſee *Galeni.*

CANGANII, (or *Ganganii*) a people who inhabited the Weſtern parts of co. Clare, prov. Munſter.

CAUCII, an antient people of Ireland, who according to Rich. Cirenceſt. inhabited the Northern parts of the co. Wicklow, and alſo the banks of the river Liffey, in co. Dublin, prov. Leinſter; the chiefs of whom were denominated *Hy Breghnan* or *O'Brenan.*

CORIONDII, a people ſuppoſed to have been the antient inhabitants of the preſent co. of Wexford, prov. Leinſter; whoſe antient chiefs were the *O'Moroghs,* and in latter ages *Mac Morroghs.* In the Iriſh hiſtory we find the M'Morroghs, frequently ſtiled kings of Leinſter; and to them the Engliſh are indebted for their firſt eſtabliſhment in this country.

DAMNII, antient inhabitants of the preſent co. Down, prov. Ulſter.

DAMNONII, a people who inhabited the antient bar. of *Mariſk,* co. Mayo, prov. Conn.

DARNII, the antient inhabitants of the co. Derry, prov. Ulſter, they are mentioned by Ptolemy.

DEASSII, a people who in antient times inhabited a diſtrict in the S. part of the co. Meath, prov. Leinſter, the chiefs of which were called *Maghcan,* and afterwards corruptly written *Æn-gus.* A chief of this diſtrict about the year 278, having rebelled againſt *Cormac M'Art* king of Meath, entered the royal palace of Taragh, and ſlew Kellach, the king's ſon; whereupon Cormac raiſed an army, ſuppreſſed the rebellion, and drove Ængus out of Meath, who with ſeveral of the Deaſſii ſettled in the co. Waterford, prov. Munſter: in which co. there is a barony called after them to this day.

DERGTENII, inhabitants antiently of the Southern coaſts of co. Cork, prov. Munſter.

EBLANII, the antient inhabitants of co. Dublin, prov. Leinſter, who formerly reſided near Dublin-bay.

ERDINII, a people formerly inhabiting the Southern parts of co. Donegal and co. Fermanagh, prov. Ulſter.

FIRCRABII, antient inhabitants of the co. Monaghan, prov. Ulſter, the chiefs of which were the M'Mahons.

FOMHO-

Fomhoraic, a people mentioned in the antient Irish poems and said to have infested the Southern coasts of Ireland, whilst it was in possession of the *Nemethæ*. They appear to have been the Punic traders, who first arrived on the coasts of the British Isles, about 500 years before the Christian æra; and during their voyages frequently made to Britain, (where they discovered the valuable tin mines of Cornwall.) It is concluded those antient navigators occasionally visited the coast of Ireland, and traded with its natives for skins and such other commodities as the country then produced: and that they obtained their appellation from the word *Femorhaicc*, which signifies sea-men.

Fomorii, see *Fomhoraic*.

Galeni, (or *Caelani*) antient inhabitants of part of co. Wicklow, prov. Leinster, the chiefs of which were the *O'Tools*.

Ganganii, see *Canganii*.

Heberii, antient inhabitants of the co. Kerry and part of co. Clare, prov. Munster. The poets have fabled that this part of the island was peopled by *Heber*, who was the son of *Milesius* and the elder brother of *Heremon*.

Hermonii, a people who inhabited the present prov. of Leinster: they are asserted to have descended from *Heremon*, a son of *Milesius* the Spaniard.

Iberi, a people mentioned by Ptolemy, who inhabited the S. coasts of co. Kerry, prov. Munster. There were other *Iberi* mentioned by the Irish writers who inhabited the N. of Ireland, in the co. Derry, between Lough Foyle and the river Ban, prov. Ulster.

Ibernii, see *Uternii*.

Lucanii, called by Ptolemy *Luccui*: they are mentioned by Rich. Cirenc. and placed by him in co. Kerry, near Dingle; they appear to have been the *Lugadii* of the Irish writers, which in a general sense comprehended all the inhabitants of the Southern coasts, from the harbour of Waterford to the mouth of the river Shannon, tho' sometimes confined to those of the co. Waterford, prov. Munster.

Lugadii, see *Lucanii*.

Menapii, a people who inhabited that part of the present co. Wicklow, prov. Leinster, which lies between the mountains and the sea.

Momonii, the antient inhabitants of the present prov. of Munster.

Nemethæ, the aboriginal inhabitants of Ireland, according to the most antient poems and histories.

Partholani, the antient inhabitants of Ireland, mentioned by the bards, and said to have been colonies prior to the arrival of the Bolgæ; but all knowledge of these people is lost, as well as that of the *Nemethæ*.

Rhobogdii, (or *Robognii*) a people who inhabited the N. of Ireland, in part of the co.'s Antrim, Londonderry and Tyrone, prov. Ulst.

Rudricii, the same as *Fircrabii*, which see.

Venicnii, the people who inhabited the country sit. near the *Venicnium-cape*, mentioned by Ptolemy: comprehending the Western coast of co. Donegal, prov. Ulster.

Vodii, antient inhabitants of co. Cork, prov. Munster.

Voluntii, an antient people who resided in part of the co. Down, prov. Ulster.

Uternii, a people mentioned by Ptolemy, who inhabited the S. parts of the co. Kerry, and the Western parts of co. Cork, prov. Munster; they appear to have been the same as the *Ibernii* of Richard of Cirencester.

APPENDIX.

APPENDIX.

No. 3.

A TABLE of Distances between the several Ports of Great-Britain, on St. George's Channel, and those of Ireland.

		Leagues			Leagues			Leagues
Fr. Land's-end, to	Cape Clear	53	From Milford-haven, to	Cape Clear	65	from Holyhead, to	Cape Clear	85
	Kinsale	49		Kinsale	50		Kinsale	69
	Cork	50		Cork	49		Cork	65
	Youghal	48		Youghal	40		Youghal	56
	Waterford	51		Waterford	30		Waterford	42
	Black-Rock	50		Black-Rock	20		Black-Rock	37
	Dublin	89		Wexford	23		Wexford	33
Liverp. Park-g from Lundy, to	Cape Clear	69		Wicklow	33		Wicklow	19
	Kinsale	53		Dublin	45		Dublin	20
	Cork	53		Drogheda	52		Drogheda	23
	Youghal	44		Dundalk	58		Dundalk	27
	Waterford	34	St. Davids-head, to	Cape Clear	66		Strangford-bay	24
	Black-Rock	27		Kinsale	51	Mull of Galloway to	Fairhead	24
	Wexford	31		Cork	45		Carrickfergus-bay	11
	Wicklow	41		Youghal	37		Strangford-bay	9
	Dublin	53		Waterford	26		Dundalk	25
Liverp. Park-g	To Dublin	43		Black-Rock	16		Drogheda	27
	Dundalk	52		Wexford	18		Dublin	33
	Drogheda	47		Wicklow	28		Wicklow	40
	To Dublin	45		Dublin	40		Wexford	57
	Dundalk	49					Canfore point	60
	Strangford-bay	42						

No. 4.

A TABLE of the Distances between the several Ports on the Coast of Ireland.

		leag.		
From Cape Clear to	Kinsale	16	From Dublin to Canfore-point	28
	Cork	20	——————— Drogheda	9
	Youghal	25	——————— Dundalk	16
	Waterford	38	——————— Strangford-bay	13
	Black-Rock	43	Strangford-bay to Carrickfergus-bay	9
From Kinsale to Cork		4	Carrickfergus-bay to Fair-head	37
From Cork to Youghal		9	Fairhead to Colodagh-head	10
——————— Waterford		20	Colodagh-head to Lough Swilly	7
——————— Black-Rock		30	Lough Swilly to Sheep-haven	6
From Youghal to Waterford		14	Sheep-haven to Tory-island	6
From Waterford to Canfore-point		10	Tory-island to Isles of Arran	9
From Canfore-point to Wexford		4	Isles of Arran to Raghlin-Isle	8
From Wexford to Wicklow		14	Raghlin-Isle to Donegal-bay	7
From Wicklow to Dublin		10	Donegal-bay to Sligo-bay	6

4 S

APPENDIX.

A P P E N D I X.
No. 5.
Circuit Roads of the Judges.
The assize Towns are printed in Italicks.

MUNSTER CIRCUIT.	
From Dublin to	*Waterford*
	Carrick
	Clonmell
	Cork
	Mill-Street
	Castle Island
	Tralee
	Castle Island
	Abbey Feale
	Newcastle
	Rathkeale
	Adair
	Limerick
	Dublin

CONNAUGHT CIRCUIT.	
From Dublin to	*Roscommon*
	Tulsk
	Elphin
	Carrick
	Boyle
	Sligo
	Ballisadare
	Coloony
	Tobercorry
	Banada
	Kilmateague
	Foxford
	Castlebar
	Balcarra
	Newbrook
	Holymount
	Kilmain
	Shrule
	Cahirmorres
	Galway
	Gort
	Crusheen
	Ennis
	Gort
	Loughrea
	Kilconnel
	Ahascragh
	Mount Talbot
	Roscommon
	Dublin

LEINSTER CIRCUIT.	
From Dublin to	*Wicklow*
	Arklow
	Gorey
	Castlebridge
	Wexford
	Ross

From Dublin to	*Kilkenny*
	Leighlin-bridge
	Carlow
	Athy
	Maryborough
	Philipstown
	Dublin

*At *Naas* generally in the Spring, and at *Athy* in Summer.

NORTH EAST CIRCUIT ULSTER.	
From Dublin to	*Drogheda*
	Dundalk
	Downpatrick
	Saintfield
	Carrickfergus
	Belfast
	Lisburn
	Lurgan
	Portadown
	Rich-hill
	Armagh
	Tynan
	Glaslough
	Monaghan
	Castleshane
	Castieblaney
	Peterborough
	Mill of Louth
	Ardee
	Navan
	Trim
	Dublin

NORTH WEST CIRCUIT ULSTER.	
From Dublin to	Kilcock
	Infield
	Kinnegad
	Mullingar
	Ballinalack
	Edgeworth'stown
	Longford
	Granard
	Cavan
	Newtownbutler
	Maguire's-bridge
	Enniskillen
	Trillick
	Omagh
	Newtownstewart
	Strabane
	Lifford
	Londonderry
	Dublin

APPENDIX.

APPENDIX.
No. 6.

A TABLE of the *First Fruits* of the Ecclesiastical Benefices in IRELAND, as taxed in the King's Books.

** We have given the Names of the following Places, as they are written in the original Record, which has been accurately copied, and was some time ago printed in a Tract entitled "VALOR BENEFICIORUM ECCLESIASTICORUM IN HIBERNIA;" as they do not follow alphabetically, an Index to the Dioceses is added at the end of the Table.

Diœcesis ARMACHANA.

Extenta & Taxatio Dignitatum & Beneficiorum Spiritualium in Diœcesi prædictâ facta per Georg. Miden, *&* Fran. Aungier *Commissionarios Regis* Jacobi *primi* 15mo *anno Regni.*

Archiepiscopus Armach. *ita taxatur ultra omniu onera & reprisas.*

	l.	s.	d.
MANER. Termonseighan	23	18	6
———Dromiskin	14	1	6
———Kilmoone	5	0	0
———Eniskeene	10	0	0
———Turlogh	0	0	0
———Donoghmore in Com. Dunen	10	0	0
———Aidtra	98	0	0
———Donoghmore in Com. Tyron	70	0	0
———Armachan.	140	0	0
Duo tertiæ Manerii de Nobber	5	0	0
R. impropriata de Athboy in Com. Miden	10	0	0
Castrum & Terræ de Canceflon	2	0	0
Priorat. St. Andreæ, vulgo le Black Abbey	0	0	0
Messuagium cum Gaidino in Villa de Drogheda	2	0	0
Proficua Spiritual. Jurisdict. Archiepiscopat.	10	0	0
In toto	400	0	0
(Archiepif. taxat. alibi, 30 Hen. VIII.	183	17	1½)
Decanatus Armach.	35	0	0
Archidiaconatus Armach.	2	0	0
Rectoria de Donoghmore	20	0	0
———Dromglafs	6	0	0
———Clonfeakle	16	0	0
———Termonmagnoike	13	0	0

	l.	s.	d.
Rectoria de Aghalow	20	0	0
———Carinteale	10	0	0
———Erylekerogh	10	0	0
———Killyshell	5	0	0
———Ballynclogg	6	0	0
———Clomwennoe, *alius* Clonnoe	6	0	0
———Donoghenrie	8	0	0
———Arbooe	6	13	4
———Derrybrochifhe, *alius* Kilnaman	13	0	0
———Tullanefken	3	6	8
———Ardtiagh	6	13	4
———Derrylowran	6	13	4
———Killdrefs	5	0	0
———Dyfertereagh	13	6	8
———Leffan	5	0	0
———Diferlhin	5	0	0
———Taulaght	3	6	8
———Ballyderry	3	6	8
———Mayheryfelta	3	6	8
———Ardmagh	25	0	0
———Creggan	18	0	0
———Levallyheglifhe	13	6	8
———Dromcree	18	0	0
———Killmore	18	0	0
———Loghgilly	20	0	0
———Derrofe	20	0	0
			Rectoria

	l.	*s.*	*d.*			*l.*	*s.*	*d.*
Rectoria de Tynan	20	0	0	Rectoria de Tawnatelee		20	0	0
————Kilclony	6	0	0	————————Mullabracke		10	0	0
————Kilfleve	20	0	0		All Sterling			

Hæc Beneficia sequentia in Com. Lud. *ita ab antiquo taxantur.*

	l.	*s.*	*d.*			*l.*	*s.*	*d.*
R. de Bewly	6	2	1	V. de Monfeildston		5	14	4½
V. de Termonfeakin	9	7	0	R. de Derver		4	19	9
V. de Donleire	4	2	0	V. de Dundalke		7	10	3½
V. de Donany	2	3	1	R. de Killincoule		5	11	9
R. de Monfieildston	11	9	0		All Sterling.			
All Irish money.								

Taxatio de antiquo facta per Commissionarios Domini Regis Henrici VIII. *anno regni sui* 30mo.

	l.	*s.*	*d.*		*l.*	*s.*	*d.*
R. de Clonemore	22	13	4	————St. Katherinæ, ibid	4	13	4
R. de Rathe	5	4	1½	R. de Knockfergus	10	0	0
R. de Carrick	4	11	4	Cant. B. Mariæ de Athird	4	0	0
V. de Moylare	5	4	1	————Sanctæ Crucis, ibid	6	6	8
R. de Killyncoule	7	9	0	————Sti. Johannis, ibid	6	13	4
R. de Derver	6	14	0	————de Stabannon	5	6	8
V. de Athird	10	10	4	Preb. de Dunben al Kilkirley	1	6	8
————Dromcar	5	16	0	————Kene	0	0	0
————Dromyn	9	14	10	R. de Heyneston	6	6	8
————Clonkin	1	7	2	V. de Carlingford	3	13	8
————Kyldymocke	1	1	1	Cant. B. Mariæ de Dundalke	5	6	8
————Stabanon	16	8	7	————S. Katherinæ, ibid	2	13	4
————Dromyskin	11	9	2	————S. Trinitatis, ibid.	5	6	8
Cantuar. Sti. Georgii de Athird	4	6	8		All Irish.		

Diœcefis C L O C H O R E N S I S.

Extenta & Taxatio Dignitatum *&* Beneficiorum Spiritualium *in Diœcesi prædictâ facta* 15mo *Jacobi primi.*

Episcopatus Clochorensis *ita taxatur.*

	l.	*s.*	*d.*			*l.*	*s.*	*d.*
In Comitatu Monaghan	140	0	0	V. de Aghaveighe		4	0	0
————Tyron.	18	0	0	R. & V. de Aghnilurgher		13	6	4
————Donegal	174	0	0	R. de Clogher		26	13	4
Abbatia Clochorensis in Com. Tyron.	18	0	0	R. de Donerave		10	0	0
				R. de Kilfkerry		6	13	4
	350	0	0	R. de Dromore		8	0	0
				R. de Tedonnagh		20	0	0
Decanatus Clocher	2	0	0	V. de Raveckmalis, *alias* Monaghan		3	6	8
Archidiaconatus	35	0	0	R. de Tahellen		6	0	0
Cancellariatus	26	13	4	V. de Ergletrough		6	0	0
Præcentoriatus	13	6	8	V. de Donnagh		6	13	4
R. & V. de Dirrefaylan	13	6	8	R. de Mucknoe		8	0	0
————Ennifmacfaugh	20	0	0	V. de Dunhemayne		7	0	0
————Bohoge	6	0	0	V. de Aghenamullen		5	0	0
————Devenifhe	13	6	8	V. de Carrickmaycrofs		4	0	0
————Mayherniecrofs	10	0	0	V. de Killeny		2	0	0
————Cleenifhe	10	0	0	V. de Mifkane		1	6	0
————Mayhericulmoney	13	6	4	V. de Mayhericlonye		3	0	0
V. de Carne	6	13	4	R. de Kilmore		4	0	0
V. de Roffirhin	1	6	8	V. de Tollcarberd		3	0	0
R. & V. de Derrevrofke	1	6	8	V. de Drumfnates		0	15	0
V. de Drommeily	10	0	0		All Sterling.			

Diœcefis

Diœcesis M I D E N S I S.

Extenta & Taxatio, 31 Hen. VIII. *facta & Taxata.*

	l.	s.	d.
Episcopatus Miden.	373	12	0½
Archidiaconatus Miden.	100	0	0

Decanatus de DULEEK.

	l.	s.	d.
R. de Admulghen	21	15	6
V. de Ballmagarve	9	9	6
V. de Tymole	2	14	4
V. de Mora	5	2	0
V. de Lecknowe, *alias* Pierstown Landy	0	17	0
R. de Rathfeigh	12	7	0
R. de Killmone	13	9	1½
V. de Stamollen	14	13	4
V. de Kilkervan	3	7	0
V. de Ardcath	6	16	3
V. de Nany	5	0	0
V. de Clonenalwoy	0	16	0
R. de Kentiston	10	12	8
V. de Ponte	6	13	4
R. de Ballygarte	8	3	10½
R. de Payneston	22	2	8

Decanatus de RATHTOUTH.

	l.	s.	d.
V. de Rathtouthe	3	17	8
V. de Trevett	5	12	8
V. de Donboyne	21	9	4
V. de Rathbeghan	5	17	0
R. de Kilbrue	13	7	1½

Decanatus de SKRYNE.

	l.	s.	d.
Vicaria de Moyclare	4	3	7½
—— Kilmore	1	13	7
—— Knockmarke	4	17	0
R. de Agher	6	17	8
V. de Galtrym	13	5	4
—— Skryne	6	18	0
—— Athlomney	6	2	0
—— Dowetilton	2	13	4
V. de Daneston	3	10	0
—— Tabelagh *alias* Taberaght	5	0	0
—— Killen	9	0	0
R. de Raperston	6	10	0
V. de Kilmessan	3	17	0
R. de Troubley	3	7	0
R. de Dunsany	4	9	8

Decanatus de TRYM.

	l.	s.	d.
V. de Athboy	23	14	2½
V. de Killowan	6	0	9
V. de Laracor	6	0	9
R. de Lescartan	9	6	0
V. de Rathmelean	5	12	0
R. de Rathmore	17	12	0

Decanatus de SLANE.

	l.	s.	d.
R. de Slane	24	6	0
R. de Nobbir	29	5	8
V. de Kilpatrick	5	17	1
R. de Drakeston	10	10	8
V. de Donamore	9	9	8
V. de Rathkenny	10	9	4
R. de Drumeonragh	21	15	11
V. de Syddan	8	11	0
R. de Kilbery	18	0	0
R. de Stacallan	10	0	0
R. de Gernoniston	14	8	6
R. de Kiilary	20	5	0
R. de Stokeston	9	3	0
R. de Kowthe	6	2	6
R. de Dunmowe	7	18	4
V. de Killary	3	10	0

Decanatus de KELLYS.

	l.	s.	d.
R. de Moynaltie	18	0	0
R. de Newton	5	6	0
R. de Cruston	3	4	10
V. de Donapatrick	7	16	0
V. de Moyaghir	8	0	0
V. de Girlie	8	16	0
R. de Kilskir	17	15	0

Decanatus de CLONARD.

	l.	s.	d.
V. de Clonard	12	18	5
R. de Castlericard	6	0	0
R. de Killagh.	4	19	8
R. de Rathwere	43	13	4
V. de Rathwere	22	6	8

Decanatus

Decanatus de MOLINGAR.

	l.	s.	d.		l.	s.	d.
V. de Molingar	5	15	0	R. de Clonfadforan	4	0	2½
V. de Rathconnyll	2	16	11	R. de Kilbridepilate	0	14	0
R. de Killagh, *alias* Kilwellagh	13	1	8	V. de Portefangan	2	8	8
R. de Lynn	1	19	8	R. de Moltefarnan	8	10	0
R. de Moleſkyr	0	10	10	V. de Delvyn	14	18	6
R. de Karryk	0	2	8	R. de Taghmone	6	18	0

Decanatus de FOURE.

	l.	s.	d.		l.	s.	d.
V. de Faghly	5	13	0	V. de Loghcrewe	4	5	4
R. de Killaloe, *alias* Killallow	11	10	0	V. de Mayne	6	17	0
V. de Rathgarth	5	2	4	R. de Moylaghe	7	5	0
V. de Diamore	2	9	11	R. de Caftlecorre	3	6	8

Decanatus de LOUGHSEUDIE.

	l.	s.	d.		l.	s.	d.
R. de Loughfeudie	16	0	0	V. de Stahalmocke	2	3	4
R. de Dyfarde	5	4	5	R. de Kilbryde-beftane	2	0	0
R. de Rathconnartie	13	15	0	R. de Newton in Fertullagh	2	3	4
V. de Rathregan	2	13	4	R. de Dyfertale	2	0	0
V. de Culmolleu	10	0	0	V. de Ardnurcher, *alias* Ballynurcher	0	0	0
R. de Trym	65	6	8	R. de Amory	2	0	0
R. de Loghbracan	6	0	0				
R. de Clonegell	10	0	0				

All Irifh Money.

Taxatio Quorundam Beneficiorum facta per Rev. in Chrifto Patrem Danielem Daren. *Epifcopum & alios Commiffionarios,* 28 Eliz. *& retornat. in Scaccarium eodem Anno.*

	l.	s.	d.		l.	s.	d.
V. de Fyrcall	20	0	0	V. de Killadory	9	0	0
R. de Killadory	18	0	0	V. de Kilcloneferte	7	0	0

All Sterling.

Diœcefis DUNENSIS.

Extenta & Taxatio &c. facta 15 Jac: I.

	l.	s.	d.		l.	s.	d.
Epifcopatus Dunenfis	25	0	0	Præb. S. Andreæ	26	6	4
Decanatus Dunenfis	13	6	8	Præb. de Talbaftown	8	0	0
Archidiaconatus	8	0	0	Proeb. de Dunfporte	2	0	0
Cancellariatus	10	0	0	V. de Bally	4	0	0
Præcentoriatus	2	0	0				

All Sterling.

Diœcefis CONNORENSIS.

Taxatio facta fuit per eofdem Commiffionarios.

	l.	s.	d.		l.	s.	d.
Epifcopatus Connorenfis	25	0	0	V. de Loughgule	2	0	0
Decanatus	1	0	0	——Skerries	2	0	0
Archidiaconatus	30	0	0	——Temaghcremay	1	0	0
Præcentoriatus	30	0	0	——Shankill	5	0	0
Cancellariatus	20	0	0	——Templepatrick	1	0	0
Thefaurariatus	13	6	8	R. de Laide	10	0	0
Præb. de Connor	12	0	0	——Culraine	26	0	0
Præb. de Magherfherkan	8	0	0	——Carrickfergus	8	0	0
Præb. de Kellnaige	20	0	0	V. de Infula	5	0	0
Piæb de Carnecaftle	13	6	8	——Ballenalmagh	1	0	0
V. de Mylton	2	0	0	——Coole	1	0	0
——Culfertrin	2	0	0	——Dumeene	0	4	0
——Singington	1	0	0	——Drumale	0	4	0
——Romoan	2	0	0	——Glinus	1	6	8

R. de Ballemartin

	£	s	d
R. de Blalemartin	2	10	0
V. de Ballwater	2	10	0
——Cramwell	2	0	0
——Donnemaught	0	10	0
——Gortfaule	1	6	0
——Ballemania	0	10	0
——Balleroberte	0	10	0
——Dawagh	0	10	0
——Carnegrame	0	10	0
——Raughlins	1	6	8
——Siliwodden	1	10	0
——Ballinderry	1	0	0
——Maghrenegall	1	0	0
——Maghrenemefke	0	10	0
——Camlin	0	10	0
——Annaghgaldanagh	1	10	0
——Lanaway	3	0	0
——Clonarine	0	6	8
——Defert	0	6	8
——Lambegg	1	10	0
R. de Emgall	0	6	8
V. de Carnemew	1	0	0
——Kilmakenett	0	6	8
——Killagh, *alias* Kiloe	3	0	0
Capella de Mylocke	0	7	0

All Sterling.

Diœcefis DERENSIS.

Extenta & Taxatio &c. facta 15 Jac. I.

	£	s	d
Epifcopatus Derenfis tem in Temporali-bus, quam in Spritualibus taxatus ad }	250	0	0
Decanatus Derenfis	50	0	0
R. de Drumchoze	8	0	0
——Ballydaigh	8	0	0
——Aghlowe	8	0	0
——Tawlaghtard	10	0	0
——Tawlaghfialegan	13	6	8
——Boyvevie	13	6	8
——Banaghcarr	8	0	0
——Connubarr	20	0	0
(Archidiaconatus de Dunboe	20	0	0)
R. de Killoyne	2	0	0
R. de Agherdowy	18	0	0
——Difertoghill	10	0	0
——Argill	10	0	0
——Mayheray	10	0	0
——Ballynefcreene	5	0	0
——Tollaghacreely	10	0	0
——Killerenaghan	3	0	0
——Difertmartin	6	0	0
V. de Killreogh	1	10	0
R. de Camus & Macofkin	13	6	8
R. de Killelaghey	3	6	8
R. de Termonanny	3	0	0
R. de Ballinefculline	6	13	4
R. five V. de Fathyn	13	6	8
R. de Clonemanye	12	0	0
R. de Donaghelantey.	10	0	0
R. & V. de Clonkay	13	6	8
——Cooledogh	10	0	0
——Movaileare	20	0	0
R. de Diferteyney	5	0	0
R. & V. de Donaghmore	20	0	0
——Clonley	20	0	0
R. de Drumraght	10	0	0
——Lambfeyll	10	0	0
——Bodoney	10	0	0
——Cappagh	13	6	8
——Teraghamingan	6	0	0
——Ardftragh	30	0	0
——Urney	13	6	8
——Donaheedy	20	0	0
——Legh Patrick	16	0	0
——Camus in Com. Tyron	3	6	8

All Sterling.

Diœcefis RAPOTENSIS.

Taxatio Dioecefis Rapoteufis *&c. facta* 15 Jacobi I.

	£	s	d
Epifcopatus Rapot.	200	0	0
Decanatus Rapot	30	0	0
R. & V. de Tabohine	33	0	0
——Ragbniohie	18	0	0
——Aghnifhe	10	0	0
——Conceall	15	0	0
——Killmacrean	6	6.	
——Tullaferne	10	0	0
——Moyvagh	5	0	0
——Clondevodogge	20	0	0
Præb. de Claudecolcath	13	13	0
——Inver, *alias* Invernayle	10	0	0
——Killemerd	6	0	0
R. & V. de Tullaghbigla	10	0	0
——Ragmunterdoyne	4	0	0
——Enifgnile	15	0	0
——Aghaninfhon	6	0	0
——Gartan	3	0	0
——Killaughty	6	0	0
——Keaelbegg	13	6	0
——Kilkaragh	5	0	0
——Glencollumkill	4	0	0
——Templecrone	4	0	0
V. de Dromhanee	20	0	0
Ecclefia Killibarrin	1	10	0

All Sterling.

Diœcesis KILMORENSIS.

Taxatio Episcopatus Kilmorensis *&c. facta* 15 Jacobi I.

	l.	s.	d.
Terræ in Com. Cavan	65	0	0
———Fermanagh	5	0	0
———Leytrim	20	0	0
———Longford	8	10	0
———Roscommon	1	0	0
———Westmidd.	0	10	0
Summa totalis Kilm. & Ard.	100	0	0
Decanatus Kilmor. confistens de			
R. de Keydie, valoris	6	0	0
V. de Kilmore, valoris	8	0	0
V. de Ballyntemple, valoris	6	0	0
Extenditur in toto ad	20	0	0
V. de Urney taxatur ad	6	0	0
R. & V. de Hanaa, *alias* Belturbet	30	0	0
V. de Drumlaghan, *alias* Bolgan	8	0	0
R. & V. Casleterra	20	0	0

	l.	s.	d
V. de Kildallon	5	0	0
———Kilshandra	15	0	0
———Drunge & Terra	15	0	0
———Kiilishedimin	10	0	0
R. & V. de Dengoone	16	0	0
V. de Tauragh	4	0	0
———Moybolge	4	0	0
———Mally and Balliclauphilip, *alias* Templecally	10	0	0
———Dim	4	0	0
———Anaghgelue	6	0	0
———Kildomfertan	8	0	0
———Killeenagh	3	6	8
———Killaffer	6	13	0
———Kinawley	10	0	0
R. de Kilcann	4	0	0
R. de Knochtyde	2	1	4
V. de Turgan	4	0	0
R. de Castleraghen	2	1	4
V. de Templepuit	13	6	8

All Sterling.

Diœcesis ARDACHANENSIS.

Extenta & Taxatio facta fuit 28mo. *Eliz.*

	l.	s.	d.
Episcopatus Ardach.	11	0	0
Decanatus ibid.	14	0	0
Archidiaconatus ibid.	2	0	0
V. de Granarde	14	0	0
———Strode	14	0	0
———Rouse	4	0	0
———Clonebronie	4	0	0
———Templemichell	4	0	0
———Clonegothe	4	0	0
———Ballycormake	4	0	0

	l.	s.	d.
V. de Clonedarrell	1	0	0
———Killoe	3	0	0
———Killess	2	0	0
———Moydowe	2	0	0
———Killacomveck	2	0	0
———Aghrye	1	0	0
———Rathreaghe	1	0	0
———Kilglass	2	0	0
———Teffyne	3	0	0

All Sterling.

In Diœc. Kilmore, *ex Lib. Visit. in Bibliotheca* Trin. Col. Dub.

	l.	s.	d.
(V. de Urny	6	0	0)
R. de Moybologe, *alias* Killinker	10	0	0
V. de Dromlane	8	0	0
In Diœc. Ardach.			
Kilbrome	2	0	0
Aghery	1	0	0

All Irish.

Diœcesis DROMORENSIS.

Extenta & Taxatio facta fuit 15mo. Jacobi I.

Episcopatus Dromorensis in temporalibus unacum Rectoria de Kilbrone, quæ extenditur ad 40s. sterl. & Rect. de Maghedrale, quæ valet 40s. sterl. & Mene decimæ de Knockaguerrin quæ valet *per annum* 20s. sterl. Extenditur ad — 50 0 0

Decanatus Dromor. confistens de Rect. & Vic. de Aghaderrick, val. 4l. sterl. & de R. & V. de St. Patrike, val. 4l. sterl. &

de R. & V. de Dromballyrome, val. 3l. 10s. & de R. & V. de Tullahih, val. 2l. 10s. & de tribus Luminaries, quæ val. 40s. sterl. & sic valet in toto — 16 0 0

Archidiaconatus Dromor. unacum R. & V. de Donaclona, val. 3l. 10s. sterl. R. & V. de Seagoe, val. 4l. R. & V. de Magherawley, val. 50s. sterl. Extenditur in toto ad — 10 0 0

Cantariatus

	l.	s.	d.
Cantariatus Dromor. taxatur unacum R. & V. de Magheralin, val. 5l. sterl. & R. & V. de Anaghilt, val. 5l. sterl. In toto.	10	0	0
Cancellariatus Dromor. unacum R. & V. de Clandallane, val. 6l. sterl. R. de Drumgath, val. 40s. sterl. in toto	8	0	0
Thesaurariatus Dromor. consistens de R. & V. de Dromore, val. 10l. sterl. R. & V. de Annaclowan, val. 5l. sterl. & V. de Drumgath, val. 20s. sterl. in toto	16	0	0
Præb. de Drommarraghe consistens de R. & V. de Drommarraghe, val. 5l. sterl. R. & V. de Shankhill, val. 6l. sterl. & R. & V. de Garvagh exceptis decimis novem Villarum ibidem, quæ sunt mensales Episcopatus, val. 3l. in toto	14	0	0
V. de Clownish	1	10	0
——Dromgnollane	1	10	0
——Donaghmore	1	6	8
——Killbroney	1	0	0

All Sterling.

Diœcesis DUBLINIENSIS.

Extenta & Taxatio facta 30mo. Hen. VIII.

	l.	s.	d.
Archiepiscopat. Dublin.	534	15	2½
Decanat. St. Patricii, ibid.	145	5	0
Præcentoriatus	51	12	8
Cancellariatus	50	5	0
Thesaurariatus	68	3	4
Archidiaconat. Dub.	42	15	8
Archidiaconat. Glandelach	34	9	0
Præb. de Kilmatalwey	13	6	8
——Swerds	32	14	0
——Yago	10	16	8
——S. Andoeni	7	9	10
——Clonmethan	28	6	8
——Tymothan	10	0	0
——Castrocknock	20	6	4
——Malahidert	18	0	0
——Tipper	16	10	0
——Monmahenock	11	15	11
——Howth	24	6	10
——Rathmichael	8	1	1
——Wicklow	10	0	0
——Maynouth	23	2	3
——Tassagard	10	1	8
——Donlavan	12	6	8
——unius portionis de Tipperkevin	5	6	8
——alterius portionis, &c.	4	0	0
——Stagonyll	1	13	4
——unius portionis de Donomore in Omaile	3	0	0
——alterius portionis, &c.	3	0	0
V. de Swerds	22	6	8
——Cowlock	5	1	8
——S. Katherinæ in vico Thomas-street, Dublin	18	16	0
R. de Cloghrane	10	0	7
V. de Donabate	7	6	8
——Luske ex parte Præcen.	14	5	10
——ex parte Thesaur.	14	12	6
R. de Baldongan	3	13	4
V. de Balrothery	11	19	10
V. de Balscaddan	4	12	4
Custos S. Stephani Dublin	6	13	4
V. de Hollywood	7	4	4
——Balmadan	4	18	0
——Killalaghan	5	6	0
——Garestown	7	11	2
——Taulagh	8	14	1
R. de Dames	1	0	4
——S. Petri de Monte	1	6	8
V. de Lucan	4	16	8
V. de Castroknock	13	6	8
R. de Hollywood	4	14	0
V. de Hollywood	2	13	4
V. de Rathmore	10	12	4
R. de Uske	0	12	0
——Delgeny	24	0	0
V. de Newcastle	2	0	0
——Bree	1	0	0
R. de Dromokey & Castle Adam	2	13	4
V. de Wicklow	3	6	8
R. de Incheboyne	13	6	8
——Silbernan in patria de O'Birnes	2	0	0
——Insula ibidem	2	0	0
V. de Larabryne	17	6	8
——Strassan	5	0	0
——Kildroght	5	12	8
——Tristledermot	12	0	0
R. de Nicholstown	9	13	6
——Norragh	20	0	0
V. de Norragh	13	6	8
R. de Timolinbegge	9	12	0
V. de Kilta	5	0	0
——Killolan	6	0	0
——Fountistown	3	10	0
——Callonestown	3	0	2
——Teaghdo	15	6	8

All Irish,

Decanatus Ecclesiæ S. Trinitatis Dub. vocat. Christ Church taxatus 25° Nov. 14mo. Jacobi I. ultra omnia onera & reprisas   70 0 0

Taxatio cæterorum Beneficiorum facta fuit 21 Junii 13mo. Jacobi I.

	l.	s.	d.
Præcentoriat.	18	0	0
Cancellariat.	22	12	6
Thesaurariatus	24	10	0
Præb. S. Michaelis	7	0	0
——S. Michani	12	11	3
——S. Johannis	11	13	4

All Sterling.

Diœcesis

APPENDIX.

Diœcefis DARENSIS.

Extenta & Taxatio facta tempore Regis Hen. VIII.

	l.	s.	d.
Epifcopatus de Kildare	69	11	4
Decanatus ibidem	8	10	1
Archidiaconatus ibidem	15	3	2
Præb. de Ballyfonan	20	4	0
———Donada	2	0	0
———Lalyaghmore	0	13	4
———Donmorkill	0	6	0
———Rathangan	40	0	0
Ecclefia Cathed. de Kildare	49	6	8
Cuftod. S. Magdalanæ, ibid.	1	4	2
V. de Kilcock	4	3	4
———Balrayne	8	4	4
———Carne	3	1	0
———Ratherny	3	8	8
———Kerogh	10	0	10
———Kill	6	13	4
———Ley	4	0	0
———Clonefhanboe	5	19	8
R. de Donmory	4	17	4
V. de Bondymgifton	6	1	5
V. de Clane	10	4	0
R. de Pollardftown	0	16	4
R. de Lyons	6	2	0
V. de Maynan	6	9	0
———Donada	1	3	0
———Donys, *alias* Downinges	9	0	0
———Deficullen	6	17	4
R. de Walterftown	3	0	0
V. de Lackagh	2	0	0
R. de Kilbrackan	3	6	8
———Ballyfax	5	0	0
———Carnalway	4	14	1
———Calloneftown	3	0	2
———Tymeghoo	1	6	8
———Naas	10	8	1
———Donnen	4	7	8
———Rathangan	12	6	8

	l.	s.	d.
R. de Knawenftown	2	16	8
———Kilmage	1	15	0
———Balimaflolk	2	0	2
———Cuftlecarbery	26	13	4
R. de Thomaftown	5	12	0
V. de Killoffy	7	15	4
V. de Ballyfas	7	7	0
Cantuaria B Mariæ in le Naas	6	17	9½
R. de Henrieftown	6	0	0
V. de Henrieftown	2	6	8
V. de Cloncurry	4	0	0
R. de Norny	4	0	0
V. de Norny	1	0	0
V. de Oughtrard	6	13	4
R. de Kilclonfert	12	0	0
R. de Hayneftown	6	0	0

All Irifh.

Taxatio aliorum Beneficiorum.
28 Eliz.

	l.	s.	d.
R. de Killadory	18	0	0
V. de Killadory	9	0	0
R. de Croghan	12	0	0
V. de Caftle-Peter, *alias* Dromcowley	10	0	0
V. de Kilclonfert	7	0	0
R. de Rathdrome, *alias* Ratheromoyne	8	0	0

Taxatio facta 14 Jac. I.

	l.	s.	d.
Præb. de Gefhill	26	13	4
V. de Gefhill ultra omnes alloc. & deductiones	14	3	0
R. de Williamftown, ultra &c.	21	9	6
R. de Prymult, ultra &c.	44	5	0
——— Caftle-Peter, ultra &c.	20	16	0
V. de Ballynekill, ultra &c.	16	13	6
——— Ardea, ultra &c.	10	3	0½
——— Oregan, ultra &c.	12	3	0½

All Sterling.

Diœcefis OSSORIENSIS.

Extenta & Taxatio facta 29mo. Hen. VIII. *per* Walterum Cowley & Jacobum Whyte *Commiffionarios,* viz.

	l.	s.	d.
Epifcopatus 100 Marks			
Decanatus Eccl. S. Kanici de Kilkenny	26	13	4
Præcentoriatus, ibidem	10	0	0
Cancellariatus	11	0	0
Thefaurariatus	11	0	0
Archidiaconatus	26	13	4
Collegium apud Kilkenny	26	13	4
Collegium five R. de Gauran	26	0	0
Præbend. de Kilmanaghe	6	13	4
———Moyne	8	0	0
———Aghcowre	8	0	0
———Killawre	8	3	4
———Blackrathe	7	0	0
———Taftoffen	4	0	0
———Clawnemonery	4	0	0

	l.	s.	d.
R. de Callan	40	0	0
V. de Callan	13	6	8
———Gauran	13	6	8
———Dongarvan	6	0	0
R. de Kildery	7	0	0
R. Sti. Martini	10	0	0
V. de Dunfert	10	0	0
V. de Kiltranyn	10	0	0
R. de Inchywologhan	13	6	8
V. de Tullyghanbroge	6	0	0
———Killmanagh	5	0	0
———Caftledwogh	10	0	0
R. de Glaifheroe	4	0	0
———Rathbeagh	10	0	0
———Cwylejahin	9	0	0

V. de

	l.	s.	d.
V. de Kilmakeare	3	0	0
———Comer	10	0	0
———Dysert	4	0	0
———Mukully	6	0	0
———Mothell	6	0	0
———Castletown	6	0	0
———Dunmore	7	0	0
R. de Rosconyll	20	0	0
V. de Tipperbrogan	2	0	0
———Killaghy	2	13	4
———Killkenny	2	13	4
R. de Cloghmantagh & Kilrush	10	0	0
R. de Aghboy *alias* Aghevo	20	0	0
V. ibidem	10	0	0
V. de Forailan	6	0	0
R. de Bondell	5	0	0
———Templenichol	4	0	0
———Kildellygly	2	0	0
———Durro vel Durrwa	6	0	0
———Eyrke	8	0	0
———Kilemoy vel Kildermey	2	0	0
V. de Gerypond	6	0	0
V. de Knocktoffre	8	0	0

	l.	s.	d.
R. de Aghbillyr	6	13	4
V. de Bollaghe	6	0	0
———Kiltoyckyghau	3	0	0
———Downky	6	0	0
———Elyt	2	0	0
R. de Kilmaboy	6	0	0
V. ibidem	4	0	0
V. de Porneflully	2	0	0
V. de Rathkeran	2	6	8
R. de Ballytarsue	3	0	0
V. de Polrwayn	6	0	0
V. de Fydowne	6	6	8
R. de Clonmore	3	10	0
R. de Beawley	4	0	0
V. de Kilpecock & Killaha	6	0	0
———Rofbarcon & Shanboghe	3	6	8
———Kilcollom	6	0	0
R. de Listerling	5	0	0
———Kilmokonoke	2	0	0
———Kilwayn & Kilbride	1	6	8
V. de Rowre	3	6	8
R. de Kilnedymock	1	0	0
R. de Delay	2	0	0

All Irish

Diœcefis FERNENSIS.

Extenta & Taxatio facta fuit 29mo. Hen. VIII.

	l.	s.	d.
Episcopatus	108	13	4
Decanatus	33	6	8
Præcentoriatus	14	18	8
Cancellariatus	32	11	8
Thefaurariatus	32	14	8
Archidiaconatus	14	9	0
Præb. de Fethard	12	5	8
———Whitchurch	4	0	0
———Rathafpoke	20	0	0
———Kilcowme & Kilroan	28	4	4
———Coulftuff	10	5	0
———Clone	3	6	8
———Crofpatrick	2	0	0
———Killawagen & Ballyelenane	10	0	0
———Tamon	28	19	7
———Kilruffe	2	0	0
Ecclefia B. Mariæ de Wexford	26	13	4
V. ejufdem	15	3	8
V. Ecclefiæ S. Patricii de Wexford	20	0	0
V. de Rathafpoke	7	6	8
V. de Rathmacknee	13	6	8
R. ejufdem	11	13	4
———Roffe	12	9	4
V. ejufdem	10	0	0
Capella Salvatoris de Roffe	1	0	0
R. de Kilmanan	16	0	0
V. ejufdem	8	0	0
V. de Thacomfhan	7	7	0
V. de Maglas	7	9	2
R. de Kilflowran	26	11	0
———Roflare	39	9	0
V. ejufdem	16	0	0
Eccl. de Killalan	4	0	0
V. de Carne	11	9	0
Capella S. Clementis	3	13	4
R. de le Ifland	10	0	0

	l.	s.	d.
V. de Kilrowan	7	6	8
R. de Tamghagher	26	11	4
V. de Kilturke	8	5	4
V. de Killmore	8	0	2
R. de Kilgorvan	2	5	0
V. de Kilcowan	4	18	4
V. de Coulftuff	2	11	0
V. de Malrancan	11	9	3
R. de Kilkevan	5	17	9
V. de Banno	5	8	0
R. de Ambroftown	3	4	0
———Donawne	2	0	0
———Ludegan	6	13	4
———Horeton	2	0	0
———Ballybraffell	5	0	0
V. de Clonmene	4	0	0
V. de Hoke	7	0	0
R. de Old Roffe	12	17	9
V. ejufdem	7	0	0
R. de Killalog	3	6	8
———Ardcroman	3	3	7
———Carnagh	1	4	0
———Ballychan	3	0	0
Capella de Tillaraght	1	4	8
Eccl. de Killefke	0	12	4
R. de Raen	1	0	0
V. de Ballybalden	0	18	0
R. de Ballyvole	0	8	1¼
———Kilpatrick	1	16	4
V. de Takillen	1	0	0
R. de Ballyhallenan	1	0	0
———Ardekenrye	1	0	0
V. de Innefcortie	2	11	4
R. de Kilvannagh	0	10	0
R. de Kilcormock	2	3	2
Eccl. Leproforum juxta Wexford	1	0	0

R. de

	l.	s.	d.
R. de Malrancan	16	0	0
V. de Killagge	13	6	6
Commendator. de Kilclogan	33	6	8
Eccl. de Doncormock	30	17	8
————S. Mich. juxta Wexford	2	0	0
Eccl. de S. Johan. juxta Wexford	16	15	0
————S. Roscarlen	1	6	8
Capella S. Mich. quæ vocatur libera capella	4	0	0
Commendat. de Ballykyock	3	6	8

All Irish.

Diœcesis LEIGHLINENSIS.

Extenta & Taxatio, de antiquo facta & Taxata.

	l.	s.	d.
Episcopatus	50	0	0
Decanatus	5	6	8
Præcentoriatus	3	0	0
Cancellariatus	5	6	8
Thesaurariatus	2	0	0
Archidiaconatus	6	13	4
Præb. de Illand	1	6	8
————Tullaghmaghma	2	0	0
————Hahold	2	13	4
V. de Carlagh	6	13	4
R. de Hurclene	5	6	8
V. de Ramore	1	6	8
V. de Tullaghfellym	6	0	0
R. de Temple Peter	2	13	4
V. de Chaliston	4	0	0
V. de Ballyellan	4	0	0
————Thomolinge	5	6	8
————Kyltenan	0	13	4
————Clonagne	0	13	4
———— Lurner	4	0	0
————Barraghe	0	13	4
R. de Misill	2	0	0
V. ejusdem	1	6	8
V. de Ballon	2	0	0
R. de Ballyenecarge	2	13	4
R. de Ballycaroghe	1	0	0
V. de Hacha	2	13	4
————Dunlekeney	5	6	8
————Leguffye	3	6	8
————Powerston	2	13	4

All Irish.

In Lexia Anglicè Queen's County.

	l.	s.	d.
V. de Galyn	4	0	0
————Cloneheyn	1	6	8
————Clonekeynagh	3	6	8
————Ballyroyne	2	13	4
————Disertdenys	4	3	4
————Killcolmabane	2	0	0
————Borres	2	0	0
————Straboo	2	13	4
(————Skenkyll	3	6	8)
————Kiltale	2	0	0
————Moyhanna	2	13	4
V. de Noyhwayle	2	0	0
————Themoke	2	0	0
————Tymgboo	4	13	4
————Ballyaquilian	1	6	8
————Rathaspucke	0	10	0
R. de Killabane	4	0	0
V. ejusdem	2	0	0
R. de Killoffen	2	13	4
V. ejusdem	1	6	8
R. de Slete	0	13	4
V. de Cloydagh	0	13	4

All Irish

Taxatio parcellæ Diœc. præd. jacentis in præd. Comitatu, facta 28mo. Eliz.

	l.	s.	d.
R. de Dysarte Eynnys	20	0	0
————Burresse	20	0	0
————Kiltelye	15	0	0
————Clonenaghe	25	0	0
————Straboe prope Shyan	18	10	0
————Ballyrone	10	2	0
————Kilcolmanbane	10	0	0
R. de Fonston, *alias* Ballintobber	10	2	0
————Moyanra	6	0	0
————Noghwall	20	0	0
————Clonkyne	20	0	0
V. ejusdem	10	0	0
Fræb. de Teckaline	3	0	0
V. de Ballintobber	5	1	0

All Sterling.

Diœcesis CASSELENSIS.

Extenta & Taxatio facta fuit per Walterum Cowley *&* Jacobum Whyte *Commissionarios,* 29mo. Hen. VIII.

	l.	s.	d.
Archiepiscopatus	66	13	4
Decanatus	12	0	0
Præcentoriatus	6	13	4
Cancellariatus	6	13	4
Thesaurariatus	10	0	0
Archidiaconatus	12	0	0

Præb

	_l._	_s._	_d._		_l._	_s._	_d._
Præb. de Mollaghynnon	10	0	0	V. de Killnerath	1	0	0
———Killbreagh	3	6	8	———Killmolan	1	0	0
———Killardry	6	0	0	———Killcount	1	0	0
———Finnor vel Fynns	8	0	0	———Callathamery	3	0	0
———Croghan	3	0	0	———Doubfeith	0	13	4
Eccl. de Knockgraffon	10	0	0	———Inchyamly	1	0	0
V. de Clogher	2	13	4	———Feihmoine	2	0	0
——— Ballyshiggan	2	13	4	———Barnenely	1	6	8
——— Ballydon	0	10	0	———Drom	2	0	0
——— Tullaghmean	1	0	0	———Loghmoid	3	6	8
Eccl. de Kilconnyll	2	13	4	———Mannabrath	0	13	4
V. de Nayreth	0	13	4	———Adnythe	0	13	4
———Villacalfe	0	13	4	———Corketenneth	3	6	8
———Collman	0	13	4	———Killeclewe	2	0	0
———Fiddert	6	0	0	———Clomoie	0	13	4
———Rathgwole	5	0	0	———Ballinsin vel Ballusin	0	13	4
———Cowlagh	2	13	4	———Matheme vel Matheyne	3	6	8
———Pepperton	2	13	4	———Rathellca	0	10	0
———Mogawry	1	6	8	———Syan	0	10	0
———Moyeshell	1	6	8	———Bolye	2	0	0
———Killmannon	2	13	4	———Kilbeacan	0	10	0
———Dysertkerane	0	10	0	———Killnesear	0	10	0
———Clonyn	2	13	4	———Garry	4	0	0
———Cronnston	1	6	8	———Killdanale	3	6	8
———Demelloge	1	6	8	———Ballynowre	1	6	8
———Killoscull	1	0	0	———Skornan	1	0	0

All Irish.

Diœcesis I M E L A C E N S I S.

Extenta & Taxatio facta fuit per Arth. Hyde & Fulc. Mounsloe _virtute Commissionis datæ_
1 Jun. 26_mo._ Eliz.

	_l._	_s._	_d._		_l._	_s._	_d._
Episcopatus	26	13	4	Eccl. de Liscormonick Rect. integra	3	1	0
Decanatus	2	13	4	V. de Kiltelly	1	1	0
Præcentoriatus	2	13	4	R. de Naharlowe	10	0	0
Archidiaconatus	5	1	0	V. ejufdem	5	1	0
Præb. de Yfirlorayfe	5	1	0	V. de Tipperary	1	1	0
V. ejufdem	1	1	0	———Toghcluggin	1	1	0
V. de Carriginlishe	8	0	9	———Ulence	2	1	0
———Caherelly	5	1	0	———Solkhoyde	5	1	0
———Luddenbegge	3	1	0	Capella de Lyfinvilly	2	1	0
———Wylleftown	1	6	8	V. de Corrigin	1	1	0
———Any	6	1	6	Eccl. de Brywyfe Rect. integra	6	1	0
———Killfillan	3	1	3	V. de Shronell	1	1	0
———Cahircorny	3	1	0	Eccl. de Clonpett	1	11	0
———Moretown	3	1	0	V. de Newcaftle	1	1	0
———Ballynarde, _alias_ Cahirfofforge	3	1	0	R. de Malte	1	1	0
———Greane	5	1	0	V. de Emiley	5	1	0
———Cluenbonnge	2	1	0				

All Sterling.

Diœcesis L I M E R I C E N S I S.

Taxatio & Extenta facta fuit per Francifcum _Epifc._ Limeric. & _alios Commiffionarios_ 2 Oct.
5_mo._ Car. I.

		_l._	_s._	_d._		_l._	_s._	_d._
Episcopatus	fterl.	40	0	0	Præb. de Tullaghbrake	3	0	0
Decanatus		13	6	8	———Effyn	5	0	0
Præcentoriatus		8	0	0	———Croyer	3	0	0
Cancellariatus		12	0	0	———Kyllydy	3	0	0
Thefaurariatus		13	6	8	———S. Monchiny	2	13	4
Archidiaconatus		36	0	0	———Ardokanny	2	0	0

4 X

Ballycayen

	l.	*s.*	*d.*		*l.*	*s.*	*d.*
Præb. de Ballycayen	fterl. 2	1	0	V. de Feodamore	5	0	1
————Donaghmore	2	0	0	————Knockomohide	2	1	0
————Dyferthe	0	13	4	Collegium de Killmalleck	13	1	0
————Kilbecan	0	13	4	————Limeric	21	3	4
V. de Browry	0	13	4	R. integra de Owrgare	6	3	4
————Mongarte	1	0	0	R. Sti. Lawrentii	0	6	8
————Kilmoclona	0	10	0	V. de Donaghmore	0	6	8
————Kyllyfyne	0	13	4	————S. Michaelis	0	5	0
————Sangole	0	13	4	————Crecoragh	2	0	0
————Clonefarre	0	10	0	————Dermacowe	2	0	0
————Kilftannel	0	13	4	————Ballytankard	1	10	0
————Cloneache	0	13	4	————Glanogra	1	0	0
————Emlaghdrenye	6	3	4	————Droghetarfney	0	5	0
————Kylldyma	0	16	8	————Dunaman	0	10	0
————S. Monchyny	1	6	8	————Ardcanny	2	0	0
Eccl. de Kyllfelly	1	6	8	————Clonecreaghe	0	5	0
————Derrygillion	0	13	4	————Clonelty	1	10	0
————Kilbride major	0	13	4	————Killady	2	0	0
————Kilbride minor	0	13	4	————Killfargus	0	10	0
————Drommen	2	0	0	————Kilfeltinan	0	5	0
————Athenefe	0	13	4	————Kilmahaloge	0	5	0
————Kyllian	0	10	0	————Ardpatrick	0	5	0
————Athletriche	2	0	0	————Adare	5	5	0
————Rathkahell	2	0	0	————Effin	1	2	6
————Killelaghe	0	13	4	Eccl. de Clonecoure	0	10	0
————Killaghillian	0	13	4	R. de Capellruffell	0	7	6
————Novo Caftro	1	0	0	R. & V. de Mahowna	0	10	0
————Gary	2	0	0	R. de Rathronan	0	10	0
————Molconriaghe	2	0	0	V. de Afkeaton	0	10	0
————Gunefkitimi	3	0	0	————Dromdeely	0	7	6
————Dowdonell	0	10	0	————Donmoylan	0	10	0
————Lifmaediry	1	0	0	————Kilbroderan	0	10	0
————Kyllcormayne	2	0	0	————Kilcolman	0	7	6
————Cormothe	3	0	0	————Caftlerobertgore	0	10	0
All Irifh, excepto Epifcopatu & Præb. de Ballycayen				————Loghill	0	10	0
V. de Kilkydy	2	1	0	————Kilmoylan	0	7	6
————Kilmure	2	1	0	All Sterling.			

Diœcefis A R D F E R T E N S I S.

Taxatio faĉta incerto tempore.

	l.	*s.*	*d.*		*l.*	*s.*	*d.*
Epifcopatus	12	13	4	Cancellariatus	2	0	0
Decanatus	3	0	0	Thefaurariatus	2	0	0
Archidiaconatus	3	0	0	Archidiaconatus de Athedo	1	10	0
Cantarariatus	2	0	0	All Sterling.			

Diœcefis W A T E R F O R D E N S I S.

Extenta & Taxatio faĉta fuit per Walterum Cowley *&* Jacobum Whyte *Commiffionarios,* 29mo. Hen. VIII.

	l.	*s.*	*d.*		*l.*	*s.*	*d.*
Epifcopatus	72	8	1	Præb. de S. Patricii de Waterford	8	0	0
Decanatus	20	0	0	Præb. de Ballygunner	0	13	4
Præcentoriatus	9	0	0	Cap. Decani infra Eccl. S. Trinit. de Waterford	14	0	0
Cancellariatus	10	0	0				
Thefaurariatus	10	0	0	Cap. S. Jacobi in diĉta Ecclefia	14	0	0
Archidiaconatus	6	0	0	Pertilar. de Monnemontre	1	7	4
Præb. de Killronan	0	10	0	————Foylinge	0	18	0
————Corbally	0	18	0	R. de Ballmakill	2	4	8
————Roffduff	0	13	4	V. de Killmedan	5	0	0
————Ballynekill	0	6	8	————Kilifh & Rathmoland	4	0	0
					R. de		

	l.	s.	d.
(R. de Dongarvan	60	0	0
V. ejufdem	30	0	0
V. de Dyfert	3	0	0
———Killmolleran	3	0	0
———Infula Brike	2	6	0
———Bellatrynn	3	10	0
———Killbarmedin	7	6	8
———Dunhill	7	6	8
V. de Novo Caflro	3	14	0
———Clonegan	3	0	0
———Gilleaghe	3	0	0
———Finwaghe	2	9	8
———Roffemyr	8	9	9½
———Fywys	3	0	6¼
———Killroffante	9	1	8
———Stradbally	12	2	9

All Irifh

Ex veteri taxatione in Bibliotheca Col. S. Trin. Dub.

	l.	s.	d.
(V. de Kilmolayte	9	16	3
Cap. de Kilrufhe	4	4	6
Praeb. de Modilrige	3	13	6
———Gloge	2	16	0
———Killgobbenet	4	10	0
Sefkyunan	4	10	0
Motalpe	4	11	9
Killaryde	2	14	6)
V. de Mothill	1	13	4

Dioecefis LISMORENSIS.

Extenta & Taxatio facta fuit per Arth. Hyde & Fulc. Mounfloe *virtute Commiffionis datae* 33mo. Eliz.

	l.	s.	d.
Epifcopat. unit. cum Waterford 1382			
Decanatus Lifmor.	13	0	0
Praecentoriatus	10	0	0
Cancellariatus	10	0	0
Thefaurariatus	6	0	0
Archidiaconatus	6	0	0
Quinquae Vicariae Chorales	20	0	0
Praeb de Tullagharton	5	0	0
———Donaghmore	5	0	0
———Kilbarmedyn	6	0	0
———Dyfert & Kiltygan	3	0	0
———Kilroffancta	4	0	0
———Modelegy	1	0	0
Praeb. de Kilgoboned	1	10	0
———Claffmore	10	0	0
———Mora	6	0	0
———Ogheteragh	5	2	0
———Moriftown, *alias* Ballymonekerick	6	0	0
V. de Remogonaghe	3	0	0
———Alba Capella	10	0	0
———Aglis	6	0	0
———Killthella	10	0	0
———Athmeane	6	0	0
———Clonethe	6	0	0
———Moycollupe	3	0	0
———Dyfert & Kilmulvemen	5	0	0
———Clonegan	2	0	0
V. de Novo Caftro	3	0	0
———Rofshufht	5	10	0
———Killroffancta taxed by order of the Court of Exchequer in Hillary term 1668	6	16	3
———Strabally	10	0	0
———Ardmore	6	0	0
———Donaghmore	3	0	0
———Kilfhronagh	5	2	0
———Rathronan	10	0	0
———Clonmell	6	0	0
———Kilallane	8	0	0
———Kilcaffe	6	0	0
———Morliere	6	0	0
———Tuburaghny	6	0	0
———Carrige	5	2	0
———Kilmurry	10	0	0
———Kilfielhan	10	0	0
———Shanrahen	3	0	0
———Tibard	5	3	0
———Newdans	5	2	0
———Deregrath	6	0	0
———Ardfynane	3	0	0
———Tullagharton	5	2	0
———Carrickmagriffen	5	2	0
———Creffe parva	1	0	0
———Dongarvan taxed by order of the Court of Exchequer in Hillary term 1668	22	10	0

All Sterling.

Dioecefis CORCAGENSIS.

Extenta & Taxatio facta 31 & 33mo. Eliz.

	l.	s.	d.
Epifcopatus per Certificationem Auditoris Generalis }	(40	0	0)
Decanatus	30	0	0
Praecentoriatus	8	0	0
Cancellariatus	2	0	0
Thefaurariatus	1	0	0
Archidiaconatus	7	1	8
Praeb. de Lifley Clerrigge	3	0	0
———Killonillie, *alias* Killemully	4	0	0
———Killbritten	1	13	4
Praeb. de			

	l.	s.	d.
Præb. de Difertmore	3	0	0
————Iniſkyine	2	5	0
————Kyllneglorie	2	5	0
————Kilaſhbeggimullan	6	0	0
Quatuor Vicarii Choral. de Corke	16	0	0
R. de Rynonrane	4	0	0
————Leighmony	4	0	0
————Rynrone	6	0	0
V. ejuſdem	3	0	0
R. de Killgobban	3	16	0
————Templetryney	4	0	0
————Rathclaryne	3	16	8
————Iniſhonan	5	6	8
V. ejuſdem	2	10	0
R. de Knockevilley	4	0	0
V. ejuſdem	2	10	0
V. de Kinſaile	3	0	0
————Kinneagh	1	10	0
————Fanlobliſhe	1	10	0
R. de Shandon	3	0	0
V. ejuſdem	3	10	0
V. de Athenowne	1	10	0
R. de Inſula parva	3	0	0
V. ejuſdem	2	0	0
V. de Ballybodan	2	0	0
————Canboye	0	10	0
————Rincurran	4	0	0
Eccl. de Rathwony	1	10	0
————Morieghmolan	2	0	0
R. de S. Trin. Civitatis Corke	1	16	8
V. ejuſdem	1	0	0
Eccl. S. Michaelis	1	0	0
————Kilſhenan & Cap. ejuſdem	3	0	0
V. de Killmowe	5	10	0
————Carmagihy			
V. de Killmocommoge	2	0	0
Eccl. de Killcoan	1	0	0
Eccl. integra de Ragherlaghen	2	0	0
————————Templeuſk	3	0	0
————————Texaſſe	3	0	0
————————Downederowe	3	0	0
V. de Clarine	4	0	0
————Leighmony	2	0	0
————Daughey	1	0	0
————Diſert Selligye	2	0	0
R. de Drinagh	2	0	0
V. ejuſdem	2	0	0
V. de Skull	6	6	8
————Killerogan	2	10	0
————Durius	1	6	8
R. de Clathoranthe	2	0	0
V. ejuſdem	2	0	0
V. de Lille Clery	2	0	0
————Roſſebegg	0	6	8
————Bullaford	5	5	0
————Powlepluck	1	10	0
————Clowneredy	0	10	0
————Killbrogan	1	10	0
————Browne	1	10	0
————Killbonane	1	0	0
————Movid	1	10	0
Una Rect. in M'Cloniſhe	1	0	0
V. ejuſdem	2	0	0
V. de Inſhykilagh	3	0	0
————Killmichell	2	0	0

All Sterling.

Diœceſis ROSSENSIS.

Extenta & Taxatio facta fuit 31 & 33mo. Eliz.

	l.	s.	d.
Epiſcopatus per Certificationem Auditoris Generalis	(10	0	0)
Decanatus	3	2	0
Præcentoriatus	2	0	0
Cancellariatus	2	0	0
Theſaurariatus	0	6	8
Archidiaconatus	3	10	0
Præb. de Inſula	1	13	4
————Dromdaleige	1	0	0
————Tymolegge	4	0	0
V. de Leſleye	6	0	0
————Kathe	6	13	4
————Killeonenaghe	5	3	4
————Crnarye *alias* Temple O Malis	2	0	0
————Kilkeran	2	0	0
————Inſula	1	13	4
————Tullaghe	2	0	0
R. de Kilmolada	3	0	0
Eccl. de Coroſſenhare, *alias* Ballymony	2	0	0
Eccl. de Kylmyne	1	5	0
R. de Tullaghe	2	0	0
————Temple O Malis	2	0	0
Eccl. de Kylmegroſſe	1	6	3
V. de Tymlaghy	4	0	0
R. de Donaghmore	1	0	0
V. ibid.	1	0	0
V. de Templekynlane	3	0	0
————Dyſert	2	0	0
————Kylegarve	3	0	0
————Arde	2	0	0
————Caſtrovenu	1	10	0
————Kilfarna	3	0	0
Una Rect. in Myſus	3	0	0
V. ibid	6	6	8
R. de Craghghe	2	10	0
V. de Craghghe	2	10	0
V. de Tullighe	2	0	0
Una Rec. de Kilcowe	0	10	0
V. ibid	1	0	0
V. de Aghadawne	6	0	0
V. de Cleere	3	0	0
R. de Kylcanyne	4	2	0
V. ibid	4	0	0
R. de Kilkateren	0	6	8
V. ibid.	0	6	8
V. de Kiltaſky	1	0	0
R. de Clanbarigkane	6	0	0
V. ibid.	6	0	0

All Sterling.

Diœceſis

Diœcesis CLONENSIS

Extenta & Taxatio facta fuit 31 & 33tio. *Eliz.*

	l.	s.	d.		l.	s.	d.
Episcopatus	10	10	0	V. de Rathgogare	3	0	0
Guardianatus Villæ & Collegii de } Youghall	100 Marks.			————Ballaghany	1	10	0
				————Eriskethe	0	13	4
Archidiaconatus Clon.	1	5	0	R. de Sandrome	7	6	8
Decanatus	3	0	0	V. ibid.	3	13	4
Præcentoriatus	3	0	0	V. de Kilholane	2	10	0
Cancellariatus	0	6	8	V. de Tyrileshe	2	0	0
Thesaurariatus	3	0	0	R. de Ballyvorane	1	0	0
Præb. de Glanmore	6	0	0	V. ibid.	0	10	0
————Ballyhowlye	3	6	8	Eccl. de Kilmaclemyne	0	13	4
————Donaghmore	2	0	0	V. de Dromodony	2	10	0
————Cowill	1	0	0	————Castlemayne	2	0	0
————Coulleny	2	10	0	————Liskarrol	5	10	0
————Subulter	0	10	0	————Browsen	4	0	0
————Lackyn	0	10	0	————Bregoghe	2	0	0
————Browsen	8	0	0	R. de Kilkorkyrane	1	0	0
————Inyskarry	2	10	0	V. ibid	0	10	0
————Kylmodonnogh	4	0	0	R. de Leter	3	6	8
Quatuor Vicarii Chorales	13	13	4	V. ibid.	3	6	8
R. & V. de Brygowne	12	0	0	R. de Drythane	5	6	8
V. de Cloanmell	1	0	0	V. ibid.	5	6	8
————Capella Roberti	1	0	0	V. de Clonesartie	5	10	0
————Ballycloghye, *alias* Lavan	0	10	0	————Reskryne	1	10	0
————Kilbryne	1	0	0	————Kilshane	1	10	0
————Ballymarter	1	5	0	————Grekenaugh	1	13	4
————Cahirulcan	0	6	8	————Garotten	1	0	0
————Bellaghathye	0	13	4	————Downaghgihie	0	6	8
————Carrigtowell	2	0	0	————Clanherkyn	0	6	8
————Templebodan, *alias* Dronmoyre	2	0	0	————Mathoha	2	0	0
————Kilcouffey	0	10	0	————Aghahbolighe	3	0	0
Eccl. de Garrybove	4	0	0	R. de Aghmaghe	6	0	0
————Beghaware	2	0	0	V. ibid.	6	0	0
V. de Kilmaghan	5	10	0	V. de Clondrethe	1	10	0
V. de Bellygory	1	10	0	————Ballyvornie	2	0	0
R. de Menshye	3	0	0	————Kilcolman	2	0	0
V. ibid.	1	10	0	————Kilmodonoghe	3	0	0
V. de Aghadda	1	10	0	R. de Killgullane	6	0	0
————Corckebegge	2	0	0	V. ibid.	6	0	0
————Rostillane	1	10	0	V. de Marshallstown	6	0	0
V. Capellæ de Rathe	1	0	0	————Clondullane	6	0	0
Eccl. de Castro Chory	2	0	0	————Carrighouane	5	10	0
Cap. de Inishinebacky	1	0	0	————Castle Lyons	5	12	0
V. de Kilbrydane	1	10	0	————Wallstown	6	0	0
R. de Siteskan	1	6	8	————Castletown	6	0	0
V. ibid	0	13	4	————Nohanne	6	10	0
R. de Aghraren	3	0	0	————Carrigleamlery	2	10	0
V. ibid.	1	10	0	R. de Rothcormock	5	10	0
Eccl. de Bellaghe	3	0	0	V. ibid.	5	10	0
————Dongory	1	0	0	V. de Knockmoryne	1	10	0
R. de Inisheullen	1	0	0	R. de Mogyley	2	0	0
Eccl. de Clonrore	5	5	0	V. ibid.	2	0	0

All Sterling.

Diœcesis LAONENSIS.

Hæc Extenta & Taxatio partim facta fuit 5mo. Car. I. *per* Rowland Delahoide *& alios Commissionarios.*

	l.	s.	d.		l.	s.	d.
Episcopatus	20	0	0	Præcentoriatus	1	6	8
Decanatus	5	6	8	Cancellariatus	6	0	0
				Thesaurariatus			

	l.	s.	d.
Thesaurariatus	2	0	0
Archidiaconatus	3	6	8
(Præb. de Clonydagad. Vasta	0	10	0
——— Tomgreny	5	0	0
——Rathblanage	1	6	8
——Eniscathie	4	0	0
——Loghcayne	3	0	0
——& R. de Dysert	2	0	0
——Tullo	3	0	0
——Clondagad	0	10	0
Rec. de Ogashine	3	0	0
——Traderry	6	0	0
——Kilmaferboy	3	0	0
——Dromclyffe, alias Ogormocke	5	0	0
——Killinboy	1	6	8
——Rath	1	6	8
——Kilkedy	1	0	0
——Obloyde	5	0	0
——Roscrey	7	0	0
——Birra	6	0	0
——Moydriney	5	0	0
——Moysse	6	13	4
Vic. de Clonrushe	0	6	8
——Irishecaltragh	0	6	8
——Castleconnell	2	0	0
——Quyn	0	10	0
——Clonee	0	13	4
——Duree	0	6	8
——Killmurrey, alias Duffkeyne	0	6	8
——Thomsynlagha	0	10	0
——Killmalyra	0	5	0
——Kylcomery	0	13	4
——Clonloghan	0	5	0
——Bonratty	1	8	4
——Clonedagard	0	10	0
——Kilfedan	0	6	8
——Killasin	0	6	8
——Kilmurrey	0	10	0
——Kitlamory	0	6	8
——Killfieragh	1	0	0
——Moartagh	0	10	0
——Killbanyhoyne	0	13	4
——Killardagh	0	10	0
——Killyferby	0	13	4
——Killmakadowen	0	10	0
——Dromcliff, alias Ocormock	0	13	4
R. & V. de Killanora	2	0	0
V. de Rathblanage	0	6	8
——Killeneboy	0	5	0
——Killidye	0	6	8

	l.	s.	d.
V. de Killeneawgh	1	0	0
——Mowsey	1	0	0
——Kneagh	1	0	0
——Killbarrayne	3	0	0
——Ardcromy	1	13	4
——Ballyngarry	0	13	4
——Uskean	1	0	0
——Burresakeyn	1	0	0
——Fynough	0	10	0
——Movdriny	3	0	0
——Oghiil	0	10	0
——Burgessebogga	0	6	0
——Roscrey	2	0	0
——Burrehin	0	6	8
——Dowcorrchin	0	5	0
R. & V. de Finglassye	0	10	0
V. de Templenohorry	0	13	4
R. & V. de Kilcomyn	0	10	0
V. de Soyanrone	0	13	0
R. & V. de Killmurrey	2	0	0
V. de Etagh	0	13	4
V. de Birra	3	0	0
R. & V. de Kilterlana	1	0	0
R. & V. de Kinity	2	0	0
V. de Rosmacrowe	0	10	0
R. de Kilclonfert Mulwore	0	13	4
——Fynagh	3	0	0
——Durragh	3	0	0
V. de Aglynecloghrane	1	0	0
V. de Ballyloghacugn	1	0	0
R. de Bannaghcayne	3	0	0
V. de Killansowlagh	0	10	0
——Cloneleagh	1	0	0
——Kilfinaghta	1	0	0
——Kilteeleigh	1	0	0
——Killokennedice	1	0	0
——Killnoe	2	0	0
——Killuran	0	15	0
——Ogonoka	2	0	0
——Moyno	0	15	0
——Kiltinanleigh	1	0	0
——Kilbraghtas	1	0	0
——Tullo	3	0	0
——Templemalie	0	15	0
——Inficronane	3	0	0
——Diferte	4	0	0
——Finagh	0	5	0
——Kilchrist	1	0	0
——Killidisarte	2	0	0
——Killmihill	1	0	0

All Sterling.

Dioecesis T U A M E N S I S.

Extenta & Taxatio facta fuit 28mo. Eliz.

	l.	s.	d.
Archiepiscopatus	50	0	0
Decanatus	6	0	0
Archidiaconatus taxat. &c. 1629	2	0	0
Præpositura Tuam.	2	0	0
Præb. de Leckaghe	6	0	0
——Kilmeamnore	0	13	4
——Keallebegge	0	13	4
——Taxsaxon, alias Templegaile	1	0	0

	l.	s.	d.
Præb. de Kylveylan	2	0	0
——Kylvyen	2	13	4
——Balla	1	0	0
Quinpue Stipendiarii infra Ecclesiam Tuam.	3	6	8
R. de Athenrye	12	0	0
V. ejusdem	5	2	0
R. de Dunmore	8	0	0
V. ejusdem	4	0	0

V. de

	l.	s.	d.
V. de Myllaghe	2	13	4
———Killofcoba	1	0	0
———Ballakillye	1	0	0
———Killareyran	2	0	0
———Kilveylan	1	6	8
———Leckaghe	1	6	8
———Kilmacrean	1	0	0
———Belleclare	0	10	0
———Killourre	0	5	0
Decanatus de Annacoyne, *alius* Enaghdune	1	15	0
Quatuor Stipendiarii, ibid.	2	13	4
V. de Ballyntogher	1	0	0
R. de Kiltullagh	1	10	0
V. ejufdem	0	15	0
V. de Kilbrenam	0	5	0
———Kilveyen	0	13	4
———Crofboyan	0	10	0
———Taghekynney	0	6	8
R. de Mayo	2	0	0
V. ejufdem	1	0	0
V. de Killmeanmore	1	0	0
———Killmeanbegge	0	13	4
———Klicoman	0	10	0
———Conga	0	5	0
———Ballenecalla	0	5	0

	l.	s.	d.
R. de Ballenrobe	2	0	0
V. ejufdem	1	0	0
V. de Enyfhboffen	0	10	0
———Knockvale	0	6	8
———Kylmayne	0	10	0
R. de Aghgoyr ex parte Archidiaconi Tuam.	2	0	0
V. de Aghgoyr	0	10	0
V. de Barrythowle	2	0	0
R. de Clancuan	2	0	0
V. ejufdem	1	0	0
V. de Coran	0	10	0
———Belagheyne	0	10	0
———Borrowfkera	0	10	0
R. de Monula	4	0	0
———Ballenegarry	1	6	8
———Killareyran	6	0	0
———Corkemore	2	0	0
———Ballencalla	1	0	0
V. de Killkeryn	1	0	0
R. de Cryfortyre	1	6	8
V. de Roffe	0	6	8
———Ballendowne	0	6	8
———Imaghyn	0	6	8
———Morrithe	0	6	8
(R. de Owle	1	0	0

All Sterling.

Diœcefis ELPHINENSIS.

Extenta & Taxatio facta fuit 28mo. Eliz. & 5mo. Car. I.

	l.	s.	d.
Epifcopatus	103	18	0
Decanatus	13	6	8
Archidiaconatus	2	13	0
Præpofitura. Elphin.	1	10	0
Præb. de Tyrebtewer	1	10	0
———Corcaghlin	2	13	4
———Artaghe	2	0	0
———Dunclyffe	4	0	0
(———Killmacallan	0	6	8)
———Clonnconnogher	3	0	0
———Ballyntubber	0	13	4
———Varan	2	0	0
———Kilbegnet	2	0	0
———Killuckyn	1	10	0
———Kilcowle	1	0	0
———Tinnenberry	4	0	0
V. de Cama	5	0	0
———Rahafker	5	1	0
———Killofalan	2	13	4
———Killean	3	0	0
———Killrowlin	0	13	4
———Taghboye	0	13	4
———Teftraragh	2	0	0
———Dyferte	0	15	0
———Kylcamroan	0	5	0
———Kiltuan	0	10	0
———Killanvoye	5	6	8
R. de Raharrowe	6	0	0
V. de Killmean	5	6	8
———Porterryne	0	5	0
———Athelegge	5	6	8
———Afhelome	0	2	0

	l.	s.	d.
V. de Ryfertenowe	0	13	4
———Ardecarne	1	10	0
———Tonnia	1	0	0
———Killyngyn	0	13	4
———Killumadan	0	5	0
———Killcowley	0	10	0
R. de Ardkerne	4	0	0
V. de Artaghe	1	0	0
———Fuard	1	0	0
———Templenylan	5	2	0
———Oaran	1	0	0
———Clongormagan	1	0	0
———Donanian	1	0	0
———Kilbegnet	1	0	0
———Ballenakallye	1	0	0
———Kilcroan	1	0	0
———Drometample	0	15	0
———Termonkeyle	0	15	0
———Kilkevyn	0	15	0
———B. Maria in Elphin	0	10	0
———Kilbryde	1	0	0
———Ballyntobber	0	6	8
———Killurrye	0	1	3
———Banflicke	1	0	0
———Killefter	0	1	0
———Killcargye	0	5	0
———Kilcowle	0	5	0
———Killuckan	0	10	0
———Ogella	0	3	4
———Shenthill	0	5	0
———Kilmacudfey	0	5	0
———Lefbride	0	6	8

V. de

	£	s	d
V. de Agherym	0	10	0
———Cloncrawne	0	3	4
———Ivernon	0	10	0
———Kilcruftan	0	5	0
———Kilglaffe	0	4	0
———Termonburye	1	3	4

	£	s	d
V. de Kiltevyn	1	0	0
———Kylgefyn	1	0	0
———Bunlyn	0	6	8
———Lifnenuffe	0	5	0
———Kilkennirran	0	3	0
———Corraghlen	0	5	0

All Sterling.

Pars Diœcefis prædictæ in Comitatu Slygoe.

	£	s	d
V. de Acanaghe	0	1	8
———Tawnoghe	0	1	4
———Kilmacallan	0	3	4
———Kilmactrana	0	1	0
———Kilvacuan	0	1	8
———Shencoghe	0	1	0
———Drom-collan	0	1	4
———Cowleha	0	0	8
———Kilraffe	0	1	8
Præb. de Duncleife	2	0	0

	£	s	d
V. ejufdem	1	0	0
V. de Killmacallan	0	3	4
———Kilmacowen	0	1	8
———Kilafpickbrowne	0	13	4
R. de Slygoe inter duos pontes	0	6	8
V. ejufdem	0	3	4
V. de Kilraghe	0	1	0
———Creeve	1	10	0
———Kilnemanagh	2	0	0

All Sterling.

Diœcefis CLONFERTENSIS.

Extenta & Taxatio facta fuit 28mo. Eliz. & 3mo. Car. I.

	£	s	d
Epifcopatus	24	0	0
Decanatus	12	0	0
Archidiaconatus	4	13	8
———Sacrifta Clonfert.	2	0	0
———Monafterii O'Gormagan			
———de Clontufkerte			
Sacrifta de Monafter. de Aghrym	2	0	0
Præb. de Kilconnell	3	0	0
———Droght	1	5	0
———Kilcuan	1	0	0
———Kiltefgill	1	0	0
———duæ Præb. de Fennor	1	10	0
———Ballytowlter	0	15	0
———Killafpickmoylan	0	6	8
———Annagcalla	1	0	0
V. de Droghte, Downenoght & Fahye	2	0	0
———Milethe	0	5	0
———Kilmaccona	1	10	0
———Kilcuan	1	10	0
———Tyrnefgayre	0	6	8
———Leckmolaffe	2	0	0
———Killeymor	1	6	8
———Kilgarrell	1	10	0
———Creaghe	1	10	0
———Kilclune	1	10	0
———Kilconnell	2	0	0
———Foynaghe	1	10	0
———Ballymawerde	1	6	8

	£	s	d
V. de Killyncofte	1	6	8
———Killovan	1	6	8
———Clankenkeryll	2	0	0
———Tenaghe	3	6	8
———Duneyre	1	17	8
———Ballenkille	2	6	8
R. de Duneyre	6	13	4
V. de Kiltefgill	1	0	0
———Leytrim	0	13	4
———Kilcoule	0	6	8
———Killrycall	0	13	4
R. de Loghereagh	18	0	0
V. ejufdem	3	0	0
V. de Killendynaa	2	0	0
———Kiltormer	0	6	8
———Kilcowan	2	0	0
———Legeirke	1	0	0
———Killuan	1	10	0
———Killeymore	1	0	0
R. de Aghryme	3	6	8
———Kilclune	2	13	4
V. de Kilcarban	0	5	0
R. integra de Killmonology	2	0	0
V. de Drunkiffe, *alias* Drunkight	0	5	0
———Killtullagh	1	0	0
———Killgerrill, *alias* Kilkerinn	0	13	4
———Killoian	1	0	0
———Teigevickennell	2	0	0

All Sterling.

Diœcefis DUANENSIS.

Extenta & Taxatio facta fuit 28mo. Eliz.

	£	s	d
Epifcopatus	13	6	8
Decanatus	2	0	0
Archidiaconatus	4	0	0
Præpofitura Duac.	2	0	0

	£	s	d
Cantarariatus	1	6	8
Thefaurariatus	1	6	8
Præb. de Dyfertkelly	1	0	0
———Kilcornan	0	12	0

Kilcryfte

Præb. de Kilcryfle	0	15	0	V. de Dronnickowe	0	10	0
———Kynmarra	1	0	0	———Stradballye	0	15	0
———Crefcornan	0	11	8	———Killeyle	1	0	0
———Ballyneddye	0	6	8	———Killeneheyne	0	13	4
R. de Kiltomys	6	0	0	———Ardrahyn	2	0	0
———Ardrahyn	5	0	0	———Dyfertkellye	1	0	0
———Beaghe	1	10	0	———Killeynan	2	0	0
V. ejufdem	0	15	0	———Kilcryfte	1	6	8
V. de Killenye	0	3	4	———Killogillyne	0	10	0
———Kynmarran	0	15	0	———Killora	1	6	8
———Dorreffe	0	8	0	———Kilcolgan	1	10	0
———Fynevara	0	13	4	———Kiltomys	1	3	4

All Sterling.

Diœcefis ALLADENSIS.

Taxatio & Extenta facta fuit 28*mo.* Eliz. & 5*mo.* Car. I.

Epifcopatus	23	6	8	V. de Killyan	0	10	0
Decanatus	4	0	0	———Rareghe	0	6	8
Archidiaconatus	1	13	4	———Dunyne	0	6	8
Præpofitura Alladenfis	6	0	0	———Kilbride	0	10	0
Præb. de Kilnaharpy	4	0	0	———Lekan	0	13	4
———Killanley	0	0	1	———Rafrannor	0	13	4
R. de Skryne	5	0	0	———Kilcomyn	0	10	0
V. ejufdem	2	0	0	———Imlaghifhell	0	13	4
R. de Caftle-Connor	4	0	0	———Kilglaffe	1	0	0
V. ejufdem	2	0	0	———Dromard	0	6	8
V. de Bellafegyre	0	16	8	———Killmacfallaghan	0	3	4
———Bellanaglys	0	13	4	———Corcaghe	0	3	4
———Kilbelada	0	13	4	R. de Tirawley	4	0	0
———Ardaghe	0	6	8	V. de Eafkagh	2	0	0
———Crofmolyne	0	13	4				

All Sterling.

Diœcefis ARCHADENSIS feu ACHONRY.

Extenta & Taxatio facta fuit 28*mo.* Eliz. & 5*mo.* Car. I.

Epifcopatus	10	0	0	V. de Killaraght	0	3	0
Decanatus	1	0	0	———Killofalvan	0	2	0
Præpofitura ibidem	0	6	8	———Imulcaddye	0	3	8
Archidiaconatus ibid. cum Vicaria de Kil-rowryn }	4	0	0	———Tuymore	0	3	0
V. de Kilvardeda	4	0	0	———Kilmorchowe	0	1	8
———Killowran	0	10	0	———Clonoghill	0	8	0
———Killefye	0	2	0	R. de Cowlaven	0	6	8
———Strade	0	4	0	V. ejufdem	0	3	8
———Killodan	0	5	0	R. de Slewloa	0	10	0
———Kilverghe	0	4	0	———Bowcowley	0	2	8
———Templemarrye	0	5	0	R. vocat. inter duos amnes	0	3	8
———Kilcolman	0	3	0	R. de Killowran	0	13	4

All Sterling.

Præbendæ præd. Diæc. ita taxatæ funt 5*mo.* Octob. 5*mo.* Car. I. *per* Rog. Jones *Militem & alios Commiffionarios.*

Præb. de Killaraght	0	0	8	Præb. de Tremoymleigh	0	0	3
———Killoran	0	1	0	———Killfry	0	0	1
———Donghorne	0	1	0	V. de Kilmeteige	2	0	0

All Sterling.

INDEX

Tabula Diœcefium.

F I N I S.